Sociology
IN OUR TIMES

Sociology
IN OUR TIMES
SECOND CANADIAN EDITION

DIANA KENDALL
BAYLOR UNIVERSITY

JANE LOTHIAN MURRAY
UNIVERSITY OF WINNIPEG

RICK LINDEN
UNIVERSITY OF MANITOBA

Nelson
Thomson Learning™

Australia • Canada • Denmark • Japan • Mexico • New Zealand • Philippines
Puerto Rico • Singapore • South Africa • Spain • United Kingdom • United States

1120 Birchmount Road
Scarborough, Ontario M1K 5G4
www.nelson.com
www.thomson.com

Statistics Canada information is used with the permission of the Minister of Industry, as
Minister responsible for Statistics Canada. Information on the availability of the wide range of
data from Statistics Canada can be obtained from Statistics Canada's Regional Offices, its
World Wide Web site at http://www.statcan.ca, and its toll-free access number 1-800-263-1136.

Canadian Cataloguing in Publication Data

Kendall, Diana Elizabeth
        Sociology in our times

2nd Canadian ed.
Includes bibliographical references and index.
ISBN 0-17-616679-3

1. Sociology.   I. Lothian Murray, Jane, 1960-   .   II. Linden, Rick.
III. Title.

HM51.K46 1999   301   C99-931673-7

Editorial Director	Michael Young
Acquisitions Editors	Jessica Mosher and Joanna Cotton
Marketing Manager	Kevin Smulan
Project Editors	Evan Turner and Toni Chahley
Production Editor	Tracy Bordian
Production Coordinator	Hedy Later
Editorial Assistant	Scott Carter
Photo Researcher	Evan Turner
Copy Editor	Erika Krolman
Proofreader	Marcia Miron
Art Director	Angela Cluer
Cover Design	Ken Phipps
Cover Image	Nello Giambi/Tony Stone Images
Compositor	Zenaida Diores
Printer	RR Donnelley & Sons Company

Printed and bound in the United States
      2   3   4   03 02 01 00

BRIEF CONTENTS

PART 1   STUDYING SOCIETY

1 The Sociological Perspective   3

2 Sociological Research Methods   31

PART 2   THE NATURE OF SOCIAL LIFE

3 Culture   65

4 Socialization   101

5 Social Structure and Interaction in Everyday Life   133

6 Groups and Organizations   165

7 Crime and Deviance   199

PART 3   SOCIAL DIFFERENCES AND SOCIAL INEQUALITY

8 Social Stratification and Class   239

9 Global Stratification   271

10 Race and Ethnicity   303

11 Sex and Gender   335

12 Aging   371

PART 4   SOCIAL INSTITUTIONS

13 The Economy and Work   401

14 Politics and Government   437

15 Families and Intimate Relationships   469

16 Education   509

17 Religion   541

18 Health, Health Care, and Disability   575

PART 5   SOCIAL DYNAMICS AND SOCIAL CHANGE

19 Population and Urbanization   605

20 Collective Behaviour and Social Change   639

CONTENTS

PART 1 STUDYING SOCIETY

1 THE SOCIOLOGICAL PERSPECTIVE 3

Putting Social Life into Perspective 4
    Why Study Sociology? 4
    The Sociological Imagination 7
    The Importance of a Global Sociological Imagination 8

The Development of Sociological Thinking 10
    Early Thinkers: A Concern with Social Order and Stability 12
    Differing Views on the Status Quo: Stability versus Change 14
    The Development of Sociology in North America 16

Contemporary Theoretical Perspectives 18
    Functionalist Perspectives 18
    Conflict Perspectives 21
    Feminist Perspectives 22
    Interactionist Perspectives 23

Chapter Review 26

2 SOCIOLOGICAL RESEARCH 31

Why Is Sociological Research Necessary? 32
    Five Ways of Knowing the World 32
    Descriptive and Explanatory Studies 34
    The Theory and Research Cycle 35

The Sociological Research Process 36
    Selecting and Defining the Research Problem 36
    Reviewing Previous Research 36
    Formulating the Hypothesis (If Applicable) 37
    Developing the Research Design 39
    Collecting the Data 40
    Analyzing the Data 40
    Drawing Conclusions and Reporting the Findings 40

Research Methods for Collecting Data 41
    Experiments 41
    Case Study: Would You Help Another Person? 41
    Surveys 45

Case Study: The Gift of Blood   47
Secondary Analysis of Existing Data   48
Case Study: Good Neighbours and Saints   49
Field Research   52
Case Study: Responding to Disaster   53
Feminist Research Methods   56
Multiple Methods of Social Research   56

Ethical Issues in Sociological Research   57
The Zellner Research   59
The Humphreys Research   59
The Ogden Case   59

Chapter Review   60

PART **2**   THE NATURE OF SOCIAL LIFE

3   CULTURE   65

Culture and Society   66
The Importance of Culture in a Changing World   66
Material and Nonmaterial Culture   68
Cultural Universals   69

Components of Culture   70
Symbols   70
Language   71
Language Diversity in Canada   74
Values   76
Norms   79

Popular Culture   80
Popular versus High Culture   80
Divergent Perspectives on Popular Culture   81

Cultural Change and Diversity   83
Cultural Change   83
Cultural Diversity   84
Culture Shock   89
Ethnocentrism   91
Cultural Relativism   92

Sociological Analysis of Culture   92
A Functionalist Perspective   92
A Conflict Perspective   92
An Interactionist Perspective   93

Cultural Patterns in the Future   94
Culture and Technology   94
A Global Culture?   95

Chapter Review   96

4 SOCIALIZATION 101

Why Is Socialization Important? **102**
Human Development: Biology and Society 103
Social Isolation 104
Child Abuse 107

Socialization and the Self **107**
Sociological Theories of Human Development 108
Psychological Theories of Human Development 113

Agents of Socialization **117**
The Family 117
The School 118
Peer Groups 119
Mass Media 120

Gender Socialization **122**

Socialization Through the Life Course **123**
Infancy and Childhood 124
Adolescence 125
Adulthood 125

Resocialization **127**
Voluntary Resocialization 127
Involuntary Resocialization 127

Socialization in the Future **127**

Chapter Review **128**

5 SOCIAL STRUCTURE AND INTERACTION IN EVERYDAY LIFE 133

Social Structure: The Macrolevel Perspective **134**

Components of Social Structure **135**
Status 135
Roles 138
Groups 141
Social Institutions 143

Societies: Changes in Social Structure **144**
Mechanical and Organic Solidarity 145
Gemeinschaft and *Gesellschaft* 145
Social Structure and Homelessness 146

Social Interaction: The Microlevel Perspective **148**
Social Interaction and Meaning 148
The Social Construction of Reality 149
Ethnomethodology 150
Dramaturgical Analysis 151
The Sociology of Emotions 154
Nonverbal Communication 155

Changing Social Structure and Interaction in the Future **159**

Chapter Review **160**

6 GROUPS AND ORGANIZATIONS 165

Social Groups 166
　　Groups, Aggregates, and Categories 166
　　Types of Groups 166

Group Characteristics and Dynamics 170
　　Group Size 170
　　Group Leadership 170
　　Group Conformity 172

Formal Organizations 176
　　Types of Formal Organizations 176
　　Bureaucracies 181
　　Shortcomings of Bureaucracies 185
　　Bureaucracy and Oligarchy 189
　　An Alternative Form of Organization 190

New Organizations for the Future 192

Chapter Review 195

7 CRIME AND DEVIANCE 199

What Is Deviance? 200

Functionalist Perspectives on Crime and Deviance 203
　　Strain Theory: Goals and the Means to Achieve Them 203
　　Opportunity Theory: Access to Illegitimate Opportunities 204
　　Control Theory: Social Bonding 205

Interactionist Perspectives on Crime and Deviance 206
　　Differential Association Theory 206
　　Labelling Theory 207

Critical Perspectives on Crime and Deviance 209
　　The Conflict Approach 209

Feminist Perspectives on Crime and Deviance 210

Crime Classification and Statistics 213
　　How the Law Classifies Crime 213
　　How Sociologists Classify Crime 213
　　Crime Statistics 217
　　Street Crimes and Criminals 220

The Criminal Justice System 227
　　The Police 227
　　The Courts 228
　　Punishment 229
　　Restorative Justice 231
　　Community Corrections 233

Crime and Deviance in the Future 234

Chapter Review 234

PART **3**   SOCIAL DIFFERENCES AND SOCIAL INEQUALITY

8   SOCIAL STRATIFICATION AND CLASS   **239**

What Is Social Stratification?   **240**

Global Systems of Stratification   **241**
    The Caste System   242
    The Class System   243

Classical Perspectives on Social Class   **244**
    Karl Marx: Relation to Means of Production   244
    Max Weber: Wealth, Prestige, and Power   245

The Canadian Class Structure   **247**
    The Upper Class   248
    The Middle Class   249
    The Working Class   250
    The Lower Class   250

Sociological Explanations of Social Inequality   **251**
    Functionalist Perspectives   251
    Conflict Perspectives   252
    The Evolutionary Approach   253

Inequality in Canada   **254**
    Distribution of Income and Wealth   254
    Consequences of Inequality   256

Poverty in Canada   **260**
    Who Are the Poor?   260
    Economic and Structural Sources of Poverty   264

Social Stratification in the Future   **265**

Chapter Review   **266**

9   GLOBAL STRATIFICATION   **271**

Wealth and Poverty in Global Perspective   **272**
    Inequality and Individuals   275

Problems in Studying Global Inequality   **275**
    The "Three Worlds" Approach   275
    The Levels of Development Approach   275

Classification of Economies by Income   **278**
    Low-Income Economies   279
    Middle-Income Economies   279
    High-Income Economies   280

The Impact of Debt and Foreign Aid   **281**
    Debt and Global Stratification   281
    Foreign Aid and Global Stratification   282

Measuring Global Wealth and Poverty   **285**
    Absolute, Relative, and Subjective Poverty   285
    The Gini Coefficient and Global Quality of Life Issues   285

Global Poverty and Human Development Issues   286
    Life Expectancy   286
    Health   287
    Education and Literacy   290

Theories of Global Inequality   290
    Development and Modernization Theories   290
    Dependency Theory   293
    World Systems Theory   295
    The New International Division of Labour Theory   296

Global Inequality in the Future   297

Chapter Review   298

10 RACE AND ETHNICITY 303

Race and Ethnicity   304
    The Social Significance of Race and Ethnicity   305
    Majority and Minority Groups   307

Components of Racial and Ethnic Conflict   308
    Prejudice   308
    Theories of Prejudice   309
    Discrimination   310
    Racism   312

Sociological Perspectives on Race and Ethnic Relations   317
    Interactionist Perspectives   317
    Functionalist Perspectives   318
    Conflict Perspectives   321
    A Feminist Perspective on Race and Gender   322

Ethnic Groups in Canada   323
    First Nations   323
    Charter Europeans   326
    Canada's Immigrants   327

Racial and Ethnic Diversity in Canada in the Future   330

Chapter Review   331

11 SEX AND GENDER 335

Sex and Gender   336
    Sex   336
    Gender   337
    The Social Significance of Gender   339
    Sexism   340

Gender Stratification in Historical Perspective   341
    Hunting and Gathering Societies   341
    Horticultural and Pastoral Societies   342
    Agrarian Societies   343
    Industrial Societies   345

Gender and Socialization   347
    Gender Socialization by Parents   348
    Peers and Gender Socialization   349
    Teachers, Schools, and Gender Socialization   351
    Sports and Gender Socialization   352
    Mass Media and Gender Socialization   353

Contemporary Gender Inequality   355
    Gender Segregation of Paid Work   355
    The Gender Wage Gap   358
    Pay Equity and Employment Equity   359
    Unpaid Work—The Second Shift   361

Perspectives on Gender Stratification   362
    Functionalist and Neoclassical Economic Perspectives   362
    Conflict Perspectives   364
    Feminist Perspectives   365

Gender Issues in the Future   366

Chapter Review   367

12 AGING   371

The Social Significance of Age   372
    Trends in Aging   372
    Age in Historical Perspective   373

Age and the Life Course in Contemporary Society   374
    Infancy and Childhood   375
    Adolescence   376
    Young Adulthood   376
    Middle Adulthood   377
    Late Adulthood   378
    Retirement   379

Inequalities Related to Aging   380
    Ageism   381
    Wealth, Poverty, and Aging   384
    Elder Abuse   385

Sociological Perspectives on Aging   386
    Functionalist Perspectives on Aging   386
    Interactionist Perspectives on Aging   387
    Conflict Perspectives on Aging   388

Living Arrangements for Older Adults   389
    Support Services, Homemaker Services, and Daycare   389
    Nursing Homes   393

Death and Dying   394

Aging in the Future   397

Chapter Review   398

PART 4   SOCIAL INSTITUTIONS

13 THE ECONOMY AND WORK   401

The Economy   402
The Sociology of Economic Life   402
Historical Changes in Economic Systems   402

Contemporary Economic Systems   407
Capitalism   407
Socialism   410
Mixed Economies   412

Perspectives on Economy and Work   412
The Functionalist Perspective   412
The Conflict Perspective   413

The Interactionist Perspective   414
The Meaning of Work   414
Job Satisfaction   415

The Social Organization of Work   415
Occupations   415
Professions   415
Managers and the Managed   417
The Lower Tier of the Service Sector and Marginal Jobs   418
Contingent Work   419
Unemployment   420
Labour Unions   422

The Global Economy in the Future   425
The End of Work?   426
The Canadian Economy   427
Global Economic Interdependence and Competition   428
Corporate Responsibility   431

Chapter Review   432

14 POWER, POLITICS, AND GOVERNMENT   437

Politics, Power, and Authority   438
Power and Authority   438

Global Political Systems   443
Monarchies   443
Authoritarian Systems   443
Totalitarian Systems   444
Democracies   444

Perspectives on Power and Political Systems   445
Functionalist Perspectives: The Pluralist Model   446
Conflict Perspectives: Elite Models   449
Critique of Pluralist and Elite Models   451
Feminist Perspectives   452

Politics and Government in Canada   453
  Political Parties   453
  Politics and the People   455

Governmental Bureaucracy   457
  Characteristics of the Federal Government Bureaucracy   457

Major Political Issues in Canada: Separatism and Self-Government   458
  The Quiet Revolution and Quebec Nationalism   458
  Aboriginal Self-Government   461

Political Issues for the Future   463

Chapter Review   465

15 FAMILIES AND INTIMATE RELATIONSHIPS   469

Families in Global Perspective   470
  Defining *Family*   470
  Family Structure   471
  Marriage Patterns   473
  Descent and Inheritance   475
  Power and Authority in Families   475

Theoretical Perspectives on Families   476
  Functionalist Perspectives   476
  Conflict Perspectives   477
  Feminist Perspectives   478
  Interactionist Perspectives   480

Developing Intimate Relationships and Establishing Families   481
  Love and Intimacy   482
  Cohabitation   483
  Marriage   484
  Housework   486

Child-Related Family Issues and Parenting   488
  Deciding to Have Children   488
  Adoption   489
  New Reproductive Techniques   489
  Single-Parenting   492

Transitions and Problems in Families   493
  Violence in Families: Wife and Child Abuse   494
  Divorce   496
  Remarriage   498

Family Diversity   499
  Gay and Lesbian Families   499
  Singlehood   502
  Aboriginal Families   502

Family Issues in the Future   504

Chapter Review   504

16 EDUCATION 509

An Overview of Education 510

Education in Historical–Global Perspective 510
    Informal Education in Preliterate Societies 510
    Formal Education in Preindustrial and Industrial Societies 511

Contemporary Education in Other Nations 513

Sociological Perspectives on Education 515
    Functionalist Perspectives 515
    Conflict Perspectives 518
    Interactionist Perspectives 521

Current Issues in Education 523
    Inequality in Public Schools versus Private Schools 523
    Dropping Out 524
    Declining Academic Standards and Functional Illiteracy 525
    Gender Bias in Schools 527
    Equalizing Opportunities for Students with Disabilities 530
    The Soaring Cost of Post-Secondary Education 532

Education in the Future 534

Chapter Review 538

17 RELIGION 541

The Sociological Study of Religion 542
    Religion and the Meaning of Life 543
    Categories of Religion 545

Sociological Perspectives on Religion 546
    The Functionalist Perspective on Religion 547
    The Conflict Perspective on Religion 548
    The Interactionist Perspective on Religion 551

World Religions 552
    Hinduism 552
    Buddhism 554
    Confucianism 555
    Judaism 555
    Islam 558
    Christianity 558

Types of Religious Organizations 559
    Ecclesia 559
    The Church–Sect Typology 559
    Cults 560

Trends in Religion in Canada 561
    Canada's Religious Mosaic 561
    Religiosity 562
    Why Have Canadians Turned Away from the Church? 563
    Fundamentalism 565
    Does Religion Make a Difference? 566
    Women in the Ministry 567

Religion in the Future 569

Chapter Review 571

18 HEALTH, HEALTH CARE, AND DISABILITY 575

Health and Medicine 576

Sociological Perspectives on Health 577
    The Functionalist Perspective on Health: The Sick Role 577
    Symbolic Interactionist Theory: The Social Construction of Illness 579
    Conflict Theory: Inequalities in Health and Health Care 582

Social Factors in Health: Age, Sex, and Social Class 582
    Age 582
    Sex 583
    Social Class 584

Race, Class, and Health: Canada's Aboriginals 586
    Health Problems Among Aboriginal Peoples in Canada 586
    Aboriginal Healing Methods 588

Disability 588
    Disability in Historical Perspective 589
    Disability in Contemporary Society 590

Social Development and Health: A Global Perspective 592
    Health Care in Canada 593
    Universal Health Care 594
    Health Care in the United States 597

Approaches to Health Care 598
    The Medical Model of Illness 598
    Alternative Approaches 598

Health Care Issues in the Future 600

Chapter Review 601

PART 5 SOCIAL DYNAMICS AND SOCIAL CHANGE

19 POPULATION AND URBANIZATION 605

Demography: The Study of Population 606
    Fertility 606
    Mortality 608
    Migration 609
    Population Composition 612
    The Baby Boom and the Baby Bust 613

Population Growth in a Global Context 617
    The Malthusian Perspective 617
    The Marxist Perspective 619

The Neo-Malthusian Perspective   619
Demographic Transition Theory   620
Demography and Public Policy   623

Urbanization and the Growth of Cities   624
Emergence and Evolution of the City   624
Preindustrial Cities   625
Industrial Cities   626
Postindustrial Cities   626

Perspectives on Urbanization and the Growth of Cities   627
Functionalist Perspectives: Ecological Models   627
Conflict Perspectives: Political Economy Models   629
Feminist Perspectives   630
Interactionist Perspectives: The Experience of City Life   631

Divided Interests: Cities, Suburbs, and Beyond   633

Population and Urbanization in the Future   634

Chapter Review   635

20 COLLECTIVE BEHAVIOUR AND SOCIAL CHANGE   639

Collective Behaviour   640
Conditions for Collective Behaviour   640
Dynamics of Collective Behaviour   641
Distinctions Regarding Collective Behaviour   642
Types of Crowd Behaviour   643
Explanations of Crowd Behaviour   645

Social Movements   652
Types of Social Movements   653
Causes of Social Movements   656
Stages in Social Movements   659

Social Change in the Future   660
The Physical Environment and Change   660
Population and Change   661
Technology and Change   662
Social Institutions and Change   663

A Few Final Thoughts   663

Chapter Review   664

GLOSSARY   666
REFERENCES   677
INDEX   713

BOXES

SOCIOLOGY AND TECHNOLOGY

Internet Cyberculture   82

The Internet and the Organization   194

Technology and Crime: Organized Crime and the Internet   216

The Digital Third World   298

Seniors and Cyberspace   382

The Digital Divide   430

The Technology Revolution in the Classroom:

    Equalizing Opportunity   536

SOCIOLOGY AND EVERYDAY LIFE

How Much Do You Know About Suicide?   7

How Much Do You Know About Altruism?   33

How Tolerant Are Canadians of Other Cultures?   67

How Much Do You Know About Child Abuse?   103

How Much Do You Know About Homelessness?   135

How Much Do You Know About Bureaucracy?   167

How Much Do You Know About Crime and Organized Crime?   201

How Much Do You Know About Poverty in Canada?   241

How Much Do You Know About Global Wealth and Poverty?   273

How Much Do You Know About Racism in Canada?   305

How Much Do You Know About Body Image and Gender?   337

How Much Do You Know About Aging?   373

How Much Do You Know About the Economy and the World of Work?   403

How Much Do You Know About Political Issues and State Institutions?   439

How Much Do You Know About the Changing Family in Canada?   471

How Much Do You Know About Education in Canada?   511

How Much Do You Know About the Impact of Religion on Education in Canada?   543

How Much Do You Know About HIV/AIDS?   577

How Much Do You Know About Immigration to Canada?   607

How Much Do You Know About Collective Behaviour, Social Change, and Environmental Issues?   641

CRITICAL THINKING

Assisting Suicide   4

The Dene Yati Project—Language Brings Families Together   76

Child Abuse Then and Now   108

The Ethics of Legislating Against Panhandling   146

Let's Make a Deal: Bargaining for Justice   230

Solving the Poverty Problem   264

Human Rights Legislation in Action   316

Will There Be a Generational War Between the Old and Young?   390

Reproductive Technology and the Future of the Family: A Feminist Critique   490

The Home-Schooling Option: Can Parents Replace Teachers?   528

A Legal Challenge to Religious Holidays in Schools   548

The Legal Response to Civil Disobedience at Clayoquot Sound   644

SOCIOLOGY AND THE MEDIA

Cultural Confusion: Advertising—The Global Marketing Hall of Shame   86

Public Awareness of Child Abuse   120

The Homeless and the Holidays   152

Dilbert and the Bureaucracy   190

"If It Bleeds, It Leads": Fear of Crime and the Media   224

Racism in the Media   310

"You've Come a Long Way, Baby"   356

The Media and Separatism   448

The Simpsons: Middle-Class Family Life   478

AIDS in the News   580

SOCIOLOGY AND THE LAW

Does the Law Require Us to Help?   38

The Case of "Normal Accidents"   178

The Rich Get Richer and the Poor Get Prison   258

Obscenity and Women's Equality   342

Labour Unions and the Law   424

Quebec and Constitutional Reform   460

AIDS and Public Health   584

Immigration and the Law in Canada   614

SOCIOLOGY IN GLOBAL PERSPECTIVE

A Look at International Trends in Suicide   10

The Grameen Bank   42

Hostility Toward Immigrants   94

Child Abuse in Asia   124

Homelessness in Japan and France   158

The Japanese Corporation   192

Street Youths, *Bosozoku,* and *Yakuza* in Japan   210

Poverty in Brazil: The Effects on Women and Children   262

Consumption and Global Poverty   276

Wealth and Poverty in Russia   282

Worldwide Racial and Ethnic Conflicts in the Twenty-First Century   320

Women and Human Rights: Female Genital Mutilation   346

Aging in Russia   394

Women and Labour Activism   428

Nationalism Around the World   464

Family Life in Japan   484

Women's Literacy in Developing Nations   532

The AIDS Epidemic in Africa   596

Immigration Policies of Canada and Other Countries   620

Environmental Hazards as a Global Concern   654

PREFACE

Welcome to the second Canadian edition of *Sociology In Our Times*! A sense of excitement is emerging in Canada as we enter a new century. Unlike ever before, people are interested in the workings not only of their own society but also of the larger world. We are coming to understand how events in other countries directly affect life in Canada. We wrote *Sociology In Our Times* to capture this excitement and to help students understand how sociological theory and research can be applied to everyday life and to the pressing social issues we face in a rapidly changing world.

In writing the second edition of *Sociology In Our Times*, we were aware that three questions are paramount in people's minds about a sociology textbook: Is this book interesting and relevant to students' lives? Is the book well organized and easy to understand? Does it show how sociological theory and research can be applied to everyday life and to the pressing social issues we face in our diverse society and rapidly changing world?

Sociology In Our Times is designed to be a cutting-edge book that highlights the relevance of sociology in at least two ways: (1) by including a diversity of classical and contemporary theory, interesting and relevant research, and lived experiences that accurately mirror the diversity in society itself; and (2) by showing students that sociology involves important questions and issues that they confront both personally and vicariously (for example, through the media).

This text speaks to a wide variety of students and captures their interests by taking into account their concerns and perspectives. The research used in this text includes the best work of classical and established contemporary sociologists, and it weaves an inclusive treatment of all people into the examination of sociology in all chapters. Although a number of introductory sociology texts give the appearance of inclusion, most existing texts were initially written with class, race, and gender neatly compartmentalized into their "appropriate" chapters and perhaps an occasional "diversity" box. Not only does that approach marginalize an increasing proportion of the students in introductory sociology classes—as well as in the Canadian population—but it also leads many students to view race, class, and gender as nothing more than variables in sociological research (e.g., statistics on welfare, crime, and homelessness). That approach downplays the significance of the interlocking nature of class, race, and gender in all topics examined by sociologists.

We encourage you to read our text and judge the writing style for yourself. We have sought to make the research accessible and engaging for both students and instructors. Readers will find that concepts and theories are presented in a straightforward and understandable way, and they will also find a wealth of concrete examples and lived experiences woven throughout each chapter. For students, this serves to clarify both the relevance and the importance of sociological theory and research.

ORGANIZATION OF THIS TEXT

Sociology In Our Times is divided into twenty chapters and five parts. In Part 1, "Studying Society," Chapter 1, "The Sociological Perspective," introduces students to the sociological imagination and traces the development of sociological thinking. The chapter sets forth the major theoretical perspectives used by sociologists in analyzing compelling social issues such as suicide. Chapter 2, "Sociological Research Methods," provides a thorough description of both quantitative and qualitative methods. Research on altruism is used to practically demonstrate to students how sociologists do research using a range of diverse methodologies.

Part 2 "The Nature of Social Life" focuses on core sociological concepts. In Chapter 3, "Culture" is spotlighted as either a stabilizing force or a force that can generate discord, conflict, and even violence in societies. Cultural diversity is discussed as a contemporary cultural issue, and unique coverage is given to popular culture and leisure and to divergent perspectives on popular culture. Chapter 4, "Socialization," looks at positive and negative aspects of socialization and presents an innovative analysis of gender socialization. Chapter 5, "Social Structure and Everyday Life," examines social structure and social interaction in detail, using homelessness as a sustained example of the dynamic interplay of structure and interaction in society. Unique to this chapter are discussions of the sociology of emotions and of personal space as viewed through the lenses of race, class, gender, and age. Chapter 6, "Groups and Organizations," analyzes groups and organizations, including innovative forms of social organization and ways in which organizational structures may differentially affect people based on race, class, gender, and age. Chapter 7, "Crime and Deviance," examines diverse perspectives on deviance, crime, and the criminal justice system. Key issues are dramatized for students through an analysis of recent research on organized crime, gangs, and the experiences of biker gang members.

Part 3, "Social Differences and Social Inequality," looks at issues of class, race/ethnicity, and sex/gender. Chapter 8, "Social Stratification and Class," addresses systems of stratification and surveys social inequality in Canada. Using child poverty as a recurring theme, the chapter analyzes the causes and consequences of inequality and poverty. Chapter 9, "Global Stratification," extends the discussion and examines differences in wealth and poverty in rich and poor nations around the world. Explanations for these differences are discussed. Chapter 10, "Race and Ethnicity," focuses on the components of racial and ethnic conflict. A thorough analysis of prejudice, discrimination, and the experiences of racial and ethnic groups are presented, along with global, racial, and ethnic issues in the future. Chapter 11, "Sex and Gender," has a special emphasis on gender stratification in historical perspective. Links between gender socialization and contemporary gender inequality are described and illustrated by lived experiences and perspectives on body image. Chapter 12, "Aging," provides a cutting-edge analysis of aging, including theoretical perspectives and inequalities experienced by people across the life course.

Part 4, "Social Institutions" focuses on the importance of social institutions and shows how problems in one area have a significant effect on others. Chapter 13, "Economy and Work," examines global economic systems, the social organization of work in Canada, unemployment, and worker resistance and activism. The chapter concludes with a discussion of the global economy in the future. Chapter 14, "Politics and Government," discusses the intertwining nature of politics and government. Political systems are examined in global perspective, and politics and government in Canada are analyzed with attention to governmental bureaucracy. The issues of race, gender, class, and sexual orientation are recurring themes in the chapter. Chapter 15, "Families and Intimate Relationships," focuses on the diversity found in Canadian families today. Chapter 16, "Education," investigates the history of education in Canada and contrasts it with systems of education in other countries. In the process, the chapter highlights issues of race, class, and gender inequalities in education in Canada. Chapter 17, "Religion," examines religion in global perspective, including a survey of world religions and how religious beliefs affect other aspects of social life. Current trends in religion in Canada are also explored, including various sociological explanations of how and why religion is a means by which people seek purpose and meaning in everyday life. Chapter 18, "Health, Health

Care, and Disability," analyzes these issues both in global perspective and in Canada.

Part 5 shifts students' focus to "Social Dynamics and Social Change." Chapter 19, "Population and Urbanization," looks at demography, global population change, and the process and consequences of urbanization. Chapter 20, "Collective Behaviour and Social Change," uses environmental activism as a sustained example to help students grasp the importance of collective behaviour and social movements in producing social change. The concluding section takes a final look at the physical environment, population, technology, social institutions, and change in the future.

UNIQUE FEATURES

The following special features are specifically designed to reflect the themes of relevance and diversity in *Sociology In Our Times*, as well as to support student learning.

Interesting and Engaging Lived Experiences Throughout Chapters

Authentic first-person accounts are used as opening vignettes and throughout each chapter to create interest and give concrete meaning to the topics being discussed. Lived experiences including racism, child abuse, environmental activism, eating disorders, altruism, disability, and ageism provide opportunities for students to examine social life beyond their own experiences and to examine class, ethnicity, gender, and age from diverse perspectives. An unusually wide range of diverse experiences—both positive and negative—is systematically incorporated to expose students to a multiplicity of viewpoints. These lived experiences were selected for their ability to speak to students, to assist them in learning concepts and theories, and to determine how they can be applied to other situations.

Focus on the Relationship Between Sociology and Everyday Life

Each chapter has a brief quiz that relates the sociological perspective to the pressing social issues presented in the opening vignette. (Answers are provided on the subsequent page.) Do official statistics accurately reflect crime rates in Canada? Does increasing cultural diversity lead to an increasing incidence of hate crimes and racism? Do welfare benefits provide enough income for recipients to live comfortably? Topics such as these will pique the interest of students.

Applying the Sociological Imagination to Contemporary Issues and the Law

Based on the latest legal research, "Sociology and the Law" boxes encourage students to think critically about the many ties between the law and sociology, and provide a springboard for discussion. Topics include child abuse, assisted suicide, obscenity and women's equality, Quebec and the Constitution, and AIDS and public health.

Using the Media to Encourage Critical Thinking

Like most people in our society, students get much of their information about the social world from the media. A significant benefit of a sociology course is the encouragement to think critically about such information. Focusing on various types of media depictions—including television news, daytime talk shows, television commercials and magazine advertisements, cartoons, movies, and mainstream and alternative presses—"Sociology and Media" boxes provide an overview of sociological topics as seen through the "eye" of the media. Topics range from "Racism in the Media" and an analysis of messages that affect women's body image to "The Electronic Church and the Internet" and news coverage of diverse topics such as advertising and people living with AIDS.

Emphasis on the Importance of a Global Perspective

In our interconnected world, the sociological imagination must extend beyond national borders. The global implications of all topics are examined throughout each chapter and in "Sociology in Global Perspective" boxes. Topics include the Grameen Bank, child abuse in Asia, poverty in Brazil, organized crime in Japan, and wealth, poverty, and aging in Russia.

Looking Ahead to Sociology in the Future

In addition to highlighting the contemporary relevance of sociology, students are encouraged to consider the sociological perspective as it might be in the future. The concluding section of Chapters 3 through 20 looks into the future and suggests how our social lives may look in the years to come. Environmental issues, homelessness, technology, population, deviance and crime, and the economy and work are among the topics discussed.

IN-TEXT LEARNING AIDS

Sociology In Our Times includes a number of pedagogical aids to promote students' mastery of sociological concepts and terminology.

- *Chapter Outlines.* A concise outline at the beginning of each chapter gives students an overview of major topics and a convenient aid for review.

- *Questions and Issues.* After the opening lived experience in each chapter, a series of introductory questions invites students to think about the major topics discussed in the chapter.

- *Integrated Running Glossary.* Major concepts and key terms are concisely defined and highlighted in bold print within the text flow to avoid disrupting students' reading. These concepts and terms are also listed at the end of the chapters and in the glossary at the back of the book.

- *End-of-Chapter Study Aids.* The Chapter Review provides a concise summary of key points and theoretical perspectives, along with a list of Key Terms. Questions for Critical Thinking encourage students to assess their knowledge of the chapter and apply insights they have gained to other issues. The Suggested Readings describe recent publications related to the chapter. This list also is a good source for book review suggestions.

NEW CHAPTERS AND FEATURES

- The second Canadian edition of *Sociology In Our Times* has expanded from seventeen to twenty chapters. "Global Stratification" (Chapter 9) is an entirely new chapter, covering issues of development and poverty. "Health, Health Care, and Disability" (Chapter 18) is also a new chapter, exploring issues surrounding the sociology of health and health care. To provide students with more comprehensive coverage of each topic, "Aging" (Chapter 12), "Education" (Chapter 16), and "Religion" (Chapter 17) have been separated into their own chapters.

- In addition to the new chapters, we have added over 400 new references that address not only the most current census data, but also new and relevant Canadian research.

- Also new and unique to this text is the acknowledgement of feminist theory as a distinct theoretical perspective. Unlike other texts, the discussion of feminist theory and methodology is not compartmentalized into only gender or family chapters, but is fully integrated throughout the text.

New "Sociology and Technology" and "Critical Thinking" Boxes

- *Sociology and Technology.* As computers become an increasingly important part of our everyday lives, they change how we communicate, how we learn, and how we conceive of ourselves in relationship to others. Topics include seniors in cyberspace, the Internet and social stratification, technology in the classroom, technology and crime, and the Internet and organizations.

- *Critical Thinking.* From human rights legislation to reproductive technology to home schooling, the Critical Thinking boxes encourage students to use their sociological knowledge to grapple with some of today's most hotly contested issues.

Internet Exercises and Net Links

Internet Exercises and Net Links, found at the end of every chapter, encourage students to explore the Internet, providing assignments that facilitate the discovery of Web sites that are directly relevant to chapter topics. Included in the Net Links are links to research articles found on the Internet. These articles are indicated with an icon and can be used for further study or in-class discussion.

What Else Is New in the Second Edition?

Chapter 1 provides a new and interesting approach to teaching sociological theory using suicide as an example of a problem that sociologists would examine. The new opening narrative introduces the topic of suicide to create interest and challenge the student to apply each of the theoretical perspectives to the social problem of suicide.

In an effort to introduce students to some of the more positive aspects of human social interaction, the new lived experience in **Chapter 2** deals with altruistic behaviour. This research methods chapter uses a unique approach to engage students in the study of methodology. Each of the different research methods are applied in case studies of research on altruism.

In **Chapter 3**, the new opening lived experience shows the diversity of Canadian culture and emphasizes how cultural differences may lead to misunderstanding. This chapter includes new information on Aboriginal culture and language, highlighting the challenges of attaining the goal of a multicultural society. A new Sociology and Technology box deals with the issue of cyberculture on the Internet, and the new Sociology and the Media box provides some fun examples of cultural misunderstanding.

Chapter 4 has a new opening lived experience that introduces the theme of how important socialization is for the well-being of children. It

gives an example of a person who was able to overcome childhood abuse.

The link in **Chapter 5** between social structure and interaction and the social problem of homelessness, which was so popular in the first edition, has been updated and expanded. A new figure demonstrating role expectations, role performance, role conflict, and role strain—featuring women students—helps students grasp these abstract concepts. A new Critical Thinking box presents many questions about how to deal with homeless people on the street—panhandlers and our young homeless, the squeegee kids.

In **Chapter 6**, a new chapter theme examines ways in which the bureaucratic form of organizations can lead to rigidity, ineffectiveness, and even disasters such as the Challenger explosion.

Chapter 7 includes new material on restorative justice and white collar crime, as well as a new Sociology and Technology box on the impact of new technology on crime and crime control.

Chapter 8 has been substantially rewritten and now focuses primarily on social stratification in Canada. It contains the most current data on poverty in Canada. The new Critical Thinking box includes a number of recommendations to deal with the problem of poverty, and challenges students to think of alternative strategies.

Chapter 9 is an exciting new chapter that examines wealth and poverty in global perspective, particularly through the eyes of the world's poor. The chapter presents the major theories of development and describes the ways in which the actions of the wealthiest countries affect the lives of people in the poorest counties. New boxes include a Critical Thinking box on consumption and world poverty, a Sociology in Global Perspective box on wealth and poverty in Russia, and a Sociology and Technology box that looks at the digital Third World. This new chapter includes tables and figures showing disparities in wealth, income, and life chances around the globe.

In **Chapter 10**, new data on race and ethnicity are set forth in this innovative chapter, which examines the components of racial and ethnic conflict. Personal narratives from individuals who have been the victims of racism are designed to have an impact on students who have difficulty understanding concepts such as prejudice, discrimination, and racism in the abstract.

Chapter 11 has a new opening lived experience that gains students' interest in the gender-related issue of body consciousness and eating dis-orders. The figures, tables, and pictures have been updated throughout. Also included is additional current feminist research in the area of gender-based inequality in Canada.

Chapter 12 now focuses exclusively on aging and issues associated with age. It features a new opening lived experience that highlights the posi-tive aspects of aging and expanded coverage of age-based problems across the life course, including those experienced by young children and adolescents.

Chapter 13 includes updated statistics and research on the Canadian economy and a new Sociology and Technology box on Internet com-merce.

Chapter 14 includes new data on women in politics around the world.

Chapter 15 has a new opening lived experi-ence that calls attention to the changing nature of families and the new demand and challenges of parenting in families of divorce. All figures and tables have been updated with the latest available information on such topics as family structure, single parenting, and stepfamilies. Feminist theory has been expanded and emphasized as a central theoretical perspective in the study of sociology of the family. The new Critical Thinking box pro-vides a feminist critique of some of the new repro-ductive technologies available to families today.

All-new **Chapter 16,** on education, contains a new opening lived experience that sets the stage for examining the importance of education in a person's life. The chapter highlights ways in which race, class, and gender differentially affect people's access to education and its outcomes. A new global section compares education in a high-income country (Japan) with that of a low-income country (Bosnia). Updated information is provided on international math and science scores, as well as on global illiteracy rates. The chapter also includes a new Critical Thinking box on home schooling and a Sociology and Technology box on the technology revolution in Canadian classrooms.

Chapter 17, on religion, is another new chapter that examines the important issue of the role of religion in educational institutions. It also contrasts the sociology of religion with theological perspectives on religion. It contains a balanced discussion on the world's religions, including how they originated, what their central teachings are, and what forms of social conflict have been found

in each. Also included is an expanded discussion of the role of women in the church, the ministry, and organized mainstream religion. A new Sociology and Technology box looks at the elec-tronic church and the Internet.

Chapter 18 is an all-new chapter on health, healthcare, and disability. The opening lived experience describes a young woman's reaction to discovering she was HIV positive and challenges many of the stereotypes concerning HIV/AIDS. This chapter provides extensive coverage on the sociology of health and medicine, including the social construction of illness and the process of medicalization, and the effects of social factors such as age, sex, and social class on health. Health care in Canada and universal health care is com-pared and contrasted with health care in the United States. *Sociology In Our Times* is the only text to incorporate a thorough discussion of health issues of Aboriginal people in Canada as well as Aboriginal healing methods. Likewise, it is the only text with a comprehensive discussion of disability.

Chapter 19 examines demography and urban life. Global population projections have been updated and a population pyramid is included that illustrates the impact of war and other social disas-ters on the age and sex structure of the Russian population. The chapter includes a discussion of how women experience city life differently from men, and it cites the latest studies on race, class, and gender in city and suburban living.

The new chapter focus question for **Chapter 20** asks students to think of reasons why collective behaviour and social movements are important for making people aware of environmental issues. A new Critical Thinking box addresses the issue of civil disobedience at Clayoquot Sound and chal-lenges students to think about how far they would go to support a social cause they valued. In addi-tion, the new Sociology and Technology box informs students of a common new form of rumour in today's culture: urban legends. At the end of the chapter, an expanded discussion is pro-vided on what the future may be like, given var-ious scenarios on changes in the physical environment, population, technology, and social institutions.

FULLY INTEGRATED SUPPORT PACKAGE FOR INSTRUCTORS AND STUDENTS

Ancillary materials that enhance teaching and learning are an important feature of a textbook. The supplements offered with *Sociology In Our Times*, Second Canadian Edition, ensure that the themes of diversity, inclusiveness, and contemporary issues are consistent with the text. These pieces work together as an effective and integrated teaching package.

Instructor's Resource Manual

The Instructor's Resource Manual provides lecture outlines, chapter summaries, and teaching tips, as well as a list of further print and video resources. In addition, guest speaker suggestions, student learning objectives, student projects, and essay questions are included. Instructors wishing to insert their own examples and references can download chapter outlines from our Web site or they may request them from Nelson Thomson Learning in ASCII format.

Test Bank

A completely revised Test Bank is available with over 2000 multiple-choice and true–false items. Each question is categorized as testing conceptual understanding, concept application, or factual knowledge, and a page reference is provided for each answer. The Test Bank is available in both print and Windows formats to facilitate the creation of your own tests.

Both the Instructor's Resource Manual and the Test Bank for the second edition were written by Keith Hampson and James Gillette of Ryerson Polytechnic University.

PowerPoint Presentation Software

PowerPoint presentation software is available to assist instructors in managing lectures. Nelson Thomson Learning has reproduced chapter objectives, key definitions, and a brief overview of the important concepts in a PowerPoint format. Instructors will have the ability to add, delete, or modify the slides according to their individual requirements.

New SocLINK CD-ROM Instructor's Presentation Tool

An exceptional resource, SocLINK contains a wide assortment of photos, figures, maps, audio and video clips, as well as easy access to the Internet. SocLINK is an ideal in-class instruction tool that allows professors to combine customized multimedia and live video with their lectures.

New Thematic Videos

Nelson Thomson Learning offers two brand-new videotapes featuring 180 minutes of excerpts compiled from the CTV Television Network archives that correspond to each chapter of the book. The segments were chosen to amplify the concepts of each chapter and provide further examples of the sociology of everyday life. An accompanying discussion guide offers a synopsis of each segment, suggestions for introducing the videos, and discussion questions.

Sociology on the Web http://sociology.nelson.com

Sociology In Our Times features a companion Web site designed for both students and instructors. Features of the Web site include online material linked directly to the text, plus a current events page, study resources, and a career centre. Instructors' resources include lecture outlines, downloadable overheads, and transparencies.

Study Guide

Created by Diane Symbaluk (of Grant MacEwan Community College), the Study Guide to accompany *Sociology In Our Times*, Second Canadian Edition, gives students further opportunity to think sociologically. Each chapter includes a chapter summary, a list of key terms and key people, a list of learning objectives, and multiple-choice and true–false questions.

ACKNOWLEDGMENTS

This edition of *Sociology In Our Times* would not have been possible without the insightful critiques of these colleagues, who have reviewed some or all of this book. Our profound thanks to each reviewer for engaging in this time-consuming process:

> Jim Barak, University of Saskatchewan
> Terry L. Hill, Lakehead University
> Jacob Peters, University of Winnipeg
> John Peters, Wilfrid Laurier University
> Alice Propper, York University
> Brian Puk, University of Saskatchewan
> Erin Steuter, Mount Allison University

We would like to express our appreciation to the many individuals at Nelson Thomson Learning involved in the development and production of the second edition of *Sociology In Our Times*. Among them, Jessica Mosher and Evan Turner for their motivation, guidance, and encouragement through the writing stage of the project. Joanna Cotton and Toni Chahley for seeing us through to completion with renewed energy and enthusiasm. Tracy Bordian for rising to the challenge of an August publication date, and putting it all together in her usual professional manner. Michael Young for ensuring that this project ran smoothly despite some changes along the way. Once again, your creativity, dedication, long hours, and hard work has made this an experience we have enjoyed and a final product that we are extremely pleased with. Thank you also to our research assistant Heather Milne for providing the most current research in a form that students can interpret.

Jane Lothian Murray would like to thank her colleagues at the University of Winnipeg, Doug Skoog, Gillian Balfour, Sandra Kirby, Lesley Murphy, Michael Weinrath, and Harry Rosenbaum for their encouragement, advice, and resources whenever needed. Rick Linden would like to thank G.N. Ramu and Rod Kueneman for their help with some of the new reference material required for this edition. Finally, we would once again like to thank our families for tolerating us when we got a little "cranky" from meeting deadlines and for inspiring us to finish so we can spend more time with them.

We invite your comments and suggestions. Send them to us care of:

> Nelson Thomson Learning
> 1120 Birchmount Rd.
> Scarborough, Ontario
> M1K 5G4

We also welcome e-mail messages at:
> jane.murray@uwinnipeg.ca
> rlinden@cc.umanitoba.ca

Jane Lothian Murray　　　　*Rick Linden*
University of Winnipeg　　　University of Manitoba

Putting Social Life into Perspective
Why Study Sociology?
The Sociological Imagination
The Importance of a Global Sociological Imagination

The Development of Sociological Thinking
Early Thinkers: A Concern
with Social Order and Stability
Differing Views on the Status
Quo: Stability versus Change
The Development of Sociology in
North America

Contemporary Theoretical Perspectives
Functionalist Perspectives
Conflict Perspectives
Feminist Perspectives
Interactionist Perspectives

"There is an impossible situation. There is no way it can be worked out. There is no reason I can see to drain & strain my children's and my friends' strength & lives, in order to maintain for me a 'life' … My 'life' revolves around a worn-out undependable body that is only a burden to me & others." (King, 1997:387)

Later—"Have made up my mind. God, please let this work. 6:45 pm—I took the toast & glass of water an hour ago … Can you believe that I spent a long time searching for the damn tea kettle to get boiling water into which to dissolve the pills? Couldn't find it. Ever resourceful, I got hot water from the coffee maker by not putting in coffee.

"I spent an hour cracking open those damn capsules with a knife, to get the powder. I have probably lost 1/3 of the stuff.

"Clea the cat is racing around. I guess she knows something is going on." (King, 1997:388)

The above excerpts are from the diary of Margaret Laurence, one of Canada's greatest writers, whose best known works include *The Stone Angel* and *The Diviners*. At the age of sixty-one and suffering from terminal cancer, Laurence took her own life. Biographer James King continues the story:

"There is a hiatus in the journal and then she made this final entry while waiting for death to arrive: 'Please, my near & dear ones, forgive me & understand. I hope this potion works. My spirit is already in another country, & my body has become a damn nuisance. I have been so fortunate.'" (King, 1997:388)

Why do people commit suicide? Can sociological research help us understand the seemingly individualistic act of taking one's own life? Do individuals (at least under some circumstances) have a right to end their own lives? Given who we are, what we know, and what we believe, our individual answers to these questions may vary. Along with others posed in this book, these questions may produce strong responses. In this chapter, suicide is used as an example of a social problem that sociologists study.

THE SOCIOLOGICAL PERSPECTIVE

People in various occupations may have different perspectives on suicide. A journalist may wonder whether a suicide is "newsworthy." Is either the deceased or the family well known? Did the suicide occur at an unusual time or location? A physician might assess the nature and extent of the physical injuries that caused death to occur. A psychiatrist might evaluate the mental state of the deceased prior to the suicide. A minister or a social worker might consider the appropriate counselling for the family. Law enforcement officers might want to determine if the death was in fact a suicide or whether charges should be brought against someone for causing or assisting in the death. As discussed in Box 1.1, assisted suicide is illegal in Canada.

What, then, is the sociologist's perspective on the problem of suicide? The sociological perspective is a point of view that helps us understand human behaviour in the larger social context in which it occurs. Accordingly, sociologists would focus on the social environment in which suicide occurs, seeking explanations by analyzing why and under what circumstances that behaviour takes place. Using existing sociological theories and methods of inquiry, sociologists would sort out probable answers from unlikely ones in their search for recurring patterns of social behaviour (see Wilson and Selvin, 1980).

Not all sociologists would apply the same theory or methods to study the issue of suicide. Some would be most interested in the demographic profiles of persons who commit suicide: their age, marital status, occupation, and any of hundreds of other statistical categories. Others might seek to document the factors that contribute to societal breakdown and result in high incidences of suicide. Sociologists constantly debate issues such as suicide, asking about its causes and effects. Both the sociological study and the related debate help society articulate and deal with a multitude of such problems.

QUESTIONS AND ISSUES

CHAPTER FOCUS QUESTION: Why is it important to use your sociological imagination when studying such issues as suicide?

How do you form a sociological perspective on issues such as suicide?

Why were early thinkers concerned with social order and stability?

Why were later social thinkers concerned with change?

What are the assumptions behind each of the contemporary theoretical perspectives?

BOX 1.1 CRITICAL THINKING

ASSISTING SUICIDE

In a recent Gallup poll, over 75 percent of people surveyed agreed with the statement "When a person has an incurable disease that causes great suffering, competent doctors should be allowed to end the patient's life through mercy killing" (C. Wood, 1994a). Although prohibited by law from doing so, many physicians are participating in physician-assisted suicides (Searles, 1995).

Under common law, suicide was a crime. It was also an offence to "aid and abet" suicide—to counsel or to help someone to commit suicide. Thus, the government was "reimbursed" for its loss of the individual, through both financial and other penalties imposed on the perpetrator and any "accomplices."

In Canada, suicide is no longer a crime. However, counselling or assisting suicide remains a criminal act in Canada, punishable by a maximum of fourteen years' imprisonment.

People can now be kept alive by machines long after there is any realistic expectation that they will ever again function independently. In such cases, friends and relatives frequently have sought legal authorization to allow the patient to die "in peace and dignity." Also,

Sue Rodriguez, who battled all the way to the Supreme Court to have physician-assisted suicide decriminalized.

many individuals have chosen to have a *living will*, which is written in advance and which directs that they not be kept alive past the point when life—without the support of medical tech-

PUTTING SOCIAL LIFE INTO PERSPECTIVE

Sociology **is the systematic study of human society and social interaction.** It is a *systematic* study because sociologists apply both theoretical perspectives and research methods (or orderly approaches) to examinations of social behaviour. Sociologists study human societies and their social interactions in order to develop theories of how human behaviour is shaped by group life and how, in turn, group life is affected by individuals.

Why Study Sociology?

Sociology helps us gain a better understanding of ourselves and our social world. It enables us to see how behaviour is largely shaped by the groups to which we belong and the society in which we live.

Most of us take our social world for granted and view our lives in very personal terms. Because of our culture's emphasis on individualism, we often do not consider the complex connections between our own lives and the larger, recurring patterns of the society and world in which we live. Sociology helps us look beyond our personal experiences and gain insights into society and the larger world order. A *society* **is a large social grouping that**

BOX 1.1

CONTINUED

nology—is no longer possible. To some people, a living will is still a form of suicide: the individual is directing that life end before the last point at which it can be maintained. In Canada, a person who turns off the life-sustaining treatment under the authority of a living will is *not* committing an offence.

Still to be resolved, however, is the issue of assisting people who have a terminal illness and who want to end their own (and perhaps their family's or friends') agony over an apparently irreversible physical deterioration—and the pain that may accompany it. Should it be up to the courts or the legislatures to decide this issue? This question was pursued all the way to the Supreme Court of Canada by Sue Rodriguez, a 42-year-old woman suffering from Lou Gehrig's disease (a degenerative, fatal disease in which the muscles weaken until eating and breathing are no longer possible). Rodriguez requested the legal right to have the assistance of a physician in ending her life. She was told that it is illegal for anyone to assist in

a suicide, even if the person wanting to die is too disabled to commit suicide on her or his own. In 1993, in a narrow decision, the Supreme Court declined Rodriguez's challenge and upheld the law prohibiting assisted suicide.

Does a person have a right to die if he or she is physically healthy? Does society have the right to say that such a person does not have that right? If a person has the right to terminate her or his own life, should that person be able to get advice and assistance regarding that decision—just as the person does for any other legal action? If the answer is yes, then does a person have the right to at least request (and does someone else have the right to provide) assistance in committing suicide? Should a perfectly healthy (in a physical sense) person have that right? These are the types of questions sociologists, lawyers, legislatures, courts, and the general public must continue to try to answer. What do you think?

Sources: Based on Humphrey, 1993; Lester and Tallmer, 1993; Health Canada, 1994; and Searles, 1995.

shares the same geographical territory and is subject to the same political authority and dominant cultural expectations, such as Canada, the United States, or Mexico. Examining the world order helps us understand that each of us is affected by *global interdependence*—a relationship in which the lives of all people are closely intertwined and any one nation's problems are part of a larger global problem.

Individuals can make use of sociology on a more personal level. Sociology enables us to move beyond established ways of thinking, thus allowing us to gain new insights into ourselves and to develop a greater awareness of the connection between our own "world" and that of other people.

According to sociologist Peter Berger (1963:23), sociological inquiry helps us see that "things are not what they seem." Sociology provides new ways of approaching problems and making decisions in everyday life. Sociology promotes understanding and tolerance by enabling each of us to look beyond our personal experiences. (See Figure 1.1.)

SOCIOLOGY AND COMMON SENSE   Many of us rely on intuition or common sense gained from personal experience to help us understand our daily lives and other people's behaviour. **Commonsense knowledge guides ordinary conduct in everyday life.** We often rely on common sense—or "what

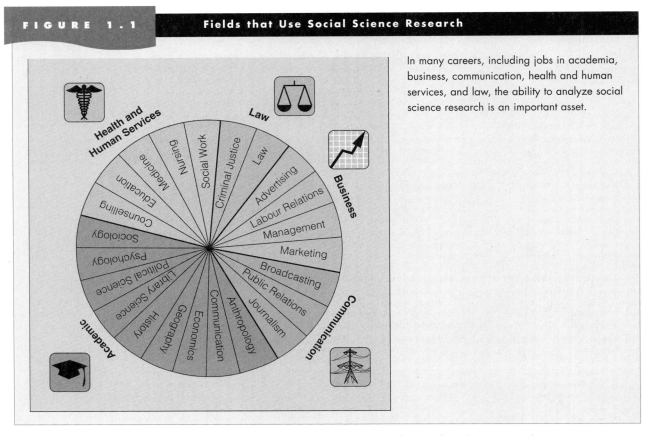

In many careers, including jobs in academia, business, communication, health and human services, and law, the ability to analyze social science research is an important asset.

Based on Katzer, Jeffrey, Kenneth A. Cook, and Wayne W. Crouch, *Evaluating Information: A Guide for Users of Social Science Research.* New York, N.Y.: McGraw-Hill. Reprinted with permission.

everybody knows"—to answer key questions about behaviour: Why do people behave the way they do? Who makes the rules? Why do some people break rules and why do others follow them?

Many commonsense notions actually are myths. A *myth* is a popular but false notion that may be used, either intentionally or unintentionally, to perpetuate certain beliefs or "theories" even in the light of conclusive evidence to the contrary. Before reading on, take the quiz in Box 1.2, which includes a number of commonsense notions about suicide.

The media are the source of much of our commonsense knowledge. Television talk show hosts and news anchors, journalists for magazines and newspapers, and authors of the many books in print all provide us with information about family life, sexual assault, homelessness, AIDS, violence, and thousands of related sociological topics. With all of this information readily available, why should we study sociology? What can we learn that is better than relying on common sense or information from an alleged expert on a talk show?

The answer is that sociologists strive to use scientific standards, not popular myths or hearsay, in studying society and social interaction. They use systematic research techniques and are accountable to the scientific community for their methods and the presentation of their findings. While some sociologists argue that sociology must be completely *objective*—**free from distorting subjective (personal or emotional) bias**—others do not think that total objectivity is an attainable or desirable goal when studying human behaviour. This issue will be discussed in Chapter 2 ("Sociological Research Methods").

The "pop" sociology of the mass media is quite different from the intellectual and academic discipline of sociology. The mass media tend to look at singular events in isolation—as individual and often bizarre occurrences. It is impossible, however, to study human behaviour in one hour on television or by reading an article in a magazine; much more is involved in studying society and social interaction. Sociologists attempt to discover patterns or commonalities in human behaviour.

BOX 1.2 SOCIOLOGY AND EVERYDAY LIFE

HOW MUCH DO YOU KNOW ABOUT SUICIDE?

TRUE	FALSE	
T	F	1. For people thinking of suicide, it is difficult, if not impossible, to see the bright side of life.
T	F	2. People who talk about suicide don't do it.
T	F	3. Once people contemplate or attempt suicide, they must be considered suicidal for the rest of their lives.
T	F	4. In Canada, suicide occurs an average of one every two hours.
T	F	5. Accidents and injuries sustained by teenagers and young adults may indicate suicidal inclinations.
T	F	6. Alcohol and drugs are outlets for anger and thus reduce the risk of suicide.
T	F	7. Older men have higher rates of both attempted and completed suicide than older women.
T	F	8. Children don't know enough to be able to intentionally kill themselves.
T	F	9. Suicide rates for Aboriginals are the highest in Canada.
T	F	10. Suicidal people are fully intent on dying.

Answers on page 8.

For example, when they study suicide, they look for patterns of behaviour even though *individuals* usually commit suicide and other *individuals* suffer as a result of these actions.

Consequently, sociologists seek out the multiple causes and effects of suicide or other social issues. They analyze the impact of the problem not only from the standpoint of suicide victims but also from the standpoint of the effects of such behaviour on all people.

The Sociological Imagination

Sociologist C. Wright Mills (1959b) described sociological reasoning as the *sociological imagination*—the ability to see the relationship between individual experiences and the larger society. This awareness enables us to understand the link between our personal experiences and the social contexts in which they occur. The sociological imagination helps us distinguish between personal troubles and social (or public) issues. *Personal troubles* are private problems of individuals and the networks of people with whom they associate regularly. As a result, those problems must be solved by individuals within their immediate social settings. For example, one person being unemployed may be a personal trouble. *Public issues* are matters beyond an individual's own control that are caused by

problems at the societal level. Widespread unemployment as a result of economic changes such as plant closings is an example of a public issue. The sociological imagination helps us place seemingly personal troubles, such as contemplating suicide or losing one's job, into a larger social context, where we can distinguish whether and how personal troubles may be related to public issues.

SUICIDE AS A PERSONAL TROUBLE Many of our individual experiences may be largely beyond our own control. They are determined by society as a whole—by its historical development and its organization. In everyday life, we do not define personal experiences in these terms. If a person commits suicide, many people consider it the result of the person's personal problems. Historical explanations of suicide focused on suicide as personal trouble, viewing the act as sinful or criminal (Evans and Farberow, 1988). Suicide was believed to be part of an evolutionary process whereby "weak-brained individuals were sorted by insanity and voluntary death" (Morselli, 1975/1881).

In the case of Margaret Laurence, her suicide note explained that her terminal illness had made life intolerable. In saying this, she expressed a typically individualistic view—that her problem was purely personal and that there was nothing she could do about it.

BOX 1.2

ANSWERS TO THE SOCIOLOGY QUIZ ON SUICIDE

1. **True.** To people thinking of suicide, an acknowledgment that there is a bright side only confirms and conveys the message that they have failed; otherwise, they, too, could have a bright side of life. Being told that "things will look better tomorrow" may cause a depressed person to feel more isolated and alone.

2. **False.** Some people who talk about suicide do kill themselves. Warning signals of possible suicide attempts include talk of suicide, the desire not to exist anymore, despair, and hopelessness.

3. **False.** Most people think of suicide for only a limited amount of time. When the crisis is over and the problems leading to suicidal thoughts are resolved, people usually cease to think of suicide as an option. However, if in the future problems arise with which the individual cannot cope, suicide may once again be an option.

4. **True.** A suicide occurs an average of every two hours in Canada; however, the rate of suicide differs with respect to the sex, race/ethnicity, and age of the individual. For example, men kill themselves more than three times as often as do women.

5. **True.** Accidents and injuries may be signs that a person is on a course of self-destruction. One study concluded that the incidence of suicide was twelve times higher among adolescents and young adults who previously had been hospitalized because of an injury.

6. **False.** Excessive use of alcohol or drugs may enhance a person's feelings of anger and frustration, making suicide a greater possibility. This risk appears to be especially high for men who abuse alcohol or drugs.

7. **True.** In Canada, as in other countries, suicide rates are highest among men over the age of 70. One theory of why this is true asserts that older women may have a more flexible and diverse coping style than older men.

8. **False.** Children do know how to intentionally hurt or kill themselves. They may learn the means and methods from television, movies, and other people. However, the Health Statistics division of Statistics Canada (the agency responsible for compiling suicide statistics) does not recognize suicides under the age of 10; they are classified as accidents, despite evidence that young children have taken their own lives.

9. **True.** The rate of suicide among Aboriginals in Canada for all age groups is 2 to 3 times higher than the rate among non-Aboriginal people. It is 5 to 6 times higher among Aboriginal youth than among non-Aboriginal youth.

10. **False.** Suicidal people often have an ambivalence about dying—they want to live and to die at the same time. They want to end the pain or problems they are experiencing, but they also wish that something or someone would remove the pain or problem so that life can continue.

Sources: Based on Levy and Deykin, 1989; Patros and Shamoo, 1989; Wickett, 1989; Leenaars, 1991; Health Canada, 1994; and Royal Commission on Aboriginal Peoples, 1995.

SUICIDE AS A PUBLIC ISSUE We can use the sociological imagination to look at the problem of suicide as a public issue—a societal problem. For example, we may use our sociological imagination to understand why suicide rates are so high in some Aboriginal communities in Canada.

Early sociologist Emile Durkheim refused to accept commonsense explanations of suicide, such as the notion that suicide is an isolated act that can be understood only by studying individual personalities or inherited tendencies. Rather he related suicide to the issue of cohesiveness (or lack of cohesiveness) in a society. In *Suicide* (1964b/1897), Durkheim documented his contention that a high suicide rate was symptomatic of large-scale social problems. In the process, he developed an approach that influences researchers to this day.

The Importance of a Global Sociological Imagination

Although existing sociological theory and research provide the foundation for sociological thinking,

Suicides of celebrities such as Kurt Cobain call our attention to significant social facts related to suicide rates in contemporary societies. Sociologists might ask questions such as why highly successful people would consider suicide.

we must reach beyond past studies that have focused primarily on North America to develop a more comprehensive global approach for the future. In the twenty-first century, we face important challenges in a rapidly changing nation and world. The world's most *developed nations* are **countries with highly industrialized economies, technologically advanced industrial, administrative, and service occupations, and relatively high levels of national and per capita (per person) income.** Examples include Australia, New Zealand, Japan, the European nations, Canada, and the United States. As compared with other countries of the world, people in the most developed nations typically have a high standard of living and a lower death rate due to good nutrition and advances in medical technology. As shown in Box 1.3, developed nations tend to have different patterns of suicide as people reach different stages in the life course.

In contrast, *developing nations* **are countries undergoing transformation from agrarian to industrial economies.** People living in these countries are more likely to work the land, and national income and per capita income remain relatively low. However, generalizations are difficult to make about developing nations because these nations vary widely in levels of economic development

and standards of living. Nations such as Mexico, Brazil, and South Korea are industrializing rapidly, but some countries in Africa and Asia remain much less developed and are among the poorest in the world. Suicide patterns in these countries vary widely from those in the most developed nations. For example, some social analysts suggest the recent increase in suicides among the Kaiowá Indians in Brazil can be linked to the loss of their land (which previously was used to grow crops to feed their families) to large, foreign-owned agribusinesses. With loss of land has come loss of culture because to the Kaiowá, land is more than a means of surviving; it is the support for a social life that is directly linked to their system of belief and knowledge (Schemo, 1996).

Throughout this text, we will examine social life in other countries—as well as in Canada—because the future of this country is deeply intertwined with the future of all nations of the world on economic, political, and humanitarian levels. We buy many goods and services that were produced in other nations, and sell much of what we produce to the people of other nations. Peace in other nations is important if we are to ensure peace within our own borders. Famine, unrest, and brutality in other regions of the world must be of concern to people in Canada. Global problems such as these contribute to the large influx of immigrants who arrive in this country annually. They bring with them a rich diversity of language, customs, religions, and previous life experiences. They also contribute to dramatic population changes that will have long-term effects on this country. Developing a better understanding of diversity and tolerance for people who are different from us is important for our personal, social, and economic well-being now and in the twenty-first century.

Whatever your race/ethnicity, class, sex, or age, are you able to include in your thinking the perspectives of people with quite dissimilar experiences and points of view? Before answering this question, a few definitions are in order. *Race* **is a term used by many people to specify groups of people distinguished by physical characteristics such as skin colour;** in fact, there are no "pure" racial types, and the concept of race is considered by most sociologists to be a myth. *Ethnicity* **refers to the cultural heritage or identity of a group and is based on factors such as language or country of origin.** *Class* **is the relative location of a person or group within a larger society, based on wealth, power, prestige, or other valued resources.** *Sex* **refers to the biological and anatomical differences between females**

BOX 1.3   SOCIOLOGY IN GLOBAL PERSPECTIVE

A LOOK AT INTERNATIONAL TRENDS IN SUICIDE

Researchers have difficulty making global comparisons regarding certain kinds of behaviour. Suicide is no exception. Frequently, suicide is discussed in Canada as if the patterns for this country are typical of all countries; however, this assumption generally is invalid.

In Canada, the two most discussed trends in suicide are the increasing suicide rate with age and the rising adolescent suicide rate among young men. How do these trends compare with other nations? Worldwide, there are three basic patterns in the variation of suicide rates:

1. an incline where the suicide rate increases regularly with age;

2. the two-peak model, where the suicide rate increases slightly in young adulthood and increases dramatically in old age;

3. one that peaks in middle age and has an inverted U-shaped curve.

Table 1 lists some countries that generally meet each of these criteria. Note that the trends for men and women are different within a number of the countries.

As Table 1 shows, several countries have suicide rates that rise with age for both sexes. In Austria and France, the peak in old age is particularly striking. For example, in Austria, the suicide rate for men aged 75 and older in 1989 was 96.0 per 100,000; in France, it was

In Japan, the suicide rate peaks for both men and women at the age of 75 and over. By contrast, in France the peak suicide rate for men is 75 and over, but the peak rate for women occurs between 45 and 54 years of age. Do these patterns provide us with insights about the intertwining of attitudes regarding gender and aging in these societies?

and males. By contrast, *gender* refers to the meanings, beliefs, and practices associated culturally and socially constructed with sex differences, referred to as femininity and masculinity (Scott, 1986:1054).

In forming your own sociological imagination and in seeing the possibilities for sociology in the twenty-first century, it will be helpful to understand the development of the discipline, beginning about one hundred years ago.

THE DEVELOPMENT OF SOCIOLOGICAL THINKING

Throughout history, social philosophers and religious authorities have made countless observations about human behaviour. However, these early thinkers primarily stated what they thought society *ought* to be like, rather than describing how society actually *was*. In light of the sweeping polit-

BOX 1.3

CONTINUED

109.0 per 100,000. In 1989 Japan had one of the highest rates of suicide for women aged 75 and older—51.6 per 100,000. Among developed nations, the second pattern—a slight peak in young adulthood and a major peak in old age—primarily describes male suicide patterns. Other nations have peak suicide rates in the middle-aged years. In Canada, the peak suicide rate for men is at age 75 and older, while 45 to 54 is the peak age range for women.

What reasons can you think of that might cause the differences discussed here? How would you analyze the data and what conclusions might you draw on the basis of these international comparisons of suicide data?

Sources: Lester, 1992; Health Canada, 1994; Leenaars et al., 1998.

TABLE 1   GLOBAL TRENDS IN SUICIDE

| | COUNTRY | |
PATTERN	MALES	FEMALES
1. Rate increases regularly with age.	Austria France Italy Japan Germany	Austria Italy Japan Germany
2. Rate peaks twice: once in young adulthood (aged 15–24, 25–34, or 35–44) and once in old age.	Australia Canada England and Wales Netherlands United States	
3. Rate peaks in middle age (aged 45–54 or 55–64).	Denmark Poland Sweden	Australia Canada France Netherlands Poland Sweden United States

ical and economic changes in the late eighteenth and early nineteenth centuries, people realized that some of the answers given by philosophers and theologians to some very pressing questions no longer seemed as relevant. Many of these questions concerned the social upheaval brought about by industrialization and urbanization that occurred first in Britain, then in Western Europe, and later in Canada and the United States.

Industrialization is the process by which societies are transformed from dependence on agriculture and handmade products to an emphasis on manufacturing and related industries. This process occurred first during the Industrial Revolution in Britain between 1760 and 1850 and soon was repeated throughout Western Europe. By the mid-nineteenth century, industrialization was well under way in North America. Massive

This opening ceremony of Expo 1986 in Vancouver reflects the increasing diversity of the Canadian population—and the need to take all people's experiences into account as we confront public issues.

economic, technological, and social changes occurred as machine technology and the factory system shifted the economic base of these nations from agriculture to manufacturing. A new social class of industrialists emerged in textiles, iron smelting, and related industries. Many people who had laboured on the land were forced to leave their tightly knit rural communities and sacrifice well-defined social relationships to seek employment as factory workers in the emerging cities, which became the centres of industrial work.

Urbanization **is the process by which an increasing proportion of a population lives in cities rather than in rural areas.** Although cities existed long before the Industrial Revolution, the development of the factory system led to a rapid increase in both the number of cities and the size of their populations. People from very diverse backgrounds worked together in the same factory. At the same time, many people shifted from being *producers* to being *consumers*. For example, families living in the cities had to buy food with their wages because they no longer could grow their own crops to consume or to barter for other resources. Similarly, people had to pay rent for their lodging because they no longer could exchange their services for shelter.

These living and working conditions led to the development of new social problems: inadequate housing, crowding, unsanitary conditions, poverty, pollution, and crime. Wages were so low that entire families—including very young children—were forced to work, often under hazardous conditions and with no job security. As these conditions became more visible, a new breed of social thinkers turned its attention to trying to understand why and how society was changing.

Early Thinkers: A Concern with Social Order and Stability

At the same time as urban problems were growing worse, natural scientists had been using reason, or rational thinking, to discover the laws of physics and the movement of the planets. Social thinkers started to believe that, by applying the methods developed by the natural sciences, they might discover the laws of human behaviour and apply these laws to solve social problems. Historically, the time was ripe for such thoughts because the Age of Enlightenment (a period that followed the "dark ages" and was characterized by reliance on scientific analysis) had produced a belief in reason and humanity's ability to perfect itself. Early social thinkers—such as Auguste Comte, Harriet Martineau, Herbert Spencer, and Emile Durkheim—were interested in analyzing social order and stability, and many of their ideas had a dramatic influence on modern sociology.

AUGUSTE COMTE The French philosopher Auguste Comte (1798–1857) coined the term *sociology* from the Latin *socius* (social, being with others) and the Greek *logos* (study of) to describe a new science that would engage in the study of society. Comte is considered by some to be the "founder of sociology." Comte's theory that societies contain *social statics* (forces for social order and stability) and *social dynamics* (forces for conflict and change)

Early in the twentieth century, sights like this 14-year-old girl working in a factory caught the attention of social thinkers and brought demands for protective child labour laws.

Auguste Comte

continues to be used in contemporary sociology, although not in these exact terms.

Comte's philosophy became known as *positivism*—a belief that the world can best be understood through scientific inquiry. Comte believed that objective, bias-free knowledge was attainable only through the use of science rather than religion. Scientific knowledge, however, was "relative knowledge," not absolute and final. Comte's positivism had two dimensions: (1) methodological— the application of scientific knowledge to both physical and social phenomena—and (2) social and political—the use of such knowledge to predict the likely results of different policies so that the best one could be chosen. For Comte, the best policies involved order and authority. He envisioned that a new consensus would emerge on social issues and that the new science of sociology would play a significant part in the reorganization of society (Jary and Jary, 1991:374).

HARRIET MARTINEAU Comte's works were made more accessible for a wide variety of scholars through the efforts of British sociologist Harriet Martineau (1802–1876). Not only did she translate and condense Comte's work, but she also was an active sociologist in her own right. Martineau studied the social customs of Britain and the United States and analyzed the consequences of industrialization and capitalism. In *Society in America* (1962/1837), she examined religion, politics, child rearing, slavery, and immigration in the United States, paying special attention to social

distinctions based on class, race, and gender. Her works explore the status of women, children, and "sufferers" (persons who were considered to be criminal, mentally ill, handicapped, poor, or alcoholic). Until recently, Martineau received no recognition in the field of sociology, partly because she was a woman in a male-dominated discipline.

HERBERT SPENCER British social theorist Herbert Spencer (1820–1903) used an evolutionary perspective to explain social order and social change. He believed that society, like a biological organism, has various interdependent parts (such as the family, the economy, and the government), which work to ensure the stability and survival of the entire society. According to Spencer, societies developed through a process of "struggle" (for existence) and "fitness" (for survival), which he referred to as the "survival of the fittest." Spencer equated this process of natural selection with progress, because only the "fittest" members of society would succeed. As a result of these ideas, he strongly opposed attempts at social reform that might interfere with the *natural selection* process and, thus, damage society by favouring its least worthy members.

Although Spencer contributed many useful concepts and terms, many of his ideas had serious flaws. For one thing, societies are not the same as biological systems; people are able to create and transform the environment in which they live. Moreover, the notion of the survival of the fittest has been used to justify class, racial-ethnic, and

Harriet Martineau

Emile Durkheim

gender inequalities and to rationalize the lack of action to eliminate harmful practices that contribute to such inequalities.

EMILE DURKHEIM French sociologist Emile Durkheim (1858–1917) disagreed with many of Spencer's views. Durkheim stressed that people are the product of their social environment and that behaviour cannot be understood fully in terms of *individual* biological and psychological traits. He believed that the limits of human potential are *socially*, not *biologically*, based.

In his work *The Rules of Sociological Method* (1964a/1895) Durkheim set forth one of his most important contributions to sociology: the idea that societies are built on social facts. **Social facts are patterned ways of acting, thinking, and feeling that exist *outside* any one individual but that exert social control over each person.** Durkheim believed that social facts must be explained by other social facts—by reference to the social structure rather than to individual attributes.

Durkheim was concerned with social order and social stability because he lived during the period of rapid social changes in Europe resulting from industrialization and urbanization. He observed that rapid social change and a more specialized division of labour produce *strains* in society. These strains lead to a breakdown in traditional organization, values, and authority and to a dramatic increase in *anomie*—**a condition in which social control becomes ineffective as a result of the loss of shared values and of a sense of purpose in society.** According to Durkheim, anomie is most likely to occur during a period of rapid social change. In *Suicide* (1964b/1897), he explored the relationship between anomic social conditions and suicide.

Durkheim's contributions to sociology are so significant that he has been referred to as "the crucial figure in the development of sociology as an academic discipline [and as] one of the deepest roots of the sociological imagination" (Tiryakian, 1978:187).

Differing Views on the Status Quo: Stability versus Change

Together with Karl Marx, Max Weber, and Georg Simmel, Durkheim established the course for modern sociology. We will look first at Marx's and Weber's divergent thoughts about conflict and social change in societies and then at Georg Simmel's microlevel analysis of society.

KARL MARX In sharp contrast to Durkheim's focus on the stability of society, German economist and philosopher Karl Marx (1818–1883) stressed that history is a continuous clash between conflicting ideas and forces. He believed that conflict—especially class conflict—is necessary in order to pro-

Karl Marx

Max Weber

duce social change and a better society. For Marx, the most important changes were economic. He concluded that the capitalist economic system was responsible for the overwhelming poverty that he observed in London at the beginning of the Industrial Revolution (Marx and Engels, 1967/1848).

In the Marxian framework, **class conflict is the struggle between the capitalist class and the working class.** The capitalist class, or *bourgeoisie,* **is composed of those who own and control the means of production.** The *means of production* **refers to the tools, land, factories, and money for investment that form the economic basis of a society.** The working class, or *proletariat,* **is composed of those who must sell their labour because they have no other means to earn a livelihood.** From Marx's viewpoint, the capitalist class controls and exploits the masses of struggling workers by paying less than the value of their labour. This exploitation results in workers' *alienation*—a **feeling of powerlessness and estrangement from other people and from oneself.** Marx predicted that the working class would become aware of its exploitation, overthrow the capitalists, and establish a free and classless society, as discussed in Chapter 8 ("Social Stratification and Class").

Marx's social and economic analyses have inspired heated debates among generations of social scientists. Although his evaluation of capitalism and his theories on the process of social change have been criticized, many of his ideas

form the foundation of contemporary conflict theory.

MAX WEBER   German social scientist Max Weber (pronounced VAY-ber) (1864–1920) also was concerned about the changes brought about by the Industrial Revolution. Although he disagreed with Marx's idea that economics is *the* central force in social change, Weber acknowledged that economic interests are important in shaping human action. Even so, he thought that economic systems were heavily influenced by other factors in a society. As we will see in Chapter 17 ("Religion"), one of Weber's most important works, *The Protestant Ethic and the Spirit of Capitalism* (1976/1904–05), evaluated the role of the Protestant Reformation in producing a social climate in which capitalism could exist and flourish.

Unlike many early analysts, who believed that values could not be separated from the research process, Weber emphasized that sociology should be *value free*—that is, research should be conducted in a scientific manner and should exclude the researcher's own personal values and economic interests (Turner, Beeghley, and Powers, 1995:192). However, Weber realized that social behaviour cannot be analyzed by the objective criteria that we use to measure such things as temperature or weight. Although he recognized that sociologists cannot be totally value free, Weber stressed that they should employ *verstehen*

(German for "understanding" or "insight") to gain the ability to see the world as others see it. In contemporary sociology, Weber's idea is incorporated into the concept of the sociological imagination (discussed earlier in this chapter).

Weber also was concerned that large-scale organizations (bureaucracies) were becoming increasingly oriented toward routine administration and a specialized division of labour, which he believed were destructive to human vitality and freedom. As we will see in Chapter 6 ("Groups and Organizations"), Weber's work on bureaucracy has had far-reaching impact.

Georg Simmel German sociologist Georg Simmel (pronounced ZIM-mel) (1858–1918) had an important influence on sociology despite the fact that he was excluded from high academic positions because of his Jewish heritage. Unlike Comte, Durkheim, Marx, and Weber—who focused on macrolevel analyses of society—Simmel primarily explored smaller social units. He thought that society is best seen as a web of patterned interactions among people. The main purpose of sociology, according to Simmel, should be to examine these interaction processes within groups. For example, he analyzed how social interactions vary depending on the size of the social group (Simmel, 1950). He concluded that interaction patterns differed between a *dyad*, a social group with two members, and a *triad*, a social group with three members. He developed *formal sociology*, an approach that focuses attention on the universal, recurring social forms that underlie the varying content of social interaction. Simmel referred to these forms as the "geometry of social life."

Like the other social thinkers of his day, Simmel analyzed the impact of industrialization and urbanization on people's lives. He concluded that class conflict was becoming more pronounced in modern industrial societies. He also linked the increase in individualism, as opposed to concern for the group, to the fact that people now had many cross-cutting "social spheres"—membership in a number of organizations and voluntary associations—rather than having the singular community ties of the past. Finally, Simmel assessed the costs of "progress" on the upper-class city dweller, who, he believed, had to develop certain techniques to survive the overwhelming stimulation of the city. Simmel's ultimate concern was to protect the autonomy of the individual in society.

The Development of Sociology in North America

From Western Europe, sociology spread in the 1890s to the United States, and in the early 1900s to Canada. It thrived in both countries as a result of the intellectual climate and the rapid rate of social change.

In the United States The first department of sociology in the United States was established at the University of Chicago in 1892. Robert E. Park (1864–1944), an original member of the Chicago School, assisted in the development of the sociology of urban life (see Chapter 19).

George Herbert Mead (1863–1931), a sociologist and social psychologist, became one of the best-known members of the Chicago School and the founder of the symbolic interaction perspective, which is discussed later in this chapter. The University of Chicago continues to be an important centre for sociological research and instruction.

In the early years, women were welcomed to sociology departments such as the University of Chicago's. However, as the departments became more established, a number of its male members became disenchanted with their own earlier radical ideas, including feminism. When many of the women were unable to gain more than a temporary foothold in academic sociology, they sought employment in the emerging field of social work. This change marked the beginning of a dual system of sex-segregated labour, whereby sociology became male-dominated and social work became female-dominated (Deegan, 1988).

Jane Addams (1860–1935) is one of the best-known early women sociologists because she founded Hull House, one of the most famous settlement houses, in an impoverished area of Chicago. Throughout her career, she actively engaged in sociological endeavours. She lectured at numerous colleges, was a charter member of the American Sociological Society, and published a number of articles and books. Although Addams was awarded a Nobel Peace Prize for her contributions to the field of social work and her assistance to the underprivileged, her sociological work was not acknowledged until recently.

The second department of sociology in the United States was founded by W.E.B. Du Bois (1868–1963) at Atlanta University. Du Bois's classic work, *The Philadelphia Negro: A Social Study*

George H. Mead

Patricia Marchak

(1967/1899), was based on his research into Philadelphia's African American community and stressed the strengths and weaknesses of a community wrestling with overwhelming social problems. Over the years, he became frustrated with the lack of progress in race relations and helped found the National Association for the Advancement of Colored People (NAACP).

IN CANADA The first sociology department in Canada was established in 1925 at McGill University in Montreal. The faculty consisted of Carl A. Dawson and Everett Hughes. Dawson modelled the McGill sociology department after the University of Chicago's, at which he was trained. Although other Canadian universities offered sociology courses through other departments, particularly history and economics, McGill had the only independent sociology department until the early 1960s (Denton and Hunter, 1995).

The University of Toronto, although equally influential in the field, had a very different approach to sociology than McGill. Sociology courses were taught as part of the department of political economy and did not form an independent department until 1963. Modelled on British sociology, the sociology taught at the University of Toronto focused on how issues of political and economic history affected Canadian society. The works of Harold A. Innis and S.D. Clark laid the

groundwork for the political economy perspective, which is central to Canadian sociology today.

By the late 1960s, sociology departments had been established across the country. The first Canadian sociology journal, the *Canadian Review of Sociology and Anthropology*, began publication in 1964. The Canadian Sociology and Anthropology Association was established in 1965 with a membership of less than 200. However, at this time, no significant government or private agency for sociological research existed in Canada, and only about a dozen books had been written by accredited Canadian sociologists (Brym and Fox, 1989).

The 1970s was a period of "Canadianization" of sociology in Canada. Prior to this time, Canadian sociology departments had tended to hire sociologists trained in the United States and to use American textbooks. During the 1970s, pressure was put on universities to hire sociologists trained in Canada. As a result, graduate programs across Canada were developed and expanded. A unique sociology was developed that focused on Canadian issues such as regionalism, ethnic relations, multiculturalism, and national identity, as well as issues common to all societies such as social inequalities created by social class, race and ethnicity, or gender. Canadian works such as John Porter's 1965 book *The Vertical Mosaic* and Patricia Marchak's *Ideological Perspectives on Canadian Society*, published in 1975, became landmarks in Canadian sociology (Denton and Hunter, 1995).

CONTEMPORARY THEORETICAL PERSPECTIVES

Given the many and varied ideas and trends that influenced the development of sociology, how do contemporary sociologists view society? Some see it as basically a stable and ongoing entity; others view it in terms of many groups competing for scarce resources; still others describe it as based on the everyday, routine interactions among individuals. Each of these views represents a method of examining the same phenomena. Each is based on general ideas as to how social life is organized and represents an effort to link specific observations in a meaningful way. Each utilizes *theory*—a set of **logically interrelated statements that attempts to describe, explain, and (occasionally) predict social events.** Each theory helps interpret reality in a distinct way by providing a framework in which observations may be logically ordered. Sociologists refer to this theoretical framework as a *perspective*—**an overall approach to or viewpoint on some subject.** The major theoretical perspectives that have emerged in sociology include the functionalist, conflict, feminist, and interactionist perspectives (see Figure 1.2). These perspectives will be used throughout this book to show you how sociologists try to understand many of the issues affecting Canadian society.

Functionalist Perspectives

Also known as *functionalism* and *structural functionalism*, **functionalist perspectives** are based on the **assumption that society is a stable, orderly system.** This stable system is characterized by *societal consensus* **whereby the majority of members share a common set of values, beliefs, and behavioural expectations.** According to this perspective, a society is composed of interrelated parts, each of which serves a function and (ideally) contributes to the overall stability of the society. Since this approach was influenced by Comte, Spencer, and Durkheim, who often drew on the work of natural scientists, early functionalists compared society to a living, evolving organism. Societies develop social structures, or institutions, that persist because they play a part in helping society survive. These institutions include the family, education, government, religion, and the economy. If anything adverse happens to one of these institutions or parts, all other parts are affected and the system

no longer functions properly. As Durkheim noted, rapid social change and a more specialized division of labour produce *strains* in society that lead to a breakdown in these traditional institutions and may result in social problems such as increased rates of crime and suicide.

TALCOTT PARSONS AND ROBERT MERTON   Talcott Parsons (1902–1979), a founder of the sociology department at Harvard University, was perhaps the most influential contemporary advocate of the functionalist perspective. He stressed that all societies must make provisions for meeting social needs in order to survive (Parsons, 1951; Parsons and Shils, 1951). For example, Parsons (1955) suggested that a division of labour (distinct, specialized functions) between husband and wife is essential for family stability and social order. The husband/father performs the *instrumental tasks*, which involve leadership and decision-making responsibilities in the home and employment outside the home to support the family. The wife/mother is responsible for the *expressive tasks*, including housework, caring for the children, and providing emotional support for the entire family. Parsons believed that other institutions, including school, church, and government, must function to assist the family and that all institutions must work together to preserve the system over time (Parsons, 1955). Although Parsons's analysis has been criticized for its conservative bias, his work still influences sociological thinking about gender roles and the family.

Functionalism was refined further by a student of Parsons, Robert K. Merton (b. 1910), who distinguished between manifest and latent functions of social institutions. **Manifest functions are intended and/or overtly recognized by the participants in a social unit.** In contrast, *latent functions* **are unintended functions that are hidden and remain unacknowledged by participants.** For example, a manifest function of education is the transmission of knowledge and skills from one generation to the next; a latent function is the establishment of social relations and networks. Merton noted that all features of a social system may not be functional at all times; *dysfunctions* **are the undesirable consequences of any element of a society.** A dysfunction of education can be the perpetuation of gender, racial, and class inequalities. Such dysfunctions may threaten the capacity of a society to adapt and survive (Merton, 1968).

Between 1945 and 1960, the functionalist perspective flourished in sociology; however, social

FIGURE 1.2   **Different Views of Society**

Is society built on consensus or conflict? How do the individual parts add up to the sum total of society? Just as astronomers get very different views of a planet depending on which bands of light they filter out, sociologists using different theoretical filters get different views of society.

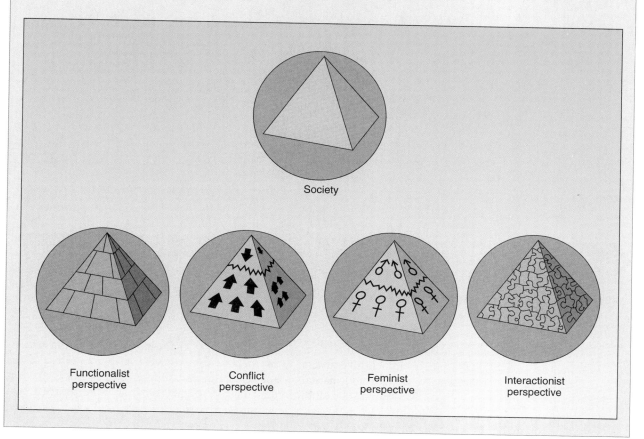

Society

Functionalist
perspective

Conflict
perspective

Feminist
perspective

Interactionist
perspective

strife during the 1960s exposed the limitations of this perspective. Critics questioned Parsons's rigid differentiation of gender roles and his assumption that the public sphere belonged to men and the private sphere to women. The functional perspective also was criticized for its tendency to legitimize the status quo without effectively examining conflict and social change. Recently, functionalism has experienced a resurgence and now is referred to by some as "neofunctionalism" (see Alexander, 1985).

Applying a Functionalist Perspective to Suicide

How might functionalists analyze the problem of suicide, which we examined at the beginning of this chapter? Although a number of possible functionalist explanations exist, we will look briefly at only one. Most functionalists emphasize the importance of shared moral values and strong social bonds to a society. When rapid social change or other disruptive conditions occur, moral values may erode, people may become more uncertain about how to act, and suicide rates may therefore increase.

In his classic study of suicide, functionalist Emile Durkheim (1964b/1897) argued that suicide rates are a reflection of the degree in a society of *social solidarity*—**that is, the state of having shared beliefs and values among members of a social group, along with intense and frequent interaction among group members.** According to Durkheim, people are most likely to kill themselves when social solidarity is either very weak or very strong.

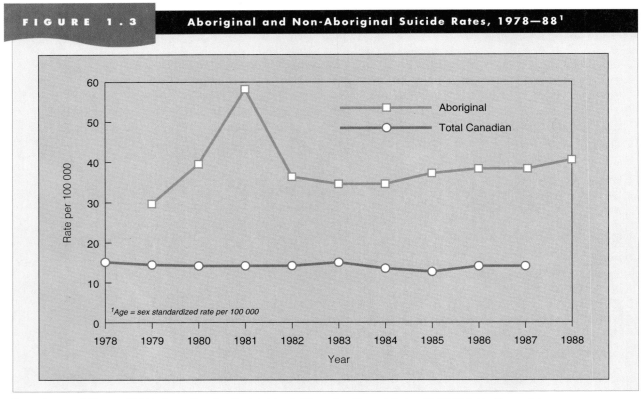

FIGURE 1.3   **Aboriginal and Non-Aboriginal Suicide Rates, 1978—88[1]**

Source: Lawrence J. Kirmayer, "Suicide Among Canadian Aboriginal People," *Transcultural Research Review*, 31 (1994):7. Used by permission.

Durkheim collected data from vital statistics for approximately 26,000 suicides and classified them according to variables such as age, sex, marital status, family size, religion, geographic location, and method of suicide. From this analysis, he was able to identify four distinct categories of suicide: egoistic, anomic, altruistic, and fatalistic. *Egoistic suicide* occurs among people who are isolated from any social group. For example, Durkheim concluded that suicide rates were relatively high in Protestant countries in Europe because Protestants were more loosely tied to the church than were Catholics. Similarly, single people had proportionately higher suicide rates than married persons because they had a low degree of social integration, which contributed to their loneliness. In contrast, *altruistic suicide* occurs among individuals who are excessively integrated into society. An example is soldiers who kill themselves after defeat in battle because they have so strongly identified with their cause that they believe they cannot live with the shame of defeat.

Durkheim recognized that the degree of social integration is not the only variable that influences the suicide rate. In keeping with the functionalist perspective, Durkheim emphasized the importance of social stability and social consensus. Rapid social change and shifts in moral values make it difficult for people to know what is right and wrong. *Anomic suicide* results from a lack of shared values or purpose and from the absence of social regulation. In contrast, excessive regulation and oppressive discipline may contribute to *fatalistic suicide*, as in the suicide of slaves.

Although Durkheim's analysis of suicide was developed in the nineteenth century, it can be used to understand suicide rates among categories of people in Canada today. For example, the rate of suicide among Aboriginal people in Canada is two to three times higher than that of non-Aboriginal people. Centuries of attempts to assimilate Aboriginal people have resulted in a weakening of traditional Aboriginal cultures. Government intervention in the form of such policies as relocating First Nations people to reserves, prohibiting traditional religious or spiritual practices, sending Aboriginal children to residential schools, and destroying Aboriginal people's economic base, have resulted in social breakdown and disorganization in many Aboriginal communities. As scholar

Kai Erikson explains, such policies sought to destroy Aboriginal communities and

> lead to injuries that are inflicted not on individuals directly but on the tissues of community life themselves—injuries that act to damage the bonds attaching people to one another, to impair the prevailing sense of group cohesion. Collective trauma works its way slowly into the awareness of those who come to suffer from it ... they learn that they are isolated and alone, living in a kind of social wasteland with no one to turn to. They have lost the solace that comes from being in a fellowship with one's kind. (Shkilnyk, 1985:xvi)

Today suicide rates are epidemic in some Aboriginal communities. Suicides due to social breakdown and normlessness are an example of what Durkheim defined as anomic suicides (Kirmayer, 1994). Using Durkheim's theoretical framework, these suicides can be best understood as indicative of social, rather than personal, problems.

The functionalist analysis of suicide (or other social problems) has been criticized for its assumption that shared values and beliefs are equally beneficial for everyone. For example, if a society values men more than women or ties being a "man" to sexual aggression, these values may contribute to the victimization of women and children. Likewise, the law-and-order solution to crime may have inherent class, race, gender, and age biases, as discussed in Chapter 7 ("Crime and Deviance"). However, proponents of functionalism point out that this perspective demonstrates the importance of social bonds for the stability of society and the well-being of individuals. For example, in communities where there is no shared sense of community, suicide rates will be higher.

Conflict Perspectives

According to **conflict perspectives, groups in society are engaged in a continuous power struggle for control of scarce resources.** Conflict theory sharply contrasts with functionalist approaches, which see society as based primarily on consensus. Conflict may take the form of politics, litigation, negotiations, or family discussions about financial matters. Simmel, Marx, and Weber contributed significantly to this perspective by focusing on the inevitability of clashes between social groups. Today, advocates of the conflict perspective view social life as a continuous power struggle among competing social groups.

MAX WEBER AND C. WRIGHT MILLS As previously discussed, Marx focused on the exploitation and oppression of the proletariat (the workers) by the bourgeoisie (the owners or capitalist class). Weber recognized the importance of economic conditions in producing inequality and conflict in society but added *power* and *prestige* as other sources of inequality. Weber (1968/1922) defined power as the ability of a person within a social relationship to carry out his or her own will despite resistance from others. Prestige ("status group" to Weber) is a positive or negative social estimation of honour (Weber, 1968/1922).

Other theorists have looked at conflict among many groups and interests (such as employers and employees) as a part of everyday life in any society. Ralf Dahrendorf (1959), for example, observed that conflict is inherent in *all* authority relationships, not just that between the capitalist class and the working class. To Dahrendorf, *power* is the critical variable in explaining human behaviour. People in positions of authority benefit from the conformity of others; those who are forced to conform feel resentment and demonstrate resistance, much as a child may resent parental authority. The advantaged group that possesses authority attempts to preserve the status quo—the existing set of social arrangements—and may use coercion to do so.

C. Wright Mills (1916–1962), a key figure in the development of contemporary conflict theory, encouraged sociologists to get involved in social reform. He contended that value-free sociology was impossible because social scientists must make value-related choices—including the topics they investigate and the theoretical approaches they adopt. He encouraged others to look beneath everyday events in order to observe the major resource and power inequalities that exist in society. He believed that the most important decisions are made largely behind the scenes by the **power elite—a small clique composed of the top corporate, political, and military officials.** Mills's power elite theory is discussed in Chapter 14 ("Power, Politics, and Government").

APPLYING CONFLICT PERSPECTIVES TO SUICIDE How might advocates of a conflict approach explain patterns of suicide among young people in Canada?

Social Class Although many other factors may be present, social class pressures can affect rates of suicide among young people. According to some conflict theorists, North American teenagers are confronted with a capitalist economy predicated on consumption and waste and on the need to achieve high levels of economic success. Some young people may perceive that they have no future because they see few educational or employment opportunities in our technologically oriented society. Some researchers suggest that young people from low-income or working-class backgrounds are among the most powerless people in society. Low levels of family income and education and financial uncertainty associated with unemployment are known risk factors associated with suicide among Canadian youth (Health Canada, 1997).

Race   Racial oppression may explain the high suicide rates of some minority groups. This fact is more glaringly reflected in the extremely high rate of suicide among some Aboriginal communities. Canadian children and youth living in Aboriginal reserve communities have a suicide rate almost five times that of children and youth in the general population (Health Canada, 1997:272). Most research has focused on individualistic reasons why some young Aboriginal people commit suicide. However, analysts using a conflict framework focus on the effect of social inequality and racial discrimination on suicidal behaviour. The *Special Report on Suicide Among Aboriginal Peoples* (Royal Commission on Aboriginal Peoples, 1995) makes frequent references to oppression as a significant factor in Aboriginal suicide. For example, Sarah MacKay of the Shibogama First Nations Council comments:

> Many reports written today about the suicides of youth ... outline in great detail the contributing factors that lead to suicide. Yet these reports fail to clearly identify the reasons why the suicides occur. The contributing factors, such as sexual abuse, family violence, alcohol and drug abuse, solvent abuse ... are only symptoms of a bigger and more devastating cycle of oppression and deprivation ... first initiated with colonial contact in 1492 ... We must stop the immoral behaviours caused by oppressions ... [That's how] to stop the suicides that are occurring amongst our youth today. (Royal Commission on Aboriginal Peoples, 1995:19)

The various conflict approaches help clarify the connections between social arrangements in society and problems such as violent crimes and suicide. However, these perspectives have been criticized for giving little attention to social stability and shared values. Critics contend that con-

Margrit Eichler

flict perspectives have lost at least some claim to scientific objectivity. Advocates of conflict perspectives respond that all social approaches have inherent biases, as will be discussed in Chapter 2 ("Sociological Research Methods").

Feminist Perspectives

In the past several decades, feminists have radically transformed the discipline of sociology. Feminist theory first emerged as a critique of traditional sociological theory and methodology. The primary criticism was that sociology did not acknowledge the experiences of women. Written by men, sociology involved the study of men and not humankind, much less women; sociology examined only half of social reality (Fox, 1989). Feminist scholar Dorothy Smith (1974) argued that sociological methods, concepts, and analyses were products of the "male social universe." If women appeared at all, it was as men saw them and not as they saw themselves. In this way, feminist sociologists argued, sociology actually contributed to the subordination and exploitation of women (Anderson, 1996). The first task of feminist sociology was to provide the missing half of social reality by generating research and theory "by, for, and about women" (Smith, 1987). In doing so, feminist sociology brought the personal problems of women, including violence against women, the poverty of women, and the invisibility of women's reproductive labour, into the public forum.

Feminist perspectives focus on the significance of gender in understanding and explaining inequalities that exist between men and women in the household, in the paid labour force, and in the realms of politics, law, and culture (Armstrong and Armstrong, 1994; Luxton, 1995; Marshall, 1995). Feminism is not one single unified approach. Rather, there are different approaches among feminist writers, namely the liberal, radical, and socialist strains (discussed in Chapter 11, "Sex and Gender"). Feminist sociology incorporates both microlevel and macrolevel analysis in studying the experiences of women. For example, some feminist theorists, such as Margrit Eichler, have used a structural approach to explain how gender inequality is created and maintained in a society dominated by men (Armstrong and Armstrong, 1994; Eichler, 1988b). Other feminist research has focused on the interpersonal relationships between men and women in terms of verbal and nonverbal communication styles, attitudes, and values in explaining the dynamics of power and social control in the private sphere (Mackie, 1995). For example, "Who eats first, sits last, or talks back reflects the micro-politics of gender" (Coltrane, 1992:104). All of these approaches share the belief that "women and men are equal and should be equally valued as well as have equal rights" (Basow, 1992). According to feminists (including many men as well as women), we live in a *patriarchy*, a hierarchical system of power in which males possess greater economic and social privilege than females (Saunders, 1999). Feminist perspectives assume that gender roles are socially created, rather than determined by one's biological inheritance, and that change is essential in order for people to achieve their human potential without limits based on gender. Feminism assumes that society reinforces social expectations through social learning: what we learn is a social product of the political and economic structure of the society in which we live (Renzetti and Curran, 1995). Feminists argue that women's subordination can end only after the patriarchal system of male dominance is replaced with a more egalitarian system.

APPLYING A FEMINIST PERSPECTIVE TO SUICIDE

In North America, females are more likely to attempt suicide, whereas males are likelier to actually take their own lives. Analysts using a feminist perspective might be more interested in determining why women, more than men, are likely to attempt suicide when they are young (under thirty years of age) and socioeconomically disadvantaged.

Despite the fact that women's suicidal behaviour has traditionally been attributed to problems in their interpersonal relationships, such as the loss of a boyfriend, lover, or husband, some analysts believe that we must examine social-structural pressures that are brought to bear on young women and how these may contribute to their behaviour, for example, cultural assumptions about women and what their multiple roles should be in the family, in education, and in the workplace. Women also experience unequal educational and employment opportunities that may contribute to feelings of powerlessness and alienation. Recent research shows there are persistent gender gaps in employment, politics, education, and other areas of social life that tend to adversely affect women more than men. Feminist theorists would suggest that the higher rate of attempted suicide among young women of all age groups may be an expression of their sense of powerlessness in a male-dominated society.

Interactionist Perspectives

Both the conflict and the functional perspectives have been criticized for focusing primarily on macrolevel analysis. A **macrolevel analysis examines whole societies, large-scale social structures, and social systems** instead of looking at important social dynamics in individuals' lives. Our final perspective, interactionism, fills this void by examining people's day-to-day interactions and their behaviour in groups. Thus, interactionist approaches are based on a **microlevel analysis, which focuses on small groups rather than large-scale social structures.**

According to *interactionist perspectives*, **society is the sum of the interactions of individuals and groups.** This approach focuses on how people act toward one another and how they make sense of those interactions. George Herbert Mead, the original force behind this perspective, emphasized that the ability to communicate in symbols is the key feature distinguishing humans from other animals. Although there are a number of loosely linked interactionist approaches, symbolic interaction is the most widely used.

SYMBOLIC INTERACTION

For *symbolic interactionists*, people create and change their social worlds through the use of mutually understood symbols. A **symbol is anything that meaningfully represents something else.** Examples of symbols include signs, gestures, written language, and shared values.

Symbolic interaction occurs when people communicate through the use of symbols; for example, a gift of food—a cake or a casserole—to a newcomer in a neighbourhood is a symbol of welcome and friendship.

Some interactionists focus on people's behaviour while others focus on the ways in which people impose their shared meanings on others. From this perspective, each person's interpretation or definition of a given situation becomes a *subjective reality* from that person's viewpoint. Individuals generally assume that their subjective reality is the same as that of others; however, this may be incorrect. Subjective reality is acquired and shared through agreed-upon symbols, especially language. If a person shouts, "Fire!" in a crowded movie theatre, for example, that language produces the same response (attempting to escape) in all of those who hear and understand it. When people in a group do not share the same meaning for a given symbol, however, confusion results; for example, people who did not know the meaning of the word *fire* would not know what the commotion was about. How people *interpret* the messages they receive and the situations they encounter becomes their subjective reality and may strongly influence their behaviour. Two branches of this approach, dramaturgical analysis and ethno-methodology, are discussed in Chapter 5 ("Social Structure and Interaction in Everyday Life").

APPLYING INTERACTIONIST PERSPECTIVES TO SUICIDE

Analysts applying an interactionist framework to the study of suicide focus on a microlevel analysis of suicidal persons' face-to-face interactions with others and the roles these others play. In our interactions with others, we define particular situations according to our own subjective reality. This applies to suicide just as it does to other types of conduct. In studying suicide, the interactionist focuses on the various meanings that are attributed to the act of suicide.

There is a great deal of variation among different cultures around the world regarding the meaning of suicide. For example, in Japan, where suicide has traditionally been accepted, the words used to describe it reflect tolerance toward suicide. In English, the word *suicide* is derived from a Latin word meaning "murder." In contrast, the Japanese have thirty-five different expressions for suicide, but none meaning self-murder (Fuse, 1997). The meaning attached to suicide in Japan is closely related to Japanese views of death. These include that death is something to be welcomed and that it

allows one to have a continuing life through one's children and their children (Wenckstern and Leenaars, 1998).

How might an interactionist perspective be applied to understand the pattern of suicide among youth in some Aboriginal communities? Once again, the interactionist perspective focuses on the meaning of suicide in attempting to understand patterns or variations in suicide rates. These patterns may be an indication of the redefinition among Aboriginal youth of the meaning of suicide. A young Aboriginal student from New Brunswick discusses how suicide is viewed by some of his peers:

> Too many [North] American Indian youths find this life devoid of meaning and worth little, whereas death is a way of finding peace and reunion with glorified ancestors. Suicide is often viewed as a brave, heroic act. Self-destructive behaviour becomes a learned and rewarded pattern. Those who die by suicide become idols of their peer group. (Royal Commission on Aboriginal Peoples, 1995:10)

From this point of view, suicide is seen as a way of gaining peer approval and acceptance. When suicide becomes defined as a brave or heroic act, we can expect an increase in suicide rates.

This helps to explain why clusters of suicide have become more common among Aboriginal Canadian youth in recent years. For example, the Inuit of the East Coast of Hudson Bay experienced a dramatic increase in suicide between 1987 and 1991. Most of this increase was the result of a cluster of suicides in 1991. Furthermore, over 90 percent of these suicides occurred in the 15–25 age group (Kirmayer, 1994:10). The interactionist perspective would view this as learned behaviour. Suicide becomes viewed by some youth as a socially acceptable solution to life's problems (Health Canada, 1997).

As this interactionist analysis of suicide makes clear, social learning is important in how we define ourselves and our relationship to others. Because interactionist perspectives focus on the microlevel of society, they help us see how individuals interact in their daily lives and interpret their experiences. However, this approach also is limited in that it basically ignores the larger social context in which behaviour takes place. If we focus primarily on the individual and small-group context of behaviour, we may overlook important macrolevel societal forces that are beyond the control of individuals,

CONCEPT TABLE 1.A

THE MAJOR THEORETICAL PERSPECTIVES

PERSPECTIVE	ANALYSIS LEVEL	NATURE OF SOCIETY
Functionalist	Macrolevel	Society is composed of interrelated parts that work together to maintain stability within society. This stability is threatened by dysfunctional acts and institutions.
Conflict	Macrolevel	Society is characterized by social inequality; social life is a struggle for scarce resources. Social arrangements benefit some groups at the expense of others.
Feminist	Macrolevel and Microlevel	Society is based on patriarchy—a hierarchical system of power in which males possess greater economic and social privilege than females.
Interactionist	Microlevel	Society is the sum of the interactions of people and groups. Behaviour is learned in interaction with other people; how people define a situation becomes the foundation for how they behave.

such as the effects of socially imposed definitions of race-ethnicity, gender, class, and age on people's lives.

Each of the sociological perspectives we have examined involves different assumptions. Consequently, each leads us to ask different questions and to view the world somewhat differently. Different aspects of reality are the focus of each approach. While functionalism emphasizes social cohesion and order, conflict and feminist approaches focus primarily on social conflict and change. In contrast, interactionism primarily examines people's interactions and shared meanings in everyday life. Concept Table 1.A reviews the major perspectives. Throughout this book, we will be using these perspectives as lenses through which to view our social world. Each approach also will be helpful in developing your own sociological imagination.

CHAPTER REVIEW

What is sociology and how can it help us to understand ourselves and others?

Sociology is the systematic study of human society and social interaction. As we explore sociology, we begin to understand how individual behaviour is largely shaped by the groups to which we belong and the society in which we live. Sociology also makes us aware of global interdependence. The sociological perspective enables us to examine individual behaviour and group interaction to find explanations for recurring patterns of social behaviour. We study sociology to understand how human behaviour is shaped by group life and, in turn, how group life is affected by individuals. Our culture tends to emphasize individualism, and sociology pushes us to consider more complex connections between our personal lives and the larger world.

What is the sociological imagination?

According to C. Wright Mills, the sociological imagination helps us understand how seemingly personal troubles, such as sexual assault victimization, actually are related to larger social forces. It requires us to include many points of view and diverse experiences in our own thinking.

What factors contributed to the emergence of sociology as a discipline?

Industrialization and urbanization increased rapidly in the late eighteenth century, and social thinkers began to examine the consequences of these powerful forces.

What did the early social thinkers contribute to the development of sociology as a unique social science?

Auguste Comte coined the term *sociology* and argued that this new discipline should apply the objective research methods of the natural sciences to the study of society. Harriet Martineau examined social customs and analyzed specific consequences of industrialization and capitalism. According to Herbert Spencer's evolutionary perspective, society—like a biological organism—is composed of interdependent parts that must work together to ensure the stability and survival of the entire society.

What are the major contributions of the early sociologists Durkheim, Marx, Weber, and Simmel?

The ideas of Emile Durkheim, Karl Marx, Max Weber, and Georg Simmel helped lead the way to contemporary sociology. Durkheim argued that societies are built on social facts, that rapid social change produces strains in society, and that the loss of shared values and purpose can lead to a condition of anomie. Marx stressed that within society there is a continuous clash between the owners of the means of production and the workers who have no choice but to sell their labour to others. According to Weber, it is necessary to acknowledge the meanings that individuals attach to their own actions. Simmel explored small social groups and argued that society was best seen as a web of patterned interactions among people.

Briefly describe the beginnings of the study of sociology in Canada.

From its origins in Europe, sociology spread to Canada in the 1920s. The first sociology department was located at McGill University in Montreal.

What are the major contemporary sociological perspectives?

The contemporary sociological perspectives incorporate much of the earlier social thinking. Functionalist perspectives assume that society is a stable, orderly system characterized by societal consensus; however, this perspective has been criticized for overlooking the importance of change in societies. By contrast, conflict perspectives argue that society is a continuous power struggle among competing groups, often based on class, race, ethnicity, or gender. Critics of conflict theory note that it minimizes the importance of social stability and shared values in society. Feminist perspectives focus on the significance of gender in understanding and explaining inequalities that exist between men and women in the household, in the paid labour force, and in politics, law, and culture. Interactionist perspectives focus on how people make sense of their everyday social interactions, which are made possible by the use of mutually understood symbols. However, this approach focuses on the microlevel of society and tends to ignore the larger macrolevel social context.

Key Terms

alienation 15
anomie 14
bourgeoisie 15
class 9
class conflict 15
commonsense knowledge 5
conflict perspectives 21
developed nations 9
developing nations 9
dysfunctions 18
ethnicity 9

functionalist perspectives 18
gender 10
global interdependence 5
industrialization 11
interactionist perspectives 23
latent functions 18
macrolevel analysis 23
manifest functions 18
means of production 15
microlevel analysis 23
objective 6
perspective 18
positivism 13
power elite 21
proletariat 15
race 9
sex 9
social facts 14
social solidarity 19
societal consensus 18
society 4
sociological imagination 7
sociology 4
symbol 23
theory 18
urbanization 12

Internet Exercises

1. Several good search engines exist on the Web. Some of the most popular search engines are:

   http://www.lycos.com
   http://www.altavista.com
   http://www.yahoo.ca

   You can use these search engines to further research the topics discussed in these chapters or to complete the exercises. Yahoo! offers a search engine specifically for Canadian-based Web sites.

   For your first exercise, go to the Yahoo! Canada uniform resource locator (URL) listed above and find the sociology section. Look at some of the sociology links. Based on these links, how do the perceptions of "what sociology is" differ from what you think sociology is, or should be? Follow some links that are not explicitly sociological. Do the authors of these Web sites seem to have an underlying sociological theory for their work (regardless of whether or not they realize it)? What connections can you draw between some of these links and the theorists you have just read about?

Professor Craig McKie of Carleton University has developed an excellent source of links for information about sociology at:

   http://www.sociosearch.com

2. Try this URL:

   http://diogenes.baylor.edu/WWWproviders/
   Larry_Ridener/DSS/DEADSOC.HTML

   This is the Dead Sociologist's Society. Many of the sociologists listed in this chapter are also on the Web site. How are Professor Ridener's views on these theorists different from the ones in this chapter? How are they the same? How does the view presented on the various theorists at the Dead Sociologist's Society compare with those found on SocioWeb, which may be found at:

   http://www.socioweb.com/~markbl/socioweb/

   How are the differences in viewpoints among these sites useful to understanding the works of these theorists? How are they detrimental to this understanding? In what ways does the World Wide Web limit or expand a person's ability to relay ideas, and how does it limit the ability to communicate?

3. Configure your newsreader software to read the newsgroups **news.newusers.questions** and **news.answers**, and follow the discussions in these groups in order to familiarize yourself with the rules and codes of conduct regarding the newsgroups. Also monitor the newsgroup **alt.sci.sociology** for a few days. How does the dialogue compare with your expectations of a sociological discussion group? Compare this to the newsgroups **alt.feminism, alt.society.labour-unions,** and **alt.society.generation-x.** Which of these newsgroups contains the livelier discussions? Which discussions most closely match what you consider to be sociology? Since anyone can post to these groups, how much do you feel the discussion in each of these groups is influenced by those outside of the realm of sociology? Do you think the influence of outsiders on sociological theory and practice is useful?

Net Links

The SocioWeb is a guide to sociological resources on the Web. It is located at:

   http://www.socioweb.com/~markbl/socioweb

A social sciences reference library is located at:

http://www.mnsfld.edu/~library/mu-scref.html

Nelson Thomson Learning has a Web site that includes study resources, chapter quizzes, degree and career information, and Web links for additional information on a variety of topics in sociology. Go to:

**http://www.thomson.com/nelson/sociology/
search.html**

Look at public issues from a conflict perspective at the Leftist and Progressive Internet Directory at:

http://www.neravt.com/left

Questions for Critical Thinking

1. How does the sociological imagination help us understand that "things are not what they seem" (Berger, 1963:23)?
2. As a sociologist, how would you remain objective and yet see the world as others see it? Would you make subjective decisions when trying to understand the perspectives of others?
3. Early social thinkers were concerned about stability in times of rapid change. In our more global world, is stability still a primary goal? Or is constant conflict important for the well-being of all humans? Use the conflict and feminist perspectives to support your analysis.
4. According to the functionalist perspective, what would happen to society if one of its institutions— say, the educational system—were to break down?

Suggested Readings

These two classics describe sociological thinking and implementation of the sociological imagination:

Peter L. Berger. *Invitation to Sociology: A Humanistic Perspective*. New York: Anchor, 1963.

C. Wright Mills. *The Sociological Imagination*. New York: Oxford University Press, 1959.

The following books examine various aspects of sociological theory in more depth:

Randall Collins. *Four Sociological Traditions*. New York: Oxford University Press, 1994.

George Ritzer. *Sociological Theory* (3rd ed.). New York: Knopf, 1992.

Dorothy Smith. *The Everyday World as Problematic: A Feminist Sociology*. Toronto: University of Toronto Press, 1987.

To find out about career possibilities in sociology, contact the Canadian Sociology and Anthropology Association, Concordia University, 1455 Boul. de Maisonneuve Ouest, Montreal, Quebec M3G 1M8. Ask for the publication *Opportunities in Sociology*.

To find out more about the problem of suicide, see:

Antoon A. Leenaars, Susan Wenckstern, Isaac Sakinofsky, Ronald J. Dyck, Michael J. Kral, and Roger C. Bland. *Suicide in Canada*. Toronto: University of Toronto Press, 1998.

E. Shneidman. *Definition of Suicide*, New York: Wiley, 1988.

CHAPTER

2

Why Is Sociological Research Necessary?
Five Ways of Knowing the World
Descriptive and Explanatory Studies
The Theory and Research Cycle

The Sociological Research Process
Selecting and Defining the Research Problem
Reviewing Previous Research
Formulating the Hypothesis (If Applicable)
Developing the Research Design
Collecting the Data
Analyzing the Data
Drawing Conclusions and Reporting the Findings

Research Methods for Collecting Data
Experiments
Case Study: Would You Help Another Person?
Surveys
Case Study: Responding to Disaster
Secondary Analysis of Existing Data
Case Study: Good Neighbours and Saints
Field Research
Case Study: The Gift of Blood
Feminist Research Methods
Multiple Methods of Social Research

Ethical Issues in Sociological Research
The Zellner Research
The Humphreys Research
The Ogden Case

On October 31, 1991, a Canadian Armed Forces Hercules transport plane with eighteen passengers and crew was preparing to land at Canadian Forces Station Alert on Ellesmere Island in the Northwest Territories. Just 800 kilometres from the North Pole, Alert is the world's most northerly permanent settlement. In the dark Arctic night, 16 kilometres short of the runway, the left wing of the Hercules struck the peak of a small mountain and the aircraft crashed onto a barren Arctic plateau. Fourteen survivors, many of them seriously injured, waited for help in the twisted wreckage.

Thirty-two hours later another Hercules, with a team of Search and Rescue Technicians (SARtechs) on board, was circling the crash site. The SARtechs were hoping conditions would allow them to parachute into the site to help the survivors. The temperature was −66°C, visibility on the ground was limited, and the winds of 35 to 40 knots were more than three times the permissible limit for parachuting. Because of the terrible weather conditions, a U.S. Air Force crew had just cancelled their attempt at a jump onto the crash site. In the back of the Canadian Hercules, Warrant Officer Arnie Macauley, the SARtech team leader, addressed his men:

"Okay, guys, you know the situation. The winds are pretty stiff. They've blown away all our marker lights ... It looks like a snowfield down there, but ground conditions are unknown. We'll be landing at a good clip. We'll try for flare illumination but I can't promise you anything.

"One more thing. Once we're down there, we're down for good. Marv will try for a supply drop, but we can expect the survival gear to be blown away. We'll have no way of extracting ourselves or the survivors ...

"That's the situation, men. We can expect casualties. I have to inform you that the jump involves a knowing risk of life. I can't ask any of you to do this."

Some of the SARtechs studied their boots, others looked out the open door into the howling void. One by one, they looked back at him. "Arnie," one said, "you know how we feel."

Good guys, Arnie thought. I hope like hell I'm doing the right thing.

Arnie checked the closures on his padded orange jumpsuit and the fasteners of his parachute harness. He pulled on his gloves. The jumpmaster clipped their static lines to the overhead cable, and the men crowded around the open door. There were six of them. They squeezed into the opening and grabbed one another by the legs, arms, waist. They would go together. (Mason Lee, 1991:229–231)

SOCIOLOGICAL RESEARCH

The rescuers completed their harrowing jump with relatively minor injuries and immediately began caring for the survivors.

Thirteen people are alive today because of the heroism of the SARtechs and the rest of the aircrew and technicians involved in this rescue. Why do people like Warrant Officer Macauley and his men risk their lives in order to save others? This question has been asked by sociologists who have studied **altruism—behaviour intended to help others and done without any expectation of personal benefit.**

In this chapter, we will see how sociological research methods can help us to understand social phenomena such as altruism. How do sociologists determine what to study? How do they go about conducting research with human subjects? What factors determine the appropriate method to use in social research? These are all questions pertaining to the process of "doing research"—questions that will be addressed in this chapter. Conducting sociological research is an interesting, exciting, and at times difficult process. Why? Because sociological research is directed at understanding human social interaction and solving problems in our social world. Sociological research offers the challenge of going as a "stranger" into a familiar world.

Several researchers have conducted studies that try to help us understand altruistic behaviour, and their work will be used to illustrate the different research methods used by sociologists. Before reading on, test your knowledge of altruism by answering the questions in Box 2.1.

QUESTIONS AND ISSUES

CHAPTER FOCUS QUESTION: How does social research add to our knowledge of human societies?

What is the relationship between theory and research?

What are the main steps in the sociological research process?

Why is it important to have different research methods?

What has research contributed to our understanding of altruism?

Why is a code of ethics for sociological research necessary?

Many Nova Scotia fishers contributed their time and equipment to help search for bodies and debris following the crash of Swissair Flight 111.

WHY IS SOCIOLOGICAL RESEARCH NECESSARY?

Sociologists obtain their knowledge of human behaviour through research, which results in a body of information that helps us move beyond guesswork and common sense in understanding society. In Chapter 1, we looked at commonsense ideas about suicide and noted that these beliefs often are incorrect. The sociological perspective incorporates theory and research to arrive at a more informed understanding of the "hows" and "whys" of human social interaction. Social research, then, is a key part of sociology.

Five Ways of Knowing the World

Sociologists try to understand social behaviour. People have always sought to bring order to the chaotic world of experience by trying to understand the social and physical realm in which they live. Understanding is the major goal of science, but this goal is shared by other fields including philosophy, religion, the media, and the arts. Our ways of knowing the world include the following:

1. *Personal experience* We have discovered for ourselves many of the things we know. If we put our tongue on a frozen doorknob, we learn that removing it can be very painful.

2. *Tradition* People hold firmly to a belief because "everyone knows" it to be true. Tradition tells us that something is correct because it has always been done that way. We accept what has always been believed rather than finding out the answers by ourselves. A person who is told by her parents and grandparents that members of another race or religion are morally and intellectually inferior does not have to discover this "truth" for herself.

3. *Authority* Experts tell us that something is true. We do not need to go to the moon to discover its mineral composition, but instead accept the judgment of space scientists. In practice, much of what we know about medicine, child rearing, crime, and many other phenomena is based on what authorities have told us.

4. *Religion* A specific type of authority is religious authority. We accept the truths that our particular scriptures and religious officials advocate. Factors as diverse as morality, diet, dress, and hair styles are based on religious authority.

5. *Science* The scientific way of knowing involves controlled, systematic observation. Scientists insist that all statements be tested and that testing procedures be open to public inspection.

Personal experience, tradition, authority, and religion are all valid sources of understanding. However, a major difficulty with these ways of knowing is that there is no way to resolve differences or disagreements between those who have had different experiences, or who believe in different religions, traditions, or authorities. For example, if two religious groups have different views concerning the activities that are permissible on the Sabbath, the role that women should play in society, or the regulation of abortion, there is no institutionalized way of reconciling these contrary positions. Scientific explanations differ from the other ways of knowing in several fundamental ways. These characteristics allow scientists to resolve differences in their understanding of the social and physical world.

First, science uses the **empirical approach, that is, its findings are based on the assumption that knowledge is best gained by direct, systematic observation.** By contrast, the **normative approach uses religion, tradition, or authority to answer important questions.** It is based on strong beliefs about what is right and wrong, and what is desirable in a society.

Second, scientific knowledge is *systematic and public.* The procedures used by scientists are organized, public, and recognized by other scientists. The scientific community will not accept claims that cannot be publicly verified. This means that both the findings and the methods by which scientists reached those findings must be open to scrutiny.

Third, science has a built-in mechanism for *self-correction.* Scientists do not claim that their findings represent eternal truths, but rather they present **hypotheses—tentative statements of the relationship between two or more concepts or variables—**that are subject to verification by themselves and by others. What is accepted as scientific truth changes over time as more evidence accumulates. By contrast, it can be very difficult to make changes in understandings based on tradition, authority, or religious belief.

Fourth, science is **objective: scientists try to ensure that their biases and values do not affect their research.** In some situations, this criterion seems easily met. For example, two scientists measuring the length of time it takes for a ball to fall from a height of three hundred feet should arrive

ANSWERS TO THE SOCIOLOGY QUIZ ON ALTRUISM

1. **False.** Durkheim and other sociologists have shown that even in complex, large-scale societies such as ours altruism has a significant role to play in maintaining the social order.

2. **True.** Studies of the rescuers of Jews during the Holocaust, freedom riders in the American South in the 1960s, and blood donation have shown that many of those showing altruism had parents with similar commitments.

3. **True.** In his participant observation study of a volunteer work crew following a severe tornado Louis Zurcher found that helping other victims acted as a form of catharsis for the men on the crew. Thus helping others can benefit both the helper and the community.

4. **False.** Researchers have found very few personality differences between altruists and those less inclined to help others.

5. **False.** In most cases there is no obligation to help those in distress.

6. **True.** The anonymity of city life apparently reduces the likelihood that a bystander will help someone in trouble.

7. **True.** In experimental situations, subjects who were the only witnesses to an emergency felt they had to intervene because nobody else knew of the victim's distress. However, those in larger groups showed concern for the victim but were also concerned about making fools of themselves by overreacting. Therefore, they often waited to see if others would respond before deciding what, if anything, they would do.

8. **False.** Prior to 1947, Canadian patients had to pay for or replace the blood they used.

9. **False.** A British survey found that only a small percentage of blood donors expected to get anything—directly or indirectly—in return.

10. **False.** Canada has a very low rate of organ donation compared with other industrial countries. Our rate of organ donation is fourteen donors per million population compared with thirty per million for Spain and twenty-two per million in the United States. As a result, a shortage of organs exists and 140 people die each year because they are unable to obtain organs to transplant.

Sources: Based on Hurst, 1999; Latane and Darley, 1970; Piliavin and Callero, 1991; Piliavin and Charng, 1990; Schwartz, 1993; Titmuss, 1971; and Zurcher, 1968.

at the same answer despite having different biases and values. However, things are not always this clear, particularly in the social sciences, and complete objectivity is not possible. Sociologists Sandra Kirby and Kate McKenna tell us that "our interaction with the social world is affected by such variables as gender, race, class, sexuality, age, physical ability ..." and conclude that "this does not mean that facts about the social world do not exist, but that what we see and how we go about constructing meaning is a matter of interpretation" (1989:25). That is, marriage may mean different things for men and for women, and people with disabilities may experience the world differently than those without disabilities. This does not mean that the observers lack objectivity, but rather that they experience social life in different ways. Because of this, researchers must always

carefully describe the methods they have used in their research so that others can decide for themselves how the researcher's subjectivity has affected his or her conclusions.

Descriptive and Explanatory Studies

Sociologists typically use two types of empirical studies: descriptive and explanatory. *Descriptive studies* **attempt to describe social reality or provide facts about some group, practice, or event.** Studies of this type are designed to find out what is happening to whom, where, and when. For example, a descriptive study of altruism might attempt to determine what percentage of people would return a lost wallet or help a stranger in dis-

FIGURE 2.1   The Theory and Research Cycle

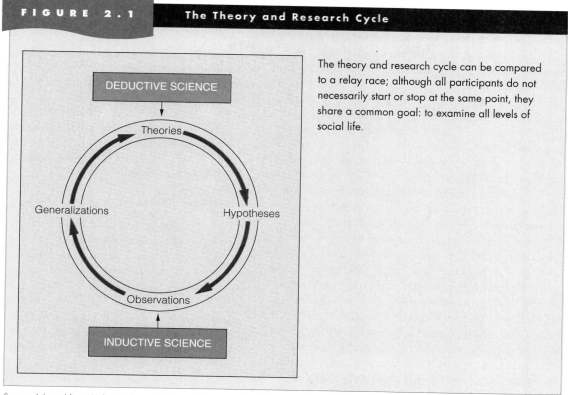

The theory and research cycle can be compared to a relay race; although all participants do not necessarily start or stop at the same point, they share a common goal: to examine all levels of social life.

Source: Adapted from Walter Wallace, *The Logic of Science in Sociology*, New York: Aldine de Gruyer, 1971.

tress. Well-known descriptive studies include the reports on the Canadian Census and the Uniform Crime Reports; however, even these "objective" studies have certain biases, as discussed in this chapter and in Chapter 7 ("Crime and Deviance"). By contrast, *explanatory studies attempt to explain cause-and-effect relationships and to provide information on why certain events do or do not occur.* In an explanatory study of altruism, we might ask, Why are some people more likely than others to offer help? or, Why do some countries rely on volunteer blood donations while others feel they must pay donors? Sociologists engage in the research process to provide answers to questions such as these.

The Theory and Research Cycle

The relationship between theory and research has been referred to as a continuous cycle, as shown in Figure 2.1 (Wallace, 1971). As we saw in Chapter 1, a theory is a set of logically interrelated statements that attempts to describe, explain, and (occasionally) predict social events. A theory attempts to explain why something is the way it

is. The theory-and-research cycle consists of deductive and inductive approaches. In the *deductive approach,* **the researcher begins with a theory and uses research to test the theory.** This approach proceeds as follows: (1) theories generate hypotheses; (2) hypotheses lead to observations (data gathering); (3) observations lead to the formation of generalizations; and (4) generalizations are used to support the theory, to suggest modifications to it, or to refute it. To illustrate, if we use the deductive method to answer the question, Why do people help others?, we start by formulating a theory about the "causes" of altruism and then test our theory by collecting and analyzing data (for example, experiments on helping behaviour or surveys to determine if men or women are more likely to offer assistance).

Theoretical knowledge is not yet well developed in the social sciences, so we lack the formal deductive theories that exist in the physical and natural sciences. However, social theories are still very helpful in examining social life and in guiding the research effort.

In the *inductive approach,* **the researcher collects information or data (facts or evidence) and** then generates theories from the analysis of that data. Under the inductive approach, we would proceed as follows: (1) specific observations suggest generalizations; (2) generalizations produce a tentative theory; (3) the theory is tested through the formation of hypotheses; and (4) hypotheses may provide suggestions for additional observations. Using the inductive approach to study altruism, we might start by simultaneously collecting and analyzing data related to helping behaviour and then generate a theory (see Glaser and Strauss, 1967; Reinharz, 1992). In fact, researchers rarely, if ever, begin with either just a theory or data. Inductive theorists need at least rudimentary theories in order to guide their data collection, and deductive theorists must refer constantly to the real world as they develop their theories. Researchers may break into the cycle at different points depending on what they want to know and what information is available. Theory gives meaning to research; research helps support theory. The actual process of research is rarely as tidy as the diagram in Figure 2.1 would suggest; instead, it typically moves back and forth from theory to data throughout the course of the inquiry.

Research helps us question assumptions we may have about social phenomena. A healthy scepticism (a feature of science) is important in research because it keeps us open to the possibility of alternative explanations. Some degree of scepticism is built into each step of the research process. With that in mind, let's explore the steps in the sociological research process.

THE SOCIOLOGICAL RESEARCH PROCESS

Suppose you were going to do some sociological research. How would you go about conducting your study? The procedure outlined here provides the guidelines for sociological research. Sociological researchers take many different paths in the course of their work. Two of these paths are shown in Figure 2.2, which is a more detailed representation of the cycle shown in Figure 2.1. Most sociological research involves the stages discussed in the rest of this section, though the order of these stages may vary from one study to another.

Selecting and Defining the Research Problem

The first step is to select a topic to research. Sometimes, a personal experience can trigger interest in a topic. You might select topics to fill gaps or challenge misconceptions in existing research or to test a specific theory (Babbie, 1992). Many sociologists choose topics related to their concerns about social policy issues. Sociologist Lesley Harman describes how she selected homeless women as the topic of her research:

> Something important began while I was teaching a course in Sociology of Deviance at York University, during the final year of my Ph.D program. I was giving a lecture on homelessness and one student asked, "What's all this about 'bag ladies'? I've never seen one and I don't think we have any in Toronto." I suggested that the fact that she lived, worked, shopped and studied in North York might have something to do with her perceptions, and that she might have a change of heart if she ventured downtown. The next week she could hardly wait to announce to the class that she had "seen one," confirming that I was right and that "there really are such things as 'bag ladies'." My interest in the cultural production of homeless women grew, and came to encompass a concern for the experience of homelessness among this increasingly visible category of women. (Harman, 1989:1)

Once a topic is selected, you must ask yourself, What do I want to know about this topic? For example, consider the issue of Good Samaritan laws discussed in Box 2.2. As a researcher, how would you approach this issue?

Reviewing Previous Research

Once you have defined your research problem, you need to review the literature (relevant books and scholarly articles). Knowledge of the existing literature is essential for a number of reasons. It helps to refine the research problem, provides possible theoretical approaches, indicates which aspects of the research topic have already been examined and where the gaps are, and identifies mistakes to avoid.

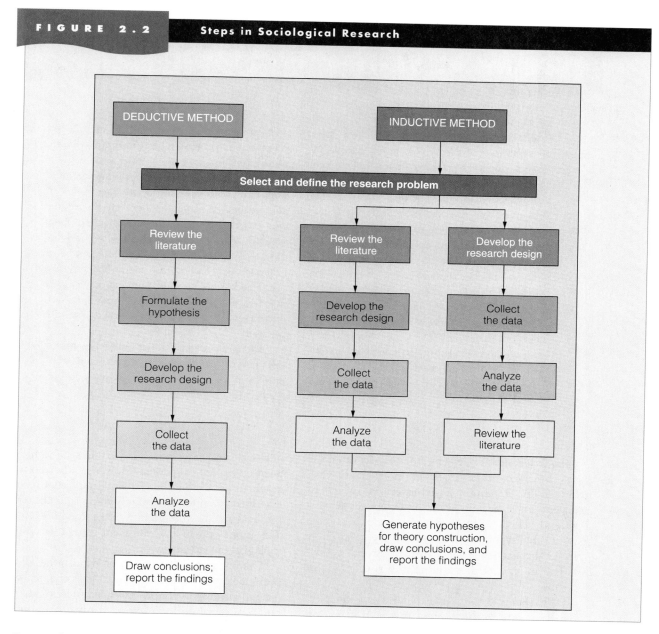

FIGURE 2.2 Steps in Sociological Research

Formulating the Hypothesis (If Applicable)

After reviewing previous research, you may formulate a hypothesis—a statement of the relationship between two or more concepts. Concepts are the abstract elements representing some aspect of the world in simplified form (such as "social integration" or "loneliness"). As you formulate your hypothesis you will need to convert concepts to variables. A **variable** is any concept with measurable traits or characteristics that can change or vary from one person, time, situation, or society to another. Variables are the observable and/or measurable counterparts of concepts. For example, "altruism" is a concept; the "percentage of the population who donate blood" is a variable.

Now you are ready to answer two important questions: What are the essential variables? and What are the relations between them? (Hoover, 1992:48). The most fundamental relationship in a hypothesis is between a dependent variable and one or more independent variables. The **independent variable** is presumed to cause or deter-

BOX 2.2   SOCIOLOGY AND THE LAW

DOES THE LAW REQUIRE US TO HELP?

Following Princess Diana's death in a Paris automobile crash in 1997, many people in Canada were surprised to learn that France has a law requiring people to help others in distress. Such laws are referred to as Good Samaritan laws after the biblical story of altruistic behaviour. Because of their failure to help the Princess, nine photographers and a press motorcyclist were placed under formal investigation—one step short of being charged—for failing to come to the aid of a person in danger. What about Canada? Does the law require that we intervene in situations where others are in danger? Will we be compensated if we are injured when trying to help others?

In most cases, the answer to these questions is no—Canadian law does little to encourage or to protect Good Samaritans. In fact, under some circumstances Canadians have been penalized for trying to help others. For example, in March 1998 a Manitoba man stopped to help three teenagers after their car had crashed. When he let them into his car, he was stabbed in the face. His attackers then tried to steal his van. Not only was the man permanently scarred, but Manitoba's public insurance corporation also made him pay the $500 deductible cost for repairing his vehicle. In other cases, people have been sued for injuries suffered by the person they had assisted.

Most provinces do have Good Samaritan laws that protect health care professionals from liability if they stop and offer assistance out-

mine a dependent variable. Sociologists often use age, sex, race, and ethnicity as independent variables. The **dependent variable is assumed to depend on or be caused by the independent variable(s)** (Babbie, 1992). Several researchers have tested the hypothesis that women are more likely to be altruistic than men. In this research gender is the independent variable and the degree of altruism is the dependent variable.

Whether a variable is dependent or independent depends on the context in which it is used. To use variables in the contemporary research process, sociologists create operational definitions. An *operational definition* is an explanation of an abstract concept in terms of observable features that are specific enough to measure the variable. Suppose, for example, your goal is to earn an "A" in this course. Your professor may have created an operational definition by defining an "A" as "having an exam average of 90 percent or above" (Babbie, 1992:G6).

Some variables can be very difficult to operationalize. For example, how do we distinguish between "criminals" and "noncriminals" when virtually all of us have broken the law? One way might be to define "criminals" as those who have been convicted of a crime. However, what do we do about people who have committed crimes, but who have been found not guilty at a trial because the evidence against them was obtained illegally? This is one of many measurement issues that criminologists must deal with.

The operational definition of altruism has also been debated. At the beginning of this chapter we defined altruism as actions intended to help others and done without any expectation of personal benefit. However, Warrant Officer Macauley and the other SARtechs were paid to rescue people and their heroism was publicly recognized. Blood donors may someday receive the benefits of a transfusion. Mother Teresa received personal satisfaction from working with the poor and may become a saint someday. Thus we must consider altruism a matter of degree rather than an attribute that some people have and others do not.

Not all social research makes use of hypotheses. If you plan to conduct an explanatory study (showing a cause-and-effect relationship), you likely will want to formulate one or more hypotheses to test theories. If you plan to conduct

BOX 2.1

CONTINUED

side a hospital or office setting. Some provinces extend this protection to all citizens who provide emergency medical services or aid. However, only Quebec *requires* people to assist others. The Quebec Charter of Human Rights and Freedoms states:

> Every human being whose life is in peril has a right to assistance. Every person must come to the aid of anyone whose life is in peril either personally or calling for aid, by giving him the necessary and immediate physical assistance, unless it involves danger to himself or a third person, or he has another valid reason.

Sources: Nairne, 1998; Quinton, 1989.

What is your view of this issue? Should we be compelled to help each other, or should we rely on people's altruism? Can the law help to encourage altruism, or is it more a function of our backgrounds and social relationships?

How could sociological research help society's understanding of this issue? How could you assess the need for Good Samaritan laws and the impact of such laws on altruistic behaviour? Do you think most people are aware that such laws are—or are not—on the books? What are public attitudes concerning the need for such laws?

---

a descriptive study, however, you will be less likely to do so, since you may want only to describe social reality or provide facts.

Developing the Research Design

During the research design phase, you will decide on one or more of the research methods— including experiments, survey research, field research, and secondary analysis of data, all of which are described in this chapter. In developing the research design, it is important to carefully consider the advantages and disadvantages of each of these methods. Your final research results will be no better than the data on which they are based, so the researcher must take great care in collecting and recording information (Robertson, 1977:43).

In developing the research design, you must also consider the units of analysis and the time frame of the study. *Units of analysis* are the *what* or *whom* being studied (Babbie, 1992). In social science research, individuals are the most typical unit of analysis. Social groups (such as families, cities, or geographic regions), organizations (such

What if one of these people suddenly had a heart attack or were stabbed by another person? Under what conditions would others intervene to help? Social research has helped us to answer this question.

as clubs, labour unions, or political parties), and social artifacts (such as books, paintings, or weddings) also may be units of analysis.

After determining the unit of analysis for your study, you must select a time frame for study. *Cross-sectional studies* are based on observations that take place at a single point in time; these studies focus on behaviour or responses at a specific moment. *Longitudinal studies* are concerned with what is happening over a period of time or at several different points in time; they focus on processes and social change. Some longitudinal studies are designed to examine the same set of people each time, while others look at trends within a general population.

Collecting the Data

Your next step is to collect the data. In the next section you will learn about the most common methods of collecting social science data: experiments, surveys, secondary analysis of existing data, and field research. No matter which of these methods is chosen, researchers must consider the reliability and validity of their data when designing a specific research project.

Reliability is the extent to which a study or research instrument yields consistent results when applied to different individuals at one time or to the same individual over time. For example, a ruler is a very reliable measure of length because it consistently gives the same results. In the social realm, an IQ test can be considered reliable if a person receives the same score when he or she takes the test more than one time. **Validity is the extent to which a study or research instrument accurately measures what it is supposed to measure.** While IQ tests are quite reliable, their validity as a measure of intelligence is more controversial. Proponents are convinced they are good measures of people's natural abilities. However, some social scientists feel the tests only measure some components of intelligence, while others criticize their use among people whose language and cultural backgrounds are different from those of the researchers who designed the tests.

Analyzing the Data

Once you have collected your data, they must be analyzed. **Analysis is the process through which data are organized so that comparisons can be made and conclusions drawn.** Sociologists use many techniques to analyze data. The process for

Conducting surveys or polls is an international means of gathering data. This investigator is conducting his research in Mexico City.

each type of research method is discussed later in this chapter. Data analysis requires considerable skill as the data do not automatically suggest a particular interpretation and the same facts can often be interpreted in several different ways.

Drawing Conclusions and Reporting the Findings

After analyzing the data, your first step in drawing conclusions is to return to your hypothesis or research objective to clarify how the data relate both to the hypothesis and to the larger issues being addressed. At this stage, you note the limitations of the study, such as problems with the sample, the influence of variables over which you had no control, or variables that your study was unable to measure.

Reporting the findings is the final stage. The report generally includes a review of each step taken in the research process in order to make the study available for *replication*—**the repetition of the investigation in substantially the same way that it originally was conducted.** Social scientists

Natural disasters such as this flood in Piedmont, Italy, may be "living laboratories" for sociologists.

generally present their findings in papers at professional meetings and publish them in academic journals and books.

RESEARCH METHODS FOR COLLECTING DATA

Experiments

An *experiment* **is a carefully designed situation in which the researcher studies the impact of certain variables on subjects' attitudes or behaviour.** Experiments are designed to create "real-life" situations, ideally under controlled circumstances, in which the influence of different variables can be modified and measured.

TYPES OF EXPERIMENTS Conventional experiments require that subjects be divided into two groups: an experimental group and a control group. The *experimental group* **contains the subjects who are exposed to an independent variable** (the experimental condition) to study its effect on them. The *control group* **contains the subjects who are not exposed to the independent variable.** The members of the two groups are matched for similar characteristics or randomly assigned to each group so that comparisons may be made between the groups. In the simplest experimental design, subjects are (1) pretested (measured in terms of the dependent variable in the hypothesis); (2) exposed to a stimulus representing an independent variable; and (3) post-tested (remeasured) in terms of the dependent variable. The experimental and control groups then are compared to see if they differ in relation to the dependent variable, and the hypothesis about the relationship of the two variables is confirmed or rejected.

In a *laboratory experiment*, subjects are studied in a closed setting so researchers can maintain as much control as possible over the research. But, not all experiments occur in laboratory settings. *Natural experiments* are real-life occurrences such as floods and other disasters that provide researchers with "living laboratories." Can you think of how you might design a field experiment to help determine the value of microcredit programs such as the one described in Box 2.3?

Case Study: Would You Help Another Person?

At 3 A.M. on March 13, 1964, Kitty Genovese was stabbed to death in the street near her home in New York City. Vincent Mosely, her attacker, assaulted her three times over a period of half an hour. At one point he left her on the street and returned a few minutes later. During the assault, Ms. Genovese screamed "Oh, my God, he stabbed me! Please help me!" However, she received no help from at least 38 neighbours who saw the attack and heard her cries for help. These neighbours did not turn away or ignore the attack; they continued to watch the murder from their apartment windows without coming to her assistance

BOX 2.2   SOCIOLOGY IN GLOBAL PERSPECTIVE

THE GRAMEEN BANK

Many rich nations, including Canada, provide foreign aid to poorer countries. Much of this aid is spent on large projects such as dams, power plants, and transportation systems. Many critics have claimed that these infrastructure projects have done little to benefit the poor people these countries are trying to help (see Chapter 9, "Global Stratification"). However, in recent years the problem of development has been approached in a new way.

Mohammad Yunus has invented a novel form of aid that directly benefits the poorest of the world's people. In the early 1970s, Yunus was the head of the economics department at Chittagong University in the newly independent country of Bangladesh. In 1974, a terrible famine killed 1.5 million Bangladeshis and changed Yunus's life. Disturbed by the contrast between the elegant economic theories he was teaching in his classes and the terrible poverty that surrounded him he decided to take his students to the affected towns and villages and try to find solutions to their poverty. On one of these visits, he met a woman who said her profit from making bamboo stools was the equivalent of only 2 cents per day. She explained to Yunus that because she had no money, she could not buy the bamboo herself even though it cost only 20 cents for a day's worth of the raw material.

Instead, she had to get it from a trader who required that she sell the stools to him for a very low price. Yunus spoke with others in the same village and found 42 self-employed people in similar circumstances who together needed a total of $27 to become self-sufficient. Yunus lent them the money and then also tried to convince local banks to lend money to the poor. The banks refused, saying that people would not repay the money and that such small sums were not worth the trouble. So, Yunus borrowed money himself and lent it to people in many different villages.

After several years of lobbying, Yunus convinced the government to allow him to set up a bank called the Grameen Bank ("rural bank" in Bengali). The bank was funded through preferential loans and through grants from international donors. Unlike most banks that lend money only to people who have money or property they can use as collateral, the Grameen Bank deals solely with the destitute. Yunus lends mainly to women, as he finds that they are more likely to give the benefits to their families and to repay the money. The bank charges interest and has several interesting requirements. For example, the bank will lend money only to groups of five borrowers. The five do not necessarily have to be in business together, but are responsible for one another's loans. The group provides both peer support

---

or calling the police. At Mosely's trial, several of these witnesses said they simply didn't want to get involved. Mosely himself said, "I knew they wouldn't do anything—they never do."

This case received worldwide attention as people tried to understand the failure of the bystanders to act. In addition to attracting public comment, the killing raised questions for researchers who sought to address the troubling questions raised by the tragedy: Why did Ms. Genovese's neighbours fail to act altruistically? Under what conditions will people be more or less likely to help others?

Among those who addressed these important issues were social psychologists Bibb Latané and John Darley (1970). They conducted initial field experiments and found that in routine situations people were very willing to help. The vast majority willingly gave directions, told inquirers the time of day, and provided change for a quarter. However, their willingness to help could be changed by manipulating simple conditions such as the wording of the request for assistance and the number of people asking for help.

Given the general willingness of the public to help in nonemergency situations, the question of

BOX 2.2

CONTINUED

and peer pressure to ensure the loans are repaid. Grameen also requires borrowers to adhere to several principles that are essentially personal commitments to things like improving sanitation practices and sending their children to school. In addition to business loans, the bank also provides housing loans.

The Grameen Bank has been phenomenally successful. About 98 percent of its loans are repaid, a much higher rate than that of other banks. The bank has expanded dramatically since it began operating in 1979. There are over two million borrowers in Bangladesh and it is lending more than half a billion dollars each year. Because of the high repayment rate, the bank is now self-sustaining. One of the bank's most recent initiatives was setting up a subsidiary, Grameen Telecom. This company lends money to rural women to buy cellphones. The women then charge other village residents to use the phones. Most villages have no regular phone connections, so there is a ready market for this service.

Yunus's idea of microcredit has spread around the globe and is operating in more than fifty countries. In Canada, there are hundreds of microcredit programs. Among the most notable are those run by Martin Connell's Calmeadow Foundation. Connell has estab-

lished several microcredit programs including the First People's Fund. Calmeadow provided half the money for this program, with First Nations communities and the five largest chartered banks sharing the remainder. The fund has now been spun off into a number of separate funds, based on reserves and run by Aboriginal people themselves.

Yunus is a very unusual bank president. He is paid only $500 per month for this job, does not own a car, and has never charged anything on a credit card. However, his work has been widely recognized and he has won countless awards and honours, including an honorary doctorate from the University of Toronto. Several observers, including U.S. President Bill Clinton, have suggested that Yunus be awarded a Nobel Prize for his revolutionary ideas and for the altruism he has shown in devoting his life to ending poverty.

What do you think would be the best way to study the impact of microcredit programs? One way would be to conduct an observational study involving extensive interviews with those who have received loans. You might also set up a field experiment in which microcredit programs were introduced into some communities that were then compared with communities that did not have the programs.

Sources: Jolis, 1996; Mitchell, 1997; Stackhouse, 1998; and Yunus, 1997.

why they often fail to respond to emergencies is difficult to understand. Latané and Darley rejected the view that this failure is due to apathy, indifference, or alienation. Instead they developed a *theoretical model* of the intervention process. Before a bystander will intervene in an emergency, he or she must notice that something is happening; interpret this event as an emergency; and decide that he or she has the personal responsibility to help. Latané and Darley proposed the hypothesis that the presence of other people will make people less likely to take each of these steps. They predicted that the presence of others would

inhibit the impulse to help for several reasons: each of the potential helpers may look to the others for guidance rather than acting quickly; potential helpers might be afraid of failing in front of other bystanders; and potential helpers may feel they are not obliged to help because one of the other bystanders could take care of the problem.

Latané and Darley did a series of experiments to test this hypothesis. Each of these experiments was scripted and designed like a short play. However, rather than entertaining, the goal of experimental research is to allow us to understand social life. One of Latané and Darley's studies was designed to simulate an emergency resembling the Kitty Genovese murder. Fifty-two university students were asked to take part in an experiment as part of a course requirement. Subjects were randomly assigned to groups of three different sizes: a two-person group (the subject and the victim); a three-person group; and a six-person group. Each of the students was seated at a table in a room, given a pair of headphones with an attached microphone, and told to listen for instructions. Over the intercom, each of the subjects was told that they were to participate in a study concerning the personal problems facing students in a high-pressure urban environment. Subjects were also told that in order to maintain their anonymity when discussing personal matters, they had been placed in individual rooms and would talk and listen to others only through an intercom. The discussion would be controlled by a mechanical switching device that would turn each student's microphone on for two minutes at a time, then turn it off while the other students were talking. Thus only one student could be heard at a time and students could not have conversations with each other. To ensure spontaneity, the experimenter would not listen to the students' discussion but would get their reactions later.

All these instructions were part of an elaborate script designed to see how the subjects would respond to an emergency, in this case an epileptic seizure by one of the respondents. The script had been acted out and tape-recorded. After receiving the instructions, each subject heard a taped simulation that began with the future seizure victim discussing his difficulties adjusting to university and to big city life. In the course of this discussion, he mentioned that he was prone to seizures during studying and exams. Each of the other people in the group, including the subject, then took their turns talking about their own adjustment problems.

The emergency occurred when it was again the victim's turn to talk. After beginning normally, he began to show obvious distress, then asked repeatedly for help, then made choking sounds and said he was going to die. After that, the intercom went quiet.

You will recall that Latané and Darley proposed the hypothesis that the presence of others would inhibit a helping response when people were faced with an emergency. The dependent variable in this experiment was the time that elapsed from the start of the victim's seizure until the subject left the experiment room to get help.

The major independent variable was the number of other people each subject believed had also heard the victim's distress.

Did the experiment support the hypothesis? Figure 2.3 shows the results. Clearly, the number of bystanders had a significant effect on the likelihood of the subject reporting the emergency. All of the subjects in the two-person groups reported the emergency compared with 85 percent of the subjects in the three-person groups and only 62 percent of the subjects in the six-person groups. The subjects in the two-person groups also responded more quickly than those in the larger groups.

What about those who failed to respond? Were they apathetic or unconcerned about the victim? You might be surprised to learn that this was not the case. Those who did not respond were clearly upset by the episode. When the researcher entered the experiment room to end the study, the subjects who had not reported the seizure were often nervous and emotionally aroused. Many asked the experimenter to confirm that the victim was "all right." While the subjects in the two-person groups clearly felt they had to intervene because nobody else knew of the victim's distress, those in the larger groups did worry about the victim but were also concerned about making fools of themselves by overreacting and about ruining the experiment. Knowledge that others also knew of the emergency made it less likely that they would resolve this conflict by helping the victim. However, according to Latané and Darley it would not be fair to say that their failure to intervene was due to apathy or a lack of concern.

Subjects in a laboratory obviously know they are participating in an experiment and may react to what they think the experiment is about or may not react realistically because they do not believe the scenario is real. This is the problem of **reactivity, which is the tendency of subjects to change their behaviour in response to the presence of the researcher or to the fact that they know they are being studied.** Latané and Darley tried to determine if their findings were due to the artificiality of the experiment. Perhaps some respondents chose not to intervene because they did not think the seizure was real. The researchers concluded this was not a problem in their study because the respondents were nervous when reporting the seizure, were surprised when they learned the true nature of the study, and made comments such as "My God, he's having a fit" during the simulated seizure.

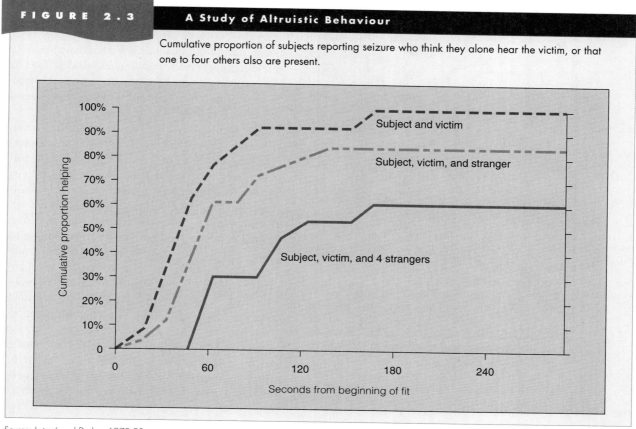

FIGURE 2.3   **A Study of Altruistic Behaviour**

Cumulative proportion of subjects reporting seizure who think they alone hear the victim, or that one to four others also are present.

Source: Latané and Darley, 1970:98.

STRENGTHS AND WEAKNESSES OF EXPERIMENTS The major advantage of the controlled experiment is the researcher's control over the environment and the ability to isolate the experimental variable. Since many experiments require relatively little time and money and can be conducted with limited numbers of subjects, it is possible for researchers to replicate an experiment several times by using different groups of subjects. Replication strengthens claims about the validity and generalizability of the original research findings (Babbie, 1992).

Perhaps the greatest limitation of experiments is that they are artificial. Social processes that occur in a laboratory setting often do not occur in the same way in real-life settings.

Experiments have several other limitations. First, the rigid control and manipulation of variables demanded by experiments do not allow for a more collective approach to data gathering that would allow input from the research subjects. Second, social scientists frequently rely on volunteers or captive audiences such as students. As a result, the subjects of most experiments may not be representative of a larger population, and the findings cannot be generalized to other groups. Third, the unnatural characteristics of laboratory experiments and of group competition in such settings may have a negative effect on subjects (Reinharz, 1992). Fourth, researchers acknowledge that experiments have the additional problem of reactivity; that is, we do not know the degree to which people are responding to the fact that they are taking part in an experiment.

Surveys

Survey research is the method of data collection most often associated with the discipline of sociology. In a **survey a number of respondents are asked identical questions through a systematic questionnaire or interview.** Researchers frequently select a representative sample (a small group of respondents) from a larger population (the total group of people) to answer questions about their attitudes, opinions, or behaviour.

THE FAR SIDE   By GARY LARSON

Chronicle Features, 1984.

"Anthropologists! Anthropologists!"

This cartoon illustrates the problem of reactivity. People may change their behaviours in response to the presence of a researcher.

Respondents **are persons who provide data for analysis through interviews or questionnaires.** The Gallup and Angus Reid polls are among the most widely known large-scale surveys. Government agencies such as Statistics Canada conduct a variety of surveys as well. Unlike many polls that use various methods of gaining a representative sample of the larger population, the census attempts to gain information from all persons in Canada. Surveys are an important research method in sociology because they make it possible to study things that are not directly observable— such as people's attitudes and beliefs—and to describe a population too large to observe directly (Babbie, 1992).

TYPES OF SURVEYS Survey data are collected by using self-administered questionnaires, personal interviews, and/or telephone surveys. A *questionnaire* **is a printed research instrument containing a series of items to which subjects respond.** Items are often in the form of statements with which the respondent is asked to "agree" or "disagree." Questionnaires may be administered by interviewers in face-to-face encounters, by telephone, or by *self-administered questionnaires*. The questionnaires typically are mailed or delivered to the respondents' homes; however, they also may be administered to groups of respondents gathered at the same place at the same time.

Self-administered questionnaires have certain strengths. They are relatively simple and inexpensive to administer, they allow for rapid data collection and analysis, and they permit respondents to remain anonymous (an important consideration when the questions are of a personal nature). A major disadvantage is the low response rate. Mailed surveys sometimes have a response rate as low as 10 percent—and a 50 percent response rate is considered by some to be minimally adequate (Babbie, 1992). The response rate usually is somewhat higher if the survey is handed out to a group, such as a school class, that is asked to fill it out on the spot.

Survey data also may be collected by interviews. An *interview* **is a data collection encounter in which an interviewer asks the respondent questions and records the answers.** Survey research often uses structured interviews, in which the interviewer asks questions from a standardized questionnaire. Structured interviews tend to produce uniform or replicable data that can be elicited time after time by different interviews.

Interviews have specific advantages. They usually are more effective in dealing with complicated issues and provide an opportunity for face-to-face communication between the interviewer and respondent. When open-ended questions are used, the researcher may gain new perspectives. The major disadvantage of interviews is the cost and time involved in conducting them.

Questionnaires may also be administered by *telephone surveys*, which are becoming an increasingly popular way to collect data for a number of reasons. Telephone surveys save time and money compared to face-to-face interviews. Some respondents may be more honest than when they are facing an interviewer. Telephone surveys also give greater control over data collection and provide greater personal safety for respondents and researchers than do personal encounters. They usually have much higher response rates than questionnaires that are mailed out.

In *computer-assisted telephone interviewing*, the interviewer uses a computer to dial random telephone numbers, reads the questions shown on the video monitor to the respondent, and then types the responses into the computer terminal. Telephone answering machines, caller identification systems, and voice mail have made telephone surveys more difficult since some people now are less accessible to researchers.

SAMPLING CONSIDERATIONS Survey research has certain built-in sampling considerations. Researchers begin by identifying the population they want to study. They then determine what constitutes a representative sample of the entire population being studied.

The *population* consists of those persons about whom we want to be able to draw conclusions (Babbie, 1992). A *sample* is the people who are selected from the population to be studied; the sample should accurately represent the larger population. A *representative sample* is a selection from a larger population that has the essential characteristics of the total population. For example, if you have to interview five students selected haphazardly from your sociology class, they would not be representative of your school's total student body. By contrast, if five hundred students were selected from the total student body using a random sampling method, they would very likely be representative of your school's students. A simple *random sample* is chosen by chance: every member of an entire population being studied has the same chance of being selected. For example, you might draw a sample of the total student body by placing all the students' names in a rotating drum and drawing names from it.

QUESTIONNAIRE CONSTRUCTION The quality of the questionnaire is central to the success of survey research. The more specific a survey question is, the more likely respondents are to interpret the question in the same way and the more easily comparable their answers will be. Questionnaires may vary in length and complexity, but in a specific study, each questionnaire must be identical in wording and in the order of items. Questions generally are pretested for reliability and validity, and they should be worded so that they are easily understood.

Most survey research relies on *closed-ended questions*, in which the respondent is asked to answer from a list of alternative responses (for example, multiple-choice questions). These responses are fairly easy to measure and compare. However, closed-ended questions sometimes fail to increase our insights into the respondents' real feelings, attitudes, and beliefs because they are forced to choose from predetermined answers that may not accurately reflect their true thoughts. By contrast, open-ended questions provide respondents with the opportunity to reply to a question in their own words (for example, "Please describe why you donate blood"). This type of question allows more flexibility in the respondent's answer, but it also makes it more difficult to measure and compare answers. Both kinds of questions should be free from biases implying that one sex, class, or age serves as the standard against which all others are measured (Eichler, 1988b; Reinharz, 1992).

Case Study: The Gift of Blood

To what degree should we be responsible for the lives of others? Should an economic value be placed on human life? Can social policy influence moral behaviour? Richard Titmuss of the University of London addressed these very important questions in his study of blood donation. Titmuss's concerns were much broader than blood; he was interested in society's spirit of altruism and he used blood donation as an indicator of social values and human relationships. He wished to understand why people would donate blood to strangers in a world that often seems characterized by self-interest and greed.

Policies regarding the donation and distribution of blood vary widely around the world. In many countries at least some donors are paid, and the collection and distribution of blood is a business. In others, including Canada and the United Kingdom, blood is not treated as a commodity to be bought and sold, but as a voluntary gift. For Titmuss, donating blood is a special kind of gift because the recipient is an anonymous stranger and because the donor may never receive anything in return. He refers to such gifts as "creative altruism" and suggests they are an important component of caring communities. In his research he wished to determine what types of people became blood donors and to ask them about their motivations for donating.

At the time of Titmuss's research, Britain's National Blood Transfusion Service did not record statistics about the age, sex, marital status, or social class of its donors. To learn about the characteristics of blood donors and their reasons for giving blood, Titmuss distributed 8000 questionnaires to current blood donors. Respondents were asked to complete the surveys and to personally return them at meetings with the researchers. Over 3800 of the questionnaires were completed and returned. This survey was only one component of the study, but it led to some important conclusions about why people are willing to give to anonymous strangers.

The British donors came from all segments of society, but were somewhat more likely to be young, male, and from the middle and upper middle classes. Most were long-service donors; over half had donated blood fifteen or more times. When asked why they had decided to become blood donors, respondents clearly supported Titmuss's hypothesis that their motivation was altruistic. They spoke of their desire to help, their awareness of the need for blood, and their sense of duty toward others. These quotations from the surveys are typical of the responses:

> I thought it just a small way to help people—as a blind person other opportunities are limited.

> At the age of 18 I decided that it was a good thing for anyone capable and healthy to donate blood for the good of other people and the advancement of medical science.

> My son was killed on the road, he was a blood donor and I knew they did their best to save him and because I know he would be pleased I am carrying on as long as I can to help someone I hope. (Titmuss, 1971:227–229)

Most donors explained their behaviour in moral terms. They felt they had responsibilities and obligations beyond their own immediate gratification. Titmuss concluded that these obligations help to sustain a feeling of community membership. You will recall from Chapter 1, "The Sociological Perspective," that Emile Durkheim discussed how preindustrial societies were held together by strong traditions and by members' shared moral beliefs and values. As societies industrialized, economic activity increasingly became the basis of the social bond. Titmuss's work demonstrates that even in complex, large-scale societies altruism plays a significant role in maintaining the social order.

STRENGTHS AND WEAKNESSES OF SURVEYS Survey research has several important strengths. First, it is useful in describing the characteristics of a large population without having to interview each person in that population. Second, survey research enables the researcher to search for causes and effects and to assess the relative importance of a number of variables. Unfortunately, Titmuss gave his surveys only to those who had donated blood, so his work does not allow us to examine the differences between donors and nondonors. The best way to study these differences would be to conduct a survey of a sample of the general population in which respondents would be asked if they had donated blood. In our analysis of the data we could then look at the effect of demographic variables (such as age, sex, and income level) and attitudinal variables on the decision to donate blood. This would allow us to determine which of these independent variables influences altruism the most and how influential each is relative to the others. Third, survey research can be useful in analyzing social change or documenting the existence of a social problem. Contemporary scholars have used survey research to provide information about problems—such as racial discrimination, sexual harassment, and sex-based inequality in employment—by documenting the fact that they are more widespread than previously thought (Reinharz, 1992).

Survey research also has several weaknesses. One is that the use of standardized questions tends to force respondents into categories in which they may or may not belong. Another weakness concerns validity. People's opinions on issues seldom take the form of a standard response ranging from "strongly agree" to "strongly disagree." Moreover, as in other types of research, people may be less than truthful, especially on emotionally charged issues or on issues such as altruism that have a strong element of social desirability. This can make reliance on self-reported attitudes and behaviour problematic.

Some scholars also have criticized the way survey data sometimes are used. The data collected are not always "hard facts" as some researchers claim. For example, survey statistics may over- or underestimate the extent of a problem and work against some categories of people more than others, as shown in Table 2.1.

Secondary Analysis of Existing Data

In *secondary analysis,* researchers use existing material and analyze data originally collected by others. Existing data sources include public

TABLE 2.1   **STATISTICS: WHAT WE KNOW (AND DON'T KNOW)**

	TOPIC		
	HOMELESSNESS	**GAY MEN**	**DOMESTIC VIOLENCE**
Research Finding	Over 200,000 people in this country are homeless.	At least 1 percent of Canadian men are exclusively homosexual.	Some surveys have reported that women are as likely as men to engage in domestic violence.
Possible Problem	Does that badly underestimate the total number of homeless people?	Does this underestimate the gay population? Is the actual figure higher?	Are the results of these surveys accurate or should we believe other data such as homicide statistics that show domestic violence is predominantly committed by males?
Explanation	The homeless are difficult to count. They may avoid interviews with census takers. The 1996 census was the first attempt to count the number of homeless in Canada. However, these numbers will not be released by Statistics Canada.	Many people are reluctant to tell interviewers the truth about their sexuality; people often are hesitant to report their sexual orientation. This may result in estimates being too low.	There may be differences in the willingness of males and females to report abusing their partners; the surveys ignore the context of the violence; and the surveys do not consider the degree of injury.

records, official reports of organizations or government agencies, and surveys conducted by researchers in universities and private corporations. Research data gathered from studies are available in data banks, such as the Inter-University Consortium for Political and Social Research, and the York University Institute for Behavioural Research. Many Canadian university libraries have recently joined the Data Liberation Initiative, which gives members of the university community access to a wide variety of databases. Other sources of data for secondary analysis are books, magazines, newspapers, radio and television programs, and personal documents. Secondary analysis is referred to as *unobtrusive research* because it includes a variety of nonreactive research techniques—that is, techniques that have no impact on the people being studied. In Durkheim's study of suicide, for example, his analysis of existing statistics on suicide did nothing to increase or decrease the number of people who *actually* committed suicide.

The following case study shows how data collected for other purposes can be used to shed light on the phenomenon of altruism.

Case Study: Good Neighbours and Saints

Sociologist Pitirim Sorokin had a remarkable life and career, and his background played an important role in shaping his work on altruism. Sorokin began life in 1889 as a poor peasant in northern Russia but by 1930 he had become the first chairman of Harvard University's sociology department. As a youth he was part of the active resistance against the Russian Czar and spent much of the time between 1906 and 1917 in jail. He was a senior official in the Kerensky government after the Czar fell, but once again became a political target when his party was replaced by the Bolsheviks, who imprisoned Sorokin for opposing Lenin. Throughout these difficult times, his strong commitment to the Orthodox church helped him to retain a positive view of life and a strong sense of duty and obligation.

Sorokin's work on altruism was driven by his view that Western culture had become increasingly negativistic. He was particularly critical of the mass media's emphasis on crime, sex scandals, and hypocrisy. In words that predated Jerry

Springer and Howard Stern by almost fifty years, Sorokin expressed his disgust with a popular culture that "dwells mainly in the region of subsocial sewers; breathes mainly their foul air; and drags down into their turbid muck everything heroic, positive, true, good and beautiful" (1950:3). He was also critical of social scientists who concentrated their efforts on studying the negative aspects of society:

> The criminal has been "researched" incomparably more thoroughly than the saint or the altruist; the idiot has been studied much more carefully than the genius; perverts and failures have been investigated much more intensely than integrated persons or heroes. In accordance with the total nature of our negativistic culture, our social science has been semi-blind about all positive types and actions and very sharp-eyed about all negative types and actions. It seems to have enjoyed moving in the muck of social sewers; it has been reluctant to move in the fresh air of high social peaks. It has stressed the pathological and neglected the sound and heroic. (1950:4)

Sorokin wanted to redress this one-sided perspective by studying altruistic behaviour. He felt that increasing the incidence of altruism was the key to transforming the culture and hoped his research on altruists would facilitate this transformation. In his book *Altruistic Love* he looked at two very different groups of people: "good neighbours" and saints. He chose these groups because of the rich secondary data that were made available to him.

In the first part of his study, rather than looking at dramatic acts of kindness or heroism, Sorokin chose to study the behaviour of ordinary people. During the 1940s, a radio program called *Breakfast in Hollywood* rewarded what it called "good neighbours" with an orchid and a citation on the show. These people were chosen from letters of recommendation sent in by listeners from across the United States. The show's producers had kept the letters on file and Sorokin was able to analyze five hundred nominations of people who had quietly served their communities with no expectation of any benefit to themselves. Data he took from these nomination letters allowed him to present a statistical picture of the individuals and their altruistic behaviour.

The majority of the good neighbours were females. Sorokin attributed this to the socialization of women into nurturing roles, to the ten-dency of men to express their altruistic spirit through financial donations rather than through direct service, and to the fact that many of the nominations were received during World War II, when millions of men were serving overseas. Most were middle-aged married people from rural communities. The vast majority were frequent church-goers. Not surprisingly, most were very optimistic, friendly people who belonged to a wide variety of community organizations.

Typical of the nominees studied by Sorokin were Mr. and Mrs. C., who helped hundreds of disabled people by contributing wheelchairs, braces, and crutches, who spent all their spare time visiting and assisting shut-ins, and who repaired and distributed used radios to those who could not afford to buy them. Like other "good neighbours" they had clearly devoted most of their free time and personal resources to helping others.

Because of the many wartime nominations, the largest category of persons helped were members of the military. Other common recipients of assistance were the sick, charitable organizations, children, and the elderly. In many respects, those helped were the opposites of their helpers—they were most often male, unmarried, and either aged or children. Many different types of help were offered including recreational and social activities, activities to help alleviate loneliness and grief, and more tangible things such as money, food, shelter, and clothing. Sorokin particularly emphasized the social functions of the good neighbours who he felt supplied a warm-hearted assistance that could never be provided by any official agency.

In the second part of his study, Sorokin turned to the lives of Catholic saints. Unlike the good neighbours, whose activities usually went unrecognized outside their communities, saints had been singled out for unique recognition by the Catholic church. For many, saints represent the epitome of selfless love and goodness. They are visible examples of the highest human qualities and are held out to other church members as examples of the highest form of altruistic love. In this study, Sorokin drew from the very rich resource provided by the twelve-volume work called *The Lives of the Saints* that provided biographical information on 3090 saints.

Unlike the good neighbours, who were predominantly female, over 80 percent of the saints were males. However, the proportion of women achieving sainthood has changed dramatically over time. From the first to the twelfth centuries, the proportion of women who became saints rarely exceeded 20 percent. Since the thirteenth century the proportion of women saints has fallen below 20 percent in only the sixteenth and seventeenth centuries, and in the eighteenth century women made up almost half the new saints. This suggests that as women moved toward becoming the social equals of men, their representation in the sainthood rose. Similarly, the proportion of saints from royal or noble backgrounds has declined, and by the nineteenth century most saints were drawn from the lower classes of peasants and urban workers.

Sorokin was able to distinguish several different paths to sainthood. The largest number (44 percent) were what he called "fortunate saints" who had loving, well-integrated families and who showed signs of religiosity and devotion to God from a very early age. They continued to show this devotion until death, so their whole lives were examples of goodness and purity. Another 37 percent achieved sainthood through martyrdom—they showed courage and devotion by not renouncing their faith despite their imminent death at a time of either religious persecution or religious war. Perhaps the most interesting finding was that 11 percent led distinctly unsaintly lives until they experienced a crisis such as sickness, a death, or an unexpected, extraordinary kindness that precipitated a complete reorientation in their lives. There were some parallels between the saints and the "good neighbours." For example, the lives of the fortunate saints were similar to many of the good neighbours, who also came from supportive families and who exhibited exemplary behaviour for most of their lives. Other good neighbours changed their lives because of inner conflicts or external precipitating factors.

While none of the good neighbours was martyred, Sorokin did find that some had run into conflicts with the law and the government in the course of doing their kind deeds. Some were conscientious objectors who refused to be drafted while others would not take part in the anticommunist witch hunts that were part of American political life after World War II.

Through his use of data collected for other purposes, Sorokin was able to tell us a great deal about the lives and work of altruistic people. However, his observation that social scientists are more interested in bad behaviour than in good works still holds true, and very few sociologists have followed his lead in studying the lives of exemplary people.

ANALYZING CONTENT Another type of secondary analysis is *content analysis*—the systematic examination of cultural artifacts or various forms of communication to extract thematic data and draw conclusions about social life. *Cultural artifacts* are products of individual activity, social organizations, technology, and cultural patterns (Reinharz, 1992:147). Among the materials studied are *written records,* such as diaries, love letters, poems, books, and graffiti; and *narratives and visual texts,* such as movies, television shows, advertisements, and greeting cards. Also studied are *material culture,* such as music, art, and even garbage; and behavioural residues, such as patterns of wear and tear on the floor in front of various exhibits at art museums to determine what exhibits are the most popular (see Webb, 1966; Reinharz, 1992). Martineau noted that more could be learned about a society in a day by studying "things" than by talking with individuals for a year (Martineau, 1988/1838:73). Researchers may look for regular patterns, such as the frequency of altruistic behaviour as a topic on television talk shows. They also may examine subject matter to determine how it has been handled, such as how the mass media handle the topic. Systematic coding and objective recording of data according to some conceptual framework are essential in content analysis.

In a recent study, sociologists Myra Ferree and Elaine Hall (1990) examined the 5413 illustrations (including photographs, drawings, and cartoons) in thirty-three introductory sociology textbooks published in the United States between 1982 and 1988. The individuals in each illustration were coded for race and sex, location in or outside the United States, and placement in one of twenty-six chapters (such as race, gender, economy, politics, and family). From their content analysis, Ferree and Hall concluded that women were not represented in the illustrations in numbers proportionate to their distribution in the population. They were particularly invisible in the chapters on politics and the economy. Although individual people of colour were shown in numerically fair proportions, they were conceptualized as essentially different and given distinctive visual roles in the text. For example, African Americans often were included to show racial integration in the United States, while Asians, Hispanics, and other racial–ethnic groups largely were depicted as living in other countries, where they provided a "comparative" perspective on the United States (Ferree and Hall, 1990:528). What do you think

Canadians have always shown a strong willingness to help in natural disasters such as the 1997 Red River flood.

the results would be of a content analysis of Canadian sociology textbooks? Would the results be similar? How would visible minorities be represented?

Strengths and Weaknesses of Secondary Analysis

One strength of secondary analysis is that data are readily available and are often inexpensive to obtain. Another is that, because the researcher usually does not collect the data personally, the chances of bias may be reduced. In addition, the use of existing sources makes it possible to analyze longitudinal data to provide a historical context within which to locate original research. However, secondary analysis has inherent problems. For one thing, the data may be incomplete, inauthentic, or inaccurate. Sorokin found that even basic data such as age at death and social class of origin were not available for many of the early saints. For another, the various sources from which content analysis is done may not be comparable with one another (Reinharz, 1992), and *coding* these data—or sorting, categorizing, and organizing the data into conceptual categories (Babbie, 1992)—may be difficult. Finally, secondary data are often collected for administrative

purposes, so the categories may not reflect variables of interest to the researcher. Sorokin could not find information about the motivation of either the good neighbours or the saints, so he could not explain why they behaved altruistically.

Field Research

Field research is the study of social life in its natural setting: observing and interviewing people where they live, work, and play. Some kinds of behaviour can be studied best by "being there"; a fuller understanding can be developed through observations, face-to-face discussions, and participation in events. Researchers use these methods to generate *qualitative* data: observations that are best described verbally rather than numerically. Although field research is less structured and more flexible than the other methods we have discussed, it also places many demands on the researcher. To engage in field research, sociologists must select the method or combination of methods that will best reveal what they want to know. For example, they must decide how to approach the target group, whether to identify themselves as researchers, and whether to participate in the events they are observing.

Observation Sociologist John Lofland (1971) has argued that the bedrock of human understanding is face-to-face contact. Sociologists who are interested in observing social interaction as it occurs may use either complete observation or participant observation. In **complete observation, the researcher systematically observes a social process but does not take part in it.** Observational research can take place just about anywhere. For example, sociologists David Karp and William Yoels (1976) became interested in why many students do not participate in discussions in university classrooms. Observers sat in on various classes and took notes that included the average number of students who participated, the number of times they talked during one class session, and the sex of the instructor and of the students who talked in class. From their observational data, Karp and Yoels found that, on average, a very small number of students are responsible for the majority of all discussion that occurs in class on any given day.

Suppose you wanted to study your own class to identify the "talkers" and the "silent ones." You would need to develop a game plan before you started to observe. A game plan typically is guided by a research question, such as, "Why don't more university students participate in class discussions?" Subjects in observation studies may not realize that they are being studied, especially if the researcher remains unobtrusive. Observation helps us view behaviour as it is taking place; however, it provides limited opportunities to learn why people do certain things. One way for researchers to remain unobtrusive is through *participant observation*—collecting systematic observations while being part of the activities of the group they are studying. Participant observation generates more "inside" information than simply asking questions or observing from the outside. As sociologist William Whyte noted in his classic participant observation study of a Boston low-income neighourhood: "As I sat and listened, I learned the answers to questions I would not have had the sense to ask" (1957:303).

Case Study: Responding to Disaster

During the spring of 1997, two of this book's authors observed altruistic behaviour first-hand when they witnessed the phenomenal response to the massive Red River floods. Tens of thousands of Manitobans devoted several weeks of their time to sandbagging; volunteers flew in from as far away as Newfoundland at their own expense to help; the Canadian military sent in over 8000 soldiers, sailors, and air force members who worked day and night to save Manitoba communities; and people from all parts of Canada donated millions of dollars to help pay for the cleanup. While the flooding was very costly and disrupted the lives of thousands of people in Manitoba and North Dakota, it was also an event that created bonds between the people involved and reinforced a sense of community.

The Manitoba experience is not unique. Natural disasters have brought people together in many parts of the world and have often shown human behaviour at its altruistic best. What motivates people to get involved in helping after natural disasters? How do groups of strangers come together and work effectively to help others? How do communities restore their cohesiveness after a tragic loss? Sociologist Louis Zurcher (1968) tried to answer these questions when he took part in the cleanup following a severe tornado that destroyed parts of Topeka, Kansas. The tornado

killed 17 persons, injured 550 others, and made 2500 people homeless.

Zurcher, a resident of Topeka, joined a volunteer work crew that spent several days cleaning up after the tornado. He joined the crew in order to help his community recover from the disaster, but he also took the opportunity to carry out an observational research study. In addition to the physical work he was doing—largely removing fallen tree limbs and trees from houses—he systematically observed what was happening and recorded these observations in detailed notes made on the scene and at the end of each work day. He supplemented these observations with unstructured interviews with members of his work crew conducted after the cleanup.

One of the most important research questions for Zurcher was why individuals gave up their time and took the risks involved in helping their fellow residents. In his interviews he found that all the volunteers in his workcrew felt they simply had to do something. The stress of living through the tornado and, for some, the guilt at having survived unscathed motivated the workers to get out and to help the community recover from the disaster. Typical of the workers' comments were those of one member of Zurcher's crew:

> ... was back at my job ... felt out of place talking about the tornado ... not yet time for talk ... felt ineffectual ... mounting sense of frustration ... wanted to do something meaningful, now, as a release for some of the feelings that had been building up inside ... not doing anything worthwhile ... try to find some way or place to be useful ... that night watch T.V. and learn that the Emergency Relief Center is calling for volunteers ... respond instinctively ... here is a place where I might be effective after all ... at Center I was told about [Zurcher's] crew and where it was ... found them and went to work. (Zurcher, 1968:285)

The crew members, most of whom did not know each other prior to the disaster, seemed to find the first day of hard work a way of working off the emotions raised by the tornado. By the end of the day, the men had begun to form a cohesive group in which each member had a specific role. This led them to look beyond their own emotions and to pay more attention to their co-workers and to the people they were helping. On the second day, the roles became more formalized and group identity became stronger as the men took on some challenging tasks. Outside social status meant little as people from a broad range of occupations worked together. The work crew quickly evolved

Case studies of homeless persons have added to our insights on the causes and consequences of this major social concern. Women often are the "invisible homeless."

from a group of strangers into a cohesive group with a well-defined division of labour and its own history, loyalty to other members, a great deal of humour, and its own specialized language. The group ended its work after the third day, but some of the men met socially for years after the disaster.

Zurcher felt that the manner in which group solidarity and cohesiveness developed in his work crew would also develop in other social settings. Following a disaster, people initially come together because of shared concerns and common experiences. However, in our complex world, a division of labour quickly evolves, and people are also bound together by their mutual dependence as they carry out specialized tasks. You will learn more about these processes in Chapter 5 ("Social Structure and Interaction in Everyday Life") when you read about Emile Durkheim's important distinction between mechanical and organic solidarity. Durkheim's insights about the change in the source of social solidarity as societies become more complex were tested by Zurcher in the real-life social laboratory provided by the Kansas tornado.

CASE STUDIES Most participant observation research takes the form of a *case study*, an in-depth, multifaceted investigation of a single event, person, or social grouping (Feagin, Orum, and Sjoberg, 1991). Case studies often involve more than one method of research, such as participant observation, unstructured or in-depth interviews, and life histories.

How do social scientists decide to do case studies? Initially, some researchers have only a general idea of what they wish to investigate. In other cases, they literally "back into" the research. They may find themselves in proximity to interesting people or situations. For example, anthropologist Elliot Liebow "backed into" his study of single, homeless women living in emergency shelters by becoming a volunteer at a shelter. As he got to know the women, Liebow became fascinated with their lives and survival strategies. Prior to Liebow's research, most studies of the homeless focused primarily on men. These studies typically asked questions like, "How many homeless are there?" and "What proportion of the homeless are chronically mentally ill?" By contrast, Liebow wanted to know more about the homeless women themselves, wondering such things as, "What are they carrying in those [shopping] bags?" (Coughlin, 1993:A8). Liebow spent the next four years engaged in participant observation research that culminated in his book *Tell Them Who I Am* (1993).

In participant observation studies, the researcher must decide whether to let people know they are being studied. After Liebow decided that he would like to take notes on informal conversations and conduct interviews with the women, he asked the shelter director and the women for permission and told them that he would like to write about them. Liebow's findings are discussed in Chapter 5 ("Social Structure and Interaction in Everyday Life"). While some social scientists gain permission from their subjects, others fear that people will refuse to participate or will change their behaviour if they know they are being observed. On the one hand, researchers who do not obtain consent from their subjects may be acting unethically. On the other hand, when subjects know they are being observed, they may alter their behaviour, so the researcher will get a misleading picture of what is happening.

The next step is to gain the trust of participants. In a participant observation study, you may wish to identify possible informants—individuals who introduce you to others, give suggestions about how to "get around" in the natural setting, and provide you with essential insider information on what you are observing.

UNSTRUCTURED INTERVIEWS   An *unstructured interview* is an extended, open-ended interaction between an interviewer and an interviewee. The interviewer has a general plan of inquiry but not a specific set of questions that must be asked, as is often the case with surveys. Unstructured interviews are essentially conversations in which interviewers establish the general direction by asking open-ended questions, to which interviewees may respond flexibly. Interviewers have the ability to "shift gears" and pursue specific topics raised by interviewees, because answers to one question are used to suggest the next question or new areas of inquiry.

Lesley Harman's (1989) study of homeless women in Ontario is an example of research that used in-depth interviews to examine the challenges homeless women face to survive in a domesticated culture. Many perplexing questions arise in deciding how to conduct unstructured interviews. Harman identified some of them as: "The dilemmas of how much closeness to develop with my subjects, how much to reveal about my own life, how much to ask about their previous lives, and how much to believe, plagued me everyday" (1989:43).

Even in unstructured interviews, researchers must prepare a few general or "lead-in" questions to get the interview started. Following the interviewee's initial responses, the interviewer may wish to ask additional questions on the same topic, probe for more information (by using questions such as, "In what ways?" or "Anything else?"), or introduce a new line of inquiry. At all points in the interview, *careful listening* is essential. It provides the opportunity to introduce new questions as the interview proceeds while simulta-

neously keeping the interview focused on the research topic. It also enables the interviewer to envision interviewees' experiences and to glean multiple levels of meaning.

Interviews and Theory Construction   In-depth interviews, along with participant observation and case studies, frequently are used to develop theories through observation. The term *grounded theory* was developed by sociologists Barney Glaser and Anselm Strauss (1967) to describe this inductive method of theory construction. Researchers who use grounded theory collect and analyze data simultaneously. For example, after in-depth interviews with 106 suicide attempters, researchers in one study concluded that half of the individuals who attempted suicide wanted both to live and to die at the time of their attempt. From these unstructured interviews, it became obvious that ambivalence led about half of "serious" suicidal attempters to "literally gamble with death" (Kovacs and Beck, 1977, quoted in Taylor, 1982:144). After asking their initial unstructured questions of the interviewees, Kovacs and Taylor decided to widen the research question from, "Why do people kill themselves?" to the broader question, "Why do people engage in acts of self damage which may result in death?" In other words, uncertainty of outcome is a common feature of most suicidal acts. In previous studies, researchers had simply assumed that in "dangerous attempts" the individual really wanted to die while in "moderate" attempts the person was ambivalent (Taylor, 1982:160).

STRENGTHS AND WEAKNESSES OF FIELD RESEARCH
Field research provides opportunities for researchers to view from the inside what may not be obvious to an outside observer. Field methods are useful when attitudes and behaviours can be understood best within their natural setting or when the researcher wants to study social processes and change over a period of time. They provide a wealth of information about the reactions of people and give us an opportunity to generate theories from the data collected (Whyte, 1989).

Through unstructured interviews, researchers gain access to "people's ideas, thoughts, and memories in their own words rather than in the words of the researcher" (Reinharz, 1992:19). Research of this type is important for the study of race, ethnicity, and gender because it lets people who previously have had no "voice" describe their experiences and provides researchers with an opportunity to explore people's views of reality.

Social scientists who believe that quantitative research methods (such as survey research) provide the most scientific and accurate means of measuring attitudes, beliefs, and behaviour often are critical of data obtained through field research. They argue that what is learned from a specific group or community cannot be generalized to a larger population. They also suggest that the data collected in natural settings are descriptive and do not lend themselves to precise measurement.

Feminist Research Methods

During the past two decades, feminist social scientists have focused a critical eye on traditional sociological research, as well as on the research methodologies and findings of other disciplines. Margrit Eichler (1988b) has identified several limitations in research that relate to gender, including androcentricity (which means approaching an issue from a male perspective or viewing women only in terms of how they relate to men); sexist language or concepts; research methods that are biased in favour of men (for example, in sampling techniques or questionnaire design); and research results that overgeneralize (which means that results that focus on members of one sex are used to support conclusions about both sexes).

Most writers on feminist research issues agree that there is no one method that can be termed *the* feminist methodology. However, qualitative methods and, in particular, in-depth interviews tend to be associated with feminist research. Although feminist research may involve the same basic methods for collecting data as other research, the way in which feminists use these methods is very different. First, women's experiences are important and, to understand them, women's lives need to be addressed in their own terms (Edwards, 1993). Feminist research is woman centred, that is, "it puts women at the center of research that is nonalienating, nonexploitive, and potentially emancipating" (Sculley, 1990:2–3). Second, the goal of feminist research is to provide explanations of women's lives that are useful to them in terms of improving their situations. It is important, therefore, to ensure that women's experiences are not objectified or treated as merely "research data." In fact, feminist sociologist Dorothy Smith (1987) suggests that "giving voice" to disadvantaged and marginalized groups in society is a primary goal of sociology. Finally, feminist research methods challenge the traditional role of the researcher as a detached, "value-free," objective observer. Rather, the researcher is seen as central to the research process and her feelings and experiences should be analyzed as an integral part of the research process (Edwards, 1993; Kirby and McKenna, 1989).

In a discussion of her study of marital rape, Raquel Kennedy Bergen has shown the need for the researcher's personal involvement in the research process. Bergen took care to ensure that the women she interviewed knew that she was supportive and interested in helping them, and was not simply exploiting their experiences for her own purposes. She was willing to share her own views and experiences with her research subjects and was careful to deal with any emotional distress that was caused by her interviews:

> During the most emotionally difficult interview, I spent a long time offering support to a woman who became extremely upset when she described her husband ... raping her in front of her child. This experience emphasized the need for researchers (especially those working on sensitive topics) to interview with conscious partiality. If I had been a detached and objective researcher merely collecting data, I might have either terminated the interview and discarded the data or possibly suggested that the woman receive outside counseling. As a feminist researcher, however, I was interacting with this woman on a personal level and her distress was deeply affecting. Thus it was not problematic for me to comfort this woman (both during and after the interview) as I had not compartmentalized my identity into counselor, researcher, and woman. (1993:208)

Multiple Methods of Social Research

What is the best method for studying a particular topic? Concept Table 2.A compares the various social research methods. It is important to understand that there is no such thing as the best research method. Each of the methodologies we have discussed in this chapter has its own strengths and weaknesses. Because of this many sociologists believe that it is best to combine multiple methods in a given study. *Triangulation* is the use of multiple approaches in a single study (Denzin, 1989). Triangulation refers not only to research methods but also to multiple data sources, investigators, and theoretical perspectives in a study. Multiple data sources include persons, situations, contexts, and time (Snow and Anderson, 1991). For example, David Snow and Leon Anderson's study of unattached homeless men and women used as their primary data sources "the homeless themselves and the array of settings, agency personnel, business proprietors, city officials, and neighbourhood activities relevant to the routines of the homeless" (1991:158). Snow and Anderson gained a detailed portrait of the homeless and their experiences and institutional contacts by tracking over seven hundred homeless individuals through a network of seven institutions with which they had varying degrees of contact.

The study also tracked a number of the individuals over a period of time and used a variety of methods, including "participant observation and informal, conversational interviewing with the homeless; participant and nonparticipant observation, coupled with formal and informal interviewing in street agencies and settings; and a systematic survey of agency records" (Snow and Anderson, 1991:158–169).

Multiple methods and approaches provide a wider scope of information and enhance our understanding of critical issues. Many researchers also use multiple methods to validate or refine one type of data by use of another type.

ETHICAL ISSUES IN SOCIOLOGICAL RESEARCH

The study of people ("human subjects") raises vital questions about ethical concerns in sociological research. Researchers are now required by a professional code of ethics to weigh the societal benefits of research against the potential physical and emotional costs to participants. Researchers are required to obtain written "informed consent" statements from the persons they study. However, these guidelines have produced many new questions, such as, What constitutes "informed consent"? What constitutes harm to a person? How do researchers protect the identity and confidentiality of their sources?

The Canadian Sociology and Anthropology Association has outlined the basic standards sociologists must follow in conducting research. Social research often involves intrusions into people's lives—surveys, interviews, field observa-

tions, and participation in experiments all involve personally valuable commodities: time, energy, and privacy. Participation in research must be voluntary. No one should be enticed, coerced, or forced to participate. Researchers must not harm the research subjects in any way—physically, psychologically, or personally. For example, the researcher must be careful not to reveal information that would embarrass the participants, or damage their personal relationships. Researchers must respect the rights of research subjects to anonymity and confidentiality.

A respondent is *anonymous* when the researcher cannot identify a given response with a given respondent. Anonymity is often extremely important in terms of obtaining information on "deviant" or illegal activities. For example, in a study on physician-assisted suicides conducted by the Manitoba Association of Rights and Liberties (Searles, 1995) ensuring the anonymity of the physicians responding to the survey was crucial because the doctors were being asked about their participation in illegal acts.

Maintaining *confidentiality* means that the researcher is able to identify a given person's responses with that person but essentially promises not to do so. Whether the researcher should reveal his or her identity is also a difficult issue. In some cases, it is useful to identify yourself as a researcher to obtain cooperation from respondents. However, there are other instances when revealing your identity can affect the content and quality of your research. It is not acceptable to use deception to obtain informed consent. For example, not informing a research subject of potential risk or harm constitutes deception. Finally, researchers have an obligation to report all of their research findings in full, including unexpected or negative findings and limitations of the research.

Sociologists are committed to adhering to these ethical considerations and to protecting research participants; however, many ethical issues arise that cannot be resolved easily. Research ethics is a difficult and often ambiguous topic. However, ethical issues cannot be ignored by researchers, whether they are sociology professors, graduate students conducting investigations for their dissertations, or undergraduates conducting a class research project.

How honest do researchers have to be with potential participants? Let's look at a specific case in point. Where does the "right to know" end and the "right to privacy" begin in this situation?

STRENGTHS AND WEAKNESSES OF SOCIAL RESEARCH METHODS

RESEARCH METHOD	STRENGTHS	WEAKNESSES
Experiments Laboratory Field Natural	Control over research Ability to isolate experimental factors Relatively little time and money required Replication possible, except for natural experiments	Artificial by nature Frequent reliance on volunteers or captive audiences Ethical questions of deception Problem of reactivity
Survey Research Questionnaire Interview Telephone survey	Useful in describing features of a large population without interviewing everyone Relatively large samples possible Multivariate analysis possible	Potentially forced answers Respondent untruthfulness on emotional issues Data that are not always "hard facts" presented as such in statistical analyses
Secondary Analysis of Existing Data Existing statistics Content analysis	Data often readily available, inexpensive to collect Longitudinal and comparative studies possible Replication possible	Difficulty in determining accuracy of some of the data Failure of data gathered by others to meet goals of current research Questions of privacy when using diaries or other personal documents
Field Research Observation Participant observation Case study Ethnography Unstructured interviews	Opportunity to gain insider's view Useful for studying attitudes and behaviour in natural settings Longitudinal/comparative studies possible Documentation of important social problems of excluded groups possible Access to people's ideas in their words Forum for previously excluded groups	Problems in generalizing results to a larger population Nonprecise data measurements Inability to demonstrate cause/effect relationships or test theories Difficult to make comparisons because of lack of structure Not representative sample

The Zellner Research

Sociologist William Zellner (1978, in Schaefer and Lamm, 1992) sought to interview the family, friends, and acquaintances of persons killed in single-car crashes that he thought might have been "autocides." Zellner wondered, Are some automobile "accidents" actually suicides? Did the individual wish to protect other people and perhaps make it easier for them to collect insurance benefits that might not be paid in suicide cases? By interviewing people who knew the victims, Zellner hoped to obtain information that would help determine if the deaths were accidental or intentional. To recruit respondents, he suggested that their participation in his study might reduce the number of accidents in the future; however, he did not mention that he suspected autocide. In each interview, he asked if the deceased had recently talked about suicide or about themselves in a negative manner.

From the data he collected, Zellner concluded that at least 12 percent of the fatal single-occupant crashes were suicides. He also learned that in a number of the crashes, other people (innocent bystanders) were killed or critically injured. Was Zellner's research unethical because he misrepresented the reasons for his study? Does the right to know outweigh the right to privacy in this situation? Other important questions also are raised in the process of social scientific investigation. Consider, for example, the following two cases.

The Humphreys Research

Laud Humphreys (1970), then a sociology graduate student, decided to study homosexuality for his doctoral dissertation. His research focused on homosexual acts between strangers meeting in "tearooms," public restrooms in parks. He did not ask permission of his subjects, nor did he inform them that they were being studied. Instead, he took advantage of the typical tearoom encounter, which involved three men: two who engaged in homosexual acts, and a third who kept a lookout for police and other unwelcome strangers. To conduct his study, Humphreys showed up at public restrooms that were known to be tearooms and offered to be the lookout. Then he systematically recorded details of the encounters that took place.

Humphreys was interested in the fact that the tearoom participants seemed to live "normal" lives apart from these encounters, and he decided to learn more about their everyday lives. To determine who they were, he wrote down their car licence numbers and tracked down their names and addresses. Later, he arranged for these men to be included in a medical survey so that he could go out and interview them personally. He wore different disguises and drove a different car so that they would not recognize him. From these interviews, he collected personal information and determined that most of the men were married and lived very conventional lives.

Humphreys probably would not have gained access to these subjects if he had identified himself as a researcher; nevertheless, the fact that he did not do so produced widespread criticism from sociologists and journalists. The police became very interested in his notes, but he refused to turn any information over to the authorities. His award-winning study, *Tearoom Trade* (1970), dispelled many myths about homosexual behaviour; however, the controversy surrounding his study has never been resolved. Do you think Humphreys's research was ethical? Would these men willingly have agreed to participate in Humphreys's research if he had identified himself as a researcher? What psychological harm might have come to these married men if people, outside of those involved in the encounters, knew about their homosexual behaviour? Ethical issues continue to arise in sociological research. A recent case involved a different sort of question from the Humphreys case.

The Ogden Case

What should social scientists do when the ethical principles of confidentiality and not harming subjects conflict with the law? In 1992, Simon Fraser University student Russel Ogden began work on his master's thesis, which was to be a study on euthanasia (mercy killing) and assisted suicide involving AIDS patients (Ogden, 1994). Both euthanasia and assisted suicide are crimes in Canada. The university's ethics committee approved his research proposal that included a promise to maintain the "absolute confidentiality" of any information provided to him by those he interviewed (Palys, 1997).

Ogden defended his M.A. thesis in 1994. Shortly afterward, he was subpoenaed to give evidence at a coroner's inquest that was investigating the possible assisted suicide of an AIDS victim. Ogden refused to testify, citing the guarantee of confidentiality he had given to his respondents. The coroner charged Ogden with contempt of court. After a lengthy legal battle, the coroner agreed that Ogden's guarantee of confidentiality was in the public good and dropped the charges. Despite this precedent, researchers do not know if other courts will support their right to maintain confidentiality, as academics do not have any legal exemption similar to that which exists between a lawyer and client. Without this exemption, decisions are made on a case by case basis. In the United States, researchers have gone to prison for refusing to testify about their research.

An interesting issue in the Ogden case is the role played by the university. Since the cornerstone of a university is the protection of academic freedom, and since Ogden's research had been approved by the university, one might have expected the university to support Ogden and to pay his legal fees. However, the $2000 the university gave him covered only part of his legal costs, and they took no responsibility for his actions. On top of this, a clause was added to the university's ethics review policy whereby researchers would be required to tell their subjects that "the researcher may be required to divulge information obtained in the course of this research to a court or other legal body." This clause subordinates ethics to law and may have a dramatic impact on the ability of social scientists to conduct research on sensitive topics (Palys and Lowman, 1998).

Ogden later sued the university for $9000 to recover his legal costs. While rejecting Ogden's claim, the judge took the unusual step of stating he felt the university's president and vice-president "demonstrated a surprising lack of courage" when they failed to support the university's principle of academic freedom because they were afraid defending Ogden would be interpreted as supporting assisted suicide. Ultimately, under a new president, Simon Fraser University accepted the recommendation of a review committee and acknowledged their responsibility in the matter. The university paid Ogden's legal fees, compensated him for lost wages, and formally apologized to him.

In this chapter, we have looked at the research process and the methods used to pursue sociological knowledge. We also have critiqued many of the existing approaches and suggested alternative ways of pursuing research. The important thing to realize is that research is the "life blood" of sociology. Without research, sociologists would be unable to test existing theories and develop new ones. Research takes us beyond common sense and provides opportunities for us to use our sociological imagination to generate new knowledge.

Our challenge today is to understand how to determine what is useful for enhancing our knowledge, to find new ways to integrate knowledge and action, and to encourage the inclusion of all people in the research process. This inclusion would be on two levels: (1) as active participants in research, to give "voice" to previously excluded people's experiences, and (2) as researchers, to help fill some of the gaps in our existing knowledge on how the research process is shaped by gender, race, class, and sexual orientation of the researcher and by the broader social and cultural context (Cancian, 1992).

CHAPTER REVIEW

What are the five ways of knowing?
The five ways of knowing are personal experience, tradition, authority, religion, and science.

What is the empirical approach to knowledge? What are the two types of empirical studies conducted by sociologists?
Sociological research is based on an empirical approach that answers questions through a direct, systematic collection and analysis of data. Sociologists generally use two types of empirical studies. Descriptive studies attempt to describe social reality or provide facts. Explanatory studies attempt to explain cause-and-effect relationships and the reasons certain events do or do not occur.

What are the inductive and deductive approaches to research?
Theory and research form a continuous cycle that encompasses both deductive and inductive approaches. With the deductive approach, the researcher begins with a theory and then collects and analyzes research to test it. With the inductive approach, the researcher collects and analyzes data and then generates a theory based on that analysis.

What are the key steps in the deductive research process?
The research process based on deduction has these key steps: (1) selecting and defining the research problem,

(2) reviewing previous research, (3) formulating the hypothesis, which involves constructing variables, (4) developing the research design, (5) collecting and analyzing the data, and (6) drawing conclusions and reporting the findings.

What are the key steps in the inductive approach to research?

A researcher taking the qualitative approach might (1) formulate the problem to be studied instead of creating a hypothesis, (2) collect and analyze the data, and (3) report the results.

What are the major sociological research methods?

Research methods are systematic techniques for conducting research. Through *experiments*, researchers study the impact of certain variables on their subjects. *Surveys* are polls used to gather facts about people's attitudes, opinions, or behaviours; a representative sample of respondents provides data through questionnaires or interviews. In *secondary analysis*, researchers analyze existing data, such as a government census, or cultural artifacts, such as a diary. In *field research*, sociologists study social life in its natural setting through participant and complete observation, case studies, unstructured interviews, and ethnography.

What is meant by triangulation?

Many sociologists use multiple methods, or triangulation, to study a particular issue. Multiple methods can provide a wider scope of data and points of view.

Key Terms

altruism 31
analysis 40
complete observation 52
content analysis 51
control group 41
deductive approach 35
dependent variable 38
descriptive studies 34
empirical approach 33
experiment 41
experimental group 41
explanatory studies 35
field research 52
hypothesis 34
independent variable 37
inductive approach 35
interview 46
normative approach 33

operational definition 38
participant observation 53
population 47
questionnaire 46
random sample 47
reactivity 44
reliability 40
replication 40
representative sample 47
respondents 46
sample 47
secondary analysis 48
survey 45
unstructured interview 55
validity 40
variable 37

Internet Exercises

1. A basic source of statistical information about Canadian society is Statistics Canada:

   http://www.statcan.ca

   You can use this Web site to search for data on a wide range of topics including births, deaths, crime, marriage, and employment. Just click "Daily News" to find a page that gives you the latest news from Statistics Canada. Near the bottom of this page click "Search the Daily Archive." This page will allow you to search for a wide range of statistical information. On the Statistics Canada homepage, "Links to other sites" will enable you to find statistical information about the provinces and other countries. The homepage also has a quiz that will enable you to test your knowledge and learn about Canada and Canadians.

2. Do some research on Mohammad Yunus and the Grameen Bank. Go to Yahoo and search for Grameen Bank. Among the sites you will find is:

   http://www.iwan.com

   This site has a number of pictures illustrating the activities of the bank. Then go to AltaVista and read some of the many stories about the bank and its founder. Go to:

   http://www.iorc.ca/reports/read_article_English. cfm?_num=264

   to read about a study by the University of Manitoba's Aminur Rahman, whose research questions some of the assumptions behind the Grameen Bank.

3. If you are interested in ethics, go to the Web site for the University of British Columbia's Centre for Applied Ethics at:

http://www.ethics.ubc.ca

This site has material on a wide range of ethical issues.

✉ Net Links

The Web site for Statistics Canada's Data Liberation Initiative gives you access to other Statistics Canada data as well as providing links to statistical agencies in many other parts of the world:

http://www.statcan.ca/english/Dli/contents.htm

Carleton University sociologist Craig McKie has designed a Web site that has a rich variety of Internet links for researchers:

http://www.socsciresearch.com/

The code of ethics of the Canadian Sociology and Anthropology Association is published on their Web site:

http://www.artsci-ccwin.concordia.ca/socanth/csaa/ csaa.html

For some online advice about college writing, go to:

http://www.cabrillo.cc.ca.us/divisions/english/290/

One of Canada's leading social research organizations is the Institute for Social Research at York University:

http://www.isr.yorku.ca/isr/index.asp

Public Agenda Online is designed to provide background information on issues for journalists:

http://www.publicagenda.org/

If you would like to read about some of the statistics used by social scientists, go to:

http://www.statsoft.com/textbook/stathome.html

Questions for Critical Thinking

1. The agency that funds the local suicide clinic has asked you to study the clinic's effectiveness in preventing suicide. What would you need to measure? What can you measure? What research method(s) would provide the best data for analysis?

2. Together with a group of students, perform a content analysis on the photographs in your textbooks. First, determine whether to sample texts from various fields of study or just one field. Try to follow the steps in the sociological research process.

3. You have been assigned a research study that examines possible discrimination against men in child custody cases. What will be the population(s) you will study? How will you sample the population(s)? How will you account for sex, race, age, income level, and other characteristics in your population(s)?

4. What are some of the major ethical issues in social research? How can we best ensure that sociological research is conducted ethically?

Suggested Readings

The following books provide in-depth information about research methods:

Earl Babbie. *The Practice of Social Research* (6th ed.). Belmont, Cal.: Wadsworth, 1992.

Therese L. Baker. *Doing Social Research* (2nd ed.). New York: McGraw-Hill, 1994.

Margrit Eichler. *Nonsexist Research Methods: A Practical Guide*. Boston: Allen & Unwin, 1988.

Sandra Kirby and Kate McKenna. *Experience Research Social Change: Methods from the Margins*. Toronto: Garamond, 1989.

Shulamit Reinharz. *Feminist Methods in Social Research*. New York: Oxford University Press, 1992. (Provides excellent information and examples of qualitative research using methods such as oral histories, content analysis, case studies, action research, and multiple-method research.)

Janice L. Ristock and Joan Pennell. *Research as Empowerment: Feminist Links, Postmodern Interruptions*. Don Mills, Ont.: Oxford University Press, 1996.

To find out more about writing a sociology term paper or report, see:

Richard Floyd. *Success in the Social Sciences: Writing and Research for Canadian Students*. Toronto: Harcourt Brace, 1995.

Margot Northey. *Making Sense: A Student's Guide to Research, Writing and Style*. Don Mills, Ont.: Oxford University Press, 1993. (Takes the reader from the initial steps of choosing a topic to doing research and writing the final paper. Describes the types of social science literature and makes suggestions about writing a research paper and preparing an oral presentation.)

CHAPTER 3

Culture and Society
   The Importance of Culture in a Changing World
   Material and Nonmaterial Culture
   Cultural Universals

Components of Culture
   Symbols
   Language
   Language Diversity in Canada
   Values
   Norms

Popular Culture
   Popular versus High Culture
   Divergent Perspectives on Popular Culture

Cultural Change and Diversity
   Cultural Change
   Cultural Diversity
   Culture Shock
   Ethnocentrism
   Cultural Relativism

Sociological Analysis of Culture
   A Functionalist Perspective
   A Conflict Perspective
   An Interactionist Perspective

Cultural Patterns in the Future
   Culture and Technology
   A Global Culture?

Crown attorney and author Rupert Ross describes the difficulties he had in learning to understand and accept the cultural traditions of the Ojibway. According to Ross this story demonstrates how easy it is to misread people who have a "different understanding" of the world (1996:51):

"My own cultural eyes have often tricked me into seeing things that Aboriginal people did not—or completely missing things they thought too obvious to point out. One of the most significant came one day when I was having coffee with an Ojibway friend. I asked her about something I often saw in the North: older couples walking along with the man twelve paces out in front, his wife bringing up the rear. I asked her how that behaviour fit with what I was being taught about equality between men and women in traditional times. She laughed, then said something like 'Rupert, Rupert, that's only your eyes again! You have to look at it the way we do!'

"She began by asking me to remember where those old people had spent their lives, to imagine walking a narrow trail through the bush with my own family. She asked me to think about who I would prefer to have out in front, my wife or myself, to be the first to face whatever dangers the bush presented. In one way, she said, it could be compared to wartime. 'Where,' she asked, 'do you put your general? Are they out in front or are they in the rear, where they have time to see and plan and react?'

"Viewed in that way, things appeared to be the opposite of what I had first supposed. Instead of occupying an inferior position, the woman was seen as the organizer and director, while the man out front was counted on for his capacity to take action under her direction. Instead of remembering the bush context in which they had lived their lives, I had put them in my own urban context where such a formation might indicate the opposite. 'So,' I said, 'she's really the general and her husband is just the foot-soldier!'

"There was a pause then, and she chuckled again, shaking her head. 'Not really,' she said. 'The problem is ... you see everything in terms of hierarchies, don't you? Why do you do that?' ... She tried to express her way then, the way she understood from the teaching of her people. In those teachings, all things have a purpose, and unless these are fulfilled, the strength of the whole is weakened. The jobs of the husband and of the

CULTURE

wife were just that, their jobs, assumed on the basis of their having different skills and capacities—different *gifts*—none of which had to be compared with each other in terms of worth or importance. Comparison itself was seen as a strange thing to do.

"As she spoke, I was flooded with recollections of other events that raised the issue of our Western dependence on hierarchies of worth and power." (Ross, 1996:52–53)

Culture **is the knowledge, language, values, customs, and material objects that are passed from person to person and from one generation to the next in a human group or society.** As previously defined, a *society* is a large social grouping that occupies the same geographic territory and is subject to the same political authority and dominant cultural expectations. While a society is made up of people, a culture is made up of ideas, behaviour, and material possessions. Society and culture are interdependent; neither could exist without the other.

To what extent does our own culture "blind" us, that is, keep us from understanding, accepting, or learning from other unique cultures? Is intolerance toward "outsiders"—people who are viewed as being different from one's own group or way of life—accepted by some people in Canada?

Culture can be an enormously stabilizing force for a society, and it can provide a sense of continuity. However, culture also can be a force that generates discord and conflict between different groups. How people view culture is intricately related to their location in society with regard to their ethnicity, class, sex, and age. From one perspective,

Canadian culture does not condone or tolerate attacks against people because of their religion, colour, disability, sexual orientation, ethnic origin, or ancestry. From another perspective, however, intolerance may be the downside of some "positive" cultural values—such as individualism, competition, and materialism—found in Canadian society. Just as attitudes of love and tolerance may be embedded in societal values and teachings, beliefs that reinforce intolerance may also be embedded in culture.

In this chapter, we examine society and culture, with special attention to the components of culture and the relationship between cultural change and diversity. We will also analyze culture from functionalist, conflict, and interactionist perspectives. Before reading on, test your knowledge of the relationship between culture and intolerance toward others by answering the questions in Box 3.1.

Shelter is a universal type of material culture, but it comes in a wide variety of shapes and forms. What might some of the reasons be for the similarities and differences you see in these cross-cultural examples?

QUESTIONS AND ISSUES

CHAPTER FOCUS QUESTION: To what extent are Canadians accepting and tolerant of cultural diversity?

What part does culture play in shaping individuals and groups?

What are the essential components of culture?

To what degree are we shaped by popular culture?

How do subcultures and countercultures reflect diversity within a society?

How do the various sociological perspectives view culture?

CULTURE AND SOCIETY

Understanding how culture affects our lives helps us develop a sociological imagination. When we meet someone from a culture vastly different from our own, or when we travel in another country, it may be easier to perceive the enormous influence of culture in people's lives. However, when we turn our sociological lens on our own society, it is more difficult to examine culture because we take our own way of life for granted.

The Importance of Culture in a Changing World

How important is culture in determining how people think and act on a daily basis? Simply stated, culture is essential for our individual sur-

HOW TOLERANT ARE CANADIANS OF OTHER CULTURES?

TRUE	FALSE		
T	F	1.	In recent years, the number of reported attacks in Canada against persons because of their race, religion, or ethnic origin has increased.
T	F	2.	It is illegal to be a member of a racist organization.
T	F	3.	Some people are born with hatred for people who are different from themselves.
T	F	4.	As the rate of immigration to Canada has increased in recent years, anti-immigrant feelings have risen.
T	F	5.	The majority of hate crimes in Canada are directed against racial minorities.
T	F	6.	Incidents of violence targeted toward African Canadians and Jews have declined in recent years.
T	F	7.	Communities with greater proportions of visible-minority immigrants are generally more tolerant of racial and ethnic differences.
T	F	8.	A recent Toronto survey found most multicultural groups felt generally well accepted.
T	F	9.	A recent national survey found that the majority of respondents accept the concept of Canada as a multicultural mosaic.
T	F	10.	Canadians generally see themselves as tolerant of other cultures and intolerant of racism.

Answers on page 68.

vival and our communication with other people. We rely on culture because we are not born with the information we need to survive. We do not know how to take care of ourselves, how to behave, how to dress, what to eat, which gods to worship, or how to make or spend money. We must learn about culture through interaction, observation, and imitation in order to participate as members of the group (Samovar and Porter, 1991a). Sharing a common culture with others simplifies day-to-day interactions. However, as our society becomes more diverse, and communication among members of international cultures more frequent, the need to appreciate diversity and to understand how people in other cultures view their world has also increased (Samovar and Porter, 1991b:65).

Just as culture is essential for individuals, it also is fundamental for the survival of societies. Culture has been described as "the common denominator that makes the actions of individuals intelligible to the group" (Haviland, 1993:30). Some system of rule making and enforcing necessarily exists in all societies. What would happen, for example, if *all* rules and laws in Canada suddenly disappeared? At a basic level, we need rules in order to navigate our bicycles and cars through traffic. At a more abstract level, we need laws to establish and protect our rights.

In order to survive, societies need rules about civility and tolerance toward others. We are not born knowing how to express kindness or hatred toward others, although some people may say, "Well, that's just human nature," when explaining someone's behaviour. Such a statement is built on the assumption that what we do as human beings is determined by *nature* (our biological and genetic makeup) rather than *nurture* (our social environment)—that is, that our behaviour is instinctive. An *instinct* is a biologically determined behaviour pattern common to all members of a species that predictably occurs whenever certain environmental conditions exist. For example, spiders do not learn to build webs. They build webs because of instincts that are triggered by basic biological needs such as protection and reproduction.

Humans do not have instincts. What we most often think of as instinctive behaviour can be attributed to reflexes and drives. A *reflex* is a biologically determined involuntary response to some physical stimulus (such as a sneeze after breathing some pepper through the nose or the blinking of an eye when a speck of dust gets in it). *Drives* are biologically determined impulses common to all members of a species that satisfy needs such as sleep, food, water, or sexual gratification. Reflexes and drives do not determine how people will behave in human societies; even the expression of these biological characteristics is channelled by culture. For example, we may be taught that the "appropriate" way to sneeze (an involuntary

BOX 3.1

ANSWERS TO THE SOCIOLOGY QUIZ ON OTHER CULTURES

1. **True.** Even though such incidents are seriously underreported in Canada, statistics indicate that the number of reported hate or bias crimes has increased in recent years.

2. **False.** As provided for in the Charter of Rights and Freedoms, individuals have the right to belong to any organization they choose to join.

3. **False.** Sociologists agree that hatred and intolerance are learned attitudes and behaviours, not genetic by-products.

4. **True.** Polls show that high rates of immigration, combined with the tightening economy, are related to an increase in anti-immigrant sentiment.

5. **True.** Recent statistics indicate that in one year, 61 percent of hate crime incidents reported to police were directed against racial minorities, 23 percent against religious minorities, 11 percent against gays or lesbians, and 5 percent against ethnic minorities.

6. **False.** Despite Canada's record of tolerance, a 1999 report showed that violent incidents directed at these two groups are on the rise.

7. **True.** According to the Economic Council of Canada's report on changing attitudes toward prejudice, the communities with more visible minorities expressed the most tolerant attitudes.

8. **False.** In a survey conducted in Toronto in which respondents were asked how well their racial or cultural group was accepted, 80 percent of those surveyed in the African Canadian community, 63 percent in the Chinese community, and 62 percent in the East Indian–Pakistani Canadian community felt there was some prejudice toward them.

9. **False.** Nearly 75 percent of 1200 Canadians surveyed in a recent poll rejected the concept of Canada as a multicultural mosaic.

10. **True.** Canadians generally see themselves as tolerant of other cultures. Yet they are also aware that racism is a serious problem in Canada. Sociologists identify this as a paradox of Canadian society.

Sources: Based on Levin and McDevitt, 1993; Gilmour, 1994; Roberts, 1995a; Henry et al., 1996; and Galloway, 1999.

response) is to use a tissue or turn our head away from others (a learned response). Similarly, we may learn to sleep on mats or in beds. Most contemporary sociologists agree that culture and social learning, not nature, account for virtually all of our behaviour patterns.

Since humans cannot rely on instincts in order to survive, culture is a "tool kit" for survival. According to sociologist Ann Swidler (1986:273), culture is a "tool kit of symbols, stories, rituals, and world views, which people may use in varying configurations to solve different kinds of problems." The tools we choose will vary according to our own personality and the situations we face. We are not puppets on a string; we make choices from among the items in our own "tool box."

Material and Nonmaterial Culture

Our cultural tool box is divided into two major parts: *material* and *nonmaterial* culture (Ogburn, 1966/1922). **Material culture consists of the** **physical or tangible creations that members of a society make, use, and share.** Initially, items of material culture begin as raw materials or resources such as ore, trees, and oil. Through technology, these raw materials are transformed into usable items (ranging from books and computers to guns and bombs). Sociologists define *technology* **as the knowledge, techniques, and tools that make it possible for people to transform resources into usable forms, and the knowledge and skills required to use them after they are developed.** From this standpoint, technology is both concrete and abstract. For example, technology includes a pair of scissors and the knowledge and skill necessary to make them from iron, carbon, and chromium (Westrum, 1991). At the most basic level, material culture is important because it is our buffer against the environment. For example, we create shelter to protect ourselves from the weather and to provide ourselves with privacy. Beyond the survival level, we make, use, and share objects that are interesting and impor-

The customs and rituals associated with weddings are one example of nonmaterial culture. What can you infer about beliefs and attitudes concerning marriage in the societies represented by these photographs?

tant to us. Why are you wearing the particular clothes you have on today? Perhaps you're communicating something about yourself, such as where you attend school, what kind of music you like, or where you went on vacation.

Nonmaterial culture **consists of the abstract or intangible human creations of society that influence people's behaviour.** Language, beliefs, values, rules of behaviour, family patterns, and political systems are examples of nonmaterial culture. A central component of nonmaterial culture is *beliefs*—the mental acceptance or conviction that certain things are true or real. Beliefs may be based on tradition, faith, experience, scientific research, or some combination of these. Faith in a supreme being, that education is the key to success, and that smoking causes cancer are examples of beliefs. We also have beliefs in items of material culture. For example, most students believe that computers are the key to technological advancement and progress.

Cultural Universals

Because all humans face the same basic needs (such as food, clothing, and shelter), we engage in similar activities that contribute to our survival. Anthropologist George Murdock (1945:124) compiled a list of over seventy *cultural universals*—**customs and practices that occur across all societies.** His categories included appearance (such as bodily adornment and hairstyles), activities (such as sports, dancing, games, joking, and visiting), social institutions (such as family, law, and religion), and customary practices (such as cooking, folklore, gift giving, and hospitality). These general customs and practices may be present in all cultures, but their specific forms vary from one group to another and from one time to another within the same group. For example, while telling jokes may be a universal practice, what is considered a joke in one society may be an insult in another.

How do sociologists view cultural universals? In terms of their functions, cultural universals are useful because they ensure the smooth and continual operation of society (Radcliffe-Brown, 1952). A society must meet basic human needs by providing food, shelter, and some degree of safety for its members so that they will survive. Children and other new members (such as immigrants) must be taught the ways of the group. A society also must settle disputes and deal with people's emotions. All the while, the self-interest of individuals must be balanced with the needs of society as a whole. Cultural universals help to fulfil these important functions of society.

From another perspective, however, cultural universals are not the result of functional necessity; these practices may have been *imposed* by members of one society on members of another. Similar customs and practices do not necessarily constitute cultural universals. They may be an indication that a conquering nation used its power to enforce certain types of behaviour on those who were defeated (Sargent, 1987). Sociologists might ask questions such as, "Who determines the dominant cultural patterns?" For example, although religion is a cultural universal, traditional religious practices of indigenous peoples (those who first live in an area) often have been repressed and even stamped out by subsequent settlers or conquerors who hold political and economic power over them.

COMPONENTS OF CULTURE

Even though the specifics of individual cultures vary widely, all cultures have four common non-material cultural components: symbols, language, values, and norms. These components contribute to both harmony and conflict in a society.

Symbols

A *symbol* **is anything that meaningfully represents something else.** Culture could not exist without symbols because there would be no shared meanings among people. Symbols can simultaneously produce loyalty and animosity, and love and hate. They help us communicate ideas such as love or patriotism because they express abstract concepts with visible objects.

For example, flags can stand for patriotism, nationalism, school spirit, or religious beliefs held by members of a group or society. They also can be a source of discord and strife among people, as evidenced by recent controversies over the Canadian flag. In 1996, a retired Canadian couple, vacationing in a Florida trailer park, decided to fly the Canadian flag on their trailer. Their neighbours, patriotic Americans, objected so strenuously that the Canadians were forced to take their flag down. One of the neighbours even claimed (mistakenly)

that it was against the law to fly a foreign flag on American soil. In 1992, a U.S. marine inadvertently held the Canadian flag upside down during the singing of "O Canada" at a World Series game. Although baseball administrators immediately apologized, Canadians were outraged and insulted by the improper display of our national symbol. This incident had a happy ending for some enterprising individuals who did a booming business at the next World Series game, selling ... upside-down American flags.

Symbols can stand for love (a heart on a valentine), peace (a dove), or hate (a Nazi swastika), just as words can be used to convey these meanings. Symbols also can transmit other types of ideas. A siren is a symbol that denotes an emergency situation and sends the message to clear the way immediately. Gestures also are a symbolic form of communication—a movement of the head, body, or hands can express our ideas or feelings to others. For example, in Canada, pointing toward your chest with your thumb or finger is a symbol for "me." We are also all aware of how useful our middle finger can be in communicating messages to inconsiderate drivers.

Symbols affect our thoughts about gender. The colour of clothing, for example, has different symbolic meaning for females and males. In a study of baby clothing, sociologist Madeline Shakin and her associates (1985) found that 90 percent of the infants they observed were dressed in colours indicating their sex. Most boys were dressed in blue or red while most girls were dressed in pink or yellow. The colour of the clothing sends implicit messages about how the child should be treated. If a female infant is wearing a pink dress, the message is, "I'm a girl. Say that I'm pretty, not that I'm handsome." Such messages about gender have long-term effects on individual and societal perceptions about how women and men should think and act.

Symbols also may affect our beliefs about race and ethnicity. Although black and white are not truly colours at all, the symbolic meanings associated with these labels permeate society and affect everyone. English-language scholar Alison Lurie (1981:184) suggests that it is incorrect to speak of "whites" and "blacks." She notes that "pinkish-tan persons ... have designated themselves the 'White race' while affixing the term 'Black' [to people] whose skin is some shade of brown or gold." The result of this "semantic sleight of hand" has been the association of pinkish-tan skin with virtue and cleanliness, and "brown or golden skin with evil, dirt and danger" (Lurie, 1981:184).

Symbols are powerful sources of communication. What messages do these two pictures communicate to you?

Language

Language **is a set of symbols that express ideas and enable people to think and communicate with one another.** Verbal (spoken) and nonverbal (written or gestured) language help us describe reality. One of our most important human attributes is the ability to use language to share our experiences, feelings, and knowledge with others. Language can create visual images in our head, such as "the kittens look like little cotton balls" (Samovar and Porter, 1991a). Language also allows people to distinguish themselves from outsiders and maintain group boundaries and solidarity (Farb, 1973).

Language is not solely a human characteristic. Other animals use sounds, gestures, touch, and smell to communicate with one another, but they use signals with fixed meanings that are limited to the immediate situation (the present) and cannot encompass past or future situations. For example, chimpanzees can use elements of Standard American Sign Language and manipulate physical objects to make "sentences," but they are not physically endowed with the vocal apparatus needed to form the consonants required for verbal language. As a result, nonhuman animals cannot transmit the more complex aspects of culture to their offspring. Humans have a unique ability to

manipulate symbols to express abstract concepts and rules and thus to create and transmit culture from one generation to the next.

LANGUAGE AND SOCIAL REALITY One key issue in sociology is whether language *creates* or simply *communicates* reality. For example, consider the terms used by organizations involved in the abortion debate: pro-life and pro-choice. Do such terms create or simply express a reality? Anthropological linguists Edward Sapir and Benjamin Whorf have suggested that language not only expresses our thoughts and perceptions but also influences our perception of reality. According to the *Sapir-Whorf hypothesis,* **language shapes the view of reality of its speakers** (Whorf, 1956; Sapir, 1961). If people are able to think only through language, language must precede thought.

If language shapes the reality we perceive and experience, some aspects of the world are viewed as important and others are virtually neglected because people know the world only in terms of the vocabulary and grammar of their own language. For example, Aboriginal languages focus on describing relationships between things rather than using language to judge or evaluate. One Aboriginal author explains, "No, we don't have any gender. It's a relationship ... The woman who cares for your heart—that's your wife. Your daughters are the ones who enrich your heart. Your sons are the ones that test your heart!" (Ross, 1996: 116). Consequently, many Aboriginal languages do not have any personal pronouns based on gender (such as words for *she* or *he*). As writer Rupert Ross explains:

> Because they don't exist there, searching for the correct ones often seems an artificial and unreasonable exercise. As a result, Aboriginal people are often as careless about getting them right as I am when speaking French and trying to remember whether a noun has "le" or "la" in front of it ... On the more humorous side, my Aboriginal friends appear heartily amused by the frenzied Western debate over whether God is a "He" or a "She." (1996:117)

According to Ross, language does have a dramatic impact on our perception of the world. He describes two very different worlds experienced by English-speaking Canadians and Aboriginal peoples:

> I've struggled for some time to find a way to express how I perceive the difference between my English-speaking world and the world my Aboriginal friends tell me is given to them by their languages. I have this sense that if you decide that the first reality is constant change, if you discard your belief in the usefulness of judgmental absolutes like "good" and "bad" and choose to speak in terms of relative movement like "towards harmony" instead, then a lot of other things change as well. You start to sit in a room differently, in a car differently, everywhere differently. (1996:125)

Similarly, Sapir and Whorf explain that the Hopi language does not contain past, present, and future tenses of verbs, or nouns for times, days, or years (Carroll, 1956); however, scholars recently have argued that this assertion is incorrect (see Edgerton, 1992). By contrast, English speakers in North America perceive time as something that can be kept, saved, lost, or wasted; therefore, "being on time" or "not wasting time" are important. Many English words divide time into units (years, months, weeks, days, hours, minutes, seconds, and milliseconds) and into the past, present, and future (yesterday, today, and tomorrow) (Samovar and Porter, 1991a).

If language does create reality, are we trapped by our language? Many social scientists agree that the Sapir-Whorf hypothesis overstates the relationship between language and our thoughts and behaviour patterns. While acknowledging that language has many subtle meanings and that the words used by people reflect their central concerns, most sociologists contend that language may *influence* our behaviour and interpretation of social reality but does not *determine* it.

LANGUAGE AND GENDER   What is the relationship between language and gender? What cultural assumptions about women and men does language reflect? Scholars have suggested several ways in which language and gender are intertwined:

- The English language ignores women by using the masculine form to refer to human beings in general (Basow, 1992). For example, the word *man* is used generically in words like *chairman* and *mankind*, which allegedly include both men and women. However, *man* can mean either "all human beings" or "a male human being" (Miller and Swift, 1993:71).

- Use of the pronouns *he* and *she* affects our thinking about gender. Pronouns show the gender of the person we *expect* to be in a particular occupation. For instance, nurses, secretaries, and schoolteachers usually are referred to as *she*, while doctors, engineers, electricians, and presidents are referred to as *he* (Baron, 1986).

- Words have positive connotations when relating to male power, prestige, and leadership; when related to women, they carry negative overtones of weakness, inferiority, and immaturity (Epstein, 1988:224). Table 3.1 shows how gender-based language reflects the traditional acceptance of men and women in certain positions, implying that the jobs are different when filled by women rather than men.

- A language-based predisposition to think about women in sexual terms reinforces the notion that women are sexual objects. Women often are described by terms such as *fox, broad, bitch, babe*, or *doll*, which ascribe childlike or even petlike characteristics to them. By contrast, men have performance pressures placed on them by being defined in terms of their sexual prowess, such as *dude, stud*, and *hunk* (Baker, 1993).

Gender in language has been debated and studied extensively in recent years, and greater awareness and some changes have been the result. For example, the desire of many women to have *Ms.* (rather than *Miss* or *Mrs.*, which indicated

TABLE 3.1   LANGUAGE AND GENDER

MALE TERM	FEMALE TERM	NEUTRAL TERM
teacher	teacher	teacher
chairman	chairwoman	chair, chairperson
policeman	policewoman	police officer
fireman	lady fireman	firefighter
airline steward	airline stewardess	flight attendant
race car driver	woman race car driver	race car driver
wrestler	lady/woman wrestler	wrestler
professor	female/woman professor	professor
doctor	lady/woman doctor	doctor
bachelor	spinster/old maid	single person
male prostitute	prostitute	prostitute
male nurse	nurse	nurse
welfare recipient	welfare mother	welfare recipient
worker/employee	working mother	worker/employee
janitor/maintenance man	maid/cleaning lady	custodial attendant

Source: Adapted from Korsmeyer, 1981:122; and Miller and Swift, 1991.

their marital status) precede their names has received a degree of acceptance in public life and the media (Tannen, 1995). Many organizations and publications have established guidelines for the use of nonsexist language and have changed titles such as *chairman* to *chair* or *chairperson*. "Men Working" signs in many areas have been replaced with ones that say "People Working" (Epstein, 1988:227). Some occupations have been given "genderless" titles, such as *firefighter* and *flight attendant* (Maggio, 1988). Yet many people resist change, arguing the English language is being ruined (Epstein, 1988).

LANGUAGE, RACE, AND ETHNICITY   Language may create and reinforce our perceptions about race and ethnicity by transmitting preconceived ideas about the superiority of one category of people over another. Let's look at a few images conveyed by words in the English language in regard to race/ethnicity.

- Words may have more than one meaning and create and reinforce negative images. Terms such as *blackhearted* (malevolent) and expressions such as "a black mark" (a detrimental fact) and "Chinaman's chance of success" (unlikely to succeed) give the words *black* and *Chinaman* negative associations and derogatory

imagery. By contrast, expressions such as "That's white of you" and "The good guys wear white hats" reinforce positive associations with the colour white.
- Overtly derogatory terms such as *nigger, kike, gook, honkey, chink, squaw, savage*, and other racial/ethnic slurs have been "popularized" in movies, music, comic routines, and so on. Such derogatory terms often are used in conjunction with physical threats against persons.
- Words frequently are used to create or reinforce perceptions about a group. For example, Aboriginal peoples have been referred to as "savages" and described as "primitive," while blacks have been described as "uncivilized," "cannibalistic," and "pagan."
- The "voice" of verbs may minimize or incorrectly identify the activities or achievements of members of various minority groups. For example, use of the passive voice in the statement "Chinese Canadians *were given* the right to vote" ignores how Chinese Canadians *fought* for that right. Active-voice verbs also may inaccurately attribute achievements to people or groups. Some historians argue that cultural bias is shown by the very notion that "Cabot discovered Canada"—given that Canada already was inhabited by people who later

became known as Aboriginal Canadians (see Stannard, 1992; Takaki, 1993).

In addition to these concerns about the English language, problems also arise when more than one language is involved.

Language Diversity in Canada

Language has been referred to as the keystone to culture because of the fact that language is the chief vehicle for understanding and experiencing one's culture (McVey and Kalbach, 1995). In recent decades, Canada has experienced rapid changes in language and culture.

BILINGUALISM In 1969 the federal government passed the Official Languages Act, making both French and English the official languages. In doing so, Canada officially became a bilingual society. However, this action by no means resolved the complex issues regarding language in our society. Canada is a linguistically diverse society consisting of Aboriginal languages, French and English, and heritage languages. Canada's two charter language groups are often referred to as "two solitudes" (Hiller, 1995). How is it possible to have a unified country when groups of people within a society cannot talk to each other? According to a recent census, 67 percent of Canadians speak English only, another 14 percent speak French only, and 17 percent are bilingual. Only 2 percent, or 473,475 Canadians, indicated they lacked the skills to converse in either French or English (Statistics Canada, 1997f). This census also indicated that bilingualism has continued to gain ground across the country. Between 1991 and 1996, the population of bilingual Canadians increased in every province except Saskatchewan (Statistics Canada, 1997f). Although French-versus-English language issues have been a significant source of conflict, bilingualism remains a distinct component of Canadian culture. As one respondent said to the Citizen's Forum on Canada's Future, a commission that toured Canada in the early 1990s and that was set up to enable Canadians to discuss the country's political future:

> Most people I talk to do not want a divided country. Nor do they deny the right of Québécois to preserve their language and culture ... having two languages doesn't split up the country, it *makes* it. Without Quebec and their French language I would feel lost as a Canadian. (1991:55)

Although it may be easy for members of the English-speaking majority to display such acceptance and tolerance of bilingualism, francophones are concerned that this policy is not enough to save their culture. Efforts to protect French language and culture have resulted in some exclusionary policies. For example, Quebec's controversial Bill 178 specifies that exterior signs on stores, restaurants, and offices are to be in French only. As the following incident demonstrates, this law has increased the tension between our two charter linguistic groups:

> I went to meet some friends at a downtown bar ... As I arrived, a solemn middle-aged man was taking photographs of the blackboard mounted on the outside steps. He was intent on a notice scrawled in chalk on the board: Today's Special—Ploughman's Lunch. This notice happened to be a blatant violation of Quebec's Bill 178 ... and the photographer was one of a number of self-appointed vigilantes who ... dutifully search the downtown streets for English language or bilingual commercial signs ... They photograph the evidence and then lodge an official complaint with the Commission de Protection de la Langue Française. (Richler, 1992:1)

As this example demonstrates, the Québécois feel that their language and culture is threatened and that these types of defensive strategies are essential to the survival of their culture.

ABORIGINAL LANGUAGES Canada's Aboriginal languages are many and diverse. These languages, tangible symbols of Aboriginal culture and group identity, are tremendously important to Canada's indigenous people. Aboriginal people's cultures are *oral cultures*, that is, cultures that are transmitted through speech rather than the written word. Many Aboriginal stories can be passed on only in the Aboriginal language in which they originated. Language is not only a means of communication, but also a link that connects people with their past and grounds their social, emotional, and spiritual vitality. Although loss of language doesn't necessarily lead to the death of a culture, it can severely handicap the transmission of that culture (Norris, 1998:8). For Aboriginal people, huge losses have already occurred as a result of the assimilist strategies of missionaries and Jesuit priests running residential schools. At these schools Aboriginal children were forbidden to speak their language. An Ojibway woman from northwestern Ontario describes her experience:

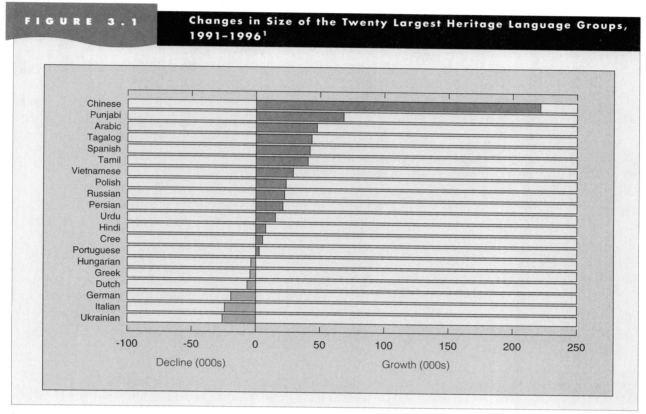

FIGURE 3.1   **Changes in Size of the Twenty Largest Heritage Language Groups, 1991–1996[1]**

[1] Single and multiple reponses are combined.

Adapted with permission from Statistics Canada, *The Daily*, Cat. no. 11-001, December 2, 1997.

Boarding school was supposed to be a place where you forgot everything about being Anishinabe. And our language too. But I said, "I'm going to talk to myself"—and that's what I did, under my covers—talked to myself in Anishinabe. If we were caught, the nuns would make us stand in a corner and repeat over and over, "I won't speak my language." (Ross, 1996:122)

Despite the efforts of Canadian Aboriginal peoples to maintain their languages, these languages are among the most endangered in the world. Only three of the approximately fifty Aboriginal languages in Canada are in a healthy state; many have already disappeared or are near extinction. In the 1996 census, only 26 percent of Aboriginal persons reported an Aboriginal language as their first language and even fewer spoke it at home (Norris, 1998.) Loss of their languages will have a profound effect on the cultural survival of Aboriginal peoples. According to Eli Taylor, a Dakota-Sioux from Manitoba:

Our native language embodies a value system about how we ought to live and relate to each other ... Now if you destroy our language, you not only break down these relationships, but you also destroy other aspects of our Indian way of life and culture, especially those that describe man's connection with nature, the Great Spirit, the order of things. Without our language, we will cease to exist as a separate people. (Fleras and Elliott, 1992:151)

Aboriginal elders, teachers, and other leaders are well aware of the gravity of the language situation and have taken steps to preserve the few remaining indigenous languages (see Critical Thinking Box 3.2). These include the introduction of Aboriginal language courses in schools and universities, Aboriginal media programming, and the recording of elders' stories, songs, and accounts of history in Aboriginal language (Ponting, 1997). According to social analyst Mary Jane Norris, if these languages vanish, "they take with them unique ways of looking at the world,

BOX 3.2   CRITICAL THINKING

THE DENE YATI PROJECT—LANGUAGE LEARNING BRINGS FAMILIES TOGETHER

In 1993, adults in the community of Lutsel'Ke in the Northwest Territories were concerned about the loss of their native Chipewyan language. Children were using their native tongue only in school during formal language classes and were speaking English in the playground and at home. "In some cases," says Joanne Barnaby, Executive Director of the Dene Cultural Institute, "when parents and grandparents spoke Dene, the children answered in English. And even some of the adults couldn't speak their language well."

Community members recognized that the loss of their language meant not only the loss of their culture, it also weakened family bonds by limiting the range of communication between children and adults. Like many Aboriginal communities, Lutsel'Ke has a very young population—of the 400-strong community members, approximately 60 are in the four to nine age group.

With the help of the Dene Cultural Institute, the community initiated a program involving extended families and activities like hunting, fishing, camping, and picnics that were conducive to Dene culture. While the responsibility to make these events happen and to speak Chipewyan during the activities rested with the

explaining the unknown and making sense of life" (Norris, 1998:8).

HERITAGE LANGUAGE GROUPS   The term *heritage language groups* refers to those groups whose language is not English, French, or one of the Aboriginal languages. In recent decades Canada has experienced a number of significant changes in the composition of its heritage languages, largely as a result of increased immigration. For example, the number of speakers of Asian languages has increased sharply (Statistics Canada, 1997f). Figure 3.1 lists recent changes in size of heritage language groups spoken in Canada.

THEORETICAL INTERPRETATIONS OF LANGUAGE DIVERSITY
How does the presence of all of these different languages affect Canadian culture? From the functionalist perspective, a shared language is essential to a common culture; language is a stabilizing force in society and is an important means of cultural transmission. Through language, children learn about their cultural heritage and develop a sense of personal identity in relation to their group. Functionalists would therefore view language diversity as potentially detrimental to Canadian culture.

Conflict theorists view language as a source of power and social control; it perpetuates inequalities between people and between groups because words are used (intentionally or not) to "keep people in their place." As linguist Deborah Tannen (1993:B5) has suggested, "The devastating group hatreds that result in so much suffering in our own country and around the world are related in origin to the small intolerances in our everyday conversations—our readiness to attribute good intentions to ourselves and bad intentions to others." Furthermore, different languages themselves are associated with inequalities. Consider this Aboriginal language instructor's comments on the lure of the English language, "It's to do with the perception of power. People associate English with prestige and power. We don't have movies in [Aboriginal language], we don't have hardcover books ... or neon signs in our language" (Martin, 1996:A8). Language, then, is a reflection of our feelings and values.

Values

Values **are collective ideas about what is right or wrong, good or bad, and desirable or undesirable in a particular culture** (Williams, 1970:27). Values do not dictate which behaviours are appropriate and which are not, but they provide us with the criteria by which we evaluate people, objects, and events. Values typically come in pairs of posi-

BOX 3.2

CONTINUED

families, the Institute and local school provided language resources and monitored the program. "Language testing showed that the children had improved proficiency in Dene," Barnaby says, "and the adults in the community reported that their children were speaking more Dene at home."

The success of the Dene Yati project went well beyond language proficiency. "It really made a difference," Barnaby explains. "Family members felt closer to one another and stronger in their culture. And the ability to make change happen made everyone feel empowered."

What do you think about this project? What can you learn from the Dene Yati project about the connections between family unit, language, and cultural transmission?

Source: Canadian Council on Social Development, "The Dene Yati Project: Language Learning Brings Families Together," in *The Progress of Canada's Children*. Ottawa: Canadian Council on Social Development, 1996:43. Adapted with permission.

tive and negative values, such as being brave or cowardly, hardworking or lazy. Since we use values to justify our behaviour, we tend to defend them staunchly (Kluckhohn, 1961).

CORE CANADIAN VALUES   Do we have shared values in Canada? Sociologists disagree about the extent to which all people in this country share a core set of values. Functionalists tend to believe that shared values are essential for societies and have conducted most of the research on core values. Between November 1990 and July 1991, approximately 400,000 Canadians participated in the Citizen's Forum on Canada's Future. The participants focused a great deal on what it meant to be Canadian. The following list summarizes the core values that emerged most strongly from participants in all regions of Canada:

1. *Equality and fairness in a democratic society.* Equality and fairness were not seen as mutually exclusive values. As one respondent said: "My hope for the future of Canada is for … a country where people feel comfortable with one another, are tolerant and understanding with one another, and where each person recognizes they have the same opportunities, responsibilities and privileges" (1991:37).

2. *Consultation and dialogue.* Canadians view themselves as people who settle their differences peaceably and in a consultative rather than confrontational manner. The view was widely held that Canadians must work together to solve their problems and remedy the apparent lack of understanding between different groups, regions, and provinces.

3. *Accommodation and tolerance.* The forum participants recognized the existence of different groups in Canadian society and their need to sustain their own culture while attaching themselves to the country's society, values, and institutions.

4. *Support for diversity.* This diversity has a number of facets, including linguistic, regional, ethnic, and cultural differences. Again, the respondents spoke of the difficulty of achieving a balance between a multicultural Canada and a secure sense of a Canadian identity.

5. *Compassion and generosity.* Forum participants deeply valued Canada's compassion and generosity as exemplified in our universal and extensive social services, health-care and pension systems, immigration policies, and commitment to regional economic equalization.

6. *Canada's natural beauty.* Canada's unspoiled natural beauty was identified as very important. The forum also recognized that this may be threatened by inadequate attention to environmental protection issues.

7. *Canada's world image: Commitment to freedom, peace, and nonviolent change.* Canada's role as a nonviolent, international peacekeeper was summed up in one respondent's comments: "Canada should not try to be a world power like the U.S.A. We should be the same kind of nation that we have always been, a peaceful and quiet nation" (1991:44).

More recently, sociologist and pollster Michael Adams examined Canadian social values as we enter the new millenium. According to Adams, the consensus on social values is breaking down as Canadians focus more on personal freedom and self-fulfilment and less on demographic factors such as age, gender, and social class. He explains that this shift has resulted in

> a culture that has few illusions about its uniformity. In the past, most Canadians had a fairly well-defined stereotype of what constituted a "Canadian." Now we have to ask ourselves, "Which one?" or "Which tribe?" "A typical Albertan? Is that Preston Manning or k.d. lang?" (1998:132)

According to Adams, when Canadians are divided according to their social values, twelve distinct social value groups emerge: three groups among those over 50, four groups among the baby boomers (aged 30 to 49), and five groups of Canadians under 30 (Generation X). The fact that there are more social value groups among the Generation Xers reflects a trend toward increasingly diverse Canadian values. Adams (1998) attributes this trend largely to the effects of advances in technology such as computers and the Internet, which allow Canadians to cross cultural boundaries and explore a diverse spectrum of values.

VALUE CONTRADICTIONS   All societies have value contradictions. *Value contradictions* are values that conflict with one another or are mutually exclusive (achieving one makes it difficult, if not impossible, to achieve another). For example, core values of morality and humanitarianism may conflict with values of individual achievement and success. In the 1990s, for example, humanitarian values reflected in welfare and other gov-

ernment aid programs have come into conflict with values emphasizing hard work and personal achievement. Similarly, despite the fact that 84 percent of Canadians feel that "people who are poor have a right to an adequate income to live on" (Bibby, 1995), they have also shown strong support for governments that have dramatically cut budgets in order to reduce financial deficits. Can you identify any value contradictions in the list of Canadian core values proposed by the Citizen's Forum?

IDEAL VERSUS REAL CULTURE   What is the relationship between values and human behaviour? Sociologists stress that a gap always exists between ideal culture and real culture in a society. *Ideal culture* refers to the values and standards of behaviour that people in a society profess to hold. *Real culture* refers to the values and standards of behaviour that people actually follow. For example, we may claim to be law-abiding (ideal cultural value) but smoke marijuana (real cultural behaviour), or we may regularly drive over the speed limit but think of ourselves as "good citizens."

Most of us are not completely honest about how well we adhere to societal values. In a study known as the "Garbage Project," household waste was analyzed to determine the rate of alcohol consumption in a U.S. city. People were asked about their level of alcohol consumption, and in some areas of the city, very low levels of alcohol use were reported. However, when their garbage was analyzed, researchers found that in more than 80 percent of these households some beer had been consumed, and in more than half occupants threw out eight or more empty beer cans a week (Haviland, 1993:11–12). Obviously, this study shows a discrepancy between ideal cultural values and people's actual behaviour.

The degree of discrepancy between ideal and real culture is relevant to sociologists investigating social change. Large discrepancies provide a foothold for demonstrating hypocrisy (pretending to be what one is not or to feel what one does not feel). These discrepancies often are a source of social problems; if the discrepancy is perceived, leaders of social movements may utilize them to point out people's contradictory behaviour. For example, preserving our natural environment may be a core value, but our behaviour (such as littering highways and lakes) contributes to its degradation, as is further discussed in Chapter 20 ("Collective Behaviour and Social Change").

Norms

Values provide ideals or beliefs about behaviour but do not state explicitly how we should behave. Norms, on the other hand, do have specific behavioural expectations. **Norms are established rules of behaviour or standards of conduct.** *Prescriptive norms* state what behaviour is appropriate or acceptable. For example, persons making a certain amount of money are expected to file a tax return and pay any taxes they owe. Norms based on custom direct us to open a door for a person carrying a heavy load. By contrast, *proscriptive norms* state what behaviour is inappropriate or unacceptable. Laws that prohibit us from driving over the speed limit and "good manners" that preclude reading a newspaper during class are examples. Prescriptive and proscriptive norms operate at all levels of society, from our everyday actions to the formulation of laws.

FORMAL AND INFORMAL NORMS Not all norms are of equal importance; those that are most crucial are formalized. *Formal norms* are written down and involve specific punishments for violators. Laws are the most common type of formal norms; they have been codified and may be enforced by sanctions. **Sanctions are rewards for appropriate behaviour or penalties for inappropriate behaviour.** Examples of *positive sanctions* include praise, honours, or medals for conformity to specific norms. *Negative sanctions* range from mild disapproval to life imprisonment. In the case of law, formal sanctions are clearly defined and can be administered only by persons in certain official positions (such as police officers and judges) who are given the authority to impose the sanctions.

Norms considered to be less important are referred to as *informal norms*—unwritten standards of behaviour understood by people who share a common identity. When individuals violate informal norms, other people may apply informal sanctions. *Informal sanctions* are not clearly defined and can be applied by any member of a group (such as frowning at someone or making a negative comment or gesture).

FOLKWAYS Norms are also classified according to their relative social importance. **Folkways are informal norms or everyday customs that may be violated without serious consequences within a particular culture** (Sumner, 1959/1906). They provide rules for conduct but are not considered to be essential to society's survival. In Canada, folkways include using underarm deodorant, brushing one's teeth, and wearing appropriate clothing for a specific occasion. Folkways are not often enforced; when they are enforced, the resulting sanctions tend to be informal and relatively mild.

Folkways are very culture specific; they are learned patterns of behaviour that can vary markedly from one society to another. In Japan, for example, where the walls of restroom stalls reach to the floor, folkways dictate that a person should knock on the door before entering a stall (you cannot tell if anyone is inside without knocking). People in Canada find it disconcerting, however, when someone knocks on the door of the stall (Collins, 1991).

MORES Other norms are considered highly essential to the stability of society. **Mores** (pronounced MOR-ays) **are strongly held norms with moral and ethical connotations that may not be violated without serious consequences in a particular culture.** Since mores are based on cultural values and are considered crucial for the well-being of the group, violators are subject to more severe negative sanctions (such as ridicule, loss of employment, or imprisonment) than are those who fail to adhere to folkways. The strongest mores are referred to as taboos. **Taboos are mores so strong that their violation is considered to be extremely offensive and even unmentionable.** Violation of taboos is punishable by the group or even, according to certain belief systems, by a supernatural force. The incest taboo, which prohibits sexual or marital relations between certain categories of kin, is an example of a nearly universal taboo.

Folkways and mores provide structure and security in a society. They make everyday life more predictable and provide people with some guidelines for appearance and behaviour. As individuals travel in countries other than their own, they become aware of cross-cultural differences in folkways and mores. For example, women from Canada travelling in Muslim nations quickly become aware of mores, based on the Sharia (the edicts of the Koran), that prescribe the dominance of men over women. In Saudi Arabia, for instance, women are not allowed to mix with men in public. Banks have branches with only women tellers—and only women customers. In hospitals, female doctors are supposed to tend only to children and other women (Alireza, 1990; Ibrahim, 1990).

LAWS   *Laws* **are formal, standardized norms that have been enacted by legislatures and are enforced by formal sanctions.** Laws may be either civil or criminal. *Civil law* deals with disputes among persons or groups. Persons who lose civil suits may encounter negative sanctions such as having to pay compensation to the other party or being ordered to stop certain conduct. *Criminal law,* on the other hand, deals with public safety and well-being. When criminal laws are violated, fines and prison sentences are the most likely negative sanctions.

Changes in law often reflect changes in culture. For example, in the 1990s, increasing awareness of hate crimes based on racial/ethnic, religious, or sexual-orientation biases has led to increasing pressure on the federal government to establish uniform reporting requirements and to increase penalties for hate crimes.

In addition to material objects, all of the nonmaterial components of culture—symbols, language, values, and norms—are reflected in the popular culture of contemporary society.

POPULAR CULTURE

Before taking this course, what was the first thing you thought about when you heard the term *culture?* In everyday life, culture often is used to describe the fine arts, literature, or classical music. When people say that a person is "cultured," they may mean that the individual has a highly developed sense of style or aesthetic appreciation of the "finer" things.

Popular versus High Culture

Some sociologists use the concepts of high culture and popular culture to distinguish between different cultural forms. These ideal types are differentiated by their content, style, expressed values, and respective audiences (Gans, 1974; DiMaggio and Useem, 1978; Bourdieu, 1984; DiMaggio, 1987). *High culture* consists of classical music, opera, ballet, live theatre, and other activities usually patronized by elite audiences, composed primarily of members of the upper middle and upper classes, who have the time, money, and knowledge assumed to be necessary for its appreciation. *Popular culture* **consists of activities, products, and services that are assumed to appeal primarily to members of the middle and working classes.** These include rock concerts, spectator sports, movies, television soap operas, and, more recently, the Internet.

Some sociological examinations of high culture and popular culture focus primarily on the link between culture and social class. French sociologist Pierre Bourdieu's (1984) *cultural capital theory* views high culture as a device used by the dominant class to exclude the subordinate classes. According to Bourdieu, people must be trained to appreciate and understand high culture. Individuals learn about high culture in upper middle- and upper-class families and in elite education systems, especially higher education. Once they acquire this trained capacity, they possess a form of cultural capital. Persons from poor and working-class backgrounds typically do not acquire this cultural capital. Since knowledge and appreciation of high culture is considered a prerequisite for access to the dominant class, its members can use their cultural capital to deny access to subordinate group members and thus preserve and reproduce the existing class structure (but see Halle, 1993).

Unlike high culture, popular culture is assumed to be far more widespread and accessible to everyone; for this reason, it is sometimes referred to as "mass culture." While the primary purpose of popular culture is entertainment, it also provides an avenue for people to express their hopes, fears, and anger. However, popular culture also may include racism, sexism, and nativism (hostility toward immigrants by native-born citizens) (Mukerji and Schudson, 1991). "Cruising the Internet" has become a new form of popular culture (see Box 3.3). Although this medium is for most Canadians a source of education and entertainment, it has also become a medium for hate groups to disseminate racist and homophobic ideology. For example, on the World Wide Web there are White Nationalist and One World Government resource pages (Chidley, 1995). For sociologists, popular culture provides a window into the public consciousness. At times the view can be disturbing.

Forms of popular culture move across cultures. In fact, popular culture is the United States' second-largest export (Rockwell, 1994), and one of its largest importers is Canada. Sadly, we often assess the quality of popular culture on the basis of whether it is a Canadian or American product. Canadian artists, musicians, and entertainers know they have "made it" when they become part of American popular culture. Of the world's 100 most-attended films in 1993, for example, 88 were produced by U.S.-based film companies. Likewise, music, television shows, novels, and street fashions from the United States have become a part of Canadian culture.

Divergent Perspectives on Popular Culture

According to many functionalist theorists, popular culture serves an important function in society: It may be the "glue" that holds society together. Regardless of their ethnicity, class, sex, or age, people are brought together (at least in spirit) to cheer teams competing in major sporting events such as the Stanley Cup or the Olympic Games. Television helps integrate immigrants into the mainstream culture, while longer-term residents become more homogenized as a result of seeing the same images and being exposed to the same beliefs and values (Gerbner et al., 1987).

Popular culture also may help us temporarily forget our everyday problems. In a recent study of Walt Disney World, anthropologist Stephen M. Fjellman (1992) found that such amusement parks allow people to forget that the outside world can be threatening. Even at night, they can walk without fear on the park's streets because virtually no crime exists and automobiles are not allowed. As Fjellman (1992:12) notes, "This freedom is enormously empowering." Various forms of popular culture provide people with opportunities to relax, be entertained, and exercise their abilities to think, feel, and remember (Fjellman, 1992).

Functionalist analysts point out, however, that popular culture also has dysfunctions. Popular culture may undermine core cultural values rather than reinforce them (see Christians, Rotzoll, and Fackler, 1987). For example, movies may glorify crime, rather than hard work, as the quickest way to get ahead. Excessive violence in music videos, movies, and television shows may be harmful to children and young people (Medved, 1992). From this perspective, popular culture may contribute to antisocial behaviour. Can you think of some forms of popular culture that might promote hatred or violence in Canada?

Conflict theorists tend to view popular culture as part of the commercial system in which it is created (see Gans, 1974; Cantor, 1980, 1987). Corporations create popular culture in the same way that any other product or service is produced. Popular culture promotes consumption of *commodities*—objects outside ourselves that we purchase to satisfy our human needs or wants (Fjellman, 1992). For example, Fjellman found that park-goers at Walt Disney World spend as much money on merchandise as they do on admissions and rides. They purchase items ranging from Magic Kingdom pencils and Mickey Mouse hats to non-Disney kitchen accessories, flowers and plants, and clothing:

Is body piercing a fad, or might it become a more lasting feature of culture? How does it reinforce or challenge "mainstream" values and norms?

> Once inside the Magic Kingdom, it is the grown-ups who relax, who drop their guards and become childlike. They buy everything in sight, shoving off much of it on their kids, wearing some of it and stashing some of it as gifts for others ... The adults themselves lose control over not only the purse strings but their very sense of self. (Fjellman, 1992:162)

From this perspective, popular culture has been turned into a commodity; people come to believe that they *need* things they ordinarily would not purchase. Their desire is intensified by marketing techniques that promote public trust in products and services provided by a corporation such as the Walt Disney Company. Sociologist Pierre Bourdieu (1984:291) referred to this public trust as *symbolic capital:* "the acquisition of a reputation for competence and an image of respectability and

BOX 3.3   SOCIOLOGY AND TECHNOLOGY

INTERNET CYBERCULTURE

So I was talking on the phone with my mother out in Minnesota the other day, and she sounded upset. "What's wrong, Mom?" I asked. "Well," she said, "I've been playing bridge on the Internet with three Frenchmen and they keep speaking French to each other and I can't understand them." When I chuckled at the thought of my card-shark mom playing bridge on the net, she took a little umbrage. "Don't laugh," she said. "I was playing bridge with someone in Siberia the other day." (Friedman, 1998:AIO)

■s there a new culture developing in cyberspace? Apparently so. The term *cyberculture* has been coined to describe this new form of popular culture. Cyberculture, which makes up a large portion of the World Wide Web, has been described as the melting pot of the world's diversity. The Internet links the world as never before, creating a global village where people from around the world can communicate with a simple click of the mouse. Through various Internet services such as chat rooms, newsgroups, and e-mail, people can connect with anyone, almost anywhere in the world. This allows for the sharing of ideas and the exchange of both material and nonmaterial cultural products.

Recent surveys report that Canada is at the leading edge of technology adoption. Among North American and European countries, Canada has the highest level of home PC use, and Canadians and Americans lead the pack for the rate of acquiring home Internet access. As a result of these advances in communication technologies, people can travel *virtually* in a cyberculture made up of networks, projects, and communities with people they have never met, in cultures they have never visited.

honourability." Symbolic capital consists of culturally approved intangibles—such as honour, integrity, esteem, trust, and goodwill—that may be accumulated and used for tangible (economic) gain. Thus, people buy products at Walt Disney World (and Disney stores throughout the country) because they believe in the trustworthiness of the item ("These children's pyjamas are bound to be flame retardant; they came from the Disney Store") and the integrity of the company ("I can trust Disney; it has been around for a long time").

Other conflict theorists suggest that corporations do not create popular culture as much as they co-opt existing popular culture for their own economic gain. As communications scholar Herbert I. Schiller (1989:30) explained:

Speech, dance, drama (ritual), music, and the visual and plastic arts have been vital ... features of human experience from earliest times. What distinguishes their situation in the industrial-capitalist era ... [is]

the relentless and successful efforts to separate these elemental expressions of human creativity from their group and community origins for the purpose of selling them to those who can pay for them.

Schiller further argues that corporate control of arenas of culture, such as museums, theatres, performing arts centres, and public broadcasting stations, has resulted in the manipulation of people's consciousness and a form of censorship.

Although numerous scholars have examined the relationship between class and popular culture, few have investigated the intertwining relationship between ethnicity, gender, and popular culture. However, sociologist K. Sue Jewell (1993) linked images found in popular culture to negative stereotypes of black women. She suggested that cultural images depicting black women as mammies or domestics, whose primary purpose is to nurture others, affect their career prospects as early as middle school, when guidance counsellors

BOX 3.3

CONTINUED

According to sociologist Michael Adams, "Thanks to virtual travel through the globalization of culture, teenagers in Toronto, Miami and Kiev often have more in common with each other than they do with their own parents" (1998:32).

Is this universal cultural connection a good thing? What possible effects do you foresee for Canadian culture? On the positive side, this new Internet culture allows for the exchange of ideas and makes foreign cultures seem familiar. This can only serve to increase global cultural understanding and tolerance.

However, on the negative side, chances are we can expect the significant influence of U.S. culture on Canadian culture to become even more pronounced through this new form of popular culture. Furthermore, the Internet is a

virtually uncensored forum for free speech. Anyone with Internet access can publish their own personal views—some of which may be racist, sexist, exploitative, or destructive. These ideas can be disseminated quickly and easily in cyberspace.

Does cyberculture open up the world? Experts on Internet culture remind us that although cyberculture may be an increasingly significant part of mainstream popular culture in Canada, we may be thinking in ethnocentric terms when assuming that this resource is readily available in all cultures. While industrialized countries are exploring sophisticated uses of the Internet, more than half of the world's population has never used a telephone.

Sources: Buckler, 1996; Hansen, 1995; and Adams, 1998.

and teachers give them little encouragement to succeed. Popular cultural icons such as Aunt Jemima, Uncle Ben (her male counterpart on rice boxes), and other "mammy trademarks" are displayed on grocery store shelves, on antique cookie jars, and in advertising campaigns. Even though Aunt Jemima's appearance has recently been changed, "racially charged imagery never fully loses its historical taint" (Staples, 1994:A14).

According to sociologists Chandra Mukerji and Michael Schudson (1991:35), a clear distinction between high culture and popular culture cannot be maintained over time. Items of popular culture—for example, jazz music, folk art—may come to be designated as high culture and aspects of high culture may become popular.

While culture may contribute to permanence and stability, changes in material and nonmaterial culture also tend to bring about dramatic changes in society.

CULTURAL CHANGE AND DIVERSITY

We have examined the nature of culture within society, the defining components of culture, and the forcefulness of popular culture. Cultures do not generally remain static, however. There are many forces working toward change and diversity. Some societies and individuals adapt to this change, while others suffer culture shock and succumb to ethnocentrism.

Cultural Change

Societies continually experience cultural change, at both material and nonmaterial levels. Moreover, a change in one area frequently triggers a change in other areas. For example, the personal computer has changed how we work and how we

With the widespread accessibility of television and the Internet, popular culture is increasingly accessible for both children and adults in their own homes. Studies show that many children spend more time watching television than they spend attending school.

think about work; today, many people work at home—away from the immediate gaze of a supervisor. Ultimately, computer technology may change the nature of boss–worker relations. Such changes are often set in motion by discovery, invention, and diffusion.

Discovery is the process of learning about something previously unknown or unrecognized. Historically, discovery involved unearthing natural elements or existing realities, such as "discovering" fire or the true shape of the earth. Today, discovery most often results from scientific research. For example, discovery of a polio vaccine virtually eliminated one of the major childhood diseases. A future discovery of a cure for cancer or the common cold could result in longer and more productive lives for many people.

As more discoveries have occurred, people have been able to reconfigure existing material and nonmaterial cultural items through invention. **Invention is the process of reshaping existing cultural items into a new form.** Guns, video games, airplanes, and the Charter of Rights and Freedoms are examples of inventions that positively or negatively affect our lives today.

When diverse groups of people come into contact, they begin to adapt one another's discoveries, inventions, and ideas for their own use. **Diffusion is the transmission of cultural items or social practices from one group or society to another** through such means as exploration, military endeavours, the media, tourism, and immigration. To illustrate, consider the comments of former Indian cabinet minister I.K. Gujral,

> My granddaughter is 4, she is always talking about bubble gum, not Indian food, or she says, "I don't like Pepsi, I like Coke." She even speaks English more than Hindi. I asked her one day why she doesn't speak to me in Hindi, and then she went to her mother and asked: "Doesn't grandfather speak English?" The other day my granddaughter said she wanted pizza. So her grandmother said she would make her a pizza. My granddaughter said, "No, no, I want Pizza Hut." (Friedman, 1998:A10).

As this example demonstrates, in today's "shrinking globe," cultural diffusion moves at a very rapid pace as countries continually seek new markets for their products (Friedman, 1998:A10). (See Box 3.4.)

When a change occurs in the material culture of a society, nonmaterial culture must adapt to that change. Frequently, this rate of change is uneven, resulting in a gap between the two. Sociologist William F. Ogburn (1966/1922) referred to this disparity as **cultural lag—a gap between the technical development of a society and its moral and legal institutions** (G. Marshall, 1994). The failure of nonmaterial culture to keep pace with material culture is linked to social conflict and problems in society. In Canada, medical treatment is a right of Canadian citizenship. In contrast, although the United States has some of the most advanced medical technology in the world, there is a lack of consensus regarding who has access to these services. The debate centres on whether medical care is a privilege for which people must pay or a right of U.S. citizenship (or noncitizen residency). The number of Americans not covered by medical insurance (about 40 million) exceeds the entire population of Canada (see Chapter 18, "Health, Health Care, and Disability").

Cultural Diversity

Cultural diversity refers to the wide range of cultural differences found between and within nations. Cultural diversity between countries may be the result of natural circumstances (such as climate and geography) or social circumstances (such as level of technology and composition of the population). Some countries—such as Sweden—are referred to as *homogeneous societies,* meaning they include people who share a common culture and are typically from similar social, religious, political, and economic backgrounds. By contrast, other countries—including Canada—are referred to as *heterogeneous societies*, meaning they include people who are dissimilar in regard to social characteristics such as nationality, race, ethnicity, class, occupation, or education (see Figure 3.2).

Immigration contributes to cultural diversity in a society. Throughout its history, Canada has been a nation of immigrants. Over the past 150 years, more than 13 million "documented" (legal) immigrants have arrived here; innumerable people also have entered the country as undocumented immigrants. Immigration can cause feelings of frustration and hostility, especially in people who feel threatened by the changes that large numbers of immigrants may produce (Fleras and Elliott, 1996). Often, people are intolerant of those who are different from themselves. When societal tensions rise, people may look for others on whom they can place blame—or single out persons because they are the "other," the "outsider," the one who does not "belong." Sociologist Adrienne Shadd described her experience of being singled out as an "other":

> Routinely I am asked, "Where are you from?" or "What nationality are you?" as if to be Black, you have to come from somewhere else. I respond that I'm "Canadian" ... I play along. The scenario usually unfolds as follows:
>
> "But where are you *originally* from?"
>
> "Canada."
>
> "Oh, *you* were born here. But where are your parents from?"
>
> "Canada."
>
> "But what about your grandparents?"
>
> As individuals delve further into my genealogy to find out where I'm "really" from, their frustration levels rise.
>
> "No, uh, I mean ... your *people*. Where do your *people* come from?"
>
> At this point, questioners are totally annoyed and/or frustrated. After all, Black people in Canada are supposed to come from "the islands," aren't they? For those of us living in large urban centres, there are constant reminders that we are not regarded as truly "Canadian." (1994:11)

Christmas trees and other holiday symbols exemplify the way in which elements from diverse cultures take on new meanings through the process of diffusion. For instance, notice the European-looking Joseph and Mary, as well as the Greek columns, in this depiction of a manger in Bethlehem. Even the traditional date chosen to celebrate the birth of Jesus (to Christians, the "light of the world") is an adaptation of an ancient pagan celebration of the winter solstice (when the light of the returning sun conquers the darkness of winter).

Have you ever been made to feel like an "outsider"? Each of us receives cultural messages that may make us feel good or bad about ourselves or may give us the perception that we "belong" or "do not belong." However, in heterogeneous societies such as Canada, cultural diversity is inevitable. In Canada, this diversity has created some unique problems in terms of defining and maintaining our distinct Canadian culture. In fact, what is unique to Canada is the number of distinct subcultures that together make up our Canadian culture.

It has been suggested that complex societies are more likely to produce subcultures. This is certainly the case in Canada, where regional, ethnic, class, language, and religious subcultures combine to produce a highly diverse society.

SUBCULTURES A *subculture* is a group of people who share a distinctive set of cultural beliefs and behaviours that differ in some significant way from that of the larger society. Although members of subcultures participate in the main-

BOX 3.4 SOCIOLOGY AND MEDIA

CULTURAL CONFUSION: ADVERTISING—THE GLOBAL MARKETING HALL OF SHAME

Selling a product in a foreign culture requires that attention be paid to cultural differences. The world's smartest advertising minds have sometimes forgotten to do so and, as the examples below demonstrate, they have consequently come off as village idiots. Costly—often amusing—mistakes have been made by advertisers who have misread cultural attitudes, sensitivities, or superstitions, or something has simply been lost in the translation to the global marketplace. Here are a few examples:

- When the makers of Coca-Cola were launching their drink in China, they found a phrase that sounded perfect: "Ko-kou-ke-la." After printing thousands of signs, the Coke masterminds discovered that they had christened their drink "Bite the wax tadpole."
- Carmaker Ford has faced several problems playing the name game. Sales of the Pinto petered out in Brazil because it turns out the

word is slang for "tiny male genitals." When this was discovered, Ford pried all the nameplates off and substituted Corcel, which means "horse."
- Ford also introduced a low-cost truck to some less-developed countries named the Fiera, a word that means "ugly old woman" in Spanish.
- General Motors introduced its Chevy Nova in South America unaware that "no va" means "It won't go" in Spanish.
- Most North Americans know the slogan for Kentucky Fried Chicken as "Finger-lickin' good." In China, after translation, the slogan became "Eat your fingers off."
- The American Dairy Council ran a "Got milk?" campaign that featured celebrities sporting milk moustaches. In converting the message to Spanish, the Council ended up asking its Mexican consumers, "Are you lactating?"

---

stream society, they tend to associate with one another more frequently and more personally than with members of other groups. Occupational groups, such as lawyers; ethnic populations such as Italian Canadians; religious groups such as Orthodox Jews; people living in small rural communities: all of these are examples of subcultures. All of these groups will develop unique beliefs, norms, and values. We next look at one subculture—the Hutterites—to see how this group interacts with the dominant Canadian culture.

THE HUTTERITES This subculture has fought for many years to maintain its distinct identity. They are the largest family-type communal grouping in the Western world, with over 20,000 members living in approximately 200 settlements (Curtis and Lambert, 1994). The Hutterites live on farms, called "colonies," in western Canada and the United States where they practise their religious beliefs and maintain a relatively closed social net-

work. Colonies strive to be self-sufficient—doing everything themselves, from making their own soap to pouring concrete and raising new buildings (Lyons, 1998).

The Hutterites are considered a subculture because their values, norms, and appearance differ significantly from those of members of the dominant culture. They have a strong faith in God and reject worldly concerns. Their core values include the joy of work, the primacy of the home, faithfulness, thriftiness, tradition, and humility. Hutterites hold conservative views of the family, believing that women are subordinate to men, birth control is unacceptable, and wives should remain at home. Children are cherished and seen as an economic asset: they help with the farming and other work.

Hutterite life is centred on the community rather than on the individual. Significant life decisions such as whether a high-school graduate will attend university are made on the basis of

BOX 3.4

CONTINUED

- "Come alive with the Pepsi Generation" was a perfectly good slogan—until it got translated into Taiwanese as: "Pepsi will bring your ancestors back from the dead."
- The makers of Coors Light beer hired an agency to develop promotional materials aimed at Hispanics in the United States. In trying to translate the ad's catchphrase "Turn it loose" into Spanish, a copywriter ended up inviting customers to "Drink Coors and get diarrhea."

The lack of cultural awareness of corporate North America is obvious in the following blunders:

- When Coca-Cola introduced its two-litre bottles in Japan, it was unaware of the fact that few Japanese refrigerators are roomy enough to store such a large bottle.
- Trying to market its cake mixes in Japan in the 1960s, Betty Crocker discovered that most Japanese homes were missing a necessary ingredient: an oven.
- When McDonald's ventured into China, corporate mascot Ronald McDonald was in tow to clown around at the launch. Talk about a bozo move: to the Chinese, the clown is a symbol of death.
- A toothpaste company ran a commercial in Southeast Asia proclaiming that its product helped whiten teeth. The problem was that the people in the local target market were in the habit of chewing betel nut in order to achieve darkly stained teeth—a social sign of prestige.

Reprinted with permission from Trish Snyder and Terri Foxman, authors of "The Global Marketing Hall of Shame" published in *Canadian Inflight Magazine* (July, 1998), 42–50.

what is best for the entire community. All aspects of day-to-day life are based on sharing, right down to eating every meal in a community hall. Members of this group also have communal rather than private property; nobody is permitted to individually own as much as a pair of shoes (Curtis and Lambert, 1994). The Hutterites also have a distinctive mode of dress that makes this subculture readily identifiable.

The Hutterites are aware that their values are distinct from those of most other Canadians and that they look different from other people; these differences, though, provide them with a collective identity and make them feel close to one another (Peter, 1987). However, the Hutterites do not attempt to achieve complete social isolation from the wider society. Although this subculture strictly adheres to centuries-old traditions, the Hutterites don't hesitate to take advantage of the twentieth century (Lyons, 1998). They are successful farmers who trade with people in the sur-

rounding communities, and they buy modern farm machinery. They also read newspapers, use home computers and telephones, and utilize the services of non-Hutterite professionals (Curtis and Lambert, 1994).

COUNTERCULTURES   Some subcultures actively oppose the larger society. A *counterculture* is a **group that strongly rejects dominant societal values and norms and seeks alternative lifestyles** (Yinger, 1960, 1982). Young people are most likely to join countercultural groups, perhaps because younger persons generally have less invested in the existing culture. Examples of countercultures include the beatniks of the 1950s, the flower children of the 1960s, the drug enthusiasts of the 1970s, and members of nonmainstream religious sects, or cults. Some countercultures (such as the Ku Klux Klan and the skinheads) even engage in revolutionary political activities.

FIGURE 3.2   **Heterogeneity of Canadian Society**

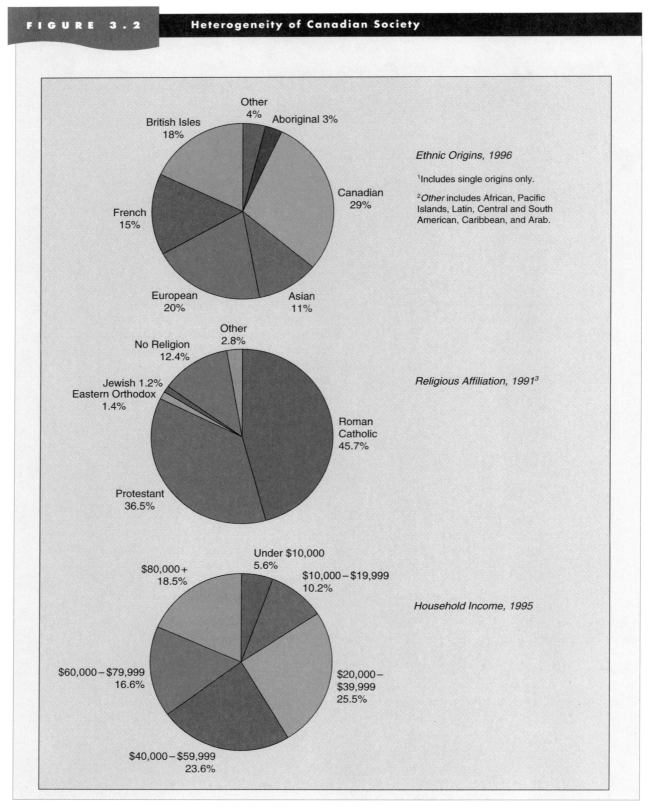

Ethnic Origins, 1996

[1]Includes single origins only.

[2]*Other* includes African, Pacific Islands, Latin, Central and South American, Caribbean, and Arab.

Religious Affiliation, 1991[3]

Household Income, 1995

Throughout history, Canada has been heterogeneous. Today, Canada is represented by a wide variety of social categories, including our religious affiliations, income levels, and ethnic origins.

Sources: "Ethnic Origins, 1996," adapted with permission from "Total Population by Ethnic Categories and Sex, for Canada, Provinces, Territories and Census Metropolitan Areas, 1996 Census," Cat. no. 930026XDB96002; "Household Income, 1995," adapted with permission from the Statistics Canada website at www.statcan.ca/english/census96/may12/t6can.htm.

Technology and tradition meet at the Fairholme Hutterite Colony as these young women try out a new digital camera at school.

One of the countercultures closely associated with hate crimes is the skinheads, sometimes referred to as "neo-Nazi skinheads," who have been present in North America since the early 1980s. Canada and the United States are not the only countries to experience these problems; as discussed in Box 3.5, Western Europe is experiencing an upswing in hate crimes against "foreigners" by neo-Nazi skinheads and others. Skinheads primarily are young, white, working-class males who express group identity by wearing boots, jeans, suspenders, green flight jackets, and chains, and by shaving their heads or sporting "burr" haircuts. Core values of "hard-core" skinheads include racial group superiority, patriotism, a belief in the traditional roles of women and men, and justification of physical violence as a means of expressing anger toward immigrants, gay men and lesbians, people of colour, and Jews (Wooden, 1995). Some skinhead groups tend to engage in relatively spontaneous outbursts of violence; others are highly organized and motivated. These groups select leaders, hold regular meetings, distribute racist propaganda, and attend rallies sponsored by groups like the Ku Klux Klan and the White Aryan Resistance (Barrett, 1987).

The skinhead counterculture in Canada consists of three main groups: the Ku Klux Klan, the Western Guard, and a third group that includes a number of smaller organizations, such as the Canadian National Socialist Party (Barrett, 1987). All of these groups share the belief that the Aryan, or white, race is superior to others morally, intellectually, and culturally and that it is their destiny to dominate society.

Canadian neo-Nazi countercultural groups also believe that the survival of white society in this country is in jeopardy because of the practice of allowing "non-Aryans" into Canada. Skinheads, consequently, have been involved in a number of violent assaults and murders. For example, in 1993 three Tamil refugees were beaten in Toronto. One died as a result of the injuries inflicted and one was paralyzed (Henry et al., 1995).

Hard-core skinheads are a countercultural group because they focus on "white power" and other racist views that contradict the norms and values of mainstream Canadian culture. However, not all skinheads share racist views; some identify themselves as SHARPS (Skinheads Against Racial Prejudice) or SARS (Skinheads Against Racism) (Wooden, 1995). Members of these groups have been attacked by hard-core skinheads because they refused to participate in violence against members of "out" groups.

Culture Shock

Culture shock is the disorientation that people feel when they encounter cultures radically different from their own and believe they cannot depend on their own taken-for-granted assumptions about life. When people travel to another society, they may not know how to respond to that setting. For example, Napoleon Chagnon (1992) was initially shocked at the sight of the Yanomamö (pronounced yah-noh-MAH-mah) tribe of South America for the first time in 1964.

Members of white extremist countercultures such as these neo-Nazi skinheads in Germany speak an international language of intolerance of those who are different from themselves.

The Yanomamö (also referred as the "Yanomami") are a tribe of about 20,000 South American Indians who live in the rain forest. Although Chagnon travelled in a small aluminum motorboat for three days to reach these people, he was not prepared for the sight that met his eyes when he arrived:

> I looked up and gasped to see a dozen burly, naked, sweaty, hideous men staring at us down the shafts of their drawn arrows. Immense wads of green tobacco were stuck between their lower teeth and lips, making them look even more hideous, and strands of dark-green slime dripped from their nostrils—strands so long that they reached down to their pectoral muscles or drizzled down their chins and stuck to their chests and bellies. We arrived as the men were blowing *ebene*, a hallucinogenic drug, up their noses. As I soon learned, one side effect of the drug is a runny nose. The mucus becomes saturated with the drug's green powder, and the Yanomamö usually just let it dangle freely from their nostrils to plop off when the strands become too heavy.
>
> Then the stench of decaying vegetation and filth hit me, and I was almost sick to my stomach. I was horrified. What kind of welcome was this for someone who had come to live with these people and learn their way of life—to become friends with them? But when they recognized Barker [a guide], they put their weapons down and returned to their

chanting, while keeping a nervous eye on the village entrances. (Chagnon, 1992:12–14)

The Yanomamö have no written language, system of numbers, or calendar. They lead a nomadic lifestyle, carrying everything they own on their backs. They wear no clothes and paint their bodies; the women insert slender sticks through holes in the lower lip and through the pierced nasal septum. Chagnon referred to the Yanomamö as a "fierce people" because they engaged in persistent aggression (such as club fighting, gang rape, and murder) within their own group and in continual warfare with outsiders (Chagnon, 1988).

When Chagnon returned to the Yanomamö in 1992, he found that they were threatened by diseases (such as malaria, venereal disease, and tuberculosis) and by environmental degradation. Seventy percent of the tribe's land in Brazil had been taken away from them, and their supplies of fish were poisoned by mercury contamination of rivers. Although the governments of Brazil and Venezuela enacted policies to save them from extinction by setting aside huge areas as a homeland for them (see Chagnon, 1992:248–255), in August 1993, about seventy of the Yanomamö were attacked and brutally killed by Brazilian gold miners in a massacre that produced a widespread outcry (Brooke, 1993a:Y3).

The distinctiveness of the Yanomamö is evident in this picture of tribe members making bread for guests.
Do you think you would experience culture shock upon encountering these people for the first time?

Ethnocentrism

Many of us tend to make judgments about other cultures in terms of our own culture. *Ethnocentrism* **is the assumption that one's own culture and way of life are superior to all others** (Sumner, 1959/1906). From a functionalist viewpoint, ethnocentrism can serve a positive function in societies by promoting group solidarity and loyalty and by encouraging people to conform to societal norms and values. For example, nationalism and patriotism encourage people to think of their own nation as "the best." International sports competitions such as the Olympic Games help to foster this idea.

On the other hand, ethnocentrism can be problematic for societies. Historically, people have regarded outsiders as "barbarians" or "primitive" because they were different. Until recently, for example, few people in the more developed nations have been interested in what indigenous peoples such as the Yanomamö might know; after all, what could nations with high levels of tech-

nology possibly learn from tribal cultures? Yet people in such cultures have devised ways to survive and flourish that constitute an important source of knowledge. Some have created methods of farming without irrigation; others hunt, fish, and gather food in the rain forest without destroying the delicate balance that maintains the ecosystem. Ethnocentrism is counterproductive when it blinds us to what other groups have to offer or when it leads to conflict, hostility, and war.

Ethnocentrism can be a problem within societies as well as between them when it leads to social isolation, prejudice, discrimination, and oppression of one group by another. People who have recently arrived in a country where their customs, dress, eating habits, or religious beliefs differ markedly from those of existing residents often find themselves the object of ridicule. Indigenous groups, such as Native Americans, also have been the target of ethnocentrism by other groups.

Recently, some sociologists have begun to study xenocentrism, or "reverse ethnocentrism."

Xenocentrism **is the belief that the products, styles, or ideas of another society are better than those of one's own culture.** Examples include the desire for German-made cars by Canadian citizens, some of whom assert that North American manufacturers cannot make a decent car any more, and the preference for American popular culture (television programs, movies, and books) over Canadian popular culture.

Cultural Relativism

An alternative to ethnocentrism is *cultural relativism*—**the belief that the behaviours and customs of a society must be viewed and analyzed within the context of its own culture.** Cultural relativism is a part of the sociological imagination; researchers must be aware of the customs and norms of the society they are studying and then spell out their background assumptions so that others can spot possible biases in their studies.

Anthropologist Marvin Harris (1974, 1985) uses cultural relativism to explain why cattle, which are viewed as sacred, are not killed and eaten in India, where widespread hunger and malnutrition exist. From an ethnocentric viewpoint, we might conclude that cow worship is the cause of the hunger and poverty in India. However, Harris demonstrates that the Hindu taboo against killing cattle is very important to their economic system. Live cows are more valuable than dead ones because they have more important uses than as a direct source of food. As part of the ecological system, cows consume grasses of little value to humans. Then they produce two valuable resources—oxen (the neutered offspring of cows), to power the ploughs, and manure (for fuel and fertilizer)—as well as milk, floor covering, and leather. As Harris's study reveals, culture must be viewed from the standpoint of those who live in a particular society.

SOCIOLOGICAL ANALYSIS OF CULTURE

Sociologists regard culture as a central ingredient in human behaviour. Although all sociologists share a similar purpose, they typically see culture through somewhat different lenses as they are guided by different theoretical perspectives in their research. What do these perspectives tell us about culture?

A Functionalist Perspective

As previously discussed, functionalist perspectives are based on the assumption that society is a stable, orderly system with interrelated parts that serve specific functions. Anthropologist Bronislaw Malinowski (1922) suggested that culture helps people meet their *biological needs* (including food and procreation), *instrumental needs* (including law and education), and *integrative needs* (including religion and art). Societies in which people share a common language and core values are more likely to have consensus and harmony. However, all societies have dysfunctions that produce a variety of societal problems. Inequalities along class, racial, and gender lines often contribute to many of these problems. When a society contains numerous subcultures, discord results from a lack of consensus about core values and a failure to educate everyone about the positive value of cultural diversity. Resolution of such problems must come from families, schools, and other organizations charged with teaching the young and maintaining order and peace.

A strength of the functionalist perspective on culture is its focus on the needs of society and the fact that stability is essential for society's continued survival. A shortcoming is its overemphasis on harmony and cooperation and a lack of acknowledgment of societal factors that contribute to conflict and strife.

A Conflict Perspective

Conflict perspectives are based on the assumption that social life is a continuous struggle in which members of powerful groups seek to control scarce resources. Values and norms help create and sustain the privileged position of the powerful in society while excluding others. As early conflict theorist Karl Marx stressed, ideas are cultural creations of a society's most powerful members. According to conflict theorists, most people are not aware that they are being dominated because they have *false consciousness,* **which means that they hold beliefs they think promote their best interests when those beliefs actually are damaging to their interests.** For example, when hate groups "blame" people located at the margins of society for society's problems, they shift attention

Many people in our society face the challenge of preserving a subcultural heritage while sharing in many of the values and norms of the dominant culture. The powwow is a means through which Aboriginal peoples can celebrate their unique culture and pass on cultural traditions to future generations.

away from persons in positions of political and economic power. Extremist groups may perpetuate the very "problem" they think exists. Thus, hate crimes may maintain the status quo by protecting the people who are responsible for making important decisions at the highest levels of society (Levin and McDevitt, 1993:234).

A strength of the conflict perspective is that it stresses how cultural values and norms may perpetuate social inequalities. It also highlights the inevitability of change and the constant tension between those who want to maintain the status quo and those who desire change. A limitation is its overemphasis on societal discord and the divisiveness of culture.

An Interactionist Perspective

Unlike functionalists and conflict theorists, interactionists do not examine the functions of culture or the ways in which culture helps maintain the status of privileged groups while excluding others from society's benefits. Interactionists instead focus on a microlevel analysis that views society as the sum of all people's interactions. From this perspective, people create, maintain, and modify culture as they go about their everyday activities. Symbols make communication with others possible because they provide us with shared meanings.

According to interactionist theory, people continually negotiate their social realities. Values and norms are not independent realities that automatically determine our behaviour. Instead, we reinterpret them in each social situation we encounter. Hard-core skinheads defy dominant group norms and accept alternative norms of violence as an appropriate response to groups they consider "inferior." This interpretation of reality is reinforced by continual interaction with other hard-core skinhead groups (Farley, 1993).

An interactionist approach highlights how people maintain and change culture through their interactions with others. However, interactionism does not provide a systematic framework for analyzing how we shape culture and how it, in turn, shapes us. It also does not provide insight into how shared meanings are developed among people, and it does not take into account the many situations in which there is disagreement on meanings. Where the functional and conflict approaches tend to overemphasize the macrolevel workings of society, the interactionist viewpoint often fails to take into account these larger social structures.

In viewing culture from any of these perspectives, the impact of ethnicity, class, gender, religion, and age must be taken into account in examining people's experiences. In Canada, people have a wide array of experiences because they come from diverse backgrounds. However, simply by living in this country, most of us share some aspects of the dominant culture. This shared culture may be as basic as our use of Canadian currency or postage stamps. It may involve a core curriculum of subjects all children are required to take in elementary school. Shared culture for many individuals is framed at the subcultural level, where, for example, members of a particular church, private club, or other organization may have similar lifestyles and hold values in common with other members of the group.

HOSTILITY TOWARD IMMIGRANTS

Hate crimes have increased in the nations of Western Europe as well as in North America in recent years. Hundreds of thousands of people fleeing economic depression or political oppression in African and Southeast Asian countries have migrated to Western Europe, where attitudes toward immigrants have changed dramatically as their numbers have grown. In many countries, immigrants were previously seen as a source of cheap labour for jobs like ditch digging or street cleaning. Today, however, in many countries (including Canada) some people see immigrant workers as competing for scarce jobs in tough economic times and as draining the welfare, education, and health-care systems. Many immigrants do not have anywhere to go, as indicated by a Liberian man who stowed away on a freighter from Nigeria to get to Western

Europe: "I don't know what to do. I can't go back [to Liberia, where civil wars have continued for a number of years]. I walk the street and I'm a dead man" (Darnton, 1993:A1).

In recent years, several political candidates in Western European nations have promised, if they are elected, to expel these "foreigners." A rising tide of racism and hate crimes waged by neo-Nazi skinheads against persons believed to be recent immigrants has bolstered their political claims that something must be done very soon. Hate speech often is based on nostalgia for a bygone era alleged to have been "comfortable, orderly, and virtually all white" (Darnton, 1993:A6). In actuality, changes in the ethnic makeup of Western Europe as nations occurred years ago; Turks, for instance, have lived for generations in Germany, as have Pakistanis in Britain.

CULTURAL PATTERNS IN THE FUTURE

As we have discussed in this chapter, many changes are occurring in our Canadian culture. Increasing cultural diversity can either cause long-simmering racial and ethnic antagonisms to come closer to the boiling point or result in the creation of a truly multicultural society in which diversity is respected and encouraged. According to our ideal culture, Canada will "prosper in diversity." The Multicultural Act has legislated cultural freedom. However, it has been suggested that this freedom is more "symbolic" than real (Roberts and Clifton, 1990). In the real culture, anti-immigration sentiment has risen in response to the estimated one-and-a-half million newcomers who have arrived in Canada over the past decade. Cultural diversity and global immigration are affecting economic and employment perceptions.

Many people accuse newcomers of stealing jobs and overutilizing the social service safety net at the Canadian taxpayers' expense.

In the decades ahead, the issue of cultural diversity will increase in importance, especially in schools. Multicultural education that focuses on the contributions of a wide variety of people from different backgrounds will continue to be an issue from kindergarten through university. Some public schools have incorporated heritage languages into their curriculum. These schools will face the challenge of embracing widespread cultural diversity while conveying a sense of community and national identity to students.

Culture and Technology

In the twenty-first century, technology will continue to profoundly affect culture. Television and radio, films and videos, and electronic communications (including the telephone, electronic mail, and fax) will continue to accelerate the flow of

BOX 3.5

CONTINUED

With dramatic increases in immigration, hate speech and crimes have skyrocketed. In Britain, the increase in tension has been particularly sharp in inner-city neighbourhoods, where most nonwhite immigrants have settled and where unemployment and recession have taken their greatest toll. The grandson of Winston Churchill publicly complained about the "relentless flow of immigrants" and noted that in the future, England would by characterized by "the muezzin ... calling Allah's faithful to the high street mosque for Friday prayers" (Schmidt, 1993:A2).

Other Western European countries, including Spain, Italy, and France, also have seen an increase in hate speech and crimes. For example, in Aravaca, a suburb of Madrid, *rapadas* (urban gang members) have shot undocumented Dominican immigrants living in abandoned buildings. Likewise, in Rome, "Nazi-skins" seek out Africans who sleep in the parks at night and beat them up, as well as burning down the residences of foreigners (Darnton, 1993:A6).

Western Europe faces a difficult, if not impossible, task if it tries to close the door to immigrants. A recent United Nations Population Fund report, for example, estimated that at least 100 million international migrants live outside the countries where they were born. The tide of people crossing borders to flee war, drought, and economic misery "could become the human crisis of our age," according to the report (quoted in Darnton, 1993:A6). Globally, then, it is very likely that immigration pressures will continue and that hate crimes will increase.

information and expand cultural diffusion throughout the world. Global communication devices will move images of people's lives, behaviour, and fashions instantaneously among almost all nations (Petersen, 1994). Increasingly, television may become people's window on the world and, in the process, promote greater integration or fragmentation among nations. Integration occurs when there is a widespread acceptance of ideas and items—such as democracy, rock music, blue jeans, and McDonald's hamburgers—among cultures. By contrast, fragmentation occurs when people in one culture disdain the beliefs and actions of other cultures, such as the rejection by fundamentalist Muslims of Western cultural values, especially as shown in North American–based television shows, music, films, and videos. As a force for both cultural integration and fragmentation, technology will continue to revolutionize communications, but most of the world's population will not participate in this revolution (Petersen, 1994).

A Global Culture?

Some scholars have suggested that a single *global culture*—a worldwide interconnection of material and nonmaterial culture without regard for national identities or boundaries—may emerge in the twenty-first century (see Featherstone, 1990). Others note that global subcultures, such as those of science, business, and diplomacy, already exist and that people are "more at home in these placeless subcultures than in any traditional culture or nation or tribe" (Anderson, 1990:23). If this assumption is correct, these subcultures would create linkages around the world with "communities of shared interest, ideology, and information" (Anderson, 1990:23). However, some analysts do not believe that such widespread acceptance of a single culture will occur.

Critics argue that the world is not developing a homogeneous global culture, rather, other cultures are becoming Westernized. Political and religious leaders in some countries oppose this process,

Multiculturalism has been described as a policy that is more symbolic than real. In recent years, Canada has experienced increasing conflict and intergroup hostility as reflected in Aboriginal peoples' struggles to gain recognition as a unique society within Canadian culture.

which they view as *cultural imperialism*—**the extensive infusion of one nation's culture into other nations.** Some view the widespread infusion of the English language into countries that speak other languages as a form of cultural imperialism. A number of countries or states within them have sought to prevent English from overtaking their native language. For example, several of India's largest states have ordered that all official government work and correspondence must be conducted in Hindi (the dominant language of northern India) (McCarroll, 1993:53). In Canada, conflict over the use of English in French-speaking Quebec is ongoing.

Perhaps the concept of cultural imperialism fails to take into account various cross-cultural influences. For example, Japanese management styles and cars are widely known in North America, and cultural diffusion of literature, music, clothing, and food has occurred on a global scale. A global culture, if it comes into existence, most likely will include components from many societies and cultures. It has been suggested that the "global culture is going to be one with a thin, fragile, and ever-shifting web of common ideas and values, and within that, incredible diversity—more diversity than there has ever been" (Anderson, 1990:25).

However, predictions of a global culture may be premature. Currently, a resurgence of *nationalism*, an ethnocentric belief that the political and economic rights of one's own nation morally supersede those of other nations, has occurred throughout the nations of Eastern Europe and the former Soviet Union. As these nations have experienced rapid change and economic decline, many people have identified more strongly with their original nationalities (as Russians, Armenians, Azerbaijanis, Georgians, or another of the hundreds of nationalities and ethnic groups in that part of the world) than as citizens of a single nation.

From a sociological perspective, the study of culture helps us not only understand our own "tool kit" of symbols, stories, rituals, and world views but also expand our insights to include those of other people of the world who also seek strategies for enhancing their lives. If we understand how culture is used by people, how cultural elements constrain or facilitate certain patterns of action, what aspects of our cultural heritage have enduring effects on our actions, and what specific historical changes undermine the validity of some cultural patterns and give rise to others, we can apply our sociological imagination not only to our own society but to the entire world (see Swidler, 1986).

CHAPTER REVIEW

What is culture?

Culture encompasses the knowledge, language, values, and customs passed from one generation to the next in a human group or society. Culture is essential for our individual survival because, unlike nonhuman animals,

Is this Japanese amusement park a sign of a homogeneous global culture or of cultural imperialism?

we are not born with instinctive information about how to behave and how to care for ourselves and others.

Culture can be a stabilizing force for society; it can provide a sense of continuity. However, culture also can be a force that generates discord, conflict, and violence.

There are both material and nonmaterial expressions of culture. Material culture consists of the physical creations of society. Nonmaterial culture is more abstract and reflects the ideas, values, and beliefs of a society.

What are cultural universals?

Cultural universals are customs and practices that exist in all societies and include activities and institutions such as storytelling, families, and laws. Specific forms of these universals vary from one cultural group to another, however.

What are the four nonmaterial components of culture common to all societies?

These components are: symbols, language, values, and norms. Symbols express shared meanings; through them, groups communicate cultural ideas and abstract concepts. Language is a set of symbols through which groups communicate. Values are a culture's collective ideas about what is or is not acceptable. Norms are the specific behavioural expectations within a culture.

What are the main types of norms?

Folkways are norms that express the everyday customs of a group, while mores are norms with strong moral and ethical connotations that are essential to the stability of a culture. Laws are formal, standardized norms that are enforced by formal sanctions.

What are high culture and popular culture?

High culture consists of classical music, opera, ballet, and other activities usually patronized by elite audiences. Popular culture consists of the activities, products, and services of a culture that appeal primarily to members of the middle and working classes.

What causes cultural change in societies?

Cultural change takes place in all societies. Change occurs through discovery and invention and through diffusion, which is the transmission of culture from one society or group to another.

How is cultural diversity reflected in society?

Cultural diversity is reflected through race, ethnicity, age, sexual orientation, religion, occupation, and so forth. A diverse culture also includes subcultures and countercultures. A subculture has distinctive ideas and behaviours that differ from the larger society to which it belongs. A counterculture rejects the dominant societal values and norms.

What are culture shock, ethnocentrism, and cultural relativism?

Culture shock refers to the anxiety people experience when they encounter cultures radically different from their own. Ethnocentrism is the assumption that one's own culture is superior to other cultures. Cultural relativism counters culture shock and ethnocentrism by viewing and analyzing another culture in terms of its own values and standards.

How do the major sociological perspectives view culture?

A functional analysis of culture assumes that a common language and shared values help to produce consensus and harmony. According to some conflict theorists, culture may be used by certain groups to maintain their privilege and exclude others from society's benefits. Symbolic interactionists suggest that people create, maintain, and modify culture as they go about their everyday activities.

What cultural changes can we expect in the twenty-first century?

While increasing cultural diversity in Canada has expanded the thinking of some individuals, it also has increased racial–ethnic antagonisms. As we look toward even more diverse and global cultural patterns in the twenty-first century, it is important to keep our sociological imaginations actively engaged.

Key Terms

counterculture 87
cultural imperialism 96
cultural lag 84
cultural relativism 92
cultural universals 69
culture 65
culture shock 89
diffusion 84
discovery 84
ethnocentrism 91
false consciousness 92
folkways 79
ideal culture 78
invention 84
language 71
laws 80
material culture 68
mores 79
nonmaterial culture 69
norms 79
popular culture 80
real culture 78
sanctions 79
Sapir-Whorf hypothesis 71
subculture 85
taboos 79
technology 68
values 76
value contradictions 78
xenocentrism 92

✹ Internet Exercises

1. To find out which Canadian cultural "tribe" you belong to visit

   http://www.environics.net/erg/

   and plot your position on the sociocultural map.

2. Go to the Alta Vista search engine

   http://www/altavista.digital.com/

   and do a search for the terms *hacker* and *warez*. Some people consider hackers to be a counterculture. Compare what you have read in this chapter about counterculture to what you find on the *hacker* and *warez* pages. What criteria of a counterculture do hackers fit? In what ways don't they fit?

3. This chapter looks at culture from functionalist, conflict, and interactionist perspectives. Visit the Postmodern Culture Journal homepage:

   http://jefferson.village.Virginia.EDU/pmc/

   and configure your newsreader software to read the newsgroup alt.postmodern. The postmodern perspective has its roots in the three perspectives you have been reading about; however, it can also be vastly different. What are some of the differences between functionalist/conflict/interactionist perspectives and the postmodern perspective?

✹ Net Links

The federal government has a Web site called "Facts on Canada" that contains information related to society and culture, including multiculturalism, French language and identity, and national cultural institutions; go to:

http://infocan.gc.ca/facts/index.html

The Department of Heritage has a site entitled "Multiculturalism" that includes current research on hate-motivated activities in Canada; go to:

http://www.pch.gc.ca/multi/html/english.html

Ethnocentrism Online has two insightful stories that demonstrate the concept of ethnocentrism; go to:

 http://www.geocities.com/CapitolHill/Lobby/8506

To read some interesting ideas about modern culture and the ideas of Marshall McLuhan, see:

R http://www.cios.org/encyclopedia/mcluhan/probe/probe.html

Questions for Critical Thinking

1. Would it be possible today to live in a totally separate culture in Canada? Could you avoid all influences from the mainstream popular culture or from the values and norms of other cultures? How would you be able to avoid any change in your culture?

2. Do fads and fashions in popular culture reflect and reinforce, or challenge and change the values and norms of a society? Consider a wide variety of fads and fashions: musical styles; computer and video games and other technologies; literature; and political, social, and religious ideas.

3. In Chapter 2, we examined sociological research and various studies on altruism. Suppose you wanted to find out why incidents of altruism were more common in some cultures than others. What might you examine in each culture? Symbols, language, values, or norms? popular culture? fads? The amount of diversity in a culture? What would be the best way to conduct your research?

4. In the twenty-first century, will there be many separate cultures in Canada, or will there be one large, diverse culture?

5. You are doing a survey analysis of neo-Nazi skinheads to determine the effects of popular culture on their views and behaviour. What are some of the questions you would use in your survey?

Suggested Readings

An interesting functionalist analysis of culture is provided by this anthropologist:

Marvin Harris. *Cannibals and Kings: The Origins of Cultures*. New York: Random House, 1977.
Marvin Harris. *Good to Eat: Riddles of Food and Culture*. New York: Simon & Schuster, 1986.

These authors analyze aspects of culture from diverse perspectives:

Michael Adams. *Sex in the Snow: Canadian Social Values at the End of the Millennium*. Toronto: Penguin, 1998.
Reginald W. Bibby. *Mosaic Madness: The Poverty and Potential of Life in Canada*. Toronto: Stoddart Publishing, 1990.
bell hooks. *Outlaw Culture: Resisting Representations*. New York: Routledge, 1994.

These books provide interesting insights on culture and demonstrate how fieldwork can be carried out in a wide variety of settings:

Napoleon A. Chagnon. *Yanamamö: The Last Days of Eden*. San Diego: Harcourt Brace Jovanovich, 1992.
Stephen M. Fjellman. *Vinyl Leaves: Walt Disney World and America*. Boulder, Colo.: Westview Press, 1992.

To find out more about subcultures, countercultures, and hate crimes, see the following:

Stanley R. Barrett. *Is God a Racist? The Right Wing in Canada*. Toronto: University of Toronto Press, 1987.
William M. Kephart and William W. Zellner. *Extraordinary Groups: An Examination of Unconventional Life-Styles* (5th ed.). New York: St. Martin's Press, 1994.

CHAPTER

4

Why Is Socialization Important?
  Human Development: Biology and Society
  Social Isolation
  Child Abuse

Socialization and the Self
  Sociological Theories of Human Development
  Psychological Theories of Human Development

Agents of Socialization
  The Family
  The School
  Peer Groups
  Mass Media

Gender Socialization

Socialization Through the Life Course
  Infancy and Childhood
  Adolescence
  Adulthood

Resocialization
  Voluntary Resocialization
  Involuntary Resocialization

Socialization in the Future

Dave Pelzer, public speaker and author of *A Child Called "It,"* describes the physical and emotional abuse he suffered at the hands of his mother during childhood:

"Before the station wagon comes to a complete stop, I dash out of the car. Mother yells for me to return. I have forgotten my crumpled lunch bag, which has always had the same menu for the last three years—two peanut butter sandwiches and a few carrot sticks. Before I bolt out of the car again, she says, 'Tell 'em ... Tell 'em you ran into the door.' Then in a voice she rarely uses with me, she states, 'Have a nice day.'

"Moments later, the school nurse leads me into her office, where we go through the normal routine. First, she examines my face and arms. 'What's that above your eye?' she asks.

"I nod sheepishly. 'Oh, I ran into the hall door ... by accident.' Again she smiles and takes a clipboard from the top of the cabinet. She flips through a page or two then bends down to show me. 'Here,' she points to the paper, 'You said that last Monday. Remember?'

"I quickly change my story, 'I was playing baseball and I got hit with the bat. It was an accident.' Accident. I am always supposed to say that. But the nurse knows better. She scolds me so I tell the truth. I always break down in the end and confess, even though I feel I should protect my mother ...

"'Oh no!' I tell myself, 'I've done something wrong ... again.' The nurse must have seen the concern in my eyes. She puts the clipboard down and hugs me. 'God,' I tell myself, 'She is so warm.' I don't ever want to let go. I want to stay in her arms forever. I hold my eyes tightly shut, and for a few moments nothing else exists. She pats my head. I flinch from the swollen bruise Mother gave me this morning. The nurse then breaks the embrace and leaves the room. I rush to put my clothes back on. She doesn't know it, but I do everything as fast as possible."

(Pelzer, 1995:5–7)

SOCIALIZATION

The process of socialization is of major significance to sociologists. Although most children are nurtured, trusted, and loved by their parents, Pelzer's experience of child abuse and neglect is not an isolated incident: Large numbers of children experience maltreatment at the hands of family members or other caregivers such as babysitters or daycare workers. Child maltreatment includes physical abuse, sexual abuse, physical neglect, and emotional mistreatment of children and young adolescents (Zuravin, 1991). Such maltreatment has a serious impact on a child's social growth, behaviour, and self-image—all of which develop within the process of socialization. Children who are abused rather than treated with respect by their parents find it difficult to develop a positive self-image and learn healthy conduct because the appropriate models of behaviour that parents normally provide are absent. In some abusive families, children may be socialized to think that maltreatment is normal interactive behaviour.

In this chapter, we examine why socialization is so crucial, and we discuss both sociological and psychological theories of human development. We look at the dynamics of socialization—how it occurs and what shapes it. Throughout the chapter, we focus on child abuse and its impact on socialization. Before reading on, test your knowledge of child abuse by taking the quiz in Box 4.1.

QUESTIONS AND ISSUES

CHAPTER FOCUS QUESTION: What happens when children do not have an environment that supports positive socialization?

What purpose does socialization serve?

How do individuals develop a sense of self?

How does socialization occur?

Who experiences resocialization?

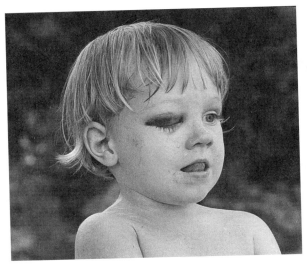

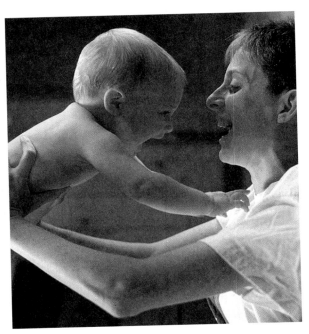

Human interaction is essential to the development of a positive self-concept; in abusive families, however, children may come to view abuse as "normal" everyday behaviour.

WHY IS SOCIALIZATION IMPORTANT?

Socialization is the lifelong process of social interaction through which individuals acquire a self-identity and the physical, mental, and social skills needed for survival in society. It is the essential link between the individual and society (Robertson, 1989). Socialization enables each of us to develop our human potential and learn the ways of thinking, talking, and acting that are essential for social living.

Socialization is essential for the individual's survival and for human development. The many people who met the early material and social needs of each of us were central to our establishing our own identity. During the first three years of our life, we begin to develop a unique identity and the ability to manipulate things and to walk. We acquire sophisticated cognitive tools for thinking and analyzing a wide variety of situations, and we learn effective communication skills. In the process, we begin a relatively long socialization process that culminates in our integration into a complex social and cultural system (Garcia Coll, 1990).

Socialization also is essential for the survival and stability of society. Members of a society must be socialized to support and maintain the existing social structure. From a functionalist perspective, individual conformity to existing norms is not taken for granted; rather, basic individual needs and desires must be balanced against the needs of the social structure. The socialization process is most effective when people conform to the norms of society because they believe this is the best course of action. In Chapter 3, we saw how people shape and are shaped by the knowledge, language, values, and customs within their cultures. Socialization enables a society to "reproduce" itself by passing on this cultural content from one generation to the next.

Although the techniques used to teach beliefs, values, and rules of behaviour are somewhat similar in many countries, the content of socialization differs greatly from society to society. How people walk, talk, eat, make love, and wage war are all functions of the culture in which they are raised. At the same time, we also are influenced by our exposure to subcultures of class, ethnicity, religion, and gender. In addition, each of us has unique experiences in our families and friendship groupings. The kind of human being that we become depends greatly on the particular society and social groups that surround us at birth and during early childhood. What we believe about ourselves, our society, and the world is largely a product of our interactions with others.

HOW MUCH DO YOU KNOW ABOUT CHILD ABUSE?

TRUE	FALSE	
T	F	1. Research suggests that older children are at greater risk of sexual abuse than younger children.
T	F	2. Child abuse only occurs in lower-class families.
T	F	3. Men are always the perpetrators of sexual abuse and very seldom the victims.
T	F	4. Infants are Canada's most likely homicide victims.
T	F	5. Neglect is not a form of child abuse.
T	F	6. In a family in which child abuse occurs, all of the children are likely to be victims.
T	F	7. It is against the law to fail to report child abuse.
T	F	8. In most cases of sexual abuse, the perpetrator is known to the child.
T	F	9. People who are the victims of child abuse are more likely to become abusers themselves.
T	F	10. Some people are "born" abusers while others learn abusive behaviour from their family and friends.

Answers on page 104.

Human Development: Biology and Society

What does it mean to be "human"? To be human includes being conscious of ourselves as individuals with unique identities, personalities, and relationships with others. As humans, we have ideas, emotions, and values. We have the capacity to think and to make rational decisions. But what is the source of "humanness"? Are we born with these human characteristics, or do we develop them through our interactions with others?

When we are born, we are totally dependent on others for our survival. We cannot turn ourselves over, speak, reason, plan, or do many of the things that are associated with being human. Although we can nurse, wet, and cry, most small mammals also can do those things. As discussed in Chapter 3, we humans differ from nonhuman animals because we lack instincts and must rely on learning for our survival. Human infants have the potential for developing human characteristics if they are exposed to an adequate socialization process.

Every human being is a product of biology, society, and personal experiences—that is, of heredity and environment or, in even more basic terms, "nature" and "nurture." How much of our development can be explained by socialization? How much by our genetic heritage? Sociologists focus on how humans design their own culture and transmit it from generation to generation through socialization. By contrast, sociobiologists assert that nature, in the form of our genetic makeup, is a major factor in shaping human behaviour. *Sociobiology* **is the systematic study of how biology affects social behaviour** (Wilson, 1975). According to zoologist Edward O. Wilson, who pioneered sociobiology, genetic inheritance underlies many forms of social behaviour such as war and peace, envy and concern for others, and competition and cooperation. Most sociologists disagree with the notion that biological principles can be used to explain all human behaviour. Obviously, however, some aspects of our physical makeup—such as eye colour, hair colour, height, and weight—largely are determined by our heredity.

How important is social influence, or "nurture," in human development? There is hardly a behaviour that is not influenced socially. Except for simple reflexes, such as dilation of the pupils and knee-jerk responses, most human actions are social, either in their causes or in their consequences. Even solitary actions such as crying or brushing our teeth are ultimately social. We cry because someone has hurt us. We brush our teeth because our parents (or dentist) told us it was important. Social environment probably has a greater effect than heredity on the way we

BOX 4.1

ANSWERS TO THE SOCIOLOGY QUIZ ON CHILD ABUSE

1. **False.** Based on Uniform Crime Report Survey results, 56 percent of reported child sexual abuse victims were 10 and under.

2. **False.** Child abuse occurs in families from all social classes. However, the research indicates a higher incidence of reported child abuse among families in low socioeconomic groups.

3. **False.** Men are not always the perpetrators of sexual abuse, and they may indeed be the victims. Many male victims of sexual abuse are abused by male abusers. However, in about 92 percent of reported sexual abuse cases, young girls and women are the victims; and in 98 percent of the cases, men are the perpetrators.

4. **True.** At a rate of 6.5 homicides per 100,000 infants, babies have a higher risk of being victims of homicide than older children, teens, or adults. The killers are most likely parents or stepparents.

5. **False.** Child abuse and child neglect are both types of child maltreatment. Neglect refers to the failure of a parent to provide minimally adequate care in terms of health, nutrition, shelter, education, supervision, affection, attention, or protection. Neglect may be as physically and mentally damaging as physical abuse.

6. **False.** In some families, one child repeatedly may be the victim of abuse while others are not. This is especially true with incest, whereby one daughter may be singled out for abuse by a father, stepfather, uncle, or other male relative.

7. **True.** In Canada, all of the provinces have mandatory reporting requirements. However, there has been inconsistent compliance with these legal mandates. All adults who believe or suspect that a child is in need of protection have a duty to report this to the authorities. Some provinces specify that professionals who are in contact with children must report suspected abuse cases or face a fine of up to $1000.

8. **True.** Recent data from police departments across Canada show that 81 percent of the child sexual assault victims knew their abuser. The largest group of offenders is stepfathers.

9. **True.** Although scholars disagree on this point, a number of studies have found that adults who were abused as children have a greater tendency to be violent and abusive than those who were not abused.

10. **False.** No one is a "born" abuser. People learn abusive behaviour from their family and friends.

Sources: Based on Wolfe, 1987; Knudsen, 1992; Jackson, 1993; Begin, 1994; Wachtel, 1994, Gunn and Linden, 1994; Rodgers and Kong, 1996; Durrant and Rose-Krasnor, 1995; and Homicide Survey, Canadian Centre for Justice Statistics, 1991–1993.

develop and the way we act. However, heredity does provide the basic material from which other people help to mould an individual's human characteristics.

Our biological and emotional needs are related in a complex equation. Children whose needs are met in settings characterized by affection, warmth, and closeness see the world as a safe and comfortable place and other people as trustworthy and helpful. By contrast, infants and children who receive less-than-adequate care or who are emotionally rejected or abused often view the world as hostile and have feelings of suspicion and fear.

Social Isolation

Social environment, then, is a crucial part of an individual's socialization. Even nonhuman primates such as monkeys and chimpanzees need social contact with others of their species in order to develop properly. As we will see, appropriate social contact is even more important for humans.

ISOLATION AND NONHUMAN PRIMATES Researchers have attempted to demonstrate the effects of social isolation on nonhuman primates raised without contact with others of their own species. In a series of laboratory experiments, psychologists

As this birthday celebration attended by four generations of family members illustrates, socialization enables society to "reproduce" itself.

Harry and Margaret Harlow (1962, 1977) took infant rhesus monkeys from their mothers and isolated them in separate cages. Each cage contained two nonliving "mother substitutes" made of wire, one with a feeding bottle attached and the other covered with soft terry cloth but without a bottle. The infant monkeys instinctively clung to the cloth "mother" and would not abandon it until hunger drove them to the bottle attached to the wire "mother." As soon as they were full, they went back to the cloth "mother" seeking warmth, affection, and physical comfort.

The Harlows' experiments show the detrimental effects of isolation on nonhuman primates. When the young monkeys later were introduced to other members of their species, they cringed in the corner. Having been deprived of social contact with other monkeys during their first six months of life, they never learned how to relate to other monkeys or to become well-adjusted adult monkeys—they were fearful of or hostile toward other monkeys (Harlow and Harlow, 1962, 1977).

If nurturing is needed for monkeys to develop normally, how much more important is it in the development of humans? We must be cautious about using nonhuman animal studies to draw inferences for human behaviour. Obviously, human beings are not monkeys. However, the Harlows' studies do show that, without socialization, monkeys do not learn normal social or emotional behaviour. And because humans rely more heavily on social learning than do monkeys, the process of socialization is even more important for us.

FERAL CHILDREN   People have always been intrigued by accounts of *feral children*, who are assumed to have been raised by animals in the wilderness, isolated from human society. The Romans, for example, believed that the alleged founders of Rome (Romulus and Remus) had been raised by a wolf.

In 1798, hunters in Aveyron, a rural area of France, reported that a boy was running naked through a forest on all fours. The "Wild Boy of Aveyron" was believed to be about 11 years old and to have lived alone in the forest for five or six years. Jean-Marc Itard, a young doctor, took the boy into his home, named him Victor, and attempted to socialize him. Victor learned to speak a few words, to eat with a knife and fork, and to get along with the doctor and his housekeeper. However, from the time Victor was found until his death at the age of 40, he never was able to develop relationships with other people (Candland, 1993). In the late-nineteenth and early-twentieth centuries, other cases of feral children were reported in India, France, and elsewhere (see Singh and Zingg, 1942; Shattuck, 1980). The children were unable to talk, were afraid of other human beings, walked on all fours or slouched over, tore ravenously at their food, and drank by lapping water (Malson, 1972). Were these tales true? Have there really been feral children?

Social scientists generally agree that it is highly unlikely that feral children actually were raised by wild animals. They suggest that the children likely were abandoned by their parents shortly before they were found by others. The children already may have been abused or isolated from most human contact before they actually were abandoned (Bettelheim, 1959). However, documented cases of child abuse and neglect indicate that human infants without adequate social interaction with other human beings are unable to develop fully "human" characteristics.

ISOLATED CHILDREN   Social scientists have documented cases of children who were deliberately raised in isolation. A look at the lives of two children who suffered such emotional abuse provides important insights into the effect of social isolation on human beings.

Anna   Born in 1932 to an unmarried, mentally impaired woman, Anna was an unwanted child. She was kept in an attic-like room in her grandfather's house. Her mother, who worked on the farm all day and often went out at night, gave Anna just enough care to keep her alive; she received no other care. Sociologist Kingsley Davis (1940) described her condition when she was found in 1938:

> [Anna] had no glimmering of speech, absolutely no ability to walk, no sense of gesture, not the least capacity to feed herself even when the food was put in front of her, and no comprehension of cleanliness. She was so apathetic that it was hard to tell whether or not she could hear. And all of this at the age of nearly six years.

When she was placed in a special school and given the necessary care, Anna slowly learned to walk, talk, and care for herself. Just before her death at the age of 10, Anna reportedly could follow directions, talk in phrases, wash her hands, brush her teeth, and try to help other children (Davis, 1940).

Genie   Almost four decades after Anna was discovered, Genie was found in 1970 at the age of 13. She had been locked in a bedroom alone, alternately strapped down to a child's potty chair or straitjacketed into a sleeping bag, since she was 20 months old. She had been fed baby food and beaten with a wooden paddle when she whimpered. She had not heard the sounds of human speech because no one talked to her and there was

Studies of feral and isolated children provide important insights into the effect of social isolation on human beings. One of the most widely known feral children was Victor, "The Wild Boy of Aveyron," shown here in an engraved portrait from Dr. Jean-Marc Itard's report of 1801.

no television or radio in her home (Curtiss, 1977; Pines, 1981). Genie was placed in a pediatric hospital where one of the psychologists described her condition:

> At the time of her admission she was virtually unsocialized. She could not stand erect, salivated continuously, had never been toilet-trained and had no control over her urinary or bowel functions. She was unable to chew solid food and had the weight, height and appearance of a child half her age. (Rigler, 1993:35)

In addition to her physical condition, Genie showed psychological traits associated with neglect, as described by one of her psychiatrists:

> If you gave [Genie] a toy, she would reach out and touch it, hold it, caress it with her fingertips, as though she didn't trust her eyes. She would rub it against her cheek to feel it. So when I met her and she began to notice me standing beside her bed, I held my hand out and she reached out and took my hand and carefully felt my thumb and fingers indi-

vidually, and then put my hand against her cheek. She was exactly like a blind child. (Rymer, 1993:45)

Extensive therapy was used in an attempt to socialize Genie and develop her language abilities (Curtiss, 1977; Pines, 1981). These efforts met with limited success: In the early 1990s, Genie was living in a board-and-care home for retarded adults (see Angier, 1993; Rigler, 1993; Rymer, 1993).

These cases are important to our understanding of the socialization process because they show that social isolation and neglect are extremely detrimental to young children. When infants are deprived of human contact, they do not develop the characteristics most of us think of as "human."

Child Abuse

What do the words "child abuse" mean to you? Many people first think of cases that involve severe physical injuries or sexual abuse. However, "child abuse" is a general term used to describe a variety of injuries inflicted by a parent or caregiver. There are three types of abuse: physical abuse or battering; neglect; and sexual abuse. It is estimated that neglect is the most frequent form of child abuse (Wachtel, 1994). Child neglect occurs when a child's basic needs—including emotional warmth and security, adequate shelter, food, health care, education, clothing, and protection—are not met, regardless of cause (Dubowitz et al., 1993:12). Neglect often involves acts of omission (where parents or caregivers fail to provide adequate physical or emotional care for children) rather than acts of commission (such as physical or sexual abuse). The cases of Anna and Genie demonstrate the devastating effect that parental neglect can have on a child's development.

What acts constitute child abuse or neglect? Throughout history and across cultures, perceptions of what constitutes abuse or neglect have differed. What might have been considered appropriate disciplinary action by parents in the past (such as following the adage "Spare the rod, spoil the child") today is viewed by many as child abuse. Still, many Canadian parents choose to use spanking as a form of discipline. Recent research on the use of corporal punishment has revealed that approximately 70 percent of Canadian parents have used physical punishment, although the majority indicate that it is ineffective to do so (Durrant and Rose-Krasnor, 1995).

Unfortunately, the federal government has yet to develop a standard definition of child abuse. Subsequently, there is a wide variety of interpretations interprovincially about what constitutes child abuse. In fact, as the debate surrounding Section 43 of the Criminal Code demonstrates (see Box 4.2), there is little agreement within Canadian society with regard to what constitutes child abuse.

SOCIALIZATION AND THE SELF

Without social contact, we cannot form a sense of self or personal identity. The *self* represents the sum total of perceptions and feelings that an individual has of being a distinct, unique person—a sense of who and what one is. This sense of self (also referred to as self-concept) is not present at birth; it arises in the process of social experience. **Self-concept is the totality of our beliefs and feelings about ourselves** (Gecas, 1982). Four components comprise our self-concept: (1) the physical self ("I am tall"), (2) the active self ("I am good at soccer"), (3) the social self ("I am nice to others"), and (4) the psychological self ("I believe in world peace"). Between early and late childhood, a child's focus tends to shift from the physical and active dimensions of self toward the social and psychological aspects (Lippa, 1994). Self-concept is the foundation for communication with others; it continues to develop and change throughout our lives (Zurcher, 1983).

Our *self-identity* is our perception about what kind of person we are. As we have seen, socially isolated children do not have typical self-identities because they have had no experience of "humanness." According to interactionists, we do not know who we are until we see ourselves as we believe others see us. We gain information about the self largely through language, symbols, and interaction with others. Our interpretation and evaluation of these messages is central to the social construction of our identity. However, we are not just passive reactors to situations, programmed by society to respond in fixed ways. Instead, we are active agents who develop plans out of the pieces supplied by culture and attempt to execute these plans in social encounters (McCall and Simmons, 1978).

BOX 4.2 **CRITICAL THINKING**

CHILD ABUSE THEN AND NOW

Childhood in Canada does not always match our idealized cultural notion that children should be loved and protected by adults. Conduct ranging from extreme indifference and neglect to physical and sexual abuse of children has been commonplace throughout history.

Historically, society has viewed children as the property of their parents—to be treated as the parents wished. In the United States in the early 1600s, the "Stubborn Child Act" specified that the parents of a rebellious or stubborn child could petition the court for permission to put the child to death (Wolfe, 1987). Even without such a law, physical beatings often have been considered appropriate discipline for children. In fact, parents who did not beat their children were considered to be neglecting their parental duties (DeMause, 1974). Parents had absolute power and control over their children. Early Roman law referred to as *patria potestas* included the right of the father to give a child away or have the child put to death.

Under an eighteenth-century English common law, *parens patriae,* the father had an obligation to exercise guardianship over minors. Children were regarded as chattel.

It is only in the past 100 years that childhood has been recognized as a distinct period. The first legal challenge to the absolute rights of parents occurred in 1870 in New York when a social worker was forced to turn to the American Society for the Prevention of Cruelty to Animals as a means of obtaining legal sanctions against the parents of a neglected child. In response, the American Society for the Prevention of Cruelty to Children was founded. Shortly thereafter, in 1891, the Children's Aid Society was established in Toronto.

One of the most contentious issues pertaining to child abuse revolves around Section 43 of the Criminal Code, which states:

> Every school teacher, parent or person standing in the place of a parent is justified in using force by way of correction

Sociological Theories of Human Development

The perspectives of symbolic interactionists Charles Horton Cooley and George Herbert Mead help us understand how our self-identity is developed through our interactions with others.

THE LOOKING-GLASS SELF According to sociologist Charles Horton Cooley (1864–1929), the **looking-glass self refers to the way in which a person's sense of self is derived from the perceptions of others.** Our looking-glass self is not who we actually are or what people actually think about us; it is based on our perception of how other people think of us (Cooley, 1922/1902). Cooley asserted that we base our perception of who we are on how we think other people see us and on whether this seems good or bad to us.

As Figure 4.1 shows, the looking-glass self is a self-concept derived from a three-step process:

1. We imagine how our personality and appearance will look to other people. We may imagine that we are attractive or unattractive, heavy or slim, friendly or unfriendly, and so on.
2. We imagine how other people judge the appearance and personality that we think we present. This step involves our *perception* of how we think they are judging us. We may be correct or incorrect!
3. We develop a self-concept. If we think the evaluation of others is favourable, our self-concept is enhanced. If we think the evaluation is unfavourable, our self-concept is diminished (Cooley, 1922/1902).

According to Cooley, we use our interactions with others as a mirror for our own thoughts and actions; our sense of self depends on how we interpret what they do and say. Consequently, our sense of self is not permanently fixed; it is always developing as we interact with others.

BOX 4.2

CONTINUED

toward a pupil or child, as the case may be, who is under his care, if the force does not exceed what is reasonable under the circumstances.

The original intention of Section 43 was the protection of the child from unreasonable force, not to sanction physical punishment by parents. However, those lobbying for the repeal of Section 43 argue that this provision gives parents the legal right to assault their children with impunity. Others argue that removing Section 43 would remove the protection that parents now have against criminal prosecution if they physically discipline their children.

"Reasonable force" is an ambiguous term. The research indicates that parents of abused children report that their actions were simply an extension of a parent's disciplinary role (Begin, 1994; Durrant, 1995).

In the Canadian courts, "reasonable force" is left for the judge to determine. In doing so, judges frequently disregard present-day attitudes. Section 43 has been used as a defence in court cases where children have been beaten black and blue. In a recent case presented to the Manitoba Court of Appeal, a judge decided that although the father had left severe bruises on his son, they were lighter than the beatings the judge had received as a child. The man was acquitted.

How do you define child abuse? Is spanking included in your definition? Can you think of circumstances where it would be acceptable for a parent to use physical discipline with their child? Do you think you will spank your children? Why? Why not?

Source: Durrant, 1995; Mitchell, 1995.

ROLE-TAKING   George Herbert Mead (1863–1931) extended Cooley's insights by linking the idea of self-concept to *role-taking*—**the process by which a person mentally assumes the role of another person in order to understand the world from that person's point of view.** Role-taking often occurs through play and games, as children try out different roles (such as being mommy, daddy, doctor, or teacher) and gain an appreciation of them.

According to Mead (1934), in the early months of life, children do not realize that they are separate from others. They do, however, begin early on to see a mirrored image of themselves in others. Shortly after birth, infants start to notice the faces of those around them, especially the significant others whose faces start to have meaning because they are associated with experiences such as feeding and cuddling. **Significant others are those persons whose care, affection, and approval are especially desired and who are most** important in the development of the self. Gradually, we distinguish ourselves from our caregivers and begin to perceive ourselves in contrast to them. As we develop language skills and learn to understand symbols, we begin to develop a self-concept. When we can represent ourselves in our own minds as objects distinct from everything else, our self has been formed.

Mead divided the self into the "I" and the "me." The "I" is the subjective element of the self that represents the spontaneous and unique traits of each person. The "me" is the objective element of the self, which is composed of the internalized attitudes and demands of other members of society and the individual's awareness of those demands. Both the "I" and the "me" are needed to form the social self. The unity of the two constitutes the full development of the individual. According to Mead, the "I" develops first, and the "me" takes form during the three stages of self development:

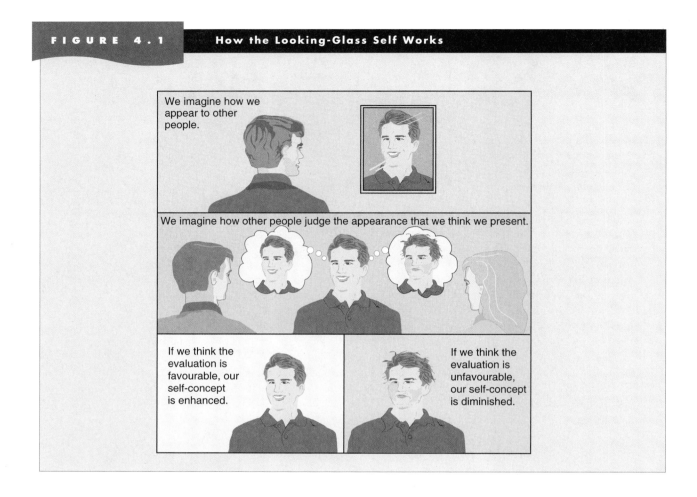

FIGURE 4.1 How the Looking-Glass Self Works

1. During the *preparatory stage*, up to about age 3, interactions lack meaning, and children largely imitate the people around them. Children may mimic family members or others nearby, but they lack understanding of the meaning of their behaviour and are simply copying others. At this stage, children are preparing for role-taking.

2. In the *play stage*, from about age 3 to 5, children learn to use language and other symbols, thus enabling them to pretend to take the roles of specific people. At first, children tend to model themselves on significant others, typically members of their families, teachers, and other caregivers with whom they spend substantial amounts of time. Later, children may play at taking the roles of others, such as "doctor, "superhero," or "bad guy." At this stage, children begin to see themselves in relation to others, but they do not see role-taking as something they have to do.

3. During the *game stage*, which begins in the early school years, children understand not only their own social position but also the positions of others around them. In contrast to play, games are structured by rules, often are competitive, and involve a number of other "players." Children now learn a system of interdependent roles and ways of relating to many people and groups. At this time, they become concerned about the demands and expectations of others and of the larger society. Mead used the example of a baseball game to describe this stage because children, like baseball players, must take into account the roles of all the other players at the same time. They must plan their responses to the predicted actions of other players based on the "big picture" of the entire situation. Mead's concept of the **generalized other refers to the child's awareness of the demands and expectations of the society as a whole or of the child's subculture.** To return

According to sociologist George Herbert Mead, the self develops through three stages. In the preparatory stage, children imitate others; in the play stage, children pretend to take the roles of specific people; and in the game stage, children become aware of the "rules of the game" and the expectations of others.

to Mead's baseball analogy, for instance, think of the 7-year-old's abstract ability to simultaneously consider the roles of other team members when the ball is hit to centre field.

Is socialization a one-way process? Not according to Mead. Socialization is a two-way process between society and the individual. Just as the society in which we live helps determine what kind of individuals we will become, we have the ability to shape certain aspects of our social environment and perhaps even the larger society.

SELF-CONCEPT AND CHILD ABUSE What happens when a child does not have a supportive environment in which to develop a positive self-concept? Interactionists suggest that a child's self-concept is defined and evaluated through interaction with significant others, who are assumed to have the best interests of the child in mind. Positive parent–child relationships, for example, are characterized by a balance between positive and negative interactions and between discipline and

emotional bonding. By contrast, child abuse occurs when there is an extreme imbalance in such interactions (Wolfe, 1987). According to interactionist analysis, although people may abuse or neglect children for many reasons, the primary "causes" are located within social interactions, especially between parent and child.

What is the relationship between childhood abuse and a person's self-concept as an adult? The dynamic interplay between individual, familial, and other social factors in relation to past events (such as exposure to abuse as a child) and present situations (such as a child who is "misbehaving") is important for understanding the long-term effects of child abuse (Wolfe, 1987; Straus et al., 1980). Consider this mother's story:

> I live in a middle-class neighborhood and have all the conveniences available to a modern-day housewife. I do not work outside the home, preferring to stay behind closed doors where it is safe. In all respects I should be a happily married woman and proud mother of two beautiful children. Unfortunately, this is not the case …

To my husband, I am an uncommunicative, frigid wife who has no desire to socialize or be sexually active with him. To my children, I am someone who barely tolerates their presence; who walks around with the belt in the hand, using it every time they step out of line, which is any time they are in my way or not being quiet; who constantly is verbally condemning them for something trivial they may have done; who violently attacks them, using my fists and wire kitchen whisks and kicking with my feet and then leaving them where they lay, crumpled in pain and misery, to wonder what they could have done to warrant such punishment ... But how can I love them and hate to be around them at the same time? ...

From the age of thirteen to the age of eighteen I was physically and sexually abused by both my mother and stepfather, and physically and sexually abused by both of my brothers, who were physically and emotionally abused also.

... How has my childhood affected my adulthood? It has deformed me. Not physically; the broken bones, cuts, and bruises have mended, the gunshot wounds have healed, leaving behind only small scars that I can cover up. It is the inner wounds that are still unhealed, visible by my inability to make friends, inability to form a close bond with my husband, and worst of all, inability to love my children in the way they were meant to be loved. For one can only teach what one has been taught, one can only give what one has been given. I was given only pain expressed in silent anger and depraved actions. Is that all I have to give to my children and my husband? I would gladly lay down my life in order to secure happiness for them. They are the innocent ones. (quoted in Fontana, 1991:23–24)

What happens in a child's socialization process that influences his or her adult behaviour? From an interactionist perspective, child abuse such as that described above can best be explained as the result of an interaction between the parent and child within a system that seldom provides alternative solutions (such as exposure to appropriate parental models, education, and social supports) or clear-cut restraints (such as laws, sanctions, and consequences) to the use of excessive force to resolve common child-rearing conflicts (Wolfe, 1987). In other words, if individuals do not learn appropriate models of parenting from their own families, then it can be difficult to learn them elsewhere.

The research suggests that parents who were abused as children may be more likely than other parents to abuse their children (Rodgers and Kong, 1996; Straus, 1994). Researcher Gordon Phaneuf (1990) describes what is often referred to as the cycle of abuse: "The vast majority of abusive parents have themselves been abused as children ... [while] previous victimization is not the cause of child abuse ... it is a significant contributing factor." In other words, children who are abused by their parents learn through their family interactions to deal with conflict through violence. This puts them at risk for committing violent acts as adults—including abusing their children (Straus, 1991).

EVALUATING INTERACTIONIST THEORIES   How useful are interactionist perspectives such as Cooley's and Mead's in enhancing our understanding of the socialization process? Certainly, this approach contributes to our understanding of how the self develops. Cooley's idea of the looking-glass self makes us aware that our perception of how we *think* others see us is not always correct. Mead extended Cooley's ideas by emphasizing the cognitive skills acquired through role-taking. He stressed the importance of play and games, as children try out different roles and gain an appreciation of them. His concept of the generalized other helps us see that the self is a social creation. According to Mead (1934:196), "Selves can only exist in definite relations to other selves. No hard-and-fast line can be drawn between our own selves and the selves of others."

As with any theoretical approach, the viewpoints of interactionists such as Cooley and Mead have certain limitations. Some conflict theorists have argued that these theories are excessively conservative because they assume that what is good for dominant group members is good for everyone. For example, sociologist Anne Kaspar (1986) suggests that Mead's ideas about the social self may be more applicable to men than women. According to Mead's theory, both the "I" and the "me" are needed to form the social self, and there is no inherent conflict between the two. By contrast, Kaspar asserts that women experience inherent conflicts between the meanings they derive from their *personal experience* and those they take from the *culture*. For many women, it is difficult to balance the idealized view of a mother as selfless, nurturing, and devoted to family with the realities of their own needs for autonomy,

Our self-concept continues to be influenced by our interactions with others throughout our lives.

during which biological explanations of human behaviour were prevalent. It also was an era of extreme sexual repression and male dominance when compared to contemporary North American standards. Freud's theory was greatly influenced by these cultural factors, as reflected in the importance he assigned to sexual motives in explaining behaviour.

Freud divided the mind into three interrelated parts: id, ego, and superego. The **id is the component of personality that includes all of the individual's basic biological drives and needs that demand immediate gratification.** The new-born child's personality is all id, and from birth, the child finds that urges for self-gratification—such as wanting to be held, fed, or changed—are not going to be satisfied immediately. The **ego is the rational, reality-oriented component of personality that imposes restrictions on the innate pleasure-seeking drives of the id.** The ego channels the desire of the id for immediate gratification into the most advantageous direction for the individual. The **superego, or conscience, consists of the moral and ethical aspects of personality.** It is first expressed as the recognition of parental control and eventually matures as the child learns that parental control is a reflection of the values and moral demands of the larger society. When a person is well adjusted, the ego successfully manages the opposing forces of the id and the superego. Figure 4.2 illustrates Freud's theory of personality.

Freud's theory has been heavily criticized by many scholars. One criticism is that his work was based on unprovable assertions. For example, according to Freud's psychoanalytic theory, most incest reports represent the sexual fantasies of alleged victims (Roth, 1993). Freud assumed that his female patients' accounts of incest were figments of their imaginations, based on their own sexual desires. Sociologist Diana E.H. Russell (1986) has argued that this assumption discounts the reality of incestuous abuse.

independence, and valued work in and outside the home (Kaspar, 1986).

How might ethnicity, class, religion, and other factors also contribute to inherent tensions between the meanings we derive from our personal experience and those we take from culture? People may be viewed as "deficient" or "poorly adjusted" if they do not accept uncritically the core values, norms, and behaviours of mainstream society. Many members of minority groups, for example, may be faced with an unhappy choice: maintain pride in one's ethnic roots and be shunned by members of the dominant group or "sell out" one's heritage in order to be accepted (Garcia Coll, 1990; Steinback, 1993; G. Williams, 1995).

Psychological Theories of Human Development

Up to this point, we have discussed sociologically oriented theories; we now turn to psychological theories that have influenced contemporary views of human development.

PSYCHOANALYTIC PERSPECTIVE Sigmund Freud (1856–1939) is known as the founder of psychoanalytic theory. He lived in the Victorian era,

PSYCHOSOCIAL DEVELOPMENT Erik H. Erikson (1902–1994) drew from Freud's theory and identified eight psychosocial stages of development. According to Erikson (1980/1959), each stage is accompanied by a crisis or potential crisis that involves transitions in social relationships:

1. *Trust versus mistrust* (birth to age 1). If infants receive good care and nurturing (characterized by emotional warmth, security, and love) from their parents, they will develop a sense

FIGURE 4.2　Freud's Theory of Personality

This illustration shows how Freud might picture a person's internal conflict over whether to commit an antisocial act such as stealing a candy bar. In addition to dividing personality into three components, Freud theorized that our personalities are largely unconscious—hidden away outside our normal awareness. To dramatize his point, Freud compared conscious awareness (portions of the ego and superego) to the visible tip of an iceberg. Most of personality—including all of the id, with its raw desires and impulses—lies submerged in our subconscious.

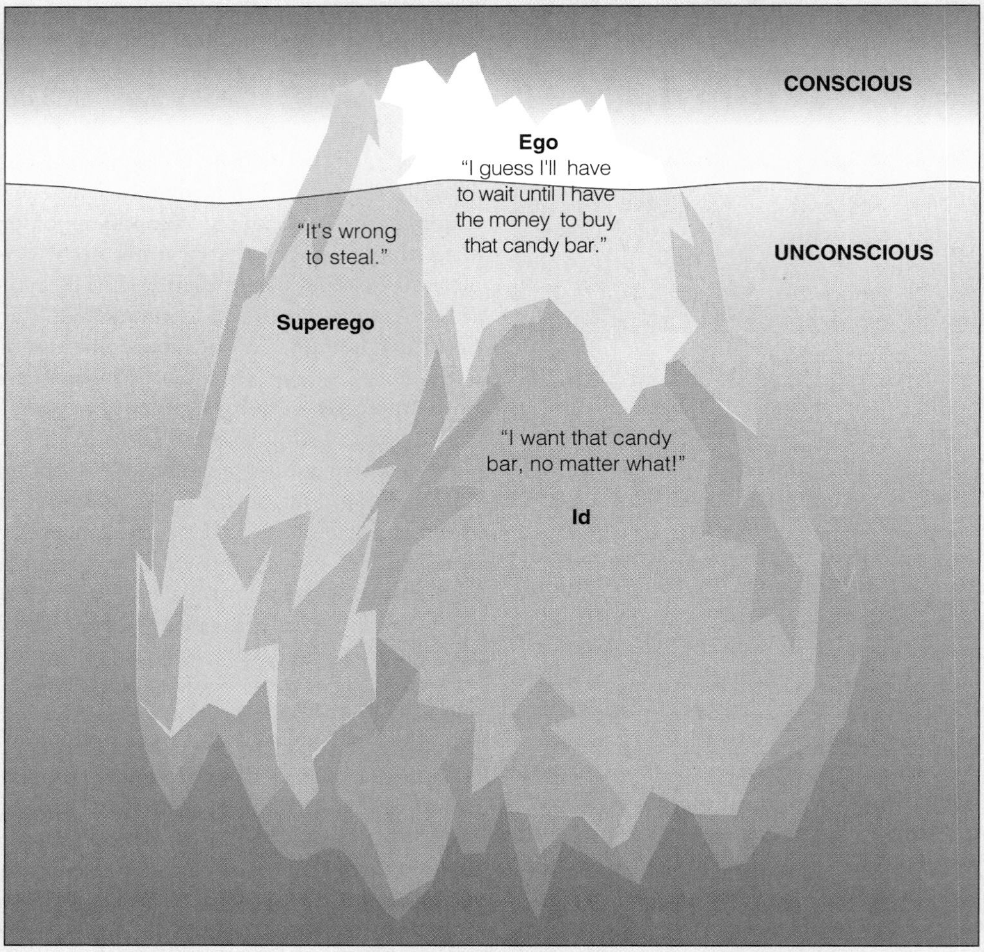

of trust. If they do not receive such care, they will become mistrustful and anxious about their surroundings.

2. *Autonomy versus shame and doubt* (ages 1 to 3). As children gain a feeling of control over their behaviour and develop a variety of physical and mental abilities, they begin to assert their independence. If they are allowed to explore their environment, children will grow more autonomous. If parents disapprove of or discourage them, children begin to doubt their abilities.

3. *Initiative versus guilt* (ages 3 to 5). If parents encourage initiative during this stage, children develop a sense of initiative. If parents make children feel that their actions are bad or that they are a nuisance, children may develop a strong sense of guilt.

4. *Industry versus inferiority* (ages 6 to 11). At this stage, children desire to manipulate

objects and learn how things work. Adults who encourage children's efforts and praise the results—both at home and at school—produce a feeling of industry in children. Feelings of inferiority result when parents or teachers appear to view children's efforts as silly or a nuisance.

5. *Identity versus role confusion* (ages 12 to 18). During this stage, adolescents attempt to develop a sense of identity. As young people take on new roles, the new roles must be combined with the old ones to create a strong self-identity. Role confusion results when individuals fail to acquire an accurate sense of personal identity.

6. *Intimacy versus isolation* (ages 18 to 35). The challenge of this stage (which covers courtship and early family life) is to develop close and meaningful relationships. If individuals establish successful relationships, intimacy ensues. If they fail to do so, they may feel isolated.

7. *Generativity versus self-absorption* (ages 35 to 55). Generativity means looking beyond oneself and being concerned about the next generation and the future of the world in general. Self-absorbed people may be preoccupied with their own well-being and material gains or be overwhelmed by "stagnation, boredom, and interpersonal impoverishment" (Erikson, 1968:138).

8. *Integrity versus despair* (maturity and old age). Integrity results when individuals have resolved previous psychosocial crises and are able to look back at their life as having been meaningful and personally fulfilling. Despair results when previous crises remain unresolved and individuals view their life as a series of disappointments, failures, and misfortunes.

Erikson's psychosocial stages broaden the framework of Freud's theory by focusing on social and cultural forces and by examining development throughout the life course. The psychosocial approach encompasses the conflicts that coincide with major changes in a person's social environment and describes how satisfactory resolution of these conflicts results in positive development. For example, if adolescents who experience an identity crisis are able to determine who they are and what they want from life, they may be able to achieve a positive self-identity and acquire greater psychological distance from their parents.

Critics have pointed out that Erikson's research was limited to white, middle-class respondents from industrial societies (Slugoski and Ginsburg, 1989). However, other scholars have used his theoretical framework to examine ethnic variations in the process of psychosocial development. Most of the studies have concluded that all children face the same developmental tasks at each stage but that ethnic minorities often have greater difficulty in obtaining a positive outcome because of experiences with racial prejudice and discrimination in society (Rotheram and Phinney, 1987). Although establishing an identity is difficult for most adolescents, one study found that it was especially problematic for children of recent South Asian immigrants who had experienced stress related to conflicting value systems and lifestyles (Kurian, 1991).

COGNITIVE DEVELOPMENT Jean Piaget (1896–1980), a Swiss psychologist, was a pioneer in the field of cognitive (intellectual) development. Cognitive theorists are interested in how people obtain, process, and use information—that is, in how we think. Cognitive development relates to changes over time in how we think.

Piaget (1954) believed that in each stage of development (from birth through adolescence), children's activities are governed by their perception of the world around them. His four stages of cognitive development are organized around specific tasks that, when mastered, lead to the acquisition of new mental capacities, which then serve as the basis for the next level of development. Piaget emphasized that all children must go through each stage in sequence before moving on to the next one, although some children move through them faster than others.

1. *Sensorimotor stage* (birth to age 2). During this period, children understand the world only through sensory contact and immediate action because they cannot engage in symbolic thought or use language. Toward the end of the second year, children comprehend *object permanence*; that is, they start to realize that objects continue to exist even when the items are out of sight.

2. *Preoperational stage* (ages 2 to 7). In this stage, children begin to use words as mental symbols and to form mental images. However, they still are limited in their ability to use logic to solve problems or to realize that physical objects may change in shape or appearance while still retaining their physical properties.

For example, Piaget showed children two identical beakers filled with the same amount of water. After the children agreed that both beakers held the same amount of water, Piaget poured the water from one beaker into a taller, narrower beaker and then asked them about the amounts of water in each beaker. Those still in the preoperational stage believed that the taller beaker held more water because the water line was higher than in the shorter, wider beaker. In this stage, children are *egocentric;* they see the world from their own perspective and do not realize that a situation may appear different to someone else.

3. *Concrete operational stage* (ages 7 to 11). During this stage, children think in terms of tangible objects and actual events. They can draw conclusions about the likely physical consequences of an action without always having to try it out. Children grow less egocentric as they begin to take the role of others and start to empathize with the viewpoints of others.

4. *Formal operational stage* (age 12 through adolescence). By this stage, adolescents are able to engage in highly abstract thought and understand places, things, and events they have never seen. They can think about the future and evaluate different options or courses of action.

Piaget provided useful insights on the emergence of logical thinking as the result of biological maturation and socialization. However, critics have noted several weaknesses in Piaget's approach to cognitive development. The theory says little about individual differences among children, nor does it account for cultural differences. In addition, as psychologist Carol Gilligan (1982) has noted, Piaget did not take into account how gender affects the process of social development.

STAGES OF MORAL DEVELOPMENT Lawrence Kohlberg (b. 1927) elaborated on Piaget's theories of cognitive reasoning by conducting a series of studies in which respondents were presented with a moral dilemma. Based on the responses, Kohlberg classified moral reasoning into three levels, each containing two specific stages (Kohlberg, 1969, 1981).

1. *Preconventional level* (ages 7 to 10). At this level, children give little consideration to the views of others. Kohlberg referred to the first stage of moral development as *punishment and obedience orientation* (punishment avoidance). Here, the child's judgment as to what is right or wrong is simply based on a fear of punishment. Stage 2 of moral development is *naive instrumental hedonism* (need satisfaction). Here, the child believes that good conduct produces pleasure and bad conduct results in unwanted consequences.

2. *Conventional level* (age 10 through adulthood). At this level, individuals are most concerned with how they are perceived by their peers. Stage 3 of moral development involves *"good-boy/nice-girl"* morality in which children believe that behaviour is good (or right) if it receives wide approval from significant others, including peers. Stage 4, *law-and-order orientation,* is based on how one conforms to rules and laws. Conforming to rules and laws is seen as being important in maintaining societal approval.

3. *Postconventional level* (few adults reach this stage). At this level, people view morality in terms of individual rights. In stage 5, *social contract orientation,* ideals and principles are seen as having value that does not depend on the approval of others; rather, rights are seen as part of a social contract. Stage 6, the final moral stage, is *universal ethical principles,* and "moral conduct" is judged by principles based on human rights that transcend government and laws.

Critics have challenged Kohlberg's concept of stages of moral development and his belief that these stages are linked to cognitive development. They also have questioned whether these stages are universal. Some researchers suggest that his "moral dilemmas" are too abstract for children. When questions are made simpler, or when children and adolescents are observed in natural (as opposed to laboratory) settings, they often demonstrate sophisticated levels of moral reasoning (Darley and Schultz, 1990; Lapsley, 1990).

GENDER AND MORAL DEVELOPMENT One of the major criticisms of Kohlberg's work came from psychologist Carol Gilligan (b. 1936), a former colleague. According to Gilligan (1982), Kohlberg's research has key weaknesses. Because all of his subjects were male, his model was based solely on male responses. Gilligan stated that there is evidence of male–female differences with regard to morality. The difference in responses does not indicate a "moral deficiency" on the part of either gender; rather, it results from different socialization and life experiences.

To correct what she perceived to be a male bias in Kohlberg's research, Gilligan (1982) examined morality in women by interviewing twenty-eight pregnant women who were contemplating having an abortion. Based on her research, Gilligan concluded that Kohlberg's stages do not reflect the ways many women think about moral problems. As a result, Gilligan identified three stages in female moral development. In stage 1, the woman is motivated primarily by selfish concerns ("This is what I want ... this is what I need"). In stage 2, she increasingly recognizes her responsibility to others. In stage 3, she makes her decision based on her desire to do the greatest good for both herself and for others. Gilligan argued that men are socialized to make moral decisions based on a justice perspective ("What is the fairest to do?") while women are socialized to make such decisions on a responsibility and care perspective ("Who will be hurt least?").

Subsequent research that directly compared women's and men's reasoning about moral dilemmas has supported some of Gilligan's assertions but not others. Most studies have found that both men and women use care-based reasoning and justice-based reasoning. Nevertheless, Gilligan's argument that people make moral decisions according to both abstract principles of justice and principles of compassion and care is an important contribution to our knowledge about moral reasoning. Studies have not confirmed, however, that women are more compassionate than men (Tavris, 1993). One study concluded that a person's level of education is a better predictor of moral reasoning than gender (Walker, 1989).

Although the sociological and psychological perspectives we have examined often have been based on different assumptions and have reached somewhat different conclusions, an important theme emerges from these models of cognitive and moral development—through the process of socialization, people learn how to take into account other people's perspectives.

AGENTS OF SOCIALIZATION

Agents of socialization are the persons, groups, or institutions that teach us what we need to know in order to participate in society. We are exposed to many agents of socialization throughout our lifetime. Here, we look at those that are most pervasive in childhood—the family, the school, peer groups, and the mass media.

The Family

The family is the most important agent of socialization in all societies. As the discussions of child abuse have demonstrated, the initial love and nurturance we receive from our families are central to our cognitive, emotional, and physical development. Furthermore, our parents are our first teachers. From infancy, our families transmit cultural and social values to us. As discussed in Chapter 15 ("Families and Intimate Relationships"), families in Canada vary in size and structure. Some families consist of two parents and their biological children, while others consist of a single parent and one or more children. Still other families reflect changing patterns of divorce and remarriage, and an increasing number are made up of same-sex partners and their children.

Functionalists emphasize that families are the primary locus for the procreation and socialization of children in industrialized nations. Most of us form an emerging sense of self and acquire most of our beliefs and values within the family context. We also learn about culture (including language, attitudes, beliefs, values, and norms) as it is interpreted by our parents and other relatives.

Families also are the primary source of emotional support. Ideally, people receive love, understanding, security, acceptance, intimacy, and companionship within families (Benokraitis, 1997). The role of the family is especially significant because young children have little social experience beyond its boundaries; they have no basis for comparison or for evaluating how they are treated by their own family.

To a large extent, the family is where we acquire our specific social position in society. From birth, we are a part of the specific ethnic, economic, religious, and regional subcultural grouping of our family. Studies show that families socialize their children somewhat differently based on ethnicity and class (Kohn, 1977; Kohn et al. 1990; Kurian, 1991; Harrison et al., 1990). Sociologist Melvin Kohn (1977; Kohn et al. 1990) has suggested that social class (as measured by parental occupation) is one of the strongest influences on what and how parents teach their children. On the one hand, working-class parents

Daycare centres have become important agents of socialization for increasing numbers of children. Today, more than 50 percent of all Canadian pre-school children are in daycare of one kind or another.

who are closely supervised and expected to follow orders at work typically emphasize to their children the importance of obedience and conformity. On the other hand, parents from the middle and professional classes, who have more freedom and flexibility at work, tend to give their children more freedom to make their own decisions and to be creative. Kohn concluded that differences in the parents' occupations were a better predictor of child-rearing practices than was social class itself.

Conflict theorists stress that socialization reproduces the class structure in the next generation. Children in poor and low-income families, for example, may be unintentionally socialized to believe that acquiring an education and aspiring to lofty ambitions are pointless because of existing economic conditions in the family (Ballantine, 1997). In contrast, middle- and upper-income families typically instil ideas of monetary and social success in children, as well as emphasizing the necessity of thinking and behaving in "socially acceptable" ways.

The School

As the amount of specialized technical and scientific knowledge has expanded rapidly, and the amount of time children are in educational settings has increased, schools continue to play an enormous role in the socialization of young people. For many people, the formal education process is an undertaking that lasts up to twenty years.

The number of one-parent families and families in which both parents work outside the home has increased dramatically, and the number of children in daycare and preschool programs also has grown rapidly. Currently, more than 50 percent of Canadian preschool children are in daycare, either in private homes or institutional settings, and this percentage continues to climb (Burke et al., 1994). Studies generally have found that daycare and preschool programs may have a positive effect on the overall socialization of children (Silverstein, 1991). These programs are especially beneficial for children from less-advantaged backgrounds in that they provide these children with valuable learning experiences not available at home. Many scholars also have found that children from all social classes and family backgrounds may benefit from learning experiences in early childhood education programs that they have not had in their homes.

Schools teach specific knowledge and skills; they also have a profound effect on children's self-image, beliefs, and values. As children enter school for the first time, they are evaluated and systematically compared with one another by the teacher. A permanent, official record is kept of each child's personal behaviour and academic activities. From a functionalist perspective, schools are responsible for (1) socialization, or teaching students to be productive members of society, (2) transmission of culture, (3) social control and personal development, and (4) the selection, training, and placement of individuals on different rungs in the society (Ballantine, 1997).

The pleasure of hanging out with friends is not the only attraction of adolescent peer groups. Peer groups contribute to our sense of belonging and self-worth regardless of our age.

In contrast, conflict theorists assert that students have different experiences in the school system, depending on their social class, their ethnic background, the neighbourhood in which they live, their gender, and other factors. According to sociologist Stephen Richer (1988), much of what happens in school amounts to teaching a *hidden curriculum* in which children learn to value competition, materialism, work over play, obedience to authority, and attentiveness. Richer's study of Ottawa classrooms indicated that success in school may be based more on students' ability to conform to the hidden curriculum than on their mastery of the formal curriculum. Therefore, students who are destined for leadership or elite positions acquire different skills and knowledge than those who will enter working-class and middle-class occupations (see Cookson and Persell, 1985).

Peer Groups

As soon as we are old enough to have acquaintances outside the home, most of us begin to rely heavily on peer groups as a source of information and approval about social behaviour (Lips, 1989). A *peer group* is a group of people who are linked by common interests, equal social position, and (usually) similar age. In early childhood, peer groups often are composed of classmates in daycare, preschool, and elementary school. In adolescence, these groups typically are people with similar interests and social activities. As adults, we continue to participate in peer groups of people with whom we share common interests and comparable occupations, income, or social position.

Peer groups function as agents of socialization by contributing to our sense of "belonging" and our feelings of self-worth. Unlike families and schools, peer groups provide children and adolescents with some degree of freedom from parents and other authority figures (Corsaro, 1992). Peer groups also teach and reinforce cultural norms while providing important information about "acceptable" behaviour. The peer group is both a product of culture and one of its major transmitters (Elkin and Handel, 1989). In other words, peer groups simultaneously reflect the larger culture and serve as a conduit for passing on culture to young people.

Is there such a thing as "peer pressure"? Individuals must earn their acceptance with their peers by conforming to a given group's own norms, attitudes, speech patterns, and dress codes. When we conform to our peer group's expectations, we are rewarded; if we do not conform, we may be ridiculed or even expelled from the group. Conforming to the demands of peers frequently places children and adolescents at cross purposes with their parents. Sociologist William A. Corsaro (1992) notes that children experience strong peer pressure even during their preschool years. For example, children frequently are under pressure to obtain certain valued material possessions (such as toys, videotapes, clothing, or athletic shoes); they then pass this pressure on to their parents through emotional pleas to purchase the desired items. In

BOX 4.3 SOCIOLOGY AND MEDIA

PUBLIC AWARENESS OF CHILD ABUSE

The media have the potential for socializing large numbers of people regarding important social problems such as child abuse. In 1992, for example, *Scared Silent: Exposing and Ending Child Abuse,* hosted by Oprah Winfrey, was the first nonnews event ever to be shown simultaneously on prime-time television by three broadcast networks.

The purpose of the film was to inform people about the nature of child abuse and to encourage them "to break the silence, to speak out, and stop further pain, injury, and death" (Rowe, 1992:11). Information about sexual, physical, and emotional abuse was provided through six true stories of intergenerational child abuse in which the victims and the perpetrators both were profiled.

The documentary, viewed by over 45 million people in North America, generated more than 112,000 telephone calls on the National Child Abuse Hotline in the five days following its airing. Local child abuse organizations also received thousands of calls.

In 1997 former NHL player Sheldon Kennedy drew widespread media attention when he announced he had been sexually abused over a period of several years by junior hockey coach Graham James. In the summer of 1998 Kennedy continued to raise public awareness by in-line skating across Canada to raise money for sexual abuse victims. In the fall of 1998, Kennedy attended a memorial service at Maple Leaf Gardens for a young man who committed suicide shortly after exposing the existence of a pedophile ring at the Gardens.

"When you get a prominent building like Maple Leaf Gardens and a prominent figure like Ken Dryden [Maple Leaf president] talking about an issue that's not talked about much, it's good," says Sheldon Kennedy (Hendley, 1998:10).

Public response to both Sheldon Kennedy and *Scared Silent* show the media's immense capacity for bringing important issues such as child abuse to our attention and providing us with information about how to prevent such violence and neglect.

"There's no question that celebrities—and sports celebrities in general—bring people in," says Sue Hunter, executive director of the Toronto Child Abuse Centre. "There's a tremendous response in our society to celebrities."

this way, adult caregivers learn about the latest fads and fashions from children, and they may contribute to the peer culture by purchasing the items desired by the children (Corsaro, 1992). Socialization is not a one-way process from adults to children. Adults also learn from children.

Mass Media

An agent of socialization that has a profound impact on both children and adults is the *mass media,* composed of large-scale organizations that use print or electronic means (such as radio, television, or film) to communicate with large numbers of people. The media function as socializing agents in several ways: (1) they inform us about events, (2) they introduce us to a wide variety of people, (3) they provide an array of viewpoints on current issues, (4) they make us aware of products and services that, if we purchase them, supposedly will help us to be accepted by others, and (5) they entertain us by providing the opportunity to live vicariously (through other people's experiences). Although most of us take for granted that the media play an important part in contemporary socialization, we frequently underestimate the enormous influence this agent of socialization may have on children's attitudes and behaviour.

Recent estimates indicate that close to 100 percent of Canadian households have at least one television. Canadian viewers watch an average of 3.3 hours of television per day (Adams, 1998). This means that the average sixteen-year-old will have spent more time watching television than attending school.

BOX 4.3

CONTINUED

In addition to providing information about social problems, the media also have the potential for sensationalizing (and perhaps trivializing) cases of alleged child abuse. In 1993, for example, Michael Jackson, the superstar pop singer, was accused of sexual abuse by a 13-year-old boy. Instantly, the media sensationalized the case under the guise of providing the public with the latest information. The allegations regarding Jackson were discussed on network news programs and television talk shows. Among the new-found (although temporary) celebrities to be interviewed were two of Michael Jackson's other young male friends, whose interviews received global coverage. They defended Jackson and stated that the accusations against him were false. They were instant celebrities because they each admitted that they had slept with Jackson without being molested (McGuigan, 1993).

When other stories such as this arise in the future, the media no doubt will continue to publicize (and perhaps sensationalize) allegations of child abuse because it is assumed that this is what people want to read about and

see. As psychologist Melvin Guyer noted, "The public gets to be puritanical and voyeuristic at the same time. Their attitude is basically, 'This food is terrible, and there's not enough of it'" (Corliss, 1993:56).

Do highly publicized cases make us more aware of child abuse, or do they trivialize the genuine problem of child abuse in our society?

Sheldon Kennedy takes a donation from a little girl in support of his skate across Canada to raise funds to build a haven for sexually abused children.

Parents, educators, social scientists, and public officials have widely debated the consequences of watching television on young people. On the one hand, television has been praised for offering numerous positive experiences to children. Some scholars suggest that television (when used wisely) can enhance children's development by improving their language abilities, concept formation skills, and reading skills and by encouraging prosocial development (Winn, 1985). On the other hand, television has been criticized for sensationalizing and trivializing violence (Adams, 1998).

Most children who watch television and movies have seen thousands of people injured or killed as a result of the aggressive behaviour of others. For example, Sylvester Stallone, Bruce Willis, and Arnold Schwarzenegger make vio-

lence look fun, sexy, and profitable. To verify this, add up the body counts in the movies listed in Table 4.1.

A person who saw all of these movies would have witnessed at least 611 killings, plus hundreds of other nonfatal injuries. The increasing level of violence in movies has been mirrored in virtually all the mass media. For example, taboos about what can be said and what can be shown on television newscasts are collapsing. From automobile accidents, to homicide victims, to airplane crash survivors, no scene is too grisly or traumatic to show viewers in the name of "the ratings."

What we see on television and in films influences many different types of conduct. For example, the Walt Disney Company removed a scene from one of its films, *The Program* (in which

TABLE 4.1	VIOLENCE IN MOVIES: RECENT BODY COUNTS

FILM	BODY COUNT
Last Action Hero	57 dead
Terminator 2	27 dead
Total Recall	76 dead
Robocop 2	81 dead
Rambo III	106 dead
Die Hard II	264 dead

Sources: Prothrow-Stith, 1991:30; and *Time*, 1993:22.

several drunken college football players lie in the middle of a busy road to prove their toughness), after three teenagers apparently attempted to imitate the scene. Unlike the movie hero, they did not walk away unharmed: one was killed, another paralyzed, and the third critically injured when hit by passing vehicles. Whether or not we are aware of it, television, films, and other forms of mass media—including newspapers, magazines, radio, musical recordings, and books—have profound influence on how we are socialized. Figure 4.3 contrasts television "reality" with its real-life counterpart.

GENDER SOCIALIZATION

If you had only one child, would you prefer for the child to be a boy or a girl? In most societies, parents prefer male children to female children based on cultural assumptions about sex differences (Steinbacher and Holmes, 1987). Is this because males inherently are superior to females? Not at all; parents acquire these gender preferences through *gender socialization,* **the aspect of socialization that contains specific messages and practices concerning the nature of being female or male in a specific group or society.** Gender socialization is important in determining what we *think* the "preferred" sex of a child should be and in influencing our beliefs about acceptable behaviours for males and females.

In some families, gender socialization starts before birth. Parents who learn the sex of the fetus through ultrasound or amniocentesis often purchase colour-coded and gender-typed clothes, toys, and nursery decorations in anticipation of

their daughter's or son's arrival. After birth, parents may respond differently toward male and female infants; they often play more roughly with boys and talk more lovingly to girls (Eccles, Jacobs, and Harold, 1990). Throughout childhood and adolescence, boys and girls typically are assigned different household chores and given different privileges (such as how late they may stay out at night).

When we look at the relationship between gender socialization and social class, the picture becomes more complex. Although some studies have found less rigid gender stereotyping in higher-income families (Seegmiller, Suter, and Duviant, 1980; Brooks-Gunn, 1986), others have found more (Bardwell, Cochran, and Walker, 1986). One study found that higher-income families are more likely than low-income families to give "male-oriented" toys (which develop visual–spatial and problem-solving skills) to children of both sexes (Serbin et al., 1990). Working-class families tend to adhere to more rigid gender expectations than middle-class families (Canter and Ageton, 1984; Brooks-Gunn, 1986).

Schools, peer groups, and the media also contribute to our gender socialization. From kindergarten through university, teachers and peers reward gender-appropriate attitudes and behaviour. Sports reinforce traditional gender roles through a rigid division of events into male and female categories. The media also are a powerful source of gender socialization; from an early age, children's books, television programs, movies, and music provide subtle and not-so-subtle messages about "masculine" and "feminine" behaviour. Gender socialization is discussed in more depth in Chapter 11 ("Sex and Gender").

Scholars may be hesitant to point out differences in socialization practices among diverse

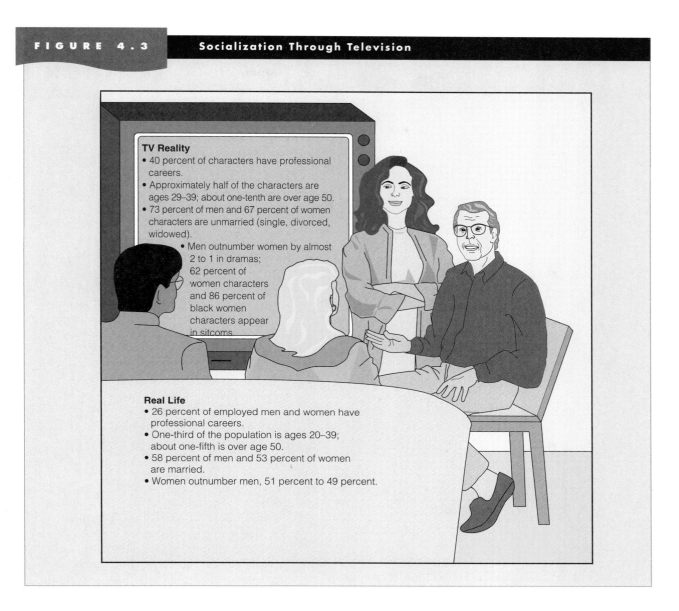

FIGURE 4.3   **Socialization Through Television**

TV Reality
- 40 percent of characters have professional careers.
- Approximately half of the characters are ages 29–39; about one-tenth are over age 50.
- 73 percent of men and 67 percent of women characters are unmarried (single, divorced, widowed).
- Men outnumber women by almost 2 to 1 in dramas; 62 percent of women characters and 86 percent of black women characters appear in sitcoms.

Real Life
- 26 percent of employed men and women have professional careers.
- One-third of the population is ages 20–39; about one-fifth is over age 50.
- 58 percent of men and 53 percent of women are married.
- Women outnumber men, 51 percent to 49 percent.

ethnic and social class groupings because such differences typically have been interpreted by others to be a sign of inadequate (or inferior) socialization practices. As discussed in Box 4.4, beliefs as to what is, and what is not, proper treatment of children vary from society to society around the world.

SOCIALIZATION THROUGH THE LIFE COURSE

Why is socialization a lifelong process? Throughout our lives, we continue to learn. Each time we experience a change in status (such as becoming a university student or getting married), we learn a new set of rules, roles, and relationships. Even before we achieve a new status, we often participate in *anticipatory socialization*—**the process by which knowledge and skills are learned for future roles.** Many societies organize social experience according to age. Some have distinct *rites of passage*, based on age or other factors, that publicly dramatize and validate changes in a person's status. In Canada and other industrialized societies, the most common categories of age are infancy, childhood, adolescence, and adulthood (often subdivided into young adulthood, middle adulthood, and older adulthood).

BOX 4.4　**SOCIOLOGY IN GLOBAL PERSPECTIVE**

CHILD ABUSE IN ASIA

How child abuse is viewed may depend on cultural values. Based on North American values, child treatment in many other nations would be defined as abuse. For example, child labour conditions in India would be considered intolerable in Canada. In India, children as young as 4 may work at looms weaving carpets for up to fifteen hours a day (without a break) to earn 5 rupees or about 15 cents. In North America, this practice would be viewed as parents "selling" their children as "child labour." In Pakistan and Bangladesh, 4- to 8-year-old boys are sold as jockeys in camel races in Saudi Arabia. Bangladeshi girls ages 8 to 10 are auctioned into sexual slavery in the slums of Karachi. Many parents consider a pretty daughter or a strong son to be a financial asset. If a girl is considered to be pretty, she is sold into prostitution; if not, she is sold to a sweatshop. Overall, millions of children live in virtual slavery, toiling for little or no pay in brothels, fields, factories, mines, or stone quarries, or as domestic help.

In cross-cultural terms, is this child abuse? In societies where poverty is endemic, the answer to this question is intertwined with the constant struggle with hunger. Cultural relativism, as discussed in Chapter 3, tells us that we should view this question from viewpoints other than our own. Some critics of child labour state that it perpetuates poverty, illiteracy, adult unemployment, and overpopulation. Others point out, however, that not working often means not eating. For example, Mohammad Sohrab, age 8, carries heavy loads of fish, rice, and vegetables from the market to shoppers' homes in Dhaka, the capital of Bangladesh, to earn the equivalent of $1 a day to support himself and his four younger brothers and sisters. Sohrab describes his life: "My mother is ill, my father

Infancy and Childhood

Some social scientists believe that a child's sense of self is formed at a very early age and that it is difficult to change this view later in life. Interactionists emphasize that during infancy and early childhood, family support and guidance are crucial to a child's developing self-concept. In some families, children are provided with emotional warmth, feelings of mutual trust, and a sense of security. These families come closer to our ideal cultural belief that childhood should be a time of carefree play, safety, and freedom from economic, political, and sexual responsibilities. However, other families reflect the discrepancy between cultural ideals and reality—children grow up in a setting characterized by fear, danger, and risks that are created by parental neglect, emotional abuse, or premature economic and sexual demands (Knudsen, 1992). Violations of the incest taboo by a parent are an example of such abuse. Consider the experiences of Mariah, a victim of childhood incest, as she described them to a psychotherapist:

When I was really little, I remember feeling a bit confused about my father. There were times when he'd hug and kiss me and tell me how special I was to him, and then there'd be other times when he'd call me "Dummy" or "Stupid Head" and yell at me to do household chores ...

When I was 6 years old my dad started touching me differently ... [He abused her sexually.] I was too afraid to turn my head to look at his face. He didn't speak to me while this happened. After he stopped moving he would gently say, "You're my special girl." So I figured that even though I was scared and uncomfortable, this was just something daddies do with their special daughters. Even so, I became very wary around my father. (quoted in Roth, 1993:2)

The father's incestuous conduct continued until Mariah left home at the age of 18 (Roth, 1993:6).

Abused children often experience low self-esteem, an inability to trust others, feelings of isolation and powerlessness, and denial of their feelings (Phaneuf, 1990). However, the manner in which parental abuse affects children's ongoing development is subject to much debate and uncer-

BOX 4.4

CONTINUED

is dead. The family will starve if I don't work. I hate to work. I want to play like other children."

Although all countries of South Asia have enacted laws against child labour, actual enforcement is lax. The ban on child labour does not cover agriculture, where about 75 percent of the child labourers are found. Officials in India estimate 20 million children, most of them below the age of 13, work in hazardous industries such as making matches, quarrying, tanning, firework-making, and carpet weaving. Child rights activists estimate the figure is closer to 55 million.

External pressures against child labour in Asia are rising. The United Nations International Labor Organization is attempting to force governments to acknowledge that child labour is a problem in their countries. Canadian child rights activist Craig Kielburger, founder of the group called Free the Children, toured Asia to speak out against child labour. This 13-year-old schoolboy from Ontario also met Prime Minister Chrétien to tell him that Canada should make a long-term commitment to protect child rights and ensure that goods imported by Canada were not the products of child labour and exploitation. Canada is exploring the possibility of "confronting the menace of child labour" by imposing restrictions on selected imports of products made by children.

Sources: Based on Moorhead, 1992; Schmetzer, 1992; Joshi, 1993; Hauser, 1996.

tainty. For example, some scholars and therapists assert that the intergenerational hypothesis—the idea that abused children will become abusive parents—is valid, but others have found little support for this hypothesis (Knudsen, 1992).

Adolescence

In industrialized societies, the adolescent (or teenage) years represent a buffer between childhood and adulthood. In Canada, no specific rites of passage exist to mark children's move into adulthood; therefore, young people have to pursue their own routes to self-identity and adulthood. Anticipatory socialization often is associated with adolescence, whereby many young people spend much of their time planning or being educated for future roles they hope to occupy. However, other adolescents (such as 15- and 16-year-old mothers) may have to plunge into adult responsibilities at this time. Adolescence often is characterized by emotional and social unrest. In the process of developing their own identities, some young people come into conflict with parents, teachers, and other authority figures who attempt to restrict their freedom. Adolescents also may find themselves caught between the demands of adulthood and their own lack of financial independence and experience in the job market. The experiences of individuals during adolescence vary according to their ethnicity, class, and gender. Based on their family's economic situation, some young people move directly into the adult world of work. However, those from upper-middle- and upper-class families may extend adolescence into their late twenties or early thirties by attending graduate or professional school and then receiving additional advice and financial support from their parents as they start their own families, careers, or businesses.

Adulthood

One of the major differences between child and adult socialization is the degree of freedom of choice. If young adults are able to support themselves financially, they gain the ability to make

A Jewish boy's bar mitzvah is an outward manifestation of his attainment of the age of religious responsibility. Many societies have similar rites of passage that publicly dramatize changes in a person's status.

more choices about their own lives. In early adulthood (usually until about age 40), people work toward their own goals of creating meaningful relationships with others, finding employment, and seeking personal fulfilment. Of course, young adults continue to be socialized by their parents, teachers, peers, and the media, but they also learn new attitudes and behaviours. For example, when we marry or have children, we learn new roles as partners or parents. Adults often learn about fads and fashions in clothing, music, and language from their children. Parents in one study indicated that they had learned new attitudes and behaviours about drug use, sexuality, sports, leisure, and ethnic issues from their university-aged children (Peters, 1985).

Workplace (or *occupational*) *socialization* is one of the most important types of adult socialization. Sociologist Wilbert Moore (1968) divided occupational socialization into four phases: (1) career choice, (2) anticipatory socialization (learning different aspects of the occupation before entering it), (3) conditioning and commitment (learning the "ups" and "downs" of the occupation and remaining committed to it), and (4) continuous commitment (remaining committed to the work even when problems or other alternatives may arise). This type of socialization tends to be most intense immediately after a person makes the transition from school to the workplace; however, this process continues throughout our years of employment. In the late 1990s, many people experience continuous workplace socialization as a result of individuals having more than one career in their lifetime (Lefrançois, 1993).

Between the ages of 40 and 60, people enter middle adulthood, and many begin to compare their accomplishments with their earlier expectations. This is the point at which people either decide that they have reached their goals or recognize that they have attained as much as they are likely to achieve.

In older adulthood, some people are quite happy and content; others are not. Erik Erikson noted that difficult changes in adult attitudes and behaviour occur in the last years of life when people experience decreased physical ability, lower prestige, and the prospect of death. Older adults in industrialized societies have experienced ***social devaluation—wherein a person or group is considered to have less social value than other groups.*** Social devaluation is especially acute when people are leaving roles that have defined their sense of social identity and provided them with meaningful activity (Achenbaum, 1978).

It is important to note that not everyone goes through passages or stages of a life course at the same age. Sociologist Alice Rossi (1980) suggests that human experience is much more diverse than life course models suggest. She also points out that young people growing up today live in a different world, with a different set of opportunities and problems, than did the young people of previous generations (Epstein, 1988). Rossi further suggests that women's and men's experiences are not identical throughout the life course and that the life course of women today is remarkably different from that of their mothers and grandmothers because of changing societal roles and expectations. Life course patterns are strongly influenced by ethnicity and social class as well.

RESOCIALIZATION

Resocialization **is the process of learning a new and different set of attitudes, values, and behaviours from those in one's previous background and experience.** It may be voluntary or involuntary. In either case, people undergo changes that are much more rapid and pervasive than the gradual adaptations that socialization usually involves.

Voluntary Resocialization

Resocialization is voluntary when we assume a new status (such as becoming a student, an employee, or a retiree) of our own free will. Sometimes, voluntary resocialization involves medical or psychological treatment or religious conversion, in which case the person's existing attitudes, beliefs, and behaviours must undergo strenuous modification to a new regime and a new way of life. For example, resocialization for adult survivors of emotional/physical child abuse includes extensive therapy in order to form new patterns of thinking and action, somewhat like Alcoholics Anonymous and its twelve-step program that has become the basis for many other programs dealing with addictive behaviour (Parrish, 1990).

Involuntary Resocialization

Involuntary resocialization occurs against a person's wishes and generally takes place within a *total institution*—**a place where people are isolated from the rest of society for a set period of time and come under the control of the officials who run the institution** (Goffman, 1961a). Military boot camps, jails and prisons, concentration camps, and some mental hospitals are total institutions. In these settings, people are totally stripped of their former selves—or depersonalized—through a *degradation ceremony* (Goffman, 1961a). Inmates entering prison, for example, are required to strip, shower, and wear assigned institutional clothing. In the process, they are searched, weighed, fingerprinted, photographed, and given no privacy even in showers and restrooms. Their official identification becomes not a name but a number. In this abrupt break from their former existence, they must leave behind their personal possessions and their family and friends. The depersonalization process con-

Recruits in this Canadian Armed Forces training exercise are resocialized through extensive, gruelling military drills and manoeuvres. What types of new values and behaviours do you think they are expected to learn?

tinues as they are required to obey rigid rules and to conform to their new environment.

After stripping people of their former identities, the institution attempts to build a more compliant person. A system of rewards and punishments (such as providing or withholding cigarettes and television or exercise privileges) encourages conformity to institutional norms. Some individuals may be rehabilitated; others become angry and hostile toward the system that has taken away their freedom. Although the assumed purpose of involuntary resocialization is to reform persons so that they will conform to societal standards of conduct after their release, the ability of total institutions to modify offenders' behaviour in a meaningful manner has been widely questioned. In many prisons, for example, inmates may conform to the norms of the prison or of other inmates, but little relationship exists between those norms and the laws of society.

SOCIALIZATION IN THE FUTURE

In the twenty-first century, the family is likely to remain the institution that most fundamentally shapes and nurtures personal values and self-identity. However, parents increasingly may feel overburdened by this responsibility, especially without societal support—such as high-quality, affordable child care—and more education in parenting skills. Some analysts have suggested that there will be an increase in known cases of child abuse and in the number of children who experience delayed psychosocial development, learning difficulties, and emotional and behavioural problems. They attribute these increases to the dramatic changes occurring in the size, structure, and economic stability of families.

A central value-oriented issue facing parents and teachers as they attempt to socialize children is the growing dominance of the mass media and other forms of technology. For example, interactive television and computer networking systems will enable children to experience many things outside their own homes and schools and to communicate regularly with people around the world. If futurists are correct in predicting that ideas and information and access to them will be the basis for personal, business, and political advancement in the twenty-first century, people without access to computers and other information technology will become even more disadvantaged. This prediction raises important issues about the effects of social inequality on the socialization process. As we enter the twenty-first century, socialization—a lifelong learning process—can no longer be viewed as a "glance in the rearview mirror" or a reaction to some previous experience. With the rapid pace of technological change, we must not only learn about the past but learn how to anticipate—and consider the consequences of—the future (Westrum, 1991).

CHAPTER REVIEW

What is socialization, and why is it important for human beings?
Socialization is the lifelong process through which individuals acquire their self-identity and learn the physical, mental, and social skills needed for survival in society. The kind of person we become depends greatly on what we learn during our formative years from our surrounding social groups and social environment.

To what degree are our unique physical and human characteristics based on heredity and to what degree are they based on social environment?

As individual human beings, we have unique identities, personalities, and relationships with others. Individuals are born with some of their unique physical and human characteristics; other characteristics and traits are gained during the socialization process. Each of us is a product of two forces: (1) heredity, referred to as "nature," and (2) the social environment, referred to as "nurture." While biology dictates our physical makeup, the social environment largely determines how we develop and behave.

Why is social contact essential for human beings?
Social contact is essential in developing a self, or self-concept, which represents an individual's perceptions and feelings of being a distinct or separate person. Much of what we think about ourselves is gained from our interactions with others and from what we perceive others think of us.

How do sociologists explain our development of a self-concept?
Charles Horton Cooley developed the image of the looking-glass self to explain how people see themselves through the perceptions of others. Our initial sense of self is typically based on how families perceive and treat us. George Herbert Mead linked the idea of self-concept to role playing and to learning the rules of social interaction. According to Mead, the self is divided into the "I" and the "me." The "I" represents the spontaneous and unique traits of each person. The "me" represents the internalized attitudes and demands of other members of society.

What are the main psychological theories on human development?
According to Sigmund Freud, the self emerges from three interrelated forces (id, ego, and superego). When a person is well adjusted, the three forces act in balance. Erik Erikson identified eight psychosocial stages of development, each of which is accompanied by a potential crisis or conflict in a person's social environment. Jean Piaget identified four cognitive stages of development; at each stage, children's activities are governed by how they understand the world around them. Lawrence Kohlberg classified moral development into six stages; certain levels of cognitive development are essential before corresponding levels of moral reasoning may occur. Carol Gilligan suggested that there are male–female differences regarding morality and identified three stages in female moral development.

What are the most important agents of socialization?
The people, groups, and institutions that teach us what we need to know in order to participate in society are

called agents of socialization. The agents include the family, schools, peer groups, the media, the workplace, and so on. Families, which transmit cultural and social values to us, are the most important agents of socialization in all societies and have these roles: (1) procreating and socializing children, (2) providing emotional support, and (3) assigning social position. Schools are another key agent of socialization; they not only teach knowledge and skills but also deeply influence the self-image, beliefs, and values of children. Peer groups contribute to our sense of belonging and self-worth; they teach and reinforce cultural norms; and they are a key source of information about acceptable behaviour. The media function as socializing agents by (1) informing us about world events, (2) introducing us to a wide variety of people, and (3) providing an opportunity to live vicariously through other people's experiences.

What factors determine socialization practices?

Social class, gender, and ethnicity are all determining factors in socialization practices. Social class is one of the strongest influences on what and how parents teach their children. Gender socialization strongly influences what we believe to be acceptable behaviour for females and males.

When does socialization end?

Socialization is ongoing throughout the life course. We learn knowledge and skills for future roles through anticipatory socialization. Parents are socialized by their own children, and adults learn through workplace socialization. Resocialization is the process of learning new attitudes, values, and behaviours, either voluntarily or involuntarily.

Key Terms

agents of socialization 117
anticipatory socialization 123
ego 113
gender socialization 122
generalized other 110
id 113
looking-glass self 108
peer group 119
resocialization 127
role-taking 109
self-concept 107
significant others 109
social devaluation 126
socialization 102
sociobiology 103

superego 113
total institution 127

✉ Internet Exercises

1. Have you ever wondered what type of personality you have? Visit the Keirsey Temperament Sorter (**http://www.davideck.com/links/keirsey1.html**) and take the personality test. How well do the results agree with what you think of yourself? Compare Keirsey's test to any of the personality tests given at The Personality Test Corner (**http://sunflower.singnet.com.sg/~tangs/Test/test.html**). Which are more accurate?

2. The World Wide Web is a form of mass media that allows one person or group to communicate a message to any number of people. Unlike most forms of mass media, there are no restrictions on what a person can say or do on a Web page. To demonstrate this, pick a prominent political figure who has been in the news lately. Go to Yahoo!'s Canadian Newspaper links page (**http://www.yahoo.ca/Regional/Countries/Canada/News_and_Media/Newspapers/**) and read about this person in any of Canada's newspapers. Then do a search for this figure using the Lycos search engine (**http://www.lycos.com**). How is the media's depiction of this figure the same as, and different from, the way this person is portrayed on various Web sites? How do the depictions of this person differ from page to page? How would reading only one of these pages bias your opinion? What are the positive and negative effects of having such a wide variety of viewpoints and interpretations of individuals and events on the World Wide Web?

3. The Canadian Society for the Prevention of Cruelty to Children (CSPCC) has its homepage at:

    http://enet.unb.calorgs/prevention_cruelty/home.htm

    What information can you find on this Web site regarding the effects of spanking on young children?

✉ Net Links

The International Society for the Prevention of Child Abuse and Neglect works toward the prevention and treatment of child abuse, neglect, and exploitation; go to:

http://www.child.cornell.edulispcan/ispcan.html

The American Psychological Association has produced a public information leaflet that includes information on what to do if you or a family member is concerned about a childhood memory of abuse; see:

 http://www.apa.org/pubinfo/mem.html

For current and expert knowledge about healthy socialization and development, visit the Voices for Children site at:

http://www.voices4children.org

To see an Internet journal on the development, care, and education of young children, go to:

http://www.ecrp.uiuc.edu

Questions for Critical Thinking

1. Consider the concept of the looking-glass self. How do you think others perceive you? Do you think most people perceive you correctly?
2. What are your "I" traits? What are your "me" traits? Which ones are stronger?
3. What are some different ways you might study the effect of toys on the socialization of children? How could you isolate the toy variable from other variables that influence children's socialization?
4. How can individuals who were abused as children be resocialized toward nurturing behaviour as adults?

Suggested Readings

These books provide in-depth information on various aspects of socialization:

Carol Gilligan. *In a Different Voice: Psychological Theory and Women's Development.* Cambridge, Mass.: Harvard University Press, 1982.

Erving Goffman. *Asylums: Essays on the Social Situation of Mental Patients and Other Inmates.* Chicago: Aldine, 1961.

Bernice Lott. *Women's Lives: Themes and Variations in Gender Learning* (2nd ed.). Pacific Grove, Cal.: Brooks/Cole, 1994.

George Herbert Mead. *Mind, Self, and Society from the Standpoint of a Social Behaviouralist.* Charles W. Morris (ed.). Chicago: University of Chicago Press, 1962; orig. pub. 1934.

To find out more about the problem of child abuse:

Sylvia Fraser. *My Father's House: A Memoir of Incest and Healing.* Toronto: Doubleday, 1987.

Connie Guberman and Margie Wolfe (eds.). *No Safe Place: Violence Against Women and Children.* Toronto: Women's Press, 1985.

Dave Pelzer. *A Child Called "It."* Deerfield Beach, Fla.: Health Communications, 1995.

David A. Wolfe. *Child Abuse: Implications for Child Development and Psychopathology.* Newbury Park, Cal.: Sage, 1987.

C H A P T E R 5

Social Structure: The Macrolevel Perspective

Components of Social Structure
Status
Roles
Groups
Social Institutions

Societies: Changes in Social Structure
Mechanical and Organic Solidarity
Gemeinschaft and Gesellschaft
Social Structure and Homelessness

Social Interaction: The Microlevel Perspective
Social Interaction and Meaning
The Social Construction of Reality
Ethnomethodology
Dramaturgical Analysis
The Sociology of Emotions
Nonverbal Communication

Changing Social Structure and Interaction in the Future

Twenty-year-old David moved to Vancouver looking for a job. He rented a bachelor apartment in the downtown core with most of his savings and set out to find a job. One evening he was robbed of all his belongings, including his life savings, which as meagre as they were, he had not bothered to deposit in the bank. David found himself without a place to stay, with his dreams in ruins. When he was interviewed, David had been homeless for three months. He was unable to go out to look for work. Demoralized, victimized, and too embarrassed to go to his family for assistance, he spent his days wandering the downtown areas of Vancouver. David describes his "drift" into homelessness:

"When I walked across the threshold of the shelter it was like someone had just hit me in the guts. I felt sick to my stomach. I'd read about homeless people but they were different, bums, and that wasn't me. Now, here I was just like them, one of them, a bum. It was a shock that has left me numb ever since. You know you're at rock bottom but you just can't shake it. You're homeless, a homeless person, that's your identity now, everything else just drops away. It's like the rest of your life never happened ... It'll probably take me months more to get out of this rut. I know I will, but it gets harder every day, you get used to it." (O'Reilly-Fleming, 1993:56)

David's activities reflect a specific pattern of social behaviour. All activities in life—including living in shelters, hostels, or "on the streets"—are social in nature. Homeless persons and domiciled persons (those with homes) live in social worlds that have predictable patterns of social interaction. **Social interaction is the process by which people act toward or respond to other people and is the foundation for all relationships and groups in society.** In this chapter, we look at the relationship between social structure and social interaction. In the process, homelessness is used as an example of how social problems occur and may be perpetuated within social structures and patterns of interaction.

Social structure is the stable pattern of social relationships that exist within a particular group or society. This structure is essential for the survival of society and for the well-being of individuals because it provides a social web of familial support and social relationships that connects each of us to the larger society. Many

SOCIAL STRUCTURE AND INTERACTION IN EVERYDAY LIFE

homeless people have lost this vital linkage. As a result, they often experience a loss of personal dignity and a sense of moral worth because of their "homeless" condition (Snow and Anderson, 1993).

In the years since 1987, the International Year of Shelter for the Homeless, there has been little improvement in the homelessness situation in Canada. In fact, a 1998 United Nations report was highly critical of Canada for failing to take care of its poor, highlighting crisis levels of homelessness, inadequate funding for women's shelters, and grossly substandard living conditions in many Aboriginal communities. Governments are now being asked to declare homelessness a national disaster.

Who are the homeless? Before reading on, take the quiz on homelessness in Box 5.1. The profile of Canada's homeless has changed dramatically in recent years. Our stereotypical image of single, alcoholic, or drug-using males, "down on their luck" is far from an accurate reflection of our country's homeless population. Now included in the homeless category are people who have never before had to depend on social assistance for food, clothing, and a roof over their heads. Today's homeless include increasing numbers of women and children, adolescents, and Aboriginal people. One of the most disturbing changes among the homeless has been the rapid growth in the numbers of homeless women and children. For example, in Toronto an average of 3600 people a day stay in emergency shelters—50 percent of whom are families with children (Canadian Public Health Association, 1997).

Also startling is the overrepresentation of Aboriginal people in Canada's homeless population. **Relative homelessness—being housed in a dwelling that fails to meet basic living standards**—is disturbingly common in both the urban and rural

Aboriginal population. Although most of the research has been done in Western Canada, large numbers of Aboriginal homeless also populate Eastern cities such as Toronto and Montreal (Beavis et al., 1997). Refugees and visible minorities are also overrepresented among the homeless (O'Reilly-Fleming, 1993).

Homeless people come from all walks of life. They live in cities, suburbs, and rural areas. Contrary to popular myth, most of the homeless are not on the streets by choice or because they were deinstitutionalized by mental hospitals (Canadian Public Health Association, 1997). Not all of the homeless are unemployed. Many homeless people hold full- or part-time jobs but earn too little to afford housing (O'Reilly-Fleming, 1993).

QUESTIONS AND ISSUES

CHAPTER FOCUS QUESTION: How is homelessness related to the social structure of a society?

What are the components of social structure?

How do societies maintain social solidarity and continue to function in times of rapid change?

Why do societies have shared patterns of social interaction?

How are daily interactions similar to being onstage?

Do positive changes in society occur through individual or institutional efforts?

All activities in life—including scavenging in garbage bins and living "on the streets"—are social in nature.

SOCIAL STRUCTURE: THE MACROLEVEL PERSPECTIVE

Social structure provides the framework within which we interact with others. This framework is an orderly, fixed arrangement of parts that together comprise the whole group or society (see Figure 5.1). At the macrolevel, the social structure of a society has several essential elements: social institutions, groups, statuses, roles, and norms.

Functional theorists emphasize that social structure is essential because it creates order and predictability in a society (Parsons, 1951). Social structure also is important for our human development. As we saw in Chapter 4, we develop a self-concept as we learn the attitudes, values, and behaviours of the people around us. When these attitudes and values are part of a predictable structure, it is easier to develop that self-concept.

Social structure gives us the ability to interpret the social situations we encounter. For example,

we expect our families to care for us, our schools to educate us, and our police to protect us. When our circumstances change dramatically, most of us feel an acute sense of anxiety because we do not know what to expect or what is expected of us. For example, newly homeless individuals may feel disoriented because they do not know how to function in their new setting. The person is likely to wonder, "How will I survive on the streets?" "Where do I go to get help?" "Should I stay at a shelter?" and "Where can I get a job?" Social structure helps people make sense of their environment, even when they find themselves on the streets. As sociologists David Snow and Leon Anderson (1993) suggest in their study of unattached, homeless men, survival strategies are the product of the interplay between the resourcefulness and ingenuity of the homeless and local political and ecological constraints.

In addition to providing a map for our encounters with others, social structure may limit our options and place us in arbitrary categories not of our own choosing. Conflict theorists maintain that there is more to the social structure than is readily visible and that we must explore the deeper, underlying structures that determine social relations in a society. Karl Marx suggested that the way economic production is organized is the most important structural aspect of any society. In capitalistic societies where a few people control the labour of many, the social structure reflects a system of relationships of domination among categories of people (for example, owner–worker and employer–employee).

Social structure creates boundaries that define which persons or groups will be the "insiders" and which will be the "outsiders." **Social marginality is the state of being part insider and part outsider in the social structure.** Sociologist Robert Park (1928) coined this term to refer to persons (such as immigrants) who simultaneously share the life and traditions of two distinct groups. Social marginality results in stigmatization. A **stigma is any physical or social attribute or sign that so devalues a person's social identity that it disqualifies that person from full social acceptance** (Goffman, 1963b). A convicted criminal, wearing a prison uniform, is an example of a person who has been stigmatized; the uniform says that the person has done something wrong and should not be allowed unsupervised outside the prison walls.

HOW MUCH DO YOU KNOW ABOUT HOMELESSNESS?

TRUE	FALSE		
T	F	1.	Many homeless people choose to be homeless.
T	F	2.	There are an estimated 20,000 homeless people in Canada.
T	F	3.	Homeless people do not work.
T	F	4.	Most homeless people are mentally ill.
T	F	5.	Older men over the age of 50 make up most of Canada's homeless population.
T	F	6.	Most homeless people are alcoholics and substance abusers.
T	F	7.	The number of homeless adolescents has increased in the past decade.
T	F	8.	Homelessness is a relatively new social problem in Canada.
T	F	9.	One out of every four homeless people is a child.
T	F	10.	Some homeless people have attended university.

Answers on page 136.

COMPONENTS OF SOCIAL STRUCTURE

The social structure of a society includes its social positions, the relationships among those positions, and the kinds of resources attached to each of the positions. Social structure also includes all of the groups that make up society and the relationships among those groups (Smelser, 1988). We begin by examining the social positions that are closest to the individual.

Status

A *status* is a socially defined position in a group or society characterized by certain expectations, rights, and duties. Statuses exist independently of the specific people occupying them (Linton, 1936); the statuses of professional athlete, rock musician, professor, university student, and homeless person all exist exclusive of the specific individuals who occupy these social positions. For example, although thousands of new students arrive on university campuses each year to occupy the status of first-year student, the status of university student and the expectations attached to that position have remained relatively unchanged for most of the twentieth century.

Does the term *status* refer only to high-level positions in society? No, not in a sociological sense. Although many people equate the term *status* with high levels of prestige, sociologists use it to refer to *all* socially defined positions—high- and low-rank. For example, both the position of director of the Department of Health and Welfare in Ottawa and that of a homeless person who is paid about five dollars a week (plus bed and board) to clean up the dining room at a homeless shelter are social statuses.

Take a moment to answer the question, "Who am I?" To determine who you are, you must think about your social identity, which is derived from the statuses you occupy and is based on your status set. A *status set* is made up of all the statuses that a person occupies at a given time. For example, Marie may be a psychologist, a professor, a wife, a mother, a Catholic, a school volunteer, an Alberta resident, and a French Canadian. All of these socially defined positions constitute her status set.

ASCRIBED AND ACHIEVED STATUS Statuses are distinguished by the manner in which we acquire them. An *ascribed status* is a social position conferred at birth or received involuntarily later in life, based on attributes over which the individual has little or no control, such as ethnicity, age, and gender. Marie, for example, is a female born to French Canadian parents; she was assigned these statuses at birth. An *achieved status* is a social position a person assumes voluntarily as a result of personal choice, merit, or direct effort. Achieved statuses (such as occupation, education, and income) are thought to be gained as a result of personal ability or successful competition. Most

---

BOX 5.1

ANSWERS TO THE SOCIOLOGY QUIZ ON HOMELESSNESS

1. **False.** This myth is an example of "blaming the victim." Homelessness is the result of a number of social factors—namely, poverty, changes in the housing market, and growing rates of unemployment.

2. **False.** Recent estimates place the number of homeless Canadians at approximately 200,000, 25 percent of whom are living in Toronto. It is very difficult to get an accurate estimate of the total number of homeless individuals in Canada given the transient status of these individuals.

3. **False.** Many homeless people are among the working poor. Minimum-wage jobs do not pay enough for an individual to support a family and pay for housing.

4. **False.** Approximately 20 percent of homeless people are mentally ill.

5. **False.** Men over the age of 50 no longer represent the majority of the homeless. The composition of the homeless population has changed significantly in the past 20 years. Now young men, teenagers, and families with children are predominant among homeless Canadians.

6. **False.** Most homeless people are not heavy drug users. Estimates suggest that about one-fourth of the homeless are substance abusers. Many of these individuals are also mentally ill.

7. **True.** The growth in this population of "street youth" has significantly altered the population of homeless Canadians. Over 70 percent of these youth report leaving home because of physical and sexual abuse.

8. **False.** Homelessness has always existed in Canada. However, the problem has grown to such proportions that the mayors of Canada's ten largest cities have declared homelessness a national disaster.

9. **True.** Children also make up the fastest growing category of homeless people in North America.

10. **True.** Some homeless people have attended university, and some have gone to graduate school. Many have completed high school.

Sources: Based on Harman, 1989; Liebow, 1993, O'Reilly-Fleming, 1993; Corelli, 1996; Canadian Public Health Association, 1997; and Branswell, 1998.

---

occupational positions in modern societies are achieved statuses. For instance, Marie voluntarily assumed the statuses of psychologist, professor, wife, mother, and school volunteer. However, not all achieved statuses are positions most people would want to attain; being a criminal, a drug addict, or a homeless person, for example, is a negative achieved status.

Ascribed statuses have a significant influence on the achieved statuses we occupy. Ethnicity, gender, and age affect each person's opportunity to acquire certain achieved statuses. Those who are privileged by their positive ascribed statuses are more likely to achieve the more prestigious positions in a society. Those who are disadvantaged by their ascribed statuses may more easily acquire negative achieved statuses.

MASTER STATUS   If we occupy many different statuses, how can we determine which is the most important? Sociologist Everett Hughes has stated

that societies resolve this ambiguity by determining master statuses. A ***master status*** **is the most important status a person occupies;** it dominates all of the individual's other statuses and is the overriding ingredient in determining a person's general social position (Hughes, 1945). Being poor or rich is a master status that influences many other areas of life, including health, education, and life opportunities. Historically, the most common master statuses for women have related to positions in the family, such as daughter, wife, and mother. For men, occupation usually has been the most important status, although occupation increasingly is a master status for many women as well. "What do you do?" is one of the first questions many people ask when meeting one another. Occupation provides important clues to a person's educational level, income, and family background. An individual's ethnicity also may constitute a master status in a society in which dominant group members single out mem-

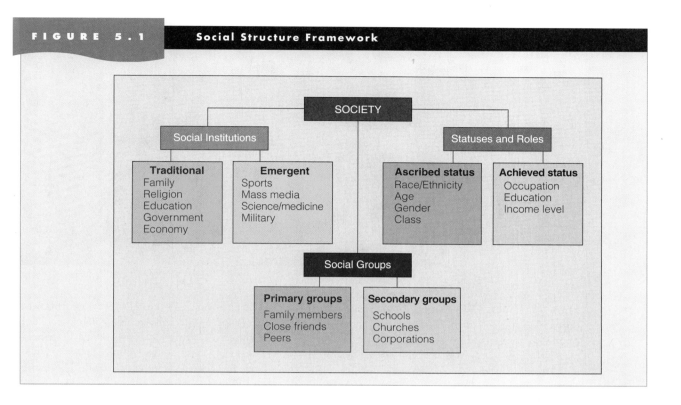

FIGURE 5.1   *Social Structure Framework*

bers of other groups as "inferior" on the basis of real or alleged physical, cultural, or nationality characteristics (see Feagin and Feagin, 1993).

Master statuses are vital to how we view ourselves, how we are seen by others, and how we interact with others. Beverley McLachlin is both a Supreme Court justice and a mother. Which is her master status? Can you imagine how she would react if attorneys arguing a case before the Supreme Court of Canada treated her as if she were a mother rather than a justice? Lawyers wisely use "Honourable Madam Justice" as her master status and act accordingly.

Master statuses confer high or low levels of personal worth and dignity on people. Those are not characteristics that we inherently possess; they are derived from the statuses we occupy. For those who have no residence, being a homeless person readily becomes a master status regardless of the person's other attributes. Homelessness is a stigmatized master status that confers disrepute on its occupant because domiciled people often believe a homeless person has a "character flaw." The circumstances under which someone becomes homeless determine the extent to which that person is stigmatized. For example, individuals who become homeless as a result of natural disasters (such as

floods or ice storms) are not seen as causing their homelessness or as being a threat to the community. Thus, they are less likely to be stigmatized. However, in cases in which homeless persons are viewed as the cause of their own problems, they are more likely to be stigmatized and marginalized by others. Twenty-six-year-old Guy, who is from Canada's East Coast, has been homeless in Vancouver for three years, during which time he has been living in shelters and looking for work. According to Guy, the homeless have to overcome a double stigma, that of being homeless and of being dependent on welfare:

> I hate going to welfare. I hate asking for money. If there's a soup kitchen I'll go to a soup kitchen. Last time I went, I went home cause my dad had died and came back here and had to get started over again. I said to this woman is there any way I can get an emergency cheque so I can get started over? She looks at me and says, "You don't deserve one. If you don't leave here I'll call the police cause you're tryin' to rip us off." I said, "I was away, my dad had died and I need to get started again." She said, "Well we need to see a death certificate." I said, "The hell with you, I don't need this shit," and I walked out. (O'Reilly-Fleming, 1993:129)

How does your perception of Sheila Copps's master status change when you compare these photographs?

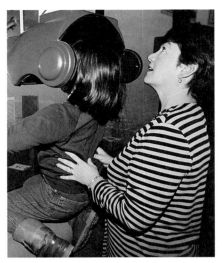

STATUS SYMBOLS   When people are proud of a particular social status they occupy, they often choose to use visible means to let others know about their position. ***Status symbols* are material signs that inform others of a person's specific status.** For example, just as wearing a wedding ring proclaims that a person is married, owning a Rolls-Royce announces that one has "made it." In North American society, people who have "made it" frequently want symbols to inform others of their accomplishments.

In our daily lives, status symbols both announce our statuses and facilitate our interactions with others. For example, medical students wear white lab jackets with plastic name tags identifying their status to all hospital personnel, patients, or visitors they encounter (Haas and Shaffir, 1995). The length and colour of a person's uniform in a hospital indicates the individual's status within the medical centre. Physicians wear longer white coats, medical students wear shorter white coats, laboratory technicians wear short blue coats, and so forth.

Status symbols for the domiciled and for the homeless may have different meanings. Among affluent persons, a full shopping cart in the grocery store and bags of merchandise from expensive department stores indicate a lofty financial position. By contrast, among the homeless, bulging shopping bags and overloaded grocery carts suggest a completely different status. Carts and bags are essential to street life; there is no other place to keep things, as shown by this description of Tamara, a homeless woman living in a city in Ontario:

I don't care much for the police. I get in fights with them a lot. They tell me to "move along" and I tell them I have a right to be there just like anyone else. One time in the subway station I was carrying two shopping bags full of clothes. I hadn't had a chance to wash them in a while, so they were a little dirty, but they were my clothes! A policeman, or it may have been a company cop, grabbed my bags and put them in the garbage. I put up a fight and told him to give them back to me. We ended up wrestling on the platform! Finally, he let his hands fall to his sides and I again demanded that he give me back my things. He went over to the garbage and took them out. (Harman, 1989:95)

For homeless women and men, possessions are not status symbols so much as they are a link with the past, a hope for the future, and a potential source of immediate cash. As Snow and Anderson (1993: 147) note, selling personal possessions is not uncommon among most social classes; members of the working and middle classes hold garage sales, and those in the upper classes have estate sales. However, when homeless persons sell their personal possessions, they do so to meet their immediate needs, not because they want to "clean house."

Roles

A role is the dynamic aspect of a status. While we *occupy* a status, we *play* a role (Linton, 1936). A ***role* is a set of behavioural expectations associated with a given status.** For example, a carpenter (employee) hired to remodel a kitchen is not expected to sit down uninvited and join the family (employer) for dinner.

Role expectation is a group's or society's definition of the way a specific role ought to be played. By contrast, **role performance is how a person actually plays the role.** Role performance does not always match role expectation. Some statuses have role expectations that are highly specific, such as that of surgeon or university professor. Other statuses, such as friend or significant other, have less structured expectations. The role expectations tied to the status of student are more specific than those for being a friend. Role expectations typically are based on a range of acceptable behaviour rather than on strictly defined standards.

Our roles are relational (or complementary); that is, they are defined in the context of roles performed by others. We can play the role of student because someone else fulfils the role of professor. Conversely, to perform the role of professor, the teacher must have one or more students.

Role ambiguity occurs when the expectations associated with a role are unclear. For example, it is not always clear when the provider–dependent aspect of the parent–child relationship ends. Should it end at age 18 or 21? When a person is no longer in school? Different people will answer these questions differently depending on their experiences and socialization, as well as on the parents' financial capability and psychological willingness to continue contributing to the welfare of their adult children.

ROLE CONFLICT AND ROLE STRAIN Most people occupy a number of statuses, each of which has numerous role expectations attached. For example, Charles is a student who attends morning classes at the university, and he is an employee at a fast-food restaurant where he works from 3:00 to 10:00 P.M. He also is Stephanie's boyfriend, and she would like to see him more often. On December 7, Charles has a final exam at 7:00 P.M., when he is supposed to be working. Meanwhile, Stephanie is pressuring him to take her to a movie. To top it off, his mother calls, asking him to fly home because his father is going to have emergency surgery. How can Charles be in all of these places at once? Such experiences of role conflict can be overwhelming.

Role conflict occurs when incompatible role demands are placed on a person by two or more statuses held at the same time. When role conflict occurs, we may feel pulled in different direc-

What are the competing demands of working parents in contemporary societies? What sociological term best describes this situation?

tions. To deal with this problem, we may *prioritize* our roles and first complete the one we consider to be most important. Or we may *compartmentalize* our lives and "insulate" our various roles (Merton, 1968). That is, we may perform the activities linked to one role for part of the day, and then engage in the activities associated with another role in some other time period or elsewhere. For example, under routine circumstances, Charles would fulfil his student role for part of the day and his employee role for another part of the day. In his current situation, however, he is unable to compartmentalize his roles.

Role conflict may occur as a result of changing statuses and roles in society. Research has found that women who engage in behaviour that is gender-typed as "masculine" tend to have higher rates of role conflict than those who engage in traditional "feminine" behaviour (Basow, 1992). According to sociologist Tracey Watson (1987), role conflict sometimes can be attributed not to the roles themselves but to the pressures people feel when they do not fit into culturally prescribed roles. In her study of women athletes in college sports programs, Watson found role conflict in the traditionally incongruent identities of being a woman and being an athlete. Even though the women athletes in her study wore makeup and presented a conventional image when they were not on the basketball court, their peers in school still saw them as "female jocks," thus leading to role conflict.

Whereas role conflict occurs between two or more statuses (such as being homeless and being a temporary employee of a social services agency), role strain takes place within one status. *Role strain occurs when incompatible demands are built into a single status that a person occupies* (Goode, 1960). For example, many women experience role strain in the labour force because they hold jobs that are "less satisfying and more stressful than men's jobs since they involve less money, less prestige, fewer job openings, more career roadblocks, and so forth" (Basow, 1992:192). Similarly, married women may experience more role strain than married men, because of work overload, marital inequality with their spouse, exclusive parenting responsibilities, unclear expectations, and lack of emotional support.

Recent social changes may have increased role strain in men. In the family, men's traditional position of dominance has eroded as more women have entered the paid labour force and demanded more assistance in child-rearing and homemaking responsibilities. High rates of unemployment have produced problems for many men whose major role in the past was centred on their occupation.

Sexual orientation, age, and occupation frequently are associated with role strain. Lesbians and gay men often experience role strain because of the pressures associated with having an identity heavily stigmatized by the dominant cultural group (Basow, 1992). Women in their thirties may experience the highest levels of role strain; they face a large amount of stress in terms of role demands and conflicting work and family expectations (Basow, 1992). Dentists, psychiatrists, and police officers have been found to experience high levels of occupation-related role strain, which may result in suicide.

Individuals frequently distance themselves from a role they find extremely stressful or otherwise problematic. *Role distancing* occurs when people consciously foster the impression of a lack of commitment or attachment to a particular role and merely go through the motions of role performance (Goffman, 1961b). People use distancing techniques when they do not want others to take

them as the "self" implied in a particular role, especially if they think the role is "beneath them." While Charles is working in the fast-food restaurant, for example, he does not want people to think of him as a "loser in a dead-end job." He wants them to view him as a university student who is working there just to "pick up a few bucks" until he graduates. When customers from the university come in, Charles talks to them about what courses they are taking, what they are majoring in, and what professors they have. He does not discuss whether the bacon cheeseburger is better than the chili burger. When Charles is really involved in role distancing, he tells his friends that he "works there but wouldn't eat there."

Role distancing is most likely to occur when people find themselves in roles in which the social identities implied are inconsistent with how they think of themselves or how they want to be viewed by others. Snow and Anderson found that role distancing was common among the homeless—especially the recently homeless. One 24-year-old man who had been homeless for only a few weeks commented:

> I'm not like the other guys who hang down at the Sally [Salvation Army]. If you want to know about the street people, I can tell you about them; but you can't really learn about street people from studying me, because I'm different. (1993:349)

These individuals often pursue employment opportunities in an effort to exit their role as a homeless person as quickly as possible.

ROLE EXIT *Role exit occurs when people disengage from social roles that have been central to their self-identity* (Ebaugh, 1988). Sociologist Helen Rose Fuchs Ebaugh studied this process by interviewing ex-convicts, ex-nuns, retirees, divorced men and women, and others who had exited voluntarily from significant social roles. According to Ebaugh, role exit occurs in four stages. The first stage is doubt, in which people experience frustration or burnout when they reflect on their existing roles. The second stage involves a search for alternatives; here, people may take a leave of absence from their work or temporarily separate from their marriage partner. The third stage is the turning point at which people realize that they must take some final action, such as quitting their job or getting a divorce. The fourth and final stage involves the creation of a new identity.

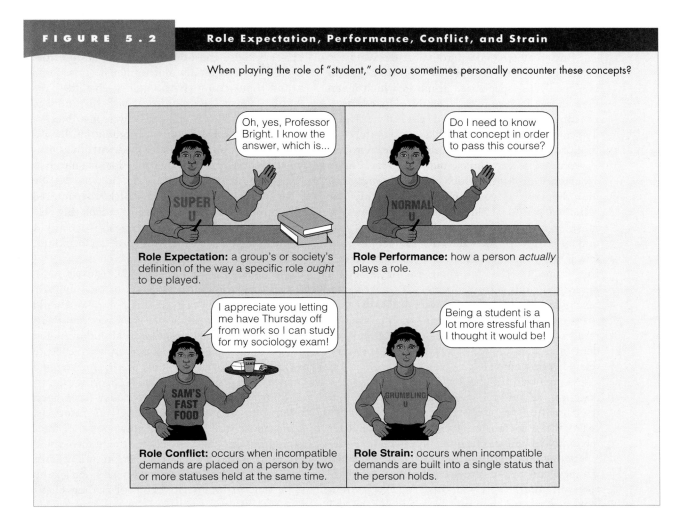

FIGURE 5.2   **Role Expectation, Performance, Conflict, and Strain**

When playing the role of "student," do you sometimes personally encounter these concepts?

Role Expectation: a group's or society's definition of the way a specific role *ought* to be played.

Role Performance: how a person *actually* plays a role.

Role Conflict: occurs when incompatible demands are placed on a person by two or more statuses held at the same time.

Role Strain: occurs when incompatible demands are built into a single status that the person holds.

Exiting the "homeless" role often is very difficult. The longer a person remains on the streets, the more difficult it becomes to exit this role. Personal resources diminish over time. Personal possessions (such as tools, clothes, and identification papers) often are stolen, lost, sold, or pawned. Work experience and skills become outdated, and physical disabilities that prevent individuals from working are likely to develop on the streets. Consider sociologist Jacqueline Wiseman's comments on the sometimes unrealistic demands placed on homeless people to exit their role:

> The goal of all institutions on the loop is to get the charge "back into the system" or "back into the real world." But, what is the concept that the professional has of these men's real world? To them rehabilitation means: "Getting a job, a room, and maintaining sobriety." ... How is he to get the job, the room, and avoid old drinking friends? How can

he change from a today-oriented, no-social-stake person to a future-oriented, middle-class person? ... How is he to feel a part of this middle-class society? (1979:229)

Of course, many of the homeless do not beat the odds and exit this role. Instead, they shift their focus from role exiting to survival on the streets.

Groups

Groups are another important component of social structure. To sociologists, a **social group consists of two or more people who interact frequently and share a common identity and a feeling of interdependence.** Throughout our lives, most of us participate in groups, from our families and childhood friends, to our university classes, to our work and community organizations, and even to society.

Primary and secondary groups are the two basic types of social groups. A *primary group* **is a small, less specialized group in which members engage in face-to-face, emotion-based interactions over an extended period of time.** Typically, primary groups include our family, close friends, and school or work-related peer groups. By contrast, a *secondary group* **is a larger, more specialized group in which members engage in more impersonal, goal-oriented relationships for a limited period of time.** Schools, churches, the military, and corporations are examples of secondary groups. In secondary groups, people have few, if any, emotional ties to one another. Instead, they come together for some specific, practical purpose, such as getting a degree or a paycheque. Secondary groups are more specialized than primary ones; individuals relate to one another in terms of specific roles (such as professor and student) and more limited activities (such as course-related endeavours).

As discussed in Chapter 1, *social solidarity,* or cohesion, relates to a group's ability to maintain itself in the face of obstacles. Social solidarity exists when social bonds, attractions, or other forces hold members of a group in interaction over a period of time (Jary and Jary, 1991). For example, if a local church is destroyed by fire and congregation members still worship together, in a makeshift setting, then they have a high degree of social solidarity.

Many of us build social networks from our personal friends in primary groups and our acquaintances in secondary groups. A *social network* **is a series of social relationships that link an individual to others.** Social networks work differently for men and women, for different ethnic groups, and for members of different social classes. Traditionally, visible minorities and women have been excluded from powerful "old-boy" social networks (Kanter, 1977; McPherson and Smith-Lovin, 1982, 1986). At the middle- and upper-class levels, individuals tap social networks to find employment, make business deals, and win political elections. However, social networks typically do not work effectively for poor and homeless individuals. Snow and Anderson (1993) found that homeless men have fragile social networks that are plagued with instability. They often do not even know each other's "real" names.

Sociological research on the homeless largely has emphasized the social isolation experienced by people on the streets. Sociologist Peter H. Rossi (1989) found that a high degree of social isolation exists because the homeless are separated from their extended family and former friends. Rossi noted that among the homeless who did have families, most either did not wish to return or believed that they would not be welcome. Most of the avenues for exiting the homeless role and acquiring housing are intertwined with the large-scale, secondary groups that sociologists refer to as formal organizations.

A *formal organization* **is a highly structured group formed for the purpose of completing certain tasks or achieving specific goals.** Many of us spend most of our time in formal organizations, such as universities, corporations, or the government. In Chapter 6 ("Groups and Organizations"), we analyze the characteristics of bureaucratic organizations; however, at this point, we should note that these organizations are a very important component of social structure in all industrialized societies. We expect such organizations to educate us, solve our social problems (such as crime and homelessness), and provide work opportunities.

Many formal organizations today have been referred to as "people-processing" organizations. For example, the Salvation Army and other caregiver groups provide services for the homeless and others in need. However, these organizations must work with limited monetary resources and at the same time maintain some control of their clientele. This control is necessary in order to provide their services in an orderly and timely fashion. According to a major at the Salvation Army,

> I'll sleep and feed almost anybody, but such help requires that they be deserving. Some people would say I'm cold-hearted, but I rule with an iron hand. I have to because these guys need to respect authority. … The experience of working with these guys has taught us the necessity of rules in order to avoid problems. (Snow and Anderson, 1993:81)

Because of rules and policies, the "Sally Ann" (as the Salvation Army sometimes is called) tends to close its doors to those who are inebriated, are chronic drunks, or are viewed as "troublemakers." Likewise, a number of the women's shelters have restrictions and regulations that some of the women feel deprive them of their personhood. One shelter used to require a compulsory gynecological examination of its residents (Golden, 1992). Another required that the women be out of the building by 7:00 A.M. and not return before

For many years, capitalism has been dominated by powerful "old-boy" social networks.

7:00 P.M. Fearful of violence among shelter residents or between residents and staff, many shelters use elaborate questionnaires and interviews to screen out potentially disruptive clients. Those who are supposed to benefit from the services of such shelters often find the experience demeaning and alienating. Nevertheless, organizations such as the Salvation Army and women's shelters do help people within the limited means they have available.

Social Institutions

At the macrolevel of all societies, certain basic activities routinely occur—children are born and socialized, goods and services are produced and distributed, order is preserved, and a sense of purpose is maintained (Aberle et al., 1950; Mack and Bradford, 1979). Social institutions are the means by which these basic needs are met. A **social institution is a set of organized beliefs and rules that establish how a society will attempt to meet its basic social needs.** In the past, these needs have centred around five basic social institutions: the family, religion, education, the economy, and the government or politics. Today, mass media, sports, science and medicine, and the military also are considered to be social institutions.

What is the difference between a group and a social institution? A group is composed of specific, identifiable people; an institution is a standardized way of doing something. The concept of "family" helps to distinguish between the two. When we talk about your family or my family, we are referring to a family. When we refer to the family as a social institution, we are talking about ideologies and standardized patterns of behaviour that organize family life. For example, the family as a social institution contains certain statuses organized into well-defined relationships, such as husband–wife, parent–child, brother–sister, and so forth. Specific families do not always conform to these ideologies and behaviour patterns.

Functional theorists emphasize that social institutions exist because they perform five essential tasks:

1. *Replacing members.* Societies and groups must have socially approved ways of replacing members who move away or die. The family provides the structure for legitimated sexual activity—and thus procreation—between adults.
2. *Teaching new members.* People who are born into a society or move into it must learn the group's values and customs. The family and the education system are essential in teaching new members.
3. *Producing, distributing, and consuming goods and services.* All societies must provide and distribute goods and services for their members. The economy is the primary social institution fulfilling this need; the government often

Whose interests are served when residential and commercial properties in a city become more upscale? How might functionalists and conflict theorists differ in their interpretations of scenes like this one?

is involved in the regulation of economic activity.

4. *Preserving order.* Every group or society must preserve order within its boundaries and protect itself from attack by outsiders. The government legitimates the creation of law enforcement agencies to preserve internal order and some form of military for external defence.

5. *Providing and maintaining a sense of purpose.* In order to motivate people to cooperate with one another, a sense of purpose is needed.

Although this list of functional prerequisites is shared by all societies, the institutions in each society perform these tasks in somewhat different ways depending on their specific cultural values and norms.

Conflict theorists agree with functionalists that social institutions originally are organized to meet basic social needs. They do not agree, however, that social institutions work for the common good of everyone in society. The homeless, for example, lack the power and resources to promote their own interests when they are opposed by dominant social groups. From the conflict perspective, social institutions such as the government maintain the privileges of the wealthy and powerful while contributing to the powerlessness of others (see Domhoff, 1983, 1990). For example, government policies in urban areas have benefited some people but exacerbated the problems of others. Urban renewal and transportation projects caused the destruction of low-cost housing and put large numbers of people "on the street" (Canadian Public Health Association, 1997). Similarly, the shift in governmental policies toward the men-

tally ill and welfare recipients resulted in more people struggling—and often failing—to find affordable housing. Meanwhile, many wealthy and privileged bankers, investors, developers, and builders benefited at the expense of the low-income casualties of those policies.

Functionalist and conflict perspectives provide a macrosociological overview because they concentrate on large-scale events and broad social features. For example, sociologists using the macrosociological approach to study the homeless might analyze how social institutions have operated to produce current conditions. By contrast, the interactionist perspective takes a microsociological approach, asking how social institutions affect our daily lives. We will discuss the microlevel perspective in detail later in this chapter.

SOCIETIES: CHANGES IN SOCIAL STRUCTURE

Changes in social structure have a dramatic impact on individuals, groups, and societies. Social arrangements in contemporary societies have grown more complex with the introduction of new technology, changes in values and norms, and the rapidly shrinking "global village." How do societies maintain some degree of social solidarity in the face of such changes? Sociologists Emile Durkheim and Ferdinand Tonnies developed typologies to explain the processes of stability and change in the social structure of societies. A *typology* is a classification scheme containing two or more mutually exclusive categories that are

Contrary to a popular myth that most homeless people are single men, today's homeless include increasing numbers of women and children.

used to compare different kinds of behaviour or types of societies.

Mechanical and Organic Solidarity

Early sociologist Emile Durkheim (1933/1893) was concerned with the question, "How do societies manage to hold together?" Durkheim asserted that preindustrial societies were held together by strong traditions and by the members' shared moral beliefs and values. As societies industrialized and developed more specialized economic activities, social solidarity came to be rooted in the members' shared dependence on one another. From Durkheim's perspective, social solidarity derives from a society's social structure, which, in turn, is based on the society's division of labour. *Division of labour* refers to how the various tasks of a society are divided up and performed. People in diverse societies (or in the same society at different points in time) divide their tasks somewhat differently, however, based on their own history, physical environment, and level of technological development.

To explain social change, Durkheim developed a typology that categorized societies as having either mechanical or organic solidarity. **Mechanical solidarity refers to the social cohesion in preindustrial societies, in which there is minimal division of labour and people feel united by shared values and common social bonds.** Durkheim used the term *mechanical solidarity* because he believed that people in such preindustrial societies feel a more or less automatic sense of belonging. Social interaction is characterized by face-to-face, intimate, primary-group relationships. Everyone is engaged in similar work, and little specialization is found in the division of labour.

Organic solidarity **refers to the social cohesion found in industrial societies, in which people perform very specialized tasks and feel united by their mutual dependence.** Durkheim chose the term *organic solidarity* because he believed that individuals in industrial societies come to rely on one another in much the same way that the organs of the human body function interdependently. Social interaction is less personal, more status-oriented, and more focused on specific goals and objectives. People no longer rely on morality or shared values for social solidarity; instead, they are bound together by practical considerations.

Gemeinschaft and *Gesellschaft*

Sociologist Ferdinand Tonnies (1855–1936) used the terms *Gemeinschaft* and *Gesellschaft* to characterize the degree of social solidarity and social control found in societies. Tonnies was especially concerned about what happens to social solidarity in a society when a "loss of community" occurs.

The **Gemeinschaft (guh-MINE-shoft) is a traditional society in which social relationships are based on personal bonds of friendship and kinship and on intergenerational stability.** These relationships are based on ascribed rather than achieved status. In such societies, people have a commitment to the entire group and feel a sense of togetherness. Tonnies used the German term *Gemeinschaft* because it means "commune" or "community"; social solidarity and social control are maintained by the community. Members have a strong sense of belonging, but they also have very limited privacy.

THE ETHICS OF LEGISLATING AGAINST PANHANDLING

Are homeless people in Canada allowed to sleep in parks and other public areas? Should homeless people be permitted to support themselves by panhandling on the street? Legal ethicist Arthur Schafer discusses the ethics of legally prohibiting homeless persons from panhandling on the street.

Beginning in the 1980s, and continuing into the 1990s, the centre of many Canadian cities experienced a dramatic increase in the number of down-and-out individuals living on the street: bag-ladies sitting in doorways or pushing their worldly goods in supermarket carts, homeless men and women huddled over heating grates during the winter, scruffy teenagers with their hands outstretched for a donation, "squeegee kids" wiping auto windshields without invitation in the expectation of payment from embarrassed motorists, beggars outside hotels and shopping malls.

Twenty years ago, an encounter with a beggar was not a common occurrence in Toronto or Winnipeg or Vancouver. Today, however, in the downtown centre of large and medium-sized Canadian cities, panhandlers seem to be ubiquitous. One is likely to encounter them on the sidewalks, on the streets, in city parks.

Cities across Canada are now moving swiftly to ban or to severely restrict panhandling. They are legislating the use of legal coercion not only against aggressive begging (which is already covered by the Criminal Code of Canada) but also against passive (peaceful) begging. For example, the city of Vancouver recently passed a law that targets squeegee kids by making it illegal to ask anyone in a stopped car for money. Violators could face fines of up to $2000. Winnipeg enacted a city-wide ban on squeegee kids, with fines of up to $1000. In Toronto, police handed out hundreds of tickets after motorists complained about aggression and topless squeegee girls.

A constitutional test-case is about to come to trial, in which the National Anti-Poverty Association challenges the validity of the City of Winnipeg's anti-panhandling by-law. If this challenge is successful, cities across Canada will be forced to rethink their enthusiasm for using legal coercion against panhandlers.

Is it good public policy to use legal coercion against peaceful panhandlers? Can it be morally right in a democratic society to prevent one person from publicly saying to another "I'm in trouble and need help?"

There is no denying that panhandling sometimes causes problems for the rest of the community. But the question that must be answered is: Are the negative consequences of peaceful panhandling so seriously harmful as to justify legal coercion that may contravene other basic social values? Is the cure (legal coercion) worse than the disease (passive panhandling)?

By contrast, the *Gesellschaft* (guh-ZELL-shoft) is a large, urban society in which social bonds are based on impersonal and specialized relationships, with little long-term commitment to the group or consensus on values. In such societies, most people are "strangers" who perceive that they have very little in common with most other people. Consequently, self-interest dominates, and little consensus exists regarding values. Tonnies selected the German term *Gesellschaft* because it means "association"; relationships are based on achieved statuses, and interactions among people are both rational and calculated.

Social Structure and Homelessness

In *Gesellschaft* societies such as Canada, a prevailing core value is that people should be able to take care of themselves. Thus, many people view the homeless as "throwaways"—as beyond help or as having already had enough done for them by society. Some argue that the homeless made their own bad decisions, which led them into alco-

BOX 5.2

CONTINUED

To defend the right peacefully to beg is not to deny that panhandling is a serious negative symptom of a deep social problem. But sweeping the existence of beggars under a coercive legal carpet is the wrong way to go about dealing with this problem.

Do we, as a society, really want to rely upon still more laws to deal with the serious social problems of poverty, homelessness, and panhandling? Are we convinced that legal coercion, with its use of physical force backed by weapons, lawyers, courts and jails, will be effective in addressing what is essentially a social problem? Are we prepared to violate fundamental rights to freedom of expression and add further burdens to the least advantaged members of our society?

We cannot expect much success if we treat panhandling as an isolated problem to be dealt with by police action. Legal prohibition may sound as if it would be a cheap and easy solution, but the messy truth is that it would, at best, provide a temporary cosmetic cover-up. To ban or to severely restrict a person's right to peacefully ask others for help would jeopardize some of the most cherished rights of a democratic society.

Passive panhandling is a nuisance, not a menace. The top-down passage of anti-pan-

handling legislation is neither good ethics nor good social policy. It should be rejected in favour of a more complex, possibly more expensive (in the short run), bottom-up approach involving such measures as income redistribution and appropriate provision of housing and social services. A social approach to passive panhandling would be more just, more humane, and ultimately more effective.

Source: Adapted with permission from Schafer, A. 1998. Down and Out in Winnipeg and Toronto: The Ethics of Legislating Against Panhandling. Ottawa: Caledon Institute of Social Policy (August).

holism or drug addiction, and should be held responsible for the consequences of their own actions. In this sense, homeless people serve as a visible example to others to "follow the rules" lest they experience a similar fate (see White, 1992).

Alternative explanations for homelessness in *Gesellschaft* societies have been suggested. Elliot Liebow (1993) notes that homelessness is rooted in poverty; homeless people overwhelmingly are poor people who come from poor families. Homelessness is a "social class phenomenon, the direct result of a steady, across-the-board lowering of the standard of living of the working class and lower class" (Liebow, 1993:224). As the standard of living falls, those at the bottom rungs of society are plunged into homelessness. The problem is exacerbated by a lack of jobs. Of those who find work, a growing number work full-time, year-round, but remain poor because of substandard wages. Households living below the poverty line use most of their income for rent—if they are able to find accommodations that they can afford at all (Corelli, 1996). Clearly, there is no simple answer to the question about what should be done to help

Sharply contrasting views of the same reality are evident in these people's views about NATO's bombing of Yugoslavia. *Right:* A Serbian Canadian protests. *Left:* A Kosovar refugee shows support of the Kosovo Liberation Army.

the homeless. Nor, as discussed in Box 5.2, is there any consensus as to what legal rights the homeless have in public areas. The answers we derive as a society and as individuals often are based on our social construction of this reality of life.

SOCIAL INTERACTION: THE MICROLEVEL PERSPECTIVE

So far in this chapter, we have focused on society and social structure from a macrolevel perspective. We have seen how the structure of society affects the statuses we occupy, the roles we play, and the groups and organizations to which we belong. We will now look at society from the microlevel perspective, which focuses on social interaction among individuals, especially in face-to-face encounters.

Social Interaction and Meaning

When you are with other people, do you often wonder what they think of you? If so, you are not alone! Because most of us are concerned about the meanings others ascribe to our behaviour, we try to interpret their words and actions so that we can plan how we will react toward them (Blumer, 1969). We know that others have expectations of us. We also have certain expectations about them. For example, if we enter an elevator that has only one other person in it, we do not expect that individual to confront us and stare into our eyes. As a

matter of fact, we would be quite upset if the person did so.

Social interaction within a given society has certain shared meanings across situations. For instance, our reaction would be the same regardless of *which* elevator we rode in *which* building. Sociologist Erving Goffman (1963b) described these shared meanings in his observation about two pedestrians approaching each other on a public sidewalk. He noted that each will tend to look at the other just long enough to acknowledge the other's presence. By the time they are about eight feet away from each other, both individuals will tend to look downward. Goffman referred to this behaviour as *civil inattention*—the ways in which an individual shows an awareness that others are present without making them the object of particular attention. The fact that people engage in civil inattention demonstrates that interaction does have a pattern, or *interaction order*, which regulates the form and processes (but not the content) of social interaction.

Does everyone interpret social interaction rituals in the same way? No. Ethnicity, gender, and social class play a part in the meanings we give to our interactions with others, including chance encounters on elevators or the street. Our perceptions about the meaning of a situation vary widely based on the statuses we occupy and our unique personal experiences. Social encounters have different meanings for men and women, and for individuals from different social classes and ethnic groups. For example, sociologist Carol Brooks Gardner (1989) found that women frequently do not perceive street encounters to be "routine" rituals. They fear for their personal safety and try to

FIGURE 5.3   **"I feel uncomfortable when I encounter homeless people."**

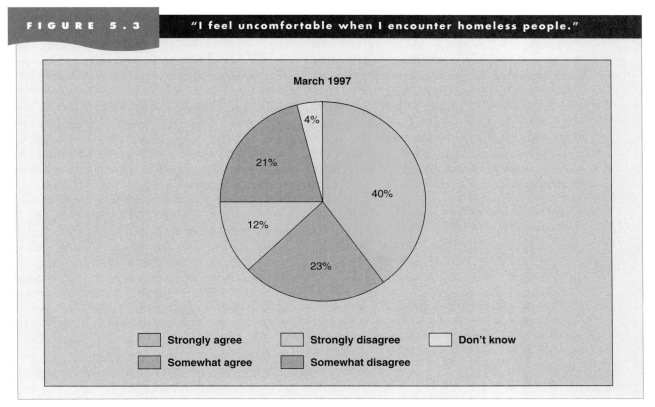

March 1997

4%
21%
40%
12%
23%

Strongly agree   Strongly disagree   Don't know

Somewhat agree   Somewhat disagree

Source: Canada Mortgage and Housing Corporation, 1998.

avoid comments and propositions that are sexual in nature when they walk down the street.

In another example, members of the dominant classes regard the poor, unemployed, and working class as less worthy of attention, frequently subjecting them to subtle yet systematic "attention deprivation" (Derber, 1983). The same can certainly be said about how members of the dominant classes "interact" with the homeless. A recent survey of Canadians' attitudes toward the homeless showed that over 60 percent of respondents felt uncomfortable when they encountered homeless people (Canada Mortgage and Housing Corporation, 1998). (See Figure 5.3.)

The Social Construction of Reality

If we interpret other people's actions so subjectively, can we have a shared social reality? Some interaction theorists believe that there is very little shared reality beyond that which is socially created. Interactionists refer to this as the **social construction of reality—the process by which our perception of reality is shaped largely by the subjective meaning that we give to an experience** (Berger and Luckmann, 1967). This meaning strongly influences what we "see" and how we respond to situations.

Our perceptions and behaviour are influenced by how we initially define situations: We act on reality as we see it. Sociologists describe this process as the *definition of the situation*, meaning that we analyze a social context in which we find ourselves, determine what is in our best interest, and adjust our attitudes and actions accordingly. This can result in a **self-fulfilling prophecy—a false belief or prediction that produces behaviour that makes the originally false belief come true** (Thomas and Thomas, 1928:72). An example would be a person who has been told repeatedly that she or he is not a good student; eventually, this person might come to believe it to be true, stop studying, and receive failing grades.

People may define a given situation in very different ways, a tendency demonstrated by sociologist Jacqueline Wiseman (1970) in her study of "Pacific City's" skid row. She wanted to know how people who live or work on skid row (a run-down area found in all cities) felt about it. Wiseman found that homeless people living on skid row evaluated it very differently from the social workers who dealt with them there. On the one hand, many of the social workers "saw" skid row as a smelly, depressing area filled with men who were "down-and-out," alcoholic, and often physically and mentally ill. On the other hand, the men who lived on skid row did not see it in such a negative light. They experienced some degree of satisfaction with their "bottle clubs [and a] remarkably indomitable and creative spirit"—at least initially (Wiseman, 1970:18). Also consider sociologist Lesley Harman's initial reaction to her field research site, a facility for homeless women in an Ontario city:

> The initial shock of facing the world of the homeless told me much about what I took for granted ... The first day I lasted two very long hours. I went home and woke up severely depressed, weeping uncontrollably. (Harman, 1989:42)

In contrast, many of the women who lived there defined the situation of living in a hostel in very different terms. For example, one resident commented, "This is home to me because I feel so comfortable. I can do what I really want, the staff are very nice to me, everybody is good to me, it's home, you know?" (1989:91). As these studies show, we define situations from our own frame of reference, based on the statuses we occupy and the roles we play.

Dominant group members with prestigious statuses may have the ability to establish how other people define "reality" (Berger and Luckmann, 1967:109). For example, the media often set the tone for our current opinions about homelessness, either with negative stories about the problems the homeless "cause" or with "human interest" stories, as discussed in Box 5.3.

Ethnomethodology

How do we know how to interact in a given situation? What rules do we follow? Ethnomethodologists are interested in the answers to these questions. **Ethnomethodology is the study of the commonsense knowledge that people use to understand the situations in which they find themselves** (Heritage, 1984:4). Sociologist Harold Garfinkel (1967) initiated this approach and coined the term: *ethno* for "people" or "folk" and *methodology* for "a system of methods." Garfinkel was critical of mainstream sociology for not recognizing the ongoing ways in which people create reality and produce their own world. Consequently, ethnomethodologists examine existing patterns of conventional behaviour in order to uncover people's *background expectancies*, that is, their shared interpretation of objects and events, as well as their resulting actions (Zimmerman, 1992). According to ethnomethodologists, interaction is based on assumptions of shared expectancies. For example, when you are talking with someone, what expectations do you have that you will take turns? Based on your background expectancies, would you be surprised if the other person talked for an hour and never gave you a chance to speak?

To uncover people's background expectancies, ethnomethodologists frequently break "rules" or act as though they do not understand some basic rule of social life so that they can observe other people's responses. In a series of *breaching experiments*, Garfinkel assigned different activities to his students to see how breaking the unspoken rules of behaviour created confusion. In one experiment, when students participating in the study were asked, "How are you?" by persons not in the study, they were instructed to respond with very detailed accounts of their health and personal problems, as in this example:

ACQUAINTANCE: How are you?

STUDENT: How am I in regard to what? My health, my finances, my school work, my peace of mind, my ...

ACQUAINTANCE (red in the face and suddenly out of control): Look! I was just trying to be polite. Frankly, I don't give a damn how you are. (Garfinkel, 1967:44)

In this encounter, the acquaintance expected the student to use conventional behaviour in answering the question. By acting unconventionally, the student violated background expectancies and effectively "sabotaged" the interaction.

The ethnomethodological approach contributes to our knowledge of social interaction by making us aware of subconscious social realities in our daily lives. However, a number of sociologists regard ethnomethodology as a frivolous approach to studying human behaviour because it does not examine the impact of macrolevel social institutions—such as the economy and education—on people's expectancies. Women's studies scholars suggest that ethnomethodologists fail to do what they claim to: look at how social realities are created. Rather, they take ascribed statuses (such as ethnicity, class, gender, and age) as "givens," not as *socially created* realities. For example, in the experiments Garfinkel assigned to his students, he did not account for how gender affected their experiences. When Garfinkel asked students to reduce the distance between themselves and a nonrelative to the point that "their noses were almost touching," he ignored the fact that gender was as important to the encounter as was the proximity of the two persons. Scholars recently have emphasized that our expectations about reality are strongly influenced by our assumptions relating to gender, ethnicity, and social class (see Bologh, 1992).

Dramaturgical Analysis

Erving Goffman suggested that day-to-day interactions have much in common with being on stage or in a dramatic production. **Dramaturgical analysis is the study of social interaction that compares everyday life to a theatrical presentation.** Members of our "audience" judge our performance and are aware that we may slip and reveal our true character (Goffman, 1959, 1963a). Consequently, most of us attempt to play our role as well as possible and to control the impressions we give to others. *Impression management,* or **presentation of self, refers to people's efforts to present themselves to others in ways that are most favourable to their own interests or image.**

For example, suppose that a professor has returned graded exams to your class. Will you discuss the exam and your grade with others in the class? If you are like most people, you probably play your student role differently depending on whom you are talking to and what grade you received on the exam. In a study at the University of Manitoba, Daniel and Cheryl Albas (1988) analyzed how students "presented themselves" or "managed impressions" when exam grades are returned. Students who all received high grades ("Ace–Ace encounters") willingly talked with one another about their grades and sometimes engaged in a little bragging about how they had "aced" the test. However, encounters between students who had received high grades and those who had received low or failing grades ("Ace–Bomber encounters") were uncomfortable. The Aces felt as if they had to minimize their own grade. Consequently, they tended to attribute their success to "luck" and were quick to offer the Bombers words of encouragement. On the other hand, the Bombers believed that they had to praise the Aces and hide their own feelings of

What kind of statement is this graduate trying to make? Is he successful at impression management? Would you identify this as *front-stage* behaviour or *back-stage* behaviour?

frustration and disappointment. Students who received low or failing grades ("Bomber–Bomber encounters") were more comfortable when they talked with one another because they could share their negative emotions. They often indulged in self-pity and relied on face-saving excuses (such as an illness or an unfair exam) for their poor performances (Albas and Albas, 1988).

In Goffman's terminology, *face-saving behaviour* refers to the strategies we use to rescue our performance when we experience a potential or actual loss of face. When the Bombers made excuses for their low scores, they were engaged in face-saving; the Aces attempted to help them save face by asserting that the test was unfair or that it was only a small part of the final grade. Why would the Aces and Bombers both participate in face-saving behaviour? In most social interactions, all role players have an interest in keeping the "play" going so that they can maintain their overall definition of the situation in which they perform their roles.

Goffman noted that people consciously participate in *studied nonobservance*, a face-saving technique in which one role player ignores the flaws in another's performance to avoid embarrassment for everyone involved. Most of us remember times when we have failed in our role and know that it

BOX 5.3 SOCIOLOGY AND MEDIA

THE HOMELESS AND THE HOLIDAYS

Why do newspaper and television stories on the homeless proliferate in November, December, and January, as shown in the figure below? Journalists may find the plight of the homeless more newsworthy during the cold winter months and the holiday season because of the stark contrast between their situation and that of the domiciled. Homeless people constitute "human interest" stories for the hol-

iday season. Members of the press barrage service providers at "soup kitchens" and homeless shelters for interviews and stories about "Jimmy G." or "Sherry P.," and volunteers are shown as they serve turkey dinners to the homeless on Thanksgiving.

From one viewpoint, the media serve an important function by keeping the public aware of the plight of homeless people. A recent tele-

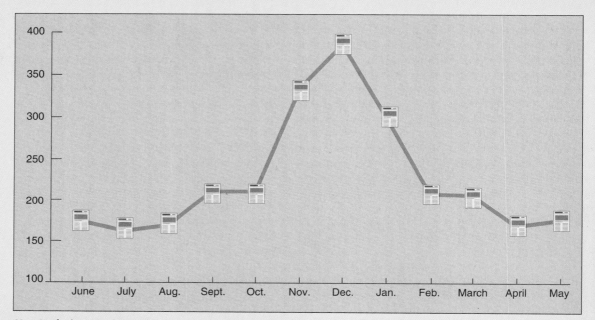

***New York Times* Stories on the Homeless, by Month, 1975–1993**
Source: Snow and Anderson, 1993; and Bunis, Yancik, and Snow, 1996.

is likely to happen again; thus, we may be more forgiving of the role failures of others.

Social interaction, like a theatre, has a front stage and a back stage. The *front stage* is the area where a player performs a specific role before an audience. The *back stage* is the area where a player is not required to perform a specific role because it is out of view of a given audience. For example, when the Aces and Bombers were talking with each other at school, they were on the "front stage." When they were in the privacy of their own residences, they were in "back stage" set-

tings—they no longer had to perform the Ace and Bomber roles and could be themselves.

The need for impression management is most intense when role players have widely divergent or devalued statuses. As we have seen with the Aces and Bombers, the participants often play different roles under different circumstances and keep their various audiences separated from one another. If one audience becomes aware of other roles that a person plays, the impression being given at that time may be ruined. For example, homeless people may lose jobs or the opportunity

BOX 5.3

CONTINUED

vision public service announcement featured homeless people in New York. The commercial begins with a voice singing, "New York, New York," the first line of a song from a popular Broadway musical that emphasized the importance of success. Next, the camera shows that the voice singing, "Start spreading the news, I'm leaving today," belongs to a homeless man sitting on a bench. Then, line by line, the rest of the song is sung by a series of homeless men and women in tattered clothing. Gradually, the disparity between being home and being homeless for the holidays (and every other day) is made vivid. Then, after one homeless person sings, "If I can make it there, I'll make it anywhere," the screen abruptly fades to black. The words to the next line of the song appear, addressing the viewer: "It's up to you, New York, New York. The Coalition for the Homeless." Similar media campaigns for the homeless have utilized billboards, newspapers, and magazines. One newspaper ad and billboard poster had a drawing of Jesus above the headline, "How can you worship a homeless man on Sunday and ignore one on Monday?"

From another viewpoint, the media perpetuate negative images and myths about the homeless. In some articles and news stories, the homeless are depicted as drug addicts, alcoholics, or con artists who choose to be homeless. Photographs of homeless women and men in alcohol- or drug-induced stupors lying on park benches, heat grates, and the street reinforce these stereotypes. After decrying the societal problems caused by the homeless, one journalist suggested quarantining homeless men on military bases. By using the money currently spent on shelters for this purpose, this writer continued, the men would receive required medical treatment and an education in ethics, philosophy, art, and music.

What do you think about the media's coverage of the homeless? Does extensive coverage during the holiday season perhaps appeal to the "guilty conscience" of individuals who have a place to live while the homeless do not?

Sources: Based on Leonard and Randell, 1992; Elliott, 1993; Hamill, 1993; Snow and Anderson, 1993; and Bunis, Yancik, and Snow 1996.

to get them when their homelessness becomes known. One woman, Kim, had worked as a receptionist in a doctor's office for several weeks but was fired when the doctor learned that she was living in a shelter. According to Kim, the doctor told her, "If I had known you lived in a shelter, I would never have hired you. Shelters are places of disease" (Liebow, 1993:53–54).

For face-saving purposes, many homeless individuals create justifications to give meaning to their actions or the settings in which they find themselves. To "salvage the self," the homeless often use one of three adages; "I'm down on my luck"; "What goes around, comes around"; and "I've paid my dues" (Snow and Anderson, 1993: 204). "I'm down on my luck" means that the role does not really fit the person, as one homeless man stated: "It ain't my fault I'm on the streets. I didn't choose to become homeless. I just had a lot of bad luck. And that ain't my fault ... It can happen to anyone, you know!" (Snow and Anderson, 1993:205). Others may salvage the self by embellishing stories about past or current occupational and financial accomplishments or sexual

Is it acceptable for men to cry? In our society, men usually learn to suppress strong displays of emotion in everyday life. In certain settings, such as in high-stakes athletic competition, crying may be seen as perfectly acceptable.

and drinking exploits. They may fantasize about the future regarding employment, money, material possessions, and women. One of the most prominent role fantasies is of becoming rich (Snow and Anderson, 1993). However, the homeless do not passively accept the roles into which they are cast. For the most part, they attempt—as we all do—to engage in impression management in their everyday life.

The dramaturgical approach helps us think about the roles we play and the audiences who judge our presentation of self. Like all other approaches, it has its critics. Sociologist Alvin Gouldner (1970) criticized this approach for focusing on appearances and not the underlying substance. Others have argued that Goffman's work reduces the self to "a peg on which the clothes of the role are hung" (see Burns, 1992) or have suggested that this approach does not place enough emphasis on the ways in which our everyday interactions with other people are influenced by occurrences within the larger society. For example, if a political official belittles the

homeless as being lazy and unwilling to work, it may become easier for people walking down a street to do likewise. Goffman's defenders counter that he captured the essence of society because social interaction "turns out to be not only where most of the world's work gets done, but where the solid buildings of the social world are in fact constructed" (Burns, 1992:380). Goffman's work was influential in the development of the sociology of emotions, a relatively new area of theory and research.

The Sociology of Emotions

Why do we laugh, cry, or become angry? Are these emotional expressions biological or social in nature? To some extent, emotions are a biologically given sense (like hearing, smell, and touch), but they also are social in origin. We are socialized to feel certain emotions, and we learn how and when to express (or not express) those emotions (Hochschild, 1983).

How do we know which emotions are appropriate for a given role? Sociologist Arlie Hochschild (1983) suggests that we acquire a set of *feeling rules*, which shape the appropriate emotions for a given role or specific situation. These rules include how, where, when, and with whom an emotion should be expressed. For example, for the role of a mourner at a funeral, feeling rules tell us which emotions are required (sadness and grief, for example), which are acceptable (a sense of relief that the deceased no longer has to suffer), and which are unacceptable (enjoyment of the occasion expressed by laughing out loud) (see Hochschild, 1983:63–68).

Feeling rules also apply to the role of student. Albas and Albas (1988) examined the rules that exist regarding the emotions or feelings students experience at exam time. They concluded that when students believe that their level of anxiety is not at the "optimal level," they will engage in *emotional labour*. This term refers to the work that students will do to suppress or enhance the intensity, duration, or direction of their emotions (in this case, anxiety). The emotional labour done by students appears overwhelmingly to be in reducing the emotion rather than enhancing it. Individuals learn the student feeling rules regarding "exam anxiety" informally through their interactions with other students (Albas and Albas, 1988).

Emotional labour may produce feelings of estrangement from one's "true" self. C. Wright

Mills (1956) suggested that when we "sell our personality" in the course of selling goods or services, we engage in a seriously self-alienating process. Hochschild uses the following case to demonstrate the potential negative effects of emotional labour:

> A businessman asked a flight attendant, "Why aren't you smiling?" She looked at him in the eye. "I'll tell you what. You smile first, and then I'll smile." The businessman smiled at her. "Good," she replied. "Now freeze and hold that for fifteen hours." Then she walked away. (Hochschild, 1983:192)

In other words, the "commercialization" of our feelings may dehumanize our work role performance and create alienation and contempt that spills over into other aspects of our life (Smith and Kleinman, 1989).

Those who are unemployed and homeless also are required to engage in emotional labour. Governmental agencies and nonprofit organizations that function as caregivers to the homeless sometimes require emotional labour (such as feelings of gratitude or penitence) from their recipients. Homeless people have been denied social services even when they were eligible and have been asked to leave shelters when they did not show the appropriate deference and gratitude toward staff members (Liebow, 1993).

Do all people experience and express emotions the same way? It is widely believed that women express emotions more readily than men. However, very little research has been conducted to determine the accuracy of this belief. In fact, women and men may differ more in the way they express their emotions than in their actual feelings (Fabes and Martin, 1991). Differences in emotional expression also may be attributed to socialization; the extent to which men and women have been taught that a given emotion is appropriate (or inappropriate) to their gender no doubt plays an important part in their perceptions (Lombardo et al., 1983).

Social class also is a determinant in managed expression and emotion management. Emotional labour is emphasized in middle- and upper-class families. Since middle- and upper-class parents often work with people, they are more likely to teach their children the importance of emotional labour in their own careers than are working-class parents, who tend to work with things, not people (Hochschild, 1983). Ethnicity is also an important factor in emotional labour. Members of minority groups spend much of their life engaged in emotional labour, because racist attitudes and discrimination make it continually necessary to manage one's feelings.

Clearly, Hochschild's contribution to the sociology of emotions helps us understand the social context of our feelings and the relationship between the roles we play and the emotions we experience. However, her thesis has been criticized for overemphasizing the cost of emotional labour and the emotional controls that exist outside the individual (Wouters, 1989). The context in which emotions are studied and the specific emotions examined are important factors in determining the costs and benefits of emotional labour.

Nonverbal Communication

In a typical stage drama, the players not only speak their lines but also convey information by nonverbal communication. In Chapter 3, we discussed the importance of language; now we will look at the messages we communicate without speaking. **Nonverbal communication is the transfer of information between persons without the use of speech.** It includes not only visual cues (gestures, appearances) but also vocal features (inflection, volume, pitch) and environmental factors (use of space, position) that affect meanings (Wood, 1994b). Facial expressions, head movements, body positions, and other gestures carry as much of the total meaning of our communication with others as our spoken words do (Wood, 1994b:151).

Nonverbal communication may be intentional or unintentional. Actors, politicians, and salespersons may make deliberate use of nonverbal communication to convey an idea or "make a sale." We also may send nonverbal messages through gestures or facial expressions or even our appearance without intending to let other people know what we are thinking.

FUNCTIONS OF NONVERBAL COMMUNICATION

Nonverbal communication often supplements verbal communication (Wood, 1994b). Head and facial movements may provide us with information about other people's emotional states, and others receive similar information from us (Samovar and Porter, 1991a). We obtain first impressions of others from various kinds of nonverbal communication, such as the clothing they wear and their body positions.

Our social interaction is regulated by nonverbal communication. Through our body posture

Nonverbal communication may be thought of as an international language. What message do you receive from the facial expression, body position, and gestures of each of these people? Is it possible to misinterpret their messages?

and eye contact, we signal that we do or do not wish to speak to someone. For example, we may look down at the sidewalk or off into the distance when we pass homeless persons who look as if they are going to ask for money.

Nonverbal communication establishes the relationship between people in terms of their responsiveness to and power over one another (Wood, 1994b). For example, we show that we are responsive toward or like another person by maintaining eye contact and attentive body posture and perhaps by touching and standing close. By contrast, we signal to others that we do not wish to be near them or that we dislike them by refusing to look them in the eye or stand near them. We can even express power or control over others through nonverbal communication. Goffman (1956) suggested that *demeanour* (how we behave or conduct ourselves) is relative to social power. People in positions of dominance are allowed a wider range of permissible actions than are their subordinates, who are expected to show deference. *Deference* is the symbolic means by which subordinates give a required permissive response to those in power; it confirms the existence of inequality and reaffirms each person's relationship to the other (Rollins, 1985).

FACIAL EXPRESSION, EYE CONTACT, AND TOUCHING

Deference behaviour is important in regard to facial expression, eye contact, and touching. This type of nonverbal communication is symbolic of our relationships with others. Who smiles? Who stares? Who makes and sustains eye contact? Who touches whom? All of these questions relate to demeanour and deference; the key issue is the status of the person who is *doing* the smiling, staring, or touching relative to the status of the recipient (Goffman, 1967).

Facial expressions, especially smiles, also reflect gender-based patterns of dominance and subordination in society. Women typically have been socialized to smile and frequently do so even when they are not actually happy (Halberstadt and Saitta, 1987). Jobs held predominantly by women (including flight attendant, secretary, elementary school teacher, and nurse) are more closely associated with being pleasant and smiling than are "men's jobs." In addition to smiling more frequently, many women tend to tilt their heads in deferential positions when they are talking or listening to others. By contrast, men tend to display less emotion through smiles or other facial expressions and instead seek to show that they are "reserved and in control" (Wood, 1994b:164).

Women are more likely to sustain eye contact during conversations (but not otherwise) as a means of showing their interest in and involvement with others. In contrast, men are less likely to maintain prolonged eye contact during conversations but are more likely to stare at other people (especially men) in order to challenge them and assert their own status (Pearson, 1985).

Eye contact can be a sign of domination or deference. For example, in a participant observation study of domestic (household) workers and their employers, sociologist Judith Rollins (1985) found that the domestics were supposed to show deference by averting their eyes when they talked to their employers. Deference also required that they present an "exaggeratedly subservient demeanour" by standing less erect and walking tentatively.

Touching is another form of nonverbal behaviour that has many different shades of meaning. Gender and power differences are evident in tactile communication from birth. Studies have shown that touching has variable meanings to parents: boys are touched more roughly and playfully, while girls are handled more gently and protectively (Condry, Condry, and Pogatshnik, 1983). This pattern continues into adulthood, with women touched more frequently than men. Sociologist Nancy Henley (1977) attributed this pattern to power differentials between men and women and to the nature of women's roles as mothers, nurses, teachers, and secretaries. Clearly, touching has a different meaning to women than to men (Stier and Hall, 1984). Women may hug and touch others to indicate affection and emotional support, while men are more likely to touch

others to give directions, assert power, and express sexual interest (Wood, 1994b:162).

PERSONAL SPACE   Physical space is an important component of nonverbal communication. Anthropologist Edward Hall (1966) analyzed the physical distance between people speaking to one another and found that the amount of personal space people prefer varies from one culture to another. ***Personal space*** **is the immediate area surrounding a person that the person claims as private.** Our personal space is contained within an invisible boundary surrounding our body, much like a snail's shell. When others invade our space, we may retreat, stand our ground, or even lash out, depending on our cultural background (Samovar and Porter, 1991a). Hall (1966) observed that North Americans have different "distance zones":

1. *Intimate distance* (contact to about 18 inches): reserved for spouses, lovers, and close friends, for purposes of lovemaking, comforting, and protecting.
2. *Personal distance* (18 inches to 4 feet): reserved for friends and acquaintances, for purposes of ordinary conversation, card playing, and similar activities.
3. *Social distance* (4 to 12 feet): marks impersonal or formal relationships, such as in job interviews and business transactions.
4. *Public distance* (beyond 12 feet): marks an even more formal relationship and makes interpersonal communication nearly impossible. This distance often denotes a status difference between dignitaries or speakers and their audience or the general public.

Hall makes the distinction between "contact" and "noncontact" cultures and emphasizes that people from different cultures have different distance zones. *Contact cultures* are characterized by closer physical distance in interaction, more frequent eye contact and touch, and greater voice volume. Representatives of contact cultures include Arabs, Southern Europeans, and the French. Canadians, Asians, and the British are examples of *noncontact cultures* who typically interact at greater distances with less eye contact and touch, and lower voice volume (Hall, 1966).

What happens to personal distance when individuals from contact and noncontact cultures interact? This question is particularly important in our multicultural society where members of different ethnic subcultures interact on a regular basis. One study examined this question by

BOX 5.4 SOCIOLOGY IN GLOBAL PERSPECTIVE

HOMELESSNESS IN JAPAN AND FRANCE

Homelessness is a problem not only in Canada and the United States but also in virtually all industrialized nations. Homeless people sleep on the sidewalks and warm air vents in Tokyo and Paris, as well as in Vancouver, Toronto, and Chicago. While many people in Canada feel fear, resentment, or compassion fatigue regarding the homeless, the Japanese and French are just becoming aware of the problem.

In Japan, volunteers feed many of the homeless to make up for the absence of any type of governmental assistance. Recently, the number of homeless people has increased significantly, even with Japan's high per capita income of over $28,000 annually. However, the Japanese economy has dipped into its deepest slump since World War II, and this recession has forced many Japanese companies to do away with their previous guarantee of lifetime employment for their workers. Layoffs and so-called voluntary retirement have produced many unemployed workers who are over the age of 50. Although the Japanese government does not keep records of the homeless, some experts estimate that persons over the age of 50 account for more than half of the homeless population. In order to have a roof over their heads, many near-homeless men rent cheap hotel rooms for as long as they can afford them. In the short term, the extremely high cost of housing in Japan makes the homeless problem even worse. If homelessness becomes a long-term problem, government initiatives will be inevitable.

observing members of a contact culture (Franco-Manitobans) and those of a noncontact culture (Anglo-Manitobans) interacting in one another's natural setting. Albas and Albas (1989) reported that the subjects, in an attempt to comply with the expectations of others, would adjust their "distance zone" when interacting with someone from a different cultural group.

Age, gender, kind of relationship, and social class also impact on the allocation of personal space. Power differentials are reflected in personal space and privacy issues. With regard to age, adults generally do not hesitate to enter the personal space of a child (Thorne, Kramarae, and Henley, 1983). Similarly, young children who invade the personal space of an adult tend to elicit a more favourable response than do older uninvited visitors (Dean, Willis, and la Rocco, 1976). The need for personal space appears to increase with age (Baxter, 1970; Aiello and Jones, 1971), although it may begin to decrease at about age 40 (Heshka and Nelson, 1972).

For some people, the idea of privacy or personal space is an unheard of luxury afforded only to those in the middle and upper classes. As we have seen in this chapter, the homeless may have no space to call their own. Some may try to "stake a claim" on a heat grate or on the same bed in a shelter for more than one night, but such claims have dubious authenticity in a society in which the homeless are assumed to own nothing and have no right to lay claim to anything in the public domain.

In sum, all forms of nonverbal communication are influenced by gender, ethnicity, social class, and the personal contexts in which they occur. While it is difficult to generalize about people's nonverbal behaviour, we still need to think about our own nonverbal communication patterns. Recognizing that differences in social interaction exist is important. We should be wary of making value judgments—the differences are simply differences. Learning to understand and respect alternative styles of social interaction enhances our personal effectiveness by increasing the range of options we have for communicating with different people in diverse contexts and for varied reasons (Wood, 1994b).

BOX 5.4

CONTINUED

Like Japan, France has experienced a high rate of homelessness caused at least in part by a downturn in the economy and massive immigration by refugees from war-torn countries. Paris has set up camps for the homeless in two underground subway stations and offers free showers in public baths. Charity groups have mobilized soup vans and expanded their shelters. A group of social workers known as the Companions of the Night has set up a meeting place where homeless people can meet and talk all night if they so desire. The homeless in Paris are highly visible as they sleep in doorways, subways, garages, and shelters. Some ride the train all night long in order to remain warm and to get some sleep. Many of the homeless in France blame their problems on a welfare state that went astray and on an over-regulated society that stifled individual initiative.

Thus far, compassion fatigue does not appear to have set in either in Tokyo or in Paris. While the French government has taken a role in ameliorating the problems faced by homeless people, the Japanese government has done little as yet. Volunteers in both countries are actively involved in working with the homeless. Do you think compassion fatigue is inevitable in all countries? Can volunteers and charities alone solve major problems such as homelessness?

Sources: Based on Greenwald, 1993; and Simons, 1993a.

CHANGING SOCIAL STRUCTURE AND INTERACTION IN THE FUTURE

The social structure in North America has been changing rapidly in recent decades. Currently, there are more possible statuses for persons to occupy and roles to play than at any other time in history. Although achieved statuses are important as we enter the twenty-first century, ascribed statuses still have a significant impact on the options and opportunities people have.

Ironically, at a time when we have more technological capability, more leisure activities and types of entertainment, and more quantities of material goods available for consumption than ever before, many people experience high levels of stress, fear for their lives because of crime, and face problems such as homelessness. In a society that can send astronauts into space to perform complex scientific experiments, is it impossible to solve some of the problems that plague us here on earth?

Individuals and groups often show initiative in trying to solve some of our pressing problems. We have recently seen the beginning of militant action by groups supporting the homeless. For example, the Ontario Coalition Against Poverty has held protest marches at the businesses of people who have objected to the presence of drop-in centres for the homeless, moved into abandoned buildings that could be used as emergency housing, and picketed the homes of government officials who have not supported the coalition's views (Philp, 1997). However, these initiatives alone will not solve all our social problems in the twenty-first century. Large-scale, formal organizations must become more responsive to society's needs.

At the microlevel, we need to regard social problems as everyone's problem; if we do not, they have a way of becoming everyone's problem anyway. When we think about "the homeless," for example, we are thinking in a somewhat misleading manner. "The homeless" suggests a uniform set of problems and a single category of poor people. Jonathan Kozol (1988:92) emphasizes that "their miseries are somewhat uniform; the squalor is uniform; the density of living space is uniform. [However, the] uniformity is in their mode of suffering, not in themselves."

What can be done about homelessness in the future? We must first become dissatisfied with explanations that see personal problems as the cause of homelessness (Burt, 1992). Many people in the past have experienced poverty, mental illness, alcoholism, physical disability, and drug addiction, but they have not become homeless. Only changes in structural factors can explain why we have a homelessness crisis in Canada today. Unless these factors are addressed, homelessness will continue to flourish and be a national disgrace. As sociologist Thomas O'Reilly-Fleming suggests:

> Within traditional approaches to homelessness our efforts are bound to fail for they make an underlying assumption that the problem is a temporary one that requires only band-aid efforts over the short term. But as the economy fails to respond, unemployment grows, welfare rolls pass the million mark and our streets are flooded with throwaway and cast off people in society. There is no end in sight, nor will there be one unless dramatic efforts are made. (1993: 168)

In sum, the future of this country rests on our collective ability to deal with major social problems at both the macrolevel and the microlevel of society.

CHAPTER REVIEW

How does social structure shape our social interactions?

The stable patterns of social relationships within a particular society make up its social structure. Social structure is a macrolevel influence because it shapes and determines the overall patterns in which social interaction occurs. Social interaction refers to how people within a society act and respond to one another. This interaction is a microlevel dynamic—between individuals and groups—and is the foundation of meaningful relationships in society. Social structure provides an ordered framework for society and for our interactions with others.

What are the main components of social structure?

Social structure comprises statuses, roles, groups, and social institutions. A status is a specific position in a group or society and is characterized by certain expectations, rights, and duties. Ascribed statuses, such as gender, class, and ethnicity, are acquired at birth or involuntarily later in life. Achieved statuses, such as education and occupation, are assumed voluntarily as a result of personal choice, merit, or direct effort. We occupy a status, but a role is a set of behavioural expectations associated with a given status. A social group consists of two or more people who interact frequently and share a common identity and sense of interdependence. A formal organization is a highly structured group formed to complete certain tasks or achieve specific goals. A social institution is a set of organized beliefs and rules that establish how a society attempts to meet its basic needs.

What are the functionalist and conflict perspectives on social institutions?

According to functionalist theorists, social institutions perform several prerequisites of all societies: replace members; teach new members; produce, distribute, and consume goods and services; preserve order; and provide and maintain a sense of purpose. Conflict theorists, however, note that social institutions do not work for the common good of all individuals. Institutions may enhance and uphold the power of some groups but exclude others, such as the homeless.

How do societies maintain stability in times of social change?

According to Durkheim, although changes in social structure may dramatically affect individuals and groups, societies manage to maintain some degree of stability. Mechanical solidarity refers to social cohesion in preindustrial societies, in which people are united by shared values and common social bonds. Organic solidarity refers to the cohesion in industrial societies, in which people perform specialized tasks and are united by mutual dependence.

How do Gemeinschaft and Gesellschaft societies differ in social solidarity?

According to Ferdinand Tonnies, the *Gemeinschaft* is a traditional society in which relationships are based on personal bonds of friendship and kinship and on intergenerational stability. The *Gesellschaft* is an urban society in which social bonds are based on impersonal and specialized relationships, with little group commitment or consensus on values.

Is all social interaction based on shared meanings?
Social interaction within a society, particularly face-to-face encounters, is guided by certain shared meanings of how we should behave. Social interaction also is marked by nonverbal communication, which is the transfer of information between people without using speech. Ethnicity, gender, and social class often influence perceptions of meaning, however.

What is the dramaturgical perspective?
According to Erving Goffman's dramaturgical analysis, our daily interactions are similar to dramatic productions. Presentation of self refers to efforts to present our self to others in ways that are most favourable to our own interests or self-image.

Why are feeling rules important?
Feeling rules shape the appropriate emotions for a given role or specific situation. Our emotions are not always private, and specific emotions may be demanded of us on certain occasions.

Key Terms

achieved status 135
ascribed status 135
dramaturgical analysis 151
ethnomethodology 150
formal organization 142
Gemeinschaft 145
Gesellschaft 146
master status 136
mechanical solidarity 145
nonverbal communication 155
organic solidarity 145
personal space 157
presentation of self 151
primary group 142
relative homelessness 133
role 138
role conflict 139
role exit 140
role expectation 139
role performance 139
role strain 140
secondary group 142
self-fulfilling prophecy 149
social construction of reality 149
social group 141
social institution 143
social interaction 132

social marginality 134
social network 142
social structure 132
status 135
status set 135
status symbol 138
stigma 134

Internet Exercises

1. Using the Lycos search engine (**http://www.lycos.com/**), set the search to "all of the words" and do a search for "homeless Canada." Visit five of the sites it identifies and try to fit the theme of the pages you choose into one of the perspectives used in the book (e.g., conflict, functionalist, interactionist). With which perspective do you feel the most comfortable?

2. Societies find ways to censure those who act outside of their norms. In addition to **alt.sci.sociology** and **alt.feminism,** also start reading **alt.psi.psychology.** How do people in these newsgroups deal with those who act outside of the norms of the group? What ways seem to work best? How does someone become familiar with the norms of a newsgroup?

3. This chapter discusses nonverbal communication. Most people who use e-mail or post to newsgroups will use emoticons—which are symbols such as ;-) and :) —to indicate emotions without having to type them out. Go to the PC Webopaedia page listing emoticons (**http://www.sandybay.com/pc-web/emoticon.htm**) to familiarize yourself with the most popular emoticons.

Net Links

To learn more about Erving Goffman's book *The Presentation of Self Everyday Life*, go to:

http:www.cfmc.com/adamb/writings/goffman.htm

What changes can we expect to see in our everyday social interactions as a result of new electronic technologies? The paper "The Presentation of Self in Electronic Life: Goffman on the Internet" addresses this question:

http://www.ntu.ac.uk/soc/psych/miller/goffman/htm

The Canadian Mortgage and Housing Corporation has current research on homeless women and homelessness among Aboriginal peoples, as well as a 1998 survey of

Canadians' attitudes toward homelessness; see:

> http://www.cmhc-schl.gc.ca/Research/Homeless/
> F-resear.html

Raising the Roof is a national charity dedicated to funding long-term solutions to homelessness in Canada. Its primary activities involve developing, finding, and/or maintaining homes for homeless people. Questions and answers, as well as current articles on homelessness, are available on this site:

> http://www.communitygates.com/raisetheroof/
> under.htm

Questions for Critical Thinking

1. Think of a person you know well who often irritates you or whose behaviour grates on your nerves (it could be a parent, friend, relative, teacher). First, list that person's statuses and roles. Then, analyze his or her possible role expectations, role performance, role conflicts, and role strains. Does anything you find in your analysis help to explain his or her irritating behaviour? (If not, change your method of analysis!) How helpful are the concepts of social structure in analyzing individual behaviour?

2. Are structural problems responsible for homelessness, or are homeless individuals responsible for their own situation?

3. You are conducting field research on gender differences in nonverbal communication styles. How are you going to account for variations in age, ethnicity, and social class?

4. When communicating with other genders, ethnic groups, and ages, is it better to express and acknowledge different styles or to develop a common, uniform style?

Suggested Readings

These books provide interesting insights on social interaction and the social construction of reality:

Peter L. Berger and Thomas Luckmann. *The Social Construction of Reality: A Treatise in the Sociology of Knowledge.* Garden City, N.Y.: Doubleday/Anchor Books, 1967.

Erving Goffman. *The Presentation of Self in Everyday Life.* New York: Doubleday, 1959.

David A. Karp and William C. Yoels. *Sociology and Everyday Life.* Itasca, Ill.: Peacock, 1986.

The process of leaving a significant role and establishing a new identity is examined in this book:

Helen Rose Fuchs Ebaugh. *Becoming an EX: The Process of Role Exit.* Chicago: University of Chicago Press, 1988.

To find out more about the problem of homelessness:

Lars Eighner. *Travels with Lizbeth.* New York: St. Martin's Press, 1993.

David A. Snow and Leon Anderson. *Down on Their Luck: A Case Study of Homeless Street People.* Berkeley: University of California Press, 1993.

Lesley D. Harman. *When a Hostel Becomes a Home: Experiences of Women.* Toronto: Garamond Press, 1989.

Thomas O'Reilly-Fleming. *Down and Out in Canada: Homeless Canadians.* Toronto: Canadian Scholars Press, 1993.

CHAPTER 6

Social Groups
    Groups, Aggregates, and Categories
    Types of Groups

Group Characteristics and Dynamics
    Group Size
    Group Leadership
    Group Conformity

Formal Organizations
    Types of Formal Organizations
    Bureaucracies
    Shortcomings of Bureaucracies
    Bureaucracy and Oligarchy
    An Alternative Form of Organization

New Organizations for the Future

Kenneth Payne describes his journey through a bureaucratic maze:
    "Since November, I have spent six to eight hours a day trying to persuade the authorities to accommodate me, but it just goes around in a circle ... It's George Orwell's Big Brother, 14 years after his book *1984* ... The bureaucracy is making me prove a negative and it turns "innocent until proven guilty" on its head ... There's no common sense here. It's an inflexible bureaucracy where nobody takes any responsibility." (Reed, 1998:A11)

What is Mr. Payne's problem? The former carpenter wants to be a school teacher. He has a degree in education and has taught as a substitute. However, he is unable to get a permanent job teaching because he has a skin disease that causes the skin on his hands to blister and peel. Why should this disqualify Mr. Payne from teaching? Because the disease has removed his fingerprints and legislators in his home state of California have passed a law requiring that all teachers be fingerprinted so their criminal records can be checked. Of course, because Mr. Payne has never had proper fingerprints, there would be nothing on file to check against even if they could read his prints. But this has not discouraged the bureaucrats. He has appealed to the state and offered to prove in other ways that he has no criminal record, but he has been unable to get an exemption from the rule.

GROUPS AND ORGANIZATIONS

W e have all been treated badly by some bureaucracy—though not perhaps to the degree of this unusual case. In fact many of us think of bureaucracies in a very negative way because of their red tape and impersonal nature. However, while bureaucracies can be inflexible and inhumane, they are also a very powerful type of social organization and are essential to modern life. They are the best way of managing large numbers of people who must accomplish a common task, so they are an essential part of our industrialized global society. Much of our lives is spent dealing with bureaucratic organizations. Most of us are born in hospitals, educated in schools, fed by restaurants and supermarket chains, entertained by communications companies, employed by corporations, and buried by funeral companies.

In this chapter, you will learn about different types of groups and organizations including bureaucracies. As social beings, we live our lives in groups and they constantly affect our behaviour. Before reading on, test your knowledge about bureaucracies by taking the quiz in Box 6.1.

QUESTIONS AND ISSUES

CHAPTER FOCUS QUESTION: How can we explain the behaviour of people who work in bureaucracies?

What constitutes a social group?

How are groups and their members shaped by group size, leadership style, and pressures to conform?

What purposes does bureaucracy serve?

What are some of the characteristics of bureaucracies?

How might an alternative form of organization differ from existing ones?

Napoleon's defeat at Waterloo in 1815 showed that massive armies could not be led in the traditional way, by a single commander responsible for everything. Subsequently, armies developed more effective organizational structures.

SOCIAL GROUPS

Three strangers are standing at a street corner waiting for a traffic light to change. Do they constitute a group? Five hundred women and men are first-year graduate students at a university. Do they constitute a group? In everyday usage, we use the word *group* to mean any collection of people. According to sociologists, however, the answer to these questions is no; individuals who happen to share a common feature or to be in the same place at the same time do not constitute social groups.

Groups, Aggregates, and Categories

As we saw in Chapter 5, a *social group* is a collection of two or more people who interact frequently with one another, share a sense of belonging, and have a feeling of interdependence. Several people waiting for a traffic light to change constitute an **aggregate—a collection of people who happen to be in the same place at the same time but have little else in common.** Shoppers in a department store and passengers on an airplane flight also are examples of aggregates. People in aggregates share a common purpose (such as purchasing items or arriving at their destination) but generally do not interact with one another, except perhaps briefly. The first-year graduate students, at least initially, constitute a **category—a number of people who may never have met one another but share a similar characteristic** (such as education level, age, ethnicity, and gender). Men and women make up categories, as do First Nations peoples, and victims of sexual or racial harassment. Categories are not social groups because the people in them usually do not create a social structure or have anything in common other than a particular trait.

Occasionally, people in aggregates and categories form social groups. People within the category known as "graduate students," for instance, may become an aggregate when they get together for an orientation to graduate school. Some of them may form social groups as they interact with one another in classes and seminars, find that they have mutual interests and concerns, and develop a sense of belonging to the group. The number and diversity of social groups within society is enormous, especially when you consider that a social group may contain as few as two members and that the purposes for which they are formed are so wide-ranging.

Social groups can change and evolve over time. For example, an aggregate or category of people over time may become a formal organization with a specific structure and clear-cut goals. A *formal organization*, you will recall, is a highly structured group formed for the purpose of achieving specific goals in the most efficient manner. Universities, factories, corporations, the military, and government agencies are examples of formal organizations. Before we examine formal organizations, we need to know more about groups in general and the ways in which they function.

Types of Groups

As you will recall from Chapter 5, groups have varying degrees of social solidarity and structure. This structure is flexible in some groups and more rigid in others. Some groups are small and personal; others are large and impersonal. We more closely identify with the members of some groups than we do others.

BOX 6.1   SOCIOLOGY AND EVERYDAY LIFE

HOW MUCH DO YOU KNOW ABOUT BUREAUCRACY?

TRUE	FALSE		
T	F	1.	Large bureaucracies have existed for about a thousand years.
T	F	2.	Because of the efficiency and profitability of the new factory bureaucracies, people were eager to leave the farms to work in the factories.
T	F	3.	Bureaucracies are deliberately impersonal.
T	F	4.	In addition to their formal structure, bureaucracies also have an "other face"—an informal structure that is also important in analyzing their operation.
T	F	5.	The rise of Protestantism helped create the social conditions favourable to the rise of modern bureaucracies.
T	F	6.	Because people in bureaucracies follow the direction of their superiors, bringing about change in large organizations is easy.
T	F	7.	One of the first modern bureaucratic organizations was the Prussian army.
T	F	8.	Businesses in Japan have developed an organizational model that is different from the one prevalent in North America.
T	F	9.	The Internet company that calls itself "the Earth's Biggest Bookstore" keeps only a small stock of books.
T	F	10.	The comic strip *Dilbert* has become popular because it is a reflection of the way many people feel about the bureaucracies in which they work.

Answers on page 168.

PRIMARY AND SECONDARY GROUPS   Sociologist Charles H. Cooley (1962/1909) used the term *primary group* to describe a small, less specialized group in which members engage in face-to-face, emotion-based interactions over an extended period of time. We have primary relationships with other individuals in our primary groups— that is, with our *significant others,* who frequently serve as role models.

In contrast, you will recall, a *secondary group* is a larger, more specialized group in which the members engage in more impersonal, goal-oriented relationships for a limited period of time. The size of a secondary group may vary. Twelve students in a graduate seminar may start out as a secondary group but eventually become a primary group as they get to know one another and communicate on a more personal basis. Formal organizations are secondary groups, but they also contain many primary groups within them. For example, how many primary groups do you think there are within the secondary group setting of your university?

INGROUPS AND OUTGROUPS   All groups set boundaries by distinguishing between insiders who are members and outsiders who are not. Sociologist William Graham Sumner (1959/1906) coined the terms *ingroup* and *outgroup* to describe people's feelings toward members of their own and other groups. An **ingroup is a group to which a person belongs and with which the person feels a sense of identity.** An *outgroup* **is a group to which a person does not belong and toward which the person may feel a sense of competitiveness or hostility.** Distinguishing between our ingroups and our outgroups helps us establish our individual identity and self-worth. Likewise, groups are solidified by ingroup and outgroup distinctions; the presence of an enemy or hostile group binds members more closely together (Coser, 1956).

Group boundaries may be formal, with clearly defined criteria for membership. For example, a country club that requires applicants for membership to be recommended by four current members, to pay a $25,000 initiation fee, and to pay $1000 per month membership dues has clearly set requirements for its members. The club may even post a sign at its entrance that states "Members Only," and use security personnel to ensure that nonmembers do not encroach on its grounds. Boundary distinctions often are reflected in symbols such as emblems or clothing. Members of the country club are given membership cards to gain access to the club's facilities or to charge food to

BOX 6.1

ANSWERS TO THE SOCIOLOGY QUIZ ON BUREAUCRACY

1. **False.** While not all sociologists agree on the specific origins of bureaucracies, many feel that modern bureaucracies began with the development of large factories in England during the nineteenth century. Large-scale organizations had existed prior to this time, but they were not organized on bureaucratic principles. As organizations grew in size, they became difficult to manage, so new organizing principles were required.

2. **False.** Commenting on the eighteenth-century factory, Charles Perrow has observed that "the unnaturalness of working for someone else's profit twelve hours a day, seven days a week was so pronounced that the early factories had to rely on criminals and paupers to do the work" (1986:49).

3. **True.** Bureaucracies are designed to be efficient and productive. In order to do this, they take a detached approach to clients and employees so that personal feelings do not interfere with organizational decisions.

4. **True.** All bureaucracies have an informal structure that is composed of activities and interactions that do not correspond with the official rules and procedures of the bureaucracy.

5. **True.** According to Max Weber, Protestantism, with its emphasis on worldliness and commitment to long-term goals, helped create the social conditions that led to the rise of the modern bureaucracy.

6. **False.** It is extremely difficult to bring about change in bureaucracies because people become comfortable with the way things have been done in the past.

7. **True.** Napoleon's defeat at Waterloo in 1815 by the allied armies of Prussia (now part of Germany), Britain, Austria, and Russia showed that mass armies could not be led in the traditional way, by a single commander responsible for everything (Stark, 1998). The Prussian military, having learned from observing Napoleon's defeat, set about designing a more effective organization. Field Marshal Helmuth von Moltke, who took command of the Prussian army in 1857, was responsible for two major innovations. He developed a general staff made up of carefully selected and trained officers who could carry out the leader's commands and he divided his army into standard-sized "divisions" that could be detached to fight as self-sufficient units. These innovations, which still guide contemporary armies, also influenced the development of industrial bureaucracies.

8. **True.** The main differences between Japanese and North American corporations are that Japanese employees can expect lifetime employment and are encouraged to participate in management decisions. This may change, however, as the recession of the nineties has led some Japanese companies to rethink their guarantee of lifetime employment.

9. **True.** While you can order over a million titles from Amazon.com, the company stocks only a few hundred titles. The rest are ordered and delivered from traditional book wholesalers.

10. **True.** Thousands of workers have posted *Dilbert* cartoons on their cubicle and office walls, and many of the ideas you see in *Dilbert* actually come from their suggestions.

Sources: Based on Perrow, 1986; Stark, 1998.

their account. They may wear sun visors and shirts with the country club's logo on them. All of these symbols denote that the bearer/wearer is a member of the ingroup. They are status symbols.

Group boundaries are not always as formal as they are in a private club. Friendship groups, for example, usually do not have clear guidelines for membership. Rather, the boundaries tend to be very informal and vaguely defined.

Ingroup and outgroup distinctions may encourage social cohesion among members, but they also may promote classism, racism, sexism, and ageism. Ingroup members typically view themselves positively and members of outgroups negatively. These feelings of group superiority, or *ethnocentrism*, are somewhat inevitable. However, members of some groups feel more free than others to act on their beliefs. If groups are

These Olympic teams graphically illustrate the concept of ingroups and outgroups. Each Olympic team can be seen as an ingroup that helps to give its members a sense of belonging and identity—feelings that are strengthened by the presence of clearly defined outgroups (competing teams).

embedded in larger groups and organizations, the large organization may discourage such beliefs and their consequences (Merton, 1968). Conversely, organizations may foster these ingroup/outgroup distinctions by denying their existence or by failing to take action when misconduct occurs. For example:

> In Winnipeg, Manitoba, recently two male employees were fired from a Canada Safeway bread plant for accusations of sexual harassment against female employees. One of the men allegedly exposed himself, stalked, and gave photographs of his anatomy to a female employee. Accusations against the other man include repeatedly making lewd and suggestive comments to female employees and inappropriately touching them. The female employee said that 10 or 12 women on the work floor have taken stress leave from work over the last five years because of the abuse. Men outnumber women on the shop floor by about eight to one. The United Food and Commercial Workers union spokesperson explained that, "the system of dealing with sexual-harassment complaints failed in this case because of the influential position one of the accused men held with the union." These incidents were not brought to the attention of the union management. Female employees say that the atmosphere at the plant discouraged women from coming forward to report incidents of harassment. (Owen, 1996)

In this case, male co-workers seem to have developed an ingroup from which the female employees were not only categorically excluded but also made the object of the group's ridicule. In a work environment, ingroups can provide support for group members. Those who are denied membership in the group, however, may find it impossible to perform their job effectively.

REFERENCE GROUPS Ingroups provide us not only with a source of identity but also with a point of reference. A *reference group* **is a group that strongly influences a person's behaviour and social attitudes, regardless of whether that individual is an actual member.** When we attempt to evaluate our appearance, ideas, or goals, we automatically refer to the standards of some group. Sometimes, we will refer to our membership groups, such as family or friends. Other times, we will rely on groups to which we do not currently belong but that we might wish to join in the future, such as a social club or a profession. We also may have negative reference groups. For many people, the Ku Klux Klan and neo-Nazi skinheads are examples of negative reference groups because most people's racial attitudes compare favourably with such groups' blatantly racist behaviour.

Reference groups help explain why our behaviour and attitudes sometimes differ from those of our membership groups. We may accept the values and norms of a group with which we identify rather than one to which we belong. We also may act more like members of a group we want to join than members of groups to which we already belong. In this case, reference groups are a source of anticipatory socialization. Many people have more than one reference group and often receive conflicting messages from them about how they should view themselves. For most of us, our reference group attachments change many times during our life course, especially when we acquire a new status in a formal organization.

GROUP CHARACTERISTICS AND DYNAMICS

What purpose do groups serve? Why are individuals willing to relinquish some of their freedom to participate in groups? According to functionalists, people form groups to meet instrumental and expressive needs. *Instrumental*, or task-oriented, needs cannot always be met by one person, so the group works cooperatively to fulfil a specific goal. Think, for example, of how hard it would be to function as a one-person football team or to single-handedly build a skyscraper. Groups help members do jobs that are impossible to do alone or that would be very difficult and time-consuming at best. In addition to instrumental needs, groups also help people meet their *expressive,* or emotional, needs, especially for self-expression and support from family, friends, and peers.

While not disputing that groups ideally perform such functions, conflict theorists suggest that groups also involve a series of power relationships whereby the needs of individual members may not be equally served. Symbolic interactionists focus on how the size of a group influences the kind of interaction that takes place among members.

We now will look at certain characteristics of groups, such as how size affects group dynamics.

Group Size

The size of a group is one of its most important features. Interactions are more personal and intense in a **small group, a collectivity small enough for all members to be acquainted with one another and to interact simultaneously.**

Sociologist Georg Simmel (1950/1917) suggested that small groups have distinctive interaction patterns that do not exist in larger groups. According to Simmel, in a **dyad—a group composed of two members—**the active participation of both members is crucial for the group's survival. If one member withdraws from interaction or "quits," the group ceases to exist. Examples of dyads include two people who are best friends, married couples, and domestic partnerships. Dyads provide members with an intense bond and a sense of unity not found in most larger groups.

When a third person is added to a dyad, a **triad, a group composed of three members,** is formed. The nature of the relationship and interaction patterns change with the addition of the third person. In a triad even if one member

Our most intense relationships occur in dyads—groups composed of two members. How might the interaction of these two people differ if they were with several other people?

ignores another or declines to participate, the group can still function. In addition, two members may unite to create a coalition that can subject the third member to group pressure to conform. A coalition is an alliance created in an attempt to reach a shared objective or goal. If two members form a coalition, the other member may be seen as an outsider or intruder. In extreme cases, certain types of harassment may be fostered in triadic relationships in which two harassers reinforce each other's behaviour and make the third member of the group the "outsider." Like dyads, triads can exist as separate entities or be contained within formal organizations.

As the size of a group increases beyond three people, members tend to specialize in different tasks, and everyday communication patterns change. For instance, in groups of more than six or seven people, it becomes increasingly difficult for everyone to take part in the same conversation; so, several conversations likely will take place simultaneously. Members also are likely to take sides on issues and form a number of coalitions. In groups of more than ten or twelve people, it becomes virtually impossible for all members to participate in a single conversation unless one person serves as moderator and facilitates the discussion. As shown in Figure 6.1, when the size of the group increases, the number of possible social interactions also increases.

Group Leadership

What role do leaders play in groups? Leaders are responsible for directing plans and activities so that the group completes its task or fulfils its goals. Primary groups generally have informal leader-

FIGURE 6.1 Growth of Possible Social Interaction Based on Group Size

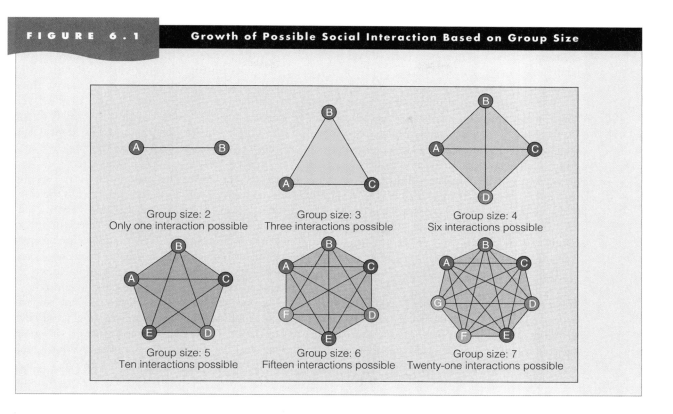

Group size: 2
Only one interaction possible

Group size: 3
Three interactions possible

Group size: 4
Six interactions possible

Group size: 5
Ten interactions possible

Group size: 6
Fifteen interactions possible

Group size: 7
Twenty-one interactions possible

ship. For example, most of us do not elect or appoint leaders in our own families. Various family members may assume a leadership role at various times or act as leaders for specific tasks. In traditional families, the father or eldest male is usually the leader. However, in today's more diverse families, leadership and power are more equally distributed, and power relationships may be quite different, as discussed in Chapter 15 ("Families and Intimate Relationships"). By comparison, leadership in secondary groups (such as colleges, governmental agencies, and corporations) involves a clearly defined chain of command with written responsibilities assigned to each position in the organizational structure.

LEADERSHIP FUNCTIONS Both primary and secondary groups have some type of leadership or positions that enable certain people to be leaders, or at least to wield power over others. From a functionalist perspective, if groups exist to meet the instrumental and expressive needs of their members, then leaders are responsible for helping the group meet those needs. *Instrumental leadership* is goal- or task-oriented; this type of leadership is most appropriate when the group's purpose is to complete a task or reach a particular goal. *Expressive leadership* provides emotional sup-

port for members; this type of leadership is most appropriate when the group is dealing with emotional issues, and harmony, solidarity, and high morale are needed. Both kinds of leadership are needed for groups to work effectively. Traditionally, instrumental and expressive leadership roles have been limited by gender socialization. Instrumental leadership has been linked with men, while expressive leadership has been linked with women. Social change in recent years has somewhat blurred the distinction between gender-specific leadership characteristics, but these outdated stereotypes have not completely disappeared (Basow, 1992).

LEADERSHIP STYLES Three major styles of leadership exist in groups: authoritarian, democratic, and laissez-faire. *Authoritarian leaders* make all major group decisions and assign tasks to members. These leaders focus on the instrumental tasks of the group and demand compliance from others. In times of crisis, such as a war or natural disaster, authoritarian leaders may be commended for their decisive actions. In other situations, however, they may be criticized for being dictatorial and for fostering intergroup hostility. By contrast, *democratic leaders* encourage group discussion and decision making through consensus building. These leaders may be praised for their expressive, supportive behaviour toward group members, but they also may be blamed for being indecisive in times of crisis.

Laissez-faire means "to leave alone." **Laissez-faire leaders are only minimally involved in decision making and encourage group members to make their own decisions**. On the one hand, laissez-faire leaders may be viewed positively by group members because they do not flaunt their power or position. On the other hand, a group that needs active leadership is not likely to find it with this style of leadership, which does not work vigorously to promote group goals (White and Lippitt, 1953, 1960).

Group Conformity

To what extent do groups exert a powerful influence in our lives? As discussed in Chapters 3 and 4, groups have a significant amount of influence over our values, attitudes, and behaviour. In order to gain and then retain our membership in groups, most of us are willing to exhibit a high level of conformity to the wishes of other group members. **Conformity is the process of maintaining or changing behaviour to comply with the norms established by a society, subculture, or other group.** We often experience powerful pressure from other group members to conform. In some situations, this pressure may be almost overwhelming.

In several studies (which would be impossible to conduct today for ethical reasons), researchers found that the pressure to conform may cause group members to say they see something that is contradictory to what they actually are seeing or to do something they otherwise would be unwilling to do. As we look at two of these studies, ask yourself what you might have done if you had been involved in this research.

ASCH'S RESEARCH Pressure to conform is especially strong in small groups in which members want to fit in with the group. In a series of experiments conducted by Solomon Asch (1955, 1956), the pressure toward group conformity was so great that participants were willing to contradict their own best judgment if the rest of the group disagreed with them.

One of Asch's experiments involved groups of undergraduate men (seven in each group) who allegedly were recruited for a study of visual perception. All of the men were seated in chairs.

However, the person in the sixth chair did not know that he was the only actual subject; all of the others were assisting the researcher. The participants first were shown a large card with a vertical line on it and then a second card with three vertical lines (see Figure 6.2). Each of the seven participants was asked to indicate which of the three lines on the second card was identical in length to the "standard line" on the first card.

In the first test with each group, all seven men selected the correct matching line. In the second trial, all seven still answered correctly. In the third trial, however, the subject became very uncomfortable when all of the others selected the incorrect line. The actual subject could not understand what was happening and became even more confused as the others continued to give incorrect responses on eleven out of the next fifteen trials.

If you had been in the position of the subject, how would you have responded? Would you have continued to give the correct answer, or would you have been swayed by the others? When Asch (1955) averaged the responses of the fifty actual subjects who participated in the study, he found that about 33 percent routinely chose to conform to the group by giving the same (incorrect) responses as Asch's assistants. Another 40 percent gave incorrect responses in about half of the trials. Although 25 percent always gave correct responses, even they felt very uneasy and "knew that something was wrong." In discussing the experiment afterwards, most of the subjects who gave incorrect responses indicated that they had known the answers were wrong but decided to go along with the group in order to avoid ridicule or ostracism. Figure 6.3 shows how group size was related to conformity.

In later studies, Asch found that if even a single assistant did not agree with the others, the subject was reassured by hearing someone else question the accuracy of incorrect responses and was much less likely to give a wrong answer himself.

One contribution of Asch's research is the dramatic way in which it calls our attention to the power that groups have to produce a certain type of conformity referred to as compliance. *Compliance* is the extent to which people say (or do) things so that they may gain the approval of other people. Certainly, Asch demonstrated that people will bow to social pressure in small-group settings. From a sociological perspective, however, the study was flawed because it involved deception about the purpose of the study and about the

FIGURE 6.2   Asch's Cards

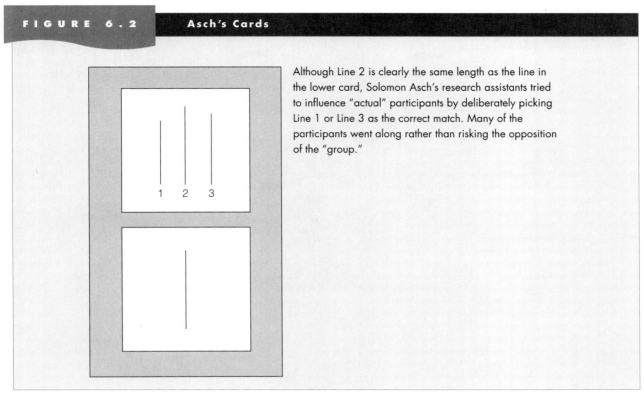

Although Line 2 is clearly the same length as the line in the lower card, Solomon Asch's research assistants tried to influence "actual" participants by deliberately picking Line 1 or Line 3 as the correct match. Many of the participants went along rather than risking the opposition of the "group."

Source: Asch, 1955.

role of individual group members. Moreover, the study included only male college students, thus making it impossible for us to generalize its findings to other populations, including women and people who were not undergraduates. Would Asch's conclusions have been the same if women had participated in the study? Would the same conclusions be reached if the study were conducted today? We cannot answer these questions with certainty, but the work of Solomon Asch and his student, Stanley Milgram, have had a lasting impact on social science perceptions about group conformity and obedience to authority.

MILGRAM'S RESEARCH How willing are we to do something because someone in a position of authority has told us to do it? How far are we willing to go in following the demands of that individual? Stanley Milgram (1963, 1974) conducted a series of controversial experiments to find answers to these questions about people's obedience to authority. *Obedience* is a form of compliance in which people follow direct orders from someone in a position of authority.

Milgram's subjects were men who had responded to an advertisement for participants in an

experiment. When the first (actual) subject arrived, he was told that the study concerned the effects of punishment on learning. After the second subject (an assistant of Milgram's) arrived, the two men were instructed to draw slips of paper from a hat to get their assignments as either the "teacher" or the "learner." Because the drawing was rigged, the actual subject always became the teacher, and the assistant the learner. Next, the learner was strapped into a chair with protruding electrodes that looked something like an electric chair. The teacher was placed in an adjoining room and given a realistic-looking but nonoperative shock generator. The "generator's" control panel showed levels that went from "Slight Shock" (15 volts) on the left, to "Intense Shock" (255 volts) in the middle, to "DANGER: SEVERE SHOCK" (375 volts), and finally "XXX" (450 volts) on the right.

The teacher was instructed to read aloud a pair of words and then repeat the first of the two words. At that time, the learner was supposed to respond with the second of the two words. If the learner could not provide the second word, the teacher was instructed to press the lever on the shock generator so that the learner would be pun-

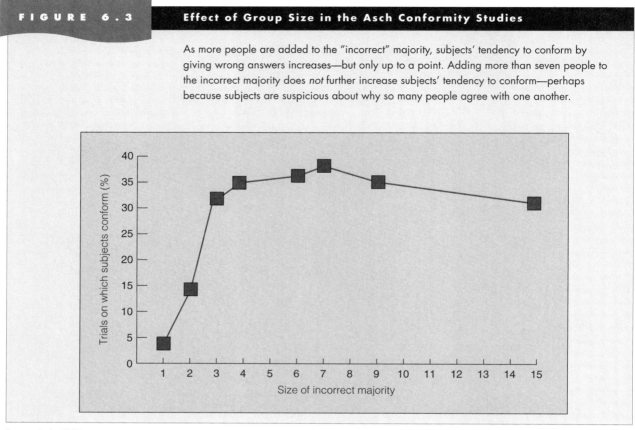

FIGURE 6.3 **Effect of Group Size in the Asch Conformity Studies**

As more people are added to the "incorrect" majority, subjects' tendency to conform by giving wrong answers increases—but only up to a point. Adding more than seven people to the incorrect majority does *not* further increase subjects' tendency to conform—perhaps because subjects are suspicious about why so many people agree with one another.

Source: Asch, 1955.

ished for forgetting the word. Each time the learner gave an incorrect response, the teacher was supposed to increase the shock level by 15 volts. The alleged purpose of the shock was to determine if punishment improves a person's memory.

What was the maximum level of shock that a "teacher" was willing to inflict on a "learner"? The learner had been instructed (in advance) to beat on the wall between himself and the teacher as the experiment continued, pretending that he was in intense pain. The teacher was told that the shocks might be "extremely painful" but that they would cause no permanent damage. At about 300 volts, when the learner quit responding at all to questions, the teacher often turned to the experimenter to see what he should do next. When the experimenter indicated that the teacher should give increasingly painful shocks, 65 percent of them administered shocks all the way up to the "XXX" (450-volt) level (see Figure 6.4). By this point in the process, the teachers frequently were sweating, stuttering, or biting on their lip. According to Milgram, the teachers (who were

free to leave whenever they wanted to) continued in the experiment because they were being given directions by a person in a position of authority (a university scientist wearing a white coat).

What can we learn from Milgram's study? The study provides evidence that obedience to authority may be more common than most of us would like to believe. None of the "teachers" challenged the process before they had applied 300 volts. Almost two-thirds went all the way to what could have been a deadly jolt of electricity if the shock generator had been real. For many years, Milgram's findings were found to be consistent in a number of different settings and with variations in the research design (Miller, 1986).

This research once again raises some questions originally posed in Chapter 2 concerning research ethics. As was true of Asch's research, Milgram's subjects were deceived about the nature of the study in which they were being asked to participate. Many of them found the experiment extremely stressful. Such conditions cannot be ignored by social scientists because subjects may receive lasting emotional scars from such research.

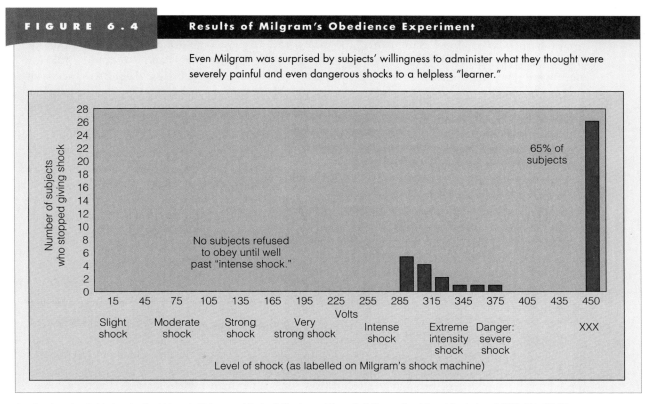

FIGURE 6.4 **Results of Milgram's Obedience Experiment**

Even Milgram was surprised by subjects' willingness to administer what they thought were severely painful and even dangerous shocks to a helpless "learner."

Graph is based on Table 2 in Stanley Milgram's "Behavioural Study of Obedience," *Journal of Abnormal and Social Psychology* (1963), Vol. 67, No. 4, p. 376. Used by permission.

It would be virtually impossible today to obtain permission to replicate this experiment in a university setting.

GROUP CONFORMITY AND SEXUAL HARASSMENT

Psychologist John Pryor (KCET, 1992) has conducted behavioural experiments on university campuses to examine the social dynamics of harassment. In one of his studies, a graduate student (who actually was a member of the research team) led research subjects to believe that they would be training undergraduate women to use a computer. The actual purpose of the experiment was to observe whether the trainers (subjects) would harass the women if given the opportunity and encouraged to do so. By design, the graduate student purposely harassed the women (who also were part of the research team), setting an example for the subjects to follow.

Pryor found that when the "trainers" were led to believe that sexual harassment was condoned and then were left alone with the women, they took full advantage of the situation in 90 percent of the experiments. Shannon Hofman, one of the

women who participated as a member of the research team, felt vulnerable because of the permissive environment created by the men in charge:

> It was very uncomfortable for me. I realized that had it been out of the experimental setting that, as a woman, I would have been very nervous with someone that close to me and reaching around me. So it kind of made me feel a little bit powerless as far as that goes because there was nothing I could do about it. But I also realized that in a business setting, if this person really was my boss, that it would be harder for me to send out the negative signals or whatever to try to fend off that type of thing. (KCET, 1992)

This research suggests a relationship between group conformity and harassment. Behaviour such as sexual harassment or racism is more likely to occur when it is encouraged (or at least not actively discouraged) by others. When people think they can get away with it, they are more likely to engage in such behaviour.

GROUPTHINK As we have seen, individuals often respond differently in a group context than they might if they were alone. Social psychologist Irving Janis (1972, 1989) examined group decision making among political experts and found that major blunders may be attributed to pressure toward group conformity. To describe this phenomenon, he coined the term **groupthink**—**the process by which members of a cohesive group arrive at a decision that many individual members privately believe is unwise.** Why not speak up at the time? Members usually want to be "team players." They may not want to be the ones who undermine the group's consensus or who challenge the group's leaders. Consequently, members often limit or withhold their opinions and focus on consensus rather than on exploring all of the options and determining the best course of action. Figure 6.5 summarizes the dynamics and results of groupthink.

The tragic 1986 launch of the space shuttle *Challenger*, which exploded 73 seconds into its flight, killing all seven crew members, has been cited as an example of groupthink. On the day preceding the launch, engineers at the company responsible for designing and manufacturing the shuttle's rocket boosters became concerned that freezing temperatures at the launch site would interfere with the proper functioning of the O-ring seals in the boosters. But when they expressed their misgivings, they were overruled by higher-level officials at the company and with NASA (the government agency that administers the U.S. space program), where executives were impatient as a result of earlier delays. A presidential commission that investigated the tragedy concluded that neither the manufacturer nor NASA responded adequately to warnings about the seals (Lippa, 1994).

You may wonder why people agreed to the launch despite their safety concerns. After all, it is one thing to doubt your judgment about the length of a line as in the Asch experiments and quite another to send seven people to their deaths. The engineers closest to the situation were almost unanimous in opposing the launch. However, the decision was ultimately made by NASA and contractor managers who were more focused on the schedule than on safety concerns. NASA managers were under great pressure to keep the shuttle flights on schedule because they feared congressional budget cuts. When the contractor suggested that the launch be delayed until air temperatures were above 53°F, NASA man-

agers responded angrily. One said "My God ... when do you want me to launch, next April?" (President's Commission, 1986:96). Another said, "I'm appalled by your recommendation" (President's Commission, 1986:94). Faced with this pressure, the contractor, who was about to begin negotiating a new billion-dollar agreement with NASA, had second thoughts. Senior managers overruled the recommendations of their engineers and recommended launch. NASA managers and the contractor managers were prepared to risk other people's lives in order to accomplish their own bureaucratic goals.

For a slightly different view of the relationship between bureaucracies and accidents such as the *Challenger* explosion, see Box 6.2.

FORMAL ORGANIZATIONS

Over the past century, the number of formal organizations has increased dramatically in Canada and other industrialized nations. Everyday life previously was centred in small, informal, primary groups, such as the family and the village. With the advent of industrialization and urbanization (as discussed in Chapter 1), people's lives became increasingly dominated by large, formal, secondary organizations. A *formal organization*, you will recall, is a highly structured secondary group formed for the purpose of achieving specific goals in the most efficient manner. Formal organizations (such as corporations, schools, and government agencies) usually keep their basic structure for many years in order to meet their specific goals.

Types of Formal Organizations

We join some organizations voluntarily and others out of necessity. Sociologist Amitai Etzioni (1975) classified formal organizations into three categories—normative, coercive, and utilitarian—based on the nature of membership in each.

NORMATIVE ORGANIZATIONS We voluntarily join normative organizations when we want to pursue some common interest or gain personal satisfaction or prestige from being a member. Voluntary membership is one of the central features of normative associations. A widely diverse range of normative organizations exists in Canada. These

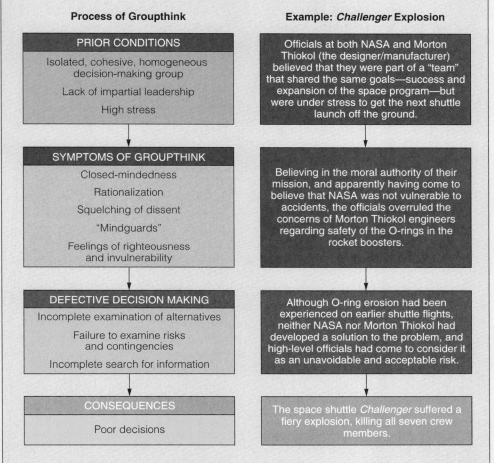

FIGURE 6.5 Janis's Description of Groupthink

In Janis's model, prior conditions such as a highly homogeneous group with committed leadership can lead to potentially disastrous "groupthink," which short-circuits careful and impartial deliberation. Events leading up to the tragic 1986 launch of the space shuttle *Challenger* have been cited as an example of this process.

Process of Groupthink

PRIOR CONDITIONS
Isolated, cohesive, homogeneous decision-making group
Lack of impartial leadership
High stress

SYMPTOMS OF GROUPTHINK
Closed-mindedness
Rationalization
Squelching of dissent
"Mindguards"
Feelings of righteousness and invulnerability

DEFECTIVE DECISION MAKING
Incomplete examination of alternatives
Failure to examine risks and contingencies
Incomplete search for information

CONSEQUENCES
Poor decisions

Example: *Challenger* Explosion

Officials at both NASA and Morton Thiokol (the designer/manufacturer) believed that they were part of a "team" that shared the same goals—success and expansion of the space program—but were under stress to get the next shuttle launch off the ground.

Believing in the moral authority of their mission, and apparently having come to believe that NASA was not vulnerable to accidents, the officials overruled the concerns of Morton Thiokol engineers regarding safety of the O-rings in the rocket boosters.

Although O-ring erosion had been experienced on earlier shuttle flights, neither NASA nor Morton Thiokol had developed a solution to the problem, and high-level officials had come to consider it as an unavoidable and acceptable risk.

The space shuttle *Challenger* suffered a fiery explosion, killing all seven crew members.

From *Introduction to Social Psychology*, 2nd ed., by R.A. Lippa. © 1994. Reprinted with permission of Wadsworth Publishing, a division of International Thomson Publishing (fax 800-730-2215).

include political parties, activist groups, religious organizations, and educational associations.

People join normative organizations for a number of reasons, some of which may be to advance a particular cause the group represents; to gain a sense of purpose and identity; or to promote social change. Many women have joined together to form women's interest groups across the country and were influential in establishing what was formerly called the National Action Committee on the Status of Women. Anti-racist coalitions are another example of an organization that fights for a particular cause, in this case to eradicate racism. Members of the environmental movement have formed various organizations such as Greenpeace and the Sierra Club to support their cause. Normative organizations have also formed to address such issues as gay rights, nuclear disarmament, animal testing, endangered species, and ozone depletion.

There are several well-known humanitarian voluntary organizations in Canada, including the Red Cross, Easter Seals, Shriners, Big Brothers and Big Sisters, and the Canadian Cancer Society.

BOX 6.2   BUREAUCRACY AND THE LAW

THE CASE OF "NORMAL ACCIDENTS"

In July 1998, relatives of the 26 men killed in the Westray mine disaster in 1992 were outraged at learning that the mine managers who they felt were responsible for the disaster would not be brought to trial. The Crown prosecutor concluded that charges should not be laid, because experts could not determine the exact cause of the mine explosion. This made it highly unlikely that the managers could be convicted of negligence. Those affected by tragedies such as Westray typically want those responsible to be brought to justice and to pay for their mistakes. However, these disasters usually occur in a bureaucratic framework that makes it almost impossible to hold anyone accountable.

Organizational sociologist Charles Perrow has coined the term "normal accident" to describe these situations. Perrow's research was motivated by his analysis of the nearly catastrophic failure of the Three Mile Island nuclear power plant in Pennsylvania. He concluded that high-risk systems have special characteristics that make accidents in them inevitable or "normal." These systems are so complex that multiple interactions of failures will occur, and these will sometimes have tragic consequences. Our bureaucracies make these sophisticated technologies possible, but they are not always able to manage these technologies safely. This does not mean that such accidents will be common, but that some will inevitably occur.

Perrow uses the analogy of a person who has an appointment for an important job interview. The person's roommate has left the coffee pot on a hot burner and cracked it. The person finds another pot, but this distraction means a delay that leaves her running a bit late. When she gets to her car, she finds that in her haste to make up for the lost time she has left her car keys—and the apartment key—in the apartment. A spare key, hidden in the hallway for emergencies, was lent to a friend the day before and hasn't been returned. A neighbour would normally lend her his car, but his car's generator is broken and is in the garage for

repair. Bus drivers went on strike that morning, and because of the strike it is impossible to get a cab quickly enough to arrive at the interview on time. What is responsible for the person missing the interview? The real answer to this is the complexity of the system. Each of the failures was trivial, but their combined effect was to hurt the person's chance of getting the job. Even though backup plans were available, they failed as well. The incident is explained by the interaction of multiple failures. Perrow concluded that we have accidents like Three Mile Island "because we have built an industrial society that has some parts, like industrial plants or military adventures, that have highly interactive and tightly coupled units. Unfortunately, some of these have high potential for catastrophic accidents" (1984:8). While better organization can help make things safer, our ability to organize cannot match the complexity of some of the things we have decided to organize.

The *Challenger* explosion discussed earlier in this chapter is an example of a normal accident. Author and pilot William Langewiesche (1998) has also used Perrow's framework to analyze the 1996 crash of a ValuJet DC-9, in which the plane caught fire in the air and crashed into the Florida Everglades, killing all 110 people on board. The actual cause of the accident was relatively simple to determine. Some chemical oxygen generators caught fire in a cargo compartment that had no fire detectors or extinguishers, and this fire led to the crash. However, the question of why the fire occurred in the first place is much more complex.

The oxygen generators belonged to ValuJet and had just been removed from another ValuJet aircraft that was being overhauled by a company called Sabre Tech. Sabre Tech was using a number of mechanics who had been hired on temporary contracts to handle a heavy workload and who were under great pressure to finish the overhaul on time. ValuJet gave Sabre Tech explicit instructions about the removal of the oxygen generators. However, when the mechanics removed the generators

BOX 6.2

CONTINUED

they did not place plastic caps over the firing pins. The work card used to guide the removal may have been partially at fault. It read "If generator has not been expended, install shipping cap on firing pin." The distinction between generators that had *expired*—which was why they were being removed—and those that were *not expended* may have been difficult for the mechanics to make. Rushing to complete the required paperwork at the end of the job, two mechanics signed that the proper work had been done. Several levels of inspectors and supervisors also certified that the caps had been installed.

Rather than being disposed of, the five boxes of generators sat around Sabre Tech's hangar for several weeks. A shipping clerk was told to clean up the area and decided to pack the boxes for shipping and send them to ValuJet headquarters. The boxes were labelled "Oxy Canisters 'Empty'" and delivered to the ValuJet flight. The ramp agent accepted the material even though ValuJet was not licensed to carry hazardous materials. The co-pilot also accepted the cargo and helped the ramp agent stack the boxes in the forward hold along with some extra tires. The boxes were not secured and movement of the boxes may have started the fire.

Several months before the accident, inspectors for the Federal Aviation Authority (FAA) became concerned about safety and maintenance problems at ValuJet and recommended that the airline be grounded and recertified. While intensive inspections continued, the FAA did not restrict ValuJet's operations. Some critics have maintained that the FAA did not take its safety mandate seriously enough and was more concerned with supporting the airline industry.

In the aftermath of the crash, the two mechanics who signed the original forms were fired; Sabre Tech lost a great deal of business; ValuJet was grounded for several months; and two senior FAA administrators lost their jobs.

Determining exactly who was to blame for the crash is extremely difficult when errors made at different levels kept interacting with other errors.

A case such as this creates dilemmas for the law. Criminal law deals only with individual responsibility, and it is very difficult to prove guilt beyond a reasonable doubt when individuals are working with complex technology within bureaucratic organizational structures. In the ValuJet case, who is responsible? The mechanics who didn't install the safety caps or discard the generators? Their supervisors who didn't train the mechanics, provide safety caps, or inspect the work? The engineers who wrote their instructions and orders in "engineer-speak"? The shipping clerk who packed the generators without knowing their danger? The ramp agent and co-pilot who accepted the cargo and loaded it improperly? The aircraft manufacturer who didn't install a fire extinguisher in the cargo hold? The airline who contracted maintenance to the lowest bidder? Or the aviation regulators who didn't properly regulate the process?

Laws based on individual actions have little to do with the reality of contemporary bureaucracy. The mechanics could not be held responsible when

> the falsification they committed was part of a larger deception—the creation of an entire pretend reality that includes unworkable chains of command, unlearnable training programs, unreadable manuals, and the fiction of regulations, checks, and controls ... [and in which] systems work in principle, and usually in practice as well, but the two may have little to do with each other. Paperwork floats free of the ground and obscures the murky workplaces where, in the confusion of real life, system accidents are born. (Langewiesche 1998:10)

Sources: Perrow, 1984; Langewiesche, 1998.

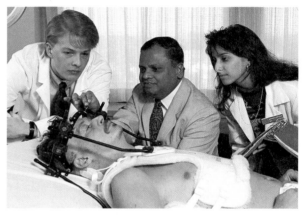

Normative organizations rely on volunteers to fulfil their goals; these volunteers (left) make Red Cross work possible in Honduras, Central America. Coercive organizations rely on involuntary recruitment; these young men (upper right) were remanded to this juvenile correctional centre (a total institution). Utilitarian organizations provide material rewards to participants; in teaching hospitals such as this (lower right), physicians, medical students, and patients all hope they may benefit from involvement with the organization.

Members volunteer their time for the good of helping others. For example, the Shriners fund twenty-two nonprofit hospitals across North America, including three for young burn victims.

Since participation in the organization is voluntary, few formal control mechanisms exist for enforcing norms on members. As a result, people tend to change affiliations rather frequently. They may change groups when personal objectives have been fulfilled or when other groups might better meet their individual needs.

COERCIVE ORGANIZATIONS Unlike normative organizations, people do not voluntarily become members of *coercive organizations*—associations people are forced to join. Total institutions, such as boot camps, prisons, and some mental hospitals, are examples of coercive organizations. As discussed in Chapter 4, the assumed goal of total institu-

tions is to resocialize people through incarceration. These environments are characterized by restrictive barriers (such as locks, bars, and security guards) that make it impossible for people to leave freely. When people leave without being officially dismissed, their exit is referred to as an "escape."

UTILITARIAN ORGANIZATIONS We voluntarily join *utilitarian organizations* when they can provide us with a material reward we seek. To make a living or earn a university degree, we must participate in organizations that can provide us these opportunities. Although we have some choice regarding where we work or attend school, utilitarian organizations are not always completely voluntary. For example, most people must continue to work even if the conditions of their employment are less than ideal.

Although telephone- and computer-based procedures have streamlined the registration process at many schools, for many students registration exemplifies the worst aspects of academic bureaucracy. Yet students and other members of the academic community depend upon the "bureaucracy" to establish and administer procedures that enable the complex system of the university to operate smoothly.

Bureaucracies

The bureaucratic model of organization remains the most universal organizational form in government, business, education, and religion. A *bureaucracy* **is an organizational model characterized by a hierarchy of authority, a clear division of labour, explicit rules and procedures, and impersonality in personnel matters.**

When we think of a bureaucracy, we may think of "buck-passing," such as occurs when we are directed from one office to the next without receiving an answer to our question or a solution to our problem. We also may view a bureaucracy in terms of "red tape" because of the situations in which there is so much paperwork and so many incomprehensible rules that no one really understands what to do. However, the bureaucracy originally was not intended to be this way; it was seen as a way to make organizations *more* productive and efficient.

As noted in Chapter 1, German sociologist Max Weber (1968/1922) was interested in the historical trend toward bureaucratization that accelerated during the Industrial Revolution. To Weber, the bureaucracy was the most "rational" and efficient means of attaining organizational goals because it contributed to coordination and control. According to Weber, *rationality* **is the process by which traditional methods of social organization, characterized by informality and spontaneity, gradually are replaced by efficiently administered formal rules and procedures.** It can

be seen in all aspects of our lives, from small colleges with perhaps a thousand students to multinational corporations employing many thousands of workers worldwide.

WHY BUREAUCRACY? While much of the rest of this chapter focuses on how bureaucracies work, it is also important to understand why they exist. The simple answer to this question is, they exist because organizations grew too large to be managed in any other way. However, large organizations existed for thousands of years before the birth of bureaucracy, so we must also consider social conditions to explain why the modern bureaucratic form of social organization arose in the nineteenth century in Europe and North America.

Sociologist Rodney Stark (1998) has provided two examples of the development of modern bureaucracies. The first is the bureaucratization of the Prussian army. Even very large armies had traditionally been controlled by a single commander. However, armies had grown so large by the nineteenth century that even a brilliant general like Napoleon was unable to directly control the actions of 600,000 troops. The scale of battle was too large for one man to manage, but the structure of armies in Napoleon's time did not allow for the effective delegation of the commander's authority. Napoleon saw his army devastated in Russia, where he lost over 400,000 men, and met his final defeat at Waterloo in 1815. The lessons of Napoleon's defeat were not lost on the Prussians.

Field Marshal Helmuth von Moltke, who took command of the Prussian army in 1857, built an army based on new organizational principles. Von Moltke developed a General Staff made up of carefully selected and highly trained officers who could operate independently in battle while still following their commander's wishes. He also borrowed an idea from the Duke of Wellington, who had defeated Napoleon at Waterloo. Wellington had divided his army into several standard-sized "divisions" that could be detached to fight as self-sufficient units. Von Moltke placed these divisions under the command of his staff officers. Prussia's quick defeat of the more experienced French army in the 1871 Franco-Prussian War validated his methods, which were quickly adopted by other nations. Von Moltke's innovations still guide contemporary armies and have also influenced the development of industrial bureaucracies.

Stark's second example was one of the pioneering corporate bureaucracies, the meat-packing empire established by Gustavus Swift. In the 1870s, the American meat industry was composed of small, local firms, and getting the meat to market was a very difficult and inefficient process. The challenge faced by wholesale butchers like Swift was that most Americans lived in the East, while most of the livestock was produced on the Great Plains. Swift came up with the idea of shipping meat in the then newly invented refrigerated railroad cars. This required that he build refrigerated storage facilities. He also needed massive packing plants to kill and process the meat. To sell the product, he set up sales and distribution systems. Swift did not raise cattle, he purchased them from ranchers, but he controlled each of the steps between purchase of the live cattle and the production of the packaged meat that would be bought by the consumer. Each step was carried out by a different division of the company. Unlike von Moltke's military divisions that were essentially complete armies, Swift's corporate divisions were based on different functions like meat packing, shipping, and sales. Each was headed by a manager who reported to a centralized corporate headquarters that was responsible for coordinating their activities. Swift's organizational model was highly successful, and his business empire is still a powerful force in the food industry. Several decades later, Henry Ford took Swift's organizational model a step further by creating the moving automobile assembly line, which has been the pattern for industrial production for nearly a hundred years (see Chapter 13, "The Economy and Work").

It seems clear that a bureaucratic structure is the key to effectively managing organizations that are large in size and scope. We can turn to the work of Max Weber to explain why the modern bureaucracy did not develop until the nineteenth century. Weber suggested that the growth of the modern bureaucracy required both cultural and structural changes that did not occur until the nineteenth century.

The cultural change was the rejection of *traditional authority* and the acceptance of *rational-legal authority* as the basis of conduct. This means that people were less willing to accept rules based on tradition, and more willing to grant legitimacy to a set of rules intended to achieve certain ends (Weber, 1947). Weber's influential work on the relationship between the rise of Protestantism and the development of capitalism (Weber, 1976) analyzes the factors that led to this change.

The structural change that facilitated the modern bureaucracy was the shift to an economic system in which people were forced to work for somebody else (Perrow, 1986). The social conditions for factory bureaucracies were established during the Industrial Revolution when peasants were forced off the farms. The former peasants became the first large labour pool for the factories, as they had no alternative but to work for whatever the owners would pay them. The system of wage employment gave the profits from the workers' labour to the factory owner while the workers were paid only a subsistence wage. This cheap labour provided a tremendous incentive for the factory owners to expand their enterprises. Owners used the capital their factories generated to mechanize the factories and they also developed the systems of specialization and standardization that most efficiently achieved the goals of productivity and profitability. Of course, breaking down production into specialized tasks required managers to coordinate activities, so the factories quickly became hierarchical organizations. The success of the factory bureaucracy was important because it encouraged other organizations to adopt the same principles. The bureaucratic form quickly spread to governments, schools, churches, and farms. Even today, we find pressure for other organizations to follow the lead of industry. Governments are continually urged to become more "business-like," and universities face pressure to become more efficient and to meet the specialized needs of industry rather than provide students with a broader education.

IDEAL CHARACTERISTICS OF BUREAUCRACY   In his study of bureaucracies, Weber relied on an ideal-type analysis, which he adapted from the field of economics. An *ideal type* **is an abstract model that describes the recurring characteristics of some phenomenon** (such as bureaucracy). Weber set forth several ideal-type characteristics of bureaucratic organizations. Although real bureaucracies often do not feature these ideal characteristics, Weber's model highlights the organizational efficiency and productivity that bureaucracies strive for.

Division of Labour   Bureaucratic organizations are characterized by specialization, and each member has a specific status with certain assigned tasks to fulfil. This division of labour requires the employment of specialized experts who are responsible for the effective performance of their duties.

In a university, for example, a distinct division of labour exists between the faculty and the administration. Faculty members primarily are responsible for teaching students and conducting research. Upper-level administrators are responsible for external relations with business and community leaders, fund-raising activities, and internal governance (such as control of the budget, allocation of space, and appointments of deans, department heads, and faculty), while lower-level administrators are responsible for the day-to-day operations of the school.

Hierarchy of Authority   In the sense that Weber described hierarchy of authority, or chain of command, it includes each lower office being under the control and supervision of a higher one. Charles Perrow (1986) has noted that all groups with a division of labour are hierarchically structured. Although the chain of command is not always followed, "in a crunch, the chain is there for those higher up to use it." Authority that is distributed hierarchically takes the form of a pyramid. Those few individuals at the top have more power and exercise more control than do the many at the lower levels. Hierarchy inevitably influences social interaction. Those who are lower in the hierarchy report to (and often take orders from) those above them in the organizational pyramid. Persons at the upper levels are responsible not only for their own actions but also for those of the individuals they supervise. Hierarchy has been described as a graded system of interpersonal relationships, a society of unequals in which

scarce rewards become even more scarce further down the hierarchy (Presthus, 1978).

In a university, student–faculty relationships are based on both hierarchical and professional authority patterns. Professors have power based on their academic credentials and knowledge. Faculty members also have some degree of academic freedom and self-governance. At the same time, they are hierarchically arranged within the faculty in ranks of instructor, assistant professor, associate professor, and full professor. In the university's vertical chain of command, they also have a position. Suppose that a student has a complaint about an instructor. The chain of command in most universities would require that the student first speak with the department head or division chair, then to the dean of the faculty, and, occasionally, even to the vice president of academic affairs, provost, or president.

Rules and Regulations   Weber asserted that rules and regulations establish authority within an organization. These rules typically are standardized and provided to members in a written format. In theory, written rules and regulations offer clear-cut standards for determining satisfactory performance. They also provide continuity so that each new member does not have to reinvent the necessary rules and regulations.

In higher education, student handbooks, catalogues, and course syllabi provide students with information about the school's rules, regulations, and academic expectations. Faculty and administrators also are provided with policy and procedures manuals that spell out their rights and obligations.

Qualification-Based Employment   Bureaucracies hire staff members and professional employees based on specific qualifications. Favouritism, family connections, and other subjective factors not relevant to organizational efficiency are not acceptable criteria for employment. Individual performance is evaluated against specific standards, and promotions are based on merit as spelled out in personnel policies.

In universities, faculty members and administrators are hired based on their academic background and technical qualifications. Many faculty members in universities have tenure or other legal guarantees against arbitrary dismissal.

Impersonality   A detached approach should prevail toward clients so that personal feelings do not interfere with organizational decisions. Officials must interact with subordinates based on their official status, not on their personal feelings about them.

Impersonality can be seen in standardization of test scores for admission to graduate and professional schools across North America, and to undergraduate programs in the United States. Standardized examinations for graduate and professional schools include the Graduate Records Exam (GRE), Law School Admission Test (LSAT), and the Medical College Admission Test (MCAT). These criteria supposedly are impartially applied, and individuals are admitted based on their ability to perform in a given academic setting. However, questions may have a class, ethnic, or gender bias, and thus make it harder for some to achieve a high score.

INFORMAL STRUCTURE IN BUREAUCRACIES

As researchers began to study how bureaucracies really operated, they found that these organizations did not always operate according to Weber's ideal principles. When we look at an organizational chart, we can easily see the official, formal structure of a bureaucracy. However, bureaucracies are more than just organization charts and rulebooks. Organizations are made up of people and people do not exist just to serve organizational goals. They bring with them their concerns about things like careers, friendships, and emotions, and these concerns lead to patterns of activities and interactions that cannot be accounted for by an organizational chart and formal rules. In addition to its formal structure, every bureaucracy has an informal structure, which has been called "bureaucracy's other face" (Page, 1946).

An organization's *informal structure* is composed of those aspects of participants' day-to-day activities and interactions that ignore, bypass, or do not correspond with the official rules and procedures of the bureaucracy. An example is an informal "grapevine" that spreads information (with varying degrees of accuracy) much faster than do official channels of communication, which tend to be slow and unresponsive. The informal structure also has been referred to as *work culture* and includes the ideology and practices of workers on the job. It is the "informal, customary values and rules [that] mediate the formal authority structure of the workplace and distance workers from its impact" (Benson, 1983:185). Workers create this work culture in order to confront, resist, or adapt to the con-straints of their jobs, as well as to guide and interpret social relations on the job (Zavella, 1987).

HAWTHORNE STUDIES AND INFORMAL NETWORKS

The existence of informal networks was first established by researchers in the Hawthorne studies, which first made social scientists aware of the effect of informal networks on workers' productivity.

In this particular study, researchers observed fourteen men in the "bank wiring room" who were responsible for making parts of switches for telephone equipment. Although management had offered financial incentives to encourage the men to work harder, the men persisted in working according to their own informal rules and sanctions. For example, they tended to work rapidly in the morning and ease off in the afternoon. They frequently stopped their own work to help another person who had fallen behind. When they got bored, they swapped tasks so that their work was more varied. They played games and made bets on the horse races and on baseball. Two competing cliques formed in the room, each with its own separate games and activities.

Why did these men insist on lagging behind even when they had been offered financial incentives to work harder? Perhaps they feared that the required productivity levels would increase if they showed that they could do more. Some of them also may have feared that they would lose their jobs if the work was finished more rapidly. One fact stood out in the study: The men's productivity level was clearly related to the pressure they received from other members of their informal networks. Those who worked too hard were called "speed kings" and "rate busters"; individuals who worked too slowly were referred to as "chiselers." Those who broke the informal norm against telling a supervisor about someone else's shortcomings were called "squealers." Negative sanctions in the form of "binging" (striking a person on the shoulder) made the workers want to adhere to the informal norms of their clique. Ultimately, the level of productivity was determined by the workers' informal networks, not by the levels set by management (Roethlisberger and Dickson, 1939; Blau and Meyer, 1987).

POSITIVE AND NEGATIVE ASPECTS OF INFORMAL STRUCTURE

Is informal structure good or bad? Should it be controlled or encouraged? Two schools of thought have emerged with regard to these questions. One approach emphasizes control (or eradication) of informal groups; the other suggests that they should be nurtured. Traditional management theories are based on the assumption that people basically are lazy and motivated by greed. Consequently, informal groups must be controlled (or eliminated) in order to ensure greater worker productivity. Proponents of this view cite the bank wiring room study as an example of the importance of controlling informal networks.

By contrast, the other school of thought asserts that people are capable of cooperation. Thus, organizations should foster informal groups that permit people to work more efficiently toward organizational goals. Chester Barnard (1938), an early organizational theorist, focused on the functional aspects of informal groups. He suggested that organizations are cooperative systems in which informal groups "oil the wheels" by providing understanding and motivation for participants. In other words, informal networks serve as a means of communication and cohesion among individuals, as well as protecting the integrity of the individual (Barnard, 1938; Perrow, 1986).

The *human relations approach*, which is strongly influenced by Barnard's model, views informal networks as a type of adaptive behaviour workers engage in because they experience a lack of congruence between their own needs and the demands of the organization (Argyris, 1960). Organizations typically demand dependent, child-like behaviour from their members and strive to thwart the members' ability to grow and achieve "maturity" (Argyris, 1962). At the same time, members have their own needs to grow and mature. Informal networks help workers to fill this void. Large organizations would be unable to function without strong informal norms and relations among participants (Blau and Meyer, 1987).

More recent studies have confirmed the importance of informal networks in bureaucracies. While some scholars have argued that women and visible minorities receive fairer treatment in larger bureaucracies than they do in smaller organizations, others have stressed that they may be categorically excluded from networks that are important for survival and advancement in the organization (Kanter, 1977; South et al., 1982; Benokraitis and Feagin, 1986; Feagin, 1991). A female firefighter describes how detrimental, and even hazardous, it is for workers to be excluded from such informal networks because of ethnicity, gender, or other attributes:

Sociologists have found that women in law enforcement are less likely than men to be included in informal networks and more likely to be harassed on the job. Are these two factors related? What steps could be taken to reduce the problems of harassment and lack of networks?

I had sort of a "Pollyanna" view of how long it would take before women were really accepted in these nontraditional, very male-dominated jobs [such as being a firefighter]. One always thinks that once I and the other women prove that we can do the job well, people will just accept us and we'll all fit in … [However,] I went to a firehouse where the men refused to eat with me. They would not talk to me. On one occasion my protective gear had been tampered with. It was always a big question as to whether in fact you have anyone there to back you up when you needed them. (KCET, 1992)

White women and visible minorities who are employed in positions traditionally held by white men (such as firefighters, police officers, and factory workers) often experience categoric exclusion from the informal structure. Not only do they lack an informal network to "grease the wheels," they also may be harassed and endangered by their co-workers. In sum, the informal structure is critical for employees—whether they are allowed to participate in it or not.

Shortcomings of Bureaucracies

As noted previously, Weber's description of bureaucracy was intentionally an abstract, idealized model of a rationally organized institution. However, the very characteristics that make up this "rational" model have a dark side that frequently has given this type of organization a bad name (see Figure 6.6). Three of the major problems of bureaucracies are (1) inefficiency and rigidity, (2) resistance to change, and (3) perpetuation of ethnic, class, and gender inequalities (see Blau and Meyer, 1987).

INEFFICIENCY AND RIGIDITY Bureaucracies experience inefficiency and rigidity at both the upper and lower levels of the organization. The self-protective behaviour of officials at the top may render the organization inefficient. One type of self-protective behaviour is the monopolization of information in order to maintain control over subordinates and outsiders. Information is a valuable commodity in organizations. Budgets and long-range plans theoretically are based on relevant information, and decisions are made based on the best available data. However, those in positions of authority guard information because it is a source of power for them—others cannot "second-guess" their decisions without access to relevant (and often "confidential") information (Blau and Meyer, 1987).

This information blockage is intensified by the hierarchical arrangement of officials and workers. While those at the top tend to use their power and authority to monopolize information, they also fail to communicate with workers at the lower levels. As a result, they often are unaware of potential problems facing the organization and of high levels of worker frustration. Meanwhile, those at the bottom of the structure hide their mistakes from supervisors, a practice that ultimately may result in disaster for the organization.

Policies and procedures also contribute to inefficiency and rigidity. Sociologists Peter M. Blau and Marshall W. Meyer (1987) have suggested that bureaucratic regulations are similar to bridges and buildings in that they are designed to withstand far greater stresses than they will ever experience. Accordingly, bureaucratic regulations are written in far greater detail than is necessary, in order to ensure that almost all conceivable situations are covered. *Goal displacement* **occurs when the rules become an end in themselves rather than a means to an end, and organizational survival becomes more important than achievement of goals** (Merton, 1968). Administrators tend to overconform to the rules because their expertise is knowledge of the regulations, and they are paid to enforce them. Officials are most likely to emphasize rules and procedures when they fear that they may lose their jobs or a "spoils system" that benefits them. They also fear

that if they bend the rules for one person, they may be accused of violating the norm of impersonality and engaging in favouritism (Blau and Meyer, 1987).

Bureaucrats may also be inflexible because they fear criticism or liability if they do not follow the rules closely. In the case of Kenneth Payne, the aspiring teacher you read about at the beginning of this chapter, bureaucrats were afraid to waive the need for fingerprints because they were wary of public concern about the possibility of sexual offenders working in the schools. Even though it made no sense to demand fingerprints from a man who had none, and even though Mr. Payne offered other ways of demonstrating he did not have a criminal record, bureaucrats were not willing to bend the rules to enable him to teach. These bureaucrats were also able to avoid taking responsibility for their stupid decision by saying that they were "just following the rules." Mistakes can be blamed on the bureaucracy rather than on the individuals who run it.

Inefficiency and rigidity occur at the lower levels of the organization as well. Workers often engage in ritualism; that is, they become most concerned with "going through the motions" and "following the rules." According to Robert Merton (1968), the term **bureaucratic personality describes those workers who are more concerned with following correct procedures than they are with getting the job done correctly.** Such workers usually are able to handle routine situations effectively but frequently are incapable of handling a unique problem or an emergency. Thorstein Veblen (1967/1899) used the term *trained incapacity* to characterize situations in which workers have become so highly specialized, or have been given such fragmented jobs to do, that they are unable to come up with creative solutions to problems. Workers who have reached this point also tend to experience bureaucratic alienation—they really do not care what is happening around them.

Sociologists have extensively analyzed the effects of bureaucracy on workers. While some may become alienated, others may lose any identity apart from the organization. Sociologist William H. Whyte, Jr. (1957) coined the term *organization man* to identify an individual whose life is controlled by the corporation. C. Wright Mills (1959a) suggested that employees become "cheerful robots" when they are controlled by an organization. Other scholars have argued that most workers do not reach these extremes.

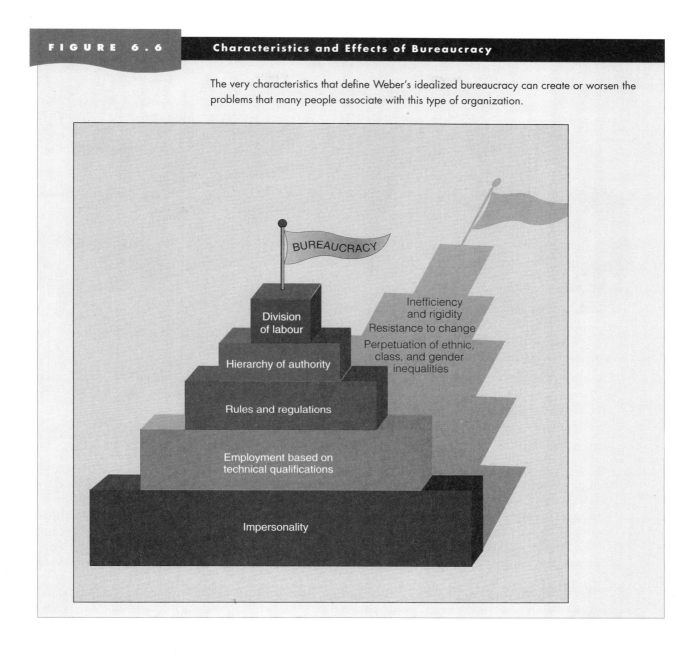

FIGURE 6.6 Characteristics and Effects of Bureaucracy

The very characteristics that define Weber's idealized bureaucracy can create or worsen the problems that many people associate with this type of organization.

BUREAUCRACY

Division of labour

Hierarchy of authority

Rules and regulations

Employment based on technical qualifications

Impersonality

Inefficiency and rigidity
Resistance to change
Perpetuation of ethnic, class, and gender inequalities

RESISTANCE TO CHANGE Once bureaucratic organizations are created, they tend to resist change. Resistance to change occurs in all bureaucratic organizations, including schools, trade unions, businesses, and government agencies. This resistance not only makes bureaucracies virtually impossible to eliminate but also contributes to bureaucratic enlargement. Because of the assumed relationship between size and importance, officials tend to press for larger budgets and more staff and office space. To justify growth, administrators and managers must come up with more tasks for workers to perform. Ultimately, the outcome pre-dicted by "Parkinson's Law" is fulfilled: "Work expands to fill the time available for its completion" (Parkinson, 1957).

Resistance to change also may lead to incompetence. Based on organizational policy, bureaucracies tend to promote people from within the organization. As a consequence, a person who performs satisfactorily in one position is promoted to a higher level in the organization. Eventually, people reach a level that is beyond their own knowledge, experience, and capabilities. This process has been referred to as the "Peter Principle": People "rise to the level of their

The "organization man" of the computer age varies widely in manner and appearance, as shown in the contrast between the blue-suited chief executive officer of IBM, Louis V. Gerstner, Jr., and this casually clad employee at Apple Computer.

incompetence" (Peter and Hull, 1969:25). However, neither the Peter Principle nor Parkinson's Law has been systematically tested by sociologists. Although each may contain some truth, if they were completely accurate, all bureaucracies would be run by incompetents.

PERPETUATION OF ETHNIC, CLASS, AND GENDER INEQUALITIES
Some bureaucracies perpetuate inequalities of ethnicity, class, and gender because this form of organizational structure creates a specific type of work or learning environment. This structure typically was created for middle- and upper-middle-class white men, who for many years were the predominant organizational participants.

Ethnic Inequalities Harish Jain has done extensive research on employment discrimination in Canada. His findings indicate that racial minorities encounter both entry-level (hiring) discrimination and post-employment (on the job) discrimination in the workplace, including lack of promotions, transfers, salary increases, and job ghettoization (Jain, 1985). Other research has found that visible minorities are more adversely affected than dominant-group members by hierarchical bureaucratic structures. These studies have been conducted in a number of organizational settings, ranging from medical schools to canning factories to corporations (see Kendall and Feagin, 1983; Zavella, 1987; and S. Collins, 1989). We will continue our discussion of the impact of organizations on visible minorities in Chapter 10 ("Race and Ethnicity").

Social Class Inequalities Like racial inequalities, social class divisions may be perpetuated in bureaucracies (Blau and Meyer, 1987). Sociologists have explored the impact of labour market conditions on the kinds of jobs and wages available to workers. The theory of a "dual labour market" has been developed to explain how social class distinctions are perpetuated through different types of employment. Middle- and upper-middle-class employees are more likely to work in industries characterized by higher wages, more job security, and opportunities for advancement. By contrast, poor and working-class employees work in industries characterized by low wages, lack of job security, and few opportunities for promotion.

Even though the "dual economy" is not a perfect model for explaining class-based organizational inequalities, it does illuminate how individuals' employment not only reflects their position in the social class but also perpetuates it. Peter Blau and Marshall Meyer (1987:160–161) conclude that "over time, then, organizational conditions reinforce social stratification ... Bureaucracies create profound differences in the life chances of the people working in them."

Gender Inequalities   Gender inequalities also are perpetuated in bureaucracies. Sociologist Rosabeth Moss Kanter (1977) analyzed how the power structure of bureaucratic hierarchies can negatively affect white women and visible minorities when they are underrepresented within an organization. In such cases, they tend to be more visible ("on display") and to feel greater pressure not to make mistakes or stand out too much. They also may find it harder to gain credibility, particularly in management positions. As a result, they are more likely to feel isolated, to be excluded from informal networks, and to have less access to mentors and to power through alliances. By contrast, affluent white men generally are seen as being "one of the group." They find it easier to gain credibility, to join informal networks, and to find sponsorships (Kanter, 1977:248–249).

Gender inequality in organizations has additional consequences. People who lack opportunities for integration and advancement tend to be pessimistic and to have lower self-esteem. They seek satisfaction away from work and are less likely to promote change at work. Believing they have few opportunities, they resign themselves to staying put and surviving at that level. By contrast, those who enjoy full access to organizational opportunities tend to have high aspirations and high self-esteem. They feel loyalty to the organization and typically see their job as a means for mobility and growth.

Bureaucracy and Oligarchy

Max Weber believed that bureaucracy was necessary because it achieved coordination and control and thus efficiency in administration (Blau and Meyer, 1987). Sociologist Charles Perrow (1986) has suggested that bureaucracy produces a high standard of living for persons living in industrialized countries because of its superiority as a "social tool over other forms of organization." Bureaucratic characteristics (such as a hierarchy

of authority, a clear division of labour, explicit rules and procedures, and impersonality in personnel matters) may contribute to organizational efficiency or they may produce gridlock.

Weber, however, was not completely in favour of bureaucracies. He believed such organizations stifle human initiative and creativity, thus producing an "iron cage." Bureaucracy also places an enormous amount of unregulated and often unperceived social power in the hands of a very few leaders. Such a situation is referred to as an oligarchy—the rule of the many by the few.

Why do a small number of leaders at the top make all of the important organizational decisions? According to German political sociologist Robert Michels (1949/1911), all organizations encounter the *iron law of oligarchy*—the tendency to become a bureaucracy ruled by the few. His central idea was that those who control bureaucracies not only wield power but also have an interest in retaining their power. In his research, Michels studied socialist parties and labour unions in Europe before World War I and concluded that even some of the most radical leaders of these organizations had a vested interest in clinging to their power. In this case, if the leaders lost their power positions, they once again would become manual labourers.

According to Michels, the hierarchical structure of bureaucracies and oligarchies go hand in hand. On the one hand, power may be concentrated in the hands of a few people because rank-and-file members inevitably must delegate a certain amount of decision-making authority to their leaders. Leaders then have access to information that other members do not have. They also have "clout," which they may use to protect their own interests, sometimes at the expense of the interests of others. On the other hand, oligarchy may result when individuals have certain outstanding qualities that make it possible for them to manage, if not control, others. The members choose to look to their leaders for direction; the leaders are strongly motivated to maintain the power and privileges that go with their leadership positions.

Is the iron law of oligarchy correct? Many scholars believe that Michels overstated his case. The leaders in most organizations do not have unlimited power. Divergent groups within a large-scale organization often compete for power, and informal networks can be used to "go behind the backs" of leaders. In addition, members routinely challenge, and sometimes remove, their leaders

Sociologist Robert Merton has pointed out that successful bureaucracies must attain a high degree of reliability of behaviour. Thus, bureaucratic structures exert pressure on officials to be "methodical, prudent, disciplined" (1968:198) and follow the rules in order to accomplish the goals of the organization. However, Merton has also shown that goal displacement can occur and for some bureaucrats the rules become an end in themselves rather than just a means to an end. When this occurs, organizations become rigid and inflexible.

Our experiences with red tape and other bureaucratic inefficiencies have been satirized by cartoonist (and disillusioned bureaucrat) Scott Adams. In the late 1980s Adams began passing his humorous scribbles and doodles around the office at Pacific Bell. Since then his cartoon *Dilbert* has become a phenomenal success and is read in over 1700 papers in 39 countries. *Dilbert* ridicules many of the worst features of bureaucracy including stupid bosses, reliance on technology instead of people, cubicles, management consultants, pointless meetings, and inflexibility. (For examples of the cartoon, go to: **http://www. unitedmedia.com/comics/dilbert**).

Readership is not the only sign that *Dilbert* strikes a responsive chord with workers. The cartoons are posted on doors, walls, and desks in thousands of offices, and many of Adams's ideas come from readers' suggestions. The British magazine *The Economist* attributes *Dilbert's* popularity to the fact that the comic strip taps into three currents that are troubling workers:

when they are not pleased with their actions. However, the concentration of power and restricted communication discussed by Michels leads to a degree of inflexibility that makes it difficult for organizations to operate effectively in today's competitive and rapidly changing environment. The company that employs Dilbert would not likely last very long in the real world (see Box 6.3). This is why the last decade has seen many attempts to create new types of complex organizations.

An Alternative Form of Organization

Many organizations have sought new and innovative ways to organize work more efficiently than the traditional hierarchical model. In the early 1980s, there was a movement in North America to *humanize bureaucracy*—to establish an organizational environment that develops rather than impedes human resources. More humane bureaucracies are characterized by (1) less rigid hierarchical structures and greater sharing of power and responsibility by all participants, (2) encourage-

ment of participants to share their ideas and try new approaches to problem solving, and (3) efforts to reduce the number of people in dead-end jobs, train people in needed skills and competencies, and help people meet outside family responsibilities while still receiving equal treatment inside the organization (Kanter, 1977, 1983, 1985). However, this movement may have been overshadowed by the perceived strengths of another organizational model.

For several decades, the Japanese model of organization has been widely praised for its innovative structure. A number of social scientists and management specialists concluded that guaranteed lifetime employment and a teamwork approach to management were the major reasons Japanese workers had been so productive since the end of World War II, when Japan's economy was in shambles. When the North American manufacturing sector weakened in the 1980s, the Japanese system was widely discussed as an alternative to the prevalent North American hierarchical organizational structure. Box 6.4 compares the characteristics of large Japanese corporations with their North American–based counterparts.

CONTINUED

1. The obsession with work as employees are forced to labour harder to compensate for the effects of downsizing;
2. Fear in the workplace as workers are laid off or see their wage increases falling far behind those of their managers; and
3. A growing cynicism about new management fads that have led to constant reorganization but that seem to have had little impact on efficiency or on job satisfaction.

Ironically, while many workers feel *Dilbert* says what they feel about stupid and uncaring managers, the leaders of many of North America's largest corporations have used the cartoons for training and corporate communications.

Sources: *The Economist*, 1997; Merton, 1968; and Whitaker, 1997. DILBERT reprinted by permission of United Features Syndicate, Inc.

LIMITATIONS   Will the Japanese organizational structure continue to work? Recently, the notion of lifetime employment has become problematic as an economic recession forced some Japanese factories to close and other companies ran out of subsidiaries willing to take on workers for "reassignment" (Sanger, 1994:E5). Also, sociologist Robert Coles (1979) has suggested that the Japanese model does not actually provide workers with more control over the corporation. While it may give them more control over their own work, production goals set by managers still must be met.

Although the possibility of implementing the Japanese model in North American-based corporations has been widely discussed, its large-scale acceptance is doubtful. Cultural traditions in Japan have focused on the importance of the group rather than the individual. Workers in North America are not likely to embrace this idea because it directly conflicts with the value of individualism so strongly held by many in this country (Krahn and Lowe, 1996). North American workers also are unwilling to commit themselves to one corporation for their entire work life. Moreover, men typically fare much better than women in Japanese corporations, in which many women have found themselves excluded from career-track positions (Brinton, 1989).

Unlike Japan, Canada and the United States have histories of labour–management disputes. Consequently, North American managers tend to oppose proposals that enhance worker participation in the decision-making process. Also, successful managers often do not make good team leaders. If managers previously have been pitted against workers in manufacturing plants, for instance, they are less likely to think that they should build consensus and encourage group decision making (Stern, 1993). Furthermore, workers sometimes equate employee participation in management with more work.

There is some evidence that the workers' concerns are justified. Welsh (1998) has reviewed several studies on the implementation of Japanese production techniques in several North American auto plants including the General Motors Saturn plant in Spring Hill, Tennessee, and the CAMI plant in Ingersoll, Ontario. These studies conclude that the notion of worker control is illusory. The plants use computerized assembly lines, and

BOX 6.4   SOCIOLOGY IN GLOBAL PERSPECTIVE

THE JAPANESE CORPORATION

How do Japanese corporations differ from their North American counterparts? The main differences are the promise of lifetime employment and the participation of Japanese employees in their company decision making.

Until recently, many large Japanese corporations guaranteed their workers permanent employment after an initial probationary period. Thus, Japanese employees often remained with the same company for their entire career, whereas their North American counterparts often changed employers every few years. Japanese workers felt obligated to remain with their company and not to leave for more pay or a better position elsewhere, as frequently occurred in Canada and the United States. Likewise, Japanese employers in the

past had an obligation not to "downsize" by laying off workers or to cut their wages. Unlike top managers in North America who gave themselves pay raises, bonuses, and so on even when their companies were financially strapped and laying off workers, Japanese managers took pay cuts. When financial problems occurred, Japanese workers frequently were reassigned or retrained by their company. Since many people retire in Japan at about age 55, the typical length of employment at one corporation for most workers is about thirty to thirty-five years.

According to advocates, the Japanese system encourages worker loyalty and a high level of productivity. Managers move through various parts of the organization and acquire

---

the workers do not control the pace of the work. Also, while there were attempts to make the workplace more egalitarian by consulting with workers and introducing work teams, the research suggests that the work teams become a means of social control. For example, if a member is sick, he or she may not be replaced and the workload must be shared by the remaining team members. Thus the team may pressure members not to miss any work, even if they are ill. The worker consultation that is part of the Japanese management philosophy had the effect of getting workers to suggest ways of speeding up the line and reducing production costs.

We are likely to see greater use of Japanese production techniques in Canada, because they have led to higher productivity, greater profits, and increased worker satisfaction (Florida and Kenney, 1991). However, the changes brought about by their introduction have so far not done nearly as much as promised to increase worker participation and improve working conditions in factories. The Japanese model represents a small step in the right direction, but we can anticipate more significant changes as we move into the twenty-first century.

NEW ORGANIZATIONS FOR THE FUTURE

What kind of "Help Wanted" ad might a company run in the twenty-first century? One journalist has suggested that a want ad in the future might read something like this: "WANTED: Bureaucracy basher, willing to challenge convention, assume big risks, and rewrite the accepted rules of industrial order" (Byrne, 1993:76). Organizational theorists have suggested a *horizontal* model for corporations in which both hierarchy and functional or departmental boundaries largely would be eliminated. Seven key elements of the horizontal corporation have been suggested: (1) work would be organized around "core" processes, not tasks; (2) the hierarchy would be flattened; (3) teams would manage everything and be held accountable for measurable performance goals; (4) performance would be measured by customer satisfaction, not profits; (5) team performance would be rewarded; (6) employees would have regular contact with suppliers and customers;

BOX 6.4

technical knowledge about the workings of many aspects of the corporation, unlike their North American counterparts who tend to become highly specialized (Sengoku, 1985). Clearly, permanent employment has its advantages for workers. They do not have to worry about losing their jobs or having their wages cut. Employers benefit by not having to compete with one another to keep workers.

Small workgroups made up of about five to fifteen workers who meet regularly with one or two managers to discuss the group's performance and working conditions are known as *quality circles*. The purpose of this team approach to management is both to improve product quality and to lower product costs. Workers are motivated to save the corporation

money because they, in turn, receive bonuses or higher wages for their efforts. Quality circles have been praised for creating worker satisfaction, helping employees develop their potential, and improving productivity (Krahn and Lowe, 1996). Because quality circles focus on both productivity and worker satisfaction, they (at least ideally) meet the needs of both the corporation and the workers. While many Japanese corporations have utilized quality circles to achieve better productivity, many North American-based corporations have implemented automation in hopes of controlling the quality of their products.

The contrasting styles of baseball players in North America and Japan reflect profound differences in organizational culture. People in North America tend to value individualism over the group, while people in Japan focus primarily on the group and deemphasize individual accomplishment in favour of teamwork and collective success.

BOX 6.5   SOCIOLOGY AND TECHNOLOGY

THE INTERNET AND THE ORGANIZATION

Do you enjoy going to the grocery store, standing in line at the checkout counter, and carrying your groceries to the car? What if you could order your groceries on the Internet and have them delivered to your home for less than what it would cost to buy them at the store? The Internet may have a major impact on the organizational structure of many businesses, including the food industry, by simplifying product distribution. One company, Peachtree, already sells groceries over the Internet (in Ontario and Quebec), and other Canadian companies are considering the idea. If large numbers of people begin to shop on the Internet, we may see what some analysts have called *disintermediation*—or removing the middleman. An Internet transaction is made directly between the producer and the consumer. The Internet will allow manufacturers to sell their products faster and more cheaply without going through wholesalers and retailers. This may have a major impact on the structure of organizations that deal with consumer goods.

The greeting card business shows us how the Internet can provide new ways of serving customer needs. For the past century, companies have designed and produced greeting cards and have sold the cards to wholesalers who distributed them to retail outlets.

Customers bought the cards, bought stamps, and mailed them to the recipient through Canada Post. A new approach has been taken by Outpost Network (**http://outpost. infospace.com**), which allows customers to order greeting cards on the Internet. The company then mails the cards to the recipient. While this approach gets rid of the need for a retailer and wholesaler, E-Greetings (**www. greetst.com**) goes further by eliminating the need to print cards. Rather than using the mail, E-Greetings designs are sent electronically over the Internet. If this method of sending greetings becomes popular, several bureaucracies will be significantly affected. Can you think through some of the consequences of such a change?

Electronic commerce has become common in areas such as banking, travel services, selling stocks, and selling goods such as automobiles, flowers, and pizza. It is much cheaper for these organizations to transact business over the Internet. What do you think will happen to the jobs of those who sell stocks and work in banks and travel agencies? How will the change affect the bureaucracies in which they work?

If disintermediation because of Internet commerce becomes a trend, there will also be a new need for electronic intermediaries who can

and (7) all employees would be trained in how to use available information effectively to make their own decisions (Byrne, 1993:76–79).

In the horizontal structure, a limited number of senior executives would still fill support roles (such as finance and human resources) while everyone else would work on multidisciplinary teams and perform core processes (such as product development or sales generation). Organizations would have fewer layers between company heads and the staffers responsible for any given process. Performance objectives would be related to the needs of customers; people would be rewarded not

just for individual performance but for skills development and team performance. If such organizations become a reality, organizational charts of the twenty-first century will more closely resemble a shamrock or an inverted pyramid than the traditional pyramid-shaped stack of boxes connected by lines.

Currently, most corporations are hybrids of vertical and horizontal organizational structures; however, a number of companies appear to be moving toward the horizontal model. If the horizontal model is widely implemented, this will constitute one of the most significant changes in

BOX 6.5

CONTINUED

provide guidance and assistance for consumers and provide marketing services and transaction assistance for producers. Are such intermediaries likely to work within traditional bureaucratic organizations? One clue to the future may come from currently successful intermediary organizations such as Amazon.com, the Internet bookseller. Amazon.com is an intermediary between publisher and consumer, but rather than being a large, formal bureaucracy, it is a virtual company with little presence outside of cyberspace. Despite calling itself "The Earth's Biggest Bookstore" with its list of over a million titles, Amazon.com keeps only a very small stock of books on hand. The rest are ordered electronically and shipped from traditional book wholesalers. Because of its low overhead costs, it can sell books more cheaply than traditional retailers. This means that many of these businesses may be in jeopardy.

Internet commerce now represents only a small portion of consumer sales. However, several factors suggest that Internet commerce will expand very rapidly: use of the Internet is growing; those who use the Internet tend to be well-educated people with high incomes who are attractive to marketers; and secure payment mechanisms are making people more comfortable about providing their credit card numbers to Internet vendors. Because of this growth, we should soon be able to get a better indication of how Internet commerce will develop and of how it will affect the structure of traditional bureaucracies.

The Internet also provides opportunities for illegal transactions. For example, the music industry is threatened by the development of technology that allows people to download music from the Internet without paying royalties to the companies or musicians. The MP3 (**http://www.mp3.com**) program can be used to download the music, which can then be played on conventional stereo systems, stored on players designed to hold MP3 music, or recorded on a custom CD. While some people use MP3 technology to purchase music online or to record songs that are in the public domain, many others use it to record illegally. The major record companies have established a consortium with IBM to try to establish a mechanism for secure Internet sales, but it will be difficult to stop those who wish to pirate music. Even if there were no illegal copying, the music industry is still threatened by the fact that Internet technology allows artists to sell their music directly to the public without going through the intermediary of the music companies.

organizational structure since the Industrial Revolution.

What is the best organizational structure for the future? Of course, this question is difficult to answer because it requires the ability to predict economic, political, and social conditions. Nevertheless, we can make the observations that, ultimately, everyone has a stake in seeing that organizations operate in as humane a fashion as possible and that channels for opportunity are widely available to all people regardless of ethnicity, gender, or class.

CHAPTER REVIEW

How do sociologists distinguish among social groups, aggregates, and categories?
Sociologists define a social group as a collection of two or more people who interact frequently, share a sense of belonging, and depend on one another. People who happen to be in the same place at the same time are considered an aggregate. Those who share a similar characteristic are considered a category. Neither aggregates nor categories are considered social groups.

How do sociologists classify groups?
Primary groups are small and personal, and members engage in emotion-based interactions over an extended period. Secondary groups are larger and more specialized, and members have less personal and more formal, goal-oriented relationships. Ingroups are groups to which we belong and with which we identify. Outgroups are groups we do not belong to or perhaps feel hostile toward.

What is the significance of group size?
In small groups, all members know one another and interact simultaneously. In groups with more than three members, communication dynamics change and members tend to assume specialized tasks.

What are the different types of leadership within groups?
Instrumental leadership is goal- or task-oriented and is an appropriate style for action-oriented groups. Expressive leadership is concerned with providing emotional support for members and works well when harmony and high morale are important for a group. Authoritarian leaders make major decisions and assign tasks to individual members. Democratic leaders encourage discussion and collaborative decision making. Laissez-faire leaders are minimally involved and encourage members to make their own decisions.

What is a bureaucracy?
A bureaucracy is a formal organization characterized by hierarchical authority, division of labour, explicit procedures, and impersonality. According to Max Weber, bureaucracy supplies a rational means of attaining organizational goals because it contributes to coordination and control.

What is "bureaucracy's other face"?
"Bureaucracy's other face" is the informal structure of daily activities and interactions that bypass the official rules and procedures. Informal networks may enhance productivity or may be counterproductive to the organization. Informal networks also may be detrimental to those who are excluded from them, typically any minority within the organization.

What are the weaknesses of bureaucracies?
There are three major shortcomings of bureaucracies. They may be inefficient and rigid, particularly when an organization's survival becomes more important than the achievement of its goals. They may resist change, which can lead to bureaucratic enlargement or incompetence. And they may perpetuate class, ethnic, and gender inequalities.

What is an oligarchy?
An oligarchy is the rule of the many by the few. In bureaucracies with an oligarchical structure, those in control have not only power but also a great interest in maintaining that power.

How does the Japanese model of management differ from the North American model?
Recent trends in North America have generated interest in more innovative bureaucratic structures. The movement to humanize bureaucracy has focused on developing, rather than impeding, human resources. The Japanese model of organization emphasizes company loyalty and a teamwork approach to management.

How are organizations likely to change in the future?
Some organizational theorists are advocating a horizontal model for bureaucracy that emphasizes teamwork, informed employee decision making, and customer satisfaction. Ultimately, all of us benefit from organizations that operate humanely and that include opportunities for all, regardless of ethnicity, gender, or class.

Key Terms

aggregate 166
authoritarian leaders 171
bureaucracy 181
bureaucratic personality 186
category 166
conformity 172
democratic leaders 171
dyad 170
expressive leadership 171
goal displacement 186
groupthink 176
ideal type 183
informal structure 184
ingroup 167
instrumental leadership 171
iron law of oligarchy 189
laissez-faire leaders 172
outgroup 167
rationality 181
reference group 169
small group 170
triad 170

Internet Exercises

1. If you belong to any groups, go to Lycos (**http://www.lycos.com/**) and search for the name of it to see if this group has a Web page. If it does, visit

it. Does the group's projected image differ greatly from the way you experience the group? Visit your university's Web page. How does the projected image of the school differ from your experience?

2. This chapter discusses the works of Max Weber. Visit the Weber section of The Dead Sociologists Page (**http://diogenes.baylor.edu/WWWproviders/ Larry_Ridener/DSS/INDEX.HTML#weber**). Compare the interpretation of Weber on this page with that in this textbook. A continuation of Weber's themes can be found in the book *The McDonaldization of Society* by George Ritzer. Visit the McDonaldization homepage (**http://www. sociology.net/mcdonald/**). After reading about the theory, think about how McDonaldization differs from Weber's theories. Is it more or less reflective of today than Weber is?

3. In his *Dilbert* comic strip, Scott Adams often satirizes corporate programs designed to make life better for a company's employees. Visit the Dilbert Archives (**http://www.unitedmedia.com/comics/ dilbert/archive/**) and read through several weeks of strips. How reflective of a typical office do you think the strip is?

4. Order music on the Internet. Go to **http://www. lycos.com** and under "shopping" go to "music." Type in the name of your favourite artist or song and see what is offered.

✉ Net Links

To read about the latest research in the area of formal organizations, see the Web site for the journal *Administrative Science Quarterly* at:

http://www.gsm.cornell.edu/ASQ/asq.html

Government is a very complex bureaucracy. To see the number of departments in the Canadian federal government, go to:

http://www.canada.gc.ca/

The Public Service Commission of Canada has an extensive bibliography of material on group leadership; go to:

http://www.psc_cfp.gc.ca/library/leadrspf.htm

Read more about Stanley Milgram's work on obedience and hear audio clips from one of his experiments at:

http://elvers.stjoe.udayton.edu/history/history.asp? RURL=http://elvers.stjoe.udayton.edu/history/ people/Milgram.html

To read an interview with George Ritzer concerning his view of the "McDonaldization" of society, go to:

http://www.mcspotlight.org/people/interviews/ ritzer_george.html

Questions for Critical Thinking

1. Who might be more likely to conform in a bureaucracy, those with power or those wanting more power?

2. Do the insights gained from Milgram's research on obedience outweigh the elements of deception and stress that were forced on his subjects?

3. The underlying rationale of Japan's participatory style of management is that the person who performs a particular job is in the best position to give advice about how the job may be improved. Would this participatory style be useful in an academic setting? What are the similarities and differences between workers in a bureaucracy and students at a college or university? What advice would you give administrators at your institution about how to improve the academic process?

4. If you were forming a company based on humane organizational principles, would you base the promotional policies on merit and performance or on affirmative action goals?

Suggested Readings

Organizations are examined from a variety of perspectives in these interesting books:

Harvey Krahn and Graham S. Lowe. *Work, Industry and Canadian Society* (3rd. ed.). Toronto: ITP Nelson, 1998.

Wallace Clement. *The Canadian Corporate Elite*. Toronto: McClelland and Stewart, 1975.

Kathy E. Ferguson. *The Feminist Case Against Bureaucracy*. Philadelphia: Temple University Press, 1984.

Richard H. Hall. *Organizations: Structures, Processes, and Outcomes*. Englewood Cliffs, N.J.: Prentice-Hall, 1991.

Rosabeth Moss Kanter. *Men and Women of the Corporation*. New York: Basic Books, 1993; orig. pub. 1977.

Gifford Pinchot and Elizabeth Pinchot. *The End of Bureaucracy and the Rise of the Intelligent Organization*. San Francisco: Berrett-Koehler, 1993.

7

What Is Deviance?

Functionalist Perspectives on Crime and Deviance
Strain Theory: Goals and the Means to Achieve Them
Opportunity Theory: Access to Illegitimate Opportunities
Control Theory: Social Bonding

Interactionist Perspectives on Crime and Deviance
Differential Association Theory
Labelling Theory

Feminist Perspectives on Crime and Deviance

Critical Perspectives on Crime and Deviance
The Conflict Approach

Feminist Perspectives on Crime and Deviance

Crime Classification and Statistics
How the Law Classifies Crime
How Sociologists Classify Crime
Crime Statistics
Street Crimes and Criminals

The Criminal Justice System
The Police
The Courts
Punishment
Restorative Justice
Community Corrections

Deviance and Crime in the Future

When most of us think of organized crime, we think of biker gangs or perhaps the Italian Mafia. In reality, however, organized crime has many faces. All organized crime groups have many things in common, including a willingness to use violence—a willingness that is evident from the following account:

Constable Peter Yuen, a member of the Metropolitan Toronto Police Service, was working undercover in a gaming house, monitoring off-track betting while police backup units waited outside. During this operation, four hooded Vietnamese gang members burst into the room and ordered the gamblers to hand over their valuables. The robbers found Yuen's police badge and ordered him to kneel with his hands behind his head. Writer Paul Kaihla, with the help of recollections and quotations from Yuen, describes the events that followed:

"'I was kicked in the face until my shirt was soaked in blood.' Then, one of the robbers forced the barrel of a .45 calibre automatic into Yuen's mouth, while another held a .357 magnum to his temple. Said Yuen: 'They were shouting that I was a traitor for serving the white authorities and that I deserved to die.' Yuen then heard a gun click and heard an assailant remark, 'Goodbye copper.' But the assault abruptly ceased when another of the robbers noticed that the building was surrounded by police. Two of the suspects were arrested at the scene, but the police ultimately chased one of Yuen's attackers into a bush area where he hid by burying himself in mud and breathing through a piece of straw. Police found him after 30 minutes using tracking dogs.

Forensic tests on the pistol showed that the gangster had indeed pulled the trigger, but that the bullet in the chamber had not fired ... Concluded Yuen, who was named Toronto's Policeman of the Year ... for his bravery during the attack: 'I have no doubt that they would have done me in if they had not been interrupted.'" (Kaihla, 1991:21)

CRIME AND DEVIANCE

The problem of organized crime is certainly not unique to Canada. This problem has existed for centuries and today such gangs operate around the world. As you will learn, organized crime is one of a wide range of behaviours that society has defined as deviant or criminal. For many years crime and deviance have been of special interest to sociologists. Many of the issues they have examined remain important today: What is deviant behaviour, and how does it differ from criminal behaviour? Why are some people considered to be "deviants" or "criminals" while others are not? In this chapter, we look at the relationship between conformity, deviance, and crime. Before reading on, take the quiz on organized crime, deviance, and crime in Box 7.1.

QUESTIONS AND ISSUES

CHAPTER FOCUS QUESTION: What are the causes and consequences of organized crime in Canada?

What is deviant behaviour?

How do sociologists explain deviant and criminal behaviour?

When is deviance considered a crime?

How do sociologists classify crime?

How does the criminal justice system deal with crime?

How can we begin to solve the crime problem in the twenty-first century?

According to sociologists, deviance is relative—in other words, it varies according to time, place, group, and circumstance. In this controlled aggression program for youth gang members in Toronto, Ontario, aggression has been defined as normative rather than deviant.

WHAT IS DEVIANCE?

How do societies determine what behaviour is acceptable and unacceptable? As discussed in previous chapters, all societies have norms that govern acceptable behaviour. If we are to live and to work with others, these rules are necessary. We must also have a reasonable expectation that other people will obey the rules. Think of the chaos that would result if each driver decided which side of the road she would drive on each day, or which stop sign he would decide to obey. Most of us usually conform to the norms our group prescribes. Of course, not all members of the group obey all the time. All of us have broken many rules, sometimes even important ones. These violations are dealt with through various mechanisms of *social control*—systematic practices developed by social groups to encourage conformity and to discourage deviance. One form of social control takes place through the process of socialization, whereby individuals *internalize* societal norms and values. A second form of social control occurs through the use of negative sanctions to punish rule-breakers and nonconforming acts. Although the purpose of social control is to ensure some level of conformity, all societies still have some degree of *deviance*—any behaviour, belief, or condition that violates cultural norms (Adler et al., 1995).

We are most familiar with *behavioural* deviance, that is, a person's intentional or inadvertent actions. For example, a person may engage in intentional deviance by drinking too much or shoplifting or in inadvertent deviance by losing the rent money at a video lottery terminal or laughing during a solemn occasion.

Although we usually think of deviance as a type of behaviour, people may be regarded as deviant if they express radical or unusual beliefs. For example, members of cults (such as Moonies and satanists) and of far-right- or far-left-wing political groups may be considered deviant when their religious or political beliefs become known to people with more conventional cultural views. For instance, schoolteachers James Keegstra and Malcolm Ross were removed from their classrooms for expressing anti-Semitic beliefs, including denying that the Holocaust actually occurred.

People may be regarded as deviant because of specific *characteristics* or *conditions* that they have had since birth (such as a physical disability or minority status in a racist society) or have acquired (such as contracting AIDS) (Adler and Adler, 1994). Sociologist Rose Weitz (1993) has suggested that persons with AIDS live with a stigma that affects their relationships with family members, friends, lovers, colleagues, and health-care workers. To avoid or reduce stigma, many people with AIDS attempt to conceal their illness, learn when and to whom they should reveal

BOX 7.1 SOCIOLOGY AND EVERYDAY LIFE

HOW MUCH DO YOU KNOW ABOUT CRIME AND ORGANIZED CRIME?

TRUE   FALSE

T   F   1. Official statistics accurately reflect the amount of crime in Canada.

T   F   2. Most organized criminals are affiliated with the Italian Mafia.

T   F   3. Organized crime exists largely to provide goods and services demanded by "respectable" members of the community.

T   F   4. Rates of murder and other violent crimes have been steadily rising for the past twenty years.

T   F   5. Because of their concern with a variety of charitable causes, biker gangs such as the Hell's Angels have become less of a social threat.

T   F   6. During Canada's great cigarette smuggling epidemic of 1992 and 1993, our major cigarette companies exported cigarettes to the United States that they knew would be smuggled back into Canada.

T   F   7. Canada's most prolific serial killer was a Hell's Angel who killed forty-three people, but served only seven years of a sentence for manslaughter.

T   F   8. Many organized crime groups are made up of people from the same ethnic group.

T   F   9. In Russia, organized crime is so pervasive that it is a threat to the future economic and political life of that country.

T   F   10. Most of the money made by organized criminals comes from gambling and loan-sharking.

Answers on page 202.

their illness, change their social networks, or work to convince others that they are still functioning social beings (Weitz, 1993). As Weitz's observation suggests, individuals considered "deviant" by one group may be conformists in another group. Organized crime gangs are no exception; members who shun mainstream cultural beliefs and values may conform routinely to codes of dress, attitude (such as defiant individualism), and behaviour (Jankowski, 1991). The Hell's Angels provide a graphic example of such conformity within a group of people who consider themselves nonconformists.

According to sociologists, deviance is *relative*— that is, an act becomes deviant when it is socially defined as such. Definitions of deviance vary widely from place to place, from time to time, and from group to group. For example, you may have played the Pick 3 lottery. To win, you must pick a three-digit number matching the one drawn by the government lottery agency. Television commercials encourage us to risk our money on this game from which the government profits. Several years ago, the same game was called the numbers racket and was the most popular form of gambling

in many low-income neighbourhoods. The two main differences between now and then are: the game used to be run by organized criminals, and these criminals paid the winners a higher share of the take than the government now does.

Deviance can be difficult to define. Good and evil are not two distinct categories. The two overlap, and the line between deviant and nondeviant can be very *ambiguous*. For example, how do we decide someone is mentally ill? What if your brother begins to behave in a strange fashion? You notice that he occasionally yells at people for no apparent reason, and keeps changing topics when you talk to him. He begins to wear clothes that don't match and phones you in the middle of the night to talk about people on the street who are threatening him. How would you respond to this change in behaviour? Would it make any difference if you knew that your brother was drinking heavily at the time or that he was under a lot of stress at work? Would it make a difference if he behaved this way once a year or twice a week? When would you decide that he had a problem and should seek help? What is the difference between someone who is eccentric and someone

BOX 7.1

ANSWERS TO THE SOCIOLOGY QUIZ ON CRIME AND ORGANIZED CRIME

1. **False.** Although official statistics provide a variety of information about crime in Canada, they reflect only crimes that are *reported* to police, not all the offences that are *committed*. Studies have shown that less than half of all crimes are reported to the police.

2. **False.** The Italian Mafia has a global influence on organized crime. However, it is one of many different organized crime groups.

3. **True.** If not for public demand for illegal drugs, gambling, tax-free liquor and cigarettes, and the other goods and services supplied by organized crime, illegal profits would largely disappear.

4. **False.** While crime rates generally rose through the 1980s, they declined steadily throughout the 1990s.

5. **False.** The Hell's Angels have used high-profile activities like toy runs for children to improve their public image. However, they are one of the most ruthless and profitable criminal organizations in North America.

6. **True.** The vast majority of cigarettes smuggled into Canada were legally manufactured here and exported into the United States. Executives of one of Canada's largest manufacturers, Imperial Tobacco, said explicitly that they wanted to ensure that their cigarettes were the ones smuggled back into Canada.

7. **True.** Yves (Apache) Trudeau was a contract killer who received a lenient sentence in exchange for information about other Montreal underworld figures. (For more on this case, see Box 7.5 on page 230.)

8. **True.** Many different nationalities are involved in Canadian organized crime, including Russian, Iranian, Chinese, Vietnamese, Colombian, Jamaican, and Italian. Restricting membership to one's own group provides a number of advantages. For one thing, interpersonal ties based on ethnic communities and language differences make it difficult for law enforcement to infiltrate the groups. The ethnic ties also facilitate the development of international crime networks.

9. **True.** After the fall of Communism, the lack of meaningful economic institutions and the failure of the criminal justice system created conditions favourable to organized crime. Organized criminals control many of the new businesses in Russia and have powerful links to the government.

10. **False.** The importation and distribution of illegal drugs is the main source of funds for organized crime.

Sources: Based on Evans and Himelfarb, 1996; Lavigne, 1987; and Stamler, 1996.

who is mentally ill? These questions reflect the difficulty we have in defining deviance.

Deviant behaviour also varies in its degree of seriousness, ranging from mild transgressions of folkways, to more serious infringements of mores, to quite serious violations of the law. Have you kept a library book past its due date or cut classes? If so, you have violated folkways. Others probably view your infraction as relatively minor; at most, you might have to pay a fine or receive a lower grade. Violations of mores—such as falsifying a university application or cheating on an examination—are viewed as more serious infractions and

are punishable by stronger sanctions, such as academic probation or expulsion. Some forms of deviant behaviour are officially defined as crimes. A **crime is an act that violates criminal law and is punishable with fines, jail terms, and other sanctions.** Crimes range from minor (such as running an illegal bingo game or disorderly conduct) to major offences (such as sexual assault and murder). A subcategory, **juvenile delinquency, refers to a violation of law by young people under the age of 18.**

When sociologists study deviance, they attempt to learn what types of behaviour are defined as deviant, who does the defining, how and why people become deviants, and how society deals with deviants (Schur, 1983). In this chapter, we present several sociological explanations of deviance. While each focuses on the role of social groups in creating deviance, these theories are quite different from one another. However, each contributes in its own way to our understanding of deviance. No one perspective provides a comprehensive explanation of all deviance. In many respects the theories presented in this chapter can be considered complementary.

FUNCTIONALIST PERSPECTIVES ON CRIME AND DEVIANCE

Strain Theory: Goals and the Means to Achieve Them

As discussed in Chapter 1, Durkheim (1964a/ 1895) introduced the concept of *anomie* to describe a social condition in which people experience a sense of futility because social norms are weak, absent, or conflicting. Sociologist Robert Merton's (1938, 1968) strain theory is based on Durkheim's assertion that the macrolevel structure of a society can produce social pressures that result in a higher rate of deviant behaviour. According to **strain theory, people feel strain when they are exposed to cultural goals that they are unable to obtain because they do not have access to culturally approved means of achieving those goals.** The goals may be material possessions and money; the approved means may include an education and jobs. When denied legitimate access to these goals, some people seek access through deviant means.

Sociologist Margaret Beare (1996a) has used Merton's strain theory to explain the involvement of Canadian Mohawks in the organized crime of smuggling in the early 1990s. In order to raise revenue and to discourage smoking, Canadian governments had for decades imposed high taxes on cigarettes. As a result, the cost of cigarettes had become much higher in this country than in the United States. To save money, many of those addicted to cigarettes turned to the contraband market. By 1993 more than one-quarter of the cigarettes consumed in Canada were purchased

illegally. In Ontario and Quebec, residents of some First Nations communities were among the major sources of these contraband cigarettes.

Because of high unemployment and lack of legitimate opportunities in most First Nations communities, deviance had become an attractive option to some community members who saw smuggling as a means of achieving the goal of financial success. Akwesasne Chief Mike Mitchell described the financial opportunity in a CBC interview:

> The money—it's unbelievable the money you can make and it's so easy ... You can buy a pack of cigarettes on the American side of the reservation for $1.58 and you go across here in Cornwall and you have to buy it for close to $7.00 a pack, same pack, within a short distance of each other, so no one is surprised that all this is happening. (cited in Beare, 1996b:272)

The business of getting the cigarettes into Canada was facilitated by a number of factors. First, Canadian cigarette manufacturers were eager to ship Canadian brands into the United States, knowing that the cigarettes would be smuggled back into Canada. Second, the location of some reserves was ideal. The Mohawk reserve at Akwesasne, for example, straddles the Ontario–Quebec and Canada–U.S. borders (see Map 7.1), and the geography of the St. Lawrence River at Akwesasne makes detection difficult. Third, First Nations peoples can purchase for personal use unlimited amounts of tax-free tobacco in the United States. While this tobacco is supposed to remain on the reserve, at the height of the smuggling epidemic much of it became part of the contraband trade. Some residents argued that they had the legal right to sell this tobacco to whoever wished to buy it. Finally, the jurisdictional disputes over law enforcement, which were so apparent during the 1990 Oka crisis in Quebec, reduced the ability of the police to work effectively. In Beare's opinion, the smuggling was also facilitated by feelings of injustice against federal and provincial governments on the part of the Mohawks, which some felt justified their deviant behaviour.

While substantial tax cuts have dramatically reduced the incidence of cigarette smuggling, the networks and expertise developed by the smugglers have remained, and many, having made linkages with other organized criminals, have turned to smuggling other commodities including drugs, alcohol, and firearms. This has helped create ille-

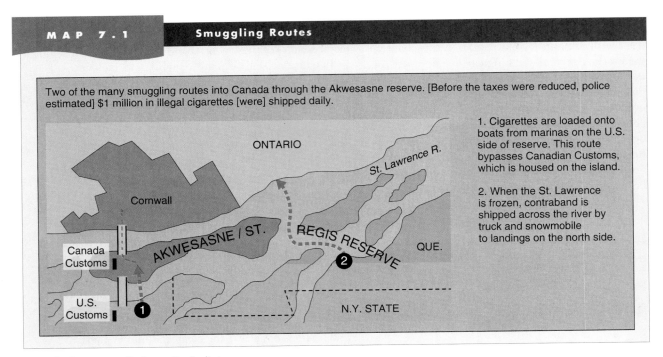

MAP 7.1 **Smuggling Routes**

Two of the many smuggling routes into Canada through the Akwesasne reserve. [Before the taxes were reduced, police estimated] $1 million in illegal cigarettes [were] shipped daily.

ONTARIO

St. Lawrence R.

Cornwall

AKWESASNE / ST. REGIS RESERVE

QUE.

Canada Customs

U.S. Customs

N.Y. STATE

1. Cigarettes are loaded onto boats from marinas on the U.S. side of reserve. This route bypasses Canadian Customs, which is housed on the island.

2. When the St. Lawrence is frozen, contraband is shipped across the river by truck and snowmobile to landings on the north side.

Reprinted with permission—The Toronto Star Syndicate.

gitimate opportunity structures on some reserves that may attract others into the world of organized smuggling.

Opportunity Theory: Access to Illegitimate Opportunities

Expanding on Merton's strain theory, sociologists Richard Cloward and Lloyd Ohlin (1960) have suggested that for deviance to occur people must have access to *illegitimate opportunity structures*—circumstances that provide an opportunity for people to acquire through illegitimate activities what they cannot get through legitimate channels. For example, members of some communities may have insufficient legitimate means to achieve conventional goals of status and wealth but have much greater access to illegitimate opportunity structures—such as theft, drug dealing, or robbery—through which they can achieve these goals. The situation at Akwesasne provided a very lucrative opportunity structure for the minority of community members who chose to use it. However, more typically, illegitimate opportunities are often situational and small-scale, as the following description an East Coast youth gave of his delinquent behaviour demonstrates:

We used to break into places. I was drunk on every one of them jobs. We never really planned

it, we just broke in. The one I remember most clearly is when we broke into the Lougheed Drive-In. I was drunk then so I can't remember everything. We just wanted to do a break, so we did a break to get more booze for the next day. It was after dark and hardly anybody was there— this was 3:00 in the morning. We busted open the door, because there's no alarm system in it— we checked all that out—we just busted the door with a crowbar. We got in there and we searched everywhere and we didn't find nothing, there wasn't no money there. Then we saw the cigarette machine so we said, "Let's take this." So the six of us picked it up and threw it in the back of the trunk—we had an old shitbox of a car—and took off. We got $35.00 out of it and around 200 packs of cigarettes. We dumped it in a field in there by Kmart on Ryerson Road. We bought a bottle of Seagram's—I know it was Seagram's because I drank half—I just drank it all down. You just get drunk, you get blackouts. You're nervous doing breaks. I never really wanted to be involved with them: mostly I just told them I'd be lookout. One time we all broke in this place: I was out watching and the boys went in, and then a cop car and two paddy wagons came down the road. I said, "Boys, the cops are coming," and I beat it. The boys all got caught. (Leyton, 1979:124)

For some people the "information super-highway" is a new avenue of illegitimate opportunity. While only a fraction of "hackers" engage in deviant behaviour, computer mischief and crime demonstrate how new opportunity structures can elicit new forms of deviance.

According to Cloward and Ohlin (1960), three different forms of delinquent subcultures—criminal, conflict, and retreatist—emerge based on the type of illegitimate opportunities available in a specific area. The criminal subculture focuses on economic gain and includes acts such as theft, extortion, and drug dealing. Sociologist Elijah Anderson (1990) suggested that the "drug economy [is an] employment agency superimposed on the existing gang network" for many young men who lack other opportunities. For young men who grow up in a gang subculture, running drug houses and selling drugs on street corners becomes a source of illegitimate opportunity. Using the money from these "jobs," they can support themselves and their families as well as purchase material possessions to impress others. When illegitimate economic opportunities are not available, gangs may become conflict subcultures that fight over turf (territory) and adopt a value system of toughness, courage, and similar status-enhancing qualities. Those who lack the opportunity or ability to join one of these gangs may turn to retreatist activities such as drinking and drug use.

Opportunity theory expands strain theory by pointing out the relationship between deviance and the availability of illegitimate opportunity structures. Some recent studies of gangs have supported this premise by pointing out that gang membership provides some women and men in low-income central-city areas with an illegitimate means to acquire money, entertainment, refuge, physical protection, and escape from living like their parents (Jankowski, 1991; Esbensen and Huizinga, 1993).

Control Theory: Social Bonding

Most theories of crime causation ask the question, Why do they do it? Control theorists reverse this question, asking, Why don't we all do it? that is, Why do people *not* engage in deviant behaviour? In an effort to answer this question, sociologist Walter Reckless (1967) developed a theory of social control, which states that certain factors draw people toward deviance while others "insulate" them from such behaviour. According to Reckless, people are drawn to deviance by poverty, unemployment, and lack of educational opportunity. They also may be influenced by members of deviant subcultures, media depictions of deviant behaviour, and their own feelings of frustration, hostility, or inferiority. However, many people do not turn to deviance because they are insulated by *outer containments* such as supportive family and friends, reasonable social expectations, and supervision by others and by *inner containments* such as self-control, a sense of responsibility, and resistance to unlawful diversions.

Extending Reckless's containment theory, Travis Hirschi (1969) developed a theory suggesting that deviant behaviour is minimized when people have strong bonds that bind them to families, school, peers, churches, and other social institutions. **Social bond theory** holds that the **probability of deviant behaviour increases when**

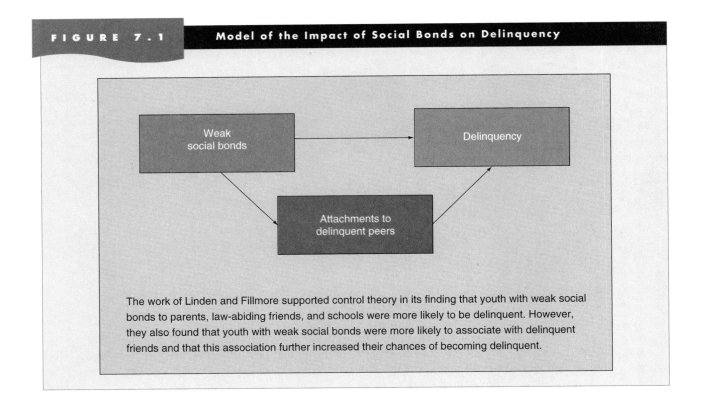

| FIGURE 7.1 | Model of the Impact of Social Bonds on Delinquency |

Weak social bonds → Delinquency

Weak social bonds → Attachments to delinquent peers

Attachments to delinquent peers → Delinquency

The work of Linden and Fillmore supported control theory in its finding that youth with weak social bonds to parents, law-abiding friends, and schools were more likely to be delinquent. However, they also found that youth with weak social bonds were more likely to associate with delinquent friends and that this association further increased their chances of becoming delinquent.

a person's ties to society are weakened or broken. According to Hirschi, social bonding consists of (1) *attachment* to other people, (2) *commitment* to conventional lines of behaviour such as schooling and job success, (3) *involvement* in conventional activities, and (4) *belief* in the legitimacy of conventional values and norms. Although Hirschi did not include females in his study, others who have replicated his study with both females and males have found that the theory appears to explain the delinquency of both (see Linden and Fillmore, 1981).

While Hirschi's theory did not differentiate between bonds to conventional and to deviant others, several researchers have modified the theory and have suggested that the probability of crime or delinquency increases when a person's social bonds are weak and when peers promote antisocial values and deviant behaviour (see Figure 7.1). Gang members may bond with one another rather than with persons who subscribe to dominant cultural values. As one gang member explains:

Before I joined the gang, I could see that you could count on your boys to help in times of need and that meant a lot to me. And when I needed money, sure

enough they gave it to me. Nobody else would have given it to me; my parents didn't have it, and there was no other place to go. The gang was just like they said they would be, and they'll continue to be there when I need them. (Jankowski, 1991:42)

INTERACTIONIST PERSPECTIVES ON CRIME AND DEVIANCE

As we discussed in Chapter 4, interactionists focus on how people develop a self-concept and learn conforming behaviour through the process of socialization. According to interactionists, deviance is learned in the same way as conformity—through interaction with others.

Differential Association Theory

More than fifty years ago, sociologist Edwin Sutherland (1939) developed a theory to explain how people learn deviance through social interaction. **Differential association theory** states that individuals have a greater tendency to deviate from societal norms when they frequently associate with persons who favour deviance over conformity. According to Sutherland, people learn the necessary techniques and the motives, drives, rationalizations, and attitudes of deviant behaviour from people with whom they associate. Peter Letkemann (1973), for example, described how a former Canadian penitentiary resident learned the now-obsolete art of safecracking:

> Prior to doing his first "can" [safe] [he] bugged an older safecracker in prison "until he finally divulged how to do it." This instruction, he added was "not like a teacher–student, it was just a matter of discussion during work."
>
> When he left the prison he went back to his regular partner and described to him what he had learned about safes. His partner said this was ridiculous but [he] persuaded him to come along: "I followed the instructions to the letter. It opened—we were both overcome with it all —the ease of it all!"
>
> This first job had been a punch job [breaking into a safe without explosives]—technically the simplest. Following this [he] and his partner "opened many doors by trial and error." ... This went on for four years; they had not yet used explosives, nor had they ever been caught punching safes. They became increasingly eager to try explosives since they found so many safes that couldn't be opened any other way.
>
> During this time, [he] was associating with other safecrackers ... He eventually asked another safecracker whether he could borrow some grease [nitroglycerine]. "I wouldn't admit that I knew nothing about it." He obtained the grease and chose a small safe, but was unsuccessful. The next day, he discussed his problem with some more experienced safecrackers. He found he had used too long a fuse and was advised to use electric knockers [detonators]. This he did with success. (Letkemann, 1973:136)

Another example of this learning of deviance—the acquisition of certain attitudes and the mastery of techniques—is provided in Box 7.2, which discusses how in Japan, younger organized crime gang members serve apprenticeships to older members of their organizations.

Differential association is most likely to result in criminal activity when a person has frequent, intense, and long-lasting interaction with others who violate the law. When there are more factors favouring violation of the law than there are

opposing it, the person is more likely to become a criminal. Ties to other deviants can be particularly important in the world of organized crime, where the willingness of peers to stand up for one another can be critical in maintaining power in the face of violent opposition from competitors. Daniel Wolf, an anthropologist who rode with the Rebels, an Edmonton biker gang, describes this solidarity:

> For an outlaw biker, the greatest fear is not of the police; rather, it is of a slight variation of his own mirror image: the patch holder [full-fledged member] of another club. Under slightly different circumstances those men would call each other "brother." But when turf is at stake, inter-club rivalry and warfare completely override any considerations of the common bonds of being a biker—and brother kills brother. None of the outlaws that I rode with enjoyed the prospect of having to break the bones of another biker. Nor did they look forward to having to live with the hate–fear syndrome that dominates a conflict in which there are no rules. I came to realize that the willingness of an outlaw to lay down his life in these conflicts goes beyond a belligerent masculinity that brooks no challenge. When a patch holder defends his colours, he defends his personal identity, his community, his lifestyle. When a war is on, loyalty to the club and one another arises out of the midst of danger, out of apprehension of possible injury, mutilation, or worse. Whether one considers this process as desperate, heroic, or just outlandishly foolish and banal does not really matter. What matters is that, for patch holders, the brotherhood emerges as a necessary feature of their continued existence as individuals and as a group. (1996:11)

Differential association theory contributes to our knowledge of how deviant behaviour reflects the individual's learned techniques, values, attitudes, motives, and rationalizations. However, critics question why many individuals who have had extensive contact with people who violate the law still conform most of the time. They also assert that the theory does not adequately assess possible linkages between social inequality and criminal behaviour.

Labelling Theory

Two complementary processes are involved in the definition of deviance. First, some people act (or are believed to act) in a manner contrary to the expectations of others. Second, others disapprove

FIGURE 7.2 **Labelling Theory**

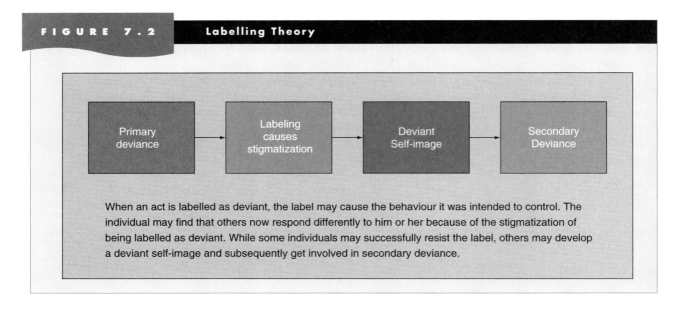

When an act is labelled as deviant, the label may cause the behaviour it was intended to control. The individual may find that others now respond differently to him or her because of the stigmatization of being labelled as deviant. While some individuals may successfully resist the label, others may develop a deviant self-image and subsequently get involved in secondary deviance.

of and try to control this contrary behaviour. Part of this social control process involves labelling people as deviants. A very important contribution to the study of deviance was made by sociologists who asked the question, "Why are some people labelled as deviants while others are not?" *Labelling theory* **suggests that deviants are those people who have been successfully labelled as such by others.** The process of labelling is directly related to the power and status of those persons who do the labelling and those who are being labelled. Behaviour, then, is not deviant in and of itself; it is defined as such by a social audience (Erikson, 1962). According to sociologist Howard Becker (1963), *moral entrepreneurs* are persons who use their own views of right and wrong to establish rules and label others as deviant. These rules are enforced on persons with less power.

William Chambliss (1973) witnessed the labelling process when he observed members of two groups of high school boys: the Saints and the Roughnecks. Both groups were "constantly occupied with truancy, drinking, wild parties, petty theft, and vandalism." Overall, the Saints committed more offences than the Roughnecks, but the Roughnecks were labelled as troublemakers by school and law enforcement officials while the Saints were seen as being likely to succeed. Unlike the Roughnecks, none of the Saints was ever arrested.

Chambliss attributed this contradictory response by authorities to the fact the Saints came from "good families," did well in school, and thus were forgiven for their "boys will be boys"–type behaviour. By contrast, the Roughnecks came from lower-income families, did poorly in school, and generally were viewed negatively. Although both groups engaged in similar behaviour, only the Roughnecks were stigmatized by a deviant label.

The concept of secondary deviance is important to labelling theory because it suggests that when people accept a negative label or stigma that has been applied to them, the label may contribute to the type of behaviour it initially was meant to control. According to sociologist Edwin Lemert (1951), *primary deviance* **is the initial act of rule breaking.** *Secondary deviance* **occurs when a person who has been labelled deviant accepts that new identity and continues the deviant behaviour.** For example, a person may smoke marijuana, not be labelled deviant, and subsequently decide to forgo such an act in the future. Secondary deviance occurs if the person smokes marijuana, is labelled a "pothead," accepts that label, and then continues to smoke marijuana.

A major contribution of labelling theory is that it calls attention to the way in which social control and personal identity are intertwined: labelling may contribute to the acceptance of deviant roles and self-images. Critics argue that this theory does not explain what causes the original acts that make up primary deviance. Nor does it provide insight into why some people accept deviant labels and others do not (Cavender, 1995).

While interactionist perspectives are concerned with how people learn deviant behaviour, identities, and social roles through interaction with others, *conflict theorists* are interested in how certain kinds of people and behaviour, and not others, come to be defined as deviant.

CRITICAL PERSPECTIVES ON CRIME AND DEVIANCE

Who determines what kinds of behaviour are deviant or criminal? According to conflict perspectives, people in positions of power maintain their advantage by using the law to protect their own interests. Conflict theorists suggest that lifestyles considered deviant by political and economic elites often are defined as illegal. They note that the activities of poor and lower-income individuals are more likely to be defined as criminal than those of persons from middle- and upper-income backgrounds. For example, those who commit welfare fraud are more likely to face criminal charges than are professionals whose misconduct is generally dealt with by disciplinary committees of their peers rather than by the criminal courts. The relative degrees of social harm caused by either of these groups seems to have little relevance in the determination of who is defined as criminal; what matters more may be the power of some groups to resist sanctions.

The Conflict Approach

Although Karl Marx wrote very little about deviance and crime, many of his ideas are found in a critical approach that has emerged from earlier Marxist and radical perspectives on criminology. The critical approach is based on the assumption that the criminal justice system protects the power and privilege of the capitalist class.

As we saw in Chapter 1, Marx based his critique of capitalism on the inherent conflict that he believed existed between the capitalists and the working class. According to Marx, social institutions (such as law, politics, and education) make up a superstructure in society that legitimizes the class structure and maintains the capitalists' superior position in it. Crime is an expression of the individual's struggle against the unjust social conditions and inequality produced by capitalism.

According to sociologist Richard Quinney (1980), people with economic and political power define as criminal any behaviour that threatens their own interests. The powerful use law to control those who are without power. For example, drug laws enacted early in the twentieth century were passed and enforced in an effort to control immigrant workers, particularly Chinese workers, who were more inclined than most other residents of Canada to smoke opium. The laws were motivated by racism more than by a real concern with drug use (Cook, 1969). By contrast, while the Canadian government passed anticombines legislation in 1889 in response to concerns expressed by labour and small business people about the growing power of monopoly capitalists, the law had no impact on major companies engaged in price-fixing and other means of limiting competition. Having symbolic anticombines laws on the books merely shored up the government's legitimacy by making it appear responsive to public concerns about big business (Smandych, 1985).

Why do people commit crimes? Some critical theorists believe that the affluent commit crimes because they are greedy and want more than they have. Corporate or white-collar crimes such as stock market manipulation, land speculation, and fraudulent bankruptcies and crimes committed on behalf of organizations often involve huge sums of money and harm many people. By contrast, street crimes such as robbery and aggravated assault generally involve small sums of money and cause harm to limited numbers of victims (Bonger, 1969). According to critical theorists, the poor commit street crimes in order to survive; they find that they cannot afford the necessary essentials such as food, clothing, shelter, and health care. Thus, some crime represents a rational response by the poor to the unequal distribution of resources in society (Gordon, 1973). Further, living in poverty may lead to violent crime and victimization *of the poor by the poor*. For example, violent gang activity may be a collective response of young people to seemingly hopeless poverty (Quinney, 1979).

In sum, the critical approach argues that criminal law protects the interests of the affluent and powerful. The way laws are written and enforced benefits the capitalist class by ensuring that individuals at the bottom of the social class structure do not infringe on the property or threaten the safety of those at the top (Reiman, 1984). However, critics assert that critical theorists have not shown that powerful economic and political elites actually manipulate criminal law making and enforcement for their own benefit. Rather, people of all classes share a consensus about the criminality of certain acts. For example, laws that

BOX 7.2 SOCIOLOGY IN GLOBAL PERSPECTIVE

STREET YOUTHS, *BOSOZOKU*, AND *YAKUZA* IN JAPAN

Criminologists have identified three categories of gangs in Japan: youth gangs, *bosozoku* (hot-rod gangs), and *yakuza* (networks of adult male criminal organizations). In Japanese society, where high levels of conformity are expected, youth groups and gangs deliberately draw public attention to their deviant status.

Youth gang members, who are between the ages of 14 and 20, want to separate themselves from mainstream society. Although these gangs may include females, the focus is on masculinity and male prowess. *Bosozoku* are males (and a very few females) aged 17 to 20, whose activities centre on nightly high-speed, high-noise, and high-risk rides on motorcycles and in customized cars as they are chased by the police. Members who reach the age of 20 are considered too old for the group and must find something else to do or join the *yakuza*, which is made up of adult men, with younger men in apprentice roles. One Japanese man, Hayashi, describes his move from the youth gang to the *yakuza*:

> My life as a *yakuza* [organized crime gang member] began with difficulty, when as a young delinquent I joined a

prohibit murder, rape, and armed robbery protect not only middle- and upper-income people but also low-income people, who frequently are the victims of such violent crimes (Klockars, 1979). While some laws do protect the rich and powerful, others reflect the interests of all citizens.

FEMINIST PERSPECTIVES ON CRIME AND DEVIANCE

Can theories developed to explain male behaviour help us understand female deviance and crime? According to some feminist scholars, the answer is no. The few early studies that were conducted on "women's crimes" focused almost exclusively on prostitution and attributed the cause of this crime to women's biological or psychological "inferiority." As late as the 1980s, researchers were still looking for unique predisposing factors that led women to commit crime, which was often seen as individual psychopathology rather than as a response to their social environment. These theories, which reinforce existing female stereotypes, have had a negative impact on both our understanding and our treatment of female offenders.

A new interest in women and deviance developed in 1975 when two books—Freda Adler's *Sisters in Crime* and Rita James Simons's *Women and Crime*—declared that women's crime rates were going to increase significantly as a result of the women's liberation movement. Although this so-called emancipation theory of female crime has been strongly criticized by subsequent analysts (Comack, 2000), Adler's and Simons's works encouraged feminist scholars (both women and men) to examine the relationship between gender, deviance, and crime more closely. While there is no single feminist perspective on deviance and crime, three schools of thought have emerged.

Liberal feminism explains women's deviance and crime as a rational response to gender discrimination experienced in work, marriage, and interpersonal relationships. Some female crimes may be attributed to women's lack of educational and job opportunities and stereotypical expectations about what roles women should have in society. For example, a woman is no more likely to be a big-time drug dealer or an organized crime boss than she is to be a corporate director (see Daly and Chesney-Lind, 1988; Simpson, 1989).

Radical feminism suggests that patriarchy (male domination over females) keeps women more tied to family and home, even if women also work full time. Based on this approach, prostitution might be explained as a reflection of society's sexual double standard, whereby it is acceptable for a

BOX 7.2

CONTINUED

gang ... I wanted to be a gambler, but for a long time after joining the family I wasn't allowed to gamble. First I helped with the cooking and cleaning ...

After some months of cleaning duty, I got a position doing *tachiban* [standing guard], but on cold winter days it was difficult. Finally, when new members joined our gang, I was able to do *zoriban* [arranging shoes in order]. These moves were important. For the first time I was not in the house, cleaning. Unless you take these steps, you could not become a card dealer ...

One must pledge total obedience. To do that you must receive sake from the boss, with a third person as a witness. It is a very important ceremony ... *Yakuza* tradition will never cease because we're different from ordinary people. That's why we joined this world. And we share the same idea that if we make one big mistake we die together. (quoted in Kaplan and Dubro, 1987:142–144)

man to pay for sex but unacceptable for a woman to accept money for such services. Although prostitution laws in Canada define both the prostitute and the customer as violating the law, women are far more likely than men to be arrested, brought to trial, convicted, and sentenced for prostitution-related offences.

Socialist feminism contends that women are exploited by capitalism and patriarchy. Because most females have relatively low-wage jobs and few economic resources, crimes such as prostitution and shoplifting become a means to earn money or acquire consumer products. Instead of freeing women from their problems, however, prostitution institutionalizes women's dependence on men and results in a form of female sexual slavery (Vito and Holmes, 1994).

Recently, some feminist scholars have observed that these schools of feminist thought have not placed sufficient emphasis on race and ethnicity in their analyses. As a result, some recent studies have focused on the simultaneous effects of race, class, and gender on deviant behaviour. Regina Arnold (1990) attributes many of the women's offences to living in families in which sexual abuse, incest, and other violence left them few choices except to engage in deviance. Economic marginality and racism also contributed to their victimization. These conclusions are reinforced by a recent study in which Elizabeth Comack exam-

ined the relationship between women's earlier victimization and their subsequent involvement in Manitoba's criminal justice system. The incidence of prior victimization was pervasive among women incarcerated in a provincial jail. To examine the problem in detail, Comack interviewed twenty-four women. The abuse suffered by the women was connected to their criminal behaviour in several ways. Some women turned to crime as a means of coping with their histories of abuse. "Meredith" had been sexually abused by her father since the age of four or five. She was in jail for fraud and had been involved in drug use and prostitution:

> Some people are violent, some people take it out in other ways, but that was my only way to release it. It was like, it's almost orgasmic, you know, you'd write the cheques, and you'd get home and you'd go through all these things and it's like, "There's so much there. I have all these new things to keep my mind off. I don't have to deal with the old issues." And so you do it. And it becomes an escape. (Comack, 1996:86)

Others break the law in the course of resisting abuse. "Janice" had been raped as a teenager and turned to alcohol as a means of coping. Serving time for manslaughter, she recounts the circumstances of the offence:

CONCEPT TABLE   7.A

THEORETICAL PERSPECTIVES ON DEVIANCE

	THEORY	KEY ELEMENTS
Functionalist Perspectives		
Robert Merton	Strain theory	Deviance occurs when access to the approved means of reaching culturally approved goals is blocked.
Richard Cloward/ Lloyd Ohlin	Opportunity theory	For deviance to occur, people must have the opportunity. Access to illegitimate opportunity structures varies, and this helps determine the nature of the deviance in which a person will engage.
Travis Hirschi	Social control/social bonding	Social bonds keep people from becoming criminals. When ties to family, friends, and others become weak, an individual is most likely to engage in criminal behaviour.
Interactionist Perspectives		
Edwin Sutherland	Differential association	Deviant behaviour is learned in interaction with others. A person becomes delinquent when exposure to lawbreaking attitudes is more extensive than exposure to law-abiding attitudes.
Howard Becker	Labelling theory	Acts are deviant or criminal because they have been labelled as such. Powerful groups often label less powerful individuals.
Edwin Lemert	Primary/secondary deviance	Primary deviance is the initial act. Secondary deviance occurs when a person accepts the label of "deviant" and continues to engage in the behaviour that initially produced the label.
Critical Perspectives		
Karl Marx Richard Quinney	Conflict approach	The powerful use law and the criminal justice system to protect their own class interests.
Feminist Perspectives		
Kathleen Daly Meda Chesney-Lind Elizabeth Comack	Feminist approach	Historically, women have been ignored in research on crime. Liberal feminism views women's deviance as arising from gender discrimination; radical feminism focuses on patriarchy; and socialist feminism emphasizes the effects of capitalism and patriarchy on women.

... well I was at a party, and this guy, older, older guy, came, came on to me. He tried telling me, "Why don't you go to bed with me. I'm getting some money, you know." And I said, "No." And then he started hitting me and then he raped me and then (pause) I lost it. Like I just, I went, I got very angry and I snapped. And I started hitting him. I threw a coffee table on top of his head and then I stabbed him, and then I left. (Comack, 1996b:96)

While abuse was strongly related to the women's law violations, Comack also found that race and class were factors contributing to the criminal behaviour of many of the women; most were Aboriginal and poor.

We have examined functionalist, interactionist, conflict, and feminist perspectives on deviance and crime (see Concept Table 7.A). These explanations help us to understand the causes and consequences of certain kinds of behaviour; however, they also make us aware of the limitations of our knowledge about deviance and crime.

CRIME CLASSIFICATION AND STATISTICS

The law divides crime into different categories. We will look first at the legal classifications of crime and then at categories typically used by sociologists and criminologists.

How the Law Classifies Crime

The law divides crime into summary conviction and indictable offences. The distinction between the two is based on the seriousness of the crime. *Indictable offences* include serious crimes such as homicide, sexual assault, robbery, and break and enter. *Summary conviction offences* are relatively minor offences, including fraudulently obtaining food from a restaurant, causing a disturbance, and wilfully committing an indecent act. Summary conviction offences are punishable by a fine of up to $2000 and/or six months in jail.

How Sociologists Classify Crime

Sociologists categorize crimes based on how they are committed and how society views the offences. We will examine four types: (1) street

crime, (2) occupational, or white-collar, and corporate crime, (3) organized crime, and (4) political crime. As you read about these types of crime, ask yourself how you feel about them. Should each be a crime? How severe should the sanctions be against each type?

STREET CRIME When people think of crime, the images that most commonly come to mind are of *street crime,* **which includes all violent crime, certain property crimes, and certain morals crimes.** Examples are robbery, assault, and break and enter. These are the crimes that occupy most of the time and attention of the criminal justice system. Obviously, all street crime does not occur on the street; it frequently occurs in the home, workplace, and other locations.

Violent crime consists of actions involving force or the threat of force against others, including murder, sexual assault, robbery, and aggravated assault. Violent crimes are probably the most anxiety-provoking of all criminal behaviour. Victims often are physically injured or even lose their lives; the psychological trauma may last for years after the event (Parker, 1995). Violent crime receives the most sustained attention from law enforcement officials and the media (see Warr, 1995). And, while much attention may be given to the violent stranger, the vast majority of violent crime victims actually are injured by someone whom they know: family members, friends, neighbours, or co-workers (Silverman and Kennedy, 1993).

Property crimes include break and enter, theft, motor vehicle theft, and arson. While violent crime receives the most publicity, property crime is much more common. In most property crimes, the primary motive is to obtain money or some other desired valuable.

Morals crimes involve an illegal action voluntarily engaged in by the participants, such as prostitution, illegal gambling, the private use of illegal drugs, and illegal pornography. Many people assert that such conduct should not be labelled as a crime; these offences often are referred to as "victimless crimes" because they involve exchanges of illegal goods or services among willing adults (Schur, 1965).

However, morals crimes can include children and adolescents as well as adults. Young children and adolescents may unwillingly become child pornography "stars" or prostitutes. Members of juvenile gangs often find selling drugs to be a lucrative business in which getting addicted and/or arrested is merely an occupational hazard.

OCCUPATIONAL AND CORPORATE CRIME Although sociologist Edwin Sutherland (1949) developed the concept of white-collar crime almost fifty years ago, it was not until the 1980s that the public really became aware of its nature. *Occupational* or *white-collar crime* **consists of illegal activities committed by people in the course of their employment or in dealing with their financial affairs.**

At the heart of much white-collar crime is a violation of positions of trust in business or government (Shapiro, 1990). These activities include pilfering (employee theft of company property or profits), soliciting bribes or kickbacks, and embezzling. In the past decade, computers have created even greater access to such illegal practices. Some white-collar criminals set up businesses for the sole purpose of victimizing the general public, engaging in activities such as land swindles, securities thefts, and consumer fraud.

In addition to acting for their own financial benefit, some white-collar offenders become involved in criminal conspiracies designed to improve the market share or profitability of their companies. This is known as *corporate crime*— **illegal acts committed by corporate employees on behalf of the corporation and with its support.** Examples include antitrust violations; false advertising; infringements on patents, copyrights, and trademarks; price-fixing; and financial fraud. These crimes are a result of deliberate decisions made by corporate personnel to enhance resources or profits at the expense of competitors, consumers, and the general public.

The cost of white-collar and corporate crimes far exceeds that of street crime. Gabor (1994) reports that tax evasion costs Canadians about $30 billion a year. In one of the world's biggest white-collar crimes, investors in Calgary's Bre-X gold-mining company lost around $5 billion when it was learned that geologist Michael de Guzman had salted core samples with gold to make a worthless mining property look like the world's biggest gold find. At the individual level, while few bank robbers get away with more than a few thousand dollars, Julius Melnitzer (a London, Ontario, lawyer) defrauded Canadian banks of $90 million in order to support his lavish lifestyle.

Corporate crimes can also be very costly in terms of lives lost and injury. Laureen Snider (1988) found that occupational accidents and ill-

Michael de Guzman (right), a geologist for the Bre-X gold-mining company, is one of those responsible for one of the world's largest stock frauds. De Guzman committed suicide by jumping from a helicopter while travelling to the Bre-X property in Indonesia.

nesses are the third leading cause of death in Canada. She attributes at least half of these deaths to unsafe and illegal working conditions. Working conditions in the mining industry, for example, have been especially dangerous. Decades ago, large numbers of Canadian miners died because their employers failed to protect them from mine hazards. Coal miners died of black lung, a condition caused by inhaling coal dust, and fluorspar miners died from the effects of inhaling silica dust in unventilated mineshafts. Not only did the mine owners fail to provide safe working conditions, but company doctors were also told not to advise the miners of the seriousness of their illnesses. The loss of 26 miners in a preventable explosion at Nova Scotia's Westray mine in 1992 suggests some mine owners have yet to put their employees' lives above profits.

One reason many employers have been reluctant to implement required safety measures is because the penalties for violating workplace health and safety laws are so light. Consider the case of Silco, an Edmonton-based construction company. A Silco employee fell to his death from a homemade man-basket attached to an unstable crane boom. The company had received three different orders to improve their safety practices earlier that year, but had ignored all of them, including a stop-work order the month of the accident. Despite Silco's obvious negligence, the company received a fine of only $6000 for its part in the employee's death (Ward, 1996).

Although people who commit occupational and corporate crimes can be arrested, fined, and sent to prison, many people do not regard such behaviour as "criminal." People who tend to condemn street crime are less sure of how their own (or their friends') financial and corporate behaviour should be judged. At most, punishment for such offences is usually a fine or a relatively brief prison sentence at a minimum-security facility. As you learned in Chapter 6, responsibility for corporate wrongdoing is often so difficult to determine that nobody is ever deemed culpable for corporate crimes.

In many corporate crimes it is more difficult to attach individual blame than in street crimes. It is far easier to determine who was responsible for a sexual assault or a robbery than to determine the specific individuals who are responsible for complex price-fixing arrangements between companies. For example, a scheme by Canada's largest flour-milling companies to fix prices on flour sold to the government for food aid to Third World countries continued for more than a decade and involved very complex business arrangements. In some respects, individual blame is legally irrelevant in most corporate crimes because usually it is the corporation that is prosecuted, not the individual manager. This, of course, makes corporate officials less accountable for their actions.

One final point that can be made about white-collar crime is that the concept also fits people who wear blue collars. Because of this, some have suggested that *occupational crime* may be a more accurate term. Many tradespeople defraud the government by doing work "off the books" in order to avoid provincial sales tax and the goods and services tax. Some blue-collar businesses have bad records of consumer fraud. Robert Sikorsky (1990) travelled across Canada and visited 152 automobile repair shops. While doing so, he documented an appalling degree of misconduct in this business. Before each visit, he disconnected the idle air control in his car, which triggered a warning light on the instrument panel. The repair needed was obvious and simple—reinsert the connector. But, more than half the shops Sikorsky visited performed unnecessary work, overcharged him for work, or lied about the work that had been done. In one case he was presented with an estimate of $570.

ORGANIZED CRIME *Organized crime* is a business operation that supplies illegal goods and services for profit. Organized crime includes drug trafficking, prostitution, liquor and cigarette smuggling, loan-sharking, money laundering, and large-scale theft, such as truck hijacking (Simon and Eitzen, 1993). No single organization controls all organized crime, but many groups operate at all levels of society. Organized crime thrives because there is great demand for illegal goods and services. This public demand has produced illicit supply systems with global connections. These activities are highly profitable, since groups that have a monopoly over goods and services the public strongly desires can set their own price. Legitimate competitors are excluded because of the illegality; illegitimate competitors are controlled by force.

The deadly nature of organized crime has been shown in Montreal, which has been the scene of a major turf war between two rival biker gangs: the Rock Machine and the Hell's Angels. The two gangs have been engaged in a battle for control of a large segment of the city's illegal drug market. During January and February of 1995, the battle took a particularly bloody turn as rival gang members died at a rate of almost one a week as a result of car bombings, shootings, and stabbings.

Along with their illegal enterprises, organized crime groups have infiltrated the world of legitimate business. Linkages between legitimate businesses and organized crime exist in banking, hotels and motels, immigration consulting, real estate, garbage collection, vending machines, construction, delivery and long-distance hauling, garment manufacturing, insurance, stocks and bonds, vacation resorts, and funeral parlours. In addition, law enforcement and government officials may be corrupted through bribery, campaign contributions, and favours intended to buy them off, although this has been much less of a problem in Canada than in many other countries.

POLITICAL CRIMES The term *political crime* refers to illegal or unethical acts involving the misuse of power by government officials, or illegal/unethical acts perpetrated against the government by outsiders seeking to make a political statement, undermine the government, or overthrow it. Government officials may use their authority unethically or illegally for material gain or political power. They may engage in graft (taking advantage of political position to gain money or property) through bribery, kickbacks, or "insider" deals that financially benefit them. For example, several members of the Mulroney

BOX 7.3 SOCIOLOGY AND TECHNOLOGY

TECHNOLOGY AND CRIME: ORGANIZED CRIME AND THE INTERNET

For a number of reasons, the fight against organized crime is very difficult. Organized crimes such as drug trafficking and living off the avails of prostitution have no victims who complain, and in others, such as extortion, the victims are too intimidated to go to the police or to testify against those who harm them. Because of the necessity of ethnic ties and the long apprenticeship needed to join organized crime groups, infiltrating these groups is difficult. The very real threat of vengeance makes it unlikely that organized gang members will testify against fellow gang members. One successful method of acquiring evidence has been electronic surveillance. Wiretaps and other listening devices have enabled justice officials to arrest and convict many high-level organized crime leaders including the notorious Mafioso John Gotti, leader of New York's Gambino family.

The rise of the Internet threatens the ability of law enforcement agencies to continue to collect information about organized crime. While the Internet is now not a very private place, new encryption technology now being developed should soon make Internet communication much more secure. Better encryption would speed the development of Internet commerce, as people would be more willing to transact business over the Internet if they knew the information they were sending was secure. However, effective encryption creates an obvious problem for law enforcement: if communications can be securely encrypted, the ability of the police to eavesdrop on organized criminals will be greatly reduced. As a result, police in North America want to restrict the sale of this software and they want the software manufacturers to provide them with the master keys to the encryption codes so that they can freely read Internet communications.

While access to these codes may be helpful for law enforcement agencies, what impact

---

government were charged with bribery, influence peddling, and abuse of public trust, and many allegations have been made that say many other senior officials were involved in these activities and in subsequent coverups (Corrado, 1996).

Other types of corruption have been costly for taxpayers, including dubious use of public funds and public property, corruption in the regulation of commercial activities (such as food inspection), graft in zoning and land use decisions, and campaign contributions and other favours to legislators that corrupt the legislative process. While some political crimes are for personal material gain, others (such as illegal wiretapping and political "dirty tricks") are aimed at gaining or maintaining political office or influence.

Some acts committed by agents of the government against persons and groups believed to be threats to national security also are political crimes. Four types of political deviance have been attributed to some officials: (1) secrecy and deception designed to manipulate public opinion, (2) abuse of power, (3) prosecution of individuals due to their political activities, and (4) official violence, such as police brutality (Simon and Eitzen, 1993).

Political crimes also include illegal or unethical acts perpetrated against the government by outsiders seeking to make a political statement or to undermine or overthrow the government. Examples include treason, acts of political sabotage, and certain types of environmental protests. During the 1960s, the Front de Libération du Québec (FLQ) tried to bring about an independent Quebec through terrorism (Corrado, 1996). Several people were killed in bombings, and in 1970 the FLQ precipitated the October Crisis by kidnapping James Cross, a British trade official, and Pierre Laporte, a provincial cabinet minister. Laporte was killed, and the federal government invoked the War Measures Act, which suspended certain civil liberties in order to deal with the crisis. While the FLQ's acts were clearly criminal, debate continues about whether the government was justified in using the War Measures Act, or whether invoking it also constituted a political

BOX 7.3

CONTINUED

would giving this access to them have on society? Bruce Phillips, Canada's privacy commissioner, feels that this would move Canada a step toward becoming a police state. In a report on this issue, Phillips has said it would be like requiring everybody to give the police a key to everybody's homes in case they needed to enter it someday and that it would likely be a violation of the Charter of Rights. Respecting these concerns, the government ultimately decided not to attempt to regulate encryption.

What do you think about this issue? Should there be an absolute right to privacy on the Internet, or does the need for the police to combat organized crime outweigh the individual's right to privacy? Should the police be able to have complete access to encryption keys or should it be regulated by the judiciary in the same way that warrants for searches and wiretaps are now regulated?

In addition to providing a means of communication for organized criminals, the Internet can be used to commit crimes in several other ways. For example, criminals themselves may break encryption programs and use confidential data transmitted by others. The Internet has proven to be a very effective way of distributing pornography, including child pornography. There are also many different types of frauds that can be committed over the Internet. You can look up some of these crimes at **www.scambusters.org** or at **www. ftc.gov/bcp/conline/pubs/alerts/ doznalrt.htm.**

Source: Phillips, 1998.

crime aimed at defeating the Quebec nationalist movement.

Crime Statistics

While citizens, police, and policy makers all wish to know how much crime there is and what forms this crime takes, those who commit crimes normally try to conceal their actions. It is always difficult to gather statistics about crime and to get access to the social worlds of criminals. Thus our information about crime will always be incomplete and we can never be certain that it is completely accurate. Our main sources of information about crime are police statistics and victimization surveys.

OFFICAL STATISTICS Our most important source of crime data is the Canadian Uniform Crime Reports (CUCR) system, which summarizes crimes reported to all Canadian police departments. The CUCR is compiled by the Canadian Centre for Justice Statistics, which is part of Statistics Canada. This system collects information on almost all Criminal Code offences as well as on violations of federal and provincial statutes. Most of our public information about crime comes from the CUCR. When we read that the homicide rate in British Columbia is higher than the national average, or that in 1997, over 2.5 million offences were reported to the police, this information is usually based on CUCR data. Figure 7.3 shows trends in violent and property crimes, and Figure 7.4 shows Canada's homicide rates. While most Canadians think that crime is increasing, these charts show that it has begun to decline over the past decade. The decline is particularly significant in the case of homicide where 1997 rates were the lowest they have been in nearly thirty years.

Crime figures should be interpreted very cautiously. While one can have confidence in homicide statistics, the accuracy of other crime statistics is less certain. Since many policy decisions by governments, as well as decisions by indi-

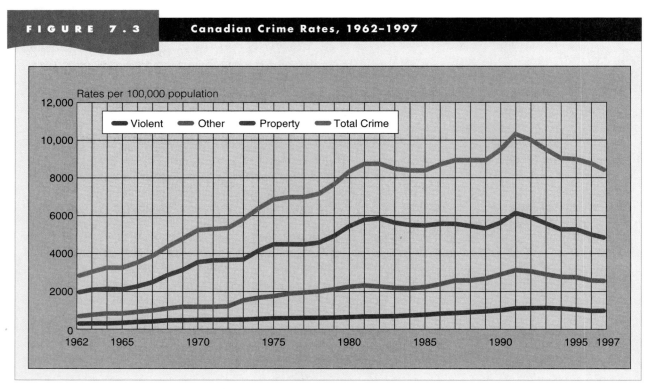

FIGURE 7.3   **Canadian Crime Rates, 1962–1997**

Reproduced by authority of the Minister of Industry, 1998, Statistics Canada, from Uniform Crime Reporting Survey, Canadian Centre for Justice Statistics, *Juristat*, Cat. no. 85-002.

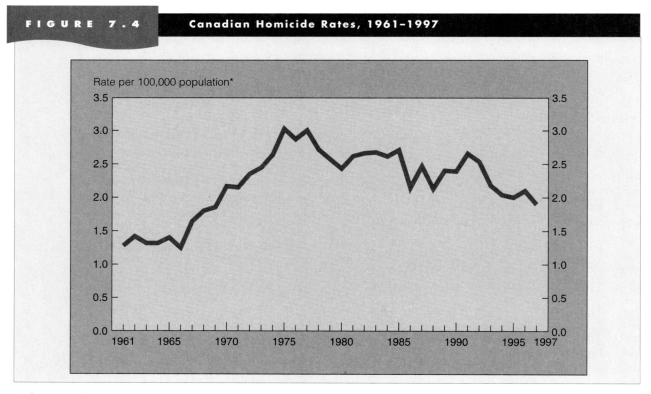

FIGURE 7.4   **Canadian Homicide Rates, 1961–1997**

As of 1971, population estimates were adjusted to reflect new methods of calculation.

Reproduced by authority of the Minister of Industry, 1998, Statistics Canada, from Homicide Survey, Policing Services Program, Canadian Centre for Justice Statistics, *Juristat*, Cat. no. 85-002.

viduals about their personal safety, are based on CUCR statistics, it is important to recognize their limitations.

The major weakness of the CUCR is that police statistics always underreport the actual amount of crime. The vast majority of offences reported in the CUCR come to the attention of the police from the reports of victims of crime, and victims do not report all crimes. Furthermore, reporting of crime is inconsistent from place to place and from time to time. Official crime rates are the result of a criminal act, a complaint by a victim or witness, and a response by the criminal justice system. A change in any of these will lead to an increase or decrease in crime rates. This makes it very difficult to make sense of crime patterns and trends.

For example, Figure 7.3 shows that rates of reported violent crimes increased significantly in Canada during the late 1980s and early 1990s. In fact, they almost doubled between 1980 and 1990. While we don't know the real number of these crimes, we do know that at least part of the increase in reported crime is due to the fact that violence against women is now reported more often than it used to be (Linden, 1994). In the mid-1980s, many provincial governments directed police in their provinces to lay charges in all suspected cases of domestic violence. The procedures have been made progressively more effective since they were first implemented. This visible support by the justice system may have encouraged more victims to report spousal assaults. The impact of these changes can be seen in Winnipeg, where the police have instituted a mandatory charging policy and where the province has set up a special family violence court to facilitate the processing of spouse abuse cases. The number of domestic violence cases dealt with by this court rose from 1444 in 1990, the first year of the court's operation, to 3387 three years later (Ursel, 1996). It is likely that this increase was entirely due to changes in the reporting and recording of domestic assaults and not to any actual increase in family violence.

Another weakness of official statistics is that many crimes committed by persons of higher socioeconomic status are routinely handled by administrative or quasi-judicial bodies or by civil courts. To avoid negative publicity, many companies prefer to deal privately with offences like embezzlement committed by their employees, and these cases are never reported to the police. As a result, many elite crimes are never classified as "crimes," nor are the business people who commit them labelled as "criminals."

VICTIMIZATION SURVEYS The weaknesses of the CUCR have led to other methods of measuring crime, the most important of which is the *victimization survey*. Because a major problem with the CUCR is the fact that many people do not report their victimization, some governments carried out surveys in which members of the public were directly asked whether they had been victims of crime. In the largest Canadian survey, less than 42 percent of the victimizations reported by respondents had been reported to the police (Evans and Himelfarb, 1996). Thus reported crimes are only the "tip of the iceberg." People told interviewers they did not report a crime because they considered the incident too minor, because they felt it was a personal matter, because they preferred to deal with the problem in another way, or because they did not feel the police could do anything about the crime. Victimization surveys provide us with information about crimes that have not been officially reported, so they provide more accurate crime statistics than do police records. However, these surveys do have some weaknesses: people may not remember minor types of victimization; they may not report honestly to the interviewer; and they do not provide any information about "victimless crimes" such as drug use and illegal gambling. Despite these flaws, victimization surveys have shed new light on the extent of criminal behaviour and are a valuable complement to other ways of counting crimes.

For example, victimization surveys have provided additional information that has helped us to understand the increase in violent crimes discussed earlier. Victimization surveys conducted as part of Statistics Canada's General Social Survey showed that despite an increase of about 25 percent in the CUCR reported assault rate between 1988 and 1993, the rate of assault victimizations reported in the survey actually declined slightly during this period (Kingsley, 1996). While both police statistics and victimization surveys have their weaknesses, you can see how analyses of data from the CUCR and from the General Social Survey allow us to tentatively conclude that assaults did not increase even though many more were reported to the police. Rather, a combination of government policies that encourage the reporting and charging of assailants in domestic violence cases and increased public attention to the problem of spousal abuse have led to increased reporting and recording of these assaults. Assaults probably did not increase—we simply did a better job of counting them.

Street Crimes and Criminals

Given the limitations of official statistics, is it possible to determine who commits crimes? We have much more information available about conventional or street crime than elite crime. Therefore, statistics do not show who commits all types of crime. Age, gender, class, and race are important factors in official statistics pertaining to street crime. These are known as *correlates of crime.* That is, they are factors associated with criminal activity. One method of testing theories of crime is to see how well they explain these correlates.

AGE AND CRIME The age of the offender is one of the most significant factors associated with crime. Arrests increase from early adolescence, peak in young adulthood, and steadily decline with age. There is some variation in this pattern—for example, violent crimes peak at a later age than property crimes—but the general pattern is almost always the same. Crime is a young person's game. Figure 7.5 shows that property crimes peak between the ages of 18 to 24, while Figure 7.6 shows that violent crimes are most common among 25- to 34-year-olds.

The relationship between age and criminality exists in every society for which we have data (Hirschi and Gottfredson, 1983). Adolescence and early adulthood are the peak times for both offending and victimization. Possible explanations for the decline in crime rates after early adulthood are the physical effects of aging, which make some criminal activity more difficult, and the realization by older chronic offenders that further arrests will result in very long jail sentences. Perhaps the best explanation for maturational reform, though, is related to the different social positions of youth and adults. Adolescents are between childhood and adult life. They have few responsibilities and no clear social role. Adolescence is also a time when young people are breaking away from the controls of their parents and others and preparing to live on their own. As we age, we begin to acquire commitments and obligations that limit our freedom to choose a lifestyle that includes crime.

GENDER AND CRIME Another consistent correlate of crime is gender. Most crimes are committed by males. Females are more likely to be victims than offenders. As with age and crime, this relationship has existed in almost all times and cultures. However, while the age distribution is remarkably stable, considerably more variation in male/female crime ratios exists in different places, at different times, and for different types of crime.

Men make up over 80 percent of those charged with crimes in Canada. As Figure 7.7 shows, the degree of involvement of males and females varies substantially for different crimes. The most important gender differences in arrest rates are reflected in the proportionately greater involvement of men in violent crimes and major property offences.

The difference between male and female crime rates has narrowed over the past three decades. Hartnagel (2000) compared the rate of male and female adults charged with a variety of offences in 1968 and in 1992, and found that crime rates for females increased much more rapidly than for males during this period. The percentage of Criminal Code offences committed by females increased from 9 percent to 18 percent. While there was virtually no change in the proportion of females charged with homicide (11 percent versus 12 percent), the proportion of women charged with serious theft (9 percent to 18 percent), fraud (11 percent to 29 percent), and minor theft (22 percent to 34 percent) changed substantially.

What has caused this change in the sex distribution of crime? One clue comes from cross-cultural data showing very large differences in sex ratios of criminal involvement in different parts of the world. While the ratio of male to female crime in North America and Western Europe is between 5:1 and 10:1, ratios as high as 20,000:1 have been reported elsewhere. The ratios are highest (meaning that male rates of crime are much higher than those of females) in countries having the greatest differences between the roles of men and women. Where women follow traditional roles in which their lives are centred exclusively on the home, their crime rates are very low. On the other hand, where women's lives are more similar to men's, their crime rates will be higher. This is consistent with the change in women's crime rates over the past several decades in Canada, where the role of women has come to resemble that of men.

While role convergence may explain some of the reduction in the gap between male and female crime rates, the rate of convergence has slowed and it does not seem likely that women will ever

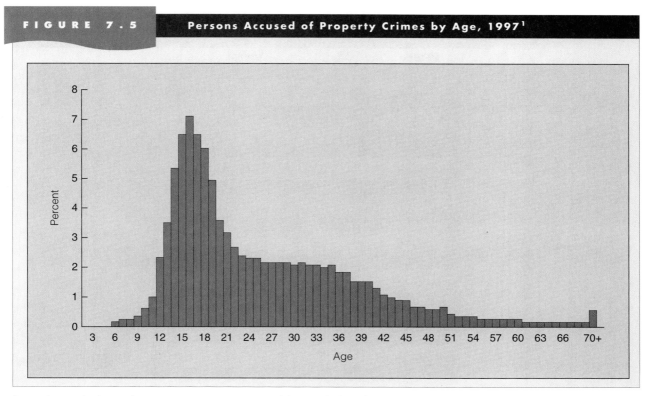

FIGURE 7.5 **Persons Accused of Property Crimes by Age, 1997[1]**

[1]Nonrandom sample of 179 police agencies representing 48 percent of the national volume of crime. The data are not nationally representative.

Reprinted by permission of Statistics Canada, 1998, "Canadian Crime Statistics, 1997," *Juristat* 18(11):12, Cat. no. 85-002-XPE.

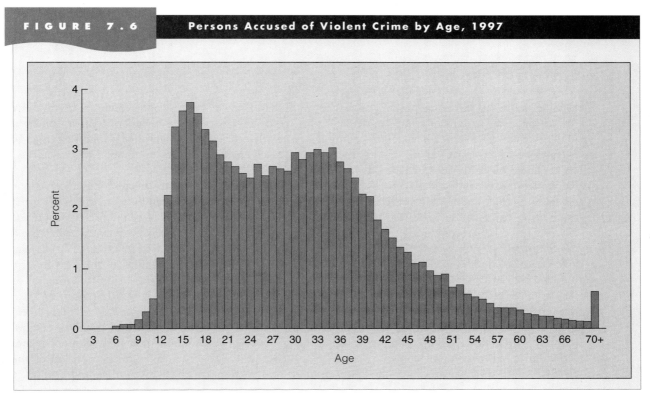

FIGURE 7.6 **Persons Accused of Violent Crime by Age, 1997**

[1]Nonrandom sample of 179 police agencies representing 48 percent of the national volume of crime. The data are not nationally representative.

Reprinted by permission of Statistics Canada, 1998, "Canadian Crime Statistics, 1997," *Juristat* 18(11):12, Cat. no. 85-002-XPE.

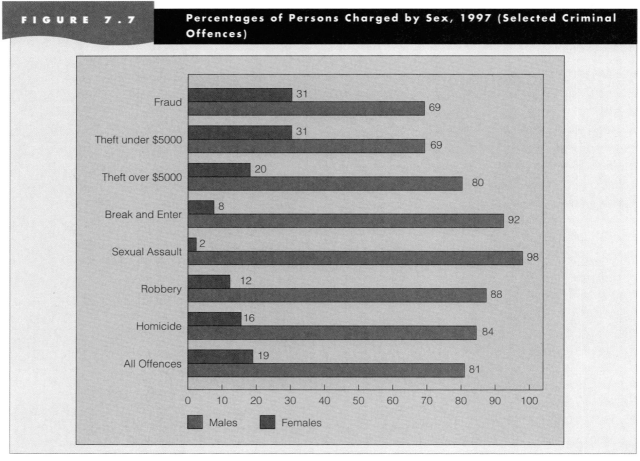

FIGURE 7.7 Percentages of Persons Charged by Sex, 1997 (Selected Criminal Offences)

Reproduced by authority of the Minister of Industry, 1998, Statistics Canada, from *Juristat*, Cat. no. 85-00XPE, volume 18, no. 11, 1997.

become as involved in crime as men, or that they will adopt male patterns of crime, particularly for violent crime. The increase in female crime has been greatest for property crimes such as theft and fraud. These two categories include offences commonly committed by females such as shoplifting, credit card fraud, and passing bad cheques, which are among the least serious property offences. Comack (2000) has concluded that this reflects the feminization of poverty rather than any convergence of men's and women's roles. As you will see in Chapter 8, the number of poor, female single parents is growing, and some of these women may commit crime in order to support themselves and their children. Thus, much of the increase in female crime may simply reflect the economic marginalization of women.

While female crime rates have increased more rapidly than male crime rates, it is important to remember that the numbers seem more dramatic

than they are because the percentage changes are based on very low numbers of female crimes in earlier decades. Women have a long way to go to reach equality in crime with men.

SOCIAL CLASS AND CRIME Criminologists have long debated the relationship between social class and crime. Many theories of crime are based on the assumption that crime is economically motivated and that poverty will lead to criminal behaviour. Unfortunately, the evidence concerning the impact of economic factors on crime is not entirely clear. We do know that persons from lower socioeconomic backgrounds are more likely to be arrested for violent and property crimes. However, we also know that these types of crimes are more likely to come to the attention of the police than are the white-collar and corporate crimes that are more likely to be committed by members of the upper class. Because the vast

| MAP 7.2 | 1997 Crime Rates per 100,000 Population (Criminal Code Excluding Traffic Offences) |

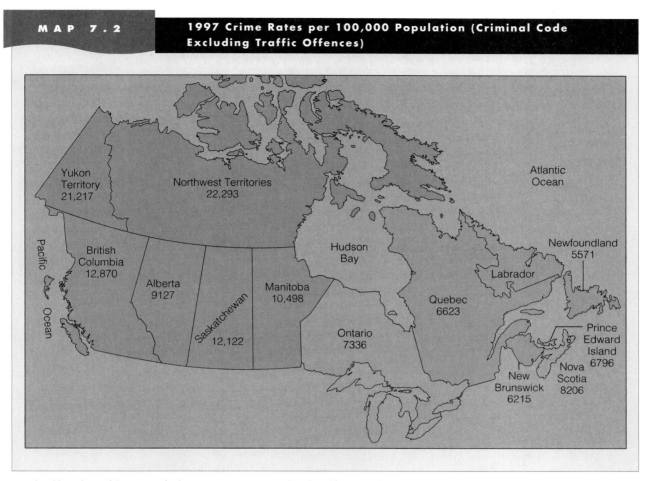

Reproduced by authority of the Minister of Industry, 1998, Statistics Canada, adapted from *Canadian Crime Statistics*, Cat. no. 85-205, page 19, 1997.

majority of white-collar and corporate crimes are never reported, we do not have the data to adequately assess the relationship between class and crime.

Before looking at some of the data on social class and crime we do have, let us briefly consider several other economic variables. Does crime increase during times of high unemployment? Do poor cities, provinces, and countries have higher crime rates than richer communities? The answer to both these questions is no. Historically, crime rates are at least as likely to rise during periods of prosperity as during recessionary times (Nettler, 1984). We are also as likely to find high crime rates in rich countries as in poor ones. The world's wealthiest countries, the United States and Japan, have very different crime rates. Compared with other countries, crime in the United States is very high and crime in Japan is very low. Within Canada, the poor provinces of Newfoundland and

New Brunswick have crime rates far lower than the rich provinces of British Columbia and Alberta (see Map 7.2). Hartnagel (2000) has concluded that the *degree of inequality*—poverty amid affluence—is a better predictor of crime than is the amount of poverty.

We know that lower-class people are overrepresented in arrest and prison admission statistics. However, we do not know if this is because lower-class people commit more crimes, or because the justice system treats them more harshly. To get closer to actual behaviour, researchers developed self-report surveys in which respondents were asked to report the number of deviant acts they had committed during a specified period of time. There is some disagreement about the conclusions that should be drawn from this research, most of which has used adolescent subjects. Some feel that self-report research shows almost no correlation between class and delinquency and crime,

BOX 7.4   SOCIOLOGY AND MEDIA

"IF IT BLEEDS, IT LEADS": FEAR OF CRIME AND THE MEDIA

Most Canadians learn about crime through the media rather than from first-hand experience. Stories on television and radio, and in newspapers, magazines, and books shape our views about crime and criminals. However, the media do not simply "report" the news. Editors and reporters select the crime news we hear about and construct the way in which this news is presented to us.

Unfortunately, the picture of crime we receive from the media is very inaccurate. For example, while most crime is property crime, most stories in the media deal with violent crime. Gabor (1994) reviewed all the crime-related stories reported over two months in an Ottawa newspaper. Over half the stories focused on violent crimes, particularly murders. However, violent crimes actually made up only 7 percent of reported crimes in Ottawa and the city averaged just six murders per year. While violent crimes were overreported, property crimes rarely received much attention, and white-collar and political crimes were almost never written about. Between 1990 and 1996 the homicide rate in Canada declined by almost 20 percent while murder coverage on CBC and

John Rosen, who was Paul Bernardo's lawyer, faces the media during Bernardo's trial.

CTV national news programs increased by 300 percent. Calgary had 12 murders in 1996, a year in which the *Calgary Herald* published 1667 murder-related stories (National Media Archive, 1997).

Why do the media misrepresent crime? The primary goal of the media is to make profits by selling advertising. Stories that attract viewers or readers will boost ratings and circulation even if these stories do not represent the reality of crime. The informal media rule, "If it bleeds,

and attributes class differences in official measures to bias in the criminal justice system (Tittle et al., 1978). However, other research (Elliott and Ageton, 1980; Thornberry and Farnworth, 1982) has supported the view that crime is more frequent in the lower class. Based on the results of these and many other studies, the most likely conclusion is that for the vast majority of people, class and crime or delinquency are not related. People from all classes break the law, at least occasionally. However, those who engage in frequent and serious offending are most likely to come from the very bottom of the class ladder—from an underclass that is severely disadvantaged economically, educationally, and socially.

This conclusion is supported by the work of several researchers who have conducted field studies among street youth in several countries including Canada, the United States, and Britain. U.S. research has focused on the role of chronic unemployment and discrimination in the development of street gangs in Hispanic (Vigil, 1990) and African American (E. Anderson, 1994) communities. Subcultures that encourage and facilitate crime have developed in response to the long-term poverty so common in many American communities. Compared to the bleak legitimate opportunities available to them, criminal opportunities, particularly from the drug trade, can be very attractive. The Canadian research involved studies of street youth in Toronto (Hagan and McCarthy, 1992) and Edmonton (Baron, 1994). These studies found that many street youth were from lower-class families and were on the streets

BOX 7.4

CONTINUED

it leads," reflects the fact that the public are fascinated by sensationalized, bloody stories such as those of mass murders or attacks against helpless senior citizens. Commenting on his experience with the media, the executive director of a provincial legal society said, "If there's no blood and gore, or there's no sex, it's not newsworthy. And if it falls into the category of being newsworthy, then they have to show the dead body. They've got to show the corpse" (McCormick, 1995:182).

The media's misrepresentation of crime has several consequences. First, Canadians greatly overestimate the amount of violent crime that is committed and have a fear of crime that is more intense than the risk of victimization justifies. One survey found that the vast majority of Canadians (75 percent) felt that most crimes are accompanied by violence, though the true figure is less than 10 percent (Doob and Roberts, 1983). Despite the significant drop in crime throughout the 1990s, a 1995 survey found that Canadians were more fearful of crime than they were in 1991 (Statistics Canada, 1998a). Our fears are reinforced by the global coverage of violence. Television can instantly bring us events from anywhere and violent crimes such as mass murders in Australia and in Scotland are reported as immediately and as thoroughly as if they had happened in our own communities.

The media also provide us with a distorted stereotype of offenders. Violent crimes are most often committed by relatives, friends, and acquaintances, not by the anonymous stranger so many of us fear. Corporate and white-collar criminals are responsible for a great deal of social harm, but their activities rarely receive much attention in the media.

Our fear of crime and our image of the criminal have an impact on government policy toward crime. Actual crime trends are irrelevant—if the public feels crime is out of control, it demands that government do something about it. While crime rates are declining, a combination of increasing media coverage of crime and pressure from a variety of interest groups has led the federal government to tighten several laws including those concerning immigration, young offenders, and firearms.

---

because of poor relationships at home and at school. Their life on the streets often leads to delinquency because of the need to survive and also because engaging in crime provides them with a sense of control they do not get in other facets of their lives.

A unique victimization survey further reinforces this conclusion. In 1993, Statistics Canada conducted the national Violence Against Women Survey, for which more than 12,000 women were interviewed (Johnson, 1996a). Several findings supported the view that violence is greatest in the lower class. First, men with high-school educations assaulted their wives at twice the rate of men with university degrees. Second, men who were out of work committed assaults at twice the rate of men who were employed. Third, men in the lowest income category (less than $15,000 a year) assaulted their wives at twice the rate of men with higher incomes. However, above this $15,000 level, there was no relationship between income and crime. This again suggests that the highest crime rates can be found at the very bottom of the economic ladder.

RACE AND ETHNICITY AND CRIME   In societies with culturally heterogeneous populations, some ethnic and racial groups will have higher crime rates than others (Nettler, 1984). For example, in the United States, African Americans and Hispanics are overrepresented in arrest data.

However, because Statistics Canada does not routinely collect data about racial and ethnic correlates of crime, we know relatively little about the situation in Canada. In addition to data about Aboriginal Canadians, which will be discussed later, there have been two recent studies dealing with minorities and crime. The first of these studies, which examined race and ethnicity in the federal prison system, found that offenders from non-Aboriginal, visible ethnic minorities were *underrepresented* in the federal correctional system's population (Thomas, 1992). Specifically, the study found that in 1989, 5.2 percent of the federal corrections population were members of ethnic minority groups, while these groups made up over 6.3 percent of the general population. The second study, which examined provincial youth and adult correctional centres in British Columbia, arrived at similar findings. Only 8.2 percent of the prison population were members of non-Aboriginal, visible ethnic minorities, yet these groups made up 13.5 percent of the province's population. Contrary to the common view that immigrants have high crime rates, only 11 percent of B.C. inmates were not born in Canada, compared with 22 percent of the population of the province.

While statistics on other minorities are limited, there are extensive data on Aboriginal peoples. This is due in part to the documentation that resulted from special inquiries held to find out whether actions toward Aboriginal people by the justice system in several provinces have been discriminatory. Many studies have demonstrated the overinvolvement of Aboriginal people (Hartnagel, 2000). A typical finding is that while Aboriginal people made up about 2 percent of the population in 1991, they made up about 24 percent of persons held in custody after being convicted of a crime (Brantingham, Mu, and Verma, 1995). In their study of Canadian homicides, Silverman and Kennedy found that Aboriginal people are involved in homicides in proportions that are at least five times greater than their representation in the population (1993). Hyde and LaPrairie (1987) showed that Aboriginal and non-Aboriginal people had different patterns, as well as different rates, of crime. Aboriginal people had more social disorder offences (many of which were alcohol-related), fewer property offences, and more violent offences. Other researchers found a great deal of variation in Aboriginal crime rates between different communities and parts of the country (Wood and Griffiths, 1996).

What is the reason for these racial and ethnic differences in crime rates? One answer is that there has often been discrimination against minority groups. The treatment of blacks in South Africa and in the southern United States throughout much of this century and the previous one are obvious examples. Discrimination against Aboriginal people in Canada, Australia, and New Zealand has also been well-documented by commissions of inquiry. Members of minority groups, who tend to be poor, may go to prison for minor offences if they are unable to pay fines. A report by the Law Reform Commission of Canada (1974) found that in 1970 and 1971 over half of all Aboriginal people admitted to Saskatchewan jails were incarcerated for nonpayment of fines. While this type of discrimination may be unintentional, it is nonetheless real. The justice system also tends to focus its efforts on the types of crimes that are committed by low-income people rather than on white-collar and corporate crimes, so members of poor minority groups may be overrepresented in crime statistics. Discrimination likely accounts for some, but not all, of the high rates of criminality of some minority groups.

To provide a further explanation, consider again the case of Canada's Aboriginal people. Their situation is, of course, unique, but the same kinds of factors may apply in other contexts. While a number of theories have been advanced to explain Aboriginal overinvolvement (Hartnagel, 1996; Wood and Griffiths, 1996), consider the following explanation, which has been drawn from conflict and social control theories. Canada's Aboriginal people have far less power and fewer resources than other Canadians. They must cope with systems of education and religion that have been imposed on them from outside their cultural communities and that are incompatible with their customs and traditions. In the past, forced attendance at residential schools and forced adoption outside the community have weakened family ties. Crippling rates of unemployment in many areas mean no job ties, and school curricula that are irrelevant to the lives of Aboriginal students mean that children do not become attached to their schools. Under these conditions, strong social bonds are difficult to develop and high rates of crime can be predicted. As Manitoba's Aboriginal Justice Inquiry concluded: "From our review of the information available to us ... we believe that the relatively high rates of crime among Aboriginal people are a result of the despair, dependency, anger, frustration and sense of injustice prevalent in Aboriginal communities, stemming from the cultural and community breakdown that has occurred over the past century" (Hamilton and Sinclair, 1991:91).

REGION AND CRIME Crime is not evenly distributed around the globe. Some countries have much higher crime rates than others, and within countries there are often significant differences among regions. Unfortunately, because different countries have such varying methods of reporting and recording crime, international comparisons are difficult. The most reliable measure for comparison is homicide rates, which are reported in a reasonably similar fashion in most countries. Canada's homicide rate of about 2 per 100,000 people is relatively low by world standards. It is about a quarter of the U.S. rate, but about one and a half times that of the United Kingdom. The highest rates of homicide are typically found in the less economically developed countries, although the high rate in the United States is a notable exception.

Major regional differences in crime rates exist within Canada. As shown in Map 7.2 (see page 223), crime rates are highest in the West and the North, and lowest in Atlantic Canada. These interprovincial differences have existed for many years.

THE CRIMINAL JUSTICE SYSTEM

The criminal justice system includes the police, the courts, and prisons. However, the term *criminal justice system* is misleading because it implies that law enforcement agencies and courts constitute one large, integrated system, when it is actually a collection of "somewhat interrelated, semi-autonomous bureaucracies," each of which possesses considerable discretion to do as it wishes (Sheley, 1991:334). *Discretion* refers to the use of personal judgment by police officers, prosecutors, judges, and other criminal justice system officials regarding whether and how to proceed in a given situation.

The Police

Most people think the main function of the police is to enforce the law. That is indeed one of their functions, but there are several others including order maintenance and the provision of social services. Order maintenance refers to keeping the peace. For example, stopping arguments, controlling the areas where skid-row alcoholics drink, and making a group of boisterous teenagers move away from the parking lot of a convenience store are all order maintenance activities. While the main concern in law enforcement is arresting a suspect, the main concern in order maintenance is restoring peace in the community. In difficult situations, arrest may be one means of doing this, but arresting someone is only a means to an end rather than an end in itself. The service role is also an important one and consists of many different activities including finding lost children, counselling crime victims, and notifying next of kin in fatal accidents.

Two questions you might ask are: Why do the police have such a broad range of responsibilities? and What, if anything, do these activities have in common? To answer the first question, there are several reasons the police have the broad responsibilities they do:

1. The police are one of the few public agencies open twenty-four hours a day.
2. In many cases, the police are serving clients that other agencies may not be interested in. The poor, the homeless, and the mentally ill may become police clients almost by default. If no other agency will gather drunks who pass out on downtown streets, the police must do it.
3. The police may not know about, or have access to, other agencies that could handle some of their cases.
4. Historically, the role of the police has been to keep the peace. Sir Robert Peel, the founder of the first municipal police force, in London, England, stressed a service-oriented philosophy, and this tradition has persisted.

The second question, What ties these diverse activities together?, is best answered by looking at two dimensions of the police role. First, the police have the *authority* (and often the duty) to intervene in situations where something must be done immediately. This authority is the same whether the incident is an armed robbery in progress, a naked man standing on a busy street screaming at people, or a complaint that someone's pet boa constrictor has just appeared in someone else's bedroom. Second, the authority is backed up by *non-negotiable force*. If someone refuses to go along with what a police officer suggests, the officer can use force (usually arrest) to back up his or her demands. Even professional caregivers may resort

Does the justice system discriminate against members of racial minority groups? CITY-TV assignment editor Dwight Drummond attends a public inquiry into his wrongful arrest during a drug bust in October 1993.

to calling the police when clients refuse to cooperate with them. Once the situation gets into the hands of the police, there may be nobody else to call so they have to resolve the situation themselves. Egon Bittner has nicely summed up the role of the patrol officer: "What policemen do appears to consist of rushing to the scene of any crisis whatever, judging its needs in accordance with canons of common sense reasoning, and imposing solutions upon it without regard to resistance or opposition" (1980:137).

Given the enormous range of activities with which the police are involved, you can see that the police have a high degree of discretion. Police managers, for one thing, have *administrative discretion* over how they organize their department and use their resources. If few resources are dedicated to commercial crime, few white-collar offenders will be apprehended. If a department rewards its members only for law-enforcement tasks, they will not do as good a job on order maintenance and service activities. Second, police officers exercise a great deal of *individual discretion* in that they often have to decide which rules to apply and how to apply them. Many of the situations in which the

police use their discretion have very low visibility. Their supervisors are unlikely to observe them or to find out many details about how individual officers use their discretion. For example, if a police officer stops a driver for speeding and the driver has alcohol on his or her breath, several outcomes are possible. The police officer may warn the person and tell them to go straight home, write a speeding ticket, or administer a breathalyzer and lay charges of impaired driving. If the officer elects not to administer the breathalyzer, the supervisor will never know how that officer has used discretion.

The use of discretion by the police is unavoidable. This is not a problem if discretion is dispensed equitably and in a manner consistent with both community standards and the rule of law. However, if it is based on extra-legal factors such as race or class, or if it is used to favour certain individuals over others, it can be considered *discriminatory* and an abuse of police powers. Issues of racial discrimination have generated the most discussion in Canada in recent years as inquiries have been held in many cities following police shootings of minority group members. But all discrimination may not be deliberate. For example, Tim Quigley has described what he calls the over-policing of Aboriginals:

> Police use race as an indicator for patrols, for arrests, detentions ... For instance, police in cities tend to patrol bars and streets where Aboriginal people congregate, rather than the private clubs frequented by white business people ... This does not necessarily indicate that the police are invariably racist (although some are) since there is some empirical basis for the police view that proportionately more Aboriginal people are involved in criminality. But to operate patrols or to allocate police on ... [this] basis ... can become a self-fulfilling prophecy: patrols in areas frequented by the groups that they believe are involved in crimes will undoubtedly discover some criminality; when more police are assigned to detachments where there is a high Aboriginal population, their added presence will most assuredly detect more criminal activity. (1994:273–274)

The Courts

Criminal courts decide the guilt or innocence of those accused of committing a crime. In theory, justice is determined in an adversarial process in which the prosecutor (a lawyer who represents the state) argues that the accused is guilty and the defence lawyer asserts that the accused is innocent. Each side presents its position, the position is debated, and evidence is introduced to support each position. Proponents of the adversarial system feel this system best provides a just decision about guilt or innocence.

The essence of the adversarial system can be seen in the defence lawyer's role, which is to do all he or she can do to help the accused. This role was described by Lord Brougham, who was the defence lawyer in an 1821 case that could have had disastrous consequences for the British government had his defence been successful:

> An advocate, in the discharge of his duty, knows but one person in all the world, and that person is his client. To save that client by all means and expedients, and at all hazards and costs to their persons, and amongst them, to himself, is his first and only duty; and in performing this duty he must not regard the alarm, the torments, the destruction which he may bring upon others. Separating the duty of a patriot from that of an advocate, he must go on reckless of the consequences, though it should be his unhappy fate to involve his country in confusion. (cited in Greenspan, 1982:201)

We can add to Lord Brougham's comment that in an adversarial system the defence lawyer is obliged to fulfil this duty to the client without concern for the client's actual guilt or innocence.

Most of those working in the courts strongly defend the adversarial system and see it as one of the cornerstones of a free and democratic society. Many of the procedures that seem to restrict the ability of the court to get at the "truth," such as the rule that accused persons cannot be forced to testify against themselves, were adopted to prevent the arbitrary use of state power against the accused. However, some critics feel that our system does not deal adequately with crime because it places more emphasis on winning than on doing what is best for the accused, for the victim, and for society. Very few people who watched the O.J. Simpson trial could disagree with at least some aspects of this criticism.

Not all Western countries use the adversarial court system. Several European countries use systems in which the judge takes a much more active role in ensuring that justice is done. Jim Hackler (1994), one of the most articulate critics of Canada's courts, has described the court process in Switzerland, for example. In Switzerland, the police investigation is directed by a magistrate and the police gather information relevant to both sides of the case. While the accused lacks some of the protection of our system, the defence has access to all information about the case and can request through the magistrate that the police gather additional information. At the trial, the judge leads the questioning and there is much more concern with getting at the truth, and less on legal constraints of the kind that exist in our system. The holistic approach to justice advocated by many Aboriginal people is another alternative to the very technical and legalistic system that now prevails in our courts. This approach takes into account the needs of the victim, the accused, and the community rather than simply applying formal legal rules and procedures.

Punishment

Punishment **is any action designed to deprive a person of things of value (including liberty) because of some offence the person is thought to have committed** (Barlow, 1987:421). Punishment can serve four functions:

1. *Retribution* imposes a penalty on the offender. Retribution is based on the premise that the punishment should fit the crime: the greater the degree of social harm, the more the offender should be punished. An individual who murders, for example, should be punished more severely than one who steals.
2. *Social protection* results from restricting offenders so they cannot commit further crimes. If someone is in prison, they are no longer a threat to those of us on the outside. However, a high rate of offending within the prison exists, so imprisonment does not necessarily put an end to criminal behaviour.
3. *Rehabilitation* seeks to return offenders to the community as law-abiding citizens. However, rehabilitation programs are not a priority for governments or prison officials and the few rehabilitation programs that exist are typically underfunded. While many Canadian prisons offer some training to inmates, the job skills that may be learned in prison typically do not transfer to the outside world, nor are offenders given much assistance in finding work that fits their skills once they are released.
4. *Deterrence* seeks to reduce criminal activity by instilling a fear of punishment. *Specific deterrence* is intended to deter the individual

BOX 7.5   CRITICAL THINKING

LET'S MAKE A DEAL: BARGAINING FOR JUSTICE

The image most of us have of the court process is that those who are arrested and charged will go to trial. This trial will be held in a courtroom packed with spectators and will be contested by highly trained and articulate lawyers arguing the fine points of law before a judge and jury. However, this image is far from the truth. Trials are relatively rare and most cases are decided by guilty pleas. A high proportion, probably the majority, of these guilty pleas result from plea bargaining.

Plea bargaining is the process of negotiating a guilty plea. Informal, private discussions are held between the defence and the prosecution in an attempt to reach a mutually agreeable outcome in which both parties receive concessions. For the accused, plea bargaining may mean that the severity of the penalty will be reduced. A negotiated guilty plea also relieves the anxiety of waiting for sentencing, as the outcome of the case is agreed on ahead of time. The accused may also wish to save the expense and publicity of a trial, especially if the likely result is convic-

tion. For the prosecution, plea bargaining saves time, which is crucial in our overloaded courts. If all cases went to trial, the backlog would be endless. It is likely that busier courts will give more lenient deals as the accused will have more bargaining power. The Crown, or prosecuting, attorney may also bargain if the prosecution's case is weak. For example, if a key witness is very reluctant to testify or would not make a good impression on a judge or jury, the prosecution may bargain to ensure the defendant does not get off.

Plea bargaining has been widely criticized on the grounds that it subverts the aims of the criminal justice system by rewarding the guilty and penalizing those who elect to maintain their innocence and go to trial. The Law Reform Commission of Canada, among other groups, has recommended its abolition. However, despite this criticism the practice continues and some argue that the system could not work without it.

Plea bargaining has been particularly criticized in cases where guilty people are given

offender from reoffending. For example, a judge may sentence a wife abuser to six months in jail to teach him not to repeat his abuse. *General deterrence* is intended to deter all of us who see the example set by the justice system. For example, a judge may decide that convenience store robberies are getting out of hand and give one offender a severe sentence to set an example for others.

There is no question that the law deters. You do not deliberately park where you know your car will be towed away, and you do not speed if you see a police car behind you. However, the law does not deter as well as we might hope because the *certainty* of being arrested and convicted for most crimes is low. Most crimes do not result in arrests and, perhaps surprisingly, most arrests do not result in convictions. It is difficult to increase

the certainty of punishment, so we try to tinker with the severity of punishment instead. Most "law and order" politicians talk about getting tough on crime by increasing penalties rather than by making punishment more certain. However, increasing the average penalty for robbery by a year will not likely reduce robbery rates if most robberies do not result in a conviction and a jail sentence.

We know less about the impact of law as a specific deterrent. That is, does serving a prison sentence make it less likely that a person will commit a crime in the future? While we do know that a large proportion of criminals are *recidivists* (repeat offenders), we do not know how many would repeat if they had not been in prison.

Most convicted criminals today are out on either *probation* (supervision in the community instead of serving a prison term) or *parole* (early

BOX 7.5

CONTINUED

light sentences in exchange for testimony against their partners in crime. The twelve-year sentence given to Karla Homolka in exchange for her testimony against Paul Bernardo is an example of this type of bargaining. While the Homolka case was controversial because of her direct involvement with Bernardo's killings, some cases are even more questionable because someone heavily involved in criminal activity receives a lenient disposition in exchange for information about others who are less involved.

Consider the case of Yves (Apache) Trudeau, for example. A former Hell's Angel, of the notorious Laval, Quebec, chapter, Trudeau is probably the most prolific killer in Canada's history. Trudeau admitted to forty-three gang-related killings and was able to negotiate a plea bargain in which the Crown accepted guilty pleas to forty-three counts of manslaughter and gave a commitment that he would be released with a new identity after

serving seven years in jail. Trudeau agreed to cooperate with the police after learning he was the target of other Hell's Angels who had already killed six members of his chapter. In exchange for police protection, a comfortable cell, and a light sentence, Trudeau agreed to tell what he knew about the operation of the Hell's Angels and other Montreal organized crime groups. Two other members of the Laval chapter, Michel Blass and Gilles Lachance, also received plea bargains in exchange for their testimony against other gang members. While the police and prosecutors would argue that plea bargaining was the only way to convict other Hell's Angels and to reduce the influence of the gang, the practice of making deals with killers raises some difficult moral and ethical questions.

What are your views about plea bargaining? Do you think that justice is served when deals are made?

Sources: Based on Griffiths and Verdun-Jones, 1994; Lavigne, 1987; and Stamler, 1996.

release from prison). If offenders violate the conditions of their probation or parole, they may be required to serve their full sentence in prison.

The disparate treatment of the poor and some racial minorities is evident in the prison system. We have seen that incarceration rates for Aboriginal people are disproportionately higher than those for whites. Disparate treatment of women also is evident. Women make up only a small minority of Canada's prison population—in 1996 there were 13,585 male inmates in federal penitentiaries compared with 277 females (Robinson et al., 1998). These small numbers mean that in some respects men are treated better than women in prison. Women's prisons, for example, offer far fewer educational and training programs than do men's prisons. The small number of women inmates makes it difficult to offer a wide range of programs. Until recently,

there was only one federal prison for women in Canada, so all female offenders receiving a sentence of two years or more were sent to Kingston rather than staying in their own provinces, closer to family and friends. Since the majority of female inmates are single parents (which is not true of male inmates), long periods of incarceration far away from home and family place a special burden on female inmates (Comack, 1996a).

Restorative Justice

For many years, we have relied on the formal justice system to deal with crime. Community members have been discouraged from participating in their own protection and have had little say in the services they received. After the victim called the police dispatcher, the police would soon arrive to take care of the problem, and if an arrest was made, case processing was left in the hands of the formal justice system. Many of those found guilty by the court were removed from the community and sent away to jail. Professionals have controlled each step in the system, and victims and other community members have had little involvement.

While most people have come to accept this as the proper way of dealing with crime, many of those who have been involved with the justice system feel it has failed them. Victims feel left out, as their role as the aggrieved party is forgotten and they are relegated to the role of witnesses. They have no control over the process; often they are not even informed about the disposition of the case. Offenders are also dealt with impersonally. Their crimes become the focus of concern, and their individual circumstances and needs are not considered. Offenders are rarely reminded of the personal harm they have done. Instead, many offenders are sent to costly prisons that result more in alienation than rehabilitation. In addition, the public is often dissatisfied with a justice system that does not respond to their concerns.

Many critics of the present justice system have advocated returning to a fundamentally different way of approaching criminal justice, to a system that is intended to restore social relationships rather than simply to punish (Church Council on Justice and Corrections, 1996). Advocates of *restorative justice* seek to return the focus of the justice system to repairing the harm that has been done to the victim and to the community. A key element of restorative justice is the involvement of the victim and other members of the community as active participants in the process. The focus of the restorative justice approach is to reconcile offenders with those they have harmed and to help communities to reintegrate victims and offenders. Restorative justice has its roots in traditional societies where the restoration of order was crucial to society's survival. In Canada, Aboriginal communities used a variety of different methods, including *circle sentencing*, to resolve disputes and are leading the way in the return to the use of restorative justice practices. In recent years, traditional practices have been revived and modified in innovative ways. Two of the most widespread contemporary restorative justice methods are *victim–offender reconciliation* and *family group conferencing.*

Victim–offender reconciliation is a program that was devised in Elmira, Ontario, in 1974 as an initiative by two individuals to persuade a judge to deal in a positive fashion with two youths who had vandalized property belonging to twenty-two different victims. Rather than a normal court disposition that may well have involved incarceration, the offence was handled in the community. Mediators worked with the victims and the offenders to reach a resolution that was acceptable to all parties. As a result, the boys had to deal personally with each of their victims and to make restitution for the damage they had caused. The restorative process gave victims a chance to have a say in what happened, and gave offenders the chance to make amends.

Family group conferencing (sometimes called community justice conferencing) is a restorative justice technique that had its origins in New Zealand and is a variation of circle sentencing. The RCMP have selected family group conferencing as one of the ways their detachments will work with communities to try to reduce crime, so use of this method of conflict resolution should become common in Canada. Family group conferencing typically applies to young offenders and normally involves the victim, the offender, and as many of their family and friends as possible. Professional or community workers may also participate. A typical family group conference involves about a dozen people. When adult offenders are involved in the process, it is more likely to involve community members than families. The goal of the conference is to allow those affected by the crime the opportunity to resolve the case in an environment that is supportive of both victim and offender. A coordinator allows all parties to speak about the case, and then leads the conference into a discussion of what might be done to repair the harm done to the victim. Victims and their family and friends outline their expectations, and offenders and their family and friends respond. Negotiation continues until a plan is agreed on and written down. The coordinator then establishes mechanisms for enforcing the plan. The family and friends of both the victim and the offender are encouraged to offer continuing help to ensure the resolution arrived at during the conference is actually carried out in the community.

Evaluations of restorative justice methods have identified concerns about the enforcement of negotiated agreements, the possible conflict with the due process rights of the accused, the potential for net-widening through including offenders who might otherwise be dealt with in less formal ways, conflicts over jurisdiction among various

In recent years, military-style boot camps have been used as an alternative to prison and long jail terms for nonviolent offenders under age 30. Critics argue that structural solutions—not stop-gap measures—are needed to reduce crime in the twenty-first century.

professional groups, and the inability to address the conditions that cause crime such as unemployment, poverty, and the breakdown of family support networks. Despite these concerns, restorative justice programs now provide us with a valuable alternative to the formal justice system.

Community Corrections

A major focus of the restorative justice approach is reducing the number of people in prison. Diversion programs and community corrections reduce the likelihood of imprisonment and replace formal consequences with more meaningful community-based sanctions. Community corrections, an important component of the restorative justice approach, shifts responsibility for corrections back to the community and minimizes the separation of the offender from society at a number of different stages in the correctional process.

Canada has a much higher rate of incarceration than most other industrialized countries. A recent study of nine countries ranked Canada third highest, following the United States and Switzerland, and ahead of (in descending order of incarceration rates) Northern Ireland, Australia, Scotland, England, Denmark, and Sweden (Mihorean and Lipinski, 1992). While our rate is double that of Sweden, it is only one-third as high as that of the United States.

Because our rates are higher than those of many other countries, some have suggested that Canada should move toward a greater use of community corrections. These dispositions include programs such as community probation, community service orders, intensive probation supervision, and bail supervision as alternatives to incarceration. The movement toward community-based sanctions has been driven by three major concerns. First, these programs are much cheaper than incarceration. It costs about $50,000 to keep a person in a federal penitentiary for a year. In its 1996 budget, the Quebec government announced that it was going to close several provincial prisons and increase the use of community-based programs as part of its program of controlling the provincial deficit. The second concern is humanitarian. Prison life is very unpleasant and it can be unfair to send people to jail for relatively minor offences. Finally, an offender may benefit from being able to maintain ties with family and community, and these ties may make subsequent involvement in crime less likely.

The move toward community corrections has been supported by federal legislation. In addition to the conventional objectives of protection of the public, deterrence, and rehabilitation, recent sentencing legislation sets out the objectives of making reparations to victims and to the community, and promoting a sense of responsibility in offenders. In announcing the legislation, the government has explicitly stated that alternatives to imprisonment should be used where appropriate (Department of Justice, 1994). The legislation also added conditional sentences to the Criminal Code. Conditional sentences allow convicted offenders to serve their sentences in the community under greater control (e.g., house arrest and electronic monitoring) and represent an important step in the direction of community corrections.

CRIME AND DEVIANCE IN THE FUTURE

Among the questions pertaining to deviance and crime facing us in the twenty-first century are: Is the solution to our "crime problem" more law and order? and, What impact will the global economy have on crime?

Although many Canadians agree that crime is one of our most important problems, they are divided over what to do about it. Some of the frustration about crime might be based on unfounded fears that the crime rate has been rising in the past few years, whereas it has actually declined. However, it is still far too high.

One thing is clear. The existing criminal justice system cannot solve the "crime problem." If most crimes do not result in arrest, most arrests do not result in convictions, and most convictions do not result in a jail term, the "lock 'em up and throw away the key" approach has little chance of succeeding. Nor does the high rate of recidivism among those who have been incarcerated speak well for the rehabilitative efforts of our existing correctional facilities. We can look to the United States to see a very expensive social experiment. Massive numbers of people are being locked up for very long periods of time and prison populations are increasing much more rapidly than in other countries. Between 1980 and 1990, the American prison population grew by 121 percent, while in Canada the increase was 14 percent (Mihorean and Lipinski, 1992). Since 1990, American prison populations have continued to increase. Several states have passed "three strikes and you're out" laws that impose a mandatory life sentence on anyone convicted of a third felony. Each inmate convicted under these laws will cost about $1.5 million to keep in prison for the rest of his or her life.

An alternative to this approach begins with the realization that the best way to deal with crime is to ensure that it doesn't happen. Instead of longer sentences, military-style boot camps or other stop-gap measures, *structural solutions*—such as more and better education and jobs, affordable housing, more equality and less discrimination, and socially productive activities—are needed to reduce street crime in the next century. The best approach for reducing delinquency and crime ultimately would be prevention: to work with young people *before* they become juvenile offenders, to help them establish family relationships, build self-esteem, choose a career, and get an education that will help them pursue that career.

Perhaps the major trend that will affect the type of crime we will see in the future is the globalization of the economy and of communications. Organized crime has spread from one country to another; the drug trade is a vast international business. With the aid of satellites and computers, financial crimes can be committed from anywhere in the world, and may be almost impossible to punish because of competing jurisdictions and different laws. The reduction of border controls in trading alliances such as the European Community makes it easier for criminals to move from one country to another.

Globalization may affect crime in many other ways. The transition to a global economy has devastated the job market in many countries. Traditional, secure manufacturing jobs have either been moved to countries in which lower wages are paid or they have disappeared altogether, and poorly paid and insecure jobs in the service sector are the jobs that remain. This loss of good jobs has, in turn, affected families and communities and may result in increased criminality. In many countries changes in taxation and social welfare policies, intended to increase global competitiveness, have increased social inequality. This inequality may also lead to crime.

CHAPTER REVIEW

What is deviance?

Deviant behaviour is any act that violates established norms. Deviance varies from culture to culture and in degree of seriousness. Crime is seriously deviant behaviour that violates written laws and that is punishable by fines, incarceration, or other sanctions.

What is the strain theory of deviance?

Strain theory focuses on the idea that the structure of a society can produce pressures that result in deviant behaviour. When denied legitimate access to cultural goals, such as a good job or nice home, people may engage in illegal behaviour to obtain them. Opportunity theory suggests that access to illegitimate opportunity structures varies, and this access helps determine the nature of deviance in which a person will engage.

How does social control theory explain crime?

According to social control theory, everyone is capable of committing crimes, but social bonding keeps many from doing so. People bond to society through their attachments to family and to other social institutions such as the church and school. When a person's bonds to society are weakened or broken, the probability of deviant behaviour increases.

How do interactionists view the causes of crime?

Differential association theory states that individuals have a greater tendency to deviate from societal norms when they frequently associate with persons who tend toward deviance instead of conformity. According to labelling theory, deviant behaviour is that which is labelled deviant. The process of labelling is related to the relative power and status of those persons who do the labelling and those who are labelled. Those in power may use their power to label the behaviour of others as deviant.

How do conflict and feminist perspectives explain deviance?

Conflict perspectives on deviance examine inequalities in society. According to the critical approach, the legal order protects those with political and economic power and exploits persons from lower classes. Feminist approaches to deviance examine the relationship between gender and deviance. Liberal feminism explains female deviance as a rational response to gender discrimination experienced in work, marriage, and interpersonal relationships. Radical feminism suggests that patriarchy (male domination of females) contributes to female deviance, especially prostitution. Socialist feminism states that exploitation of women by patriarchy and capitalism is related to their involvement in criminal acts such as prostitution and shoplifting.

What are the major types of crime?

Street crime, which includes violent crimes, property crimes, and morals crimes, is a major type of crime. Another is occupational, or white-collar, crimes, which are illegal activities committed by people in the course of their employment or financial dealings. Other major types are corporate crimes, which are illegal acts com-

mitted by company employees on behalf of the corporation and with its support; organized crime, which is a business operation that supplies illegal goods and services for profit; and political crimes, which are illegal or unethical acts involving the misuse of power by government officials or illegal or unethical acts perpetrated against the government by those seeking to make a political statement, undermine the government, or overthrow it.

What are our main sources of crime statistics?

Official crime statistics are taken from the Canadian Uniform Crime Reporting survey, which lists crimes reported to the police. We also collect information about crime through victimization surveys that interview households to determine the incidence of crimes, including those not reported to police. Studies show that many more crimes are committed than are officially reported.

How are age, sex, and social class related to crime?

Age is a key factor in crime. Persons under 25 have the highest rates of crime. Persons arrested for assault and homicide generally are older, and white-collar criminals usually are older because it takes time to acquire the professional position and skill needed to commit occupational crime. Women have much lower rates of crime than men. Persons from lower socioeconomic backgrounds are more likely to be arrested for violent and property crimes; corporate crime is more likely to occur among upper socioeconomic classes.

How is discretion used in the justice system?

The criminal justice system includes the police, the courts, and prisons. These agencies often have considerable discretion in dealing with offenders. The police often use discretion in deciding whether to act on a situation. Prosecutors and judges use discretion in deciding which cases to pursue and how to handle them.

Key Terms

corporate crime 214
crime 202
deviance 200
differential association theory 206
illegitimate opportunity structures 204
juvenile delinquency 202
labelling theory 208
occupational or white-collar crime 214
organized crime 215
political crime 215
primary deviance 208

punishment 229
secondary deviance 208
social bond theory 205
social control 200
strain theory 203
street crime 213

Internet Exercises

1. Go to the Statistics Canada Web pages that list the national crime rate by type of offence (**http://www. statcan.ca/english/Pgdb/State/Justice/legal02.htm**) and the province-by-province breakdown of crime rates (**http://www.statcan.ca/english/Pgdb/State/ Justice/legal04a.htm**). Compare the province in which you live with other provinces, and then with the national average, with respect to different crimes.

2. Go to one of the search engines such as AltaVista or Excite and find articles containing the word *hacker*. Read some of the articles and decide which deviance theory (or theories) best describes how analysts and commentators view hackers and hacking.

3. Governments in Canada have begun to place a higher priority on the prevention of crime. The Web page of the National Crime Prevention Council (**http://www.crime-prevention.org/ncpc**) has a section called Prevention Databases. Look at three of the programs in the Urban Safety category. Do you think these programs have the potential to reduce crime in your community? Do you know of any similar activities in your community?

4. In 1867 and 1868 three murders took place in a small settlement on Salt Spring Island in the British colony of British Columbia. An Aboriginal man, Tshuanahusset, was found guilty of one of the murders despite considerable evidence that he did not commit the crime. Go to the Who Killed William Robinson Web site at (**http://web.uvic.ca/history-robinson**) to find an extensive collection of documents relating to the life, times, and death of one of the victims. Use these documents to decide if you think the conviction of Tshuanahusset was fair.

Net Links

To read about restorative justice issues, visit the site of Transformative Justice Australia at:

http://www.tja.com.au/

Blueline magazine is intended for police audiences and looks at a variety of issues concerning Canadian policing; go to:

http://www.blueline.ca/

Many jurisdictions still have outdated or strange laws on their books. Read some of them at:

http://www.dumblaws.ca

Look at Canada's Criminal Code. You can read the way each offence is defined and look at the maximum penalties at:

http://insight.mcmaster.ca/org/efc/pages/cc/cc.html

Read recent news about criminal justice and Canadian research in policing and corrections at the Web site of the Solicitor General of Canada:

http://www.sgc.gc.ca/ehome.htm

Questions for Critical Thinking

1. What factors account for the increase in organized crime throughout the world? How can society best deal with this type of crime?
2. Should so-called victimless crimes, such as prostitution and recreational drug use, be decriminalized? Do these crimes harm society?
3. Several commissions have recommended that Aboriginal people have a separate justice system. Do you agree? How do you think such a system would operate?
4. As a sociologist armed with a sociological imagination, how do you propose to deal with the problem of crime in Canada? What programs would you suggest enhancing? What programs would you reduce?

Suggested Readings

These books provide additional insights on many of the crime and justice issues discussed in this chapter:

Margaret Beare. *Criminal Conspiracies: Organized Crime in Canada*. Toronto: Nelson Canada, 1996.

James Dubro. *Mob Rule: Inside the Canadian Mafia*. Toronto: Macmillan, 1985.

Thomas Fleming. *The New Criminologies in Canada: State, Crime and Control*. Toronto: Oxford University Press, 1985.

Thomas Gabor. *Everybody Does It! Crime by the Public*. Toronto: University of Toronto Press, 1994.

Curt T. Griffiths and Simon N. Verdun-Jones. *Canadian Criminal Justice* (2nd ed.). Toronto: Harcourt Brace and Company, 1994.

James C. Hackler. *Crime and Canadian Public Policy.* Scarborough: Prentice Hall, 1994

Allen C. Hamilton and C. Murray Sinclair. *Report of the Aboriginal Justice Inquiry of Manitoba, Vol. 1.* Winnipeg: Queen's Printer, 1994.

Holly Johnson. *Dangerous Domains: Violence Against Women in Canada.* Toronto: Nelson Canada, 1996.

Leslie W. Kennedy and Vincent F. Sacco. *Crime Counts: A Criminal Event Analysis.* Toronto: Nelson Canada, 1997.

Yves Lavigne. *Hell's Angels: Taking Care of Business.* Toronto: Ballantine Books, 1987.

Rick Linden. *Criminology: A Canadian Perspective* (4th ed.). Toronto: Harcourt Brace and Company, 2000.

Chris McCormick. *Constructing Danger: The Mis/Representation of Crime in the News.* Halifax: Fernwood Publishing, 1995.

Robert Silverman and Leslie Kennedy. *Deadly Deeds: Murder in Canada.* Scarborough: Nelson Canada, 1993.

Laureen Snider. *Bad Business: Corporate Crime in Canada.* Scarborough: Nelson Canada, 1993.

Daniel Wolf. *The Rebels: A Brotherhood of Outlaw Bikers.* Toronto: University of Toronto Press, 1991.

CHAPTER 8

What Is Social Stratification?

Global Systems of Stratification
    The Caste System
    The Class System

Classical Perspectives on Social Class
    Karl Marx: Relation to Means of Production
    Max Weber: Wealth, Prestige, and Power

The Canadian Class Structure
    The Upper Class
    The Middle Class
    The Working Class
    The Lower Class

Sociological Explanations of Social Inequality
    Functionalist Perspectives
    Conflict Perspectives
    The Evolutionary Approach

Inequality in Canada
    Distribution of Income and Wealth
    Consequences of Inequality

Poverty in Canada
    Who Are the Poor?
    Economic and Structural Sources of Poverty

Social Stratification in the Future

Sally is a 29-year-old single mother who lives with her 8-year-old son Sean in Toronto. She is one of many Canadians who have experienced downward mobility—moving from a comfortable middle-class lifestyle to a life of poverty. Sally talks about her life in a motel, her struggle to survive, and the impact of poverty on her young son:

"He just hates it. He's not used to living like this. My son always had the best of everything; now from the best of everything he's got nothing ... Everytime I look at Sean I think no, I can't let myself down or this kid's even gonna suffer more. This kid's seen more in his eight years. At his age I'd never seen half of this ... This is no place for a child at all. There's prostitutes. I hear a lot of fights ... I look at myself and Sean and I think at eight years old I'd had no worries ... If Sean needs a pair of shoes or boots, well, I got him a pair of boots for $4 over there [the Goodwill Store] and a jacket. I had to say 'Well Sean, you need your winter coat, your winter boots so like no, I can't buy this kind of meat and no, I can't buy jam 'cause we need that for your winter boots.'" (O'Reilly-Fleming, 1993:147–148)

SOCIAL STRATIFICATION AND CLASS

When we examine social stratification and social inequality in Canada, it becomes apparent that Sally and Sean's situation is not unique. Poverty affects people's lives, their sense of self, and their most important relationships with others. The emotional, physical, and social toll that poverty takes is most apparent among children. The evidence suggests that the years spent in childhood poverty will have long-term consequences for the life chances of children like Sean. The most recent estimates indicate that, apparently, 1.5 million of Canada's children are growing up poor (Ross, 1998). Children represent more than one-quarter of our poor and the child poverty rate in Canada is the second highest in the industrialized world, topped only by that of the United States (Duffy and Mandell, 1996). In 1989, the House of Commons unanimously resolved "to seek to achieve the goal of eliminating poverty among Canadian children by the year 2000" (Hughes, 1995:779). At that time, just over 15 percent of Canadian children were living in poverty (see Figure 8.1). Today the child poverty rates have risen to over 20 percent. What factors have contributed to this disturbing pattern? In this chapter we will attempt to answer this question by examining more closely the relationship between social stratification, social inequality, and child poverty.

Before reading on, test your knowledge of poverty in Canada by taking the quiz in Box 8.1.

QUESTIONS AND ISSUES

CHAPTER FOCUS QUESTION: How are the lives of Canadians affected by social stratification?

How do prestige, power, and wealth determine social class?

What role does ownership of resources play in a conflict perspective on class structure?

How are social stratification and poverty linked?

What is the extent of social inequality in Canada?

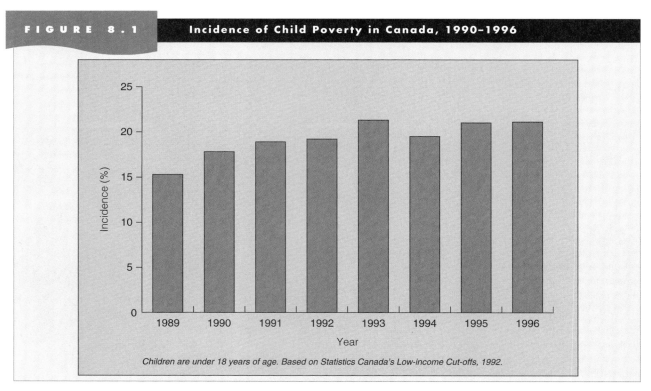

FIGURE 8.1 — Incidence of Child Poverty in Canada, 1990–1996

Children are under 18 years of age. Based on Statistics Canada's Low-income Cut-offs, 1992.

Prepared by the Centre for International Statistics at the Canadian Council on Social Development, using data from Statistics Canada, Cat. no. 13-569-XPB.

WHAT IS SOCIAL STRATIFICATION?

Social stratification is the hierarchical arrangement of large social groups based on their control over basic resources (Feagin and Feagin, 1997). Stratification involves patterns of structural inequality that are associated with membership in those groups as well as the ideologies that support inequality (Rothman, 1993). Sociologists examine the social groups that make up the hierarchy in a society and seek to determine how inequalities are structured and persist over time (Jary and Jary, 1991).

Max Weber's term *life chances* describes the extent to which persons have access to important scarce resources such as food, clothing, shelter, education, and employment. According to sociologists, more-affluent people typically have better life chances than the less affluent because they have greater access to quality education, safe neighbourhoods, high-quality nutrition and health care, and an extensive array of other goods and services. In contrast, persons with low- and poverty-level incomes tend to have limited access

People's life chances are enhanced by access to important societal resources such as education. How will the life chances of students who have the opportunity to pursue a university degree differ from those of young people who do not have the chance to go to university?

HOW MUCH DO YOU KNOW ABOUT POVERTY IN CANADA?

TRUE	FALSE		
T	F	1.	Winning the war on poverty is an unrealistic goal.
T	F	2.	Individuals over the age of 65 have the highest rate of poverty.
T	F	3.	Men account for two out of every three impoverished adults in Canada.
T	F	4.	Most poor children live in female-headed, single-parent households.
T	F	5.	The Canadian cities with the highest rates of child poverty are Winnipeg, Montreal, and Saskatoon.
T	F	6.	Poverty is predominantly a rural phenomenon.
T	F	7.	A large proportion of people receiving social assistance are able to work.
T	F	8.	Children living in poverty are more likely to be abused and/or neglected.
T	F	9.	A number of people living below the official poverty line have full-time jobs.
T	F	10.	Welfare benefits provide enough income for recipients to live comfortably.

Answers on page 242.

to these resources. *Resources* are anything valued in a society, ranging from money and property to medical care and education; they are considered to be scarce because of their unequal distribution among social categories. If we think about the valued resources available in Canada, Sally's life chances are readily apparent. As one analyst suggested, "Poverty narrows and closes life chances. The victims of poverty experience a kind of arteriosclerosis of opportunity. Being poor not only means economic insecurity, it also wreaks havoc on one's mental and physical health" (Ropers, 1991:25). Our life chances are intertwined with our class, race, gender, and age.

All societies distinguish among people by age. Young children typically have less authority and responsibility than older persons. Older persons, especially those without wealth or power, may find themselves at the bottom of the social hierarchy. Similarly, all societies differentiate between females and males: women often are treated as subordinate to men. Age and gender are examples of *ascribed status*—that is, a status that is assigned to an individual, typically at birth. Ascribed status is not chosen or earned and cannot be changed. Can you think of other ascribed statuses you may have?

Individuals are also ranked on the basis of *achieved status*—a changeable status that is achieved on the basis of how well an individual performs in a particular role. Examples of achieved statuses are occupational statuses such as

accountant, lawyer, professor, as well as other earned roles such as mother, husband, Olympic athlete, or armed robber. There is an element of choice in each of these roles. Can you identify your achieved statuses? The degree of significance of achieved and ascribed statuses will vary in different systems of stratification.

GLOBAL SYSTEMS OF STRATIFICATION

Around the globe, one of the most important characteristics of systems of stratification is their degree of flexibility. Sociologists distinguish among such systems based on the extent to which they are open or closed. In an *open system*, the boundaries between levels in the hierarchies are more flexible and may be influenced (positively or negatively) by people's achieved statuses. Open systems are assumed to have some degree of social mobility. **Social mobility is the movement of individuals or groups from one level in a stratification system to another** (Rothman, 1993). This movement can be either upward or downward. **Intergenerational mobility is the social movement experienced by family members from one generation to the next.** By contrast, **intragenerational mobility is the social movement of individuals within their own lifetime.** In a *closed system*, the boundaries between levels in the

BOX 8.1

ANSWERS TO THE SOCIOLOGY QUIZ ON POVERTY

1. **False.** Statistics Canada estimated that the cost of bringing all poor people out of poverty in 1996 would have been $17.8 billion. According to the National Council of Welfare that is a huge but not outrageous amount of money relative to government spending in Canada.

2. **False.** As a group, children have a higher rate of poverty than the elderly. Government programs such as old age security are indexed to inflation, while many of the programs for the young have been scaled back or eliminated. However, many elderly individuals do live in poverty.

3. **False.** Women, not men, account for two out of three impoverished adults in Canada. Reasons for this include the lack of job opportunities for women, lower pay for women than men for comparable jobs, lack of affordable daycare for children, sexism in the workplace, and a number of other factors.

4. **False.** In 1996, 730,000 poor children were living in two-parent families, compared with 673,000 in female-headed single-parent households. However, the *rate* of poverty is highest for female-headed single-parent families.

5. **True.** In these three cities, one-quarter of preschool-aged children are poor.

6. **False.** Images of poverty as a rural phenomenon are out of date. In 1996, 57 percent of all poor families in Canada lived in a city with a population of 500,000 or more.

7. **False.** According to one widely held stereotype, the poor are lazy and do not want to work. In reality only a fraction of welfare recipients are able-bodied adults who are capable of working. Rather than looking at the structural characteristics of society, people cite the alleged personal attributes of the poor as the reason for their plight.

8. **True.** A literature review on poverty and child abuse concluded that poverty debilitates families and can be a "catalyst and intensifier of child maltreatment" (Volpe, 1989:12).

9. **True.** Many of those who fall below the official poverty line are referred to as the "working poor" because they work full time but earn such low wages that they are considered to be impoverished.

10. **False.** Welfare payments across Canada fall far below the low-income cut-offs.

Sources: Based on Harman, 1995; Lochhead and Shillington, 1996; National Council of Welfare, 1998; and Volpe, 1989.

hierarchies of social stratification are rigid, and people's positions are set by ascribed status.

Open and closed systems are ideal-type constructs; no actual stratification system is completely open or closed. The systems of stratification we will examine—caste and class—are characterized by different hierarchical structures and varying degrees of mobility. Let's examine these systems of stratification to determine how people acquire their positions in each and what potential for social movement they have.

The Caste System

Caste is a closed system of social stratification. A **caste system is a system of social inequality in which people's status is permanently determined at birth based on their parents' ascribed charac-**

teristics. Vestiges of caste systems exist in contemporary India and South Africa.

In India, caste is based in part on occupation; thus, families typically perform the same type of work from generation to generation. By contrast, the caste system of South Africa was based on racial classifications and the belief of white South Africans (Afrikaners) that they were morally superior to the black majority. Until the 1990s, Afrikaners controlled the government, the police, and the military by enforcing *apartheid*—**the separation of the races.** Blacks were denied full citizenship and restricted to segregated hospitals, schools, residential neighbourhoods, and other facilities. Whites held almost all of the desirable jobs; blacks worked as manual labourers and servants.

In a caste system, marriage is *endogamous*, meaning that people are allowed to marry only within their own group. In India, parents tradi-

"Social stratification" may seem to be an abstract concept, but it is an everyday reality for these individuals spending the night at a shelter.

tionally have selected marriage partners for their children. In South Africa, interracial marriage was illegal until 1985.

Cultural beliefs and values sustain caste systems. In India, the Hindu religion reinforced the caste system by teaching that people should accept their fate in life and work hard as a moral duty. Caste systems grow weaker as societies industrialize; the values reinforcing the system break down, and people start to focus on the types of skills needed for industrialization.

As we have seen, in closed systems of stratification, group membership is hereditary, and it is almost impossible to move up within the structure. Custom and law frequently perpetuate privilege and ensure that higher-level positions are reserved for the children of the advantaged (Rothman, 1993:171).

The Class System

The *class system* is a type of stratification based on the ownership and control of resources and on the type of work people do (Rothman, 1993). At least theoretically, a class system is more open than a caste system because the boundaries between classes are less distinct than the boundaries between castes. In a class system, status comes at least partly through achievement rather than entirely by ascription. **Class refers to the relative location of a person or group within a larger society, based on wealth, power, prestige, or other valued resources.**

In class systems, people may become members of a class other than that of their parents through both intergenerational and intragenerational mobility, either upward or downward. *Horizontal mobility* occurs when people experience a gain or loss in position and/or income that does not produce a change in their place in the class structure. For example, a person may get a pay increase and a more prestigious title but still not move from one class to another. In contrast, movement up or down the class structure is *vertical mobility*. Martin, a commercial artist who owns his own firm, is an example of vertical, intergenerational mobility:

> My family came out of a lot of poverty and were eager to escape it … My [mother's parents] worked in a sweatshop. My grandfather to the day he died never earned more than $14 a week. My grandmother worked in knitting mills while she had five children … My father quit school when he was in eighth grade and supported his mother and his two sisters when he was twelve years old. My grandfather died when my father was four and he basically raised his sisters. He got a man's job when he was twelve and took care of the three of them. (quoted in Newman, 1993a:65)

Martin's mobility reflects the ideal of upward mobility, according to which we can move beyond our origins and become more "successful" than our parents.

People also may experience downward mobility for any number of reasons, including a lack of jobs, lower wages and employment instability, marriage to someone with fewer resources and less power than oneself, and changing social conditions (Ehrenreich, 1989; Newman, 1988, 1993a). Laura, who was born in the 1950s and who grew up believing that hard work translated into success, instead has found that she has experienced downward mobility:

> I'll never have what my parents had. I can't even dream of that. I'm living a lifestyle that's way lower than it was when I was growing up and it's depressing. You know it's a rude awakening when you're out in the world on your own … Even if you are a hard worker and you never skipped a beat, you followed all the rules, did everything they told you you were supposed to do, it's still horrendous. They lied to me. You don't get where you were supposed to wind up. At the end of the road it isn't there. I

worked all these years and then I didn't get to candy land. The prize wasn't there, damn it. (quoted in Newman, 1993a:3)

In Canadian society we are socialized to believe that hard work is the key to personal success. Conversely, we are also taught that individuals who fail, who do not achieve success, do so as a result of their own personal inadequacies. Poverty is attributable to personal defect and it is up to the individual to find a way to break the "cycle of poverty." Do you agree? Or do you think structural factors in Canadian society affect the degree of success individuals achieve? Anthropologist Katherine Newman (1993a:11) has identified several social and structural factors that affect the level of material success an individual achieves. She attributes the downward mobility experienced by Laura and others of her generation to "escalating housing prices, occupational insecurity, blocked mobility on the job, and the cost-of-living squeeze that has penalized the boomer generation, even when they have more education and better jobs than their parents." Ascribed statuses such as race/ethnicity, gender, and religion also affect people's social mobility. We will look at the ideals versus the realities of social mobility as we continue to examine the class structure in Canada.

CLASSICAL PERSPECTIVES ON SOCIAL CLASS

Early sociologists grappled with the definition of class and the criteria for determining people's location within the class structure. Both Karl Marx and Max Weber viewed class as an important determinant of social inequality and social change, and their works have had a profound influence on contemporary class theory.

Karl Marx: Relation to Means of Production

For Karl Marx, class position is determined by people's work situation, or relationship to the means of production. As previously discussed, Marx suggested that capitalistic societies are made up of two classes—the capitalists and the workers. The capitalist class, or *bourgeoisie,* consists of those who own the means of production—the land and capital necessary for factories and mines, for example. The *working class,* or *prole-* *tariat,* consists of those who must sell their labour to the owners in order to earn enough money to survive (see Figure 8.2).

According to Marx, class relationships involve inequality and exploitation. The workers are exploited as capitalists maximize their profits by paying workers less than the resale value of what they produce but do not own. This exploitation results in worker *alienation—a feeling of powerlessness and estrangement from other people and from oneself.* As mechanization reduces the cost of producing products and machines replace many workers, the newly created surplus of workers becomes a "reserve army"—a readily available source of cheap labour that can be used by capitalists as a "weapon" against employees who demand pay raises or better working conditions. The presence of the reserve army keeps wages low and creates even greater profits for members of the capitalist class.

In Marx's view, the capitalist class maintained its position at the top of the class structure by control of the society's *superstructure,* which is composed of the government, schools, churches, and other social institutions that produce and disseminate ideas perpetuating the existing system of exploitation.

As discussed in Chapter 1, Marx predicted that the exploitation of workers by the capitalist class ultimately would lead to *class conflict—the struggle between the capitalist class and the working class.* According to Marx, when the workers realized that capitalists were the source of their oppression, they would overthrow the capitalists and their agents of social control, and this would lead to the end of capitalism. The workers would then take over the state and create a more egalitarian society.

Why has no workers' revolution occurred? According to sociologist Ralf Dahrendorf (1959), capitalism may have persisted because it has changed significantly since Marx's time. Individual capitalists no longer own and control factories and other means of production; today, ownership and control largely have been separated. For example, contemporary multinational corporations are owned by a multitude of stockholders but run by paid officers and managers. Similarly, many (but by no means all) workers have experienced a rising standard of living, which may have contributed to a feeling of complacency. Moreover, some people have become so engrossed in the process of consumption—including acquiring more material possessions and going on outings to shopping malls, movie the-

FIGURE 8.2 **Marx's View of Stratification**

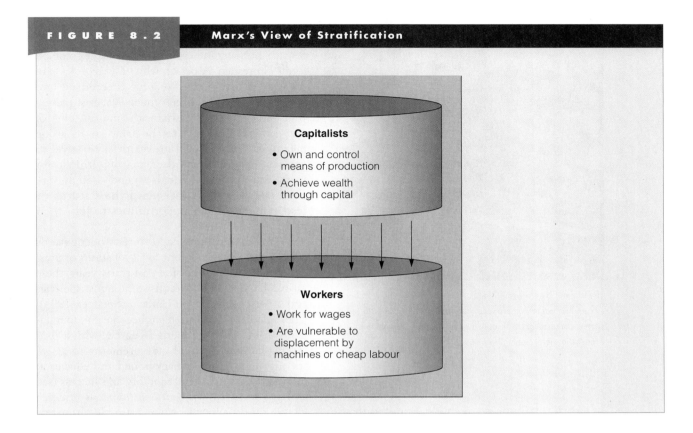

atres, and amusement parks such as Disney World—that they are less likely to engage in workers' rebellions against the system that has brought them a relatively high standard of living (Gottdiener, 1997). During the twentieth century, workers have also pressed for salary increases and improvements in the workplace through their activism and labour union membership (see Chapter 13). They have also gained more legal protection in the form of workers' rights and benefits such as worker's compensation insurance for job-related injuries and disabilities (Dahrendorf, 1959). For these reasons, and because of a myriad of other complex factors, the workers' revolution predicted by Marx never came to pass. However, the failure of his prediction does not mean that his analysis of capitalism and his theoretical contributions to sociology are without validity.

Marx had a number of important insights into capitalist societies. First, he recognized the economic basis of class systems (Gilbert and Kahl, 1993). Second, he noted the relationship between people's location in the class structure and their values, beliefs, and behaviour. Finally, he acknowledged that classes may have opposing (rather than complementary) interests. For example, capitalists' best interests are served by a

decrease in labour costs and other expenses and a corresponding increase in profit; workers' best interests are served by well-paid jobs, safe working conditions, and job security.

Marx's views make us aware of macrolevel economic conditions that may influence large numbers of oppressed people to recognize their common condition and to act politically to change it. According to political scientist Michael Parenti (1994:66), the absence (thus far) of a class revolution does not mean that workers are not exploited by capitalists or that people's class position does not mould the conditions of their lives. People who work for a living do fight back; struggles between the classes are continual even if they do not result in revolution as Marx predicted (Parenti, 1994).

Max Weber: Wealth, Prestige, and Power

Max Weber agreed with Marx's assertion that economic factors are important in understanding individual and group behaviour. However, Weber emphasized that no one factor (such as economic divisions between capitalists and workers) was suf-

The attempt by workers to improve their place in the stratification system has led to numerous labour strikes. Here, Ontario public sector workers fight with police in an attempt to move their protests to the provincial legislature.

ficient for defining people's location within the class structure. As a result, he developed a multidimensional approach to social stratification that focused on the interplay among wealth, prestige, and power in determining a person's class position.

Wealth **is the value of all of a person's or family's economic assets, including income, personal property, and income-producing property.** Weber placed people who have a similar level of wealth and income in the same class. For example, he identified a privileged commercial class of *entrepreneurs*—wealthy bankers, shipowners, professionals, and merchants who possess similar financial resources. He also described a class of *rentiers*—wealthy individuals who live off their investments and do not have to work. According to Weber, entrepreneurs and rentiers have much in common. Both are able to purchase expensive consumer items, control other people's opportunities to acquire wealth and property, and monopolize costly status privileges (such as education) that provide contacts and skills for their children.

Weber divided those who work for wages into two classes: the middle class and the working class. The middle class consists of white-collar workers, public officials, managers, and professionals. The working class consists of skilled, semiskilled, and unskilled workers.

Prestige **is the respect with which a person or status position is regarded by others.** Fame, respect, honour, and esteem are the most common forms of prestige. A person who has a high level of prestige is assumed to receive deferential and respectful treatment from others. Weber suggested that individuals who share a common level of social prestige belong to the same status group regardless of their level of wealth. They tend to socialize with one another, marry within their own group of social equals, spend their leisure time together, and safeguard their status by restricting outsiders' opportunities to join their ranks (Beeghley, 1996).

As you might expect, different occupations have significantly different levels of status or prestige (see Table 8.1). For the past thirty years, these ratings have been fairly consistent across societies and among subgroups in Canada (Spencer, 1993). These prestige rankings have become the foundation for status attainment research, which uses sophisticated statistical measurements to assess the influence of family background and education on people's occupational mobility and success (see Curtis et al., 1993). *Status attainment research* focuses on the process by which people ultimately reach their position in the class structure. Based largely on studies of men, this research uses the father's occupation and the son's education and first job as primary determinants of the eventual class position of the son. Obviously, family background is the central factor in this process because the son's education and first job are linked to the family's economic status. In addition, the family's location in the class system is related to the availability of social ties that may open occupational doors for the son.

Although they have been widely employed in sociological research, status attainment models have several serious limitations. One is the focus of this research on the occupational prestige of traditionally male jobs and the exclusion of women's work, which often has been unpaid. A woman's social class position typically has been linked to that of her father or husband, irrespective of her own work. Moreover, the status attainment model is unable to account for power differentials rooted in inequalities based on race, ethnicity, or gender.

Power **is the ability of people or groups to achieve their goals despite opposition from others.** The powerful shape society in accordance with their own interests and direct the actions of others (Tumin, 1953). Social power in modern

TABLE 8.1 | **PRESTIGE RATINGS FOR SELECTED OCCUPATIONS 1993 AND 1963**

Respondents were asked to evaluate a list of occupations according to their prestige; the individual rankings were averaged and then converted into scores, with 1 the lowest possible score and 99 the highest possible score (Gilbert and Kahl, 1993).

	SCORE			SCORE	
OCCUPATION	1993	1963	OCCUPATION	1993	1963
Physician	86	93	Police officer	60	72
Lawyer	75	89	Electrician	51	76
University professor	74	90	Mail carrier	47	66
Dentist	72	88	Garbage collector	28	39
Accountant	65	81	Janitor	22	48
Elementary school teacher	64	82	Shoe shiner	9	34

Source: Hodge, Siegel, and Rosis, 1964; and National Opinion Research Center, 1993.

societies is held by bureaucracies; individual power depends on a person's position within the bureaucracy. Weber suggested that the power of modern bureaucracies was so strong that even a workers' revolution (as predicted by Marx) would not lessen social inequality (Hurst, 1992).

Wealth, prestige, and power are separate continuums on which people can be ranked from high to low. Individuals may be high in one dimension while being low in another. For example, people may be very wealthy but have little political power (for example, a recluse who has inherited a large sum of money). They also may have prestige but not wealth (for instance, a university professor who receives teaching excellence awards but lives on a relatively low income). In Weber's multidimensional approach, people are ranked in all three dimensions.

Although power, wealth, and prestige are independent of one another, one may be used to acquire the others. Wealth, for example, can be used to gain power or prestige; the "charitable rich" in Canada acquire prestige by their financial contributions to and voluntary activities on behalf of nonprofit groups, such as symphony orchestras, museums, hospitals, and charities (Odendahl, 1990). Similarly, people may use their prestige to gain wealth. For example, celebrity athletes and entertainers often make their fortunes by endorsing products.

Weber's analysis of social stratification contributes to our understanding by emphasizing that people behave according to both their economic interests and their values. He added to Marx's insights by developing a multidimensional explanation of the class structure and identifying additional classes. Both Marx and Weber emphasized that capitalists and workers are the primary players in a class society, and both noted the importance of class to people's life chances. However, they saw different futures for capitalism and the social system. Marx saw these structures being overthrown; Weber saw the increasing bureaucratization of life even without capitalism.

THE CANADIAN CLASS STRUCTURE

How many social classes exist in Canada? No broad consensus exists about how to characterize the class structure in this country. In fact, many Canadians do not like to talk about social class. Some even deny that class distinctions exist, leading social analysts to refer to class as the "last dirty secret" (see Forcese, 1986). Most people like to think of themselves as middle-class; it puts them in a comfortable position—neither rich nor poor. Sociologists differ in the methods used to determine people's relative positions in the class structure.

Three methods may be used to determine people's placement in the class structure: the subjective, the reputational, and the objective. In the

FIGURE 8.3   **Weber's Multidimensional Approach to Social Stratification**

According to Max Weber, wealth, power, and prestige are separate continuums. Individuals may rank high in one dimension and low in another, or they may rank high or low in more than one dimension. Also, individuals may use their high rank in one dimension to achieve a comparable rank in another.

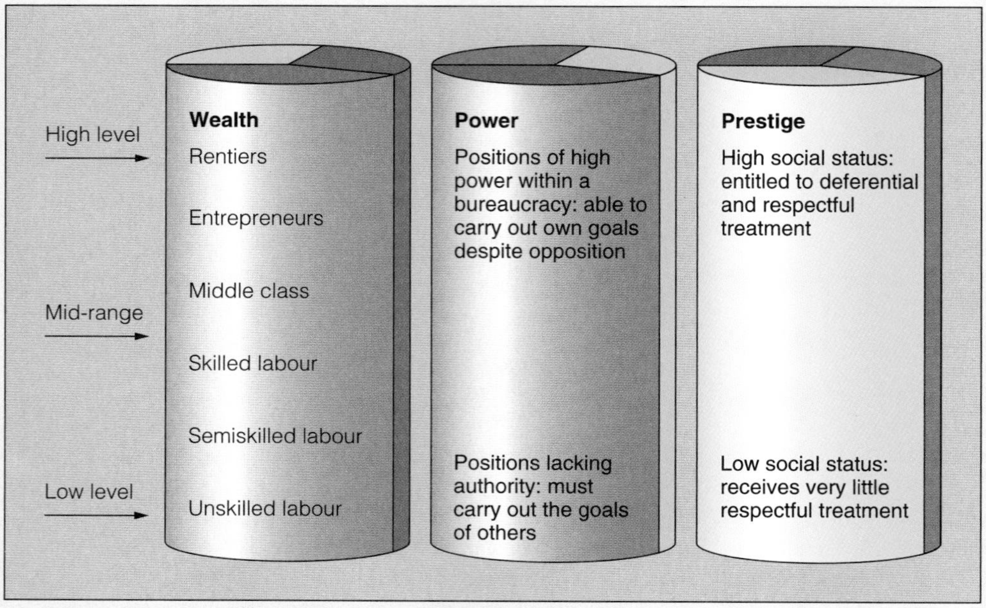

High level →	**Wealth**	**Power**	**Prestige**
	Rentiers	Positions of high power within a bureaucracy: able to carry out own goals despite opposition	High social status: entitled to deferential and respectful treatment
	Entrepreneurs		
Mid-range →	Middle class		
	Skilled labour		
	Semiskilled labour		
Low level →	Unskilled labour	Positions lacking authority: must carry out the goals of others	Low social status: receives very little respectful treatment

subjective method, people are asked to locate themselves in the class structure. However, when Canadians are questioned about their social class, most will say, in effect, that "there is no such thing as social class in Canada. We're all equal" (Spencer, 1993:166). In the *reputational method,* people are asked to place other individuals in their community (based on their reputation) into social classes. Using the *objective method,* researchers assign individuals to social classes based on predetermined criteria (occupation, source and amount of income, amount of education, and type and area of residence, for example). Analysts often use **socioeconomic status (SES), a combined measure that attempts to classify individuals, families, or households in terms of indicators such as income, occupation, and education,** to determine class location.

The Upper Class

The upper class is the wealthiest and most powerful class in Canada. Approximately 3 to 5 percent of the population is included in this class, whose members own substantial income-pro-

ducing assets and operate at both the national and international level. People in this class have an influence on the economy and society far beyond their numbers (Clement, 1975).

Some models further divide the upper class into upper-upper ("old money") and lower-upper ("new money") categories (Warner and Lunt, 1941; Coleman and Rainwater, 1978). Only 1 percent of the population are members of the upper-upper class. They come from prominent families, which possess great wealth that they have held for several generations. Canada has some of the wealthiest families in the world. For example, the net worth of the Thomson family was recently estimated at $14 billion (Forbes, 1998; see Table 8.2). Family names—such as Bronfman, Eaton, and Weston—are well known and often held in high esteem. Persons in the upper-upper class tend to have strong feelings of ingroup solidarity. They belong to the same exclusive clubs and support high culture (such as the opera, symphony orchestras, ballet, and art museums). Their children are educated at private schools such as Upper Canada College in Toronto and at prestigious universities; many acquire strong feelings of

The death of a homeless man at Queen's Park in Toronto is a disturbing reminder of Canada's growing underclass—individuals who are poor, unemployed, and caught in an existence characterized by deprivation.

privilege from birth. Children of the upper class are often socialized to view themselves as different from others; they also learn that they are expected to marry within their own class (Warner and Lunt, 1941; Baltzell, 1958; Mills, 1959a; Domhoff, 1970, 1983).

Members of the lower-upper class may be extremely wealthy but have not attained as much prestige as members of the upper-upper class. The "new rich" have earned most of their money in their own lifetimes as entrepreneurs, presidents of major corporations, sports or entertainment celebrities, or top-level professionals. Some members of the lower-upper class aspire to gain the respect of the upper-upper class members. In the early 1990s, for example, American-billionaire real estate developer Donald Trump purchased a 118-room Florida estate and entertained members of the upper-upper class in hopes of being invited to join the elite Palm Beach Bath and Tennis Club. After Trump was shunned by club members, he disdainfully remarked to a journalist that the old-line rich are "frivolous and boring" (Kunen, 1990:31).

The Middle Class

This is the largest group: an estimated 40 to 50 percent of Canada's population is in this class. Once again, this group is sometimes divided into the upper-middle class and the lower-middle class. Persons in the upper-middle class often are highly educated professionals who have built careers as physicians, lawyers, stockbrokers, or corporate managers. Others derive their income from family-owned businesses. A combination of three factors qualifies people for the upper-middle class: university degrees, authority and independence on the job, and high incomes. Of all the class categories, the upper-middle class is the one that is most shaped by formal education.

In past decades, a high-school diploma was necessary to qualify for most middle-class jobs. Today, the community college degree has supplemented the high school diploma as an entry-level job requirement in a number of middle-class occupations such as medical technicians, nurses, legal and medical assistants, lower-level managers, semiprofessionals, and nonretail salesworkers. Traditionally, most middle-class occupations have been relatively secure and provided more opportunities for advancement (especially with increasing levels of education and experience) than working-class positions. Recently, however, four factors have diminished the chances for material success for this class: (1) escalating housing prices, (2) occupational insecurity, (3) blocked mobility on the job, and (4) the cost-of-living squeeze that has penalized younger workers, even when they have more education and better jobs than their parents (Newman, 1993). Consider, for example, Brenda and Amancio Irizarry, who are struggling to get by on a combined pretax income of $38,000 a year. Although they make more money than their parents did, the Irizarrys cannot afford to buy a house, have no savings, and have never taken a

TABLE 8.2	MAJOR CANADIAN ENTREPRENEURS AMONG THE WORLD'S RICHEST PEOPLE: THEIR PRINCIPAL BUSINESSES AND ESTIMATED WEALTH, 1998	
NAME	**PRINCIPAL BUSINESS**	**WEALTH ($billion)**
Kenneth Roy Thomson	Newspapers, Thomson Corp.	14.4
Three Irving brothers	Gas stations, oil refineries	4
Charles Bronfman	Seagram Co.	3.3
Israel Asper	CanWest Global Communications	1.8

Reprinted by permission of *Forbes Magazine*. © Forbes Inc., 1998. Figures have been converted to Canadian dollars.

vacation together. They are working hard to send their daughter, Michelle, to a community college. As Mrs. Irizarry explains:

> We didn't have a college fund for Michelle. You see commercials on television saying to start [saving] when the baby is born. But because of the unforeseen things that happen in life, it's impossible to save money. (quoted in Jones, 1995:9)

Michelle appreciates her parents' efforts but eventually wants much more for herself:

> I don't want to live like this the rest of my life … I mean, they have morals and are trying to make it. But unless they hit the Lotto, this is how it's going to be the rest of their lives. And that's sad, to think that's it. This is as good as it's going to get. (quoted in Jones, 1995:9)

Michelle has not given up; she is determined to become a social worker and have a nice place to live (Jones, 1995). As this example suggests, class distinctions between the middle and working classes are less clear than those between other classes due to overlapping characteristics (Gilbert and Kahl, 1998).

The Working Class

The core of this class is composed of people who hold relatively unskilled blue-collar and white-collar jobs. Members of the working class include clerks, salespeople, and some members of the service sector who have jobs involving routine, mechanized tasks, which typically involve a short period of on-the-job training. Also included in the working class are *pink-collar occupations*— **relatively low-paying, nonmanual, semiskilled positions primarily held by women,** such as day-

care workers, checkout clerks, cashiers, and waitpersons. An estimated 30 percent of the Canadian population is in the working class.

How does life in the working-class family compare with that of individuals in middle-class families? Working-class families earn less than middle-class families and have less financial security, especially because of layoffs and plant closings in some parts of the country. Few members have training beyond a high-school diploma, and many have less, which makes job opportunities scarce for them in a "high-tech" society (Gilbert and Kahl, 1998).

The Lower Class

The lower class account for about 20 percent of the Canadian population. Included in this group are the working poor and the underclass. Members of the working poor live from just above to just below the poverty line; they typically hold unskilled jobs, seasonal migrant employment in agriculture, lower-paid factory jobs, and service jobs (such as counter help at restaurants). Employed single mothers often belong to this class; consequently, children are overrepresented in this category. Visible minorities, Aboriginal peoples, and recent immigrants are also overrepresented among the working poor (Ross, Shillington, and Lochhead, 1994). For the working poor, living from paycheque to paycheque makes it impossible to save money for emergencies such as periodic or seasonal unemployment, which is a constant threat to any economic stability they may have.

People in the under class are poor, seldom employed, and caught in long-term deprivation that results from low levels of education and income and high rates of unemployment. Some

FIGURE 8.4   Stratification Based on Education, Occupation, and Income

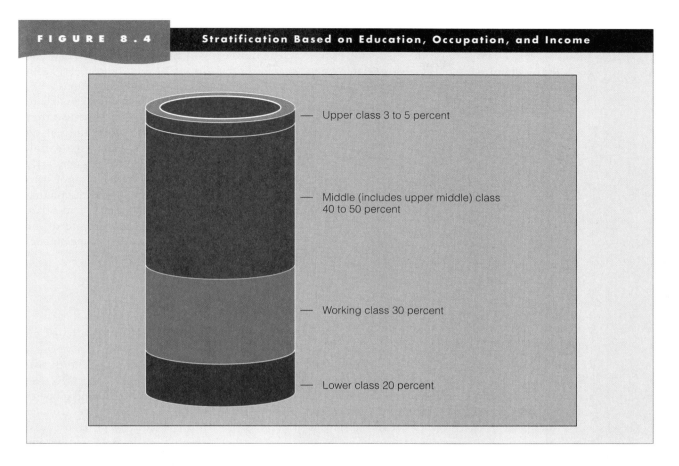

— Upper class 3 to 5 percent

— Middle (includes upper middle) class
40 to 50 percent

— Working class 30 percent

— Lower class 20 percent

are unable to work because of age or disability; others experience discrimination based on race/ethnicity. Single mothers are overrepresented in this class because of the lack of jobs, affordable child care, and many other impediments to the mother's future and that of her children. People without a "living wage" often must rely on the welfare system for survival.

While some young people are hopeful that they can acquire well-paid, meaningful jobs that will help them escape poverty, others view their futures with pessimism and uncertainty. They may have levelled aspirations, as author Jay MacLeod (1988) learned when he asked members of two male teenage peer groups from underclass families what their lives would be like in twenty years. Three of them replied (in separate interviews):

Stoney: Hard to say, I could be dead tomorrow. Around here, you gotta take life day by day.

Boo-Boo: I dunno. I don't want to think about it. I'll think about it when it comes.

Shorty: Twenty years? I'm gonna be in jail. (MacLeod, 1988:61)

Those who discussed work saw it solely as a means to an end—money (MacLeod, 1988).

SOCIOLOGICAL EXPLANATIONS OF SOCIAL INEQUALITY

Why are all societies stratified? The functionalist perspective sees inequality as an inevitable and even necessary feature of society. The conflict perspective, influenced by Karl Marx, sees inequality as avoidable, unnecessary, and the source of most human conflict. Gerhard Lenski (1966) has offered a third approach that combines elements of both functionalism and conflict theory.

Functionalist Perspectives

Fifty years ago, Kingsley Davis and Wilbert Moore developed a theory of social stratification that has been debated ever since. Davis and Moore (1945) suggested that social inequality is not only universal but also functionally necessary for all societies. How can social inequality be beneficial to a society? The *Davis–Moore thesis*, which has become the definitive functionalist explanation for social inequality, can be summarized as follows:

1. All societies have important tasks that must be accomplished and certain positions that must be filled.
2. Some positions are more important for the survival of society than others.
3. The most important positions must be filled by the most qualified people.
4. The positions that are the most important for society and that require scarce talent, extensive training, or both, must be the most highly rewarded.
5. The most highly rewarded positions should be those that are functionally unique (no other position can perform the same function) and on which other positions rely for expertise, direction, or financing.

Davis and Moore use the physician as an example of a functionally unique position. Doctors are very important to society and require extensive training, but individuals would not be motivated to go through years of costly and stressful medical training without incentives to do so. The Davis–Moore thesis assumes that social stratification results in *meritocracy*—**a hierarchy in which all positions are rewarded based on people's ability and credentials.**

An important contribution of the Davis–Moore thesis is that it directs attention to the distribution of social prestige based on occupation. Yet occupational prestige rankings may not actually be based on the importance of a position to society. The highest ratings may be given to professionals—such as physicians and lawyers—because they have many years of training in their fields and some control of their own work, not because these positions contribute the most to society. According to some scholars, members of the medical profession have created a professional monopoly that has contributed significantly to their income and prestige throughout most of the twentieth century (see Freidson, 1970, 1986; Starr, 1982).

Critics have suggested that the Davis–Moore thesis ignores inequalities based on inherited wealth and intergenerational family status (Rossides, 1986). The thesis assumes that economic rewards and prestige are the only effective motivators for people, and fails to take into account other intrinsic aspects of work, such as self-fulfilment (Tumin, 1953). It also does not adequately explain how such a reward system guarantees that the most qualified people will gain access to the most highly rewarded positions.

What about people who have not been able to maximize their talents and skills because they were born in impoverished circumstances and received a substandard education (see Kozol, 1991)? The functionalist approach generally ignores such questions because it does not consider structural factors (such as racial discrimination, lack of job opportunities, and inadequate funding of schools) that may contribute to the persistence of inequality in society. Some conflict approaches attempt to fill this gap.

Conflict Perpectives

Conflict approaches, especially those based on Marxist theories, identify ownership or nonownership of the means of production as the distinguishing feature of classes. From this perspective, classes are social groups organized around property ownership and control of the workplace. Conflict theory is based on the assumption that social stratification is created and maintained by one group in order to protect and enhance its own economic interests. Societies are organized around classes in conflict over scarce resources. Stratification exists only because the rich and powerful are determined to hang on to more than their share of scarce resources. Inequality results from the more powerful exploiting the less powerful.

From a conflict perspective, people with economic and political power are able to shape and distribute the rewards, resources, privileges, and opportunities in society for their own benefit. Conflict theorists do not believe that inequality serves as a motivating force for people; they argue that powerful individuals and groups use ideology to maintain their favoured positions at the expense of others. A stratified social system is accepted because of the dominant ideology of the society, the set of beliefs that explain and justify the existing social order (Marchak, 1975). Core values in Canada emphasize the importance of material possessions, hard work and individual initiative to get ahead, and behaviour that supports the existing social structure. These same values support the prevailing resource distribution system and contribute to social inequality.

Conflict theorists note that laws and informal social norms also support inequality in Canada. For the first half of the twentieth century, for example, both legalized and institutionalized segregation and discrimination reinforced employment discrimination and produced higher levels of economic inequality. Although laws have been passed to make these overt acts of discrimination illegal, many forms of discrimination still exist in educational and employment opportunities.

The Evolutionary Approach

Gerhard Lenski (1966) developed a theory of power and privilege to explain social stratification and inequality. Lenski's theory, referred to as the *evolutionary approach,* combined elements from both conflict theory and functionalism. Lenski focused on the concept of ruling elites in society and how they managed to maintain control over society's wealth and power (Krahn, 1995b).

Lenski begins with the idea that people generally are more rewarded by fulfilling their own wants and ambitions rather than by addressing the needs of others. He acknowledged that it may be possible to socialize human beings so that they do not behave in this way, but he also pointed out that it remains an almost universal feature of social life. Most of the things that people want (wealth, power, prestige) are scarce. In other words, the demand exceeds the supply. Therefore, some conflict over how these limited resources are distributed is inevitable. The result is social inequality. Sometimes this inequality is functional for a society. However, Lenski points out, forms of stratification persist long after their functional benefit has ended. As a result, most societies are much more stratified than they need to be (Robertson, 1977).

Lenski traced the evolution of social stratification and argued that the type and form it takes is related to the society's means of economic production or technological base. Lenski shows how the nature of stratification varies from one type of society to another.

Hunting and Gathering Societies People in these societies depend on materials taken directly from nature for their food, clothing, and shelter. Their technology consists of primitive tools such as digging sticks, bows and arrows, traps, and fishing equipment. Members of these societies are nomadic—as soon as local resources are used up, they move on in pursuit of more. In simple hunting and gathering societies, the few resources of the society are distributed primarily on the basis of need. There is no surplus wealth, and therefore no opportunity for some people to become wealthier than others. Consequently, hunting and gathering societies are the least stratified, especially in the dimensions of property and power. The main criteria for inequality in these societies are age and sex. But the overall stratification system is simple and fairly egalitarian.

Simple Horticultural Societies As societies became more technologically complex, more resources were produced than were needed to fulfil the basic needs of the society. Further, it is possible to accumulate property in horticultural societies because people are not having to move when resources are depleted. In these societies "specialists," such as producers of harpoons, canoes, drums, or art appear for the first time. With increasing specialization comes increased inequality as some roles are assigned more prestige or power than others. In horticultural and pastoral societies a surplus product is available and chieftainships emerge as powerful families obtain control over surplus—an advantage also known as resources *privilege*. As a result, differences in property, power, and prestige among members become more prevalent.

Agricultural Societies These societies are much larger and richer, and much more specialized and stratified than simple horticultural societies. The primary reason for these differences is related to technological advancement—specifically the production of metal tools. The metal plough dramatically increased yields from farming. Because a small number of farmers can produce enough food to support a large number of people, a relatively small portion of the population needs to be involved in food production. The most important consequence of increased productivity is the creation of permanent armies and elaborate governmental structures. In simple horticultural societies a great deal of wealth is based on the accumulation of wives. With advances in production, it becomes profitable to own people in order to gain the surplus wealth from their labour. It is in these societies that slavery first appears. In agricultural societies the status of heredity rises dramatically. Cattle, land, slaves, and even primitive forms of money can be passed from one generation to another. Therefore, each generation can accumulate more wealth through inheritance. These societies are the first to exhibit hereditary classes and very marked inequalities of power, property, and prestige. The ruling elites accumulated wealth at the expense of the less privileged. The result is that the society becomes divided into strata (Robertson, 1977).

INDUSTRIAL SOCIETIES In their earliest form, industrial societies had similar stratification systems to those of agricultural societies. However, as a result of industrialization and increasingly complex technology, the trend toward increasing inequality was reversed (Lenski, 1966). Industrial societies became less stratified than agricultural societies and this trend has continued.

The specific cause of this reversal was that the owners of the means of production, the ruling elite, could no longer control the production process directly and were forced to rely on educated managers and specialized technical workers to maintain production. This change curtailed the power of the ruling classes. Individuals and groups were introduced to ideas of democracy, which led them to demand a larger share of the profits they were helping to produce (Krahn, 1995). The ruling elite gave in to these demands because they could not produce without the educated, skilled workers. Furthermore, industrialized societies are much more productive—therefore there is more wealth to divide (Lenski, 1966; Robertson, 1977). In industrial societies the importance of ascribed status is diminished while achieved status is emphasized.

INEQUALITY IN CANADA

Throughout human history, people have argued about the distribution of scarce resources in society. Disagreements often centre on whether the share we get is a fair reward for our efforts and hard work (Braun, 1991). Recently, however, social analysts have pointed out that the old maxim—the rich get richer—continues to apply in Canada and across North America. To understand how this happens, we first must take a closer look at the distribution of income and wealth in this country.

Distribution of Income and Wealth

Money is essential for acquiring goods and services. People without money cannot purchase food, shelter, clothing, legal services, education, and the other things they need or desire. Money—in the form of both income and wealth—is very unevenly distributed in Canada. Among the industrialized nations of North America and Europe, Canada has one of the worst records of income inequality, second only to the United States (McQuaig, 1993).

Income Income is the economic gain derived from wages, salaries, income transfers (governmental aid such as social assistance, Canada Pension Plan payments), and ownership of property (Beeghley, 1996). Economist Paul Samuelson has noted that, "If we made an income pyramid out of a child's blocks, with each layer portraying $500 of income, the peak would be far higher than Mount Everest, but most people would be within a few feet of the ground" (quoted in Samuelson and Nordhaus, 1989:644).

Dennis Gilbert and Joseph Kahl (1998:93) compare the distribution of income to a "national pie that has been sliced into portions, ranging in size from stingy to generous, for distribution among segments of the population." One way of measuring income inequality is to divide the population into five equal groups called *quintiles*, and to indicate the share of total income received by each group. As shown in Figure 8.5, in 1996 the wealthiest 20 percent of households received over 40 percent of the total income "pie," while the poorest have received less than 5 percent of all income (Statistics Canada, 1996f). The top 10 percent had average incomes, over 10 times greater than the poorest 10 percent (Campaign 2000, 1998). Figure 8.5 also reveals the remarkable stability of income distribution over time.

There is considerable regional variation in income in Canada. As shown in Map 8.1, the average family income is highest in Ontario, British Columbia, and Alberta and lowest in the Atlantic provinces.

Income distribution also varies by race/ethnicity. Table 8.3, which shows the average incomes of the largest nineteen ethnic groups in Canada, demonstrates that race and ethnicity are important determinants of social position. People of Jewish origin rank first with average incomes of $37,146, more than double the income of both Aboriginal peoples and Latin Americans, who rank lowest (Driedger, 1996). The categories that have the lowest average incomes are almost exclusively visible minorities. Recent statistics indicate that in 1995, 36 percent of the visible minority

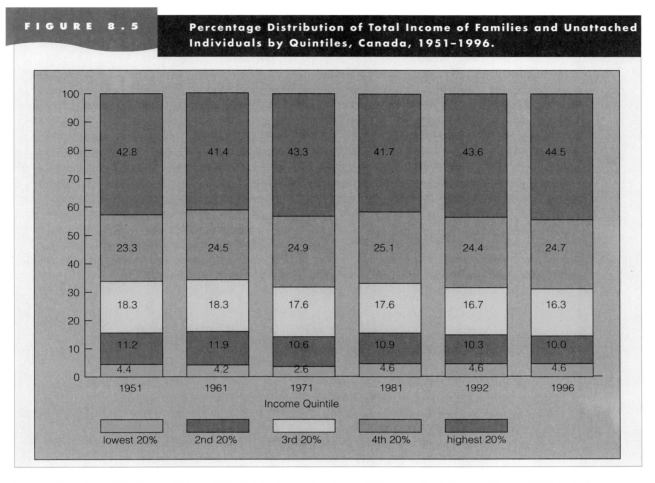

FIGURE 8.5 Percentage Distribution of Total Income of Families and Unattached Individuals by Quintiles, Canada, 1951–1996.

Reproduced by authority of the Minister of Industry, 1996, Statistics Canada, from *Income Distribution by Size in Canada*, Cat. no. 13-207; Centre for International Statistics at the Canadian Council on Social Development, Statistics Canada, *Income Distributions by Size in Canada*, 1996, Cat. no. 13-207.XPB.

population were in the low-income group, compared with 20 percent in the general population (Statistics Canada, 1998i). It is also clear from the data that Aboriginal peoples are particularly disadvantaged. For example, the average income of an Aboriginal person in Canada is less than two-thirds of the average income of a non-Aboriginal (Lochhead and Shillington, 1996; Frideres, 1993).

WEALTH Income is only one aspect of wealth. Wealth includes property such as buildings, land, farms, houses, factories, and cars, as well as other assets such as money in bank accounts, corporate stocks, bonds, and insurance policies. Wealth is computed by subtracting all debt obligations and converting the remaining assets into cash. For most people in Canada, wealth is invested primarily in property that generates no income, such as a house or a car. In contrast, the wealth of an

elite minority often is in the form of income-producing property.

Research on the distribution of wealth in Canada reveals that wealth is more unevenly distributed among the Canadian population than is income. For the upper class, wealth often comes from inheritance. The majority of the wealthiest people in Canada are inheritors, with some at least three or four generations removed from the original fortune (Dyck, 1996). The combined wealth of a small number of Canada's richest individuals and families, shown in Table 8.2, is over $23 billion. Clearly, a limited number of people own or control a very large portion of the wealth in Canada. In fact, the wealthiest quintile accounts for more than 50 percent of the wealth in Canada. Furthermore, Antonious and Crowley (1986) reported that more than two-thirds of the largest Canadian corporations were controlled by

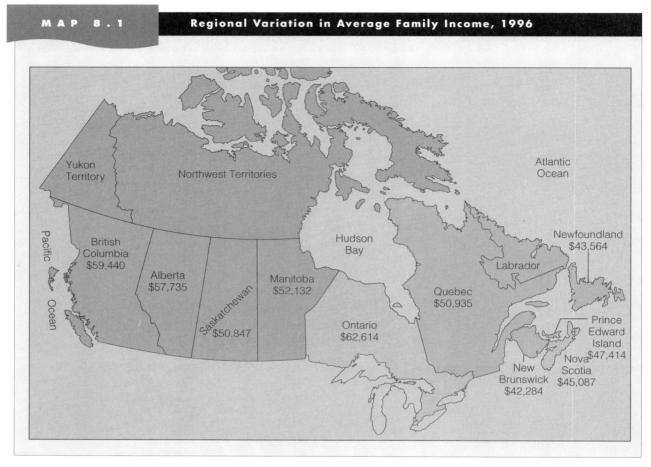

MAP 8.1 Regional Variation in Average Family Income, 1996

Prepared by the Centre for International Statistics at the Canadian Council on Social Development using data from Statistics Canada, *Income Distributions by Size in Canada*, 1996, Cat. no. 13-207-XPB. Used by permission.

a single owner. At least half of these owners were families. Richardson's (1990) analysis of corporate ownership in Canada reported similar findings. He noted that over three-quarters of the assets of Canada's largest nonfinancial corporations were controlled by only 17 large business enterprises. Eleven of the 17 enterprises were controlled by a single owner.

Whether we consider distribution of income or wealth, though, it is relatively clear that social inequality is a real, consistent, and enduring feature of life in Canadian society (Harman, 1995).

Consequences of Inequality

Income and wealth are not simply statistics; they are intricately related to our individual life chances. Persons with a high income or substantial wealth have more control over their lives. They have greater access to goods and services; they can afford better housing, more education,

and a wider range of medical services. Similarly, as discussed in Box 8.2, those with greater access to economic resources fare better when dealing with the criminal justice system (Reiman, 1979; Gabor 1994; Linden, 1995). Persons with less income, especially those living in poverty, must spend their limited resources on the basic necessities of life.

HEALTH AND NUTRITION People who are wealthy and well educated and who have high-paying jobs are much more likely to be healthy than are poor people. As people's economic status increases, so does their health status. The poor have shorter life expectancies and are at greater risk for chronic illnesses such as diabetes, heart disease, and cancer, as well as for infectious diseases such as tuberculosis. (See Chapter 18, "Health, Healthcare, and Disabilities.")

Children born into poor families are at much greater risk of dying during their first year of life.

TABLE 8.3

MEAN WAGE INCOMES OF CANADIAN EMPLOYED MALE POPULATION AGED 20–60 BY ETHNIC GROUP, 1981 AND 1991

	ANNUAL INCOME	
OCCUPATION	1981	1991
Jewish	$19,054	$37,146
Ukrainian	17,109	34,110
German	16,887	31,506
Dutch	16,461	30,888
Multiple British/French*	16,556	30,649
British	17,360	30,420
Multiple non British/French*	16,190	29,928
Polish	17,095	29,656
Italian	15,588	29,550
Other European	15,776	28,458
French	15,389	27,222
Portuguese	14,776	29,926
Chinese	14,120	26,392
South Asian	—	25,718
Other E/SE Asian	—	24,080
Black/Caribbean	14,442	23,346
Arab/West Asian	—	21,284
Aboriginal	—	18,779
Latin American	—	16,460

* Multiple British/French refers to individuals who have both British and French ethnic origins.

** Multiple non British/French refers to individuals having mixed ethnic origins that do not include French or English.

Reproduced by authority of the Minister of Industry, 1996, Statistics Canada, from 1981, and 1991 Census of Canada.

Some die from disease, accidents, or violence. Others are unable to survive because they are born with low birth weight, a condition linked to birth defects and increased probability of infant mortality (Canadian Institute of Child Health, 1994; and Health Canada, 1997). Low birth weight in infants is attributed, at least in part, to the inadequate nutrition received by many low-income pregnant women. Most of the poor do not receive preventive medical and dental checkups; many do not receive adequate medical care after they experience illness or injury. Furthermore, many high-poverty areas lack an adequate supply of doctors and medical facilities. The higher death rates among Aboriginal peoples in Canada are partly attributable to unequal access to medical care and nutrition.

Although the precise relationship between class and health is not known, analysts suggest that people with higher incomes and greater wealth tend to smoke less, exercise more, maintain a healthy body weight, and eat nutritious meals. As a category, affluent people tend to be less depressed and face less psychological stress, conditions that tend to be directly proportional to income, education, and job status (Ross and Roberts, 1997).

Good health is basic to good life chances, and adequate amounts of nutritious food are essential for good health. Hunger is related to class position and income inequality. After spending 60 percent of their income on housing, low-income families are often unable to provide enough food for their children. Consider the following comments by a mother on her attempts to manage her food budget:

I remember opening up the fridge just to see what was in there. There was a green pepper, an onion in the drawer and a bag of frozen rhubarb in the freezer,

BOX 8.2 SOCIOLOGY AND LAW

THE RICH GET RICHER AND THE POOR GET PRISON

How does social class affect the likelihood of being sent to prison? Are there different sets of rules operating in the criminal justice system—one for the rich and one for the poor? According to Jeffery Reiman, author of *The Rich Get Richer and the Poor Get Prison: Ideology, Class and Criminal Justice* (1979), economic power is the central factor in determining whether a person will go to prison for a criminal offence. Reiman supports this premise with data that reveals that in the United States the prison populations are overwhelmingly from the ranks of society's disadvantaged. He states:

> For the same criminal behavior, the poor are more likely to be arrested; if arrested, they are more likely to be charged; if charged, more likely to be convicted; if convicted, more likely to be sentenced to prison; and if sentenced, more likely to be given longer prison terms than members of the middle and upper classes. In other words, the image of the criminal population one sees in our nation's jails and prisons is an image distorted by the shape of the criminal justice system itself. It is the face of

evil reflected in a carnival mirror, but it is no laughing matter. (1979:97)

What effect does social class play in the processing of accused persons in the Canadian criminal justice system? According to criminologist Thomas Gabor, the justice system in Canada also favours the middle and upper classes—those who have the financial resources to protect their best interests. For example, in the case of young offenders, police are more likely to refer lower-class youths to juvenile court. Youth from wealthier homes are more likely to be dealt with informally. Poor defendants are less likely to be able to afford bail and are therefore more likely to remain in jail until their case goes to trial (this may be several months). The poor must rely on legal-aid lawyers who have large caseloads and little time to prepare cases for trial. The sentencing stage also favours individuals of higher social standing. Crimes committed by middle- and upper-class persons—for example, embezzlement, fraud, and income tax evasion—usually earn lighter sentences than those more likely to be committed by the poor (e.g., robbery and burglary).

and that was all the food we had in the entire house. We used to eat peanut butter by the spoonful, if we had any peanut butter. We used to make rhubarb soup. And we'd throw in whatever we could find. (Canadian Council on Social Development, 1996:21)

In 1994, over 50,000 Canadian children experienced hunger due to lack of food or money. Lack of adequate nutrition has been linked to children's problems in school. The number of food banks in Canada has grown from 1 in 1981 to more than 300 in 1996 (Canadian Council on Social Development, 1998). This increase clearly indicates that many Canadians are unable meet their nutritional needs (Kitcher et al., 1991; Oderkirk, 1992).

EDUCATION Educational opportunities and life chances are directly linked. Some functionalist theorists view education as the "elevator" to social mobility. Improvements in the educational achievement levels (measured in number of years of schooling completed) of the poor, visible minorities, and women have been cited as evidence that students' abilities now are more important than their class, race, or gender. From this perspective, inequality in education is declining, and students have an opportunity to achieve upward mobility through achievements at school (see Hauser and Featherman, 1976).

Functionalists generally see the education system as flexible, allowing most students the opportunity to attend university if they apply themselves (Ballantine, 1993).

BOX 8.2

In short, white-collar criminals have been very successful in ensuring that their interests are reflected in the law and its enforcement. According to criminologist Rick Linden, the crimes committed by higher-status criminals are much less likely to be labelled criminal:

> A storekeeper who sells a turkey labelled 12 kg which actually weighs 11 kg may not be prosecuted; if he or she actually is, the charge will be breach of a regulatory offence with relatively minor penalties. However, someone caught stealing a kilogram of turkey meat will be charged with the criminal offence of theft. Doctors who fraudulently bill provincial health insurance plans are usually disciplined by their professional body, while someone who fraudulently receives welfare is subject to criminal prosecution. (1995:219)

It is evident that social class plays a significant role in terms of the type of punishment, if any, offenders receive for their crime.

However, as Gabor notes, other factors such as the type and severity of the offence are also important considerations:

> Even poor people are selectively punished. The poor people we find in prisons have been incarcerated for murder, robbery, theft, burglary, drug offences and the like; they are rarely punished for assaulting their wives, abusing their children, or stealing from their employers. Thus, the type of infraction one commits, too, is important in the selection of people for legal proceedings. (1994:290)

Arrest, detention, and sentencing decisions are extremely complex and involve a number of legal (prior record, severity of offence, type of offence) and non-legal (social class, age, demeanour, gender) factors. Therefore, although we can say that social class affects an individual's chances of going to prison, it is difficult to determine the degree of influence this non-legal factor has.

Source: Gabor, 1994; Reiman, 1979; Linden, 1995

In contrast, most conflict theorists stress that schools are agencies for reproducing the capitalist class system and perpetuating inequality in society (Bowles and Gintis, 1976; Bowles, 1977). From this perspective, education perpetuates poverty. Parents with limited income are not able to provide the same educational opportunities for their children as are families with greater financial resources. Author Jonathan Kozol (1991, quoted in Feagin and Feagin, 1994:191) documented the effect of educational inequality on students:

> Kindergartners are so full of hope, cheerfulness, high expectations. By the time they get into fourth grade, many begin to lose heart. They see the score, understanding they're not getting what others are getting … They see suburban schools on television … They begin to get the point that they are not valued much in our society. By the time they are in junior high, they understand it. "We have eyes and we can see; we have hearts and we can feel … We know the difference."

Poverty exacts such a toll that many young people will not have the opportunity to finish high school, much less enter university, which subsequently affects job prospects, employment patterns, and potential earnings. As a report by the National Council of Welfare indicated, "To be born poor in Canada does not make it a certainty that you will live poor and die poor—but it makes it very likely" (quoted in Singh Bolaria, and Wotherspoon, 1991:470).

POVERTY IN CANADA

When many people think about poverty, they think of people who are unemployed or on welfare. However, many hardworking people with full-time jobs live in poverty. The most common measure used to establish the poverty line is the low-income cut-offs used by Statistics Canada. According to this measure, any individual or family that spends more than 56 percent of their income on the necessities of life—food, clothing, and shelter—is considered to be living in poverty. There is no single cut-off line for all of Canada because living costs vary by family size and place of residence. In 1997, the income cut-offs for a family of four ranged from $22,639 in rural areas to $32,759 in cities of more than 500,000. Based on these low-income cut-offs, nearly 5.2 million children, women, and men—one in every six Canadians—were living in poverty in 1996 (National Council of Welfare, 1998).

When sociologists define poverty, they distinguish between absolute and relative poverty. **Absolute poverty exists when people do not have the means to secure the most basic necessities of life.** This definition comes closest to that used by the federal government. Absolute poverty often has life-threatening consequences, such as when a homeless person freezes to death on a park bench. By comparison, **relative poverty exists when people may be able to afford basic necessities but still are unable to maintain an average standard of living** (Harman, 1995). Regardless of how it is

defined, poverty is primarily about deprivation, as this woman's comments reveal:

> There are times when I am so scared that I'm not going to find a job, I think, "What the hell is wrong with me?" ... I can get scared to death ... I have periods of insomnia. I'll get very short tempered with my husband and with the children. (Burman, 1998:195)

> If I say "no" to the children, they feel very depressed when they see other children taking things to school. The children feel very disappointed. They kind of lose love for you. They think that you don't love them. (Women for Economic Survival, 1984:23)

Who Are the Poor?

Poverty in Canada is not randomly distributed, but rather is highly concentrated among certain groups of people—specifically, women, children, persons with disabilities, and Aboriginal peoples. When people belong to more than one of these categories, for example, Aboriginal children, their risk of poverty is even greater.

AGE   Today, children are at much greater risk of living in poverty than are adults aged 16 to 64 (National Council of Welfare, 1998). A generation ago, persons over age 65 were at greatest risk of being poor; however, increased government transfer payments and an increase in the number of elderly retiring with private pension plans have led to a

The "feminization of poverty" refers to the fact that two out of three impoverished adults in North America are women. Should we assume that poverty is primarily a women's issue? Why or why not?

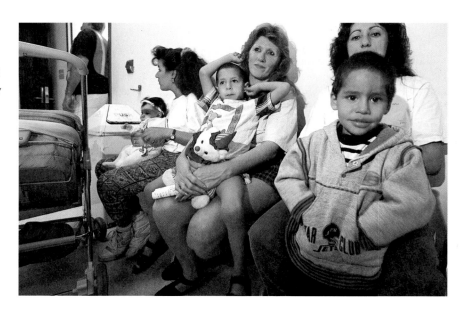

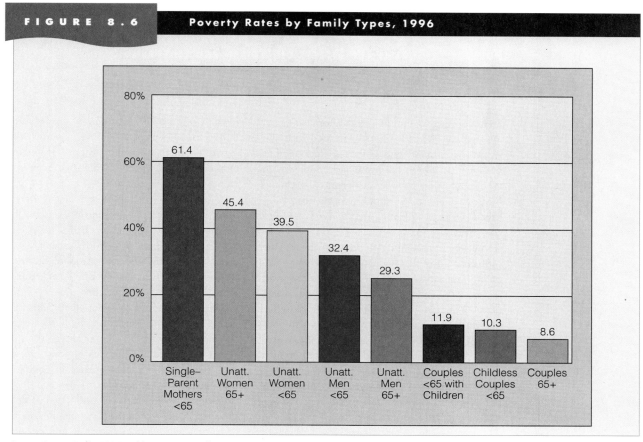

FIGURE 8.6 Poverty Rates by Family Types, 1996

Source: Poverty Profile 1994, Table 4, Poverty Profile 1996. Poverty Rates by Family Types, Health Canada. Ottawa: National Council of Welfare, Spring 1998. Reproduced by permission of the Minister of Public Works and Government Services, 1999.

decline in poverty among the elderly. Even so, older women are twice as likely as older men to be poor.

The age category most vulnerable to poverty today is the very young. While the overall poverty rate in 1996 was about 17.9 percent, the rate for children under the age 18 was 21.1 percent (Statistics Canada, 1997b; Canadian Council on Social Development, 1998). This means more than 1.5 million Canadian children are living in poverty (Ross, 1998). A large number of children hover just above the official poverty line. The precarious position of Aboriginal children is even more striking. Approximately 51 percent of Aboriginal children (both on and off reserves) are living in poverty (Shillington, 1991).

Children as a group are poorer now than they were at the beginning of the 1980s, and this is true whether they live in one- or two-parent families. The majority of poor children live in two-parent families in which one or both parents are employed. However, children in single-parent households headed by women are much likelier to be living in poverty. Despite the promise to alle-

viate child poverty by the year 2000 made by the House of Commons in 1989, the future for poor children does not look bright. These children are poor because their parents are poor, and one of the main reasons for poverty among adults is a lack of good jobs. Government cuts to unemployment insurance benefits and employment programs will affect not only those who need these services but also the children of these individuals.

GENDER About two-thirds of all adults living in poverty in Canada are women. As Figure 8.6 shows, in 1996, single-parent families headed by women had a 61 percent poverty rate compared with a rate of 12 percent for two-parent families. Furthermore, women are among the poorest of the poor. Poor single mothers with children under 18 are the worst off, living $9,604 below the poverty line in 1996. Sociologist Diana Pearce (1978) coined a term to describe this problem: the *feminization of poverty* refers to the trend in which **women are disproportionately represented among individuals living in poverty.** Women

BOX 8.3   SOCIOLOGY IN GLOBAL PERSPECTIVE

POVERTY IN BRAZIL: THE EFFECTS ON WOMEN AND CHILDREN

According to the United Nations, most of the roughly 100 million homeless people in the world are women and children, and another 600 million live in impoverished conditions in inadequate and unhealthy shelters. The United Nations Center for Human Settlement published a report indicating that of the 1.3 billion people living in poverty, 70 percent are women and girls. They referred to this as the global feminization of poverty, further indicating that women and girls are also the most rapidly growing group of impoverished. Some 50,000 people—mostly women and children—die daily because of poor shelter, polluted water, and bad sanitation. The report estimated that if housing could be brought up to a minimum standard, there would be 5 million fewer deaths and 2 million fewer disabilities per year. Women are relegated to homelessness or squatter-status in many parts of the world where they cannot legally own or inherit land, cannot obtain bank loans, receive much

lower wages than men, and often are abandoned to raise children on their own. Women are often also the prime targets of political upheavals, making up 70 to 80 percent of the world's 23 million refugees.

What is life like for these women? Persons in all nations have hopes and dreams for their children and grandchildren. Doralice Moreira de Souza is a 47-year-old woman whose hands are gnarled from years of cutting a daily quota of five tons of sugar cane in Conceicao de Macabu, Brazil. She has a dream for Alan, her 10-year-old grandson: "I would like him to study, so that when he grows up, he won't end up like a slave like me." However, Alan's life chances already are seriously limited because of economic conditions and labour exploitation in his country. Today, slavery flourishes in rural and other isolated areas of Brazil—on sugarcane plantations and ranches, in gold mines, and in the charcoal industries of the Amazon. The sugarcane fields

---

have a higher risk of being poor because they bear the major economic burden of raising children as single heads of households but earn only 70 cents for every dollar a male worker earns—a figure that has changed little over four decades. More women than men are unable to obtain regular, full-time, year-round employment, and the lack of adequate, affordable daycare exacerbates this problem (Schellenberg and Ross, 1997). As discussed in Box 8.3, the feminization of poverty is a global phenomenon.

While some women are victims of chronic poverty, others are among the "new poor" who have experienced "event-driven poverty" as a result of marital separation, divorce, or widowhood (Bane, 1986). Sociologist Lenore Weitzman (1985) has suggested that no-fault divorce laws have placed many women in financial jeopardy because supposedly "equal" settlements did not take into account women's lesser earning capabilities, especially if they had been out of the work-

force taking care of young children at home. A recent Statistics Canada report indicated that women's incomes (adjusted for family size) dropped by about 23 percent one year after they divorced or separated. Men, on the other hand, reported a 10 percent *gain* in income during the same time period (Statistics Canada, 1997c). Five years after the marriage breakup, women's incomes were still 5 percent *below* their earlier level. In contrast, men's incomes *increased* by an average of 15 percent five years after the breakup (Statistics Canada, 1997c).

Certain groups of women experience "multiple jeopardy," a term used to refer to the even greater risk of poverty faced by women who are immigrants, disabled, visible minorities, or Aboriginal (Gerber, 1990).

RACE/ETHNICITY   According to some stereotypes, most of the poor and virtually all welfare recipients are visible minorities. Such stereotypes are

CONTINUED

in which Doralice works are harvested by farm workers who toil from sunup to sundown and sleep in hammocks strung in cow stalls. Their employer, an alcohol distillery owner, does not pay wages for their work. Workers instead receive scrip, which they can redeem for food. Because landowners need to ensure that they will have a readily available supply of cheap labour, they bind labourers by encouraging them to run up unpayable debts at company-owned stores or canteens. As a Rio de Janeiro prosecutor looking into labour law violations stated, "In the 19th century, the chains were metal. Today, the chains are debt—the worker has to repay his transportation, his tools, his food" (Brooke, 1993b:3).

What is life like for the children living in poverty in Brazil? In the Brazilian slum areas both adults and children rummage through garbage dumps to find enough decaying food to keep themselves alive, and hordes of homeless children roam the streets, begging, stealing, shining shoes—anything to survive. These children are considered by middle- and upper-class Brazilians as part of the "dangerous classes" because they threaten the status quo. Since there are no social institutions in this country to provide for these children, one monstrous "solution" has been to kill them. Each year the Brazilian police and death squads murder about 2000 children. These murders are often preceded by ritual torture.

As these tragic examples demonstrate, poverty is the world's deadliest disease. How should First World nations respond to global world poverty?

Source: Based on Brooke, 1993b; Henslin and Nelson, 1996; and Osterman, 1995.

---

perpetuated because a disproportionate percentage of the impoverished in Canada are Aboriginal persons and recent immigrants. Aboriginal people in Canada are among the most severely disadvantaged persons. About one-half live below the poverty line, and some live in conditions of extreme poverty. The average income for Aboriginal persons is just over $17,000—34 percent below the national average income of $26,000 (Statistics Canada, 1998i). Also, the unemployment rate for Aboriginal persons in Canada ranges from 40 to 60 percent, while the national average is about 10 percent. In short, "to be Native in Canada is to face a strong likelihood of poverty" (Harman, 1995:259).

PERSONS WITH DISABILITIES Awareness that persons with disabilities are discriminated against in the job market has increased in recent years. As a result, they now constitute one of the recognized "target groups" in efforts to eliminate discrimination in the workplace. People with disabilities have more opportunities to work today than they had a decade ago. Today although over 50 percent of people with disabilities are in the labour force, many continue to be excluded from the workplace, not because of the disability itself, but because of environmental barriers in the workplace (Schellenberg and Ross, 1997). The effects of this systemic discrimination continue to be felt by disabled persons, as they are still, as a group, vulnerable to poverty (Fawcett, 1996). As discussed in Chapter 18 ("Health, Healthcare, and Disability"), adults with disabilities have significantly lower incomes than nondisabled Canadians. Recent estimates indicate that close to half of employed persons with disabilities had incomes below $10,000 (Ross, Shillington, and Lochhead, 1994). Once again, when gender and disability are combined, we find that women with disabilities are doubly disadvantaged (Fawcett, 1996).

BOX 8.4 CRITICAL THINKING

SOLVING THE POVERTY PROBLEM

In 1996, the International Year for the Eradication of Poverty, the National Council of Welfare made four recommendations to address the issue of poverty in Canada. The Council indicated that in order to achieve any dramatic reductions in poverty, it would be necessary for all levels of government to change their priorities and their attitudes toward poor people. The recommendations directed at "mounting and winning the war on poverty" were outlined as follows:

1. *Government should make a special effort to promote realistic portraits of poor people.* A faltering economy and family breakups have added greatly to the ranks of the poor in recent years. In this context, it is wrong to condone false and degrading stereotypes of poor people.
2. *Governments should look to tax expenditures rather than cuts in social programs as the prime means for reducing their deficits.* Governments should stop cutting social programs that provide help to the least fortunate members of our society. It is unfair to ask poor people to "pay their share" of the cost of deficit reduction.
3. *Governments should agree to work collectively to fight poverty.* It makes sense for governments to work together rather than passing on their own financial problems to other governments. In the early 1980s the federal government started putting pressure on provincial governments with a series of cuts to cost-shared programs. Many provinces offset the effects of these costs by cutting funds to local governments, school districts, and hospitals.
4. *Governments should add fighting poverty to their list of immediate economic priorities.* Given the resources available to govern-

Economic and Structural Sources of Poverty

Poverty has both economic and structural sources. The low wages paid for many jobs is the major cause: over half of all families living in poverty are headed by someone who is employed either full or part time (National Council of Welfare, 1998). In 1972, minimum-wage legislation meant that a worker who worked 40 hours a week, 52 weeks a year could earn a yearly income 20 percent over the poverty line. By today's standards, the same worker would have to earn over $10 per hour simply to reach the poverty line. Minimum wages across Canada range from just over $5 per hour to a high of approximately $7 per hour. In other words, a person with full-time employment in a minimum-wage job cannot keep a family of four above the official poverty line (Campaign 2000, 1998).

Structural problems contribute to both unemployment and underemployment. Automation in the industrial heartland of Quebec and Ontario has made the skills and training of thousands of workers obsolete. Many of these workers have become unemployable and poor. Corporations have been deinvesting in Canada, and millions of people have lost their jobs as a result. Economists refer to this displacement as the *deindustrialization of North America* (Bluestone and Harrison, 1982). Even as they have closed their Canadian factories and plants, many corporations have opened new facilities in other countries where "cheap labour" exists because people of necessity will work for lower wages. **Job deskilling—a reduction in the proficiency needed to perform a specific job that leads to a corresponding reduction in the wages for that job**—has resulted from the introduction of computers and other technology (Hodson and Parker, 1988). The shift from manufacturing to service occupations has resulted in the loss of higher-paying positions and their replacement with lower-paying and less secure positions that do not offer the wages, job stability, or advance-

BOX 8.4

CONTINUED

ments, there is no reason that fighting poverty should have to wait while governments grapple with reducing the deficit, lowering interest rates, or creating jobs. The reality is that poor people cannot wait five, ten, or twenty years for their concerns to be addressed. (National Council of Welfare, 1996:86)

The question of how to solve the problem of poverty has been debated for the past two decades. A lack of consensus exists regarding both the definition of the problem and the possible solutions for it. While the political debates rage on, many thousands of lives are being unalterably damaged. Sociologist Thomas O'Reilly-Fleming discusses one of these young lives:

When I interviewed a young homeless family, their daughter ... drew a stark

depiction of three figures crowded in a tiny black box. It was her depiction of life for the homeless in a motel ... Leaving the interview, to face a Christmas with no toys, no Christmas tree, and a macaroni dinner, she inquired innocently as she hugged me "Isn't there anyone who looks after little children in Canada?" (O'Reilly-Fleming 1993:178)

Do you think the federal and provincial governments are doing enough to allieviate poverty in Canada? What progress has been made since 1996 in "winning the war on poverty"? To what extent has the government followed through on the recommendations by the National Council of Welfare?

---

ment potential of the disappearing manufacturing jobs. Consequently, there are simply not enough good jobs available in Canada to enable families to lift themselves out of poverty. In addition, the lack of affordable high-quality daycare for women who need to earn an income means that many jobs are inaccessible, especially to women who are single parents. The problems of unemployment, underemployment, and poverty-level wages are even greater for visible minorities and young people (Ross, Shillington, and Lochhead, 1994).

SOCIAL STRATIFICATION IN THE FUTURE

Will social inequality in Canada increase in the twenty-first century? Many social scientists predict that existing trends point to an increase. First, the purchasing power of the dollar has stagnated or

declined since the early 1970s. As families started to lose ground financially, more family members (especially women) entered the labour force in an attempt to support themselves and their families (Ross, Shillington, and Lochhead, 1994). Economist Robert Reich (1993:145) has noted that the employed have been travelling on two escalators—one going up and the other going down—in recent years. The gap between the earnings of workers and the income of managers and top executives has widened (Feagin and Feagin, 1997).

Second, wealth continues to become more concentrated at the top of the Canadian class structure. As the rich have grown richer, more people have found themselves among the ranks of the poor. Structural sources of upward mobility are shrinking while the rate of downward mobility has increased. The main problem in redistributing wealth and income in Canada is that the middle and upper classes may have to accept less so that others can have more (Krahn, 1995b). This is a tough, if not impossible, sell in a society like Canada, in which the ability to acquire material goods is as highly valued as it is.

Are we sabotaging our future if we do not work constructively to eliminate poverty? It has been said that a chain is no stronger than its weakest link. If we apply this idea to the problem of poverty, it is to our advantage to see that those who cannot find work or do not have a job that provides a living wage receive adequate training and employment. Children of today, the adults of tomorrow, need education, health care, and safety as they grow up.

Reich (1993) emphasizes that the growth in single-parent lower-income families cannot continue to be used as an explanation for the widening gap between the rich and the poor. He argues instead that the persistence of economic inequality is related to profound global economic changes. In this chapter, we have focused primarily on social stratification in Canada; however, in Chapter 9 ("Global Stratification"), we examine the connections between wealth and poverty in the developed nations (such as Canada and the United States) and in the less developed nations of the world.

As mentioned at the beginning of this chapter, the House of Commons established a goal of eliminating poverty among children by the year 2000. Are we getting any closer to reaching these goals? Canada's response to poverty has been contradictory. One would expect that in working toward eliminating poverty action would be taken to address the structural causes of poverty—high unemployment and an inadequate set of child and family social policies. Instead, the federal government has cut federal social supports (such as subsidized daycare, unemployment benefits, and family allowance) (Campaign 2000, 1998), leaving families to bear the burden of poverty. Box 8.4 discusses a number of recommendations made by the National Council of Welfare to address the issue of poverty in Canada.

As Canadians, we take pride in our international reputation for fairness and compassion. The United Nations has ranked Canada as one of the best countries in the world to live. However, the United Nations has also been harshly critical of Canada over its treatment of the poor. Almost one-fifth of the children in this country continue to grow up poor, in circumstances that seriously jeopardize their chances of becoming happy and

productive citizens. As Marsden and Robertson state in their report *Children in Poverty: Toward a Better Future,*

> Children are the future of any society. There is no sounder investment in Canada's future than an investment in our children. It is disturbing ... that the necessity of solving child poverty must be justified in monetary or "bottom line" terms. Nevertheless, if that is required, the figures speak for themselves—but poor children cannot." (Marsden and Robertson, 1991:6)

CHAPTER REVIEW

What is stratification, and how does it affect our daily life?
Stratification is the hierarchical arrangement of large social groups based on their control over basic resources. People are treated differently based on where they are positioned within the social hierarchies of class, race, gender, and age.

What are the major systems of stratification?
Stratification systems include caste and class. The caste system is a closed system in which people's status is determined at birth and is based on their parents' position in society. The class system, which exists in Canada, is a type of stratification based on ownership of resources and on the type of work people do. Class systems are characterized by unequal distribution of resources and by movement up and down the class structure through social mobility.

How did classical sociologists such as Karl Marx and Max Weber view social class?
Karl Marx and Max Weber acknowledged social class as a key determinant of social inequality and social change. For Marx, people's relationship to the means of production determines their class position. Weber developed a multidimensional concept of stratification that focuses on the interplay of wealth, prestige, and power.

What is the functionalist view of social inequality?
According to the Davis–Moore thesis, stratification exists in all societies, and some inequality is not only inevitable but also necessary for the ongoing functioning of society. The positions that are most impor-

tant within society and that require the most talent and training must be highly rewarded.

What is the conflict view of social inequality?

Conflict perspectives on inequality are based on the assumption that social stratification is created and maintained by one group in order to enhance and protect its own economic interests. Conflict theorists measure inequality according to people's relationships with others in the production process.

What are some of the consequences of inequality in Canada?

The stratification of society into different social groups results in wide discrepancies in income and wealth and in variable access to available goods and services. People with high incomes or wealth have a greater opportunity to control their own lives. People with lower incomes have fewer life chances and must spend their limited resources to acquire basic necessities.

How do sociologists define poverty?

Sociologists distinguish between absolute poverty and relative poverty. Absolute poverty exists when people do not have the means to secure the basic necessities of life. Relative poverty exists when people may be able to afford basic necessities but still are unable to maintain an average standard of living.

Who are the poor in Canada?

Age, gender, race/ethnicity, and disability tend to be factors in poverty. Children have a greater risk of being poor than do the elderly, while women have a higher rate of poverty than do men. Although whites account for approximately two-thirds of those below the poverty line, Aboriginal peoples and visible minorities account for a share of the impoverished in Canada that is disproportionate to their numbers. As the gap between rich and poor and between employed and unemployed widens, social inequality clearly will increase in the future if we do nothing.

Key Terms

absolute poverty 260
alienation 242
apartheid 242
capitalist class 243
caste system 242
class conflict 244
class system 243
class 193
feminization of poverty 261
intergenerational mobility 241

intragenerational mobility 241
job deskilling 264
life chances 240
meritocracy 252
pink-collar occupations 250
power 246
prestige 246
relative poverty 260
social mobility 241
social stratification 240
socioeconomic status (SES) 248
wealth 246

Internet Exercises

1. Visit the homepage for the Canadian Council on Social Development at:

   http:www.ccsd.ca

   From here go to Free Statistics and see what information you can find on the life chances of children in lower-income and higher-income families.

2. There is talk about a widening gap between rich and poor in this country and in the world. Think about the vast amount of information you have been able to gather using the Internet thus far. Some argue that the biggest gap of the twenty-first century will be between the information "haves" and "have nots." What do you think? What aspects of the way in which information is presented on the Internet would lead you to believe that access to the World Wide Web is liberating and empowering? Are there any reasons to believe that access to all of the information on the World Wide Web does little, if anything, to enlighten and educate individuals?

   The most spectacular example of the gap between the information "haves" and "have nots" is Bill Gates, the founder of Microsoft. To see how wealthy Gates is today, go to:

   http://webho.com/WealthClock

   Remember, this clock is in American dollars, so you must multiply by 1.4 to get the Canadian value.

Net Links

The Canadian Council on Social Development is one of the leading organizations speaking for Canada's poor; see:

http://www.ccsd.ca

Campaign 2000 is an initiative to end child poverty in Canada; see:

http://www.web.net/~rpopham/campaign2000/

To see Forbes' listing of the world's billionaires, including home country, net worth, source of income, and brief biographies, go to:

http://www.forbes.com/tool/toolbox/billnew/1998.asp

For a discussion on how families—especially those with low incomes—have fared in the job market in recent years, review the executive summary of *Left Poor by the Market: A Look at Family Poverty and Earnings* by Grant Schellenberg and David P. Ross:

http://www.ccsd.ca/es_left.htm

Does family income affect the healthy development of young children? David P. Ross and Paul Roberts of the Canadian Council on Social Development address this question in their research article, which is available at:

http://www.ccsd.ca/p211fi.htm

Questions for Critical Thinking

1. Based on the functionalist model of class structure, what is the class location of each of your ten closest friends or acquaintances? What is their location in relation to yours? to one another? What does their location tell you about friendship and social class?
2. Should employment be based on merit, need, or affirmative action policies?
3. What might happen in Canada in the future if the gap between rich and poor continues to widen?

Suggested Readings

These texts provide more in-depth information about social stratification:

Wallace Clement. *The Canadian Corporate Elite: An Analysis of Economic Power.* Toronto: McClelland & Stewart, 1975.

Dennis Forcese. *The Canadian Class Structure.* Toronto: McGraw-Hill Ryerson, 1986.

Charles E. Hurst. Social Inequality: Forms, Causes, and Consequences. Boston: Allyn & Bacon, 1992.

John Porter. *The Vertical Mosaic: An Analysis of Social Class and Power in Canada.* Toronto: University of Toronto Press, 1965.

A wide diversity of viewpoints on the intertwining of race, class, and gender in social stratification are found in this reader:

James E. Curtis, Edward Grabb, and Neil Guppy (eds). *Social Inequality in Canada: Patterns, Problems, Policies* (2nd ed.). Scarborough, Ont.: Prentice-Hall, 1993.

For more information on poverty in Canada, see:

David P. Ross, Richard Shillington, and Clarence Lochhead. *The Canadian Fact Book on Poverty.* Ottawa: Canadian Council on Social Development, 1994.

CHAPTER 9

Wealth and Poverty in Global Perspective
Inequality and Individuals

Problems in Studying Global Inequality
The "Three Worlds" Approach
The Levels of Development Approach

Classification of Economies by Income
Low-Income Economies
Middle-Income Economies
High-Income Economies

The Impact of Debt and Foreign Aid
Debt and Global Stratification
Foreign Aid and Global Stratification

Measuring Global Wealth and Poverty
Absolute, Relative, and Subjective Poverty
The Gini Coefficient and Global Quality of Life
Issues

Global Poverty and Human Development Issues
Life Expectancy
Health
Education and Literacy

Theories of Global Inequality
Development and Modernization Theories
Dependency Theory
World Systems Theory
The New International Division of Labour Theory

Global Inequality in the Future

The following is an excerpt from a letter a mother in the Philippines wrote to her daughters explaining her commitment to political activism:

"Today, both of you are in University. In less than five years, you will join the ranks of the 40–50 percent unemployed and underemployed Filipinos. If you are lucky and do find jobs, you will painfully experience the discrepancy between the daily cost of living at 354 pesos and the minimum wage pegged by the government at 150 pesos. I won't be surprised if you find yourselves in the 70 percent of the population considered below the poverty line and the 40 percent below the food threshold. Even now, that is what we see happening.

"I fear that very soon, even the environment will no longer be a dependable support system. What with biologically dead rivers, contaminated drinking water, and depleted marine resources because of the mine tailings spewed by mining companies, the likes of Marcopper and its Canadian partner, Placer Dome, what with dry rice fields that have to be abandoned due to the lack of water for irrigation brought about by open pit mining operations of giant establishments ... What with 2/3 of the whole Cordillera region apportioned to Australian, American and Canadian mining companies ...

"This government has launched a grandiose plan it calls Philippines 2000. President Fidel Ramos ... wants to take the Philippines down the road to NIChood (Newly Industrialized Country) by the year 2000. That is why our agricultural lands which 75 percent of our population was tilling have now been converted into industrial enclaves, called Regional Industrial Centers. Is it any wonder, then, that thousands of peasants have been displaced?

"... The road is long that leads to progress—too long in fact, that hope could easily be snuffed out. But this one thing I can say, Mitzi May and Lily Joyce: I HAVE NOT LOST HOPE. This is why I have opted to leave you for a while—to join the many hopeful Filipinos who have put their lives on the line. And I will continue to put my life on the line for as long as this insensitive government rides roughshod on our people's God-given rights."

(Sharon Ruiz-Duremdes, Anglican Church of Canada)

Y ou might be surprised to learn that of all the narratives that we used to open the twenty chapters in this book, this was the most difficult to find. The world's poorest people have no voice. Even researchers who study global stratification rarely let them tell their own stories. Books are

GLOBAL STRATIFICATION

full of statistics that tell the stories of nations that cannot feed their citizens and of researchers' compassionate descriptions of the lives of people living at the margins of survival. However, the poor themselves remain faceless. If not for the haunting images of famine or civil war that we see on television news programs or the occasional story about problems in low-income countries on the radio or in the newspaper, most of us would know nothing about the over one billion people who live out their lives in abject poverty. They are even more invisible to those managing the global corporations and the international organizations whose decisions have life and death consequences for those at the bottom of the global stratification system.

Even the quotation we did select is not really representative of the world's poor. The mother writing to her children is educated, articulate, and a member of an activist political organization. While her country, the Philippines, is poor, it is far wealthier than many other nations. However, her letter does articulate many of the problems of people in developing countries including unemployment, foreign control of resources, environmental degradation, economic restructuring, and political discontent.

Poverty and inequality know no political boundaries or international borders. In this chapter we examine global stratification and inequality, and discuss the perspectives that have been developed to explain this problem. It is often difficult to connect the lives of people living in poverty in distant countries to our own lives in one of the world's wealthiest countries. When television shows us thousands of people starving in Somalia or babies being treated for dehydration at aid stations in Rwanda, it is sometimes hard to realize that the people we see are individual human beings just like you and your friends. The global stratification system determines who will live long, prosperous lives like those of most Canadians and who will live short, mis-

erable lives, eking out a marginal existence in subsistence agriculture and subject to the vagaries of rain, floods, and political instability.

Why do these inequities persist? In this chapter you will learn about some of the reasons the life prospects of billions of people remain so dismal. When you read the explanations of global stratification, you should remember that these are not just dry academic theories. Rather, these are the ideas shaping the way governments and international organizations such as the United Nations deal with this very complex and difficult problem. As you will see, decisions based on the wrong theories can be disastrous for the poor.

Before reading on, test your knowledge of global wealth and poverty by taking the quiz in Box 9.1.

QUESTIONS AND ISSUES

CHAPTER FOCUS QUESTION: *What is global stratification, and how does it contribute to economic inequality?*

How are global poverty and human development related?

What is modernization theory, and what are its stages?

How do conflict theorists explain patterns of global stratification?

What is world systems theory?

How is the new system of global trade affecting people in poor countries?

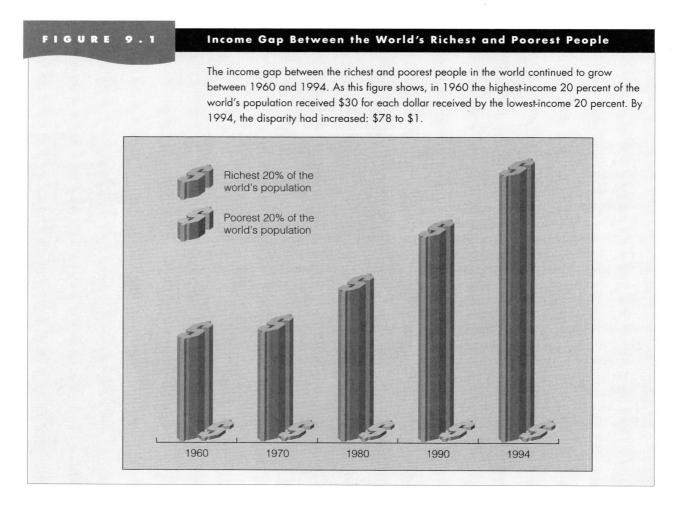

FIGURE 9.1   **Income Gap Between the World's Richest and Poorest People**

The income gap between the richest and poorest people in the world continued to grow between 1960 and 1994. As this figure shows, in 1960 the highest-income 20 percent of the world's population received $30 for each dollar received by the lowest-income 20 percent. By 1994, the disparity had increased: $78 to $1.

Richest 20% of the world's population

Poorest 20% of the world's population

1960   1970   1980   1990   1994

WEALTH AND POVERTY IN GLOBAL PERSPECTIVE

What do we mean by global stratification? *Global stratification* refers to the unequal distribution of wealth, power, and prestige on a global basis, resulting in people having vastly different lifestyles and life chances both within and among the nations of the world. Just as Canada is divided into classes, the world is divided into unequal segments characterized by extreme differences in wealth and poverty. For example, the income gap between the richest and the poorest 20 percent of the world population continues to widen (see Figure 9.1). When we compare social and economic inequality *within* other nations, we find gaps that are more pronounced than they are in Canada. *Developed (high-income) nations* are countries characterized by highly industrialized economies; technologically advanced industrial, administrative, and service occupations; and a relatively high level of national and per capita (per person) income. In contrast, *developing (low-income) nations* are countries that are undergoing the transformation from an agrarian to an industrial economy and have lower levels of income. Within some nations the poorest one-fifth of the population has an income that is only a slight fraction of the overall per capita income for that country. For example, in Brazil, Guatemala, and Honduras, less than 3 percent of total national income accrues to the poorest one-fifth of the population (World Bank, 1996).

Between 1960 and 1994, the gap in global income differences between rich and poor countries continued to widen. In 1960, the wealthiest 20 percent of the world's population had more than 30 times the income of the poorest 20 percent. By 1994, the wealthiest 20 percent of the world's population had 78 times the income of the poorest 20 percent (United Nations Development Programme, 1997).

BOX 9.1 SOCIOLOGY AND EVERYDAY LIFE

HOW MUCH DO YOU KNOW ABOUT GLOBAL WEALTH AND POVERTY?

TRUE	FALSE	
T	F	1. Because of foreign aid and the globalization of trade, the gap between the incomes of people in the poorest countries and the richest countries has narrowed over the past several decades.
T	F	2. Although the percentage of the world's people living in absolute poverty has declined over the past decade, the total number of people living in poverty has increased.
T	F	3. The richest fifth of the world's population receives about 50 percent of the total world income.
T	F	4. The political role of governments in policing the activities of transnational corporations has expanded as companies' operations have become more globalized.
T	F	5. Most analysts agree that the World Bank was created to serve the poor of the world and their borrowing governments.
T	F	6. In low-income countries, the problem of poverty is unequally shared between men and women.
T	F	7. Income and standard of living have increased significantly for most Russians as the transition from a centrally planned economy to a market orientation has taken place in recent years.
T	F	8. Poverty levels have declined somewhat in East Asia, the Middle East, and North Africa in recent years.
T	F	9. The majority of people with incomes below the poverty line live in the rural areas of the world.
T	F	10. Poor people in low-income countries meet most of their energy needs by burning wood, dung, and agricultural wastes, which increases health hazards and environmental degradation.

Answers on page 274.

However, when examining the income gap, it is important to note that economic inequality is not the only dimension of global stratification. For example, in an earlier study on world poverty, Swedish economist Gunnar Myrdal (1970:56) distinguished between social and economic inequality:

> Social inequality is clearly related to status and can perhaps best be defined as an extreme lack of social mobility and a severely hampered possibility of competing freely … Economic inequality … is related to differences in wealth and income … But there is a close relation between the two, since *social inequality stands as a main cause of economic inequality, while, at the same time, economic inequality supports social inequality.*

Social inequality, which may result from factors such as discrimination based on race, ethnicity, gender, or religion, exacerbates problems of eco-nomic inequality. According to Myrdal, social inequality is a main cause of the poverty of a nation. Therefore, a society must have greater social equality among its citizens as a precondition for the entire country getting out of poverty.

Many people have sought to address the issue of world poverty and to determine ways in which resources can be used to meet the urgent challenge of poverty. However, not much progress has been made on this front (Lummis, 1992) despite a great deal of talk and billions of dollars in "foreign aid" flowing from high-income to low-income nations. The notion of "development" has become the primary means used in attempts to reduce social and economic inequalities and to alleviate the worst effects of poverty in the less industrialized nations of the world. Often, the nations that have been unable to reduce or eliminate poverty are chastised for not establishing the necessary social and economic reforms to make

BOX 9.1

ANSWERS TO THE SOCIOLOGY QUIZ ON GLOBAL WEALTH AND POVERTY

1. **False.** Since 1960, the gap between the incomes of the richest 20 percent of the world's population and the poorest 20 percent has been steadily growing. The ratio of the income of the top 20 percent of the population to that of the poorest 20 percent rose from 30 to 1 in 1960 to 78 to 1 in 1994 (United Nations Development Programme, 1997).

2. **True.** Data from the World Bank indicate that the percentage of the world's people living in absolute poverty has declined since the mid-1980s, particularly in Asia. However, other regions have not reduced the incidence of poverty to the same degree, and the total number of people living in poverty has risen to approximately 1.4 billion in the mid-1990s (World Bank, 1996).

3. **False.** According to the United Nations Development Programme (1996), the richest fifth receive more than 80 percent of total world income.

4. **False.** As companies have globalized their operations, governmental restrictions have become less effective in controlling their activities. Transnational corporations have very little difficulty sidestepping governmental restrictions based on old assumptions about national economies and foreign policy. For example, Honda is able to circumvent import restrictions that the governments of Taiwan, South Korea, and Israel have placed on its vehicles by shipping vehicles made in Ohio to those locations (Korten, 1996).

5. **False.** Some analysts point out the linkages between the World Bank and the transnational corporate sector on both the borrowing and lending ends of its operation. Although the bank is supposedly owned by its members' governments and lends money only to governments, many of its projects involve vast financial dealings with transnational construction companies, consulting firms, and procurement contractors (see Korten, 1996).

6. **True.** In almost all low-income countries (as well as middle- and high-income countries), poverty is a more chronic problem for women due to sexual discrimination, resulting in a lack of educational and employment opportunities (Hauchler and Kennedy, 1994).

7. **False.** Not all Russians have shared equally in the transition to the market economy (see Box 9.3 on pages 282 and 283, "Sociology in Global Perspective").

8. **True.** These have been the primary regions in which poverty has decreased somewhat and infant mortality rates have fallen. Factors such as economic growth, oil production, foreign investment, and overall development have been credited with the decrease in poverty in East Asia, the Middle East, and North Africa (United Nations DPCSD, 1997).

9. **True.** The majority of people with incomes below the poverty line live in the rural areas of the world; however, the number of poor people residing in urban areas is growing rapidly (United Nations DPCSD, 1997).

10. **True.** Poor people in low-income countries meet most of their energy needs by burning wood, dung, and agricultural wastes. Although these fuels are inefficient and harmful to health, many low-income people cannot afford appliances, connection charges, and so forth. In some areas, electric hookups are not available (United Nations DPCSD, 1997).

change possible. However, as other social analysts have suggested,

> The *problem* of inequality lies not in poverty, but in excess. "The problem of the world's poor," defined more accurately, turns out to be "the problem of the world's rich." This means that the solution to the problem is not a massive change in the culture of poverty so as to place it on the path of development, but a massive change in the culture of superfluity in order to place it on the path of counterdevelopment. It does not call for a new value system forcing the world's majority to feel shame at their traditionally moderate consumption habits, but for a new value system forcing the world's rich to see the shame and vulgarity of their overconsumption habits, and the double vulgarity of standing on other people's shoulders to achieve those consumption habits. (Lummis, 1992:50)

Vast inequalities in income and lifestyle are shown in this photo of slums and nearby upper-class housing in Rio de Janeiro, Brazil. Do similar patterns of economic inequality exist in other nations?

As this statement suggests, the increasing interdependency of all the world's nations was largely overlooked or ignored until increasing emphasis was placed on the global marketplace and the global economy. The linkage between consumption and global poverty is explored in more detail in Box 9.2.

Inequality and Individuals

Nothing illustrates the disparity between rich and poor better than the difference between the wealth amassed by a few individuals and the poverty of the poorest nations. The 225 richest people in the world have a net worth of more than $1.3 trillion. This is equal to the annual incomes of the poorest 2.5 billion people. Only 4 percent of this amount ($53 billion) is required each year to achieve reproductive health care for all women, and basic education, basic medical care, and adequate food, water, and sanitation for all. The wealth of the three richest people (Microsoft owner Bill Gates, investor Warren Buffett, and the oil-rich Sultan of Brunei) is greater than the gross domestic product of the 48 least developed countries (United Nations Development Programme, 1998).

PROBLEMS IN STUDYING GLOBAL INEQUALITY

One of the primary problems encountered by social scientists studying global stratification and social and economic inequality is what terminology should be used to refer to the distribution of resources in various nations. During the past twenty-five years, major changes have occurred in the way that inequality is addressed by organizations such as the United Nations. Most definitions of *inequality* are based on comparisons of levels of income or economic development, whereby countries are identified in terms of the "three worlds" or upon their levels of economic development.

The "Three Worlds" Approach

After World War II, the terms "First World," "Second World," and "Third World" were introduced by social analysts to distinguish among nations on the basis of their levels of economic development and the standard of living of citizens. The term was also related to the competing sides in the Cold War that followed World War II. First World countries included the advanced industrial countries such as Britain, France, Germany, Japan, and Canada that were aligned with the United States. Second World countries were the Communist industrial countries such as Poland, Czechoslovakia, and China that were aligned with the Soviet Union. According to social analysts, although the quality of life in Second World nations was not comparable to that of life in the First World, it was far greater than that of people living in the Third World—the poorest countries, with little or no industrialization and the lowest standards of living, shortest life expectancies, and highest rates of mortality. The majority of these countries were either colonies or economic dependencies, or had emerged from colonial status. The language of the "three worlds" was closely linked to terminology based on levels of development.

The Levels of Development Approach

Among the most controversial terminology used for describing world poverty and global stratifica-

BOX 9.2 CRITICAL ISSUES IN GLOBAL STRATIFICATION

CONSUMPTION AND GLOBAL POVERTY

The United Nations *Human Development Report* has played a major role in drawing attention to the need to eradicate poverty. The 1998 edition of the report focused on the way in which some aspects of consumption have affected global stratification. Excessive consumption in developed countries threatens the environment, depletes natural resources, and wastes money that might otherwise provide for the needs of the desperately poor in developing countries.

Global consumption is concentrated among the wealthy. The wealthiest 20 percent of the world's people account for 86 percent of private consumption, while the poorest 20 percent account for only 1.3 percent (see Figure 9.2). While some argue that money now used to buy luxuries might be better spent on the world's poor, others would claim that conspicuous consumption does buy happiness for those who can afford it. Though very limited, the evidence does not support the view that consumption beyond basic needs necessarily makes people happier. According to the *Human Development Report*, the percentage of Americans who describe themselves as

FIGURE 9.2 Share of World Consumption[1]

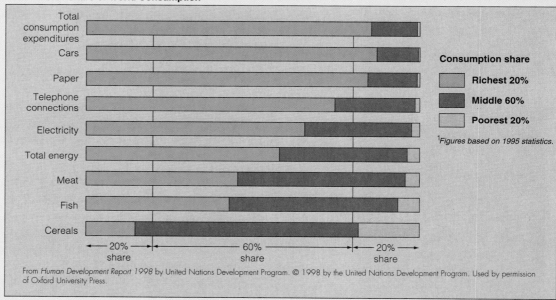

From *Human Development Report 1998* by United Nations Development Program. © 1998 by the United Nations Development Program. Used by permission of Oxford University Press.

tion has been the language of development. Terminology based on levels of development includes concepts such as developed nations, developing nations, less developed nations, and underdevelopment. Let's look first at the contemporary origins of the idea of "underdevelopment" and "underdeveloped nations."

Following World War II, the concepts of *underdevelopment* and *underdeveloped nations* emerged out of the Marshall Plan (named after U.S.

Secretary of State George C. Marshall), which provided massive sums of money in direct aid and loans to rebuild the European economic base destroyed during World War II. Given the Marshall Plan's success in rebuilding much of Europe, U.S. political leaders decided that Southern Hemisphere nations that had recently been released from European colonialism could also benefit from a massive financial infusion and rapid economic development. Leaders of the

BOX 9.2

"happy" peaked in 1957 even though consumption has more than doubled since that time. Unfortunately, as we spend more, we find more things to spend on. If we are able to keep up with the Joneses next door, we shift our horizons to the rich and famous whose lifestyles we know about from newspapers and television. When American consumers were asked in 1986 how much they would need to earn to "fulfil all their dreams" the answer was $50,000. By 1994 this had increased to $102,000 (United Nations Development Programme, 1998). Theoretically at least, our wants are limitless.

But surely, some argue, the world's needs are so great that channelling some of the money people in rich nations now spend on excessive consumption would not make a difference in the lives of the world's poor. Surprisingly, the amount of money required to meet some basic human needs is not that great. *The Hindu*, an Indian newspaper, has put these needs in perspective:

> Consumers in Europe and the U.S. spend $17 billion every year on pet foods. Yet, the world cannot find the additional $13 billion that is needed every year to provide basic health services to all people in developing countries. Consumers in Europe and the U.S.

annually spend $12 billion on perfumes. This is the additional amount needed to meet the basic reproductive health needs of the women in developing countries. Consumers in Europe spend $11 billion every year buying ice cream, which is more than the extra $9 billion required to provide universal access to drinking water and sanitation in the developing countries. (*The Hindu*, 1998:25)

Excessive consumption hurts the poor in another way. Rising consumption is harmful to the environment, and the poor are more vulnerable to environmental damage than the wealthy. Environmental degradation in high-income countries will hurt some people, particularly those whose incomes depend on agriculture. But in these countries there are many alternative sources of food and money to help restore the environment. However, environmental degradation in countries where people depend on subsistence agriculture can mean malnutrition and starvation for huge numbers of people.

As we consume more, there is less for people in poor countries. Do you think we should continue to increase our consumption at their expense, or should we accept the challenge of setting new directions for consumption in the twenty-first century?

Source: United Nations Development Programme, 1998; The Hinou, 1998.

developed nations argued that urgent problems such as poverty, disease, and famine could be reduced through the transfer of finance, technology, and experience from the developed nations to less developed countries. From this viewpoint, economic development is the primary way to solve the poverty problem: Hadn't economic growth brought the developed nations to their own high standard of living? Moreover, "self-sustained development" in a nation would require

that people in the less developed nations accept the beliefs and values of people in the developed nations, so the development movement had an explicitly political component.

Ideas regarding *underdevelopment* were popularized by President Harry S. Truman in his 1949 inaugural address. According to Truman, the nations in the Southern Hemisphere were "underdeveloped areas" because of their low *gross national product* (GNP)—a term that refers to all

In 1997, people around the world were saddened by the death of Mother Teresa, who had dedicated her life to ministering to the poor and unfortunate in low-income nations, especially India. According to Mother Teresa, people who are not poor have much that they could learn from the poor.

the goods and services produced in a country in a given year, plus the income earned outside the country by individuals or corporations. If nations could increase their GNP, then social and economic inequality among the citizens within the country could also be reduced. Accordingly, Truman believed that it was necessary to assist the people of economically underdeveloped areas to raise their *standard of living*, by which he meant material well-being that can be measured by the quality of goods and services that may be purchased by the per capita national income (Latouche, 1992). Thus, an increase in the standard of living meant that a nation was moving toward economic development, which typically included the increased exploitation of natural resources by industrial development. According to social scientist Serge Latouche (1992:250–251), measuring social and economic conditions on the basis of standard of living ultimately denigrates the culture and way of life in some societies:

> While the hope of a satisfactory life is a very human concern, the obsession with this sort of "standard of living" is very recent. Interest in salary levels on the part of wage earners and as a general social preoccupation dates from the industrial era … In fact, looking at the world in terms of "standard of living" is like looking through dark glasses; they make the rich variety of colours disappear, turning all differences into shades of the same colour.

What has happened to the issue of development since the post-World War II era? After several decades of economic development fostered by organizations such as the United Nations and the World Bank, it became apparent by the 1970s that improving a country's GNP did not tend to reduce the poverty of the poorest people in that country. In fact, global poverty and inequality were increasing, and the initial optimism of a speedy end to underdevelopment faded. Although many developing countries had achieved economic growth, it was not shared by everyone in the nation. For example, the poorest 40 percent of the Brazilian population receives less than 7 percent of the total national income, whereas the richest 20 percent of the population receives more than 65 percent (Elliott, 1994).

Why did inequality increase even with greater economic development? Many attribute this to the actions of the industrialized countries. Later in this chapter we will consider the impact of foreign aid programs and policies to control debt on the economies of developing nations. Other analysts in the developed nations began to link growing social and economic inequality on a global basis to relatively high rates of population growth taking place in the underdeveloped nations. Organizations such as the United Nations and the World Health Organization stepped up their efforts to provide family planning services to the populations so that they could control their own fertility.

CLASSIFICATION OF ECONOMIES BY INCOME

An alternative way of describing the global stratification system is simply to measure a country's per capita income. The World Bank classifies nations into three economic categories: *low-income economies* (a GNP per capita of $1100 or less in 1994), *middle-income economies* (a GNP per capita of more than $1100 but less than $13,500 in 1994), and *high-income economies* (a GNP per capita of $13,500 or more in 1994).

Based on the assumption that economic development is the primary way to reduce poverty in low-income nations, the United Nations has funded projects such as this paper company in Nepal.

Low-Income Economies

About half of the world's population lives in the fifty-one low-income economies, where most people engage in agricultural pursuits, reside in nonurban areas, and are impoverished (World Bank, 1996). As shown on Map 9.1, low-income economies are found primarily in countries in Asia and Africa. Included are such nations as Rwanda, Mozambique, Ethiopia, Nigeria, Cambodia, Vietnam, Afghanistan, and Bangladesh. Countries such as Armenia and Bosnia-Herzegovina are among the low-income economies in Eastern Europe. Latin American nations with low-income economies include Honduras and Nicaragua.

Among those most affected by poverty in low-income economies are women and children. Mayra Buvinić, chief of the women in development program unit at the Inter-American Development Bank, describes the plight of one Nigerian woman as an example:

> On the outskirts of Ibadan, Nigeria, Ade cultivates a small, sparsely planted plot with a baby on her back and other visibly undernourished children nearby. Her efforts to grow an improved soybean variety, which could have improved her children's diet, failed because she lacked the extra time to tend the new crop, did not have a spouse who would help her, and could not afford hired labor. (Buvinić, 1997:38)

According to Buvinić, Ade's life is typical of many women worldwide who face obstacles to increasing their economic power because they do not have the time to invest in the additional work that could bring in more income.

Additionally, many poor women worldwide do not have access to commercial credit and have been trained only in traditionally female skills that produce low wages. All these factors have contributed to the *global feminization of poverty,* whereby women around the world tend to be more impoverished than men (Durning, 1993). Despite the fact that women have made some gains in terms of well-being, the income gap between men and women continues to grow wider in the low-income, developing nations.

Middle-Income Economies

About one-third of the world's population resides in the fifty-seven nations with middle-income economies (a GNP per capita of more than $1100 but less than $13,500 in 1994). The World Bank divides middle-income economies into lower middle-income ($1100 to $4300) and upper middle-income ($4300 to $13,500). Countries classified as lower middle-income include the Latin American nations of Bolivia, Colombia, Guatemala, El Salvador, and Panama. However, even though these countries are referred to as "middle-income," more than half of the people residing in countries such as Bolivia and Guatemala live in poverty, defined as below $90 per month in 1994 dollars (World Bank, 1996).

Other lower middle-income economies include the former Soviet Union, Poland, and Romania. These areas had centrally planned (i.e., socialist)

MAP 9.1 High-, Middle-, and Low-Income Economies in Global Perspective

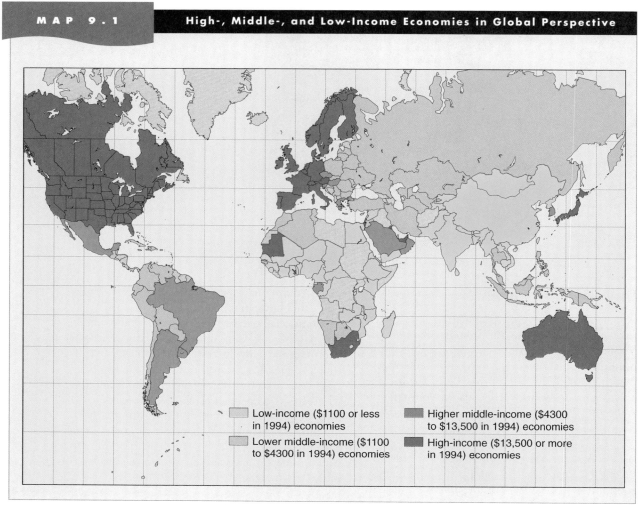

Low-income ($1100 or less in 1994) economies

Lower middle-income ($1100 to $4300 in 1994) economies

Higher middle-income ($4300 to $13,500 in 1994) economies

High-income ($13,500 or more in 1994) economies

Source: World Bank, *World Development Report 1996: From Plan to Market.* New York: Oxford University Press for the World Bank, 1996. Reprinted by permission.

economies until dramatic political and economic changes occurred in the late 1980s and early 1990s. Since then, these nations have been going through a transition to a market economy. Some nations have been more successful than others in implementing key elements of change and bringing about a higher standard of living for their citizens. Among other factors, high rates of inflation, the growing gap between the rich and the poor, low life-expectancy rates, and homeless children have been visible signs of problems in the transition toward a free-market economy in countries such as Russia (see Box 9.3).

Compared with lower middle-income economies, nations having upper middle-income economies typically have a somewhat higher standard of living and export diverse goods and services, ranging from manufactured goods to raw materials and fuels. Nations with upper middle-income economies include Brazil, South Africa, Chile, Hungary, and Mexico. Although these nations are referred to as middle-income economies, they have extremely high levels of indebtedness, leaving them with few resources for fighting poverty or developing their economies.

High-Income Economies

High-income economies are found in twenty-five nations, including Canada, the United States, Japan, Australia, Portugal, Ireland, Israel, Italy, Norway, and Germany. Nations with high-income economies continue to dominate the world economy, despite the fact that shifts in the global marketplace have affected some workers who have found themselves without work due to *capital*

In developing nations such as Turkey, many families support themselves by creating hand-made products such as rugs. The loom in this living room is a common sight throughout Turkey.

flight—the movement of jobs and economic resources from one nation to another—and *deindustrialization*—closing plants and factories because of their obsolescence or the fact that workers in other nations are being hired to do the work more cheaply (see Chapter 13, "The Economy and Work").

The only significant group of middle- and lower-income economies to close the gap with the high-income, industrialized economies over the past few decades have been the nations of East Asia. South Korea has recently been reclassified from a middle-income to a high-income economy. China has experienced a 270 percent increase in per capita income over the past seventeen years. But some analysts wonder if the East Asian "miracle" is over (Crossette, 1997). Differences in the rate of growth between G-7 countries (Canada, United States, Britain, France, Germany, Italy, and Japan) and the nations in East Asia, the Pacific, and South Asia are shown in Figure 9.3.

Despite its recent economic growth, the East Asian region remains home to approximately 350 million poor people.

THE IMPACT OF DEBT AND FOREIGN AID

Debt and Global Stratification

The gap between rich and poor countries has grown over the past forty years for many reasons. One is the problem of debt, which has made it virtually impossible for some countries to move out of poverty. Private banks, governments, and international organizations have lent more money to poor countries than these countries can afford to pay back, especially when cyclical reductions in commodity prices have dramatically reduced their incomes. Much of the borrowed money was spent on military hardware and other nonproductive investments, so little went to building the productive capacity that would have allowed the poor countries to develop. As a result of the debt crisis, many countries were forced by the International Monetary Fund and the World Bank to restructure their economies by cutting back on social spending, devaluing their currencies, and reducing the funds spent on economic development. In many respects these governments have lost whatever power they once had to control their own economic destinies because they must follow the dictates of the lenders. This happened to most Latin American economies during the 1980s and to many East Asian and Eastern European economies during the late 1990s.

In many countries, the consequences of this externally imposed structural adjustment have been disastrous. Debt repayment takes money that could otherwise be used to provide social services and health care and to expand the country's economic base. In addition, debt repayment and economic restructuring have caused massive unemployment, reduced incomes, and soaring prices that have led to drastically reduced living standards, declines in investment, and political instability. This has represented a major setback in the progress of development. The problem has been summarized by Michel Chossudovsky:

BOX 9.3 SOCIOLOGY IN GLOBAL PERSPECTIVE

WEALTH AND POVERTY IN RUSSIA

All the most famous people in the world breed horses. Here in Russia, we have lots of rich people. They will start breeding horses at some point, especially when they get tired of gambling in Moscow casinos. Then they will come to me. (quoted in LeVine, 1997:A4)

The speaker is Daud Naloyev, a horse breeder who is trying to lure newly wealthy Russians to come to Club Erdan, his stable, and purchase horses.

The boys huddling behind the statue of Catherine the Great on Nevsky Prospekt appeared for a moment to be blowing up balloons. But the balloons were plastic bags, and the boys were not exhaling air but breathing in glue. Spotted by a policeman, they tried to scramble away, but one, who appeared to be about 8, was collared ... [In Russia] vagrant children, some homeless, wander about looking for handouts, for pockets to pick, glue to sniff, vodka

to guzzle, a sex partner to rob. (*Dallas Morning News*, 1997:A40)

The foregoing is a journalist's description of the *besprizorniki* ("the neglected ones") who roam the streets of Russia, where about 60 percent of families with three or more children are poor.

As Russia and other countries in the former Soviet Union continue making the transition from centrally planned economies to a market orientation, significant changes are taking place in the daily lives of many men, women, and children.

The economic transition has brought about greater disparity of wages, income, and wealth. Increasing inequality also raises the rate of poverty, at least in the short term. Although analysts attribute rising inequality to a wide variety of factors, some of the most commonly cited concerns include the time lags involved in the shift of various sectors of the economy to a market orientation, the widening income gap between regions and between urban and rural areas, corruption among some

The movement of the global economy is "regulated" by "a world wide process of debt collection" which constricts the institutions of the national state and contributes to destroying employment and economic activity. In the developing world, the burden of external debt has reached two trillion dollars: entire countries have been destabilized as a consequence of the collapse of national currencies, often resulting in the outbreak of social strife, ethnic conflicts and civil war (1997:15) ... Internal purchasing power has collapsed, famines have erupted, health clinics and schools have been closed down, hundreds of millions of children have been denied the right to a primary education. In several regions of the developing world, the reforms have been conducive to resurgence of infectious diseases including tuberculosis, malaria, and cholera. (1997:33)

Many countries, particularly those in sub-Saharan Africa, have no chance of progressing economically unless the burden of debt repayment is eased by the richer debtholder countries.

Foreign Aid and Global Stratification

Few of us have not been moved by the compelling images of starving people in developing countries where droughts or floods have destroyed the annual harvest. Most of us support the emergency exports of food to these countries in order to prevent famine. However, some analysts have begun to ask whether this type of aid hurts more than it helps. For example, consider the recent history of Somalia, now one of the world's poorest and the most politically unstable countries. While

BOX 9.3

CONTINUED

politicians and business leaders, higher rates of foreign investment in some economic sectors than in others, and radical decentralization of the budget, which has substantially reduced income transfers from the wealthiest to the poorest people (World Bank, 1996).

People's lifestyles and life chances have been affected by the economic transition. Think about women, for example. Under the former system, women were expected to work full time, but they received free daycare and health care from the state. Although women are no longer seen as having a socially imposed duty to be employed outside their own home, many work full time out of economic necessity. Currently, large numbers of employed women with young children find themselves without affordable child care facilities and with a deteriorating health care system. Feeding and clothing families, which are typically viewed as "women's responsibilities" in Russia and other nations, are more difficult tasks given the recent economic uncertainties and hardships experienced by many people, particularly women who are single parents.

Russian men are also being deeply affected by economic changes and the growing gap between the rich and the poor. Although some men have garnered fortunes and are enjoying lavish lifestyles that were largely unknown under the former economic system, most others have not fared as well. For example, male life expectancy fell by six years between 1990 and 1994 (from 64 to 58 years), while women's life expectancy dropped by three years (from 74 to 71 years). Two primary reasons given for declining life expectancy are a significant increase in substance abuse, especially alcohol, and a decline in the quality of and access to medical care in recent years (World Bank, 1996).

Will the transition to a market economy gradually reduce poverty and increase life chances in Russia and other former Soviet Union nations? Only time will tell, but the political and economic crisis of the late 1990s suggests the process will take many years.

Somalia's troubles are commonly blamed on drought and clan rivalries, some analysts feel that economic restructuring and food aid are the real causes (Chossudovsky, 1997). Because of droughts and other internal problems, food aid to Somalia increased dramatically from the mid-1970s to the mid-1980s. This donated food was sold into local markets very cheaply and undercut the price of locally grown food. At the same time, a currency devaluation demanded by the International Monetary Fund as a condition for restructuring Somalia's foreign debt made the cost of farm equipment and fuel more expensive. The combined result of the financial restructuring and the lower food prices was the virtual destruction of Somalia's agricultural system. While we normally think that a shortage of food is the cause of starvation, the global oversupply of grain may actually be contributing to famine by destroying the agricultural base of developing countries, making them vulnerable to future food shortages (Chossudovsky, 1997).

Foreign aid can also be damaging to low-income countries in other ways. First, aid can be tied to specific projects or objectives that may meet the interests of the donor country more than the interests of the recipients. For example, military aid will do little to help the lives of the poor and may do them great harm. Similarly, aid devoted to large infrastructure projects such as dams may cause more problems than it solves. Second, aid may be given to achieve political objectives. For example, the Soviet Union provided extensive aid to Cuba to maintain an ally just off the coast of the United States. The United States did the same thing in countries of strategic interest, including several Latin American countries. In these situations, aid is dependent on the

FIGURE 9.3 **Economic Growth**

Substantial gains in economic growth were experienced by some East Asian, Pacific, and South Asian nations over the past decade, as compared with the slower rate of growth among the more-developed G-7 nations. However, some analysts wonder if the East Asian "miracle" is over.

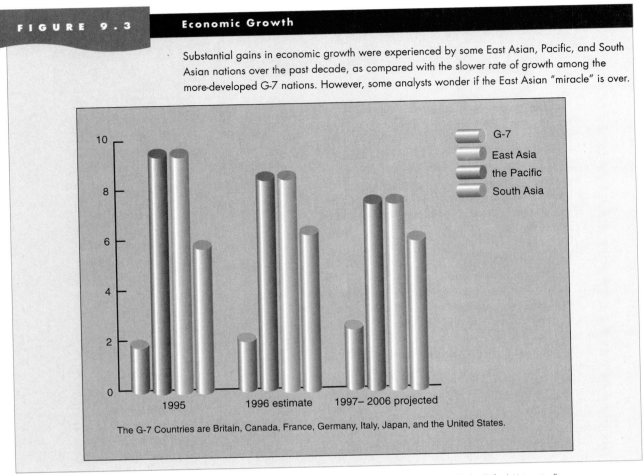

The G-7 Countries are Britain, Canada, France, Germany, Italy, Japan, and the United States.

Reprinted with permission from the World Bank, *World Development Report 1996: From Plan to Market.* New York: Oxford University Press for the World Bank, 1996.

low-income country's continuing political support for the activities of the donor country. This can severely constrain the power of governments to make decisions based on their own interests. Third, even when aid is targeted to individuals, it may not filter down to the poor. For example, donor countries may intend food aid to be distributed to the poor without payment, but elites may simply take the food, sell it, and keep the money.

The other problem is that there is not enough aid to help low-income countries solve health, nutrition, and employment problems. According to the head of the United Nations Children's Fund, foreign aid donations from the world's wealthiest countries declined by 30 percent between 1992 and 1997 despite the enormous growth of their economies over that time (Stackhouse, 1999). This has meant major reductions of assistance to the most needy countries. Canada has been one of the countries that have

reduced aid donations over the past decade. Although Canada has a target of donating 0.7 percent of its gross domestic product (GDP) to foreign aid, the amount donated in 1998 was only 0.25 percent of GDP.

Thus there is not enough aid, and the aid that is provided is often not spent very effectively. However, there are signs of change. Many aid agencies have changed their focus away from large infrastructure programs such as dams and railroads to programs that focus directly on the poor. New ideas include using labour-intensive technologies and other strategies to create employment; providing basic social services such as health care, nutrition, and education; and giving assistance directly to the poorest people in low-income countries (Martinussen, 1997). Above all, the poor themselves must have a say in aid programs and should be empowered to make decisions about how aid money is spent. Otherwise foreign aid can be a double-edged sword that creates more problems than it solves. Not only do the poorest countries need more help from the industrialized world, but the aid that is provided needs to be administered in a manner than recognizes the needs of the countries receiving aid.

MEASURING GLOBAL WEALTH AND POVERTY

Absolute, Relative, and Subjective Poverty

How is poverty defined on a global basis? Isn't it more a matter of comparison than an absolute standard? According to social scientists, defining poverty involves more than comparisons of personal or household income; it also involves social judgments made by researchers. From this point of view, *absolute poverty*—previously defined as a condition in which people do not have the means to secure the most basic necessities of life—would be measured by comparing personal or household income or expenses with the cost of buying a given quantity of goods and services. The World Bank (1996) has defined absolute poverty as living on less than a dollar a day. Similarly, *relative poverty*—which exists when people may be able to afford basic necessities but are still unable to maintain an average standard of living—would be measured by comparing one person's income with the incomes of others. Finally, *subjective poverty* would be measured by comparing the actual income against the income earner's expectations and perceptions. However, for low-income nations in a state of economic transition, data on income and levels of consumption are typically difficult to obtain and often ambiguous when they are available. Defining levels of poverty involves several dimensions: (1) how many people are poor, (2) how far below the poverty line people's incomes fall, and (3) how long they have been poor (is the poverty temporary or long-term?) (World Bank, 1996).

The Gini Coefficient and Global Quality of Life Issues

The World Bank uses as its measure of income inequality what is known as the *Gini coefficient,*

Workers in this toy factory in Zhuhal, China, make toys that are often marketed in high-income nations such as the United States.

which ranges from zero (meaning that everyone has the same income) to 100 (one person receives all the income). Using this measure, inequality has increased in nations such as Bulgaria, the Baltic countries, and the countries of the former Soviet Union to levels similar to those in the most unequal industrial market economies, such as the United States. Stark contrasts also exist in countries such as India, where abject poverty is found side by side with lavish opulence in Calcutta. Note the sharp contrast in lifestyle on one Calcutta street:

> On one side is the Tollygunge Club, 40 hectares of landscaped serenity with an 18-hole golf course, a driving range, riding stables, tennis courts, and two covered swimming pools ... On the other side stands the M.R. Bangur Hospital, a sooty building with a morgue [that sometimes takes] the corpses of paupers who die in Calcutta's streets. (Watson, 1997: F1)

This street is symbolic of the sharp chasm that divides the eleven million people who live in Calcutta. In fact, some analysts believe that the scale of poverty in southern and eastern Asia is most visible in the big-population states of India and China. It is estimated that 652 million of Asia's people are poor and that 448 million of them live in India alone, where there are more than twice as many poor people as in sub-Saharan Africa (Watson, 1997).

Similar disparities between the rich and the poor can be seen in nations throughout the world. For example, in Montrouis, Haiti, Club Med runs a resort featuring pristine beaches, an Olympic-size swimming pool, and all the amenities that affluent tourists expect from a luxury resort. However, just a short walk away from Club Med, open markets have raw meat crawling with flies, and homeless, malnourished people sleep nearby on the ground. But Club Med staff members and tourists at the resort seldom see the other side of Montrouis: Most never leave the compound except when they are going to and from the air-port (Emling, 1997b). In other regions of Haiti as well, starvation and disease are a way of life for most inhabitants. Haiti is the poorest nation in the Western Hemisphere, and recent droughts have further reduced that country's ability to feed people. It is estimated that 40 percent of Haitian children are chronically malnourished, and an estimated 80 percent of all Haitians eat fewer than 2,200 calories a day (Emling, 1997a). Lack of rain has greatly reduced crops that previously fed families, who often live in grass or stone huts "the size of a typical office building elevator" (Emling, 1997a:A17).

GLOBAL POVERTY AND HUMAN DEVELOPMENT ISSUES

Most of the early work on global stratification focused on incomes as a measure of well-being. However, income disparities are not the only factor that defines poverty and its effect on people. Work by prominent economists such as Amaryta Sen and Mahbub ul Haq has led to a shift toward human welfare as a measure of development.

In 1990, the United Nations Development Programme introduced the Human Development Index (HDI), establishing three new criteria—in addition to GDP—for measuring the level of development in a country: life expectancy, education, and living standards. According to the United Nations, human development is "the process of increasing people's options to lead a long and healthy life, to acquire knowledge, and to find access to the assets needed for a decent standard of living" (Pietilä and Vickers, 1994:45).

Table 9.1 shows the difference between Canada and several other countries on the Human Development Index. The World Bank calculates that 37 percent of the population in low- and middle-income countries (1.6 billion people) lack the essentials of well-being, whereas only 21 percent (900 million people) are "income poor," as defined by the bank's poverty line.

While Canadians can be justifiably proud that they have been at the top of the Human Development Index through much of the 1990s, the picture is not completely positive. The United Nations Development Programme also publishes a Human Poverty Index for industrial countries that measures the percentage of people not expected to survive to age 60, the percentage of the population that is functionally illiterate, the population below the poverty line, and the percentage of the labour force that has suffered long-term unemployment. Rankings on this index are shown in Table 9.2. You can see that Canada ranks only tenth on this index, because of a high rate of functional illiteracy and a high proportion of the population with incomes below the poverty level. The United Nations has been critical of the quality of life among Canada's Aboriginal people, who rank far below other Canadians on the Human Development Index.

Life Expectancy

Although some advances have been made in middle- and low-income countries regarding life expectancy, major problems still exist (see Figures 9.4a–9.7d). On the positive side, average life expectancy has increased by about a third in the past three decades and is now more than seventy years in twenty-three countries (United Nations, 1997a). On a less positive note, the average life expectancy at birth of people in middle-income countries remains about twelve years less than that of people in high-income countries. Moreover, the life expectancy of people in low-income nations is as much as twenty-three years less than that of people in high-income nations. Especially striking are the differences in life expectancies in high-income economies and low-income economies such as sub-Saharan Africa, where estimated life expectancy has dropped significantly in many countries, largely because of HIV/AIDS (see Chapter 18, "Health, Health Care, and Disability").

One major cause of shorter life expectancy in low-income nations is the high rate of infant mor-

TABLE   9.1   **HUMAN DEVELOPMENT INDEX**

COUNTRY	RANK	INDEX	PER CAPITA GDP[1]
Canada	1	.960	21,916
France	2	.946	21,176
Norway	3	.943	22,427
United States	4	.943	26,977
Japan	8	.940	21,064
Mexico	49	.855	6,769
Thailand	59	.838	7,742
Brazil	62	.809	5,928
Turkey	69	.782	5,516
Russia	72	.769	4,531
China	106	.650	2,935
Kenya	137	.463	1,438
India	139	.451	1,422
Nigeria	142	.391	1,270
Sierra Leone	174	.185	625

[1]In comparing GDP, the *Human Development Report* uses purchasing power parities (PPP) in international dollars. PPP is a measure that accounts for different levels of purchasing power within different countries.

From *Human Development Report 1998* by United Nations Development Program. © 1998 by the United Nations Development Program. Used by permission of Oxford University Press.

tality. Low-income countries typically have higher rates of illness and disease, and they do not have adequate health care facilities. Malnutrition is a common problem among children, many of whom are underweight, stunted, and have anemia—a nutritional deficiency with serious consequences for child mortality. Consider this journalist's description of a child she saw in Haiti:

> Like any baby, Wisly Dorvil is easy to love. Unlike others, this 13-month-old is hard to hold.
>
> That's because his 10-pound frame is so fragile that even the most minimal of movements can dislocate his shoulders.
>
> As lifeless as a rag doll, Dorvil is starving. He has large, brown eyes and a feeble smile, but a stomach so tender that he suffers from ongoing bouts of vomiting and diarrhea.
>
> Fortunately, though, Dorvil recently came to the attention of U.S. aid workers. With round-the-clock feeding, he is expected to survive.
>
> Others are not so lucky. (Emling, 1997a:A17)

The world's poorest 600 million people suffer from chronic malnutrition, and over 40 million people die each year from hunger-related diseases (Kidron and Segal, 1995). To put this figure in perspective, the number of people worldwide dying from hunger-related diseases is the equivalent of over 300 jumbo-jet crashes a day with no survivors, and half the passengers are children (Kidron and Segal, 1995). However, some progress has been made. Since the 1960s life expectancy has increased by sixteen years and infant mortality has been cut in half in the developing world. Basic immunization—a simple measure—saves more than 3 million lives each year (United Nations Development Programme, 1998).

Health

Health is defined by the World Health Organization as "a state of complete physical, mental and social well-being and not merely the absence of disease or infirmity" (Smyke, 1991:2). Because of their poverty, many people in low-income nations are far from having physical, mental, and social well-being. Of the 4.4 billion people who live in developing countries, 2.6 billion lack access to proper sanitation, 1.3 billion do not have safe water, 1 billion do not have adequate shelter, 880 million have no access to modern health services, and 841 million are malnourished (United Nations Development Programme, 1998). About 17 million people die each year from diarrhea, malaria, tuberculosis, and

TABLE 9.2	HUMAN POVERTY INDEX (HPI) FOR INDUSTRIAL COUNTRIES

Countries	HUMAN POVERTY INDEX Human poverty index for industrial countries		DEPRIVATION IN SURVIVAL People not expected to survive to age 60 (%) 1995	DEPRIVATION IN KNOWLEDGE People who are functionally illiterate (% age 16–65) 1995	DEPRIVATION IN INCOME Population below the income poverty line (%) 1990	SOCIAL EXCLUSION Long-term unemployment, 12 months or more (as % of total labour force) 1995	Real GDP per capita (PPP$) rank
	Value (%)	HPI (rank)					
Sweden	1	6.8	8	7.5	6.7	1.5	13
Netherlands	2	8.2	9	10.5	6.7	3.2	10
Germany	3	10.5	11	14.4	5.9	4.0	8
Norway	4	11.3	9	—	6.6	1.3	2
Italy	5	11.6	9	—	6.5	7.6	9
Finland	6	11.8	11	—	6.2	6.1	14
France	7	11.8	11	—	7.5	4.9	7
Japan	8	12.0	8	—	11.8	0.6	4
Denmark	9	12.0	12	—	7.5	2.0	3
Canada	10	12.0	9	16.6	11.7	1.3	5
Belgium	11	12.4	10	18.4	5.5	6.2	6
Australia	12	12.5	9	17.0	12.9	2.6	11
New Zealand	13	12.6	10	18.4	9.2	1.3	16
Spain	14	13.1	10	—	10.4	13.0	17
United Kingdom	15	15.0	9	21.8	13.5	3.8	12
Ireland	16	15.2	9	22.6	11.1	7.6	15
United States	17	16.5	13	20.7	19.1	0.5	1

Source: United Nations Development Programme, 1998.

From *Human Development Report 1998* by United Nations Development Program. © 1998 by the United Nations Development Program. Used by permission of Oxford University Press.

other infectious and parasitic illnesses (Hauchler and Kennedy, 1994). According to the World Health Organization, infectious diseases are far from under control in many nations due to such factors as unsanitary or overcrowded living conditions. Despite the possible eradication of diseases such as poliomyelitis, leprosy, guinea-worm disease, and neonatal tetanus in the near future, at least thirty new diseases—for which there is no treatment or vaccine—have recently emerged. Among these are AIDS and Ebola, both of which were unknown twenty-five years ago (see Chapter 18, "Health, Healthcare, and Disability").

Some middle-income countries are experiencing rapid growth in degenerative diseases such as cancer and coronary heart disease, and many more deaths are expected from smoking-related diseases. Despite the decrease in tobacco smoking in high-income countries, there has been an increase in per capita consumption of tobacco in low- and middle-income countries, many of which have been targeted for free samples and promotional advertising by U.S. tobacco companies (United Nations Development Programme, 1997).

FIGURE 9.4   Global Health Trends

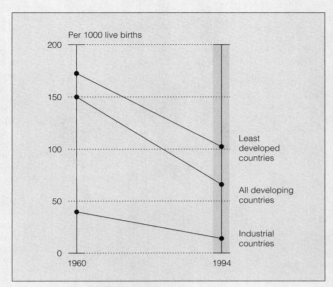

9.4.a   TRENDS IN INFANT MORTALITY

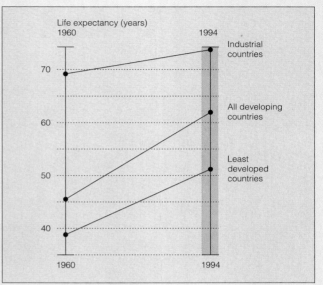

9.4.b TRENDS IN LIFE EXPECTANCY

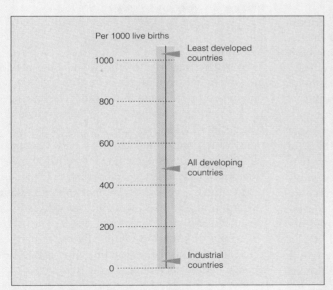

9.4.c MATERNAL MORTALITY, 1990

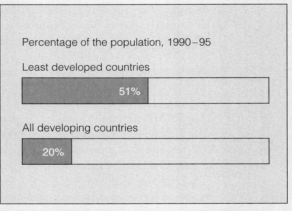

9.4.d PEOPLE WITHOUT ACCESS TO HEALTH SERVICES

Malnutrition is a widespread health problem in many low-income nations.

Education and Literacy

According to the Human Development Report (United Nations Development Programme, 1997), education is fundamental to reducing both individual poverty and national poverty. As a result, school enrolment is used as one measure of human development. The United Nations Educational, Scientific and Cultural Organization (UNESCO) defines a *literate* person as "someone who can, with understanding, both read and write a short, simple statement on their everyday life" (United Nations, 1997a:89). Based on this definition, people who can write only their name, a memorized phrase, or with figures are not considered literate. The adult literacy rate in low-income countries is about half that of the high-income countries, and for women the rate is even lower (United Nations, 1997a). Women constitute about two-thirds of those who are illiterate: there are approximately 74 literate women for every 100 literate men (United Nations, 1997). Literacy is crucial for women because it has been closely linked to decreases in fertility, improved child health, and increased earnings potential (Hauchler and Kennedy, 1994).

THEORIES OF GLOBAL INEQUALITY

Why is the majority of the world's population growing richer while the poorest 20 percent—over one billion people—are so poor that they are effectively excluded from even a moderate standard of living? Social scientists have developed many theories, which view the causes and consequences of global inequality somewhat differently. We will examine the development approach and modernization theory, dependency theory, world systems theory, and the new international division of labour theory. Modernization theory is part of the functionalist tradition, while the other perspectives are rooted in the conflict approach. These approaches are depicted in Figure 9.5.

Development and Modernization Theories

According to some social scientists, global wealth and poverty are linked to the level of industrialization and economic development in a given society. These theorists maintain that low-income nations have progressed less than the wealthier

This poster symbolizes the massive financial aid that was provided by the United States after World War II to help rebuild the European economic base that had been destroyed during the war. Based on the success of the Marshall Plan, many political and economic leaders believe that the problems of today's underdeveloped nations could be reduced in a similar manner.

industrial countries. They feel that industrialization and economic development are essential steps that nations must go through in order to reduce poverty and improve the living conditions of their citizens. These theorists also believe that although the process by which a nation industrializes may vary somewhat, industrialization almost inevitably brings with it a higher standard of living in a nation and some degree of social mobility for individual participants in the society. Family status, race/ethnicity, and gender are said to become less significant in industrialized nations than in agrarian-based societies. As societies industrialize, they also urbanize as workers locate their residences near factories, offices, and other places of work. Consequently, urban values and folkways overshadow the beliefs and practices of the rural areas. Analysts using a development framework typically view industrialization and economic development as essential steps that nations must go through in order to reduce poverty and increase life chances for their citizens.

Earlier in the chapter, we discussed the post-World War II Marshall Plan, under which massive financial aid was provided to the European nations to help rebuild infrastructure lost in the war. Based on the success of this infusion of cash in bringing about modernization, President Truman and many other politicians and leaders in the business community believed that it should be possible to help so-called underdeveloped nations modernize in the same manner.

The most widely known development theory is *modernization theory*—a perspective that links global inequality to different levels of economic development and suggests that low-income economies can move to middle- and high-income economies by achieving self-sustained economic growth. According to modernization theory, the low-income, less-developed nations can improve their standard of living only with a period of intensive economic growth and accompanying changes in people's beliefs, values, and attitudes toward work. As a result of modernization, the values of people in developing countries supposedly become more similar to those of people in high-income nations.

Perhaps the most widely known modernization theory is that of Walt W. Rostow (1971, 1978). To Rostow, one of largest barriers to development in low-income nations was the traditional cultural values held by people, particularly fatalistic beliefs such as viewing extreme hardship and economic deprivation as inevitable and unavoidable facts of life. Fatalistic people do not see any need to work in order to improve their lot in life: It is predetermined for them, so why bother? According to modernization theory, poverty can be attributed to people's cultural failings, which are further reinforced by governmental policies interfering with the smooth operation of the economy.

Rostow suggested that all countries go through four stages of economic development with identical content, regardless of when these nations started the process of industrialization. He compares the stages of economic development to an airplane ride. The first stage is the *traditional stage*, in which very little social change takes place, and people do not think much about changing their current circumstances. According to Rostow, societies in this stage are slow to change because the people hold a fatalistic value system, do not subscribe to the work ethic, and save very little money. The second stage is the *take-off stage*—a period of economic growth accompanied by a growing belief in individualism, competition, and

FIGURE 9.5   **Approaches to Studying Global Inequality**

What causes global inequality? Social scientists have developed a variety of explanations, including the four theories shown here.

Modernization Theory: Low-income, less-developed countries can move to middle- and high-income economies by achieving self-sustained economic growth.

Dependency Theory: Global poverty can at least partially be attributed to the fact that low-income countries have been exploited by high-income economies; the poor nations are trapped in a cycle of dependency on richer nations.

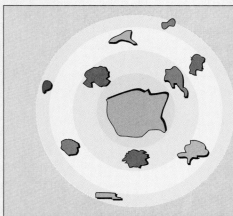

World Systems Theory: How a country is incorporated into the global capitalist economy (e.g., a core, semiperipheral, or peripheral nation) is the key feature in determining how economic development takes place in that nation.

The New International Division of Labour Theory: Commodity production is split into fragments, each of which can be moved (e.g., by a transnational corporation) to whichever part of the world can provide the best combination of capital and labour.

achievement. During this stage, people start to look toward the future, to save and invest money, and to discard traditional values. According to Rostow's modernization theory, the development of capitalism is essential for the transformation from a traditional, simple society to a modern, complex one. With the financial help and advice of the high-income countries, low-income countries eventually will be able to "fly" and enter the third stage of economic development. In the third

stage, the country moves toward *technological maturity*. At this point, the country improves its technology, reinvests in new industries, and embraces the beliefs, values, and social institutions of the high-income, developed nations. In the fourth and final stage, the country reaches the phase of *high mass consumption* and a corresponding high standard of living.

Modernization theory has had both its advocates and its critics. According to proponents of this approach, studies have supported the assertion that economic development occurs more rapidly in a capitalist economy. In fact, the countries that have been most successful in moving from low- to middle-income status typically have been those most centrally involved in the global capitalist economy. For example, the nations of East Asia have successfully made the transition from low-income to higher-income economies through factors such as a high rate of savings, an aggressive work ethic among employers and employees, and the fostering of a market economy.

Critics of modernization theory point out that it tends to be Eurocentric in its analysis of low-income countries, which it implicitly labels as backward (see Evans and Stephens, 1988). In many respects modernization was equated with westernization, as modernization theorists assumed that the problems of low-income countries would only be alleviated once they adopted Western values, culture, and economic models. Modernization theory does not take into account the possibility that all nations do not industrialize in the same manner. For example, Anton Allahar (1989) points out that leading industrial countries such as the United States, Britain, and Japan followed very dissimilar paths to industrialization. Thus we might also assume that the modernization of low-income nations in the late-twentieth and early-twenty-first centuries will require novel policies, sequences, and ideologies that are not accounted for in Rostow's approach (see Gerschenkron, 1962). The theory also does not tell us what actually causes the move from one stage to another, but simply assumes they are natural stages that must be followed as societies advance economically and socially.

One of the most influential critics of modernization theory was Andre Gunder Frank (1969). Frank's research in Latin America convinced him that modernization theory was badly flawed. While Rostow felt that all societies had to move in a linear fashion from underdevelopment to industrialization, Frank pointed out that underdevelopment was not an original stage, but a condition created by the imperial powers that had created dependency through actions such as the deindustrialization of India, the damage incurred by African societies during the years of the slave trade, and the destruction of Indian civilizations in Central and Latin America (Hettne, 1995). All societies were *un*developed at one time, but not all became *under*developed. While some countries moved from being underdeveloped to develop-

ment, others moved from being undeveloped to a condition of underdevelopment in which they were dependent on other nations. These dependent countries had structures and institutions that effectively blocked any further development (Allahar, 1989).

Frank's critique of modernization theory was also a critique of the social policies that grew out of the theory. Rostow was a particular target, because he had been an adviser to U.S. President John Kennedy and as such had been instrumental in shaping U.S. policy in Latin America during the 1960s. Frank and others felt that the Western powers, particularly the United States, were imposing their views of development through both political and military means. Modernization theory was linked to the fight against communism. Because communism was an obstacle on the road to modernization, it was necessary to persuade or force countries to adopt alternative forms of government. The inadequacies of modernization theory, and the political injustices that resulted from policies based on the theory moved the next generation of development theorists to *dependency theory*, an approach that was based on the conflict perspective.

Dependency Theory

According to dependency theorists, rich countries have an interest in maintaining the dependent status of poor countries, as this ensures them a source of raw materials and an essentially captive market for manufactured goods exported to the dependent nations. Business and political leaders in the poor nations find it in their interests to accept dependence and willingly work with the advanced nations to impose policies that maintain the dependent relationship. Any surpluses created in the dependent country will be taken by the affluent capitalist country rather than being used to build up production infrastructure or raise the standard of living in the dependent nations. For these reasons, dependency theorists believe that many countries can never reach the sustained economic growth patterns of the more advanced capitalist economies.

Dependency theory states that global poverty can at least partially be attributed to the fact that the low-income countries have been exploited by the high-income countries. Analyzing events as part of a particular historical process—the expansion of global capitalism— dependency theorists see the greed of the rich

A variety of factors—such as foreign investment and the presence of transnational corporations—has contributed to the economic growth of nations such as Singapore.

countries as a source of increasing impoverishment of the poorer nations and their people. Dependency theory disputes the notion of the development approach—and modernization theory specifically—that economic growth is the key to meeting important human needs in societies. In contrast, the poorer nations are trapped in a cycle of structural dependency on the richer nations due to their need for infusions of foreign capital and external markets for their raw materials, which makes it impossible for the poorer nations to pursue their own economic and human development agendas. Frank and other scholars believed that the best way for low-income countries to move ahead was to break their links with the industrialized countries and to establish independent socialist governments.

Dependency theory has been most often applied to the newly industrializing countries (NICs) of Latin America, whereas scholars examining the NICs of East Asia have found that dependency theory has little or no relevance to economic growth and development in that part of the world. Therefore, dependency theory has had to be expanded to encompass transnational economic linkages that affect developing countries, including foreign aid, foreign trade, foreign

direct investment, and foreign loans. On the one hand, in Latin America and sub-Saharan Africa, transnational linkages such as foreign aid, investments by transnational corporations, foreign debt, and export trade have been significant impediments to development within a country. On the other hand, East Asian countries such as Hong Kong, Taiwan, South Korea, and Singapore have also had high rates of dependency on foreign aid, foreign trade, and interdependence with transnational corporations but have still experienced high rates of economic growth despite dependency. According to sociologist Gary Gereffi (1994), differences in outcome are probably associated with differences in the timing and sequencing of a nation's relationship with external entities such as foreign governments and transnational corporations.

Dependency theory makes a positive contribution to our understanding of global poverty by pointing out that "underdevelopment" is not necessarily the cause of inequality. Rather, this theory points out that exploitation not only of one country by another but of countries by transnational corporations may limit or retard economic growth and human development in some nations.

What remains unexplained is how some East Asian countries had successful "dependency management" whereas many Latin American countries did not (Gereffi, 1994). In fact, from the mid-1980s to the mid-1990s, the annual economic growth in East Asia (excluding Japan) has averaged 8.5 percent, which is four times the rate of the West (Tanzer, 1996). This growth slowed dramatically at the end of the 1990s and it remains to be seen if the East Asian "economic miracle" will continue.

While dependency theory has made a significant contribution to our understanding of global stratification, even its proponents feel it is no longer adequate. In addition to the problem of explaining the success of the East Asian economies that were closely linked with global capitalist structures, the dependency theorists' faith in development through socialist revolution has been shaken by the failure of many socialist economies including that of the Soviet Union (Frank, 1981). Also, most have concluded that the global economy is so pervasive that it is impossible for low-income countries to disconnect themselves from the industrialized world and proceed with their own development (Martinussen, 1997).

World Systems Theory

Drawing on Karl Marx's ideas about global imperialism and capitalist exploitation, world systems theory suggests that what exists under capitalism is a truly global system held together by economic ties. From this approach, global inequality does not emerge solely as a result of the exploitation of one country by another. Instead, economic domination involves a complex world system in which the industrialized, high-income nations benefit from other nations and exploit the citizens of those nations. This theory is most closely associated with sociologist Immanuel Wallerstein (1979, 1984), who believed that a country's mode of incorporation into the capitalist work economy is the key feature in determining how economic development takes place in that nation. According to **world systems theory, the capitalist world economy is a global system divided into a hierarchy of three major types of nations—core, semiperipheral, and peripheral—in which upward or downward mobility is conditioned by the resources and obstacles that characterize the international system.**

Core nations are dominant capitalist centres characterized by high levels of industrialization and urbanization. Core nations such as the United States, Japan, and Germany possess most of the world's capital and technology. Even more importantly for their position of domination, they exert massive control over world trade and economic agreements across national boundaries. Some cities in core nations are referred to as *global cities* because they serve as international centres for political, economic, and cultural concerns. New York, Tokyo, and London are the largest global cities, and they are often referred to as the "command posts" for the world economy (Sassen, 1991, 1995).

Most low-income countries in Africa, South America, and the Caribbean are *peripheral nations*—**nations that are dependent on core nations for capital, have little or no industrialization (other than what may be brought in by core nations), and have uneven patterns of urbanization.** According to Wallerstein (1979, 1984), the wealthy in peripheral nations benefit from the labour of poor workers and from their economic relations with core nation capitalists, whom they uphold in order to maintain their own wealth and position. At a global level, uneven economic growth results from capital investment by core nations. Disparity between the rich and the poor

within the major cities in these nations is increased in the process. The United States/Mexico border is an example of disparity and urban growth: Transnational corporations have built *maquiladora* plants just over the border in Mexico so that goods can be assembled by low-wage workers to keep production costs down. Because of a demand for a large supply of low-wage workers, thousands of people have moved from the rural regions of Mexico to urban areas along the border in hope of earning a higher wage. This influx has pushed already overcrowded cities far beyond their capacity. Many people live on the edge of the city in shantytowns made from discarded materials or in low-cost rental housing in central-city slums because their wages are low and affordable housing is nonexistent (Flanagan, 1995). In fact, housing shortages are among the most pressing problems in many peripheral nations. According to most world systems theorists, it will be very difficult for peripheral countries to change their structural position in the capitalist world economy (Wallerstein, 1979).

Semiperipheral nations **are more developed than peripheral nations but less developed than core nations.** Nations in this category typically provide labour and raw materials to core nations within the world system. These nations constitute a midpoint between the core and peripheral nations that promotes the stability and legitimacy of the three-tiered world economy. These nations include South Korea and Taiwan in East Asia, Mexico and Brazil in Latin America, India in South Asia, and Nigeria and South Africa in Africa. Only two global cities are located in semiperipheral nations: São Paulo, Brazil, which is the centre of the Brazilian economy, and Singapore, which is the economic centre for a multicountry region in Southeast Asia (Friedmann, 1995). According to Wallerstein, semiperipheral nations exploit peripheral nations, just as the core nations exploit both the semiperipheral and the peripheral.

Not all social analysts agree with Wallerstein's (1979, 1984) perspective on the hierarchical position of nations in the global economy. However, most scholars acknowledge that nations throughout the world are influenced by a relatively small number of cities and transnational corporations that have prompted a shift from an international to a more global economy (see Knox and Taylor, 1995; Wilson, 1997). Even Wallerstein (1991) acknowledges that world systems theory is an "incomplete, unfinished cri-

Michael Jordan makes more money for endorsing Nike shoes than the combined salaries of thousands of the workers who manufacture the shoes.

tique" for long-term, large-scale social change that influences global inequality.

The New International Division of Labour Theory

Although the term *world trade* has long implied that there is a division of labour between societies, the nature and extent of this division have been reassessed in the late 1990s based on the changing nature of the world economy. According to the **new international division of labour theory, commodity production is being split into fragments that can be assigned to whichever part of the world can provide the most profitable combination of capital and labour.** Consequently, the new international division of labour has changed the pattern of geographic specialization between countries, whereby high-income countries have become dependent on low-income countries for labour. The low-income countries, especially, provide transnational corporations with a situation in which they can pay lower wages and taxes and face fewer regulations regarding workplace conditions and environmental protection (Waters, 1995).

This new division of labour is part of a global economy based on free trade among countries.

Multilateral trade agreements such as the General Agreement on Tariffs and Trade (GATT) and the North American Free Trade Agreement (NAFTA) have allowed the freer transfer of goods and services among countries, and global corporations now view the whole world both as potential markets and as potential locations for production.

These trade liberalization agreements would appear to be beneficial for poor countries, as the movement of production into developing countries brings jobs to countries with chronically high unemployment. However, few of the profits remain in these countries. For example, a study of garment manufacturing in Bangladesh found that less than 2 percent of the final value of the product went to production workers and that 1 percent went to the local producer. The rest of the money went to profit those who owned the company, and to pay expenses such as shipping and storage costs, and customs duties and sales taxes in high-income countries (Chossudovsky, 1997). There is little hope of higher wages for workers, as the jobs are unskilled and can quickly be moved to another poor country if workers begin to put pressure on the companies.

Overall, a global manufacturing system has emerged in which transnational corporations establish labour-intensive, assembly-oriented export production, ranging from textiles and clothing to technologically sophisticated exports such as computers, in middle- and lower-income nations (Gereffi, 1994). At the same time, manufacturing technologies are shifting from the large-scale, mass-production assembly lines of the past toward a more flexible production process involving microelectronic technologies. Even service industries—such as processing insurance claims forms—that were formerly thought to be less mobile have become exportable through electronic transmission and the Internet. The global nature of these activities has been referred to as *global commodity chains*, a complex pattern of international labour and production processes that results in a finished commodity ready for sale in the marketplace.

This type of commodity chain is most common in labour-intensive consumer goods industries such as toys, garments, and footwear (Gereffi, 1994). Athletic footwear companies such as Nike and Reebok and clothing companies like The Gap and Liz Claiborne are examples of this model. Since these products tend to be labour intensive at the manufacturing stage, the factory system is typically very competitive and globally decentralized. Workers in commodity chains are often exploited by low wages, long hours, and poor working conditions. In fact, most workers cannot afford the products they make. Tini Heyun Alwi, who works on the assembly line of the shoe factory in Indonesia that makes Reebok sneakers, is an example: "I think maybe I could work for a month and still not be able to buy one pair" (quoted in Goodman, 1996: F1). Since Tini earns only 2,600 Indonesian rupiah ($1.28) per day working a ten-hour shift six days a week, her monthly income would fall short of the retail price of the athletic shoes (Goodman, 1996).

Sociologist Gary Gereffi (1994:225) explains the problem with studying the new global patterns as follows:

> The difficulty may lie in the fact that today we face a situation where (1) the political unit is *national*, (2) industrial production is *regional*, and (3) capital movements are *international*. The rise of Japan and the East Asian [newly industrializing countries] in the 1960s and 1970s is the flip side of the "deindustrialization" that occurred in the United States and much of Europe. Declining industries in North America have been the growth industries in East Asia.

As other analysts suggest, these changes have been a mixed bag for people residing in these countries. For example, Indonesia has been able to woo foreign business into the country, but workers have experienced poverty despite working full time in factories making such consumer goods as Nike tennis shoes (Gargan, 1996). As employers feel pressure from workers to raise wages, clashes erupt between the workers and managers or owners. Similarly, the governments in these countries fear that rising wages and labour strife will drive away the businesses, leaving behind workers who have no other hopes for employment and become more impoverished than they previously were. What will be the future of global inequality given this current set of conditions in countries such as Indonesia?

GLOBAL INEQUALITY IN THE FUTURE

As we have seen, social inequality is a major issue within and among the countries of the world. Even in high-income nations where wealth is highly concentrated, many poor people coexist with the affluent. In middle- and low-income countries, there are small pockets of wealth in the midst of poverty and despair.

What are the future prospects for greater equality across and within nations? Not all social scientists agree on the answer to this question. Depending on their theoretical framework, social analysts may describe either an optimistic or a pessimistic scenario for the future.

In some regions, persistent and growing poverty continues to undermine human development and future possibilities for socioeconomic change. In many poor countries, economic development has stalled. In fact, in about one hundred countries incomes today are lower than they were ten years ago (United Nations Development Programme, 1998). Gross inequality has high financial and quality of life costs to people, even among those who are not the poorest of the poor. In the future, continued population growth, urbanization, and environmental degradation threaten even the meagre living conditions of those residing in low-income nations. From this perspective, the future looks dim not only for people in low- and middle-income countries but also for those in high-income countries, who will see their quality of life diminish as natural resources are depleted, the environment is polluted, and high rates of immigration and global political unrest threaten the elevated standard of living that many have enjoyed in the second half of the twentieth century. According to some social analysts, transnational corporations and financial institutions such as the World Bank and the International Monetary Fund will further solidify their control over a globalized economy, which will transfer the power to make significant choices to these organizations and away from the people and their governments. As a result, further loss of resources and means of livelihood will affect people and countries around the globe. Adding to the problem, industrialized countries have cut back on foreign aid despite their increased wealth.

On the other hand, a more optimistic scenario is also possible. With modern technology and worldwide economic growth, it might be possible to reduce absolute poverty and to increase people's opportunities. Among the trends cited by the Human Development Report (United Nations Development Programme, 1996) that have the potential to bring about more sustainable patterns of development are the socioeco-

BOX 9.4 SOCIOLOGY AND TECHNOLOGY

THE DIGITAL THIRD WORLD

There is little doubt that information and communications technologies are changing our world. However, there is considerable debate about the impact of these technologies on the poor. Some feel that the ability to share information from around the globe will hasten the development of low-income countries, as they will be able to become knowledge societies that can compete with the industrialized nations. The new technologies will allow them to rapidly streamline their governments and industries, and their competitive advantage in wages will allow them to attract business from richer nations. Technology can also speed the pace of educational reform and help to build a more participatory civil society through the sharing of information and ideas. However, a more common view is that the move to a world linked by new information and communications technology will lead to a greater polarization between the rich who can exploit the new technologies and the poor who do not even have access to them. In other words, the poor will likely be excluded from the global information society—and this includes the poor in industrialized countries, as the "digital Third World" does not follow international borders. The Internet is accessible to only about 2 percent of the world's people (Hammann, 1998), and these are disproportionately high-income residents of high-income countries.

Why is it unlikely that the information revolution will reduce global stratification? There are many barriers to the spread of information and communications technology. The major obstacle is cost. To become part of the "digital world" low-income countries must build very expensive communications infrastructures. For example, while Canada has 57 phone lines per 100 people, countries such as China, India, Kenya, and Pakistan have just one. The costs of installing a phone line in places like rural Africa are about $5000, and existing phone lines in most low-income countries cannot handle the transmission speeds necessary to use the Internet effectively (Wresch, 1996). In a world in which global communications and access to the Internet are becoming critical to business and trade, countries that cannot afford to build communications networks or to train people in how to use computers will be at a great competitive disadvantage. It is most unlikely that countries that are deeply in debt and have other pressing needs such as health care and nutrition will be able to create a communications

nomic progress made in many low- and middle-income countries over the past thirty years as technological, social, and environmental improvements have occurred. For example, technological innovation continues to improve living standards for some people. Fertility rates are declining in some regions (but remain high in others, where there remains grave cause for concern about the availability of adequate natural resources for the future). Health and education may continue to improve in lower-income countries. However, if positive change is to continue, the practices of global corporations, foreign aid donors, and international lending organizations must begin to focus on the needs of low-income

countries rather than solely on the perceived demands of the marketplace.

We will continue to focus on issues pertaining to global inequality in subsequent chapters as we discuss such topics as race, gender, education, health and medicine, population, urbanization, social change, and the environment.

CHAPTER REVIEW

What is global stratification, and how does it contribute to economic inequality?

BOX 9.4

CONTINUED

infrastructure without a great deal of help. It is hard to conceive of the "wired classroom" in a country that cannot afford to build schools or train teachers.

A second reason for the lack of Internet access in most parts of the world is language. The vast majority of content on the Internet is in English. Without multilingual sites, the name, the World Wide Web, will never be accurate. A Web that is dominated linguistically by English and technologically and culturally by the United States will never reflect the point of view of people in low-income countries. (For a rare example of an Internet site that uses several African languages, see the Channel Africa site at **http://www.channelafrica.org/currenta.shtml**).

A final reason for lack of access is government censorship. Most totalitarian countries are afraid of the free flow of information. It is easier to restrict the freedom of people who are unable to share ideas with each other and with people in other countries. As a result, many governments, including China, Algeria, and Afghanistan, have restricted their citizens' access to new forms of communications technology.

While low-income countries continue to fall further behind in the development of information technology, some small steps have been taken to reduce the gap. One model project has been undertaken by Canada's International Development Research Centre (IDRC). Project Acacia is an international effort led by the IDRC to provide sub-Saharan communities with the ability to apply information and communication technologies to their own social and economic development (for more information, go to **http://www.idrc.ca/acacia/acacia_e.htm**). Its partners in the project include the African Information Society Initiative, which is trying to provide an African perspective on the opportunities and challenges of that continent in an emerging information age. The project has placed a priority on working with rural and disadvantaged communities, and particularly with women and youth groups in these communities.

While this project is promising, it is a very small step toward the solution of a very large problem. Much more must be done if low-income countries are to build on-ramps to the information superhighway.

Global stratification refers to the unequal distribution of wealth, power, and prestige on a global basis, which results in people having vastly different lifestyles and life chances both within and among the nations of the world. Today, the income gap between the richest and the poorest 20 percent of the world population continues to widen, and within some nations the poorest 20 percent of the population has an income that is only a slight fraction of the overall per capita income for that country.

Why is it difficult to study global inequality?

Terminology is a major problem in studying global inequality. Most definitions of inequality are based on comparisons of levels of income or economic development, whereby countries are identified in terms of the "three worlds" or upon their levels of economic development. Today, many sociologists use the World Bank's classification of nations into three economic categories: low-income economies, middle-income economies, and high-income economies.

How are global poverty and human development related?

Income disparities are not the only factor that defines poverty and its effect on people. The United Nation's Human Development Index measures the level of development in a country through indicators such as life expectancy, infant mortality rate, proportion of underweight children under age five (a measure of nourishment and health), and adult literacy rate for low-income, middle-income, and high-income countries.

What is modernization theory, and what stages did Rostow believe all societies go through?

Modernization theory is a perspective that links global inequality to different levels of economic development and suggests that low-income economies can move to middle- and high-income economies by achieving self-sustained economic growth. According to Rostow, all countries go through four stages of economic development: (1) the traditional stage, in which very little social change takes place; (2) the take-off stage, a period of economic growth accompanied by a growing belief in individualism, competition, and achievement; (3) technological maturity, a period of improving technology, reinvesting in new industries, and embracing the beliefs, values, and social institutions of the high-income, developed nations; and (4) the phase of high mass consumption, accompanied by a high standard of living.

How does dependency theory differ from modernization theory?

Dependency theory states that global poverty can at least partially be attributed to the fact that the low-income countries have been exploited by the high-income countries. Whereas modernization theory focuses on how societies can reduce inequality through industrialization and economic development, dependency theorists see the greed of the rich countries as a source of increasing impoverishment of the poorer nations and their people.

What is world systems theory, and how does it view the global economy?

According to world systems theory, the capitalist world economy is a global system divided into a hierarchy of three major types of nations: core nations are dominant capitalist centres characterized by high levels of industrialization and urbanization; peripheral nations are those countries that are dependent on core nations for capital, that have little or no industrialization (other than what may be brought in by core nations), and that have uneven patterns of urbanization; and semiperipheral nations are more developed than peripheral nations but less developed than core nations.

What is the new international division of labour theory?

The new international division of labour theory is based on the assumption that commodity production is split into fragments that can be assigned to whichever part of the world can provide the most profitable combination of capital and labour. This division of labour has changed the pattern of geographic specialization among countries, whereby high-income countries have become dependent on low-income countries for labour. The low-income countries provide transnational corporations with a situation in which they can pay lower wages and taxes and face fewer regulations regarding workplace conditions and environmental protection.

Key Terms

core nations 295
dependency theory 293
modernization theory 291
peripheral nations 295
semiperipheral nations 295

Internet Exercises

1. Visit the homepage for UNICEF (the United Nations Children's Fund):

   http://www.unicef.org/

   What types of issues can you access through this page's links? Click on several of the links. Would some—or even all—of them be helpful in studying the consequences of poverty among the world's children?

2. One of the sites maintained by UNICEF on the Internet is the State of the World's Children:

   http://www.unicef.org/sowc(plus the last two digits of the most recent year)

   Access this site and its links to lived experiences (under "news features") and data (under "fact sheets"). Compare the status of children in low-income nations as shown on this site's pages with that of children in Canada in terms of absolute, relative, and subjective poverty.

3. Go to the site of the Canadian International Development Agency (CIDA) at:

   http://www.acdi-cida.gc.ca/index-e.htm

   What are Canada's priorities in giving aid? What regions of the world are most important to those directing aid programs? Do you think CIDA's programs are more concerned with Canada's needs and priorities or with the needs and priorities of the countries receiving the aid?

🕮 Net Links

The United Nations Development Programme has done an excellent job in focusing public attention on global inequality issues. To find out more about the world's poorest people and to learn what can be done to help them, visit the Programme's Web site at:

> http://www.undp.org/index5.html

World Factbook 1998 contains demographic information from around the globe; go to:

> http://www.odci.gov/cia/publications/factbook

United Nations Development Report

> http://www.undp.org/

Women's International Net looks at international development issues from a woman's perspective; go to:

> http://welcome.to/winmagazine

A number of reports from the World Bank are available at:

> http://www.worldbank.org/

Boycotts have been held against Nike and Reebok because of their treatment of workers in low-income countries. Read about boycotts at:

> http://cyberzone.net/wharton/CVX/Nike/
> index2.html

Questions for Critical Thinking

1. You have decided to study global wealth and poverty. How would you approach your study? What research methods would provide the best data for analysis? What might you find if you compared your research data with popular presentations—such as films and advertising—of everyday life in low- and middle-income countries?

2. How would you compare the lives of poor people living in central cities and rural areas of Canada with those of people living in the low-income nations of the world? In what ways are their lives similar? In what ways are they different?

3. Should Canadian foreign policy include provisions for reducing poverty in other nations of the world? Should our domestic policy include provisions for reducing poverty in Canada? How are these issues similar? How are they different?

4. Using the theories discussed in this chapter, devise a plan to alleviate poverty. Assume that you have the necessary wherewithal, including wealth, political power, and natural resources. Share your plan with others in your class and create a consolidated plan that represents the best ideas and suggestions presented.

Suggested Readings

For more information on issues such as economic development and the global economy, the following books are recommended:

Michel Chossudovsky. *The Globalization of Poverty*. Penang: Third World Network, 1997.

James M. Cypher and James L. Dietz. *The Process of Economic Development*. New York: Routledge, 1997.

David C. Korten. *When Corporations Rule the World*. West Hartford, Conn: Kumarian Press, 1995.

John Martinussen. *Society, State, and Market: A Guide to Competing Theories of Development*. Halifax: Fernwood Books, 1997.

United Nations Development Programme. *Human Development Report, 1997*. New York: Oxford University Press, 1997.

Malcolm Waters. *Globalization*. New York: Routledge, 1995.

World Bank. *World Development Report 1996: From Plan to Market*. New York: Oxford University Press, 1996.

Race and Ethnicity
    The Social Significance of Race and Ethnicity
    Majority and Minority Groups

Components of Racial and Ethnic Conflict
    Prejudice
    Theories of Prejudice
    Discrimination
    Racism

Sociological Perspectives on Race and Ethnic Relations
    Interactionist Perspectives
    Functionalist Perspectives
    Conflict Perspectives

A Feminist Perspective on Race and Gender

Ethnic Groups in Canada
    First Nations
    Charter Europeans
    Canada's Immigrants

Racial and Ethnic Diversity in Canada in the Future

In the following personal narrative, Valerie Bedassigae Pheasant discusses her experiences with racism and the impact of these experiences on both her mother and herself:

"I sat on the banister railing for what felt like an eternity, watching my mother. As silently as I crept to watch, I left. I wondered why she did not dance for us. That was the first and only time I saw my mother dance with abandon. What I did see was a gradual freezing of her emotions and a treacherous walk with silence. Her metamorphosis had happened before our eyes and we were unable to stop it. Why didn't she yell at them? Why didn't she tell them—no? Where did the fire go? When was it that the dancing stopped?

"The cocoon that encased my mother was woven by inside thoughts that constricted her more strongly than anything tangible in the human world. Inside thoughts reacting to outside action generated towards our family's Nativeness. Blatant racist remarks and statements by women who did not care to know us. Each word, each comment diminished her capacity to speak—she moved slower and slower ... My mother liked to play bingo at the church hall occasionally. I went with her ... It was hard to find seats. We found some. We looked around at the other women at the table. Nobody said hello. They looked and I looked back ... The other women talked amongst themselves in what resembled a huddle. They glanced furtively in our direction. We sat and waited—I watched. Whispers. Whispers coming from the huddle. Whispers that called out, too loud, clanging in my ears, 'Smells like Indians!' Instinctively, I breathed in deeply. Did they mean us? I could see them staring at us. My mother's head was down. Tears? I knew it was us. We moved to another table. We do not speak about what was said about us. We do not recognize them. We cannot give them more power. My anger grows. My mother's spirit staggers." (1994:35–36)

RACE AND ETHNICITY

Canada is a diverse and complex society composed of racially and ethnically different groups. Our country has a reputation as a tolerant and compassionate country whose success in race and ethnic relations has received worldwide admiration. Canadians profess to be colour-blind: the refrain "race doesn't matter here" is widely endorsed (James and Shadd, 1994:47). Is it surprising, therefore, to read the above personal narrative, in which it is suggested that Aboriginal people in Canada experience racism as part of their everyday life? As Fleras and Elliott comment, "From afar, Canada looks idyllic; up close, the picture changes. Dig deeper and one can unearth a country that has little to boast about in the treatment of minorities" (1996:17). In this chapter racism will be central to the discussion of race and ethnicity. One of the most important and reliable sources of data on racism is the victims who have experienced it directly (Henry et al., 1996). Therefore, we will explore the subjective impact of race and ethnicity on people's lives—and examine whether those effects are changing. Before reading on, test your knowledge about racism in Canada by taking the quiz in Box 10.1.

QUESTIONS AND ISSUES

CHAPTER FOCUS QUESTION: How significant is race in Canadian society?

How do race and ethnicity differ?

What are the causes of prejudice?

How does discrimination differ from prejudice?

How are racial and ethnic relations analyzed from a sociological perspective?

What are the unique experiences of racial and ethnic groups in Canada?

Golf star Tiger Woods's mother is one-half Chinese and one-half Thai, and his father had one white, one Native, and two black grandparents. Woods calls himself a "Cablinasian" to reflect this diverse background. Racial intermarriage is steadily increasing in Canada, the United States, and Britain. What will this mean for the concept of race in the future?

RACE AND ETHNICITY

What is "race"? Some people think it refers to skin colour (the Caucasian "race"); others use it to refer to a religion (the Jewish "race"), nationality (the British "race"), or the entire human species (the human "race") (Marger, 1997). A **race is a category of people who have been singled out as inferior or superior, often on the basis of physical characteristics such as skin colour, hair texture, and eye shape** (Newman, 1995).

A number of difficulties arise when thinking in terms of race. First, race is defined by perceived skin colour: white or nonwhite (S. Lee, 1993). While one category exists for "whites" (who vary considerably in actual skin colour and physical appearance), all of the remaining categories are considered "nonwhite." This classification system, which took hold in such predominantly "white" countries as Canada, the United States, and Europe, is now outdated because of the increased presence in these countries of ethnic groups who fit neither category (Starr, 1987, 1992).

Second, use of the term *race* implies that racial purity exists. Although we may assume that we can distinguish between people on the basis of racially defined physical characteristics, biology confirms that most Canadians, like people all over the world, are genetically mixed. The combined effects of migration, immigration, and intermarriage have made it impossible to identify distinct characteristics that are attributable to specific races (Martin and Franklin, 1983). Consider the difficulty Lawrence Hill had in defining his "race":

> Even as a boy, I sensed that terms such a "mulatto," "half-Black" and "part-Black" denied my fullness as a person. I recognized the absurdity of calling somebody "one-half" or "one-quarter" or "one-eighth" Black ... One couldn't assign this colour to the heart and that colour to the liver. And at the same time, a person like me couldn't be all white and not Black, or all Black and not White, unless society imposed one colour on me. (1994:47)

The true diversity of the population is not revealed when multiracial individuals in Canada are placed in vague categories such as "other" (S. Lee, 1993). The concept of race is a social creation rather than a biological reality. Nevertheless, individuals like Lawrence Hill struggle to define themselves according to arbitrary racial classifications in an attempt clarify their identity.

The third problem with thinking in terms of race is that official racial classifications may create a sense of group membership or "consciousness of kind" for people within a somewhat arbitrary classification. When people of European descent were classified as "white," some began to see themselves as different from those classified as "nonwhite." Consequently, Jewish, Italian, and Irish immigrants may have felt more a part of the northern European white mainstream in the late nineteenth and early twentieth centuries. Whether Chinese Canadians, Japanese Canadians, and Filipino Canadians come to think of themselves collectively as "Asian Canadians" because of official classifications remains to be seen (S. Lee, 1993).

How do you classify yourself with regard to race? For an increasing number of people, this is a difficult question to answer. What if you were asked about your ethnic origin or your ethnicity? The Canadian census, unlike that of the United States, collects information on ethnic origin

HOW MUCH DO YOU KNOW ABOUT RACISM IN CANADA?

TRUE	FALSE	
T	F	1. There is only one kind of racism in Canada.
T	F	2. The majority of Canadians view racism as a significant social problem.
T	F	3. Racism in Canada is a result of immigration of non-whites.
T	F	4. Racism occurs only in times of economic decline and recession.
T	F	5. Policies of multiculturalism are insufficient to address the problems of racism.
T	F	6. No civil rights movement existed in Canada.
T	F	7. Affirmative action programs directed at hiring visible minorities are a form of reverse discrimination.
T	F	8. Visible minorities are the likeliest victims of racism.
T	F	9. Incidents of anti-Semitism (racism directed at Jews) have increased in the past decade.
T	F	10. Slavery has never existed in Canada.

Answers on page 306.

rather than race. Race refers only to physical characteristics, but the concept of ethnicity refers to cultural features. These features may include language, religion, national origin, distinctive foods, a common heritage, music, dress, or any other distinctive cultural trait. An **ethnic group, then, is a collection of people who, as a result of their shared cultural traits and a high level of interaction, regard themselves and are regarded as a cultural unit** (Robertson, 1977). As Table 10.1 demonstrates, in 1996 over ten million Canadians—roughly 36 percent of all Canadians—reported multiple ethnic origins (Statistics Canada, 1998h). As a result, collecting data on ethnic origin is not a simple task.

Ethnic groups share five main characteristics: (1) *unique cultural traits,* such as language, clothing, holidays, or religious practice, (2) *a sense of community,* (3) *a feeling of ethnocentrism,* (4) *ascribed membership from birth,* and (5) *territoriality,* or a tendency to occupy a distinct geographic area by choice or for protection.

Although the distinction between ethnicity and race appears obvious—one is cultural, the other biological—they are often used interchangeably. Many people, for example, believe that people of Jewish origin constitute a race, although their distinctiveness pertains to cultural characteristics, primarily religious beliefs, as well as a history of persecution.

The Social Significance of Race and Ethnicity

How important are race and ethnicity in Canada? According to sociologists Augie Fleras and Jean Leonard Elliott:

> Most Canadians appear ambivalent about the race concept. The concept carries a negative connotation that conflicts with the virtues of an achievement-oriented, upwardly mobile society. Many dislike the underlying message of race: That is, the most important thing about a person is an accident of birth, something beyond control, and that alone should determine job status, and privilege. (1996:37)

It is easy to suggest that race is insignificant if one is not a member of a racial minority. But, whether we like to acknowledge it or not, race does matter. It matters because it provides privilege and power for some. Fleras and Elliott discuss the significance of being white and enjoying what has sometimes been referred to as *white privilege:*

> Think for a moment about the privileges associated with whiteness, many of which are taken for granted and unearned by accident of birth. Being white means you can purchase a home in any part of town and expect cordial treatment rather than commu-

BOX 10.1

ANSWERS TO THE SOCIOLOGY QUIZ ON RACISM

1. **False.** Racism takes many forms. The more subtle forms of racism such as institutional or systemic racism remain prevalent in Canadian society.

2. **True.** A recent poll indicated that 75 percent of Canadians consider racism a serious social problem.

3. **False.** The argument here is that if immigration is curbed, racism will decrease. However, even before Canada began allowing large-scale immigration, racism existed in the relationship between white colonial settlers and Aboriginal peoples.

4. **False.** Racism has been practised systematically in Canada since this country was formed—even in times of economic prosperity. For example, in the early 1950s, despite an economic boom, Chinese and Japanese citizens were regarded as "enemy aliens."

5. **True.** To expect that programs supporting cultural retention can also achieve racial equality and harmony is unrealistic.

6. **False.** In the 1940s and 1950s organizations such as the Windsor Council on Group Relations, the National Unity Association of Chatham-Dresden-North Buxton, and the Negro Citizens' Association of Toronto fought segregation in housing and employment, as well as fighting racist immigration laws.

7. **False.** For affirmative action policies to be a form of reverse discrimination, they would have to require employers to discriminate against better-qualified whites and give an unfair advantage to visible minorities. Affirmative action is directed not at discrimination, but at elimination of a long history of employment practices that result in preferential treatment toward white candidates.

8. **False.** In Canada both Aboriginal people and visible minorities are subjected to racism. Which group is victimized more is difficult to measure.

9. **True.** In the past decade, the League for Human Rights of B'nai B'rith has monitored the number and types of anti-Semitic incidents that have occurred in all regions of Canada. They report a significant increase in anti-Semitic incidents of all kinds.

10. **False.** Slavery was introduced in Canada by the French in 1608. Sixteen legislators in the first Parliament of Upper Canada owned slaves. Slavery existed in Quebec, New Brunswick, Nova Scotia, and Ontario until the early nineteenth century.

Source: Henry et al., 1995; Fleras and Elliott, 1996.

nity grumblings about the neighborhood "going to pot." Being white saves you the embarrassment of going into a shopping mall with fears of being followed, frisked, monitored, or finger printed. Being white means you can comment on a variety of topics without someone impugning your objectivity or motives. You can speak your mind with little to lose if things go wrong. Being white enables you to display righteous anger in dealing with colleagues, yet not incur snide remarks about "aggression" or "emotional stability" ... Being white gives you the peace of mind that your actions are not judged as a betrayal or a credit to your race. Finally, being white provides the satisfaction of cruising around late at night without attracting unnecessary police attention. (1996:35)

Ethnicity, like race, is a basis of hierarchical ranking in society and an "extremely critical determinant of who gets 'what there is to get' and in what amounts" (Marger, 1994:18). John Porter (1965) described Canada as a "vertical mosaic," made up of different ethnic groups wielding varying degrees of social and economic power, status, and prestige. Porter's analysis of ethnic groups in Canada revealed a significant degree of ethnic stratification with some ethnic groups heavily represented in the upper strata, or elite, and other groups heavily represented in the lower strata. The dominant group holds power over other (subordinate) ethnic groups. Ethnic stratification is one dimension of a larger system of structured social inequality, as examined in Chapter 8.

TABLE 10.1   **SELECTED ETHNIC ORIGINS OF CANADIANS,[1] 1996**

	CANADA	
Total population	**28,528,125**	**Percentage**
Single origins[2]	*18,303,625*	*64*
British Isles origins[3]	3,267,520	11
French origins[4]	2,683,840	9
Western European origins	1,126,095	4
Northern European origins	167,285	0.6
Eastern European origins	867,055	3
Southern European origins	1,376,935	5
Other European origins	205,525	0.7
Arab origins	188,435	0.6
West Asian origins	106,870	0.3
South Asian origins	590,145	2
East and Southeast Asian origins	1,217,450	4
African origins	137,315	0.4
Pacific Island origins	5,765	0.002
Latin, Central, and South American origins	118,640	0.4
Caribbean origins	305,290	1
Aboriginal origins[5]	477,630	2
Canadian origins[6]	5,326,995	19
Other origins[7]	80,840	0.2
Multiple origins[8]	*10,224,495*	*36*

1. Ethnic origin refers to the ethnic or cultural group(s) to which the respondent's ancestors belonged. Ethnic origin pertains to the ancestral roots or background of the population, and should not be confused with citizenship or nationality.

2. A single response occurs when the respondent provides only one ethnic origin.

3. British Isles includes single responses of English, Irish, Scottish, Welsh, or other British, as well as multiple "British Isles only" responses—that is, a combination of English, Irish, Scottish, Welsh, or other British.

4. French origins include single responses of French or Acadian, as well as multiple responses of French and Acadian.

5. Aboriginal includes the single response of Inuit, Métis, and North American Indian.

6. Caution should be used in comparing data for "Canadian" ethnic origin between censuses.

7. Includes American, Australian, New Zealander, Québécois, and Other not included elsewhere.

8. A multiple response occurs when the respondent provides two or more ethnic groups.

Source: Statistics Canada, "Single and Multiple Origin Responses, *1996 Census.*" Adapted from "The Nation Series Package No. 6: Ethnic Origin and Visible Minority Population," Cat. no. 93F0026XDB96000. Used by permission.

Majority and Minority Groups

The terms *majority group* and *minority group* are widely used, but what do they actually mean? To sociologists, a **majority (or dominant) group is one that is advantaged and has superior resources and rights in a society** (Feagin and Feagin, 1996). In Canada, whites with northern European ancestry (often referred to as Euro-Canadians, white Anglo-Saxon Protestants, or WASPs) are considered the majority group. A **minority (or subordinate) group is one whose** members, because of physical or cultural characteristics, are disadvantaged and subjected to unequal treatment by the dominant group and who regard themselves as objects of collective discrimination (Wirth, 1945). While we all belong to an ethnic group or groups, not everyone belongs to a minority group. All visible minorities and white women are considered minority group members in Canada. The term **visible minority refers to an official government category of non-white non-Caucasian individuals.** Included in this category are Chinese, Japanese, Koreans,

Filipinos, Indo-Pakistanis, West Asians and Arabs, Southeast Asians, blacks, Latin Americans, and Pacific Islanders (Statistics Canada, 1998h). Aboriginal people form a separate category. The 1996 census was the first census to collect data on persons who are members of visible minorities. This was an important objective due to the increasing number of recent immigrants from China, Asia, and Africa. In 1996, 3.2 million Canadians—over 11 percent of the Canadian population—identified themselves as members of a visible minority (Statistics Canada, 1998h).

Although the terms *majority group* and *minority group* are widely used, their actual meanings are not clear. In the sociological sense, *group* is misleading because people who merely share ascribed racial or ethnic characteristics do not constitute a group. Further, *majority* and *minority* have meanings associated with both numbers and domination. Numerically speaking, *minority* means that a group is smaller in number than a dominant group. However, in countries such as South Africa and India, this has not historically been true. Those running the country were of a race (in South Africa) or caste (in India) with far fewer members than the masses that they ruled. Consequently, the use of these terms from a standpoint of dominance is more accurate. In this context, majority and minority refer to relationships of advantage/disadvantage and power/exploitation. Many sociologists prefer to use the terms *dominant group* and *subordinate group* because they more precisely reflect the importance of power in the relationships (Feagin and Feagin, 1996).

COMPONENTS OF RACIAL AND ETHNIC CONFLICT

Prejudice

Prejudice is a negative attitude based on preconceived notions about members of selected groups. Prejudice partially stems from our attempts to create some order in our lives by classifying others. However, prejudices (pre + judgments) are judgments that are irrational and rigid insofar as they are supported by little or no direct evidence. Prejudice can be directed against a range of social or personal characteristics including social class, gender, sexual orientation,

occupation, religion, political affiliation, age, race, or ethnicity. These attitudes may be either felt or expressed. *Racial prejudice* involves beliefs that certain racial groups are innately inferior to others or have a disproportionate number of negative traits.

STEREOTYPES Prejudice is often reinforced by *stereotypes*—overgeneralizations about the appearance, behaviour, or other characteristics of all members of a group. Although all stereotypes are hurtful, negative stereotypes are particularly harmful to minorities. As Fleras and Elliott comment, "Power and privilege provide a protective layer. For minorities, however, stereotyping is a problem. Each negative image or unflattering representation reinforces their peripheral position within an unequal society" (1996:69). Consider the following conversation:

> *Sabra:* So, you think I'm not like the rest of them ...
>
> *Alex:* Well, when I see you, I don't see your colour. I don't see you as a South Asian. You're not like the rest of them ...
>
> *Sabra:* Oh, so, I'm more like you and less like, should I say it, "a real South Asian." You see, although you are not saying it, your statement reveals that you have some preconceived ideas of South Asians, the people I'm supposed to be so unlike. This means that whatever your preconceived ideas are of South Asians, they make South Asians less acceptable, less attractive, and less appealing to you than I. Well, this is not just stereotyping, this is racist stereotyping. (Desai, 1994:191)

How do people learn of stereotypes? As Box 10.2 illustrates, the media are a major source of racial and ethnic stereotypes. One study reported that children were aware of media stereotypes at a young age, indicating that the news media tend to reinforce negative stereotypes regarding visible minorities. One young girl commented, "You always see black people doing drugs and carrying around drugs, shooting people and stealing things" (CNN Interactive, 1998:2).

Another source of stereotypes is ethnic jokes, which portray minorities in a derogatory manner, not necessarily intentionally, but because such humour by definition is simplistic and prone to exaggeration. Take a moment and think of an ethnic joke you have heard. Do you think this joke is harmful? Would you tell the joke to a member of the minority group that the joke is about? If not, chances are that you have some level of awareness that these jokes are damaging. Consider the comments of Paul, a student in a race and ethnic relations course at a Canadian university:

> If I laugh at a joke that uses a Black ... because I associate a stereotype with what has been said, I am a bigot. For example, what do you call a Black guy in a new car? A thief. Funny, eh? No, the joke itself is not funny, but it makes reference to a stereotype about Blacks that they're all thieves, which I do find funny ... That kind of joke is not funny. It does not point out a funny stereotype of a certain race ... it is pure malice and cruelty against a specific group. The fact that it was Blacks mattered little. Am I a bigot? I don't know what I am anymore. (James, 1995:107)

ETHNOCENTRISM   Prejudice is often present in *ethnocentrism,* which, as discussed in Chapter 3, **is the belief in the superiority of one's own culture compared with that of others.** Ethnocentrism involves the evaluation of all groups and cultures in terms of one's own cultural standards and values. What is wrong with believing that your cultural values are preferable to those of others? Such a belief is, after all, a source of pride. The problem with ethnocentrism is that your standards are used as a frame of reference for negatively evaluating the behaviour of other groups. Not surprisingly, these groups will be evaluated negatively as backward, immoral, primitive, or irrational. In short, although ethnocentrism promotes group cohesion and morale, it is also a major source of intergroup hostility and conflict.

Theories of Prejudice

Are some people more prejudiced than others? Some theories focus on how individuals may transfer their internal psychological problems onto an external object or person (Feagin and Feagin, 1996). Others look at factors such as social learning and personality types.

The *frustration-aggression hypothesis* states that people who are frustrated in their efforts to achieve a highly desired goal will respond with a pattern of aggression toward others (Dollard et al., 1939). The object of their aggression becomes the *scapegoat*—**a person or group that is incapable of offering resistance to the hostility or aggression of others** (Marger, 1997). Scapegoats often are used as substitutes for the actual source of the frustration. For example, members of subordinate racial and ethnic groups often are blamed for societal problems (such as unemployment or an economic recession) over which they have no control.

According to some interactionists, prejudice results from *social learning;* in other words, it is learned from observing and imitating significant others, such as parents and peers. Initially, children do not have a frame of reference from which to question the prejudices of their relatives and friends. When they are rewarded with smiles or laughs for telling derogatory jokes or making negative comments about outgroup members, children's prejudiced attitudes may be reinforced. In the following commentary, a university student discusses his prejudiced beliefs:

> I don't fancy myself as a redneck who goes around killing Blacks à la KKK, nor do I participate in Gay-bashing or any other type of physical outbursts aimed at any particular race or ethnic group. Where I am prejudiced is through all the stereotypes. Women and Chinese people can't drive. Pakistanis smell bad. Blacks are thieves and smell bad. Italians either build houses or kill people for a living.
>
> Most of these stereotypes were fed to me over time by my parents and my older brother. I didn't know what the word stereotype meant then. I took these "phrases of wisdom" as truths and they altered my view of people. Prejudice is learned, not instinctive. (James, 1995:60)

Psychologist Theodore W. Adorno and his colleagues (1950) concluded that highly prejudiced individuals tend to have an *authoritarian personality,* **which is characterized by excessive conformity, submissiveness to authority, intolerance, insecurity, a high level of superstition, a propensity for stereotyping, and rigid thinking** (Adorno et al., 1950). This personality, moreover, is most likely to develop in a family environment in which dominating parents who are anxious about status use physical discipline but show very little love in raising their children (Adorno et al., 1950). Other scholars have linked prejudiced attitudes to traits such as being submissive to authority, extreme anger toward outgroups, and conservative religious and political beliefs (Altemeyer, 1981, 1988; Weigel and Howes, 1985).

MEASURING PREJUDICE   To measure levels of prejudice, some social scientists use the concept of

The media are one of the most powerful sources of information in society, influencing the way we look at the world, how we understand it, and the manner in which we experience and relate to it. In other words, the media provide a "window on the world." For many Canadians, the media are the primary source of information about racial and ethnic groups. For example, the media relay information about who racial minorities are, what they want, why, how they propose to achieve their goals, and with what consequences for Canadian society. Racial minorities have accused Canada's mass media of slanted coverage; descriptions of the coverage have ranged from unfair and inadequate to racist. The following are examples of how B.C. journalist Doug Collins has discussed visible minorities and Aboriginal peoples in his columns in the *North Shore News*:

> The result is that Vancouver is becoming a suburb of Asia; Toronto, once the Queen City of English Canada, has become the tower of Babel, with every race except ours bawling for special rights and receiving them. Montreal is a target for the enlightened folk of Haiti. And the politicians wouldn't care if voodooism became the leading religion.
>
> The Third World is occupying the classrooms of much of the Lower Mainland. This is clear from the statistics and the pictures on TV. Hardly a White face in sight. Which should tell you something about why we have to have free lunches. But no one wants to say it.
>
> What saving the country boils down to is handing out more dough to the French and the ever-squawking Indians who know they are dealing with dummies and never had it so good until we turned up and showed them the wheel.

---

social distance, **which refers to the extent to which people are willing to interact and establish relationships with members of racial and ethnic groups other than their own** (Park and Burgess, 1921). Sociologist Emory Bogardus (1925, 1968) developed a scale to measure social distance in specific situations. Using the scale, he asked respondents to answer yes or no to the following seven questions with regard to members of various racial and ethnic groups:

1. I would marry or accept as a close relative.
2. I would accept as a close friend.
3. I would accept as a next-door neighbour.
4. I would accept in my school or church.
5. I would accept in my community but would not have contact with.
6. I would accept as a resident of my country but not in my community.
7. I would not accept at all even as a resident of my country.

He concluded that some groups were consistently ranked as more desirable than others for close interpersonal contact. More recently, analysts have found that whites who accept racial stereotypes desire greater social distance from people of colour than do whites who reject negative stereotypes (Krysan and Farley, 1993). While the Bogardus social distance scale has been used in numerous studies around the world, use of the scale for social distance research in Canada has been limited.

Discrimination

While prejudice refers to attitudes and beliefs, discrimination refers to the process by which these negative attitudes are put into practice. *Discrimination* **involves actions or practices of dominant group members (or their representatives) that have a harmful impact on members of a subordinate group** (Feagin and Feagin, 1997).

BOX 10.2

CONTINUED

The issue is whether the Holocaust took place. In other words, whether the Hitler regime deliberately set out to kill all the Jews it could get its hands on, and that 6,000,000 died as a result. More and more, I am coming to the conclusion that it [the Holocaust] didn't. (Darling thoughts that could land a guy in jail in this free country of ours!)

The response to these articles has been mixed. Although a complaint against Collins was filed with the British Columbia Press Council, the council dismissed it. In 1993, the British Columbia Organization to Fight Racism (BCOFR) was appalled when it learned that the Governor General of Canada had presented Collins with an award that honours Canadians who have made a significant contribution to their fellow citizens, their community, or Canada. Collins was described as a "controversial columnist for the *North Shore News* who forces people to think for themselves and re-evaluate commonly held opinions." Finally, in 1999, the B.C. Human Rights Tribunal ordered Collins to pay a $2000 fine to businessman Harry Abrams for exposing Jews to hatred in contravention of the Human Rights Act.

What do you think? Is there an effective way to reconcile the apparently contradictory goals of freedom of expression and freedom from discrimination? If not, perhaps we need to re-examine which of these goals should take priority.

Source: Doug Collins, quotations from various articles in the *North Shore News*, North Vancouver, B.C. © North Shore News. Reprinted by permission.

For example, people who are prejudiced toward South Asian, Jewish, or Aboriginal people may refuse to hire them, rent an apartment to them, or allow their children to play with them. In these instances, discrimination involves the differential treatment of minority group members not because of their ability or merit, but because of irrelevant characteristics such as skin colour or language preference. Discriminatory actions vary in severity from the use of derogatory labels to violence against individuals and groups. Discrimination takes two basic forms: *de jure*, or legal discrimination, which is encoded in laws; and *de facto*, or informal discrimination, which is entrenched in social customs and institutions. De jure discrimination has been supported with explicitly discriminatory laws such as the Chinese Exclusionary Act, which restricted immigration to Canada on the basis of race, or the Nuremberg laws passed in Nazi Germany, which imposed restrictions on Jews. The Indian Act provides another example of *de jure* discrimination. According to the Act, status Indian women lost their "status rights" if they married someone who was not a status Indian, while status Indian men did not. An amendment to the Indian Act in 1985 ended this legalized sex discrimination. Section 15 of the Charter of Rights and Freedom prohibits discrimination on the basis of race, ethnicity, or origin. As a result, many cases of de jure discrimination have been eliminated. De facto discrimination is more subtle and less visible to public scrutiny and, therefore, much more difficult to eradicate.

Prejudice and discrimination do not always go hand in hand—discrimination can exist without prejudice, and prejudice may flourish without expressing itself in discriminatory action (Fleras and Elliott, 1996). This was demonstrated in a classic study conducted in the early 1930s. Richard LaPiere travelled around the United States with a Chinese couple, stopping at over 250 restaurants and hotels along the way. The per-

---

FIGURE 10.1   Merton's Typology of Prejudice and Discrimination

	Prejudiced attitude?	Discriminatory behaviour?
Unprejudiced nondiscriminator	No	No
Unprejudiced discriminator	No	Yes
Prejudiced nondiscriminator	Yes	No
Prejudiced discriminator	Yes	Yes

---

vasive anti-Oriental prejudice of the time led LaPiere to assume that the travellers would be refused service in most of the hotels and restaurants at which they intended to stop. However, LaPiere was wrong—only one establishment refused service to LaPiere and his friends. Several months later LaPiere sent letters to all the establishments they had visited, asking if they would serve "members of the Chinese race" as guests in their establishments. Ninety-two percent of the establishments that had earlier accepted LaPiere and his guests replied that Chinese people would not be welcome. This study is one of many examples of sociological research that reveals the discrepancy between what people say and what they do (Robertson, 1977).

As shown in Figure 10.1, sociologist Robert Merton (1949) identified four combinations of attitudes and responses. *Unprejudiced nondiscriminators* are not personally prejudiced and do not discriminate against others. These are individuals who believe in equality for all. *Unprejudiced discriminators* may have no personal prejudices but still engage in discriminatory behaviour because of peer group pressure or economic, political, or social interests—for example, an employee who has no personal hostility toward members of certain groups but is encouraged not to hire them by senior management. *Prejudiced nondiscriminators* hold personal prejudices but do not discriminate due to peer pressure, legal demands, or a desire for profits. Such individuals are often referred to as "timid bigots" because they are reluctant to translate their attitudes into action (especially when prejudice is considered to be "politically incorrect"). Finally, *prejudiced discriminators* hold personal prejudices and actively discriminate against others—for example, the landlord who refuses to rent an apartment to an Aboriginal couple and then readily justifies his actions on the basis of racist stereotypes.

Racism

Racism is a complex phenomenon that displays itself in a number of different forms. In his book *Is God a Racist?: The Right Wing in Canada*, Stanley Barrett discusses one of the less recognizable forms:

> If racists as a category all wore horns, the battle against them would be a great deal easier ... The type that chilled me the most, in fact, was not the hard-nosed bully who wanted to kick somebody's teeth in, but rather the highly educated man, wealthy and sophisticated, who sat sipping his cognac while elaborating on the nobility of the

Members of white supremacy groups such as the Ku Klux Klan are rednecked racists; they often use members of subordinate racial and ethnic groups as scapegoats for societal problems over which they have no control.

white race and the necessity of excising the "mud people" from our midst. (1987:16)

Racism involves elements of prejudice, ethnocentrism, stereotyping, and discrimination. For example, racism is present in the belief that some racial or ethnic groups are superior while others are inferior; this belief is a prejudice. Racism may be the basis for unfair treatment toward members of a racial or ethnic group. In this case the racism involves discrimination. Fleras and Elliott (1996) developed the most inclusive definition of racism, which incorporates both racial prejudice and discrimination. They define **racism as "an organized set of beliefs about the innate inferiority of some racial groups, combined with the power to transform these ideas into practices that deny or exclude equality of treatment on the basis of race"** (1996:98). Fleras and Elliott (1996) make distinctions between a number of different types of racism.

REDNECKED RACISM *Rednecked racism* **is overt racism and may take the form of public statements about the "inferiority" of members of a racial or ethnic group.** Instances of rednecked racism are readily available in Canada. Racist, white supremacist groups including the White Aryan Nation, the Western Guard, and the Ku Klux Klan are active in Canada. These groups have relied on violence to create an environment of fear and hatred against minorities throughout Canada and the United States. According to

Warren Kinsella (1994), white hate groups disseminate their propaganda primarily through telephone hotlines, the Internet, and disinformation campaigns by hatemongers. White supremacist groups perceive themselves as the "saviours of the White race and Western Christian civilization" (Barrett, 1987:90). (See Chapter 3 for more on hate groups.)

White supremacist groups are not the only rednecked racists in Canada. Barrett (1987) suggests that the ideology of these right-wing groups may reflect the opinions of other Canadians. A 1988 survey of racist attitudes in Canada found that 19 percent of Canadians agree with "research findings" that assert Asians' superiority to whites, who were, in turn, "found" superior to blacks. In addition, 13 percent of those surveyed indicated they would exclude nonwhite groups from immigrating to Canada; 7 percent would not vote for a black political candidate; and 9 percent would not vote for a Chinese candidate (Henry et al., 1996). Research suggests that this type of racism is becoming increasingly unacceptable in Canadian society, and few people today will tolerate the open expression of racism. Both the Charter of Rights and Freedoms, as previously mentioned, and human rights legislation (see Box 10.3) have served to limit the expression of racist ideology or active racial discrimination. In Canada, overt acts of discrimination are now illegal. While blatant forms of racism have dissipated to some extent, less obvious expressions of bigotry and stereotyping remain prevalent in our society.

The decision by the RCMP to allow Sikh officers to wear turbans in uniform resulted in subliminal racism. Racist pins and calendars with turban-clad mounties appeared across Canada, and 250,000 Canadians signed a petition protesting that the turbans were "unCanadian."

Although the Charter and human rights legislation were designed to eliminate racism, they may have had the unintentional effect of "moving racism into the closet." As Fleras and Elliott explain, "Racist slurs ('those kind of people ... ') are now couched in a way that allows us to talk around or disguise our criticism of others by using somewhat more muted (polite) tones" (1996:74).

POLITE RACISM *Polite racism is an attempt to disguise a dislike of others through behaviour that appears to be nonprejudicial.* This type of racism may be operating when members of visible minority groups are ignored or turned down for jobs or promotions on a regular basis. A number of studies over the past two decades have examined the extent of racial prejudice and discrimination in the workplace. In the well-known study *Who Gets Work?* by Henry and Ginzberg (1984), black and white job seekers with similar job qualifications were sent to apply for entry positions advertised in a major newspaper. After several hundred applications were received and interviews held, it was revealed that whites received job offers three times more often than did black job applicants. In addition, telephone callers with accents, particularly those from South Asia and the Caribbean, were often screened out when they phoned to inquire about a job vacancy. This study was replicated in 1989 and the findings were much more favourable, with blacks slightly favoured in job offers: 20 compared with 18 offers to whites. However, individuals with accents were still more

likely to be screened out prior to being selected for an interview (Economic Council of Canada, 1991).

SUBLIMINAL RACISM *Subliminal racism involves an unconscious criticism of minorities.* Subliminal racism is not directly expressed, but is demonstrated in opposition to progressive minority policies (such as Canada's immigration policy) or programs (such as employment equity or affirmative action). For example, refugees are not condemned in blunt racist terminology, but their entry into Canada is viewed by some as taking unfair advantage of Canada's generosity. The decision by the Royal Canadian Mounted Police (RCMP) to allow Sikh officers to wear turbans while on duty resulted in petitions tabled in the House of Commons, which were signed by 250,000 Canadians and which protested "that a handful of Sikhs wearing turbans would crack up the RCMP" (Henry et al., 1996:136). The petitioners said they had nothing against Sikhs, but that turbans were "unCanadian," "an affront to majority values," "excessively demanding," and "too costly," among other things. Racist pins and calendars with depictions of turban-clad Mounties began appearing across Canada (Henry et al., 1996).

Subliminal racism, more than any other type of racism, demonstrates the ambiguity concerning racism. Values that support racial equality are publicly affirmed, while at the same time resentment at the prospect of moving over and making space for newcomers is also present. Subliminal

TABLE 10.2 **THE FACES OF RACISM**

	WHAT: CORE SLOGAN	WHY: DEGREE OF INTENT	HOW: STYLE OF EXPRESSION	WHERE: MAGNITUDE AND SCOPE	WHEN: LOCUS OF EXPRESSION
Rednecked Racism	"X" get out	conscious	personal and explicit	personal	interpersonal
Polite Racism	"Sorry, the job is taken."	moderate	discreet and subtle	personal	interpersonal
Subliminal Racism	"I'm not racist, but ..."	ambivalent	oblique	cultural	value conflicts
Institutional Racism	"X need not apply."	deliberate	blatant	institutional	rewards and entitlements
Systemic Racism	"We treat everyone the same here."	unintentional	impersonal	societal	rules and procedures

Source: Fleras and Elliott, 1996:84.

racism enables individuals to maintain two apparently conflicting values—one rooted in the egalitarian virtues of justice and fairness, the other in beliefs that result in resentment and selfishness (Fleras and Elliott, 1996).

INSTITUTIONALIZED RACISM *Institutionalized racism* is made up of the rules, procedures, and practices that directly and deliberately prevent minorities from having full and equal involvement in society. These actions are routinely carried out by a number of dominant group members based on the norms of the immediate organization or community (Feagin and Feagin, 1996).

In 1991, the Canadian Civil Liberties Association (CCLA) examined institutionalized discrimination in employment agencies. The CCLA randomly selected agencies in four cities in Ontario and asked whether the agencies would agree to refer only white people for the jobs that needed to be filled. Eleven of the fifteen agencies surveyed agreed to accept discriminatory job orders. The following are examples of the agencies' responses:

It is discrimination, but it can be done discreetly without anyone knowing. No problem with that.

That's no problem. It's between you and me. I don't tell anyone; you don't tell anyone.

You are paying to see the people you want to see.

Absolutely—definitely ... that request is pretty standard here.

That's not a problem. Apperance means a lot, whether it's colour or overweight people. (quoted in Henry et al., 1996:142)

What happens in actual cases of agencies using such discriminatory employment practices? Recently a complaint laid with the Ontario Human Rights Commission against two employment agencies in Toronto drew public attention to this issue. A settlement was reached in which the agencies agreed to develop policies against accepting discriminatory job requests, and employees received training in race relations and employment equity. Institutions can no longer openly discriminate against minorities without attracting legal sanctions, negative publicity, or consumer resistance (Fleras and Elliott, 1996).

SYSTEMIC RACISM *Systemic racism* refers to practices that have a harmful impact on subordinate group members even though the organizationally prescribed norms or regulations guiding these actions initially were established with no intent to harm. Institutions may have standards that have the unintended effect of excluding members of minority groups (Fleras and Elliott, 1996). For example, occupations such as police officer and firefighter had minimum weight, height, and educational requirements for job applicants. These criteria resulted in discrimination because they favoured white applicants over members of many minority groups, as well as males over females. Other examples of systemic racism include the requirement of a college or university degree for

BOX 10.3   CRITICAL THINKING

HUMAN RIGHTS LEGISLATION IN ACTION

Human rights legislation is grounded on the premise that all human beings are full and equal persons. As such, all persons have a fundamental right to life and freedom, equality, and dignity in all life pursuits. What legal recourse do individuals have who experience a violation of these basic human rights? How effective is present human rights legislation in curtailing these violations? These questions can be addressed by examining legal cases that have been brought forward by minority claimants under the provisions of human rights legislation in Canada.

In the first example, a claim of racial discrimination was made against a Victoria restaurant and the Victoria police by a black citizen of Canada. The complainant, born in St. Vincent, holds master's degrees from two Canadian universities and works as a health coordinator in British Columbia. While visiting Victoria, the complainant, a registered guest at a motor inn, went into the restaurant at the inn and sat down at the only available table. All other tables were occupied by nonblack patrons. He placed his order with a waiter, but

within five minutes was informed by a waitress that he would have to move so that she could seat two other persons at his table. He refused to move because he could see no other table available and because he had not, as yet, received his order. The police were called. Victoria police questioned him about his citizenship, threatened him with deportation, searched and handcuffed him, and then took him to jail and locked him up for eight hours. The complainant brought his case to the B.C. Human Rights Council, which found that the only reasonable inference that could be drawn was that the complainant was the subject of racial discrimination. The complainant was awarded $2000 for humiliation, embarrassment, and damage to his self-respect in the settlement of his claim against both the restaurant and the police. Do you think the amount awarded is sufficient compensation for the harm done in this case? Do you think this amount will deter future racist actions on the part of the organizations sanctioned? If not, what do you think an appropriate settlement would be?

nonspecialized jobs, employment regulations that require people to work on their Sabbath, and the policy of only recognizing university degrees and trade diplomas obtained in North America.

Systemic racism is normally reflected in statistical underrepresentation of certain groups within an institution or organization. For example, a given group may represent 15 percent of the general population but only 2 percent of those promoted to upper management positions in a large company. Efforts to eliminate this kind of disproportionate representation are the focus of employment equity legislation. The target groups for employment equity in Canada are visible minorities, women, persons with disabilities, and Aboriginal peoples. Strategies include modified admissions tests and requirements, enhanced recruitment of certain target groups, establish-

ment of hiring quotas for particular minority groups, or specialized training or employment programs for specific target groups. The most recent analysis of employment equity programs indicates that these programs have had the most significant effect on women and Aboriginal peoples, while people with disabilities have made the fewest gains. As for members of visible minorities, although they have higher levels of education on average than do other Canadians and very high labour force participation rates, they continue to be concentrated in low-status, low-paying occupations (Henry et al., 1996). It is important to note that effects of systemic discrimination on specific visible minority groups in Canada vary substantially, with blacks experiencing the greatest disadvantage in income and Asian groups, the least (Boyd, 1992).

BOX 10.3

CONTINUED

This case demonstrates that under human rights legislation the employer (the restaurant) is held responsible for the discriminatory acts of employees. In other words, what appeared to be a case of individual discrimination or racism was treated as an act of institutional racism. Thus, the onus is on those who control organizations to ensure that their employees respect the human rights of all persons. Do you agree?

A second and somewhat parallel case involves a claim filed with the Canadian Human Rights Commission that alleged institutional discrimination on the part of the RCMP. A Chinese Canadian, who was born in Halifax, filed a complaint of racial discrimination under the (federal) Canadian Human Rights Act, because an RCMP officer, who had stopped him for a driving offence, asked him whether he was a Canadian citizen and whether he was born in Canada. An internal

RCMP investigation following the lodging of the complaint revealed that the RCMP officer in question customarily interrogated members of visible ethnic minorities in the same way when he stopped them for speeding. The commission found that the officer's action was not an isolated case, but represented accepted RCMP practice. The commission concluded that the RCMP discriminated against suspects on the basis of racial origin and that such discrimination was unjustifiable. The commission ordered the RCMP to cease the practice in question and to issue a directive to this effect to all members of the force. The commission also recommended that the RCMP provide educational instruction to members of the force on the right to equal treatment of citizens from visible minorities. The RCMP was ordered to pay the complainant $250 for hurt and affront to dignity. What do you think of the penalty in this case?

Source: Adapted with permission from Kallen, 1991.

SOCIOLOGICAL PERSPECTIVES ON RACE AND ETHNIC RELATIONS

Interactionist, functionalist, and conflict analysts examine race and ethnic relations in different ways. Functionalists focus on the macrolevel intergroup processes that occur between members of majority and minority groups in society. Conflict theorists analyze power and economic differentials between the dominant group and subordinate groups. Interactionists examine how microlevel contacts between people may produce either greater racial tolerance or increased levels of hostility.

Interactionist Perspectives

What happens when people from different racial and ethnic groups come into contact with one another? In the *contact hypothesis*, interactionists point out that contact between people from divergent groups should lead to favourable attitudes and behaviour when certain factors are present. Members of each group must (1) have equal status, (2) pursue the same goals, (3) cooperate with one another to achieve their goals, and (4) receive positive feedback when they interact with one another in positive, nondiscriminatory ways (Allport, 1958; Coakley, 1994). For example, does participation in interracial sports teams promote intergroup cohesion and reduce prejudice? Scholars have found that increased contact may have little or no effect on existing prejudices and, in some circumstances, can even lead to an

The members of this adult education class are learning English as their second language. What type of assimilation does this represent?

increase in prejudice and conflict. If racial tension between players on teams is high enough, violence may erupt (Edwards, 1973; Lapchick, 1991). Why might sports contribute to prejudice? Sports events are highly competitive, and prejudice may be aggravated by the actions of players or spectators.

What happens when individuals meet someone who does not conform to their existing stereotype? Frequently, they ignore anything that contradicts the stereotype or interpret the situation to support their prejudices (Coakley, 1994). For example, a person who does not fit the stereotype may be seen as an exception—"You're not like other (persons of a particular race)."

When a person is seen as conforming to a stereotype, he or she may be treated simply as one of "you people." Former Los Angeles Lakers basketball star Earvin "Magic" Johnson (1992: 31–32) described how he was categorized along with all other African Americans when he was bused to a predominantly white school:

On the first day of [basketball] practice, my teammates froze me out. Time after time I was wide open, but nobody threw me the ball. At first I thought they just didn't see me. But I woke up after a kid named Danny Parks looked right at me and then took a long jumper. Which he missed.

I was furious, but I didn't say a word. Shortly after that, I grabbed a defensive rebound and took the ball all the way down for a basket. I did it again and a third time, too.

Finally Parks got angry and said, "Hey, pass the [bleeping] ball."

That did it. I slammed down the ball and glared at him. Then I exploded. "I knew this would happen!" I said. "That's why I didn't want to come to this [bleeping] school in the first place!"

"Oh, yeah? Well, you people are all the same," he said. "You think you're gonna come in here and do whatever you want? Look, hotshot, your job is to get the rebound. Let us do the shooting."

The interaction between Johnson and Parks demonstrates that when people from different racial and ethnic groups come into contact with one another, they may treat one another as stereotypes, not as individuals. Eventually, Johnson and Parks were able to work out most of their differences. "There's nothing like winning to help people get along," Johnson explained (1992:32).

Interactionist perspectives make us aware of the importance of intergroup contact and the fact that it may either intensify or reduce racial and ethnic stereotyping and prejudice.

Functionalist Perspectives

How do members of subordinate racial and ethnic groups become a part of the dominant group? To answer this question, early functionalists studied immigration and patterns of majority and minority group interaction.

ASSIMILATION   *Assimilation* is a process by which members of subordinate racial and ethnic groups become absorbed into the dominant culture. To some analysts, assimilation is functional because it

BOX 10.4

CONTINUED

Conflict between Protestants and Catholics in Northern Ireland has continued for hundreds of years. Here, Londonderry Protestants approach the Catholic Bogside neighbourhood as tensions rise in August 1996.

in those days. Dresden, home of the historic Uncle Tom's cabin, made national headlines in 1954 when Blacks tested the local restaurants after the passage of the Fair Accommodation Practices Act and found that two openly refused to serve them. This came as no surprise, given that for years certain eateries, hotels, and recreational clubs were restricted to us, and at one time Blacks could only sit in designated sections of movie theatres (usually the balcony) if admitted at all. (Shadd, 1991:1)

One of the most blatant examples of segregation in Canada is the federal government reserve system for status Indians, which resulted in segregation of Aboriginal peoples on reserves in remote areas across the country.

Although legally sanctioned forms of racial segregation have been all but eliminated, de facto segregation, which is enforced by custom, still exists. Although functionalist explanations provide a description of how some early white ethnic immigrants assimilated into the cultural mainstream, they do not adequately account for the persistent racial segregation and economic inequality experienced by minority group members.

Conflict Perspectives

Why do some ethnic groups continue to experience subjugation after many years? Conflict theorists focus on economic stratification and access to power in their analysis of race and ethnic relations.

INTERNAL COLONIALISM   Conflict theorists use the term *internal colonialism* to refer to a situation in which members of a racial or ethnic group are conquered or colonized and forcibly placed under the economic and political control of the dominant group. Groups that have been subjected to internal colonialism often remain in subordinate positions longer than groups that voluntarily migrated to North America.

Aboriginal peoples in Canada were colonized by Europeans and others who invaded their lands and conquered them. In the process, Aboriginal peoples lost property, political rights, aspects of their culture, and often their lives (Das Gupta, 1995). The capitalist class acquired cheap labour and land through this government-sanctioned racial exploitation. The effects of past internal colonialism are reflected today in the number of Aboriginal people who live in extreme poverty on government reserves (Das Gupta, 1995).

The experiences of internally colonized groups are unique in three ways: (1) they have been forced to exist in a society other than their own; (2) they have been kept out of the economic and political mainstream, so that it is difficult for them to compete with dominant group members; and (3) they have been subjected to severe attacks on their own culture, which may lead to its extinction (Blauner, 1972).

The internal colonialism model is rooted in historical foundations of racial and ethnic inequality in North America. However, it tends to view all voluntary immigrants as having many more opportunities than do members of colonized groups. Thus, this model does not explain the continued exploitation of some immigrant groups, such as Chinese, Filipinos, and Vietnamese, and the greater acceptance of others, primarily those from northern Europe (Cashmore, 1996).

THE SPLIT-LABOUR-MARKET THEORY Who benefits from the exploitation of visible minorities? Dual or split-labour-market theory states that both white workers and members of the capitalist class benefit from the exploitation of visible minorities. *Split labour market* refers to the division of the economy into two areas of employment: a primary sector or upper tier, composed of higher-paid (usually dominant group) workers in more secure jobs, and a secondary sector or lower tier, made up of lower-paid (often subordinate group) workers in jobs with little security and hazardous working conditions (Bonacich, 1972, 1976). According to this perspective, white workers in the upper tier may use racial discrimination against nonwhites to protect their positions. These actions most often occur when upper-tier workers feel threatened by lower-tier workers hired by capitalists to reduce labour costs and maximize corporate profits. In the past, immigrants were a source of cheap labour that employers could use to break strikes and keep wages down. Agnes Calliste (1987) applied the split-labour-market theory in her study, "Sleeping Car Porters in Canada." Calliste found a doubly submerged split labour market, with three levels of stratification in this area of employment. While "white" trade unions were unable to restrict access to porter positions on the basis of race, they were able to impose differential pay scales. Consequently, black porters received less pay than white porters, even though they were doing the same work. Furthermore, the labour market was doubly submerged because black immigrant workers from the United States received even less pay than both black and white Canadian porters. Throughout history, higher-paid workers have responded with racial hostility and joined movements to curtail immigration and thus do away with the source of cheap labour (Marger, 1997).

Proponents of the split-labour-market theory suggest that white workers benefit from racial and ethnic antagonisms. However, these analysts typically do not examine the interactive effects of race, class, and gender in the workplace.

A Feminist Perspective on Race and Gender

The term *gendered racism* refers to the interactive effect of racism and sexism in the exploitation of women of colour. According to social psychologist Philomena Essed (1991), women's particular position must be explored within each racial or ethnic group, because their experiences will not have been the same as the men's in each grouping.

All workers are not equally exploited by capitalists. Gender and race or ethnicity are important in this exploitation. For example, jobs are race-typed and gender-typed. Consider a registered nurse and a custodian in a hospital. What race and gender are they likely to be? Did a white woman and a man of colour come to mind? Most jobs have similar race and gender designations. Often, the jobs people hold are linked to their class, race, and gender. Consequently, the effect of class on our life chances is inseparable from the effects of our gender and race or ethnicity. The split labour market, then, involves not only class but also race, ethnicity, and gender (Amott and Matthaei, 1991). Historically, the high-paying primary labour market has been monopolized by

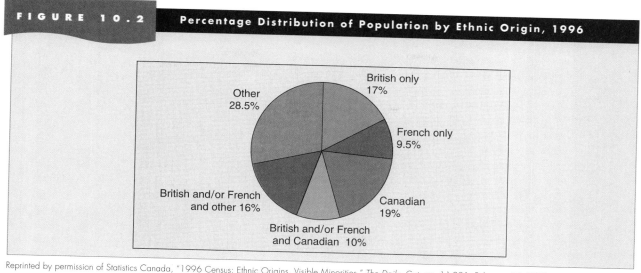

FIGURE 10.2 — Percentage Distribution of Population by Ethnic Origin, 1996

British only 17%

French only 9.5%

Other 28.5%

British and/or French and other 16%

British and/or French and Canadian 10%

Canadian 19%

Reprinted by permission of Statistics Canada, "1996 Census: Ethnic Origins, Visible Minorities," *The Daily*, Cat. no. 11-001, February 17, 1998.

white men. People of colour and most white women more often hold lower-tier jobs. Below that tier is the underground sector of the economy, characterized by illegal or quasi-legal activities such as drug trafficking, prostitution, and working in sweatshops that do not meet minimum wage and safety standards. Many undocumented workers and some white women and people of colour attempt to earn a living in this sector (Amott and Matthaei, 1991).

ETHNIC GROUPS IN CANADA

At the turn of the century, the Canadian population was predominantly made up of French Canadians (30.7 percent) and British Canadians (57 percent). As Figure 10.2 indicates, in 1996 approximately one-third of Canada's population claimed ethnic origins other than French, British, or Canadian. Given the diversity of our population, imposing any kind of conceptual order on a discussion of ethnic groups in Canada is difficult. A detailed historical account of the unique experiences of each group is beyond the scope of this chapter. Instead, we will look briefly at some of the unique ethnic groups in Canada. In the process, we will examine a brief history of racism with respect to each group.

First Nations

Canada's Aboriginal peoples are believed to have migrated to North America from Asia an esti-

mated 40,000 years ago (Dyck, 1996). Aboriginal peoples are an extremely diverse group. Today, the term *Native, First Nations,* or *Aboriginal* refers to approximately fifty-five sovereign peoples including the Inuit, Cree, Micmac, Blackfoot, Iroquois, and Haida. Other categories of Aboriginal peoples are status Indians (those Indians with legal rights under the Indian Act), nonstatus Indians (those without legal rights), Métis, and Inuit. Those who settled in the southern part of Canada, the Yukon, and the Mackenzie Valley, can be termed *North American Indians.* Those located in the eastern Arctic and northern islands, who were formerly referred to as Eskimos, are now referred to as *Inuit.* A third category, *Métis,* who mostly live on the Prairies, are descendants of Indian and non-Indian unions (primarily French settlers and Indian women).

When European settlers arrived on this continent, the Aboriginal inhabitants' way of life was changed forever. Experts estimate that between one and twelve million Aboriginal people lived in North America at this time; however, their numbers had been reduced to less than 240,000 by 1900 (Churchill, 1994). What factors contributed to this drastic depopulation?

GENOCIDE, FORCED MIGRATION, AND FORCED ASSIMILATION Aboriginal people have been the victims of genocide and forced migration. Many Native Americans either were massacred or died from European diseases (such as typhoid, smallpox, and measles) and starvation (Wagner and Stearn, 1945; Cook, 1973). In battle,

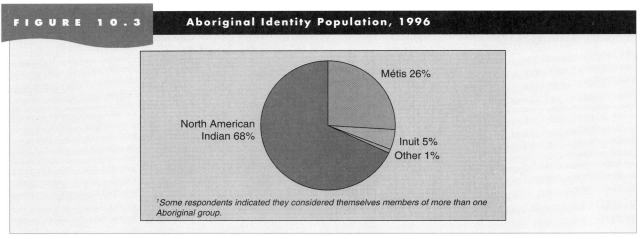

FIGURE 10.3 **Aboriginal Identity Population, 1996**

Métis 26%

North American
Indian 68%

Inuit 5%
Other 1%

¹Some respondents indicated they considered themselves members of more than one
Aboriginal group.

Reprinted by permission of Statistics Canada, "1996 Census: Aboriginal Data," adapted from *The Daily*, Cat. no. 11-001, January 13, 1998.

Aboriginal people often were no match for the Europeans, who had the latest weaponry (Amott and Matthaei, 1991). Europeans justified their aggression by stereotyping Aboriginals as "savages" and "heathens" (Takaki, 1993).

Entire nations were forced to move in order to accommodate the white settlers. The "Trail of Tears" was one of the most disastrous of the forced migrations to occur in North America. In the coldest part of the winter of 1832, over half of the Cherokee Nation died during or as a result of their forced relocation from the southeastern United States to the Indian Territory in Oklahoma (Thornton, 1984). The colonization of the Aboriginal population was far less brutal in Canada than in the United States. However, it is not clear whether this more benign conquest left Aboriginals in Canada any better off than their counterparts in the United States in the long run (Weinfeld, 1995:48).

Indian rights were clearly defined in the Royal Proclamation of 1763, which divided up the territory acquired by Britain. In a large area called Indian Territory, the purchase or settlement of land was forbidden without a treaty. This is sometimes called the principle of "voluntary cession" (Dyck, 1996:154). The government broke treaty after treaty as it engaged in a policy of wholesale removal of indigenous nations in order to clear the land for settlement by Anglo-Saxon "pioneers" (Green, 1977; Churchill, 1994). The 1867 Constitution Act gave jurisdiction over Indians and lands reserved for the Indians to the federal government. The Canadian government then passed the Indian Act of 1876, which provided for federal government control of almost every aspect of Indian life. The regulations under the Act included prohibitions against owning land, voting, and purchasing and consuming alcohol. Later provisions prevented Aboriginal people from leaving reserves without permission and a ticket from the agent (Bolaria and Li, 1988). It is clear that the Indian Act was designed to promote assimilation; Aboriginal peoples were to adopt the cultural attitudes and norms of the dominant culture and give up their own cultural traditions (including their values, customs, and language).

Aboriginal children were placed in residential boarding schools to facilitate their assimilation into the dominant culture. The Jesuits and other missionaries who ran these schools believed that Aboriginal peoples should not be left in their "inferior" natural state and considered it their mission to replace Aboriginal culture with Christian beliefs, values, rituals, and practices (Bolaria and Li, 1988). Many Aboriginal children who attended these schools were sexually, physically, and emotionally abused. They were not allowed to speak their language or engage in any of their traditional cultural practices. The coercive and oppressive nature of this educational experience is one of the most blatant examples of institutionalized racism (Henry et al., 1996:62).

ABORIGINAL PEOPLES TODAY In 1996, almost 800,000 individuals reported that they were North American Indian, Métis, or Inuit—about 3 percent of Canada's total population (Statistics Canada, 1998). Figure 10.3 displays the composition of this population.

There are several tribal groups, living in nearly 600 bands. Although the majority of registered Indians live on reserves, the majority of the total Aboriginal population lives off reserves. The

TABLE 10.3	DISTRIBUTION BY PROVINCE AND TERRITORY OF THOSE REPORTING ABORIGINAL ORIGINS, 1996

	ABORIGINAL POPULATION				
	Total[1]	North American Indian [2,3]	Métis	Inuit	Percentages of Provincial and Territorial Populations
Canada	**799,010**	**554,290**	**210,190**	**41,080**	
Newfoundland	14,205	5,430	4,685	4,265	2.6
Prince Edward Island	950	825	120	15	0.7
Nova Scotia	12,380	11,340	860	210	1.4
New Brunswick	10,250	9,180	975	120	1.4
Quebec	71,415	47,600	16,075	8,300	1.0
Ontario	141,525	118,830	22,790	1,300	1.3
Manitoba	128,685	82,990	46,195	360	11.7
Saskatchewan	111,245	75,205	36,535	190	11.4
Alberta	122,840	72,645	50,745	795	4.6
Yukon	6,175	5,530	565	110	20.1
Northwest Territories	39,690	11,400	3,895	24,600	61.9

1. The total of North American Indian, Métis, and Inuit does not equal the total Aboriginal population because 6,415 persons reported identifying with more than one group.

2. Single and multiple responses have been combined.

3. Users should note that the counts for North American Indian may be affected by the incomplete enumeration of 177 Indian reserves and settlements in the 1996 Census, depending on the geographic area under study.

Reprinted by permission of Statistics Canada, "1996 Census: Aboriginal Data," *The Daily*, Cat. no. 11-001, January 13, 1998.

Aboriginal population is unevenly distributed across Canada, with the heaviest concentrations of Aboriginal Canadians in western and northern Canada, as Table 10.3 indicates.

Aboriginal peoples are the most disadvantaged racial or ethnic group in Canada in terms of income, employment, housing, nutrition, and health. The life chances of Aboriginal peoples who live on reservations are especially limited. They have the highest rates of infant mortality and death by exposure and malnutrition. They also have high rates of tuberculosis, alcoholism, and suicide. The overall life expectancy of Aboriginal people in Canada is ten years less than that of non-Aboriginals; this is largely due to poor health services and inadequate housing on reserves (Dyck, 1996). Aboriginal peoples also have had very limited educational opportunities (the functional illiteracy rate for Aboriginal peoples is 45 percent compared with the overall Canadian rate of 17 percent), and they have a very high rate of unemployment (their jobless rate averages nearly 70 percent) (Henry et al., 1996).

In spite of the odds against them, many Aboriginal peoples resist oppression. National organizations like the Assembly of First Nations, Inuit Tapirisat, the Native Council of Canada, and the Métis National Council have been instrumental in bringing the demands of those they represent into the political and constitutional arenas. Of these demands, the major ones have been and still are self-government, Aboriginal rights, and the resolution of land claims (see Frideres, 1993). Meanwhile, Aboriginal women's groups such as the Native Women's Association of Canada have publicized the harmful conditions (including child sexual abuse, incest, and wife battering) that exist on reserves.

One of the first major successes in the quest for self-determination is the creation of Nunavut (which means "our land"). The vision of Nunavut came to be in 1993 when the Nunavut Land Claims Agreement was signed. Under the terms of this agreement, the Inuit have received title to 350,000 square kilometres of land in the Northwest Territories, including mineral rights to 36,000 square kilometres. The agreement also provides financial compensation of $1.14 billion. The territorial government is controlled by the Inuit with the assistance of a system of cooperatives and the Inuit Broadcasting Corporation. Nunavut is a positive step for the Inuit in establishing their rights of self-determination over their unique culture.

Charter Europeans

WHITE ANGLO-SAXON PROTESTANTS (BRITISH CANADIANS)

Whereas Aboriginal peoples have been among the most disadvantaged peoples, white Anglo-Saxon Protestants (WASPs) have been the most privileged group in this country. Although many English settlers initially came to North America as indentured servants or as prisoners, they quickly emerged as the dominant group, creating a core culture (including language, laws, and holidays) to which all other groups were expected to adapt. Most WASPs do not think of themselves as belonging to a particular race or ethnic group. As one young woman commented, "I don't think of myself as white, I don't feel superior. I just felt normal" (quoted in Fleras and Elliott, 1996:35). The experience of being a WASP in Canadian society is an experience of privilege. But few Canadians are likely to acknowledge this privileged status—nor that it is derived from skin colour. Even fewer are prepared to concede that whiteness is directly related to the underprivileged status of others (Fleras and Elliott, 1996). The following student's comments, however, reflect a definite awareness of what it means to be a white Anglo-Saxon male:

> I am a member of a majority group that has a great deal of power ... It is White culture that I experience day to day and the very fact that discrimination is rarely an issue for me personally results in my own racial identity becoming an invisible thing. The powerful people within my experience, directly or indirectly—the politician, the employer, the teacher, the social worker—are invariably White. I know that my race will not be an issue with most of the people I must deal with, as I know we will have a commonality from the start. Being in the majority in all three origins [White, English, Canadian], there is also a good chance that either culturally, ethnically or both, our backgrounds will be similar. Neither will I expect my values or behavior to be an issue because I fit into the "norm." (quoted in James, 1995:47)

Class, Gender, and WASPs Like members of other racial and ethnic groups, not all WASPs are alike.

Social class and gender affect their life chances and opportunities. For example, members of the working class and the poor do not have political and economic power; men in the capitalist class do. Likewise, WASP women have not always had the same rights as the men of their group. Women historically were viewed as the property of men and were denied equal protection under the law and the right to vote. In short, while WASP women have the privilege of a dominant racial position, they do not have the gender-related privileges of men (Amott and Matthaei, 1991).

FRENCH CANADIANS

The European colonization of Canada began with the exploration and settlement of New France. In 1608, the first permanent settlement in New France was established at Quebec City, by Samuel de Champlain. At this time France's North American empire extended from Hudson Bay to Louisiana.

Following the British conquest of the French in Canada in the Seven Years' War (1756–1763), Canada became a British dominion and the French found themselves in an inferior position (Weinfeld, 1995). The French were able to maintain French civil law, language, and religion; however, the overall economic, social, and political power passed to English Canada.

The British North America Act (1867) formally acknowledged the rights and privileges of the French and British as the founding or charter groups of Canadian society. With Confederation, it was assumed that in the future French- and English-speaking groups would co-exist and complement one another. However, during the period between Confederation and World War II, the French struggled for cultural survival because English-speaking Canadians controlled the major economic institutions in both English Canada and Quebec.

During the period known as the Quiet Revolution (1960–1966), Quebec nationalism grew sharply. Under the leadership of newly elected Premier Jean Lesage in 1960, Quebec began undergoing a rapid process of modernization. During this time the authority of the Catholic Church over the educational system was reduced as the Quebec government established a department of education. More French Canadians began pursuing higher education, particularly in business and science. The church also lost some of its influence over moral issues, which was reflected in a declining birth rate and an increase in common-law marriages. Finally, nonfrancophone

Life chances are extremely limited for Aboriginal peoples who live in Aboriginal communities. These boys are participating in the pole twist—a traditional Inuit game. Despite their athletic prowess, it is unlikely that they will become members of professional sports teams.

immigrants were challenging French culture by choosing to learn English and having their children learn English, rather than French. The result? Francophones came to view their language and culture as endangered. As a result, they rejected their Canadian identity and adopted a distinctly Québécois identity.

In 1976, René Lévesque's Parti Québécois government introduced Bill 101, a controversial law that established French as the sole official language in Quebec. In 1980, the Lévesque government held a referendum on whether to negotiate a relationship of "sovereignty association" with Canada. The proposal was rejected, but the matter was not resolved (see Chapter 14). A second referendum, held on October 30, 1995, also ended in a loss for the sovereignists, but this time by a narrow margin of only 1 percent.

French Canadians Today   Today approximately 25 percent of the Canadian population is francophone, 85 percent of which is located in Quebec. Many Quebec nationalists now see independence or separation as the ultimate protection against cultural and linguistic assimilation, as well as the route to economic power. As political scientist Rand Dyck comments,

[G]iven its geographic concentration in Quebec and majority control of a large province, and given their modern-day self-consciousness and self-confidence, the French fact in Canada cannot be ignored. If English Canada wants Quebec to remain a part of the country, it cannot go back to the easy days of pre-1960 unilingualism. (1996:185)

French Canadians have at least forced Canada to take its second language and culture seriously, which is an important step toward attaining cultural pluralism.

Canada's Immigrants

Home to approximately five million foreign-born immigrants, Canada is well described as a land of immigrants. According to the 1996 census, over three-quarters of immigrants arriving in Canada today are members of a visible minority group (Statistics Canada, 1998h). Canada's policies toward some of these groups have been far from exemplary. In fact, initial Canadian immigration policies have been described as essentially racist in orientation, assimilationist in intent, and segregationist in content (Fleras and Elliott, 1996). A "racial pecking order" sorted out potential immigrants on the basis of racial characteristics and capacity for assimilation (Lupul, 1988). As much energy was expended in keeping out certain "types" as was put into encouraging others to settle (Whitaker, 1991). A preferred category was that of *white ethnics*—a term coined to identify immigrants who came from European countries other than England, such as Scotland, Ireland, Poland, Italy, Greece, Germany, Yugoslavia, and Russia and other former Soviet republics. Immigration from "white" countries was encouraged to ensure the British character of Canada. With the exception of visa formalities, this category of "preferred" immigrants was virtually exempt from entry restrictions. On the other hand, Jews and Mediterranean populations required special permits for entry, and Asian populations were admitted grudgingly, mostly to serve as cheap labour for Canadian capitalist expansion. The restrictions regarding the Chinese, Japanese, and Jews highlighted the racist dimension of Canada's early immigration policies (Satzewich, 1991).

CHINESE CANADIANS   The initial wave of Chinese immigration began in the 1850s, when Chinese men were "pushed" from China by harsh economic conditions and "pulled" to Canada by the promise of gold in British Columbia and employment opportunities. Nearly 16,000 Chinese were brought to Canada at this time to lay track for the Canadian Pacific Railway. The work was brutally hard and dangerous, living conditions were appalling, food and shelter were insufficient, and due to scurvy and smallpox there was a high fatality rate. These immigrants were "welcomed" only as long as there was a shortage of white workers. However, they were not permitted to bring their wives and children with them or to have sexual relations with white women, because of the fear they would spread the "yellow menace" (Henry et al., 1995). After the railroad was built, the welcome mat was quickly rolled up.

The Chinese were subjected to extreme prejudice and were referred to by derogatory terms such as "coolies," "heathens," and "Chinks." Some were attacked by working-class whites who feared they would lose their jobs to Chinese immigrants. In 1885 the federal government passed its first anti-Chinese bill, the purpose of which was to limit Chinese immigration. Other hostile legislation included a range of racist exclusionary policies including prohibiting the Chinese from voting, serving in public office, serving on juries, participating in white labour unions, and working in the professions of law and pharmacy. In 1888, a head tax was imposed on all Chinese males arriving in Canada. In 1903, the tax was raised to $500 from $100 in a further attempt to restrict entry to Canada (Satzewich, 1991). Not until after World War II were these discriminatory policies removed from the Immigration Act. After immigration laws were further relaxed in the 1960s, the second and largest wave of Chinese immigration occurred, with immigrants coming primarily from Hong Kong and Taiwan (Henry et al., 1995).

JAPANESE CANADIANS Japanese immigrants began arriving in Canada in large numbers after Chinese immigration tapered off. Like Chinese immigrants two decades earlier, the Japanese were viewed as a threat by white workers and became victims of stereotyping and discrimination.

In 1907 an organization known as the Asiatic Exclusion League was formed with the mandate of restricting admission of Asians to Canada. Following the arrival of a ship carrying over a thousand Japanese and a few hundred Sikhs, the league carried out a demonstration that precipitated a race riot. A "gentlemen's agreement,"

As more Chinese Canadians have made gains in education and employment, many have also made a conscious effort to increase awareness of Chinese culture and to develop a sense of unity and cooperation. This Chinese Dragon parade exemplifies this desire to maintain traditional celebrations.

negotiated in 1908, permitted entry only of certain categories of Japanese on a fixed quota basis.

Japanese Canadians experienced one of the most vicious forms of discrimination ever sanctioned by Canadian law. During World War II, when Canada was at war with Japan, nearly 23,000 people of Japanese ancestry (13,300 of whom were Canadian-born) were placed in internment camps because they were seen as a security threat (Takaki, 1993). They remained in the camps for more than two years despite the total lack of evidence that they posed a danger to this country. Many of the camps were situated in remote locales in British Columbia, Alberta, and Manitoba; they had guard towers, and were surrounded by barbed-wire fences. This action was a direct violation of the citizenship rights of Japanese Canadians. Only the Japanese were singled out for such harsh treatment; German immigrants avoided this fate even though Canada was at war with both Japan and Germany. Four decades after these events, the Canadian government issued an apology for its actions and agreed to pay $20,000 to each person who had been placed in an internment camp (Henry et al., 1995).

SOUTH ASIANS South Asians also had to deal with discriminatory immigration laws. One of these

FIGURE 10.4

Place of Birth of Immigrants by Period of Immigration, 1996

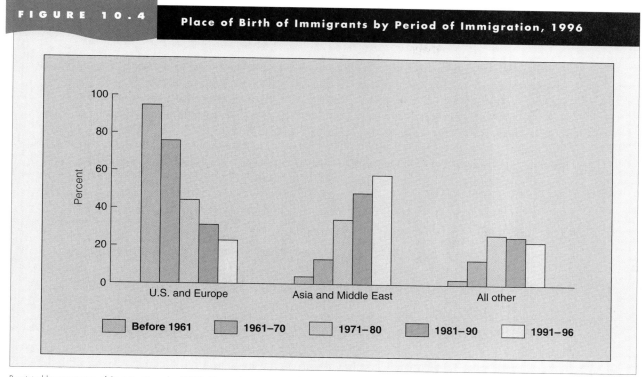

Reprinted by permission of Statistics Canada, "1996 Census: Immigration and Citizenship," adapted from *The Daily*, Cat. no. 11-001. November 4, 1997, p. 3.

laws was the "continuous passage" rule of 1908, which specified that South Asians could immigrate only if they came directly from India and did not stop at any ports on the way. This law made it almost impossible for them to enter the country, since no ships made direct journeys from India. South Asians who did manage to immigrate to Canada faced hostile employers and distrustful citizens. Their property and businesses were frequently attacked, and they were denied citizenship and the right to vote in British Columbia until 1947 (Henry et al., 1995).

JEWISH CANADIANS   In 1942, Canada closed its doors to Jews fleeing Hitler and the Holocaust. A ship carrying Jewish refugees from Europe attempted to land in Halifax and was denied entrance. During the 1930s Canada admitted fewer Jewish refugees as a percentage of its population than any other Western country. Jews who did immigrate experienced widespread discrimination in employment, business, and education. Other indicators of anti-Semitism included restrictions on where Jews could live, buy property, and attend university. Signs posted along Toronto's beaches warned "No dogs or Jews

allowed." Many hotels and resorts had policies prohibiting Jews as guests (Abella and Troper, 1982, quoted in Henry et al., 1995:74). Despite the discrimination and racism to which Jews were subjected, Jewish Canadians today have attained a level of education and income considerably above the Canadian average.

IMMIGRATION TRENDS FROM 1929 TO THE PRESENT
The Great Depression, which began in 1929, prompted the implementation of restrictive measures to further limit new immigrants to those from the preferred groups.

Changes to the Immigration Act in 1962 opened the door to immigration on a nonracial basis. Education, occupation, and language skills replaced race or national origin as the criteria for admission. In 1967, a *points system* was introduced whereby immigrants were rated according to the totals of points given for the following: job training, experience, skills, level of education, knowledge of English or French, degree of demand for the applicant's occupation, and job offers (Isajaw, 1999). This new act opened the doors to those from previously excluded countries. As Figures 10.4 and 10.5 show, Canadian immigra-

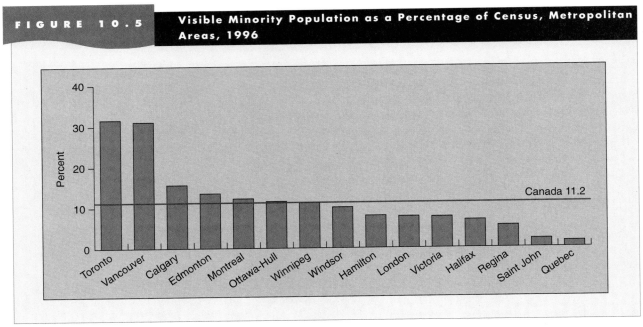

FIGURE 10.5 Visible Minority Population as a Percentage of Census, Metropolitan Areas, 1996

Source: Statistics Canada, "1996 Census: Visible Minority Population."

tion patterns changed dramatically because of this new immigration policy. Prior to 1960, the majority of immigrants were from the United States or Europe; by 1996, the percentage of immigrants from these countries had fallen to just over 20 percent. In contrast, prior to 1960, immigrants from Asia and the Middle East accounted for less than 2 percent of immigrants to Canada, but by 1996, this figure had risen to almost 60 percent. However, while changes in Canada's immigration laws altered Canada's ethnic composition, the domination of the Euro-Canadian majority in the stratification system has not been altered significantly. While Euro-Canadian and French-Canadian groups have been able to achieve upward mobility into middle- and upper-class social positions, the lower status of many visible minority groups has been virtually unchanged.

RACIAL AND ETHNIC DIVERSITY IN CANADA IN THE FUTURE

Racial and ethnic diversity is increasing in Canada. This changing demographic pattern is largely the result of the elimination of overtly racist immigration policies and the opening up of immigration to Third World countries. Canada

has evolved from a country largely inhabited by whites and Aboriginal peoples to a country made up of people from more than seventy countries. Today, almost two-thirds of racial-minority immigrants come from Asia. The number of Latin American immigrants is expected to grow fourfold in the new century (Henry et al., 1996). Almost all immigrants to Canada live in cities. Recent immigrants are especially attracted to Canada's three largest cities. In fact, nearly three-quartres of immigrants who came here between 1991 and 1996 chose to live in Toronto, Montreal, or Vancouver (see Figure 10.5). In the year 2001, nearly half of the population of Toronto and nearly two-fifths of the population of Vancouver will be composed of visible minorities. Furthermore, visible minorities will make up close to 12 percent of the total population of Canada, in contrast to 6.3 percent in 1986.

What effect will these changes have on racial and ethnic relations? Several possibilities exist. On the one hand, conflict between whites and people of colour may become more overt and confrontational. Certainly, the concentration of visible minorities will mean that these groups will become more visible than ever in some Canadian cities. Increasing contact may lead to increased intergroup cohesion and understanding, or it may bring on racism or prejudice. The rapid political changes and the global economic recession of the 1990s have made people fearful about their future and may cause some to blame "foreigners" for their problems. Interethnic tensions among members of subordinate groups in urban areas may increase as subordinate groups continue to face economic deprivation and discrimination. People may continue to use *sincere fictions*—personal beliefs that reflect larger societal mythologies, such as "I am not racist" or "I have never discriminated against anyone"—even when these are inaccurate perceptions (Feagin and Vera, 1995). Concerns about violence, crime, welfare, education, housing, and taxes may be encompassed in the larger issue of race (Edsall and Edsall, 1992).

On the other hand, there is reason for cautious optimism. Throughout Canadian history, subordinate racial and ethnic groups have struggled to gain the freedom and rights that previously were withheld from them. Today, employment equity programs are alleviating some of the effects of past discrimination against minority groups as well as addressing systemic and institutional forms of racism that exist in employment. Movements made up of both whites and visible minorities continue to oppose racism in everyday life, to seek to heal divisions among racial groups, and to teach children about racial tolerance (Rutstein, 1993). Many groups hope not only to affect their own countries but also to contribute to worldwide efforts to end racism (Ford, 1994). Norman Buchignani explains the need to end racism:

> Racism is a moral issue, which reflects on Canadian society at large. Like sexism, racism ties us morally and intellectually to centuries-old legitimations and patterns of subordination which simply have no morally justifiable place in today's world. The persistence of racism diminishes us all. (1991:200)

The challenge of trying to keep together a nation composed of people divided by ethnicity, language, and even region, is a monumental task—one that will not be resolved in the near future (Rosenburg, 1995). Nevertheless, the elimination of racial/ethnic conflict should be an important government and public priority.

CHAPTER REVIEW

How do race and ethnicity differ?
A race is a category of people who have been singled out as inferior or superior, often on the basis of physical characteristics such as skin colour, hair texture, or eye shape. An ethnic group is a collection of people who, as a result of their shared cultural traits and high level of mutual interaction, regard themselves as a cultural unity.

Why are race and ethnicity important?
Race and ethnicity are ingrained in our consciousness. They often form the basis of hierarchical ranking in society and determine who gets what resources: employment, housing, education, and social services.

What are majority and minority groups?
A majority or dominant group is an advantaged group that has superior resources and rights in society. A minority or subordinate group is a disadvantaged group whose members are subjected to unequal treatment by the majority group. The terms dominant and subordinate reflect the importance of power in relationships.

What is prejudice?
Prejudice is a negative attitude based on preconceived notions about members of selected groups. Prejudice is often reinforced by stereotypes and is present in ethnocentric attitudes.

How do sociologists explain prejudice?
According to the frustration-aggression hypothesis of prejudice, people frustrated in their efforts to achieve a highly desired goal may respond with aggression toward others, who then become scapegoats. Another theory of prejudice focuses on the authoritarian personality, which is marked by excessive conformity, submissiveness to authority, intolerance, insecurity, superstition, and rigid thinking. According to social learning theory, prejudice is learned from significant others, such as parents and close friends.

What is discrimination, and how does it differ from prejudice?
Discrimination involves actions or practices of dominant group members that have a harmful impact on members of a subordinate group. Whereas prejudice involves attitudes, discrimination involves actions. Discriminatory actions range from name-calling to violent actions. Discrimination can be either de jure (encoded in law) or de facto (informal).

What is racism and what forms does it take?
Racism refers to an organized set of beliefs about the innate inferiority of some racial groups combined with the power to discriminate on the basis of race. There are many different ways in which racism may manifest itself, including rednecked racism, polite racism, subliminal racism, institutional racism, and systemic racism.

How do sociologists view racial and ethnic group relations?

Interactionists suggest that increased contact between people from divergent groups should lead to favourable attitudes and behaviour when members of each group (1) have equal status, (2) pursue the same goals, (3) cooperate with one another to achieve goals, and (4) receive positive feedback when they interact with one another. Functionalists stress that members of subordinate groups become absorbed into the dominant culture. Conflict theorists focus on economic stratification and access to power in race and ethnic relations.

How have the experiences of various ethnic groups in Canada differed?

Aboriginal people suffered greatly from the actions of European settlers, who seized their lands and made them victims of forced assimilation strategies and migration. White Anglo-Saxon Protestants are the most privileged group in Canada, although social class and gender affect their life chances. White ethnics, whose ancestors migrated from southern and eastern European countries, gradually have made their way into the mainstream of Canadian society. The struggle of francophones, the majority of whom live in Quebec, to receive recognition of their language and culture has been ongoing and is reflected in the increasing identification of Québécois with the separatist movement.

How have Canada's immigration policies, past and present, affected the composition of Canada's ethnic population?

Canada's early immigration policies were described as racist and included exclusionary policies directed at Asian populations including Chinese, Japanese, and South Asians as well as Jews. "White ethnics" who came from European countries comprised the preferred category of immigrants. Changes to the Immigration Act in 1962 involving the implementation of a points system opened the door to immigration on a nonracial basis.

Key Terms

assimilation 318
authoritarian personality 309
discrimination 310
ethnic group 305
ethnic pluralism 319
ethnocentrism 309
institutionalized racism 315
internal colonialism 321
majority (dominant) group 307
minority (subordinate) group 307
polite racism 314
prejudice 308
race 304
racial prejudice 308
racism 313
rednecked racism 313
scapegoat 309
segregation 320
social distance 310
split labour market 322
stereotypes 308
subliminal racism 314
systemic racism 315
visible minority 307

Internet Exercises

1. March 21 is the International Day for the Elimination of Racial Discrimination. Visit the Heritage Canada Web site at **www.march21.com.** What recommendations can you find on how to deal with racial violence?

2. Using the Alta Vista search engine (**http://altavista.digital.com/**), do a search for the term ethnic struggle. What types of sites do you come to? What are the differences in the way the concept of ethnic struggle is discussed in the textbook versus how it is talked about on the Internet?

3. Because of the nature of the Internet, it is possible for anyone with an idea to publish on it, providing he or she has access to a computer. Go to Deja News (**http://www.dejanews.com**) and run a search on white power. How are the racist arguments on the Internet the same as traditional arguments? How are they different? How do people react to these comments on the Internet?

Net Links

For highlights from the *Report of the Royal Commission on Aboriginal Peoples*, go to:

http://www.inac.gc.ca/rcap/report/index.html

For additional information on First Nations peoples, go to the Aboriginal Web Links site at:

http://www.johnco.com/native/#13

"The Crosspoint" is the Internet's largest collection of links in the field of human rights, anti-racism, and anti-facism; see:

http://www.magenta.nl/crosspoint

For a thorough overview of anti-Semitism in Canada, review Dr. Karen Mock's article "Perspectives on Racism: Anti-Semitism in Canada":

(R)   http://www1.ca.nizkor.org/hweb/people/m/mock_k aren/perspectives-on-racism.html

"Hate on the Internet" by Dr. K. Mock and Lisa Armony, B'nai B'rith Canada, outlines the growth of hate on the Internet, debates the pros and cons of Internet regulations of hate propaganda, and suggests other responses to the presence of hate on the Internet; go to:

(R)   http://www.media-awareness.ca/eng/issues/ internet/resource/mock.htm

Questions for Critical Thinking

1. Do you consider yourself defined more strongly by your race or by your ethnicity? How so?
2. Given that minority groups have some common experiences, why is there such deep conflict between certain minority groups?
3. What would need to happen in Canada, both individually and institutionally, for a positive form of ethnic pluralism to flourish in the twenty-first century?

Suggested Readings

For an in-depth analysis of race and ethnic relations, these texts are excellent:

W.W. Isajiw. *Understanding Diversity: Ethnicity and Race in the Canadian Context*. Toronto: Thomson Educational Publishing, 1999.

Carl E. James and Adrienne Shadd (eds.). *Talking About Difference: Encounters in Culture, Language and Identity*. Toronto: Between the Lines, 1994.

Peter S. Li (ed.). *Race and Ethnic Relations in Canada*. Toronto: Oxford University Press, 1990.

Martin N. Marger. *Race and Ethnic Relations: American and Global Perspectives*. Belmont, Cal.: Wadsworth, 1994.

These recent books provide excellent discussions on racism in Canada:

Stanley R. Barrett. *Is God a Racist? The Right Wing in Canada*. Toronto: University of Toronto Press, 1987.

Augie Fleras and Jean Leonard Elliott. *Unequal Relations: An Introduction to Race, Ethnic and Aboriginal Dynamics in Canada* (2nd ed.). Scarborough, Ont.: Prentice-Hall, 1996.

Frances Henry, Carol Tator, Winston Mattis, and Tim Rees. *The Colour of Democracy: Racism in Canadian Society*. Toronto: Harcourt Brace, 1995.

Carl James. *Seeing Ourselves: Exploring Race, Ethnicity, and Culture*. Toronto: Thompson Publishing, 1995.

Ormond McKague (ed.). *Racism in Canada*. Saskatoon: Fifth House, 1991.

For additional information on the experiences of specific racial and ethnic groups:

Menno Boldt. *Surviving as Indians: The Challenge of Self-Government*. Toronto: University of Toronto Press, 1993.

James S. Frideres (ed.). *Native Peoples in Canada: Contemporary Conflicts* (4th ed.). Scarborough, Ont.: Prentice-Hall, 1993.

Sex and Gender
Sex
Gender
The Social Significance of Gender
Sexism

Gender Stratification in Historical Perspective
Hunting and Gathering Societies
Horticultural and Pastoral Societies
Agrarian Societies
Industrial Societies

Gender and Socialization
Gender Socialization by Parents
Peers and Gender Socialization
Teachers, Schools, and Gender Socialization
Sports and Gender Socialization
Mass Media and Gender Socialization

Contemporary Gender Inequality
Gender Segregation of Paid Work
The Gender Wage Gap
Pay Equity and Employment Equity
Unpaid Work—The Second Shift

Perspectives on Gender Stratification
Functionalist and Neoclassical Economic
  Perspectives
Conflict Perspectives
Feminist Perspectives

Gender Issues in the Future

An estimated 5 percent of Canadian women have an eating disorder. Another 10 to 20 percent have symptoms of eating disorders (Marble, 1995). Approximately 95 percent of those who develop eating disorders are women. Men are not immune to these pressures though they respond in a very different manner than women. An estimated 83,000 Canadian youths—mostly young men—take muscle-building steroids (Nemeth et al., 1994). A recent study of weight and eating disorders indicated that dissatisfaction with weight and shape is a common complaint among many university women (Hesse-Biber, 1996). Consider the story of this young Bishop's University student's struggle with anorexia:

"It was March 1995, I was 17 and in my graduating year of high school when I decided that I wanted to lose weight—10 pounds, maybe 15, certainly not more than 20. I was five eight and 155 pounds. I wanted to impress the boys in university and I thought being thin would help. So I went on a diet.

"People with eating disorders do not wake up one morning and say to themselves, 'I am not going to eat any more' or 'I think I will start bingeing and purging.' Nobody called me fat or told me life would be perfect if I lost 50 pounds. I can't pinpoint one event that directly led to my disorder. I just needed something to depend on, something to think about and to put all my effort into. I just happened to find dieting at the wrong time. It was comforting to take a break from the changes and worries in my life to concentrate on what I was, or wasn't, going to eat that day. It was also nice to pat myself on the back every time I resisted eating.

"By June graduation I was down to 130 pounds. I was satisfied but afraid I might regain weight, so I kept dieting. When I entered university that fall, I weighed 120 pounds. I had heard about the Frosh 15, the 15 pounds on average that university students supposedly gain in the first year. I decided that I, dieter extra ordinaire, would not become part of that statistic ... At Christmas I returned home to a horrified family. I wasn't just thin, I was emaciated. But aside from my looks I still seemed to have it all together. I was an honours student when I entered university and had an 82 percent average after my first semester. I had made lots of friends and had balanced my social and academic obligations. Except for the state of my health, I was a success story.

"When I went back to university in January, my life dissolved both emotionally and physically. I cried at least twice a day, although never in public. I couldn't get up for class. I couldn't even walk up the stairs without sitting down to take a rest. Every single moment was a fight between me and every cell in my body—cells that were begging me to give in and nourish them ... I know that I could not continue living that way but I saw no alternative. Losing the anorexia nervosa felt like losing everything." (Rutherford, 1998: 107–108).

Eating disorders are strongly linked to social and cultural pressures. In our society, thinness is associated with beauty, happiness, and success. We live in a culture in which the body is a means of assessing an individual's value or worth. A person's weight may be "fair game" for jokes even in an era when remarks about race, sex, or religion are considered unacceptable (Wolf, 1990). Discrimination against people on the basis of appearance has been referred to as one of the last acceptable forms of prejudice (Stolker, 1992). People who deviate significantly from existing weight and appearance norms often are devalued and objectified by others. *Objectification* is the process of treating people as if they were objects or things, not human beings. We objectify people when we judge them on the basis of their physical appearance, rather than on the basis of their individual qualities or actions (Schur, 1983). In our society, objectification of women is especially common (see Table 11.1).

Studies suggest that both men and women may have negative perceptions about their body size, weight, and appearance (Marble, 1995; Nemeth et al., 1994). Many men compare themselves unfavourably to muscular bodybuilders and believe that they need to gain weight or muscularity, which for some is associated with masculinity and power (Basow, 1992; Klein, 1993). For women, however, body image is an even greater concern. Women may compare themselves unfavourably to slender stars of film and television and believe that they need to lose weight. Men are less likely to let concerns about appearance affect how they feel about their own competence, worth, and abilities; among women, dislike of their bodies may affect self-esteem and feelings of self-worth (Mintz and Betz, 1986).

Why do women and men feel differently about their bodies? Cultural differences in appearance norms may explain women's greater concern; they tend to be judged more harshly, and they know it (Wolf, 1990). Throughout their lives, men and women receive different cultural messages about body image, food, and eating. Men are encouraged to eat while women are made to feel guilty about eating (Basow, 1992). Sociologist Sharlene Hesse-Biber (1996:11) refers to this phenomenon as the *cult of thinness*, in which people worship the "perfect" body and engage in rituals such as dieting and exercising with "obsessive attention to monitoring progress—weighing the body at least once a day and constantly checking calories." The main criterion for joining the cult of thinness is being female (Hesse-Biber, 1996).

Body image is only one example of the many socially constructed differences between men and women—differences that relate to gender (a social concept) rather than to a person's biological make-up, or sex. In this chapter, we examine the issue of gender: what it is and how it affects us. Before reading on, test your knowledge about gender and body image by taking the quiz in Box 11.1.

No wonder many women are extremely concerned about body image; even billboards communicate cultural messages about their appearance.

QUESTIONS AND ISSUES

CHAPTER FOCUS QUESTION: How do expectations about female and male appearance reflect gender inequality?

How do a society's resources and economic structure influence gender stratification?

What are the primary agents of gender socialization?

How does the contemporary workplace reflect gender stratification?

How do functionalist, conflict, and feminist perspectives on gender stratification differ?

SEX AND GENDER

The word *sex* often is used to refer to the biological attributes of men and women (Epstein, 1988). *Gender* often is used to refer to the distinctive qualities of men and women (masculinity and femininity) that are culturally created (Epstein, 1988; Marshall, 1994).

Sex

Sex **refers to the biological and anatomical differences between females and males.** At the core of these differences is the chromosomal informa-

tion transmitted at the moment a child is conceived. The mother contributes an X chromosome and the father either an X (which produces a female embryo) or a Y chromosome (which produces a male embryo). At birth, male and female infants are distinguished by *primary sex characteristics:* **the genitalia used in the reproductive process.** At puberty, an increased production of hormones results in the development of *secondary sex characteristics:* **the physical traits (other than reproductive organs) that identify an individual's sex.** For women, these include larger breasts, wider hips, and narrower shoulders, a layer of fatty tissue covering the body, and menstruation. For men, they include development of enlarged genitals, a deeper voice, greater height, a more muscular build, and more body and facial hair (see Lott, 1994:17–32).

These changes produce an acute awareness of sexuality. During this time, many young people become aware of their *sexual orientation*—**a preference for emotional–sexual relationships with members of the opposite sex (heterosexuality), the same sex (homosexuality), or both (bisexuality)** (Lips, 1993). Some researchers believe that sexual orientation is rooted in biological factors that are present at birth (Pillard and Weinrich, 1986); others believe that sexuality has both biological and social components and is not preordained at birth (Golden, 1987).

Sex is not always clear-cut. Occasionally, a hormone imbalance before birth produces a

BOX 11.1 SOCIOLOGY AND EVERYDAY LIFE

HOW MUCH DO YOU KNOW ABOUT BODY IMAGE AND GENDER?

TRUE FALSE

T	F	1. Most people have an accurate perception of their own physical appearance.
T	F	2. Recent studies show that up to 95 percent of men express dissatisfaction with some aspect of their bodies.
T	F	3. Many young girls and women believe that being even slightly overweight makes them less feminine.
T	F	4. Physical attractiveness is a more central part of self-concept for women than for men.
T	F	5. Virtually no men have eating problems such as anorexia and bulimia.
T	F	6. Thinness has always been the "ideal" body image for women.
T	F	7. Women bodybuilders have gained full acceptance in society.
T	F	8. In school, boys are more likely than girls to ridicule people about their appearance.
T	F	9. Canada has laws prohibiting employment discrimination on the basis of weight.
T	F	10. Young girls and women very rarely die as a result of anorexia or bulimia.

Answers on page 338.

hermaphrodite—a person in whom sexual differentiation is ambiguous or incomplete (Renzetti and Curran, 1995). Hermaphrodites tend to have some combination of male and female genitalia. In one case, for example, a chromosomally normal (XY) male was born with a penis just one centimetre long and a urinary opening similar to that of a female (Money and Ehrhardt, 1972). Some people may be genetically of one sex but have the gender identity of the other. That is true for a *transsexual,* **a person who believes that he or she was born with the body of the wrong sex.** Some transsexuals take hormone treatments or have a sex change operation to alter their genitalia in order to achieve a body congruent with their own sense of sexual identity (Basow, 1992).

Western societies acknowledge the existence of only two sexes; some other societies recognize three—men, women, and *berdaches* (or *hijras* or *xaniths*), biological males who behave, dress, and work and are treated in most respects as women. The closest approximation of a third sex in Western societies is a *transvestite,* **a male who lives as a woman or a female who lives as a man but does not alter the genitalia.** Although transvestites are not treated as a third sex, they often "pass" for members of that sex because their appearance and mannerisms fall within the range of what is expected from members of the other sex (Lorber, 1994).

Gender

Gender **refers to the culturally and socially constructed differences between females and males found in the meanings, beliefs, and practices associated with "femininity" and "masculinity."** Although biological differences between women and men are very important, most "sex differences" actually are socially constructed "gender differences" (Gailey, 1987). According to sociologists, social and cultural processes, not biological "givens," are most important in defining what females and males are, what they should do, and what sorts of relations do or should exist between them (Ortner and Whitehead, 1981; Lott, 1994). Sociologist Judith Lorber (1994:6) summarizes the importance of gender:

> Gender is a human invention, like language, kinship, religion, and technology; like them, gender organizes human social life in culturally patterned ways. Gender organizes social relations in everyday life as well as in the major social structures, such as social class and the hierarchies of bureaucratic organizations.

Virtually everything social in our lives is *gendered:* people continually distinguish between males and females and evaluate them differently (Mackie, 1995). Gender is an integral part of the daily experiences of both women and men (McDaniel, 1991).

BOX 11.1

ANSWERS TO THE SOCIOLOGY QUIZ ON BODY IMAGE AND GENDER

1. **False.** Many people do not have a very accurate perception of their own bodies. For example, many young girls and women think of themselves as fat when they are not. Some young boys and men tend to believe that they need well-developed chest and arm muscles, broad shoulders, and a narrow waist.

2. **True.** In recent studies, up to 95 percent of men believed they needed to improve some aspect of their bodies.

3. **True.** More than half of all adult women in North America are currently dieting, and over three-fourths of normal-weight women think they are too fat. Recently, very young girls have developed similar concerns. For example, 80 percent of Grade 4 girls in one study were watching their weight.

4. **True.** Women have been socialized to believe that being physically attractive is very important. Studies have found that weight and body shape are the central determinants of women's perception of their physical attractiveness.

5. **False.** Some men do have eating problems such as anorexia and bulimia. These problems have been found especially among gay men and male fashion models and dancers.

6. **False.** The "ideal" body image for women has changed a number of times. A positive view of body fat has prevailed for most of human history; however, in the twentieth century in North America, this view has given way to "fat aversion."

7. **False.** Although bodybuilding among women has gained some degree of acceptance, women bodybuilders still are expected to be very "feminine" and not to overdevelop themselves.

8. **True.** Boys are especially likely to ridicule girls whom they perceive to be "unattractive" or overweight.

9. **False.** To date Canada has no laws that specifically prohibit employment discrimination on the basis of weight.

10. **False.** Although the exact number is not known, many young girls and women do die as a result of starvation, malnutrition, and other problems associated with anorexia and bulimia. These are considered life-threatening behaviours by many in the medical profession.

Sources: Based on Lips, 1993; Fallon, Katzman, and Wooley, 1994; Kilbourne, 1994; and Seid, 1994.

A microlevel analysis of gender focuses on how individuals learn gender roles and acquire a gender identity. **Gender role refers to the attitudes, behaviour, and activities that are socially defined as appropriate for each sex and are learned through the socialization process** (Lips, 1993). For example, in Canadian society, males traditionally are expected to demonstrate aggressiveness and toughness while females are expected to be passive and nurturing. **Gender identity is a person's perception of the self as female or male.** Typically established between 18 months and 3 years of age, gender identity is a powerful aspect of our self–concept (Cahill, 1986; Lips, 1993). Although this identity is an individual perception, it is developed through interaction with others. As a result, most people form a gender identity that matches their biological sex: most biological females think of themselves as female,

and most biological males think of themselves as male. Body consciousness is a part of gender identity (Basow, 1992). **Body consciousness is how a person perceives and feels about his or her body;** it also includes an awareness of social conditions in society that contribute to this self-knowledge (Thompson, 1994). Consider, for example, these comments by Steve Michalik, a former Mr. Universe:

I was small and weak, and my brother Anthony was big and graceful, and my old man made no bones about loving him and hating me … The minute I walked in from school, it was, "You worthless little s--t, what are you doing home so early?" His favorite way to torture me was to tell me he was going to put me in a home. We'd be driving along … and we'd pass a building with iron bars on the windows, and he'd stop the car and say to me, "Get out. This is the

TABLE   11.1   ☐ THE OBJECTIFICATION OF WOMEN

GENERAL ASPECTS OF OBJECTIFICATION	OBJECTIFICATION BASED ON CULTURAL PREOCCUPATION WITH "LOOKS"
Women are responded to primarily as "females," while their personal qualities and accomplishments are of secondary importance.	Women often are seen as the objects of sexual attraction, not full human beings—for example, when they are stared at.
Women are seen as being "all alike."	Women are seen by some as depersonalized body parts—for example, "a piece of ass."
Women are seen as being subordinate and passive, so things can easily be "done to a woman"—for example, discrimination, harassment, and violence.	Depersonalized female sexuality is used for cultural and economic purposes—such as in the media, advertising, fashion and cosmetics industries, and pornography.
Women are seen as easily ignored, dismissed, or trivialized.	Women are seen as being "decorative" and status-conferring objects, to be sought (sometimes collected) and displayed by men and sometimes by other women.
	Women are evaluated according to prevailing, narrow "beauty" standards and often feel pressure to conform to appearance norms.

Source: Edwin M. Schur, *Labeling Women Deviant: Gender, Stigma, and Social Control* © 1983 Temple University Press. Reprinted by permission, The McGraw-Hill Companies.

home we're putting you in." I'd be standing there sobbing on the curb—I was maybe eight or nine at the time. (quoted in Klein, 1993:273)

As we grow up, we become aware, as Michalik did, that the physical shape of our bodies subjects us to the approval or disapproval of others. While being small and weak may be considered positive attributes for women, they are considered negative characteristics for "real men."

A macrolevel analysis of gender examines structural features, external to the individual, that perpetuate gender inequality. These structures have been referred to as *gendered institutions*, meaning that gender is one of the major ways by which social life is organized in all sectors of society. Gender is embedded in the images, ideas, and language of a society and is used as a means to divide up work, allocate resources, and distribute power. For example, every society uses gender to assign certain tasks—ranging from child rearing to warfare—to females and to males.

These institutions are reinforced by a *gender belief system* that includes all of the ideas regarding masculine and feminine attributes that are held to be valid in a society. This belief system is legitimated by religion, science, law, and other societal values (Lorber, 1994). For example, gendered belief systems may change over time as gender

roles change. Many fathers take care of young children today, and there is a much greater acceptance of this change in roles. However, popular stereotypes about men and women, as well as cultural norms about gender-appropriate appearance and behaviour, serve to reinforce gendered institutions in society (Deaux and Kite, 1987).

The Social Significance of Gender

Like ethnicity, gender is a social construction with important consequences in everyday life. Just as stereotypes regarding race/ethnicity have built-in notions of superiority and inferiority, gender stereotypes hold that men and women are inherently different in attributes, behaviour, and aspirations. Stereotypes define men as strong, rational, dominant, independent, and less concerned with their appearance. Women are stereotyped as weak, emotional, nurturing, dependent, and anxious about their appearance.

The social significance of gender stereotypes is illustrated by eating problems. The three most common eating problems are anorexia, bulimia, and obesity. With *anorexia*, a person has lost at least 25 percent of body weight due to a compulsive fear of becoming fat (Lott, 1994). With *bulimia*, a person binges by consuming large quan-

The way society views women's role in war illustrates how gender belief systems change over time as gender roles change.

tities of food and then purges the food by induced vomiting, excessive exercise, laxatives, or fasting (Renzetti and Curran, 1992). With *obesity*, individuals are 20 percent or more above their desirable weight, as established by the medical profession. For a 5-foot-4-inch woman, that is about twenty-five pounds; for a 5-foot-10-inch man, about thirty pounds (Burros, 1994:1).

Sociologist Becky W. Thompson argues that, based on stereotypes, the primary victims of eating problems are presumed to be white, middle-class, heterosexual women. However, such problems also exist among women of colour, working-class women, lesbians, and some men. According to Thompson, explanations regarding the relationship between gender and eating problems must take into account a complex array of social factors, including gender socialization and women's responses to problems such as racism and emotional, physical, and sexual abuse (Thompson, 1994; see also Heywood, 1998).

Bodybuilding is another gendered experience. *Bodybuilding* is the process of deliberately cultivating an increase in mass and strength of the skeletal muscles by means of lifting and pushing weights (Mansfield and McGinn, 1993). In the past, bodybuilding was predominantly a male activity; musculature connoted power, domination, and virility (Klein, 1993). Today, an increasing number of women engage in this activity. As gendered experiences, eating problems, and bodybuilding have more in common

than we might think. Historian Susan Bordo (1993) has noted that the anorexic body and the muscled body are not opposites; instead, they exist on a continuum because they are united against a "common platoon of enemies: the soft, the loose; unsolid, excess flesh." The *body* is objectified in both compulsive dieting and bodybuilding (Mansfield and McGinn, 1993:53).

Sexism

Sexism **is the subordination of one sex, usually female, based on the assumed superiority of the other sex.** Sexism directed at women has three components: (1) negative attitudes toward women, (2) stereotypical beliefs that reinforce, complement, or justify the prejudice, and (3) discrimination—acts that exclude, distance, or keep women separate (Lott, 1994).

Can men be victims of sexism? Although women are more often the target of sexist remarks and practices, men can be victims of sexist assumptions. As social psychologist Hilary M. Lips (1993:11) notes, "Sexism cuts both ways; for example, the other side of the prejudiced attitude that [usually bars] women from combat positions in the military is the attitude that it is somehow less upsetting to have male soldiers killed than to have female soldiers killed."

Like racism, sexism is used to justify discriminatory treatment. When women participate in what is considered gender-inappropriate endeavours in the workplace, at home, or in leisure activities, they often find that they are the targets of prejudice and discrimination. Obvious manifestations of sexism are found in the undervaluing of women's work, in hiring and promotion practices that effectively exclude women from an organization or confine them to the bottom of the organizational hierarchy, and in the denial of equal access for women to educational opportunities (Armstrong and Armstrong, 1994). Some people feel that pornography serves to perpetuate sexism by portraying women as objects. Box 11.2 addresses how the law in Canada deals with this complex issue. Women who attempt to enter nontraditional occupations (such as firefighting, welding, and steelworking) or professions (such as dentistry and architecture) often encounter hurdles that men do not face. Women may experience discrimination because they are perceived to be "out of place." Consider the following comments from a male steelworker in Hamilton regarding the hiring of female steelworkers:

> It's dirty, heavy, it's no climate for a woman. The men's world is a little rougher than the women's. Physically a man is in better shape. Men are more mechanically minded … There is nothing wrong with women, it's just that sometimes with heavy work … if you take the overall picture, masculinity has always been the man's. It doesn't mean that he has more brains because that is not true, but muscularity. I think that women should be outside. It is no place for women. I hate it. (Livingston and Luxton, 1995:190)

Sexism is interwoven with *patriarchy*—a hierarchical system of social organization in which cultural, political, and economic structures are controlled by men. By contrast, *matriarchy* is a hierarchical system of social organization in which cultural, political, and economic structures are controlled by women; however, few (if any) societies have been organized in this manner (Lengermann and Wallace, 1985). Patriarchy is reflected in the way men may think of their position as men as a given while women may deliberate on what their position in society should be. As sociologist Virginia Cyrus (1993:6) explains, "Under patriarchy, men are seen as 'natural' heads of households, political candidates, corporate executives, university presidents, etc. Women, on the other hand, are men's subordinates, playing such supportive roles as housewife, mother, nurse, and secretary." Gender inequality

and a division of labour based on male dominance are nearly universal, as we will see in the following discussion of the origins of gender-based stratification.

GENDER STRATIFICATION IN HISTORICAL PERSPECTIVE

How do tasks in a society come to be defined as "men's work" or "women's work"? Three factors are important in determining the gendered division of labour in a society: (1) the type of subsistence base, (2) the supply of and demand for labour, and (3) the extent to which women's child-rearing activities are compatible with certain types of work. *Subsistence* refers to the means by which a society gains the basic necessities of life, including food, shelter, and clothing (Nielsen, 1990). The three factors vary according to a society's *technoeconomic base*—the level of technology and the organization of the economy in a given society. Four such bases have been identified: hunting and gathering societies, horticultural and pastoral societies, agrarian societies, and industrial societies, as shown in Table 11.2.

Hunting and Gathering Societies

The earliest known division of labour between women and men is in hunting and gathering societies. While the men hunt for wild game, women gather roots and berries (Nielsen, 1990). A relatively equitable relationship exists because neither sex has the ability to provide all of the food necessary for survival. When wild game is nearby, both men and women may hunt (Basow, 1992). When it is far away, hunting becomes incompatible with child rearing (which women tend to do because they breast-feed their young), and women are placed at a disadvantage in terms of contributing to the food supply (Lorber, 1994). In most hunting and gathering societies, women are full economic partners with men; relations between them tend to be cooperative and relatively egalitarian (Chafetz, 1984). Little social stratification of any kind is found because people do not acquire a food surplus.

A few hunting and gathering societies remain, including the Bushmen of Africa, the aborigines of Australia, and the Yanomamö of South America. However, some analysts predict that

BOX 11.2   SOCIOLOGY AND LAW

OBSCENITY AND WOMEN'S INEQUALITY

Is pornography harmful? If so, who does it harm? Is all pornographic material obscene or just some of it? Does it result in exploitation and further objectification of women in our society? In the Canadian courts, the jury on these issues is still out.

The Criminal Code originally defined obscene material as that which involves, "the undue exploitation of sex." What exactly constitutes "undue exploitation of sex"? This is yet to be resolved in the courts, despite millions of dollars of litigation dating back forty years to when the legislation was originally enacted. Until recently, judges had the responsibility of assessing what was decent and what was indecent in obscenity cases. In other words, obscenity was in the eye of the beholder and varied with the times.

This changed in 1992 with the landmark Supreme Court of Canada case R vs. Butler. David Butler, the owner of a Winnipeg pornography shop, was charged with 250 counts of possessing and trafficking in obscene hardcore videos and magazines. Owning and distributing obscene material carries a maximum

penalty of two years in jail. Butler was acquitted on 242 counts and convicted on eight. Unsatisfied with this result, Butler appealed his convictions up to the Supreme Court of Canada, arguing that pornographic material is protected from prosecution because of the guarantee of freedom of expression in the Charter of Rights and Freedoms.

The outcome of the Butler case was influenced by the Women's Legal Education and Action Fund (LEAF). In an official brief, LEAF asked the Supreme Court to uphold the obscenity law on the basis that some forms of pornography promoted violence against women. However, as LEAF acknowledged, the research evidence is ambiguous—it neither proves nor disproves this claim.

The Supreme Court agreed with LEAF and in a unanimous decision, upheld the obscenity law and the court's rights to censor pornographic material that is defined as obscene. However, according to Justice Sopinka, who authored the Supreme Court ruling, only the worst types of pornography should be outlawed "not because it offends against morals

these groups will cease to exist within the next century (Lenski, Lenski, and Nolan, 1991). Aboriginal peoples in Canada had very successful hunting and gathering societies prior to European inhabitation. Sadly, few cultures have been able to maintain this egalitarian system.

Horticultural and Pastoral Societies

In horticultural societies, which first developed ten to twelve thousand years ago, a steady source of food becomes available. People are able to grow their own food because of hand tools, such as the digging stick and the hoe. Women make an important contribution to food production because hoe cultivation is compatible with child care. A fairly

high degree of gender equality exists because neither sex controls the food supply (Basow, 1992).

When inadequate moisture in an area makes planting crops impossible, *pastoralism*—the domestication of large animals to provide food—develops. Herding primarily is done by men, and women contribute relatively little to subsistence production in such societies. In some herding societies, women have relatively low status; their primary value is their ability to produce male offspring so that the family lineage can be preserved and enough males will exist to protect the group against attack (Nielsen, 1990).

Social practices contribute to gender inequality in horticultural and pastoral societies. Male dominance is promoted by practices such as menstrual taboos, bridewealth, and polygyny (Nielsen, 1990). *Polygyny*—the marriage of one man to multiple wives—contributes to power differences

BOX 11.2

CONTINUED

but because it is perceived by public opinion to be harmful to society, particularly women (Verberg, 1994:26). If an obscene work threatened the equality of women, censorship was justified.

A more explicit definition of obscenity resulted from Butler's Supreme Court challenge. First, any material that mixes explicit sex and violence, or includes children, should be ruled obscene. Second, materials that involve explicit sex and degradation are obscene if they are deemed to encourage violence or other harm against women. Finally, other sexually explicit material is permissible.

The ruling in the Butler decision has resulted in increasingly liberal interpretations of obscenity laws. Why? Now in order to obtain a conviction on an obscenity charge, the prosecution has to prove that a certain work causes harm. This is a defence counsel's dream: as one Toronto criminal lawyer comments, "Dirty pictures don't cause anything" (Kaihla, 1994:30).

What do you think? In a downtown Toronto shop called "Books," an entire wall is devoted to bondage videos. One of the selections is entitled *Women Ruled by Men*. On the cover are two nude women strapped back to back by a series of chains. One of them has what looks like a horse's bit in her mouth, held there by a strap around her head. Another selection features "Sir Michael" in a dungeon with whips and chains hanging from the wall, pulling open the negligee of a young women gagged with heavy, knotted rope. The cover reads "Join Sir Michael as he teases, torments, humiliates and disciplines some of the most beautiful and submissive women who have fallen under his powerful will" (Kaihla, 1994:30).

Are these videos harmful? How would you go about proving this in a court of law?

Source: Kaihla, 1994; Verberg, 1994; Busby 1999.

between women and men. A man with multiple wives can produce many children who will enhance his resources, take care of him in his "old age," and become heirs to his property (Nielsen, 1990). *Menstrual taboos* place women in a subordinate position by segregating them into menstrual huts for the duration of their monthly cycle. Even when women are not officially segregated, they are defined as "unclean." *Bridewealth*—the payment of a price by a man for a wife—turns women into property that can be bought and sold. The man gives the bride's family material goods or services in exchange for their daughter's exclusive sexual services and his sole claim to their offspring.

In contemporary horticultural societies, women do most of the farming while men hunt game, clear land, work with arts and crafts, make tools, participate in religious and ceremonial activities, and engage in war (Nielsen, 1990). A combination of horticultural and pastoral activities is found in some contemporary societies in Asia, Africa, the Middle East, and South America. These societies are characterized by more gender inequality than in hunting and gathering societies but less than in agrarian societies (Nielsen, 1990:36–39).

Agrarian Societies

In agrarian societies, which first developed about eight to ten thousand years ago, gender inequality and male dominance become institutionalized. The most extreme form of gender inequality developed about five thousand years ago in societies in the fertile crescent around the Mediterranean Sea (Lorber, 1994). Agrarian societies rely on agriculture—farming done by animal-drawn or energy-powered plows and equipment. Because agrarian tasks require more labour and

TABLE 11.2	TECHNOECONOMIC BASES OF SOCIETY			
	HUNTING AND GATHERING	**HORTICULTURAL AND PASTORAL**	**AGRARIAN**	**INDUSTRIALIZED**
Change from Prior Society	—	Use of hand tools, such as digging stick and hoe	Use of animal-drawn plows and equipment	Invention of steam engine
Economic Characteristics	Hunting game, gathering roots and berries	Planting crops, domestication of animals for food	Labour-intensive farming	Mechanized production of goods
Control of Surplus	None	Men begin to control societies	Men who own land or herds	Men who own means of production
Inheritance	None	Shared—patrilineal and matrilineal	Patrilineal	Patrilineal
Control over Procreation	None	Increasingly by men	Men—to ensure legitimacy of heirs	Men—but less so in later stages
Women's Status	Relative equality	Decreasing in move to pastoralism	Low	Low

Source: Adapted from Judith Lorber, *Paradoxes of Gender* © 1994 Yale University Press. Reprinted by permission.

greater physical strength than horticultural ones, men become more involved in food production. It has been suggested that women are excluded from these tasks because they are viewed as too weak for the work and because child-care responsibilities are considered incompatible with the full-time labour that the tasks require (Nielsen, 1990).

Why does gender inequality increase in agrarian societies? Scholars cannot agree on an answer; some suggest that it results from private ownership of property. When people no longer have to move continually in search of food, they can acquire a surplus. Men gain control over the disposition of the surplus and the kinship system, which serves men's interests (Lorber, 1994). The importance of producing "legitimate" heirs to inherit the surplus increases significantly, and women's lives become more secluded and restricted as men attempt to ensure the legitimacy of their children. Premarital virginity and marital

fidelity are required; indiscretions are punished (Nielsen, 1990). Other scholars argue that male dominance existed before the private ownership of property (Firestone, 1970; Lerner, 1986).

The division of labour between women and men is very distinct in contemporary agrarian societies in places such as Burma and parts of the Middle East. There, women's work takes place in the private sphere (inside the home) and men's work occurs in the public sphere, providing them with more recognition and greater formal status.

Four practices in agrarian societies contribute to the subordination of women. *Purdah*, found primarily among Hindus and Muslims, requires the seclusion of women, extreme modesty in apparel, and the visible subordination of women to men. Women must show deference to men by walking behind them, speaking only when spoken to, and eating only after the men have finished a meal (Nielsen, 1990).

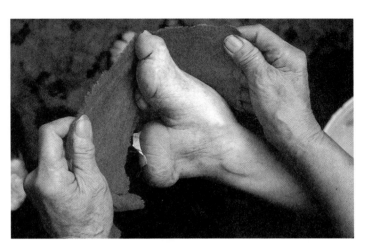

Footbinding, which was practised in China until the early twentieth century, contributed to the subordination of women.

Footbinding is the custom of thwarting the growth of a female's feet that was practised in China beginning around A.D. 1000 and continuing into the early twentieth century. The toes of young girls are bent under and continually bound tighter to the soles of their feet. As a result, women may experience extreme pain as their toenails grow into their feet or develop serious infections due to lack of blood circulation (Dworkin, 1974).

Suttee (most common in parts of India) is the sacrificial killing of a widow upon the death of her husband. Although some women allegedly choose to make this sacrifice, others are tied to their husband's funeral pyre. The practice is justified on the basis that the widow's sins in a former life are responsible for her husband's death. However, the actual purpose is to ensure that the husband's male relatives, rather than the widow, inherit his property (Nielsen, 1990:43–44).

Genital mutilation is a surgical procedure performed on young girls as a method of sexual control (Nielsen, 1990). The mutilation involves cutting off all or part of a girl's clitoris and labia, and in some cases stitching her vagina closed until marriage (Simons, 1993b). Often justified on the erroneous belief that the Koran commands it, these procedures are supposed to ensure that women are chaste before marriage and have no extramarital affairs after marriage. Genital mutilation has resulted in the maiming of many females, some of whom died as a result of hemorrhage, infection, or other complications. It is still practised in more that twenty-five countries. Box 11.3 discusses genital mutilation of women around the world.

In sum, male dominance is very strong in agrarian societies. Women are secluded, subordinated, and mutilated as a means of regulating their sexuality and protecting paternity. Most of the world's population currently lives in agrarian societies in various stages of industrialization.

Industrial Societies

An *industrial society* is one in which factory or mechanized production has replaced agriculture as the major form of economic activity (Nielsen, 1990:49). As societies industrialize, the status of women tends to decline further. Industrialization in Canada created a gap between the nonpaid work performed by women at home and the paid work that increasingly was performed by men and unmarried girls (Krahn and Lowe, 1993; Armstrong and Armstrong, 1994). When families needed extra money, their daughters worked in the textile mills until they married. Once married, women were expected to leave the paid work force. In 1931, for example, only 3.5 percent of married Canadian women were in the paid labour force (Baker and Lero, 1996). As it became more difficult to make a living by farming, many men found work in the factories, where their primary responsibility often was supervising the work of women and children. Men began to press for a clear division between "men's work" and "women's work," as well as corresponding pay differentials (higher for men, lower for women).

In Canada, the division of labour between men and women in the middle and upper classes became much more distinct with industrialization (Vanier Institute of the Family, 1994). The men were responsible for being "breadwinners," the women were seen as "homemakers." In this new "cult of domesticity" (also referred to as the "cult of true womanhood"), the home became a private, personal sphere in which women created a haven for the family (Mandell and Momirov, 1999).

BOX 11.3 SOCIOLOGY IN GLOBAL PERSPECTIVE

WOMEN AND HUMAN RIGHTS: FEMALE GENITAL MUTILATION

The little girl, entirely nude, is immobilized in the sitting position on a low stool by at least three women. One of them has her arms tightly around the little girl's chest, two others hold the child's thighs apart by force, in order to open the vulva. The child's arms are tied behind her back, or immobilized by two other women guests. Then the old woman takes her razor and excises the clitoris. The infibulation follows: the operator cuts with her razor from top to bottom of the small lip and then scrapes the flesh from the inside of the large lip. The nymphotomy and scraping are repeated on the other side of the vulva. The little girl howls and writhes in pain, although strongly held down. The operator wipes the blood from the wound and the mother, as well as the guests, "verify" her work, sometimes putting their fingers in. The opening left for urine and menstrual blood is minuscule. Then the practitioner applies a paste and ensures the adhesion of the large lips by means of acacia thorn, which pierces one lip and passes through into the other. She sticks in three or four in this manner down the vulva. These thorns are then held in place either by means of a sewing thread or horsehair. Paste is again put on the wound. Exhausted, the little girl is then dressed and put on a bed. The operation lasts from 15 to 20 minutes according to the ability of the old woman and the resistance put up by the child. (Tomasevski, 1993:85)

Now in her early thirties, Selma recalls enduring this procedure in Sudan at age 8, screaming and resisting to no avail: "They held me down. It was painful. I had some anesthetic, but I felt it all" (Rowley, 1994:A9).

As we enter the twenty-first century, the traditional ritual of female genital mutilation is performed on an estimated 6000 girls a day around the world, despite the efforts of some governments to stamp it out. The World Health

---

Those who supported the cult of domesticity argued that women were the natural keepers of the domestic sphere and that children were the mother's responsibility. Meanwhile, the "breadwinner" role placed enormous pressure on men to support their families—being a good provider was considered to be a sign of manhood. However, this gendered division of labour increased the economic and political subordination of women (Bernard, 1995). As a result, many women focused their efforts on acquiring a husband who was capable of bringing home a good wage. Single women and widows and their children tended to live a bleak existence, crowded into rundown areas of cities, where they were unable to support themselves on their meagre wages.

While industrialization was a source of upward mobility for many whites, most racial and ethnic minorities were left behind. The cult of domesticity, for example, was distinctly white and middle or upper class. White families with the financial means to do so hired domestic servants to do much of the household work. In the early 1900s, many black women (as well as white non-English-speaking European women) were employed as household servants (Das Gupta, 1999). Consequently, the cult of true womanhood not only increased women's dependence on men but also became the source of discrimination against women from visible minority groups.

As people moved from a rural, agricultural lifestyle to an urban existence, body consciousness increased. People who worked in offices often became sedentary and exhibited physical deterioration from their lack of activity. As gymnasiums were built to fight this lack of physical fitness, a new image of masculinity developed. Whereas the "burly farmer" or "robust workman" previously had been the idealized image of masculinity, now the middle-class man who exercised and lifted

BOX 11.3

CONTINUED

Organization estimates that between 85 million and 110 million women have had their genitals mutilated. Although the practice occurs primarily in twenty-eight African nations and in some areas of Asia, cases of genital mutilation among families of recent immigrants from Africa and Asia have been reported in the United States, Canada, Europe, and Australia. In Egypt in 1998, three girls were reported to have died during the procedure.

In 1993, attorney Linda Weil-Curiel made the following statement at the Paris trial of a mother accused of allowing the mutilation of her daughter (a practice brought to France by African immigrants): "This is butchery invented to control women ... It's a form of violence we would never allow here against white girls. If immigrants cut off a girl's ear in the name of tradition, there would be an outcry. But here the sex of a future woman is cut off and people are willing to defend it or turn away" (quoted in Simons, 1993b:A4).

Some view genital mutilation as a deeply embedded ritual that must be understood in terms of the culture involved. These practices may be perpetrated on young girls because of centuries-old customs dictating that girls must be kept chaste and that, without the ritual, they will not get a husband and their family will not get a dowry. A spokesperson for the World Health Organization noted that respect for other cultures is needed but that such practices must be challenged when they threaten people's health. What do you think? In 1998, the United Nations launched an International campaign to eradicate female genital mutilation. Do you support this campaign? When this practice occurs in Canada, should the parents be charged with child abuse, or should they be excused because of their cultural background?

Sources: Based on Simons, 1993b; Tomasevski, 1993; Greenhouse, 1994; and Rowley, 1994.

weights came to embody the ideal of masculinity (Klein, 1993).

In the late nineteenth century, middle-class women began to become preoccupied with body fitness (Bordo, 1993; Seid, 1994). As industrialization progressed and food became more plentiful, the social symbolism of body weight and size changed. Previously, it had been considered a sign of high status to be somewhat overweight, but now a slender body reflected an enhanced social status. To the status-seeking middle-class man, a slender wife became a symbol of the husband's success. Historian Susan Bordo (1993:193) has suggested that "social power had come to be less dependent on the sheer accumulation of material wealth and more connected to the ability to control and manage the labor and resources of others. At the same time, excess body weight came to be seen as reflecting moral or personal inadequacy, or lack of will" (see also Banner, 1983). Today,

women's bodies (even in bodybuilding programs) are supposed to be "inviting, available, and welcoming" while men's bodies should be "self-contained, active and invasive" (MacSween, 1993:256).

In sum, from hunting and gathering societies to contemporary industrial societies, women's status relative to men has declined. Today, patriarchy and male dominance remain pervasive. These existing patterns of inequality are perpetuated through the process of gender socialization.

GENDER AND SOCIALIZATION

We learn gender-appropriate behaviour through the socialization process. Our parents, teachers, friends, and the media all serve as gendered institutions that communicate to us our earliest, and

Are children's toys a reflection of their own preferences and choices? How do toys reflect gender socialization by parents and other adults?

often most lasting, beliefs about the social meanings of being male or female and thinking and behaving in masculine or feminine ways. Some gender roles have changed dramatically in recent years; others remain largely unchanged over time.

Many parents prefer boys to girls because of stereotypical ideas about the relative importance of males and females to the future of the family and society (Achilles, 1996). Although some parents prefer boys to girls because they believe old myths about the biological inferiority of females, research suggests that social expectations also play a major role in this preference. We are socialized to believe that it is important to have a son, especially as a first or only child. For many years, it was assumed that a male child could support his parents in their later years and carry on the family name.

Across cultures, boys are preferred to girls, especially when the number of children that parents can have is limited by law or economic conditions. For example, in China, which strictly regulates the allowable number of children to one per family, a disproportionate number of female fetuses are aborted (Basow, 1992). In India, the practice of aborting female fetuses is widespread, and female infanticide occurs frequently

(Achilles, 1996). As a result, both India and China have a growing surplus of young men who will face a shortage of women their own age (Shenon, 1994).

In North America, some sex selection no doubt takes place through abortion. However, most women seek abortions because of socioeconomic factors, problematic relationships with partners, health-related concerns, and lack of readiness or ability to care for a child (or another child) (Lott, 1994).

Gender Socialization by Parents

From birth, parents act toward children on the basis of the child's sex. Baby boys are perceived to be less fragile than girls and tend to be treated more roughly by their parents. Girl babies are thought to be "cute, sweet, and cuddly" and receive more gentle treatment (MacDonald and Parke, 1986). When girl babies cry, parents respond to them more quickly, and parents are more prone to talk and sing to girl babies (Basow, 1992). However, one study ("The Favored Infants," 1976) found ethnic–racial variations within cultures of these socialization patterns.

Children's clothing and toys reflect their parents' gender expectations. Boys' clothing, for example, is more "masculine" and functional and features male activities and characters (baseball players and superheros) while girls' clothing is more "feminine" and dainty (floral fabrics, lace, and bows) and has female characters. Gender-appropriate toys for boys include blocks and building sets, trucks and other vehicles, sports equipment, and war toys such as guns and soldiers (Richardson and Simpson, 1982). Girls' toys include "Barbie" dolls, play makeup, and home-making items. Parents' choices of toys for their children are not likely to change in the near future. A group of university students in a recent study was shown slides of toys and asked to decide which ones they would buy for girls and boys. Most said they would buy guns, soldiers, jeeps, carpenter tools, and red bicycles for boys; girls would get baby dolls, dishes, sewing kits, jewellery boxes, and pink bicycles (Fisher-Thompson, 1990).

Boys are encouraged to engage in gender-appropriate behaviour; they are not to show an interest in "girls'" activities. For example, one father was dismayed when he bought his 4-year-old son a Ninja Turtle shaving kit, only to see the little boy head straight for the bathroom, sit on the edge of the tub, and start to shave his legs (*Austin American–Statesman*, 1994).

Differential treatment leads to differential development. A doll or a stuffed animal in a girl's hand calls for "hugging, stroking, and tender loving care"; a ball in a boy's hand "demands bouncing, throwing, and kicking" (Lott, 1994:40). When children are old enough to help with household chores, they often are assigned different tasks. Maintenance chores (such as mowing the lawn) are assigned to boys while domestic chores (such as shopping, cooking, and cleaning the table) are assigned to girls. Chores also may become linked with future occupational choices and personal characteristics. Girls who are responsible for domestic chores such as caring for younger brothers and sisters may learn nurturing behaviours that later translate into employment as a nurse or schoolteacher. Boys may learn about mechanics and other types of technology that lead to different career options.

Just as appropriate "masculine" or "feminine" behaviour is learned through interaction with parents and other caregivers, inappropriate behaviour such as eating problems can be learned from parents. Nicole Annesi tells how she learned about binging and purging from her mother:

I was seven years old the first time I was exposed to my mother's bulimia. It was after dinner one evening. After Mom and I cleared the table … she quickly disappeared into the bathroom … What was unusual about these visits was that they became consistent. After each meal Mom would visit the bathroom and come out a few minutes later looking pale, yet refreshed …

So after the dishes were cleared away that evening, I disappeared into the bathroom. I hid in the tub, behind the navy blue, opaque curtain … like clockwork, in she came. I peered between the curtains to find my mother bent over the toilet, like she was going to get sick or something. And then I watched her … She placed a popsicle stick down her throat and made herself sick. How weird, I thought to myself. Mom comes into the bathroom every night to stick one of these doctor sticks down her throat! …

I began to do some thinking myself … I knew when I got sick, afterwards my stomach would flatten out. I felt lighter. So one day after school I ate a bag of Pecan Sandies. I stuffed myself until I couldn't swallow. Afterwards I made my way to the upstairs bathroom and locked the door behind me. I turned on the faucet so that nothing could be heard

From an early age, a number of societal influences encourage us to learn gender-appropriate behaviour.

… That day I became a seven-year-old bulimic. (Annesi, 1993:91–93)

Many parents are aware of the effect that gender socialization has on their children and make a conscientious effort to provide nonsexist experiences for them. For example, one study found that mothers with nontraditional views encourage their daughters to be independent (Brooks-Gunn, 1986). Many fathers also take an active role in socializing their sons to be thoughtful and caring individuals who do not live by traditional gender stereotypes. However, peers often make nontraditional gender socialization much more difficult for parents and children (see Rabinowitz and Cochran, 1994).

Peers and Gender Socialization

Peers help children learn prevailing gender role stereotypes, as well as gender-appropriate and –inappropriate behaviour. During the school years, same-sex peers have a powerful effect on how children see their gender roles (Maccoby and Jacklin, 1987); children are more socially acceptable to their peers when they conform to gender stereotypes (Martin, 1989).

Male peer groups place more pressure on boys to do "masculine" things than female peer groups place on girls to do "feminine" things (Fagot, 1984). For example, girls wear jeans and other "boy" clothes, play soccer and softball, and engage in other activities traditionally associated with males. But, if a boy wears a dress, plays hopscotch with girls, and engages in other activities associated with being female, he will be ridiculed by his peers. This distinction between the relative value of boys' and girls' behaviours strengthens the cultural message that masculine activities and behaviour are more important and more acceptable (Wood, 1994b).

During adolescence, peers often are more influential agents of gender socialization than adults. Peers are thought to be especially important in boys' development of gender identity (Maccoby and Jacklin, 1987). Male bonding that occurs during adolescence is believed to reinforce masculine identity (Gaylin, 1992) and to encourage gender-stereotypical attitudes and behaviour (Huston, 1985; Martin, 1989). For example, male peers have a tendency to ridicule and bully others about their appearance, size, and weight. One woman painfully recalled walking down the halls at school when boys would flatten themselves against the lockers and cry, "Wide load!" At lunchtime, the boys made a production of watching her eat lunch and frequently made sounds like pig grunts or moos (Kolata, 1993). Because peer acceptance is so important for both males and females during their first two decades, such actions can have very harmful consequences for the victims.

As young adults, men and women still receive many gender-related messages from peers. Among university students, for example, peers play an important role in career choices and the establishment of long-term, intimate relationships. Male peers may pressure other men to participate in "male bonding" rituals that are derogatory toward women (DeKeseredy and Kelly, 1995). For example, fraternity initiations may require pledges to participate in behaviour ranging from "showing their manhood" to gang rapes (O'Sullivan, 1993). Some of the research suggests that male peers are often unable to show a man how to effectively interact intimately with other people (Tannen, 1990; DeKeseredy and Kelly, 1995).

Peer groups for both women and men on university campuses are organized largely around gender relations (Holland and Eisenhart, 1990). In a study that followed a number of women students at two universities, anthropologists Dorothy C. Holland and Margaret A. Eisenhart (1990) found that the peer system propelled women into a world of romance in which their attractiveness to men counted most; the women were subjected to a "sexual auction block." While peers initially did not influence the women's choices of majors and careers, they did influence whether the women continued to pursue their initial goals, changed their course of action, or were "derailed" (Holland and Eisenhart, 1981, 1990).

If Holland and Eisenhart's research can be generalized to other colleges and universities, peer pressure often is at its strongest in relation to appearance norms. As other researchers have shown, peer pressure can strongly influence a person's body consciousness. Women in university often feel pressure to be very thin, as Karen explains:

"Do you diet?" asked a friend [in my first year of university], as I was stuffing a third homemade chocolate chip cookie in my mouth. "Do you know how many calories there are in that one cookie?"

Stopping to think for a moment as she and two other friends stared at me, probably wanting to ask me the same question, I realized that I really didn't even know what a calorie was …

From that moment, I'd taken on a new enemy, one more powerful and destructive than any human can be. One that nearly fought me to the death—my death …

I just couldn't eat food anymore. I was so obsessed with it that I thought about it every second … In two months, I'd lost thirty pounds … Everyone kept telling me I looked great …

I really didn't realize that anything was wrong with me … There were physical things occurring in my body other than not having my period anymore. My hair was falling out and was getting thinner … I would constantly get head rushes every time I stood up … When my friends would all go out to dinner or to a party I stayed home quite often, afraid that I might have to eat something, and afraid that my friends would find out that I didn't eat. (Twenhofel, 1993:198)

Feminist scholars have concluded that eating problems are not always psychological "disorders" (as they are referred to by members of the medical profession). Instead, eating (or not eating) may be a strategy for coping with problems such as unrealistic social pressures about slenderness (see Orbach, 1978; Chernin, 1981; Hesse-Biber, 1996) and/or social injustices caused by racism, sexism, and classism in society (Thompson, 1994).

Teachers, Schools, and Gender Socialization

From kindergarten through university, schools operate as gendered institutions. Teachers provide important messages about gender through both the formal content of classroom assignments and informal interaction with students. Sometimes, gender-related messages from teachers and other students reinforce gender roles that have been taught at home; however, teachers also may contradict parental socialization. During the early years of a child's schooling, the teacher's influence is very powerful; many children spend more hours per day with their teachers than they do with their own parents.

One of the messages teachers may communicate to students is that boys are more important than girls. Research spanning the past twenty years shows that unintentional gender bias occurs in virtually all educational settings. **Gender bias consists of showing favouritism toward one gender over the other.** Researchers consistently find that teachers devote more time, effort, and attention to boys than to girls (Sadker and Sadker, 1994). Males receive more praise for their contributions and are called on more frequently in class, even when they do not volunteer. Very often, boys receive attention because they call out in class, demand help, and sometimes engage in disruptive behaviour (Sadker and Sadker, 1994). Teachers who do not negatively sanction such behaviour may unintentionally encourage it. In a Toronto secondary school classroom, a teacher asked students to use a stopwatch to measure the speaking time of male and female students in the class. The students themselves were shocked to learn that males were speaking 75 to 80 percent of the time (Gaskell et al., 1995). Boys learn that when they yell out an answer without being called on, their answer will be accepted by the teacher; girls learn that they will be praised when they are compliant and wait for the teacher to call on them. If they call out an answer, they may be corrected with comments such as, "Please raise your hand if you want to speak" (Sadker and Sadker, 1994).

The content of teacher–student interaction is very important. In a multiple-year study of more than one hundred Grade 4, Grade 6, and Grade 8 students, education professors Myra and David Sadker (1984) identified four types of teacher comments: praise, acceptance, remediation, and criticism. They found that boys typically received more of all four types of teacher comments than did girls. Teachers also gave more precise and penetrating replies to boys; by contrast, teachers used vague and superficial terms such as "OK" when responding to girls. Because boys receive more specific and intense interaction from teachers, they may gain more insights than girls into the strengths and weaknesses of their answers and thus learn how to improve their responses.

Teacher–student interactions influence not only students' learning but also their self-esteem (Sadker and Sadker, 1985, 1986, 1994). A comprehensive study of gender bias in schools suggested that girls' self-esteem is undermined in school through such experiences as (1) a relative lack of attention from teachers, (2) sexual harassment by male peers, (3) the stereotyping and invisibility of females in textbooks, especially in science and math texts, and (4) test bias based on assumptions about the relative importance of quantitative and visual-spatial ability, as compared with verbal ability, that lessen girls' chances of being admitted to the university of their choice and awarded scholarships. White males may have better self-esteem because they receive more teacher attention than all other student groups (Sadker and Sadker, 1994).

Teachers also influence how students treat one another during school hours. Many teachers use sex segregation as a way to organize students, resulting in unnecessary competition between females and males (Eyre, 1992). In addition, teachers also may take a "boys will be boys" attitude when females complain of sexual harassment. Even though sexual harassment is prohibited by law, and teachers and administrators are obligated to investigate such incidents, the complaints may be dealt with superficially. If that happens, the school setting can become a hostile environment rather than a site for learning (Sadker and Sadker, 1994).

Most problems that exist in prekindergarten through high school also are found in colleges and universities. University professors often pay more attention to men than women in their classes.

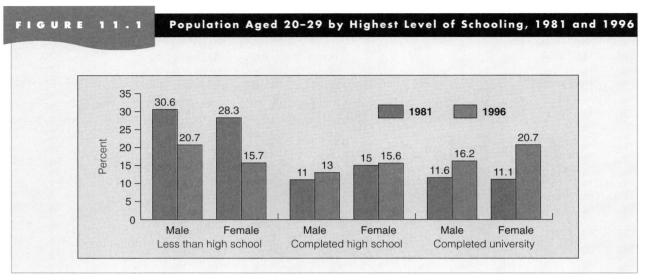

FIGURE 11.1 Population Aged 20–29 by Highest Level of Schooling, 1981 and 1996

Reprinted by permission of Statistics Canada, adapted from *The Daily*, Cat. no. 11-001, March 17, 1998.

Women are also subjected to a number of "exclusionary tactics," such as being called on less frequently and receiving less encouragement than men, or being interrupted, ignored, or devalued (Wylie, 1995). Researchers have found that women university professors (approximately 22 percent of university teachers) encourage a more participatory classroom environment and do a better job of including both women and men in their interactions (Statham, Richardson, and Cook, 1994). However, a study, which has come to be known as the "Chilly Climate Report" conducted at the University of Western Ontario, found that the university classroom is a "chilly" climate for women students, who often experience a drop in self-esteem as a result of their academic experiences. One graduate student reported that she felt "totally demoralized ... a failure ... I forget, even now, that I used to be seen as a powerful person. I lost my sense of personal power and self worth in the four years I was there" (Backhouse et al., 1995:127).

Despite these obstacles, young Canadian women are more likely to earn a university degree than their male counterparts. As shown in Figure 11.1, in 1996 almost 21 percent of women in their 20s obtained a university degree compared with approximately 16 percent of men in the same age group (Statistics Canada, 1998g). This is a relatively recent trend. It was not until 1988 that women's enrolment in university surpassed men's (Wylie, 1995).

Most fields of study retain a male or female orientation, even though there has been a blending of fields of study in recent years. The proportion of women has been increasing in many traditionally male fields (including physics, meteorology, engineering, architecture, and dentistry), yet remains comparatively small. Men still constitute the majority of majors in architecture, engineering, computer technology, and physical sciences, and at the graduate level, the number of women degree recipients in these disciplines declines dramatically. The mix of men and women is relatively equal in some of the fields that lead to high-paying jobs such as law, medicine, and optometry (Wannell and Caron, 1996). These recent trends should be reflected in further reductions in earnings gaps between men and women.

Sports and Gender Socialization

Children spend more than half of their nonschool time in play and games, but the type of games played differs with the child's sex. Studies indicate that boys are socialized to participate in highly competitive, rule-oriented games with a larger number of participants than games played by girls. Girls have been socialized to play exclusively with others of their own age, in groups of two or three, in activities such as hopscotch and jump rope that involve a minimum of competitiveness (Adler et al., 1995).

From elementary school through high school, boys are encouraged to play competitive sports

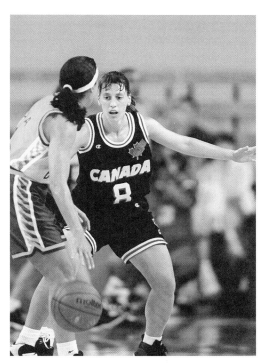

Women athletes juggle contradictory statuses. According to one study, women university basketball players "did athlete" on the court and "did woman" after the game.

According to sociologist Judith Lorber (1994:41), "Sports illustrate the ways bodies are gendered by social practices and how the female body is socially constructed to be inferior." Most sports are rigidly divided into female and male events. Assumptions about male and female physiology and athletic capabilities influence the types of sports in which members of each sex are encouraged to participate. For example, women who engage in activities that are assumed to be "masculine" (such as bodybuilding) may either ignore their critics or attempt to redefine the activity or its result as "feminine" or womanly (Duff and Hong, 1984; Klein, 1993). Some women bodybuilders do not want their bodies to get "overbuilt." They have learned that they are more likely to win women's bodybuilding competitions if they look and pose "more or less along the lines of fashion models" (Klein, 1993:179). How strongly some female gymnasts internalize this idealized body image was reflected by the death of 22-year-old Christy Henrich, a former nationally ranked gymnast. At the time of her death, she weighed less than sixty pounds, the victim of anorexia and bulimia; her mother said, "[Christy] was going to do whatever it took, no matter what the price. She could endure any pain" (quoted in Amdur, 1994:B9).

Mass Media and Gender Socialization

The media are a powerful source of gender stereotyping. While some critics argue that the media simply reflect existing gender roles in society, others point out that the media have a uniquely persuasive ability to shape ideas. Think of the impact that television has on children who are estimated to spend one-third of their waking time watching it. Children from working-class families spend significantly more time in front of the television than those from the middle class (Basow, 1992).

From children's cartoons to adult shows, television programs are sex-typed and white-male oriented. More male than female roles are shown, and male and female characters act in strikingly different ways. Males are typically more aggressive, constructive, and direct and are rewarded for their actions. In contrast, females are depicted as acting deferentially toward people or as manipulating them through helplessness or seductiveness to get their way (Basow, 1992). Because adver-

such as hockey and football. For males, competitive sports becomes a means of "constructing a masculine identity, a legitimate outlet for violence and aggression, and an avenue for upward mobility" (Lorber, 1994:43). Patricia Adler and her colleagues' participant observation study (1995) of two elementary school classrooms indicated that the most important factor affecting the boys' popularity or social status was athletic ability. Recently, more girls have started to play soccer, hockey, and baseball, and in the future, even more girls and women will participate in sports formerly regarded as exclusively "male" activities. However, even with these changes, women athletes have to manage a contradictory status of being both "women" and "athletes." One study found that women university basketball players dealt with this contradiction by dividing their lives into segments. On the basketball court, the women "did athlete": they pushed, shoved, fouled, ran hard, sweated, and cursed. Off the court, they "did woman": after the game, they showered, dressed, applied makeup, and styled their hair, even if they were only getting in a van for a long ride home (Watson, 1987).

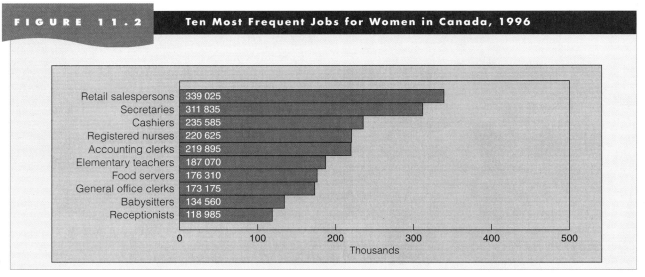

FIGURE 11.2   Ten Most Frequent Jobs for Women in Canada, 1996

Job	Number
Retail salespersons	339 025
Secretaries	311 835
Cashiers	235 585
Registered nurses	220 625
Accounting clerks	219 895
Elementary teachers	187 070
Food servers	176 310
General office clerks	173 175
Babysitters	134 560
Receptionists	118 985

Thousands

Reprinted by permission of Statistics Canada, adapted from *The Daily*, Cat. no. 11-001, March 17, 1998.

tisers hope to appeal to boys, who constitute more than half of the viewing audience for some shows, many programs feature lively adventure and lots of loud noise and violence. Even educational programs such as *Sesame Street* and *Barney* may perpetuate gender stereotypes. Most of the characters on these shows have male names and masculine voices and participate in "boy's activities."

While attempts have been made by media "watchdogs" and some members of the media itself to eliminate sexism in children's programming, adult daytime and prime-time programs (which children frequently watch) have received less scrutiny. Soap operas are a classic example of programs that stereotype gender. In them, women are depicted as emotional, nurturing, and unable to make a decision; men are forceful and more oriented toward problem solving. Daytime talk shows such as *Oprah* may trivialize important issues of sex and gender under the guise of letting people air their grievances and opinions and of having experts who set the record straight (Basow, 1992).

In prime-time television, a number of significant changes in the past three decades have reduced gender stereotyping; however, men still outnumber women as leading characters. Men, for the most part, have been police officers, detectives, attorneys, doctors, and businessmen. In recent years, women in professional careers have been overrepresented, which may give the erroneous impression that most women in the workforce are in executive, managerial, and professional positions; in the "real world," most employed women work in low-paying, low-status

jobs (see Figure 11.2). In most programs, women's appearance is considered very important and frequently is a topic of discussion in the program itself. Advertising reinforces the notion that women can never be too young or too thin, as discussed in Box 11.4.

Advertising—whether on television and billboards or in magazines and newspapers—can be very persuasive. The intended message is clear to many people: if they embrace traditional notions of masculinity and femininity, their personal and social success is assured; and if they purchase the right products and services, they can enhance their appearance and gain power over other people. For example, the $20-billion-per-year cosmetics industry uses ads depicting the "truly feminine woman" as needing a "plethora of beauty aids to help her look younger and more attractive to men" (Wolf, 1990). Such ads may play an important role in adult gender socialization.

A knowledge of how we develop a gender-related self-concept and learn to feel, think, and act in feminine or masculine ways is important for an understanding of ourselves. Examining gender socialization makes us aware of the impact our parents, sibling, teachers, friends, and the media have on our own perspectives about gender. However, the gender socialization perspective has been criticized on several accounts. Childhood gender-role socialization may not affect people as much as some analysts have suggested. For example, the types of jobs people take as adults may have less to do with how they were socialized in childhood than it does with how they are

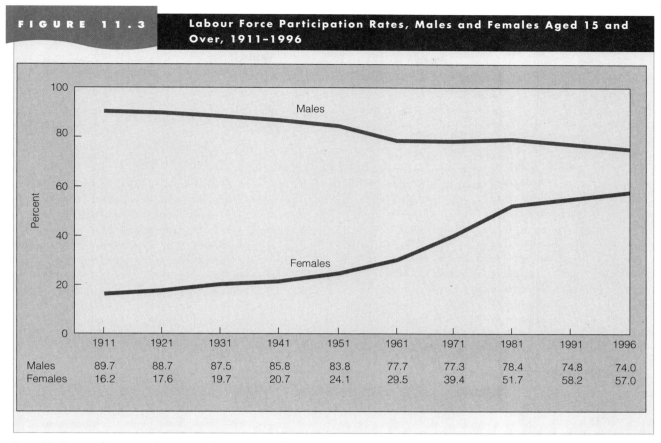

Prepared by the Centre for International Statistics. © The Vanier Institute of the Family. 1996 figures from Akyeampoing, 1996. Used by permission.

treated in the workplace. From this perspective, women and men will act in ways that bring them the most rewards and produce the fewest punishments (Reskin and Padavic, 1994). Also, gender socialization theories can be used to blame women for their own subordination (Eitzen and Baca Zinn, 1995). For example, if we assume that women's problems can all be blamed on women themselves, existing social structures that perpetuate gender inequality will be overlooked. We will now examine some of those structural forces.

CONTEMPORARY GENDER INEQUALITY

According to feminist scholars, women experience gender inequality as a result of economic, political, and educational discrimination (Luxton, 1980; Smith, 1987; Curtis et al., 1999). Women's position in the Canadian workforce reflects their overall subordination in society.

Gender Segregation of Paid Work

One of the most significant changes in Canadian society in recent decades has been the dramatic rise in the number of women in the paid workforce. As shown in Figure 11.3, in 1950 only 24 percent of all adult women in Canada worked outside of the home for pay. By 1996, this figure had jumped to 57 percent. Among the most significant factors contributing to these changes in the labour force are women's rising educational levels, the rise in single-parent families, and the economic demand for dual-income families (Lowe, 1999).

Not only are more Canadian women working today, but they are employed in a much wider range of occupations than ever before. In the past two decades women have been successful in breaking down barriers to some of the high-paying, prestigious, traditionally "male" professions such as medicine, law, and corporate management (Creese and Beagan, 1999:202). For example, in 1996, women accounted for 30 percent of general practitioners and specialist physi-

BOX 11.4   SOCIOLOGY AND MEDIA

"YOU'VE COME A LONG WAY, BABY"

In a television commercial, two little French girls are shown dressing up in the feathery finery of their mothers' clothes. They are exquisite little girls, flawless and innocent, and the scene emphasizes both their youth and the natural sense of style often associated with French women. (The ad is done in French, with subtitles.) One of the girls, spying a picture of the other girl's mother, exclaims breathlessly, "Your mother, she is so slim, so beautiful? Does she eat?" The daughter, giggling, replies, "Silly, just not as much," and displays her mother's helper, a bottle of diet pills. "Aren't you jealous?" the friend asks. Dimpling, shy, yet self-possessed, deeply knowing, the daughter answers, "Not if I know her secrets." (Bordo, 1993:99)

Women are bombarded with such advertisements and commercials for weight-loss products and programs. This ad is especially problematic, however, because it suggests that very young girls should begin learning to control their weight by the use of some "secret" (Bordo, 1993:99). Viewers must use their imagination about how the mother looks, but

the message is clear: Her "slim … beautiful" appearance can belong to any woman who purchases this product. According to media scholar Jean Kilbourne (1994:395):

> The current emphasis on excessive thinness for women is one of the clearest examples of advertising's power to influence cultural standards and consequent individual behavior. Body types, like clothing styles, go in and out of fashion, and are promoted by advertising … The images in the mass media constantly reinforce the latest ideal—what is acceptable and what is out of date … Advertising and the media indoctrinate us in these ideals, to the detriment of most women.

Today's ideal body type is unattainable except for the thinnest 5 percent of all women. Clearly, the dramatic increase in eating problems in recent years cannot be attributed solely to advertising and the mass media; however, their potential impact on young girls and women in establishing role models with whom to identify is extremely important (Kilbourne, 1994:398).

Recurring themes in advertising campaigns directed at women include the need for diet

cians, up from 18 percent in 1982 (Statistics Canada, 1998k). Social analyst John Kettle indicated that women are now filling the majority of new managerial and professional jobs. Using Statistics Canada data, he found that between 1975 and 1996 the Canadian economy produced 1.3 million additional management jobs and 1.2 million professional jobs. Women filled 57 percent of the managerial jobs and 65 percent of the professional jobs (Kettle, 1998b). Despite this progress, the majority of Canadian women continue to be employed in a much narrower range of occupations which are lower-paying, low-status, traditionally female jobs. Almost 70 percent of all

working women are employed in just four occupational sectors: teaching, nursing and health-related occupations, clerical, or sales and service.

Gender-segregated work refers to the concentration of women and men in different occupations (Lowe, 1999). In 1996, for example, almost 80 percent of all clerical jobs in Canada were held by women (see Table 11.3). In the same year, men were overrepresented in jobs in the natural sciences, engineering, and mathematics—making up 80 percent of the professionals in these fields (Creese and Beagan, 1999). The term *female job ghetto* refers to the unequal rewards and opportunities built into the labour market on the basis of

BOX 11.4

CONTINUED

products and the fear of fat, reinforced by the theme of guilt (Kilbourne, 1994:404). The messages in these ads may even be contradictory. Virginia Slims cigarette advertisements say, "You've come a long way, baby!" even though they are marketing an addictive and unhealthy product (Kilbourne, 1994:413). In one ad, a slim, elegant African American woman holds up a lighted cigarette. The caption states, "Decisions are easy. When I get to a fork in the road, I eat." The ad suggests that this woman can make decisions easily; she can eat and not experience negative consequences simply because she smokes a particular brand of cigarettes. Nor are such ads new; for most of this century, cigarettes have been marketed to women and young girls as a way to control their weight. In 1928, for example, Lucky Strike cigarette ads stated, "To keep a slender figure, no one can deny ... reach for a Lucky instead of a sweet" (Kilbourne, 1994:413).

As women have attempted to gain power and freedom, advertising has worked to reduce the political to the personal. If people buy the right products and get their individual acts together, everything will be fine. As Kilbourne (1994) notes, "The advertisers will

never voluntarily change, because it is profitable for women to feel terrible about themselves. Thus, we need to educate everyone to be critical viewers of advertising and the mass media."

Sources: Based on Barthel, 1988; Moog, 1990; Bordo, 1993; and Kilbourne, 1994.

the employee's gender. Women in job ghettos often have limited access to the more challenging, higher-paying occupations dominated by men because many of these professions set up success criteria that are male-biased (Canadian Committee on Women in Engineering, 1992, cited in Lowe, 1999).

Gender-segregated work affects both men and women. Men often are kept out of certain types of jobs. Those who enter female-dominated occupations often have to justify themselves and prove that they are "real men." They have to fight stereotypes ("Is he gay? Lazy?") about why they are interested in such work (Williams, 1993:3). Even

if these assumptions do not push men out of female-dominated occupations, they affect how the men manage their gender identity at work. For example, men in occupations such as nursing emphasize their masculinity, attempt to distance themselves from female colleagues, and try to move quickly into management and supervisory positions (Williams, 1989, 1993).

Although the degree of gender segregation in parts of the professional labour market has declined since the 1970s (Sokoloff, 1992), racial-ethnic segregation has remained deeply embedded in the social structure. However, the relationship between visible minority status and occupational

TABLE 11.3	DISTRIBUTION OF EMPLOYMENT IN CANADA, BY OCCUPATION AND GENDER, 1996		
OCCUPATION	PERCENTAGE OF WOMEN	PERCENTAGE OF MEN	WOMEN AS A PERCENTAGE OF EMPLOYMENT
Managerial/administrative	12.7	14.0	44.9
Natural Sciences/engineering/ mathematics	0.8	5.8	20.2
Social Sciences/religion	0.2	2.0	57.5
Teaching	6.6	3.0	64.6
Doctors/dentists	0.5	0.9	32.1
Nursing/other health related	9.1	1.2	86.1
Artistic/literary/recreational	2.3	2.4	44.4
Clerical	25.0	5.3	79.7
Sales	10.2	9.9	46.1
Service	17.5	10.9	57.1
Primary industries	2.2	6.5	21.5
Manufacturing	5.1	18.0	19.0
Construction	0.3	8.9	2.6
Transportation	0.8	6.3	9.3
Material handling/other crafts	1.7	5.1	22.0

Reprinted by permission of Statistics Canada, adapted from *The Labour Force: Annual Averages*, Statistics Canada, 1996, Cat. no. 13-217.

status is complex and varies by gender. Although visible minority males are overrepresented in both lower- and higher-status occupations, nonwhite women are heavily overrepresented in lower-paying, low-skilled jobs (Krahn and Lowe, 1993).

Workplace gender segregation is not unique to Canada. For example, in Sweden, the country with the highest rate of women's paid labour force participation in the world, gender segregation is even greater (Borchorst and Siim, 1987). Across cultures, men are less active than women in crossing the gender barrier in employment (Kauppinen-Toropainen and Lammi, 1993).

Occupational gender segregation contributes to stratification in society. Job segregation is structural; it does not occur simply because individual workers have different abilities, motivations, and material needs. As a result of gender and racial segregation, employers are able to pay many visible minority males and females less money, promote them less often, and provide fewer benefits. If they demand better working conditions or

wages, workers often are reminded of the number of individuals (members of Marx's "reserve army") who would like to have their jobs.

The Gender Wage Gap

Occupational segregation contributes to a second form of discrimination—the *wage gap,* a term used to describe the disparity between women's and men's earnings. It is calculated by dividing women's earnings by men's to yield a percentage, also known as the *earnings ratio* (Lowe, 1999). Male–female wage differences reveal that gender is a major source of inequality in the workforce. Figure 11.4 shows that there has been some improvement in this earnings ratio in recent decades, but the progress has been slow. In 1996, women who worked full time for the whole year still earned only 73 cents for each dollar earned by their male counterparts (Statistics Canada, 1999a). Marital status has a dramatic impact on

What stereotypes are associated with men in female-oriented occupations? With women in male-oriented occupations? Do you think such stereotypes will change in the near future?

the wage gap. In 1996, *single* women earned 93 cents for every dollar earned by single men. *Married* women, on the other hand, earned only 69 cents for every dollar earned by a married man (Statistics Canada, 1998c). As shown in Table 11.4, the gender wage gap exists for all levels of education. Although higher education clearly narrows the wage gap between men and women, a woman with a university degree earns approximately $13,000 less than a man with a university degree. Once again, this gap is attributable to occupation segregation. The majority of female university students enrol in degree programs in education, health professions, fine arts, and the humanities, while males continue to dominate in the fields of science and engineering. Even within occupations that require specialized educational credentials, the wage gap does not disappear—for every dollar earned by men, women earned: 66 cents as dentists, 68 cents as lawyers, and 77 cents as university professors (Statistics Canada, 1998c).

Because women's overall pay relative to men's has increased by about a penny a year for the past ten years, it might seem that women's earnings have taken a noticeable move upwards. However, this decrease in the wage gap can be partially attributed to the fact that men's earnings have declined since the 1970s while women's have climbed slowly (Krahn and Lowe, 1998).

Pay Equity and Employment Equity

A number of strategies have been implemented in an attempt to achieve greater gender equality in the labour market. *Pay equity* attempts to raise the value of the work traditionally performed by women. *Employment equity* strategies focus on ways to move women into higher-paying jobs traditionally held by men (Creese and Beagan, 1999). Since the 1980s the federal government,

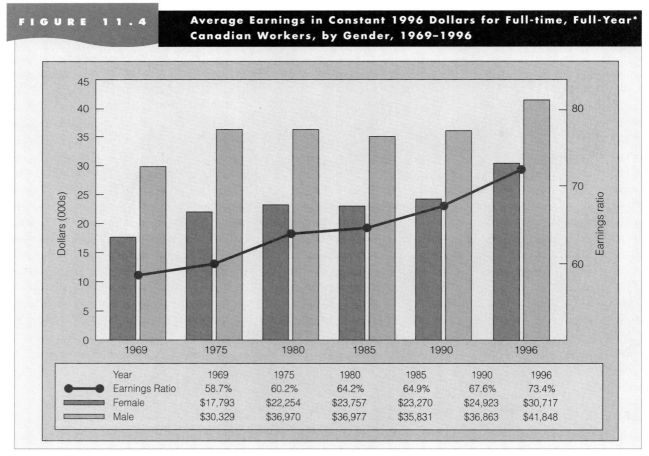

FIGURE   11.4   Average Earnings in Constant 1996 Dollars for Full-time, Full-Year* Canadian Workers, by Gender, 1969–1996

Year	1969	1975	1980	1985	1990	1996
Earnings Ratio	58.7%	60.2%	64.2%	64.9%	67.6%	73.4%
Female	$17,793	$22,254	$23,757	$23,270	$24,923	$30,717
Male	$30,329	$36,970	$36,977	$35,831	$36,863	$41,848

*Full-time = 30 or more hours weekly; full-year = 49–52 weeks annually (50–52 weeks prior to 1981). Earnings ratio: female earnings as a percentage of male earnings.

Reprinted by permission of Statistics Canada, adapted from *Earnings of Men and Women in 1996*, Cat. no. 13-217.

some provincial governments, and a number of private companies have implemented pay equity and employment equity policies (Lowe, 1999).

Pay equity or, as it is sometimes called **comparable worth** reflects the belief that wages ought to reflect the worth of a job, not the gender or race of the worker (Kemp, 1994). How can the comparable worth of different kinds of jobs be determined? One way is to compare the actual work of women's and men's jobs and see if there is a disparity in the salaries paid for each. To do this, analysts break a job into components—such as the education, training, and skills required, the extent of responsibility for others' work, and the working conditions—and then allocate points for each (Lorber, 1994). For pay equity to exist, men and women in occupations that receive the same number of points should be paid the same. In short, pay equity promotes the principle of equal pay for work of equal value.

A second strategy for addressing inequality in the workplace is **employment equity**—a strategy to eliminate the effects of discrimination and to fully open the competition for job opportunities to those who have been excluded historically (Krahn and Lowe, 1998). The target groups for employment equity are visible minorities, persons with disabilities, Aboriginal peoples, and women. In comparison with pay equity, which addresses wage issues only, employment equity covers a range of employment issues such as recruitment, selection, training, development, and promotion. Employment equity also addresses issues pertaining to conditions of employment such as compensation, layoffs, and disciplinary action (Boyd, 1995). The 1986 Employment Equity Act covers only employers within the federal government, including federal Crown corporations, banks, and companies that have federal government contracts. This represents only about 11 percent of

TABLE 11.4 **AVERAGE ANNUAL EARNINGS, BY EDUCATION AND GENDER, FULL-TIME FULL-YEAR WORKERS, 1995**

EDUCATIONAL ATTAINMENT	WOMEN	MEN	WOMEN'S EARNINGS AS A PERCENTAGE OF MEN'S
Less than Grade 9	20,637	29,634	69.6
Some secondary school	21,971	33,735	65.1
Secondary school graduate	25,760	35,650	72.3
Some postsecondary	27,399	37,859	72.4
Postsecondary certificate/diploma	28,840	39,710	72.6
University degree	42,584	55,976	76.1
Total	29,700	41,610	73.1

Reprinted by permission of Statistics Canada, adapted from *Earnings of Men and Women in 1995*, Cat. no. 13-217XPB.

the Canadian labour force (Boyd, 1995:24). Although these policies represent a start in the right direction, male resistance and poor regulation and enforcement have resulted in minimal progress toward gendered employment equity.

Unpaid Work—The Second Shift

As previously discussed, the first big change in the relationship between family and work occurred with the Industrial Revolution and the rise of capitalism. The cult of domesticity kept many middle- and upper-class women out of the workforce during this period. Working-class and poor women primarily were the ones who had to deal with the work/family conflict. Today, however, the issue spans the entire economic spectrum (McQuillan and Belle, 1999). The typical married woman in Canada combines paid work in the labour force and family work as a homemaker.

Even with dramatic changes in women's workforce participation, the sexual division of labour in the family remains essentially unchanged. While most married women now share responsibility for the breadwinner role, many men do not accept their share of domestic responsibilities (Armstrong, 1993; Marshall, 1995; Luxton, 1995; McQuillan and Belle, 1999). The 1996 Census was the first census to include questions on unpaid work. The results indicated that even when women work full time in the paid workforce, most maintain primary responsibility for unpaid work, which includes child care, elder care, housework, shopping, and food preparation (Creese and

Beagan, 1999). Among couples without children, the woman does about 60 percent more housework than her male partner (see Figure 11.5). This gap is even more pronounced in families with children, in which women spend more than twice as much time on domestic work. Consequently, many women have a "double day" or "second shift" because of their dual responsibilities for paid and unpaid work (Hochschild, 1989). Working women have less time to spend on housework; if husbands do not participate in routine domestic chores, some chores simply do not get done or get done less often.

Although some kinds of housework can be put off, the needs of children often cannot be ignored or delayed. When children are ill or school events cannot be scheduled around work, parents (especially mothers) may experience stressful role conflicts ("Shall I be a good employee or a good mother?"). Consider the following scenario of a mother trying to balance the often conflicting demands of working and parenting her young daughter:

A few weeks ago, Camille Allen tried to get a jump on the day by leaving earlier than usual to her human resources job at the Canadian Imperial Bank of Commerce in Toronto. The change in timetable didn't suit her seven-year-old daughter, who burst into tears when her mother got ready to go. "She's not usually like that and her Dad was there, but she wanted me to take her to school," Allen says. "She wailed and wailed and I kind of peeled her off me at the front door." Allen, 41, got in her van and drove

FIGURE 11.5   **Mean Hours of Housework per Week by Gender and Presence of Children**

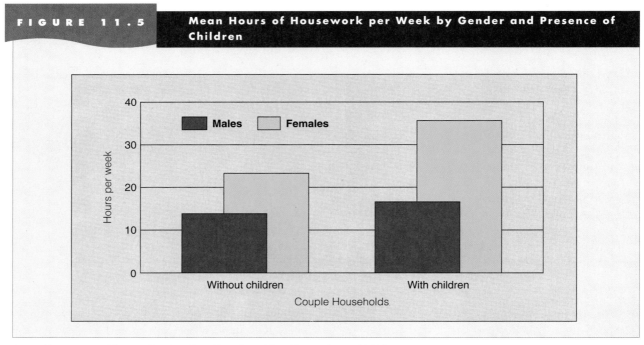

Reprinted by permission of Statistics Canada, adapted from *General Social Survey*, Cat. no. 11-612.

off with her daughter's cries still ringing in her head. "I got close to the highway and I thought, 'You know what? This just isn't worth it.' So I turned around, went home, waited around for half an hour and took her to school." (Chisholm et al., 1999)

Many working women care not only for themselves, their husbands, and their children but also for elderly parents or in-laws. Some analysts refer to these women as "the sandwich generation"— caught between the needs of their young children and elderly relatives. Many women try to solve their time crunch by forgoing leisure time and sleep. When Arlie Hochschild interviewed working mothers, she found that they talked about sleep "the way a hungry person talks about food" (1989:9).

What can be done to address the gendered division of unpaid work? Strategies include improved government supports such as low-cost daycare and better maternity and paternity leave provisions. Employers also need to create more "family friendly" programs such as on-site daycare, flex-time, and family leave, as well as decreasing demands for overtime. Finally, although men are involved in a greater share of the unpaid work in the home than ever before, the division of labour is still far from equal. Until significant changes are made in the distribution of unpaid work, gender

segregation in lower-paying jobs will likely remain a reality for most Canadian women (Creese and Beagan, 1999: 208).

PERSPECTIVES ON GENDER STRATIFICATION

Sociological perspectives on gender stratification vary in their approach to examining gender roles and power relationships in society. Some focus on the roles of women and men in the domestic sphere; others note the inequalities arising from a gendered division of labour in the workplace. Still others attempt to integrate both the public and private spheres into their analyses.

Functionalist and Neoclassical Economic Perspectives

As seen earlier, functionalist theory views men and women as having distinct roles that are important for the survival of the family and society. The most basic division of labour is biological: men are physically stronger while women are the only ones able to bear and nurse children. Gendered belief systems foster assumptions about appropriate behaviour for men and women and may have an impact on the types of work women and men perform.

THE IMPORTANCE OF TRADITIONAL GENDER ROLES

According to functional analysts such as Talcott Parsons (1955), women's roles as nurturers and caregivers are even more pronounced in contemporary industrialized societies. While the husband performs the *instrumental* tasks of providing economic support and making decisions, the wife assumes the *expressive* tasks of providing affection and emotional support for the family. This division of family labour ensures that important societal tasks will be fulfilled; it also provides stability for family members.

This view has been adopted by a number of conservative analysts. George F. Gilder (1986) argues that traditional gender roles are important not only for individuals but also for the economic and social order of society. He asserts that relationships between men and women are damaged when changes in gender roles occur, and family life suffers as a consequence. According to Gilder, women provide for the socialization of the next generation; if they do not, society's moral fabric will decay, resulting in higher rates of crime, violence, and drug abuse. From this perspective, the traditional division of labour between men and women is the natural order of the universe (Kemp, 1994).

THE HUMAN CAPITAL MODEL

Functionalist explanations of occupational gender segregation are similar to neoclassical economic perspectives, such as the human capital model (Horan, 1978; Kemp, 1994). According to this model, individuals vary widely in the amount of human capital they bring to the labour market. *Human capital* is acquired by education and job training; it is the source of a person's productivity and can be measured in terms of the return on the investment (wages) and the cost (schooling or training) (Stevenson, 1988; Kemp, 1994).

From this perspective, what individuals earn is the result of their own choices (the kinds of training, education, and experience they accumulate, for example) and of the labour market need (demand) for and availability (supply) of certain kinds of workers at specific points in time. For example, human capital analysts argue that women diminish their human capital when they leave the labour force to engage in childbearing and child-care activities. While women are out of the labour force, their human capital deteriorates from nonuse. When they return to work, women earn lower wages than men because they have fewer years of work experience and have "atrophied human capital" because their education and training may have become obsolete (Kemp, 1994:70).

Other neoclassical economic models attribute the wage gap to such factors as (1) the different amounts of energy men and women expend on their work (women who spend much energy on their family and household have less to put into their work), (2) the occupational choices women make (choosing female-dominated occupations so that they can spend more time with their families), and (3) the crowding of too many women into some occupations (suppressing wages because the supply of workers exceeds demand) (Kemp, 1994).

EVALUATION OF FUNCTIONALIST AND NEOCLASSICAL ECONOMIC PERSPECTIVES

Although Parsons and other functionalists did not specifically endorse the gendered division of labour, their analysis views it as natural and perhaps inevitable. However, critics argue that problems inherent in traditional gender roles, including the personal role strains of men and women and the social costs to society, are minimized by this approach. For example, men are assumed to be "money machines" for their families when they might prefer to spend more time in child-rearing activities. Also, the woman's place is assumed to be in the home, an assumption that ignores the fact that many women hold jobs due to economic necessity.

In addition, the functionalist approach does not take a critical look at the structure of society (especially the economic inequalities) that make educational and occupational opportunities more available to some than to others. Furthermore, it fails to examine the underlying power relations between men and women or to consider the fact that the tasks assigned to women and to men are unequally valued by society (Kemp, 1994). Similarly, the human capital model is rooted in the premise that individuals are evaluated based on their human capital in an open, competitive market where education, training, and other job-enhancing characteristics are taken into account. From this perspective, those who make less money (often men of visible minority groups and all women) have no one to blame but themselves. According to sociologist Alice Kemp (1994:76):

The disparity between women's and men's earnings is even greater for women of colour. Feminists who analyze ethnicity, class, and gender suggest that equality will occur only when all women are treated more equitably.

If women have children to care for, it is a situation they freely chose and will have to work out for themselves. That jobs and professions have been structured to reflect men's lives and circumstances is seldom recognized; instead women are conceptualized as somehow different from men in their motivations and preference for income.

Critics note that, instead of blaming people for their choices, we must acknowledge other realities. Wage discrimination occurs in two ways: (1) The wages are higher in male-dominated jobs, occupations, and segments of the labour market, regardless of whether women take time for family duties, and (2) in any job, women and members of some minority groups will be paid less (Lorber, 1994).

Conflict Perspectives

According to many conflict analysts, the gendered division of labour within families and in the workplace results from male control of and dominance over women and resources. Differentials between men and women may exist in terms of economic, political, physical, and/or interpersonal power. The importance of a male monopoly in any of these arenas depends on the significance of that type of power in a society (Richardson, 1993). In hunting and gathering and horticultural societies, male dominance over women is limited because all members of the society must work in order to survive (Collins, 1971; Nielsen, 1990). In agrarian societies, however, male sexual dominance is at its peak. Male heads of household gain a monopoly not only on physical power but also on economic power, and women become sexual property.

Although men's ability to use physical power to control women diminishes in industrial societies, men still remain the heads of household and control the property. In addition, men gain more power through their predominance in the most highly paid and prestigious occupations and the highest elected offices. In contrast, women have the ability to trade their sexual resources, companionship, and emotional support in the marriage market for men's financial support and social status; as a result, however, women as a group remain subordinate to men (Collins, 1971; Nielsen, 1990).

All men are not equally privileged; some analysts argue that women and men in the upper classes are more privileged, because of their economic power, than men in lower-class positions and members of some minority groups (Lorber, 1994). In industrialized societies, persons who occupy elite positions in corporations, universities, the mass media, and government or who have great wealth have the most power (Richardson, 1993). However, most of these are men.

Conflict theorists in the Marxist tradition assert that gender stratification results from private ownership of the means of production; some men not only gain control over property and the distribution of goods but also gain power over women. According to Friedrich Engels and Karl Marx, marriage serves to enforce male dominance. Men of the capitalist class instituted monogamous marriage (a gendered institution) so that they could be certain of the paternity of their offspring, especially sons, whom they wanted to inherit their wealth. Feminist analysts have examined this theory, among others, as they have sought to explain male domination and gender stratification.

Feminist Perspectives

Feminism—the belief that women and men are equal and that they should be valued equally and have equal rights—is embraced by many men as well as women. Gender is viewed as a socially constructed concept that has important consequences in the lives of all people (Craig, 1992). According to sociologist Ben Agger (1993), men can be feminists and propose feminist theories; both women and men have much in common as they seek to gain a better understanding of the causes and consequences of gender inequality.

Feminist perspectives vary in their analyses of the ways in which norms, roles, institutions, and internalized expectations limit women's behaviour. Taken together, they all seek to demonstrate how women's personal control operates even within the constraints of a relative lack of power (Stewart, 1994). Although subordination and oppression have significant consequences in women's lives, feminist theorists note that these are not the *only* features of women's lives (Fine, 1987, 1989). We will now look at the main types of feminist theory and examine the focus of each.

LIBERAL FEMINISM In liberal feminism, gender equality is equated with equality of opportunity. Liberal feminism strives for sex equality through the elimination of laws that differentiate people by gender. The roots of women's oppression lie in women's lack of equal civil rights and educational opportunities. Only when these constraints on women's participation are removed will women have the same chance of success as men. This approach notes the importance of gender-role socialization and suggests that changes need to be made in what children learn from their families, teachers, and the media about appropriate masculine and feminine attitudes and behaviour. Liberal feminists fight for better child-care options, a woman's right to choose an abortion, and elimination of sex discrimination in the workplace.

RADICAL FEMINISM According to radical feminists, male domination causes all forms of human oppression, including racism and classism (Tong, 1989). Radical feminists often trace the roots of patriarchy to women's childbearing and child-rearing responsibilities, which make them dependent on men (Firestone, 1970; Chafetz, 1984). In the radical feminist view, men's oppression of women is deliberate, and ideological justification for this subordination is provided by other institutions such as the media and religion. For women's condition to improve, radical feminists claim, patriarchy must be abolished. If institutions currently are gendered, alternative institutions—such as women's organizations seeking better health care, daycare, and shelters for victims of domestic violence and sexual assault—should be developed to meet women's needs.

SOCIALIST FEMINISM Socialist feminists suggest that women's oppression results from their dual roles as paid *and* unpaid workers in a capitalist economy. In the workplace, women are exploited by capitalism; at home, they are exploited by patriarchy (Kemp, 1994). Women are easily exploited in both sectors; they are paid low wages and have few economic resources. Gendered job segregation is "the primary mechanism in capitalist society that maintains the superiority of men over women, because it enforces lower wages for women in the labour market" (Hartmann, 1976:139). As a result, women must do domestic labour either to gain a better-paid man's economic support or to stretch their own wages (Lorber, 1994). According to socialist feminists, the only way to achieve gender equality is to eliminate capitalism and develop a socialist economy that would bring equal pay and rights to women.

FEMINIST PERSPECTIVES ON EATING PROBLEMS As noted earlier, feminist analysts suggest that eating problems are not just individual "disorders" but relate to the issue of subordination (see Orbach, 1978; Fallon, Katzman, and Wooley, 1994). This analysis focuses on the relationship between eating problems and patriarchy (male dominance) in the labour force and family. Eating problems cannot be viewed solely as psychological "disorders" but rather are symbolic of women's personal and cultural oppression. Anorexia and bulimia reflect women's (and sometimes men's) denial of other problems, disconnection from other people, and disempowerment in society (Peters and Fallon, 1994:353).

Feminist scholars have begun to look at ways in which race/ethnicity may be linked to eating problems (Root, 1990). In contrast, most early research focused on the problems of white, middle- to upper-class females; women from minority groups were, at most, mentioned in a footnote (for example, see Brumberg, 1988). In a recent study of women with eating problems, sociologist Becky Thompson (1992, 1994) found that more than half the women from minority groups had been victims of sexual abuse, racism, anti-Semitism, and/or homophobia. However, she suggests that it is impossible to determine a single explanation about socialization and eating problems among visible minority women.

Eating problems also may be associated with social class and sexual orientation. For example, some lower-class women may view binge eating as a momentary reprieve from poverty and other worries. Some lesbians may develop eating problems in rebellion against cultural expectations that attempt to force heterosexuality or at least heterosexual values on them, in sharp contradiction to their own sexual identities (Thompson, 1994). Two feminist studies comparing lesbian and heterosexual women found that both groups are influenced by cultural pressures to be thin but that lesbians tend to be more satisfied with their bodies and to desire a somewhat higher ideal weight (Brand, Rothblum, and Solomon, 1992; Herzog et al., 1992). Gay men, on the other hand, may be more prone to eating problems because of the importance some place on low body weight and/or physical attractiveness (see Shisslak and Crago, 1992).

Feminist perspectives focus on the prevention of eating problems and a re-evaluation of existing therapies. However, feminist authors Naomi Wolf (1990) and Susan Faludi (1991) have suggested that the current social order may have a vested interest in promoting, rather than preventing, eating problems among women. Wolf (1994) argues that emphasis on thinness is a response to the threat posed by women's efforts to gain courage, self-esteem, and a sense of effectiveness. By contrast, dieting leads to passivity, anxiety, and low self-esteem—traits valued in women by the dominant culture.

Feminists argue that to prevent eating problems—as well as other mental and physical problems of women—societal changes are needed. These changes relate to work (such as equal pay, and the elimination of sexual harassment and discrimination) and the family (child-care programs and deterrence of sexual violence, for example) (Wolf, 1990; Shisslak and Crago, 1994). As Thompson (1994:5) notes:

Most women are relegated to sex-segregated jobs that pay them less well than men are paid for comparable work. What is typically referred to as the "glass ceiling" in employment is actually a euphemism for real men's bodies blocking most women's advancement. These barriers, coupled with educational systems that still steer girls away from mathematics, science, and competitive sports, help explain why adolescent girls' self-esteem declines as boys' self-esteem increases. In this context, eating problems signal women's many hungers—for recognition, achievement, and encouragement. It is no surprise that appetites and food take on a metaphorical significance in a society in which women typically are responsible for food preparation and yet are taught to deny themselves ample appetites.

EVALUATION OF CONFLICT AND FEMINIST PERSPECTIVES

Conflict and feminist perspectives provide insights into the structural aspects of gender inequality in society. While functionalist approaches focus on the characteristics of individuals, the conflict and feminist approaches emphasize factors external to individuals that contribute to the oppression of women. These approaches also examine the ways in which the workplace and the home are gendered.

Conflict theory has been criticized for emphasizing the differences between men and women without taking into account their commonalities. Feminist approaches have been criticized for their emphasis on male dominance without a corresponding analysis of the ways in which some men also may be oppressed by patriarchy and capitalism. Some theorists in men's studies have attempted to overcome this deficit by exploring how gender domination includes "men's subordination and denigration of other men as well as men's exploitation of women" (Brod, 1987; Kimmel and Messner, 1992; Lorber, 1994:4).

GENDER ISSUES IN THE FUTURE

In the past thirty years, women have made significant progress in the labour force (Creese and Beagan, 1999). Laws have been passed to prohibit sexual discrimination in the workplace and in schools. Affirmative action programs have made women more visible in education, government, and the professional world. More women are entering the political arena as candidates instead of as volunteers who "answer the telephone and lick stamps" in the campaign offices of male candidates (Lott, 1994:341).

Many men have joined movements to raise their consciousness not only about men's concerns but also about the need to eliminate sexism and gender bias. Many men realize that what is harmful to women also may be harmful to men. For example, women's lower wages in the labour force suppress men's wages as well; in a two-pay-cheque family, women who are paid less contribute less to the family's finances, thus placing a greater burden on men to earn more money.

In the midst of these changes, many gender issues remain unresolved. In the labour force, gender segregation may increase if the number of female-dominated jobs—such as information clerk, nurse's aide, and fast-food restaurant worker—continues to grow. If men lose jobs in the blue-collar sector as factories relocate to other countries or close entirely, they may seek jobs that primarily have been held by women. Although this situation might lead to less gender segregation, the loss of desirable jobs ultimately is not in anyone's interest (Reskin and Padavic, 1994:172). As men see the number and quality of "men's jobs" shrink, they also may become more resistant to women's entry into what have customarily been male jobs (Reskin and Padavic, 1994).

The pay gap between men and women should continue to shrink, but this may be due in part to decreasing wages paid to men (Armstrong and Armstrong, 1994). Employers and governments will continue to implement family-leave policies, but these will not relieve women's domestic burden in the family. The burden of the "double day" or "second shift" has led many women to work part time in an attempt to reconcile family–work contradictions. This choice increases or maintains occupational segregation, low pay with minimal or no benefits, and marginalized treatment (Gee, 1995). The burden of the "second shift" will likely preserve women's inequality at home and in the workplace for another generation.

CHAPTER REVIEW

How do sex and gender differ?
Sex refers to the biological categories and manifestations of femaleness and maleness; gender refers to the socially constructed differences between females and males. In short, sex is what we (generally) are born with; gender is what we acquire through socialization.

How do gender roles and gender identity differ from gendered institutions?
Gender role encompasses the attitudes, behaviours, and activities that are socially assigned to each sex and that are learned through socialization. Gender identity is an individual's perception of self as either female or male. Gendered institutions are those structural features, external to the individual, that perpetuate gender inequality.

How does the nature of work affect gender equality in societies?
In most hunting and gathering societies, fairly equitable relationships exist because neither sex has the ability to provide all of the food necessary for survival. In horticultural societies, hoe cultivation is compatible with child care, and a fair degree of gender equality exists because neither sex controls the food supply. In agrarian societies, male dominance is very apparent; agrarian tasks require more labour and physical strength, and women often are excluded from these tasks because they are viewed as too weak or too tied to child-rearing activities. In industrialized societies, a gap exists between nonpaid work performed by women at home and paid work performed by men and women.

What are the key agents of gender socialization?
Parents, peers, teachers and schools, sports, and the media are agents of socialization that tend to reinforce stereotypes of appropriate gender behaviour.

What causes gender inequality in Canada?
Gender inequality results from economic, political, and educational discrimination against women. In most workplaces, jobs are either gender segregated or the majority of employees are of the same gender. While the degree of gender segregation in the professional workplace has declined since the 1970s, racial and ethnic segregation remains deeply embedded.

How is occupational segregation related to the pay gap?
Many women work in lower-paying, less prestigious jobs than men. This occupational segregation leads to a disparity, or pay gap, between women's and men's earnings. Even when women are employed in the same job as men, on average they do not receive the same, or comparable, pay.

How do functionalists and conflict theorists differ in their view of division of labour by gender?

According to functional analysts, women's roles as caregivers in contemporary industrialized societies are crucial in ensuring that key societal tasks are fulfilled. Whereas the husband performs the instrumental tasks of economic support and decision making, the wife assumes the expressive tasks of providing affection and emotional support to the family. According to conflict analysis, the gendered division of labour within families and the workplace—particularly in agrarian and industrial societies—results from male control and dominance over women and resources.

How do the various feminist perspectives explain gender inequality?

Although feminist perspectives vary in their analyses of women's subordination, they all advocate social change to eradicate gender inequality. In liberal feminism, gender equality is connected to equality of opportunity. In radical feminism, male dominance is seen as the cause of oppression. According to socialist feminists, women's oppression results from their dual roles as paid and unpaid workers.

Key Terms

body consciousness 338
employment equity 360
feminism 365
gender 337
gender bias 351
gender identity 338
gender role 338
hermaphrodite 337
matriarchy 341
patriarchy 341
pay equity 360
primary sex characteristics 336
secondary sex characteristics 336
sex 336
sexism 340
sexual orientation 336
transsexual 337
transvestite 337
wage gap 358

Internet Exercises

1. Visit the newsgroup **alt.feminism**. What are some of the issues that concern feminists today? What issues seem to be Internet-specific? What portion of the people posting to this site are men? How, if at all, do you think the ratio between male and female posters to this group affects the debate? Should men be allowed to post to this newsgroup at all?

2. A famous cartoon shows two dogs sitting at computer keyboards and typing away on the Internet. The caption underneath reads "On the Internet no one knows if you are a dog." It is said that the same rules apply to gender. From Lycos (**http://lycos.com**), do a search on the term *chat room*. Visit a chat room and observe the conversation. Are there differences between the way men and women speak? How easy would it be for you to pass yourself off as a member of the opposite sex? Would you ever consider doing this? Why or why not? Based on your observation of a chat room, is there a difference between what can and what does happen in terms of gender-bending activity?

3. Visit the National Organization for Women (NOW) homepage (**http://www.now.org**). Based on your reading there, how closely does the philosophy of this feminist organization fit one of the feminist theory models outlined in this chapter? Visit one of the Canadian feminist organizations listed on the Feminism and Women's Resources page (**http://www.ibd.nrc.ca/~mansfield/feminism/**). How does the philosophy of this organization compare with that of NOW? What model of feminist theory would this organization fit?

4. Visit the National Eating Disorder Information Centre at **www.nedic.on.cal**. What information can you find about eating disorders and weight dissatisfaction among males and females? What comparisons can be made?

Net Links

Status of Women Canada (SWC) is a federal government agency that promotes gender equality and full participation of women in the economic, social, cultural, and political life of the country. SWC focuses in three areas: improving women's economic autonomy and well-being, eliminating violence against women and children, and advancing women's human rights; go to:

http://www.swc-cfc.gc.ca/direct.html

Women's International Net is an online magazine about women all over the world; go to:

http://www.geocities.com/Wellesley/3321

Canadian Women's Internet Association (CWIA) contains hundreds of links to sites relevant to women, with a special focus on Canadian content; go to:

http://women.ca

What role does gender play in computer culture? Diane Currie of the University of British Columbia addresses this question in "The Construction of Gender at UBC Computing Services"; go to:

http://www.women.ca/compgend.html

Questions for Critical Thinking

1. Do the media reflect societal attitudes on gender, or do the media determine and teach gender behaviour? (As a related activity, watch television for several hours and list the roles women and men play in the shows watched and in the advertisements.)
2. Review the concept of cultural relativism discussed in Chapter 3. Should the Canadian government and human rights groups such as Amnesty International protest genital mutilation in those countries in which it is practised, and should the government withhold any funding or aid destined for those nations until they cease the practice?
3. Examine the various academic departments at your university. What is the gender breakdown of the faculty in selected departments? What is the gender breakdown of undergraduates and graduates in those departments? Are there major differences among the social sciences, science, and humanities departments? What can you come up with to explain your observations?

Suggested Readings

These well-written books provide in-depth information on various issues raised in this chapter:

Sandra L. Bem. *The Lenses of Gender: Transforming the Debate on Sexual Inequality.* New Haven, Conn.: Yale University Press, 1993.

Michael S. Kimmel and Michael A. Messner (eds.). *Men's Lives.* New York: Macmillan, 1992.

Claire M. Renzetti and Daniel J. Curran. *Women, Men, and Society.* Boston: Allyn & Bacon, 1995.

Women's and men's work is examined in this interesting book:

Pat Armstrong and Hugh Armstrong. *The Double Ghetto: Canadian Women and Their Segregated Work.* Toronto: McClelland & Stewart, 1994.

The unequal treatment of females in schools and universities is explored in these books:

Jane Gaskell and Arlene McLaren. *Women and Education.* Calgary: Detselig, 1992.

Bernice Lott. *Women's Lives: Themes and Variations in Gender Learning* (2nd ed.). Pacific Grove, Cal.: Brooks/Cole, 1994.

Stephen Richer and Lorna Weir. *Beyond Political Correctness: Toward the Inclusive University.* Toronto: University of Toronto Press, 1995.

Bestsellers dealing with feminism, appearance norms, and communication between women and men include these books:

Deborah Tannen. *You Just Don't Understand: Women and Men in Conversation.* New York: Morrow, 1990.
————. *Talking From 9 to 5.* New York: Morrow, 1994.

Naomi Wolf. *The Beauty Myth: How Images of Beauty Are Used Against Women.* New York: Morrow, 1990.

For additional information on the bodybuilding subculture:

Alan M. Klein. *Little Big Men: Bodybuilding Subculture and Gender Construction.* Albany: State University of New York Press, 1993.

Leslea Newman (ed.). *Eating Our Hearts Out: Personal Accounts of Women's Relationship to Food.* Freedom, Cal.: The Crossing Press, 1993.

CHAPTER 12

The Social Significance of Age
  Trends in Aging
  Age in Historical Perspective

Age and the Life Course in Contemporary Society
  Infancy and Childhood
  Adolescence
  Young Adulthood
  Middle Adulthood
  Late Adulthood
  Retirement

Inequalities Related to Aging
  Ageism
  Wealth, Poverty, and Aging
  Elder Abuse

Sociological Perspectives on Aging
  Functionalist Perspectives on Aging
  Interactionist Perspectives on Aging
  Conflict Perspectives on Aging

Living Arrangements for Older Adults
  Support Services, Homemaker Services, and
     Daycare
  Nursing Homes

Death and Dying

Aging in the Future

"We're a new generation. When we grew up, anybody fifty or sixty was considered old. I remember as a young boy, thirteen, fourteen, attending the twenty-fifth wedding anniversary of my mother and father. Everybody was dancing and singing and having a wonderful time. I remember saying to myself: 'What are they so happy about? They're on the verge of dying.' They were maybe fifty-five.

"There's a new breed now. I'm going to be seventy-nine [soon] and I don't for a second consider myself old. I still play a good game of golf, and I exercise and swim and am active in business ... I have more vitality than those who call me an old man. You turn around and want to know who the hell they're talking about." (quoted in Terkel, 1996:9)

These are the words of Jack Culberg, 79, a former CEO of several large corporations. His views on growing older are typical of a new breed that is willing to face challenges. Rod Dawson offers another example. Here he describes a nine-day Outward Bound canoe trip:

"A million reasons not to go.

"At age 66 would I be able to keep up? I didn't feel old—on the other hand—neither did I feel young. Three major surgeries for cancer had taken a lot of the zip and vinegar out of me. I feared walking that lonesome road to another year—a year that might not be there for me. Maybe I can do it? Maybe I can't? ...

"Wednesday. Just before dinner we were dropped off for our 'solo.' Each participant was given a plastic tarp, rope, food, matches, sleeping bag and mattress to spend 24 hours alone on an isolated piece of shore ... Wrapped in a garment of morning mist, time marched forward with an immeasurable cadence and before I was ready 24 hours had passed ...

"On the solo and while paddling the next day, I met myself, my regrets, my hopes, my fears. It was Friday afternoon, paddling bow in the lead canoe I dipped my cup into the lake, drank, looked around and breathed deeply. One year ago this very day I lay in a hospital bed, alive because of surgeons' skills and a frightening array of painful medical technology. The contrast between then and now was so overwhelming that tears ran down my cheeks." (Dawson, n.d.:26–27)

AGING

Eventually, all of us will be affected by aging. **Aging is the physical, psychological, and social processes associated with growing older** (Atchley, 1997). As the experiences of Jack Culberg and Rod Dawson suggest, the psychological and social processes associated with aging can be at least as important as the physical processes in determining how we will spend our older years.

In some societies, including Canada, older people are the targets of prejudice and discrimination based on myths about aging. For example, older people may be seen as incompetent solely on the basis of their age. Although some older people may need assistance from others and support from society, many others are physically, socially, and financially independent. In this chapter, we examine the sociological aspects of aging. We will also examine how older people seek dignity, autonomy, and empowerment in a society that often devalues people who do not fit the ideal norms of youth, beauty, physical fitness, and self-sufficiency. Before reading on, test your knowledge about aging and age-based discrimination by taking the quiz in Box 12.1.

QUESTIONS AND ISSUES

CHAPTER FOCUS QUESTION: Given the fact that aging is an inevitable consequence of living (unless an individual dies young), why do many people in Canada devalue older persons?

How does functional age differ from chronological age?

How does age determine a person's roles and statuses in society?

What factors contribute to successful aging?

What actions can be taken to bring about a more equitable society for older people?

THE SOCIAL SIGNIFICANCE OF AGE

"How old are you?" This is one of the most frequently asked questions in our society. Beyond indicating how old or young a person is, age is socially significant because it defines what is appropriate for or expected of people at various stages. Moreover, while it is an ascribed status, age is one of the few ascribed statuses that changes over time. Thus behaviour that is considered appropriate at one stage of a person's life may be considered odd or unusual at another stage. For example nobody thinks it is unusual if a person in her twenties goes in-line skating. However, if her seventy-five-year-old grandfather does the same thing, he may receive some odd looks and even media coverage because he is defying norms regarding age-appropriate behaviour.

When people say "Act your age," they are referring to *chronological age*—a person's age based on date of birth (Atchley, 1994). In everyday life, however, we gain a general idea of a person's age based on *functional age*—observable individual attributes such as physical appearance, mobility, strength, coordination, and mental capacity that are used to assign people to age categories (Atchley, 1994). Because we typically do not have access to other people's birth certificates to learn their chronological age, we often use visible characteristics—such as youthful appearance or gray hair and wrinkled skin—as our criteria for determining whether someone is "young" or "old." As historian Lois W. Banner (1993:15) suggests, "Appearance, more than any other factor, has occasioned the objectification of aging. We define someone as old because he or she looks old." Feminist scholars have noted that functional age works differently for women and men—as they age, men may be viewed as distinguished or powerful whereas when women grow older they are thought to be "over the hill" or grandmotherly (Banner, 1993).

Trends in Aging

You are used to thinking about people getting older, but you may not have realized that societies can also age. Today, older Canadians make up more than one-tenth of the population. This makes Canada's population one of the oldest in the world, and population projections suggest that

Many older persons seek dignity, autonomy, and empowerment in a society that values youth, beauty, physical fitness, and self-sufficiency.

Canadian society will age even more in the next fifty years (see Figure 12.1).

In 1981 the median age (the age at which half the people are younger and half are older) in Canada was 30. In 2001 it is expected to be 38. This substantial increase—eight years in two decades—is partly the result of the baby boomers (people born between 1946 and 1964) moving into middle age, and partly the result of more people living longer. As shown in Figure 12.2, the number of older people (age 65 and above) increased dramatically between 1901 and 1991 (McKie, 1993). Especially fast growing has been the population over age 85.

Referred to by some analysts as the *greying of Canada*, the aging of the Canadian population resulted from an increase in life expectancy combined with a decrease in birth rates (McKie, 1994). **Life expectancy is the average length of time a group of individuals of the same age will live.** Based on the death rates in the year of birth, life expectancy shows the average length of life of

BOX 12.1 SOCIOLOGY AND EVERYDAY LIFE

HOW MUCH DO YOU KNOW ABOUT AGING?

TRUE	FALSE	
T	F	1. Most older persons have serious physical or mental disabilities.
T	F	2. Women in Canada have a longer life expectancy than men.
T	F	3. Scientific studies have documented the fact that women age faster than men.
T	F	4. The majority of older people have incomes below the poverty line.
T	F	5. Studies show that advertising no longer stereotypes older persons.
T	F	6. Older Canadians tend to be much less happy than those who are younger.
T	F	7. The majority of older people live alone.
T	F	8. Retirement has been a distinct part of life for hundreds of years.
T	F	9. Men over 65 years of age are much more likely to be married than are women over 65 years of age.
T	F	10. The image of older people presented in the media has become much more negative over the past two decades.

Answers on page 374.

a *cohort—*a group of people born within a specified period of time. Cohorts may be established on the basis of one-, five-, or ten-year intervals; they may also be defined by events taking place at the time of their birth, such as the "Depression era" babies or baby boomers (Moody, 1994). For the cohort born in 1996, for example, life expectancy at birth was 81 for females and 76 for males. Figure 12.3 outlines the sex differences in life expectancy.

At the turn of the century, about 5 percent of the Canadian population was over age 65; in 1981, that number had risen to approximately 10 percent. As Figure 12.2 shows, in 1991, approximately 12 percent of the population was age 65 or over. By the year 2031, according to projections, about 22 percent of the population will be at least 65 (Norland, 1994).

Since the beginning of the twentieth century, life expectancy has steadily increased as industrialized nations developed better water and sewage systems, improved nutrition, and made tremendous advances in medical science. Economic development that contributed to the lower death rate also was a force in lowering the birth rate. In industrialized nations, children came to be viewed as an economic liability: they could not contribute to the family's financial well-being and had to be supported.

The current distribution of the Canadian population is depicted in the "age pyramid" in Figure 12.4. If, every year, the same number of people are born as in the previous year and a certain number die in each age group, the plot of the population distribution should be pyramid-shaped. As you will note, however, Figure 12.4 is not a perfect pyramid, but rather reflects declining birth rates since the baby boom. This has resulted in fewer young people (see Chapter 19, "Population and Urbanization").

As a result of changing population trends, research on aging has grown dramatically in the past fifty years. *Gerontology* is the study of aging and older people. A subfield of gerontology, *social gerontology* is the study of the social (nonphysical) aspects of aging, including such topics as the societal consequences of an aging population and the personal experience of aging. According to gerontologists, age is viewed differently from society to society and changes over time.

Age in Historical Perspective

People are assigned to different roles and positions based on the age structure and role structure in a particular society. *Age structure* is the number of persons at each age level within the society; *role structure* is the number and type of positions available to them (Riley and Riley, 1994). Over the years, the age continuum has been chopped up into finer and finer points. Two hundred years ago, people divided the age spectrum into "babyhood," a *very* short childhood, and then adulthood. What we would consider "childhood" today was very

BOX 12.1

ANSWERS TO THE SOCIOLOGY QUIZ ON AGING

1. **False.** In Canada, approximately 46 percent of people 65 or over have a disability—the majority of which are classified as mild or moderate disabilities.
2. **True.** In 1996, female life expectancy (at birth) was 81 years, compared with 76 years for males.
3. **False.** No studies have documented that women age faster than men. However, some scholars have noted a "double standard" of aging that places older women at a disadvantage with respect to older men because women's worth in the North American culture is defined in terms of physical appearance.
4. **False.** The 1994 poverty rate for seniors was 18 percent, which is down from 33 percent reported in 1980. However, females are at a greater risk of living in poverty than males.
5. **False.** Studies have shown that advertisements frequently depict older people negatively—for example, as sickly or silly. However, this is changing (see Question 10).
6. **False.** Several surveys have shown that people 65 and over are actually more satisfied with their lives than are younger Canadians.
7. **False.** The majority of older persons live with others. In Canada, only about 14 percent of men and 34 percent of women over 65 live alone.
8. **False.** Retirement is a relatively modern invention. The first government pension plan was established in Germany in 1899. Canada adopted a pension system in 1927, but retirement was not common until after World War II when benefits were improved.
9. **True.** In 1991, 77 percent of men and 43 percent of women over 65 were married. The reason for this is that women live longer than men. This means that men are unlikely to be widowed, while women are likely to outlive their spouses.
10. **False.** Analysis of books, magazines, advertisements, and television shows has shown that in recent years media images of older people have become more positive and less likely to give stereotypical and negative portrayals.

Sources: Novak, 1997; Rodgers and Kong, 1996; Statistics Canada, 1992a; Norland, 1994; McPherson, 1998; and Chen and Zhou, 1994.

different two hundred years ago when agricultural societies needed a large number of strong arms and backs to work on the land to ensure survival. When 95 percent of the population had to be involved in food production, categories such as toddlers, preschoolers, preteens, teenagers, young adults, the middle-aged, or older persons did not exist.

If the physical labour of young persons is necessary for society's survival, then young persons are considered "little adults" and are expected to act like adults and do adult work. Older persons also are expected to continue to be productive for the benefit of the society for as long as they are physically able. In pre-industrial societies, persons of all ages help with the work, and little training is necessary for the roles that they fill. During the seventeenth and eighteenth centuries in North America, for example, older individuals helped with the work and were respected because they were needed—and because few people lived that

long (Gratton, 1986). The presence of large numbers of older people is a modern phenomenon and their place in society is still evolving.

AGE AND THE LIFE COURSE IN CONTEMPORARY SOCIETY

In industrialized societies, the skills necessary for many roles are more complex and the number of unskilled positions is more limited. Consequently, children are expected to attend school and learn the necessary skills for future employment rather than perform unskilled labour. Further, older persons are expected to retire so that younger persons can take their places. However, when older persons have fewer productive roles to fill, inequality may increase. For example, the trend in recent years to "downsize" the workforce has contributed

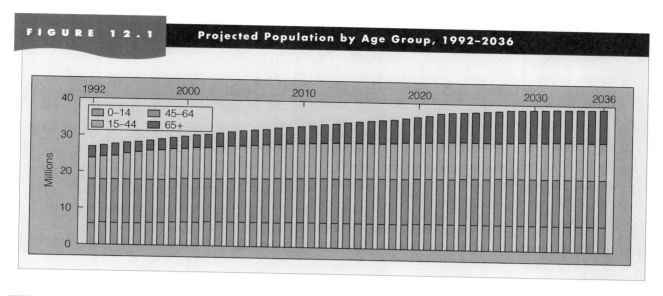

FIGURE 12.1 Projected Population by Age Group, 1992–2036

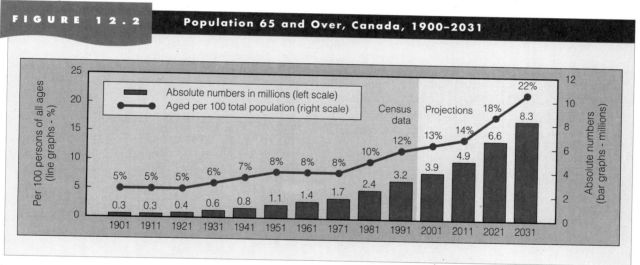

FIGURE 12.2 Population 65 and Over, Canada, 1900–2031

to pressure on some older workers to retire early, thereby saving employers money and preserving jobs for young workers. Such "early retirement" is not always voluntary and may pose significant economic risks for individuals who find that they cannot live on their pensions and that employment is not available because employers won't hire older workers.

In North America, age differentiation is based on narrowly defined categories, such as infancy, childhood, adolescence, young adulthood, middle adulthood, and later adulthood. These narrowly defined age categories have had a profound effect on our perceptions of people's capabilities, responsibilities, and entitlements. What is considered appropriate for or expected of people at various ages is somewhat arbitrarily determined and pro-

duces *age stratification*—**the inequalities, differences, segregation, or conflict between age groups** (Atchley, 1997). We will now examine some of those strata.

Infancy and Childhood

Infancy (birth to the age of 2) and childhood (ages 3 to 12) are times of dependency. Infants and children are among the most powerless people in society. Historically, children were seen as the property of their parents, who could do with them as they pleased (Tower, 1996). During this period, family support and guidance are crucial factors in the development of a healthy and well-adjusted young person.

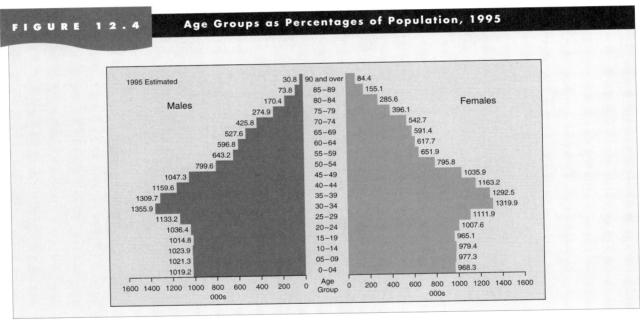

FIGURE 12.3 — Evolution of Life Expectancy by Age and Sex, Canada, 1921–1996

Year	Males — At Birth — Females	
1921	58.8	60.6
1926	60.5	62.3
1931	60.0	62.1
1941	63.0	66.3
1951	66.4	70.9
1961	68.4	74.3
1971	69.4	76.5
1981	71.9	79.0
1991	73.9	80.5
1996	75.7	81.4

FIGURE 12.4 — Age Groups as Percentages of Population, 1995

1995 Estimated

Males	Age Group	Females
30.8	90 and over	84.4
73.8	85–89	155.1
170.4	80–84	285.6
274.9	75–79	396.1
425.8	70–74	542.7
527.6	65–69	591.4
596.8	60–64	617.7
643.2	55–59	651.9
799.6	50–54	795.8
1047.3	45–49	1035.9
1159.6	40–44	1163.2
1309.7	35–39	1292.5
1355.9	30–34	1319.9
1133.2	25–29	1111.9
1036.4	20–24	1007.6
1014.8	15–19	965.1
1023.9	10–14	979.4
1021.3	05–09	977.3
1019.2	0–04	968.3

000s

Sources: Fig. 12.1: Statistics Canada, *Canadian Social Trends*, 1993; 12.2: Norland, 1994; 12.3: Norland, 1994; 12.4: McVey and Kalbach, 1995. Fig. 12.2, population statistics for 1995–2016 adapted from Statistics Canada, "Annual Demographic Statistics," Cat. no. 91-213, and "Population Projections for Canada, Provinces and Territories, 1993–2016," Cat. no. 91-250.

Adolescence

In contemporary industrialized countries, adolescence roughly spans the teenage years, although some analysts place the lower and upper ages at 15 and 24 (Corr, Nabe, and Corr, 1994). Compared with pre-industrial societies in which 7-year-old children were expected to do adult work, adolescence today is a period in which the individual is neither treated as a child nor afforded full status as an adult (Chudacoff, 1989). Adolescents are expected to continue their education and perhaps hold a part-time job while they do so.

Young Adulthood

Young adulthood, which follows adolescence and lasts to about age 39, is socially significant because, during this time, people are expected to get married, have children, and get a job. For some young adults, this may be easier than for others. As discussed in earlier chapters, ethnicity

Today many retired persons have good health and the resources to enjoy an active life.

and gender strongly influence people's opportunities to engage in these activities. Today, age may be less of a determinant of when people enter or leave the basic social structures of work, education, and family.

Middle Adulthood

Prior to the twentieth century, life expectancy in Canada was only about 47 years, so the concept of middle adulthood—people between the ages of 40 and 65—did not exist until fairly recently. Normal changes in appearance occur during these years; although these changes have little relationship to a person's health or physical functioning, they are socially significant to many people (Lefrançois, 1993). In going through these changes, people are experiencing *senescence* (primary aging) in the form of molecular and cellular changes in the body. Wrinkles and gray hair are visible signs of senescence. Less-visible signs include arthritis and a gradual dulling of the senses of taste, smell, touch, and vision. Typically, reflexes begin to slow down, but the actual nature and extent of the changes vary greatly from person to person.

People may experience a change of life in this stage. Women undergo *menopause*—the cessation of the menstrual cycle caused by a gradual decline

in the body's production of the "female" hormones estrogen and progesterone. Menopause typically occurs between the mid-forties and the early fifties and signals the end of a woman's childbearing capabilities. Some women may experience irregular menstrual cycles for several years, followed by hot flashes, retention of body fluids, swollen breasts, and other aches and pains. Other women may have few or no noticeable physical symptoms. The psychological aspects of menopause often are as important as any physical effects. In one study, Anne Fausto-Sterling (1985) concluded that many women respond negatively to menopause because of negative stereotypes associated with menopausal and postmenopausal women. These stereotypes make the natural process of aging in women appear abnormal when compared with men's aging process. Actually, many women experience a new interest in sexual activity because they no longer have to worry about the possibility of becoming pregnant.

Men undergo a *climacteric* in which the production of the "male" hormone testosterone decreases. Some have argued that this change in hormone levels produces nervousness and depression in men. However, it is not clear whether these emotional changes are due to biological changes or to a more general "midlife crisis" in which men assess what they have accomplished (Benokraitis, 1993). While these biological changes may have a liberating effect on some people, they also may reinforce societal stereotypes of older people, especially women, as "sexless."

Along with primary aging, people in middle adulthood also experience *secondary aging*, which occurs as a result of environmental factors and lifestyle choices. For example, smoking, drinking heavily, and engaging in little or no physical activity are factors that affect the aging process. People who live in regions with high levels of environmental degradation and other forms of pollution are also at greater risk of aging more rapidly and having chronic illnesses and diseases associated with these external factors.

On the positive side, middle adulthood for most people represents the time during which (1) they have the highest levels of income and prestige, (2) they leave the problems of child rearing behind them and are content with their spouse of many years, and (3) they may have grandchildren who give them another tie to the future. Even so, persons in middle adulthood know that, given society's current structure, their status may begin to change significantly when they reach the end of that period of their lives.

Late Adulthood

Late adulthood is generally considered to begin at age 65—the "normal" retirement age. *Retirement* is the institutionalized separation of an individual from an occupational position, with continuation of income through a retirement pension based on prior years of service (Atchley, 1994). Retirement means the end of a status that long has been a source of income and a means of personal identity. Perhaps the loss of a valued status explains why many retired persons introduce themselves by saying, "I'm retired now, but I was a (banker, lawyer, plumber, supervisor, and so on) for forty years."

Some gerontologists subdivide late adulthood into three categories: (1) the "young-old" (ages 65–74), (2) the "old-old" (ages 75–85), and (3) the "oldest-old" (over age 85) (see Moody, 1994). Although these are somewhat arbitrary divisions, the "young-old" are less likely to suffer from disabling illnesses, while some of the "old-old" are more likely to suffer such illnesses (Belsky, 1990). A recent study found, however, that the prevalence of disability among those 85 and over decreased during the 1980s due to better health care.

The rate of biological and psychological changes in older persons may be as important as their chronological age in determining how they are perceived by themselves and others. As adults grow older, they actually become shorter, partly because bones that have become more porous with age develop curvature. A loss of three inches in height is not uncommon. As bones become more porous, they also become more brittle; simply falling may result in broken bones that take longer to heal. With age, arthritis increases, and connective tissue stiffens joints. Wrinkled skin, "age spots," gray (or white) hair, and midriff bulge appear; however, people may use Oil of Olay, Clairol, or Buster's Magic Tummy Tightener in the hope of avoiding looking older (Atchley, 1997).

Older persons also have increased chances of heart attacks, strokes, and cancer. Some diseases affect virtually only persons in late adulthood. Alzheimer's disease (a progressive and irreversible deterioration of brain tissue) is an example; about 55 percent of all organic mental disorders in the older population are caused by Alzheimer's (Atchley, 1997). Persons with this disease have an impaired ability to function in everyday social roles. Eventually, they cease to be able to recognize people they have always known and lose all sense of their own identity. Finally, they may revert to a speechless, infantile state such that others must feed them, dress them, sit them on the toilet, and lead them around. The disease has no known cause and, currently, there is no cure. Over a quarter million Canadians suffer from Alzheimer's disease and related dementias. By the year 2030, it is estimated that this number will grow to three-quarters of a million.

The time and attention needed to care for someone who has Alzheimer's disease or who simply no longer can leave home without help can be staggering. Daniel Heinrichs, a full-time caregiver for his wife, explains what caring for Norah was like:

> My wife Norah was afflicted with Alzheimer's disease. She could no longer function as a person in our marriage. Slowly I had to take over the various duties she had performed. After that I took over her financial affairs. Then I had to care for her personally: choosing, buying, and looking after clothing, dressing and undressing her, combing her hair, and feeding her. Slowly our conversation ceased. She could not think rationally any more. She could not understand the words that were being used, and she did not know the names of objects she saw. She no longer knew who I was either. "Norah is gone, there is nothing left of your marriage. You need to look after yourself again," is advice that I have heard and felt. Fortunately, I did not yield to this advice. Despite all of Norah's disabilities, we continued to have a rich and enjoyable experience together. I learned to communicate with Norah in other ways. How I spoke the words said more than their actual meaning. She watched for the smile on my face and the fun in my voice. My disposition had more effect on her than my words. She let me put my arm around her and hold her hands whenever I desired, or needed to do so ... Now Norah is gone, but I'm glad that I stayed with her "... till death do us part." (Heinrichs, 1996:48)

Fortunately, most older people do not suffer from Alzheimer's and are not incapacitated by their physical condition. Only about 5 percent of older people live in nursing homes, about 10 percent have visual impairment, and about 50 percent have some hearing loss (Naeyaert, 1990; Lou, 1990; Novak, 1993). Although most older people experience some decline in strength, flexibility, stamina, and other physical capabilities, much of that decline does not result simply from the aging process and is avoidable; with proper exercise, some of it is even reversible (Lefrançois, 1993).

Along with physical changes come changes in the roles played by older adults. One that most people enjoy is being a grandparent. An extended family is a great source of pleasure for many older Canadians. Grandparenting is an interesting role because it "has no clearly defined responsibilities, expectations, or rights" (McPherson, 1998:209). This gives members of younger and older generations the opportunity to build relationships that are to their mutual benefit. Some of the benefits of having grandparents are described in the following comments by Grade 3 students about the role of a grandmother (Huyck, cited in McPherson, 1998:213):

> When they read to us they don't skip words and they don't mind if it is the same story.

> They don't have to be smart, only answer questions like why dogs hate cats, and how come God isn't married.

> Grandmas are the only grownups who have got time—so everybody should have a grandmother, especially if you don't have television.

Some of the physical and psychological changes that come with increasing age can cause stress. According to Erik Erikson (1963), older people must resolve a tension of "integrity versus despair." They must accept that the life cycle is inevitable, that their lives are nearing an end, and that achieving inner harmony requires accepting both one's past accomplishments and past disappointments. Mark Novak interviewed several older people about what he termed "successful aging." One respondent, Joanne, commented:

> For me getting older was very painful at first because I resisted change. Now I'm changed, and it's okay. I would say I have a new freedom ... I thought I had no limits, but for me a great learning [experience] was recognizing my limits. It was a complete turnover, almost like a rebirth. I guess I've learned we're all weak really. At least we should accept that—being weak—and realize, "Hey, I'm only a fragile human being." (Novak, 1995:125)

Like many older people, Joanne has worked to maintain her dignity and autonomy.

Despite its negative aspects, aging has many positive dimensions and most older people are quite content with their lives. Many are financially secure with home mortgages paid off and no children remaining at home. This gives them a great deal of personal freedom. Most report they are in good or excellent health (Norland, 1994). Northcott found that older Edmonton residents were actually happier with their lives than younger respondents (1984). A national study conducted by Health and Welfare Canada (1998) found that older people were much less likely than younger people to report that their lives were stressful and the vast majority (92 percent) reported that they were pretty happy or very happy.

Retirement

Retirement is a recent invention. The first national pension system was established by Otto von Bismark in Germany in 1889. In Canada the Old Age Pension Act was introduced in 1927 to provide a basic income to needy retired people. This was the beginning of a shift in the burden of retirement from the individual to the state. However, payments were minimal in the early days, and retirement did not become common until the amount paid to retirees by public pension plans increased. The pension system became more generous when coverage was made universal in 1951 and as benefits were improved between 1951 and 1975 (Northcott, 1997).

Pensions are one of the most important factors affecting retirement plans. Currently, all working people in Canada are covered by the Canada or Quebec Pension Plans and all those over 65 receive additional money through the Old Age Security pension, though some or all of this may be taxed back from higher-income recipients. About 1.4 million lower income Canadians also receive the benefits of the Guaranteed Income Supplement program. These programs are responsible for the reduction in poverty among older people shown in Figure 12.5. Many people also have their own company pension plans and others have invested in registered retirement savings plans (RRSPs). Most government workers belong to pension plans compared with only about one-third of those employed in the private sector (Statistics Canada, 1996e).

Retirement plays an increasingly important part in the lives of Canadians. When the first retirement laws were passed, the retirement age (usually 70) was much higher than the average life expectancy. As a result, most people never retired, and for those who did, the retirement years were typically short. Today, however, only a small percentage of people over 65 remain in the labour market. Since the retirement age has been declining and life expectancy has been increasing, the retirement years will likely make up an increasing proportion of people's lives in the future. The average age at retirement is 61 for men and 59 for women (Monette, 1996), and the average retiree can expect to live another twenty years.

Retirement can represent a major transition for people, as they lose a source of income, identity, lifestyle, and friends that they may have had for most of their adult lives. This is especially true of high-status workers who achieve a great deal of satisfaction from their jobs. Jack Culberg explains the difficulties of the transition:

> When you suddenly leave [the corporate jungle], life is pretty empty. I was sixty-five, the age people are supposed to retire. I started to miss it quite a bit. The phone stops ringing. The king is dead. You start wanting to have lunch with old friends. At the beginning, they're nice to you, but then you realize that they're busy, they're working. They've got a job to do and just don't have the time to talk to anybody where it doesn't involve their business. I could be nasty and say, "Unless they make a buck out of it"—but I won't ... You hesitate to call them. (quoted in Terkel, 1996:9–10)

As Culberg's statement indicates, people tend to think of age in narrowly defined categories and reaching "retirement age" places many of them out of the mainstream. To ease this transition, researchers suggest that people plan ways of remaining occupied and engaged in society. Those who are involved with activities such as volunteer work and hobbies that can be continued after retirement are happier and healthier than those who have few retirement interests and who withdraw from social life. Research has shown that people do adjust successfully to retirement and they have few problems adapting to their new social status and lifestyle (McPherson, 1998). Many retirees say they are busier after retirement than before; the difference is that they stay busy doing things they choose to do rather than things they are obliged to do.

Along with the difficulties of changing status from worker to retiree, the major threats to successful retirement are finances and health. Financially, the government provides most Canadians with sufficient resources to meet basic needs for food and shelter. However, if you want to travel, move to escape harsh winters, buy gifts for grandchildren, and do the other things that bring satisfaction to many retired people you will need to save money to supplement the government pension. This can be done through employer-sponsored pension plans or registered retirement savings plans. In either case, the mathematics of compound interest mean that this must be done as early in life as possible. Unfortunately, many Canadians have not learned this lesson; a 1999 poll showed that 11 percent of Canadians actually expected to finance their retirement through lottery winnings (Dube, 1999). Since the odds of winning the 6/49 lottery are about 14 million to one, this is not really a sound financial plan. The same poll also pointed out the costs of neglecting retirement planning, as 38 percent of retired Canadians reported that they did not have sufficient funds to maintain the lifestyle they had envisioned when they retired.

Health is another major determinant of successful retirement. Poor health has many consequences. An individual may lose his or her freedom and independence because of illness. Poor health may also be isolating, as it limits the physical and social activities that are so important to older people.

How can you increase your chances of enjoying a long and happy retirement? The answer is that you should begin to look after your physical and financial health as early in life as possible. Proper diet, moderate drinking, not smoking, regular medical checkups, maintaining your fitness, and investing for your older years will help to ensure many years of successful retirement.

INEQUALITIES RELATED TO AGING

In previous chapters, we have seen how prejudice and discrimination may be directed toward individuals based on ascribed characteristics—such as ethnicity or gender—over which they have no control. The same holds true for age.

In some respects, older people are treated very well in Canada. Most have adequate incomes and all have access to publicly funded medical care. Housing for older people is often subsidized, and many businesses offer discounts for people who are over 65. At the same time, however, many older people feel their biggest problem is that other people have negative views of aging and of the capabilities of older people.

Ageism

Stereotypes regarding older persons reinforce *ageism*—**prejudice and discrimination against people on the basis of age, particularly when they are older persons** (Butler, 1975). Ageism against older persons is rooted in the assumption that people become unattractive, unintelligent, asexual, unemployable, and mentally incompetent as they grow older (Comfort, 1976).

Ageism is reinforced by stereotypes, whereby people have narrow, fixed images of certain groups. One-sided and exaggerated images of older people are used repeatedly in everyday life. Older persons often are stereotyped as thinking and moving slowly; as bound to themselves and their past and, therefore, unable to change and grow; and as being unable to move forward and often moving backward (Belsky, 1990). They are viewed as cranky, sickly, and lacking in social value (Atchley, 1994); as egocentric and demanding; as shallow and enfeebled; and as aimless and absent-minded (Belsky, 1990).

The media contribute to negative images of older persons, many of whom are portrayed as doddering, feebleminded, wrinkled, and laughable men and women, literally standing on their last legs (Lefrançois, 1993). This is especially true with regard to advertising. In one survey, 40 percent of respondents over age 65 agreed that advertising portrays older people as unattractive and incompetent (Pomice, 1990). According to the advertising director of one magazine, "Advertising shows young people at their best and most beautiful, but it shows older people at their worst" (quoted in Pomice, 1990:42). Of older persons who do appear on television, most are male; only about one in ten characters appearing to be age 65 or older is a woman, conveying a subtle message that older women especially are unimportant (Pomice, 1990).

Stereotypes also contribute to the view that women are "old" ten or fifteen years sooner than men (Bell, 1989). The multibillion-dollar cos-

For many years, advertisers have bombarded women with messages about the importance of a youthful appearance. Increasingly, men, too, are being targeted by advertising campaigns that play on fears about the "ravages" of aging.

metics industry helps perpetuate the myth that age reduces the "sexual value" of women but increases it for men. Men's sexual value is defined more in terms of personality, intelligence, and earning power than physical appearance. For women, however, sexual attractiveness is based on youthful appearance. By idealizing this "youthful" image of women and playing up the fear of growing older, sponsors sell thousands of products that claim to prevent the "ravages" of aging.

Fortunately, in recent years there appears to have been a change in the media coverage of older persons. Analysis of books, magazines, advertisements, and television shows has shown that media images of older people have recently become more positive (Chen and Zhou, 1994; Novak, 1997). Features such as the "Aging Dangerously" segment on CBC radio's *This Morning* program draw attention to the contributions, talents, and stamina of older persons rather than offering stereotypical and negative portrayals.

Despite some changes in media coverage of older people, many younger individuals still hold

BOX 12.2   SOCIOLOGY AND TECHNOLOGY

SENIORS AND CYBERSPACE

Do you know a grandparent or other older person who will not use a bank machine or who can't understand why there is so much fuss about computers? If so, this fits the stereotype many of us hold that seniors are far behind the rest of us in their use of technology. While older people are not usually among the first to adopt new technology, recent studies concerning their use of computers and the Internet have shown that they are rapidly catching up to other age groups. In fact, seniors are the fastest growing group of Internet users (Philbeck, 1997).

In the early days of personal computing few seniors used computers. Because many of them had retired, they did not learn to use computers on the job and the early technology was difficult to use. However, computers are now much more user-friendly, requiring neither lengthy training nor consultants on stand-by. There is even technology that enables older persons with disabilities such as blindness or arthritis to use computers.

Many seniors start using the Internet in order to communicate by e-mail with children and grandchildren living in other parts of the country. However, they have many other uses. Chat rooms and other forms of e-mail can help to replace friends who have died and keep in touch with those who have moved away. Internet shopping can help those who have difficulty going out. Surfing the Internet can help to alleviate the boredom felt by some older persons. One senior describes her experience with the Internet:

> From my desk chair I now tracked elephants in Africa, listened to the national anthem of Greece, read the *New York Times* ... But most of all, the people. Relatives and long-time, long-distance friends who used to be in touch only on holidays, were now "talking" with me

negative stereotypes of "the elderly." In one study, William C. Levin (1988) showed photographs of the same man (disguised to appear as ages 25, 52, and 73 in various photos) to a group of college students and asked them to evaluate these (apparently different) men for employment purposes. Based purely on the photographs, the "73-year-old" was viewed by many of the students as being less competent, less intelligent, and less reliable than the "25-year-old" and the "52-year-old."

These attitudes have serious consequences. Many older people who find themselves unemployed due to layoffs or plant closures often find it very difficult to find new jobs. Both employers and employment counsellors say that there is age-related bias against older workers (Underhill et al., 1997; Lipovenko, 1997). The situation is particularly difficult for workers who have never acquired the technological skills demanded by employers. Many of these people simply give up their search for employment when faced with dis-

crimination by employers. Others are forced to accept low salaries or jobs that do not fully utilize their skills.

Although not all people act on appearances alone, Patricia Moore, an industrial designer, found that many do. At age 27, Moore disguised herself as an 85-year-old woman by donning age-appropriate clothing and placing baby oil in her eyes to create the appearance of cataracts. With the help of a makeup artist, Moore supplemented the "aging process" with latex wrinkles, stained teeth, and a gray wig. For three years, "Old Pat Moore" went to various locations, including a grocery store, to see how people responded to her:

> When I did my grocery shopping while in character, I learned quickly that the Old Pat Moore behaved—and was treated—differently from the Young Pat Moore. When I was 85, people were more likely to jockey ahead of me in the checkout line. And even more interesting, I found that

BOX 12.2

CONTINUED

regularly on the computer. I soon made myself at home in a chat-room for seniors only and met people from all over the United States and beyond—"seniornetters" ... who also had exchanged their typewriters for cyberspace.

What a zany, caring bunch! It was obvious that the Internet was rescuing many seniors from what otherwise would be isolated lives. Some were housebound due to illness or the illness of a spouse. Others sought relief from boredom, or relished just plain fun and good conversation. Friendships (yes, real ones), blossomed through this medium and, with appropriate precautions, I dared travel to meet in person some of those whom I had met online.

Sources: Patterson, 1998; and Philbeck, 1997.

My mother, nearing 90, remains convinced that the folks I meet via computer all belong to the Mafia and warns me regularly about "those Internet people." I try to break the news gently that I am one of "those Internet people." (Patterson, 1998)

Recent research has shown that Internet use may even have health benefits: a psychological study found that Internet-using older persons showed gains in a cognitive ability test that is part of the Geriatric Depression Scale (Philbeck, 1997).

Some Web sites for seniors are:
http://www.seniornet.org/
http://www.hc-sc.gc.ca/seniors-aines/
http://www.eurolinkage.org/

when it happened, I didn't say anything to the offender, as I certainly would at age 27. It seemed somehow, even to me, that it was okay for them to do this to the Old Pat Moore, since they were undoubtedly busier than I was anyway. And further, they apparently thought it was okay, too! After all, little old ladies have plenty of time, don't they? And then when I did get to the checkout counter, the clerk might start yelling, assuming I was deaf, or becoming immediately testy, assuming I would take a long time to get my money out, or would ask to have the price repeated, or somehow become confused about the transaction. What it all added up to was that people feared I would be trouble, so they tried to have as little to do with me as possible. And the amazing thing is that I began almost to believe it myself ... I think perhaps the worst thing about aging may be the overwhelming sense that everything around you is letting you know that you are not terribly important anymore. (Moore with Conn, 1985:75–76)

If we apply our sociological imagination to Moore's study, we find that "Old Pat Moore's" experiences reflect what many older persons already know—it is other people's *reactions* to their age, not their age itself, that places them at a disadvantage.

Many older people buffer themselves against ageism by continuing to view themselves as being in middle adulthood long after their actual chronological age would suggest otherwise. In one study of people aged 60 and over, 75 percent of the respondents stated that they thought of themselves as middle-aged and only 10 percent viewed themselves as being old. When the same people were interviewed again ten years later, one-third still considered themselves to be middle-aged. Even at age 80, one out of four men and one out of five women said that the word *old* did not apply to them; this lack of willingness to acknowledge having reached older age is a consequence of ageism in society (Belsky, 1990).

Wealth, Poverty, and Aging

Many of the positive images of aging and suggestions on how to avoid the most negative aspects of ageism are based on an assumption of class privilege. Older people are seen as being able to afford travel, exercise classes, social activities such as ballroom dancing or golf, and that they have available the time and facilities to engage in pursuits that will "keep them young." However, many older people have meagre incomes, have saved little, or are in poor health. In addition, those who are isolated in rural areas or in low-income areas of central cities do not have the same opportunities to follow popular recommendations about successful aging (Stoller and Gibson, 1997:76). For these people aging is not so much a matter of seeking to defy one's age but rather of simply surviving in a society where they do not have sufficient financial resources and where they are devalued because of their age.

How have older people as a group fared economically in recent decades? There is no easy answer to this question. The elderly comprise an extremely heterogeneous group. Some of Canada's wealthiest individuals are old. At the same time, a significant number of this country's older citizens are poor or near poor. The image of our elderly population living the "high life" on the backs of our younger population is a myth that only serves to perpetuate ageism.

In order to accurately assess the economic situation of older people, it is necessary to address two questions. First, has the economic situation of older Canadians improved? The answer is yes—rather dramatically. The income of people over the age of 65 has improved in the past two decades. In fact, the income for Canadians aged 65 and over has risen faster than that of the rest of the population since the early 1970s.

The second question is whether older Canadians are able to maintain a satisfactory standard of living. The answer to this question is more complex. If we compare wealth (all economic resources of value, whether they produce cash or not) with income (available money or its equivalent in purchasing power), we find that older people tend to have more wealth but less income than younger people. For example, older people are more likely to own a home that has increased substantially in market value; however, some may not have the available cash to pay property taxes, to buy insurance, and to maintain the property (Moody, 1994). In short, although some older Canadians are able to

maintain a reasonable standard of living, they do not have higher incomes than the rest of the population.

It is important to remember that although the economic situation of seniors has improved, 15 percent of all people over the age of 65 have low incomes. Changes to government income transfer programs, expansion of tax-sheltered RRSPs, and increased investment returns have reduced the incidence of low income among older people in Canada since the early 1970s (Ng, 1994). Furthermore, while income has risen in the past few years for older people in general, certain groups still have incomes below the poverty line in old age. Older people from lower-income backgrounds, people who cannot speak English or French, people with limited education, Aboriginal people, and people in small towns tend to have low incomes. Very old people, women, and unattached individuals (Figure 12.5) often live below the poverty line.

THE FEMINIZATION OF POVERTY

One conclusion stands out from all the facts and figures [about aging and poverty]: Poverty in old age is largely a woman's problem, and is becoming more so every year. (National Council of Welfare, c.f. Novak, 1993:239)

The poverty rate for elderly women is double the poverty rate for elderly men. *Unattached* elderly women are at the greatest risk of poverty with a rate that is double that of married elderly women (see Figure 12.5). In 1996 more than one-half of women living alone had incomes below the low-income cut-off (Health Canada, 1998). Why do women have such low incomes in old age? According to the National Council of Welfare, "after a lifetime spent taking care of their spouses and children, these women who had no opportunity to become financially self-sufficient are now abandoned by the generation that benefited most from their work" (quoted in Novak, 1993:239).

Although middle-aged and older women make up an increasing portion of the workforce, they are paid substantially less than men their age, receive raises at a slower pace, and still work largely in gender-segregated jobs (see Chapter 11). As a result, women do not garner economic security for their retirement years at the same rate that men do. These factors have contributed to the economic marginality of the current cohort of older women.

FIGURE 12.5 Poverty Rate, People 65 and Older, 1994

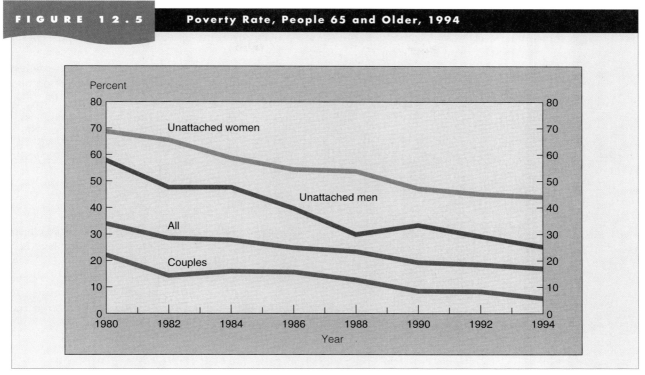

Source: National Council of Welfare, *Poverty Profile 1994*. Cat. no. 467-1/4-1994E. Reproduced with the permission of the Minister of Public Works and Government Services Canada, 1999.

In a recent study, gerontologists Melissa A. Hardy and Lawrence E. Hazelrigg (1993) found that gender was more directly related to poverty in older persons than was ethnicity, educational background, or occupational status. Hardy and Hazelrigg (1993) suggested that many women who are now age 65 or over spent their early adult lives as financial dependents of husbands or as working nonmarried women trying to support themselves in a culture that did not see women as the heads of households or sole providers of family income. Because they were not viewed as being responsible for the family's financial security, women were paid less. Therefore, older women may rely on inadequate income replacement programs originally designed to treat them as dependents. Furthermore, women tend to marry men who are older than they are, and women live longer than men. Consequently, nearly half of all women over age 65 are widowed and living alone on fixed incomes. The result? According to the National Council of Welfare, "after fifty years or so of unpaid, faithful service a women's only reward is likely to be poverty" (quoted in Novak, 1993:241).

Young women today will be much better equipped to deal with the financial pressures of old age as a result of a number of structural changes in Canadian society. The majority of women are working in the paid labour force, they have begun to enter male-dominated professions, and more of them belong to private pension plans (Connelly and MacDonald, 1990).

Elder Abuse

Abuse and neglect of older persons has received increasing public attention in recent years, due both to the increasing number of older people and to the establishment of more vocal groups to represent their concerns. ***Elder abuse* refers to physical abuse, psychological abuse, financial exploitation, and medical abuse or neglect of people age 65 or older** (Patterson and Podnieks, 1995).

The elderly are often referred to as "hidden victims" of intimate violence (DeKeseredy, 1996). It is difficult to determine the extent of abuse of older persons. Many victims are understandably reluctant to talk about it. One study used a cross-

Canada telephone survey of elderly persons living in private houses (Podnieks, 1989). Four percent of a randomly selected sample reported some form of abuse. Although this may appear to be a small percentage, 4 percent of all seniors living in private dwellings translates into 98,000 Canadians. Many cases of abuse are chronic or repetitive. Podnieks reported that only 25 percent of the victims of elder abuse had reported the incident to the police. In only one case was a criminal charge laid. The most common reasons for not reporting the incident were that it was not serious enough to report to the police or it was a private family matter. The research indicates that elder abuse tends to be concentrated among those over age 75 (Steinmetz, 1987). In most cases the abuse is inflicted by a relative and is approximately equally distributed between children or grandchildren and spouses (Patterson and Podnieks, 1995). Almost two-thirds of the victims were men even though there are far more women in the elderly population. Abusers usually live with the victim and have often cared for the victim for a long time.

Elder abuse traditionally has been associated with high levels of impairment on the part of the older person (Harris, 1990), but studies have found little evidence to support that conclusion (Pedrick-Cornell and Gelles, 1982). Sociologist Karl Pillemer found that there was no support for another common misconception: that dependency on the part of the older person leads to abuse. In fact, victims of abuse were more likely than nonvictims to report that they lived with a person with serious health, emotional, or alcohol abuse problems. Furthermore, the abusers are very likely to be dependant on the older person for housing and financial assistance (Pillemer, 1985).

Although the risk of criminal victimization is much lower for individuals over the age of 65 than for their younger counterparts, older people report more fear of crime. For example, the Canadian Urban Victimization Survey found that almost 60 percent of people over 65 indicated that they felt unsafe walking alone at night (Johnson, 1990). Older unattached women with low incomes and fair-to-poor health reported the most fear of criminal victimization (Podnieks,1989). There are a number of factors that may lead to this fear. According to Novak, "loss of social networks due to retirement, widowhood, and staying home may lead to increased fear of crime" (1993:8). Furthermore, cases of abuse and neglect of older people are highly dramatized in the media because of their extremely disturbing nature.

However, the media coverage may also serve to create a fear of victimization that does not fit the facts regarding elder abuse. Finally, the consequences of victimization may be more serious. A young person who is knocked down by a stranger may get up unharmed, while an older person may be seriously hurt in a similar incident.

SOCIOLOGICAL PERSPECTIVES ON AGING

Sociologists and social gerontologists have developed a number of explanations of the social effects of aging. Some of the early theories were based on a microlevel analysis of how individuals adapt to changing social roles. More recent theories have used a macrolevel approach to examine the inequalities produced by age stratification at the societal level.

Functionalist Perspectives on Aging

Functionalist explanations of aging focus on how older persons adjust to their changing roles in society. According to sociologist Talcott Parsons (1960), the roles of older persons need to be redefined by society. He suggested that devaluing the contributions of older persons is dysfunctional for society; older persons often have knowledge and wisdom to share with younger people.

How does society cope with the disruptions resulting from its members growing older and dying? According to *disengagement theory,* older persons make a normal and healthy adjustment to aging when they detach themselves from their social roles and prepare for their eventual death (Cumming and Henry, 1961). Gerontologists Elaine C. Cumming and William E. Henry (1961) noted that disengagement can be functional for both the individual and society. The withdrawal of older persons from the workforce, for example, provides employment opportunities for younger people. Disengagement also facilitates a gradual and orderly transfer of statuses and roles from one generation to the next; an abrupt change would result in chaos. Retirement, then, can be thought of as recognition for years of service and acknowledgment that the person no longer fits into the world of paid work (Williamson, Duffy Rinehart, and Blank, 1992). The younger workers who move into the vacated positions have received more up-to-date training—for example, the computer skills that are taught to most younger people today.

Critics of this perspective object to the assumption that all older persons want to disengage while they still are productive and gain satisfaction from their work. Disengagement may be functional for organizations but not for individuals. A corporation that has compulsory retirement may be able to replace higher-paid, older workers with lower-paid, younger workers but retirement may not be beneficial for some older workers. Contrary to disengagement theory, a number of studies have found that activity in society is *more* important as people get older.

Interactionist Perspectives on Aging

Interactionist perspectives examine the connection between personal satisfaction in a person's later years and a high level of activity. **Activity theory states that people tend to shift gears in late middle age and find substitutes for previous statuses, roles, and activities** (Havighurst, Neugarten, and Tobin, 1968). From this perspective, older people have the same social and psychological needs as middle-aged people and thus do not want to withdraw unless restricted by poor health or disability.

Whether they invest their energies in grandchildren, travelling, hobbies, or new work roles, social activity among retired persons is directly related to longevity, happiness, and health (Palmore, 1981). Psychologist and newspaper columnist Eda LeShan observed a difference in the perceptions of people who do and do not remain active:

The Richardsons came for lunch: friends we hadn't seen for twenty years … Helen and Martin had owned and worked together in a very fine women's clothing shop … Having some mistaken notion they were getting too old and should retire and "enjoy themselves," they sold the business ten years ago.

During lunch, Larry and I realized we were dealing with two seriously depressed people, in excellent health but with no place to go. When Larry asked Helen what she'd been doing, she replied bitterly, "Who has anything to do?" Martin said sadly he was sorry he gave up tennis ten years ago; if he'd kept it up he could still play …

We were embarrassed to indicate we were still so busy that we couldn't see straight. They seemed genuinely shocked that we had no plans to retire at seventy-one and seventy-four. (LeShan, 1994:221–222)

Studies have confirmed LeShan's suggestion that healthy people who remain active have a higher level of life satisfaction than do those who are inactive or in ill health (Havighurst, Neugarten, and Tobin, 1968). Among those whose mental capacities decline later in life, deterioration is most rapid in people who withdraw from social relationships and activities.

A variation on activity theory is the concept of *continuity*—that people are constantly attempting to maintain their self-esteem and lifelong principles and practices and that they simply adjust to the feedback from and needs of others as they grow older (Williamson, Duffy Rinehart, and Blank, 1992). From this perspective, aging is a continuation of earlier life stages rather than a separate and unique period. Thus, values and behaviours that have been important to an individual previously will continue to be so as the person ages. People also may turn to their ethnic culture to help them deal with physical changes, role changes, and bereavement issues in their later years. For example, studies have found that the church serves an important function in reducing loneliness, providing support systems, and enhancing self-image in older African-American persons (Gelfand, 1994).

Other interactionist perspectives focus on role and exchange theories. Role theory poses the question, What roles are available for older people? Some theorists have noted that industrialized, urbanized societies typically do not have roles for older people (Cowgill, 1986). Analysts examining the relationship between ethnicity and aging have found that many older persons are able to find active roles within their own ethnic group. While their experiences may not be valued in the larger society, they are esteemed within their ethnic subculture because they provide a rich source of knowledge of ethnic lore and history. For example, Mildred Cleghorn, an 80-year-old Aboriginal woman, passes on information to younger people by use of dolls:

I decided … to show that we were all not the same, by making dolls that said we were just as different as our clothes are different. I made four dolls … representing the four tribes there—then seven more … for the tribes living here. Now, over the years, I have

What happens as we grow older? Activity theory assumes we will find substitutes for our previous roles and activities. Disengagement theory assumes we will detach ourselves from social roles and prepare for death. Which scenario do you prefer for your future?

a collection of forty-one fabric dolls, all different tribes. The trouble is there are thirty-two more to go! (quoted in Mucciolo, 1992:23)

Cleghorn's unique knowledge about the various First Nations has been a valuable source of information for young Aboriginal people who otherwise might be unaware of the great diversity found among First Nations peoples. According to sociologist Donald E. Gelfand (1994), older people can "exchange" their knowledge for deference and respect from younger people.

Conflict Perspectives on Aging

Conflict theorists view aging as especially problematic in contemporary capitalistic societies. As people grow older, their power tends to diminish unless they are able to maintain wealth. Consequently, those who have been disadvantaged in their younger years become even more so in late adulthood. Women age 75 and over are among the most disadvantaged because they often must rely solely on government support payments, having outlived their spouses and sometimes their children (Harrington Meyer, 1990).

Underlying the capitalist system is an ideology that assumes that all people have equal access to the means of gaining wealth and that poverty results from individual weakness. When older people are in need, they may be viewed as not having worked hard enough or planned adequately for their retirement. The family and the private sector are seen as the "proper" agents to respond to their needs. To minimize the demand for governmental assistance, these services are made punitive and stigmatizing to those who need them (Atchley, 1994). Class-based theories of inequality assert that government programs for older persons stratify society on the basis of class. Feminist approaches claim that these programs perpetuate inequalities on the basis of gender and ethnicity in addition to class (Harrington Meyer, 1994).

Conflict analysis draws attention to the diversity in the older population. Differences in social class, gender, and ethnicity divide older people just as they do everyone else. Wealth cannot forestall aging indefinitely, but it can soften the economic hardships faced in later years. The conflict perspective adds to our understanding of aging by focusing on how capitalism devalues older people, especially women. Critics assert, however, that this approach ignores the fact that industrialization and capitalism have greatly enhanced the longevity and quality of life for many older persons.

If we apply our sociological imagination to problems associated with aging, we find that these are not isolated situations shared by only a few

What does the concept of nursing homes imply about the ability of residents to live out their lives with dignity and respect?

people. Individuals cannot solve all of the problems associated with growing older or, in some cases, becoming a person with a disability. Some older persons initially may not see commonalities between their experiences and those of persons with a disability; however, if they have a problem that overlaps both categories, their perceptions may change. Eda LeShan (1994) explains:

> People like me sometimes need a hard lesson. Having just recently moved … I looked forward eagerly to swimming at the local YMCA … I was sure many of the members would be old ladies like me … Much to my surprise I discovered I had two choices: Either I would have to climb down a ladder, which I couldn't do because of arthritic feet, or I could paddle about in the "old people's pool," which was small and kept at 87 degrees. I am, at seventy, one helluva good swimmer. I just can't deal with ladders, and the hot pool was too debilitating and had no room for swimming laps. I got my membership fee back …
>
> What do you know—I am one of the disabled! Unfortunately we imperfect humans often have to experience something ourselves before we get the full significance of a problem. (LeShan, 1994:132–133)

LIVING ARRANGEMENTS FOR OLDER ADULTS

Many frail, older people live alone or in a family setting where care is provided informally by family or friends. Relatives (especially women) provide most of the care (Glazer, 1990). Many women caregivers are employed outside the home; some are still raising a family. Recently, the responsibilities of informal caregivers have become more complex. For frail, older persons, for example, family members often are involved in nursing regimes—such as chemotherapy and tube-feeding—that previously were performed in hospitals (Glazer, 1990). Only about 7 percent of frail, older persons are currently in nursing homes (Priest, 1993). As you would expect, the older people are the more likely it is that they will live in institutions. Very few people under 75 are in nursing homes, compared with over 40 percent of people aged 85 and over.

Support Services, Homemaker Services, and Daycare

Support services help older individuals cope with the problems in their day-to-day care. For older persons, homemaker services perform basic chores (such as light housecleaning and laundry); other services (such as Meals on Wheels) deliver meals to homes. Some programs provide balanced meals at set locations, such as churches, synagogues, or senior centres.

Daycare centres also have been developed to help older persons maintain as much dignity and autonomy as possible. These centres typically provide transportation, activities, some medical personnel (such as a licensed practical nurse) on staff, and nutritious meals.

Support services and daycare for older persons can be costly, but they are far less expensive than institutional care. Even intensive services that

BOX 12.3 CRITICAL THINKING

WILL THERE BE A GENERATIONAL WAR BETWEEN THE OLD AND THE YOUNG?

Canadians enjoy retirement, and why not? Most retirees are having the time of their lives: long, lazy summers at the cottage, gambling jaunts to Vegas in the winter, golf all year round ...

Retirement as we know it—ten or twenty years of fun, partly at public expense, as a reward for showing up at work during our adult lives—is doomed. The happy coincidence of generous governments and the postwar economic and population boom that made it possible has come undone. The web of government-sponsored seniors' programmes that pays retirees largely from the taxes of those still working has become unsustainable ...

Funding leisure in later life must become a personal responsibility, not a social obligation. Retirees must stop insisting that they have a right to siphon money from their kids to help make their golden years enjoyable. (Taylor, 1995:18)

■s Peter Shawn Taylor correct? Will our social welfare system go bankrupt when the baby boomers reach retirement age? Will young people be impoverished by their parents and grandparents? Let us look at how the system works and its likely future.

Much of Canada's social welfare system has been designed to support the young and the old. An informal social contract between generations obliges the working-age population to support dependent children and older adults. In exchange, these workers received support during their own childhoods and could expect to receive support in their old age.

After World War II, governments in most industrial countries placed a priority on providing old-age pensions for seniors. Figure 12.5 shows that this effort was successful: between 1980 and 1994 the proportion of people over 65 who were poor dropped from 33 percent to 18 percent. However, in the mid 1970s people began to worry that increasing numbers of elderly and increasing entitlements would cause the collapse of the Old Age Security program (Myles, 1999).

This led people such as Taylor to suggest that the social contract between generations has been broken and that young people will have to pay far more to support older people than they will ever receive in return. The huge numbers of aging baby boomers, who themselves supported a relatively small number of older people and who are responsible for building up much of our national debt, will have to be supported in their old age by a much smaller number of workers.

The debate over the possibility of intergenerational conflict flourished during the eighties and nineties when unemployment rates were high, particularly for young people, and when massive social service cuts were pitting one group against the other. This was symbolized by seniors activist Solange Denis, who confronted then prime minister Mulroney on Parliament Hill in 1985 and helped to force him to back down on planned cuts to pensions. Because of their political power, older people suffered fewer cuts to social programs than other vulnerable groups such as children and single-parent families (Gray, 1997).

The tension between the generations is increased by public images such as the one in the quotation at the beginning of this box that

BOX 12.3

CONTINUED

suggest older people are living the good life while younger people struggle to find jobs and to pay off student loans. Those concerned with this issue have suggested that benefits be cut, that the age for payment of government pensions be raised, or that monthly premiums be raised to ensure that sufficient funds are available when the baby boomers begin to retire. You know from reading this chapter that this stereotype does not reflect the lives of the many older persons who have very modest incomes. However, the image of the affluent senior living off the backs of younger people has the potential to create divisions within Canadian society.

Those readers who will not retire for several decades should not be too concerned about the gloomy future predicted by Taylor. Several European countries already have high proportions of older persons and are able to support old-age-security programs without seeing signs of intergenerational hostility. Also, a number of factors should help to alleviate the problem before it turns into a crisis. First, because of declining fertility rates, fewer resources will be required to look after children and it will be easier to direct resources to older people (Easterlin, 1991). Second, governments have begun to take action that will lessen the future burden on our pension system. Even in the most pessimistic scenarios, a pension crisis is still several decades away and planning now can help avoid trouble in the future. In 1983, the United States passed a law delaying payment of Social Security. The minimum age will begin rising from 65 in 2002 to 67 in 2027. More recently, the 1999 increase in Canada Pension Plan contributions will help to ensure

that pensions are still available for all Canadians in the future. Finally, many older persons will be well off and paying high levels of tax on their retirement income. Many also contribute significant amounts of volunteer labour, so older people do not just take from their children and grandchildren.

With good planning, much can also be done to alleviate a possible crisis in health care. Measures such as community support programs are discussed in this chapter. Others include taking measures to improve health. In fact, older people have responded well to government health-promotion efforts focused on diet, exercise, and lifestyle, and have led the way in adopting healthier lifestyles. This should help reduce their use of the health care system. Health care officials can also deal with the problems of inappropriate referrals and repeat visits to doctors adding significant costs to the system by reducing their numbers without affecting public health. Finally, we can develop policies that address the fact that a large proportion of health care costs occur in the final six months of life. These costs include keeping the dying patient in an acute care facility, ordering tests and life-support in order to prolong life even when it is clear that the patient is dying. Many dying patients could be well cared for in hospices or chronic care hospitals, rather than in more expensive acute care hospitals.

What do you think about this issue? Are you prepared to pay to support your parents and grandparents? What should our politicians do to prepare Canada for the future?

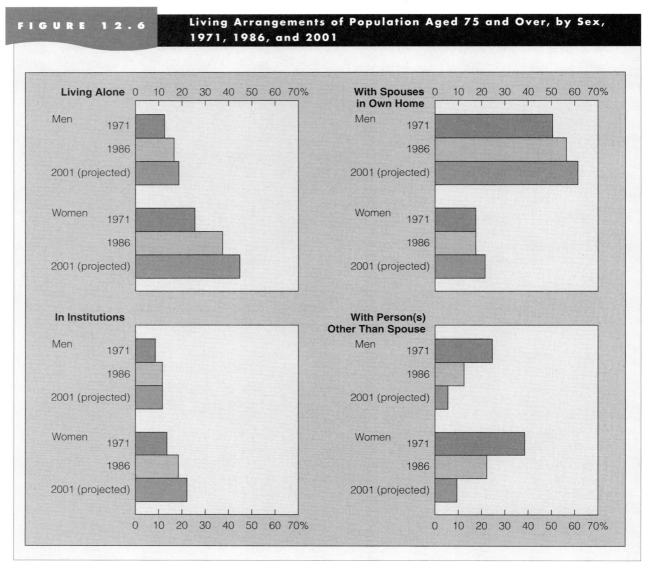

FIGURE 12.6   Living Arrangements of Population Aged 75 and Over, by Sex, 1971, 1986, and 2001

Adapted from Statistics Canada, *Canadian Social Trends 1996*, Cat. no. 11-008, 1993. Used by permission.

provide the support to allow older persons with serious physical problems to live in their homes may cost only 25 percent of that of a nursing home. More importantly, these services allow older persons to live in a familiar environment and to retain much of their independence.

A Victoria, British Columbia, program illustrates how a carefully planned program can save money and enhance the quality of life of older persons (Novak, 1997). The Quick Response Team (QRT) was designed to deal with patients who have been admitted to hospital because of medical emergencies such as broken bones and strokes. After the emergency has been dealt with,

the acute care hospital can do little more for the patient. Many patients are, however, unable to return home because they are unable to care for themselves. The QRT arranges for community support for these patients. The nature of these supports depends on the patient's needs and can include live-in homemaker services, transportation, home nursing, meals-on-wheels, physiotherapy, and household equipment such as walkers and bath seats. Because it costs about $1000 per day to keep a patient in an acute care hospital, programs such as the QRT can be a very cost-effective way of providing high-quality services to older persons.

Most of us rely on informal support networks to help us through difficult times. When our needs become greater or our informal supports weaken, as they do with some older persons, we need to find formal support networks to replace them. Programs such as QRT can be effective because they recognize that older persons often have multiple needs and several different types of support must be coordinated if they are to be effective.

Nursing Homes

Nursing homes can be defined as any institution that offers medical care for chronically ill older people but that is not a hospital (Novak, 1977:148). They are the most restrictive environment for older persons.

Why do people live in nursing homes? Many nursing home residents have major physical and/or cognitive problems that prevent them from living in any other setting or do not have available caregivers in their family. Women are more likely to enter nursing homes because of their greater life expectancy, higher rates of chronic illness, and higher rates of widowhood.

Some people adjust very well to life in a nursing home. However, for many others the transition to an institutional setting can be very stressful. Mortality rates are higher after admission to nursing homes. In part, this is due to the fact that the sickest older people enter these institutions. However, researchers have concluded that institutionalization itself can lower levels of well-being and can accelerate mortality (Novak, 1997). Cases of neglect, excessive use of physical restraints, overmedication of patients, and other complaints have been rampant in many of the homes. Author Betty Friedan (1993:516) stresses that even the best-run nursing homes "deny the personhood of age [because they] reify the image of age as inevitable decline and deterioration."

One solution to this problem is to reduce the number of admissions to nursing homes by providing higher levels of support that will enable people to remain in the community. However, there will always be people whose physical or mental condition makes institutional care necessary. Gerontologists have found that nursing homes can do many things to reduce the negative effects of institutionalization by making life in the institution as much like life outside as possible (MacLean and Bonar, 1983). One is ensuring that patients are always treated with respect and allowed as much freedom of choice as possible.

Older persons and persons with disabilities both seek to be fully accepted as participants in everyday life, as this seniors protest demonstrates.

Patients should also have programs that allow them to remain active, and they should be allowed to maintain the daily, monthly, and yearly rhythms of life (Novak, 1997). It is also important for patients to have a normal social life and to have enough of their own possessions that the institution becomes their home and not just a place where they are forced to stay.

Contrasting views of nursing home life that illustrate some of these points are expressed by two nursing home residents (NACA, 1992):

My eyesight and ability to walk are very bad. I have a hard time getting around. But I am feeling alright because I have enough money, thanks to my pension, and I am in a home where people look after me. I don't have any family but like being here because everybody is a friend.

They take care of me here but they don't do it the same as I would myself. I can't take care of myself because I'm all crippled up. Sometimes I think this place is run more for the convenience of the staff than for the residents. I resent having to go to bed early just to suit them ... I have only $90 a month to get by on. That is not very much. It is very hard for me to take a car or a bus to go anywhere.

AGING IN RUSSIA

Since the breakup of the Soviet Union in 1991, Russia has been struggling to make the transition from communism to capitalism. Faced with a crumbling economy and an ineffective government, and plagued by corruption and organized crime, the Russian economy has been failing and the country has been unable to pay its debts or provide for its citizens. Under the communist regime, older persons were provided for by the state. While they were not particularly well-off by Canadian standards, they had basic medical care and the security of a state pension. Today, the health care system is in crisis and pensioners are in desperate financial trouble.

The political change in Russia had a dramatic impact on the structure of the Russian population (see Figure 12.7). As the economic and political structure changed, birth rates dropped and death rates rose. Death rates are particularly high for working-age males, many of whom die prematurely because of accidents, homicide, and alcohol consumption. In 1994 mortality rates for males 15 to 64 were twice as high as they had been in 1986. For the first time in Russian history, the number of deaths is higher than the number of births (DaVanzo and Adamson, 1997).

The decline in births in the 1990s shown in Figure 12.7 represents the continuation of a long-term trend that was interrupted by mid-1980s government incentives to have children during that period (DaVanzo and Adamson, 1997). The reduction in births means that the average age of the population is rising and that fewer working-age people are supporting

FIGURE 12.7 Birth and Death Rates in Russia, 1959–1995

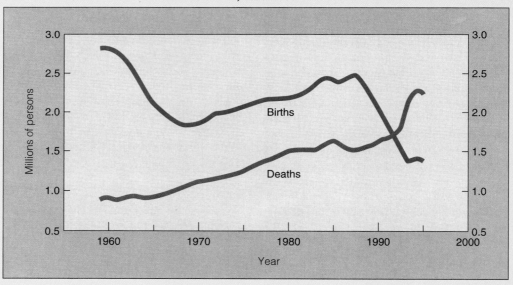

DEATH AND DYING

Historically, death has been a common occurrence at all stages of the life course. Until the twentieth century, the chances that a newborn child would live to adulthood were very small. Poor nutrition, infectious diseases, accidents, and natural disasters took their toll on men and women of all ages. In contemporary, industrial societies, however, death is looked on as unnatural because it largely has been removed from everyday life. Most deaths now occur among older persons and in institutional settings. The association of death with the

BOX 12.4

CONTINUED

larger numbers of older persons. While the proportion of the population aged 65 and over is lower than that of many countries including Canada, the average age of the Russian working population is among the highest in the world and will continue to increase over the next several decades.

As you have seen in Box 12.3, the increasing ratio of old persons to young persons does not pose a serious problem for Canadians, but Russia faces far greater difficulties. With its economy in ruins, its workers often going unpaid, and its government essentially bankrupt, continuing to provide services to older people will be very hard. Because of inflation caused by a series of financial crises, the value of pensions once worth the equivalent of $75 per month has dropped to less than $30 per month. Often pensions are not paid at all for months at a time because of the government's monetary problems (Nickles, 1998). The pension system is threatened by a reduction in workers' contributions because of high unemployment and because many employers have stopped making their required contributions to the plan (United Nations, 1997b). This dismal situation is made worse by the fact that part of the transition to capitalism involved removing price subsidies from food and other essential commodities. This means that while the value of pensions was dropping, the price of basic commodities has been increasing.

Older people will also be hurt by the decline in Russia's health care system. DaVanzo and Adamson conclude that the system is in crisis:

As the command economy crumbled, the public-health sector plunged into financial crisis. The system found itself in an emerging market environment without the capacity to function successfully in it. Left without proper funding, health-care facilities were forced to abandon new construction, renovation, and other basic investments. Cost cutting necessitated switching to cheaper technologies, which proved insufficient to maintain needed levels of care. Available funds were frequently diverted to current needs. As a result, the health status of the Russian population is deteriorating, and diseases long thought to be eliminated or controlled ... are now spreading again. (1997:6)

Under these conditions, older people will be victims of diseases such as tuberculosis that are now becoming epidemic in Russia, and also will not have adequate treatment for the diseases and disabilities that afflict the elderly in all societies.

The cause of Russia's difficulties was summed up by Natalia Rimachevskaya, a Russian delegate to a United Nations conference, who said: "[T]he old principles and social structures had been destroyed but nothing new had really been created" (United Nations, 1997b). As usual, the burden of difficulties such as these fall most heavily on those who are vulnerable, including children and older people.

Source: Fig. 12.7 Reprinted by permission from Anatoly Vishevski; "Family, Fertility, and Demographic Dynamics in Russia: Analysis and Forecast" in Julie Da Vanzo (ed.), *Russia's Demographic Crisis.*" Santa Monica, CA: Rand, 1996, CF-124-CRES,32.

aging process has contributed to ageism in our society; if people can deny aging, they feel they can deny death (Atchley, 1994).

In the past, explanations for death and dying were rooted in custom or religious beliefs; today, they have been replaced by medical and legal explanations and definitions, and ongoing medical and legal battles.

The Canadian courts have not yet successfully resolved a number of controversial issues that relate to the right to die with dignity. Should parents of incompetent persons in permanent vegetative states have the legal right to refuse medical treatment? Should individuals suffering from an incurable, terminal illness have the right to decide when their life should end? In 1993, the Supreme Court of Canada considered this question in the case of Sue Rodriguez, a British Columbia woman suffering from Lou Gehrig's disease. The court decided that the right to life, liberty, and security of the person (as outlined in the Charter of Rights and Freedoms) does not include the right to take action that will end one's life. Furthermore, the court decided that prohibition of physician-assisted suicide did not constitute cruel and unusual treatment. However, the lack of consensus over this complex issue was reflected in a strong dissenting vote expressed by four of the nine justices. Justice Beverley McLachlin wrote:

> The denial to Sue Rodriguez of a choice available to others cannot be justified. Such a denial deprived Sue Rodriguez of her security of the person (the right to make decisions concerning her own body which affect only her own body) in a way that offended the principles of fundamental justice. (quoted in Bolton, 1995:391)

After the Supreme Court declined her challenge for a legal physician-assisted suicide, Rodriguez took her own life with the help of an anonymous doctor and NDP MP and right-to-die advocate Svend Robinson. Currently, the Criminal Code specifies that anyone who counsels or "aids and abets" a suicide is guilty of an indictable offence and subject to 14 years in prison (McGovern, 1995). The patient's consent can not be used as a defence.

A related issue concerns the legality of a doctor hastening the death of a terminally ill patient. Ethical guidelines allow doctors to remove life support with the consent of the patient or of the patient's family if the patient is incapable of responding. After life support is removed, doctors may administer pain-killing drugs to make the patient comfortable even if these drugs may hasten death. However, Halifax doctor Nancy Morrison was charged with murder over her role in the 1996 death of a patient who was near death and in terrible pain. Dr. Morrison administered two drugs that were not painkillers, but which would stop the patient's heart. After a colleague reported the occurrence to police, the hospital was raided by sixty police officers and Dr. Morrison was arrested on a charge of first degree murder. The charges were subsequently dismissed by a judge who did not think that the Crown

could prove its charges. However, the case has led to a major debate about proper medical practice.

There is no national standard for determining when life support measures should be ended. Thousands of people are in some kind of permanent vegetative state today, and many thousands more are faced with terminal illnesses. As a result, many people have chosen to have a say in how their own lives might end by signing a *living will*—a document stating their wishes about the medical circumstances under which their life should be terminated. Most provinces recognize living wills. Many issues pertaining to the quality of life and to death with dignity may remain unresolved as we enter the twenty-first century. We can be sure, however, that the debate about the right to die will continue. The number of deaths in Canada will increase from about 200,000 per year now to 500,000 per year in 2039 as the lives of the baby boomers end (Kettle, 1998a).

How do people cope with dying? There are three widely known frameworks for explaining how people cope with the process of dying: the *stage-based approach*, the *dying trajectory*, and the *task-based approach*. The *stage-based approach* was popularized by psychiatrist Elisabeth Kübler-Ross (1969), who proposed five stages: (1) denial ("Not me!"), (2) anger ("Why me?"), (3) bargaining ("Yes me, but … "—negotiating for divine intervention), (4) depression and sense of loss, and (5) acceptance. She pointed out that these stages are not the same for all people; some of them may exist at the same time. Kübler-Ross (1969:138) also stated that "the one thing that usually persists through all these stages is hope."

Kübler-Ross's stages were attractive to the general public and the media because they provided common responses to a difficult situation. On the other hand, her stage-based model also generated a great deal of criticism. Some have pointed out that these stages have never been conclusively demonstrated or comprehensively explained.

The second approach, the *dying trajectory*, focuses on the perceived course of dying and the expected time of death. For example, a dying trajectory may be sudden, as in the case of a heart attack, or it may be slow, as in the case of lung cancer. According to the dying-trajectory approach, the process of dying involves three phases: the acute phase, characterized by the expression of maximum anxiety or fear; the chronic phase, characterized by a decline in anxiety as the person confronts reality; and the terminal phase, characterized by the dying person's withdrawal from others (Glaser and Strauss, 1968).

Finally, the *task-based approach* is based on the assumption that the dying person can and should go about daily activities and fulfil tasks that make the process of dying easier on family members and friends, as well as on the dying person. Physical tasks can be performed to satisfy bodily needs, whereas psychological tasks can be done to maximize psychological security, autonomy, and richness of experience. Social tasks sustain and enhance interpersonal attachments and address the social implications of dying. Spiritual tasks help people to identify, develop, or reaffirm sources of spiritual energy and to foster hope (Corr, Nabe, and Corr, 1994). In the final analysis, however, how a person dies is shaped by many social and cultural factors. According to social gerontologists Nancy Hooyman and H. Asuman Kiyak (1996:417), "the dying process is shaped by an individual's own personality and philosophy of life, by the specific illness, and by the social context (e.g., whether at home surrounded by family who encourage the expression of feelings, or isolated in a hospital)."

In recent years, the process of dying has become an increasingly acceptable topic for public discussion. Such discussions helped further the hospice movement in the 1970s (Weitz, 1995). A **hospice is a homelike facility that provides supportive care for patients with terminal illnesses.** The hospice philosophy asserts that people should participate in their own care and have control over as many decisions pertaining to their life as possible. Pain and suffering should be minimized, but artificial measures should not be used to sustain life. This approach is family based and provides support for family members and friends, as well as for the person who is dying (see Corr, Nabe, and Corr, 1994). Although the hospice movement has been very successful, critics claim that the movement has exchanged much of its initial philosophy and goals for social acceptance and financial support (Finn Paradis and Cummings, 1986; Weitz, 1995).

AGING IN THE FUTURE

The size of the older population in Canada will increase dramatically in the early decades of the twenty-first century. By the year 2031, there will be an estimated 8 million persons aged 65 and older, compared with 3.2 million in 1991. Because of decreasing birth rates, over the next sixty years most of the population growth will occur in the older age cohorts. More people will survive to age 85, and more will even reach the 95-and-over cohort (Norland, 1994). These estimates point out the importance of developing ways of assisting people to live full and productive lives as they grow older.

In the twenty-first century, approximately one in every four people will be 65 or over. How will this affect life in Canada? First, there will be a much greater demand on social resources and programs that provide support to the elderly. Some have suggested that unless steps are taken to meet the health care needs of millions of additional older people, our society will face a monumental health care crisis in the next century. However, others have stressed that changes in the health care system, like changes in the population, occur gradually. Therefore, the health care system will have a long time to adjust to the increasing demands of the next century (Barer et al., 1995).

One of the most positive consequences of the "graying of Canada" is that there will be considerably less age segregation. The younger population today has limited contact with older people. When the elderly comprise one-quarter of the population, there will be much more interaction between individuals of all age groups. This increased information regarding older people and the effects of aging should lead to dramatic decreases in both ageism and negative stereotypes of old age.

Who will assist persons with needs they cannot meet themselves? Family members in the future may be less willing or able to serve as caregivers. Women, the primary caregivers in the past, are faced with not just double but *triple* workdays if they attempt to combine working full-time with caring for their children and assisting older relatives. Even "superwomen" have a breaking point—no one has unlimited time, energy, and will to engage in such demanding activities for extended periods of time.

As biomedical research on aging and disabilities continues, new discoveries in genetics may eliminate life-threatening diseases and make early identification of others possible. Technological advances in the diagnosis, prevention, and treatment of Alzheimer's disease may revolutionize people's feelings about growing older (Butler, 1987; Atchley, 1997). Advances in medical technology may lead to a more positive outlook on aging and disability.

If these advances occur, will they help everyone or just some segments of the population? This is a very important question for the future. As we have seen, many of the benefits and opportunities of living in a highly technological, affluent society are not available to all people. Classism, racism, sexism, and ageism all serve to restrict individuals' access to education, medical care, housing, employment, and other valued goods and services in society.

For older persons the issues discussed in this chapter are not merely sociological abstractions; they are an integral part of their everyday lives. Older people have resisted ageism through organizations such as the New Horizons Program, the Senior's Independence Program, and the Gray Panthers.

CHAPTER REVIEW

What is aging, and what is the study of aging called?
Aging refers to the physical, psychological, and social processes associated with growing older. Gerontology is the study of aging and older people. Social gerontology is the study of the social (nonphysical) aspects of aging, including the consequences of an aging population and the personal experience of aging.

How do views of aging differ in preindustrial and industrialized societies?
In preindustrial societies, people of all ages are expected to share the work, and the contributions of older people are valued. In industrialized societies, however, older people are often expected to retire so that younger people may take their place.

What are ageism and elder abuse, and how are these perpetrated in society?
Ageism is prejudice and discrimination against people on the basis of age, particularly against older persons. Ageism is reinforced by stereotypes of older people. Elder abuse includes physical abuse, psychological abuse, financial exploitation, and medical abuse or neglect of people aged 65 or older. Passive neglect is the most common form of abuse.

How do functionalist and interactionist explanations of aging differ?

Functionalist explanations of aging focus on how older persons adjust to their changing roles in society; gradual transfer of statuses and roles from one generation to the next is necessary for the functioning of society. Activity theory, a part of the interactionist perspective, states that people change in late middle age and find substitutes for previous statuses, roles, and activities. This theory asserts that people do not want to withdraw unless restricted by poor health or disability.

Key Terms

activity theory 387
ageism 381
age stratification 375
aging 371
chronological age 372
cohort 373
disengagement theory 386
elder abuse 385
functional age 372
hospice 397
life expectancy 372
social gerontology 373

✺ Internet Exercises

1. Much of the Internet seems to serve people in their twenties and thirties. However, a number of sites are designed for older people. Use Yahoo Canada (**http://ca.yahoo.com**, then go to Society and Culture) to find sites aimed at older people. What types of sites can you find? Do these sites differ from sites geared to younger people?

2. Go to the SeniorNet site at **http://www. seniornet.org/**. Describe some of the efforts that are being made to educate seniors about computer use. Do you think the site will help in accomplishing its goal of using computer technology to enhance the lives of seniors and enabling them to share their knowledge and wisdom with others? What organizations are helping sponsor this site? Why do you think they are doing this?

3. One of the largest and best-known organizations for older persons is the Canadian Association for Retired Persons. Go to their Web site at:

http://www.fifty-plus.net/

What kinds of issues seem to interest people who belong to this organization? Find the links between CARP's home page and its sites for activities.

Compare what you find with the various sociological perspectives on aging set forth in this chapter.

4. To see some of the obstacles faced by older persons with limited mobility, go to the Design for Ageing Network at: **http://dan.interact.nl/**. Go to the Obstacle Course to see how poor design can impede older people as well as others with disabilities.

🕸 Net Links

Several universities, including the University of Manitoba, have research centres focusing on aging. See how sociologists approach aging and pick up other Net links at:

http://www.umanitoba.ca/centres/aging/

For data about Canada's seniors, see the Canada's Seniors at a Glance Web site:

http://www.hc-sc.gc.ca/seniors-aines/seniors/pubs/poster/seniors/page1e.htm

The federal government is responsible for support programs for seniors. To learn about Canada's pension and old security programs; go to:

http://www.hrdc-drhc.gc.ca/isp/common/home.html

Go to the Web site of the Canadian Association of Retired Persons:

http://www.fifty-plus.net/about/index.dhtml?url=main.dhtml

Questions for Critical Thinking

1. Is it necessary to have a mandatory retirement age?
2. How will the size of the older population in Canada affect society in the twenty-first century?
3. Analyze your grandparents (or other older persons you know well or even yourself if you are older) in terms of disengagement theory and activity theory. Which theory seems to provide the most insight? Why?
4. Find media examples presenting aging in a positive and a negative light.

Suggested Readings

Texts and readers that give insightful coverage of aging and diversity include:

Robert C. Atchley. *Social Forces and Aging: An Introduction to Social Gerontology* (7th ed.). Belmont, Cal.: Wadsworth, 1994.

Susan McDaniel. *Canada's Aging Population.* Toronto: Butterworths, 1986.

Barry D. McPherson. *Aging as a Social Process: An Introduction to Individual and Population Aging.* Toronto: Harcourt Brace.

Harry R. Moody. *Aging: Concepts and Controversies.* Thousand Oaks, Cal.: Pine Forge Press, 1994.

Mark Novak. *Aging and Society* (3rd ed.). Toronto: ITP Nelson, 1997.

Eleanor Palo Stoller and Rose Campbell Gibson. *Worlds of Difference: Inequality in the Aging Experience.* Thousand Oaks, Cal.: Pine Forge Press, 1994.

To learn more about aging in global perspective:

Steven M. Albert and Maria G. Cattell. *Old Age in Global Perspective: Cross-Cultural and Cross-National Views.* New York: G.K. Hall, 1994.

The Economy
    The Sociology of Economic Life
    Historical Changes in Economic Systems

Contemporary Economic Systems
    Capitalism
    Socialism
    Mixed Economies

Perspectives on Economy and Work
    The Functionalist Perspective
    The Conflict Perspective

The Interactionist Perspective
    The Meaning of Work
    Job Satisfaction

The Social Organization of Work
    Occupations
    Professions
    Managers and the Managed
    The Lower Tier of the Service Sector
        and Marginal Jobs
    Contingent Work
    Unemployment
    Labour Unions

The Global Economy in the Future
    The End of Work?
    The Canadian Economy
    Global Economic Interdependence and Competition
    Corporate Responsibility

Wilfred Popoff was the associate editor of Saskatoon's *Star Phoenix* until Conrad Black's Hollinger Corporation purchased the newspaper in early 1996 and immediately reduced the size of its staff. Popoff (1996:A22) describes how he, a senior employee with more than 30 years of service, was dismissed:

"I can only attribute my sudden firing, within several months of possible retirement, a dignified retirement I had seen so many others receive, to total abandonment of common civility, a phenomenon more and more prevalent today. You see, I was fired not because of anything I did or didn't do, but because of the need to cut costs in the quest for fantastic profits. And how the affair was stage-managed tells more than one wishes to know about the uncivil environment surrounding contemporary capitalism.

"On a Friday afternoon all employees, about 300 in all, received a terse letter from the boss commanding attendance at a meeting in a hotel the following morning. The arrangement was reminiscent of military occupations portrayed in countless movies. The vanquished are summoned to the market square where officers of the occupying army register all people and direct them to various camps. In our case the officers were employees of a consulting firm, also strangers, who directed employees to various rooms, separating survivors from those marked for elimination. Of course, I was in the second group, although none of us knew what fate awaited us. Eventually the boss entered, gripped the lectern and read a brief statement: We were all finished, the decision was final.

"Not only were we finished, our place of work a few blocks away had been locked up, incapacitating our entry cards, and was under guard. We could never go back except to retrieve our personal belongings, and this under the watchful eye of a senior supervisor and one of the newly retained guards. I felt like a criminal. In my time I had managed large portions of this company, had represented it the world over and, until the previous day, had authority to spend its money. Now I couldn't be trusted not to snitch a pencil or note pad ... The current phenomenon known as downsizing is threatening to hurt capitalism by depriving it of the very thing it needs most: a market. This, however, speaks to the stupidity of capitalism today, not its abandonment of civility. But perhaps there is a connection."

THE ECONOMY AND WORK

Many Canadians have faced unemployment over the past decade because of slow economic growth and deficit cutting by governments. However, Popoff and his colleagues at the *Star Phoenix* lost their jobs for another reason that has become very common: corporate cost-cutting. Although the paper had been quite profitable under its previous owners, new owner Conrad Black wished to cut costs and increase profits so he and other shareholders would receive a greater return on their investment. Firing staff is often the quickest route to short-term profits, so the termination consultants were called.

Unemployment shows the linkage between the economy and work. Changes in the economy affect the lives of most people. Those who lose their jobs will feel an acute sense of financial and personal loss. For many people, work helps define who they are. The first question usually asked of someone with whom one is speaking for the first time is, Where do you work? or What do you do for a living? Job loss may cause people to experience financial crises that could include the loss of their cars and homes to bankruptcy and foreclosure, as well as bringing on personal problems such as depression and divorce.

In this chapter, we will discuss the economy and the world of work—how people feel about their work, how the work world is changing, and what impact these changes may have on university students and other current and future workers. We will also look at how workers have sought better wages and working conditions through unions and at how unions have affected work in contemporary society. Before reading on, test your knowledge about the economy, work, and workers by taking the quiz in Box 13.1.

QUESTIONS AND ISSUES

CHAPTER FOCUS QUESTION: How is work in Canada affected by changes in the economy?

How do economics and sociology overlap?

What are the key assumptions of capitalism and socialism?

What contributes to job satisfaction and to work alienation?

Why does unemployment occur?

How do workers attempt to gain control over their work situation?

How will the nature of work change in the future?

In the wake of the Industrial Revolution, many thoughtful observers were dismayed by the mechanization of work and its effects on the dignity of workers. Filmmaker Charlie Chaplin bitingly satirized the new relationship between workers and machines in the classic *Modern Times*.

THE ECONOMY

The *economy* **is the social institution that ensures the maintenance of society through the production, distribution, and consumption of goods and services.** *Goods* are tangible objects that are necessary (such as food, clothing, and shelter) or desired (such as VCRs and electric toothbrushes). *Services* are intangible activities for which people are willing to pay (such as dry cleaning, a movie, or medical care). While some services are produced by human labour (the plumber who unstops your sink, for example), others primarily are produced by capital (such as communication services provided by a telephone company). *Labour* consists of the physical and intellectual services, including training, education, and individual abilities, that people contribute to the production process (Boyes and Melvin, 1994). *Capital* is wealth (money or property) owned or used in business by a person or corporation. Obviously, money, or financial capital, is needed to invest in the physical capital (such as machinery, equipment, buildings, warehouses, and factories) used in production.

The Sociology of Economic Life

While economists focus on the complex workings of economic systems (such as monetary policy, inflation, and the national debt), sociologists who study the economy focus on interconnections among the economy, other social institutions, and the social organization of work. At the macrolevel, sociologists may study the impact of multinational corporations on industrialized and developing nations. At the microlevel, sociologists might study people's satisfaction with their jobs. To better understand the Canadian economy, we will examine how economic systems came into existence and how they have changed over time.

Historical Changes in Economic Systems

In all societies, the specific method of producing goods is related to the technoeconomic base of the society. In each society, people develop an economic system, ranging from simple to very complex, for the sake of survival.

PREINDUSTRIAL ECONOMIES Hunting and gathering, horticultural and pastoral, and agrarian societies are all preindustrial economic structures (previously discussed in Chapter 8, "Social Stratification and Class"). Most workers engage in *primary sector production*—**the extraction of raw materials and natural resources from the environment.** These materials and resources typically are consumed or used without much processing.

The *production* units in hunting and gathering societies are small; most goods are produced by family members. The division of labour is by age and gender. The potential for producing surplus

BOX 13.1 SOCIOLOGY AND EVERYDAY LIFE

HOW MUCH DO YOU KNOW ABOUT THE ECONOMY AND THE WORLD OF WORK?

TRUE FALSE

T	F	1. Most factory workers are aware of the part their work plays in the overall production process.
T	F	2. Sociologists have developed special criteria to distinguish professions from other occupations.
T	F	3. Workers' skills usually are upgraded when new technology is introduced in the workplace.
T	F	4. Many of the new jobs being created in the service sector pay poorly and offer little job security.
T	F	5. Women are more likely than men to hold part-time jobs.
T	F	6. Labour unions probably will not exist in the twenty-first century.
T	F	7. It is possible for a person to start with no money and to build a personal forture worth more than $110 billion in less than twenty years.
T	F	8. New office technology has made it possible for clerical workers to function with little or no supervision.
T	F	9. Unions were established in Canada with the full cooperation of industry and government who recognized the need to protect the interests of workers.
T	F	10. Assembly lines are rapidly disappearing from all sectors of the Canadian economy.

Answers on page 404

goods increases as people learn to domesticate animals and grow their own food. In horticultural and pastoral societies, the economy becomes distinct from family life. The distribution process becomes more complex with the accumulation of a *surplus* such that some people can engage in activities other than food production. In agrarian societies, production is related primarily to producing food. However, workers have a greater variety of specialized tasks, such as warlord or priest; for example, warriors are necessary to protect the surplus goods from plunder by outsiders (Hodson and Sullivan, 1990). Surplus goods are distributed through a system of *barter*—the direct exchange of goods or services considered of equal value by the traders. However, bartering is limited as a method of distribution; equivalencies are difficult to determine (how many fish equal one rabbit?) because there is no way to assign a set value to the items being traded. As a result, *money*, a medium of exchange with a relatively fixed value, came into use in order to facilitate the distribution of goods and services in society. Most commercial enterprises operated on a small scale, and the vast majority of the population still lived in small rural communities. This changed dramatically with the advent of industrialization.

INDUSTRIAL ECONOMIES At the beginning of the twentieth century, the majority of workers in Canada and in most other countries were farmers (Drucker, 1994). However, industrialization brought about a sweeping transformation in the nature of work. By the end of the century, only 3 percent were agriculture workers, and other primary sector workers were equally rare. Industrialization dramatically changed the system of production and the distribution of goods and services. Drawing on new forms of energy (such as steam, gasoline, and electricity) and technology, factories became the primary means of producing goods. Wage labour became the dominant form of employment relationship; workers sold their labour to others rather than working for themselves or with other members of their family. In a capitalist system, this means that the product belongs to the factory owner and not to those whose labour creates that product.

Most workers engage in *secondary sector production*—**the processing of raw materials (from the primary sector) into finished goods.** For example, steel workers process metal ore; auto workers then convert the ore into automobiles, trucks, and buses. In industrial economies, work becomes specialized and repetitive, activities

BOX 13.1

ANSWERS TO THE SOCIOLOGY QUIZ ON THE ECONOMY AND THE WORLD OF WORK

1. **False.** Most factory workers view their work as fragmented and specialized, and they do not understand what part their work plays in the overall production process.

2. **True.** Professions are defined by five characteristics that distinguish them from other occupations: (1) abstract, specialized knowledge, (2) autonomy, (3) self-regulation, (4) authority over clients and subordinate occupational groups, and (5) a degree of altruism.

3. **False.** Jobs often are deskilled when new technology (such as bar code scanners or computerized cash registers) is installed in the workplace. Some of the workers' skills are no longer needed because a "smart machine" now provides the answers (such as how much something costs or how much change a customer should receive). Even when new skills are needed, the training is usually minimal.

4. **True.** Many of the new jobs being created in the service sector, such as nurse's aide, child-care worker, hotel maid, and fast-food server, offer little job security and low pay.

5. **True.** Women account for nearly 70 percent of part-time workers.

6. **False.** Sociologists who have examined organized labour generally predict that unions will continue to exist. However, their strength may wane in the global economy because companies having to deal with strong unions may move production to other countries where labour is less powerful.

7. **True.** Bill Gates, founder of Microsoft, turned his idea for a computer operating system into a personal fortune that in 1999 was worth $110 billion (see the Bill Gates Net Worth Page at http://web.quuxwm.orc/~evan/bgnw.html).

8. **False.** Clerical workers still work under supervision; however, they may not even know when they are being observed because of new technology. For example, a supervisor may examine a clerk's work on a computer network without the employee knowing about it, and an airline reservationist's supervisor may listen in on selected conversations with customers.

9. **False.** The struggle to unionize in Canada was always difficult and often bloody. Governments often worked with employers to make union organizing difficult.

10. **False.** According to some scholars, assembly lines will remain a fact of life for businesses ranging from fast-food restaurants to high-tech semiconductor plants.

Sources: Based on Garson, 1989; Zuboff, 1988; Hodson and Sullivan, 1990; Feagin and Feagin, 1994; and Rifkin, 1995.

become bureaucratically organized, and workers primarily work with machines instead of with one another.

This method of production is very different from craftwork, where individual artisans perform all steps in the production process. Think of the difference between a skilled artisan, who creates a wide variety of intricate metal castings from handmade sand mouldings, and a relatively unskilled foundry worker who operates a moulding machine. The transition from craft to assembly line in the metalwork trade is described by Craig Heron:

> By the 1920s ... the role of the artisan in the foundry had been reduced to only those few tasks which could not be turned over to machines and handymen ... As early as 1909, Josiah Beare, a

young union moulder in Hamilton, told a workmate: "Jim, I have worked too hard in my time; the pace is set too fast for the average man to keep up, and I am a nervous wreck"; he died six weeks later of [what was referred to as] "heart trouble." Half a century later Joe Davidson, future leader of [the union for] Canada's postal workers, arrived in Hamilton as an experienced Scottish moulder and discovered "the more intense style of working" at Canada Iron Foundries; in nearby Dundas, he found, "The motto was 'produce or else' and every day was a mad race, the men working like beasts." (Heron, 1993:10)

The craft workers were forced out and their jobs were taken over by machines and by unskilled labourers. The work was broken up into simple tasks that labourers repeated hour after hour. This

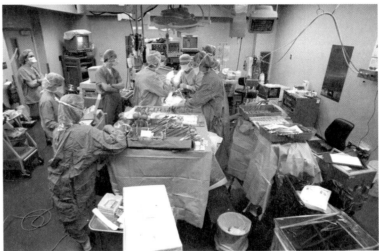

The nature of work is markedly different in the three main types of economies. In pre-industrial economies, most workers are directly involved in extracting raw materials and natural resources from the environment. The development of a surplus leads to bartering and the use of money as a medium of exchange. In industrial economies, production and distribution of goods are much more complex and work tends to become specialized and repetitive. In post-industrial economies, workers increasingly are involved in providing services such as health care rather than in manufacturing goods.

was much less costly than using craftspeople who completed a finished product because more goods are produced in a shorter time on an assembly line and because labourers received a lower wage than more skilled workers. However, workers lost control over their workplaces and some began to see themselves as part of the machinery, not as human beings.

In many countries, industrialization had a major impact on women's lives. In preindustrial times much of the production took place within the household and men and women often worked together. Factories separated production from the household, causing a gendered division of labour. Men became responsible for the family's income and women for domestic tasks. In Canada, however, home-based production had never been widespread outside the agricultural sector. The

resource-based economy was already male-oriented, so industrialization brought little change to the role of women (Cohen, 1993).

Working conditions were very harsh in the early days of industrialization. Hours were long, wages were low, and workers had no pensions, no vacation, and no overtime pay. The comments of a member of a parliamentary committee that investigated working conditions in the 1880s show how child labour was exploited:

Many children of tender age, some of them not more than nine years old, were employed in cotton, glass, tobacco and cigar factories ... Some of them worked from six o'clock in the morning till six in the evening, with less than an hour for dinner, others worked from seven in the evening till six in the morning. (quoted in Rinehart, 1996)

By 1950, unionized industrial workers had gained better working conditions, better wages, and significant political power. However, many of these gains were lost by the end of the century as manufacturing jobs disappeared in the *postindustrial economy.*

POSTINDUSTRIAL ECONOMIES During the first half of the twentieth century, Canada shifted from a primary sector economy to one focused on manufacturing and service industries. By 1951, 47 percent of Canadian workers were employed in the service sector, an additional 31 percent were employed in manufacturing, and the remaining 22 percent worked in primary industries. However, manufacturing has steadily declined in importance as production has shifted offshore to low-wage countries and we have moved to a service-based company. By 1996, only 5 percent of workers remained in primary industries, while 20 percent were employed in manufacturing and construction. Fully 74 percent worked in service industries (Krahn and Lowe, 1998). We now have what has been called a *postindustrial economy.* A **postindustrial economy is based on the provision of services rather than goods.** These services are the primary source of livelihood for workers and profit for owners and corporate shareholders. The service sector includes a wide range of activities, such as fast-food service, transportation, communication, health care, education, real estate, advertising, sports, and entertainment.

A number of factors created the service economy. Mechanization and technological innovation have allowed fewer workers to produce more in both the manufacturing and primary sectors. Sophisticated manufacturing processes require technologists rather than semiskilled workers; robots have replaced assembly line workers; and tractors and factory ships have enabled farmers and fishers to produce far more than their predecessors. The expansion of our economy and the increased leisure time available have increased the demand for a wide variety of services. Finally, much of the low-skill production is now done offshore, where wages are much cheaper, leaving components such as design, sales, and marketing in North America, Europe, and Japan.

Challenging, well-paid jobs in the service sector have grown dramatically, and highly skilled "knowledge workers" in this sector have benefited from the postindustrial economy. However, these benefits have not been felt by those who do routine production work, such as manufacturing and data entry, and workers who provide personal services, including restaurant workers and sales clerks. The positions filled by these workers form a second tier where labour is typically unskilled and poorly paid. Many jobs in the service sector emphasize productivity, often at the expense of workers. Fast-food restaurants are a case in point, as the manager of a McDonald's explains:

> As a manager I am judged by the statistical reports which come off the computer. Which basically means my crew labour productivity. What else can I really distinguish myself by? ... O.K., it's true, you can over spend your [maintenance and repair] budget; you can have a low fry yield; you can run a dirty store, every Coke spigot is monitored. Every ketchup squirt is measured. My costs for every item are set. So my crew labour productivity is my main flexibility ... Look, you can't squeeze a McDonald's hamburger any flatter. If you want to improve your productivity there is nothing for a manager to squeeze but the crew. (quoted in Garson, 1989:33–35)

"McDonaldization" is built on many of the ideas and systems of industrial society, including bureaucracy and the assembly line (Ritzer, 1993).

Class conflict and poverty may well increase in postindustrial societies (see Touraine, 1971; Thompson, 1983). Recently, researchers also have found that employment in the service sector remains largely gender segregated and that skills degradation, rather than skills upgrading, has occurred in many industries where women hold a large number of positions (Steiger and Wardell, 1995). Machines and off-shore production have eliminated many of the well-paying manufacturing jobs that were formerly available to young people with low levels of education and training. These people now work in lower-paying service sector jobs. A recent Statistics Canada study showed that this change has been particularly hard on young men between the ages of 18 and 24 with full-time jobs whose earnings declined by 20 percent between 1977 and 1997 (Gadd, 1998). Over the same period, earnings for young women declined by 9 percent, but their incomes levelled off during the 1990s. Many young men have been stuck in entry-level jobs with few prospects for advancement or for additional training. It is too early to tell whether these young men will become more prosperous as they move on in their careers or whether the wage restructuring is permanent.

However, analysts studying these data did not think that many would ever move into a more favourable job situation.

To gain a better understanding of how our economy works today, we now turn to an examination of contemporary economic systems and their interrelationship in an emerging global economy.

CONTEMPORARY ECONOMIC SYSTEMS

During the twentieth century, capitalism and socialism have been the principal economic models in industrialized countries. Sociologists often use two criteria—property ownership and market control—to distinguish between types of economies. Keep in mind, however, that no society has a purely capitalist or socialist economy.

Capitalism

Capitalism **is an economic system characterized by private ownership of the means of production, from which personal profits can be derived through market competition and without government intervention.** Most of us think of ourselves as "owners" of private property because we own a car, a stereo, or other possessions. However, most of us are not capitalists; we are consumers who *spend money* on the things we own, rather than *making money* from them. Capitalism is not simply the accumulation of wealth, but is the "use of wealth … as a means for gathering more wealth" (Heilbroner, 1985:35). Relatively few people control the means of production, and the rest are paid to work for these capitalists. "Ideal" capitalism has four distinctive features: (1) private ownership of the means of production, (2) pursuit of personal profit, (3) competition, and (4) lack of government intervention.

PRIVATE OWNERSHIP OF THE MEANS OF PRODUCTION

Capitalist economies are based on the right of individuals to own income-producing property such as land, water, mines, and factories and to "buy" people's labour. The early Canadian economy was based on the sale of *staples*—goods associated with primary industries including lumber, wheat, and minerals. Economist Harold Innis (1930) showed how the early Canadian economy was driven by the demands for raw materials by the colonial powers of France and Britain. This began early in Canada's history; in 1670 a British royal charter gave the privately held Hudson's Bay Company exclusive control over much of what is now western Canada, which was the source of the very lucrative fur trade. This was *commercial capitalism* in which fortunes were made by merchants who controlled the trade in these raw materials. Inventions such as the steam engine and the spinning jenny led to factory production and the dramatic transformation to *industrial capitalism*. Industrial capitalism did not just alter the production of goods and services, it changed the very nature of European and North American societies. Urbanization, the growth of the modern nation state, and the struggle for democracy can all be traced to the growth of industrial capitalism (Krahn and Lowe, 1998).

In the early stages of industrial capitalism (1850–1890), virtually all of the capital for investment was individually owned, and a few individuals and families controlled all the major trade and financial organizations in Canada. Under early monopoly capitalism (1890–1940), most ownership rapidly shifted from individuals to huge *corporations*—**large-scale organizations that have legal powers, such as the ability to enter into contracts and buy and sell property, separate from their individual owners.** During this period, major industries came under the control of a few corporations owned by shareholders. For example, the automobile industry in North America came to be dominated by the "Big Three"—General Motors, Ford, and Chrysler. Industrial development in Canada lagged behind that of many other countries as business focused on exporting raw materials and importing finished products. Many of the industries that did establish themselves in Canada were branch plants of large American and British corporations whose profits flowed back to their home countries. Economist Kari Levitt (1970) was among the first to show how this foreign private investment posed a threat to Canadian sovereignty as fundamental economic decisions were made outside the country and did not necessarily take Canadian interests into account.

In advanced monopoly capitalism (1940–present), ownership and control of major industrial and business sectors have become increasingly concentrated. *Economic concentration* is the degree to which a relatively small number of corporations controls a disproportionately large share of a nation's economic resources. There are about 400,000 corporations in Canada; the top 100 control 67 percent of Canadian business assets, while the other 399,900 account for the remaining 33 percent of these assets. The level of corporate concentration in Canada is far higher than that of our major trading partners, the United States, Germany, and Japan (Richardson, 1992).

Today, *multinational corporations—large companies that are headquartered in one country and have subsidiaries or branches in other countries*—play a major role in the economies and governments of many nations. Multinational corporations also are referred to as *transnational corporations* because they sell and produce goods abroad. These corporations are not dependent on the labour, capital, or technology of any one country and may move their operations to countries where wages and taxes are lower and potential profits are higher. Corporate considerations of this kind help to explain why many jobs formerly located in Canada have been moved to developing nations where workers will accept jobs at significantly less pay than would Canadians because there are few employment opportunities.

PURSUIT OF PERSONAL PROFIT A tenet of capitalism is the belief that people are free to maximize their individual gain through personal profit; in the process, the entire society will benefit from their activities (Smith, 1976/1776). Economic development is assumed to benefit both capitalists and workers, and the general public also benefits from public expenditures (such as for roads, schools, and parks) made possible through an increase in business tax revenues.

During the period of industrial capitalism, however, specific individuals and families (not the general public) were the primary recipients of profits. For many generations, descendants of some of the early industrial capitalists have benefited from the economic deeds (and misdeeds) of their ancestors. For example, much of the Seagram distillery's fortune was based on the profits made from bootlegging during Prohibition. In early monopoly capitalism, some stockholders derived massive profits from companies that held near-monopolies on specific goods and services. In advanced (late) monopoly capitalism, profits have become even more concentrated as a few large corporations control more of the market through expansion and the acquisition of competitors. Ownership of these companies is more broadly held among Canadians through pension plans and mutual funds, but these small shareholders *do not control* the companies.

COMPETITION In theory, competition acts as a balance to excessive profits. When producers vie with one another for customers, they must be able to offer innovative goods and services at competitive prices. However, from the time of early industrial capitalism, the trend has been toward less, rather than more, competition among companies; profits are higher when there is less competition. In early monopoly capitalism competition was diminished by increasing concentration *within* a particular industry. Today, Microsoft Corp. so dominates certain areas of the computer software industry that it has virtually no competitors in those areas. In 1998, the U.S. government filed an antitrust suit against Microsoft accusing the company of unlawfully trying to monopolize the Internet browser market.

How do large companies restrict competition? One way is by temporarily setting prices so low that weaker competitors are forced out of business. Ultramar, which owns 1400 gasoline stations in Quebec and Atlantic Canada, started a gasoline price war that saw gas prices in Quebec fall from 63 to 19.9 cents per litre in 1996. One Nova Scotia independent station owner complained that Ultramar was charging him 50 cents a litre for wholesale gasoline, while it was retailing its own gasoline at a nearby station for 42.9 cents per litre. While this provides a temporary benefit to consumers, it reduces competition by forcing small retailers out of the market. The large companies recoup their losses when the competition has disappeared. Similarly, Netscape was dominant in the Internet browser market until Microsoft began giving its own browser away free in order to secure a larger share of the market for its own products.

What appears to be competition among producers *within* an industry actually may be "competition" among products, all of which are produced and distributed by relatively few corporations. Much of the beer in Canada is produced by Molson and Labatt, who use a wide variety of different brand names for their products. An *oligopoly exists when several companies overwhelmingly control an entire industry*. An example is the music industry, in which a few giant companies are behind many of the labels and artists known to consumers (see Table 13.1). More specifically, a *shared monopoly exists when four or fewer companies supply 50 percent or*

TABLE 13.1 | **THE MUSIC INDUSTRY'S BIG FIVE**

COMPANY	PARENT COMPANY COUNTRY	PERCENTAGE OF CANADIAN MARKET	LEADING ARTISTS
Universal/ Polygram	United States	30	Shania Twain U2 Beck The Tragically Hip
Warner Music	United States	18	Alanis Morissette The Barenaked Ladies Celine Dion
Sony	Japan	16	Lauryn Hill Will Smith Bruce Springsteen
EMI	United Kingdom	14	Garth Brooks the Rolling Stones the Beastie Boys
BMG Music	Germany	10	Prairie Oyster Sarah McLachlan Run DMC Moist

These five foreign-owned companies share almost 90 percent of Canada's record business. They have a similar share of the market throughout much of the world—a market worth $38 billion in annual sales.

Sources: Biagi, 1994:248; Biagi, 1998:149.

more of a particular market (Eitzen and Baca Zinn, 1995).

In advanced monopoly capitalism, mergers also occur *across* industries: corporations gain near-monopoly control over all aspects of the production and distribution of a product by acquiring both the companies that supply the raw materials and the companies that are the outlets for its products. For example, an oil company may hold leases on the land where the oil is pumped out of the ground, the plants that convert the oil into gasoline, and the individual gasoline stations that sell the product to the public. By acting as producers, wholesalers, and retailers, companies such as Ultramar are able to maintain control over their markets and their competition.

Corporations with control both within and across industries often are formed by a series of mergers and acquisitions across industries. These corporations are referred to as **conglomerates— combinations of businesses in different commercial areas, all of which are owned by one holding company**. Media ownership is a case in point: companies such as Time Warner and Paramount Communications have extensive holdings in radio and television stations, cable television companies, book publishing firms, and film production and distribution companies, to name only a few. Similarly, a small number of companies control most of Canada's newspapers.

The government, the business community, and the public do not seem disturbed by the fact that these major media outlets are run by a small number of Canada's wealthiest businessmen. While the government and the business community seem content with this control of the media by a few rich white males, do you think they would accept the same degree of control of the media by feminists, trade unions, or religious fundamentalists?

Competition is reduced over the long run by **interlocking corporate directorates—members of the board of directors of one corporation who also sit on the board(s) of other corporations**. Interlocking directorates diminish competition by producing interdependence. Individuals who serve on multiple boards often are able to forge cooperative arrangements that benefit their corporations

Gasoline price wars benefit consumers. However, they may also be part of a strategy in which major companies put smaller competitors out of business.

but not necessarily the general public. When several corporations are controlled by the same financial interests, they are more likely to cooperate with one another than to compete. Canadian business has a very high degree of integration at the board level, with the five big banks serving as the principal centres linking the different corporate sectors (Richardson, 1992).

LACK OF GOVERNMENT INTERVENTION   Proponents of capitalism say that ideally capitalism works best without government intervention in the marketplace. This policy of laissez-faire was advocated by economist Adam Smith in his 1776 treatise *An Inquiry into the Nature and Causes of the Wealth of Nations*. Smith argued that when people pursue their own selfish interests, they are guided "as if by an invisible hand" to promote the best interests of society (see Smith, 1976/1776). Today, terms such as *market economy* and *free enterprise* often are used, but the underlying assumption is the same: that free market competition, not the government, should regulate prices and wages.

However the "ideal" of unregulated markets benefiting all citizens has been seldom realized. Individuals and companies in pursuit of higher profits have run roughshod over weaker competitors, and small businesses have grown into large monopolistic corporations. Accordingly, government regulations were implemented in an effort to curb the excesses of the marketplace brought about by laissez-faire policies. While its effectiveness can be debated, Canada has a Competitions

Bureau with the mandate of ensuring that corporations compete fairly.

Ironically, much of what is referred to as government intervention has been in the form of aid to business. Canadian governments have always been intimately involved with business. To encourage settlement of the West, the government gave subsidies and huge tracts of land to the Canadian Pacific Railway to encourage the construction of a national railway. Many corporations receive government assistance in the form of public subsidies and protection from competition by tariffs, patents, and trademarks. Government intervention in the 1990s has included billions of dollars in tax credits for corporations, large subsidies or loan guarantees to manufacturers, and subsidies and tariff protection for farmers. Overall, most corporations have gained much more than they have lost as a result of government involvement in the economy.

Socialism

Socialism **is an economic system characterized by public ownership of the means of production, the pursuit of collective goals, and centralized decision making.** Like "pure" capitalism, "pure" socialism does not exist. Karl Marx described socialism as a temporary stage en route to an ideal communist society. Although the terms *socialism* and *communism* are associated with Marx and often are used interchangeably, they are not identical. Marx defined communism as an economic system characterized by common ownership of all economic resources (G. Marshall, 1994). In *The Communist Manifesto* and *Das Kapital*, he predicted that the working class would become increasingly impoverished and alienated under capitalism. As a result, the workers would become aware of their own class interests, revolt against the capitalists, and overthrow the entire system (see Turner, Beeghley, and Powers, 1995). After the revolution, private property would be abolished and capital would be controlled by collectives of workers who would own the means of production. The government (previously used to further the interests of the capitalists) no longer would be necessary. People would contribute according to their abilities and receive according to their needs (Marx and Engels, 1967/1848; Marx, 1967/1867). Over the years, state control was added as an organizing principle for communist societies. This structure is referred to as a system of "state socialism." The reasons state socialism in the former Soviet Union did not evolve into a communist economic system are discussed in the following sections.

PUBLIC OWNERSHIP OF THE MEANS OF PRODUCTION In a truly socialist economy, the means of production are owned and controlled by a collectivity or the state, not by private individuals or corporations. Prior to the early 1990s, the state owned all the natural resources and almost all the capital in the Soviet Union. In the 1980s, for example, state-owned enterprises produced more than 88 percent of agricultural output and 98 percent of retail trade, and owned 75 percent of the urban housing space (Boyes and Melvin, 1994). At least in theory, goods were produced to meet the needs of people. Access to housing and medical care was considered a right.

Leaders of the former Soviet Union and some Eastern European nations decided to abandon government ownership and control of the means of production because the system was unresponsive to the needs of the marketplace and offered no incentive for increased efficiency (Boyes and Melvin, 1994). Shortages and widespread unrest led to the reform movement headed by Soviet President Mikhail Gorbachev in the late 1980s.

In the 1990s, Russia and other states in the former Soviet Union have attempted to privatize ownership of production. In *privatization*, resources are converted from state ownership to private ownership; the government takes an active role in developing, recognizing, and protecting private

One of the twentieth century's most important leaders was Mikhail Gorbachev, who began reforms that led to the end of the socialist economy in the former USSR.

property rights (Boyes and Melvin, 1994). However, this has proven difficult and the Russian economy almost completely collapsed in 1998. The transition to a capitalist economy will take decades.

PURSUIT OF COLLECTIVE GOALS Ideal socialism is based on the pursuit of collective goals, rather than on personal profits. Equality in decision making replaces hierarchical relationships (such as between owners and workers or political leaders and citizens). Everyone shares in the goods and services of society, especially necessities such as food, clothing, shelter, and medical care based on need, not on ability to pay. In reality, however, few societies can or do pursue purely collective goals.

CENTRALIZED DECISION MAKING Another tenet of socialism is centralized decision making. In theory, economic decisions are based on the needs of society; the government is responsible for facilitating the production and distribution of goods and services. Central planners set wages and prices to ensure that the production process works. When problems such as shortages and unemployment arise, they can be dealt with quickly and effectively by the central government (Boyes and Melvin, 1994).

Centralized decision making is hierarchical. In the former Soviet Union, for example, broad economic policy decisions were made by the highest authorities of the Communist Party, who also held political power. The production units (the enterprises and farms) at the bottom of the structure had little voice in the decision-making process. Wages and prices were based on political priorities and eventually came to be completely unrelated to actual supply and demand. At the same time as some factories kept producing goods that nobody wanted, there were chronic shortages of other goods.

The collapse of state socialism in the former Soviet Union was due partly to the declining ability of the Communist Party to act as an effective agent of society and partly to the growing incompatibility of central planning with the requirements of a modern economy (see Misztal, 1993). While the socialist system as practised in the Soviet Union was not sustainable, privatization has proven difficult. Only a few years after centralized decision making was abolished in Russia, people are faced with soaring unemployment and crime rates, and the prices of goods and services have risen greatly. The armed motorcades of Communist Party leaders from the past have been replaced by the limousines of business people with their armed escorts. Organized criminal groups have muscled their way into business and trade; many workers feel their future is very dim. According to a 30-year-old machinist in Moscow: "I was raised in a country that cared about its workers … Life used to be simple, but we had a deal. We worked hard, and the company took care of the rest" (Specter, 1994:A6).

Mixed Economies

As we have seen, no economy is truly capitalist or socialist; most economies are mixtures of both. A *mixed economy* combines elements of a market economy (capitalism) with elements of a command economy (socialism). Sweden and France have mixed economies, sometimes referred to as *democratic socialism*—an economic and political system that combines private ownership of some of the means of production, governmental distribution of some essential goods and services, and free elections. Government ownership in Sweden, for example, is limited primarily to railroads, mineral resources, a public bank, and liquor and tobacco operations (Feagin and Feagin, 1994). Compared with capitalist economies, however, the government in a mixed economy plays a larger role in setting rules, policies, and objectives.

The government also is heavily involved in providing services such as medical care, child care, and transportation. In Sweden, for example, all residents have health insurance, housing subsidies, child allowances, paid parental leave, and daycare subsidies. National insurance pays medical bills associated with work-related injuries, and workplaces are specially adapted for persons with disabilities. College tuition is free, and public funds help subsidize cultural institutions such as theatres and orchestras ("General Facts on Sweden," 1988; Kelman, 1991). While Sweden has a very high degree of government involvement, all industrial countries have assumed many of the obligations to provide support and services to its citizens. However, there are very significant differences in the degree to which these services are provided among these countries. For example, Canada provides medical care to all its citizens, but over 40 million Americans have no health insurance at all (see Chapter 18, "Health, Health Care, and Disability"). While Canada is much closer to a welfare state than the United States, the benefits provided by our government are less than those provided in most Western European countries.

PERSPECTIVES ON ECONOMY AND WORK

Functionalists, conflict theorists, and interactionists view the economy and the nature of work from a variety of perspectives. In this section, we examine functionalist and conflict views; in the next section, we focus on the interactionist perspective on the social organization of work.

The Functionalist Perspective

Functionalists view the economy as a vital social institution because it is the means by which needed goods and services are produced and distributed. When the economy runs smoothly, other parts of society function more effectively. However, if the system becomes unbalanced, such as when demand does not keep up with production, a maladjustment occurs (in this case, a surplus). Some problems may be easily remedied in the marketplace (through "free enterprise") or through government intervention (such as buying and storing excess production of butter and cheese). However, other problems, such as periodic *peaks* (high points) and *troughs* (low points) in the business cycle, are more difficult to resolve. The *business cycle* is the rise and fall of economic activity relative to long-term growth in the economy (McEachern, 1994).

From this perspective, peaks occur when "business" has confidence in the country's economic future. During a peak, or *expansion* period, the economy thrives: plants are built, raw materials are ordered, workers are hired, and production increases. In addition, upward social mobility for workers and their families becomes possible. For example, some workers hope their children will not have to follow their footsteps into the factory. Ben Hamper (1992:13) describes how GM workers felt:

> Being a factory worker in Flint, Michigan, wasn't something purposely passed on from generation to generation. To grow up believing that you were brought into this world to follow in your daddy's footsteps, just another chip-off-the-old-shoprat, was to engage in the lowest possible form of negativism. Working the line for GM was something fathers did so that their offspring wouldn't have to.

The dream of upward mobility is linked to peaks in the business cycle. Once the peak is reached, however, the economy turns down because too large a surplus of goods has been produced. In part, this is due to *inflation*—a sustained and continuous increase in prices (McEachern, 1994). Inflation erodes the value of people's money, and they no longer are able to purchase as high a percentage of the goods that have been produced. Because of this lack of demand, fewer goods are produced, workers are laid off, credit becomes difficult to obtain, and people cut back on their purchases even more, fearing unemployment. Eventually, this produces a distrust of the economy, resulting in a *recession*—a decline in an economy's total production that lasts six months or longer. To combat a recession, the government lowers interest rates (to make borrowing easier and to get more money back into circulation) in an attempt to spur the beginning of the next expansion period.

The Conflict Perspective

Conflict theorists view business cycles and the economic system differently. From a conflict perspective, business cycles are the result of capitalist greed. In order to maximize profits, capitalists suppress the wages of workers. As the prices of the products increase, the workers are not able to purchase them in the quantities that have been produced. The resulting surpluses cause capitalists to reduce production, close factories, and lay off workers, thus contributing to the growth of the reserve army of the unemployed, whose presence helps to reduce the wages of the remaining workers. For example, many businesses, including most supermarket chains, have forced wages down by hiring large numbers of part-time workers and by negotiating pay cuts for full-time employees. Companies justify this on the grounds of meeting the lower wages paid by competitors. The practice of contracting out—governments and corporations hiring outside workers to do some jobs rather than using existing staff—has become a favourite cost-cutting technique. In today's economy, it is easy to find someone who will do the work more cheaply than existing employees whose seniority and wages have increased over time, often because of the efforts of unions.

Much of the pressure to reduce costs has come from shareholders, and many observers have seen the firing or deskilling of workers as symptoms of class warfare. The rich are benefiting at the expense of the poor. The rich have indeed thrived; those with large amounts of capital have seen their fortunes increase dramatically. However, the largest shareholders in many companies are pension plans whose assets belong to workers from the private and public sectors; so, in essence some workers have lost their jobs to enhance the retirement benefits of other workers. Bob Bertram, vice president of the Ontario Teachers Pension Plan, puts the matter very succinctly:

> We believe the board of directors is representing us as owners and they have a duty to maximize share wealth for us. If it's not going to be looking after our interests first and foremost, then we will invest elsewhere … Companies aren't put together to create

jobs. The No.1 priority is creating shareholder wealth. (Ip, 1996:B1)

Alienation is an important part of conflict theory. Alienation occurs when workers' needs for self-identity and meaning are not met and when work is done strictly for material gain, with no accompanying sense of personal satisfaction. According to Marx, workers dislike having very little power and no opportunities to make workplace decisions. This lack of control contributes to an ongoing struggle between workers and employers. Job segmentation, isolation of workers, and the discouragement of any type of pro-worker organizations (such as unions) further contribute to feelings of helplessness and frustration. Some occupations may be more closely associated with high levels of alienation than others. Also, contemporary pressures to reduce the labour force and cut payroll costs have likely increased the levels of alienation of Canadian workers.

THE INTERACTIONIST PERSPECTIVE

Sociologists who focus on microlevel analyses are interested in how the economic system and the social organization of work affect people's attitudes and behaviour. Interactionists, in particular, have examined the meaning of work in people's lives and have studied the factors that contribute to job satisfaction.

The Meaning of Work

Does work play a role in defining our humanity, or is it just something we have to do to put bread on the table? Some critics view work as dehumanizing, oppressive, and alienating. In his book *The End of Work* Jeremy Rifkin (1995) tells us that only by working less can people be free. He feels that less work and more leisure will lead to greater personal fulfillment and will allow people the time to rebuild communities that have been weakened by the pressures of work and the market economy.

Others take the view that people find both moral meaning and a sense of personal identity through their work. Sociologist Robert Wuthnow (1996) found that when people were asked about their most important reason for working, the most common response was "the money." However,

when asked what they most preferred in a job, 48 percent chose "a feeling of accomplishment," and only 21 percent chose "high income." Wuthnow found that even for many lower-level employees, work is not just a source of money, but also a vital part of their identity. Work is important in several ways: people are connected to their communities through their work; they share personal friendships in their work settings; and work gives them a sense of accomplishment. Murial Johnson, one of Wuthnow's interview subjects, has three jobs but spends most of her work time as a security guard at a city convention centre. She takes pride in the job because she has been able to do it well. According to Wuthnow, Johnson

> says she has earned the "respect and liking" of other employees to the point that she is often called on to serve in a supervisory capacity. She takes pride in having organizational skills. When a big event takes place, or when there is a special crisis ... she can be counted on to make things work. (Wuthnow, 1996:219)

However, Wuthnow also found that in a rapidly changing world, many people are redefining the relationship between work and other parts of their lives and this can create uncertainty and dissatisfaction. This redefinition is also apparent in a study by Arlie Hochschild (1997). Hochschild found that many of the women she interviewed found more satisfaction with work than with other parts of their lives. Many worked long hours because they liked to work, not because of economic necessity. In fact, many used work as a refuge from the stresses and strains of the contemporary family. Of course, these long hours spent at work, whether out of choice or necessity, only make family problems worse (see Chapter 15, "Families and Intimate Relationships").

In an interesting contrast to Rifkin's view of a better future in which work plays a less important role in people's lives, William Julius Wilson (1996) studied inner-city neighbourhoods to see what happens when work actually disappears. He found that the impact has been devastating to individuals and to the community. To Wilson, a person without work is incomplete. They lack the system of concrete goals and expectations, and the daily discipline and regularities that work provides. Without work, it is difficult for the urban poor to take control of their lives.

However, even proponents of the view that work has moral meaning recognize that not all jobs allow the same degree of satisfaction and personal fulfillment. Assembly-line work can be particularly alienating:

> Basically, I stand there all day and slash the necks of chickens. You make one slash up on the skin of the neck and then you cut around the base of the neck so the next person beside you can crop it ... The chickens go in front of you on the line and you do every other chicken or whatever. And you stand there for eight hours on one spot and do it. (Armstrong and Armstrong, 1983:128)

Job Satisfaction

According to interactionists, work is an important source of self-identity for many people; it can help people feel positive about themselves or it can cause them to feel alienated. *Job satisfaction* refers to people's attitudes toward their work, based on (1) their job responsibilities, (2) the organizational structure in which they work, and (3) their individual needs and values (Hodson and Sullivan, 1990). Studies have found that worker satisfaction is highest when employees have some degree of control over their work, when they are part of the decision-making process, when they are not too closely supervised, and when they feel that they play an important part in the outcome (Kohn et al., 1990). The reasons contract administrator Beth McEwen gives for liking her job, for example, bear this out:

> I've worked for employers who couldn't care if you were gone tomorrow—who let you think your job could be done by anyone because 100,000 people out there are looking for work. But here, there's always someone to help you if you need assistance, and they're open to letting you set out your own job plan that suits what they're after and what you're trying to accomplish. They know every person goes about a job in a different way. (quoted in Maynard, 1987:121)

Job satisfaction often is related to both intrinsic and extrinsic factors. Intrinsic factors pertain to the nature of the work itself, while extrinsic factors include such things as vacation and holiday policies, parking privileges, on-site daycare centres, and other amenities that contribute to workers' overall perception that their employer cares about them.

THE SOCIAL ORGANIZATION OF WORK

Occupations

Occupations are categories of jobs that involve similar activities at different work sites (Reskin and Padavic, 1994). There are hundreds of different types of occupations. Historically, occupations have been classified as blue collar and white collar. Blue-collar workers primarily were factory and craftworkers who did manual labour; white-collar workers were office workers and professionals. However, contemporary workers in the service sector do not easily fit into either of these categories; neither do the so-called pink-collar workers, primarily women, who are employed in occupations such as preschool teacher, dental assistant, secretary, and clerk (Hodson and Sullivan, 1990).

Professions

What occupations are professions? Athletes who are paid for playing sports are referred to as "professional athletes." Dog groomers, pest exterminators, automobile mechanics, and nail technicians (manicurists) also refer to themselves as professionals. Although sociologists do not always agree on exactly which occupations are professions, they do agree that the number of people categorized as "professionals" has grown dramatically since World War II. According to sociologist Steven Brint (1994), the contemporary professional middle class includes most doctors, natural scientists, engineers, computer scientists, accountants, economists, social scientists, psychotherapists, lawyers, policy experts of various sorts, professors, at least some journalists and editors, some clergy, and some artists and writers.

CHARACTERISTICS OF PROFESSIONS *Professions* are high-status, knowledge-based occupations. Sociologists use five criteria to determine which occupations classify as professions (Freidson, 1970, 1986; Larson, 1977):

1. *Abstract, specialized knowledge.* Professionals have abstract, specialized knowledge of their field, based on formal education and interaction with colleagues. Education provides the credentials, skills, and training that allow pro-

Professionals are expected to share their knowledge and display concern for others. These surgeons have volunteered their services to people in Ecuador.

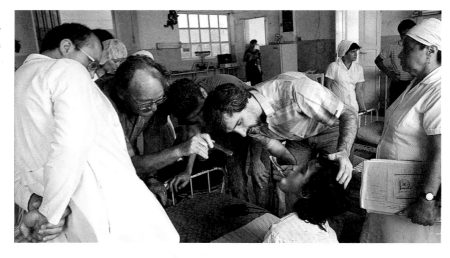

fessionals to have job opportunities and to assume positions of authority within organizations (Brint, 1994).

2. *Autonomy.* Professionals are autonomous in that they can rely on their own judgment in selecting the relevant knowledge or the appropriate technique for dealing with a problem. Consequently, they expect patients, clients, or students to respect that autonomy.

3. *Self-regulation.* In exchange for autonomy, professionals theoretically are self-regulating. All professions have licensing, accreditation, and regulatory associations that set professional standards and that require members to adhere to a code of ethics as a form of public accountability.

4. *Authority.* Because of their authority, professionals expect compliance with their directions and advice. Their authority is based on mastery of the body of specialized knowledge and on their profession's autonomy: professionals do not expect the client to argue about the professional advice rendered.

5. *Altruism.* Ideally, professionals have concern for others. The term *altruism* implies some degree of self-sacrifice whereby professionals go beyond self-interest or personal comfort so that they can help a patient or client (Hodson and Sullivan, 1995). Professionals also have a responsibility to protect and enhance their knowledge and to use it for the public interest.

In the past, job satisfaction among professionals generally has been very high because of relatively high levels of income, autonomy, and authority. In the future, professionals may either become the backbone of a postindustrial society or suffer from "intellectual obsolescence" if they cannot keep up with the knowledge explosion (Leventman, 1981).

Many professions exist under legislation that gives their members a monopoly on the provision of particular services, and these professions use their power to resist attempts by others to provide these services. For example, in the health care field, doctors have used their professional associations to protect their right to control the practice of medicine. Chiropractors, midwives, and other alternative health care practitioners have been fighting for decades to have governments recognize their right to practice and to be paid under provincial health care legislation. The role of nurse practitioners is currently under debate in several provinces as health care officials look for cheaper ways of providing health care services. Similarly, lawyers actively opposed the attempt by companies of nonlawyers to represent people accused of traffic offences.

Women have made significant gains in the professions. For example, Catherine Marshall found that the number of women employed in traditionally male-dominated professions in Canada rose by 42 percent between 1981 and 1986, compared with a 9 percent increase for men (Marshall, 1990). This increase continued throughout the next decade. From 1981 to 1986, women's share of employment rose from 17 percent to 36 percent among doctors, from 8 percent to 22 percent among dentists, and from 16 percent to 42 percent among lawyers (Marshall, 1990; Human Resources Development Canada, 1999). These percentages will continue to grow as women make up over half of the students now studying in many professional schools. In 1971, women received 9 percent of law degrees and 13 percent of medical degrees. By 1993 these had increased to 51 percent of law degrees and 44 percent of medical degrees (Krahn and Lowe, 1998).

Managers and the Managed

A wide variety of occupations are classified as "management" positions. The generic term *manager* often is used to refer to executives, managers, and administrators (Hodson and Sullivan, 1990). At the upper level of a workplace bureaucracy are *executives*, who control the operation of their organizations. *Administrators* often work for governmental bureaucracies or organizations dealing with health, education, or welfare (such as hospitals, colleges and universities, and nursing homes) and usually are appointed. *Managers* typically have responsibility for workers, physical plants, equipment, and the financial aspects of a bureaucratic organization. Women have increasingly gained access to management positions at this level, especially in middle management positions. In 1993, 42 percent of those working in management and administrative positions in Canada were women, up from 29 percent in 1982 and 6 percent in 1971 (Statistics Canada, 1994b).

MANAGEMENT IN BUREAUCRACIES   Managers are essential in contemporary bureaucracies in which work is highly specialized and authority structures are hierarchical (see Chapter 6). Managers often control workers by applying organizational rules. Workers at each level of the hierarchy take orders from their immediate superiors and perhaps give orders to a few subordinates. Upper-level managers typically are responsible for coordination of activities and control of workers. The *span of control*, or the number of workers a manager supervises, is affected by the organizational structure and by technology. Some analysts believe hierarchical organization is necessary to coordinate the activities of a large number of people; others suggest that it produces apathy and alienation among workers (Blauner, 1964). Lack of worker control over the labour process was built into the earliest factory systems through techniques known as scientific management (Taylorism) and mass production (Fordism).

SCIENTIFIC MANAGEMENT (TAYLORISM)   At the beginning of the twentieth century, industrial engineer Frederick Winslow Taylor revolutionized management with a system he called *scientific management*. In an effort to increase productivity in factories, Taylor did numerous *time-and-motion* studies of workers he considered to be reasonably efficient. From these studies, he broke down each task into its most minute components to determine the "one best way" of doing each of them. Workers then were taught to perform the tasks in a concise series of steps. Skilled workers became less essential since unskilled workers could be trained by management to follow routinized procedures. The process of breaking up work into specialized tasks and minute operations contributed to the *deskilling* of work and shifted much of the control of knowledge from workers to management (Braverman, 1974). As this occurred, workers increasingly felt powerless (Westrum, 1991).

The *differential* piece-rate system, a central component of scientific management in which workers were paid for the number of units they produced, further contributed to the estrangement between workers and managers. Taylor believed that this system would reduce the antagonism workers felt about direct supervision and control by managers. However, just the opposite often tended to occur: workers felt distrustful and overworked because managers often increased the number of pieces required when workers met their quotas. Overall, scientific management amplified the divergent interests of management and workers rather than lessening them (Zuboff, 1988). Management became even more removed from workers with the advent of mass production.

MASS PRODUCTION THROUGH AUTOMATION (FORDISM)
Fordism, named for Henry Ford, the founder of the Ford Motor Company, incorporated hierarchical authority structures and scientific management techniques into the manufacturing process (Collier and Horowitz, 1987). Assembly lines, machines, and robots became a means of *technical control* over the work process (Edwards, 1979). The *assembly line*, a system in which workers perform a specialized operation on an unfinished product as it is moved by conveyor past their workstation, increased efficiency and productivity. On Ford's assembly line, for example, a Model T automobile could be assembled in one-eighth the time formerly required. Ford broke the production process of the Model T into 7882 specific tasks (Toffler, 1980).

This fragmentation of the labour process meant that individual workers had little to do with the final product. There is a huge difference between a craftsperson helping to build a complete automobile and an assembly-line worker repeating the same task hundreds of times each shift. The assembly line also allowed managers to control the pace of work by speeding up the line when they wanted to increase productivity. As productivity increased, however, workers began to grow increasingly alienated as they saw themselves becoming robot-like labourers (Collier and Horowitz, 1987). However, dramatically increased productivity allowed Ford to give pay raises, which kept workers relatively content, while his own profits steadily rose. Without mass consumers there could be no mass production; Ford recognized that better wages would allow the workers to buy his products.

The role of contemporary managers was strongly influenced by the development of the assembly line and mass production techniques, which made it possible to use interchangeable parts in a variety of products. According to sociologist George Ritzer (1993), the assembly line and machine technology have even come to dominate work settings such as fast-food restaurants. Burger King, for example, uses a conveyor belt to cook hamburgers, and food is produced in assembly line fashion. McDonald's has a soft-drink dispenser with a sensor that shuts off when the glass is full so that the employee does not have to make this decision (Ritzer, 1993). What do managers do in such a highly rationalized, technically controlled setting? Their task is limited because the restaurant's system is designed to be error-free. George Cohon, the president of McDonald's of Canada, describes how the system works:

> A McDonald's outlet is a machine that produces, with the help of unskilled machine attendants, a highly polished product. Through painstaking attention to total design and facilities planning, everything is built integrally into the technology of the system. The only choice open to the attendant is to operate it exactly as the designers intended. (*Globe and Mail*, 1990:B80)

Of course, managers also hire workers, settle disputes, and take care of other tasks, but in many work settings, automation has dramatically deskilled their jobs (Garson, 1989; Zuboff, 1988; Ritzer, 1993).

Automation also has contributed to increased surveillance of employees. With computer networks, managers can measure productivity without employees even realizing it. Truckers are tracked by satellite tracking systems, and the work of many call centre workers can be monitored by a single supervisor. Whereas early forms of management involved direct supervision of workers, technology now makes it possible for a limited number of managers to control many more workers (see Zuboff, 1988).

The Lower Tier of the Service Sector and Marginal Jobs

Positions in the lower tier of the service sector are characterized by low wages, little job security, few chances for advancement, and higher unemployment rates. Typical lower-tier positions include janitor, waitress, messenger, sales clerk, typist, file clerk, farm labourer, and textile worker.

According to the employment norms of this country, a job should (1) be legal, (2) be covered by government work regulations, such as minimum standards of pay, working conditions, and safety standards, (3) be relatively permanent, and (4) provide adequate pay with sufficient hours of work each week to make a living (Hodson and Sullivan, 1990). However, many lower-tier service sector jobs do not meet these norms and therefore are marginal. **Marginal jobs differ from the employment norms of the society in which they are located**; examples in the Canadian labour market are service and household workers.

SERVICE AND HOUSEHOLD WORKERS Service workers often are viewed by customers as subordinates or personal servants. Frequently, they are required to wear a uniform that reflects their status as a clerk, food server, maid, or porter. In 1991, more than 3 million workers in Canada were employed in the retail trade and other consumer services. Occupational segregation by gender (see Chapter 11) and by age is clearly visible in personal service industries. Thirty-two percent of working women were employed in this sector, compared with 21 percent of men (Statistics Canada, 1992b). Younger workers are more likely than older people to work in this sector, as they pay for their studies with part-time work or use these low-level positions as a means of entering the labour force.

Robots at this Honda factory exemplify the deskilling of jobs through automation. What are managers' responsibilities in workplaces such as this?

and Latin America (see Chapter 9, "Global Stratification")

Although "high-tech" occupations (such as engineering and computer technology) are viewed by some as the wave of the future, many jobs in this field are marginal. Assembly line jobs in high-tech industries often are boring, low-paying, and hazardous. These industries also are more likely to export jobs to other regions of the country or to developing nations, where labour costs are lower. The term *global assembly line* is used to describe situations in which corporations hire workers, usually girls and young women, in developing nations at very low wages to work under hazardous conditions. Despite the grim work environment such jobs represent a temporary respite from grinding poverty for many workers (Ehrenreich and Fuentes, 1981; Women Working Worldwide, 1991).

To gain the same benefits of "cheap labour," some Canadian companies hire women who have recently migrated to this country. While many work for low wages in factories, their lack of language and job skills, and the shortage of affordable child care makes these women vulnerable to companies that will hire them as *homeworkers*, that is, they perform the work these companies require at home. As such, they are not protected by employment standards legislation. Many expensive fashion labels sell clothing that is made by homeworkers who are paid less than the minimum wage. A 1991 study of Chinese-Canadian garment workers in Toronto found that their hourly wages averaged $4.50, they did not get vacation pay or overtime, and their employers did not make contributions on their behalf to unemployment insurance or to the Canada Pension Plan (Dagg and Fudge, 1992).

Contingent Work

Contingent work is part-time work or temporary work that offers advantages to employers but that can be detrimental to the welfare of workers. Contingent work is found in every segment of the workforce, including colleges and universities, where tenure-track positions are fewer in number than in the past and a series of one-year, non-tenure-track appointments at the lecturer or instructor level has become a means of livelihood for many professionals. The federal government is part of this trend, as is private enterprise. For example, the health care field continues to undergo significant change, as governments try to

Household service work has shifted. Once done by domestics who worked full-time with one employer, it is now usually performed by part-time workers who may work several hours a week in several different homes. Household work is marginal: it lacks regularity, stability, and adequacy. The jobs are excluded from most labour legislation, the workers are not unionized, and employers sometimes flout the rules and regulations that do apply. The jobs typically have few benefits.

INTERNATIONALIZATION OF MARGINAL JOBS   Some manufacturing jobs also may be marginalized, especially those in peripheral industries such as garment or microelectronics manufacturing that operate in markets where prices are subject to sudden, intense fluctuations and where labour is a significant part of the cost of the goods sold (Hodson and Sullivan, 1990). Companies such as sportswear manufacturer Nike have moved much of their production to low-wage countries in Asia

Occupational segregation by race and gender is clearly visible in personal service industries, such as restaurants and fast-food chains. Women and visible minorities are disproportionately represented in marginal jobs such as waitperson or fast-food server—jobs that do not meet societal norms for minimum pay, benefits, or security.

cut health costs. Nurses, personal care home-workers, and others in this field increasingly are employed through temporary agencies as their jobs are contracted out.

Employers benefit by hiring workers on a part-time or temporary basis. They are able to cut costs, maximize profits, and have workers available only when they need them. As some companies have cut their workforce, or downsized, they have replaced regular employees who had higher salaries and full benefit packages with part-time and hourly employees who receive lower wages and no benefits. Although some people voluntarily work part-time (such as through job sharing and work sharing), many people are forced to do so because they lack opportunities for full-time employment. Sociologist Harvey Krahn (1995a) found that between 1976 and 1994, the number of part-time jobs increased at an average rate of 6.9 percent annually, whereas the rate was only 1.5 percent for full-time jobs. By 1999 nearly 18 percent of the labour force worked part-time.

A Statistics Canada survey reveals that most *part-time workers* are young people and that women are much more likely than men to hold part-time jobs. Women account for nearly 70 percent of all part-time workers. More than one-third of part-time workers wanted full-time employment. The proportion of part-time workers who want full-time work has tripled in the past two decades (Schellenberg, 1997).

Temporary workers make up the fastest-growing segment of the contingent workforce, and the number of agencies that "place" them has increased dramatically in the last decade. The agencies provide workers on a contract basis to employers for an hourly fee; workers are paid a portion of this fee.

In 1994, almost one million Canadians (9 percent of all employees) were temporary workers (Krahn, 1995a). Men and women were equally likely to hold temporary employment. Temporary workers usually have lower wages and fewer benefits than permanent, full-time employees in the same field. Many employers enjoy the flexibility provided by temporary employees. In examining this perspective, Zeidenberg (1990) interviewed Kathy Sayers, the co-owner of a Vancouver technical writing company that relies heavily on temporary employees, and found, in the case of this enterprise, that

> When the [economic] downturn hits, International Wordsmith will be ready and able to retrench quickly and wait out the storm. It won't have a big payroll to cut, nor high overhead costs. "It takes a load off your mind and lets you sleep easier," says Sayers, "when your company has a plan to deal with a change in the economic weather." When the economy perks up … the partners will quickly hire more temporary employees for stints lasting weeks or months. (Zeidenberg, 1990:31)

While employers find it easier to cope with changes in the economy using such methods, their temporary employees have no economic security and can find themselves quickly unemployed during economic hard times.

Unemployment

To many Canadians, unemployment rates are just numbers we see in the news every month. However, behind the statistics lie countless individual tragedies. The story of Wilfred Popoff in the chapter introduction shows the personal devastation of losing a job. When an entire community is affected, the consequences can be far-reaching. A 1998 newspaper article on unemployment in Port Hardy, British Columbia, began with the statement "This picturesque Vancouver Island coastal town is on a deathwatch" (Howard, 1998:A4). Already high, the suicide rate increased dramatically in the town following the closing of a copper mine, a reduction in logging

Workers in developing nations—often women or young girls—make or assemble a number of products sold in North America and other developed nations. Workers in China make many Nike products; in the United States, Nike employees are primarily involved in nonmanufacturing work, including research, design, and retailing.

activity, and a sharp decline in salmon stocks. With a population of only 5500, Port Hardy had 5 suicides and 24 attempted suicides in a nine-month period. Those who killed themselves were young to middle-aged adults—in other words, members of the group whose prospects were most affected by the community's poor employment prospects. While suicide is the most serious consequence of a community's loss of jobs, hundreds of communities, particularly in the Maritimes and Newfoundland, are disappearing due to the loss of so many of their young people to other provinces, as traditional resource-related jobs in the fishery and mining industries have disappeared.

There are three major types of unemployment—cyclical, seasonal, and structural. *Cyclical unemployment* occurs as a result of lower rates of production during recessions in the business cycle. Although massive layoffs initially occur, some of the workers eventually will be rehired, largely depending on the length and severity of the recession. *Seasonal unemployment* results from shifts in the demand for workers based on conditions such as the weather (in agriculture, the construction industry, and tourism) or the season (holidays and summer vacations). Both of these types of unemployment tend to be relatively temporary in nature.

By contrast, structural unemployment may be relatively permanent. *Structural unemployment* arises because the skills demanded by employers do not match the skills of the unemployed or because the unemployed to not live where the jobs are located (McEachern, 1994). This type of unemployment often occurs when a number of plants in the same industry are closed or new technology makes certain jobs obsolete. For example, workers previously employed in the Nova Scotia coal industry or in the Ontario steel industry found that their job skills did not transfer to other types of industries when their mines and plants closed. Workers who lose their jobs when a factory closes down or moves or when their positions or shifts are abolished experience *worker displacement*. One study found that the most frequent reasons for displacement in Canada were the closure or relocation of a plant and reductions in workload. Several years after displacement, almost two-thirds of these workers had new jobs, often at lower rates of pay, while the remaining third had either left the workforce or were still unemployed (Picot and Wannell, 1990). Structural unemployment often results from *capital flight*—the investment of capital in foreign facilities, as previously discussed. Today, many workers fear losing their jobs, exhausting their unemployment benefits, and not being able to find another job.

The *unemployment rate* **is the percentage of unemployed persons in the labour force actively seeking jobs.** The unemployment rate is not a complete measure of unemployment because it does not include those who have become discouraged and have stopped looking for work, nor does it count students, even if they are looking for jobs. Unemployment rates vary by year, region, gender, race, age, and with the presence of a disability.

- *Yearly variations.* The Canadian unemployment rate reached a post–World War II high in the early 1980s, when it climbed above 11 percent. For most of the 1990s the rate was above 10 percent. In May 1999, 8.3 percent of the workforce was unemployed.

- *Regional differences.* Canada's regions have widely different rates of unemployment. Newfoundland has traditionally been the highest, with rates that are frequently above 20 percent. Rates in the other Atlantic provinces and in Quebec are also usually higher than the Canadian average. British Columbia, Alberta, and Ontario often have the lowest rates as their economies have been the most successful at creating jobs.

- *Gender.* Male and female unemployment rates have been very similar for the past two decades. While women formerly had higher rates than men, their rates have recently been slightly lower than those of male workers (Statistics Canada, 1994b).

- *Race.* Data from the 1986 census showed that visible minorities (a category that does not include Aboriginals) had an unemployment rate that was only slightly higher than the national average. However, despite higher levels of education, their average employment income was lower than for Canadians overall. Aboriginal Canadians had rates of unemployment that were more than double the national average (Moreau, 1994).

- *Age.* Youth have higher rates of unemployment than older persons. Unemployment rates for people aged 15 to 24 are as much as 50 percent higher than the overall unemployment rate. The gap between youth and other workers grew throughout the 1990s.

- *Presence of a disability.* People with disabilities were much less likely to be employed than other Canadians. According to a 1990 study by David Gower (1990), while 640,000 disabled persons aged 15 to 64 were employed, their employment rate was only about two-thirds that of the nondisabled population. Even those with jobs were often underemployed in jobs below their qualifications.

Canada's unemployment rates have historically been higher than those of most other industrial countries. In the late 1990s these rates remained much higher than those of the United States and Japan. However, unemployment has risen to unusually high levels in many European countries in recent years, and, by comparison, Canada's rates are low.

Labour Unions

Workers have used a number of methods to improve their work environment and gain some measure of control over their own work-related activities. Many have joined labour unions to gain strength through collective actions.

Tired of toiling for the benefit of capitalists instead of for themselves, some workers banded together to form labour unions in the middle of the nineteenth century. Craftspeople such as printers, tailors, and blacksmiths were the first to organize, and their efforts led to the passage of the Trade Unions Act in 1872, which legalized union activity in Canada. A *labour union* **is a group of employees who join together to bargain with an employer or a group of employers over wages, benefits, and working conditions.**

During the period of monopoly capitalism, as industries such as automobile and steel manufacturing shifted to mass production, workers realized that they needed more power to improve poor working conditions. The suppression of the Winnipeg General Strike in 1919 and the employment crisis during the Depression of the 1930s had devastated unions. Those that remained were largely based in the United States and usually organized to benefit specific trades such as bricklayers and carpenters. One of the most important events in Canadian labour history was the United Automobile Workers (UAW) strike against General Motors in 1937 in Oshawa, Ontario (Abella, 1974). At the beginning of 1937, there was no union at the Oshawa plant, and workers had suffered their fifth consecutive wage cut while General Motors had announced record profits. When the company announced

Unions have often been negatively portrayed in the media. This stereotyping can make it more difficult for unions to obtain support from the public.

that the assembly line would be speeded up to produce 32 units per hour instead of the 27 it had been producing, the men stopped work and organizers started a Canadian chapter of the UAW.

An unusual feature of the strike was the involvement on behalf of GM of the premier of Ontario, Mitchell Hepburn. He hoped to crush the strike and stop the spread of industrial unions in Ontario. His fear of unions is clear from the following statement, which he made at a press conference (Abella, 1974:106):

We now know what these [union] agitators are up to. We are advised only a few hours ago that they are working their way into the lumber camps and pulp mills and our mines. Well, that has got to stop and we are going to stop it! If necessary we'll raise an army to do it.

Hepburn did raise an army. He recruited hundreds of men into the provincial police; the newcomers were irreverently called "Hepburn Hussars" and "Sons of Mitches." Despite the premier's efforts, the union won the strike and received a contract that became a model for unions throughout Canada. This also marked the beginning of *industrial unionism,* in which all workers in a particular industry, covering a wide variety of different trades, belonged to a single union. This gave the workers a great deal of bargaining power because a strike could shut down an entire industry.

Industrial unions faced a long struggle to organize. Relations between workers and managers were difficult and violence against workers was often used to fight unionization. Ultimately, organizers were successful, and unions have been credited with gaining an eight-hour workday and a five-day work week, health and retirement benefits, sick leave and unemployment insurance, and workplace health and safety standards for many

employees. Most of these gains have occurred through *collective bargaining*—negotiations between employers and labour union leaders on behalf of workers. In some cases, union leaders have called strikes to force employers to accept the union's position on wages and benefits. While on strike, workers may picket in front of the workplace to gain media attention, to fend off "scabs" (nonunion workers) who might take over their jobs, and in some cases to discourage customers from purchasing products made or sold by their employer. Studies documenting strikes and lockouts reveal that their incidence has fluctuated widely over the past three decades. During the 1970s and 1980s, Canada's record of labour problems was much higher than in most other industrial countries. However, during the 1990s strike activity diminished significantly as the recession and corporate restructuring made it unlikely that a successful strike would mean major gains for workers, many of whom were happy to even have a job. Many recent strikes have been a result of workers trying to protect their jobs during a time of cutbacks. Labour relations in the health care field have been particularly difficult in a number of provinces, as governments have been trying to reduce health costs by cutting people or by contracting out services to lower-paying private companies. The number of strikes increased once again in 1998 and 1999 as unions sought to regain some of the wages and benefits they had lost during the cutbacks over the previous decade.

Union membership, which has grown dramatically throughout this century, grew particularly quickly during the two world wars, when labour shortages and economic growth made union expansion easy, and in the 1970s when governments allowed public servants to unionize (Krahn and Lowe, 1993). However, union membership declined during the 1980s and 1990s as economic

BOX 13.2 SOCIOLOGY AND LAW

LABOUR UNIONS AND THE LAW

Labour unions have existed in Canada since the 1800s, when groups of craft workers began to organize in an effort to earn higher wages and achieve better working conditions. The law discouraged collective bargaining (under common law, collective action by workers was treated as criminal conspiracy) and unions had almost no influence until the 1872 Trade Unions Act removed many of these restrictions. Subsequently, labour unions grew in size and strength as factory workers banded together to bargain with management. However, union influence remained limited, and union activity was often violently repressed by employers and governments.

In collective bargaining, union and management face each other as equals; only in this way can an equitable agreement be reached. When management does not meet the union's demands, the members of the union may strike—walk off the job in order to cripple the employer's production (or, in the case of services such as airlines, curtail the service). The extent to which a strike is successful depends on many factors, including the percentage of workers who stop working, the number of replacements who can be hired, the surplus of goods the employer has on hand to "weather"

the strike, and the ability of the striking workers to survive economically. A strike is, in effect, a duel between the union and management. Who prevails, and to what extent, depends on who "blinks" or wears out first.

The legislative framework governing collective bargaining is critical in ensuring its fairness. Canada's labour laws did not support a system of full-scale collective bargaining until the end of World War II. Since labour law is a provincial matter, it is difficult to impose national policies. However, during the war, Prime Minister Mackenzie King recognized the importance of labour stability and in 1944 used the federal government's extraordinary wartime powers to pass the National War Labour Order, which dramatically liberalized labour relations. While the legislation was no longer valid after the war, it was used as a model by the federal and most provincial governments when postwar labour laws were drafted.

The postwar legislation established the rights of workers to join and form unions and to bargain collectively with their employer under fair conditions. Governments also restricted the rights of workers and employers in order to avoid work stoppages. Strikes and lockouts were prohibited during the period of a collective agreement, and a provision was

recessions and massive layoffs in government and industry have reduced the numbers of unionized workers and severely weakened the bargaining power of unions. You have seen that jobs have shifted from manufacturing and manual work to the service sector where employees have been less able to unionize. While white-collar workers in the public sector such as teachers and civil servants have successfully organized, white-collar workers in the private sector remain largely unorganized. For example, only 4 percent of workers in banks and other financial services belong to unions. Women now make up nearly half of all union membership and have accounted for most of the growth in union membership over the past decade. In 1998, 30 percent of all female paid workers were unionized, compared with

32 percent of male paid workers (Statistics Canada, 1994b).

The rate of union membership among workers in Canada is higher than in Japan and the United States, but far lower than in most Western European countries. About 90 percent of all workers in Sweden belong to unions, as do 50 percent in Great Britain, almost 40 percent in Germany, and about 33 percent in Switzerland and Japan. Thirty years ago, the union membership rate in the United States was the same as in Canada, but it is now less than half. American industry has been very antiunion, and state and federal laws have not protected the rights of workers to unionize (see Box 13.2).

In most industrialized countries, collective bargaining by unions has been dominated by men.

BOX 13.2

CONTINUED

made for compulsory mediation and/or concil-iation during disputes. This legislation had a significant impact on the union movement; union membership increased dramatically and collective bargaining began to play a vital role in the labour market.

Union membership in the United States has declined dramatically compared with Canada. At least some of this difference can be attrib-uted to labour law. First, it is more difficult for U.S. workers to unionize. American law requires a certification campaign before workers vote on unionization. During this cam-paign, employers are able to use a variety of methods to discourage unionization. In Canada, certification as a union can be accomplished if the union simply signs up a majority of workers as members. Second, American workers have less power than Canadian workers to force employers to bar-gain in good faith. Third, in the United States many companies have moved their businesses and factories to states whose laws discourage unionization. In Canada, provincial laws are still relatively consistent.

While unions are stronger in Canada than in the United States, the power of labour is still quite limited. This is illustrated by the Anti-Inflation Act of 1975–1978. To control infla-tion and to ensure labour stability, the federal government introduced legislation that sus-pended collective bargaining and imposed wage controls on all Canadian workers even though this meant the denial of previously won bargaining rights. Once this precedent had been set, governments were not reluctant to restrict bargaining of public sector workers during times of economic difficulty. Federal government salaries were virtually frozen during most of the 1990s, and many provin-cial governments demanded wage rollbacks from employees in order to balance their bud-gets, including (in 1993) the labour-backed NDP government in Ontario. Many private sector employers eagerly followed the example set by federal and provincial governments. As a result of wage cuts and freezes, the incomes of Canadian families declined significantly between 1990 and 1996.

Sources: Panitch and Swartz (1993); and Wieler (1986).

However, in many countries, including Sweden, Germany, and Austria, women workers have made important gains as a result of labour union partici-pation, as discussed in Box 13.3

Difficult times may lie ahead for unions; the growing diversity of the workforce; the increase in temporary and part-time work, the threat of global competition, the ease with which jobs can be moved from one country to another, and the replacement of jobs with technology are just a few of the challenges that lie ahead. As our economy becomes increasingly service-based, an important challenge for unions will be organizing the lower tier of service sector workers. Companies like McDonald's and Wal-Mart have strongly resisted attempts to organize unions. McDonald's has gone so far as to close outlets where staff have sought to

unionize. The first successful certification of a McDonald's union in North America occurred in Squamish, British Columbia.

The next decade will be a critical time for the labour movement. How do you think union leaders can change their organizations to meet the new realities of the world of work?

THE GLOBAL ECONOMY IN THE FUTURE

Will the nature of work change in the twenty-first century? What are Canada's future economic prospects? What about the global economy?

These two young women are employees of the first McDonald's in North America to be certified as a union.

Although sociologists do not have a crystal ball with which to predict the future, some general trends can be suggested.

The End of Work?

Corporations around the world eliminated millions of jobs in the 1990s for a variety of different reasons. Only the most efficient companies can flourish in an era when the globalization of trade means that competition can now come from anywhere in the world. Downsizing has also become fashionable, and even profitable companies feel pressure to reduce costs. Perhaps most importantly, technology has enabled workers to be replaced with machines. Because of these trends, economist and futurist Jeremy Rifkin (1995) thinks that work as we know it is coming to an end. Rifkin feels that we are moving into a postindustrial, information-based economy in which factory work, clerical work, middle management, and many other traditional jobs are falling victim to technology. Bank machines and Internet banking are replacing tellers; robots are replacing factory workers; and electronic scanners are replacing cashiers. When agriculture became mechanized, displaced workers found jobs in industry, and when industry turned to computers, service jobs were available. However, the information age does not hold the same potential for jobs. Some *knowledge workers*— the engineers, technicians, and scientists who are leading us into the information age—will gain, but

there may be little work for the rest of us. We will have an elite workforce, not a mass workforce. The elites will be well paid; Microsoft's Bill Gates is but one of a number of people who have made astonishing fortunes in the computer industry. However, the majority have not received the benefits of the postindustrial society. Many people do not have jobs, and those with jobs have seen declines in their purchasing power. Nathan Gardels fears that the unemployed face economic irrelevance: "We don't need what they have and they can't buy what we sell" (quoted in Rifkin, 1995:215).

Two questions arise from Rifkin's analysis. First, what does society do with the millions of people who may not be needed by employers? Second, how do we persuade the top 20 percent, who are receiving the benefits of productivity gains, to share them with the bottom 80 percent who are bearing the burden of change? One possible answer to the first question is to gradually shorten the workweek to 30 hours for the same pay using productivity gains to pay the bill. Earlier technological revolutions resulted in reduced hours of work—from eighty hours per week in the nineteenth century to the current level of forty hours per week. Leisure, rather than formal work, would become the focus of people's lives. Reductions in the workweek have been used in many places to save jobs. Several provincial governments avoided layoffs by requiring employees to take mandatory unpaid days off, and one local of the Canadian Automobile Workers agreed to cut overtime in order to hire new workers. In 1998 France passed legislation reducing the work week to 35 hours in order to reduce the unemployment rate. However, in many segments of the economy, hours are becoming longer rather than shorter. This is particularly true of high-level employees who are now continuously connected to work by cellular phones, faxes, and computers.

The second possibility is to redefine what we now consider work. Rifkin suggests that countries should turn to the nonprofit *civil sector*—community service activities now largely carried out by volunteers—as a source of jobs. The civil sector includes activities such as social services, health care, education, the arts, and assisting the disadvantaged. Not only would this create jobs, but it would strengthen our communities. Recognizing these benefits, the government of Quebec has implemented programs to encourage welfare and unemployment insurance recipients to take jobs in *l'économie sociale* (Rifkin's civil sector). This may become a model for other provinces.

What incentives exist to encourage those benefiting from increased productivity to change? The after-tax purchasing power of Canadians has declined during the past decade and the lack of jobs means that the number of potential customers may decline. Recall that Henry Ford recognized that only well-paid workers could buy his cars. Many economists blame the depression of the 1930s on the failure of business leaders to recognize that they had to share the benefits of increased productivity with their workers (Rifkin, 1995). The same threat may now exist if people do not have adequate incomes; nobody will be able to purchase the goods and services created by our new technology.

Increased inequality may also destabilize society. As British journalist Victor Keegan has observed, "A world in which the majority of people are disenfranchised will not be a pleasant or safe place for the rich minority" (1996:D4). The United States, which has the greatest disparity between rich and poor in the industrialized world, now incarcerates about 2 percent of its adult male population (Epstein, 1996), yet still has a much higher crime rate than most other industrialized countries. Recent riots in Jakarta, Indonesia, were begun by young people who were angry at the growing gap between rich and poor and at their own lack of opportunity (Stackhouse, 1996). Rifkin argues that the rich can either use some of their gains to create a fortress economy or they can use the same money to prevent it.

Edward Luttwak has contrasted these two different approaches to the distribution of wealth:

> When I go to a gas station in Japan, five young men wearing uniforms jump on my car. They not only check the oil but also wash the tires and wash the lights. Why is that? Because government doesn't allow oil companies to compete by price, and therefore they have to compete by service ... I pay a lot of money for the gas.
>
> Then I come to Washington, and in Washington gas is much cheaper. Nobody washes the tires, nobody does anything for me, but here, too, there are five young men ... standing around, unemployed, waiting to rob my car. I still have to pay for them, through my taxes, through imprisonment, through a failed welfare system ... But in Japan at least they clean my car. (1996:24)

Also, the public, unions, and some politicians have begun to protest the growing trend toward paying executives enormous salaries while their workers are being laid off or having their wages cut. Public pressure may eventually force a redistribution of the costs and benefits of the shift to a new economy. Blaming World War II on economic crises, policymakers built a postwar economy designed to promote both growth and equity (Epstein, 1996). The resulting decades of stability and prosperity may help serve as a model for the future.

Many disagree with Rifkin's view that work is coming to an end. They argue that while the nature of work has changed in our postindustrial society, there are now more jobs, not fewer. In North America millions of new jobs have been created over the past decade and some futurists feel that this technology-led growth will continue. However, Rifkin's scenario is a plausible one and his work points out the way in which fundamental changes in our economy can affect all of us.

The Canadian Economy

Many of the trends we have examined in this chapter will produce dramatic changes in the organization of the economy and work in the next century. Canadian industry will continue to compete with companies around the globe for a share of international trade, and the jobs that go with this trade. As globalization and the technological revolution continue, workers increasingly may be fragmented into two major labour market divisions: (1) those who work in the innovative, pri-

BOX 13.3   SOCIOLOGY IN GLOBAL PERSPECTIVE

WOMEN AND LABOUR ACTIVISM

*We are learning to use the system, and well
we should for it has certainly used us.*
—Tish Sommers

Even among the most industrialized nations in the world—such as Sweden, Great Britain, the United States, Germany, and Canada—almost all union negotiators are men. The issues most often brought forward by these negotiators are those affecting "all" workers, often to the exclusion of issues that primarily affect women. Take, for example, the issue of the shorter workweek. Most women who do not have child-rearing responsibilities, as well as most men, want a shorter *workweek*, while most women who have child-rearing responsibilities prefer a shorter *workday* so that they can share child-care duties with other persons.

In recent years, however, some women union members in industrialized countries have become much more savvy at "using the system." Initially, most improvements in women's work opportunities came through legislation. Subsequently, collective bargaining

provided a new vehicle through which women could press for needed changes. For example, through labour–management negotiations, workers have bargained for higher safety standards in the workplace than those required by law. However, struggles over what are perceived to be "women's issues" often produce conflict among union leaders. Many male union leaders typically saw such issues as just that—"women's issues." Ironically, some of their perceptions began to change as they became more aware that some of the health and safety problems in many factories, mines, and other work settings also affected men.

European unions have made many advances in dealing with some of these problem areas. For example, German and Austrian unions have been instrumental in instituting inspection systems to identify work hazards. In Germany and Sweden, unions have bargained for relief from "repetitive motion" injuries such as carpal tunnel syndrome (a hand and wrist disorder associated with exces-

---

mary sector and (2) those whose jobs are located in the growing secondary, marginal sector (see Box 13.4, "The Digital Divide"). Knowledge will increasingly become the factor that differentiates the rich from the poor. In the innovative sector, increased productivity will be the watchword as corporations respond to heightened international competition. In the marginal sector, alienation will grow as temporary workers, sometimes professionals, look for avenues of upward mobility or at least a chance to make their work life more tolerable.

Labour unions will be increasingly less able to help workers unless the unions embark on innovative programs to recruit new members, improve their image, and recover their former political clout (Hodson and Sullivan, 1990). The participation of women in the labour force will continue to increase, and women will continue to make inroads into the professions and senior levels of management. Part-time work, job sharing, and

work from the home—the "electronic cottage" will likely continue to grow.

Global Economic Interdependence and Competition

Borderless markets and industries defy political boundaries. For example, Japanese cars may be produced in Canada and the United States using components that can be made virtually anywhere in the world. Capital and jobs can move very rapidly, so governments have much less power to intervene in markets.

Most futurists predict that multinational corporations will become even more significant in the global economy of the twenty-first century. As they continue to compete for world market share, these corporations will become even less aligned with the values of any one nation. Those who advocate

BOX 13.3

CONTINUED

sive use of computer keyboards and type-writers) for thousands of women computer operators. Men in the manufacturing sector also benefited from the negotiations because their work is repetitive and may lead to back, leg, hand, and eye injuries. The important role that unions can play in improving workplace health has been demonstrated in Saskatchewan where it was shown that safety was improved by giving workers greater control over their jobs.

Canadian women have had some success in attaining leadership roles and serving on the national boards of unions. As a result, women's issues, including pay equity and maternity leave, have recently been addressed in collective bargaining.

Women workers in industrialized nations currently fare much better than their counterparts in other parts of the global economy. In many situations, workers have been denied the right to organize and unionize in free trade zones and home-based production industries. Some nations have no labour laws dealing with minimum wages, maternity benefits, equal pay, and leave; others have not enforced existing laws. In some Asian countries, for example, women migrant workers who are exempt from many regulations do most of the back-breaking, repetitive work on plantations. Because they are brought in from another cultural context, they often experience triple discrimination based on race, class, and gender. In the global economy, many working women and men lack not only union representation but also basic human rights.

Sources: Based on Cook, Lorwin, and Daniels, 1992; National Safety Council, 1992; Sass, 1986; and Tomasevski, 1993.

increased globalization typically focus on its potential impact on developed countries, not on the effect it may have on the 80 percent of the world's population that resides in less developed and developing countries. Persons in developing countries may become increasingly resentful when they are bombarded with media images of Western affluence and consumption. Billions of "have nots" may feel angry at the "haves"—including the employees and managers of multinational companies living and working in their midst (P. Kennedy, 1993).

The chasm between rich and poor nations probably will widen in the twenty-first century as developed countries purchase fewer raw materials from developing countries and more products and services from one another. This change will take place because raw materials of all sorts are no longer as important to manufacturers in developed nations. Oil, for example, may become less important as a power source with the development of solar power and other types of energy. Initial losers

in the global marketplace may be the Arab states of the Middle East, where economies will become less stable and elites and workers much poorer when the petroleum age comes to an end (P. Kennedy, 1993).

In recent years, the average worker in Canada and other developed countries has benefited from global economic growth more than have workers in less developed and developing countries. More than a billion of the world's people live in abject poverty. For many, this means attempting to survive on less than $370 a year (Kennedy, 1993). According to a recent United Nations Report, the total wealth of the world's 358 billionaires equals the combined incomes of the poorest 45 percent of the world's population—2.3 billion people (United Nations Development Program, 1996). While some countries, including many in Southeast Asia and Latin America, will begin to enter the developed world, others, particularly in Africa, will continue to fall farther behind the rest

BOX 13.4   SOCIOLOGY AND TECHNOLOGY

THE DIGITAL DIVIDE

Many people feel that in our postindustrial society, knowledge will be what differentiates the rich from the poor. Because of the key role played by technology, access to computers and to the Internet is critical to gaining this knowledge. However, this access is affected by social class—the "digital divide" refers to the gap created by children and adults from lower-class backgrounds having less access to computers than those from higher classes. Access is also affected by place of residence, as computers and Internet access are more prevalent in cities than in rural areas. Governments, community organizations, and corporations are placing more and more information on the Internet and less in other channels of communi-

cation, so the digital divide is becoming more and more important. For example, if the number of job vacancies posted on the Internet continues to increase, those without computer access will also not have access to these jobs. Also, if government policy information is channelled through the Internet, those without access will not be able to participate in policy decisions.

There are several ways of reducing the digital divide. Increasing the number of computers and improving computer instruction in the schools would help ensure that all young people are on an equal footing. Community computer networks, or FreeNets, provide Internet access to those who cannot afford

of the world (see Chapter 9, "Global Stratification").

The impact of globalization on Canada has been the subject of an interesting debate, part of which concerns whether our economy has benefited from agreements such as the North American Free Trade Agreement (NAFTA), which involves Canada, the United States, and Mexico. We know that the economies of Canada and the United States are becoming more closely linked. The amount of trade is steadily increasing and the border has become almost irrelevant to business. Those looking for opportunities to expand business are increasingly looking south rather than east or west. For example, the Manitoba government placed a high priority on building a four-lane highway south to the United States, while parts of the Trans-Canada Highway in Manitoba remain with only two lanes. This is symbolic of the fact that most of our provincial economies are more dependent on exports to other countries than on exports to other provinces.

The economic consequences of NAFTA will not be known for decades. Critics complained that NAFTA would bring an end to medicare and to our social safety net and would dramatically reduce environmental standards. During the first

few years following the 1989 implementation of the agreement with the United States that preceded NAFTA, a great number of manufacturing jobs were lost, just as opponents of the deal had predicted. However, these were also years when Canada's economy was in a recession, and when high interest rates and the high value of the Canadian dollar made our exports uncompetitive. More recently, as a result of low interest rates, a low dollar, and more competitive industry, Canada is exporting far more to the United States than we import and export-related jobs are creating economic growth. We do not know if the future will bring increased prosperity to all three countries, or whether factors like the low wages paid to workers in Mexico and the southern United States will result in jobs permanently moving out of Canada.

Regardless of the impact of globalization on individual countries, the process will almost inevitably continue. A global workplace is emerging in which telecommunications networks will link workers in distant locations, and the skills of some professionals will transcend the borders of their own countries. For example, there is a demand for the services of international law specialists, engineers, and software designers across countries. One result of this has been a "brain

BOX 13.4

CONTINUED

commercial access charges. Libraries are now a major access provider, and many provinces have provided funding to provide Internet access through their library systems. The federal government has funded a Community Access Program with the goal of providing Internet access in 5000 rural and remote communities by the year 2000.

The digital divide also has international implications. Some observers feel that Internet lines and data-transmission facilities may soon be a better indicator of development than roads, bridges, and railroad lines. In a knowledge-based global economy the countries that develop the fastest will be those that build a strong communications infrastructure (or what some call an "infostructure") and provide high-technology training for their workforce. Countries that lack this communications technology and expertise will be bypassed in the global economy. Not surprisingly, the industrialized countries are in the best position to benefit from the information-based economy. These countries are home to 84 percent of the world's mobile phones, 91 percent of fax machines, and 97 percent of Internet host computers.

Sources: Ditchburn, 1998; and Tapscott, 1998.

drain" of skilled technical specialists to the United States where jobs are plentiful, wages are higher, and taxes lower. One area that has been particularly hit hard is medicine. There are currently almost 10,000 Canadian doctors living in the United States and from 1994 to 1996 17,000 Canadian nurses also moved there. Even as nations become more dependent on one another, they also will become more competitive in the economic sphere.

The need to stay competitive with low wage countries has had an impact on all Canadians. By threatening to close plants and move elsewhere, corporations have forced drastic wage cuts. Meat packer Maple Leaf Foods rolled back wages in Burlington and Winnipeg, and closed its Edmonton plant when workers rejected similar reductions. Even more significantly, there is great pressure on governments to adjust taxation and social policies so business remains competitive. Business leaders argue that if Canada's tax rates are higher than those of other countries, particularly those of our main trading partner, the United States, corporations will not locate here and we will steadily lose jobs and people. This international pressure limits the freedom of our government to act in the best interests of all its citizens. It would be very difficult for the Canadian govern-

ment to raise taxes on business or on wealthy Canadians in order to redistribute income to the poor, because this would make us less competitive with the low tax rates of the United States. This means that governments are steadily losing the ability to set national policies in the face of opposition from global market forces and from multinational corporations that operate without concern for national boundaries. The impact of globalization has been particularly acute in countries that lack the resources to provide a basic manufacturing infrastructure and a minimally trained labour force. In many of these countries there has been an almost complete collapse of jobs and people can barely maintain a subsistence standard of living (see Chapter 9, "Global Stratification").

Corporate Responsibility

The growing power of corporations and the globalization of trade raises issues about the social role of corporations. To whom should corporations be responsible? Do businesses owe anything to the communities in which they operate? Should corporations spend resources helping to build a better society or should they only be responsible for raising wealth for their shareholders? This issue is of concern to the general public. Surveys in many countries have shown that a large majority feel social responsibility is important and prefer to do business with responsible corporations. However, a 1997 Angus Reid poll showed that 45 percent of Canadians felt that corporations were becoming less responsible (Pratt, 1997).

Milton Friedman, winner of the Nobel prize for economics, has set out one side of this issue. Friedman (1970) believes that the only responsibility of business is to engage in activities designed to increase its profits.

> There is one and only one social responsibility of business—to use its resources and engage in activities designed to increase its profits so long as it stays within the rules of the game. (1970:125)

According to this view, corporations should not be concerned about their social responsibilities but only about maximizing the money they make for shareholders. Thus investing in communities, training workers, protecting the environment, and producing safe products should not be of concern unless doing these things will make the corporation more profitable. Businesses that maximize their profits will provide the jobs and investment that are essential to strong communities. However, it is up to other organizations including government and the voluntary sector to ensure that other community needs are looked after.

Others feel that corporate responsibility should go beyond enriching shareholders. Courtney Pratt, the former president of Canadian resources company Noranda, has strongly advocated that corporations exercise greater social responsibility (1997). He argues that corporations must be concerned with profit, but that they should also be committed to creating a better society. According to Pratt, there is no conflict between profits and taking an active role in improving society; he feels business can "do well by doing good" (1997:4). Only by helping build strong communities can businesses ensure that they have effective employees and the kind of economically prosperous society that provides a good climate for business.

As globalization reduces the power of governments, corporate citizenship will become an important issue in the future. If corporations are only economic entities and do not contribute to the public good, it will be much more difficult to resolve social issues such as youth unemployment, income disparities, and the full participation of women and minorities in Canadian society.

CHAPTER REVIEW

What is the primary function of the economy?
The economy is the social institution that ensures the maintenance of society through the production, distribution, and consumption of goods and services.

What are the three sectors of economic production?
In primary sector production, workers extract raw materials and natural resources from the environment and use them without much processing. Industrial societies engage in secondary sector production, which is based on the processing of raw materials (from the primary sector) into finished goods. Postindustrial societies engage in tertiary sector production by providing services rather than goods.

How do the three major contemporary economic systems differ?
In the twentieth century, capitalism, socialism, and mixed economies have been the main economic systems in industrialized countries. Capitalism is characterized by ownership of the means of production, pursuit of personal profit, competition, and limited government intervention. Socialism is characterized by public ownership of the means of production, the pursuit of collective goals, and centralized decision making. In mixed economies, elements of a capitalist, market economy are combined with elements of a command, socialist economy.

What are the functionalist, conflict, and interactionist perspectives on the economy and work?
According to functionalists, the economy is a vital social institution because it is the means by which needed goods and services are produced and distributed. Business cycles represent the necessary rise and fall of economic activity relative to long-term economic growth. Conflict theorists view business cycles as the result of capitalist greed. In order to maximize profits, capitalists suppress the wages of workers who, in turn, cannot purchase products, making it necessary for capitalists to reduce production, close factories, lay off workers, and adopt other remedies that are detrimental to workers and society. Interactionists focus on the microlevel of the economic system, particularly on the social organization of work and its effects on workers' attitudes and behaviour.

How do occupations differ in the primary and secondary labour market?
The primary labour market consists of well-paying jobs with good benefits that have some degree of security

and the possibility of advancement. The secondary labour market consists of low-paying jobs with few benefits and very little job security or possibility of advancement.

What is a labour union?

A labour union is a group of employees who join together to bargain with an employer or a group of employers over wages, benefits, and working conditions.

How has globalization affected Canadian workers?

The need to stay competitive with low wage countries has kept wages down. If workers insist on higher wages, companies can simply close their factories and move production to another country. On the positive side, increased trade has created jobs in Canada.

Key Terms

capitalism 407
conglomerates 409
contingent work 419
corporations 407
democratic socialism 412
economy 402
interlocking corporate directorate 409
labour union 422
marginal jobs 418
mixed economy 412
multinational corporations 408
occupations 415
oligopoly 408
postindustrial economy 406
primary sector production 402
professions 415
secondary sector production 403
shared monopoly 408
socialism 410
unemployment rate 422

Internet Exercises

1. Visit the Adam Smith Institute (**http://www.cyberpoint.co.uk/asi/**). Read through some of Adam Smith's writings. How do his ideas about capitalism compare with the way you see capitalism operating today?

2. Use Lycos (**http://www.lycos.com**) to search for "labour unions Canada." What union seems to be the most well represented on the Internet? Visit the

global LabourStart page (**http://www.solinet.org/LEE/labour04.html**). Do you think that the Internet can bring labour unions from around the world together? What effect would a global union have on the world economy, and on the way in which business operates?

3. Go to the Statistics Canada site (**http://www.statcan.ca**) Go to the *The Daily News*. Search *The Daily* archives. Enter the search term "unemployment." Find the latest issue of *The Daily* that lists the monthly release of unemployment statistics. What is the current annual rate of unemployment? What provinces have the highest rates of unemployment? What is the *employment* rate? Does this show a different picture of working Canadians than the unemployment rate?

Net Links

For a left-wing perspective on economic and labour issues, go to the Canadian Centre for Policy Alternatives at:

> **http://www.policyalternatives.ca/**

For a right-wing perspective on economic and labour issues, go to the Fraser Institute at:

> **http://www.fraserinstitute.ca/**

For a look at the changing nature of work in Canada, read the Government of Canada's Collective Reflection on the Changing Workplace at:

> **http://www.reflection.gc.ca/**

Ⓡ

LabourNet uses computer communications as a means of building an international labour movement; see:

> **http://www.labournet.ca/**

For a wide range of information on labour and the labour force in Canada, go to the Web site of Human Resources Development Canada (the government department responsible for employment matters) at:

> **http://www.hrdc-drhc.gc.ca/arb/arb-home.html**

Questions for Critical Thinking

1. If you were the manager of a computer software division, how might you encourage innovation among your technical employees? How might you encourage efficiency? If you were the manager of a

fast-food restaurant, how might you increase job sat-isfaction and decrease job alienation among your employees?

2. Using Chapter 2 as a guide, design a study to deter-mine the degree of altruism in certain professions. What might be your hypothesis? What variables would you study? What research methods would pro-vide the best data for analysis?

3. What types of occupations will have the highest prestige and income in 2020? The lowest prestige and income? What, if anything, does your answer reflect about the future of the Canadian economy?

4. Many occupations will change or disappear in the future. Think of a specific occupation or profession and consider its future. For example, what will be the role of the librarian when books, journals, and abstracts are all instantly accessible on the Internet?

Suggested Readings

A very good general book on the sociology of work is:

Harvey J. Krahn and Graham S. Lowe. *Work, Industry, and Canadian Society.* Scarborough, Ont.: Nelson Canada, 1993.

These books provide more information about capi-talism:

Peter L. Berger. *The Capitalist Revolution: Fifty Propositions About Prosperity, Equality, and Liberty.* New York: Basic Books, 1986.

Harry Braverman. *Labour and Monopoly Capital: The Degradation of Work in the Twentieth Century.* New York: Monthly Review Press, 1974.

Karl Marx. *Selected Writings in Sociology and Social Philosophy.* Thomas B. Bottomore and Maximilian Rubel (eds.). New York: McGraw-Hill, 1964.

Books that provide interesting insights on the sociology of work include:

Patrick Burman. *Killing Time, Losing Ground: Experiences of Unemployment.* Toronto: Wall and Thompson, 1988.

Barbara Garson. *The Electronic Sweatshop: How Computers Are Transforming the Office of the Future into the Factory of the Past.* New York: Penguin Books, 1989.

Ben Hamper. *Rivethead: Tales from the Assembly Line.* New York: Time Warner, 1992.

Jeremy Rifkin. *The End of Work.* New York: G.P. Putnam's Sons, 1995.

Studs Terkel. *Working: People Talk About What They Do All Day and How They Feel About What They Do.* New York: Ballantine Books, 1985.

Scholarly works on labour unions include:

Irving Abella. *On Strike: Six Key Labour Struggles in Canada 1919-1949.* Toronto: James Lewis and Samuel, 1974.

Berch Berberoglu (ed.). *The Labor Process and the Control of Labor: The Changing Nature of Work Relations in the Late Twentieth Century.* Westport, Conn.: Praeger, 1993.

Politics, Power, and Authority
        Power and Authority

Global Political Systems
        Monarchies
        Authoritarian Systems
        Totalitarian Systems
        Democracies

Perspectives on Power and Political Systems
        Functionalist Perspectives: The Pluralist Model
        Conflict Perspectives: Elite Models
        Critique of Pluralist and Elite Models
        Feminist Perspectives

Politics and Government in Canada
        Political Parties
        Politics and the People

Governmental Bureaucracy
        Characteristics of the Federal Government
        Bureaucracy

Major Political Issues in Canada: Separatism and
Self-Government
        The Quiet Revolution and Quebec Nationalism
        Aboriginal Self-Government

Political Issues for the Future

Compared with most other nations, Canada has had a very peaceful political history. However, there have been instances of political violence. During the 1960s and early 1970s, a group called the Front de Libération du Quebec (FLQ) committed a number of terrorist acts, which culminated in the kidnapping of a British diplomat and the murder of a Quebec cabinet minister. One of the intellectual leaders of the FLQ was Pierre Vallières. In *White Niggers of America*, a book he wrote in prison following his arrest for the murder of a woman who died in one of the terrorists bomb attacks carried out by the FLQ, Vallières outlined some of the grievances of the Quebec separatists:

"In writing this book I claim to do no more than bear witness to the determination of the workers of Quebec to put an end to three centuries of exploitation, of injustices borne in silence, of sacrifices accepted in vain, of insecurity endured with resignation; to bear witness to their new and increasingly energetic determination to take control of their economic, political, and social affairs and to transform into a more just and fraternal society this country, Quebec, which is theirs, this country where they have always been the overwhelming majority of citizens and producers of the "national" wealth, yet where they never have enjoyed the economic power and social freedom to which their numbers and labor entitle them." (1971:17)

While this sounds much like the rhetoric of present-day separatists, the FLQ was different because its members also adhered to a revolutionary Marxist ideology, which they used to justify their violence. Vallières, who saw himself as a political prisoner, rather than as a "common criminal," described the two goals of his movement in this way:

"The FLQ is ... the armed avant-garde of the exploited classes of Quebec: the workers, the farmers, the petty white-collar workers, the students, the unemployed, and those on welfare—that is, at least 90 percent of the population. The FLQ is struggling not only for the political independence of Quebec, but also and inseparably for the revolution, a total revolution which will give all power to the workers and students in a free, self-administering, and fraternal society. Only a total revolution will make it possible for the Québécois, in collaboration with the other peoples of the earth, to build a Quebec that is truly free, truly sovereign." (1971:258–259)

While few now share Vallières's views about the need for a violent revolution, many Quebeckers still dream of independence. Feeling their culture threatened by the influence of English-speaking

POWER, POLITICS, AND GOVERNMENT

North America, separatists believe they can only fulfil their destiny as a distinct "people" through political independence. While the separatists lost the October 1995 referendum by the narrowest of margins and were supported by a large majority of French-speaking voters, the feelings of Quebeckers remain ambivalent. For example, a poll conducted after the referendum found that two-thirds of Quebeckers wanted their province to remain part of the country. However, the same poll showed that 55 percent would vote for separation. These data reflect Quebec comedian Yvon Deschamps's perception that what Québécois really want is an independent Quebec within a strong and united Canada. They also suggest that some flexibility from the other provinces concerning Quebec's place in Canada would ensure that our country stays together, as many Quebeckers would clearly prefer constitutional reform to separation.

Interestingly, Vallières himself reflected the different strains of Québécois political thought. After his release from prison, he disavowed violence and became a member of the separatist Parti Québécois. However, he left that party, feeling it had become too conservative in economic matters. Late in his life, Vallières was horrified by the ethnic violence in the former Yugoslavia and prior to his death in 1998 he rejected separatism, fearing it would lead to ethnic and linguistic apartheid.

This chapter is about political and state institutions. Political institutions are concerned with the exercise of power, and state institutions are the means through which that power is exercised. Modern nations face tremendous political challenges. Resolving the place of Quebec in (or out) of Confederation is but one of the political issues facing Canadians. In this chapter, we will discuss some of these issues and describe the political system through which Canadians will deal with them. We will also examine other systems of government. Before reading on, test your knowledge about political issues and state institutions by taking the quiz in Box 14.1.

QUESTION AND ISSUES

CHAPTER FOCUS QUESTION: Can the aspirations of Aboriginal people and French-speaking Quebeckers be accommodated within the Canadian political system?

What is the relationship between power and authority? Why do people accept authority?

What are the major political systems?

Whose interests are reflected in political decisions?

How is government shaped by political parties and political attitudes?

Why is nationalism such an important force in the world today?

What is the place of democracy in the twenty-first century?

Tension between anglophone and francophone Montrealers has increased since the 1995 referendum. Many separatists are angry at the English and ethnic voters who refused to support independence.

POLITICS, POWER, AND AUTHORITY

Politics is the social institution through which power is acquired and exercised by some people and groups. In contemporary societies, the government is the primary political system. *Government* is the formal organization that has the legal and political authority to regulate the relationships among members of a society and between the society and those outside its borders. Some social scientists refer to government as the *state*—the political entity that possesses a legitimate monopoly over the use of force within its territory to achieve its goals.

Power and Authority

Power is the ability of persons or groups to carry out their will even when opposed by others (Weber, 1968/1922). Through the use of power, people's actions are channelled in one direction rather than another on the assumption that meeting some collective goal is more important than satisfying individual needs and wishes. Consequently, power is a *social relationship* that involves both leaders and followers. Power also is a dimension in the structure of social stratifica-

tion. Persons in positions of power control valuable resources of society—including wealth, status, comfort, and safety—and are able to influence the actions of others by awarding or withholding those resources (Dye and Zeigler, 1993).

The most basic form of power is force or military might. Initially, force may be used to seize and hold power. Max Weber suggested, however, that force is not the most effective long-term means of gaining compliance, because those who are being ruled do not accept as legitimate those who are doing the ruling. Consequently, most leaders do not want to base their power on force alone; they seek to legitimize their power by turning it into authority.

Authority **is power that people accept as legitimate rather than coercive.** People have a greater tendency to accept authority as legitimate if they are economically or politically dependent on those who hold power. They also may accept authority more readily if it reflects their own beliefs and values (Turner, Beeghley, and Powers, 1995). *Legitimation* refers to the process by which power is institutionalized and given a moral foundation to justify its existence. Weber outlined three *ideal types* of authority—charismatic, traditional, and rational-legal—each of which has a different basis of legitimacy and a different means of administration.

CHARISMATIC AUTHORITY According to Weber, *charismatic authority* **is power legitimized on the basis of a leader's exceptional personal qualities** or the demonstration of extraordinary insight and accomplishment, which inspire loyalty and obedience from followers. To Weber, charismatic individuals are able to "identify themselves with the central facts or problems of people's lives [and through the force of their personalities] communicate their inspirations to others and lead them in new directions" (Turner, Beeghley, and Powers, 1995:214–215). Charismatic leaders may be politicians, soldiers, and entertainers, among others (Shils, 1965; Bendix, 1971).

From Weber's perspective, a charismatic leader may be either a tyrant or a hero. Thus, charismatic authority has been attributed to such diverse historical figures as Jesus Christ, Napoleon, Julius Caesar, Adolf Hitler, Winston Churchill, and Martin Luther King, Jr. Among the most charismatic leaders in Canadian politics have been Pierre Trudeau and Lucien Bouchard. Bouchard's personal appeal almost led to a separatist victory in the 1995 referendum, which,

BOX 14.1 SOCIOLOGY AND EVERYDAY LIFE

BOX 14.1 SOCIOLOGY AND EVERYDAY LIFE

HOW MUCH DO YOU KNOW ABOUT POLITICAL ISSUES AND STATE INSTITUTIONS?

TRUE   FALSE

TRUE	FALSE		
T	F	1.	Organizations in which authority is based on the charismatic qualities of particular leaders can be unstable, and these kinds of organizations often fail.
T	F	2.	In Canada, our constitutional right to freedom of speech means that any kind of pornography or hate literature can be legally distributed.
T	F	3.	While authoritarian governments still exist in many countries, democratic government has become more widespread throughout the world during the past decade.
T	F	4.	In Canada, members of the governing party are free to vote against the government in Parliament whenever they wish.
T	F	5.	Canada's Aboriginal peoples have been able to vote in federal elections since 1867, the year of Confederation.
T	F	6.	Governments tend to make their decisions based on a broadly representative sampling of the opinions of all citizens.
T	F	7.	Canada has had a female prime minister.
T	F	8.	Canada is one of the few nations in the world that has had as its official Opposition in Parliament a political party dedicated to the breakup of the country.
T	F	9.	A higher proportion of Canadians vote in federal elections than do the citizens of other industrialized countries.
T	F	10.	Under most proposals for Aboriginal self-government, Aboriginal groups in Canada would have total control over their territory and would be considered sovereign nations.

Answers on page 440.

under the distinctly uncharismatic Jacques Parizeau, looked to be heading for defeat.

Since women seldom are permitted to assume positions of leadership in patriarchal political and social structures, they are much less likely to become charismatic leaders. Famous women who had charismatic appeal include Joan of Arc, Mother Teresa, Indira Gandhi of India, Evita Perón of Argentina, and Margaret Thatcher of the United Kingdom. Kim Campbell's strong performance as Minister of Justice and her personality gave her a charismatic appeal, which, in turn, helped her to win the leadership of the Progressive Conservative Party and become Canada's first woman prime minister. However, the fleeting nature of such appeal was illustrated in the 1993 election when the campaign performance of Campbell and her party was too weak to overcome the negative feelings Canadians held about the government of her predecessor, Brian Mulroney. The Conservatives were reduced to only two seats in Parliament and their future as a party was threatened.

Charismatic authority generally tends to be temporary and unstable; it derives primarily from individual leaders (who may change their minds, leave, or die) and from an administrative structure usually limited to a small number of faithful followers. For this reason, charismatic authority often becomes routinized. The **routinization of charisma occurs when charismatic authority is succeeded by a bureaucracy controlled by a rationally established authority or by a combination of traditional and bureaucratic authority** (Turner, Beeghley, and Powers, 1995). According to Weber (1968/1922:1148), "It is the fate of charisma to recede ... after it has entered the permanent structures of social action." However, charisma cannot always be successfully transferred to organizations; many organizations, particularly religious ones, fail when the leader departs.

TRADITIONAL AUTHORITY   In contrast to charismatic authority, **traditional authority is power that is legitimized by respect for long-standing custom.** In preindustrial societies, the authority of tradi-

BOX 14.1

ANSWERS TO THE SOCIOLOGY QUIZ ON POLITICAL ISSUES AND STATE INSTITUTIONS

1. **True.** Many political and religious movements that are held together by the personal qualities of their leader fail when the leader dies, retires, or is found to be "ordinary."

2. **False.** While the Canadian Charter of Rights and Freedoms does guarantee the freedom of speech, all freedoms are subject to "reasonable limits." Our courts have interpreted this to allow governments some powers of censorship.

3. **True.** The movement toward democratic government speeded up dramatically with the fall of the Berlin Wall in 1989 and the subsequent breakup of the Soviet Union. A number of countries in Africa and in Central and South America have also become democracies since that time.

4. **False.** In the United States members of Congress who belong to the same party as the president often vote against the president. However, in Canada party discipline is imposed on those who vote against their leader.

5. **False.** Aboriginal people did not have voting rights in federal elections until 1960.

6. **False.** Special interest groups and various elites in society have far more influence on government policy than do average citizens.

7. **True.** Kim Campbell was prime minister of Canada in 1993. When Brian Mulroney retired from politics, Campbell took over the leadership of the Progressive Conservative Party and automatically became prime minister. However, she was defeated in an election held a few months later, so we have still never had a woman elected prime minister.

8. **True.** In 1993 the Bloc Québécois won the second highest number of seats in the federal election and become the official opposition. The main purpose of the Bloc is to promote the separation of Quebec from Canada.

9. **False.** Canada's voter turnout rate is substantially higher than that of the United States, but lower than that of most other industrialized countries.

10. **False.** Some Aboriginal groups, including some Quebec Mohawks, do argue that they have the status of sovereign nations, but most Aboriginal people have a more limited view of self-government.

Sources: Boldt, 1993; and Dyck, 1996.

tional leaders, such as kings, queens, pharaohs, emperors, and religious dignitaries, usually is grounded in religious beliefs and established practices. For example, British kings and queens historically have traced their authority from God. Members of subordinate classes obey a traditional leader's edicts out of economic and political dependency and sometimes personal loyalty. However, custom and religious beliefs are sufficient to maintain traditional authority for extended periods of time only as long as people share similar backgrounds and accept this type of authority as legitimate.

Weber noted that traditional authority may be either patriarchal or patrimonial. In systems of *patriarchy*, men are assumed to have authority in the household and in other small groups. In systems of *patrimony*, traditional authority rests in larger social structures that require administrators

(such as personal aides who are loyal to the ruler) to carry out edicts. Although patrimonial systems largely have become extinct (or ceremonial, as in the case of the English monarchy), patriarchal systems remain a source of authority. One of the ironies of modern life occurred, for example, in the Persian Gulf War when military women from several countries including Canada risked their lives for countries (Kuwait and Saudi Arabia) where women are not allowed to drive vehicles or to vote (Eisenstein, 1994).

As societies industrialize, traditional authority is challenged by a more complex division of labour and by the wider diversity of people who now inhabit the area as a result of migration. In industrialized societies, people do not share the same viewpoint on many issues and tend to openly question traditional authority. As the division of labour becomes more complex, political

Two solitudes: Quebec Premier Lucien Bouchard and Prime Minister Jean Chrétien are the two people responsible for Canada's future as a nation. Does the body language in this photo suggest that cooperation is likely?

and economic institutions become increasingly interdependent (Durkheim, 1933/1893).

Weber predicted that traditional authority would inhibit the development of capitalism. He stressed that capitalism cannot fully develop when rules are not logically established, when officials follow rules arbitrarily, and when leaders are not technically trained (Weber, 1968/1922; Turner, Beeghley, and Powers, 1995). Weber believed that capitalism worked best in systems of rational-legal authority.

RATIONAL-LEGAL AUTHORITY   According to Weber, *rational-legal authority* **is power legitimized by law or written rules and regulations.** Rational-legal authority is also called *bureaucratic authority.* As you will recall from Chapter 6, bureaucracies are characterized by a clear-cut division of labour, hierarchy of authority, formal rules, impersonal enforcement of rules, and job security based on a person's technical qualifications. In rational-legal authority, power is legitimized by procedures; if leaders obtain their positions in a procedurally correct manner (such as by election or appointment), they have the right to act.

In Canada, our political system gives rational-legal authority to the office of the prime minister, for example, by specifying the procedures by which persons hold the office as well as its duties and limitations. Rational-legal authority also is held by other elected or appointed government officials and by officers in a formal organization. However, authority is invested in the *office*, not in the *person* who holds the office. For example,

when the Conservatives lost the 1993 federal election, Kim Campbell passed on the power of the office of prime minister to Jean Chrétien and no longer had any involvement in government.

In a rational-legal system, bureaucracy is the apparatus responsible for creating and enforcing rules in the public interest. Weber believed that rational-legal authority was the only means by which to attain "efficient, flexible, and competent regulation under a rule of law" (Turner, Beeghley, and Powers, 1995:218). Weber's three types of authority are summarized in Concept Table 14.A.

The "rule of law" differs in various situations and organizations. For example, the unique needs of the military as a specialized society separate from civilian society are used as a justification for policies that, in civilian life, would be a violation of rights. For example, in most military forces a soldier can be tried and imprisoned for not showing up for work. This penalty far exceeds that which most of you would expect to receive if you missed a day of school or work, but reflects the need for discipline during times of combat.

Are all citizens guaranteed certain liberties and rights? The Charter of Rights and Freedoms, which is entrenched in the Canadian Constitution, guarantees Canadians *fundamental freedoms,* including the freedoms of the press, speech, assembly, and religion; *democratic rights,* including the right to vote; *mobility rights,* which guarantee Canadians the right to live in any province; *legal rights,* including the presumption of innocence and the right to a fair trial; and *equality rights* prohibiting discrimination on the basis of

CONCEPT TABLE 14.A

WEBER'S THREE TYPES OF AUTHORITY

Max Weber's three types of authority are shown here in global perspective. Charismatic authority is exemplified by former prime minister Indira Gandhi of India. Sultan Ali Mirah, leader of Ethiopia's Afar Liberation Front, is an example of traditional authority sanctioned by custom. Australian Supreme Court justices (shown here at the opening of Parliament in Perth, Australia) represent rational-legal authority, which depends on established rules and procedures.

	DESCRIPTION	**EXAMPLES**	
Charismatic	Based on leaders' personal qualities Temporary and unstable	Napoleon Adolf Hitler Indira Gandhi	
Traditional	Legitimized by long-standing custom Subject to erosion as traditions weaken	Patrimony (authority resides in traditional leader supported by larger social structures, as in old British monarchy) Patriarchy (rule by men occupying traditional positions of authority, as in the family)	
Rational-legal	Legitimized by rationally established rules and procedures Authority resides in the office, not the person	Modern British Parliament Canadian prime minister, Parliament, federal bureaucracy	

race, age, gender, sexual orientation, or religion (Dyck, 1996). These rights normally cannot be violated by government or the state, and the courts have the power to invalidate legislation that violates a citizen's rights and freedoms. However, Canadian courts have considerable discretion, as rights are not absolute but subject to "reasonable limits." That is, governments can pass laws that may violate citizens' rights if the courts find it reasonable for the government to do so. For example, the court has found it reasonable for governments to limit the freedoms of Holocaust deniers and pornographers. On the other hand, governments have the power to overrule the Charter and the courts through the "notwithstanding clause," which governments can use to pass legislation that conflicts with some parts of the Charter. The notwithstanding clause was used, for example, by the Quebec government to maintain its laws limiting English-language signs after the Supreme Court of Canada ruled these laws unconstitutional.

GLOBAL POLITICAL SYSTEMS

Political systems as we know them today have evolved slowly. In the earliest societies, politics was not an entity separate from other aspects of life. As we will see, however, all groups have some means of legitimizing power.

Hunting and gathering societies do not have political institutions as such because they have very little division of labour or social inequality. Leadership and authority are centred in the family and clan. Individuals acquire leadership roles due to personal attributes such as great physical strength, exceptional skills, or charisma (Lenski, Lenski, and Nolan, 1991).

Political institutions first emerged in agrarian societies as they acquired surpluses and developed greater social inequality. Elites took control of politics and used custom or traditional authority to justify their position. When cities developed circa 3500–3000 B.C.E., the *city-state*—a city whose power extended to adjacent areas—became the centre of political power. Both the Roman and Persian empires comprised a number of city-states, each of which had its own monarchy. Thus, in these societies, political authority was decentralized. After each of these empires fell, the individual city-states lived on.

Nation-states, as we know them, began to develop in Spain, France, and England between the twelfth and fifteenth centuries (see Tilly, 1975). A *nation-state* is a unit of political organization that has recognizable national boundaries and citizens who possess specific legal rights and obligations. Nation-states emerge as countries develop specific geographic territories and acquire greater ability to defend their borders. Improvements in communication and transportation make it possible for people in a larger geographic area to share a common language and culture. As charismatic and traditional authority are superseded by rational-legal authority, legal standards come to prevail in all areas of life, and the nation-state claims a monopoly over the legitimate use of force (Kennedy, 1993).

Approximately 190 nation-states currently exist throughout the world. The four main types of political systems found in nation-states are monarchies, authoritarian systems, totalitarian systems, and democracies.

Monarchies

A *monarchy* is a political system in which power resides in one person or family and is passed from generation to generation through lines of inheritance. Monarchies are most common in agrarian societies and are associated with traditional authority patterns. However, the relative power of monarchs has varied across nations, depending on religious, political, and economic conditions. *Absolute monarchs* claim a hereditary right to rule (based on membership in a noble family) or a divine right to rule (in other words, a God-given right to rule that legitimizes the exercise of power). In *limited monarchies*, rulers depend on powerful members of the nobility to retain their thrones. Unlike absolute monarchs, limited monarchs are not considered to be above the law. In *constitutional monarchies*, the royalty serve as symbolic rulers or heads of state while actual authority is held by elected officials in the national parliaments. In such present-day monarchies as the United Kingdom, Sweden, Japan, and the Netherlands, members of royal families primarily perform ceremonial functions.

Authoritarian Systems

An *authoritarian* political system is one controlled by rulers who deny popular participation in government. A few authoritarian regimes have been absolute monarchies in which rulers claimed a hereditary right to their position. Today, Saudi Arabia and Kuwait are examples of authoritarian absolute monarchies. *Dictatorships*, in which power is gained and held by a single individual, also are authoritarian in nature. Pure dictatorships are rare: all rulers need the support of the military and the backing of business elites to maintain their position. *Military juntas* result when military officers seize power from the government, as has happened in recent years in Nigeria, Chile, and Haiti. Authoritarian regimes may be relatively short-lived; some nations may move toward democracy while others may become more totalitarian.

Totalitarian Systems

A *totalitarian* political system is one in which the state seeks to regulate all aspects of people's public and private lives. Such systems rely on modern technology to monitor and control people; mass propaganda and electronic surveillance are widely used to influence people's thinking and control their actions. One example of a totalitarian regime was the National Socialist (Nazi) party in Germany during World War II, where military leaders sought to control all aspects of national life, not just government operations. Other examples include the former Soviet Union and contemporary Iraq under Saddam Hussein's regime.

To keep people from rebelling, totalitarian governments enforce conformity: people are denied the right to assemble for political purposes; access to information is strictly controlled; and secret police enforce compliance, creating an environment of constant fear and suspicion. Economic class is another factor in totalitarian control. For example, the Nazi party gained support from members of the middle class who wanted to maintain the status quo while enhancing their own position. By contrast, in the former Soviet Union, the working class sought to eliminate class distinctions, a belief that fit well with Soviet ideology of collective ownership. Sometimes, the relationship between political and economic systems is complex. For example, the People's Republic of China today appears to be readying itself for global competition by embracing some aspects of capitalism (and consumerism) while maintaining strict control over its citizens and blocking their efforts to embrace democracy as it did so ruthlessly in 1989 at Tiananmen Square (see Arendt, 1973; Soper, 1985; McLeod, 1994; Piturro, 1994).

Democracies

A *democracy* is a political system in which the people hold the ruling power either directly or through elected representatives. In an ideal-type democracy, people would actively and directly rule themselves. *Direct participatory democracy* requires that citizens be able to meet regularly to debate and decide the issues of the day. Historical examples of direct democracy might include ancient Athens or a town meeting in colonial New England; however, the extent to which such meetings actually reflected the wishes of most

people has been the subject of scholarly debate. Moreover, the impracticality of involving an entire citizenry in direct decision making becomes evident in nations containing millions of adults. If all thirty million people in Canada came together in one place for a meeting, for example, they would occupy an area of 30 square kilometres, and a single round of five-minute speeches would require hundreds of years. At this rate, people would be born, grow old, and die while waiting for a single decision to be made. Even an electronic town hall meeting in which people were linked through the telephone, television, or the Internet would be enormously complicated to organize.

In most democratic countries, including Canada, people have a voice in the government through *representative democracy*, whereby citizens elect representatives to serve as bridges between themselves and the government. In a representative democracy, elected representatives are supposed to convey the concerns and interests of those they represent, and the government is expected to be responsive to the wishes of the people. Elected officials are held accountable to the people through elections.

However, representative democracy is not always equally accessible to all people in a nation. Throughout Canada's history, for example, members of subordinate groups have been denied full participation in the democratic process. Aboriginals, women, East Asians, and South Asians have in the past been prohibited from voting. Today, the Charter of Rights and Freedoms guarantees that all Canadians have the right to democratic participation.

Even representative democracies are not all alike. Compared to the winner-takes-all elections in Canada, which are decided by who wins the most votes in each constituency, many European elections are based on a system of *proportional representation*, meaning that each party is represented in the national legislature according to the *proportion* of votes received by each political party. For example, a party that won 40 percent of the vote would receive 40 percent of the seats in a legislative body, and a party receiving 20 percent of the votes would receive 20 percent of the seats. (By contrast, in the 1993 Canadian federal election, the Progressive Conservatives won two seats with 16 percent of the total vote, while the Bloc Québécois won 54 seats with only 14 percent of the vote. This was because the Progressive Conservative votes were scattered across the country, while the Bloc Québécois votes were all concentrated in francophone Quebec ridings.) Systems based on proportional representation increase the power of minority parties because these parties still have a chance of gaining representation in the legislature even though they would not have sufficient strength to win any particular constituency. Israel has a system that encourages a wide range of minority parties, and an election is usually followed by a long period of negotiation before a coalition is formed representing a majority of seats in the country's parliament, the Knesset. This bargaining can give a great deal of power to small parties representing only a fraction of the population, as their participation in a coalition may determine which of the two major parties forms the government.

The specific form of representative democracies also varies. Canada is a *constitutional monarchy* whose head of state is the Queen, a hereditary ruler who is represented in Canada by the governor general. The governor general is appointed by the Queen but recommended by the prime minister, and has a role that is largely ceremonial, as our elected parliament actually governs the country. By contrast, the United States and France are *republics*, whose heads of state are elected and share governing power with the legislature.

Another major difference between Canada and the United States is that our system is a *parliamentary* one in which the prime minister is the leader of the party that wins the most seats in the House of Commons. This system is based on parliamentary discipline, which ensures that the policies favoured by the prime minister will become law. If government members oppose these policies, they have the opportunity to debate them in private caucus meetings, but they are normally bound to vote with the government in the House. Party discipline can be harsh; in 1996, John Nunziata was expelled from the Liberal Party by Prime Minister Jean Chrétien for voting against the government's budget. By contrast, U.S. legislators often vote against their party's program.

When Canada adopted the British parliamentary system, the Fathers of Confederation also implemented an important feature of the American system—both Canada and the United States are *federations*, with a division of power between the central government and provincial or state governments. Other countries, including Israel and Italy, are *unitary states*, which means they have a single central political authority. While John A. Macdonald, our first prime minister, would have preferred a centralized unitary state, this was opposed by Quebec and the Maritimes, which wished to protect their distinctive identities. The British North America Act of 1867 established the distribution of powers between federal and provincial governments.

Some countries have one-party democracies that appear to be democratic because they hold periodic elections. However, the outcome of these elections is a foregone conclusion; voters get to select from candidates belonging to only one party. For example, in the former Soviet Union, all candidates belonged to the Communist party; in Iraq, all candidates are aligned with Saddam Hussein's Baathist party.

During the past decade, democracy has spread very rapidly, particularly in formerly Communist states. Communism was a one-party system that often maintained its power through repressive means. Since the fall of the Berlin Wall in 1989, the countries of the former Soviet bloc in Eastern Europe, as well as others such as Nicaragua and Zambia have established democratic governments. While Communist governments remain in a number of countries including China and Cuba, pressures for democratization are strong around the globe.

If nothing else, the economic and social success of the democratic states serves as a model for those wishing to reform their own governments. Historically and today, capitalism is best served by a democratic system and most countries initiating reforms are moving to capitalism. Full control over property and free markets are necessary and these are not compatible with an absolutist state. The global revolution in communications has also facilitated democratization. Nondemocratic governments may wish to keep their citizens cut off from developments elsewhere in the world. However, satellite television, fax machines, and the Internet make it impossible to control or close off communications, and global culture, including democratic ideals, continues to spread.

PERSPECTIVES ON POWER AND POLITICAL SYSTEMS

Is political power in Canada concentrated in the hands of the few or distributed among the many? Sociologists and political scientists have suggested many different answers to this question; however, two prevalent models of power have emerged: pluralist and elite.

Functionalist Perspectives: The Pluralist Model

The pluralist model is rooted in a functionalist perspective, which assumes that people share a consensus on central concerns, such as freedom and protection from harm, and that the government serves important functions in society that no other institution can fulfil. According to Emile Durkheim (1933/1893), the purpose of government is to socialize people to become good citizens, to regulate the economy so that it operates effectively, and to provide the necessary services for citizens. Contemporary functionalists state the four main functions of government as follows: (1) maintaining law and order, (2) planning and directing society, (3) meeting social needs, and (4) handling international relations, including warfare.

If government at national, provincial, and local levels is responsible for these functions, what role do people play in the political system? What keeps the government from becoming all-powerful? What happens when people do not agree on specific issues or concerns? Functionalists suggest that divergent viewpoints lead to a system of political pluralism in which the government functions as an arbiter between competing interests and viewpoints. According to the *pluralist model,* **power in political systems is widely dispersed throughout many competing interest groups** (Dahl, 1961). Many of these are *special interest groups*—**political coalitions made up of individuals or groups that share a specific interest they wish to protect or advance with the help of the political system** (Greenberg and Page, 1993). Examples of special interest groups include the Business Council on National Issues, the Canadian Labour Congress, the National Action Committee on the Status of Women, and the Assembly of First Nations.

Some feel that pressure group activity is increasingly replacing individual and party activity in Canada's political system. Our country is so large and so diverse that we have always had a highly pluralistic society, and political scientist Rand Dyck (1996) predicts that pluralism will become even more important in the future. Our ethnic diversity is growing (see Chapter 10), and groups representing women, French-speaking Quebeckers, Aboriginal peoples, ethnic

In addition to direct contact with legislators, special interest groups like the "gun lobby" try to influence policymaking by mobilizing constituents and stirring up public opinion. Recent years have seen a proliferation of single-issue groups like those on both sides of the gun control issue. The strong feelings of gun owners are shown in this Ottawa rally.

Canadians, and many others are challenging the elitism of the past. Interest groups are now part of our political culture and their influence has been enhanced through legislation such as the Charter of Rights and Freedoms, which guarantees them a voice in political affairs.

While a pluralistic system ensures the voice of many groups will be heard, it does not always work as fairly as political theorists might wish. For example, there are many more groups representing business interests than there are groups representing the interests of the lower class (Dyck, 1996). While this does not mean that government actions always reflect the interests of the powerful, it does mean that the weak must work much harder to be heard. Another potential problem with a highly pluralistic system is that if people turn away from broad social values to those of particular economic, cultural, racial, and gender groups—a process known as *identity politics*—society may become too fragmented. Signs of a

Canada played a very important role in the international campaign to eliminate land mines. In this photo, Prime Minister Chretién, Foreign Affairs Minister Axworthy, and Jody Williams of the International Campaign to Ban Landmines destroy Canada's last landmine.

backlash to this fragmentation can be seen in the success of the Reform Party in Alberta during the 1993 federal election, which was largely a response to the concern of right-wing voters with the power of less conservative special interest groups (Harrison, Johnston, and Krahn, 1996). The challenge ahead is to build a society that embraces all minorities while retaining a sense of national community.

KEY ELEMENTS   Political scientists Thomas R. Dye and Harmon Zeigler (1993) have summarized the key elements of pluralism as follows:

- Decisions are made on behalf of the people by leaders who engage in a process of bargaining, accommodation, and compromise.
- Competition among leadership groups (such as in business, labour, education, law, medicine, consumer organizations, and government) protects people by making the abuse of power by any one group more difficult. These groups often operate as veto groups that attempt to protect their own interests by keeping others from taking actions that would threaten those interests.
- People can influence public policy by voting in elections, participating in existing special

interest groups, or forming new ones to gain access to the political system.
- Power is widely dispersed in society. Leadership groups that wield influence on some decisions are not the same groups that may be influential in other decisions.
- Public policy is not always based on majority preference; rather, it reflects a balance among competing interest groups.

From a pluralist perspective, representative democracy (coupled with the checks and balances provided by our legal system, and the division of governmental powers between a central government and smaller units such as provinces and municipalities) ensures that no one group can overpower the others and that individual rights are protected.

SPECIAL INTEREST GROUPS   Special interest groups help people advocate their own interests and further their causes. Of the thousands of special interest groups in Canada, some (such as consumer groups) seek a collective good while others (such as the cigarette manufacturers' lobby) have a relatively narrow focus. Broad categories of special interest groups include banking, business, education, energy, the environment, health,

BOX 14.2 SOCIOLOGY AND MEDIA

THE MEDIA AND SEPARATISM

The mass media have a major influence on politics. Most of us are aware that the media can distort events; this is particularly true of television, which is Canadians' main source of political information. Television news is very brief—items rarely last more than a minute or two—and producers try to show pictures that are interesting, exciting, and visually appealing. This means that any political messages must be short and simple. Since most political issues are very complex, they are inevitably oversimplified and distorted by television.

Media bias is a particular problem when reporters favour one side of a political debate. This has been the case in the battle over Quebec separatism. Many of those who work in Quebec's French-language media are ardent nationalists and their stories reflect their polit-

ical views. Another problem is that owners can impose their views on reporters. For example, Pierre Péladeau was one of Quebec's wealthiest and most influential publishers. When he was accused of rebuking the staff of one of his papers for their stories praising Jews, Péladeau's defence was that he was not anti-Semitic, but that he wanted his papers to focus on stories about francophones. Since Quebec Jews are typically English-speaking, stories about them should not take up too much space in his papers.

On the other side, the English-language media are very much opposed to the sovereignty of Quebec and their work reflects a pro-unity position. That the French and English media in Quebec can differ dramatically in their reporting of the same event was shown in their coverage of a June 1996 rally of federal-

labour, persons with a disability, religious groups, retired persons, women, and those espousing a specific ideological viewpoint; obviously, many groups overlap in interests and membership. Within each of these categories are numerous subgroups. In education, for example, different special interest groups represent teachers, parents, school administrators, universities, professors, vocational and technical schools, and students. Despite their claims to objectivity, members of the media also represent interest groups. Box 14.2 shows how the media portray different sides in the separatism debate.

Special interest groups also are referred to as *pressure groups* (because they put pressure on political leaders) and *lobbies*. The term *lobby* derives from the tradition of interest groups' representatives (*lobbyists*) cornering legislators in the lobbies and hallways of legislative buildings (Greenberg and Page, 1993). Lobbies often are referred to in terms of the organization they represent or the single issue on which they focus—for example, the "gun lobby" and the "dairy lobby."

Lobbying can be conducted as either an inside or an outside game. The *inside game* refers to situa-

tions in which interest group representatives are in direct contact with officials in the government and try to build influence on the basis of personal relationships. This method is typically used by corporations who often hire former government officials to lobby their former colleagues. In the *outside game*, interest groups attempt to pressure officials by mobilizing their constituents to telephone or write letters demanding a specific course of action, by stirring up public opinion, and by getting their membership involved in activities to make their wishes known (Greenberg and Page, 1993). This method is often used by more broadly based groups such as environmentalists or anti-abortion groups.

Advocates of the pluralist model point out that special interest groups provide a "voice" for people who otherwise might not be heard by elected officials at the national, provincial, and local level. However, many special interest groups have specific economic stakes in public policy. Professional groups (such as the Canadian Bankers' Association) wield power with policymakers on issues that they feel may affect their economic well-being (such as increased competition in the

BOX 13.2

CONTINUED

ists on Parliament Hill in Ottawa. *The Gazette,* Montreal's leading English-language newspaper, reported that 12,000 people had attended a federalist "love-in." Their front-page photo showed a girl in front of the flag-waving crowd. In the girl's hand was a sign saying "Separation: It's Over." Contrast this with *Le Devoir,* a French-language paper, which reported that 6000 people had attended the rally. On the front page was a photo of a protester wearing a Lucien Bouchard mask and carrying a cane. Another man appeared to be kicking him in the leg. The spin the media put on events, as in this case, makes it difficult to separate reality from media bias.

The importance of the media in the battle for the hearts, minds, and votes of Quebeckers is indicated by the ongoing controversy over the role of the Canadian Broadcasting Corporation (CBC) in the unity debate. In 1967, the Liberal government gave the CBC the explicit mandate of promoting national unity and the Canadian identity. This led at times to political interference by the federal government in coverage by Radio-Canada, the French-language network of the CBC. While national unity has since been removed from the CBC's mission, the media remain an important part of our national debate.

Sources: Panitch and Swartz, 1993; and Wieler, 1986.

banking industry). As discussed in Chapter 13, labour unions have asserted their claims in the hope of protecting the jobs of their members and gaining maximum wages and benefits.

Over the past two decades, special interest groups have become more involved in "single-issue politics," in which political candidates often are supported or rejected solely on the basis of their views on a specific issue—such as abortion, gun control, gay and lesbian rights, or the environment. Single-issue groups derive their strength from the intensity of their beliefs; leaders have little room to compromise on issues. Some of these groups have been very effective; about a decade ago, a quickly organized group of seniors was able to make the government back down on its plans to change the law that provided automatic cost-of-living increases to old age pensioners.

Interest groups have also been effective on the international level. In recent years, Canada played a major role in passing two important international agreements. The first was to ban the use of land mines; the second was to set up a permanent war crimes tribunal. While these agree-

ments were signed by governments, citizens' groups in many different countries were instrumental in convincing those governments to take action. The 1997 Nobel Peace Prize was awarded to one of these groups, the International Campaign to Band Landmines, which coordinated the activities of over 1000 nongovernmental organizations in more than sixty countries. These efforts culminated in the land mines treaty that was signed in Ottawa in 1997.

Conflict Perspectives: Elite Models

Although conflict theorists acknowledge that the government serves a number of important purposes in society, they assume that government exists for the benefit of wealthy or politically powerful elites who use the government to impose their will on the masses. According to the *elite model,* **power in political systems is concentrated in the hands of a small group of elites and the masses are relatively powerless.** Early Italian sociologists Vilfredo Pareto (1848–1923) and Gaetano Mosca (1858–1941) were among the first to show that concentration of power may be inevitable within societies. Pareto first used the term *elite* to refer to "the few who rule the many" (G. Marshall, 1994). Similarly, Karl Marx claimed that under capitalism, the government serves the interests of the ruling (or capitalist) class that controls the means of production.

KEY ELEMENTS   Elite models are based on the following assumptions (Dye and Zeigler, 1993):

- Decisions are made by the elite, which possesses greater wealth, education, status, and other resources than do the "masses" it governs.

- Consensus exists among the elite on the basic values and goals of society; disagreements arise only over the means to achieve those values and goals. However, most people in a society do not necessarily share the elite consensus on these important social concerns.

- The masses have little influence over the elite and public policy. The masses are seen as uninterested in and uninformed about the issues facing society; the elite is in the best position to make important decisions.

- Power is highly concentrated at the top of a pyramid-shaped social hierarchy; those at the top of the power structure come together to set policy for everyone.

- Public policy reflects the values and preferences of the elite, not the preferences of the people. The elite uses the media to shape the political attitudes of the masses.

From this perspective, a few of the "best and brightest" among the masses may rise to elite positions by acquiring the requisite education, experience, leadership skills, and other attributes of the elite (Dye and Zeigler, 1993). However, those who do not share the attitudes, political philosophy, gender, or race of the elites will not succeed in this way.

C. WRIGHT MILLS AND THE POWER ELITE   Sociologist C. Wright Mills (1959a) was among the first to formulate and test ideas concerning power elites. Mills examined the power structure of the United States and concluded that a power elite occupied the upper echelon of the power pyramid. The *power elite* is composed of leaders at the top of business, the executive branch of the federal government, and the military. Of these three, Mills speculated that the "corporate rich" (the highest-paid officers of the biggest corporations)

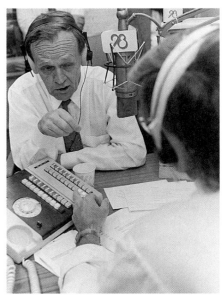

Political leaders often avoid contact with "average voters." When was the last time you saw a prime minister at a public forum or press conference where his policies could be challenged? This is one of Prime Minister Chrétien's rare visits to an open-line radio show.

were the most powerful because of their unique ability to parlay the vast economic resources at their disposal into political power. At the middle level of the pyramid, Mills placed the legislative branch of government, special interest groups, and local opinion leaders. The bottom (and widest layer) of the pyramid is occupied by the unorganized masses who are relatively powerless and vulnerable to economic and political exploitation.

Mills emphasized that individuals who make up the power elite have similar class backgrounds and interests; many of them also interact on a regular basis. Members of the power elite are able to influence many important decisions, including federal spending. Other researchers (Hunter, 1953) have identified elites who control decision making at local community levels; so, the view of elite domination can be extended to all levels of government.

G. WILLIAM DOMHOFF AND THE RULING CLASS   According to sociologist G. William Domhoff (1978), the *ruling class* is made up of the corporate rich, who make up less than 1 percent of the population. Domhoff uses the term *ruling class* to signify a relatively fixed group of privileged people who wield sufficient power to constrain political processes and serve underlying capitalist interests. By contrast, *governing power* refers to the everyday operation of the political system; who *governs* is much less important than who *rules*.

Like Mills, Domhoff asserted that individuals in the upper echelon are members of a business class that owns and controls large corporations. The intertwining of the upper class and the corporate community produces economic and social cohesion. Economic interdependence among members of the ruling class is rooted in common stock ownership and is visible in interlocking corporate directorates that serve as a communication network (Domhoff, 1983; Clement, 1975). Members of the ruling class also are socially linked with one another. They attend the same schools, belong to the same clubs, and frequently socialize together. Consider the example of Power Corporation, which is controlled by Paul Desmarais, who is a close friend of former prime ministers Pierre Trudeau and Brian Mulroney, and of Prime Minister Jean Chrétien—in fact, Desmarais's son is married to Chrétien's daughter. A wide variety of senior politicians and government bureaucrats move back and forth between senior Power Corporation positions and government service. With these contacts, Desmarais certainly has no difficulty in having his views heard by those responsible for Canada's governmental policy. Fox and Ornstein (1986) have documented an extensive network of links between large corporations and the federal Cabinet, the Senate, and the federal bureaucracy. These links grew over the three decades they studied. They found far fewer links between provincial governments and the corporate world.

According to Domhoff (1983), the corporate rich influence the political process in three ways. First, they affect the candidate selection process by helping to finance campaigns and providing favours to political candidates. Second, through participation in the special interest process, the corporate rich are able to obtain favours, tax breaks, and favourable regulatory rulings. Finally, the corporate rich in Canada may gain access to the policy-making process through their appointments to governmental bodies such as the Senate. While the economic elites are not in agreement on all issues, they do agree on the need to ensure an economic climate that favours their continuing accumulation of wealth. Fox and Ornstein conclude that the state is not simply an instrument or tool of the capitalists, but that there are important

structural connections between the state and corporations that often help capitalists shape legislation to their benefit.

Today, some members of the ruling class influence international politics through their involvement in banking, business services, and law firms that have a strong interest in overseas sales, investments, or raw materials extraction (Domhoff, 1990). The power of transnational corporations has become an important factor in class analyses of the modern state.

CLASS CONFLICT PERSPECTIVES Most contemporary elite models are based on the work of Karl Marx; however, there are divergent viewpoints about the role of the state within the Marxist (or class conflict) perspective. On the one hand, *instrumental Marxists* argue that the state invariably acts to perpetuate the capitalist class. From this perspective, capitalists control the government through special interest groups, lobbying, campaign financing, and other types of "influence peddling" to get legislatures and the courts to make decisions favourable to their class (Miliband, 1969; Domhoff, 1970). In other words, the state exists only to support the interests of the dominant class (Marger, 1987).

On the other hand, *structural Marxists* contend that the state is not simply a passive instrument of the capitalist class. Because the state must simultaneously preserve order and maintain a positive climate for the accumulation of capital, not all decisions can favour the immediate wishes of the dominant class (Quadagno, 1984; Marger, 1987). For example, at various points in the history of this country, the state has had to institute social welfare programs, regulate business, and enact policies that favour unions in order to placate people and maintain "law and order." Ultimately, however, such actions serve the long-range interests of the capitalists by keeping members of subordinate groups from rebelling against the dominant group (O'Connor, 1973).

Critique of Pluralist and Elite Models

Pluralist and elite models share some basic assumptions about the nature of power and its distribution. Both models assume that decisions are made through interactions among key actors from the upper echelons of larger-scale organizations and institutions in society. Both models agree that these leaders are not everyday citizens and that

TABLE 14.1	WOMEN IN PARLIAMENT, VARIOUS COUNTRIES, 1999
Sweden	42.7
Denmark	37.4
Norway	36.4
Netherlands	36.0
Finland	33.5
Germany	30.9
South Africa	29.6
Canada	**20.6**
United Kingdom	18.4
United States	13.3
Italy	11.1
France	10.9

Source: Julian Nundy, "French Women to Get Greater Role in Government," *The Globe and Mail*, 5 March 1993:A13. Reprinted by permission of the author.

public policy usually reflects the interests of these organizations (Dye and Zeigler, 1993).

Pluralist and elite models each make a unique contribution to our understanding of power. The pluralist model emphasizes that many different groups, not just elected officials, compete for power and advantage in society. This model also shows how coalitions may shift over time and how elected officials may be highly responsive to public opinion on some occasions (Eitzen and Zinn, 1995). However, critics counter that the pluralist model is naive in its assumption that diverse interest groups balance one another out. They note that our system only has the appearance of pluralism and that it is, in fact, remarkably elitist for a society that claims to value ordinary people's input (Domhoff, 1983). A wide disparity exists between the resources and political clout of big business and those of interest groups that represent infants and children or persons with disabilities, for example. According to critics, consensus is difficult, if not impossible, in populations consisting of people from different classes, religions, and racial-ethnic and age groups.

Mills's power elite model highlights the interrelationships of the economic, political, and military sectors of society and makes us aware that the elite may be a relatively cohesive group. Similarly, Domhoff's ruling class model emphasizes the role of elites in setting and implementing policies that benefit the capitalist class. Power elite models call

our attention to a central concern in contemporary Canadian society: the ability of democracy and its ideals to survive in the context of the increasingly concentrated power held by capitalist oligarchies (see Chapter 13).

One important critique of elite models is that social change does not always favour the dominant groups in our society. For example, women have won many battles over the past two decades despite the degree of control that males have had over the corporate and political spheres. The success of the women's movement supports the pluralist claim that nonelites can organize to force change.

Feminist Perspectives

Political theorists have focused much of their attention on class issues. British sociologist Mary McIntosh (1978) was among the first to argue that gender issues were also important. McIntosh felt that the state supported a system in which women were controlled in the household, where they performed unpaid labour that helped supply a cheap workforce for the capitalist system. Until they achieved some political power, women would inevitably be subordinated by the patriarchal state.

Women have long been excluded from the political process. The Elections Act of 1903 said that "No woman, criminal, or lunatic can vote," and Canadian women were not permitted to vote in federal elections until 1918. Most provinces began allowing women to vote at around this time, though in Quebec women were not enfranchised until 1940. With the vote, women also received the right to run for election. However, few ran, and even fewer were successful. Only 27 women were elected to the federal Parliament between 1921 and 1968. Since that time, significant progress has been made; 21 percent of the Members of Parliament (MPs) elected in 1997 were women (see Table 14.1). But women have not yet reached the highest political positions. While Canada has had one woman prime minister (Kim Campbell) and two provincial premiers, only one of these three, Catherine Callbeck of Prince Edward Island, was actually elected to the position. Women have been much more successful at the municipal level; many of Canada's mayors are women. The low representation of women in Canadian political office is typical of most western countries. The major exception is the Scandinavian countries where women make up over 35 percent of the membership of the national parliaments. The issue is not simply one of representation. The absence of women in our legislatures has meant that many gender-related issues have not received sufficient attention. Issues like daycare policy, pay equity, the feminization of poverty, and violence against women and children have only recently begun to receive the attention they deserve. In theory, male legislators, whose constituents are over 50 percent women, could have pursued these issues. But for many years they did not.

POLITICS AND GOVERNMENT IN CANADA

The Canadian political process consists of formal elements, such as the duties of the prime minister and the legislative process, and informal elements, such as the role of political parties in the election process. We now turn to an examination of these informal elements, including political parties, political socialization, and voter participation.

Political Parties

A *political party* is an organization whose purpose is to gain and hold legitimate control of government; it usually is composed of people with similar attitudes, interests, and socio-economic status. A political party (1) develops and articulates policy positions, (2) educates voters about issues and simplifies the choices for them, and (3) recruits candidates who agree with those policies, helps those candidates win office, and holds the candidates responsible for implementing the party's policy positions. In carrying out these functions, a party may try to modify the demands of special interest groups, build a consensus that could win majority support, and provide simple and identifiable choices for the voters on election day. Political parties create a *platform*, a formal statement of the party's political positions on various social and economic issues.

The party that wins the most seats in an election forms the government; the party with the next largest number of seats becomes the official Opposition. Since Confederation, two political parties, the Liberals and the Progressive Conservatives, have dominated the Canadian political system. Although one party may control the government for several terms, at some point the voters elect the other party and control shifts. From time to time, other parties have gained some strength. At various times the New Democratic Party (NDP) and the Social Credit Party had some political strength, but neither had enough seats to form the official Opposition. However, in the 1993 election, the Progressive Conservatives were reduced to only two seats. The Bloc Québécois, a party that favours Quebec separation, became the official Opposition and the Reform Party, which mainly represents politically disaffected Western Canadians, also won significant representation. These two new parties retained their representation in the 1997 election, though this time the Reform Party became the opposition.

IDEAL TYPE VERSUS REALITY   Ideally, political parties will offer clear alternatives to the electorate— alternatives that reflect the aspirations, concerns, and viewpoints of the population. For several reasons, this is usually not the case. First, the two major parties rarely offer voters clear policy alternatives. Most voters view themselves as being close to the centre of the political spectrum (extremely liberal being the far left of that spectrum and extremely conservative being the far right). Although the definitions of liberal and conservative vary over time, *liberals* tend to focus on equality of opportunity and the need for government regulation and social safety nets. By contrast, *conservatives* are more likely to emphasize economic restraint and freedom from government

When people move from one country to another, they learn new political attitudes, values, and behaviour. This citizenship ceremony was held in Quebec City during National Citizenship Week. What role do you think these new Canadians will play in Quebec politics?

interference (Greenberg and Page, 1993). However, because most voters consider themselves moderates, neither party has much incentive to move very far from the middle. Parties like the NDP and Reform, which choose to maintain some ideological purity, run the risk of being marginalized and are very unlikely to win a national election. While these parties have not won electoral power, they have been successful in having their ideas implemented. During the 1960s and 1970s, many of the social policies advocated by the NDP were implemented by Liberal and Progressive Conservative governments. More recently, the Reform Party has been much more successful in having its deficit-cutting agenda implemented by federal and provincial governments than it has been in convincing Canadians it should be given the power to run the country.

This staying near the centre of the political spectrum and the co-optation of opposing parties' policy ideas mean that Canadian elections tend to be fought over issues of leadership rather than of fundamental political principles. The most notable recent exception to this is instructive. A major issue of the 1988 election was the Canada–U.S. free trade agreement; a pact removing the barriers to the sale of goods and services between Canada and the United States. The Progressive Conservatives, who ultimately won the election, strongly supported the Canada–U.S. Free Trade Agreement, while their main opponents, the Liberals, opposed it. However, when the Liberals did eventually take power in 1993

they quickly "studied" the North American Free Trade Agreement (NAFTA), the successor to the earlier pact, which was also negotiated by the Conservatives and opposed by the Liberals, expressed their support for it, and since then have been ardent free traders, seeking to expand NAFTA to Chile. (See Chapter 13, "The Economy and Work.")

The second reason the two major political parties do not offer clear alternatives that reflect the viewpoints of the population is that most political parties are dominated by active elites who are not representative of the general population. Many represent special interests and tend to come from the upper echelons of society. Thus the poor, women, and racial minorities have not been included in drafting party policy or in selecting party leaders. One study (Lele et al., 1979) looked at attendance at Liberal, Progressive Conservative, and NDP conventions and found that none of them had participation that was representative of the Canadian population. Similarly, Members of Parliament are disproportionately male and from the upper and middle classes (Guppy et al., 1987). Many people involved in politics today tend to work outside the traditional party structure, often in single-issue interest groups. Organizations like the National Action Committee for the Status of Women, Greenpeace, and various Aboriginal groups have been very effective in advancing their agendas and in getting grassroots involvement without attaching themselves to a particular political party.

Finally, our electoral system effectively limits the degree to which a diversity of views will be reflected in our legislatures. In those political systems with proportional representation (discussed earlier in this chapter), minority parties have a much greater chance of electing candidates to the legislature. It is interesting to speculate on what impact proportional representation would have on our political system.

Despite the fact that the Liberals and Progressive Conservatives may not have all of the ideal characteristics of political parties, they have both flourished—at least until the Conservatives were decimated in the 1993 election. Whether the Bloc Québécois and the Reform Party retain their current representation, or whether the Progressive Conservatives will regain their role as a major political force, remains to be seen.

Politics and the People

Why do some people vote and others do not? How do people come to think of themselves as being conservative, moderate, or liberal? Key factors include individuals' political socialization, attitudes, and participation.

POLITICAL SOCIALIZATION   *Political socialization* is the process by which people learn political attitudes, values, and behaviour. For young children, the family is the primary agent of political socialization, and children tend to learn and hold many of the same opinions as their parents. By the time children reach school age, they typically identify with the political party (if any) of their parents (Burnham, 1983). As they grow older, other agents of socialization including peers, teachers, and the media begin to affect children's political beliefs. Over time, these other agents may cause people's political attitudes and values to change, and they may cease to identify with the political party of their parents. Even for adults, political socialization continues through the media, friends, neighbours, and colleagues in the workplace.

POLITICAL ATTITUDES   In addition to the socialization process, people's socioeconomic status affects their political attitudes, values, beliefs, and behaviour. For example, individuals who are very poor or who are unable to find employment tend to believe that society has failed them and therefore are often indifferent toward the political system

(Zipp, 1985; Pinderhughes, 1986). Believing that casting a ballot would make no difference to their own circumstances, they do not vote.

In general, voters tend to select candidates and political parties based on social and economic issues they consider important to their lives. *Social issues* are those relating to moral judgments or civil rights, ranging from abortion rights to equal rights for homosexuals. Other social issues include the rights of people of colour and persons with a disability, capital punishment, and gun control. Persons with a liberal perspective on social issues, for example, tend to believe that women have the right to an abortion (at least under certain circumstances), that criminals should be rehabilitated and not just punished, and that the government has an obligation to protect the rights of subordinate groups. Conservatives tend to believe in limiting individual rights on social issues and to oppose social programs that they see as promoting individuals on the basis of minority status rather than merit. Based on these distinctions, Liberals and New Democrats are more likely to seek passage of social programs that make the government a more active participant in society, promoting social welfare and equality. By contrast, Progressive Conservative and Reform Party members are more likely to act according to the belief that government should limit its involvement in social issues.

Economic issues fall into two broad categories: (1) the amount that should be spent on government programs and (2) the extent to which these programs should encourage a redistribution of income and assets. Those holding liberal political views believe that without government intervention, income and assets would become concentrated in the hands of even fewer people and that the government must act to redistribute wealth, thus ensuring that everyone gets a "fair slice" of the economic "pie." In order to accomplish this, they envision that larger sums of money must be raised and spent by the government on such programs. Conservatives contend that such programs are not only unnecessary but also counterproductive. That is, programs financed by tax increases decrease people's incentive to work and to be innovative, and make people dependent on the government.

You will remember that the main parties tend toward the centre and that their policies are often not ideologically distinct on either social or economic issues. The Progressive Conservatives, who ideologically favour spending restraint, ran up the largest budget *deficits* in Canadian history before they were voted out of office in 1993. The Liberals, on the other hand, after winning the election, implemented the largest budget *cuts* in Canadian history in order to reduce the deficit, despite the impact of these cuts on the social programs that have traditionally received their support. The immediate demands of political reality are often more important in determining government policy than is political philosophy.

Social class is correlated with political attitudes. People in the upper classes tend to be more conservative on economic issues and more liberal on social issues. Upper-class conservatives generally favour equality of opportunity but do not want their own income and assets taxed heavily to abolish poverty or societal problems that they believe some people bring upon themselves. Most of Canada's social programs faced opposition from corporate and upper-class interests, and some of these groups led the call for cuts to these programs in the 1990s. By contrast, people in the lower classes tend to be conservative on social issues, such as capital punishment or abortion rights, but liberal on economic issues, such as increasing the minimum wage and expanding social programs.

Despite these tendencies, there is probably less of a connection between voting behaviour and social class in Canada than in many other industrialized countries. The Liberal Party has typically attracted voters from all classes, while the NDP gets a high proportion of its support from skilled and unskilled labour. Even so, more voters from the skilled and unskilled labour classes usually vote for other parties than they do for the New Democrats. In fact, Canadian voters tend to be somewhat fickle at the polls and frequently switch parties. For example, comparing the 1988 and 1993 federal elections, more voters switched parties than voted for the same party they had chosen in the earlier election (Pammett, 1993).

Why is the association between class and voting so low in Canada? Canadian voters appear to be influenced more by individual leaders or particular issues and events than by loyalties to a particular party's philosophy. This conclusion is supported by the results of one study (Clarke et al., 1991) in which it was found that class, gender, ethnicity, religion, community size, and age all had some effect on Canadians' voting preferences, but much less than such political variables as prior voting record, concern about immediate issues, and the image of the party leader.

Another reason for the weak connection between class and voting is that the mainstream parties, particularly the Liberals, have been able to incorporate many of the reforms suggested by more class-based parties into their own platforms. For example, government medical care, which was introduced in Saskatchewan by the CCF (Cooperative Commonwealth Federation) party—now the New Democratic Party—was subsequently adopted by the Liberals, who implemented it at the national level.

Finally, sociologist Rick Ogmundson (1975) explained the weak link between class and voting as resulting from what he called the *subjective class vote*. Using survey data, he found that people often believed they were voting for a party that reflected their interests, even though more objective measures of the party's position indicated that this was not the case. According to Ogmundson and Ng (1982), the subjective class vote in Canada was about as high as it was in the United Kingdom, which is usually thought to have a high degree of class politics. Ogmundson's work is supported by research showing that support for the NDP was more strongly related to belief in class ideology, including support for unions and an egalitarian philosophy than it was to the actual class position of the voters (Nakhaie and Arnold, 1996).

POLITICAL PARTICIPATION Democracy has been defined as a government "of the people, by the people, and for the people." Accordingly, it would stand to reason that "the people" would actively participate in their government at any or all of four levels: (1) voting, (2) attending and taking part in political meetings, (3) actively participating in political campaigns, and (4) running for or holding political office. Participation is important as elections are the means through which citizens can make their views known to politicians. Participation also helps to legitimate the political process; those who vote share a responsibility for, and an interest in, the outcome of the election. In Canada, the participation rate for federal elections has declined from 75 percent in 1988 to 67 percent in 1997. The participation rate is slightly higher for provincial elections and much lower for municipal elections. While our 67 percent participation rate means that most Canadians do get involved in the electoral process, many western industrial countries have even higher rates. For example, in Western European countries participation rates are normally 80 to 90 percent. The

The swearing-in of the new cabinet in June 1997. In our system of parliamentary democracy, power rests in the hands of the prime minister and the cabinet. Individual members of Parliament have little influence on government policy.

United States has one of the lowest voter participation rates of all Western nations. Less than 50 percent of eligible voters participated in the 1996 U.S. elections.

Why do many eligible voters in North America stay away from the polls? During any election, some voting-age persons do not go to the polls due to illness, disability, lack of transportation, or absenteeism. However, these explanations do not account for why many other people do not vote. According to some analysts, people may not vote because they are satisfied with the status quo or because they are apathetic and uninformed, and being uninformed, they lack a basic understanding of both public issues and the basic process of government. Surveys of voters typically show that the majority of Canadians have little knowledge of the candidates or the issues. This lack of knowledge makes it difficult for many people to cast a meaningful ballot, so they simply stay away from the polls.

By contrast, others argue that people stay away from the polls because they feel alienated from politics at all levels of government—federal, provincial, and local. They believe that government does not care about issues that concern them and that only the elites or special interest groups have any influence.

Participation in politics is influenced by gender, age, race/ethnicity, and socioeconomic status (SES). The rate of participation increases as

a person's SES increases. One explanation for the higher rates of political participation at higher SES levels is that higher levels of education may give people a better understanding of government processes, a belief that they have more at stake in the political process, and greater economic resources to contribute to the process.

GOVERNMENTAL BUREAUCRACY

When most people think about political power, they overlook one of its major sources—the governmental bureaucracy. As previously discussed, Weber's rational-legal authority finds its contemporary embodiment in bureaucratic organizations. Negative feelings about bureaucracy are perhaps strongest when people are describing the "red tape" and "faceless bureaucrats" in government with whom they must deal (see Chapter 6). But who are these "faceless bureaucrats," and what do they do?

Characteristics of the Federal Government Bureaucracy

Bureaucratic power tends to take on a life of its own. During the nineteenth century, the government had a relatively limited role. The scope of government was extended greatly during the Great Depression in the 1930s to deal with labour–management relations, public welfare, and regulation of financial markets. With dramatic increases in technology and increasing demands from the public that the government "do something" about problems facing society, the government has grown still more in recent decades. Today, even with reductions in size, the federal bureaucracy employs more than two hundred thousand people.

Our federal government is divided into departments such as Finance, National Defence, Foreign Affairs, Human Resources Development, and Health. While the number of departments varies as governments change, there are usually between twenty and twenty-five, and each is headed by a minister who is a member of the prime minister's cabinet. The prime minister and the cabinet make up the political executive. Most decisions come from cabinet, and the power of MPs who are not ministers is quite limited. Ministers do not usually have any expertise in their area of responsibility, so they rely very heavily on members of their departmental bureaucracy for advice. Even strong ministers may have difficulty imposing their ideas on a bureaucracy consisting of thousands of people with a great deal of expertise, who have permanent jobs in their departments, and who have seen many ministers come and go.

The governmental bureaucracy has been able to perpetuate itself and expand because many of its employees have highly specialized knowledge and skills and cannot be replaced easily by outsiders. Also, Canada decided almost a century ago to rely on a professional civil service rather than follow a *political patronage* system in which civil servants are replaced when a new party assumes power. In the United States, a change in the president can mean that thousands of changes will be made at the senior levels of the U.S. bureaucracy. In Canada it is rare to see more than one or two senior officials lose their jobs during such transitions.

While patronage is not an issue within the civil service, the government bases many of its appointments on party loyalty rather than on the principle of merit. Appointments to the Senate are perhaps the most obvious example, but appointments to the judiciary and to a wide variety of regulatory boards and commissions are also based on political ties. While opposition parties loudly complain about patronage, when they get into power they have always followed the same practices as their predecessors.

A major issue concerning our government bureaucracy is the extent to which it represents Canadian society. Traditionally, the civil service, like other sectors of our society, has been controlled by white, English-speaking males. The first major change to this was the involvement of francophones. The Official Languages Act of 1969 mandated a bilingual government and most senior officials are, as a result, required to be fluent in both official languages. Francophones were given preference in hiring and promotion until the imbalance was redressed, and language training was required for many unilingual government employees. The federal civil service now has a higher proportion of francophones than does the Canadian population.

Women now make up almost half the civil service. While they are still underrepresented in senior management positions, women have made substantial gains in recent years. For example, Jocelyne Bourgon was until recently the clerk of the Privy Council, the top position in the civil service, and pay equity programs have ensured that women are fairly paid. The federal government has also passed employment equity legislation, the aim of which is to increase the representation in the federal public service of women, Aboriginals, people with disabilities, and visible minorities.

MAJOR POLITICAL ISSUES IN CANADA: SEPARATISM AND SELF-GOVERNMENT

The Quiet Revolution and Quebec Nationalism

Because of our former colonial status and the dissatisfaction of many Quebec nationalists with the current political structure, constitutional matters have been much more prominent in Canada than in most other countries. The following review of events from the early 1960s onwards will set the stage for the very close results of the 1995 referendum on separation. They are events that even after the referendum continue to play a major role in the political, economic, and social life in Canada.

Aboriginal leaders have played a prominent role in Canadian politics during the past decade. As questions of self-government, Aboriginal rights, and land claims have been considered, two of the most important leaders have been Grand Chief Phil Fontaine of the Assembly of First Nations and Elijah Harper, who was formerly a member of the Manitoba legislature and the federal parliament.

The constitutional crises of recent years were set in motion by the Quiet Revolution, which began in Quebec in the 1960s. The term of Premier Jean Lesage (1960–1966) saw a dramatic change. Prior to 1960, Quebec had been a very traditional society. The Catholic Church and the family were at the core of French-Canadian society, and economic power was in the hands of English Canadians. In a very short time Quebec underwent a dramatic transformation into a secular, urban society with a modern educational system, public health and welfare programs, and a provincially controlled electric power system. A new sense of nationalism was used as a core ideology to justify the expanded role of the state. This nationalism was clearly expressed in the 1962 Liberal campaign slogan *maîtres chez nous* ("masters in our own house"). Economic and social reform would strengthen French culture. The state would replace the church at the heart of Quebec society. To pursue its agenda of renewal, the Quebec government began demanding, and receiving, more control over matters traditionally managed by the federal government.

As Quebec became more like the rest of North America in most other respects, language came to be its major distinguishing factor, assuming both a real and a symbolic role in the province's political future. English was the language of business in the province, and French-Canadian owners and managers were rare. In a series of legislative steps beginning in the 1960s, the provincial government moved to ensure that French became the language of business. The goal was stated clearly in the White Paper (that is, a government policy document) that preceded a major piece of language legislation, Bill 101, which was adopted in 1977:

> The Quebec that we wish to build will be essentially French. The fact that the majority of the population is French will be distinctly visible: at work, in communications, in the country. It is also a country where the traditional division of powers, especially in matters concerning the economy, will be modified: the use of French will not be generalized simply to hide the predominance of foreign powers over Francophones; this usage will accompany, will symbolize a reconquest by the Francophone majority of Quebec of the hold which returns to it on the levers of the economy. (cited in Cook, 1995:133)

By any measure, the Quiet Revolution has been a success. A large body of legislation now protects the French language in Quebec. Regulations requiring immigrant children to attend French-language schools and restrictions on the use of English on commercial signs have

BOX 14.3   SOCIOLOGY AND LAW

QUEBEC AND CONSTITUTIONAL REFORM

Pierre Trudeau attempted several times to achieve a constitutional arrangement that was acceptable to Quebec and the other provinces. Among the critical issues were (1) the division of powers between the federal and provincial governments—most provinces, particularly Quebec, wanted more power decentralized to the provinces; (2) language rights, with Quebec wanting the power to limit individual rights on language matters; and (3) a formula for amending the constitution—Quebec wanted a veto over constitutional changes that might affect the French language and culture. The election of René Lévesque's separatist government in 1976 further complicated the already difficult negotiations over these matters. Following the failure of the Yes side in Quebec's first referendum on sovereignty-association in 1980, Trudeau repatriated Canada's constitution from Britain in 1982. While the 1982 Constitution Act, including the Charter of Rights, applied to Quebec, the government of Quebec had not consented to it.

In 1984 Brian Mulroney, another prime minister from Quebec, sought to modify the constitution to make it acceptable to Quebec. For his part, Quebec's Premier Robert Bourassa set out the following five demands for his province's inclusion:

- recognition of Quebec as a distinct society,
- increased control over immigration,
- participation in Supreme Court appointments,
- a veto on constitutional changes, and
- the ability to opt out of national programs operating in areas that fall within provincial jurisdiction.

Despite some reservations, in 1987 the provincial premiers all agreed to support these demands in the Meech Lake Accord. Prior to implementation, the Accord had to be passed by all provincial legislatures within a three-year period. A great deal of public debate took place during this period; many opponents were concerned the Accord gave Quebec and other provinces too much power, while others complained of insufficient consultation with the public, and that the interests of groups such as Aboriginals and women had not been

reinforced the dominant role of the French language in Quebec. Quebeckers have gained control over the economy and other major social institutions including culture, politics, and government.

While the transformation of Quebec was remarkably rapid, it was not rapid enough for some. Nationalist groups, which began to emerge in the 1960s, saw independence as the only means by which Quebec could fulfil its destiny. At the same time, another vision was offered by Quebeckers like Pierre Trudeau who felt that Quebec's aspirations could best be fulfilled within Canada. For Trudeau, cultural survival did not depend on political sovereignty; a strong federal government, which actively promoted bilingualism, was the best guarantee that French would survive in a predominantly English North America. As prime minister, Trudeau in 1969 brought in the Official Languages Act, which

made the federal public service bilingual. This provided opportunities for francophones and helped to ensure that Canadians in all parts of the country could receive services in either language. The government also began to encourage French immersion programs in schools in English Canada.

These changes met with vociferous resistance among some English Canadians. Consider matters from the perspective of those opposed to bilingualism. As Quebec was becoming more autonomous and less bilingual, the need for bilingualism was being promoted throughout the rest of the country (Dyck, 1996). Unilingual anglophone civil servants had to learn French if they wished to be promoted and bilingualism was clearly a major part of the federal political agenda. Many felt that Quebec was blackmailing the federal government at the expense of the other provinces. With extreme Quebec nationalists on

BOX 14.3

CONTINUED

advanced by the Accord. Ultimately, the Accord failed when Elijah Harper, an Aboriginal member of the Manitoba legislature, did not allow its passage. Harper opposed the Accord because it gave Quebec recognition as a distinct society and with it the special status that Aboriginal people had sought for themselves. Aboriginal people were not opposed to Quebec's demands, but were frustrated because their own demands had been ignored.

The Mulroney government made a second attempt at bringing Quebec into the constitutional fold. Following a broad process of consultation, the provincial premiers once again met with their federal counterparts to discuss constitutional reform. The resulting Charlottetown Accord included four major components:

- a Canada clause that recognized Quebec as a distinct society,

- a reformed and elected Senate,
- recognition of the inherent right of Aboriginals to self-government, and
- increased decentralization of federal powers.

The Accord was defeated in a national referendum in 1992. Dyck (1996) attributes the defeat as much to public hostility against politics and politicians as to the substance of the Accord. Many people felt that politicians should be more concerned with economic and social issues than with esoteric matters such as the federal–provincial division of powers and constitutional amending formulae. Ironically, the failure of the Charlottetown Accord meant that constitutional issues would remain on the national agenda for years to come.

Sources: Cook, 1995; and Dyck, 1996.

one side and those in the rest of Canada who were tired of "having French forced down their throats" on the other, the stage was set for several decades of constitutional debate (see Box 14.3).

Aboriginal Self-Government

Canada's constitutional debate has focused on the role of our "two founding peoples"—the English and the French. Aboriginal peoples have strongly objected to this view of Canadian history. Anthropologist Olive Dickason, a Métis, has pointed out that when the Europeans first came to North America, fifty-five Aboriginal First Nations were on the continent. Each of these nations had its own government, territory, culture, and language. But Aboriginal objections to the notion of two founding peoples do not focus only on the historical issue of which groups were here first.

The more important concern is which groups will have political power in the future. Quebec claims a special status that entitles it to certain powers to govern its own people, and also certain rights within the federation such as having three Quebec members of the Supreme Court. Aboriginal peoples also claim a unique status based on their position as Canada's First Nations and have, because of that position, pursued their right to self-government.

While the issue of self-government is extremely complex, some background will help in understanding the broad issues involved. In 1763, the British government issued a royal proclamation that formed the basis for the negotiation of treaties with Aboriginal groups. Without a background in European law, Aboriginal peoples did not realize that title to the land had passed to the Crown. They were, however, still entitled to the

The need for federal assistance following the 1997 ice storm in Ontario and Quebec demonstrates the need for a strong central government in our complex society.

use and benefit of that land through their "aboriginal title" (Boldt, 1993). Following Confederation, Aboriginal peoples came under the control of the government. The mechanism for this control, the Indian Act, was passed in 1876 and gave government bureaucrats almost total control over Aboriginal peoples. The Act even went so far as to define a "person" as "an individual other than an Indian" (Hamilton and Sinclair, 1991).

The consequences of the Indian Act were profound. For example, Aboriginal children were forced to attend residential schools (which meant that generations of children were not raised by their families); traditional religious practices were restricted; Aboriginal people did not fully control their own land and could not sell agricultural products off the reserve; and the government imposed a "pass system," which restricted the right of Aboriginal peoples to travel off their reserves. Aboriginal peoples did not have full voting rights in federal elections until 1960. As sociologist Menno Boldt has observed, contemporary "Indian powerlessness has its roots in Canada's Indian policies" (1993:xvii).

In the 1960s, the federal government began to review its policies concerning Aboriginal peoples. A White Paper, tabled in 1969, proposed assimilation of Aboriginal peoples. Treaties were to be dropped, reserves were to become like neighbouring non-Aboriginal communities, and Aboriginal rights and Aboriginal land titles were to be discarded. The "Aboriginal problem" would disappear, it was thought, if Aboriginal people

became, in Pierre Trudeau's words, "Canadians as all other Canadians" (Boldt, 1993). Reaction to this paper marked a watershed in Aboriginal politics. A national campaign, which ultimately forced the government to drop its proposals, became a countrywide movement and several pan-Indian organizations, including the Assembly of First Nations, were formed (Hamilton and Sinclair, 1991). Rather than accepting the federal government's assimilationist model, Aboriginal leaders embraced nationalism. Self-government, Aboriginal rights, and land claims became the rallying points of the movement.

Some Aboriginal leaders, particularly among the Mohawks, view their bands as separate nations that have sovereign control over their lands. However, most proponents of Aboriginal self-government take the more limited view that their First Nations status gives them the "inherent" right to self-government within the Canadian federation (Boldt, 1993). They feel their status as Canada's first people, who were never conquered and who signed voluntary treaties with the Crown, entitles them to the right of self-determination and to protection of their culture and customs. These rights are not *granted* by the Canadian government, but are inherently theirs. On the other hand, the positions of the federal and the provincial governments have been that the right to self-determination could only be extended as powers delegated to Aboriginal people by government through legislation or constitutional change. Further, the powers that would be granted by government would extend only to powers now held by municipal governments rather than the much broader powers sought by Aboriginal peoples. It is difficult to predict where the current process of ending the colonial rule of Aboriginals will lead. One major change occurred in 1999, when Inuit took over government of the newly created Nunavut Territory, encompassing over 350,000 square kilometres of land in the Eastern Arctic. While the federal government accepted the inherent nature of Aboriginals' right to self-government in 1995 and are committed to dismantling the Department of Indian Affairs and Northern Development, the future form of self-government is not at all clear—not even among Aboriginal people themselves. Also, many problems must be solved along the way, including decisions about how the growing number of urban Aboriginals will be included, the applicability of the Canadian Charter of Rights and Freedoms to Aboriginal communities, and sources of funding for this new order of government. The possible separation of Quebec also creates some interesting issues. While the separatists argue strongly for their right to self-determination and their recognition as a "people," they do not accept that Aboriginal people in the resource-rich northern part of Quebec have the same right.

Future developments in self-government will be guided by the 1996 report of the Royal Commission on Aboriginal Peoples. The principles that guided the work of the Commission are the reality of societal and cultural difference; the right to self-government; the nature of Aboriginal nationhood; and the requirement for adequate land, resources, and self-reliant Aboriginal economies. The Commission concluded that history and law give all Aboriginal peoples of Canada the inherent right to govern themselves. By virtue of this right, Aboriginal peoples are entitled to negotiate freely the terms of their relationship with Canada and to establish governmental structures that they consider appropriate for their needs. This report has set the stage for future negotiations between federal and provincial governments and First Nations.

POLITICAL ISSUES FOR THE FUTURE

Economic agreements such as the North American Free Trade Agreement and the European Union are helping to create a single market for capital and services, and will inevitably lead to closer relationships between the countries involved. At the same time, budget cuts have reduced the role of federal governments in providing services to their citizens, and globalization of financial markets has dramatically reduced the ability of governments to control their own economic destinies. This has led many people to ask if the governments of modern nation-states will become obsolete in the twenty-first century. Although there has been some erosion of the powers of developed nations and an increase in the transnational nature of politics and the economy, scholars like Paul Kennedy (1993:134) argue that

> the nation-state remains the primary locus of identity for most people; regardless of who their employer is and what they do for a living, individuals pay taxes to the state, are subject to its laws, serve (if need be) in its armed forces, and can travel only by having its passport. Moreover, as new challenges emerge ... people turn instinctively (at least in the democracies) to their own governments to find "solutions."

However, the nature of the new challenges facing many governments makes it increasingly difficult for them to control events. For example, how do nations deal with terrorism within their borders, such as the 1995 bombing in Oklahoma City that resulted in the deaths of more than 150 people, including many infants and children at an on-site daycare centre, and the terrorist attacks carried out in England by the Irish Republican Army? In the aftermath of tragedies such as these, governments' responsibility for protecting citizens but not violating their basic freedoms was widely examined in national debates that inevitably will continue into the twenty-first century.

Likewise, how are nations to deal with the proliferation of arms and nuclear weapons in other countries? Will some of the missiles and warheads fall into the hands of terrorists? What should be done with the masses of nuclear waste being produced? No easy answers are forthcoming. International agencies, such as the United Nations, the World Bank, and the International Monetary Fund, face many of the same problems that individual governments do—including severe economic constraints and extreme differences of opinion among participants. Without some form of effective international control, it will be impossible to ensure that future generations are pro-

BOX 14.4 SOCIOLOGY IN GLOBAL PERSPECTIVE

NATIONALISM AROUND THE WORLD

Historian Ramsay Cook has observed that "Everyone belongs somewhere. Yet much of the conflict in the history ... of mankind has been about who belongs where" (Cook, 1995:9). Cook goes on to discuss the role of nationalism in justifying one's place in the world. Nationalism, he says, is a "doctrine asserting that humanity is naturally divided into groups with common characteristics and that by virtue of those collective traits they have a right to exercise control—sovereignty—over the particular place" (1995:9). Most Canadians have heard Lucien Bouchard and other Quebec separatists state that the Québécois constitute a "people" who must have sovereignty over their territory if their destiny is to be fulfilled. The desire for separation from Canada in Quebec is a manifestation of nationalism.

Quebec nationalists are not the only people trying to take control of what they see as their territory. Punjabis in India, Tamils in Sri Lanka, and Palestinians in the Middle East are just a few of the hundreds of nationalist groups active in the world today. Authority or justification for their claims is usually given to or provided by God, language, culture, or history. However, what ultimately decides things is power. This power may be political—the Czech Republic and Slovakia separated after a democratic vote—but more typically, it is military, as with the Iraqis and the Turks who in this way prevented the Kurds from establishing a separate homeland.

Nationalism can be a unifying force—many countries, including Germany and Italy, were formed in the late nineteenth century through the unification of smaller states with similar language and cultural backgrounds. Diverse groups were brought together under a common flag. However, nationalism can also be divisive—and often deadly. Societies based on national identity can easily become intolerant of those who do not share the same ethnicity, religion, or culture. Millions have died at the hands of oppressive nationalists. Historically, most wars have been between countries; today they are almost all within countries.

tected from environmental threats such as global warming, and water and air pollution.

While international agreements are necessary, it is likely that these agreements will be reached in different ways and involve different participants than in the past. The way in which hundreds of groups came together with governments to create the treaty banning land mines is increasingly becoming a model for involving more grassroots organizations in such negotiations. The Internet has made it much easier for such widely scattered organizations to work effectively together.

Another issue that will continue to trouble many countries is nationalism. Can Canada make an accommodation with Quebec? How will European countries adapt to the loss of national powers within the European Community? Will groups continue to make war to support their nationalistic aspirations? (Some of the more troubling aspects of nationalism are discussed in Box 14.4.) The issues surrounding nationalism must be resolved if we are to continue to move toward the dream of a peaceful world.

The twenty-first century will be a challenging one for politicians and for the citizens they represent. Can countries like Russia and Mexico, with their very weak democracies, cope with the conflicts inherent in the transition to a market economy? Will politicians around the globe be able to manage the changes that lie ahead when actions occurring elsewhere may profoundly affect their cultures, economies, and political systems? Even countries that wish to close themselves off

BOX 14.4

CONTINUED

Successful nationalist movements often carry with them the seeds of their own destruction. Yugoslavia is a case in point. Prior to 1989, the diverse elements of the country had been held together by the Communist regime. However, when the Communist domination of Eastern Europe ended, the Croats and Muslims in Yugoslavia decided to break away from the Serb-dominated Communist government and created the independent states of Croatia and Bosnia-Herzegovina. However, after years of living within the common boundaries of Yugoslavia, each of the new countries had significant ethnic minorities within its borders. These minorities in turn claimed their independence and the ensuing carnage has cost hundreds of thousands of lives and has added the words "ethnic cleansing" to our vocabulary. Ethnic cleansing is a chilling final solution to the minority problem—you simply kill or expel every man, woman, and child of a different religious or cultural background who has the misfortune of remaining within your territory.

War has become a means of expressing national identities, and grievances dating back hundreds or even thousands of years have become the justification for brutal mass murder. As large nation-states become less relevant in an era of globalization and homogenization, they lose their ability to unify. People search for a collective identity at the local level. Unfortunately, this identity is often grounded on exclusion—those who are not like us are not tolerated.

Where this will lead is uncertain. It is difficult to imagine the nationalist process continuing indefinitely. Fewer than 200 countries now exist; if every linguistic group became a nation, there would be about 8000 countries.

Source: Cook, 1995.

to outside influences must still be involved in global trade and will be unable to control what is seen, read, and heard by their citizens because of the communications revolution. Can they restore people's faith in the ability of the political system to deal with issues such as jobs, crime, and social services before voters become too cynical and critical to care which party manages their country?

CHAPTER REVIEW

What is power?
Power is the ability of persons or groups to carry out their will even when opposed by others.

What is the relationship between power and politics?
Politics is the social institution through which power is acquired and exercised by some people or groups. Government is the formal organization that has the legal and political authority to regulate the relationships among members in a society.

What are the three types of authority?
Max Weber identified three types of authority. Charismatic authority is based on a leader's exceptional personal qualities. Traditional authority is based on respect for custom. Rational-legal authority is based on law or written rules and regulations.

What are the main types of political systems?
There are four main types of contemporary political systems. In a monarchy, one person is the ruler of the

nation. In authoritarian systems, rulers tolerate little or no public opposition and generally cannot be removed from office by legal means. In totalitarian systems, the state seeks to regulate all aspects of society and to monopolize all societal resources in order to control completely both public and private life. In a democracy, the powers of the government are derived from the consent of all the people.

What are the pluralist and elite perspectives on power?

According to the pluralist (functionalist) model, power is widely dispersed throughout many competing interest groups. People influence policy by voting, joining special interest groups and political campaigns, and forming new groups. According to the elite (conflict) model, power is concentrated in a small group of elites, while the masses are relatively powerless.

Key Terms

authoritarian system 443
authority 438
charismatic authority 438
democracy 444
elite model 449
government 438
monarchy 443
pluralist model 446
political party 453
political socialization 455
politics 438
power 438
power elite 450
rational-legal authority 441
routinization of charisma 439
special interest groups 446
state 438
totalitarian system 444
traditional authority 439

Internet Exercises

1. Many forums discuss politics on the Internet. Read some of the material on Canadian politics at **http://www.yahoo.ca/Regional/ Countries/Canada/Government/Politics/Political_ Opinion**. Then go to the CNN AllPolitics page (**http://www.AllPolitics.com/**); visit the dialogue section and choose a topic that interests you. Are there differences between the way politics are presented on the American sites as opposed to the Canadian sites? Which direction do most of the people who are posting on the Canadian and American sites lean politically?

2. There are many political parties in Canada, and most use the Internet to convey their message. Visit the sites of the most prominent parties on following pages:

> The Liberal Page
> (**http://www.liberal.ca/cgi-win/core.exe**)
> The NDP Page (**http://www.ndp.ca/**)
> The Progressive Conservative Page
> (**http://www.pcparty.ca/**)
> The Bloc Québécois Page
> (**http://blocquebecois.org**)
> The Reform Party Page
> (**http://www.reform.ca**)
> The Communist Party of Canada Page
> (**http://www.communist-party.ca**)
> The Green Party (**http://green.ca/**)

How does the popularity and funding of a party affect the type of page design a party uses for its Web site? How do the different pages reflect the interests of the parties? Do some of the parties reflect regional interests, or do they all attempt to reflect Canadian interests as a whole?

3. Visit PeaCon:

(http://www.uni-muenster.de/PeaCon/)

This site contrasts military studies with peace studies. What types of issues are focused on by the military site? By the peace site?

4. The latest initiative to globalize world trade is the Multilateral Agreement on Investment (MAI). This initiative has been very controversial, and many groups around the world have opposed it. You can read the arguments supporting the agreement at the Web site of the Organization for Economic Development and Cooperation:

http://www.oecd.org/daf/cmis/mai/maindex.htm

Opposing arguments are given at the Council of Canadians Web site at:

http://www.canadians.org/mai.html

After reading this material, what impact do you think further globalization might have on Canada's sovereignty?

✺ Net Links

See the International Campaign to Ban Landmines at:

http://www.icbl.org

See Mines Action Canada at:

http://www.minesactioncanada.com

Two very important developments on the road to self-government are the Royal Commission on Aboriginal Peoples at:

http://www.inac.gc.ca/rcap/index.html

and the Nisga'a Land Agreement at:

http://www.aaf.gov.bc.ca/aaf/treaty/nisgaa/nisgaa.htm

The Web site of the Department of Indian and Northern Affairs, including the government's response to the Royal Commission on Aboriginal People is available at:

http://www.inac.gc.ca/index_e.html

Toronto lawyer Bill Henderson maintains an exceptionally useful Web site with links to a wide variety of sites dealing with Aboriginal people and issues at:

http://www.bloorstreet.com/300block/aborl.htm

The International Institute for Democracy and Electoral Assistance has a Web site that discusses women in politics. It has some interesting material on the representation of women in parliaments; go to:

http://www.idea.int/women/

For a large collection of Canadian government information on the Internet, go to:

http://dsp-psd.pwgsc.gc.ca/dsp-psd/Reference/cgii_index-e.html

Questions for Critical Thinking

1. Who is ultimately responsible for decisions and policies that are made in a democracy such as Canada, the people or their elected representatives?
2. How would you design a research project that studies the relationship between campaign contributions to elected representatives and their subsequent voting records? What would be your hypothesis? What kinds of data would you need to gather? How would you gather accurate data?
3. How does your school (or workplace) reflect a pluralist or elite model of power and decision making?
4. How is it possible to be a liberal on some issues and a conservative on others? Do you tend to be both liberal and conservative?

Suggested Readings

These books examine politics from a sociological perspective:

G. William Domhoff. *The Power Elite and the State: How Policy Is Made in America*. New York: Aldine de Gruyter, 1990.

Anthony M. Orum. *Introduction to Political Sociology: The Social Anatomy of the Body Politic* (3rd ed.). Englewood Cliffs, N.J.: Prentice-Hall, 1988.

In-depth information about politics and government is provided in this political science text:

Rand Dyck. *Canadian Politics: Critical Approaches* (2nd ed.). Toronto: Nelson Canada, 1996.

Two books that are helpful in understanding Aboriginal political issues are:

Menno Boldt. *Surviving as Indians: The Challenge of Self-Government*. Toronto: University of Toronto Press, 1993.

Olive Dickason. *Canada's First Nations*. Toronto: McClelland and Stewart, 1992.

For a good overview of Quebec separatism and related issues, you can read:

Ramsay Cook. *Canada, Quebec and the Uses of Nationalism* (2nd ed.). Toronto: McClelland and Stewart, 1995.

Marcel Rioux. *Quebec in Question*. Toronto: James Lorimer and Company, 1971.

Families in Global Perspective
    Defining *Family*
    Family Structure
    Marriage Patterns
    Descent and Inheritance
    Power and Authority in Families

Theoretical Perspectives on Families
    Functionalist Perspectives
    Conflict Perspectives
    Feminist Perspectives
    Interactionist Perspectives

Developing Intimate Relationships and Establishing Families
    Love and Intimacy
    Cohabitation
    Marriage
    Housework

Child-Related Family Issues and Parenting
    Deciding to Have Children
    Adoption
    New Reproductive Technologies
    Single Parenting

Transitions and Problems in Families
    Violence in Families: Wife and Child Abuse
    Divorce
    Remarriage

Family Diversity
    Gay and Lesbian Families
    Singlehood
    Aboriginal Families

Family Issues in the Future

CHAPTER 15

Author Robert Mason Lee's discussion of his family exemplifies the increasing complexity of modern-day family life:

"I'll be travelling at Christmas, as many men travel, to be with the girl of my dreams. She is as excited about this as I am: when I sent her the E-mail informing her of my flight plans, she replied, 'Yippee!' But she didn't linger over the mushy stuff. 'It's lunch time, Gotta go, XOXOXOXO.'

"My girl has to run when it's lunch time, because she is still only nine years old. As her father, I find myself surprised that hers has become the most constant relationship of my adult life. It wasn't supposed to be that way. The plan was to marry, start a family, and become a constant for my children. Instead, I started a family, obtained a divorce, and now find that my child has become a constant for me. Christmas is the time of year that reveals the anchors in our lives, and I no longer go home to my parents for Christmas. Yet, as an adult, my child doesn't come home to me. Instead, I go home to my child.

"Jacqueline loves nothing more than a party, and there will be a party on Christmas Eve, where the lines of marriage, remarriage, blood and love will weave a pattern of Celtic complexity. I know, for example, that my present girlfriend will have a high old time with my daughter's younger sister by my first wife's second marriage, because they are both so naughty ... It is the one time of the year when everyone gets together like this, and it is all on account of the children.

"When the party winds down, I'll be putting my daughter to bed with visions of sugarplums; on Christmas morn, I'll be there to open gifts. I've done neither of these since she was an infant ... Until now ours has been the typically divided Christmas of the typically divided home—I got Jacqueline either just before, or just after, the big day. We adapted our own traditions to make all of this seem normal.

"Although she had never previously heard of such a thing, she jumped on my worldly knowledge that Santa could be recalled for a "post-Christmas" delivery. In fact, it made sense that Santa would do such a thing, with so many kids of divorce around." (Mason Lee, 1998:A14)

FAMILIES AND INTIMATE RELATIONSHIPS

Fifty years ago, the majority of Canadian families consisted of two adults in a permanent union that produced three to five children. Other kinds of families were the exception. Today when we think of families, we think of diversity and change, and exceptions are the rule (Vanier Institute of the Family, 1998). The experiences of the family in the above narrative certainly are not unique. Children are experiencing the separation of their parents at increasingly earlier ages. Separation and divorce, remarriage, and blended or reconstituted families are a reality for many Canadians. Despite these changes, family life continues to be a source of great personal satisfaction and happiness. A recent opinion poll indicated that over 85 percent of respondents felt family life was becoming more important (Gregg and Posner, 1990).

In this chapter, we examine the diversity and complexity of families and intimate relationships. In the process, we will focus on issues such as changing patterns of marriage and divorce, work versus parenting demands, and other problems facing contemporary families. Before reading on, test your knowledge about the changing family by taking the quiz in Box 15.1.

QUESTIONS AND ISSUES

CHAPTER FOCUS QUESTION: How is social change affecting the Canadian family?

Why is it difficult to define family?

How do marriage patterns vary across cultures?

What are the key assumptions of functionalist, conflict, feminist, and interactionist perspectives on families?

What significant trends affect many Canadian families today?

Why do some analysts argue that the family as we know it will become extinct in the twenty-first century?

Despite the idealized image of "the family," North American families have undergone many changes in the past century as exemplified by the case of Carol Hoard and newborn K.C., who was conceived after his father Ron died from a heart attack. The new reproductive technologies available today raise many questions about how we define "a family."

FAMILIES IN GLOBAL PERSPECTIVE

Defining *Family*

What is a family? Although we all have a family of some form or another, and we all understand the concept of family, it is not an easy concept to define. More than ever, this term means different things to different people. For example, Hutterite families in Canada live in communal situations, in which children from about the age of three spend most of their days in school. The children also eat their meals in a communal dining hall, away from their parents. In this case, the community is the family as opposed to a traditional nuclear family.

Native peoples in Canada also tend to have a much broader idea of family membership. Children are often cared for by relatives in the extended family. A social worker may define a family as consisting of parents and children only. Some Aboriginal parents may be perceived as neglecting their children, when the parents feel they are safe and well cared for by "their family"— that is, by uncles, grandparents, or other relatives (Ward, 1998).

Similarly, gay men and lesbians often form unique family forms. Many gay men and lesbians have *families we choose*—social arrangements that include intimate relationships between couples and close familial relationships with other couples and with other adults and children (Kirby and Robinson, 1998). According to sociologist Judy Root Aulette (1994), "families we choose" include both blood and legal ties, but they also include *fictive kin*—persons who are not actually related by blood but are accepted as family members. For example, fictive kin are included in this woman's plans for procreation:

> When I go to have a kid, I'm not gonna have my sisters as godparents. I'm gonna have people around me, that are gay. No, I call on my inner family—my community, or whatever—to help me with my life. So there's definitely a family. (quoted in Weston, 1991:108)

In a society as diverse as Canada, talking about "a family" as though a single type of family exists or ever did exist is inaccurate. In reality, different groups will define their family lives in unique ways, depending on a number of factors such as their socioeconomic background, immigrant status, religious beliefs, or cultural practices and traditions (Baker, 1996).

For many years, a standard sociological definition of *family* has been a group of people who are related to one another by bonds of blood, mar-

HOW MUCH DO YOU KNOW ABOUT THE CHANGING FAMILY IN CANADA?

TRUE	FALSE	
T	F	1. The number of common-law relationships has increased dramatically over the past fifteen years.
T	F	2. Men are as likely as women to be single parents.
T	F	3. One out of every two marriages ends in divorce.
T	F	4. Polygamy, being married to more than one person at the same time, is against the law in Canada.
T	F	5. The incidence of reported spousal assault has increased dramatically in the past decade.
T	F	6. People marry at a much later age now than they did several decades ago.
T	F	7. Nearly 25 percent of all marriages are dual-earner marriages.
T	F	8. Test-tube babies are grown entirely outside the mother's womb.
T	F	9. People who marry young are more likely to divorce than those who marry later in life.
T	F	10. Most people who divorce marry again.

Answers on page 472.

riage, or adoption and who live together, form an economic unit, and bear and raise children (Benokraitis, 1997). Many people believe that this definition should not be expanded—that social approval should not be extended to other relationships simply because the persons in those relationships wish to consider themselves a family. However, others challenge this definition because it simply does not match the reality of family life in contemporary society (Eichler, 1981; Lynn, 1996; Vanier Institute of the Family, 1998). Today's families include many types of living arrangements and relationships, including single-parent households, unmarried couples, lesbian and gay couples, and multiple-generation families that include grandparents, parents, and children, for example. Historically, the state has played a significant role in determining what a family is, and family benefits have been available only to those families that fit a strictly legal definition of family. More recently a number of legal challenges have been launched in Canada regarding the definitions of *marriage* and *spouse* by same-sex couples who, because they are not legally married, have been denied the rights and benefits accorded to other families. To accurately reflect the reality of family life, we need an encompassing definition of what constitutes a family. Accordingly, we will define *families* as **relationships in which people live together with commitment, form an economic unit and care for any young, and consider**

their identity to be significantly attached to the group. Sexual expression and parent–children relationships are a part of most, but not all, family relationships (based on Benokraitis, 1997; Lamanna and Riedmann, 1997).

In our study of families, we will use our sociological imagination to see how our personal experiences are related to the larger happenings in our society. At the microlevel, each of us has our own "biography," based on our experience within a family; at the macrolevel, our families are embedded in a specific social context that has a major impact on them (Aulette, 1994). We will examine the institution of the family at both of these levels, starting with family structure and characteristics.

Family Structure

EXTENDED AND NUCLEAR FAMILIES Sociologists distinguish between extended and nuclear families based on the number of generations that live within a household. An *extended family* is a **family unit composed of relatives in addition to parents and children who live in the same household.** These families often include grandparents, uncles, aunts, or other relatives who live in close proximity to the parents and children, making it possible for family members to share resources. In horticultural and agricultural societies, extended families are extremely important;

ANSWERS TO THE SOCIOLOGY QUIZ ON THE CHANGING FAMILY IN CANADA

1. **True.** Between 1981 and 1995, the number of common-law families almost tripled. Common-law families now represent almost 12 percent of Canadian families.
2. **False.** Eighty-two percent of single-parent families in Canada are headed by a mother.
3. **False.** Current estimates are that about one-third of marriages will end in divorce.
4. **True.** Monogamy is the only legally sanctioned form of marriage.
5. **True.** This trend is in part the result of the implementation of "zero tolerance" policies, which direct that charges be laid in all domestic violence cases.
6. **True.** In 1996 the average marrying age was 27 for women and 29 for men. In 1971 it was 22 for women and 25 for men.
7. **False.** Approximately 62 percent of all marriages in Canada are dual-earner marriages—marriages in which both spouses are in the labour force.
8. **False.** Test-tube babies are babies conceived by fertilizing an egg removed from a woman with a sperm in a laboratory, and then implanting the fertilized egg (embryo) into the woman.
9. **True.** Those who marry at an early age have a higher rate of divorce than those marrying later.
10. **True.** An estimated 76 percent of divorced men and 64 percent of divorced women remarry and the majority do so within three years of their divorce.

Sources: Balakrishnan et al., 1987; Statistics Canada, 1995; Gorlick, 1995; Oderkirk and Lochhead, 1995; Richardson, 1996; Statistics Canada, 1996c, Statistics Canada, 1998d.

having a large number of family members participate in food production may be essential for survival. Today, extended family patterns are found in Latin America, Africa, Asia, and some parts of Eastern and Southern Europe (Busch, 1990).

A *nuclear family* is a family composed of one or two parents and their dependent children, all of whom live apart from other relatives. A traditional definition specifies that a nuclear family is made up of a "couple" and their dependent children; however, this definition became outdated as a significant shift occurred in the family structure. As shown in Figure 15.1, in 1996, about 51 percent of all households were composed of married couples with children under the age of 18. The second-largest family type, at 29 percent, were married couples without children living at home. This group consisted of childless couples and couples whose children no longer lived at home (empty-nesters) (Statistics Canada, 1997e).

Nuclear families are smaller than they were twenty years ago; whereas the average family size in 1971 was 3.7 persons, in 1996 it was 3.1 persons (Statistics Canada, 1997e). This decrease has been largely attributed to decisions to postpone or forego childbearing and to increases in separation and divorce rates.

"Bob and Ruth! Come on in .... Have you met Russell and Bill, our 1.5 children?"

The Far Side © 1988; Distributed by Universal Press Syndicate. Reprinted with permission.

FIGURE 15.1   **Family Structure**

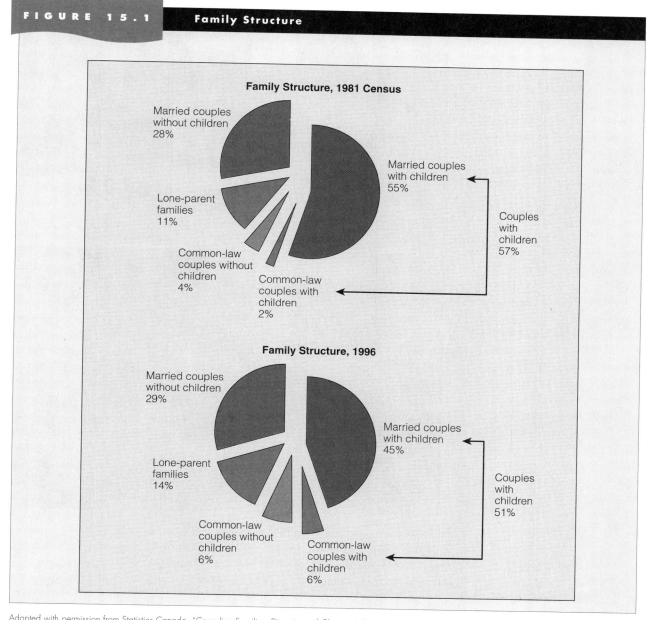

Adapted with permission from Statistics Canada, "Canadian Families: Diversity and Change," Cat. no. 12F0061XFE.

Marriage Patterns

Across cultures, families are characterized by different forms of marriage. **Marriage is a legally recognized and/or socially approved arrangement between two or more individuals that carries certain rights and obligations and usually involves sexual activity.**

In Canada, the only legally sanctioned form of marriage is **monogamy—a marriage to one person at a time.** For some people, marriage is a lifelong commitment that ends only with the death of a partner.

Members of some religious groups believe that marriage is literally "forever"; if one spouse dies, the surviving spouse is precluded from marrying anyone else. For others, marriage is a commitment of indefinite duration. Through a pattern of marriage, divorce, and remarriage, some people practise *serial monogamy*—a succession of marriages in which a person has several spouses over a lifetime but is legally married to only one person at a time.

Polygamy is the concurrent marriage of a person of one sex with two or more members of the opposite sex (G. Marshall, 1994). The most

While the relationship between a husband and wife is based on legal ties, relationships between parents and children may be established either by blood ties or by legal ties.

prevalent form of polygamy is *polygyny*—**the concurrent marriage of one man with two or more women.** Polygyny has been practised in a number of societies, including by some in parts of Europe until the Middle Ages. More recently, some marriages in Islamic societies in Africa and Asia have been polygynous; however, the cost of providing for multiple wives and numerous children makes the practice impossible for all but the wealthiest men.

Polygyny brings prestige to the men through their wives' work and the children they produce. Some researchers assert that women also benefit from polygyny because agricultural and domestic work can be shared among wives, and educated women can have children but remain independent from their husbands (Mackintosh, 1979). Others argue that polygyny is an oppressive practice, existing only for the purpose of men's sexual advantage and continuation of the oppression of women (see Thiam, 1986).

The second type of polygamy is *polyandry*—**marriage of one woman with two or more men.** Polyandry is very rare; when it does occur it usually takes place in societies in which men greatly outnumber women because of high rates of female infanticide. Polyandry often involves the marriage of a woman to two or more brothers. For example, among the Nayar and Toda in South India in the late nineteenth century, a woman who married a man also became the wife of his brothers (even those born after the marriage began). Everyone lived in the same household and rotated sexual privileges. The oldest brother was considered to be the legal father of the first two or three children; other brothers became the legal fathers of subsequent children. Even after marriage, women were considered members of their mother's household, and the children's lineage was traced through the mother's side of the family (Cassidy and Lee, 1989).

Descent and Inheritance

Even though a variety of marital patterns exist across cultures, virtually all forms of marriage establish a system of descent so that kinship can be determined and inheritance rights established. In preindustrial societies, kinship is usually traced through one parent (unilineally). The most common pattern of unilineal descent is *patrilineal descent*—a system of tracing descent through the father's side of the family. Patrilineal systems are set up in such a manner that a legitimate son inherits his father's property and sometimes his position upon the father's death. In nations such as India, where boys are seen as permanent patrilineal family members and girls are seen only as temporary family members, girls tend to be considered more expendable than boys (O'Connell, 1994). Even with the less common pattern of *matrilineal descent*—a system of tracing descent through the mother's side of the family—women may not control property. However, inheritance of property and position usually is traced from the maternal uncle (mother's brother) to his nephew (mother's son). In some cases, mothers may pass on their property to daughters.

In contrast, in industrial societies, kinship usually is traced through both parents (bilineally). The most common form is *bilateral descent*—a system of tracing descent through both the mother's and father's sides of the family.

In Canada, we have bilateral descent for determining kinship and inheritance rights, but patrilineal descent for surnames—children usually take the father's last name. The surname taken by a man's wife and their children has traditionally been the husband's family name, which symbolized that he had become the head of the new household. This tradition has recently changed in Quebec, where the law requires new wives to retain their family names. They may add their names to their husband's with a hyphen, but their children must use both names. Elsewhere in Canada, many women are choosing to retain their own family name (Baker, 1996).

Power and Authority in Families

Descent and inheritance rights are intricately linked with patterns of power and authority in families. A *patriarchal family* is a family structure in which authority is held by the eldest male (usually the father). The male authority figure acts as head of the household and holds power and authority over the women and children as well as over other males. A *matriarchal family* is a family structure in which authority is held by the eldest female (usually the mother). In this case, the female authority figure acts as head of the household. Although there has been a great deal of discussion about matriarchal societies, scholars have found no historical evidence to indicate that true matriarchies ever existed.

The most prevalent pattern of power and authority in families is patriarchy. Across cultures, men are the primary (and often sole) decision makers regarding domestic, economic, and social concerns facing the family. The existence of patriarchy may give men a sense of power over their own lives, but it also can create an atmosphere in which some men feel greater freedom to abuse women and children (O'Connell, 1994). According to some feminist scholars and journalists, hostility and violence perpetrated by men against women and children is the result of patriarchal attitudes, economic hardship, rigid gender roles, and societal acceptance of aggression (Lynn and O'Neill, 1995; Smith, 1996). As discussed later, the majority of domestic violence cases involve male perpetrators and female victims, although women can also perpetrate acts of violence against men.

An *egalitarian family* is a family structure in which both partners share power and authority equally. In egalitarian families, issues of power and authority may be frequently negotiated as the roles and responsibilities within the relationship change over time. For example, it is much easier to maintain an egalitarian relationship when a family is composed of a couple. When children are introduced, many couples experience difficulties in maintaining an equal distribution of power and authority as work and household responsibilities change.

Recently, a trend toward more egalitarian relationships has been evident in a number of countries as women have sought changes in their legal status and increased educational and employment opportunities. Some degree of economic independence makes it possible for women to delay marriage or to terminate a problematic marriage (Ward, 1998). Among gay and lesbian couples, power and authority issues also are important. While some analysts suggest that legalizing marriage among gay couples would reproduce more egalitarian relationships, others argue that such marriages would reproduce inequalities in power and authority found in conventional heterosexual relationships (Robinson, 1997; Kirby and Robinson, 1998).

To this point, we have examined a variety of marriage and family patterns found around the world. Regardless of the exact patterns followed by families, virtually all share certain common purposes and may have somewhat similar consequences for individual members.

THEORETICAL PERSPECTIVES ON FAMILIES

The *sociology of family* is the subdiscipline of sociology that attempts to describe and explain patterns of family life and variations in family structure. Functionalist perspectives emphasize the functions that families perform at the macrolevel of society, while conflict and feminist perspectives focus on families as a primary source of social inequality. By contrast, interactionists examine microlevel interactions that are integral to the roles of different family members.

Functionalist Perspectives

Functionalists emphasize the importance of the family in maintaining the stability of society and the well-being of individuals. According to Emile Durkheim, marriage is a microcosmic replica of the larger society; both marriage and society involve a mental and moral fusion of physically distinct individuals (Lehmann, 1994). Durkheim also believed that a division of labour contributed to greater efficiency in all areas of life—including marriages and families—even though he acknowledged that this division imposed significant limitations on some people.

Talcott Parsons was a key figure in developing a functionalist model of the family. According to Parsons (1955), the husband/father fulfils the *instrumental role* (meeting the family's economic needs, making important decisions, and providing leadership) while the wife/mother fulfils the *expressive role* (running the household, caring for children, and meeting the emotional needs of family members).

Contemporary functionalist perspectives on families derive their foundation from Durkheim

and Parsons. Division of labour makes it possible for families to fulfil a number of functions that no other institution can perform as effectively. In advanced industrial societies, families serve four key functions:

1. *Sexual regulation.* Families are expected to regulate the sexual activity of their members and thus control reproduction so that it occurs within specific boundaries. At the macrolevel, incest taboos prohibit sexual contact or marriage between certain relatives. For example, virtually all societies prohibit sexual relations between parents and their children and between brothers and sisters. However, some societies exclude remotely related individuals such as second and third cousins from such prohibitions. Sexual regulation of family members by the family is supposed to protect the *principle of legitimacy*—the belief that all children should have a socially and legally recognized father (Malinowski, 1964/1929).

2. *Socialization.* Parents and other relatives are responsible for teaching children the necessary knowledge and skills to survive. The smallness and intimacy of families makes them best suited for providing children with the initial learning experiences they need.

3. *Economic and psychological support.* Families are responsible for providing economic and psychological support for members. In preindustrial societies, families are economic production units; in industrial societies, the economic security of families is tied to the workplace and to macrolevel economic systems. In recent years, psychological support and emotional security have been increasingly important functions of the family (Chafetz, 1989).

4. *Provision of social status.* Families confer social status and reputation on their members. These statuses include the ascribed statuses with which individuals are born, such as race/ethnicity, nationality, social class, and sometimes religious affiliation. One of the most significant and compelling forms of social placement is the family's class position and the opportunities (or lack thereof) resulting from that position. Examples of class-related opportunities include access to quality health care, higher education, and a safe place to live.

Functionalist explanations of family problems examine the relationship between family troubles and a decline in other social institutions. Changes

Functionalist theorists believe that families serve a variety of important functions that no other social institution can adequately fulfil. In contrast, conflict and feminist analysts believe that the functionalist perspective is idealistic and inadequate for explaining problems in contemporary families.

in the economy, in religion, in the educational system, in the law, or in government programs all can contribute to family problems. For example, when Tony Bardolino was laid off from his job due to a recession, he was unable to find work for about a year; his wife, Marianne, describes the consequences:

> So he took this job as a dishwasher in this restaurant. It's one of those new kind of places with an open kitchen, so there he was, standing there washing dishes in front of everybody. I mean, we used to go there to eat sometimes, and now he's washing the dishes and the whole town sees him doing it. He felt so ashamed, like it was such a comedown, that he'd come home even worse than when he wasn't working. (quoted in Rubin, 1994:219)

Media depictions of how members of working-class families may attempt to deal with the frustrations of everyday life are discussed in Box 15.2.

Functionalists assert that erosion of family values may occur when the institution of religion becomes less important in everyday life. Likewise, changes in law (such as recognition of "no fault" divorce) contribute to high rates of divorce and dramatic increases in single-parent households. According to some functionalists, children are the most affected by these trends because they receive less nurturance and guidance from their parents (see Popenoe, 1993).

Conflict Perspectives

Both conflict and feminist analysts view functionalist perspectives on the role of the family in society as idealized and inadequate. Rather than operating harmoniously and for the benefit of all members, families are sources of social inequality and conflict over values, goals, and access to resources and power (Benokraitis, 1993).

The foundation of conflict views of the family appeared in the works of Frederich Engels, a friend and colleague of Karl Marx. In his classic work *The Origin of the Family, Private Property and the State* (1972), which was first published in 1884, Engels argued that the family in a capitalist society is an exploitive social institution that is primarily responsible for the oppression of women. Conflict theorists view the relationship between husbands and wives as similar to the relationship between capitalists and their workers. Women are dominated by men in the home in the same manner that workers are dominated by capitalists and managers in factories. Just as workers exchange their labour for a wage, so do wives exchange their domestic labour for the economic support of their husbands. While childbearing and care for family members in the home contributes to capitalism, these activities also reinforce the subordination of women through unpaid (and often devalued) labour. As a result, husbands—like capitalists—enjoy more power and privilege within the family. Engels predicted that the oppression of women would end when women moved out of the private sphere of the home and into the paid workforce. As discussed in Chapter 11, ("Sex and Gender"), women's oppression has not disappeared as a result of the dramatic increases in the number of women in the paid workforce. In many ways, it has become more prevalent as women struggle with issues of gender inequality in pay and benefits, job advancement,

BOX 15.2 SOCIOLOGY AND MEDIA

THE SIMPSONS: MIDDLE-CLASS FAMILY LIFE

In one episode of *The Simpsons*, the popular animated television series, Marge Simpson (the wife and mother) reads a "checklist for family problems" to Homer (the husband and father):

MARGE: Do you need a beer to fall asleep?

HOMER: Thank you, that'd be nice.

MARGE: Do you ever hide beer around the house?

[Homer removes a beer from the top of the commode in the bathroom.]

MARGE: Do you ever fantasize that you are someone else?

[Homer looks in the mirror, humming the tune "Can-Can."]

MARGE: Homie, I'd like you to do something for me. I want you to give up beer for a month.

HOMER: You got it! No deer for a month.

MARGE: Did you say "beer" or "deer"?

HOMER: Deer.

In this exchange, Marge represents the dutiful working-class wife who hopes to get her husband to drink less. Homer blissfully ignores her hints and suggestions because he finds that beer relaxes him after a stressful day at work. On other occasions, Homer talks with Bart (the son) and Lisa (the oldest daughter) about his drinking:

HOMER: ... Daddy has to go to a beer-drinking contest today.

BART: Think you'll win?

HOMER: Son, when you participate in sporting events, it's not whether you win or lose, it's how drunk you get.

BART: Gotcha ...

The fictional Simpson family is one of the most popular working-class families of all time; however, several decades ago, *The Simpsons* could never have been shown on television. The earliest family comedies (such as *Father*

and balancing career and home responsibilities. Other conflict analysts are concerned with the effect that class conflict has on the family. The exploitation of the lower classes by the upper classes contributes to family problems such as high rates of divorce and overall family instability.

Feminist Perspectives

Feminist theory has contributed to radical changes in the sociological study of families. Feminist theorists have been primarily responsible for redefining the concept of "the family," focusing on the diversity of family arrangements. Some feminist scholars reject the "monolithic model of the family" (Eichler, 1981:368), which idealizes one family form: the family with a male bread-winner and stay-at-home wife and children as the normal household arrangement. Feminist theorists argue that limiting our concept of family to this traditional form means ignoring or denigrating

diverse family forms, such as single-parent families, childless families, gay or lesbian families, and stepfamilies (Mackie, 1995:50). Roles within the family are viewed by feminist theorists as primarily socially constructed rather than biologically determined. Feminist scholars have challenged a number of common assumptions about family life and the roles we fulfil within families. For example, they question whether all "real" women want to be mothers, or whether the inequality between traditional husbands and wives is "natural" (Duffy, 1988:11).

In contrast to conflict theory, which focuses on class and property arrangements as the source of inequality within the family, feminist perspectives on inequality focus on *patriarchy*—**a hierarchical system of social organization in which cultural, political, and economic structures are controlled by men.** From this viewpoint, men's domination over women existed long before private ownership of property and capitalism (Mann, 1994). Women's subordination is rooted in patriarchy

BOX 15.2

CONTINUED

Knows Best, The Adventures of Ozzie and Harriet, and *Leave It to Beaver*) idealized the white middle-class nuclear family and depicted the father as a superdad. The children were respectful as compared with Bart, who says exactly what is on his mind. These early shows offered endless images of "adoring and endearing couples who were blessed with squeaky-clean kids" (Medved, 1992:129); they created a powerful and lasting vision of how the nuclear family is *supposed to be.* Unlike Homer Simpson, the male characters in 1950s and 1960s family shows were never shown consuming alcoholic beverages.

Beginning in the late 1960s and early 1970s, some situation comedies based on working-class families depicted fathers quite differently from the superdads of the middle-class. Working-class fathers were more likely to have a few beers or to talk about being "hung over" from their "night out with the boys." Working-class fathers routinely were depicted as inept or made the butt of jokes. As for Homer Simpson, his bumbling but well-intentioned behaviour has endeared him to many viewers, who feel that his character captures the essence of many men's existences. Similarly, many women identify with the overworked and underappreciated Marge Simpson, who, even as a cartoon character, realistically shows that raising a family can be a tough but rewarding experience. *The Simpsons* reflects a working-class, "we-stick-together-and-survive-on-our-own" ethic.

Sources: Based on Cantor and Cantor, 1992; Coontz, 1992; Duffy, 1992; and Medved, 1992.

and men's control over women's labour power (Hartmann, 1981). Although the division of labour may appear to be an equal pooling of contributions within the family unit, feminist scholars view women as giving much but receiving less in return. According to sociologist Patricia Mann, "Male power in our society is expressed in economic terms even if it does not originate in property relations; women's activities in the home have been undervalued at the same time as their labor has been controlled by men" (Mann, 1994:42). The power discrepancy and economic dependency created in a patriarchal family system was demonstrated in sociologist Meg Luxton's study of families in Flin Flon, Manitoba. Consider this husband's comments: "You'd never work like I do. That's hard work, real work that earns money. And that money keeps you alive. Don't you forget it" (Luxton, 1980:164). As these comments reveal, men may feel that they have earned special privileges as a result of their breadwinner status. On the other hand, a woman's economic dependence means that her needs become secondary in the family (Luxton, 1980).

Many women resist male domination. Women can control their reproductive capabilities through contraception and other means, and they can take control of their labour power from their husbands by working for wages outside the home (Mann, 1994). However, men are often reluctant to relinquish their status as family breadwinner. Why? Although only 15 percent of families in Canada are supported solely by a male breadwinner (Bradbury, 1996), many men continue to construct their ideal of masculinity around this cultural value (Livingston and Luxton, 1995).

Feminist perspectives on families primarily focus on the problems of dominance and subordination inherent in relationships. Specifically, feminist theorists have acknowledged what has been described as the "dark side of the family," focusing on research efforts on issues such as child abuse, wife abuse, and violence against the elderly (Johnson, 1996b). Feminist explanations take into account the unequal political relationship between women and men in families and outside of families (Comack, 1996b; Smith, 1985). Some feminist analysts explain wife abuse as a conscious strategy used by men to control women and perpetuate gender inequality (Harris, 1991; Smith, 1996). According to Lisa Freedman, the reason men batter women, simply put, is:

> ... because they can ... Their perceived role as the "head of the household" tells them that they can batter in order to "control" their spouses. And though society does not encourage battering, social institutions do tacitly condone it. (Freedman, 1985)

To remedy problems such as wife battering, the subordination of women in all areas of society would have to be eliminated. A starting point might be the elimination of factors fostering violence, such as media images that "convey strong messages that men are sexual predators and sexually dominant in their relationships with women" (Johnson, 1996b:7). These messages serve to "glorify and romanticize assaults and other violent behavior" (Aulette, 1994:329).

A feminist analysis of families provides not only a theoretical perspective, but also a broad movement for social change. Supported by a variety of advocacy groups and networks, feminists have brought women's private problems such as wife abuse, and the financial difficulties of economically dependent wives, into the public arena (Cheal, 1991). Feminist sociology seeks to enhance the status of women in society by validating the contributions, experiences, and viewpoints of women in all institutions, including the family (Gee, 1994).

Interactionist Perspectives

Early interactionists viewed the communication process in families as integral to the roles that different family members play. Interactionists examine the roles of husbands, wives, and children as they act out their own part and react to the actions of others. From this perspective, what people think, as well as what they say and do, is very important in understanding family dynamics.

According to sociologists Peter Berger and Hansfried Kellner (1964), interaction between marital partners contributes to a shared reality. Although newlyweds bring separate identities to a marriage, over time they construct a shared reality as a couple. In the process, the partners redefine their past identities to be consistent with new realities. Development of a shared reality is a continuous process, taking place not only in the family but in any group in which the couple participates together. Divorce is the reverse of this process; couples may start with a shared reality and, in the process of uncoupling, gradually develop separate realities (Vaughan, 1985).

Interactionists explain family relationships in terms of the subjective meanings and everyday interpretations people give to their lives. Sociologist Jessie Bernard (1982/1973) pointed out that women and men experience marriage differently and that a marriage contains two marriages: "his marriage" and "her marriage." While a husband may see his marriage very positively, his wife may feel less positive about her marriage, and vice versa. Researchers have found that husbands and wives may give very different accounts of the same event. For example, Bernard found that husbands tended to underestimate the frequency of lovemaking, while wives tended to overestimate it (Bernard, 1972).

How do interactionists view problems within the family? Some focus on the terminology used to describe these problems, examing the extent to which words convey assumptions or "realities" about the nature of the problem. For example, violence between men and women in the home often is referred to as *spouse abuse* or *domestic violence*. However, these terms imply that women and men play equal roles in the perpetration of violence in families, overlooking the more active part men usually play in such aggression. In addition, the term *domestic violence* suggests that this is the "kind of violence that women volunteer for, or inspire, or provoke" (Jacobs, 1994:56). Some scholars and activists use terms such as *wife battering* or *wife abuse* to highlight the gendered nature of such behaviour (see Macleod, 1987). However, others argue that *battered woman* suggests a "woman who is more or less permanently black and blue and helpless" (Jacobs, 1994:56).

Analysts using a social constructionist approach note that definitions concerning family violence are not only socially constructed but also have an effect on how people are treated. In one study of a shelter for battered women, analysts found that workers made decisions about whom to assist and how to assist them based on their own understanding of what constitutes a "real" battered woman (Loseke, 1992). In fact, the term

CONCEPT TABLE 15.A

THEORETICAL PERSPECTIVES ON FAMILIES

	FOCUS	KEY POINTS	PERSPECTIVE ON FAMILY PROBLEMS
Functionalist	Role of families in maintaining stability of society and individuals' well-being	In modern societies, families serve the functions of sexual regulation, socialization, economic and psychological support, and provision of social status.	Family problems are related to changes in social institutions such as the economy, religion, education, and law/government.
Conflict	Families as sources of conflict and social inequality	Families both mirror and help to perpetuate social inequalities based on class and gender.	Family problems reflect social patterns of dominance and subordination.
Feminist	Families are patriarchal institutions	Women's subordination is rooted in patriarchy and men's control over women's labour power.	Family problems such as child abuse, wife abuse, and elder abuse are the result of attempts to control women and perpetuate gender inequality.
Interactionist	Family dynamics, including communication patterns and subjective meanings people assign to events	Interactions within families create a shared reality.	How family problems are perceived and defined depends on patterns of communication, the meanings people give to roles and events, and individuals' interpretations of family interactions.

"stitch rule" is used by some shelter workers in reference to the belief that if a person does not require stitches, she is not hurt (DeKeseredy and Hinch, 1991).

Concept Table 15.A summarizes these sociological perspectives on the family. Taken together, these perspectives on the social institution of families help us understand both the good and bad sides of familial relationships. Now we shift our focus to love, marriage, intimate relationships, and family issues in Canada.

DEVELOPING INTIMATE RELATIONSHIPS AND ESTABLISHING FAMILIES

It has been said that we are "in love with love." Why is this so? Perhaps the answer lies in the fact that our ideal culture emphasizes *romantic love*, which refers to a deep emotion, the satisfaction of significant needs, a caring for and acceptance of

In Canada, the notion of romantic love is deeply intertwined with our beliefs about how and why people develop intimate relationships and establish families. Not all families share this concern for romantic love.

the person we love, and involvement in an intimate relationship (Lamanna and Riedmann, 1997).

Love and Intimacy

How have Canadians viewed love and intimacy in the past? During the Industrial Revolution in the late nineteenth century, people came to view work and home as separate spheres in which different feelings and emotions were appropriate (Coontz, 1992). The public sphere of work—men's sphere—emphasized self-reliance and independence. In contrast, the private sphere of the home—women's sphere—emphasized the giving of services, the exchange of gifts, and love. Accordingly, love and emotions became the domain of women, and work and rationality the domain of men (Lamanna and Riedmann, 1997).

Although the roles of women and men have changed dramatically in the twentieth century, they still do not always share the same perspectives about romantic love. Moreover, they typically do not express their feelings in the same manner. According to sociologist Francesca Cancian (1990), women tend to express their feelings verbally, whereas men tend to express their love through nonverbal actions, such as running an errand for someone or repairing a child's

broken toy. Women may not always interpret men's routine actions as signs of love—a fact that deeply frustrates many men, as one noted when he was asked how he showed his love for his wife.

> What does she want? Proof? She's got it, hasn't she? Would I be knocking myself out to get things for her—like to keep up this house—if I didn't love her? Why does a man do things like that if not because he loves his wife and kids? I swear, I can't figure out what she wants. (quoted in Rubin, 1976:146)

Told of his response, his wife said, "It's not enough that he supports us and takes care of us. I appreciate that, but I want him to share things with me. I need him to tell me his feelings" (quoted in Rubin, 1976:146).

Love, intimacy, and sexuality are closely intertwined. Intimacy may be psychic ("the sharing of minds") or sexual, or both. Although sexuality is an integral part of many intimate relationships, perceptions about sexual activities vary from one culture to the next and from one era to another. For example, kissing is found primarily in Western cultures; many African and Asian cultures view kissing negatively (Reinisch, 1990).

Scholars have suggested that there are six dominant sexual standards in North America (Altman, 1982; Kelly, 1992; Aulette, 1994):

1. *Heterosexual:* Sexual attraction should be limited to members of the opposite sex.
2. *Romantic:* Sex and love should go together.
3. *Marital:* Marriage should include sex; sex outside of marriage is designated as premarital or extramarital sex.
4. *Two-person:* Sex must involve two (but no more than two) people.
5. *Coital:* Sexual intercourse should occur between a man and a woman, with coitus being the ultimate sexual act.
6. *Orgasmic:* People should experience orgasm as the climax of sexual interactions; if not, something is wrong.

These dominant sexual ideologies continue to have a strong impact on how people think and feel about sexual conduct. In recent years, the sociological aspects of human sexuality have been examined in a subdiscipline known as *sociology of sexuality*—the "study of sexual attitudes and behavior, the contexts in which these occur, and the social organization of sexual relations at the individual, community, and societal level" (Schneider and Gould, 1987:23).

For over forty years, the work of biologist Alfred C. Kinsey was considered the definitive research on human sexuality, even though some of his methodology had serious limitations. More recently, the National Opinion Research Center at the University of Chicago conducted the National Health and Social Life Survey (see Laumann et al., 1994; Michael et al., 1994). Based on interviews with more than 3400 men and women aged 18 to 59, this random survey tended to reaffirm the significance of the dominant sexual ideologies. Most respondents reported that they engaged in heterosexual relationships, although 9 percent of the men said they had had at least one homosexual encounter resulting in orgasm. While 6.2 percent of men and 4.4 percent of women said that they were at least somewhat attracted to others of the same gender, only 2.8 percent of men and 1.4 percent of women identified themselves as gay or lesbian. According to the study, persons who engaged in extramarital sex found their activities to be more thrilling than those with their marital partner, but they also felt guilty. Persons in sustained relationships such as marriage or cohabitation found sexual activity to be the most satisfying emotionally and physically.

Cohabitation

Cohabitation **refers to a couple's living together without being legally married.** Many couples choose to live together before marrying or as an alternative to marriage. Although cohabitation or living together is a relatively new alternative to traditional marriage in Canada, in some parts of the world, especially Africa, Latin America, and Sweden, it has been practised for hundreds of years (Cunningham and Antill, 1995).

Attitudes about cohabitation have changed in the past two decades. In Canada, it has become increasingly popular. The census defines *common-law* partners as two persons of the opposite sex who are not legally married, but live together as husband and wife. The growth of common-law families is the strongest of all family structures (Statistics Canada, 1997). Since the early eighties, the number of persons living common-law has nearly tripled, going from 700,000 in 1981 to two million in 1995 (Statistics Canada, 1997e). Almost half of these common-law-couple families included children, whether born to the current union or brought to the family from previous unions. The proportion of people in common-law unions varies considerably by province (see Figure 15.2). In Quebec, one in four couples lives common-law, making it the province with the highest rate of common-law families.

The increase in cohabitation is thought to be associated with many recent social changes influencing family behaviours and attitudes. These include the massive entry of women into the labour market, the dissociation between sexuality and marriage and between fertility and marriage, the decline in religious practice, and the redefinition of the roles and expectations of spouses (Turcotte and Bélanger, 1997).

Those most likely to cohabit are young adults between the ages of 25 and 29. In 1996, one out of every six Canadians in this age group lived in a common-law union (Statistics Canada, 1997e). Cohabitation is even more common among Canadian university and college students, an estimated 25 percent of whom report having cohabited at some time. While "living together" is often a prelude to marriage for young adults, common-law unions are also becoming a popular alternative both to marriage and to remarriage following divorce or separation (Stout, 1994; Dumas, 1997).

For couples who plan to get married eventually, cohabitation usually follows the *two-stage marriage* pattern set out by anthropologist Margaret Mead, who argued that dating patterns in North America are not adequate preparation for marriage and parenting responsibilities. Instead, Mead suggested that marriage should occur in two stages, each with its own ceremony and responsibilities. In the first stage, the *individual marriage*, two people would make a serious commitment to each other but agree not to have children during this stage. In the second stage, the *parental marriage*, the couple would decide to have children and to share responsibility for their upbringing (Lamanna and Riedmann, 1997).

Today, some people view cohabitation as a form of "trial marriage." For others, however, cohabitation is not a first step toward marriage. Studies have found that cohabiting partners are often not as committed to their relationship as married couples are. Couples who cohabit do not face the same legal difficulties as divorcing couples. Furthermore, their relationship is regarded socially as less permanent than marriage. Studies have shown that fewer than half of such relationships culminate in marriage (McDaniel, 1994). However, if the cohabiting couple has children they are less likely to separate (Wu, 1995).

Does cohabitation contribute to marital success? Some studies have found that cohabitation

BOX 15.3   SOCIOLOGY IN GLOBAL PERSPECTIVE

FAMILY LIFE IN JAPAN

Traditionally, Japanese women have been socialized to fulfil the "good wife/wise mother" role and find satisfaction primarily in marriage and motherhood. Although Japan is experiencing many social changes, traditional values still dictate that a Japanese girl is not a woman until she marries. Popular culture supports this ideal as well. For example, smiling newlyweds and wistful brides routinely are featured in magazine ads for wedding halls.

Japanese women who currently are in the 40–50 age cohort were taught *amae*—the belief that a very strong bond should exist between a mother and her children because the dependence a child learns for the mother can be transferred to the group as the child grows older. As a result, many of these mothers gave almost twenty-four-hour-a-day care and attention to their children, including picking them up immediately when they cried and always being there for them.

However, after the children leave home, many Japanese mothers feel that they have lost their sense of purpose *(ikigai)* and begin to search for something else to occupy their time.

After years of diapering babies, overseeing homework, and meeting all of the needs of their children, many women lack self-confidence and marketable skills. Consequently, middle age becomes a time of crisis. While some take classes to widen their horizons, others may turn to drinking, out of fear of rejection or feelings of depression and boredom. At this time, some husbands are at the height of their careers and are working long hours or entertaining clients.

Today, many younger women in Japan are employed. Like women in Canada, however, they often have a second shift of housework averaging three hours a day as compared with their husbands' eight minutes a day. However, traditional roles increasingly are being challenged by women (and some men) in Japan. Many more children now are entrusted to child-care centres, whereas in the past it was unthinkable to have strangers take care of one's children. As is true with many changes in Japanese society today, the long-term effects of this change are as yet unknown.

has little or no effect on marital adjustment, emotional closeness, satisfaction, and intimacy (White, 1987). However, other evidence suggests that couples who cohabit report poorer-quality relationships than married couples (Ward, 1998). In a study that examined the relationship between cohabiting before marriage and the likelihood of divorce, researchers concluded that those who had cohabited were both less satisfied with their marriage and less committed to the institution of marriage than those who married without having first cohabited (Baker, 1996). The researchers theorized that cohabitation may contribute to people's individualistic attitudes and values while making them more aware that alternatives to marriage exist (Axinn and Thornton, 1992; Thomson and Colella, 1992).

Marriage

Despite the prevalence of divorce in our society, marriage continues to be an extremely popular institution. This was reflected in a recent survey of nearly 4000 Canadian high school students. Eighty-five percent of the teens indicated that they planned to marry and 86 percent expected their marriages to last a lifetime (Bibby and Posterski, 1992). Are these unrealistic expectations? Not at all. Despite debates regarding the demise of the institution of marriage, the fact remains that the majority of Canadians will marry at some point in their lives. Furthermore, although marriages today experience many problems, for better or worse, the majority of marriages in Canada do last a lifetime (Vanier Institute of the Family, 1998).

Why do people get married? Couples get married for a variety of reasons. Some do so because

BOX 15.3

CONTINUED

Although Japanese women have been socialized to fulfil the "good wife/wise mother" role in the past, many Japanese women currently are employed and face the same "double shift" as many Canadian women.

Sources: Based on Kitano and Chi, 1986–87; Shorto, 1991; Kitano et al., 1992; Benokraitis, 1993; and Jung, 1994.

they are "in love," desire companionship and sex, want to have children, feel social pressure, are attempting to escape from a bad situation in their parents' home, or believe that they will have more money or other resources if they get married. These factors notwithstanding, the selection of a marital partner actually is fairly predictable. Most people in Canada tend to choose marriage partners who are similar to themselves. **Homogamy refers to the pattern of individuals marrying those who have similar characteristics, such as race/ethnicity, religious background, age, education, or social class.** However, homogamy provides only the general framework within which people select their partners; people are also influenced by other factors. For example, some researchers claim that people want partners whose personalities match their own in significant ways. Thus, people who are outgoing and friendly may

be attracted to people with those same traits. However, other researchers claim that people look for partners whose personality traits differ from but complement their own.

Regardless of the individual traits of marriage partners, research indicates that communication and emotional support are crucial to the success of marriages. Common marital problems include lack of emotional intimacy, poor communication, and lack of companionship. One study concluded that for many middle- and upper-income couples, women's paid work was critical to the success of their marriages. People who have a strong commitment to their work have two distinct sources of pleasure—work and family. For members of the working class, however, work may not be a source of pleasure. For all women and men, balancing work and family life is a challenge (Baker and Lero, 1996).

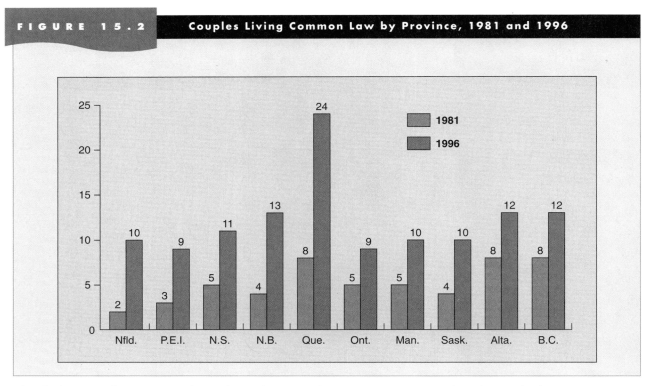

FIGURE 15.2 Couples Living Common Law by Province, 1981 and 1996

Adapted with permission from Statistics Canada, "Families: Number, Type, and Structure," Cat. no. 93-312; and "Families: Social and Economic Characteristics," Cat. no. 93-320.

Housework

Thirty years ago, most Canadian families relied on one wage-earner. Today over 60 percent of all families in Canada are *dual-earner families—* **families in which both partners are in the labour force** (see Figure 15.3). Most women who are employed hold full-time, year-round jobs. Even when their children are very young, most working mothers are employed full time. Moreover, as discussed in Chapter 11, many married women leave their paid employment at the end of the day and go home to perform hours of housework and child care. Difficulty in balancing work and family is the defining feature of family life today. Parents must make difficult decisions—decisions often driven by economic necessity—between the amount of time they spend at work and the amount of time they can be at home with their children (Canadian Council on Social Development, 1996). Sociologist Arlie Hochschild (1989) refers to this as the *second shift*—**the domestic work that employed women perform at home after they complete their workday on the job.** Thus, many women today contribute to the economic well-being of their families and also meet many, if not all, of the

domestic needs of family members by cooking, cleaning, shopping, taking care of children, and managing household routines. According to Hochschild, the unpaid housework women do on the second shift amounts to an extra month of work each year. Furthermore, women assume more responsibility for housework as the number of children in the family increases. This pattern is consistent regardless of whether the woman is employed full time or part time (Marshall, 1995). Across race, class, and culture, numerous studies have confirmed that domestic work remains primarily women's work (Canadian Council on Social Development, 1996) (see Box 15.3 for a discussion of housework in Japan).

In recent years, more husbands have attempted to share some of the household and child-care responsibilities, especially in families in which the wife's earnings are essential to family finances (Ward, 1998). In contrast, husbands who see themselves as the primary breadwinners are less likely to share housework with their wives. Even when husbands share some of the household responsibilities, however, they typically spend much less time at these activities than do their wives (Canadian Council on Social Development, 1996). Women and men perform different house-

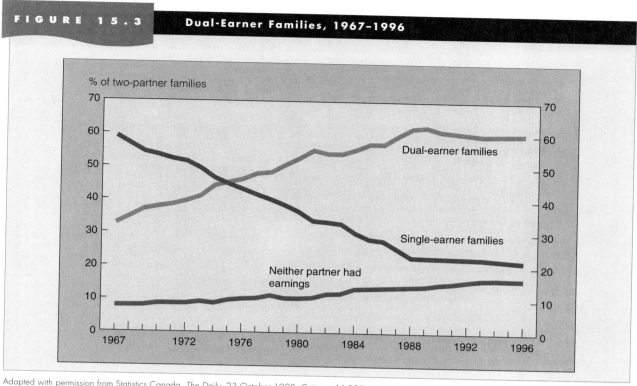

FIGURE 15.3   **Dual-Earner Families, 1967–1996**

Adapted with permission from Statistics Canada, *The Daily*, 23 October 1998. Cat. no. 11-001.

hold tasks, and the deadlines for their work vary widely. Recurring tasks that have specific times for completion (such as bathing a child or cooking a meal) tend to be the women's responsibility, whereas men are more likely to do the periodic tasks that have no highly structured schedule (such as mowing the lawn or changing the oil in the car) (Hochschild, 1989; Marshall, 1994). Many men are also more reluctant to perform undesirable tasks such as scrubbing the toilet or diapering a baby, or to give up leisure pursuits in order to contribute more time to household tasks.

Couples with more egalitarian ideas about women's and men's roles tend to share more equally in food preparation, housework, and child care (Wright et al., 1992). For some men, the shift to a more egalitarian household occurs gradually, as Wesley, whose wife works full time, explains:

> It was me taking the initiative, and also Connie pushing, saying "Gee, there's so much that has to be done." At first I said, "But I'm supposed to be the breadwinner," not realizing she's also the bread-winner. I was being a little blind to what was going on, but I got tired of waiting for my wife to come home to start cooking, so one day I surprised the

Juggling housework, child care, and a job in the paid workforce are all part of the average day for many women. Why does sociologist Arlie Hochschild believe that many women work a "second shift"?

hell out [of] her and myself and the kids, and I had supper waiting on the table for her. (quoted in Gerson, 1993:170)

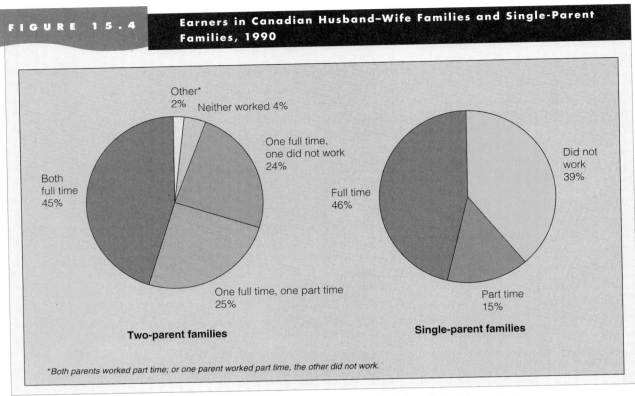

FIGURE 15.4   **Earners in Canadian Husband–Wife Families and Single-Parent Families, 1990**

Other*
2%
Neither worked 4%

One full time,
one did not work
24%

Both
full time
45%

One full time, one part time
25%

Two-parent families

Did not
work
39%

Full time
46%

Part time
15%

Single-parent families

Both parents worked part time; or one parent worked part time, the other did not work.

Source: Canadian Council on Social Development, *The Progress of Canada's Children*, Ottawa: CCSD, 1996. Reprinted by permission.

Women employed full time who are single parents probably have the greatest burden of all; they have complete responsibility for the children and the household, often with little or no help from ex-husbands or relatives.

CHILD-RELATED FAMILY ISSUES AND PARENTING

Deciding to Have Children

Not all couples become parents. Those who decide not to have children often consider themselves to be "child-free," while those who want to have children but cannot do so may consider themselves "childless." Research on voluntary childlessness in Canada reveals that one-third of childless couples decide before marriage that they do not want children (Veevers, 1980, 1991). Couples remain childless for a number of reasons including the view that pregnancy is a form of illness, or a condition that reduces one's sexual appeal; the association of motherhood with

dependency or incompetence; and the interference of children with career advancement, travelling, and marital stability. Do couples need to have children to be happy? According to the research, the answer is no. Studies have found that child-free couples report greater marital satisfaction than do couples with children (Ramu, 1984). However, despite this fact, childless couples experience higher rates of divorce. Although only about 20 percent of couples are childless, between 50 to 70 percent of divorces in Canada are obtained by childless couples (Adams, 1990). The decision not to have children often comes in conflict with our society's *pronatalist* bias, which assumes that having children is the norm and can be taken for granted, and, therefore, those who choose not to have children believe they must justify their decision to others (Lamanna and Riedmann, 1997).

Some couples experience involuntary infertility, whereby they want to have a child but they are physically unable to do so. **Infertility is defined as one year of attempting to achieve pregnancy without success** (Achilles, 1996). Infertility has become increasingly common in recent years. Research suggests that fertility problems originate in females in approximately 30 to 40 percent of cases and with males in about 40 percent of cases; in the other approximately 20 percent of the cases, the cause is unknown (Gabriel, 1996). A leading cause of infertility is sexually transmitted diseases, especially those cases that develop into pelvic inflammatory disease (Gold and Richards, 1994). It is estimated that about half of infertile couples who seek fertility treatment can be helped (Gabriel, 1996).

According to sociologist Charlene Miall (1986), women who are involuntarily childless engage in "information management" to combat the social stigma associated with childlessness. Their tactics range from avoiding people who make them uncomfortable to revealing their infertility so that others will not think of them as "selfish" for being childless. People who are involuntarily childless may choose to become parents by adopting a child.

Adoption

Adoption is a legal process through which the rights and duties of parenting are transferred from a child's biological and/or legal parents to new legal parents. This procedure gives the adopted child all of the rights of a biological child. In most adoptions, a new birth certificate is issued, and the child has no future contact with the biological parents. In Canada, adoption is regulated provincially. Therefore, adopted persons' access to information regarding their "biological parents" varies, as does their desire to access this information (Jackson, 1993).

Matching children who are available for adoption with prospective adoptive parents can be difficult. The available children have specific needs, and the prospective parents often set specifications on the type of child they want to adopt. Thousands of children are available for adoption each year in North America, but many prospective parents seek out children in developing nations such as Romania, South Korea, and India. The primary reason is that the available children in Canada are thought to be "unsuitable." They may have disabilities or illnesses, or their undesirability may be due to their being nonwhite (most prospective parents are white) or too old (Zelizer, 1985). In addition, fewer infants are available for adoption today than in the past because better means of contraception exist; abortion is more readily available; and more single parents decide to keep their babies. Consequently, the demand

Dual-earner marriages are a challenge for many children as well as their parents. While parents are at work, latchkey children often are at home alone.

for adoptive children is growing, while the supply of children available for adoption is shrinking. In Canada, there are three applicants for each public adoption and almost as many for private adoptions. In addition, in 1990, an estimated 2000 to 5000 Canadians were actively pursuing international adoptions. This trend toward private adoptions (which are more costly) means that adoption is increasingly becoming a parenting option available only to wealthy families (Vanier Institute of the Family, 1994).

New Reproductive Technologies

The availability of a variety of reproductive technologies is having a dramatic impact on traditional concepts of the family and parenthood. Since the first "test tube" baby was born in 1985, there has been an explosion of research, clinical practice, and experimentation in the area of reproductive technology. Procedures used in the creation of new life such as artificial insemination and in vitro fertilization, are referred to as methods of assisted reproduction (Achilles, 1996). These procedures, in particular, have raised some controversial ethical issues in terms of what role medical science should play in the creation of human life (Eichler, 1996).

BOX 15.4 CRITICAL THINKING

REPRODUCTIVE TECHNOLOGY AND THE FUTURE OF THE FAMILY: A FEMINIST CRITIQUE

Reproductive technology is burgeoning, and so is discussion about it by sociologists, legal experts, feminists, and philosophers. Many—but especially doctors, lawyers, and scientists—are willing to sing the praises of reproductive technology, yet they seldom stop to consider its implications for our future. The general rules appear to be: (1) what can be done should be done, and (2) if it is possible to manipulate human reproduction, then human reproduction should be manipulated.

What are some of the potential effects of reproductive technologies on human relationships? Sociologist Christine Overall considers this question in the context of the different assisted reproductive technologies available:

Fetal Sex Preselection: This term refers to various means that have been proposed for the purpose of determining, at the time of conception, the sex of the fetus. Many questions are raised with respect to fetal sex preselection: Are individuals ever justified in making use of these techniques to determine the sex of their child? If so, when and why are they justified, and if not, why are they not justified? Also, would widespread use of sex preselection techniques result in a change in the sex ratio: that is, if people could choose, would far more males than females be born? Would the use of these procedures produce a decrease in population, since people would, from the start, get

exactly the number and kind of children they want? Parents would no longer need to have "just one more child" to obtain a child of the desired sex.

The use of fetal sex preselection appears to imply that children are wanted, not for their own sake—that is, for their individual characters and abilities—but rather for the sake of the gender they represent.

Prenatal Diagnosis: This term refers to the use of such techniques as ultrasound tests, chorionic villi sampling, and amniocentesis. These procedures provide information about possible birth defects in the fetus, as well as its sex. The issue with these technologies is, will a fetus found to be defective be aborted? Can a woman freely choose to continue the pregnancy if she so desires, or is pressure exerted on her to have an abortion? A consequence of using these procedures may be that the autonomy of the woman is not increased but decreased.

Although there can be no doubt that these procedures will permit the birth of more and more healthy babies, some fear that the widespread use of prenatal diagnosis and fetal surgery will mean that in the future many children born with handicaps will tend to be regarded as unfortunate mistakes who should have been eliminated before birth.

Artificial insemination is the oldest, simplest, and most common type of assisted reproduction. It has been suggested that the word "artificial" is misleading and that a more accurate term for this procedure would be "alternative insemination" (Achilles, 1996:349).

There are several complex issues concerning the moral, legal, and social implications of artificial insemination. In most cases the woman is given no information about the donor and the

donor is not told if a pregnancy has occurred. The result of this anonymity is that neither mother nor the individuals conceived through donor insemination will have access to information regarding the biological father. With the exception of Quebec and Yukon, the laws in all provinces and territories do not provide legal protection for the participants in this procedure. In Quebec, a child born through artificial insemination is legally considered to be the child of the *social* father, that is,

BOX 15.4

CONTINUED

Surrogate Motherhood: In cases where a woman for a variety of reasons is unable to sustain a pregnancy, she may choose to hire a woman—referred to as a surrogate—to carry her child. Once again many complex questions arise when considering this procedure. What happens if the baby is born with a defect or is not the sex the couple wanted? Does the commissioning couple have to accept "damaged goods"? What is the fate of a child for whom no one wants to take responsibility? What if the surrogate mother produces not one baby but two. While the commissioning couple seem to be getting double for their money, what if they only want one? Are they entitled to both children?

One of the most serious legal complications that has so far arisen with some frequency in surrogate arrangements is that some mothers are unwilling to surrender the child after it is born. The other side of the coin is that some couples have been known to change their minds about taking the baby they have ordered, if their circumstances change. If the surrogate mother also does not want the baby, it is an unwanted child.

Women who seek work as surrogate mothers are often poor and uneducated. For them, surrogacy may appear to be a sort of last resort. In becoming surrogates, they take on work that denies their individuality, that values them only to the extent that they are successful and healthy reproductive machines. Although the practice of surrogate motherhood appears to increase our reproductive freedom by allowing some infertile women and men (at least those who are wealthy) to acquire a baby, in fact, because of its highly commercialized form, it diminishes at least some women's reproductive freedom and control. For, as the popular press has so aptly suggested, surrogacy amounts to no more than a depersonalized rent-a-womb arrangement.

New reproductive technology generates many conflicts and contradictions. It has the potential to be both an asset and a liability for the future of human relationships. Perhaps the main source of this ambiguity is the question of power that it raises. If women and men, both as individuals and collectively, share control over reproductive technology, it may be put to uses that benefit us all. But if, as now seems to be the case, most people are able to exert very little control over research into the development and applications of reproductive technology, it may be a real threat to our hopes for a humane future.

Adapted with permission from Overall, 1991.

the father who reared the child; in the Yukon, donors are protected from possible action by offspring or donor sperm recipients (Achilles, 1996).

The term *test-tube baby* is often used incorrectly to describe babies conceived through *in vitro fertilization*. An actual test-tube baby would require conception, gestation, and birth to occur outside of a woman's body. To date, this technology has not been developed (Achilles, 1996). In vitro (Latin for "in glass") fertilization involves removing an egg from a woman, fertilizing the egg with the sperm in a petri dish, and then implanting the fertilized eggs (embryos) into the woman. Critics of in vitro fertilization have suggested that the success rate of this procedure is no better than the probability of an infertile couple's having a child without medical intervention.

Another alternative available to couples with fertility problems is the use of a surrogate, or substitute, mother to carry a child for them. There are two types of surrogacy. In *traditional surrogacy* the surrogate is artificially inseminated with the father's sperm. In this case, the egg is the surrogate's. The child is biologically related to the surrogate and the father. This type of surrogacy is typically used in cases were the woman is infertile or when there is a risk of passing on a serious genetic disorder from mother to child. In the second type of surrogacy, *gestational surrogacy*, the sperm and the eggs from the infertile couple are transferred to the surrogate using an assisted reproductive technology (such as in vitro fertilization). With gestational surrogacy the surrogate carries the child but is not biologically or genetically related to it. The genetic parents are the man and woman whose eggs and sperm were donated to the surrogate.

All of this may be very confusing. One of the many reasons we have so much difficulty with these new reproductive technologies is because they are just that—new. They are new to our society and also new to our concept of the family. In fact, we have yet to develop accurate terminology to incorporate all of these new alternatives. Consider the comments of sociologist Christine Overall:

> Thanks to reproductive technology, a baby could, potentially, have five different parents: its genetic mother and genetic father, who supply the ovum and the sperm; its carrying mother, who gestates the embryo produced by the union of the ovum and sperm; and finally, its social mother and father, the individuals who rear the child produced by the carrying mother. (Overall, 1991:473)

In light of all the assisted reproductive technologies available, what does the term "parent" mean? How many "parents" does the child have? Is "mother" an accurate term for the gestational surrogate mother? The practice of surrogate motherhood also raises important questions about the position of women in society and about women's relationships to men and to their offspring (Overall, 1991).

In June 1996, legislation was tabled in an effort to address many of the serious ethical, legal, and emotional issues regarding new reproductive technologies. This bill proposed outlawing several reproductive technologies such as surrogate motherhood. The bill also prohibits sex selection for nonmedical reasons; buying and selling of human eggs, sperm, and embryos; and attempts to create animal–human hybrids. The laws pertaining to surrogacy are still evolving and so far are inadequate in addressing the complexities of these new family relationships. The new reproductive technologies available to families today involve serious ethical, social, legal, religious, and emotional considerations (see Box 15.3). However, these new reproductive technologies have enabled some infertile couples to become parents. For them, the benefits far outweigh the costs.

Single Parenting

Single parenting is not a new phenomenon in Canada. However, one of the most significant changes in Canadian families is the dramatic increase in single-parent families. In 1996, there were over 1.1 million single-parent families, an increase of 33 percent from 1986. The majority (82 percent) of these families are headed by a female (Oderkirk and Lochhead, 1995). In the past, most single-parent families were created when one parent died. Today, as shown in Figure 15.5, the major causes of single parenthood for women are divorce and separation (Canadian Council on Social Development, 1996). Recent estimates suggest that up to one-third of all Canadian mothers will be single parents at some stage in their lives (Marcil-Gratton, 1993).

Even for a person with a stable income and a network of friends and family to help with child care, raising a child alone can be an emotional and financial burden. According to sociologists Sara McLanahan and Karen Booth (1991), children in mother-only families are more likely than children in two-parent families to have poor academic achievement, higher school absentee and dropout rates, higher early marriage and parenthood, higher divorce rates, and more drug and alcohol abuse. Does living in a one-parent family cause all of this? Certainly not! Many other factors—including poverty, discrimination, unsafe neighbourhoods, and high crime rates—contribute to these problems.

Lesbian mothers and gay fathers are counted in some studies as single parents; however, they often share parenting responsibilities with same-sex partners. Due to *homophobia* (hatred and fear of homosexuals and lesbians), lesbian mothers and gay fathers are more likely to lose custody to a heterosexual parent in divorce cases (Arnup, 1995; Epstein, 1996; Robinson et al., 1998). In any case, many gay men in the United States and Canada are fathers. Some gay men are married natural fathers, others are single gay men who

In recent years, many more fathers and mothers alike have been confronting the unique challenges of single parenting.

have adopted children on their own, and still others are gay couples who have adopted children. Very little research exists on gay fathers; what does exist tends to show that noncustodial gay fathers try to maintain good relationships with their children (Bozett, 1988).

Single fathers who do not have custody of their children may play a relatively limited role in the lives of those children. Others struggle to maintain a relationship with their children. Author Robert Mason Lee describes how important his relationship with his daughter is to him, despite the fact that he is separated from her as a result of divorce:

> A man's love affair with his daughter has more in common with his love for a woman than most would care to admit—although not sexual, it is physical, passionate, and true. She calls me up just to say her "kiss box" is empty. We spend long hours on the phone making smooching noises. We bring to each other our most intimate concerns, a fervent heart, absolute trust. I like nothing better than to watch her when she's sleeping. I indulge her shamelessly. (Mason Lee, 1998:A14)

While some single fathers remain actively involved in their children's lives, others may become "Disneyland daddies" who spend time with their children in recreational activities and buy them presents for special occasions but have a very small part in the children's day-to-day lives. Sometimes, this limited role is by choice, but more often, it is caused by workplace demands on

time and energy, the location of the ex-wife's residence, and the limitations placed on the visitation arrangements.

Currently, men head about 18 percent of lone-parent families; among many of the men, a pattern of "involved fatherhood" has emerged (Gerson, 1993). For example, in a study of men who became single fathers because of their wives' deaths, desertion, or relinquishment of custody, sociologist Barbara Risman (1987) found that the men had very strong relationships with their children.

TRANSITIONS AND PROBLEMS IN FAMILIES

Families go through many transitions and experience a wide variety of problems, ranging from separation and divorce, to unplanned pregnancy, to family violence. These all-too-common experiences highlight two important facts about families: (1) for good or ill, families are central to our existence, and (2) the reality of family life is far more complicated than the idealized image found in the media and in many political discussions. Whereas some families provide their members with love, warmth, and satisfying emotional experiences, other families may be hazardous to the individual's physical and mental well-being. Because of this dichotomy in family life, sociologists have described families as both a "haven in a

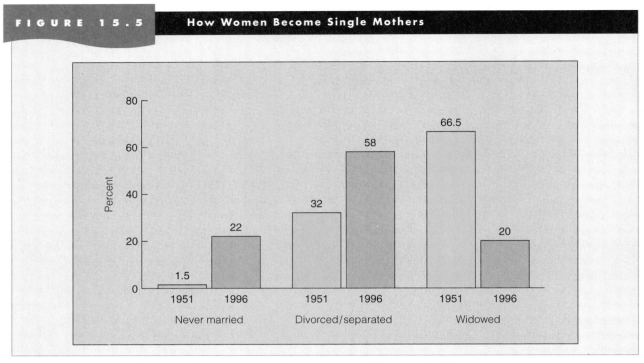

FIGURE 15.5   How Women Become Single Mothers

Source: Reprinted with permission from Statistics Canada, adapted from *The Daily*, Cat. no. 11-001, October 23, 1998.

heartless world" (Lasch, 1977) and a "cradle of violence" (Gelles and Straus, 1988).

Violence in Families: Wife and Child Abuse

Violence between men and women in the home is often referred to as spouse abuse or domestic violence. *Spouse abuse* refers to any intentional act or series of acts—whether physical, emotional, or sexual—that causes injury to a female or male spouse (Wallace, 1996). According to sociologists, spouse abuse refers not only to people who are married but also to those who are cohabiting or involved in a serious relationship, as well as those individuals who are separated or living apart from their former spouse (Wallace, 1996). As discussed in Chapter 4, *child abuse* refers to physical or sexual abuse and/or neglect by a parent or caregiver.

How much do we know about violence in families? Violence against spouses and children is clearly an extreme form of family dysfunction. However, sociologists have difficulty studying family violence because it is often hidden from outsiders and not reported to law enforcement authorities. This is particularly true in cases of child abuse because the powerlessness of children

in the family assures that most incidents remain hidden (Rodgers and Kong, 1996). Statistics on the incidence of familial child abuse capture only those cases that come to the attention of official agencies. Data on the extent of wife assault in Canada is more extensive and is based on police reports and findings from self-report studies such as the 1993 Violence Against Women (VAW) survey. Reports from these sources of information indicate that:

- Three in 10 women currently or previously married have experienced at least one incident of physical or sexual violence at the hands of a marital partner.
- In almost 40 percent of violent marriages, the children witnessed violence against their mothers. In over half of these cases, their mothers were physically injured.
- Women living in common-law relationships are much more likely to experience violence at the hands of their spouse than are legally married women.

Children who are raised in an environment of violence suffer profoundly, even if they are not the direct targets. Their own physical and emotional needs are often neglected and they may learn by example to deal with conflict through violence

Are you being hurt by your
husband or boyfriend?

Do you feel trapped
or scared?

**Wife assault
is a crime.**

**You can
get help.**

Ontario
Women's
Directorate

Although public awareness of domestic violence has
increased in recent years, society is far from finding an
effective solution for this pressing social problem.

(Canadian Council on Social Development,
1996).

Only within the last few decades have various
forms of domestic violence been defined as intolerable criminal offences. Historically, domestic
abuse was seen as a private family matter. For centuries the law permitted the male head of the
house to use force against his wife and children.
The expression "rule of thumb," which comes
from English common law, referred to the authorization a man had to beat his wife with a stick as
long as it was no thicker than his thumb.

Why has our society been slow to respond to
the problem of domestic violence, whether in the
form of child abuse, spouse abuse, or both? Until
recently, individuals and law enforcement officials
have followed a policy of *nonintervention,* which
was based on a strong reluctance to interfere in
other people's family matters. Police reacted to

calls for assistance with frustration or apathy,
viewing responses to "domestic" calls as a waste of
valuable time and resources. The general perception was that battered women could simply leave
an abusive relationship if they wanted to.

The women's movement was largely responsible for bringing the issue of wife abuse into the
public and political arenas in the 1970s. During
the same period, child sexual abuse was "discovered" and found to be much more extensive than
ever imagined (Rodgers and Kong, 1996:116).
This growing awareness led to the organization of
shelters for victims of family violence and to
changes in the criminal justice system's response
to spousal assault and child abuse. The first step in
providing protection against domestic violence
occurred in the early 1980s, when police forces
across Canada were given directives making it
mandatory for them to lay charges where there are
reasonable grounds to believe an assault has
occurred. Before these policies were implemented,
the onus was on the abused spouse to lay charges.
Many victims of spousal abuse refused to have
their spouses charged because they feared pro-
voking them to further violence. In 1983, the
sexual assault laws were changed so that men
could be charged with sexually assaulting their
wives. At the same time the Canada Evidence
Act was revised to permit wives to testify against
their husbands (Johnson, 1996a). Finally, in order
to provide better protection to children, the legislation was enacted encompassing a range of sexual
offences against children (Rodgers and Kong,
1996).

Despite legislative changes and efforts to
change attitudes, violence continues to be a much
too common occurrence in families. The research
indicates that many incidents of child and spousal
abuse remain hidden in the private domain of the
family home. According to criminologist Holly
Johnson:

> Unlike crimes that occur outside the milieu of the
> family, victims are living with their assailants; they
> often have strong emotional, financial, and physical
> bonds; many share children; and very often they
> want the relationship to continue. All of these fac-
> tors create complications for both victims and police
> officers called to the scene of the crime. (1996a:215)

In short, there are no easy solutions to a problem
as complex as family violence.

Although differences in power and privilege
between women and men do not inevitably result

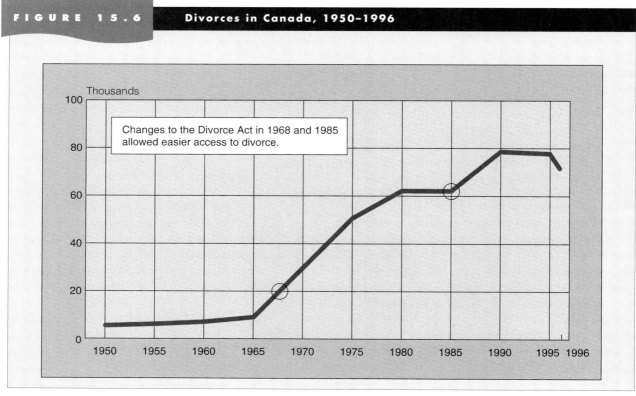

FIGURE 15.6   Divorces in Canada, 1950–1996

Changes to the Divorce Act in 1968 and 1985 allowed easier access to divorce.

Reprinted with permission in from Statistics Canada, *The Daily*, October 14, 1997.

in violence, gender-based inequalities can still produce sustained marital conflicts. In any case, a common consequence of marital strife and unhappiness is divorce.

Divorce

Divorce is the legal process of dissolving a marriage that allows former spouses to remarry if they so choose. Prior to 1968 it was difficult to obtain a divorce in Canada. A divorce was granted only on the grounds of adultery. In 1968 the grounds for divorce were expanded to include marital breakdown (i.e., desertion, imprisonment, or separation of three or more years) and marital offences (physical or mental cruelty). As shown in Figure 15.6 the divorce rate increased dramatically as a result of the wider grounds for divorce (McKie, Prentice, and Reid, 1983). In 1985 the Divorce Act introduced "no fault" provisions that made marital breakdown the sole ground for divorce. In addition, the waiting period for divorce on the grounds of marriage breakdown was reduced to one year. Once again the divorce rate jumped following the implementation of a shorter waiting

period. The amendments resulted in a record 96,200 divorces in 1987. Under no-fault divorce laws, proof of "blameworthiness" is no longer necessary. However, when children are involved, the issue of "blame" may assume greater importance in the determination of parental custody.

Have you heard statements such as "One out of every two marriages ends in divorce"? Statistics might initially appear to bear out this statement. In 1997, for example, 159,350 Canadian couples married and 67,408 divorces were granted (Statistics Canada, 1998d). However, comparing the number of marriages with the number of divorces from year to year can be misleading. The couples who are divorced in any given year are very unlikely to come from the group that married that year. In addition, in years when the economy is in a recession people may delay getting married but not divorced (McVey and Kalbach, 1995). Some people also may go through several marriages and divorces, thus skewing the divorce rate. The likelihood of divorce goes up with each subsequent marriage in the serial monogamy pattern.

In order to accurately assess the probability of a marriage ending in divorce it is necessary to use what is referred to as a *cohort approach*. This approach establishes probabilities based on assumptions about how the various age groups (cohorts) in society might behave, given their marriage rate, their age at first marriage, and their responses to various social, cultural, and economic changes. Canadian estimates based on a cohort approach are that 30 to 40 percent of marriages will end in divorce (Richardson, 1996).

CAUSES OF DIVORCE Why do divorces occur? As you will recall from Chapter 2, sociologists look for correlations (relationships between two variables) in attempting to answer questions such as this. Existing research has identified a number of factors at both the macro- and microlevel that make some couples more or less likely to divorce. At the macrolevel, societal factors contributing to higher rates of divorce include changes in social institutions, such as religion, the family, and the legal system. Some religions have taken a more lenient attitude toward divorce, and the social stigma associated with divorce has lessened. Further, as we have seen in this chapter, the family institution has undergone a major change that has resulted in less economic and emotional dependency among family members—and thus reduced a barrier to divorce. And, as Figure 15.6 demonstrates, the liberalization of divorce laws in Canada has had a dramatic impact on the divorce rate.

At the microlevel, a number of factors contribute to a couple's "statistical" likelihood of becoming divorced. Some of the primary social characteristics of those most likely to get divorced include:

- Marriage at an early age (15–19) (Balakrishnan et al., 1993)
- A short acquaintanceship before marriage (Grover, 1985)
- Disapproval of the marriage by relatives and friends (Goode, 1976)
- Limited economic resources and low wages (Nett, 1993)
- A high-school education or less (although deferring marriage to attend college may be more of a factor than education per se) (Burch and Madan, 1987)
- Parents who are divorced or have unhappy marriages (Goode, 1976)
- The presence of children (depending on their gender and age at the beginning of the marriage) (Rankin and Maneker, 1985; Morgan,

Lye, and Condran, 1988; Martin and Bumpass, 1989)

The interrelationship of these and other factors is complicated. For example, the effect of age is intertwined with economic resources; persons from families at the low end of the income scale tend to marry earlier than those at more affluent income levels. Thus, the question becomes whether age itself is a factor or whether economic resources are more closely associated with divorce.

CONSEQUENCES OF DIVORCE Divorce may have a dramatic economic and emotional impact on family members. Few children want their parents to divorce, no matter how unhappy the marriage is. Divorce for children results in the most significant changes they have experienced in their lifetimes—new relationships with each parent, often new residences, changing schedules to accommodate visitation privileges, and, in some cases, a new parental figure. Author Robert Mason Lee describes his daughter's reaction to her parents' divorce:

> The adult world of falling in and out of love, of emotions blowing fire and ice, of uncoupling and recoupling, is unknown to her. For some years it was fun to have two houses, two families, two Santas. But now she wishes that all her houses would be united. (Mason Lee, 1998:A14)

The exact number of children affected by divorce in Canada is difficult to determine because no official information is available on out-of-court custody decisions. In 1996, approximately 60,000 Canadian children were involved in custody disputes. In seven out of ten of these cases, the mother was awarded custody (Doyle Driedger, 1998; Robinson, 1998). Parental joint custody is also an option for some divorcing couples. When joint custody is a voluntary arrangement and when there is motivation to make it work, it has benefits for both children and parents (Richardson, 1996). Joint custody allows the children to maintain regular contact with both parents, which can ease the adjustment to the marriage breakup, and give parents more time to adjust to their new lives. However, this arrangement may also create unique problems for children. Siblings six-year-old Kimberley, eight-year-old Ann Marie, and eleven-year-old Philippe talk about the impact of divorce on their lives:

Kimberley: I remember Daddy used to tuck me in at night and I remember I was still waiting and he didn't because that was when he first divorced.

Ann Marie: Now we are living far from Daddy and we only get to see him a little bit of time.

Philippe: The divorce is bad because I don't always like to go from one to the other and back again. I like being with both at the same time. It gets complicated. (quoted in Doyle Driedger, 1998:41)

For most children, divorce is a difficult experience. In fact, Rhonda Freeman, director of *Families in Transition*, a Toronto divorce support service, comments, "In 25 years, I have yet to meet a child who has no effects" (Doyle Driedger, 1998:40). Today, more than one-third of all divorced mothers have below-poverty-level incomes. As discussed in previous chapters, divorce is one of the major factors contributing to the feminization of poverty, because many divorced mothers attempt to support themselves and their children on low-wage jobs and whatever child support, if any, they get from their ex-husbands.

Divorce not only changes relationships for the couple involved but also for other relatives. In some divorces, grandparents feel that they are the big losers. To see their grandchildren, the grandparents have to keep in touch with the parent who has custody. In-laws are less likely to be welcome and may be seen as being on the "other side" simply because they are the parents of the ex-spouse. Recently, some grandparents have sued for custody of minor grandchildren. They generally have not been successful except in cases where questions existed about the emotional stability of the biological parents or the suitability of a foster care arrangement.

The consequences of divorce are not entirely negative. There is no doubt that some children are better off after their parents divorce. Sociologist Susan McDaniel emphasizes that "Many are relieved that they no longer live in abusive families, with fear and violence and squabbling" (quoted in Doyle Driedger, 1998:40). For some people, divorce may be an opportunity to terminate destructive relationships. For others, it may represent a means to achieve personal growth by enabling them to manage their lives and social relationships and establish their own identity. Consider the comments of this separated, single mother of two:

It was amazing once I got my affairs in order and got my apartment. It was like the clouds parted and the sun came out. It was so amazing. I think it was the best thing that I ever did for myself. Through that whole marriage I don't think I had this much self-esteem. Everybody says, Oh, it's a tragedy. It's not a tragedy. It's a growing thing. It probably could have happened sooner. I'm glad it didn't happen later. I probably would have been a wreck. (quoted in Lynn, 1996:56)

Elizabeth Church (1996) suggests that, given the divorce rate in Canada, divorce should no longer be viewed as a deviant act, but should, rather, be considered a normal part of many people's lives. She stresses that viewing divorce in this way does not deny that divorce and remarriage cause significant upheaval in people's lives. Both divorce and remarriage are generally very painful and difficult events for some members of the family (Church, 1996:86).

Remarriage

Remarriage has been described as "the triumph of hope over experience" (Spencer, 1993:223). Most people who divorce get remarried (McVey and Kalbach, 1995) and most divorced people remarry others who have been divorced. For example, approximately one in five men and women who were legally married during the early 1990s had been married before (Statistics Canada, 1997e). Remarriage rates, however, vary by gender. At all ages, a greater proportion of men than women remarry, but both often do so relatively soon after their divorce (an estimated 76 percent of men and 64 percent of women *will* remarry)(Gorlick, 1995). Remarriage is also effected by age level and level of education. Among women, the older a woman is at the time of divorce, the lower the likelihood of her remarrying. Women who have not graduated from high school and have young children tend to remarry relatively quickly; by contrast, women with a university degree and without children are less likely to remarry (Nett, 1993). Some of these remarriages involved children from a previous relationship, thus creating stepfamilies or *blended families,* which consist of a husband and wife, children from previous marriages, and children (if any) from the new marriage. In Canada, an estimated 7 percent of children under the age of 12 live in a stepfamily (Cheal, 1996).

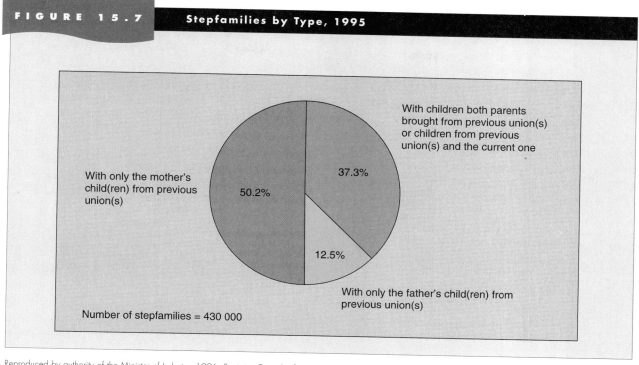

FIGURE 15.7 Stepfamilies by Type, 1995

With children both parents brought from previous union(s) or children from previous union(s) and the current one

37.3%

With only the mother's child(ren) from previous union(s)

50.2%

12.5%

With only the father's child(ren) from previous union(s)

Number of stepfamilies = 430 000

Reproduced by authority of the Minister of Industry, 1996, Statistics Canada, from *1996 General Social Survey,* Cat. no. 11-612.

Despite the increasing number of stepfamilies, they have been largely ignored in discussions of the family. In fact, the 1995 General Social Survey was one of the first to include the category "stepfamily" when collecting data to profile Canadian families. Figure 15.7 outlines the different types of stepfamilies.

At least initially, levels of family stress in stepfamilies may be fairly high because of rivalry among the children and hostility directed toward stepparents or ex-spouses (Church, 1996). As Hazel, a new stepparent, explains:

> Laura [ex-wife] would come over after school to visit with the children [Hazel's stepchildren] during the times the children were living with us. I felt really uncomfortable about having her in the house when I wasn't home … I would sit at work imagining that she was going through my kitchen cupboards, and it bothered me so much that George told Laura he didn't want her in the house unless we were there. So then she got mad and refused to come into the house at all and would stay in the car and honk the horn for Kathleen and Noel to come out. They got angry with me and told their father that I was unreasonable and I ended up feeling like the wicked stepmother. (quoted in Church, 1996:91)

In spite of these problems, however, many blended families succeed. The family that results from divorce and remarriage typically is a complex binuclear family in which children may have a biological parent and a stepparent, biological siblings and stepsiblings, and an array of other relatives including aunts, uncles, and cousins (Church, 1996).

According to sociologist Andrew Cherlin (1992), the norms governing divorce and remarriage are ambiguous. Because there are no clear-cut guidelines, people must make decisions about family life (such as whom to invite to birthday celebrations or weddings) based on their own beliefs and feelings about the people involved.

FAMILY DIVERSITY

Gay and Lesbian Families

Lesbians and gay men grow up in families, establish long-lasting, committed, emotional relationships, and sometimes become parents. Nevertheless, until recently, discussions of gay and lesbian relationships and families have been

Adoption is a complex legal process for most parents; it can be even more complicated for gay and lesbian couples.

excluded from discussions of the family. In fact, these relationships were considered by many as threatening to notions of the traditional family. Lesbians and gay men were viewed as existing entirely outside families, and many people felt that recognition of gay and lesbian relationships would result in the demise of "the family." Notions of the family that are limited to unions between members of the opposite sex are also considered *heterosexist*—**an attitude in which heterosexuality is considered the only valid form of sexual behaviour, and gay men, lesbians, and bisexuals are inferior to heterosexual people.**

In Canada, the law grants particular rights, benefits, and privileges to heterosexual relationships, especially legally married partners. Gay and lesbian couples have been prohibited from legally marrying, sponsoring their partner's immigration to Canada, obtaining custody of their children, jointly adopting children, or receiving spousal benefits and survivors pensions. This lack of recognition has had emotional, legal, and economic consequences for same-sex families (O'Brien and Weir, 1995).

Since the advent of the gay liberation movement in the 1970s, there has been a growing recognition and acceptance of homosexual relationships as family relationships (Eichler, 1997). Recently, some gay and lesbian activists have sought recognition of *domestic partnerships*— **household partnerships in which an unmarried couple lives together in a committed, sexually intimate relationship and is granted the same rights and benefits as those accorded married**

heterosexual couples (Gerstel and Gross, 1995). Benefits such as health and life insurance are extremely important to *all* couples. As Gayle, a lesbian, points out: "It makes me angry that [heterosexuals] get insurance benefits and all the privileges, and Frances [her partner] and I take a beating financially. We both pay our insurance policies, but we don't get discounts that other people get and that's not fair" (quoted in Sherman, 1992:197).

Despite the failure of the law to recognize gay marriages, many lesbian and gay couples consider themselves married and living in lifelong commitments. To make their commitment public, some couples exchange rings and vows in church, such as the Metropolitan Community Church in Toronto. Other couples, like Gayle and Frances, do not feel the need to be married. As Gayle says,

> Within my home I feel married to Frances, but I don't consider us "married." The marriage part is still very heterosexual to me. One of the reasons I don't like to associate with marriage is because heterosexual marriage seems to be in trouble. It's like booking a passage on the Titanic. Frances is my life partner; that's how I'm accustomed to thinking of her. (quoted in Sherman, 1992: 189–190)

In contrast to stereotypes of same-sex relationships as short-term, promiscuous, and noncommittal, research on homosexual relationships indicates that partnerships lasting twenty years or more are not uncommon (Peplau, 1991). In fact, the breakup rates of married or cohabiting heterosexual couples and lesbian and gay couples have been found to be approximately equal (O'Brien and Weir, 1995). However, studies have found that lesbian and gay relationships are more egalitarian than heterosexual relationships. This finding is in part attributable to the fact that in virtually all lesbian and gay relationships both partners are wage earners (Eldridge and Gilbert, 1990; Sum Quod Sum Foundation, 1997).

An increasing number of lesbian and gay males form families with children. This may occur in a variety of ways. In many cases, lesbian mothers and gay fathers may have children from a previous marriage or relationship. However, not all children in same-sex families are products of previous heterosexual relationships. Lesbian women may become pregnant through artificial insemination. Lesbian mothers and gay fathers may also form families through fostering or adoption. Unlike many heterosexual families in which both mother and father have genetic links to their children, gay and lesbian families always have a nonbiological parent. These nonbiological parents are often not regarded as parents either socially or legally. For example, nonbiological parents may not be granted admission to parent–teacher interviews, or may be denied permission to make important medical decisions for their children if the biological parent is unavailable. Anne, a lesbian mother, describes one of her encounters with the medical profession:

> You can tell the doctor three times, "Talk to me like I'm his mother; so is she," and they don't get it. Sometimes they really say, "I don't know what you're talking about." [And we'll answer,] "We're two lesbians, we're both the mother." "Huh. No, I'll talk to the one with the dress, that's safe." (quoted in Epstein, 1996:123)

Increasingly, younger lesbians and gay males are acknowledging their homosexuality and seeking acceptance from parents and other relatives. The reactions of family members range from support and acceptance to anger, denial, and rejection. These negative responses have led some researchers to conclude that families can be hazardous to the emotional and physical well-being of gay and lesbian youth. This hazard is reflected in the alarmingly high suicide rates for gay adolescents. Many families will continue to deny their child's sexual orientation years after they have "come out." One lesbian woman describes how her partner's family describes her:

Secondary-school systems are being pressured to address issues of family diversity in the classroom. In Surrey, British Columbia, a battle is being fought over the censorship of books about same-sex families.

> Her family didn't acknowledge our relationship. I would always be introduced as Chris's friend, or *our* friend even, but nothing real. But you understand that, you live with that. It became more of a personal issue when there was a kid there and I got referred to as the aunt or the live-in nanny. It would be sort of a joke, just to deal with her [mother's] own discomfort, I expect. (Epstein, 1996:122)

An encouraging sign of change is the growing number of parents who are accepting their child's sexual orientation. Canadian organizations such as *Parents and Friends of Lesbians and Gays* work to educate parents about homosexuality and assist gay youth in maintaining positive relationships with their families (O'Brien and Weir, 1995).

Recently, several high-profile court challenges have pushed the public debate toward considering gay and lesbian spouses and families as such (Eichler, 1997). For example, in 1992, the Ontario Human Rights Commission agreed that spousal benefits should be granted to the same-sex partner of a civil servant. In 1995, gay and lesbian couples in Ontario won the right to adopt the biological children of their partners. In 1998, B.C. courts ruled that both biological and nonbiological parents in same-sex families have the same legal rights regarding their children. Most recently, the Supreme Court of Canada declared

Ontario's Family Support Act unconstitutional because its definition of a spouse excludes men and women involved in same-sex relationships. This landmark decision is expected to place an estimated 1000 laws across the country into question (Gatehouse, 1999). Slowly, the laws are being challenged and much will likely change over the next decade.

Singlehood

While marriage at increasingly younger ages was the trend in Canada during the first half of the twentieth century, by the 1960s the trend had reversed, and many more adults were remaining single. In 1971, close to half of Canadians aged 20 to 24 were already married. In 1996, almost 90 percent of Canadians aged 20 to 24 were single (Statistics Canada, 1997). Currently, approximately 25 percent of households in Canada are one- or single-person households. However, this estimate includes people who are divorced, widowed, and those who have never married. Given the fact that nine out of ten Canadians marry at some time in their lives, single status is often temporary. Only an estimated 10 percent of the population will remain single throughout their lives (Nett, 1993).

Some never-married singles remain single by choice. Reasons include more opportunity for a career (especially for women), the availability of sexual partners without marriage, the belief that the single lifestyle is full of excitement, and the desire for self-sufficiency and freedom to change and experiment (Stein, 1976, 1981). Some scholars have concluded that individuals who prefer to remain single hold more individualistic values and are less family-oriented than those who choose to marry. Friends and personal growth tend to be valued more highly than marriage and children (Alwin, Converse, and Martin, 1985; Nett, 1993).

Other never-married singles remain single out of necessity. For some people, being single is an economic necessity: they simply cannot afford to marry and set up their own household. Structural changes in the economy have limited the options of many working-class young people. Even some university and college graduates have found that they cannot earn enough money to set up a household separate from that of their parents. Consequently, a growing proportion of young adults are living with one or both parents (Boyd and Norris, 1999).

Aboriginal Families

It is difficult to discuss Aboriginal families given the fact that Aboriginal peoples in Canada are by no means a homogeneous group. Aboriginal peoples are composed of many distinct nations with different histories, cultures, economic bases, and languages (Das Gupta, 1995). However, in all Aboriginal families the extended family was seen as central to both the individual and the community. The concept of family was defined very broadly. For example, to the Ojibwa, *family* referred to individuals who worked together and were bound together by responsibility and friendship as well as kinship ties. Family size averaged between 20 and 25 persons (Shkilnyk, 1985). A bandmember describes the economic cooperation and sharing that once existed within the Ojibwa family:

> Trapping kept the family together because everyone in the family had something to do; the man had to lay traps and check them; the woman skinned the animals, cooked, and looked after the kids. The grandparents helped with the kids; they taught them manners, how to behave, and told them stories about our people. The kids, if they were old enough, had work to do. (Shkilnyk, 1985:81)

Under this cooperative family system Aboriginal families were extremely successful in ensuring the survival and well-being of their members.

Four hundred years after contact with the European settlers, the current state of family disruption is evident when you consider the following data. The proportion of Aboriginal children who are removed from their homes as a result of parental abuse or neglect is ten times that of non-Aboriginal children; the proportion of Aboriginal children who commit suicide is seven times the rate of non-Aboriginal children; wife abuse among Aboriginal peoples is said to be at least seven times the national average; and mass disclosures of previously hidden sexual and physical abuse of Aboriginal children are being made (Timpson, 1995:9).

How did this happen? Sociologist Tania Das Gupta (1995) explains that the destruction of the traditional Aboriginal family was the result of interventionist strategies employed by the Canadian church and state. Families were displaced from their traditional lands, moved to reserves, and denied access to the resources that were central to the economic survival of the extended family unit. Aboriginal children were removed from their families and placed in residential schools (where they were often sexually and physically abused) or adopted by non-Aboriginal families. Generations of Aboriginal children were separated from their families and their communities, and this separation also served to sever links with Aboriginal culture and languages.

After generations of cultural and spiritual destruction, Aboriginal peoples are now reclaiming their culture. They have also united behind the goal of self-government, especially in the areas of social services and child welfare (Das Gupta, 1995). Aboriginal peoples believe in maintaining the ties between children and their natural parents, as well as caring for children within their Aboriginal communities. This they see as essential to the rebuilding of Aboriginal families in Canada. Many Aboriginal communities are striving to return to the practices and values that traditionally nourished Aboriginal family life: respect for women and children, mutual responsibility, and, above all, the general creed of sharing and caring (Royal Commission of Aboriginal Peoples, 1995:81).

FAMILY ISSUES IN THE FUTURE

As we have seen, families and intimate relationships have changed dramatically during the twentieth century. Some people believe the family as we know it is doomed. Others believe that a return to traditional values will save this important social institution and create greater stability in society. Family diversity is perceived by some as an indication that Canadian families are in "decline" or "crisis." However, as sociologist Ellen Gee reminds us, "Family diversity is the norm in Canadian society, past and present. Only for a short period in history … did Canadian families approach uniformity, centered around near-universal marriage and parenthood, family "intactness" and highly differentiated gender roles" (1995:80). The diversity in Canadian families has simply taken on new forms, with increases in common-law unions, gay and lesbian families, and single-parent and blended families.

One of the most notable changes in the past fifty years has been the increase in dual-wage earner families. The labour force participation rate of women, particularly married women, has increased dramatically. However, regardless of women's labour force participation, women are still primarily responsible for child care and domestic chores (Canadian Council on Social Development, 1996). The absence of adequate affordable child care and inflexible work hours and parental leave policies means that work is structured in ways that are not "user friendly" for family life (Gee, 1995:102). A challenge for families in the next century is to find ways to reconcile family and work contradictions. As gender roles continue to change, we can expect to see a greater degree of egalitarianism within the family.

Despite the fact that most Canadian families are made up of two wage earners, many families are still unable to make ends meet. The result is that over one million Canadian children live in families with incomes below the poverty line. Children living with a single-parent mother are the hardest hit—they are five times more likely to live in poverty than those living with two parents. According to sociologist David Cheal, "Poverty in Canada today can no longer be regarded as a minor anomaly in an otherwise progressive society" (1998:1). Canada has the second highest rate of child poverty among industrialized countries. The situation of poor families is unlikely to change in the near future without significant changes in government support and tax incentives for families with children.

One of the most disturbing issues concerning the family, and one that will continue to affect the quality and stability of family relationships in the future, is family violence. The latter part of this century has been marked by the "discovery" of the dark side of the family—child abuse (including physical, sexual, and emotional abuse), wife abuse, and elder abuse. As Elizabeth Comack notes:

> The ideal of the family as a "private domain" and a "resting place" or "sanctuary" has been shattered by the finding that violence in the home is a frequent occurrence in contemporary society, and that violence between adults is systematically and disproportionately directed against women. (Comack, 1996a:155)

Armed with the knowledge that the family is not immune to this violence, the challenge of the next century is to find effective strategies to reduce the incidence of family violence.

The final issue to consider in the twenty-first century is the impact of new reproductive technologies on families. As Margrit Eichler comments, "There is probably no other recent social development which has a potentially more far-reaching impact on the very nature of the family, on our understandings as to what it means to be a parent, and on the rights and obligations attached to this status" (1988a:280). New reproductive technologies have the capacity to revolutionize family life. Whether or not people will choose to take advantage of the possibilities, and whether or not governments will allow certain services to be delivered, remains to be seen (Baker, 1996).

Regardless of problems facing families in the twenty-first century, the family remains the central institution in the lives of most Canadians. A recent national opinion poll found that over three-quarters of Canadians regard the family as the most important thing in their lives—more important than their career or religion. Ninety-two percent of the respondents with young children at home indicated that the family is becoming *more* important to them. Finally, an overwhelming majority demonstrated their faith in the family by indicating that they want to marry and have children (although fewer children) (Vanier Institute of the Family, 1998). Individuals in families are now freer to establish the kinds of family arrangements that best suit them.

CHAPTER REVIEW

What is a family?
Families may be defined as relationships in which people live together with commitment, form an economic unit and care for any young, and consider their identity to be significantly attached to the group.

What is the difference between extended families and nuclear families?
An extended family is a family unit composed of relatives in addition to parents and children who live in the same household. A nuclear family is a family composed of one or two parents and their dependent children, all of whom live apart from other relatives.

What pattern of marriage is legally sanctioned in Canada?
Monogamy is a marriage to one person at a time. In Canada, monogamy is the only form of marriage sanctioned by law.

What are the functionalist, conflict, feminist, and interactionist perspectives on families?
Functionalists emphasize the importance of the family in maintaining the stability of society and the well-being of the individuals. Functions of the family include sexual regulation, socialization, economic and psychological support, and provision of social status. Conflict and feminist perspectives view the family as a source of social inequality and an arena for conflict over values, goals, and access to resources and power. Interactionists explain family relationships in terms of the subjective meanings and everyday interpretations people give to their lives.

How are Canadian families changing?
Families are changing dramatically in Canada. Cohabitation has increased significantly in the past two decades. With the increase in dual-earner marriages, women increasingly have been burdened by the second shift—the domestic work that employed women perform at home after they complete their workday on the job. The number of single-parent families has also increased dramatically in recent decades.

What is divorce, and what are some of its causes?
Divorce is the legal process of dissolving a marriage. At the macrolevel, changes in social institutions may contribute to an increase in divorce rates; at the microlevel, factors contributing to divorce include age at marriage, length of acquaintanceship, economic resources, education level, and parental marital happiness. Divorce has contributed to greater diversity in family relationships, including stepfamilies or blended families and the complex binuclear family.

What are some of the diverse family forms in Canada today?
Although all families share certain characteristics, each family is unique. An increasing number of Canadians are choosing to remain single—currently approximately 25 percent of households are single households. Lesbians and gay men establish long-lasting committed relationships and sometimes become parents. These families have received increasing recognition and acceptance both legally and socially in recent decades. Aboriginal families, although diverse, view the extended family as central to both the individual and the community. Aboriginal peoples believe that maintaining the ties between children and their natural parents and caring for children within their Aboriginal community are essential to rebuilding Aboriginal families in Canada.

Key Terms

bilateral descent 475
cohabitation 483
domestic partnerships 500
dual-earner families 486
egalitarian family 475
extended family 471
families 471
family we choose 470
heterosexist 500
homogamy 485
homophobia 497
infertility 488
marriage 473
matriarchal family 475
matrilineal descent 475
monogamy 473
nuclear family 472
patriarchal family 475
patriarchy 478
patrilineal descent 475
polyandry 474
polygamy 473
polygyny 474
second shift 486
sociology of family 476

Internet Exercises

1. The Internet is a good place for grassroots activism because it allows people from all over the world with similar concerns to interact with one another. Domestic violence is a concern all over the world. Using AltaVista(**http://www.altavista.digital.com/**), do a search on the term *domestic violence*. Two of the sites that should come up are the Domestic Violence Hotlines site, and the Domestic Violence: Shelters, Hotlines, and Related Services site. Visit these sites and follow some of the links to others. How can these sites help victims of violence? How can they help other centres set up aid for victims?

2. Something that has become very popular on the Internet in recent years is genealogy. Use any search engine to do a search on your last name. How many other people's names come up? To the best of your knowledge, are any of them related to you?

3. Visit the Child & Family Canada page (**http://www.cfc-edc.ca/**). Find the discussion of the influence of media on children. What conclusion can you draw from this material?

Net Links

The Vanier Institute of the Family provides the most comprehensive information on Canadian families on the Child and Family Web site; go to:

http://www.cfc-efc.ca/docs/00000001.htm

PFLAG (Parents and Friends of Lesbians and Gays) is a national organization promoting the health and well-being of gay, lesbian, and bisexual persons and their families and friends; see:

http://www.pflag.ca

Vis-à-vis, Canada's national newsletter on family violence, discussed important information on programs and initiatives aimed at reducing violence in the family. The final issue was published in the summer of 1996. Back issues are available at:

http://www.ccsd.ca/visavis.html

The executive summary of the Royal Commission on New Reproductive Technologies entitled "Proceed with Care" includes a detailed examination and recommendations of how new reproductive technologies should be handled in Canada; go to:

http://www.ualberta.ca/~ethics/bb-nrtex.htm

Questions for Critical Thinking

1. In your own thinking, what constitutes an ideal family? How might functionalist, conflict, feminist, and interactionist perspectives describe the ideal family?

2. Suppose you wanted to find out about women's and men's perceptions about love and marriage. What specific issues might you examine? What would be the best way to conduct your research?

3. Discuss the changes Canadian families are experiencing today. Are these changes an indication that the family as we know it is about to *become* extinct?

4. Could the following be considered families?
   - man, women, no children; married but living apart
   - woman, woman, child of one woman; living together. Women are a same-sex couple.
   - man, his biological child and woman (not his wife) with whom he has a sexual relationship; living together
   - four adults; sharing household for many years. None are a same-sex couple.

Suggested Readings

These comprehensive textbooks offer in-depth information on families and intimate relationships:

Nijole V. Benokraitis. *Marriage and Families: Changes, Choices, and Constraints.* Englewood Cliffs, N.J.: Prentice-Hall, 1997.

Margrit Eichler. *Family Shifts: Families, Policies, and Gender Equality.* Don Mills, Ont.: Oxford University Press, 1997.

G.N. Ramu. *Marriage and the Family in Canada Today.* Scarborough, Ont.: Prentice Hall, 1993.

These books provide new insights on the diversity of family life:

K. Ishwaran. *Family and Marriage: Cross-Cultural Perspectives.* Toronto: Thompson Educational Publishing, 1992.

Marion Lynn. *Voices: Essays on Canadian Families.* Scarborough Ont.: Nelson, 1996.

Nancy Mandell and Ann Duffy. *Canadian Families Diversity, Conflict, and Change.* Scarborough, Ont.: ITP Nelson, 1995.

A historical perspective on Canadian families may be found in:

Jane Ursel. *Private Lives, Public Policy: 100 Years of State Intervention in the Family.* Toronto: Women's Press, 1992.

For additional information about family problems, see:

Arlie Russell Hochschild. *The Second Shift: Working Parents and the Revolution at Home.* New York: Viking/Penguin, 1989.

An Overview of Education

Education in Historical–Global Perspective
        Informal Education in Preliterate Societies
        Formal Education in Preindustrial and Industrial
            Societies

Contemporary Education in Other Nations

Sociological Perspectives on Education
        Functionalist Perspectives
        Conflict Perspectives
        Interactionist Perspectives

Current Issues in Education
        Inequality in Public Schools versus Private Schools
        Dropping Out
        Declining Academic Standards and Functional
            Illiteracy
        Gender Bias in Schools
        Equalizing Opportunities for Students with
            Disabilities
        The Soaring Cost of Postsecondary Education

Education in the Future

Consider these comments made by the parent of a child in Grade 4 at a Toronto public school:

"Basically, we're disappointed with the Toronto Board of Education and have to supplement like crazy. She goes to the local school and brings home so-called creative homework, but they never learn grammar or spelling. We've had our son in a private school and they actually learn to like homework and want to achieve. The difference between the private and public system is played out in our house, and what we see doesn't say good things about the public schools."

Another parent is less critical of the school system, saying his sons are enrolled in Kumon, a private tutoring program, as a form of enrichment:

"It's a matter of customizing education for your kids. You mix it all up— swimming, piano lessons, math. Part of it involves looking ahead for your kids, and I tell mine that either they develop solid math skills or learn to say, 'Would you like fries with that?' The world is increasingly divided, and you have to prepare your kids to end up on the right side of the big divide." (Krueger, 1997:21)

EDUCATION

Both of these parents are discussing strategies to help their child "get a head start" in the race for success through educational attainment. More than ever before, education—in particular, higher education—is regarded as the key to success. Increasingly, we hear of parents opting out of the public school system altogether, placing their children in private schools, charter schools, or home schooling or "supplementing" with specialized extra-curricular programming such as computer camps, mini-universities, or private tutoring, in an effort to ensure that their child "makes it." It is apparent that only parents with the financial resources (i.e. middle- and upper-income families) can afford these programs. What effect will this have on students from low-income families? Although most social scientists agree that schools are supposed to be places where people acquire knowledge and skills, not all of them agree on how a wide array of factors—including class, race, gender, age, religion, and family background—affects individuals' access to educational achievement or to the differential rewards that accrue at various levels of academic achievement. Canada has become a "schooled society" (Guppy and Davies, 1998), and the education system has become a forum for competition. All children in Canada have an equal opportunity to participate in elementary and secondary public schools. Does this mean that all students have an equal opportunity to succeed in school? In this chapter we will explore the issue of educational inequality in Canada as well as looking at other problems facing contemporary elementary, secondary, and higher education. Before reading on, test your knowledge about education in Canada by taking the quiz in Box 16.1.

QUESTIONS AND ISSUES

CHAPTER FOCUS QUESTION: How do race, class, and gender affect people's access to and opportunities in education?

How do educational goals differ in various countries?

What are the key assumptions of functionalist, conflict, and interactionist perspectives on education?

What major problems are being faced by Canadian schools today?

The first schools in Canada, typically one-room schoolhouses, combined children of all ages. Attendance was sparse and students rarely went beyond Grades 3 or 4.

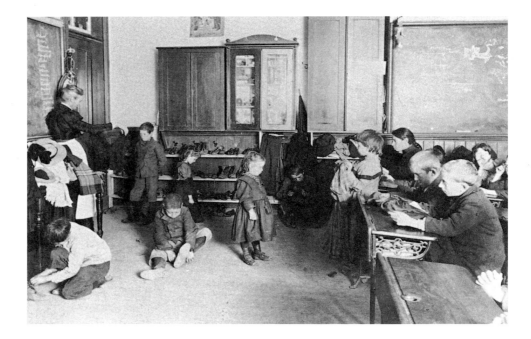

AN OVERVIEW OF EDUCATION

Education is the social institution responsible for the systematic transmission of knowledge, skills, and cultural values within a formally organized structure. Education is a powerful and influential force in contemporary societies. As a social institution, education imparts values, beliefs, and knowledge considered essential to the social reproduction of individual personalities and entire cultures (Bourdieu and Passeron, 1990). Education grapples with issues of societal stability and social change, reflecting society even as it attempts to shape it. Whereas early socialization is primarily informal and takes place within our families and friendship networks, socialization then passes to the schools and other, more formalized organizations created for the specific purpose of educating people. Today, education is such a significant social institution that an entire subfield of sociology—the *sociology of education*—is devoted to its study.

How did education emerge as such an important social institution in contemporary, industrialized nations? To answer this question, we begin with a brief examination of education in historical–global perspective.

EDUCATION IN HISTORICAL–GLOBAL PERSPECTIVE

Education serves an important purpose in all societies. At the microlevel, people must acquire the basic knowledge and skills they need to survive in society. At the macrolevel, the social institution of education is an essential component in maintaining and perpetuating the culture of a society across generations. *Cultural transmission—the process by which children and recent immigrants become acquainted with the dominant cultural beliefs, values, norms, and accumulated knowledge of a society*—occurs through informal and formal education. However, the process of cultural transmission differs in preliterate, preindustrial, and industrial nations.

Informal Education in Preliterate Societies

Preliterate societies have no written language and are characterized by very basic technology and a simple division of labour. People in these societies acquire knowledge and skills through *informal education—learning that occurs in a sponta-*

BOX 16.1 SOCIOLOGY AND EVERYDAY LIFE

HOW MUCH DO YOU KNOW ABOUT EDUCATION IN CANADA?

TRUE	FALSE	
T	F	1. Canada has the highest ratio of university students per 100,000 population of any developed nation.
T	F	2. Women and men earn about the same number of doctoral degrees in Canada each year.
T	F	3. Children of parents with high levels of education are more likely to pursue postsecondary education.
T	F	4. Aboriginal peoples are underrepresented among postsecondary graduates relative to their presence in the overall population.
T	F	5. Since the early 1990s the number of jobs requiring a university degree or postsecondary diploma has increased dramatically.
T	F	6. Students from low socioeconomic status families are more likely to have difficulty in school.
T	F	7. More young men than young women in Canada have university degrees.
T	F	8. Over half the Aboriginal population in Canada does not have a high school diploma.
T	F	9. Most Canadians today have a postsecondary education.
T	F	10. By international standards, expenditures on education in Canada are low.

Answers on page 512.

neous, unplanned way. For example, a boy might learn skills such as hunting, gathering, fishing, and farming from his father, whereas a girl might learn from her mother how to plant, gather, and prepare food, or how to take care of younger sisters and brothers. Such informal education often occurs through storytelling or ritual ceremonies that convey cultural messages and provide behavioural norms.

Formal Education in Preindustrial and Industrial Societies

Although *preindustrial societies* have a written language, few people know how to read and write, and formal education is often reserved for the privileged. Education becomes more formalized in preindustrial and industrial societies. *Formal education is learning that takes place within an academic setting such as a school, which has a planned instructional process and teachers who convey specific knowledge, skills, and thinking processes to students.* Perhaps the earliest formal education occurred in ancient Greece and Rome, where philosophers such as Socrates, Plato, and Aristotle taught elite males the necessary skills to become thinkers and orators who could engage in the art of persuasion (Ballantine, 1997). During

the Middle Ages, the first colleges and universities were developed under the auspices of the church. The history of education in Canada began with attempts by Jesuit priests and missionaries to "civilize" Aboriginal children and the children of the colonists. During this time, the church was central to the institution of education. Many of Canada's oldest universities and colleges were founded by churches. The oldest, King's College of Nova Scotia, was founded in 1789. Laval University was founded in 1852 by the Jesuits (Gaskell, 1994).

The Renaissance and the Industrial Revolution had a profound effect on education. During the Renaissance, the focus of education shifted from human depravity to the importance of developing well-rounded and liberally educated people. With the rapid growth of industrial capitalism and factories during the Industrial Revolution, it became necessary for workers to have basic skills in reading, writing, and arithmetic. However, from the Middle Ages until the end of World War I, only the sons of the privileged classes were able to attend European universities. Agriculture was the economic base of society, and literacy for people in the lower classes was not deemed important.

As societies industrialize, the need for formal education of the masses increases significantly. In Canada, the school reformers of the late 1800s

BOX 16.1

ANSWERS TO THE SOCIOLOGY QUIZ ON EDUCATION IN CANADA

1. **True.** Canada has the most university students (7197) per 100,000 population. The United States is second, with 5653 students per 100,000 population, followed by New Zealand (4232) and South Korea (4208).

2. **False.** Men earn 65 percent of doctorates, whereas women earn 35 percent. In the physical sciences, however, men earn 80 percent of the doctoral degrees, as compared to 20 percent for women.

3. **True.** Young adults (aged 26 to 35) were three times more likely to earn postsecondary credentials if their parents had a postsecondary education than if their parents had not completed high school.

4. **True.** While they represent close to 4 percent of the total population in Canada, Aboriginal peoples represent only 1.2 percent of university graduates and 2.8 percent of community college graduates.

5. **True.** Since 1990, the number of jobs requiring a university degree or postsecondary diploma has increased by 1.3 million. The number of jobs available for people without these credentials has decreased by 800,000. In short, the more education you have, the more likely it is that you will find a job.

6. **True.** For example, students from the lowest socioeconomic group score lower on tests of academic performance, are more likely to have to repeat a grade, and are more likely to require remedial education.

7. **False.** In 1996, 21 percent of women aged 20 to 29 had a university degree, compared with 16 percent of men the same age.

8. **True.** Fifty-four percent of the Aboriginal population aged 15 and over have not graduated from high school, compared with 35 percent of the non-Aboriginal population.

9. **False.** Despite rapid increases in participation rates in higher education almost 60 percent of Canadians do not have any formal education beyond high school.

10. **False.** Canada spends approximately 7 percent of the gross national product (GNP) on education, which places Canada first among developed countries along with Finland and Norway.

Sources: Statistics Canada, 1998g, 1995b, 1997h; CMEC, 1998.

were concerned that the "classical curriculum did not reflect the realities of the new economic order ... education, thus, began to be viewed as essential for national economic growth" (Gilbert, 1989:105). Ontario school reformer Egerton Ryerson promoted free schooling for all children, arguing that sending rich and poor children to the same schools would bring people closer together and create more harmony (Tepperman, 1994). By the early 1900s, mass education had taken hold in Canada, as the provinces established free, tax-supported elementary schools that were readily available to children throughout the country. **Mass education refers to providing free, public schooling for wide segments of a nation's population.**

As industrialization and bureaucratization intensified, managers and business owners demanded that schools educate students beyond Grades 3 or 4 so that well-qualified workers would be available for rapidly emerging "white-collar" jobs in management and clerical work (Bailyn, 1960). In addition to educating the next generation of children for the workplace, public schools were also supposed to serve as the primary agents of socialization for millions of European immigrants arriving in Canada seeking economic opportunities and a better life. By the 1920s, educators had introduced the "core" curriculum: courses such as mathematics, social sciences, natural sciences, and English. This core is reflected in the contemporary "back to basics" movement, which calls for teaching the "three R's" (reading, 'riting, and 'rithmetic) and enforcing stricter discipline in schools.

Contemporary education in Canada attempts to meet the needs of the industrial and postindustrial society by teaching a wide diversity of students a myriad of topics ranging from history and science to computer skills, how to balance a

Schools in Japan emphasize conformity even at an early age. Many Japanese people believe that high-quality education is a crucial factor in their country's economic success.

cheque book, and AIDS prevention. According to sociologists, many functions performed by other social institutions in the past are now under the auspices of the public schools. Many teachers feel that their job description encompasses too many divergent tasks. According to Ruth Prale, an elementary reading specialist,

> A teacher today is a social worker, surrogate parent, a bit of disciplinarian, a counselor, and someone who has to see to it that they eat. Many teachers are mandated to teach sex education, drug awareness, gang awareness. And we're supposed to be benevolent. And we haven't come to teaching yet! (quoted in Collins and Frantz, 1993:83)

At all levels of education in Canada, from kindergarten through graduate school, controversy exists over *what* should be taught, *how* it should be taught, and *who* should teach it. Do other countries have similar questions regarding their educational systems? Let's take a brief look at how educational systems are organized in Japan and Bosnia.

Contemporary Education in Other Nations

In this section we will examine schools in two nations that frequently show up in the media. Because Canada, the United States, and Japan are often compared to each other in the global marketplace, social analysts frequently compare the educational systems of these high-income countries. Similarly, since Bosnia is known for racial–ethnic factions and problems with racism, social analysts often examine how Bosnian schools handle ethnic and religious discord.

EDUCATION IN JAPAN   Like other countries, Japan did not make public education mandatory for children until the country underwent industrialization. During the Meiji Period (1868–1912), feudalism was eliminated, and Japan embarked on a new focus on youth and "bureaucratic" universal education (White, 1994). In hopes of catching up with the West, Japanese officials created an educational system and national educational goals. Education was viewed as a form of economic and national development and as a means of identifying talent for a new technological elite (White, 1994).

Today, Japanese educators, parents, students, and employers all view education as a crucial link in Japan's economic success. Japanese schools not only emphasize conformity and nationalism; they also highlight the importance of obligation to one's family and of learning the skills necessary for employment. Beginning at about three years of age, many Japanese toddlers are sent to cram schools (*jukus*) to help them qualify for good preschools.

In both cram schools and public schools, students learn discipline and thinking skills, along with physical activities such as karate and gymnastics to improve agility. By the time children reach elementary school, they are expected to engage in cooperative activities with their classmates. In some schools, children are responsible for preparing, serving, and cleaning up after the midday meal. At the end of the day, children may be seen cleaning the chalkboards and even mopping the floors, all as a part of the spirit of cooperation they are being taught.

In Japan, the middle-school years are especially crucial: students' futures are based on the academic status track on which they are placed while in middle school. Moreover, the kind of job they will hold in the future depends on the university or vocational–technical school they attend, which in turn depends on the high school they attend. By the third year of middle school, most students are acutely aware of their academic future and how their lives and friendships change as they go through the educational process:

> Middle school was fun; I was with my friends and I could throw myself into sports and I didn't have to study very hard. I couldn't be sure which of my friends would be with me in high school. Now that I am in high school, I know these will be my friends for life—they've been with me through very tough times. (White, 1994:77)

Up until high school, the student population of a school typically reflects the neighbourhoods in which children live. However, at the high school level, entrance to a particular school is based on ability: some Japanese students enter vocational schools that teach them skills for the workplace; others enter schools that are exclusively for the university-bound. Many analysts have noted the extent to which most Japanese vocational schools provide state-of-the-art equipment and instruction in fields with wide employment opportunities. Consequently, graduates of most vocational high schools do not have problems finding relatively well-paid employment upon graduation.

Typically, the instruction in Japanese high schools for the university-bound is highly structured, and all students are expected to respond in unison to questions posed by the teacher. Students are expected to be fluent in more than one language; many Japanese high schools teach English, particularly vocabulary and sentence construction. Science and math courses are challenging, and Japanese students often take courses such as algebra and calculus several years before their North American counterparts. Students must be prepared for a variety of university entrance examinations because each college and university gives its own test, and all tests occur within a few weeks of each other.

Girls and young women in Canada would likely feel stifled by the lack of educational opportunities experienced by their counterparts in Japan. Although there have been some changes, many parents and educators still believe that a good junior college education is all that young women need in order to be employable and marriageable (White, 1994). At the college and university level, the absence of women as students and professors is especially pronounced. Although a woman recently became the first-ever female president of a state-run university (Nara Women's University) in Japan, women account for fewer than 5 percent of all presidents of colleges and universities (Findlay-Kaneko, 1997). Moreover, lack of child-care facilities within the universities remains a pressing problem for women students and faculty in Japanese higher education.

Young men also experience extreme pressures in the Japanese system. In fact, high rates of school truancy occur as tens of thousands of students balk at going to school, and still others experience school-related health problems such as stomach ulcers, allergy disorders, and high blood pressure (White, 1994).

EDUCATION IN BOSNIA To understand education in contemporary Bosnia, it is important to consider the country's recent history. Located in Eastern Europe and frequently the topic of Canadian newspaper headlines because of ongoing ethnic strife, the nation of Bosnia-Herzegovina has sought to maintain its schools throughout violent clashes among its three principal ethnic groups: Muslims, Eastern Orthodox Serbs, and Roman Catholic Croats. Despite the existence of a formal peace agreement between these groups since 1995, animosities remain strong.

Recently, journalists and social scientists have found that each of the principal ethnic groups has taken control over how its children are educated and how cultural ideas are presented to them. Many schools identify and educate students by their ethnic background. For example, in history classes, students are segregated into ethnically distinct classrooms and taught different versions of history, language, and art, depending on their own ethnic and religious identity (Hedges, 1997). The fact that schools with integrated classrooms have seen an increase in conflicts between students from different ethnic groups undoubtedly contributes to this. According to one Serbian sociologist, his teenage daughter came home in tears because of comments made in her class about the Serbian "aggressors": "She would not return to school for 10 days. Many of her friends now cross

Although schools may contribute to social control in society, today's school officials find control increasingly difficult to maintain. This Toronto school has implemented a cooperative program operated by staff and students.

the line at the edge of the city to take classes in schools run by the Bosnian Serbs to avoid ridicule and harassment" (quoted in Hedges, 1997:A4).

What will happen in the future is unknown. However, the case of Bosnian education illustrates how difficult it is for teaching and learning to take place in an environment where there is little consensus about a shared sense of values, history, and what is important for the future. How much consensus exists in Canada regarding education? Let's examine that question, using three theoretical perspectives.

SOCIOLOGICAL PERSPECTIVES ON EDUCATION

Sociologists have divergent perspectives on the purpose of education in contemporary society. Functionalists believe that education contributes to the maintenance of society and provides people with an opportunity for self-enhancement and upward social mobility. Conflict theorists argue that education perpetuates social inequality and benefits the dominant class at the expense of all

others. Interactionists focus on classroom dynamics and the effect of self-concept on grades and aspirations. Each of these perspectives can provide valuable insights.

Functionalist Perspectives

Functionalists view education as one of the most important components of society. According to Emile Durkheim, education is crucial for promoting social solidarity and stability in society: education is the "influence exercised by adult generations on those that are not yet ready for social life" (Durkheim, 1956:28) and helps young people travel the great distance that it has taken people many centuries to cover. In other words, we can learn from what others already have experienced. Durkheim also asserted that *moral education* is very important because it conveys moral values—the foundation of a cohesive social order. He believed that schools are responsible for teaching a commitment to the common morality.

From this perspective, students must be taught to put the group's needs ahead of their individual desires and aspirations. Contemporary functionalists suggest that education is responsible for teaching values.

Sociologists Jonathon H. Turner, Leonard Beeghley, and Charles H. Powers summarize some of Durkheim's ideas on the functions of education:

> The commitment to the common morality must be learned in schools, where the teacher operates as the functional equivalent of the priest. The teacher gives young students an understanding of and a reverence for the nature of the society and the need to have a morality that regulates passions and provides attachments to groupings organized to pursue societal goals. Such educational socialization must assure that the common morality is a part of the students' motivational needs ... their cognitive orientations ... and their self-control processes. (1995:46)

Functionalists emphasize that "shared" values should be transmitted by schools from kindergarten through university. However, not all analysts agree on what those shared values should be or what functions education should serve in contemporary societies. In analyzing the values and functions of education, sociologists using a functionalist framework distinguish between manifest and latent functions. Manifest functions and latent functions are compared in Figure 16.1.

FIGURE 16.1 Manifest and Latent Functions of Education

Manifest functions—open, stated, and intended goals or consequences of activities within an organization or institution. In education, these are:

- socialization
- transmission of culture
- social control
- social placement
- change and innovation

Latent functions—hidden, unstated, and sometimes unintended consequences of activities within an organization. In education, these include:

- matchmaking and production of social networks
- restricting some activities
- creation of a generation gap

MANIFEST FUNCTIONS OF EDUCATION Some functions of education are *manifest functions*—previously defined as open, stated, and intended goals or consequences of activities within an organization or institution. Education serves five major manifest functions in society:

1. *Socialization.* From kindergarten through university, schools teach students the student role, specific academic subjects, and political socialization. In kindergarten, children learn the appropriate attitudes and behaviour for the student role (Ballantine, 1997). In primary and secondary schools, students are taught specific subject matter appropriate to their age, skill level, and previous educational experience. At the university level, students focus on more detailed knowledge of subjects they have previously studied and are exposed to new areas of study and research. Throughout their schooling, students receive

political socialization in the form of history and civics lessons.

2. *Transmission of culture.* Schools transmit cultural norms and values to each new generation and play an active part in the process of assimilation, whereby recent immigrants learn dominant cultural values, attitudes, and behaviour so that they can be productive members of society. However, questions remain as to *whose* culture is being transmitted. Because of the great diversity in Canada today, it is virtually impossible to define a single culture.

3. *Social control.* Schools are responsible for teaching values such as discipline, respect, obedience, punctuality, and perseverance. Schools teach conformity by encouraging young people to be good students, conscientious future workers, and law-abiding citizens. The teaching of conformity rests primarily

with classroom teachers, as Adele Jones, a high-school math teacher, explains:

> I tell kids from the start that I'm not out to fail them, but they've got to understand certain concepts in order to go on to college. If they do four things, they'll do fine: pay attention in class, do their homework, study, and ask questions. They need to understand that quizzes count, that coming to class shows a commitment to learn, that doing homework, studying for tests, and participating in class tell me they want to learn ... I set my standards high so my kids can do likewise; is it therefore my fault if they choose not to do the work? (Jones, 1994:23)

4. *Social placement.* Schools are responsible for identifying the most qualified people to fill the positions available in society. As a result, students are channelled into programs based on individual ability and academic achievement. Graduates receive the appropriate credentials to enter the paid labour force.

5. *Change and innovation.* Schools are a source of change and innovation. As student populations change over time, new programs are introduced to meet societal needs; for example, sex education, drug education, and multicultural studies have been implemented in some schools to help students learn about pressing social issues. Innovation in the form of new knowledge is required in colleges and universities. Faculty members are encouraged—and sometimes required—to engage in research and to share the results with students, colleagues, and others. In medical schools, for example, innovative technologies (such as new drugs) and new techniques (such as gene splicing) are developed and tested.

LATENT FUNCTIONS OF EDUCATION All social institutions, including education, have *latent functions*—previously defined as hidden, unstated, and sometimes unintended consequences of activities within an organization or institution. Education serves at least three latent functions:

1. *Restricting some activities.* Early in the twentieth century, all provinces passed *mandatory education laws* that require children to attend school until they reach a specified age (usually the age of 16) or complete a minimum level of formal education (generally completion of Grade 8). The assumption was that an educated citizenry and workforce are necessary for the smooth functioning of democracy and capitalism. Out of these laws grew one latent function of education, which is to keep students off the street and out of the full-time job market for a number of years, thus helping keep unemployment within reasonable bounds (Braverman, 1974).

2. *Matchmaking and production of social networks.* Because schools bring together people of similar ages, social class, and race/ethnicity, young people often meet future marriage partners and develop social networks that may last for many years.

3. *Creation of a generation gap.* Students may learn information in school that contradicts beliefs held by their parents or their religion. Debates over the content of textbooks and library books typically centre on information that parents deem unacceptable for their children. When education conflicts with parental attitudes and beliefs, a generation gap is created if students embrace the newly acquired perspective.

Functionalists acknowledge that education has certain dysfunctions. Some analysts argue that education systems in Canada are not promoting the high-level skills in reading, writing, science, and mathematics that are needed in the workplace and the global economy. For example, mathematics education in Canada does not compare favourably with that found in many other industrialized countries (see Table 16.1). In the 1996 Third International Math and Science Study—a comprehensive study of science and math achievement by students in forty-one countries—Canadian nine-year-olds scored lower on the math exam than did students in at least twelve other nations, including Singapore, Korea, Japan, and Hong Kong (*Time*, 1997:67). However, analysts do not agree on what these score differences mean. For example, Japanese students may outperform their Canadian counterparts because their schools are more structured, and teachers focus on drill and practice (Celis, 1994). Educators David C. Berliner and Bruce J. Biddle (1995) believe that data on cross-cultural differences in educational attainment actually involve comparisons of "apples" and "oranges": They found that the International Math and Science Study compares the achievement of Grade 8 Japanese students who have already taken algebra with the achievement of North American students, who typically take such courses a year or two later. Among Canadian students who had already completed an

TABLE 16.1	INTERNATIONAL MATH AND SCIENCE SCORES	

Results of the 1996 Third International Math and Science Study (selected nations).

COUNTRY	MATH SCORE	SCIENCE SCORE
Singapore	626	547
Korea	611	597
Japan	597	574
Hong Kong	587	533
Netherlands	577	557
Czech Republic	567	557
Austria	559	565
Slovenia	552	546
Ireland	550	539
Hungary	548	532
Australia	546	562
United States	545	565
Canada	**532**	**549**
Scotland	520	536

Source: *Time*, 1997b.

algebra course, most did at least as well as their Japanese counterparts on the mathematics exam (Barlow and Robertson, 1994). Are Canadian schools dysfunctional if students are not taking algebra courses sooner? According to some functionalists, limited academic demands placed upon students are a dysfunctional aspect of public schools in this country.

Conflict Perspectives

Conflict theorists do not believe that public schools reduce social inequality in society; rather, they believe that schools often perpetuate class, racial–ethnic, and gender inequalities as some groups seek to maintain their privileged position at the expense of others (Apple, 1980; Ballantine, 1997; Curtis, Grabb, and Guppy, 1999).

CULTURAL CAPITAL AND CLASS REPRODUCTION

Although many factors—including intelligence, family income, motivation, and previous achievement—are important in determining how much education a person will attain, conflict theorists argue that access to quality education is closely related to social class. From this approach, education is a vehicle for reproducing existing class

relationships. According to French sociologist Pierre Bourdieu, the school legitimates and reinforces the social elites by engaging in specific practices that uphold the patterns of behaviour and the attitudes of the dominant class. Bourdieu asserts that students from diverse class backgrounds come to school with differing amounts of *cultural capital*—**social assets that include values, beliefs, attitudes, and competencies in language and culture** (Bourdieu and Passeron, 1990). Cultural capital involves "proper" attitudes toward education, socially approved dress and manners, and knowledge about books, art, music, and other forms of high and popular culture. Middle- and upper-income parents endow their children with more cultural capital than do working-class and poverty-level parents. Because cultural capital is essential for acquiring an education, children with less cultural capital have fewer opportunities to succeed in school. For example, standardized tests that are used to group students by ability and to assign them to classes often measure students' cultural capital rather than their "natural" intelligence or aptitude. Thus, a circular effect occurs: Students with dominant cultural values are more highly rewarded by the educational system; in turn, the educational system teaches and reinforces those values that sustain the elite's position in society.

In her study of working-class women who returned to school after dropping out, sociologist Wendy Luttrell (1997:113–114) concluded that schools in the United States play a critical role in class reproduction and determining people's self concept and identity:

> School denied but at the same time protected certain students' unearned advantages related to class, gender, and skin color in ways that made the women doubt their own value, voice, and abilities … [When] the women were degraded by teachers and school officials for their speech, styles of dress, deportment, physical appearance, skin color, and forms of knowledge, they learned to recognize as "intelligent" or "valuable" only the styles, traits, and knowledge possessed by the economically advantaged students[:] … white, middle-class … behaviors and [appearance] … and urban or suburban mannerisms and styles of speech. Most important, [it was assumed that] those who possessed such cultural capital [were] entitled to their superior positions.

TRACKING AND SOCIAL INEQUALITY   Closely linked to the issue of cultural capital is how tracking in schools is related to social inequality. Conflict theorists who study ability grouping focus on how the process of tracking affects students' educational performance. Ability grouping, which is based on the assumption that it is easier to teach students with similar abilities, is often used in elementary schools. However, class-based factors also affect which children are most likely to be placed in "high," "middle," or "low" groups, often referred to by such innocuous terms as "Blue Birds," "Red Birds," and "Yellow Birds." In middle school, junior high, and high school, most students experience *tracking—* **the assignment of students to specific courses and educational programs based on their test scores, previous grades, or both.** Ruben Navarrette, Jr. (1997:274–275), talks about his experience with tracking:

> One fateful day, in the second grade, my teacher decided to teach her class more efficiently by dividing it into six groups of five students each. Each group was assigned a geometric symbol to differentiate it from the others. There were the Circles. There were the Squares. There were the Triangles and Rectangles.
>
> I remember being a Hexagon.

> I remember something else, an odd coincidence. The Hexagons were the smartest kids in the class. These distinctions are not lost on a child of seven. Even in the second grade, my classmates and I knew who was smarter than whom. And on the day on which we were assigned our respective shapes, we knew that our teacher knew, too.
>
> As Hexagons, we would wait for her to call on us, then answer by hurrying to her with books and pencils in hand. We sat around a table in our "reading group," chattering excitedly to one another and basking in the intoxication of positive learning. We did not notice, did not care to notice, over our shoulders, the frustrated looks on the faces of Circles and Squares and Triangles who sat quietly at their desks, doodling on scratch paper or mumbling to one another.
>
> We knew also that, along with our geometric shapes, our books were different and that each group had different amounts of work to do. The Circles had the easiest books and were assigned to read only a few pages at a time. Not surprisingly, the Hexagons had the most difficult books of all, those with the biggest words and the fewest pictures, and we were expected to read the most pages.
>
> The result of all of this education by separation was exactly what the teacher had imagined that it would be: Students could, and did, learn at their own pace without being encumbered by one another. Some learned faster than others. Some, I realized only [later], did not learn at all.

In junior high and in high school, students continue to be tracked into specific courses and educational programs. At the secondary level, the streaming consists of separating students into three streams: technical and vocational programs, general-level programs, and university entrance programs.

According to conflict analysis, streaming actually works to perpetuate inequality rather than to encourage individual achievement according to ability. Much research challenges the efficacy of tracking and instead points out its discriminatory biases. For one thing, as education scholar Jeannie Oakes has noted, streaming defines half of all students as below average (1985:86–89). What factors determine which "track" a student is placed in? Student records, test scores, dress, appearance, parental background, sex, and ethnicity combine in very complex ways to affect teacher expectations and evaluations of student potential (Gomme, 1995). In addition, a considerable amount of research suggests that socioeconomic background has as much to do with tracking as does individual merit (Bowles and Gintis, 1976; Oakes, 1985; Porter, 1987). Students in lower tracks tend to come from lower-class and minority backgrounds. In contrast, students from affluent families typically are placed in university-bound streams. Oakes (1985:86–89) also found that tracking affects students' perceptions of classroom goals and achievements, as the following statements from high- and low-track students suggest:

> I want to be a lawyer and debate has taught me to dig for answers and get involved. I can express myself. (High-Track English)

> To understand concepts and ideas and experiment with them. Also to work independently. (High-Track Science)

> To behave in class. (Low-Track English)

> To be a better listener in class. (Low-Track English)

> I have learned that I should do my questions for the book when he asks me to. (Low-Track Science)

Perceptions of the students on the "low tracks" reflect the impact that years of tracking and lowered expectations can have on people's educational and career aspirations. Often, the educational track—vocational or university-bound—on which high school students are placed has a significant influence on their future educational and employment opportunities. Although the stated purpose of tracking systems is to permit students to study subjects that are suitable to their skills and interests, most research reveals that this purpose has not been achieved (Oakes, 1985). Moreover, some social scientists believe that tracking is one of the most obvious mechanisms through which poor and minority students receive a diluted academic program, making it much more likely that they will fall even further behind their white, middle-class counterparts (see Miller, 1995). The research also indicates that streaming is particularly detrimental to the educational experiences of some ethnic minorities (Baril and Mori, 1991). Shamai (1992) examined the educational attainment of different ethnic groups in Canada and found that Aboriginal people, Ukrainians, French, and Italians have lower-than-average years of schooling. Aboriginal peoples are the most disadvantaged group, with over

50 percent having less than a secondary education and less than 5 percent ever going to college or university (Statistics Canada, 1998g). People from Jewish, Chinese, and Japanese backgrounds have higher-than-average educational attainment and are much more likely to attend university.

Awareness of these effects has resulted in numerous destreaming initiatives across the country. For example, in 1993 the Ontario Ministry of Education and Training began a destreaming program of one grade per year starting with Grade 9. These initiatives were met with some opposition by parents, teachers, and school boards, who were concerned that children will receive lower-quality education in destreamed classrooms. However, the benefits of destreaming may outweigh the costs, when we consider the perceptions and lowered expectations of students on the "low tracks," brought on by years of tracking.

Instead of enhancing school performance, tracking systems may result in students dropping out of school or ending up in dead-end situations because they have not taken the courses required to go to university.

THE HIDDEN CURRICULUM According to conflict theorists, the *hidden curriculum* is the transmission of cultural values and attitudes, such as conformity and obedience to authority, through implied demands found in rules, routines, and regulations of schools (Snyder, 1971). Although students from all social classes are subjected to the hidden curriculum, working-class and poverty-level students may be affected the most adversely (Cookson and Hodges Persell, 1985; Polakow, 1993; Ballantine, 1997). In a study of five elementary schools located in different communities, significant differences were found in the manner in which knowledge was transmitted to students even though the curriculum was organized similarly (Anyon, 1980). Schools for working-class students emphasize procedures and rote memorization without much decision making, choice, and explanation of why something is done a particular way. Schools for middle-class students stress the processes (such as figuring and decision making) involved in getting the right answer. Schools for affluent students focus on creative activities in which students express their own ideas and apply them to the subject under consideration. Schools for students from elite families work to develop students' analytical powers and

According to conflict theorists, the hidden curriculum in schools makes low-income students aware that they will be expected to follow rules when they work for others throughout their adult lives.

critical thinking skills, applying abstract principles to problem solving.

Through the hidden curriculum, schools make working-class and poverty-level students aware that they will be expected to take orders from others, arrive at work on time, follow bureaucratic rules, and experience high levels of boredom without complaining (Richer, 1988). Over time, these students may be disqualified from higher education and barred from obtaining the credentials necessary for well-paid occupations and professions (Bowles and Gintis, 1976). Educational credentials are extremely important in societies that emphasize *credentialism*—**a process of social selection in which class advantage and social status are linked to the possession of academic qualifications** (Collins, 1979; G. Marshall, 1994). Conflict theorists point out that the credentials required for a job often bear little resemblance to the actual skills and responsibilities of the job. Why then are degrees so important? The answer is that without them access to prestigious, high-paying jobs is limited. In other words, credentials serve a gatekeeping function, allowing professional groups such as doctors, lawyers, and accountants to exclude anyone without the proper education, thus keeping wages high and regulating the labour market (Collins, 1979). The result is a process of social selection in which class advantage and social status are linked to the possession of academic credentials (Collins, 1979; Marshall, 1994). According to conflict theorists, credentialism is not driven by an actual need for increased knowledge, but rather by the desire on the part of the members of professional groups to protect their own vested interests, namely income, prestige, autonomy, and power.

Credentialism is closely related to *meritocracy*—**previously defined as a social system in which status is assumed to be acquired through individual ability and effort** (Young, 1994). Persons who acquire the appropriate credentials for a job are assumed to have gained the position through *what they know*, not *who they are* or *whom they know*. According to conflict theorists, the hidden curriculum determines in advance that the most valued credentials will primarily stay in the hands of the elites. Therefore, Canada is not actually as meritocratic as some might claim.

Interactionist Perspectives

Unlike functionalist analysts, who focus on the functions and dysfunctions of education, and conflict theorists, who focus on the relationship between education and inequality, interactionists focus on classroom communication patterns and educational practices such as labelling that affect students' self-concept and aspirations.

LABELLING AND THE SELF-FULFILLING PROPHECY

Chapter 7 explained that *labelling* is the process whereby a person is identified by others as possessing a specific characteristic or exhibiting a certain pattern of behaviour (such as being deviant). According to interactionists, the process of labelling is directly related to the power and status of those persons who do the labelling and those who are being labelled. In schools, teachers and administrators are empowered to label children in various ways, including grades, written comments on deportment (classroom behaviour), and placement in classes. For example, based on standardized test scores or classroom performance, educators label some children as "special ed" or low achievers, whereas others are labelled as average or "gifted and talented." For some students, labelling amounts to a *self-fulfilling prophecy*—previously defined as an unsubstantiated belief or prediction resulting in behaviour that makes the originally false belief come true (Merton, 1968). A classic form of labelling and self-fulfilling prophecy occurs through the use of IQ (intelligence quotient) tests, which claim to measure a person's inherent intelligence, apart from any family or school influences on the individual. In many school systems, IQ tests are used as one criterion in determining student placement in classes and ability groups.

USING LABELLING THEORY TO EXAMINE THE IQ DEBATE

The relationship between IQ testing and labelling theory has been of special interest to sociologists. In the 1960s, two social scientists conducted an experiment in an elementary school where they intentionally misinformed teachers about the intelligence test scores of students in their classes (Rosenthal and Jacobson, 1968). Despite the fact that the students were randomly selected for the study and had no measurable differences in intelligence, the researchers informed the teachers that some of the students had extremely high IQ test scores, whereas others had average to below-average scores. As the researchers observed, the teachers began to teach "exceptional" students in a different manner from other students. In turn, the "exceptional" students began to outperform their "average" peers and to excel in their classwork. This study called attention to the labelling effect of IQ scores.

However, experiments such as this also raise other important issues: What if a teacher (as a result of stereotypes based on the relationship between IQ and race) believes that some students of colour are less capable of learning? Will that teacher (often without realizing it) treat such students as if they are incapable of learning? In their controversial book *The Bell Curve: Intelligence and Class Structure in American Life*, Richard J. Herrnstein and Charles Murray (1994) argue that intelligence is genetically inherited and that people cannot be "smarter" than they are born to be, regardless of their environment or education. According to Herrnstein and Murray, certain racial–ethnic groups differ in average IQ and are likely to differ in "intelligence genes" as well. For

example, they point out that, on average, people living in Asia score higher on IQ tests than white Americans and that African Americans score 15 points lower on average than white Americans. Based on an all-white sample, the authors also concluded that low intelligence leads to social pathology such as high rates of crime, dropping out of school, and winding up poor. In contrast, high intelligence typically leads to success, and family background plays only a secondary role.

Many scholars disagree with Herrnstein and Murray's research methods and conclusions. Two major flaws found in their approach were as follows: (1) the authors used biased statistics that underestimate the impact of hard-to-measure factors such as family background, and (2) they used scores from the Armed Forces Qualification Test, an exam that depends on how much schooling people have completed. Thus, what the authors claim is immutable intelligence is actually acquired skills (Weinstein, 1997). Despite this refutation, the idea of inherited mental inferiority tends to take on a life of its own when people want to believe that such differences exist (Duster, 1995; Hauser, 1995; Taylor, 1995). According to researchers, many African American and Mexican American children are placed in special education classes on the basis of IQ scores when the students were not fluent in English and thus could not understand the directions given for the test. Moreover, when children are labelled as "special ed" students or as being *learning disabled*, these terms are social constructions that may lead to stigmatization and become a self-fulfilling prophecy (Carrier, 1986; Coles, 1987).

Labelling students based on IQ scores has been an issue throughout the twentieth century. Immigrants from Southern and Eastern Europe—particularly from Italy, Poland, and Russia—who arrived in this country at the beginning of the twentieth century typically had lower IQ scores on average than did Northern European immigrants who had arrived earlier from nations such as Great Britain. For many of the white ethnic students, IQ testing became a self-fulfilling prophecy: teachers did not expect them to do as well as children from a Northern European (WASP) family background and thus did not encourage them or give them an opportunity to overcome language barriers or other educational obstacles. Although many students persisted and achieved an education, the possibility that differences in IQ scores could be attributed to linguistic, cultural, and educational biases in the tests was largely ignored (Feagin and Feagin, 1997). Debates over the possible intellectual inferiority of white ethnic groups are unthinkable today, but arguments pertaining to African Americans and IQ continue to surface in the United States.

A self-fulfilling prophecy can also result from labelling students as gifted. Gifted students are considered to be those with above-average intellectual ability, academic aptitude, creative or productive thinking, or leadership skills (Ballantine, 1997). When some students are labelled as better than others, they may achieve at a higher level because of the label. Ironically, such labelling may also result in discrimination against these students. For example, according to law professor Margaret Chon (1995:238), the "myth of the superhuman Asian" creates a self-fulfilling prophecy for some Asian American students:

> When I was in college, I applied to the Air Force ROTC program ... I was given the most complete physical of my life [and] I took an intelligence test. When I reported back to the ROTC staff, they looked glum. What is it? I thought. Did the physical turn up some life-threatening defect? ... It turned out I had gotten the highest test score ever at my school ... Rather than feeling pleased and flattered, I felt like a sideshow freak. The recruiters were not happy either. I think our reactions had a lot to do with the fact that I did not resemble a typical recruit. I am a woman of East Asian, specifically Korean, descent ... They did not want me in ROTC no matter how "intelligent" I was.

According to Chon, painting Asian Americans as superintelligent makes it possible for others to pretend they do not exist: "Governments ignore us because we've already made it. Schools won't recruit us because we do so well on the SATs ... Asian Americans seem almost invisible, except when there is a grocery store boycott—or when we're touted as the model minority" (Chon, 1995: 239–240).

Labelling and the self-fulfilling prophecy are not unique to U.S. and Canadian schools. Around the globe, students are labelled by batteries of tests and teachers' evaluations of their attitudes, academic performance, and classroom behaviour. Other problems in education, ranging from illiteracy and school discipline to unequal school financing and educational opportunities for students with disabilities, are concerns in elementary and secondary education in many countries.

CURRENT ISSUES IN EDUCATION

Public schools in Canada today are a microcosm of many of the issues and problems facing the country. Canada is the only advanced industrialized country without a federal ministry of education—a fact that has made it difficult to coordinate national educational and teaching standards. Each province enacts its own laws and regulations, with local school boards frequently making the final determination regarding curriculum. Accordingly, no general standards exist as to what is to be *taught* to students or how, although many provinces have now adopted standards for what (at a minimum) must be *learned* in order to graduate from high school. Countries such as France have an education ministry that is officially responsible for every elementary school in the nation. Countries such as Japan have a centrally controlled curriculum, whereas in nations such as England, national achievement tests are administered by the government, and students must pass them in order to advance to the next level of education (Lemann, 1997).

Inequality in Public Schools versus Private Schools

Often, there is a perceived conflict between public schools and private schools for students and financial resources. However, far more students and their parents are dependent on public schools than on private ones for providing a high-quality education. Enrolment in Canadian elementary and secondary education (Grades K through 12) totals approximately 5.5 million students. Over 90 percent of elementary and secondary students are educated in public schools. About 6 percent of all students are educated in private schools, and approximately 1 percent of all students attend private schools with tuition of more than $5000 a year (Statistics Canada, 1999b).

Private secondary boarding schools tend to be reserved for students from high-income families and for a few lower-income or minority students who are able to acquire academic or athletic scholarships that cover their tuition, room and board, and other expenses. The average cost for seven-day tuition and room and board at secondary boarding schools is nearly $20,000 a year, whereas the cost of day-school tuition can be as high as $8000.

Among parents whose children attend private secondary schools, an important factor for a majority of the parents is the emphasis on academics that they believe exists in private (as opposed to public) schools. Another important factor for many of the parents is the moral and ethical standards that they believe private secondary schools instil in students. Overall, many families believe that private schools are a better choice for their children because they feel that these schools are more academically demanding, motivate students to learn, provide more stringent discipline, and do not have many of the inadequacies found in public schools (Peterson's Educational Center, 1996). However, according to some social analysts, there is little to substantiate the claim that private schools (other than elite academies attended by the children of the wealthiest and most influential families) are inherently better than public schools (Institute for Social Research, 1995).

Dropping Out

Although the overall school dropout (or school leaver) rate has significantly decreased in recent decades, about 15 percent of people under the age of 24 still leave school before earning a high school diploma. Ethnic and class differences are important factors in the data on dropout rates. For example, Aboriginal students have a dropout rate of over 40 percent. Recent immigrants to Canada were much less likely to drop out before they had completed high school. The dropout rate also varies by region—Prince Edward Island had the highest proportion of school dropouts in 1995 at 21 percent, while Saskatchewan and Alberta had the lowest at 11 percent (Clark, 1997).

Why do students drop out? According to a survey on school leavers by S.N. Gilbert and B. Orok (1993), male school leavers identified a preference for work over school, boredom, financial pressures, and problems with teachers as the most important reasons for quitting school. In a recent study by sociologist Howard Pinderhughes, one high school dropout summed up his reasons for leaving school:

> I never liked school. The teachers all hated my guts because I didn't just accept what they had to say. I was kind of a wiseass, and that got me in trouble. But that's not why they kept kicking me out of

school. Either I didn't come to school or I got in fights when I did come. It got so I got a reputation that people heard about and there was always some kid challengin' me. (quoted in Pinderhughes, 1997:58)

Other students may view school as a waste of time, as this student's comments bear out:

> I thought [school] was a big waste of time. I knew older guys who had dropped out of the tenth grade and within a couple of years were makin' cash money as a mechanic or carpenter. My brothers did the same thing. I didn't think I was learnin' no skill that I could get a job in school. I wasn't very good in school. It was pretty damn boring. So I left. (quoted in Pinderhughes, 1997:58)

Female school leavers also identified boredom and a preference for work as important reasons for leaving school. However, they also cited problems with school work and pregnancy/marriage as factors involved in their decision to quit school.

Students who drop out of school may be skeptical about the value of education in improving their job opportunities. On leaving school, many dropouts have high hopes of making money and enjoying their new freedom. However, these feelings often turn to disappointment when they find that few jobs are available and that they do not meet the educational requirements for any of the "good" jobs that exist (Pinderhughes, 1997). Increasingly, high school completion or higher is the minimum level of education needed for entry-level jobs. As shown in Table 16.2, leaving high school before graduation dramatically increases the likelihood of unemployment, particularly among women. In 1995, female dropouts had an unemployment rate of 30 percent, as compared to a rate of only 10 percent for women who had completed high school and pursued additional education or training. Students who drop out of school may lack the basic capabilities needed to retrain and learn new skills. Given the rapid technological change occurring in the Canadian economy, the ability to continue to learn throughout a lifetime has become increasingly important (Clark, 1997). Almost half of the respondents in Gilbert and Orok's survey of school leavers (1993) indicated they were unhappy that they had left school, mainly because they now recognized the value of an education. In fact, many of the individuals reported that they intended to "drop back in" to school and com-

| TABLE 16.2 | LABOUR FORCE PARTICIPATION AND UNEMPLOYMENT RATES OF HIGH-SCHOOL DROPOUTS AND GRADUATES, 1995 |

		HIGH SCHOOL-GRADUATES	
	HIGH-SCHOOL DROPOUTS	Without further education or training	With further education or training
		%	%
Labour force participation rates[1]			
Total	81	85	84
Men	91	92	84
Women	63	77	84
Unemployment rates[2]			
Total	21	13	11
Men	17	14	11
Women	30	11	10

[1]Percentage of people who were either working or unemployed and actively looking for work and available for work.

[2]Percentage of labour force participants who were unemployed and actively looking for work and available for work.

Reprinted with permission from Statistics Canada, "Higher Unemployment Among School Leavers," adapted from *Canadian Social Trends*, Cat. no. 11-008, Spring 1997.

plete the educational requirements necessary to get a better job. However, findings from a follow-up survey conducted in 1995 indicated that only one-quarter of school leavers had returned to high school. After having left, most found that work and family responsibilities got in the way of completing their high school diplomas.

Although critics of the public education system point to high dropout rates as proof of failure in the public education system, these rates have steadily declined in Canada since the 1950s when over 70 percent of students did not complete high school (Fennell, 1993).

Declining Academic Standards and Functional Illiteracy

Across Canada, thousands of parents are expressing their concerns that the public school system is doing a poor job of teaching their children (Fennell, 1993). Although parents may have always been difficult to please, over the past twenty years, an increasing number are dissatisfied with the quality of their children's education (see Table 16.3). The performance of Canadian students on recent international tests of English, math, and science continues to raise public concerns that Canadian students are "failing to make the grade" in comparison with other industrialized

countries. A recent public opinion poll found that Canadians overwhelmingly supported a "back to basics" approach in which the fundamentals of literacy and numeracy would be taught (Canadian Education Association, 1999).

How do students feel about the quality of their education? A 1993 survey of 500 university students indicated that only 52 percent of respondents felt that high school had prepared them properly for university. According to one University of Toronto engineering student, not enough emphasis was placed on the fundamentals of reading and writing (Fennell, 1993). Postsecondary institutions and employers were also disillusioned with the level of preparedness they were finding in high school graduates (Canadian Education Association, 1999). The result is that many universities across the country have implemented remedial math and English classes to bring students up to the skill level they need to complete their degrees.

Much of the blame for declining standards in the 1980s and early 1990s has been directed at educational reforms focusing on *child-centred education*—a system of learning that encourages children to progress at their own rate. Critics of child-centred education argue that because this system did not impose clear standards it is unaccountable and produces students who cannot read

TABLE 16.3 — **PARENTS' DISSATISFACTION WITH CHILDREN'S EDUCATION, 1973, 1978, 1992**

Are you satisfied or dissatisfied with the education children are getting today?

CANADA

	SATISFIED	DISSATISFIED	DON'T KNOW
1992	35%	56%	9%
1978	34	53	13
1973	51	41	8

REGIONAL BREAKDOWN (1992)

Atlantic	41	54	6
Quebec	37	55	8
Ontario	30	61	10
Prairies	49	45	6
B.C.	25	63	12

Note: Percentages may not add up to 100, due to rounding. Reprinted with permission—The Toronto Star Syndicate.

TABLE 16.4 — **GRADE 8 TEST-SCORE PERCENTAGE DECLINES, 1966–1991***

Vocabulary	−2%
Mathematics	−6%
Reading Comprehension	−9%
Writing Skills	−11%

* Based on periodic tests of Grade 8 students from all provinces except Quebec, conducted by Nelson Canada.

Source: *Nelson Canada.*

and write. Critics of child-centred teaching methods also pointed to the declining skill level of students. For example, a recent test of Grade 8 students across Canada found that students' skills had declined in vocabulary, mathematics, reading, and writing between 1966 and 1991 (see Table 16.4).

As further evidence of declining academic standards, social analysts cite the rate of functional illiteracy in this country. ***Functional illiteracy* is the inability to read and/or write at the skill level necessary for carrying out everyday tasks.** Everyday tasks would include reading a newspaper, filling out a form, or following written instructions. Sixteen percent of adult Canadians do not have the skills to handle most of the written material they see every day, that is, they are functionally illiterate. An additional 24 to 26 percent can use reading materials only to carry out simple reading tasks. They do not have the

reading skills to cope with unfamiliar and more complex reading materials. In other words, they can read, but not well (Statistics Canada, 1996d). Overall, Canada has a high rate of adult literacy compared with the seven other countries surveyed in the 1994 International Adult Literacy Survey (Statistics Canada, 1994a). However, Canada also had the largest proportion of youth with poor literacy skills (10 percent). A report by the Economic Council of Canada estimated that more than one million functionally illiterate young people will graduate from Canada's schools over the next ten years (Fennell, 1993). Illiteracy is a global problem as well as a national one (see Table 16.5). Low rates of literacy for women in lower-income countries are a reflection of how different countries view education and gender (see Box 16.3).

As a result of the concerns with declining standards and illiteracy, school boards across the

TABLE 16.5	NATIONS WITH THE LOWEST LITERACY RATES

COUNTRY	LITERACY RATE
Niger	13.6%
Burkina Faso	19.2%
Eritrea	20.0%
Mali	31.0%
Sierra Leone	31.4%
Afghanistan	31.5%
Senegal	33.1%
Burundi	35.3%
Ethiopia	35.5%
Guinea	35.9%

Source: Russell, Joel, "Early Lessons," *Hispanic Business* (June 1997):96–102. Reprinted by permission, Hispanic Business Inc., 425 Pine Ave., Goleta, CA 93117-3709.

Illiteracy is a problem across all age categories. Today, many adults are enrolled in classes that will help them learn to read, write, and speak English.

country have been revising their curriculum to place a greater emphasis on the core subject areas of reading, mathematics, and science. Educators are also returning to more objective criteria and expectations, and to more traditional teaching methods. The curriculum in most provinces has specified outcomes and objectives for age and grade levels. Some provinces are also moving away from the practice of passing children from grade to grade with their peers, regardless of their achievement level. Educators in the public school system are also returning to an emphasis on testing and evaluation. In addition to increasing the amount of testing at the classroom level, the majority of provinces have introduced tests to assess system-wide performance levels. Final

exams in high school, which were virtually eliminated in the 1970s and 1980s, are now mandatory in nine provinces (Canadian Education Association, 1999). Given their dissatisfaction with the public school system, some parents are moving away from traditional public schools and trying alternatives such as home schooling or charter schools (see Box 16.2).

Gender Bias in Schools

Gender bias in schools is an area of concern that has received increased scrutiny in recent years. In Chapter 11, we examined ways in which gender bias in schools has a negative impact on female students. Although most women in Canada have

BOX 16.2 CRITICAL THINKING

THE HOME-SCHOOLING OPTION: CAN PARENTS REPLACE TEACHERS?

Olga Hymers, mother of four, discusses her family's experience with home-schooling:

> My husband, Percy, and I embarked on this venture four years ago for a variety of reasons, including a measure of disillusionment with the public-school system and a strong feeling we could do as well on our own ... So why do we teach our children at home? We love the satisfaction, freedom and creativity of working together. Percy works at a lumber mill, which means shifts that conflict with traditional school hours. Home schooling gives him more time to spend with the children. And for me, home schooling provides a feeling of satisfaction ... So far, the benefits of home schooling have outweighed the costs. But visions of designing our own curriculum, spending leisurely days at museums, libraries, and art galleries, and of teaching our children more than the regular school system offers have all gone by the wayside. Now, our goal is far more realistic:

to teach our children in a relaxed learning environment and keep them on a par with their traditionally schooled peers. (Hymers, 1997:31)

At the start of every school year, a number of children do not head off to the classroom. Instead, they stay with a parent who will be teaching them at home what others learn at school. Despite the fact that the home-schooled still account for only a small percentage of school-aged children, their numbers have increased every year since the early 1980s. According to provincial ministries of education, in 1996–97, the number of children registered as being home-schooled totalled approximately 17,500 or about 0.4 percent of the total student enrolment in Canada. Home-schooling organizations have reported higher numbers, placing the number of students studying at home at 30,000 to 40,000, or approximately 1 percent of the total student enrolment. Home-schooling is especially popular in the Western provinces, particularly in Alberta and British Columbia. Increased public acceptance and

greater educational opportunities than those living in developing nations, their educational opportunities are not equal to those of males in their social class (Gaskell and McLaren, 1987). According to the *A Cappella Papers*, a series of reports outlining the concerns of young women in Grades 6 to 12, the education system—curricula, standards, and social environment—does not always provide a supportive atmosphere for girls and may undermine their confidence. One female student commented, "Some teachers listen to you—the ones that care. In some subjects (math and science) they're more concerned with the boys than the girls." (Canadian Council on Social Development, 1996).

Through reading materials, classroom activities, and treatment by teachers and peers, female students learn that they are less important than male students (Gaskell, McLaren, and Novogrodsky, 1995; Orenstein, 1995). For example, teachers

generally interact with and encourage boys more in class, and they send subtle messages concerning their lower expectations of girls in such areas as science and mathematics (Gaskell et al., 1995). Over time, differential treatment undermines females' self-esteem and discourages them from taking math and science, which are usually dominated by male teachers and students (Raffalli, 1994). Teachers tend to encourage boys to be problem solvers and to ask them more complicated questions than they ask girls. As a result, females tend to take fewer courses in these areas or drop them because they find them uninteresting (Gaskell et al., 1995). Further evidence suggests that teachers and guidance counsellors encourage women to make educational and occupational choices that are consistent with traditional gender roles. The results of the gender bias in education are clearly evident at the postsecondary level: as shown in Table 16.6, in 1997 women received only 21 percent of the

BOX 16.2

CONTINUED

the introduction of more flexible legislation may have contributed to this growth.

Parents home-school for a variety of reasons. This arrangement is ideal for those who wish to incorporate their beliefs and values into the curriculum, who are concerned that not enough learning takes place in the classroom, and who prefer their child to learn in an informal, family setting. According to supporters of home-schooling, the benefits for children are many: they may, for example, learn at their own pace, pursue special interests, make the most of individual strengths and weaknesses, and avoid the competition and peer pressure of the classroom. Home-schooling may also be the solution for a child who, for whatever reason, does not fit in a regular classroom and is falling behind academically, socially, or both.

Critics, however, are quick to point out areas of concern: the average parent's ability to cover all areas of the curriculum, the avail-

ability of appropriate program materials, and the potential absence of social interaction. And, although every province monitors home-schoolers for compliance with its Education Act, no province has regulations regarding the qualifications of parents to teach.

Home-schooling is not for everyone. Relatively few people are able to invest the required vast amount of time, effort, and energy into teaching their children at home. Fewer still have the required knowledge—particularly at the secondary level—and instructional capability necessary to carry out the job well. Those who do, however, feel that they are raising healthy, well-adjusted children in a positive, family-oriented environment. What do you think of this alternative form of schooling? Given some of the issues facing the public education system today, will this become a popular choice for an increasing number of Canadian parents?

Source: Adapted with permission from Luffman, 1998.

degrees awarded in engineering and applied sciences and just over 30 percent of the degrees awarded in mathematics and the physical sciences.

Studies show that gender bias pervades the overall academic environment. At least partly due to the school environment, girls labelled as "gifted and talented" routinely deny their intelligence, feeling that academic achievement might keep them from being popular with others (see Eder, 1985; Eder and Parker, 1987). Ashley Reiter, a first-place winner in a national mathematics competition, described her middle school years as a "smart girl's torture chamber":

No one would speak to me. I wouldn't even go into the cafeteria for lunch. Long tables stretched the length of the whole room, but wherever I sat, people acted as if I wasn't in the right place ... So I ... would go to the library ... It was definitely not cool to be smart in seventh and eighth grade, especially

for a girl. Some kids thought they would lose their reputation just by speaking to someone smart. (quoted in Sadker and Sadker, 1994:93)

Some analysts suggest that girls receive subtle cues from teachers and parents that lead them to attribute success to *effort*; boys learn to attribute success to their *intelligence* and *ability*. Conversely, girls attribute their own failure to lack of ability; boys attribute failure to lack of effort (Sadker and Sadker, 1994). Other analysts argue that girls—and some boys—who are high achievers may be the victims of *anti-intellectualism*—hostility or opposition toward persons assumed to have great mental ability or toward subject matter thought to necessitate significant intellectual ability or knowledge for its comprehension.

In recent studies, sociologists have concluded that more research is needed on how gender bias affects both female and male students and that

TABLE 16.6	UNIVERSITY DEGREES GRANTED BY FIELD OF STUDY, BY SEX, 1997

	1997	PERCENTAGES
Canada	171,736	
Male	72,120	42%
Female	99,616	58%
Social sciences	65,806	
Male	28,066	43%
Female	37,740	57%
Education	27,405	
Male	7,911	29%
Female	19,494	71%
Humanities	21,190	
Male	7,951	
Female	13,239	
Health professions and occupations	12,901	
Male	3,425	27%
Female	9,476	73%
Engineering and applied sciences	12,613	
Male	10,004	79%
Female	2,609	21%
Agriculture and biological sciences	11,627	
Male	4,716	41%
Female	6,911	58%
Mathematics and physical sciences	9,612	
Male	6,665	69%
Female	2,947	31%
Fine and applied arts	5,136	
Male	1,672	33%
Female	3,464	67%
Arts and sciences	5,446	
Male	1,710	31%
Female	3,736	69%

Reprinted by permission from Statistics Canada, adapted from the CANSIM database, series no. 00580602.

more forums are needed in schools and elsewhere to allow people to discuss how education contributes to sexism and a limited view of masculinity and femininity that directly affects individuals and their academic accomplishments (see Thorne, 1993; Eder, 1995; Orenstein, 1995).

Equalizing Opportunities for Students with Disabilities

Another recent concern in education has been how to provide better educational opportunities for students with disabilities.

Slowly, methodically, Brent Hoey is learning to print his first name. Several of his classmates have no trouble making well-formed letters, but Brent struggles with his until he reaches the last one. Triumphantly, he crayons a clearly legible "t," and throws up his arms in glee. Although he has Down's Syndrome, Brent is thriving in a regular kindergarten class at Canadian Martyrs Elementary School in Newmarket, Ontario. As the class moves on to other activities, Brent jumps up to practise for his part in a play called *The Gingerbread Man*. His lines have been simplified, allowing him to participate with other neophyte thespians pretending to be hungry farm animals and a crafty fox. "People have said to me, 'There are places for kids like him,'" says his mother. "But he is doing well here. To have him stacking and sorting cans in a special education class would just be criminal." (Chisholm, 1995:52)

Until recently, children like Brent, as well as those with other physical and mental disabilities, were segregated—either placed in special classes in public schools or sent away to specialized schools (Chisholm, 1995:52). As discussed in Chapter 18, the term *disability* has a wide range of definitions (see Shapiro, 1993). For the purposes of this chapter, disability is regarded as any physical and/or mental condition that limits students' access to, or full involvement in, school life. As recently as 1994, eleven-year-old Emily Eaton, a Grade 4 student, was placed in a segregated classroom in a public school in a small community in Ontario because the teachers and the school board officials had decided that her severe cerebral palsy made it extremely difficult for her to learn in a regular classroom environment. The parents disagreed, believing that the regular classroom was the best learning environment for their daughter. The courts agreed with the parents, finding that "Emily had a constitutional right to attend school with fully able children [and that] segregating Emily because of her disability— against her parents' wishes and without establishing that she would be better off in a segregated classroom—was no different than segregating her on the basis of race or gender" (Chisholm, 1995:53).

As this case demonstrates, the barriers facing students with disabilities are slowly being removed or surmounted by new legislation (Nagler, 1997). Today most people with disabilities are no longer prevented from experiencing the full range of academic opportunities. Under various provincial human rights guidelines and the Charter of Rights and Freedoms, all children with disabilities are guaranteed a free and appropriate public education. This means that local school boards must make the necessary efforts and expenditures to accommodate special needs students.

Many schools have attempted to *mainstream* children with disabilities by *inclusion programs* under which the special education curriculum is integrated with the regular education program and each child receives an *individualized education plan* that provides annual educational goals (Nagler, 1997). Inclusion means that children with disabilities work with a wide variety of people; over the course of a day, children may interact with their regular education teacher, the special education teacher, a speech therapist, an occupational therapist, a physical therapist, and a resource teacher, depending on the child's individual needs. According to 1995 statistics, over 70 percent of children with disabilities are integrated into mainstream schools. Only fifteen years ago, more than 80 percent of these children were placed in segregated schools. This dramatic change reflects growing acceptance of the fact that children with a range of disabilities often thrive in an integrated learning environment.

Although much remains to be done, recent measures to enhance education for children with disabilities has increased the inclusion of many young people who were formerly excluded or marginalized in the educational system. But the problem of equal educational opportunities does not end at the elementary and high school level for students with disabilities. If these students complete high school and continue on to university, they find new sets of physical and academic barriers that limit their access to higher education. Sociology professor Mark Nagler, who has cerebral palsy, recalls the academic barriers he faced obtaining his Ph.D.:

My parents made me aware that many people would make fun of my condition and that both kids and adults might create embarrassing situations ... The former chairperson of a Sociology Graduate Department at a prominent university told me I should go home and live with my parents as I would never make it as a professor. Twenty-eight years later I am still proving him wrong. (Nagler, 1997:6)

Prior to the late 1980s students in wheelchairs found it difficult, if not impossible, to attend postsecondary schools. Author Connie Panzarino (1994:219), who was born with the rare disease spinal muscular atrophy type III, explains how difficult it was to attend university without being able to take a shower:

I received a letter from the Disabled Students Office informing me that the administration had to indefinitely put off installing wheelchair-accessible showers. "How the Hell am I supposed to stay healthy if I can't stay clean?" I thought to myself ... Several of the disabled students had already fallen while trying to take showers or baths in the undersized, nonregulation tubs in our bathrooms. My Hoyer bathtub lift would not fit into these tubs.

BOX 16.3 SOCIOLOGY IN GLOBAL PERSPECTIVE

WOMEN'S LITERACY IN DEVELOPING NATIONS

Education is a powerful agent of progress. Literacy is the most basic and necessary of learning skills.

—Maria Luisa Jauregui de Gainza, literacy specialist, UNESCO (quoted in Ballara, 1992)

Women's literacy has been referred to as the "challenge of the decade." *Functional illiteracy* refers to a lack of basic literacy and numeracy skills that are essential for proper functioning—such as the ability to read or write or to make sense of written material (Ballara, 1992:1). Organizations such as the United Nations believe that the education of women in developing nations is a high priority not only for national development but also for the well-being of children and families.

An estimated 95 percent of all illiterate people are concentrated in the developing nations of Southeast Asia and sub-Saharan Africa. Here, one-third of all women are illiterate, as compared with one-fifth of the men. In the least-developed nations, 79 percent of adult women are illiterate. Even with organizations such as the United Nations Educational, Scientific and Cultural Organization (UNESCO) attempting to eradicate illiteracy, the problem remains.

Many factors stand in the way of women's literacy, including religious beliefs that subordinate women and emphasize a traditional gen-

---

After Panzarino called a "shower strike" in which students with and without disabilities refused to take a bath until something was done about the showers, the university constructed accessible showers for each wheelchair-accessible dorm room (Panzarino, 1994). Today, building codes have been changed to require educational institutions to be accessible (Nagler, 1997). Many colleges and universities have provided relatively inexpensive accommodations to make facilities more accessible to students with disabilities. However, some educational institutions find it financially prohibitive to install ramps and/or elevators. In these settings, teachers often change classrooms in order to provide access to students who have mobility impairments. Despite these efforts, students with disabilities continue to be underrepresented at the postsecondary level. Recent statistics indicate that although persons with disabilities make up 7 percent of the total postsecondary student population in 1991, they represented less than 4 percent of 1990 university graduates. They did, however, account for 6.5 percent of community college graduates (Wannell and Caron, 1994).

The Soaring Cost of Post-Secondary Education

Who attends college or university? What sort of college or university do they attend? Even for students who complete high school, access to colleges and universities is determined not only by prior academic record but also by the ability to pay.

Postsecondary education has been described as the dividing line of the modern labour market. Today, more than ever before, employers want employees with a university degree, college diploma, or some other form of postsecondary educational certificate. As shown in Figure 16.2,

BOX 16.3

CONTINUED

dered division of labour, such as "care of children, maintenance of the household, care of older family members and the ill, servicing their husband and his relevant kin, maintenance of the network of familial ties, and servicing of the community" (Ballara, 1992:x). Religions that confine women's activities to domestic tasks and stress their role as wives and mothers often limit their access to education and produce feelings of low self-esteem and isolation.

Ultimately, the main reason most women (and men) are illiterate is poverty; daily survival becomes far more important than learning how to read or compute math problems. Some analysts have found that schools in the poorest developing nations are becoming even more impoverished. Some countries have a two-tier system: (1) in rural areas, a grossly inadequate school system that may be state-run or attached to a local temple or mosque, where religious education is often the primary goal; and (2) in urban areas, a better school system that may be patterned after Western schools such as those found in England or France and that serves the children of the nation's elite population.

Is there hope for the future? Media campaigns and numerous projects are actively seeking to promote literacy. Perhaps a greater awareness of the problem is the first step toward eradication of it. Are the problems of women in developing nations in any way related to your life? Using your sociological imagination, can you think of ways in which their "fate" might be intertwined with yours?

Sources: Based on Ballara, 1992; and Ballantine, 1997.

for most Canadians, higher education will result in better employment and higher earnings. However, in order to obtain a university education, students must have the necessary financial resources. What does a university education cost? In Canada, postsecondary education is funded by the federal and provincial governments, and by parents and students through personal savings (Clark, 1998). As governments cut their funding to higher education, an increasing financial burden is falling on the shoulders of students and their parents. To make matters worse, the cost of attending university has increased dramatically over the past twenty years. Increases in tuition fees have outstripped the rate of inflation every year since 1983. A prominent investment company estimated the cost of one year of undergraduate studies at almost $9000. The Canadian Federation of Students indicated that the cost may be closer to $15,000 when living expenses are included. According to the Federation chairman,

"More than ever, getting into the system depends not just on ability, but on how much money a person has" (Farren, 1998:45). Despite the soaring cost of postsecondary education, the percentage of young people attending university continued to rise in the first years of the 1990s. However, undergraduate enrolment has declined over the past five consecutive years, an indication that for some students the cost of a university education has become prohibitive.

How do students afford this increasingly costly education? The 1995 National Graduates Survey explored this question with nearly 43,000 recent graduates. Both college and university graduates identified employment earnings and student loan programs as their primary sources of funding. Parents ranked a close third for university graduates. Scholarships, fellowships, grants, and bursaries were rarely identified as a significant source of funding (Statistics Canada, 1997d). Approximately half of college and university stu-

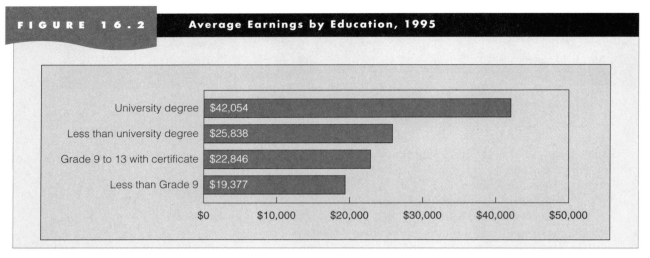

FIGURE 16.2   Average Earnings by Education, 1995

University degree	$42,054
Less than university degree	$25,838
Grade 9 to 13 with certificate	$22,846
Less than Grade 9	$19,377

$0 $10,000 $20,000 $30,000 $40,000 $50,000

Reprinted by permission from Statistics Canada, 1998. "1996 Census: Sources of Income, Earnings and Total Income, and Family Income." *The Daily* (May 12).

dents indicated that they relied on student loans to finance their education. Students graduating from college in 1995 owed close to $10,000 at the end of their studies. University students receiving bachelor's degrees in the same year owed, on average, close to $13,000 on graduation (Clark, 1998).

A substantial proportion of postsecondary students opt for community college because of the lower costs. However, the overall enrolment of low-income students in community college has dropped as a result of increasing costs and also because many students must work full time or part time to pay for their education. As a result, many students drop out before they have completed a two-year program. In contrast, students from more affluent families are more likely to attend prestigious public universities or private colleges outside of Canada, where tuition fees alone may be more than $20,000 per year (Fennell, 1993).

According to some social analysts, a university education is a bargain—even at about $90 a day for private schools or $35 for public schools—because for their money students receive instruction, room, board, and other amenities such as athletic facilities and job placement services. However, other analysts believe that the high cost of a university education reproduces the existing class system: Students who lack money may be denied access to higher education, and those who are able to attend college or university tend to receive different types of education based on their ability to pay. For example, a community college student who receives an associate's degree or completes a certificate program may be prepared for a

position in the middle of the occupational status range, such as a dental assistant, computer programmer, or auto mechanic (Gilbert, 1998). In contrast, university graduates with four-year degrees are more likely to find initial employment with firms where they stand a chance of being promoted to high-paying management and executive positions. Although higher education may be a source of upward mobility for talented young people from poor families, the Canadian system of higher education is sufficiently stratified that it may also reproduce the existing class structure (Gilbert, 1998; Barlow and Robertson, 1994; Davies, 1999).

EDUCATION IN THE FUTURE

This chapter ends as it began by noting that education will remain an important institution in the twenty-first century. Also remaining, however, will be the controversies that we have discussed—controversies that your generation will attempt to resolve. Questions will remain about what should be taught, not only in terms of preparing your children for their adult lives and the world of work but also with regard to the values to which you want your child exposed. The debate over what should be taught is not limited to moral issues; rather, it includes the entire curriculum. If, as critics assert, academic achievement in Canada compares unfavourably with the level of achievement by students in many other countries, what can be done to change the situation?

Soaring costs at both public and private institutions of higher education are a pressing problem for today's university students and their parents. What factors have contributed to the higher overall costs of obtaining a university degree?

In recent decades, the Canadian public has been demanding greater accountability for student outcomes (Dunning, 1997). A number of policy initiatives have been introduced in the public school system that should result in an improvement in the quality of education. At the elementary and secondary level there has been a shift toward increased emphasis on curriculum standards and more testing and provincial exams. In addition, *compensatory education programs*, including preschool, remedial, and extra education programs, which provide additional learning assistance to disadvantaged children, have been designed to address the effects of poverty, deprivation, and disadvantage on school performance (Guppy, 1995). Although these programs were tried and failed twenty years earlier, more recent compensatory programs have produced more favourable results.

Some elected officials, business leaders, and educators have shifted their focus to other ways of improving education. Some are advocating school-voucher programs, which give parents the choice of what school their child will attend. This strategy would make it possible for low-income children to leave behind the problems of the inner-city public schools and find better educational opportunities elsewhere. The question remains, however: What happens to those who remain in the inner-city public schools?

The charter school movement has as its focus the creation of public schools that are free from many of the bureaucratic rules that often limit classroom performance. These schools operate under a charter contract negotiated by the school's organizers (often parents or teachers)

and the local school board that oversees the provisions of the contract. A charter school is freed from the day-to-day bureaucracy of a larger school district and may provide more autonomy for individual students and teachers. However, critics of the charter school movement argue that it takes money away from conventional schools.

A final alternative, home-schooling, has been chosen by some parents who hope to avoid the problems of public school while providing a quality education for their children. Today, an estimated 30,000 to 40,000 children are educated in home-school programs. An association of home-schoolers now provides communication links for parents and children, and technological advances in computers and the Internet have made it possible for parents and children involved in home-schooling to access information and communicate with one another. However, critics question the knowledge and competence of typical parents to educate their own children at home, particularly in rapidly changing academic subjects such as science and computer technology.

Increasingly, information technologies are being accepted as an integral part of education. Since 1993, the federal government has spent over $25 million to create the SchoolNet system—a student-friendly Web site that links students with experts in a variety of fields, as well as with students and teachers across the country. The objective of SchoolNet is to bring every school in Canada online by the year 2000. The effects of the introduction of computer technologies to the classroom remain to be seen. While some experts argue that it will transform the way

THE TECHNOLOGY REVOLUTION IN THE CLASSROOM: EQUALIZING OPPORTUNITY

Technology itself is not new, but its importance as an educational issue has exploded in the past few years as computers have moved into classrooms and workplaces. No longer simply an object of study for those who wish to pursue "technical" careers, technology—particularly computer technology—has become an essential educational tool. Like reading or writing, it is now recognized as a prerequisite for student success. Word processing, simulations, and computerized data analysis have become as standard in schools as typewriters and adding machines a generation ago. In fact, the technological revolution is moving at such a rapid pace that any review of "current" activities is certain to be obsolete by the time it is read.

Canada was one of the first countries in the world to link its entire student body to the information highway. In 1995 Newfoundland became the first province with full Internet access, linking all schools to the World Wide Web and the Internet; by 1997, virtually all schools in the country had access to the Internet via the SchoolNet national electronic network. Despite overall reductions in education budgets, most provinces have introduced systematic plans to expand the role of technology in the curriculum, primarily through the acquisition of computer hardware and software for classroom use.

A number of provinces have set specific targets for classroom computer acquisition. For example, British Columbia announced a five-year plan in 1995 to have one computer in place for every three secondary students and every six elementary students, and Nova Scotia has set a goal of one computer for every ten students by the year 2000. To help the provinces meet these objectives, Industry Canada's "Computers in the Schools" program has moved thousands of used computers, software, and other technologies from industry into Canadian classrooms. In co-operation with

Today computers are essential learning tools in most Canadian classrooms. Proponents of computers in schools see them as a powerful way to equalize opportunities for all students. What do you think are the negative aspects of using computers to teach in schools?

BOX 16.4

CONTINUED

provincial and territorial governments and the private sector, the program had placed more than 20,000 computers and 40,000 pieces of software in schools and libraries by 1997.

Once in place, computers are being used to train teachers as well as students, and to offer computer training and Internet access to the community. Human Resources Development Canada has set up the Office of Learning Technologies (OLT) expressly to provide funding support to innovative learning opportunities using new technologies.

Proponents of computers in schools see them as a powerful tool for levelling the playing field in Canadian classrooms. Their capacity to retrieve information is nearly limitless, and equally available in urban, rural and remote locations; they can be equipped with features that allow many children with disabili-

ties to work alongside their classmates; and they increase understanding within Canada and internationally by allowing students to connect with individuals and classrooms across the country and around the world.

Nevertheless, there are those who have reservations about the expanding role of computer technology in schools. Some parents and teachers continue to fear that, in the face of reduced school budgets, students may find themselves facing machines more frequently than teachers. They also express concern about the quality and suitability of information available on the Internet. Educators stress the importance of teaching students the skills to evaluate that information, since, at this point, the Internet does not impose standards equivalent to those of the publishing industry, or exercise the judgement of a school librarian.

Excerpted with permission from *Education in Canada: An Overview* by Paula Dunning (Toronto: Canadian Education Association, 1997).

students learn, others view "high tech" teaching as simply the latest panacea in education.

What will education be like in the future? School enrolments will continue to grow and diversify as baby boomers continue to have children, and immigration to Canada creates an increasingly diverse population of students. The challenge for the next century lies in finding ways to facilitate learning in a pluralistic school system—by meeting the distinct cultural, linguistic, and religious traditions of a diverse student population.

A further challenge for educational systems in the twenty-first century is to make education more accessible to all disadvantaged groups in Canadian society. Considerable progress has been made in diminishing the educational disparities among women and men and among most visible minority groups. Although differences remain in terms of types of education and fields of study, women now have outcomes superior to men on

many measures of educational attainment (Guppy and Davies, 1998). Similarly, the educational attainment of many visible minority groups are among the highest in Canada. However, although Aboriginal peoples and persons with disabilities have improved their educational levels in recent decades, progress remains slow. Finally, social class continues to be the most persistent and enduring source of educational inequality at all levels of education from preschool through university.

Recent trends suggest that access to education is becoming more restricted as a result of funding cuts at both the provincial and federal levels. Course availability is diminished as school curricula are pared down to "core" subjects, and the specialized services of speech pathologists, physiotherapists, and psychologists are being cut, leaving some children—such as special needs children, children from low-income families, and children from new immigrant families—without the services they need to help them achieve their full

Will distance learning courses change the face of the typical college or university classroom? What do you believe education will be like in the future?

potential in the school system (Canadian Council on Social Development, 1996). At the postsecondary level, tuition fees are rising at a rate that has made university and college educations unaffordable for low-income students. If education is one of the key factors in promoting individual and collective prosperity, then we must strive to improve educational opportunities to all Canadians (Guppy and Davies, 1998).

CHAPTER REVIEW

What is education?
Education is the social institution responsible for the systematic transmission of knowledge, skills, and cultural values within a formally organized structure.

What is the functionalist perspective on education?
According to functionalists, education has both manifest functions (socialization, transmission of culture, social control, social placement, and change and innovation) and latent functions (keeping young people off the streets and out of the job market, matchmaking and producing social networks, and creating a generation gap).

What is the conflict perspective on education?
From a conflict perspective, education is used to perpetuate class, racial–ethnic, and gender inequalities through tracking, ability grouping, and a hidden curriculum that teaches subordinate groups conformity and obedience.

What is the interactionist perspective on education?
Interactionists examine classroom dynamics and study ways in which practices such as labelling may become a self-fulfilling prophecy for some students, such that these students come to perform up—or down—to the expectations held for them by teachers.

What percentage of students drop out before completing high school?
Approximately 15 percent of people under the age of 24 left school before earning a high school diploma. There are, however, significant ethnic and class differences in dropout rates.

Are academic standards in the Canadian education system declining? Why?
According to both parents and recent international tests of math, science, and English, Canadian students are failing to make the grade in comparison with other industrialized countries. Much of the blame for these declining standards has been directed at child-centred education—a system of learning that encourages children to progress at their own rate.

What is functional illiteracy, and what is the rate of functional illiteracy in Canada?
Functional illiteracy is the inability to read and/or write at the skill level necessary for carrying out everyday tasks. The 1994 International Adult Literacy Survey indicated that 16 percent of adult Canadians are functionally illiterate. Furthermore, Canada has the highest rate of youth with poor literacy skills among the leading industrialized nations.

What controversies persist in education?
Gender bias in the classroom, unequal educational opportunities for students with disabilities, and the soaring cost of a university education are among the pressing issues in education in Canada today.

Key Terms

credentialism 521
cultural capital 518
cultural transmission 510
education 510
formal education 511
functional illiteracy 526
hidden curriculum 520
informal education 510
mass education 512
meritocracy 521
tracking 519

📧 Internet Exercises

In order to effectively use the Internet exercises in this book, it will be necessary to have both a Web browser and newsreader software. If you are using Netscape 2.0 or greater, or Microsoft Internet Explorer 3.0 or greater, you have a newsreader built into your software. Please consult the computing centre at your school if you need assistance with these programs.

1. The Canadian Education Association has a Web site at:

   http://www.acea.ca

   What information can you find on recent trends in education in Canada?

2. Canada's SchoolNet is designed to promote the effective use of information technology among Canadians by helping schools and public libraries connect to the Internet. Visit SchoolNet's home page at:

   http://www.schoolnet.ca

   and explore what subject areas are available under Learning Resources. What sociology Web sites can you locate in Learning Resources?

📧 Net Links

National Adult Literacy Database is a national database of adult literacy programs, resources, services, and activities across Canada. It also links with other services and databases in North America and overseas; go to:

   http://www.nald.ca

The Canadian Teachers' Federation is an excellent source of information on teaching in Canada as well as current issues facing schools; see:

   http://www.ctf-fce.ca

The Canadian Federation of Students represents about half a million students at over 60 universities, colleges, and technical institutes across Canada. Its Web site has been established to offer students, the general public, media, and government officials information on the issues facing college and university students today; go to:

   http://www.cfs-fcee.ca

The United Nations Educational, Scientific, and Cultural Organization's (UNESCO) Education Information Service provides global educational news, statistics, updates on programs and activities, and current publications on education; see:

   http://www.unesco.org/education/

In the on-line publication *Education—A Right or a Privilege?*, student journalists from across the world report on the right to education; see:

   http://www.unesco. org/education/cfa/ contest/index.htm

Questions for Critical Thinking

1. What are the major functions of education for individuals and for societies?
2. Why do some theorists believe that education is a vehicle for decreasing social inequality whereas others believe that education reproduces existing class relationships?
3. Why does so much controversy exist over what should be taught in Canadian public schools?
4. How are the values and attitudes you learned from your family reflected in your beliefs about education?

Suggested Readings

This book provides more information about the sociology of education:

Jeanne H. Ballantine. *The Sociology of Education: A Systematic Analysis* (4th ed.). Englewood Cliffs, N.J.: Prentice-Hall, 1997.

Further readings on the controversy over IQ include the following:

Russell Jacoby and Naomi Glauberman (eds.). *The Bell Curve Debate: History, Documents, Opinions.* New York: Times Books, 1995.

Elaine Mensh and Harry Mensh. *The IQ Mythology: Class, Race, Gender, and Inequality.* Carbondale: Southern Illinois University Press, 1991.

Comprehensive discussions on problems in today's schools may be found in the following studies:

Maude Barlow and Heather-jane Robertson. *Class Warfare: The Assault on Canada's Schools.* Toronto: Key Porter Books, 1994.

Neil Guppy and Scott Davies. *Education in Canada: Recent Trends and Future Challenges.* Ottawa: Statistics Canada, 1998.

The Sociological Study of Religion
    Religion and the Meaning of Life
    Categories of Religion

Sociological Perspectives on Religion
    The Functionalist Perspective on Religion
    The Conflict Perspective on Religion
    The Interactionist Perspective on Religion

World Religions
    Hinduism
    Buddhism
    Confucianism
    Judaism
    Islam
    Christianity

Types of Religious Organizations
    Ecclesia
    The Church–Sect Typology
    Cults

Trends in Religion in Canada
    Canada's Religious Mosaic
    Religiosity
    Why Have Canadians Turned Away from the
        Church?
    Fundamentalism
    Does Religion Make a Difference?
    Women in the Ministry

Religion in the Future

For most of Canada's history religion played a major role in the development and maintenance of educational institutions. Religious instruction was considered an essential component of "becoming educated." Which religion was to be taught was relatively simple—it was Christianity in either its Catholic or Protestant form. Today, things are not that simple—while the majority of Canadians are Christians, with Catholics making up 46 percent and Protestants 33 percent, other religions such as Hinduism, Islam, Buddhism, Confucianism, Sikhism, and others too numerous to mention are now part of our Canadian mosaic (Statistics Canada, 1996a). Currently, there is no consensus among Canadians regarding what role religion should play in education.

Should students receive religious instruction in the classroom? If so, which religions should be included? Should prayer be offered in schools? Should participation in prayer be voluntary or compulsory? In our multi-ethnic society, these questions are becoming increasingly difficult to answer. Some parents feel that religious instruction is necessary, suggesting that secularization in the public school system is contributing to a declining morality.

Albertans Dick and Joanne Barendregt teach their children at home. While home-schooling is relatively common in Canada, the Barendregts are part of a growing network of parents who do not register their children or allow provincial officials to monitor their children's education because they feel this would interfere with their religious freedom. The couple decided to educate their children at home after they found that one of their children's textbooks had a section on evolution that conflicted with their religious views.

Joanne Barendregt feels that "in two or three years, they're going to regulate what we feed our children ... and after that it will be our reproductive systems." She goes on to say that "we feel the highest calling a girl can have is to be a wife and mother first. We teach that that is their purpose ... We are not changing. You [society] have changed. You're trying to destroy our [religious] heritage." Her husband says they will not register with the government because "we will not have a partnership with a government that promotes and allows homosexuality to continue, and abortion." (Mitchell, 1999:A7)

The Barendregts feel that religious instruction is a vital part of education. However, others feel that the educational system must be separate from religion and that the curriculum should be based on secular concerns.

RELIGION

Proponents of this point of view suggest that in our multicultural society no religion should be espoused or endorsed. How can schools teach religious values that might conflict with the values and customs of a significant number of students? How might students and teachers who come from diverse religious and cultural backgrounds feel about instruction or organized prayer in public schools? Rick Nelson, a teacher in the public school system, explains his concern about the potential impact of religion in his classroom:

"I think it really trivializes religion when you try to take such a serious topic with so many different viewpoints and cover it in the public schools. At my school we have teachers and students who are Hindu. They are really devout, but they are not monotheistic. I am not opposed to individual prayer by students. But when there is a group prayer, who's going to lead the group?" (CNN, 1994)

This argument is only one in a lengthy history of debates about the appropriate relationship between religion and other social institutions. In education, for example, controversies have arisen over topics such as the teaching of creationism versus evolutionism, moral education, sex education, school prayer, and the subject matter of textbooks and library books.

What role does religion play in Canada's school systems today? The simple answer is that religion plays almost no role in the public school system. Most of those who wish to combine education with religious instruction must do so through private schooling. However, education falls within provincial jurisdiction, and some provinces provide public funding to Roman Catholic separate schools (Holmes, 1998). For example, Saskatchewan and Ontario fully fund Roman Catholic schools, but do not support schools operated by members of other religious denominations. On the other hand, Manitoba and British Columbia do not use religion as a criterion, but provide funding to a wide variety of private schools (many of which are religious schools) based on academic criteria. Ontario's situation is quite interesting, as the teaching of the Christian religion in the public school system, which was once mandatory, is now forbidden. At the same time Roman Catholic schools are fully funded. This means that the Protestant majority cannot teach its religion in the public schools, while the Catholic minority has its own funded system.

All other minorities and Protestants who wish a religious-based education receive no provincial support (Holmes, 1998).

As the issue of religious education suggests, religion can be a highly controversial topic. One group's deeply held beliefs or cherished religious practices may be a source of irritation to another. As we begin a new century, religion is a source of both stability and conflict throughout the world (Kurtz, 1995). In this chapter, we examine how religion influences life in Canada and in other areas of the world. Before reading on, test your knowledge about how religion affects public education in this country by taking the quiz in Box 17.1 on page 543.

Debates about what children should be taught in schools have taken place throughout the history of Canadian public education. The issue of teaching creationism versus evolution in science classrooms is only one example of the intersection of religion and education.

QUESTIONS AND ISSUES

CHAPTER FOCUS QUESTION: What is the relationship between society and religion, and what role does religion play in people's everyday lives?

What are the key components of religion?

How do functionalist, conflict, and interactionist perspectives on religion differ?

What are the central beliefs of the world's religions?

How do religious bodies differ in organizational structure?

What is the future of religion in Canada?

THE SOCIOLOGICAL STUDY OF RELIGION

What is religion? *Religion* **is a system of beliefs, symbols, and rituals, based on some sacred or supernatural realm, that guides human behaviour, gives meaning to life, and unites believers into a community** (Durkheim, 1947/1912). For many people, religious beliefs provide the answers for seemingly unanswerable questions about the meaning of life and death. Religion is one of the most significant social institutions in society. As such, it consists of a variety of elements, including beliefs about the sacred or supernatural, rituals, and a social organization of believers drawn together by their common religious tradition (Kurtz, 1995). This system of beliefs seeks to

bridge the gap between the known and the unknown, the seen and the unseen, and the sacred ("holy, set apart, or forbidden") and the secular (things of this world). Most religions attempt to answer fundamental questions such as those regarding the meaning of life and how the world was created. Most religions also provide comfort to persons facing emotional traumas such as illness, suffering, grief, and death. According to sociologist Lester Kurtz (1995:9), religious beliefs are typically woven into a series of narratives, including stories about how ancestors and significant others had meaningful experiences with supernatural powers. Moreover, religious beliefs are linked to practices that bind people together and to rites of passage such as birth, marriage, and death. People with similar religious beliefs and practices often bind themselves together in a moral community (such as a church, mosque, temple, or synagogue) where they can engage in religious beliefs and practices with similarly minded people.

Given the diversity and complexity of religion, how is it possible for sociologists to study this social institution? Most sociologists studying religion are committed to the pursuit of "disinterested scholarship," meaning that they do not seek to make value judgments about religious beliefs or to determine whether particular religious bodies are "right" or "wrong." However, many acknowledge that it is impossible to completely rid themselves of those values and beliefs into which they were socialized (Bruce, 1996). Therefore, for the most part, sociologists study religion by using sociological methods such as historical analysis, experimentation, participant observation, survey

HOW MUCH DO YOU KNOW ABOUT THE IMPACT OF RELIGION ON EDUCATION IN CANADA?

TRUE	FALSE	
T	F	1. Provincial governments in Canada do not fund separate religious schools.
T	F	2. Virtually all contemporary sociologists have advocated the separation of moral teaching from academic subject matter.
T	F	3. The federal government has limited control over how funds are spent by school districts because most of the money comes from the provinces, thus questions of religion in the schools are decided at the provincial level.
T	F	4. Enrolment in parochial schools has decreased in Canada as interest in religion has waned.
T	F	5. In Canada, the public school system recognizes only Christian religious holidays.
T	F	6. The number of children from religious backgrounds other than Christian and Judaic has grown steadily in public schools over the past three decades.
T	F	7. Debates over textbook content focus only on elementary education because of the vulnerability of young children.
T	F	8. Increasing numbers of parents are instructing their own children through home-schooling because of their concerns about what public schools are (or are not) teaching their children.
T	F	9. Most members of the baby boom generation have no religious affiliation today because they received no religious instruction in school.
T	F	10. Prayer in public schools in Canada is offered on a voluntary basis.

Answers on page 544.

research, and content analysis that can be verified and replicated (Roberts, 1995). As a result, most studies in the sociology of religion focus on tangible elements that can be *seen*, such as written texts, patterns of behaviour, or individuals' opinions about religious matters, and that can be studied using standard sociological research tools. According to sociologist Keith A. Roberts (1995:28), beliefs constitute only a small part of a sociological examination of religion:

> The sociological approach focuses on religious groups and institutions (their formation, maintenance, and demise), on the behavior of individuals within these groups (e.g., social processes that affect conversion, ritual behavior), and on conflicts between religious groups (such as Catholic vs. Protestant, Christian vs. [Muslim], mainline denomination vs. cult). For the sociologist, beliefs are only one small part of religion.

How does the sociological study of religion differ from the theological approach? Unlike the sociological approach, which focuses primarily on the visible aspects of religion, *theologians* study specific religious doctrines or belief systems, including answers to questions such as, What is the nature of God or the gods? and What is the relationship among supernatural power, human beings, and the universe? Many theologians primarily study the religious beliefs of a specific religion (such as Christianity, Judaism, Buddhism, or Hinduism), denomination (such as Catholic or Anglican), or religious leader so that they can interpret this information for laypersons who seek answers for seemingly unanswerable questions about the meaning of life and death.

Religion and the Meaning of Life

Religion seeks to answer important questions such as why we exist, why people suffer and die, and what happens when we die. Sociologist Peter Berger (1967) referred to religion as a *sacred canopy*—a sheltering fabric hanging over people that gives them security and provides answers for the questions of life. However, this sacred canopy requires that people have **faith**—unquestioning

BOX 17.1

ANSWERS TO THE SOCIOLOGY QUIZ ON RELIGION AND EDUCATION

1. **False.** Schools operated by the Catholic Church are provincially funded in several provinces.

2. **False.** Obviously, contemporary sociologists hold strong beliefs and opinions on many subjects. However, most of them do not think it is their role to advocate specific stances on a topic such as religion. Early sociologists were less inclined to believe that they had to be "value-free." For example, Durkheim strongly advocated that education should have a moral component and that schools had a responsibility to perpetuate society by teaching a commitment to the common morality.

3. **True.** Under the terms of the British North America Act, education is a provincial responsibility. Public school revenue comes from local funding through property taxes and provincial funding from a variety of sources. The federal government is responsible for maintaining schools for Aboriginal people, running a military college, funding adult education programs, and over-seeing educational programs in federal penitentiaries.

4. **False.** In recent years, just the opposite has happened. As parents have begun feeling that their children were not receiving the type of education the parents desired for them in public schools, parochial schools have flourished. Most religions have established their own parochial schools.

5. **True.** This is normally the case, although, as you will learn, some schools have also recognized Jewish holidays. However, this has resulted in conflict, as other religious groups also want to see their religious holidays formally recognized.

6. **True.** Although about 83 percent of Canadians aged 18 and over describe their religion as one of the forms, or denominations, of Christianity, the number of those who either adhere to no religion or who are Jewish, Muslim/Islamic, Sikh, Buddhist, or Hindu has increased significantly.

7. **False.** Attempts to remove textbooks occur at all levels of schooling. A recent case involved the removal of Chaucer's "The Miller's Tale" and Aristophanes' *Lysistrata* from a high school curriculum.

8. **True.** Some parents choose home-schooling for religious reasons. Others embrace it for secular reasons, including fear for their children's safety and concerns about the quality of public schools.

9. **False.** Most baby boomers did receive religious instruction, either in private schools or in public schools where prayer and Bible reading took place.

10. **True.** Parents must sign consent forms for their children to participate in prayers in public schools.

Sources: Based on Johnson, 1994; Ballantine, 1993; Greenberg and Page, 1993; Kosmin and Lachman, 1993; Roof, 1993; Sullivan, 1993; and Gibbs, 1994.

belief that does not require proof or scientific evidence. Science and medicine typically rely on existing scientific evidence to respond to questions of suffering, death, and injustice, whereas religion seeks to explain such phenomena by referring to the sacred. According to Emile Durkheim (1995/1912), the *sacred* refers to those aspects of life that are extraordinary or supernatural—in other words, those things that are set apart as "holy." People feel a sense of awe, reverence, deep respect, or fear for that which is considered sacred. Across cultures and in different eras, many things have been considered sacred, including invisible gods, spirits, specific animals or trees, altars, crosses, holy books, and special words or songs that only the initiated could speak or sing

(Collins, 1982). Those things that people do not set apart as sacred are referred to as the *profane—* the everyday, secular, or "worldly" aspects of life (Collins, 1982). Sacred beliefs are rooted in the holy or supernatural, whereas secular beliefs have their foundation in scientific knowledge or everyday explanations. For example, in the educational debate over creationism and evolutionism, advocates of creationism view their belief as founded in sacred (Biblical) teachings, but advocates of evolutionism argue that their beliefs are based on provable scientific facts.

In addition to beliefs, religion also comprises symbols and rituals. According to anthropologist Clifford Geertz (1966), religion is a set of cultural symbols that establishes powerful and pervasive

Devout Muslims around the world kneel in prayer at specific times of day. Muslims are among the fastest-growing religious groups in North America.

moods and motivations to help people interpret the meaning of life and establish a direction for their behaviour. People often act out their religious beliefs in the form of **rituals—regularly repeated and carefully prescribed forms of behaviour that symbolize a cherished value or belief** (Kurtz, 1995). Rituals range from songs and prayers to offerings and sacrifices that worship or praise a supernatural being, an ideal, or a set of supernatural principles. For example, Muslims bow toward Mecca, the holy city of Islam, five times a day at fixed times to pray to God, whereas Christians participate in the celebration of communion to commemorate the life, death, and resurrection of Jesus Christ. Rituals differ from everyday actions in that they involve very strictly determined behaviour. The rituals involved in praying or in observing communion are carefully orchestrated and must be followed with precision. According to sociologist Randall Collins (1982:34), "In rituals, it is the forms that count. Saying prayers, singing a hymn, performing a primitive sacrifice or a dance, marching in a procession, kneeling before an idol or making the sign of the cross—in these, the action must be done the right way."

Rituals are one of the sets of rules that are part of religious life. The importance of rituals and other religious regulations can be understood if you recall that the purpose of religion is to provide explanations of fundamental questions such as death and the meaning of life. Rodney Stark has pointed out that religions do more for humans

than "supply them with answers to questions of ultimate meaning. The assumption that the supernatural exists raises a new question: *What does the supernatural want or expect from us?*" (1998:386). Thus religions also provide the faithful with rules about how they must act if they are to please the gods. These rules can be justified in religious terms, and those who share the religious faith see them as legitimate.

Categories of Religion

Although it is difficult to establish exactly when religious rituals first began, anthropologists have concluded that all known groups over the past hundred thousand years have had some form of religion (Haviland, 1993). Religions have been classified into four main categories based on their dominant belief: simple supernaturalism, animism, theism, and transcendent idealism (McGee, 1975). In very simple preindustrial societies, religion often takes the form of **simple supernaturalism—the belief that supernatural forces affect people's lives either positively or negatively.** This type of religion does not acknowledge specific gods or supernatural spirits but focuses instead on impersonal forces that may exist in people or natural objects. For example, simple supernaturalism has been used to explain mystifying events of nature, such as sunrises and thunderstorms, and ways that some objects may bring a person good or bad luck. By contrast, **animism is the belief that plants, animals, or other elements of the natural**

Throughout the world, people seek the meaning of life through traditional and nontraditional forms of religion. These Italian spiritual seekers are meeting together at a Mayan ruin in quest of harmonic convergence.

world are endowed with spirits or life forces that have an impact on events in society. Animism is associated with early hunting and gathering societies in which everyday life is not separated from the elements of the natural world (Albanese, 1992).

The third category of religion is *theism*—a belief in a god or gods. Horticultural societies were among the first to practise *monotheism*—a belief in a single, supreme being or god who is responsible for significant events such as the creation of the world. Three of the major world religions—Christianity, Judaism, and Islam—are monotheistic. By contrast, Hinduism, Shinto, and a number of the indigenous religions of Africa are forms of *polytheism*—a belief in more than one god. By contrast, the fourth category of religion, transcendent idealism, is a *nontheistic religion*—a religion based on a belief in divine spiritual forces such as sacred principles of thought and conduct, rather than a god or gods. Transcendent idealism focuses on principles such as truth, justice, affirmation of life, and tolerance for others, and its adherents seek an elevated state of consciousness in which they can fulfil their true potential.

SOCIOLOGICAL PERSPECTIVES ON RELIGION

Religion as a social institution is a powerful, deeply felt, and influential force. Sociologists study the social institution of religion because of the importance that religion holds for many people. They also want to know more about the influence of religion on society, and vice versa. For example, some people believe that the introduction of prayer or religious instruction in public schools would have a positive effect on the teaching of values such as honesty, compassion, courage, and tolerance because these values could be given a moral foundation. However, society has strongly influenced the practice of religion in Canada as a result of court rulings and laws that have limited religious activities in public settings, including schools.

The major sociological perspectives have different outlooks on the relationship between religion and society. Functionalists typically emphasize the ways in which religious beliefs and rituals can bind people together. Conflict explanations suggest that religion can be a source of false consciousness in society. Interactionists focus on the meanings that people give to religion in their everyday life.

The Functionalist Perspective on Religion

Emile Durkheim was one of the first sociologists to emphasize that religion is essential to the maintenance of society. He suggested that religion was a cultural universal found in all societies because it met basic human needs and served important societal functions.

DURKHEIM ON RELIGION In *The Elementary Forms of the Religious Life* (1947/1912:47), Durkheim defined religion as "a unified system of beliefs and practices relative to sacred things, that is to say, things set apart and forbidden—beliefs and practices which unite into one single moral community all those who adhere to them." According to Durkheim, all religions share three elements: (1) beliefs held by adherents, (2) practices (rituals) engaged in collectively by believers, and (3) a moral community based on the group's shared beliefs and practices pertaining to the sacred.

For Durkheim, the central feature of all religions is the presence of sacred beliefs and rituals that bind people together in a collectivity. In his studies of the religion of the Australian Aborigines, for example, Durkheim found that each clan had established its own sacred totem, which included kangaroos, trees, rivers, rock formations, and other animals or natural creations. To clan members, their totem was sacred; it symbolized some unique quality of their clan. People developed a feeling of unity by performing ritual dances around their totem, which caused them to abandon individual self-interest. Durkheim suggested that the correct performance of the ritual gives rise to religious conviction. Religious beliefs and rituals are *collective representations*—group-held meanings that express something important about the group itself (McGuire, 1992:177). Because of the intertwining of group consciousness and society, functionalists suggest that religion is functional because it meets basic human needs.

FUNCTIONS OF RELIGION From a functionalist perspective, religion has three important functions in any society: (1) providing meaning and purpose to life, (2) promoting social cohesion and a sense of belonging, and (3) providing social control and support for the government.

Meaning and Purpose Religion offers meaning for the human experience. Some events create a profound sense of loss on both an individual basis (such as injustice, suffering, and the death of a loved one) and a group basis (such as famine, earthquake, economic depression, or subjugation by an enemy). Inequality may cause people to wonder why their own personal situation is no better than it is. Most religions offer explanations for these concerns. Explanations may differ from one religion to another, yet each tells the individual or group that life is part of a larger system of order in the universe (McGuire, 1992). Some (but not all) religions even offer hope of an afterlife for persons who follow the religion's tenets of morality in this life. Such beliefs help make injustices in this life easier to endure.

In a study of religious beliefs among baby boomers (born between 1946 and 1964), religion and society scholar Wade Clark Roof (1993) found that a number of people had returned to organized religion as part of a personal quest for meaning. Roof notes that they were looking "for something to believe in, for answers to questions about life," as reflected in this woman's comments:

> Something was missing. You turn around and you go, is this it? I have a nice husband, I have a nice house; I was just about to finish graduate school. I knew I was going to have a very marketable degree. I wanted to do it. And you turn and you go, here I am. This is it. And there were just things that were missing. I just didn't have stimulation. I didn't have the motivation. And I guess when you mentioned faith, I guess that's what was gone. (quoted in Roof, 1993:158)

Social Cohesion and a Sense of Belonging By emphasizing shared symbolism, religious teachings and practices help promote social cohesion. An example is the Christian ritual of communion, which not only commemorates a historical event but also allows followers to participate in the unity ("communion") of themselves with other believers (McGuire, 1997). All religions have some forms of shared experience that rekindle the group's consciousness of its own unity.

Religion has played an important part in helping members of subordinate groups develop a sense of social cohesion and belonging. For

BOX 17.2   CRITICAL THINKING

A LEGAL CHALLENGE TO RELIGIOUS HOLIDAYS IN SCHOOLS

Like millions of other young Canadians, 14-year-old Aysha Bassuny returns to school this [September]. But the Ottawa Board of Education has delayed the start of her school year for two days so that Jewish students can observe the Jewish New Year—Rosh Hashanah. Bassuny is one of many in Ottawa's Islamic community who are angry that the board has refused to consider extending them a similar courtesy by closing schools for two Muslim holy days. "It's not fair," says Bassuny, a Grade 10 student at suburban Brookfield High School, who wears the traditional Islamic head scarf, the hijab. "I have to miss school for my holy days and the Jewish kids don't. You cannot have it for one group and not the other."

In July 1995 Islamic Schools Federation of Ontario, which represents independent Muslim schools, launched a lawsuit against the Ottawa Board of Education alleging that the rights of Muslims to freedom of conscience and religion under the Charger of Rights have been undermined by the board's actions. The lawsuit argued that schools with significant numbers of Muslim students should be required to observe two important Islamic holidays. The Islamic Schools Federation chose to sue the Ottawa Board of Education as a test case, believing that a victory there would set a precedent for the rest of the country.

The dispute began in April 1994, when the Ottawa board agreed to what seemed at the time to be a modest request from Ottawa's Jewish community—to delay the start of the school year so that Jewish students could observe Rosh Hashanah without missing the

---

example, in the late 1980s and early 1990s, Russian Jewish immigrants to Canada have found a sense of belonging in some congregations. Even though they did not speak the language of their new country, they had religious rituals and a sense of history in common with others in the congregation. Korean immigrants are forming their own congregations in Canada. In Calgary, the Baptist minister at a church with a congregation made up of 1500 Korean Calgarians, comments, "The church is more than a Christian institution, it is also a means of cultural fellowship. It is a place to feel comfortable. They are in a strange country and here there is friendship" (Nemeth et al., 1993:33). Shared experiences such as these strengthen not only the group but also the individual's commitment to the group's expectations and goals (McGuire, 1997).

Social Control and Support for the Government   How does religion help bind society together and maintain social control? All societies attempt to maintain social control through systems of rewards and punishments. Sacred symbols and beliefs establish powerful, pervasive, long-lasting motivations based on the concept of a general order of exis-

tence (Geertz, 1966). In other words, if individuals consider themselves to be part of a larger order that holds the ultimate meaning in life, they will feel bound to one another (and past and future generations) in a way that otherwise might not be possible (McGuire, 1997).

Religion also helps maintain social control in society by conferring supernatural legitimacy on the norms and laws in society. In some societies, social control occurs as a result of direct collusion between the dominant classes and the dominant religious organizations. Niccolo Machiavelli, an influential sixteenth-century statesman and writer, wrote that it was "the duty of princes and heads of republics to uphold the foundations of religion in their countries, for then it is easy to keep their people religious, and consequently well conducted and united" (quoted in McGuire, 1997:235). As discussed in Chapter 14, absolute monarchs often have claimed a divine right to rule.

The Conflict Perspective on Religion

KARL MARX ON RELIGION   For Marx, *ideologies*—"systematic views of the way the world ought to

BOX 17.2

CONTINUED

first two days of school. According to Jewish community leader Ron Singer, the request was entirely reasonable, because it did not mean a permanent change in the school year: the Jewish calendar is based on the cycles of the moon, and Rosh Hashanah coincides with the opening of school only once every 40 years.

On the other side of the issue, the lawyer for the Islamic Schools Federation of Ontario said that the problem was "the recognition of two religions, Christian and Jewish, and the rejection of another, Muslim."

Those involved in the dispute recognized that, if taken to its logical extreme, the rapid growth of Canada's Muslim, Buddhist, Hindu, and Sikh communities could lead to a school year with as many as 15 religious holidays. At the time, one school board member conceded that it was "a tough problem," and one that an increasingly multicultural society would be unable to avoid. Ultimately, the lawsuit was rejected by the Ontario Divisional Court and in July 1997 the Ontario Appeal Court refused to hear an appeal. This means that Ontario schools are not required to recognize the holidays of minority religious groups. Do you think it is fair that Christian holidays are recognized while the holidays of other religions are not?

Adapted with permission from Luke Fisher, "A Holy War Over Holidays," *Maclean's*, August 12, 1994.

be"—are embodied in religious doctrines and political values (Turner, Beeghley, and Powers, 1995:135). These ideologies also serve to justify the status quo and retard social change. The capitalist class uses religious ideology as a tool of domination to mislead the workers about their true interests. For this reason, Marx wrote his now famous statement that religion is the "opiate of the masses." People become complacent because they have been taught to believe in an afterlife in which they will be rewarded for their suffering and misery in this life. Although these religious teachings soothe the masses' distress, any relief is illusory. Religion unites people under a "false consciousness," according to which they believe they have common interests with members of the dominant class (Roberts, 1995b).

From a conflict perspective religion also tends to promote strife between groups and societies. The conflict may be *between* religious groups (for example, anti-Semitism), *within* a religious group (for example, when a splinter group leaves an existing denomination), or between a religious group and *the larger society* (for example, the conflict over religion in the classroom). Conflict theorists assert that, in attempting to provide meaning and purpose in life while at the same time promoting the status quo, religion is used by the dominant classes to impose their own control over society and its resources (McGuire, 1992). Many feminists object to the patriarchal nature of most religions; some advocate a break from traditional religions, while others seek to reform religious language, symbols, and rituals to eliminate the elements of patriarchy (Renzetti and Curran, 1992).

MAX WEBER ON RELIGION Whereas Marx believed that religion retarded social change, Weber argued just the opposite. For Weber, religion could be a catalyst to produce social change. In *The Protestant Ethic and the Spirit of Capitalism* (1976/1904–1905), Weber asserted that the religious teachings of John Calvin were directly related to the rise of capitalism. Calvin emphasized the doctrine of *predestination*—the belief that, even before they are born, all people are divided into two groups, the saved and the damned. Only God knows who will go to heaven (the elect) and who will go to hell. Because people cannot know whether they will be saved, they look for earthly signs that they are among

The shared experiences and beliefs associated with religion have helped many groups maintain a sense of social cohesion and a feeling of belonging in the face of prejudice and discrimination.

the elect. According to the Protestant ethic, those who have faith, perform good works, and achieve economic success are more likely to be among the chosen of God. As a result, people work hard, save their money, and do not spend it on worldly frivolity; instead they reinvest it in their land, equipment, and labour (Chalfant, Beckley, and Palmer, 1994).

The spirit of capitalism grew in the fertile soil of the Protestant ethic. Even as people worked ever harder to prove their religious piety, structural conditions in Europe led to the Industrial Revolution, free markets, and the commercialization of the economy—developments that worked hand in hand with Calvinist religious teachings. From this viewpoint, wealth was an unintended consequence of religious piety and hard work. With the contemporary secularizing influence of wealth, people often think of wealth and material possessions as the major (or only) reason to work. Although no longer referred to as the "Protestant" ethic, many people still refer to the "work ethic" in somewhat the same manner that Weber did.

Like Marx, Weber was acutely aware that religion could reinforce existing social arrangements, especially the stratification system. The wealthy can use religion to justify their power and privilege: it is a sign of God's approval of their hard work and morality. As for the poor, if they work hard and live a moral life, they will be richly rewarded in another life. The Hindu belief in reincarnation is an example of religion reinforcing the stratification system. Because a person's social position in the current life is the result of behaviour in a former life, the privileges of the upper

class must be protected so that each person may enjoy those privileges in another incarnation.

Does Weber's thesis about the relationship between religion and the economy withstand the test of time? Recently, sociologist Randall Collins reexamined Weber's assertion that the capitalist breakthrough occurred just in Christian Europe and concluded that this belief is only partially accurate. According to Collins, Weber was correct that religious institutions are among the most likely places within agrarian societies for capitalism to begin. However, Collins believes that the foundations for capitalism in Asia, particularly Japan, were laid in the Buddhist monastic economy in late medieval Japan. Collins (1997:855) states that "the temples were the first entrepreneurial organizations in Japan: the first to combine control of the factors of labor, capital, and land so as to allocate them for enhancing production." Due to an ethic of self-discipline and restraint on consumption, high levels of accumulation and investment took place in medieval Japanese Buddhism. Gradually, secular capitalism emerged from temple capitalism as new guilds arose that were independent of the temples, and the gap between the clergy and everyday people narrowed through property transformation brought about by uprisings of the common people and wars with outside entities. Moreover, the capitalist dynamic in the monasteries was eventually transferred to the secular economy, opening the way to the Industrial Revolution in Japan. From the works of Weber and Collins, we can conclude that the emergence of capitalism through a religious economy happened in several parts of the

According to Marx and Weber, religion serves to reinforce social stratification in a society. For example, according to Hindu belief, a person's social position in their current life is a result of behaviour in a former life.

world, not just one, and that it occurred in both Christian and Buddhist forms (Collins, 1997).

The Interactionist Perspective on Religion

Thus far, we have been looking at religion primarily from a macrolevel perspective. Interactionists focus their attention on a microlevel analysis that examines the meanings that people give to religion in their everyday life.

RELIGION AS A REFERENCE GROUP For many people, religion serves as a reference group to help them define themselves. Religious symbols, for example, have meaning for large bodies of people. The Star of David holds special significance for Jews, just as the crescent moon and star do for Muslims and the cross does for Christians. For individuals, a symbol may have a certain meaning beyond that shared by the group. For instance, a symbol given to a child may have special meaning when he or she grows up and faces war or other crises. It may not only remind the adult of a religious belief but also create a feeling of closeness with a relative who is now deceased. It has been said that the symbolism of religion is so very powerful because it "expresses the essential facts of our human existence" (Collins, 1982:37).

HIS RELIGION AND HER RELIGION Not all people interpret religion in the same way. In virtually all religions, women have much less influence on the establishment of social definitions of appropriate gender roles both within the religious community and in the larger community (McGuire, 1992).

Therefore, women and men may belong to the same religious group, but their individual religion will not necessarily be a carbon copy of the group's entire system of beliefs. In fact, according to McGuire (1997), women's versions of a certain religion probably differ markedly from men's versions. For example, whereas an Orthodox Jewish man may focus on his public ritual roles and his discussion of sacred texts, Orthodox Jewish women have few ritual duties and are more likely to focus on their responsibilities in the home. Consequently, the meaning of being Jewish may be different for women than for men.

Religious symbolism and language typically create a social definition of the roles of men and women. For example, religious symbolism may depict the higher deities as male and the lower deities as female. Sometimes, females are depicted as negative, or evil, spiritual forces. For example, the Hindu goddess Kali represents men's eternal battle against the evils of materialism (Daly, 1973). Historically, language has defined women as being nonexistent in the world's major religions. Phrases such as "for all men" in Catholic and Anglican services gradually have been changed to "for all"; however, some churches retain the traditional liturgy. Although there has been resistance, especially by women, to some of the terms, overall inclusive language is less common than older male terms for God (Briggs, 1987). (See Table 17.1.)

Many women resist the subordination they have experienced in organized religion. They have worked to change the existing rules that have excluded them or placed them in a clearly subordinate position.

TABLE 17.1	GENERED IMAGES OF GOD

Question: Which of the following images do you associate with God? (You may select more than one.)

IMAGE	PERCENT SURVEYED WHO IMAGE GOD THIS WAY
Master	48.3
Father	46.8
Judge	36.5
Redeemer	36.2
Creator	29.5
Friend	26.6
King	20.6
Healer	8.3
Lover	7.3
Liberator	5.5
Mother	3.2
Spouse	2.6

Sources: National Opinion Research Centre, *General Social Survey*, 1989, 156–159; and Renzetti and Curran, 1998.

WORLD RELIGIONS

Although there are many localized religions throughout the world, those religions classified as *world religions* cover vast expanses of the Earth and have millions of followers. Six world religions—Hinduism, Buddhism, Confucianism, Judaism, Islam, and Christianity—have more than four billion adherents—almost 75 percent of the world population. These six religions are compared in Table 17.2.

Hinduism

We begin with Hinduism because it is believed to be one of the world's oldest current religions, having originated along the banks of the Indus River in Pakistan between 3500 and 4500 years ago. Since Hinduism began before written records were kept, modern scholars have only limited information about its earliest leaders and their teachings (Kurtz, 1995). Unlike most other world religions, Hinduism does not have a specific founder or worship a single god and is considered by many people to be *polytheistic* because its adherents believe that there are many gods. Hindu beliefs and practices have been preserved through an oral tradition and expressed in texts and hymns known as the *Vedas* (meaning "knowledge" or "wisdom"); however, this religion does not have a "sacred" book, such as the Judeo-Christian Bible or the Islamic Qur'an (Sharma, 1993). Consequently, Hindu beliefs and practices emerged over the centuries across the subcontinent of India in a variety of forms, reflecting the influence of the various regional cultures (Kurtz, 1995). Since Hinduism has no scriptures that are thought to be inspired by a god or gods and is not based on the teachings of any one person, religion scholars refer to it as an *ethical religion*—a system of beliefs that calls upon adherents to follow an ideal way of life. For most Hindus, this is partly achieved by adhering to the expectations of the caste system (see Chapter 8).

Central to Hindu teachings is the belief that individual souls (*jivas*) enter the world and roam the universe until they break free into the limitless atmosphere of illumination (*moska*) by discovering their own *dharma*—duties or responsibilities. According to Hinduism, individual *jivas* pass through a sequence of bodies over time as they undergo a process known as reincarnation (*samsara*)—an endless passage through cycles of life, death, and rebirth until the soul earns liberation

TABLE 17.2   MAJOR WORLD RELIGIONS

	CURRENT FOLLOWERS	FOUNDER/ DATE	BELIEFS
Christianity	1.7 billion	Jesus Christ; 1st century C.E.	Monotheistic. Jesus is the Son of God. Through good moral and religious behaviour (and/or God's grace), people achieve eternal life with God.
Islam	950 million	Muhammad; ca. 610 C.E.	Monotheistic. Muhammad received the Qu'ran (scriptures) from God. On Judgment Day, believers who have submitted to God's will, as revealed in the Qu'ran will go to an eternal Garden of Eden.
Hinduism	719 million	No specific founder; ca. 1500 B.C.E.	Polytheistic. Brahma (creator), Vishnu (preserver), and Shiva (destroyer) are divine. Union with ultimate reality and escape from eternal reincarnation are achieved through yoga, adherence to scripture, and devotion.
Buddhism	309 million	Siddhartha Gautama; 6th to 5th centuries B.C.E.	Nontheistic. Through meditation and adherence to the Eightfold Path (correct thought and behaviour), people can free themselves from desire and suffering, escape the cycle of eternal rebirth, and achieve nirvana (enlightenment).
Judaism	18 million	Abraham, Isaac, and Jacob; ca. 2000 B.C.E.	Monotheistic. God's nature and will are revealed in the Torah (Hebrew scripture) and in His intervention in history. God has established a covenant with the people of Israel, who are called to a life of holiness, justice, mercy, and fidelity to God's Law.
Confucianism	5.9 million	K'ung Fu-Tzu (Confucius); 6th to 5th centuries B.C.E.	Neither polytheistic nor monotheistic. The sayings of Confucius (collected in the *Analects*) stress the role of virtue and order in the relationships between individuals, their families, and society.

Source: National Opinion Research Centre, *General Social Survey* (1989): 156–159. Reprinted by permission.

(Kurtz, 1995). The soul's acquisition of each new body is tied to the law of *karma* (deed or act), which is a doctrine of the moral law of cause and effect. The present condition of the soul—how happy or unhappy it is, for example—is directly related to what it has done in the past, and its present thoughts and decisions are the ultimate determinants of what its future will be. The ultimate goal of Hindu existence is entering the state of *nirvana*—becoming liberated from the world by uniting the individual soul with the universal soul (*Brahma*).

Hinduism has been devoid of some of the social conflict experienced by other religions. Since Hinduism is based on the assumption that there are many paths to the "Truth" and that the world's religions are alternative paths to that goal, Hindus typically have not engaged in religious debates or "holy wars" with those holding differing beliefs. One of the best-known Hindu leaders of modern times was Mohandas ("Mahatma") Gandhi, the champion of India's independence movement, who was devoted to the Hindu ideals of nonviolence, honesty, and

Worshippers at this Buddhist temple in Los Angeles celebrate the Thai New Year.

courage (Sharma, 1995). However, some social analysts note that Hinduism has been closely associated with the perpetuation of the caste system in India. Although people in the lower castes are taught to live out their lives with dignity, even in the face of poverty and despair, they may also come to believe that their lowly position is the acceptable and appropriate place for them to be—which allows the upper castes to exploit them (Kurtz, 1995).

The Hindu religion is almost as diverse as the wide array of people who adhere to its teachings. It is estimated that there are more than 700 million Hindus in the world today, with 95 percent of them residing in India, over 80 percent of whose population is Hindu (Sharma, 1993).

Buddhism

When Buddhism first emerged in India some twenty-five hundred years ago, it was thought of as a "new religious movement," arising as it did around the sixth century B.C.E. ("before the Common Era") after many earlier religions had become virtually defunct. Buddhism's founder, Siddhartha Gautama of the Sakyas (also known as Gautama Buddha), was born about 563 B.C.E. into the privileged caste. His father was King Suddhodana (who was more like a feudal lord than a king because many kingdoms existed on the Indian subcontinent during that era).

According to historians, the king attempted to keep his young son in the palace at all times so that he would neither see how poor people lived nor experience the suffering present in the outside world. As a result, Siddhartha was oblivious to social inequality until he began to make forays beyond the palace walls and into the "real" world, where he observed how other people lived. On one excursion, he saw a monk with a shaven head and became aware that some people withdraw from the secular world and live a life of strict asceticism. Later, Siddhartha engaged in intense meditation underneath a bodhi tree in what is now Nepal, eventually declaring that he had obtained Enlightenment—an awakening to the true nature of reality (Kurtz, 1995). From that day forward, Siddhartha was referred to as *Buddha*, meaning the "Enlightened One" or the "Awakened One," and spent his life teaching others how to reach nirvana (Smith, 1991).

Through the efforts of a series of invaders, Buddhism had ceased to exist in India by the thirteenth century but had already expanded into other nations in various forms. *Theravadin Buddhism*, which focuses on the life of the Buddha and seeks to follow his teachings, gained its strongest toehold in Southeast Asia. *Mahayana Buddhism* is centred in Japan, China, and Korea and focuses primarily on meditation and the Four Noble Truths:

1. Life is *dukkha*—physical and mental suffering, pain, or anguish that pervades all human existence.
2. The cause of life's suffering is rooted in *tanha*—grasping, craving, and coveting.
3. One can overcome *tanha* and be released into Ultimate Freedom in Perfect Existence (nirvana).
4. Overcoming desire can be accomplished through the Eightfold Path to Nirvana. This path is a way of living that avoids extremes of indulgence and suggests that a person can live in the world but not be worldly. The path's eight steps are *right view* (proper belief), *right intent* (renouncing attachment to the world), *right speech* (not lying, slandering, or using abusive talk), *right action* (avoiding sexual indulgence), *right livelihood* (avoiding occupations that do not enhance spiritual advancement), *right effort* (preventing potential evil from arising), *right mindfulness*, and *right concentration* (overcoming sensuous appetites and evil desires). (Smith, 1991; Matthews, 1995)

The third major branch of Buddhism—*Vajrayana*—incorporates the first two and some aspects of Hinduism and was adopted in Tibet in the seventh century (Albanese, 1992). Like Hinduism, the teachings of Buddhism—and specifically those of the Dalai Lama, the Tibetan Buddhist leader—emphasize the doctrine of *ahimsa,* or nonharmfulness, and discourage violence and warfare. It is believed that Buddhism may have suppressed caste-related tensions resulting from the vast economic inequality found in early India (Kurtz, 1995).

Confucianism

Confucianism—which means the "family of scholars"—started as a school of thought or a tradition of learning before its eventual leader, Confucius, was born (Wei-ming, 1995). Confucius (the Latinized form of K'ung Fu-tzu) lived in China between 551 and 479 B.C.E. and emerged as a teacher at about the same time that the Buddha became a significant figure in India.

Confucius—whose sayings are collected in the *Analects*—taught that people must learn the importance of *order* in human relationships and follow a strict code of moral conduct, including respect for others, benevolence, and reciprocity (Kurtz, 1995). A central teaching of Confucius was that humans are by nature good and that they learn best by having an example or a role model. As a result, he created a *junzi* ("chun-tzu"), or model person, who has such attributes as being upright regardless of outward circumstances, being magnanimous by expressing forgiveness toward others, being directed by internal principle rather than external laws, being sincere in speech and action, and being earnest and benevolent. Confucius wanted to demonstrate these traits, and he believed that he should be a role model for his students. The junzi's behaviour is to be based on the Confucian principle of *Li*, meaning righteousness or propriety, which refers both to ritual and to correct conduct in public. One of the central attributes exhibited by the junzi is *ren (jen)*, which means having deep empathy or compassion for other humans (Matthews, 1995).

Confucius established the foundation for social hierarchy—and potential conflict—when he set forth his Five Constant Relationships: *ruler–subject, husband–wife, elder brother–younger brother, elder friend–junior friend,* and *father–son*. In each of these pairs, one person is unequal to the other, but both are expected to carry out specific responsibilities to the other (Matthews, 1995). Confucius taught that due authority is not automatic; it must be earned. The subject does not owe loyalty to the ruler or authority figure if that individual does not fulfil his or her end of the bargain.

Confucianism is based on the belief that Heaven and Earth are not separate places but rather are a continuum in which both realms are constantly in touch with each other. According to this approach, those who inhabit Heaven are ruled over by a supreme ancestor and are the ancestors of those persons who are on Earth. These forefathers are eventually joined by those who are currently on Earth; therefore, death is nothing more than the promotion to a more honourable estate.

Until the Communist takeover and establishment of the People's Republic of China, Confucianism was the official religion of China. After the takeover, political leaders sought to replace Confucianism, Taoism, and Buddhism with Maoism—belief in the teachings of the Chinese Communist leader—but the Confucian influence remains in East Asian countries such as Japan, Korea, Taiwan, and Singapore.

We now move from the Eastern religions (Hinduism, Buddhism, and Confucianism) that tend to be based on ethics or values more than on a deity or Supreme Being to the Western religions (Judaism, Christianity, and Islam) that are founded on the Abrahamic tradition and place an emphasis on God and a relationship between human beings and a Supreme Being. The original locations of all six of these religions are shown on Map 17.1.

Judaism

Although Judaism has fewer adherents worldwide than some other major religions, its influence is deeply felt in Western culture. Today, there are an estimated 18 million Jews residing in about 134 countries worldwide; however, the majority reside in the United States or Israel (Wright, 1997).

Central to contemporary Jewish belief is monotheism, the idea of a single God, called Yahweh, the God of Abraham, Isaac, and Jacob. The Hebrew tradition emerged out of the relationship of Abraham and Sarah, a husband and wife, with Yahweh. According to Jewish tradition, the God of the Jews made a covenant with Abraham and Sarah—His chosen people—that He would protect and provide for them if they swore Him love and obedience. When God

Orthodox Jews at the Wailing Wall in Jerusalem—a wall that holds special significance for all Jews—express their faith in God and in the traditions of their ancestors.

Confucianism is based on the ethical teachings formulated by Confucius, shown here in a portrait created by a Manchu prince in 1735.

appeared to Abraham in about the eighteenth century B.C.E., He encouraged Abraham to emigrate to the area near the Sea of Galilee and the Dead Sea (what is now Israel), leaving behind the ancient fertile crescent of the Middle East (present-day Iraq).

The descendants of Abraham and Sarah migrated to Egypt, where they became slaves of the Egyptians. In a vision, God's chosen leader, Moses, was instructed to liberate His chosen people from the bondage and slavery imposed upon them by the Pharaoh. After experiencing a series of ten plagues, the Pharaoh decided to free the slaves. The tenth and final plague had involved killing all of the firstborn in the land of Egypt—human beings and lower animals, as well—except the firstborn children of the Hebrews, who had put the blood of a lamb on the doorposts of their houses so that they would be passed over. This practice inspired the Jewish holiday Passover, which commemorates God's deliverance of the Hebrews from slavery in Egypt during the time of Moses. It is believed that the first Passover took place in Egypt in about 1300–1200 B.C.E. (Matthews, 1995).

Wandering in the desert after their release, the Hebrews established a covenant with God, who promised that if they would serve Him exclusively,

He would give the Hebrews a promised land and make them a great nation. Known as the Ten Commandments (or *Decalogue*), the covenant between God and human beings was given to Moses on top of Mount Sinai. The Ten Commandments and discussions of moral, ceremonial, and cultural laws are contained in four books of the Torah: Exodus, Leviticus, Numbers, and Deuteronomy. The Torah, also known as the Pentateuch, is the sacred book of contemporary Judaism.

The Jewish people believe that they have a unique relationship with God, affirmed on the one hand by His covenant and on the other by His law. Judaism has three key components: God (the deity), Torah (God's teachings), and Israel (the community or holy nation). Although God guides human destiny, people are responsible for making their own ethical choices in keeping with His law; when they fail to act according to the law, they have committed a sin. Also fundamental to Judaism is the belief that one day the Messiah will come to earth, ushering in an age of peace and justice for all.

Today, Jews worship in synagogues in congregations led by a *rabbi*—a teacher or ordained interpreter and leader of Judaism. The Sabbath is observed from sunset Friday to sunset Saturday, based on the story of Creation in Genesis, espe-

MAP 17.1   Original Locations of the World's Major Religions

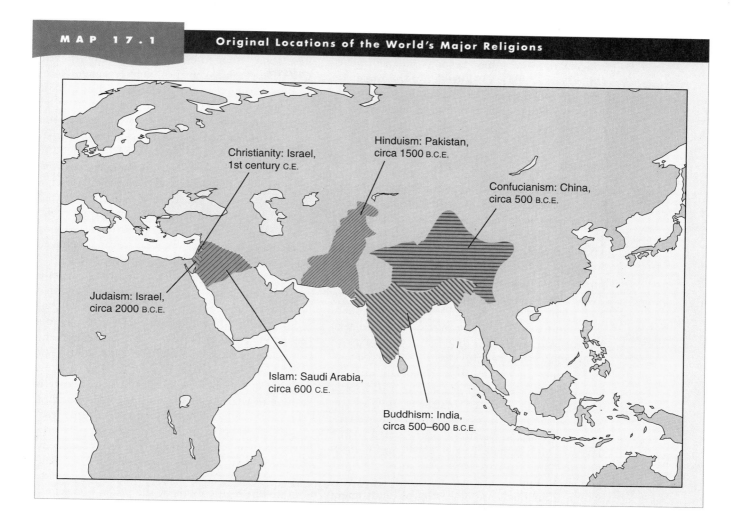

Christianity: Israel, 1st century C.E.

Hinduism: Pakistan, circa 1500 B.C.E.

Confucianism: China, circa 500 B.C.E.

Judaism: Israel, circa 2000 B.C.E.

Islam: Saudi Arabia, circa 600 C.E.

Buddhism: India, circa 500–600 B.C.E.

cially the belief that God rested on the seventh day, after He had created the world in the first six. Worship services consist of readings from scripture, prayer, and singing. Jews celebrate a set of holidays distinct from Canadian dominant cultural religious celebrations. The most important holidays in the Jewish calendar are Rosh Hashana (New Year), Yom Kippur (Day of Atonement), Hanukkah (Festival of Lights), and Pesach (Passover).

Today, Judaism has three main branches—Orthodox, Reform, and Conservative. Orthodox Judaism follows the traditional practices and teachings, including eating only kosher foods prepared in a designated way, observing the traditional Sabbath, segregating women and men in religious services, and wearing traditional clothing. Reform Judaism, which began in Germany in the nineteenth century, is based on the belief that the Torah is binding only in its moral teachings and that adherents should no

longer be required to follow all of the Talmud, the compilation of Jewish law setting forth the strict rabbinic teachings on practices such as food preparation, rituals, and dress. In some Reform congregations, gender-segregated seating is no longer required.

Conservative Judaism emerged between 1880 and 1914 with the arrival of many Jewish immigrants in the United States from countries such as Russia, Poland, Rumania, and Austria. Seeking freedom and an escape from persecution, these new arrivals settled in major cities such as New York and Chicago, where they primarily became factory workers, artisans, or small shopkeepers. Conservative Judaism, which became a middle ground between Orthodox and Reform Judaism, teaches that the Torah and Talmud must be followed and that *Zionism*—the movement to establish a Jewish homeland in Israel—is crucial to the future of Judaism. In Conservative synagogues, worship services are typically performed in

Hebrew. Men are expected to wear head coverings, and women have roles of leadership in the congregation; some may become ordained rabbis (Matthews, 1995). Despite being the target of centuries of religious hatred and discrimination, Judaism persists as one of the world's influential religions.

Islam

Like Judaism, Islam is a religion in the Abrahamic tradition; both religions arose through sons of Abraham—Judaism through Isaac and Islam through Ishmael. Islam, whose followers are known as Muslims, is based on the teachings of its founder, Muhammad, who was born in Mecca (now in Saudi Arabia) in about 570 C.E. According to Muhammad, followers must adhere to the five Pillars of Islam: (1) believing that there is no god but Allah, (2) participating in five periods of prayer each day, (3) paying taxes to help support the needy, (4) fasting during the daylight hours in the month of Ramadan, and (5) making at least one pilgrimage to the Sacred House of Allah in Mecca (Matthews, 1995).

The Islamic faith is based on the Qur'an—the holy book of the Muslims—as revealed to the Prophet Muhammad through the Angel Gabriel at the command of God. According to the Qur'an, it is up to God, not humans, to determine which individuals are deserving of punishment and what kinds of violence are justified under various conditions.

The Islamic notion of *jihad*—meaning "struggle"—is a core belief. The Greater Jihad is believed to be the internal struggle against sin within a person's heart, whereas the Lesser Jihad is the external struggle that takes place in the world (Ferguson, 1977; Kurtz, 1995).

Today, more than 19 percent of the world's population considers itself to be Muslim. Most of the more than one billion adherents of this religion reside in the Middle East, but most people residing in northern Africa and western Asia also consider themselves to be Muslim. Other large populations of Muslims are located in Pakistan, India, Bangladesh, Indonesia, and the southern regions of the former Soviet Union.

Christianity

Along with Judaism and Islam, Christianity follows the Abrahamic tradition, tracing its roots to Abraham and Sarah. Although Jews and Christians share common scriptures in the portions of the Bible known to Christians as the "Old Testament," they interpret them differently. The Christian teachings in the "New Testament" present a world view in which the old covenant between God and humans, as found in the Old Testament, is obsolete in light of God's offer of a new covenant to the followers of Jesus Christ, whom Christians believe to be God's only son.

As described in the New Testament, Jesus was born to the virgin Mary and her husband, Joseph. After a period of youth in which He prepared himself for the ministry, Jesus appeared in public and went about teaching and preaching, including performing a series of miracles—events believed to be brought about by divine intervention.

The central themes in the teachings of Jesus are the kingdom of God and standards of personal conduct for adherents of Christianity. Jesus emphasized the importance of righteousness before God and of praying to the Supreme Being for guidance in the daily affairs of life (Matthews, 1995).

One of the main teachings of Christianity is linked to the unique circumstances surrounding the death of Jesus. Just prior to His death, Jesus and His disciples held a special supper, now referred to as "the last supper," which is commemorated in contemporary Christianity in the sacrament of Holy Communion. Afterward, Jesus was arrested by a group sent by the priests and scribes for claiming to be king of the Jews. After being condemned to death by political leaders, Jesus was executed by crucifixion, which made the cross a central symbol of the Christian religion. According to the New Testament, Jesus died, was placed in a tomb, and on the third day was resurrected—restored to life—establishing that He is the son of God. Jesus then remained on earth for forty days, after which He ascended into heaven on a cloud. Two thousand years later, many Christian churches teach that one day Jesus will "come again in glory" and that His second coming will mark the end of the world as we know it (Cox, 1995).

Today, almost one-third of the world's population (between 1.5 and 2 billion) refer to themselves as Christians. The majority of Christians live in North or South America or in Europe. According to Kurtz (1995), a sociological analysis of Christianity would reveal that it became the dominant religion not necessarily due to its theology but because of its alliance with the power structures of Western civilization, beginning with

Women play an active role in the spiritual life of Muslims, as reflected by this photo taken at the Dome of the Rock mosque in Jerusalem.

the fourth-century conversion of Roman Emperor Constantine and following with its expansion into Western Europe during the Middle Ages. Missionary movements helped to spread Christianity outward from Europe to other regions of the world in the nineteenth century, as missionaries also conquered land, cultures, and the economic and political resources of indigenous populations (Kurtz, 1995). As Christianity moved across cultures, it underwent dramatic transformations and became, in actuality, a tremendous variety of "Christianities" rather than just one highly integrated body of religious beliefs and practices (Kurtz, 1995).

TYPES OF RELIGIOUS ORGANIZATIONS

Religious groups vary widely in their organizational structure. While some groups are large and somewhat bureaucratically organized, others are small and have a relatively informal authority structure. Some require total commitment from their members; others expect members to have only a partial commitment. Sociologists have developed typologies or ideal types of religious organization to enable them to study a wide variety of religious groups. The most common categorization sets forth four types: ecclesia, church, sect, and cult.

Ecclesia

Some countries have an official or state religion known as the *ecclesia*—**a religious organization that is so integrated into the dominant culture that it claims as its membership all members of a society.** Membership in the ecclesia occurs as a result of being born into the society, rather than by any conscious decision on the part of individual members. The linkages between the social institutions of religion and government often are very strong in such societies. Although no true ecclesia exists in the contemporary world, the Anglican church (the official church of England), the Lutheran church in Sweden and Denmark, the Catholic church in Spain, and Islam in Iran and Pakistan come fairly close.

The Church–Sect Typology

To help explain the different types of religious organizations found in societies, Ernst Troeltsch (1960/1931) and his teacher, Max Weber (1963/1922), developed a typology that distinguishes between the characteristics of churches and sects (see Table 17.3). Unlike an ecclesia, a church is not considered to be a state religion; however, it may still have a powerful influence on political and economic arrangements in society. A *church* **is a large, bureaucratically organized religious body that tends to seek accommodation with the larger society in order to maintain some degree of control over it.** Church membership largely is based on birth; children of church mem-

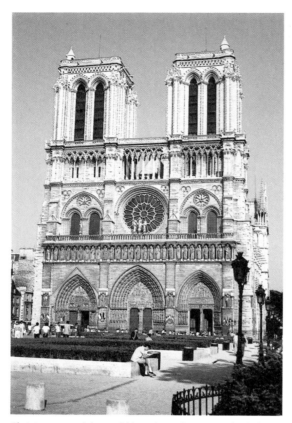

Christians around the world have been drawn to cathedrals such as Notre-Dame de Paris (built between 1163 and 1257) to worship God and celebrate their religious beliefs.

bers typically are baptized as infants and become lifelong members of the church. Older children and adults may choose to join the church, but they are required to go through an extensive training program that culminates in a ceremony similar to the one that infants go through. Leadership is hierarchically arranged, and clergy generally have many years of formal education. Churches have very restrained services that appeal to the intellect rather than the emotions (Stark, 1992). Religious services are highly ritualized; they are led by clergy who wear robes, enter and exit in a formal processional, administer sacraments, and read services from a prayer book or other standardized liturgical format.

Midway between the church and the sect is a *denomination*—a large, organized religious body characterized by accommodation to society but frequently lacking the ability or intention to dominate society (Niebuhr, 1929). Denominations have a trained ministry, and while involvement by lay members is encouraged more than in the church, their participation usually is limited to particular activities, such as readings or prayers. Denominations tend to be more tolerant and less likely than churches to expel or excommunicate members. This form of organization is most likely to thrive in societies characterized by religious pluralism—a situation in which many religious groups exist because they have a special appeal to specific segments of the population. Because of its diversity, Canada has more denominations than most other countries.

A *sect* is a relatively small religious group that has broken away from another religious organization to renew what it views as the original version of the faith. Unlike churches, sects offer members a more personal religion and an intimate relationship with a supreme being, depicted as taking an active interest in the individual's everyday life. Whereas churches use formalized prayers, often from a prayer book, sects have informal prayers composed at the time they are given. Also, whereas churches typically appeal to members of the upper classes, and denominations to members of the middle and upper classes, sects seek to meet the needs of people who are low in the stratification system—that is, the masses (Stark, 1992).

According to the church–sect typology, as members of a sect become more successful economically and socially, their religious organization also is likely to focus more on this world and less on the next. If some members of the sect do not achieve financial success, they may feel left behind as other members and the ministers shift their priorities. Eventually, this process will weaken some organizations, and people will split off to create new, less worldly versions of the group, which will be more committed to "keeping the faith." Those who defect to form a new religious organization may start another sect or form a cult (Stark and Bainbridge, 1981).

Cults

A *cult* is a religious group with practices and teachings outside the dominant cultural and religious traditions of a society. Although many people view cults negatively, all major religions and some denominations (such as the Mormons) started as cults. Cult leadership is based on charismatic characteristics of the individual, including an unusual ability to form attachments with others (Stark, 1992). An example is the religious movement started by Reverend Sun Myung

TABLE 17.3 **CHARACTERISTICS OF CHURCHES AND SECTS**

CHARACTERISTIC	CHURCH	SECT
Organization	Large, bureaucratic organization, led by a professional clergy	Small, faithful group, with high degree of lay participation
Membership	Open to all; members usually from upper and middle classes	Closely guarded membership, usually from lower classes
Type of Worship	Formal, orderly	Informal, spontaneous
Salvation	Granted by God, as administered by the church	Achieved by moral purity
Attitude toward Other Institutions and Religions	Tolerant	Intolerant

Moon, a Korean electrical engineer who believed that God had revealed to him that Judgment Day was rapidly approaching. Out of this movement, the Unification church, or "Moonies," grew and flourished, recruiting new members through their personal attachments to present members (Stark, 1992). Some recent cult leaders have not fared well, including Jim Jones, whose ill-fated cult ended up committing mass suicide in Guyana, and David Koresh of the also ill-fated Branch Davidians in Waco, Texas.

Are all cults short-lived? Over time, most cults disappear. However, others undergo transformation into sects or denominations. For example, cult leader Mary Baker Eddy's Christian Science church has become an established denomination with mainstream methods of outreach. Some researchers view cults as a means of reviving religious practice when existing churches do not provide satisfaction to those seeking a spiritual home.

TRENDS IN RELIGION IN CANADA

Canada's Religious Mosaic

Canada has been described as a "monopolized mosaic." Until the end of the nineteenth century, Canada was a country with a religious population made up almost entirely of Protestants and

Catholics. The Roman Catholic Church was the dominant religious force during the early settlement of Canada, a situation that continued well into the nineteenth century. With the arrival of the United Empire Loyalists from the American colonies in the 1780s, the Protestant population in Canada became larger than the French-Catholic population. The turning point, with respect to the dominance of the Protestant churches, occurred after World War II. Their combined share declined from 51 percent in 1951 to 36 percent in 1991, and the most rapid decline occurred during the most recent decade (McVey and Kalbach, 1995). Changes in the population of the major religious groups in Canada are illustrated in Figure 17.1. In 1996, Catholics, at 46 percent of the population, were the largest religious group in Canada.

Other religions than Christianity were practised in Canada prior to European colonization. Aboriginal peoples were excluded from the earliest census collections. Even so, in 1891, almost 2 percent of Canadians reported practising religions other than Christianity. In 1996, almost 6 percent of Canadians were affiliated with "other" religions, including Eastern Orthodox, Judaism, and Eastern non-Christian religions such as Islam, Buddhism, Hinduism, Sikhism, and parareligious groups (see Table 17.4). Eastern non-Christian religious populations have grown significantly since the 1960s as a result of the liberalization of immigration law in Canada, as have the numbers of those who fall under the category "no religion," going from 56,679 in 1951 to almost 3.4 million in 1991 (McVey and Kalbach, 1995). Does this mean that Canadians are rejecting religion? An answer to this question can be found by examining other recent trends in religion in Canada.

Religiosity

As we have seen, religion in Canada is very diverse. Pluralism and religious freedom are among the cultural values most widely espoused. However, is Canada a religious society? The answer depends on how you look at things. Nationally, church attendance, public confidence in church leadership, and church influence have all gradually declined since the late 1940s.

Religious affiliation has been tracked through the census, the annual General Social Survey (GSS), and opinion polls. Over the past fifty years, attendance at religious services has declined precipitously (Clark, 1998). A 1946 Gallup poll reported that 67 percent of Canadian adults had attended religious services during the previous week. By 1996, the General Social Survey found that attendance at weekly religious services had declined to only 20 percent. A generation ago, most Canadians attended religious services; today only a small minority attend.

In recent years different denominations have seen different rates of decline (Clark, 1998). The 1996 GSS found that 24 percent of Roman Catholics attended weekly services, a marked drop from 37 percent attendance in 1986. Nearly one in three Roman Catholics did not attend church at all in 1996 compared with one in seven in 1986. During the same period attendance in the mainline Protestant churches (United, Anglican, Presbyterian, and Lutheran) dropped from 17 percent to 14 percent. However, members of conservative Protestant denominations (Baptist, Pentecostal) have maintained 50 percent to 60 percent attendance rates. While 30 percent of Canadians claim affiliation with the mainline Protestant denominations compared with 8 percent for the conservative denominations, the latter now have more people who are regular participants than do the mainline churches (Posterski and Barker, 1993). Most other religions (including Judaism, Hinduism, Buddhism, and Sikhism) have also seen serious declines in the percentage of people attending services, although some have seen a stabilization or even an increase in the number of members because of immigration.

This mass wedding ceremony of thousands of brides and grooms brought widespread media attention to the Reverend Sun Myung Moon and the Unification Church, which many people view as a religious cult.

While attendance rates have declined for all age groups, the drop has been particularly large for younger people. Thirty-four percent of those 65 years of age and over are regular church attenders, compared with only 12 percent of 15- to 24-year-olds. This loss of young members does not bode well for the future of Canadian churches, as the vast majority of regular adult church attendees had also been regular attenders in childhood. This means that as older members die, there will likely be fewer and fewer people taking their places in the pews.

On the other hand, despite the decline in involvement with the institutional church, the vast majority of Canadians still report a religious affiliation and affirm that they believe in God. However, both of these measures have also declined in recent years. In 1961, only 1 percent of Canadians reported no religious affiliation; by 1996, this had increased to 13 percent (Clark, 1998). In 1975, 89 percent of Canadians reported that they believed in God compared with 81 percent in 1995 (Bibby, 1995). Despite these declines, the vast majority of Canadians still have religious affiliations and beliefs. This view is further supported by a 1993 poll that found that 75 percent of Canadians expressed a belief in the death and the resurrection of Jesus, the basic tenet of Christianity. Almost one-third of the adult population claimed to pray daily and more than half reported reading the Bible or other religious literature at least occasionally (Nemeth et al., 1993).

In addition to their religious beliefs, Canadians also show an interest in other aspects of spirituality. Table 17.5 shows that most Canadians believe that some people have psychic powers; that supernatural and evil forces exist; that there is life after death; and that some people have

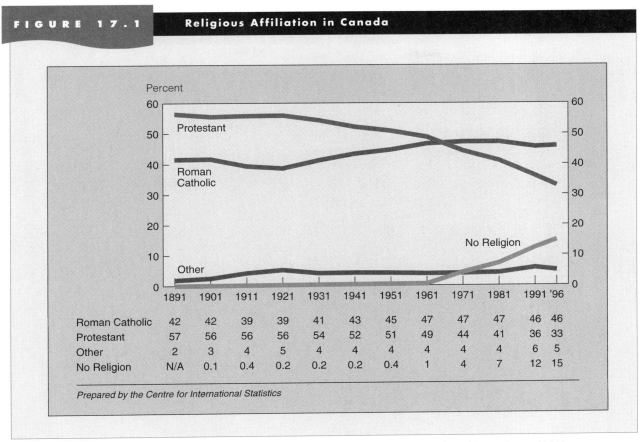

FIGURE 17.1   **Religious Affiliation in Canada**

	1891	1901	1911	1921	1931	1941	1951	1961	1971	1981	1991	'96
Roman Catholic	42	42	39	39	41	43	45	47	47	47	46	46
Protestant	57	56	56	56	54	52	51	49	44	41	36	33
Other	2	3	4	5	4	4	4	4	4	4	6	5
No Religion	N/A	0.1	0.4	0.2	0.2	0.2	0.4	1	4	7	12	15

Prepared by the Centre for International Statistics

Sources: Vanier Institute of the Family, 1994. Reprinted by permission. 1996 figures from Statistics Canada, *General Social Survey*, Cat. no. 11-612. Used by permission.

extrasensory perception. A significant minority believe that astrology has some merit; that it is possible to make contact with the spirit world; that they have experienced God; and that they will be reincarnated after death.

The results of these surveys lead us to an interesting paradox. Church attendance has dramatically declined despite the fact that most Canadians report some religious affiliation, express a belief in God, and believe in other spiritual aspects of life. It should be noted that people have not rejected the churches completely. Most still rely on the organized church for services such as baptisms, weddings, and funerals. However, they are not regular participants in religious activities, choosing instead to adopt what researcher Reginald Bibby calls "religious fragments"—isolated beliefs, isolated practices, and isolated services (1987). They receive spiritual sustenance from their religions, but they also draw from alternatives such as astrology, extrasensory perception, and New Age practices such as crystals that serve

as adjuncts to traditional religious practice. Theologian Tom Harper sums up this approach to religion:

> There is a huge spiritual quest going on. There's a lot of attempts at quick fixes and spiritual junk food as well. But even the silly fringe is part of it ... People seem intuitively aware that something is missing in their lives, and there's a reaction against traditional religion. (quoted in McDonald, 1994:42)

Why Have Canadians Turned Away from the Church?

Bibby concludes that people have moved from religious commitment to religious consumption. These religious consumers look at the church as simply one of many different options for solving their spiritual or worldly problems. Even those with a high degree of religious commitment may not feel church attendance is the best way to

TABLE 17.4	POPULATION BY RELIGION, 1981 AND 1991			
	1981		**1991**	
TOTAL POPULATION	24,083,495	100.0%	26,994,045	100.0%
Catholic	11,402,605	47.3	12,335,255	45.7
Roman Catholic	11,210,385	46.5	12,203,620	45.2
Ukrainian Catholic	190,585	0.8	128,390	0.5
Other Catholic	1,630	0.0	3,235	0.0
Protestant	9,914,575	41.2	9,780,715	36.2
United Church	3,758,015	15.6	3,093,120	11.5
Anglican	2,436,375	10.1	2,188,110	8.1
Presbyterian	812,105	3.4	636,295	2.4
Lutheran	702,900	2.9	636,205	2.4
Baptist	696,845	2.9	663,360	2.5
Pentecostal	338,790	1.4	436,435	1.6
Other Protestant	1,169,545	4.9	2,127,190	7.9
Eastern non-Christian	305,890	1.3	747,455	2.8
Islam	98,165	0.4	253,260	0.9
Buddhist	51,955	0.2	163,415	0.6
Hindu	69,505	0.3	157,010	0.6
Sikh	67,715	0.3	147,440	0.5
Other eastern non-Christian	18,550	0.1	26,330	0.1
Eastern Orthodox	361,565	1.5	387,395	1.4
Jewish	296,425	1.2	318,065	1.2
Parareligious groups	13,450	0.1	28,155	0.1
No religious affiliation	1,783,530	7.4	3,386,365	12.5
Other religions	5,465	0.0	10,640	0.0

*Based on sample data, which exclude institutional residents.

Reproduced by authority of the Minister of Industry, 1996, Statistics Canada, from *Religions in Canada*, Cat. no. 93-319.

express that commitment. As one of Bibby's respondents commented:

> I've been through a great deal in life and my faith is very strong. But I believe that one is closer to God in their own home and garden than a church. I see going to church these days as "keeping up with the Joneses." (Bibby, 1987:83)

No simple explanations can account for this change. It is apparent, though, that organized religion no longer seems relevant to the lives of many Canadians. Comments of two participants in one of Bibby's more recent studies illustrate this view: "I don't see religion as having much power at all in today's affairs" and "The major issues of the day seem to me to have little to do with religion and

morality; economic and political factors are far more important" (1993:59). Our culture has become more individualistic and people are less likely to accept without question the dictates of the church.

When it has tried to address contemporary issues, the church has often had problems. For example, several Protestant denominations have had major conflicts over the role of homosexuals in the church. Debates over issues ranging from the tolerance of homosexuality to the ordination of homosexual ministers have led to splits within local congregations and to major divisions at the national level. Not only have these moral issues been divisive, but they have also distracted the churches from other activities. Some churches, notably the United Church, have tried to become more socially relevant by focusing on social justice issues, but this strategy has not attracted new members (Bibby, 1993) and may have driven older members away from the church.

Many women have also felt marginalized by the church, and their alienation may have contributed to the decline in attendance. While the role of women in Canadian society has changed dramatically over the past thirty years, some churches are still very patriarchal organizations. These practices can be difficult or impossible to change, as traditional gender roles are part of the core religious ideology of some churches. You saw in Table 17.1 that people hold gendered images of God. We also know that in many denominations only males are allowed to become priests or ministers and women are expected to play a very traditional role supporting the males who are leaders of their religion. The quote from Joanne Barendregt in the opening to this chapter illustrates the fundamentalist view that a woman's sacred duty is submission to her husband. While some women welcome this role, this subordination is seen as unacceptable to many others who do not feel comfortable in a male-dominated church. The failure by many denominations to address the concerns of women may have serious consequences, as women are normally more likely to participate in church activities than are men.

The image of the church has also suffered from thousands of charges of child sexual abuse by ministers and priests. While these incidents have taken place in a wide variety of contexts, the abuse was most pervasive in residential settings such as the church-run schools that were established for Aboriginal children during the first half of this century. Over 125,000 children attended these schools before the system was closed in the 1980s, and by 1999 more than one thousand abuse complaints had been laid against church officials who worked in the schools (Cheney et al., 1998). The problem was not limited to the abuse of Aboriginal youth; the first major scandal grew out of offences committed by members of the Christian Brothers order at Newfoundland's Mount Cashel orphanage. The image of the church was further damaged by the fact that in many cases senior church officials knew about the problem, did little or nothing to stop it, and tried to cover it up. Few church leaders have been willing to take responsibility for the problem or even to apologize to those whose lives were destroyed by people who were entrusted with their physical and spiritual care. These incidents make it more difficult for the churches to speak credibly on moral issues.

Finally, we can look at the special case of Quebec. According to sociologist S.D. Clark (1962), in few countries of the Western world has religion had more influence on the nature of community as it has in Canada. The early development of French and English Canada was strongly influenced by religious principles. This was particularly apparent in Quebec, where all social institutions came under the influence of the Roman Catholic Church. For example, much of the education system was directly run by the church. Throughout most of Quebec's history, the Catholic Church was politically powerful and dominated the province's social and moral life.

However, following the Quiet Revolution in the mid-1960s (see Chapter 14, "Power, Politics, and Government"), the influence of the Roman Catholic Church in Quebec dwindled rapidly. Weekly church attendance dropped from a remarkable high of 90 percent in the 1940s (Bibby, 1993), to less than 30 percent by 1990 and continues to decline. As Quebec was transformed into a secular society, the church lost its influence in fields such as education and social services. The decline of the church represented a break with the past that was accompanied by such major shifts as the birth of the separatist political movement. Policies of the Roman Catholic Church, such as the prohibitions on birth control, premarital sex, abortion, and divorce and the refusal to ordain women priests, also turned people away. The reduced influence of the church is shown by the fact that the province with the highest proportion of Roman Catholics (Quebec) also has Canada's highest rate of common-law marriage (see Chapter 15, "Families and Intimate Relationships").

Fundamentalism

The rise of a new fundamentalism has occurred at the same time as a number of mainline denominations have been losing membership. The term *religious fundamentalism* refers to a conservative religious doctrine that opposes intellectualism and worldly accommodation in favour of restoring a traditional otherworldly focus. In Canada, fundamentalism has been gaining popularity, primarily among Protestants, but also among Roman Catholics and Jews. Whereas "old" fundamentalism usually appealed to people from lower-income, rural backgrounds, the "new" fundamentalism appears to have a much wider

TABLE 17.5	SPIRITUAL BELIEFS OF CANADIANS	

	PERCENTAGE AGREEING	
	TEENS	**ADULTS**
God exists	81	83
Divinity of Jesus	80	75
Some people have psychic powers	69	59
Supernatural forces exist	66	*
Life after death	64	68
Evil forces exist	64	*
Astrology	53	34
Extrasensory perception	52	59
Contact within the spirit world	44	39
I have experienced God	34	46
I will be reincarnated	32	27

*Figures unavailable.

Reprinted by permission of Donald Posterski, *Where's a Good Church?* Winfield, B.C.: Wood Lake Books, Inc. 1993.

following among persons from all socio-economic levels, geographical areas, and occupations. "New-right" fundamentalists have been especially critical of *secular humanism*—a belief in the perfectibility of human beings through their own efforts rather than through a belief in God and a religious conversion. As you read in the chapter introduction, fundamentalists feel that instead of offering children a proper Christian education, the public schools are teaching things that seem to the child to prove their parents' lifestyle and religion are inferior and perhaps irrational (Carter, 1994:52). The new-right fundamentalists claim that banning the teaching of Christian beliefs in the classroom while teaching things that are contrary to their faith is an infringement on their freedom of religion (Jenkinson, 1979). As we have seen in this chapter, the debate continues over what should be taught and what practices (such as Bible reading and prayer) should be permitted in public schools. The selection of textbooks and library materials is an especially controversial issue. Starting in the 1960s, books considered to have racist and sexist biases were attacked by civil rights activists and feminists. Soon thereafter, challenges were brought by conservative religious groups to protest the use of books that they alleged had "factual inaccuracies" (such as a criticism of the free enterprise system) or morally objectionable subject matter or language (see Hefley, 1976; Shor, 1986; Wong, 1991; Bates, 1994). This debate, along with the message of fundamentalism, has been transformed into an international issue because of the growth of the electronic church and the Internet, as discussed in Box 17.3.

Does Religion Make a Difference?

Research looking at the impact of religion on attitudes and behaviour has had mixed results. Bibby (1998) has concluded that religiosity has little impact on personal characteristics such as happiness and contentment. While religion may help some people to be happy and content, many others find the same level of satisfaction through other means. He also found that people with strong religious beliefs were no different from other Canadians in terms of relationships with other people, compassion, and tolerance of others (Bibby, 1995). However, a recent Statistics Canada study found that weekly church attendees were much more likely to feel satisfied with their lives and much less likely to feel their lives were stressful than nonattenders (Clark, 1998).

Religiosity also affects other aspects of behaviour. All religions have ethical codes that govern personal and social behaviour. While it would be naive to equate religious with "good" and nonreligious with "bad," there is some evidence that religious commitment does influence people's conduct with regard to a variety of what might be called moral issues. For example, religiosity does reduce involvement in delinquent and criminal behaviour (Linden, 2000). However, this relationship is complex—it is greatest where there is a strong religious community (Stark et al., 1982); to some extent it is mediated by one's relationships with family and friends (Elifson et al., 1983); and it has more impact on behaviour that is not universally condemned by other segments of society, such as illegal drug use, than on behaviour such as theft and assault that most other social institutions also disapprove of (Linden and Currie, 1977).

Religiosity is also associated with marital stability. Weekly church attenders place more importance on marriage and children than those who do not attend church, although the differences are not large. Church attenders also have longer and happier marriages than nonattenders, and the marriages of church attenders are less than half as likely to break down than the marriages of nonattenders. Attenders are also much less likely to have lived common-law prior to marriage (Clark, 1998).

What about the impact of religion on health? In many small-scale societies, the same individual—the healer or *shaman*—was responsible for both physical and spiritual needs. After many years of separateness or even conflict, some people are once more trying to reintegrate medicine and religion. The increasing popularity of alternative medicine has led to an openness to nontraditional approaches, and opinion polls show that many people (including some doctors) believe that religious faith can help cure disease and, therefore, use prayer as medical therapy (Sloan et al., 1999).

Many researchers have attempted to test the relationship between religion and medical outcomes. In a somewhat humorous attempt to test the hypothesis, the eminent British scientist Sir Francis Galton sought to determine if prayer could increase longevity. He assumed that nobody in England received more prayers for longevity than the British royal family. People sang "God Save the Queen [or King]" and regularly expressed concerns for their rulers in their prayers. Recognizing that the upper-class lifestyle of royalty made them more likely to live longer, Galton knew he had to compare them with other wealthy people. He selected for his comparison group wealthy lawyers, determining that nobody would pray that lawyers live longer lives. Contrary to his hypothesis, he found that the lawyers lived longer and concluded that prayer had little efficacy in this regard.

Other, more serious studies have found that priests, monks, and nuns have less illness and live longer than members of the general population. However, these studies lack validity because they do not control for the lower exposure of those in religious orders to a variety of risk factors. Similarly, studies of Israelis living on secular and religious kibbutzim that found that the religious Jews lived longer than those who were nonreligious did not control for risk factors such as smoking, blood cholesterol, and marital status (Sloan et al., 1999).

In their review of several dozen studies in this area, Sloan and his colleagues (1999) concluded that the evidence of an association between religiosity and health is weak and inconsistent. However, if it does not affect physical health, there is evidence that religion can play a role in comforting the sick. For example, one study found that 40 percent of a group of hospitalized adults reported that their religious faith was the most important factor in their ability to cope with their illness (Johns Hopkins, 1998).

Women in the Ministry

I believe in God, the Father Almighty, Creator of Heaven and Earth, and in Jesus Christ, His only Son. (MacDonald, 1996:47)

A woman can't represent Christ. Men and women are totally different—that's not my fault—and Jesus chose men for his disciples. (MacDonald, 1996:47)

The above quotations relate to two issues that are becoming increasingly important to women in today's society: the gender inclusiveness of Christianity and Judaism and the absence of women in significant roles within religious institutions. These contentious issues are leading many women to reject mainstream religion in search of a spirituality that reflects the experiences of both women and men. In churches, synagogues, and even Buddhist Zendos, women are demanding an end to the traditions that do not reflect their historic role and their ongoing stake in the divine. Some women are choosing alternative spiritual belief systems, while others are working from within the church to create change. The battles

BOX 17.3 SOCIOLOGY AND TECHNOLOGY

IN THE MEDIA AGE: THE ELECTRONIC CHURCH AND THE INTERNET

In a single telecast, I preach to millions more than Christ did in His entire lifetime.
—Billy Graham (quoted in Roberts, 1995:360)

Television and the Internet are having an impact on religion in the United States and Canada. Although television has been used as a medium of communication by ministers since the 1950s, the *electronic church* has far surpassed most people's wildest estimates by becoming a multimillion-dollar industry with audiences ranging from 10 million to 130 million in the United States.

When religious services were first televised, many were church services conducted by a local congregation and carried by a regional television station primarily for the benefit of shut-ins and those who had no "church home" in the community. In the 1950s and early 1960s, the few nationally televised religious programs featured people like the Rev. Bishop Fulton J. Sheen, an established spokesperson for the Roman Catholic Church, or evangelists such as Billy Graham who were televised conducting a revival or "crusade" in some remote part of the world.

By comparison, most contemporary televangelists are entrepreneurs whose success hinges on presenting a message that "sells well" and generates the extremely large sums of money needed to keep the "television ministry" profitable. Rather than attempting to change viewers' beliefs, many televangelists attempt simply to confirm them. In the 1970s and 1980s, televangelists like Jerry Falwell, Oral Roberts, Jim and Tammy Faye Bakker, James Robison, Jimmy Swaggart, and Pat Robertson offered audiences a sense of belonging; for a certain sum of money, people could become "members" of the "700 Club" or "partners" in the "P.T.L. (Praise the Lord) Club" with Jim and Tammy Faye Bakker. Even while some televangelists were discredited because of sexual or financial misconduct or, as in the case of Jim Bakker, convicted of felonies, others took their place not only to proclaim the "gospel" but also to become spokespersons for a conservative political agenda. While televangelists have a great deal of impact in the United States, they have not been as successful in Canada. According to Reginald Bibby (1998), fewer than 5 percent of Canadians regularly watch

---

have been intense and polarizing. In 1992, the Church of England allowed the ordination of women priests. In response, a British vicar made a point of telling the media that he would "burn the bloody bitches" (MacDonald, 1996:47).

Despite opposition, some advances have been made. In the United States, there are at least 300 priestless Roman Catholic parishes. The majority are headed by women, specifically nuns (Wallace, 1991). In the year 2000, close to 25 percent of Christian pastors in the United States may be women. In 1994, the Vatican flatly rejected female ordination and more gender-neutral language in the Catholic Church. Given the dominance of the Roman Catholic Church in Canada, the growth in the proportion of female clergy here is likely to be more gradual (Currie and

Stackhouse, 1996). Nonetheless, 25 percent of ordained United Church ministers and approximately 10 percent of Anglican priests in Canada are women (Nason-Clark, 1993). The Baptist and Presbyterian Churches in Canada have begun to ordain women as well. However, once ordained, these women still face an uphill battle: they continue to be offered junior positions, are paid lower wages, and are not promoted to more prestigious posts (Nason-Clark, 1993). Not all religions are resistant to women in the clergy. For example, Reform Judaism has ordained women as rabbis since the early 1970s. Aboriginal Canadian religions have traditionally given status to women in spiritual leadership.

According to Raymond Currie and John Stackhouse (1996), there is little doubt that the

BOX 17.3

CONTINUED

religious services on television, which is much less than the 29 percent who watched or listened to services on television and radio in 1958. Further, most of those who did watch religious programs on television also attended church services regularly. This means that television has not become an electronic church replacing more traditional forms of worship. Only a few televangelists such as David Mainse have become nationally known in Canada, and none have any political influence.

By comparison, the Internet is just beginning to have an impact on religion. Some religious groups now have begun to use it to spread their message. For example, the Catholic Information Center on the Internet (**http://www.catholic.net**) was established to provide a wide range of services including a review of recent Church-related news stories; discussions of Church teachings; and a solicitation to inactive Catholics to become reinvolved with the Church. While the Internet is a good

way for mainline churches to get their message out, it also provides a means for newer spiritual groups to try to attract new followers. For example, the Fishgoat's Leaves of Wonder site (**http://www.gatewest.net/~dem/low/low.html**) provides information about Wicca and Magick for those who might have an interest in paganism.

While the Internet may be a useful tool for religious groups, it raises new questions and concerns because controlling what young people read on the Internet is almost impossible. Some religious groups have begun pressing for limits to the type of information available on this network, or at least to limits on young people's access to certain types of information. How do you think religious organizations should respond to this problem? Is censorship of the Internet either possible or desirable?

Sources: Based on Hadden and Swann, 1981; Frankl, 1987; Hadden and Shupe, 1988; McGuire, 1992; Kosmin and Lachman, 1993; Tidwell, 1993; Bates, 1994; and Roberts, 1995b.

future role of religion will depend significantly on the ability of religious institutions to respond to the changing role of women in society.

RELIGION IN THE FUTURE

Religious debates, particularly over issues such as secularization and fundamentalism, no doubt will continue well into the twenty-first century. However, in many parts of the world we are seeing not only the creation of new religious forms, but also a revitalization of traditional forms of religious life (Kurtz, 1995).

One example of this change is **liberation theology—the Christian movement that advocates**

freedom from political subjugation within a traditional perspective and the need for social transformation to benefit the poor and downtrodden (Kurtz, 1995). Although liberation theology initially emerged in Latin America as people sought to free themselves from the historical oppression of that area, this perspective has been embraced by a wide variety of people, ranging from Africans and African American Christians to German theologians and some feminists.

Another change in the nature of theology is found in some feminist movements that have turned to pagan religions and witchcraft as a means of countering what they consider the patriarchal structure and content of the world's religions. For instance, the *Goddess movement* encompasses a variety of countercultural beliefs

Storefront missions such as this seek to win religious converts and offer solace to people in low-income central-city areas.

based on paganism and feminism rooted in acknowledgment of the legitimacy of female power as a "beneficent and independent power" (Christ, 1987:121).

What significance will religion have in the future? Religion will continue to be important in the lives of many people. Moreover, the influence of religion may be felt even by those who claim no religious beliefs of their own. In many nations, the rise of *religious nationalism* has led to the blending of strongly held religious and political beliefs. The rise of religious nationalism is especially strong in the Middle East, where Islamic nationalism has spread rapidly and where the daily lives of people, particularly women and children, have been strongly affected (Juergensmeyer, 1993). Similarly, in Canada the influence of religion will be evident in ongoing political battles over social issues such as school prayer, abortion, gay and lesbian rights, and family issues. On the one hand, religion may unify people; on the other, it may result in tensions and confrontations among individuals and groups.

We began this chapter with a discussion of the place of religion in our educational system. It is clear that this role is diminishing. Numerous recent incidents have forced the issue of what is acceptable in schools and what is not. For example, to promote a multicultural environment, several schools in Toronto decided to exclude all references to Christian symbols or doctrine from their annual Christmas celebrations. One Toronto high school renamed its Christmas assembly a "holiday assembly" and eliminated all references

to Christianity. Another school banned the singing of religious Christmas carols on the grounds that references to Christianity would upset the non-Christian children (over 30 percent of Toronto's school population). As discussed in Box 17.2, the issue of which religious holidays are recognized in public schools is being played out in the courts. The overall effect of such incidents has been the increased secularization of the public school system. For example, in 1990 the Ontario Court of Appeal ruled against religious instruction in public elementary schools because it violates an individual's rights to freedom of religion (Fleras and Elliott, 1992). In 1995, Newfoundlanders voted to eliminate church-run schools in favour of a public, nondenominational education system. Newfoundland was at that time the only province in Canada that still had a church-run educational system.

The changing role of religion in education is but one example of the declining influence of organized religion in Canadian society. In many respects, the church in Canada is facing a bleak future. Despite an interest in the supernatural and a continued identification with religious traditions, church attendance and church membership continue to decline. In addition to these problems, which it shares with most other denominations, the Roman Catholic Church faces an additional difficulty in that the number of priests and nuns has declined dramatically. Fewer than two hundred men enter the priesthood in Canada each year, a figure that is only one-sixth the number of those who entered in 1962. Over half of Canadian nuns and priests are over 65 years of age (Jackman, 1999). These facts make it plain that this is an organization in decline and that church renewal, including the attracting of young new members, will be difficult.

One might think that with Canada's high rate of immigration from a wide variety of countries (see Chapter 10, "Race and Ethnicity") membership in religions such as Islam and Hinduism would be growing rapidly. However, this has not been the case for two reasons. First, many immigrants are Christian and are adding to the ethnic and religious diversity within the dominant religious groups (Posterski and Barker, 1993). Second, growth has been slowed because many young people from these other faith groups have been marrying outside their faith (Bibby, 1998). Children resulting from these marriages may attend Protestant or Catholic churches, or the family may drop all participation in religious activities.

Some see hope for the future in our aging population (see Chapter 12, "Aging"). They feel that as the baby boomers age, they are likely to search for spiritual meaning and some may turn back to the religions of their youth. However, the baby boomers are used to institutions that respond to their demands and the mainstream churches may prove to be unresponsive. As a result, they may look for the answers and the support they need elsewhere. Thus far there is little evidence that the church is meeting these needs and membership continues to stagnate.

As we have seen in this chapter, the debate continues over what religion is, what it should do, and what its relationship to other social institutions such as education should be. It will be up to your generation to understand other religions and to work for greater understanding among the diverse people who make up our country and the world. But some religious leaders see reason for hope, as one scholar explains:

> [People] know that religion, for all its institutional limitations, holds a vision of life's unity and meaningfulness, and for that reason it will continue to have a place in their narrative. In a very basic sense, religion itself was never the problem, only social forms of religion that stifle the human spirit. The sacred lives on and is real to those who can access it. (Roof, 1993:261)

CHAPTER REVIEW

What is religion, and what purpose does it serve in society?

Religion is a system of beliefs, symbols, and rituals, based on some sacred or supernatural realm, that guides human behaviour, gives meaning to life, and unites believers into a community.

What is the functionalist perspective on religion?

According to functionalists, religion has three important functions in any society: (1) providing meaning and purpose to life, (2) promoting social cohesion and a sense of belonging, and (3) providing social control and support for the government.

What is the conflict perspective on religion?

From a conflict perspective, religion can have negative consequences in that the capitalist class uses religion as a tool of domination to mislead workers about their true interests. However, Max Weber believed that religion could be a catalyst for social change.

What is the interactionist perspective on religion?

Interactionists focus on a microlevel analysis of religion, examining the meanings people give to religion and the meanings they attach to religious symbols in their everyday life.

What are the major types of religious organizations?

Religious organizations can be categorized as ecclesia, churches, denominations, sects, and cults.

What are the major world religions?

The major world religions are Buddhism, Hinduism, Confucianism, Judaism, Islam, and Christianity. More than 75 percent of the world's population is represented in these religions.

What impact does religion have on attitudes and behaviour?

Research looking at the impact of religion on attitudes and behaviour has had mixed results. Religiosity reduces involvement in delinquent and criminal behaviour, though this relationship is complex. Religious people had longer and happier marriages than non-religious people. Religion and prayer appear to have little impact on health, though they play a strong role in comforting the sick.

Will religion continue as a major social institution?

Religion in Canada is clearly in decline and the prognosis for the future is not bright. However, Canadians still have a strong interest in spiritual matters and continue to identify with the Church. If it is to take advantage of these factors, the Church must find new ways to become relevant to the daily lives of Canadians.

Key Terms

animism 545
church 559
cult 560
denomination 560
ecclesia 559
faith 543
liberation theology 569
monotheism 546
nontheistic religion 546
polytheism 546
profane 544
religion 542
rituals 545
sacred 544
sect 560
simple supernaturalism 545
theism 546

Internet Exercises

In order to effectively use the Internet exercises in this book, it will be necessary to have both a Web browser and newsreader software. If you are using Netscape 2.0 or greater, or Microsoft Internet Explorer 3.0 or greater, you have a newsreader built into your software. Please consult the computing centre at your school if you need assistance with these programs.

1. Go to the Yahoo Canada Web site at:

   http://ca.yahoo.com

   In the Society and Culture section of the home page, go to Religion. Then go to Canada Only, then to Faiths and Practices. Find two nontraditional faiths or beliefs that you are not familiar with and go to their Web sites. What are some of the fundamental principles of these faiths?

2. Go to the Virtual Religion Index at:

   http://religion.rutgers.edu/links/vrindex.html

   What Web sites can you find referenced at this site that will tell you about the religious practices of North America's Aboriginal peoples?

3. Several of the world religions discussed in this chapter are now represented at Web sites. Reach the BuddhaNet at

   http://www2.hawkesbury.uws.edu.au/BuddhaNet/budnetp.htm

   Here you may find links to the "Bhuddhazine," insight meditation, and dhamma data. Taking into account the images and topics conveyed by these Web pages, what do they tell you about Buddhism as a religion? How does that compare with the treatment of Buddhism in this chapter?

4. Al-Islam maintains a Web site at

   http://www.al-islam.org

   Read some of the "New Muslims Stories" available at this site. Again, compare what you find at this site with what is set forth in the text. What do these pages tell you about Islam?

Net Links

To look up links related to research on religion, go to the Virtual Religion Index at:

http://religion.rutgers.edu/links/vrindex.html

To see the Web site of the World Council of Churches, go to:

http://www.wcc-coe.org/wcc/english.html

Much of civilization's greatest art was commissioned by religious organizations. Visit the Vatican's Sistine Chapel with its ceiling painted by Michelangelo at:

http://www.kfki.hu/~arthp/tours/sistina/index.html
http://www.science.wayne.edu/~mcogan/Humanities/Sistine/index.html

Read about the PBS documentary on the first Christians at:

http://www.pbs.org/wgbh/pages/frontline/shows/religion

Questions for Critical Thinking

1. What are the major functions of religion and education for individuals and for societies? Why do these functions overlap in Canada? How would you design a research project to study the everyday effects of fundamentalist religion on everyday life? What kinds of data would be most accessible?

2. How is religion a force for social stability? How is it a force for social change?

3. If Durkheim, Marx, and Weber were engaged in a discussion about religion, on what topics might they agree? On what topics would they disagree?

Suggested Readings

These books provide more information on religion in Canada:

Reginald Bibby. *Fragmented Gods: The Poverty and Potential of Religion in Canada.* Toronto: Irwin, 1996.

W.E. Hewitt (ed.). *The Sociology of Religion: A Canadian Focus.* Toronto: Butterworths, 1993.

Useful books on the world's religions include the following:

Lester Kurtz. *Gods in the Global Village: The World's Religions in Sociological Perspective.* Thousand Oaks, Cal.: Pine Forge, 1995.

Warren Matthews. *World Religions.* St. Paul, Minn.: West, 1995.

Arvind Sharma (ed.). *Our Religions.* San Francisco: HarperSanFrancisco, 1993.

Huston Smith. *The World's Religions: Our Great Wisdom Traditions.* San Francisco: HarperSanFrancisco, 1991.

C H A P T E R

18

Health and Medicine

Sociological Perspectives on Health
    The Functionalist Perspective on Health: The Sick Role
    Symbolic Interactionist Theory: The Social Construction
        of Illness
    Conflict Theory: Inequalities in Health and Health Care

Social Factors in Health: Age, Sex, and Social Class
    Age
    Sex
    Social Class

Race, Class, and Health
    Health Problems Among Aboriginal Peoples in
        Canada
    Aboriginal Healing Methods

Disability
    Disability in Historical Perspective
    Disability in Contemporary Society

Social Development and Health: A Global Perspective
    Health Care in Canada
    Universal Health Care
    Health Care in the United States

Approaches to Health Care
    The Medical Model of Illness
    Alternative Approaches

Health Care Issues in the Future

Rae Lewis-Thornton describes her experience with HIV/AIDS in the following way:

"The day I found out [I was HIV positive] I was so calm ... I walked out of the ... Red Cross office and into the ... sunshine, flagged a cab and went back to work. I worked late that night ... I was 24. I'd just been given a death sentence ... I am the quintessential Buppie. I'm young ... Well educated. Professional. Attractive. Smart. I've been drug and alcohol-free all my life. I'm a Christian. I've never been promiscuous. Never had a one-night stand. And I am dying of AIDS.

"I've been living with the disease for nine years, and people still tell me that I am too pretty and intelligent to have AIDS. But I do. I discovered I was HIV-positive when I tried to give blood at the office. I have no idea who infected me or when it happened. Still, there is one thing I am absolutely certain of; I am dying now because I had one sexual partner too many. And I'm here to tell you one is all it takes." (Lewis-Thornton, 1994:63)

As we enter the twenty-first century, AIDS is among the most significant global/human problems we face, taking its toll on individuals, families, cities, and nations. The disease known as AIDS (acquired immuno-deficiency syndrome) is caused by HIV, the human immunodeficiency virus, which gradually destroys the immune system by attacking the white blood cells, making the person with HIV more vulnerable to other types of illnesses. While we do not know the actual number of people infected with HIV—some countries do not have adequate diagnostic equipment or centralized reporting systems—the United Nations estimated in 1998 that over 33 million people were infected with HIV and that 2.5 million people died of AIDS in 1997. Some countries are being devastated by HIV/AIDS; in Botswana and Zimbabwe more than 25 percent of the adult population is infected. In Canada an estimated 44,000 Canadians had HIV in 1994 and more than 10,000 had died of AIDS by 1997 (Archibald, 1997). Map 18.1 outlines the global distribution of the HIV virus. The number of victims is growing by about 10 percent each year.

AIDS is also a significant global/human problem because it may be a major species-threatening phenomenon with a potentially devastating impact on the world's population (Robertson, 1992:133). This threat is particularly significant in sub-Saharan Africa. In 1998 the region experienced 5500 deaths from AIDS each day, and there were four million new cases of the disease (UNAIDS, 1998). Half of all new infections are among 15- to 24-year-olds and many newborns are being infected by

HEALTH, HEALTH CARE, AND DISABILITY

their mothers, which means that the disease will destroy much of Africa's hope for the future. The average life expectancy in many countries has dropped by as much as 17 years, and the cost of providing even minimal treatment for the disease is taking away many of the hard-won economic gains some countries have achieved in the past decade. Clearly, the problem of AIDS illustrates how sociology can be applied to what, at first glance, appears to be a purely medical phenomenon. As sociologist Karen Grant explains, AIDS is a social phenomenon as much as a disease: "AIDS demonstrates that disease not only affects health, but one's definition of self, relations with others, and behaviours. As well, AIDS has had a significant impact on social institutions. The health-care system has been most directly affected, requiring assessments of the adequacy of research, treatment modalities, and health care facilities. Legal scholars and legislators have wrestled with issues of privacy and human rights protections for people with AIDS. AIDS has resulted in social and sexual mores and lifestyles being reassessed. AIDS has challenged stereotypes and forced some people to reconsider their prejudices" (Grant, 1993:395).

In this chapter, we will explore the dynamics of health and health care. In the process, we will periodically focus on HIV/AIDS and on both its present and potential impact on society. While we will use HIV/AIDS as an example throughout this chapter, you should be aware that globally several other causes of death are more common. In 1997, there were 52 million deaths around the world. About 2.5 million of them were due to HIV/AIDS compared with 17.3 million due to infectious and parasitic diseases; 15.3 million caused by circulatory diseases; 6.2 million due to cancer; 2.9 million resulted from respiratory diseases; and 3.6 million were due to perinatal conditions (World Health Organization, 1998). Before reading on, test your knowledge about HIV/AIDS by taking the quiz in Box 18.1.

QUESTIONS AND ISSUES

CHAPTER FOCUS QUESTION: What effect has HIV/AIDS had on the health of the global population?

Why is HIV/AIDS referred to as a global/human problem?

In what ways do sociological factors influence health and disease?

How do functionalist, symbolic interactionist, and conflict models differ in their analyses of health?

How does social inequality affect health and health care?

What are some of the consequences of disability?

What is the state of the health care system in Canada today and how could it be improved?

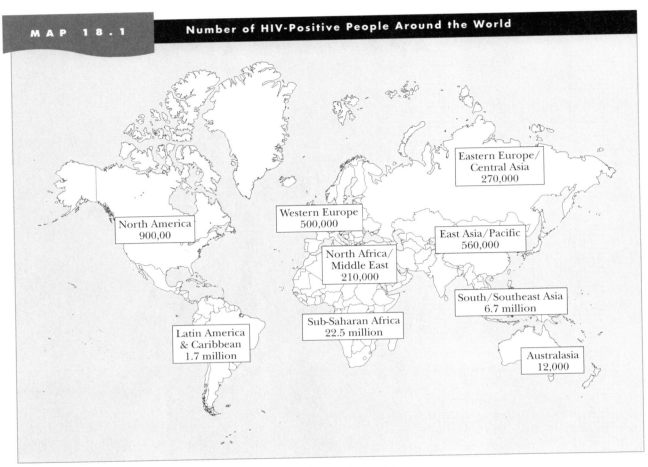

MAP 18.1   Number of HIV-Positive People Around the World

Eastern Europe/
Central Asia
270,000

Western Europe
500,000

North America
900,00

East Asia/Pacific
560,000

North Africa/
Middle East
210,000

South/Southeast Asia
6.7 million

Latin America
& Caribbean
1.7 million

Sub-Saharan Africa
22.5 million

Australasia
12,000

Source: UNAIDS, 1998. Available online: http://www.unaids.org/index.html. Reprinted by permission.

HEALTH AND MEDICINE

What does the concept of health mean to you? If you were asked whether you are healthy, how would you respond? Although the definition of health may at first appear obvious, consensus on its definition remains elusive. At one time health was considered to be simply the absence of disease. The World Health Organization (WHO) provides a more inclusive definition of **health, calling it the state of complete physical, mental, and social well-being.** In other words, health involves not only the absence of disease, but also a positive sense of wellness. You may know individuals who are ill but who consider life more fulfilling and satisfying than some disease-free people. Health, as the WHO's definition makes clear, has several dimensions; physical, social, and psychological factors are all important. It does not, therefore, depend solely on the absence of

disease or sickness. Health is also socially defined and therefore varies over time and between cultures (Farley, 1992). For example, in our society obesity is viewed as unhealthy, while in other times and places it has signalled prosperity and good health.

Medicine is an institutionalized system for the scientific diagnosis, treatment, and prevention of illness. Medicine forms a vital part of the broader concept of **health care, which is any activity intended to improve health.** As it has developed in North American culture, medicine typically is used when there is a failure in health. When people become sick, they seek medical attention to make them healthy again. As the definition of medicine suggests, medicine and health can go hand in hand. Medicine and the larger category of health care have undergone many changes over time. Most recently the field of *preventive medicine*—medicine that emphasizes a healthy lifestyle in order to prevent poor health

TRUE	FALSE	
T	F	1. Worldwide, most people with AIDS are gay men.
T	F	2. In Canada, it is against the law to knowingly transmit the HIV virus.
T	F	3. HIV, the virus that transmits AIDS, is spreading rapidly among women in some nations.
T	F	4. Nearly 50 percent of people who are HIV-positive worldwide are under the age of 25.
T	F	5. Infants who are born HIV-positive do not live past infancy or early childhood.
T	F	6. People can get AIDS from sharing toilets, toothbrushes, eating utensils, or razors.
T	F	7. People infected with HIV may not show any physical symptoms for ten years or longer and can infect others without realizing it.
T	F	8. Many people with AIDS die of the disease.
T	F	9. In Canada, the majority of new HIV cases occur among homosexual men.
T	F	10. One of the major concerns of AIDS activists is reducing the stigmatization of HIV/AIDS victims.

Answers on page 578.

before it occurs, is receiving increasing attention (Appelbaum and Chambliss, 1997).

SOCIOLOGICAL PERSPECTIVES ON HEALTH

The Functionalist Perspective on Health: The Sick Role

One of the most influential contributions to the development of the sociology of health from a functionalist perspective is Talcott Parsons's work on the sick role. Functionalists view society as a complex, stable system. Therefore, the normal state of affairs is for people to be healthy and to contribute to their society. Parsons viewed illness as dysfunctional both for the individual who is sick and for the larger society (Parsons, 1951). Sick people may be unable to fulfil their necessary social roles, such as parenting, maintaining a home, or working in the paid labour force. Due to this inability, illness can cause the social system to malfunction. Societies must, therefore, establish boundaries that define who is legitimately sick. Furthermore, those who are sick are expected to get well so that they can once again contribute to the healthy functioning of the social system. According to Parsons, all societies have a *sick*

role—patterns of behaviour defined as appropriate for people who are sick. He developed a model to describe the characteristics of the sick role:

1. The sick person is exempt from normal social responsibilities. For example, when you are sick you are not expected to go to work or school.
2. The sick person is exempt from responsibility for his or her condition. In other words the sickness must be the result of an accident or other circumstances beyond the individual's control. Individuals should not be blamed or punished because sickness is not their fault.
3. The sick person must want to get well. The sick role is considered to be a temporary role and the person who does not do everything in his or her power to return to a healthy state is no longer a legitimately sick person and may be considered a hypochondriac, a careless person, or a malingerer.
4. The sick person should seek competent help and cooperate with health care practitioners to hasten his or her recovery.

Critics of Parsons's model, and more generally of the functionalist view of health and illness, argue that it places too much responsibility for illness upon the sick people themselves, neglecting the fact that often the actions of other people may be the cause of someone's illness. For example, a

BOX 18.1

ANSWERS TO THE SOCIOLOGY QUIZ ON HIV/AIDS

1. **False.** Although AIDS has taken a devastating toll on the gay population in North America, the World Health Organization estimates that about 75 percent of the people with AIDS world-wide were infected through heterosexual intercourse.

2. **False.** No specific law forbids this behaviour. However, in 1995 a Newfoundland man who knowingly infected 19 women was sentenced to 11 years and 3 months in jail after pleading guilty to a charge of criminal negligence causing bodily harm. Also, in 1998 the Supreme Court of Canada ruled that a person could be charged with assault if they did not tell their sexual partners they had HIV/AIDS or other sexually transmitted diseases.

3. **True.** HIV has been spreading rapidly among women. Estimates place the number of HIV-infected women at more than 1 million in Africa alone. In Canada women accounted for 19 percent of HIV cases in 1996.

4. **True.** AIDS is found disproportionately among young people, a consequence of the fact that they are more likely either to engage in sexually promiscuous behaviour and/or to be intravenous drug users.

5. **False.** Some children who were born HIV-positive are now reaching their teens. Some of these children have shown no symptoms of AIDS-related illnesses; others have experienced continual medical problems.

6. **False.** AIDS is caused by HIV (human immunodeficiency virus), which is transmitted to men or women through unprotected (vaginal, anal, or oral) sexual intercourse with an infected partner (either male or female), through sharing a contaminated hypodermic needle with someone who is infected, through exposure to contaminated blood or blood products (usually from a transfusion), and through the passing on of the virus by an infected woman to her child during pregnancy, childbirth, or breast-feeding.

7. **True.** Without an HIV antibody test (which indicates whether a person's body has begun making antibodies in response to the virus), it may be impossible for an individual to tell whether he or she has been infected with HIV. And, for those who have taken this test, it can take from three to six months from the time a person is infected for the virus to show up on the test.

8. **False.** People do not actually die of AIDS; they die because HIV makes their bodies so weak they cannot fight off diseases such as pneumonia, tuberculosis, yeast infections, and Kaposi's sarcoma and other forms of cancer. Technically, AIDS is a syndrome, not a disease.

9. **False.** In 1996, 49 percent of victims were injection drug users and 37 percent were men who had sex with men.

10. **True.** Many AIDS victims have suffered hostility and discrimination as a result of their illness. Educational programs and political lobbying by AIDS activists have tried to reduce this stigmatization.

Sources: Based on Albert and Williams, 1998; Weeks, 1992; Gross, 1993; *JAMA*, 1994; Land, 1994; Singer and Deschamps, 1994; and Waldram et al., 1995.

child may be born with Fetal Alcohol Syndrome as a result of the mother consuminig alcohol while pregnant. Individuals living in poverty may become sick because of inadequate food and shelter (see Chapter 8, "Social Stratification and Class").

Critics of the sick role theory also point out that it is more applicable to individuals with acute illnesses than to those with either chronic illnesses or disabilities that may not be reversible. **Acute illness is illness of limited duration from which** the patient recovers or dies. Examples include chicken pox, the flu, pneumonia, and appendicitis. The term *chronic illness* **is applied to a long-term or permanent condition that may or may not be fatal.** Examples of chronic conditions are multiple sclerosis, muscular dystrophy, arthritis, and cystic fibrosis. Patients with terminal conditions, such as Lou Gehrig's disease, who want to get well once they have been diagnosed, may be criticized for failing to both to accept the reality of their situations and to adapt to daily limitations and disabili-

This AIDS memorial in Toronto is a striking reminder that AIDS has taken a toll on individuals, families, cities, and nations. In some countries, AIDS is a significant cause of population mortality.

ties (Nancarrow Clarke, 1996). Also, contrary to the functionalist view, individuals may be blamed for their illness, as people who contract HIV or lung cancer often are.

Symbolic Interactionist Theory: The Social Construction of Illness

Symbolic interactionists attempt to understand the specific meanings and causes that we attribute to particular events. In studying health, interactionists focus on the fact that the meaning that social actors give their illness or disease will affect their self-concept and their relationships with others. The interactionist approach is illustrated by society's response to AIDS.

We often try to explain disease by blaming it on those who are ill. This reduces the uncertainty of those of us who fear the disease; nonsmokers who learn that a cancer victim had a two-pack-a-day habit feel comforted that the guilty have been punished and that the same fate is unlikely to befall them. Because of the association of their disease with promiscuous homosexuality and intravenous drug use, victims of AIDS have particularly suffered from blame. How is a person's self-concept affected when they are diagnosed with AIDS? How does this diagnosis affect the relationships the person has with others in his or her social world?

In the case of AIDS, the social definition of the illness has had as profound an impact on the AIDS patient as the medical symptoms. According to Giddens (1996:123), AIDS is an example of illness as stigma. As indicated in Chapter 5, a *stigma* is any physical or social attribute or sign that so devalues a person's social identity that it disqualifies that person from social acceptance. Unlike other illnesses—the ones that provoke sympathy or compassion—an illness that is seen primarily as infectious is perceived as dishonourable or shameful. The result is that sufferers are rejected by the healthy population. Children with AIDS have been driven from their schools; homes of people with AIDS have been burned by those afraid of getting the disease; employees have been fired; and medical professionals have refused treatment to AIDS patients. All of this has happened despite the fact that AIDS cannot be transmitted by casual, everyday contact. However, as the case of AIDS clearly demonstrates, the social definition of an illness may have no basis in medical fact. The incidents of hostility and discrimination directed at individuals with AIDS nevertheless have a profound impact on their self-concept, social relationships, and ability to cope with the illness. The role of the media in shaping the way in which society defines an illness is discussed in Box 18.2.

THE SOCIAL DEFINITION OF HEALTH AND ILLNESS: THE PROCESS OF MEDICALIZATION

Because of their biological characteristics, most of us would agree that conditions such as heart disease, tuberculosis, and cancer are illnesses. You have seen in our discussion of the social construction of illness so far that even in these cases there is a subjective component to the way illness is defined. This subjective component is very important when we look at conditions that are more ambiguous than cancer

BOX 18.2 SOCIOLOGY AND MEDIA

AIDS IN THE NEWS

At the age of 13, Ryan White learned that he had contracted HIV through blood products used to treat his hemophilia. When school officials told White he could not return to school because of HIV, he fought back and eventually was readmitted. White also temporarily became a celebrity.

> We had been in the news so much that reporters were practically part of the family. They came from all over the place, even Japan. I felt like I was growing up with some of them. They followed us into the bathroom to see if we were telling the truth when we said we shared toothpaste and glasses. They stood by the kitchen sink and asked Mom if she was doing dishes by hand so she could use bleach on mine ...

> We talked to some reporters more often than we visited with our friends and relatives. (quoted in White and Cunningham, 1992:120–121)

Why did journalists pay so much attention to Ryan White and his plight?

Journalists have the ability to transform events—such as White's illness and battle with the school—into news. However, HIV poses unique problems for journalists. Gay men (a stigmatized category) were among the first to be identified with the problem. To report on HIV transmitted by gay men, journalists must refer to blood, semen, sex, and death, all of which are viewed by some media elites as being beyond good taste. Because of these problems, some journalists divided persons with HIV into two categories: "innocent vic-

---

or a broken bone. For example: a child who has difficulty learning may be diagnosed as having attention deficit disorder (ADD); a man who occasionally behaves strangely may be called mentally ill; and a woman going through menopause may be defined as having a hormonal deficiency disease. Alternatively, we could view these conditions as part of the range of normal human behaviour. The child might be seen as a poor student, the man as a bit odd, and the woman as a person going through the normal aging process. The way we view these individuals will depend on our cultural perspectives, which can change over time.

The term *medicalization* **refers to the process whereby an object or a condition becomes defined by society as a physical or psychological illness.** This process usually entails the application of medical technology in the diagnosis and treatment of the condition (Grant, 1993). Conrad and Schneider (1992) found that medicalization is typically the result of a lengthy promotional campaign conducted by interest groups, often culminating in legislative or other official changes that institutionalize a medical treatment for the new "disease." The interest groups may include scientists acting on the results of their research; those

who have the disease, and who may be seeking either a cure or a socially acceptable excuse for their behaviour; and members of the medical industry interested in increasing their profits.

Women's health issues such as those having to do with childbirth, menopause, PMS, and contraception have been particularly susceptible to medicalization (Reissman, 1983; Findlay and Miller, 1994), and this process has not necessarily served the interests of women. A 1989 paper by the American Society for Plastic and Reconstructive Surgery provides an extreme example of the subjective nature of disease. This society, the major professional organization representing plastic surgeons, wanted the U.S. government to loosen its restrictions on the use of breast implants. The society based its case on the view that having small breasts constituted a disease. They alleged that this disease resulted in "feelings of inadequacy, lack of self-confidence, distortion of body image, and a total lack of well-being due to a lack of self-perceived femininity" (cited in Weitz, 1996:123). Of course, the "disease" could be cured if the victims received expensive, often dangerous breast implants from the plastic surgeons. In Chapter 11, "Sex and Gender," you read about the

BOX 18.2

CONTINUED

tims" such as Ryan White who acquire the virus through blood transfusions or other means considered beyond their control, and "sources" of the problem, including gay and bisexual men, intravenous drug users, and prostitutes. This way of thinking suggests that we withhold compassion from those whose behaviours may have caused or contributed to their deaths. On these grounds we would never mourn the passing of a heart attack victim who did not exercise, worked under stress, or ate foods high in cholesterol. Persons with lung cancer owing to smoking should be disdained; persons with back injuries from lifting should be despised; the person who sees

the ice but nonetheless slips on it should be left in agony where he landed ... This is more than logically ridiculous. It is morally reprehensible. (Fisher, 1993:27–30)

The novel that was the basis for the hit play *Rent* dealt with gay victims of AIDS. However, producers of the play changed the focus to a heterosexual couple with AIDS because they felt the audience would not accept a play that was primarily about homosexuals.

Do you think media coverage of HIV/AIDS divides people into innocent victims and guilty parties? What role should the media play, if any, in disseminating information about HIV/AIDS to the public?

Sources: Based on Molotch and Lester, 1974; Colby and Cook, 1991; White and Cunningham, 1992; Fisher, 1993; Hernandez, 1994; and Gideonse, 1998.

low self-esteem felt by women that is often the result of sexism in our society. Having done so, it will not be difficult to imagine the harm that the plastic surgeons' lobbying effort encouraging women to think of their biologically normal bodies as "diseased" might have on women's self-image.

Conrad and Schneider (1980) emphasize that many behaviours that were at one time defined as "badness" have been redefined as "sicknesses" or "illnesses." Peter Conrad (1975) describes how the disruptive behaviour of children in schools became medicalized. Until a medical condition was established and given the name attention deficit-hyperactivity disorder (ADHD), children who had difficulty sitting still, concentrating, or who were impulsive and full of energy were labelled "active" or "energetic," or they were called "problem children" (Conrad, 1975). Regardless of the label, this behaviour was not treated as a medical condition. In the early 1970s the medical profession started to intervene in treating these "deviant" children. The "discovery" of the illness now known as attention deficit disorder (ADD) coincided with the development of Ritalin, a drug that suppresses hyperactive behav-

iours. As a result, medication became the accepted treatment for this condition. For schools, the social construction of this illness results in fewer disruptive students and more manageable classrooms. Furthermore, it creates a large new patient population for the medical profession and a profitable new market for the pharmaceutical industry. For the children whose problem behaviour is organically based, Ritalin enables them to concentrate and function better in the classroom. However, for children whose disruptive behaviour is a reflection of their acting "like children" rather than symptomatic of ADD, it results in unnecessary medication.

Just as conditions can be medicalized, so can they be *demedicalized*. For many years, homosexuality was defined as a mental illness, and gays and lesbians were urged to seek psychiatric treatment. Conrad and Schneider (1992) have described the successful fight by gay activists to convince the American Psychiatric Association to remove homosexuality from the association's psychiatric diagnostic manual. At the same time women's groups have been trying to demedicalize childbirth and menopause, and to redefine them as natural processes rather than as illnesses.

Conflict Theory: Inequalities in Health and Health Care

The conflict approach to health and illness considers the political and social forces that affect health and the health care system and the inequities that result from these forces. Among the issues of concern for conflict theorists are the ability of all citizens to obtain health care; the impact of race, class, and gender on health and health care; the relative power of doctors compared with other health workers; the dominance of the medical model of health care; and the role of profit in the health care system.

While we will consider several of these issues throughout this chapter, the role of conflict in the provision of health care is clearly illustrated in the debate over the allocation of money for research and treatment for different diseases. There is competition among those concerned with different diseases; money spent doing research on cancer cannot be spent on heart disease. Conflict also exists among those who take different approaches to research and treatment of a particular disease. Should funds be spent on treatment or prevention? Should nontraditional treatment methods be studied or is the medical model the only legitimate way of responding to disease?

Understandably, groups representing victims of particular types of diseases have lobbied governments and medical groups to give their problem a higher priority and more funding. Thus the priority given to research, prevention, and medical care for particular types of diseases may reflect the power of lobby groups as well as the seriousness of the problem. AIDS activists have been particularly successful in having their concerns reflected in policy. Homosexuals have worked together to form a lobby that has had a powerful impact on securing government support and funding for AIDS research and treatment. As you will learn from reading Box 18.3, AIDS activists have also been very concerned with reducing the stigmatization of HIV/AIDS victims.

Women with breast cancer saw that AIDS research received about ten times the funding of breast cancer research and have also organized to increase their share of research funding. The incidence of breast cancer has risen dramatically over the past four decades; the chances that a Canadian woman will get this type of cancer have risen from 1 in 20 in 1960 to 1 in 8 in the 1990s (Driedger, 1997). However, death rates from the disease are now at their lowest level in four decades, a decline analysts attribute to the increased mammography screening for early detection of the cancer (Statistics Canada, 1997a). Despite this decline, breast cancer remains a major cause of death for women and little is known about its causes.

SOCIAL FACTORS IN HEALTH: AGE, SEX, AND SOCIAL CLASS

We often think of health in only physical terms. However, the health of any group is a product of the interaction of a wide range of physiological, psychological, spiritual, historical, sociological, cultural, economic, and environmental factors (Waldram et al., 1995). In this section, we will see how these factors affect the health of people of different ages, genders, and classes in Canada. A basic premise of conflict theory is that groups compete with one another for access to scarce resources. Conflict theorists would predict that because of this competition, the quality of health and health care will vary by age, sex, and class. As with other social issues you have studied so far, there are dramatic differences in the health of people in these different social categories.

Age

Rates of illness and death are highest among the old and the young. Mortality rates drop shortly after birth and begin to rise significantly during the middle years. After 65, rates of chronic illness and mortality increase rapidly. This has obvious implications for individuals and their families, but also has an impact on Canadian society.

Canada is an aging society (see Chapter 19, "Population and Urbanization"). Today, about 12 percent of the population is 65 or over; by 2036 this will double to about 25 percent. Because health care costs are high for some older people, these costs will begin to rise dramatically after 2010 when the first baby boomers turn 65. This concern with future costs is one of the factors behind the current attempts by provincial and federal governments to restructure the operation of health care. For example, the number of cases of one of the most debilitating conditions among the elderly, *senile dementia*—a term for diseases, such as Alzheimer's, that involve a progressive impairment of judgment and memory—is forecast to triple by 2031 to nearly 800,000 people (Lipovenko, 1997). Many of these people will require costly institutional care unless changes are made to improve the support available for home care and group homes.

Sex

Prior to this century, women had shorter life expectancies than men because of high mortality rates during pregnancy and childbirth. Preventive measures have greatly reduced this cause of female mortality and women now live longer than men. Females born in Canada in 1996 could expect to live about 81 years compared with 76 years for males (Statistics Canada, 1998b). Ingrid Waldron (1994) has identified three factors leading to this sex difference in mortality rates. First, differences in gender roles in our society mean that females are less likely than males to engage in risky behaviour such as drinking alcohol and using drugs, driving dangerously, and engaging in violent activities such as fights. Males are also more likely than females to work in dangerous occupations such as commercial fishing, mining, and construction. Second, females are more likely to make use of the health care system and so may have problems identified at an earlier, more treatable stage than men, who are more reluctant to consult doctors. Third, it is likely that biological differences contribute, as females have higher survival rates than males at every stage from fetus to old age.

Some health experts have predicted that as the social roles played by females become more like those of males, the mortality gap will narrow. Women in traditionally male-dominated occupations, such as farming and policing, face the same risks as their male counterparts, and the number of such women is steadily increasing. Also, as female rates of behaviour such as smoking and illicit drug use approach those of males, females have begun to pay the price in illness and early death. About three decades ago smoking among women began to increase steadily. Predictably, rates of lung cancer among women have risen by more than 400 percent since 1969, while rates for men are dropping (National Cancer Institute of Canada, 1997). Also, Leviathan and Cohen (1985) studied life expectancy in Israeli kibbutz society, where the social roles of men and women are very similar. They found that sex differences in mortality on the kibbutz were only 4.5 years, compared with 7.1 years for the general population of Israel.

Alzheimer's disease is a tragedy for the afflicted individuals and for their families. As our population ages, such debilitating conditions will also increasingly place a burden on our health care system and on the taxpayers who fund it.

Because women live longer than men, many of us assume that women are also healthier. In fact, while men die sooner, women have higher rates of disease and disability. While men at every age have higher rates of fatal diseases, women have higher rates of nonfatal chronic conditions (Waldron, 1994).

One of the interesting issues relating to womens' health concerns the lack of medical research on women. For example, many of the largest and most influential studies of diseases that affect both sexes, such as heart disease, have excluded women. Despite this limitation, these studies have become the basis for the diagnosis and treatment of both sexes even though there may be differences between them. Protests by women's groups have led to change in this area, and some funding agencies now require researchers to include both men and women subjects unless there are clear reasons for limiting the study to one sex. However, the fact remains that a great deal of existing medical knowledge is based on the earlier male-centred research.

BOX 18.3 SOCIOLOGY AND LAW

AIDS AND PUBLIC HEALTH

In 1993, London, Ontario, resident Charles Ssenyonga was charged with criminal negligence causing bodily harm and aggravated sexual assault for knowingly passing AIDS on to several women. At least twenty women had contracted HIV through having unprotected sex with him. Ssenyonga died during his trial, so we don't know what verdict would have been rendered, though in a similar case the Newfoundland Court of Appeal imposed a sentence of eleven years and three months on Raymond Mercer, who had pleaded guilty to criminal negligence causing bodily harm for knowingly infecting women with HIV/AIDS. Canada has no specific law against knowingly infecting others with a sexually transmittable disease, though such laws do exist in several other countries including Australia and in many American states.

Ssenyonga knew in 1985 that he likely had HIV. AIDS was epidemic in his home country of Uganda and one of his former girlfriends there had died of the disease. On several occasions doctors suggested he get tested for HIV; however, he refused and assured his doctors that he was always careful to protect his partners during intercourse. In fact, he was HIV-positive and was having unprotected sex with multiple partners. In early 1989 two of his victims reported him to public health authorities. The Middlesex–London health unit did nothing for a month, then advised Ssenyonga to be tested. In March of 1989 both Ssenyonga and the

health department received confirmation of his infection. A restraining order forbidding him to have sex was issued at the request of public health officials. Despite this and despite his assurances to health officials that he would practise only safe sex, he continued to infect more women.

The public health system could not protect Ssenyonga's victims from HIV/AIDS. Doctors who suspected he had the virus could not require him to be tested, and after his diagnosis confirmed that he was HIV-positive his sexual behaviour could not be controlled.

Controlling the spread of HIV has been very controversial. The normal steps taken in dealing with infectious diseases include routine testing for infection, reporting the names of those who have positive tests, tracing contacts to determine who might have been infected, and informing them they have been exposed to the disease. Quarantine has even been used to prevent the spread of disease; in the 1940s and 1950s many Canadians were kept in hospitals so they could not pass on tuberculosis. In Ontario, twelve diseases including syphilis, gonorrhea, and tuberculosis are defined as virulent, and people with these diseases can be forced to stay in a hospital or jail for up to four months for treatment. However, HIV/AIDS is not included in this category. Because it is incurable, health authorities have reasoned, it does not make sense to force victims to have treatment. When Dr. Richard Schabas,

Social Class

The poor have worse health and die earlier than the rich. This is also true of poor and rich countries; illness and mortality rates are far higher in less developed countries than in developed nations. Even within the industrialized world, people in countries with the most equal distribution of income (Norway and Sweden) have the best health as measured by life expectancy (Nancarrow Clarke, 1996). In Canada, males

living in the highest-income neighbourhoods have a life expectancy of almost 6 more years than males in the lowest-income neighbourhoods. For women the difference is about 2 years (Trovato, 1994). There are similar differences between people in the highest- and lowest-income neighbourhoods for other health indicators.

In 1994–1995 and 1996–97, the National Population Health Survey found that low-income Canadians were much more likely to experience

BOX 18.3

CONTINUED

Ontario's medical officer of health, suggested classifying HIV/AIDS as a virulent disease in order to control rare, irresponsible victims like Ssenyonga who knowingly spread the disease, AIDS activists responded with furious protests. Dr. Schabas was burned in effigy and was given police protection when he received death threats.

Why is HIV/AIDS treated differently from other serious communicable diseases? One reason is the societal reaction to victims of the disease. Homosexual men, who have been the main victims of the disease in North America, have had justifiable fears that AIDS testing and reporting would result in discrimination against them. For example, some U.S. school districts wished to use HIV tests to identify and fire gay teachers, and insurance companies were anxious to cancel the policies of victims. Most Canadian provincial human rights codes do not protect homosexuals from discrimination in matters such as housing and employment. To AIDS activists and civil libertarians, Dr. Schabas's suggestion that AIDS victims could be involuntarily detained raised the possibility of homophobic governments locking up large numbers of gay men simply because they were ill. Because of the social consequences of an HIV-positive diagnosis, testing and notification procedures are generally voluntary and almost

all testing is done anonymously or with the consent of the person being tested.

Clearly there are weaknesses in our current system of controlling AIDS. However, the argument has been made that actions like mandatory testing and reporting or quarantining some AIDS victims will drive those at risk of AIDS underground, thus increasing the chances of further transmission. If there was a chance that HIV-positive people could be publicly identified, those at risk might choose to avoid the health care system altogether. In addition, these kinds of coercive control measures would be costly in financial as well as human terms, and would not likely be effective as a general public health measure (Hodgson, 1989).

What are your views on this controversial issue? Should all known partners of HIV victims be informed of their risk? Because medical advances such as AZT treatment for HIV-infected pregnant women and protease inhibitors dramatically reduce HIV levels, should more effort go into identifying those with HIV so that they can be treated? Can societal attitudes be changed so that the consequences of being labelled an HIV/AIDS victim are less severe? Should it be a crime to knowingly spread HIV, or should the problem be dealt with outside the criminal courts?

Sources: Callwood, 1995; Burr, 1997; and Weston and Jeffery, 1994.

major chronic diseases such as emphysema, high blood pressure, and stomach ulcers than those with middle- and upper-incomes. People under 75 in the low-income group in 1994–1995 were also twice as likely to die as those with higher incomes (Statistics Canada, 1998b). The National Longitudinal Survey of Children and Youth found that children from low-income families were twice as likely as those from families in the highest income category to have functional health problems (see Figure 18.1).

While poverty is correlated with poor health, government policy can help reduce its effects. Providing the poor with access to medical advice and treatment through universal medicare is one way of doing this. A five-year study comparing cancer survival rates for the poorest one-third of Toronto residents who all had government-funded health care, with their counterparts in Detroit, who typically had little or no health insurance, shows the impact of ensuring the poor have adequate health care (Gorey et al., 1997). Survival

In the summer of 1997, 650 people met in Kingston, Ontario, for the first World Conference on Breast Cancer. The major political goal of the conference was "to do for breast cancer what happened to AIDS in the 1980s—to put breast cancer on the centre stage" (Driedger, 1997).

rates were higher in Toronto for 12 of the 15 most common types of cancer. For many of these types of cancer, survival rates after 5 years were 50 percent higher among the poor in Toronto than among those in Detroit. The benefits of government-funded care go particularly to the poor, as this study found no differences among middle- or high-income patients in the two countries.

If access to medical care does improve the health of the poor, why then are Canada's poor still less healthy than its middle and upper classes? The answer is that medical care cannot compensate for the other disadvantages of poverty such as poor housing, hazardous employment, inadequate diet, greater exposure to disease, and the psychological stresses of poverty. The poor are more likely to become injured or sick because of these conditions, so their health is worse despite the availability of care once the medical problem has occurred. The poor may also lack knowledge of preventive strategies and services. For example, college- or university-educated women are twice as likely as women who have not graduated from high school to have mammograms. This means that less-educated women are at higher risk of dying of breast cancer.

RACE, CLASS, AND HEALTH: CANADA'S ABORIGINALS

We have looked at some aspects of the relationship between class and health. The experience of Canada's Aboriginal people clearly illustrates how the disadvantages of race interact with those of class to cause health problems. While the economic disadvantages and the prejudice suffered by Aboriginal people are worse than they are for most other groups of Canadians, the poverty and discrimination that affect Aboriginal people's health also affect the health of some other minority groups.

Health Problems Among Aboriginal Peoples in Canada

Aboriginal people have a history of serious health problems that begins with their early contact with Europeans. *Epidemics—sudden, significant increases in the numbers of people contracting a disease*—of contagious diseases such as tuberculosis, measles, smallpox, and influenza broke out in the early years of this contact. These epidemics were partly due to the fact that Aboriginals had no immunity to these European diseases. They were also caused by new patterns of trade that led to contact with more diverse groups of people than had occurred before European settlement. A critical mass of population is necessary to sustain an epidemic, and trade led to higher population densities around trading posts. Tuberculosis epidemics were particularly devastating in the late nineteenth century, as Aboriginal people were moved to reserves. Crowded and lacking proper sanitation and hygiene facilities, the reserves were ideal settings for the spread of disease, and mortality rates for tuberculosis remained high until the 1950s. The epidemics were very dramatic, but death rates from diseases such as typhoid fever and puerperal fever caused by poor sanitation in the settlements were also high (Waldram et al., 1995).

While their mortality rates have improved significantly since the middle of this century, Aboriginal people still die earlier than other Canadians. Infant mortality rates among Aboriginal people, moreover, are twice the Canadian average and life expectancy is 9 years less than average for Aboriginal men and 7 years less for Aboriginal women, who also have higher than average rates of hospital admission and dis-

FIGURE 18.1 | **Children with Lower Functional Health by Average Household Income[1]**

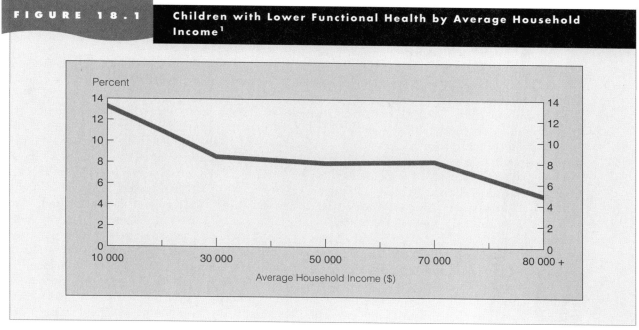

[1]Statistics Canada has based functional health on eight attributes: vision, hearing, speech, mobility, dexterity, cognition, emotion, and pain and discomfort.

Note: Two-parent families with children aged 4–11.

Prepared by the Canadian Council on Social Development, using the *National Longitudinal Survey of Children and Youth, 1994–1995*. Reprinted by permission.

ease (Wotherspoon, 1994). While infectious diseases among Aboriginals have been brought under control (though their rates remain higher than those of other Canadians), their health problems are now chronic diseases such as heart disease, respiratory problems, and diabetes. HIV/AIDS is now beginning to affect the Aboriginal community. The B.C. Aboriginal HIV/AIDS Task Force reported that while Aboriginal people made up less than 5 percent of the province's population, they made up 16 percent of those testing HIV-positive. The problem was particularly acute for Aboriginal women, who were eight times more likely to contract HIV than were non-Aboriginal women.

What are the reasons for the poorer health of Aboriginal people? A major factor is poverty. You have seen in Chapter 8, "Social Stratification and Class," that Aboriginal people are among the poorest in Canada and suffer from the poor nutrition and other social conditions that go with poverty. The complexity of these problems is shown in a study of the food supply of three northern Manitoba Cree communities (Campbell et al., 1997). The use of traditional food obtained from fishing and hunting was common but limited by the fact that 50 percent of the respondents did not have an active hunter or fisher in the household. Because the communities are isolated, food is up to twice as expensive as in the more accessible communities of Thompson and Winnipeg. The costs of a well-balanced diet may be too high for some families who do not have an adequate supply of traditional food, so health problems due to nutritional deficiencies are a concern.

Many of the diseases that affect Aboriginal people can also be traced to the inadequate housing, crowding, and poor sanitary conditions common on reserves and in other communities where they live. The isolation of many Aboriginal communities is also a factor; an illness that could be easily treated in a city hospital can be fatal in a community 500 miles from the nearest doctor.

Aboriginal people also have high rates of violent death and suicide. Rates of homicide are 6 times higher than the Canadian average for Aboriginal men and 4 times higher for women; rates of suicide are 3 times higher for men and twice as high for women than the Canadian averages (Mao et al., 1992). Rates of adolescent suicide are particularly high; the images of gasoline-sniffing young Innu from Davis Inlet in Labrador seen by most of us on television were a vivid and haunting illustration of this problem.

Accidental death rates are also higher: Aboriginal people are three times more likely than other Canadians to die as a result of motor vehicle accidents and twice as likely to die by drowning (Wotherspoon, 1994). These kinds of accidental deaths are often associated with the high rates of alcohol and drug abuse that are serious problems in many Aboriginal communities. These problems in turn are a consequence of the marginal role Aboriginal play in Canadian society.

Finally, the legacy of colonialism still affects Aboriginal people's health problems. Anastasia Shkilnyk (1985), who studied the Ojibwa community of Grassy Narrows in northwestern Ontario, attributes the high rates of suicide and violent death and health problems on the reserve to colonial actions such as the destruction of Aboriginal language and religion, the family breakdown caused by enforced attendance at residential schools, and the forced relocation of the community by the Department of Indian Affairs. Environmental destruction by local industries that dumped methyl mercury into the lakes and rivers around the reserve was another contributor. This toxic substance had a direct impact on the health of Grassy Narrows residents and also had an indirect impact by destroying the traditional fishery that was the foundation of the community's way of life.

Aboriginal Healing Methods

Aboriginal cultural and healing traditions are holistic and deal with the interactions between spirit, mind, and body. However, the Western medical model of medicine has been as dominant in Aboriginal communities as it has in the rest of Canada. Janice Acoose-Pelletier describes the problems this has created:

> When a Native person is admitted to a hospital, a number of other problems arise because we have our own ways of dealing with illness and care of the sick. Most hospitals don't recognize this or simply don't care ... Non-native medical personnel do not understand that healing, to many Native people, concerns whole communities or families ... To become well and whole again, the sick person must have faith and confidence in the healing process. For Native people, this is difficult and frustrating because in many cases they can't even communicate with doctors ... Doctors are just not aware of the cultural dif-

ferences between Natives and non-Natives regarding disease and care of the sick. (cited in Anderson, 1994:320–321)

Though traditional healing practices fell into disuse for many years, they are now becoming popular again for several reasons. First, medical and government authorities have responded to Aboriginal demands that culturally appropriate healing methods should be available. The introduction and acceptance of these methods, however, has been mixed. Some hospitals and clinics now have Aboriginal healers and combine traditional and Western treatment methods. For example, a plaque in a Kenora, Ontario, hospital reads: "We believe traditional Native healing and culture have a place in our provision of health care services to the Native people" (Waldram et al., 1995). Second, Aboriginal groups are gaining greater control over the delivery of medical services in their communities. These changes are almost certainly indicators of a future in which there will be greater involvement of Aboriginal people in the health care system and more integration of the traditional and Western medical traditions.

Finally, these holistic methods are important, in part for the treatment of alcohol and drug problems, but also in the treatment of other illnesses and injuries. Frideres (1994) suggests there is evidence that this restoration of Native control over their health care will also lead to improved health among Aboriginal people. Researchers in many parts of the world, moreover, have found that many traditional medicines are effective, and pharmaceutical companies now market many products (including aspirin) with the same chemical composition as traditional herbal remedies.

DISABILITY

What is a disability? There are many different definitions. In business and government, it often is defined in terms of work—for instance, "an inability to engage in gainful employment." Medical professionals tend to define it in terms of organically based impairments—the problem being entirely within the body (Albrecht, 1992). However, not all disabilities are visible to others nor do they necessarily limit people physically. An alternative definition of **disability** as a physical or

Does life expectancy take on a different meaning for persons with chronic disabilities? While he was still in college, British theoretical physicist Stephen Hawking learned he had Lou Gehrig's disease (amyotrophic lateral sclerosis). Hawking, nevertheless, went on to develop a quantum theory of gravity that forever changed our view of the universe and, as a result, he is considered one of the leading figures in modern cosmology.

health condition that stigmatizes or causes discrimination helps us view disability as residing primarily (although not exclusively) in social attitudes and in social and physical environments (Weitz, 1995). In other words, disability is socially created through everyday experiences that create barriers for individuals with disabilities. According to Blackford (1996), the social system and its planners have failed to provide the universal access that would allow people with disabilities to participate fully in all aspects of life. For example, in an elevator, the buttons may be beyond the reach of persons using a wheelchair. In this context, disability derives from the fact that certain things have been made inaccessible to some people (Weitz, 1995). Michael Oliver (1990) used the term *disability oppression* to describe the barriers that exist for disabled persons in Canadian society. These include economic hardship (from such things as the additional costs of accessibility devices, transportation, and attendant care; or employment discrimination), inadequate government assistance programs, and negative social attitudes toward disabled persons. According to disability rights advocates, disability must be thought of in terms of how society causes or contributes to the problem—not in terms of what is "wrong" with the person with a disability.

Disability in Historical Perspective

Historically, different societies dealt with disabilities on the basis of their culture, values, and technology. For example, in the Neolithic period, some persons with disabling illnesses had a hole drilled in their skull to provide an escape route for the evil spirits that were assumed to cause the problem (McElroy and Townsend, 1989; Albrecht, 1992). During the Middle Ages, disabilities were seen as an expression of God's displeasure, so the clergy dealt with medical problems.

The mode of subsistence in a society is a major determinant of the social responses to the various types of disabilities. In some hunting and gathering societies, impairments are viewed as punishment for past transgressions, and people with disabilities may be banished or killed; in others, they are fully integrated into the group (Albrecht, 1992). In pastoral societies, the migratory life inherent in continually moving herds of cattle, sheep, or goats to new locations for grazing may have serious consequences for those with an immobilizing disability. By contrast, in horticultural and agrarian societies, in which people settle down to cultivate crops and raise domestic animals, fewer stigmas are associated with disabilities

(Albrecht, 1992). At the same time, however, as stable communities are developed, epidemics related to poor sanitation and overcrowding are more likely to occur. For example, during the early stages of industrialization, urban density, lack of adequate sanitation, and poverty all contribute to a rise in the rate of chronic illness and physical disability (Albrecht, 1992).

Disability in Contemporary Society

An estimated 4.2 million or 15.5 percent of the population in Canada have one or more physical or mental disabilities. (For more information on the disabilities of Canadians aged 15 to 65, see Table 18.1) This number is increasing for several reasons. First, with advances in medical technology, many people who formerly would have died from an accident or illness now survive, although with an impairment. Second, as more people live longer, they are more likely to experience diseases (such as arthritis) that may have disabling consequences (Albrecht, 1992). Third, persons born with serious disabilities are more likely to survive infancy because of medical technology. However, less than 15 percent of persons with a disability today were born with it; accidents and disease account for most disabilities in this country.

Although anyone can become disabled, some people are more likely to be or to become disabled than others. Aboriginal people have higher rates of disability than whites, especially rates of more serious disabilities; persons with lower incomes also have higher rates of disability (Bolaria and Bolaria, 1994). However, "disability knows no socioeconomic boundaries. You can become disabled from your mother's poor nutrition or from falling off your polo pony," says Patrisha Wright, a spokesperson for the Disability Rights Education and Defense Fund (quoted in Shapiro, 1993:10).

For persons with chronic illness and disability, life expectancy may take on a different meaning. Knowing that they likely will not live out the full life expectancy for persons in their age cohort, they may come to "treasure each moment," as does James Keller, a baseball coach:

> In December 1992, I found out I have Lou Gehrig's disease—amyotrophic lateral sclerosis, or ALS. I learned that this disease destroys every muscle in the body, that there's no known cure or treatment and

that the average life expectancy for people with ALS is two to five years after diagnosis.

> Those are hard facts to accept. Even today, nearly two years after my diagnosis, I see myself as 42-year-old career athlete who has always been blessed with excellent health. Though not an hour goes by in which I don't see or hear in my mind that phrase "two to five years," I still can't quite believe it. Maybe my resistance to those words is exactly what gives me the strength to live with them and the will to make the best of every day in every way. (Keller, 1994)

Environment, lifestyle, and working conditions all may contribute to either temporary or chronic disability. For example, air pollution in automobile-clogged cities leads to a higher incidence of chronic respiratory disease and lung damage, which may result in severe disability in some people. Eating certain types of food and smoking cigarettes increase the risk for coronary and cardiovascular diseases (Albrecht, 1992). In contemporary industrial societies, workers in the second tier of the labour market (primarily recent immigrants, white women, and visible minorities) are at the greatest risk for certain health hazards and disabilities. Employees in data processing and service-oriented jobs also may be affected by work-related disabilities. The extensive use of computers has been shown to harm some workers' vision; to produce joint problems such as arthritis, low-back pain, and carpal tunnel syndrome; and to place employees under high levels of stress that may result in neuroses and other mental health problems (Albrecht, 1992).

Nearly one out of six people in Canada have a "chronic health condition which, given the physical, attitudinal, and financial barriers built into the social system, makes it difficult to perform one or more activities generally considered appropriate for persons of their age" (Nessner, 1994). Can a person in a wheelchair have equal access to education, employment, and housing? If public transportation is not accessible to those in wheelchairs, the answer certainly is no. As disability rights activist Mark Johnson put it, "Black people fought for the right to ride in the front of the bus. We're fighting for the right to get on the bus" (quoted in Shapiro, 1993:128).

Living with disabilities is a long-term process. For infants born with certain types of congenital (present at birth) problems, their disability first acquires social significance for their parents and caregivers. In a study of children with disabilities

TABLE 18.1 DISABLED PERSONS IN CANADA, AGES 15–65, 1990–1991

CHARACTERISTIC	PERCENTAGE
Nature of disability	
Mobility	52
Agility	50
Cognitive disability (includes intellectual, mental health, or learning disability)	32
Hearing	25
Vision	9
Speaking	8
Type of disability	
Severe	14
Moderate	32
Mild	54
Age	
15–34 years	29.4
35–54 years	43.2
55–64 years	27.4
Marital status	
Never married	24
Married/common law	61
Divorced	7
Separated	4
Widowed	4
Employment status	
Unemployed	52
Employed	48
Level of schooling	
University degree	6
High-school diploma	19
Some post-secondary	35

*Note: Totals do not add up to 100 as disabled persons may have more than one disability.

Reproduced by permission of Statistics Canada, adapted from *Report on Canadian Health and Disability Survey*, Cat. no. 82-555.

in Israel, sociologist Meira Weiss (1994) challenged the assumption that parents automatically bond with infants, especially those born with visible disabilities. She found that an infant's appearance may determine how parents view the child. Parents are more likely to be bothered by external, openly visible disabilities than by internal or disguised ones; some of the parents are more willing to consent to or even demand the death of an "appearance-impaired" child (Weiss, 1994). According to Weiss, children born with internal (concealed) disabilities at least initially are more acceptable to parents because they do not violate the parents' perceived body images of their children. Weiss's study provides insight into the social significance people attach to congenital disabilities.

Many disability rights advocates argue that persons with a disability have been kept out of the mainstream of society. They have been denied equal opportunities in education by being consigned to special education classes or special schools. For example, people who grow up deaf often are viewed as disabled; however, many members of the deaf community instead view themselves as a "linguistic minority" that is part of a unique culture (Lane, 1992; Cohen, 1994). They believe they have been restricted from entry into schools and the workforce, not due to their own limitations, but by societal barriers. Why are disabled persons excluded? Susan Wendell offers an explanation:

> In a society which idealizes the body, the physically disabled are often marginalized. People learn to identify with their own strengths (by cultural standards) and to hate, fear, and neglect their own weaknesses. The disabled are not only de-valued for their de-valued bodies; they are constant reminders to the able-bodied of the negative body—of what the able-bodied are trying to avoid, forget, and ignore ... In a culture which loves the idea that the body can be controlled, those who cannot control their bodies are seen (and may see themselves) as failures. (1995:458)

Among persons who acquire disabilities through disease or accidents later in life, the social significance of their disability can be seen in how they initially respond to their symptoms and diagnosis, how they view the immediate situation and their future, and how the illness and disability affect their lives. According to Wendell:

> Disabled people can participate in marginalizing ourselves. We can wish for bodies we do not have, with frustration, shame, self-hatred. We can feel trapped in the negative body; it is our internalized oppression to feel this. Every (visibly or invisibly) disabled person I have talked to has felt this; some never stop feeling it. (1995:458)

When confronted with a disability, most people adopt one of two strategies—avoidance or vigilance. Those who use the avoidance strategy deny their condition so as to maintain hopeful images of the future and elude depression; for example, some individuals refuse to participate in rehabilitation following a traumatic injury because they want to pretend that it does not exist (Weitz, 1995). By contrast, those using the vigilant strategy actively seek knowledge and treatment so that they can respond appropriately to the changes in their bodies (Weitz, 1995).

The combination of a disability and society's reaction to the disability has an impact on the lives of many people. The disabled often suffer from stereotyping: movies, for example, are given to depicting villains as individuals with disabilities (think of *Nightmare on Elm Street* and its sequels and the villains in the Batman movies). Charitable organization fundraising campaigns may contribute to the perception of the disabled as persons who are to be pitied. Prejudice against persons with disabilities may result in either subtle or overt discrimination. It may also be the reason they have difficulty finding employment. While the role of disabled persons in the Canadian labour force has expanded in recent years, compared with nondisabled adults a much smaller proportion of the disabled population is employed. Even when persons with a disability find jobs, they typically earn less than nondisabled persons (H.A.L.S., 1991). Greater inclusion of people with disabilities is a challenge Canadians must accept if we are to achieve our cultural goal of equality for all citizens.

SOCIAL DEVELOPMENT AND HEALTH: A GLOBAL PERSPECTIVE

Earlier in this chapter you learned how poverty and colonialism have affected the health of Canada's Aboriginal people. These factors also operate on a global scale. For example, Hunt (1989) attributes the rapid spread of diseases such as HIV/AIDS in Africa to the underdevelopment and dependency that is the legacy of colonialism. While one of the specific causes of HIV transmission is Africa's labour market that concentrates male migrant workers in a few locations far from their families, the underlying roots of this health problem lie in the economic and social marginalization of most African people.

The difference between rich and poor countries is dramatically reflected in infant mortality rates. While 6 out of every 1000 infants in Canada die before their first birthday, infant mortality rates in the world's poorest countries are far higher. Rwanda, Haiti, and Pakistan, for instance, have infant mortality rates of 119, 109, and 104 per 1000 live births. Life expectancy is correspondingly low; for persons born in Canada in 1996, life expectancy at birth was about 79 years, compared with less than 45 years in many poor African nations. Most deaths in less-developed countries are caused by infectious and parasitic diseases that are now rare in the industrialized world.

While statistics paint a grim picture of health in the developing world, a UNICEF report on the health of the world's children puts the situation in even starker terms (1997). Over eight million children each year die of the childhood diseases of measles, diarrhea, malaria, pneumonia, and mal-

A nurse interviews a mother at a rural health clinic in Sierra Leone. With the support of the World Health Organization, these clinics were established to reduce infant mortality and to improve the health of mothers and their children.

nutrition. As Monica Sharman and James Tulloch tell us, "Children in rich countries do not die from the common, preventable diseases of childhood. Children in poor countries do" (1997:1).

Tremendous progress has nevertheless been made in saving the lives of children over the past fifteen years. Steps such as immunization, oral rehydration therapy for diarrhea, and iodizing salt save as many as five million children each year. Sharman and Tulloch say this progress "must be ranked as one of the great achievements of the second half of the twentieth century" (1997:2). However, there continue to be millions of child deaths that could be prevented through simple measures such as improved sanitation, clean water, improved preventive measures such as immunization, and the provision of better local health services.

Of course, not only children in poor countries are dying. Each year 585,000 women die of complications arising from pregnancy and childbirth. Virtually all of these deaths take place in poor countries.

As we have noted, AIDS is becoming an epidemic in developing countries but little has been done to prevent its spread in these countries. (See Box 18.4 for more on the spread of AIDS in Africa, particularly Uganda.) While 90 percent of people currently infected with HIV live in the developing world, only 8 percent of the $18 billion a year spent on treatment, prevention, and research goes to these countries (Piot, 1997). Even worse, the new methods of treatment that have successfully extended the lives of those with AIDS in the developed world are unaffordable in developing countries where average annual incomes are only a fraction of the cost of these treatments.

Health Care in Canada

In 1998 the United Nations once again ranked Canada the best place in the world to live. This prestigious designation is in part based on an assessment of Canada's national health care system. Unquestionably, this system ranks among the best in the world.

Though cherished by Canadians and envied by many in other countries, some critics feel that Canada's health care system is in danger of "wasting away" because of budget cuts (Armstrong and Armstrong, 1996), and people in many communities across the country have been protesting hospital closures and health care funding cuts. In 1996, government funding for health care fell for the first time since the birth of medicare (Canadian Press, 1997). While the drop was a small one, it has raised even greater concern among those who fear our health care system is deteriorating. Public opinion polls demonstrate this concern. An international health survey found that in 1988 only 5 percent of Canadians felt their health care system required major rebuilding. By 1998, 23 percent felt that major changes were needed (Blendon, et al., 1998). Other surveys have shown similar declines in satisfaction (*Maclean's*, 1996). The reason for this dissatisfaction is illustrated by the following complaint about an occurrence that is becoming frequent. The complaint was made to Ontario's Patient Care Hotline by a patient who was released from hospital too soon after a serious operation:

> They wanted to discharge me but everything still hurt. I was still weak, weak, weak and there was something very wrong. But never mind, they were telling me I was fine and that it was time for me to

Government home-care workers march at the Manitoba legislature in April of 1997, protesting the provincial government's plans to contract out their services to private companies. Public opposition to this privatization convinced the government to scale back their plans to a small trial project. Later in the year, the government found that privatization would not save any money and returned all responsibility for home care to government workers.

go home. I was so sick on that day I couldn't hold my head up, couldn't get out of bed or get dressed and I was heaving on and off.

Following release, the patient remained bedridden at home for a month and then was readmitted when a home-care nurse became concerned with the patient's condition:

> They took me to emergency. They found a massive infection ... They operated that evening ... I was in hospital in intensive care for 2 months and on the medical ward for 3 weeks. They told my friend I might pass away. (Armstrong et al., 1997:72)

There is, however, some cause for optimism about the future of our health care system in that Canadians still highly value their system and are determined to ensure its survival. Public pressure may stop the erosion of health services. Several provinces have begun to put new money into health care, and the premiers of all provinces demanded that the federal government place health care funding at the top of the spending priority list. In the 1999 budget, the federal government began restoring some of the money it had cut from health budgets.

Universal Health Care

Canadians have not always had a *universal health care system,* **that is, one in which all citizens receive medical services paid for through taxation revenues.** Prior to the early 1960s Canadians had a "user pay" system, in which people had to pay for health care directly out of their pockets. Individuals who did not have health insurance and who required expensive medical procedures or long-term care or who developed a chronic illness often suffered severe financial losses. Today, under our universal system, if you are sick, you have the right to receive quality medical care regardless of your ability to pay. Individuals do not pay doctor or hospital costs directly, but they are responsible for at least part of the costs of other medical services such as prescription drugs and ambulances.

While the idea of universal health care was first introduced in Canada by Liberal Party leader Mackenzie King in 1919, it took almost five decades for this platform proposal to be implemented. This long delay was due in part to the fact that, constitutionally, health care is a provincial responsibility, and all changes had to be approved by the provinces. Legislation providing universal hospital insurance—but not fees for doctors' services—was passed in 1958. Responding to

TABLE 18.2 LIFE SPAN AND HEALTH CARE EXPENDITURE

COUNTRIES IN ORDER OF LIFE EXPECTANCY	LIFE EXPECTANCY AT BIRTH, 1996 IN YEARS	TOTAL EXPENDITURE ON HEALTH, % OF GDP, 1997	EXPENDITURE ON HEALTH PER CAPITA, 1997[1]
Japan	80.3	7.3	$1741
Canada	78.5	9.3	2095
Australia	78.2	8.3	1805
France	78.1	9.6	2051
U.K.	76.9	6.7	1347
Germany	76.8	10.4	2339
U.S.	76.1	13.6	4090

[1]Adjusted for cost of living differences.

Reprinted by permission of Gerard Anderson, *Highlights of the 1998 Multinational Comparisons of Health Care.* New York, NY: The Commonwealth Fund, 1998.

concerns about the quality of health care in Canada, in 1961 the federal government established the Royal Commission on Health Services. The commission identified many problems in Canada's health care system, including high infant mortality, high incidence of sickness, insufficient numbers of trained personnel, gaps in health insurance, and inequality in health care for the poor (Jarvis, 1994). The commission recommended that the provincial and federal governments introduce a program to remove the economic barriers that prevented many Canadians from accessing necessary medical care.

Acting on its own, the government of Saskatchewan in 1962 implemented a provincial health insurance plan despite opposition from doctors, who went on strike in protest against the program. The strike was not successful, as the vast majority of citizens supported the government, which maintained health services by importing doctors from Great Britain. The Saskatchewan program proved itself to be viable in the years that followed the strike, and by 1972 all Canadian provinces and territories had coverage for medical and hospital services.

Health care is a provincial responsibility, and each province has its own medical insurance plan. However, the federal government contributes a significant amount of money to the provinces for health care and enforces basic standards that each province must follow. Provincial plans must meet the following five requirements:

1. *Universality*—all Canadians should be covered on uniform terms and conditions;
2. *Comprehensiveness*—all necessary medical services should be guaranteed, without dollar limit, and should be available solely on the basis of medical need;
3. *Accessibility*—reasonable access should be guaranteed to all Canadians;
4. *Portability*—benefits should be transferable from province to province; and
5. *Public administration*—should be operated on a nonprofit basis by a public agency or commission. (Grant, 1993:401)

Although Canada's health care system continues to rank among the best in the world, it has its critics. The system has been subjected to drastic cuts in funding that have led to reduced resources and services. Canada still spends over 9 percent of its gross domestic product on health care. While this is low in comparison with the rate in the United States (see Table 18.2), it is higher than that of many other industrialized countries and it amounts to a sizable expenditure. For example, Canada's 1996 health care expenditures were $75 billion (Canadian Press, 1997). Of this amount, $52 billion came from government funding, while the remainder came from individuals and medical insurance companies for services not covered by medicare.

Related to the issue of increasing costs and declining resources is the problem of overutiliza-

BOX 18.4   SOCIOLOGY IN GLOBAL PERSPECTIVE

THE AIDS EPIDEMIC IN AFRICA

RAKAI, UGANDA: From the shadows of this mud hut, the gaunt and weary young man stares outside at the pigs playing in the dust under the banana palms. His chest is covered with open sores; skin rashes have left his ebony arms looking as if they are covered in chalk; his army fatigues hang loosely around his waist.

Outside, Charles Lawanga glances toward his ailing second son and lowers his voice. Last year, when the Ugandan army gave him his medical furlough, his son was sick, but at least he could walk, says Lawanga.

Lawanga's brows are furrowed; he has the face of a man who is watching his son die. His eyes sharpen when he hears that an American journalist knows many of the Western doctors working on the disease. He knows that the United States is a country of immense wealth, and that the medicine that will save his country and his son will probably come from there. Tears gather in his brown eyes, and he asks, "When will it come? When will there be the cure?" (Shilts, 1988:621)

In the mid-1990s, Uganda has the highest number of recorded HIV cases in Africa—

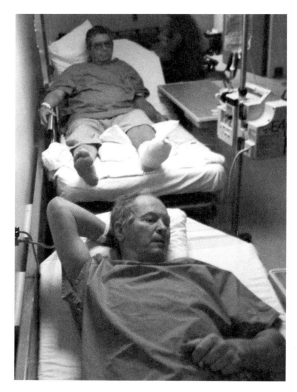

One of the consequences of cutbacks to Canada's health care system has been hospital overcrowding. These patients spent two days in an emergency room hallway because no rooms were available.

tion of health care services by the Canadian public. Utilization surveys have indicated that Canadians began to use health services more extensively following the introduction of medicare. According to sociologist Karen Grant:

> Canadians have an almost insatiable appetite for medical services, because they do not pay for health services when received, and because they have no knowledge of the actual costs of care, they inappropriately use the system. Frequenting emergency rooms for routine care is perhaps the most common illustration of this problem. (Grant, 1993:401)

While members of the public may not always make the most economical choices, many of the costs of our system are controlled by doctors, who prescribe drugs, admit patients to hospitals, determine patients' lengths of stay in hospital, order tests and examinations, determine the course of treatment that will be used, and recommend follow-up visits. Since patients will do almost anything to ensure their health and since they do not pay directly, they have no incentive to question doctors' recommendations. For many years the number of doctors has been increasing faster than the rate at which the population is growing. This has resulted in decreases in the number of patients per doctor and has led to doctors having to see

BOX 18.4

CONTINUED

around 1.5 million. AIDS has touched virtually all families in this country, and much of the stigma of this syndrome has diminished because it is now so widespread. Average life expectancy in Uganda is predicted to fall from 59 years to 32 years by 2010.

Will a cause for HIV be found? A vaccine or a cure? What impact will AIDS have on world population size? Currently, it is impossible to assess the demographic impact of AIDS; not enough is known about the patterns of transmission of the current strains of HIV. In Africa (as compared with North America), HIV appears to have been in the population longer, and it infects women and men about equally. Africans are highly vulnerable to AIDS because of malnutrition, rapid population growth, and a continually changing ecological situation.

Should Canada and other developed nations take an active role in trying to limit the AIDS epidemic in sub-Saharan Africa? Why or why not?

Sources: Shilts, 1988; Ehrlich and Ehrlich, 1991; Lorch, 1993; Obbo, 1993; *Audubon*, 1994; Gibson, 1994; and Weitz, 1996.

patients more frequently or suffer a loss of income. Reducing the economic control of doctors while ensuring that treatment decisions are made on medical, not economic, grounds is one of the major challenges of taxpayer-funded health care systems.

A final criticism of the Canadian health care system is its costly and often wasteful focus on hospitals and doctors. From the beginning, there has been an imbalance in our national health care system in its emphasis on acute care and its lack of recognition of and funding for community care (Crichton et al., 1997). Cheaper forms of noninstitutional health care such as home-care services are not subject to national standards, so these services vary widely from province to province and may not be available even when they are the most cost-effective type of care. Thus, people who need minimal care may be taking up expensive acute care hospital beds costing over $1000 per day because community alternatives are not available. The focus on physicians and hospitals can also be costly because it comes at the expense of preventive measures.

Health Care in the United States

The United States is the only industrialized country without a health care system that provides universal coverage to all its citizens. In fact, the United States does not really have a health care system at all; what it has is a mixture of private and public health care providers with no centralized control. While Canada and western European countries treat health care as a basic human right, the United States sees it as a market commodity. Most Americans receive health care coverage through private insurance programs that are sometimes paid for or subsidized by their employers. However, many Americans cannot afford to buy insurance and others may be denied coverage because of medical conditions. Some of those who do not have insurance may be covered by government-funded Medicare and Medicaid programs. Medicare covers Americans over 65 and some people with permanent disabilities. Medicaid provides coverage to a minority of those below the poverty line. Approximately 16 percent of the U.S. population—44 million people—have no medical coverage. An even larger number are inadequately covered and the expenses incurred in treating a serious medical condition such as cancer, a heart attack, or long-term disability can lead to financial ruin.

Despite the lack of universal coverage, per capita health care costs in the United States are much higher than in Canada. In 1997, for example, adjusted per capita costs in the United

States of $4090 were roughly double the per capita cost of $2095 in Canada for that year (see Table 18.2). Much of this difference is due to the efficiency of Canada's national nonprofit government insurance system compared with the fragmented U.S. system with its large number of different health care insurers and providers, each anxious to maximize profits and each adding its overhead costs to the final bill. Overhead costs are also greater because the United States imposes no central controls on hospital construction, and, as a result, the country has about a third more hospital beds than it requires. Finally, the salaries of health care workers, particularly doctors, are much lower in Canada than in the United States.

In an effort to address the inadequacies of the existing system, a national health care reform plan was proposed by the Clinton administration in 1993 (Weitz, 1996). However, a massive lobbying effort by the health care industry, fearful of losing some of its profits, ensured that this proposal was not successful. Even if it had been adopted, though, coverage provided by the plan would have fallen far short of Canadian standards.

In the debate over health care reform, many U.S. politicians and health care lobbyists were highly critical of Canada's "socialized" health care. They claimed that Clinton's plan would lead to the treatment delays and inferior care alleged to characterize the Canadian system. Are these critics correct? Do Canadians have an inferior system that forces people to travel to the United States to get proper treatment? The answer to these questions is no. Despite the higher costs of U.S. health care, Canadians are healthier than Americans and have better access to health care. Canada has a lower rate of infant mortality and longer life expectancy than the United States; these two indicators are often used as broad measures of the quality of health care. A wide variety of studies demonstrate the superiority of our health care system. Earlier in this chapter, you read about a study showing that poor Canadians had much higher cancer survival rates than poor Americans. Another study comparing the outcomes of ten different surgical procedures for elderly persons in Manitoba with those in the New England states reported that long-term survival rates were higher in Canada than in the United States for nine of the ten procedures studied (Roos et al., 1992). These differences are recognized by the public as Canadians are more satisfied with their health care than are Americans with theirs (Blendon et al., 1998).

APPROACHES TO HEALTH CARE

The Medical Model of Illness

The medical model has been the predominant way of thinking about illness in Western industrialized societies for many years. The medical model can best be described by considering its five basic assumptions: that illness is "(1) deviation from normal, (2) specific and universal, (3) caused by unique biological forces, (4) similar to the breakdown of a machine whose parts can be repaired, and (5) defined and treated through a neutral scientific process" (Weitz, 1996:129). One consequence of this model has been that our society has vested great power in the hands of doctors, who are seen to be the experts in diagnosing and treating illness. Doctors have gone to great lengths to protect this view and their role at the centre of the health care system. For example, they have actively resisted those with conflicting views such as midwives, advocates of natural healing methods, and those more concerned with preventing disease than with treating it.

Alternative Approaches

Despite the many successes of modern medicine such as heart pacemakers, arthroscopic surgery, and lung transplants, the medical model of illness is losing some of its dominance. While medical care is an important part of the health care system, Canadians are recognizing that their health needs cannot be met by medical services alone and that more medical care does not necessarily lead to better health (Grant, 1993). In 1986, the federal government explicitly adopted a health promotion policy, which emphasized prevention of disease, and promoted healthy lifestyles and an increase in informal and community-based care (Crichton et al., 1997). The cost crisis in medicare has led the federal government to implement programs in support of this approach that emphasize environment and lifestyle in health promotion. For example, education about the hazards of smoking combined with more effective legislation against the use and advertising of tobacco products can improve public health and save the money now used to treat victims of smoking-related diseases such as emphysema and lung cancer. Responsibility for health care is shifting

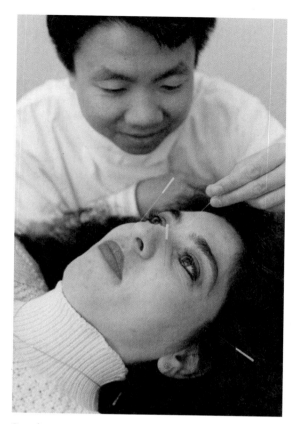

Canadians are increasingly using alternative health care methods such as acupuncture.

away from the government and the health care system and toward the individual and the family.

Issues of cost and benefit to patients have also led to a move toward community-based care in most provinces. Programs such as home care, community health clinics, and alternative care for the elderly have saved costs by reducing the need for more expensive hospital care (Crichton et al., 1997). Many of these community programs also enhance people's quality of life by allowing them to remain in their communities.

The popularity of the holistic health care movement is a further indication of the move toward a new definition of health. Holism has a long history and reflects the orientations of many ancient therapeutic systems including that of Canadian Aboriginals. Modern scientific medicine has been widely criticized for its focus on diseases and injuries rather than on the prevention of illness and the promotion of overall well-being. Advocates of holistic medicine say the medical model looks at problems in a mechanical fashion without considering their context, while the holistic approach emphasizes the interdependence

of body, mind, and environment (Northcott, 1994).

Holism is adaptable to more traditional medical practice and is being adopted by some medical doctors and nurses as well as by practitioners of alternative health care including chiropractors, osteopaths, acupuncturists, and naturopathic doctors. Supporters of the holistic health movement encourage people to take greater individual responsibility for their health and health care, especially with regard to diseases and disabilities that are the products of lifestyle. This approach also urges health care providers to pay more attention to clients in diagnosing and treating illness, and to develop a greater sensitivity to cultural differences in the ways in which people define and react to illness.

The holistic approach also emphasizes the role of social factors in illness. This view is now beginning to receive support in research done by traditional practitioners. For example, an article published in the *Journal of the American Heart Association* found that middle-aged men with high levels of despair had a 20 percent greater chance of developing atherosclerosis—narrowing of the arteries—than more optimistic men with similar physiological risk factors. This was a difference in the risks for heart disease as great as that between a nonsmoker and a pack-a-day smoker (Cable News Network, 1997). Research on the health of older adults has also shown that nonmedical factors such as isolation, the death of a family member or a friend, and the loss of status after retirement have a major influence on health. Thus, programs for the elderly must deal with these issues as well as with physical problems (Crichton et al., 1997).

Alternative approaches will continue to challenge traditional medicine's preoccupation with illness and disease and its focus on treatment by conventional biomedical means into the next century (Alix, 1995). The 1994–1995 National Population Health Survey found that many Canadians were making use of alternative medicine. While about 15 percent of those surveyed said they had consulted an alternative practitioner within the previous year, only 2 percent of them said they had relied exclusively on an alternative practitioner within the previous year. Since only 2 percent relied exclusively on alternative medicine, it seems that this form of health care is being used as a complement to traditional medicine rather than as a replacement. Of the groups surveyed, college- and university-educated young adults were most likely to use alternative health care. Also, women were more likely than men to use alternative health care.

While its use appears to be growing, some types of alternative medicine are being criticized. Psychologist Barry Beyerstein has recently repeated the most pointed criticism, saying that some of the claims of alternative medical practice have not been empirically verified. He blames the acceptance of such claims on the fact that most people know little about science:

> ... even an elementary understanding of chemistry should raise strong doubts about the legitimacy of homeopathy; a passing familiarity with human anatomy would suggest that "subluxations" of the vertebrae cannot cause all the diseases that chiropractors believe they do; and a quite modest grasp of physiology should make it apparent that a coffee enema is unlikely to cure cancer. But when consumers have not the foggiest idea of how bacteria, viruses, carcinogens, oncogenes, and toxins wreak havoc on bodily tissues, then shark cartilage, healing crystals, and pulverized tiger penis seem no more magical than the latest breakthrough from the biochemistry laboratory. (1997:150)

Beyerstein does, however, see some benefits in alternative medicine. It has, he says, added a comforting human component to a medical world that has become increasingly impersonal and technological. Many alternative healers offer sound advice about prevention and a healthy lifestyle, and some alternative practices do have strong scientific backing. However, he fears that some alternatives can divert sick people from more effective treatment. Consumers of health care will need to be sufficiently well informed about the variety and nature of the options available to make sound treatment choices in the future. These options will certainly grow in number as alternative therapies become more widely accepted and as some become integrated with conventional medicine.

HEALTH CARE ISSUES IN THE FUTURE

Health and health care have changed dramatically in this century, and will continue to change in the years to come. Scientific developments such as the mapping of human genes and the new reproductive technologies have already begun to affect our lives. These changes will improve the lives of many but will also create some very difficult social and ethical problems that will continue to be debated for years to come. To give but one example, the ability to determine the sex of our children may lead to an imbalance between males and females. This would have a major impact on courtship and marriage as some in the larger sex group would have no chance to marry, while those in the smaller group would be very much in demand. Can you predict some of the possible consequences this might have on family structure and social relationships?

Unless there is a major shift in the economy, Canadians have likely seen the last of the major cuts to the health care system. However, the evolution from hospital-based care to prevention and community care will continue. This change can potentially be a positive one. For example, most of you have many years to live before you reach old age, but think ahead to that time. If you become unable to perform some household tasks such as cooking and cleaning, would you prefer to sell your home and move into institutional care or to receive daily home-care visits that would enable you to continue living independently? The political power of the aging baby boomers (see Chapter 12) and the cost of caring for growing numbers of elderly people will force governments to give more serious attention to home-care programs.

However, there is one worry—the shift to community-based health care will not improve matters unless governments put adequate resources into community care. The deinstitutionalization of the mentally ill in the 1970s and 1980s illustrates this danger. Ending the warehousing of mentally ill people in institutions was a good thing. However, rather than providing sufficient funding for community services for the deinstitutionalized patients, governments spent the savings on other things. As a result, many former patients became a burden on their communities and were themselves put at risk because the proper support was not available. If home care is not properly funded, the burden of care will be transferred from the state to relatives who already have busy lives (Armstrong et al., 1997). More than one in eight Canadians is already providing care to people with long-term health problems. Many of these caregivers have reported that providing this help has hurt their jobs, finances, or health (Statistics Canada, 1997f). While many of the caregivers surveyed were willing and able to provide support, government assistance will be necessary for those caregivers who lack the resources to do it alone and for individuals who do not have a network of family and friends to assist them.

While the health of Canadians will likely continue to improve in the future, at the global level there is great cause for concern. You have already read about the impact of AIDS on people living in developing nations and about the precarious health of many of the world's children. Medical authorities now also fear the return of infectious diseases such as cholera, malaria, and tuberculosis that were once controlled by antibiotics and vaccines, and by public health programs like improved sanitation. The reasons for the renewed threat from these diseases include environmental change, the public health consequences of poverty in the developing world, and the fact that global travel has helped bacteria and viruses move easily from one place to another (Taylor, 1997).

The resurgence of diseases such as malaria and tuberculosis, and the rapid spread of HIV/AIDS show that health is a social issue as much as it is a medical one. Social factors such as economic inequality, geographic mobility, societal values, human settlement patterns, and the overuse of pesticides and antibiotics all contribute to the spread of disease. Improving the health of the world's population will require social change as well as improved ways of treating the sick.

CHAPTER REVIEW

What is health?
Health is often defined as a state of complete physical, mental, and social well-being.

What is the relationship between health care, medicine, and preventive medicine?
Medicine is an institutionalized system for the scientific diagnosis, treatment, and prevention of illness. Medicine forms a vital part of the broader concept of health care, which is any activity intended to improve health. Preventive medicine is medicine that emphasizes a healthy lifestyle that will prevent poor health before it occurs.

What are the functionalist, conflict, and interactionist perspectives on health and health care?
Functionalists view society as a complex, stable system; therefore, the normal state of affairs is for people to be healthy and to contribute to their society. Illness is seen as dysfunctional for both the individual who is sick and for society. Sickness may result in an inability on the part of the sick person to fulfil his or her necessary social roles. Symbolic interactionists attempt to understand the specific meanings and causes that we attribute to particular events. In studying health, interactionists focus on the fact that the meaning that social actors give their illness or disease will affect their self-concept and their relationships with others. The interactionist approach is illustrated by society's response to AIDS. The conflict approach to health and illness considers the political and social forces that affect health and the health care system, and the inequities that result from these forces. Among the issues of concern for conflict theorists are the ability of all citizens to obtain health care; the impact of race, class, and gender on health and health care; the relative power of doctors compared with other health care workers; the dominance of the medical model of health care; and the role of profit in the health care system.

How do age, sex, and social class affect health?
Rates of illness and death are highest among the old and the young. Mortality rates drop shortly after birth and begin to rise significantly during the middle years. After 65, rates of chronic illness and mortality increase rapidly. While in earlier times women had shorter life expectancies than men because of high mortality rates due to complications arising from pregnancy and childbirth, women now live longer than men. Females born in Canada in 1994 could expect to live about 81 years compared with 75 years for males. However, women have higher rates of disease and disability. While men at every age have higher rates of fatal disease, women have higher rates of nonfatal chronic conditions. The poor have worse health and die earlier than the rich. The same goes for countries: illness and mortality rates are far higher for less developed countries than for developed nations. Within the industrialized world, citizens of those countries with the most equal distribution of income (Norway and Sweden) have the best health as measured by life expectancy.

What is a disability?
A disability is a physical or health condition that stigmatizes or causes discrimination.

What is the difference between a universal health care system and one in which the user pays for health services?
Canadians have a universal health care system in which all Canadians receive medical services that are paid for through the tax system. If you are sick, you have the right to receive quality medical care regardless of your

ability to pay. Prior to the early 1960s Canadians had a "user pay" system, which meant that many people had to pay for health care directly out of their pockets. Individuals without health insurance who required expensive medical procedures, long-term care, or who developed a chronic illness often suffered severe financial losses. The United States has a user pay system.

Key Terms

acute illness 578
chronic illness 578
disability 588
epidemics 586
health 576
health care 576
medicalization 580
medicine 576
preventive medicine 576
senile dementia 582
sick role 577
universal health care system 594

✿ Internet Exercises

1. Health Canada is the federal government agency responsible for health matters. Go to the Health Canada Web site (**http://www.hwc.ca/links.english.html**). This site discusses current government activities in health promotion. What are the government's priorities? How do you think they have changed over the past decade?

2. Visit the Web page of the American Council on Science and Health (**http://acsh.org**). What types of health concerns are reflected in this page? The Council says its priority is to distinguish between real and artificial health care risks. Do any of its views differ from those you have read about in other sources?

3. *The Progress of Nations* is an annual report from UNICEF. Visit its Web site (**http://unicef.org/pon96/**). According to the 1996 report, have health conditions been improving around the world? Is there cause for optimism?

✿ Net Links

Read about a wide variety of diseases including HIV/AIDS at the Web site of the Centres for Disease Control and Prevention:

http://www.cdc.gov/nchstp/hiv_aids/pubs/facts.htm

Health Canada has established a comprehensive database on health and healthcare issues called the Canadian Health Network; see

http://www.Canadian-health-network.ca

For recent information about the problems of HIV/AIDS, see the Web site of the Joint United Nations Program on HIV/AIDS:

http://www.unaids.org

Learn about the global effort that aims to reduce deaths and illnesses among women and infants, especially in developing countries, at the Safe Motherhood Initiative:

http://www.safemotherhood.org

For comparative health care data from a variety of countries, see the International Program in Health Policy section of the Commonwealth Fund Web site:

http://www.cmwf.org

The article by Gail Fawcett entitled "Canada's Untapped Workplace Resource: People with Disabilities" deals with the issue of barriers to employment faced by disabled persons; go to:

http://www.ccsd.ca/perception/per_214a.htm

The Council of Canadians with Disabilities advocates for the right of Canadians with disabilities to be centrally involved in the decision-making processes that affect their lives, and for the removal of barriers to their full participation in matters affecting their lives. The organization has a Web site at:

http://www.pcs.mb.ca~ccd/

Questions for Critical Thinking

1. How do you think governments should balance their needs for financial savings and the public need for quality health care? Should everyone receive unlimited health services regardless of cost, or should priorities be set based on provincial and federal budgets?

2. What is the best way for society to deal with diseases like lung cancer and HIV/AIDS that sometimes can be controlled by changing people's behaviour?

3. What is the role of alternative therapies in health care? Have you or your friends or relatives made use of alternative treatments?

4. In your view what constitutes a disability? Do you think disabled persons can participate more fully in society?

Suggested Readings

Terry Albert and Gregory Williams. *The Economic Burden of HIV/AIDS in Canada*. Ottawa: Canadian Policy Research Networks, 1998.

Gary L. Albrecht. *The Disability Business: Rehabilitation in America*. Newbury Park: Sage, 1992.

Pat Armstrong and Hugh Armstrong. *Wasting Away: The Undermining of the Canadian Health Care System*. Toronto: Oxford University Press, 1996.

Juanne Nancarrow Clarke. *Health, Illness and Medicine in Canada*. Toronto: McClelland and Stewart, 1990.

James B. Waldram, D. Ann Herring, and T. Kue Young. *Aboriginal Health in Canada: Historical, Cultural, and Epidemiological Perspectives*. Toronto: University of Toronto Press, 1995.

Rose Weitz. *The Sociology of Health, Illness, and Health Care: A Critical Approach*. Belmont: Wadsworth, 1995.

World Health Organization. *Fifty Facts from the World Health Report 1998*. Available: http://www.who.int/whr/1998/factse.htm

CHAPTER 19

Demography: The Study of Population
> Fertility
> Mortality
> Migration
> Population Composition
> The Baby Boom and the Baby Bust

Population Growth in a Global Context
> The Malthusian Perspective
> The Marxist Perspective
> The Neo-Malthusian Perspective
> Demographic Transition Theory
> Demography and Public Policy

Urbanization and the Growth of Cities
> Emergence and Evolution of the City
> Preindustrial Cities
> Industrial Cities
> Postindustrial Cities

Perspectives on Urbanization and the Growth of Cities
> Functionalist Perspectives: Ecological Models
> Conflict Perspectives: Political Economy Models
> Feminist Perspectives
> Interactionist Perspectives: The Experience of City Life

Divided Interests: Cities, Suburbs, and Beyond

Population and Urbanization in the Future

Moving to a new country and a new culture can be difficult, but the transition is easier for those who have support from others who share the same experiences. Consider the contrasting lives of two women—one described and one quoted—below. The following excerpt is from an interview with the child of a Sikh woman:

"My mother had it hard when I was growing up. We had a small rented farm in the Okanagan Valley, where there were then very few Sikhs. I made friends with Canadians at school. Since I knew English fluently I often talked with the neighbours, as did my father. Mother wasn't so lucky. She never learned English well enough to communicate easily, so never really had any good Canadian friends. There were so few other Sikh families around that she had little contact with them either. For her, the family was everything." (Buchignani, Indra, and Srivastiva, 1985:76)

In the next excerpt a woman who moved from Hong Kong to a Canadian city with a large middle-class Chinese community talks about her Chinese friends in Canada:

"I feel we have more in common with each other. We often get together and reminisce about our lives in Hong Kong. We also laugh about our ignorance of Canadian culture and the little faux pas that we get ourselves into. Other times, we exchange information about schools, dentists, and other practical knowledge. Or we marvel at the high price we now pay for little things such as cooking wares and stockings. I have a feeling of solidarity when I talk to these people. They understand where I'm coming from." (Man, 1996:290)

POPULATION AND URBANIZATION

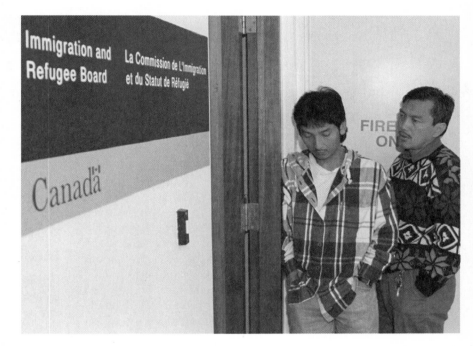

The presence of others from one's former home plays a large role in determining where new immigrants settle in Canada. This has meant that cities such as Toronto and Vancouver have very high proportions of recent immigrants, while other communities have almost none. This is just one example of the impact that immigration has on our society. However, immigration is just one of the *demographic factors* that are changing Canada and the rest of the world. The phenomena of births, deaths, and the movement of people interact to affect us all in very complex ways.

In this chapter, we will explore the dynamics of population growth and urban change. In the process we will periodically focus on immigration and its importance to Canadian society. Before reading on, test your knowledge about the causes and consequences of immigration by taking the quiz in Box 19.1.

QUESTIONS AND ISSUES

CHAPTER FOCUS QUESTION: What are the major social processes affecting Canada's population?

What causes global population growth?

How are people affected by population changes?

What has been the impact of the baby boom on Canada's population?

How do ecological/functionalist models and political economy/conflict models differ in their explanation of urban growth?

What is meant by the experience of urban life, and how do sociologists seek to explain this experience?

What are the best-case and worst-case scenarios regarding population and urban growth in the twenty-first century, and how might some of the worst-case scenarios be averted?

Canada has a long history of immigration. In this photo, the Netherland's ambassador welcomes a shipload of Dutch immigrants to Canada in 1947.

DEMOGRAPHY: THE STUDY OF POPULATION

Although population growth has slowed in Canada, the world's population of 6 billion in 1999 is increasing by 78 million people per year (United Nations, 1998). By 2050 there will be an estimated 9 billion people in the world (United Nations, 1998). Virtually all of this growth will come in the less developed nations of the world. The population in many of the developed nations may actually decrease over this period. This means that people in different parts of the world face dramatically different futures. While many people in developing countries face starvation because of rapidly increasing populations, Canadians have a much different problem. Because of very low birth rates, our population is aging and there are concerns about how a relatively small number of young workers will support large numbers of elderly people.

Why does the population grow rapidly in some nations? What are the consequences of low birth rates in industrialized countries? What impact does immigration have on immigrants and on the country of destination? What effect might a widespread AIDS crisis have on world population? How large will our cities be in twenty years? These questions are of interest to scholars who specialize in the study of *demography*—the subfield of sociology that examines population size, composition, and distribution. Many sociological studies use demographic analysis as a component in the research design.

Increases or decreases in population can have a powerful impact on the social, economic, and political structures of societies. Demographers define *population* as a group of people who live in a specified geographic area. Only three variables can change a population: *fertility* (births), *mortality* (deaths), and *migration* (movement from one place to another).

Fertility

Fertility is the actual level of childbearing for an individual or a population. The level of fertility in a society is based on biological and social factors, the primary biological factor being the number of women of childbearing age (usually between ages 15 and 45). Other biological factors affecting fertility include the general health and level of nutrition of women of childbearing age. Social factors influencing the level of fertility include the roles available to women in a society and prevalent viewpoints regarding what constitutes the "ideal" family size.

Based on biological capability alone, most women could produce twenty or more children during their childbearing years. *Fecundity* is the potential number of children that could be born if every woman reproduced at her maximum biological capacity. Fertility rates are not as high as fecundity rates because people's biological capabilities are limited by social factors such as practising voluntary abstinence and refraining from sexual intercourse until an older age, as well as by con-

BOX 19.1 SOCIOLOGY AND EVERYDAY LIFE

HOW MUCH DO YOU KNOW ABOUT IMMIGRATION TO CANADA?

TRUE	FALSE	
T	F	1. Immigrants usually become a drain on the taxpayer because they have high rates of welfare use.
T	F	2. Immigrants are not evenly distributed across the country, because many prefer to settle in large cities.
T	F	3. Most immigrants to Canada are refugees.
T	F	4. Canada has had rates of immigration in the past that were higher than current rates.
T	F	5. There is no limit to the number of family-sponsored immigrants who are allowed into Canada.
T	F	6. Immigrants have lower rates of crime than other Canadians.
T	F	7. If we do not maintain rates of immigration that are high by world standards, our population will eventually decline.
T	F	8. About 3 percent of Canada's population was not born in Canada.
T	F	9. Canada welcomed hundreds of thousands of Jewish refugees fleeing Nazi persecution during World War II.
T	F	10. Most countries of the world have open immigration and citizenship policies like those of Canada.

Answers on page 608.

traception, voluntary sterilization, abortion, and infanticide (Davis and Blake, 1956). Additional social factors affecting fertility include significant changes in the number of available partners for sex and/or marriage (as a result of war, for example), increases in the numbers of women of childbearing age in the workforce, and high rates of unemployment.

In some countries, governmental policies also affect the fertility rate. For example, China's one-child policy requires that IUDs (intrauterine devices) be used by women of childbearing age with one child, sterilization (most often performed on women) for couples with two children, and abortions for women pregnant without authorization. According to estimates, more than thirty million abortions, sterilizations, and IUD insertions occur each year in China. In some cases, Chinese birth control officials have been coercive in their efforts to control population in that nation (see Mosher, 1994). A preference for male children, especially when parents are permitted only one child, has led to practices, such as female infanticide, which are creating an imbalance in sex ratios. The Chinese Academy of Social Sciences says that the male–female ratio is now 120 to 100. This means that one in six males will never be able to find a wife (Kesterton, 1999).

The most basic measure of fertility is the **crude birth rate—the number of live births per 1000 people in a population in a given year**. In 1996, the crude birth rate in Canada was less than 13 per 1000, compared with a post-World-War-II high of 28 per 1000 in 1956 and around 40 per 1000 at the time of Confederation. This measure is referred to as a "crude" birth rate because it is based on the entire population and is not "refined" to incorporate significant variables affecting fertility, such as age, marital status, religion, or race/ethnicity.

In most parts of the world, women are having fewer children. Crude birth rates in Japan, Italy, and Spain are just over 9 per 1000; in the United Kingdom and France they are 13 per 1000 (about the same as Canada), and in the United States they are 15 per 1000. However, families are much larger in underdeveloped, agricultural regions of the world where children's labour is essential to a family's economic survival, and child mortality rates in those regions are still very high. Countries

BOX 19.1

ANSWERS TO THE SOCIOLOGY QUIZ ON IMMIGRATION

1. **True.** Immigrants are less likely to be on welfare than people born in Canada. A study by the Economic Council of Canada using the 1986 census found that the proportion of welfare recipients among recent immigrants (12.5 percent) was smaller than among people born in Canada (13.8 percent). Immigrants are more highly educated and more likely to be working than native-born Canadians.

2. **True.** A high proportion of immigrants live in Toronto, Vancouver, and Montreal.

3. **True.** This figure varies from year to year, but, for example, in 1994, only 8 percent of immigrants to Canada were refugees.

4. **True.** Immigration rates fluctuate widely and at times in the past they have been much higher than they are today.

5. **True.** Each year the government determines the number of family-sponsored immigrants who will be admitted.

6. **True.** Immigrants were significantly underrepresented in the population of those incarcerated in the federal correctional system in 1989 and 1991.

7. **True.** Birth rates in Canada are currently below replacement level. When the baby boom generation begins to die (after 2025), Canada will lose population unless we give entry to about 250,000 immigrants each year.

8. **True.** About 17 percent of Canadian residents were born in other countries.

9. **True.** While most Canadians are proud of this country's record in accepting refugees, our policies were not always as liberal as they are today. Very few Jewish refugees were admitted to Canada during the Holocaust.

10. **True.** Canada has one of the highest rates of legal immigration in the world. Most countries discourage immigration and many will not give citizenship to anyone not born to parents who themselves are citizens of that country.

Sources: Based on Abella and Troper, 1982; Beaujot, 1991; Economic Council of Canada, 1991; Gordon and Nelson, 1993; Matas, 1995; McVey and Kalbach, 1995; and Statistics Canada, 1998j.

with high crude birth rates (more than 40 per 1000) include Nigeria, Somalia, and Ethiopia (Central Intelligence Agency, 1998).

Mortality

The primary cause of world population growth in recent years has been a decline in *mortality*—the **incidence of death in a population**. The simplest measure of mortality is the *crude death rate*—the **number of deaths per 1000 people in a population in a given year**. Mortality rates have declined dramatically in the last two hundred years. In 1867, the crude death rate in Canada was 21 deaths per 1000—half what it had been one hundred years earlier. By 1995 the death rate had dropped to 7 per 1000. This decline has been due the fact that infectious diseases such as malaria, polio, cholera, tetanus, typhoid, and measles have been virtually eliminated by improved nutrition, sanitation, and personal

hygiene and by vaccination. As the burden of communicable diseases has steadily declined, the major causes of death in the developed world are now chronic and degenerative diseases such as heart disease and cancer. Table 19.1 illustrates this trend in Canada.

While mortality rates have dropped significantly in the less developed and developing nations, they are still two or three times higher than those of developed countries. In many countries, infectious diseases remain the leading cause of death; in some areas, mortality rates are increasing rapidly as a result of HIV/AIDS and a resurgence of tuberculosis (see Chapter 18, Health, Health Care, and Disability").

In addition to the crude death rate, demographers often measure the *infant mortality rate*—**the number of deaths of infants under 1 year of age per 1000 live births in a given year**. The infant mortality rate is an important reflection of a society's level of preventive (prenatal) medical

Women tend to have more children in agricultural regions of the world, such as Kenya, where children's labour is essential to the family's economic survival and child mortality rates are very high.

care, maternal nutrition, childbirth procedures, and neonatal care for infants, and it is often used by sociologists as a measure of the level of a country's social development. The impact of modernization on infant mortality rates has been dramatic. In 1921 the infant mortality rate in Canada was 102 deaths per 1000 live births; by 1996 it had declined to 5.6 per 1000 live births (Statistics Canada, 1998j). This can be compared with rates of 7 per 1000 in the United States, 6 in the United Kingdom, and 4 in Japan.

Underdeveloped countries with high birth rates also have high infant mortality rates. For example, the infant mortality rates for Afghanistan, Ethiopia, and Haiti are (respectively) 143, 125, and 99 per 1000 live births (Central Intelligence Agency, 1998).

Infant mortality rates and crude death rates are high among Canada's Aboriginal population, who suffer severe social disadvantages compared with the rest of the population, and who often lack access to health care services (see Chapter 18, "Health, Health Care, and Disability").

Our declining mortality rates have led to substantial increases in *life expectancy*, which is an estimate of the average lifetime in years of people born in a specific year. For persons born in Canada in 1996, for example, life expectancy at birth was about 79 years. Within Canada, life expectancy is lower for Aboriginal people. On average, Aboriginals live about 7 years less than the non-Aboriginal population, though this difference has been reduced in the past decade. Life expectancy

also varies by sex; for example, females born in Canada in 1996 could expect to live about 81 years as compared with 76 years for males (Statistics Canada, 1996c).

Migration

Migration **is the movement of people from one geographic area to another for the purpose of changing residency.** Migration affects the size and distribution of population in a given area. In Canada, people are not evenly distributed throughout the country; most Canadians live in densely populated areas while much of the country is sparsely populated. *Density* is the number of people living in a specific geographic area. Density may be measured by the number of people who live per room, per block, or per square mile.

Migration may be either international (movement between two nations) or internal (movement within national boundaries). When people migrate internationally, demographers refer to the country they leave as their *country of origin*; the country they enter is known as their *country of destination*.

Migration involves two types of movement: immigration and emigration. *Immigration* **is the movement of people into a geographic area to take up residency,** while *emigration* **is the movement of people out of a geographic area to take up residency elsewhere.**

TABLE 19.1	LEADING CAUSES OF DEATH, CANADA, 1880–81 AND 1996		
RANK	**1880–81***	**RANK**	**1996**
1	Consumption (Tuberculosis)	1	Cancer
2	Diphtheria	2	Heart disease
3	Lung disease	3	Stroke
4	Old Age	4	Obstructive lung disease
5	Brain disease	5	Accidental injury
6	Heart & blood disease	6	Pneumonia/Flu
7	Scarlet fever	7	Suicide
8	Croup	8	Diabetes
9	Bowel disease	9	Arterial disease
10	Debility	10	Central nervous system disease

*Includes P.E.I., N.B., N.S., Que., Ont., Man., B.C., and the Territories.

1880 data: Reprinted by permission of Statistics Canada, adapted from *Mortality—Summary List of Cases, 1991*, Cat. no. 84-209; 1996 data: Reprinted by permission from Mark Nicols, "Men's Health," *Maclean's*, February 22, 1999.

INTERNAL MIGRATION   Internal migration has occurred throughout Canada's history and has significantly changed the distribution of our population over time. In the late nineteenth and early twentieth centuries, a major population shift occurred as Canada was transformed from a rural to an urban nation. At the time of Confederation, about 80 percent of the population resided in rural areas; today, almost 80 percent are urban. While Canada is now an urban country, the degree of urbanization among the provinces varies, ranging from 82 percent of the population of Ontario to only 40 percent of Prince Edward Island residents (McVey and Kalbach, 1995).

Along with movement from rural to urban areas, we have also seen extensive migration from one province to another. Between 1981 and 1991 British Columbia and Ontario attracted the most internal migrants. All other provinces except Alberta lost more internal migrants than they gained. The provinces with the highest rates of loss were Newfoundland, Saskatchewan, and New Brunswick.

Many factors cause people to move from one part of the country to another. Better job opportunities in other parts of the country is a major cause of movement from rural to urban areas, and the booming economies of British Columbia, Alberta, and Ontario have drawn migrants from provinces with fewer opportunities. For decades, people from the Atlantic provinces have moved west in search of work. The impact of this migration can be seen in Fort McMurray, Alberta. This city is effectively Newfoundland's fifth largest community. One in every three of Fort McMurray's 40,000 residents is a Newfoundlander (Sytnick, 1998). While jobs explain many of our internal migration patterns, other reasons for internal migration are climate and lower living costs, which tend to be particularly important for retired persons.

INTERNATIONAL MIGRATION   People migrate either voluntarily or involuntarily. *Pull* factors at the international level, such as a democratic government, religious freedom, employment opportunities, or a more temperate climate, may draw voluntary immigrants into a nation. *Push* factors at the international level, such as political unrest, violence, war, famine, plagues, and natural disasters, may encourage people to leave one area and relocate elsewhere. Involuntary, or forced, migration usually occurs as a result of political oppression, such as when Jews fled Nazi Germany in the 1930s or when Haitians left their country to escape the Cedras regime in the 1990s. Slavery is the most striking example of involuntary migration; the ten to twenty million Africans transported forcibly to the Western Hemisphere prior to 1800 did not come by choice.

FIGURE 19.1 Annual Levels of Canadian Immigration, 1900-1997

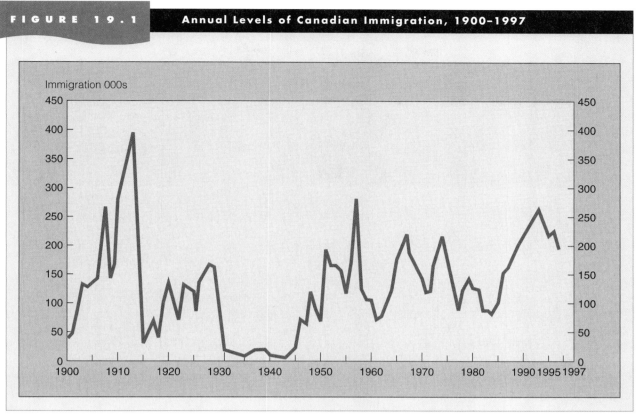

Sources: Jean Dumas, *Rapport sur l'état de la population du Canada*, 1990, Statistics Canada, Cat. no. 91-209 (Ottawa: Minister of Supply and Services, 1990), p. 2; Roderic Beaujot, K.G. Basavarajappa, and Ravi B.P. Verma, *Current Demographic Analysis: Income of Immigrants in Canada*, Statistics Canada, Cat. no. 91-527 (Ottawa: Minister of Supply and Services, 1988), p. 7. Adapted from *Population Change in Canada* by R. Beaujot.

Most of Canada's thirty million people are immigrants or the descendants of immigrants. Thus, immigration has been a critical factor in the country's growth and development. Our immigration policy is one of the most open in the world, and we have much higher rates of legal immigration than almost any other country. Immigrants make up over 17 percent of Canada's population (Statistics Canada, 1998j). This compares with 8 percent for the United States and 3 percent for Britain. Australia, with 22 percent of its population born elsewhere, is one of the few countries in which the percentage is higher than in Canada (Mitchell, 1997a).

Figure 19.1 shows that Canadian immigration levels throughout the last century have fluctuated a great deal. Economic conditions, wars, pressures from refugees, and changes in government policies have all contributed to these shifts. Following the end of an economic depression in 1896, the government began to promote immigration to encourage settlement of the West. In the years

before World War I as many as 400,000 people per year immigrated to Canada, a number which has never been exceeded. Most of these immigrants were European and many of them settled the farms, towns, and cities of the Prairie provinces. The beginning of World War I caused a precipitous decline in immigration. While numbers rose again after the war, the Great Depression and World War II meant very low levels of immigration for almost twenty years. During this period more people left Canada than arrived here. Immediately after World War II, immigration rates again climbed. Canada built a large industrial capacity during the war, and the postwar economy was very strong. Skilled foreign workers were needed to help with the expansion. Political instability and economic difficulty in Europe meant that many people were willing to leave to find a better life elsewhere. The postwar immigration peak in 1956–57 was the result both of Canada's acceptance of great numbers of refugees who were escaping the unsuccessful Hungarian

Political unrest, violence, and war are "push" factors that encourage people to leave their country of origin. Shown here, a shipload of Liberian refugees awaiting political asylum in Ghana, and Bosnian refugees fleeing Serb-held parts of Sarajevo. Civil wars cause massive population movement.

Revolution and of its providing a home for British subjects leaving Egypt following the Suez crisis.

As discussed in Chapter 10 ("Race and Ethnicity") Canada's immigration regulations permitted discrimination on the basis of racial and ethnic origin until the early 1960s (see Box 19.2). At various times, Chinese, Japanese, and South Asians were prohibited from immigrating to Canada, and the 1953 Immigration Act allowed the government to bar entry on the grounds of race, ethnicity, or even "peculiar customs, habits, modes of life or methods of holding property" (Beaujot, 1991:109). Preference was given to whites, particularly those of British origin. These discriminatory restrictions were lifted in 1962, and from then on the face of immigration changed dramatically. Compare the source countries of immigrants arriving in 1957 with those of immigrants who came in 1991–1996, as shown in Table 19.2. Whereas, in 1957, the vast majority of immigrants were whites from northern Europe, in 1991–1996 immigrants to Canada came from all over the world and represented many different ethnic groups and cultures. While this diversity would not have been possible under the old rules, the factors "pushing" immigrants have also changed. For the past thirty years, most western European countries have had very strong economies, low unemployment rates, and stable governments. Living under these conditions, people have had little reason to emigrate. At the same time, conditions in many other parts of the world are less favourable, so emigration to Canada is seen positively. Most of the countries from which we drew immigrants between 1991–1996 had some combination of political turmoil, war, or poverty.

For most of the 1990s the number of immigrants coming to Canada has remained relatively stable at between 200,000 and 250,000 persons. This is the result of government policy aimed at achieving a stable population in the future in the face of declining birth rates and an aging population.

Population Composition

Changes in fertility, mortality, and migration affect the *population composition*—the biological and social characteristics of a population, including age, sex, ethnic origin, marital status, education, occupation, income, and size of household.

One measure of population composition is the *sex ratio*—the number of males for every hundred females in a given population. A sex ratio of 100 indicates an equal number of males and females. If the number is greater than 100, there are more males than females; if it is less than 100, there are more females than males. In Canada, the sex ratio in 1991 was 97, which means there were about 97 males per 100 females. Although approximately 106 males are born for every 100 females, higher male mortality rates mean there are more females than males in the population. This difference is particularly great among people over 65 years of age.

For demographers, sex and age statistics are significant population characteristics. They are key predictors of fertility and mortality rates, and the age distribution of a population has a direct bearing on the demand for schooling, health, employment, housing, and pensions. The distribution of a population can be depicted in a *popula-*

TABLE 19.2   CANADIAN IMMIGRANTS' COUNTRIES OF ORIGIN, 1957 AND 1991–1996

RANK	1857 COUNTRY	% OF TOTAL IMMIGRATION	RANK	1991–1996 COUNTRY	% OF TOTAL IMMIGRATION
1	U.K.	38.6	1	Hong Kong	10.5
2	Hungary	11.2	2	China	8.5
3	Germany	10.0	3	India	6.9
4	Italy	9.8	4	Philippines	6.9
5	Netherlands	4.2	5	Sri Lanka	4.3
6	U.S.	3.9	6	Poland	3.6
7	Denmark	2.7	7	Taiwan	3.1
8	France	2.0	8	Vietnam	3.1
9	Austria	2.0	9	U.S.	2.8
10	Greece	1.9	10	U.K.	2.4

Reprinted with permission from Rose Zgodzinski, "Where Immigrants Came From." *The Globe and Mail* (June 20, 1996):A2; and reproduced by authority of the Minister of Industry, 1997, Statistics Canada, from *The Daily*, Cat. no. 11-001E, November 4.

tion pyramid—**a graphic representation of the distribution of a population by sex and age**. Population pyramids are a series of bar graphs divided into five-year age cohorts; the left side of the pyramid shows the number or percentage of males in each age bracket; the right side provides the same information for females.

The age/sex distribution in Canada and other developed nations such as France (see Figure 19.2) does not have the appearance of a pyramid, but rather is more rectangular or barrel-shaped. This shows a population that has a low birth rate and an increasing number of older people. You can see in Figure 19.2 that a developing nation such as Iran has a population distribution that fits the classic population pyramid. Iran has high fertility and mortality rates, which means a large number of children and few older people. The population pyramid for Russia has some unusual features that have been caused by catastrophic events such as the two World Wars, the Civil War of 1917–1922, famine in the 1920s and 1930s, and the recent dramatic decline in birth rates. For example, the large number of males killed during World War II gave Russia the lowest male-to-female ratio in the world. The irregularities in Russia's population pyramid will affect patterns of population growth and aging for decades to come (Institut National d'Etudes Demographiques, 1999). (Population pyramids for Canada are shown later in this chapter in Figure 19.4.)

As societies modernize, there is a time lag between the decrease in the death rate and a corresponding decrease in the birth rate. During this time lag, populations often grow very rapidly. The rate of population growth in a society is determined by a combination of fertility, mortality, and migration. The age and sex composition of the population affects each of these processes. If a large number of young people are in their prime reproductive years, the crude birth rate will rise because a large number of children will be produced relative to the total population. In a population with a relatively small proportion of young people and a high proportion of older people, a substantial number of deaths will occur each year because of the large number of individuals moving into the higher-risk years. Thus, even if the society has a high life expectancy, the crude death rate will be higher because of the proportion of older people. Young adults are more likely to migrate than older persons, a factor that also affects the size of a specific population.

The Baby Boom and the Baby Bust

One very simple fact will help you to understand many things about Canadian society: every year you get one year older, and, more importantly, so does everyone else. Until recently, the age struc-

BOX 19.2 SOCIOLOGY AND LAW

IMMIGRATION AND THE LAW IN CANADA

Canadians can be proud of having welcomed immigrants from around the globe. However, the record has not been consistently good; at times in the past our immigration policy has been exclusionary and racist.

Shortly after the turn of the century, some Canadians began to express concerns about immigration from East Asia (China) and South Asia (India). The first Chinese immigrated to Canada in the 1850s; many were recruited to work as labourers on the construction of the Canadian Pacific Railway. South Asians began to immigrate to Canada in 1903. While the numbers of both groups were small, these immigrants were treated very poorly and subjected to discrimination. British Columbia, where the two groups were largely concen-

trated, passed a number of laws restricting the rights of Chinese and Japanese. For example, the Chinese and Japanese were denied the right to vote in 1872 and 1895 respectively, and many restrictions were imposed on their right to work. The federal government levied a head tax on the Chinese in 1885 to restrict their immigration and in 1923 passed the Chinese Immigration Act, which virtually disallowed new immigration from East Asia.

While these measures now seem appalling, Canada's behaviour was no worse than that of most other Western countries, which also had very restrictive immigration policies. Many leading scientists of the day backed the view that Anglo-Saxons were biologically superior,

ture of the population was something of a hidden factor. While age differences among individuals were obvious, researchers and planners often failed to recognize the impact of changes in the *age structure* of the population.

One of the most significant demographic changes in Canadian history was the *baby boom*—the dramatic increase in births that occurred between 1946 and 1966. The boom was caused by young couples who married and began having families in the years immediately following the war. The high birth rates of the baby boom were followed by the *baby bust*, which saw birth rates fall to the very low levels where they remain today. While many demographic changes are subtle and take place over a long period of time, the baby boom was a rapid reversal of a long-term downward trend in birth rates. This increase is shown in Figure 19.3. By the end of the boom in 1966, one-third of all the people in Canada had been born in the preceding fifteen years.

The baby boom and the baby bust have had a dramatic impact on the age structure, which can be seen in the series of population pyramids in Figure 19.4. The top pyramid shows the population of Canada toward the end of the baby boom

in 1961. There are large numbers of young people because of the boom. The relatively small number of people aged 15 to 24 is the result of low birth rates during the Depression and World War II. In the 1981 pyramid, we can see the consequences of the baby boom and the drop in fertility rates that followed. This drop is called the "baby bust." The pyramid for 2006 shows an increased number of older people as the oldest baby boomers approach 60. Finally, in the 2031 pyramid, mortality has begun to affect the baby boomers, and the survivors are now 65 to 85 years of age.

The baby boom has had a profound impact on virtually every aspect of our society. To help understand the impact of the baby boom, think of it as a twenty-year bulge in the population pyramid. Each year, this bulge moves one year up the pyramid as the baby boom cohort ages. You can easily track this bulge in the population pyramids in Figure 19.4. Some demographers have used the analogy of a pig that has been swallowed by a python to describe the way in which the baby boom generation has moved up the population pyramid. It is interesting to compare Canada's demographic structure with those of other countries. For example, you can see from Figure 19.2

BOX 19.2

CONTINUED

and the admission of other races was seen as a danger to these white democracies.

Many Canadians are also unaware that for many years our immigration policy restricted the admission of Jews. This was because of anti-Jewish sentiment and because Jews settled in urban areas and rejected the rural settlement preferred by the government. Even during World War II, when millions of Jews were being exterminated in Europe, Canada would not open its doors to Jewish refugees. No country made the immigration of Jews a priority during the Holocaust, but Canada's record was particularly poor. Between 1933

and 1945 Canada admitted fewer than 5000 Jews, whereas during the same period 200,000 were allowed into the United States and 70,000 into the United Kingdom. Despite significant and vocal support among Canadians for taking action to save Jewish refugees, Prime Minister Mackenzie King and his cabinet refused. The attitude of the government is summed up in the words of a senior Canadian official who was speaking with journalists in early 1945. When asked how many Jews would be admitted to Canada following the war, his response was "None is too many" (Abella and Troper, 1982:xxi).

Sources: Based on Abella and Troper, 1982; Ghosh and Kanungo, 1992; and Statutes of Canada, 1910 c. 27.

---

that Iran, which is a developing society, has a constant baby boom—it is continually adding young people to its population as its population rapidly expands. On the other hand, France did not have a baby boom after the war, so its age structure is quite different from Canada's. The age structure of many European countries is much like that of France. Besides Canada, the only other countries that had a baby boom were Australia and the United States.

The baby boom has transformed society in many different ways. Because it has always been the largest age group, the baby boom generation has had a tremendous impact. Beginning in the late 1940s, many businesses saw their markets expand. Manufacturers of baby food, diapers, and children's toys flourished, and obstetricians were in great demand. As the cohort aged, school construction increased dramatically and teaching jobs were plentiful. By the mid-1960s university enrolments began to climb and many new universities opened to meet the demand. You will recall from Chapter 7 ("Crime and Deviance") that crime rates also began to increase at this time. This is because the baby boomers had entered the 15 to 24 age group during which criminal behaviour is

most common. In the mid-1970s house prices rose quickly in most Canadian cities, as the baby boomers began to settle down and raise families.

Because of the baby bust, many of these changes reversed themselves in the 1980s. Schools that had been built to house the soaring numbers of children in the 1960s were forced to close twenty years later and school boards spent decades dealing with an oversupply of teachers. By the 1990s both university enrolments and crime rates had begun to decline. In most parts of Canada, house prices have dropped or remained stable for much of the past decade. Radio stations that had catered to the baby boomers when they were young began to play "golden oldies" to keep this large audience. Corporations that had targeted youthful consumers have begun to reorient their products and their advertising to appeal to an older market. Clothing manufacturers are now offering their products in "relaxed fit" sizes as middle-aged spread begins to hit the baby boomers, and fast food chains are developing products to appeal to older people. The sight of a television commercial showing Ronald McDonald on a golf course is a sure sign of the consumer power of the baby boom generation. In fact golf,

FIGURE 19.2   Population Pyramids for Russia, Iran, and France

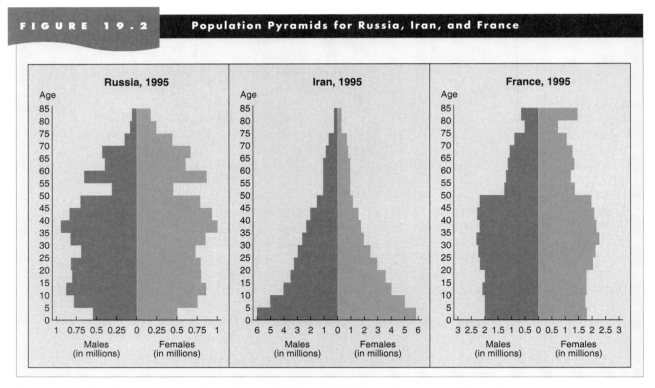

From *Population: An Introduction to Concepts and Issues*, 6th ed., by J.R. Weeks. © 1996. Reprinted by permission of Wadsworth Publishing, a division of International Thomson Publishing. Fax 800-730-2215.

and other modestly active forms of recreation such as travel, gardening, and birdwatching are replacing more active sports like tennis and downhill skiing in popularity as the baby boomers begin to slow down in middle age.

What of the future? The baby boom cohort is now entering middle age and the first of its members will reach 65 in the year 2012. As you have read in Chapter 12 ("Aging"), our society will soon begin to have a much higher proportion of older persons than it does today. In 1971, about 8 percent of Canadians were 65 and over; by 2011 the percentage will be 16 percent; and by 2036 it will likely stabilize at almost 25 percent. There will be about 9 million Canadians over 65, compared with the current 3.7 million.

The aging of our population is causing concern in a number of areas. Since the elderly are the biggest users of health care, governments are trying to get health costs under control before the baby boomers start reaching the age at which they will begin to have serious health concerns. Those responsible for the Canada Pension Plan have increased premiums and decreased some benefits so the Plan can stay in operation (see Chapter 12, "Aging").

One final trend worth noting is the *baby boom echo*—the children of the baby boomers. You can see this echo in Figure 19.4, which shows a relatively large cohort following about twenty years behind the baby boom. Even though the baby boomers had far fewer children than their parents (about 1.66 children per family compared with more than 3 children for their parents), there were so many of them that their children are having a significant impact. The leading edge of the echo generation were about 19 years old in 2000, so they will have an impact on such things as high school and university enrolments and crime rates over the next two decades.

THE BABY BOOM AND IMMIGRATION POLICY   One consequence of our current low birth rate is possible depopulation. Fertility of 2.1 children per woman is needed to ensure the replacement of a population. Two children will replace the parents, and the additional 0.1 compensates for deaths that occur before potential parents reach reproductive age. This level of fertility will eventually lead to a stable population with zero population growth except for that caused by migration. In Canada, our fertility is now less than 1.7 children

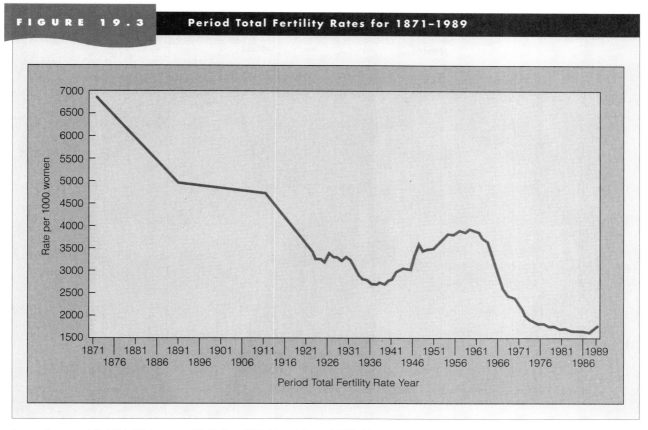

FIGURE 19.3 Period Total Fertility Rates for 1871–1989

Sources: Romaniuc, 1994:121–22; Beaujot and McQuillan, 1982:54; and Dumas, 1990b:18.

per woman, which will not provide replacement of our population. If this level of fertility remains constant for the next several decades, Canada will begin losing population when the baby boomers begin to die. You can see this in the 2031 population pyramid in Figure 19.4. At present, besides losing population through death, we also lose about 60,000 each year to emigration.

As Figure 19.1 shows, during the 1990s Canada admitted between 200,000 and 250,000 immigrants annually. This number was chosen because demographers have calculated that to stabilize the population we need about 250,000 immigrants a year. Thus, the baby bust has had an important impact on our immigration policies.

POPULATION GROWTH IN A GLOBAL CONTEXT

What are the consequences of global population growth? Scholars do not agree on the answer to this question. Some biologists have warned that Earth is a finite ecosystem that cannot support the 9 billion people expected on the planet by 2050; however, some economists have predicted that free-market capitalism is capable of developing innovative ways to solve such problems, and religious opponents of birth control assure us that God will provide. This debate is not a new one; for several centuries, strong opinions have been voiced about the effects of population growth on human welfare.

The Malthusian Perspective

English clergyman and economist Thomas Robert Malthus (1766–1834) was one of the first scholars to systematically study the effects of population. According to Malthus, the population, if left unchecked, would exceed the available food supply. He argued that the population would increase in a geometric (exponential) progression (2, 4, 8, 16 ...), while the food supply would

FIGURE   19.4   Population by Age and Sex, Canada, 1961 and 1981 (Census), 2006 and 2031

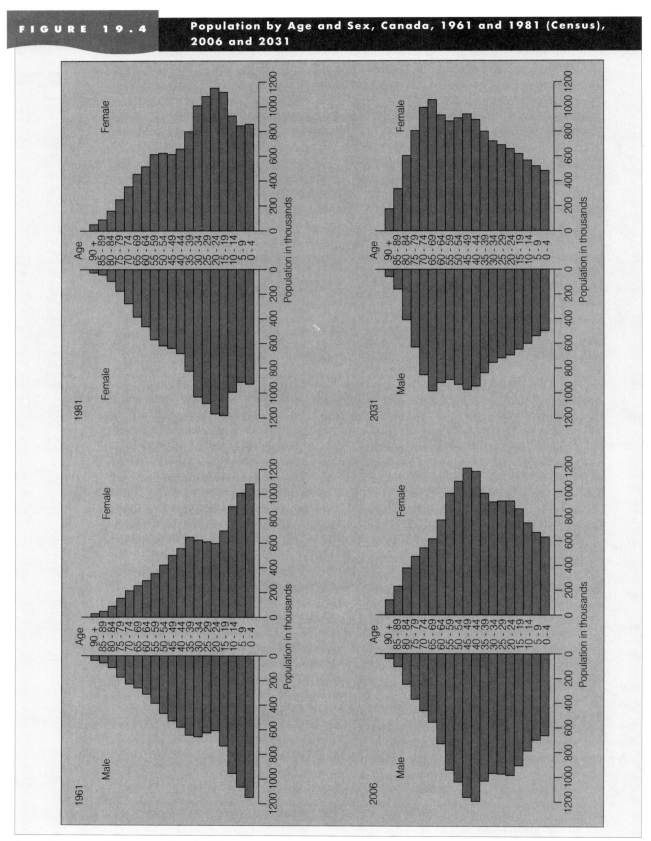

Reprinted by permission of Statistics Canada, adapted from *Population Projections for Canada, Provinces and Territories 1984–2006*, Cat no. 91-520; and from *1961 Census Bulletin* 1.2-2.

increase only by an arithmetic progression (1, 2, 3, 4 ...). In other words, a *doubling effect* occurs: two parents can have four children, sixteen grandchildren, and so on, but food production increases by only one acre at a time. Thus, population growth inevitably surpasses the food supply, and the lack of food ultimately ends population growth and perhaps eliminates the existing population (Weeks, 1992). Even in a best-case scenario, overpopulation results in poverty.

However, Malthus suggested that this disaster might be averted by either positive or preventive checks on population. *Positive checks* are mortality risks such as famine, disease, and war; *preventive checks* are limits to fertility. For Malthus, the only acceptable preventive check was *moral restraint*; people should practise sexual abstinence before marriage and postpone marriage as long as possible in order to have only a few children.

The Marxist Perspective

According to Karl Marx and Friedrich Engels, the food supply is not threatened by overpopulation; technologically, it is possible to produce the food and other goods needed to meet the demands of a growing population. Marx and Engels viewed poverty as a consequence of the exploitation of workers by the owners of the means of production.

From this perspective, overpopulation occurs because capitalists desire to have a surplus of workers (an industrial reserve army) so as to suppress wages and force workers concerned about losing their livelihoods to be more productive. Marx believed that overpopulation would contribute to the eventual destruction of capitalism: unemployment would make the workers dissatisfied, resulting in a class consciousness based on their shared oppression and in the eventual overthrow of the system. In a socialist regime, enough food and other resources would be created to accommodate population growth.

Marx and Engels made a significant contribution to the study of demography by suggesting that poverty, not overpopulation, is the most important issue with regard to food supply in a capitalist economy. Although Marx and Engels offer an interesting counterpoint to Malthus, some scholars argue that the Marxist perspective is self-limiting because it attributes the population problem solely to capitalism. In actuality, nations with socialist economies have demographic trends similar to those in capitalist societies.

The Neo-Malthusian Perspective

More recently, *neo-Malthusians* (or "new Malthusians") have re-emphasized the dangers of overpopulation. To neo-Malthusians, the earth is "a dying planet" with too many people and too little food, and environmental degradation. From the time of Christ to 1840, the doubling time of the population was 1250 years, while at current growth rates the earth's population will double every 42 years (Grindstaff and Trovato, 1994). Overpopulation and rapid population growth result in global environmental problems, ranging from global warming and rain forest destruction to famine and vulnerability to epidemics such as AIDS (Ehrlich, Ehrlich, and Daily, 1995). Environmental problems will worsen as countries such as India and China, with their large populations, modernize and begin to use resources at a rate closer to that of industrialized countries.

Throughout history, population growth and epidemic diseases have interacted to shape human destiny. People are extremely vulnerable to disease if they already are debilitated from inadequate nutrition, unclean water supplies, poor medical care, and lack of sanitation.

Are the neo-Malthusians correct? Will population increases leave many populations vulnerable to mass death through starvation and disease? Some possible outcomes are found in the work of Thomas Homer-Dixon, a University of Toronto political scientist who is often placed in the neo-Malthusian camp. Homer-Dixon feels that increases in population and resource consumption will lead to significant environmental changes including scarcities of soil, water, and climatic instability (1993). The strains caused by these scarcities may lead to unrest, including war, revolution, ethnic violence, and riots. The gloominess of this scenario is tempered by the fact that Homer-Dixon does not feel that population disaster is inevitable. Human social and technical ingenuity can overcome or at least delay the consequences of population increase. For example, despite decades of predictions that China will be unable to support its population, the average caloric intake in China has been rising as the country has massively increased its production of food. Unfortunately, there is no guarantee that solutions to the predicted problems will be found. Ingenuity itself is a function of a country's social institutions, and in many countries these institutions are too fragmented or too lacking in human and physical resources to solve their problems. In

BOX 19.3 SOCIOLOGY IN GLOBAL PERSPECTIVE

IMMIGRATION POLICIES OF CANADA AND OTHER COUNTRIES

Canadian immigration laws and policies are among the most open in the world. Each year Canada accepts just under 1 percent of our population as immigrants and all have the right to obtain citizenship. Israel takes in about 2 percent of its population annually, while the other two leading destination countries for immigrants, Australia and the United States, each accept less than one-half of a percent of their populations. Most of the world's countries accept few or no immigrants, though many do accept refugees, at least on a temporary basis. Receiving countries react to immigration in three different ways.

The first is *differential exclusion*, according to which immigrants are allowed in certain areas of society, chiefly the labour market, but denied access to other areas such as health

care, education, and social benefits. Immigrants in these countries are primarily refugees and guest workers who are admitted for specified periods to do work that members of the resident population cannot or will not perform. Germany, for example, imports workers from many countries, especially Turkey. Citizenship is based on ethnicity. German ancestry entitles an immigrant to automatic citizenship. However, naturalization of non-Germans is extremely rare. The result of this is the permanent marginalization of people who are essentially permanent residents but who cannot become citizens. Currently, eight million residents of Germany were born elsewhere or are children of guest workers. Almost none of these people have been allowed to become citizens. Japan, which has strongly

addition, political turmoil has been an obstacle; unrest has kept many countries in sub-Saharan Africa from progressing and, without major reform, their future is gloomy. For the same reasons, Homer-Dixon is more pessimistic about the future of India than of China because, he feels, India's social institutions are endangered by religious and caste cleavages. Also, India's population is growing much more rapidly than China's, so any economic gains are lost to increased population. Ultimately, the future of humanity will depend on both national and international action to solve the problems created by population growth and environmental damage.

Demographic Transition Theory

Some scholars who disagree with the neo-Malthusian viewpoint suggest that the theory of demographic transition offers a more accurate picture of future population growth. **Demographic transition is the process by which some societies have moved from high birth and death rates to relatively low birth and death rates as a result of**

technological development. Although demographic transition theory initially was applied to population changes brought about by the Industrial Revolution in western Europe and North America, it recently has emerged as a dominant perspective in contemporary demography (Weeks, 1992). Demographic transition is linked to four stages of economic development (see Figure 19.5):

- *Stage 1: Preindustrial societies*. Little population growth occurs because high birth rates are offset by high death rates. Children are viewed as an economic asset because of their ability to work, but infant and child mortality rates are high due to lack of sanitation and poor nutrition. Life expectancy is around 30 years.
- *Stage 2: Early industrialization*. Significant population growth occurs because birth rates remain relatively high while death rates decline. Improvements in health, sanitation, and nutrition produce a substantial decline in infant mortality rates. Overpopulation is likely to occur because more people are alive than the society has the ability to support. However,

BOX 19.3

CONTINUED

emphasized the need for ethnic purity, has similar policies, but has treated its immigrant workers much more harshly than has Germany. Ethnic Koreans, many of whom are third- and fourth-generation Japanese, have suffered severe discrimination.

The second immigration model is *assimilationist*, whereby immigrants are incorporated into the host society through a one-sided process of change. Immigrants are expected to become the same as the majority. Canada used to follow this policy, but today France probably follows this model the most closely. Immigrants to France can obtain citizenship after five years of residence, and children born in France automatically become citizens at 18 years of age unless they give up this right. All citizens are expected to accept the French language and culture. This is sometimes referred to as the "melting-pot approach."

The third model is *pluralism*, according to which immigrants are encouraged to form ethnic communities that can have equal rights while retaining their diversity in language, culture, and other matters. Citizenship is readily given to legal immigrants, and even to children of illegal immigrants. Canada has a multicultural policy that actively supports the rights of ethnic communities.

Source: Castles, Stephen, "Trois Siecles de Depopulation Amerindienne," in Louise Normandeau and V. Piche (eds.), *Les Populations Amerindienne et Inuit du Canada*, Montreal, QC: Presse de l'Universite de Montreal, 1995. Reprinted by permission.

FIGURE   19.5   The Demographic Transition

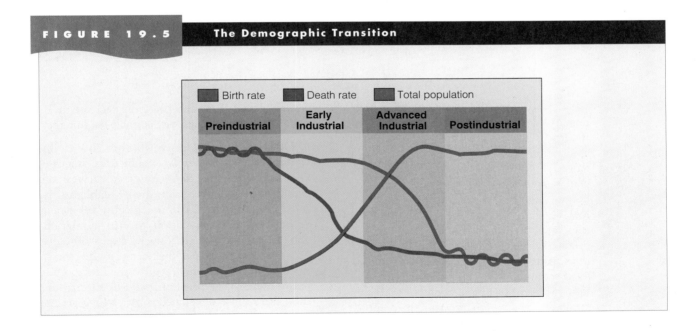

BOX 19.4 SOCIOLOGY AND MEDIA

IMMIGRATION AND THE MEDIA

Just after the turn of the century, a great deal of hostility was directed at nonwhite immigrants. The media actively promoted this racism by publishing inflammatory articles about racial minorities. These articles not only affected public opinion, but were also used by legislators to justify laws that targeted minority immigrants. The writing of Judge Emily Murphy of Edmonton, the first woman judge in the British Empire, was particularly influential. Her series of five articles, published in *Maclean's* magazine, shaped Canada's drug laws throughout the 1920s; their effects live on in our present narcotics legislation. These articles also shaped the attitudes of Canadians toward nonwhite immigrants by attributing the drug

An opium addict

The keeper of an opium den

These photographs appeared in Judge Murphy's book *The Black Candle* (Murphy, 1922), which, like her articles published in *Maclean's* in the 1920s, were used by legislators to justify laws that targeted minority immigrants.

social institutions continue to promote high fertility. Many developing nations—especially in Africa, Asia, and Latin America—currently are in this stage.

- *Stage 3: Advanced industrialization and urbanization.* Very little population growth occurs because both birth rates and death rates are low. The birth rate declines as couples control their fertility through contraception and become less likely to adhere to religious directives against their use. Children are not viewed as an economic asset; they consume income rather than producing it. Societies in this stage attain zero population growth—the point at which no population increase occurs from year to year.
- *Stage 4: Postindustrialization.* Birth rates continue to decline as more women gain full-time employment and the cost of raising children continues to increase. The population grows very slowly, if at all, because the decrease in birth rates is coupled with a stable death rate.

Debate continues as to whether this evolutionary model accurately explains the stages of population growth in all societies. Advocates note that demographic transition theory highlights the relationship between technological development and a slowing of population growth—a relationship that makes Malthus's predictions obsolete. Scholars also point out that demographic transitions occur at a faster rate in now-developing nations than they previously did in the nations that already are developed. Critics suggest that demographic transition theory best explains development in Western societies. Many regions of the Third World may never achieve a steady growth in social and economic wealth unless fertility levels first decline, so other routes to population control must be found.

BOX 19.4

CONTINUED

problem to Chinese and black "villains" who, according to Judge Murphy, were trying to spread the drug habit in order to seduce white women and to destroy the Anglo-Saxon way of life.

Judge Murphy felt that nonwhite immigrants were a threat to the Canadian way of life. In *Maclean's,* she wrote of a detective who had a special talent for smelling cooked opium. Two of the detective's cases involved a "Chinaman," a beautiful young girl he found smoking opium under a piano case, and a "negro" smoking opium in a wardrobe with a "white woman on either side of him." Her articles were illustrated with photographs of opium smokers (almost all of whom were women and/or nonwhite men) and cartoons (which were also racially demeaning). Each article featured a caricature of a Chinese opium smoker with smoke coming out of each ear.

She saw the Chinese drug pedlar as one who was perhaps unknowingly carrying out the wishes of his superiors who were trying to bring about the "downfall of the white race." The "Negroes coming into Canada," she wrote "have similar ideas."

The same conspiratorial view was advanced by other media. For example, in 1911, the Montreal *Herald* responded to the immigration of 58 black women domestics from Guadeloupe by reporting that the "dark-skinned domestics were the advanced guard for others to follow."

That these views were so freely expressed in the media certainly made it easy for politicians and members of the public to follow the same racist line. The views, moreover, help to explain why Canada had racially based immigration policies for much of this century.

Sources: Based on Calliste, 1993/94; Murphy, 1922; and Cook, 1969.

Timothy Weiskel (1994) has pointed out that we should not expect that developing countries will follow the same path as Western nations, as they have very different demographic histories and their population dynamics operate within very different historical, cultural, and economic circumstances. Weiskel notes that women's status and education, along with active family planning programs, have been more important than overall economic growth as causes of declining fertility.

The increased education of women in developing nations is one of the reasons the rate of population growth in these countries has slowed in recent decades. Once the average education of women gets beyond Grade 8, fertility rates decline. The global fertility rate is now 2.7 births per woman compared with 5 births per woman in the early 1950s. This decline has been most dramatic in Asia and Latin America where fertility rates have dropped by almost 50 percent to about 2.6

per woman in the last 25 years. However, they remain at 5.1 per woman in Africa (United Nations, 1998).

Demography and Public Policy

China has dramatically reduced its rate of population growth because of its one-child-per-family policy, not because of technological advances and urbanization—80 percent of the Chinese population still resides in rural areas. China's one-child policy is an example of public policy that is based on demographic knowledge. The Chinese government recognized that with more than one billion people, the country could not continue to sustain high birth rates. To avoid the consequences of overpopulation suggested by Malthus, they developed a number of policies to convince couples to have only one child. This is a very harsh measure (if successful, it would mean that Chinese society would no longer have brothers, sisters, aunts, uncles, or cousins), which conflicts with both the strong value placed on the family in Chinese society and with the practical need for several children to help support the parents in old age. However, the government decided that the health of the nation was more important than the rights of Chinese citizens to have the number of children they wished.

We have discussed some of the ways in which Canada must change its policies to cope with the health and retirement demands of the aging baby boomers. While many government policies are related to population trends, it might surprise you to learn that demographic analysis has played a large part in French/English politics over the past three decades.

Traditionally, Quebec has constituted about one-third of Canada's population. For many years, it had a higher birth rate than the other provinces. This meant increasing numbers of French-speaking Quebeckers—what some have called "the revenge of the cradle"—and it ensured a strong political voice for Quebec and helped maintain the dominance of the French language in Quebec. However, following the Quiet Revolution in the 1960s in Quebec (see Chapter 14, "Power, Politics, and Government"), the influence of the Catholic Church diminished and the province became increasingly secular. The birth rate declined dramatically, to a level far lower than that of most other provinces, reaching a low of 1.4 children per family in 1985 (Romaniuc, 1994). Like the rest of Canada, Quebec sought to make up for this shortage of births by increasing immigration. However, to the dismay of the Quebec government, many immigrants to Quebec chose to learn English rather than French. The French-speaking population continued to drop and, in response, the government passed Bill 101, which restricted the use of English and which required immigrants to send their children to French-language schools. Much of the nationalism in Quebec can be explained by Quebeckers' fears that the French language and culture will disappear in the vast North American sea of English. In 1996, Quebec's share of the Canadian population dropped below 25 percent for the first time since Confederation.

While the French/English question will remain with us in some form for some time, demographic trends may create other sources of policy debate and political division. For example, most of the political and economic power in Canada has been centred in Ontario and Quebec. With the shift in jobs and population to Western Canada (British Columbia and Alberta together now have more jobs than Quebec), we can anticipate that the West will begin to demand that its interests be reflected more broadly in national policies.

URBANIZATION AND THE GROWTH OF CITIES

Urban sociology **is a subfield of sociology that examines social relationships and political and economic structures in the city.** According to urban sociologists, a *city* is a relatively dense and permanent settlement of people who secure their livelihood primarily through nonagricultural activities. The census term that defines our cities is *census metropolitan area*, or CMA. A CMA is "a very large urban area, together with adjacent urban and rural areas that have a high degree of economic and social integration with that urban area" (Statistics Canada, 1991:117). Canada has 25 CMAs, which in 1996 ranged in size from about 4.4 million people in Toronto to 129,000 in Saint John.

Although cities have existed for thousands of years, only about 3 percent of the world's population lived in cities two hundred years ago, as compared with almost 50 percent today. In Canada, the population is even more concentrated: almost 80 percent of us live in areas defined as urban; about 60 percent in CMAs; and about 30 percent in the three major metropolitan areas of Toronto, Montreal, and Vancouver. Canada has become steadily more urbanized since Confederation, when our population was roughly 16 percent urban (Stone, 1967). To understand the process by which increasing numbers of people have become urban residents, we first need to examine how cities began.

Emergence and Evolution of the City

Cities are a relatively recent innovation when compared with the length of human existence. The earliest humans are believed to have emerged anywhere from 40,000 to one million years ago, and permanent human settlements are believed to have first begun about 8000 B.C.E. However, some scholars date the development of the first city

Toronto's Highway 401 at rush hour illustrates the development of postindustrial cities in which people commonly commute long distances to work.

between 3500 and 3100 B.C.E., depending largely on whether a formal writing system is considered a requisite for city life (Sjoberg, 1965; Weeks, 1992; Flanagan, 1995).

According to sociologist Gideon Sjoberg (1965), three preconditions must be present in order for a city to develop:

1. *A favourable physical environment*, including climate and soil favourable to the development of plant and animal life and an adequate water supply to sustain both
2. An *advanced technology* (for that era) that could produce a social surplus in both agricultural and nonagricultural goods
3. A *well-developed social organization*, including a power structure, in order to provide social stability to the economic system

Based on these prerequisites, Sjoberg places the first cities in the Middle Eastern region of Mesopotamia or in areas immediately adjacent to it at about 3500 B.C.E. However, not all scholars concur; some place the earliest city, in Jericho (located in present-day Jordan), at about 8000 B.C.E. with a population of about six hundred people (see Kenyon, 1957). As Sjoberg points out, however, Jericho had no known formal writing system; therefore, a political structure and an economy (both essential to the establishment of a city) would not have been able to function effectively (see also Childe, 1957).

The earliest cities were not large by today's standards. The population of the larger Mesopotamian centres was between five and ten thousand (Sjoberg, 1965). The population of ancient Babylon (probably founded around 2200 B.C.E.) may have grown as large as 50,000 people; Athens may have held 80,000 people (Weeks, 1992). Four to five thousand years ago, cities with at least 50,000 people existed in the Middle East (in what today is Iraq and Egypt) and Asia (in what today is Pakistan and China), as well as in Europe. About 3500 years ago, cities began to reach this size in Central and South America.

Preindustrial Cities

The largest preindustrial city was Rome; by 100 C.E., it may have had a population of 650,000 (Chandler and Fox, 1974). With the fall of the Roman Empire in 476 C.E., the nature of European cities changed. Seeking protection and survival, those persons who lived in urban settings typically did so in walled cities containing no more than 25,000 people. For the next six hundred years the urban population continued to live in walled enclaves, as competing warlords battled for power and territory during the "dark ages." Slowly, as trade increased, cities began to tear down their walls. Some walled cities still exist; Quebec City is the only walled city on this continent.

Preindustrial cities were limited in size by a number of factors. For one thing, crowded conditions and a lack of adequate sewage facilities increased the hazards from plagues and fires, and death rates were high. For another, food supplies were limited. In order to generate food for each city resident, at least fifty farmers had to work in the fields (Davis, 1949), and animal power was the only means of bringing food to the city. Once foodstuffs arrived in the city, there was no effective way to preserve them. Finally, migration to the city was difficult because people were bound to the land and because travel was arduous.

In spite of these problems, many preindustrial cities had a sense of *community*—a set of social relationships operating within given spatial boundaries or locations that provide people with a sense of identity and a feeling of belonging. The cities were full of people from all walks of life, both rich and poor, and they felt a high degree of social integration. You will recall that Ferdinand Tonnies (1940/1887) described such a community as a *Gemeinschaft*—a society in which social relationships are based on personal bonds of friendship and kinship and on intergenerational stability, such that people have a commitment to the entire group and feel a sense of togetherness. In this type of society the person who sells you groceries may also be your neighbour, an elder in your church, and a relative by marriage. When you visit the store, your grocery purchase will be handled in a very personal fashion. By contrast, an industrial city was classified by Tonnies as a *Gesellschaft*—a society characterized by impersonal and specialized relationships, with little long-term commitment to the group or consensus on values (see Chapter 5). In *Gesellschaft* societies, even neighbours are "strangers" who feel they have little in common with one another. Your transaction at the grocery store will be handled much more formally in this type of society.

Canadian communities arose as settlement extended to new parts of this large country. Until the building of the Canadian Pacific Railway, much of Canada was accessible only by water, so most of our settlements, including those that have grown into large cities, were in areas with access to waterways. Transportation routes were particularly important for a colony whose main function was sending large quantities of raw materials such as timber, wheat, and beaver pelts overseas to European markets. Virtually all of our large cities are located on oceans, lakes, or large rivers.

Industrial Cities

The Industrial Revolution changed the nature of the city. Factories sprang up rapidly as production shifted from the primary, agricultural sector to the secondary, manufacturing sector. With the advent of factories came many new employment opportunities not available to people in rural areas. In fact, factories required a concentration of population to act as a labour force. Emergent technology, including new forms of transportation and agricultural production, made it easier for people to leave the countryside and move to the city. Between 1700 and 1900, the population of many European cities mushroomed. Although the Industrial Revolution did not start in North America until the mid-nineteenth century, the effect was similar. Between 1871 and 1911 the population of Toronto grew by 700 percent and that of Montreal by 450 percent (Nader, 1976). By 1911 both cities had roughly 500,000 people and were on their way to becoming major metropolises. A **metropolis is one or more central cities and their surrounding suburbs that dominate the economic and cultural life of a region.** A *central city* is the **densely populated centre of a metropolis.**

The growth of cities during the industrial period was something of a mixed blessing. As cities grew in size and density, overcrowding, poor sanitation, and lack of a clean water supply often led to the spread of epidemic diseases and contributed to a high death rate. In Europe, mortality rates were higher in cities than in rural areas until the nineteenth century, and this remains the case in many cities in the developing world today.

Postindustrial Cities

Since the 1950s, postindustrial cities have emerged in technologically advanced countries, the economies of which have gradually shifted from secondary (manufacturing) production to tertiary (service and information-processing) production. As more traditional industries such as textile manufacturing, steel producing, and many different types of light manufacturing have become obsolete or moved to other countries with lower wages, cities have had to either change or face decline. For example, cities in New Brunswick have been economically devastated by the loss of many jobs in traditional industries such as shipbuilding and railroad maintenance, as well as in resource industries associated with the fishing industry. The province has tried to counteract these losses by moving into the technologically based field of telephone call centres, which perform tasks such as telephone marketing and airline-reservation handling.

Postindustrial cities are dominated by "light" industry, such as computer software manufacturing; information-processing services, such as airline and hotel reservation services; educational complexes; medical centres; convention and entertainment centres; and retail trade centres and shopping malls. Most families do not live in close proximity to a central business district. Technological advances in communication and transportation make it possible for middle- and upper-income individuals and families to have more work options and to live greater distances from the workplace. Some futurists feel that communications technology, along with the retirement plans of the baby boomers, may soon lead to a degree of deurbanization. People who do not have to be physically present in the city centre each day may find a rural or semirural lifestyle an attractive alternative to the commuting and high housing prices that are a part of life in a large city.

PERSPECTIVES ON URBANIZATION AND THE GROWTH OF CITIES

Functionalist Perspectives: Ecological Models

Functionalists examine the interrelations among the parts that make up the whole; therefore, in studying the growth of cities, they emphasize the life cycle of urban growth. Like the social philosophers and sociologists before him, University of Chicago sociologist Robert Park (1915) based his analysis of the city on *human ecology*—the study of the relationship between people and their physical environment. According to Park (1936), economic competition produces certain regularities in land use patterns and population distributions. Applying Park's idea to the study of urban land use patterns, sociologist Ernest W. Burgess (1925) developed the concentric zone model, an ideal construct that attempted to explain why some cities expand radially from a central business core.

CONCENTRIC ZONE MODEL Burgess's *concentric zone model* is a description of the process of urban growth that views the city as a series of circular areas or zones, each characterized by a different type of land use, that developed from a central core (see Figure 19.6a). *Zone 1* is the central business district and cultural centre (retail stores, financial institutions, hotels, and theatres, for

example), in which high land prices cause vertical growth in the form of skyscrapers. *Zone 2* is the zone of transition. As the city expanded, houses formerly occupied by wealthy families were divided into rooms that now are rented to recent immigrants and poor persons; this zone also contains wholesale light manufacturing and marginal business (such as secondhand stores, pawnshops, and taverns). *Zone 3* contains working-class residences and shops and ethnic enclaves, such as Little Italy. *Zone 4* is composed of homes for affluent families, single-family residences of white-collar workers, and shopping centres. *Zone 5* is a ring of small cities and towns populated by persons who commute to the city to work and by wealthy people living on estates.

Two important ecological processes are involved in the concentric zone theory: invasion and succession. **Invasion is the process by which a new category of people or type of land use arrives in an area previously occupied by another group or land use** (McKenzie, 1925). For example, Burgess noted that recent immigrants and low-income individuals "invaded" Zone 2 which were formerly occupied by wealthy families. **Succession is the process by which a new category of people or type of land use gradually predominates in an area formerly dominated by another group or activity** (McKenzie, 1925). In Zone 2, for example, when some of the single-family residences were sold and subsequently divided into multiple housing units, the remaining single-family owners moved out because the "old" neighbourhood had changed. As a result of their move, the process of invasion was complete and succession had occurred.

Invasion and succession theoretically operate in an outward movement: those who are unable to "move out" of the inner rings are those without upward social mobility, so that the central zone ends up being primarily occupied by the poorest residents—except when gentrification occurs. **Gentrification is the process by which members of the middle and upper-middle classes move into the central city area and renovate existing properties.** Centrally located, naturally attractive areas are the most likely candidates for gentrification. To urban ecologists, gentrification is the solution to revitalizing the central city. To conflict theorists, gentrification creates additional hardships for the poor by depleting the amount of affordable housing available and "pushing" them out of the area (Flanagan, 1995).

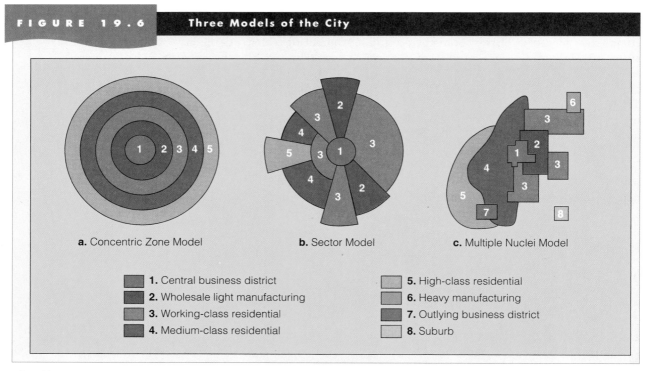

Adapted from Harris and Ullman, 1945.

The concentric zone model demonstrates how economic and political forces play an important part in the location of groups and activities, and it shows how a large urban area can have internal differentiation (Gottdiener, 1985). However, the model is most applicable to older cities that experienced high levels of immigration early in the twentieth century (Queen and Carpenter, 1953). No city, including Chicago (on which the model is based), entirely conforms to this model.

THE SECTOR MODEL   In an attempt to examine a wider range of settings, urban ecologist Homer Hoyt (1939) studied the configuration of 142 cities. Hoyt's *sector model* emphasizes the significance of terrain and the importance of transportation routes in the layout of cities. According to Hoyt, residences of a particular type and value tend to grow outward from the centre of the city in wedge-shaped sectors, with the more expensive residential neighbourhoods located along the higher ground near lakes and rivers or along certain streets that stretch in one direction or another from the downtown area (see Figure 19.6b). By contrast, industrial areas tend to be located along river valleys and railroad lines. Middle-class residential zones exist on either side of the wealthier neighbourhoods. Finally, lower-

class residential areas occupy the remaining space, bordering the central business area and the industrial areas.

THE MULTIPLE NUCLEI MODEL   According to the *multiple nuclei model* developed by urban ecologists Chauncey Harris and Edward Ullman (1945), cities do not have one centre from which all growth radiates, but rather they have numerous centres of development based on specific urban needs or activities (see Figure 19.6c). As cities began to grow rapidly, they annexed formerly outlying and independent townships that had been communities in their own right. In addition to the central business district, other nuclei developed around activities such as an educational institution, a medical complex, or a government centre. Residential neighbourhoods may exist close to or far away from these nuclei. A wealthy residential area may be located near a high-priced shopping centre, for instance, while less-expensive housing must locate closer to industrial and transitional areas of town. This model fits some urban areas such as Toronto, which has large nuclei such as the business district of North York. It also applies to a number of communities such as Edmonton, which have nuclei around universities. However, critics suggest that it does not provide insights about uniformity of land use patterns among cities and relies on an after-the-fact explanation of why certain activities are located where they are (Flanagan, 1995).

DIFFERENCES BETWEEN CANADIAN AND U.S. CITIES

The models of urban growth discussed above were developed to explain the growth of U.S. cities. They do not fit preindustrial cities (most of which have their slums on the outskirts of the city rather than in the central core) nor do they fit cities such as those in Europe that were relatively large before they industrialized. Because they developed on the same continent and at about the same time, there are many similarities between Canadian and American cities, but the models probably do not apply as well to Canadian cities, which differ from U.S. cities in the following important ways (Gillis, 1995; Wolfe, 1992):

1. Canadian cities are higher in density, which means they have less urban sprawl. It is cheaper to provide services in compact cities, and commuting to work is far easier.

2. The core areas of Canadian cities are much healthier than those in the United States. In many U.S. cities, residents have moved to the suburbs to avoid crime, high taxes, and other inner-city problems. This has created what some observers refer to as "doughnut cities," with poor central core areas that have no industry, no job opportunities, poor schools, deteriorated housing, and no tax base to help improve things. The strength of our urban core is a major reason Canadian cities have much lower crime rates than American cities.

3. Urban Canadians rely on public transit more than do Americans, though both countries are far behind European cities in public transit use. Because of this, our cities are less divided by freeways than American urban areas.

4. Racial tension has been far less pronounced in Canada than in the United States, where it has led to many problems including urban riots and "white flight" to the suburbs.

5. Canadian and U.S. public housing policies have been very different. With a few exceptions, such as Toronto's Regent Park and Montreal's Jeanne Mance, governments in Canada have not built large-scale, high-rise developments. Public housing in Canada has taken the form of small, infill projects in established neighbourhoods. These are small housing developments typically consisting of small apartment buildings or row housing. Thus we have not faced the problem of large numbers of economically disadvantaged people crowded into areas that can easily be neglected by the rest of society.

Conflict Perspectives: Political Economy Models

Conflict theorists argue that cities do not grow or decline by chance. Rather, they are the product of specific decisions made by members of the capitalist class and political elites. These far-reaching decisions regarding land use and urban development benefit the members of some groups at the expense of others (see Castells, 1977/1972). Karl Marx suggested that cities are the arenas in which the intertwined processes of class conflict and capital accumulation take place; class consciousness and worker revolt were more likely to develop when workers were concentrated in urban areas (Flanagan, 1995).

CAPITALISM AND URBAN GROWTH

According to political economy models, urban growth is influenced by capital investment decisions, power and resource inequality, class and class conflict, and government subsidy programs. Members of the capitalist class choose corporate locations, decide on sites for shopping centres and factories, and spread the population that can afford to purchase homes into sprawling suburbs located exactly where the capitalists think they should be located (Feagin and Parker, 1990).

Business involvement in urban development is nothing new. Winnipeg became a major transportation centre because of its location at the junction of the Red and Assiniboine Rivers. However, because of Winnipeg's flooding problems, the small community of Selkirk was originally chosen for the route of the Canadian Pacific Railway (CPR). After several years of intense lobbying by Winnipeg's political and business leaders, along with promises of subsidies to the CPR, the line was built through Winnipeg in 1881. According to Bellan (1978), Sir Donald Smith, the man who drove the last spike to finish the transcontinental railway, was instrumental in having the route shifted to Winnipeg. A key figure in building the CPR, Smith was also the largest shareholder in the Hudson's Bay Company, which owned a large block of land in the centre of Winnipeg. During the land boom that followed the announcement of the railway's new route, the

According to conflict theorists, members of the capitalist class make decisions that limit the choices of ordinary citizens, such as how affordable or unaffordable their housing will be. However, scenes like this show that tenants may become active participants in class conflict over the usage of urban space.

Hudson's Bay Company made millions of dollars selling this land.

Today, a small number of financial institutions and developers finance and construct most of Canada's major and many of its smaller urban development projects, including skyscrapers, shopping malls, and suburban housing projects, across the country. These decision makers set limits on the individual choices of the ordinary citizen with regard to real estate, just as they do with regard to other choices (Feagin and Parker, 1990). They can make housing more affordable or totally unaffordable for many people. Ultimately, their motivation rests not in benefiting the community, but rather in making a profit; the cities they produce reflect this mindset.

One of the major results of these urban development practices is *uneven development*—the tendency of some neighbourhoods, cities, or regions to grow and prosper while others stagnate and decline (Perry and Watkins, 1977). An example of this is the movement of middle- and upper-class people to the suburbs, which reduces the tax base of the city core. Conflict theorists argue that uneven development reflects inequalities of wealth and power in society. The problem not only affects areas in a state of decline but also produces external costs, even in "boom" areas, that are paid for by the entire community. Among these costs are increased pollution, traffic congestion, and rising rates of crime and violence. According to sociologist Mark Gottdiener (1985:214), these costs are "intrinsic to the very core of capitalism, and those who profit the most

from development are not called upon to remedy its side effects."

Feminist Perspectives

Feminist perspectives have only recently been incorporated in urban studies (Garber and Turner, 1995). From this perspective, urbanization reflects the workings not only of the political economy but also of patriarchy.

GENDER REGIMES IN CITIES According to sociologist Lynn M. Appleton (1995), different kinds of cities have different *gender regimes*—prevailing ideologies of how women and men should think, feel, and act; how access to social positions and control of resources should be managed; and how relationships between men and women should be conducted. The higher density and greater diversity found in central cities serve as a challenge to the patriarchy found in the home and workplace in lower-density, homogeneous areas such as suburbs and rural areas because central cities offer a broader range of lifestyle choices, some of which do not involve traditional patriarchal family structures. For example, cities are more likely than suburbs to support a subculture of economically independent females. Thus the city may be a forum for challenging patriarchy; all residents who differ in marital status, paternity, sexual orientation, class and/or race/ethnicity tend to live in close proximity to one another and may hold and act upon a common belief that both public and private patriarchy should be eliminated (Appleton, 1995).

Interactionist Perspectives: The Experience of City Life

Interactionists examine the *experience* of urban life. How does city life affect the people who live in a city? Some analysts answer this question positively; others are more negative about the effect of urban living on the individual.

SIMMEL'S VIEW OF CITY LIFE According to German sociologist Georg Simmel (1950/1905), urban life is highly stimulating and it shapes people's thoughts and actions. Urban residents are influenced by the quick pace of city life and the pervasiveness of economic relations in everyday life. Due to the intensity of urban life, people become somewhat insensitive to events and individuals around them. When city life requires you to interact with hundreds of different people every day, you cannot become personally involved with each of them so most of your contacts will be impersonal. Urbanites are wary of one another because most interactions in the city are economic rather than social. Simmel suggests that attributes such as punctuality and exactness are rewarded but that friendliness and warmth in interpersonal relations are viewed as personal weaknesses. Some people act in a reserved way to cloak deeper feelings of distrust or dislike toward others. However, Simmel did not view city life as completely negative; he also pointed out that urban living could have a liberating effect on people because they had opportunities for individualism and autonomy (Flanagan, 1995).

URBANISM AS A WAY OF LIFE Based on Simmel's observations on social relations in the city, early Chicago School sociologist Louis Wirth (1938) suggested that urbanization is a "way of life." *Urbanism* refers to the distinctive social and psychological patterns of life typically found in the city. According to Wirth, the size, density, and heterogeneity of urban populations typically result in an elaborate division of labour and in spatial segregation of people by race/ethnicity, social class, religion, and/or lifestyle. In the city, primary group ties largely are replaced by secondary relationships; social interaction is fragmented, impersonal, and often superficial ("Hello! Have a nice day"). Even though people gain some degree of

freedom and privacy by living in the city, they pay a price for their autonomy, losing the group support and reassurance that comes from primary group ties.

From Wirth's perspective, people who live in urban areas are alienated, powerless, and lonely. A sense of community is obliterated and replaced by "mass society"—a large-scale, highly institutionalized society in which individuality is supplanted by mass messages, faceless bureaucrats, and corporate interest.

Simmel and Wirth share an *environmental determinism* that assumes that the physical environment of the city determines the behaviour of urban dwellers. Their work has contributed to the commonly held view that cities are cold, anonymous, and unfriendly places (Kennedy, 1983). However, other researchers claim that the rural/urban contrast is too simplistic and ignores the wide diversity of lifestyles found in urban areas. This view has led to research into the reasons for the different ways in which urban residents have responded to their environment.

GAN'S URBAN VILLAGERS In contrast to Wirth's gloomy assessment of urban life, sociologist Herbert Gans (1982/1962) suggested that not everyone experiences the city in the same way. Based on research conducted in the west end of Boston, Gans concluded that many residents develop strong loyalties and a sense of community in central city areas that outsiders may view negatively. People make choices about the lifestyle they wish to lead based on their personal characteristics, the most important of which are social class and stage in the life cycle. According to Gans, there are five major categories of adaptation among urban dwellers. *Cosmopolites* are students, artists, writers, musicians, entertainers, and professionals who live in the city because they want to be close to its cultural facilities. *Unmarried people and childless couples* live in the city because they want to be close to work and entertainment. *Ethnic villagers* live in ethnically segregated neighbourhoods; some are recent immigrants who feel most comfortable within their own group. The *deprived* are poor individuals with dim future prospects; they have very limited education and few, if any, other resources. The *trapped* are urban dwellers who can find no escape from the city; this group includes persons left behind by the process of invasion and succession, downwardly mobile individuals who have lost their former position in society, older persons who have nowhere else to

These photographs represent three of the ways people adapt to city life described by Herbert Gans. Cosmopolites choose to live in the city to enjoy cultural facilities such as Toronto's Roy Thomson Hall. Ethnic villagers live in the tightly knit neighbourhood enclaves, such as this Chinese neighbourhood in Richmond, British Columbia. Trapped residents can find no escape from the city, as exemplified by this homeless person in Toronto.

go, and individuals addicted to alcohol or other drugs. Transient people in the inner city are most likely to suffer the urban ills described by Wirth, but this is because of residential instability, and not simply an inevitable result of urbanization. Gans concluded that the city is a pleasure and a challenge for some urban dwellers and an urban nightmare for others.

GENDER AND CITY LIFE   Do women and men experience city life differently? According to scholar Elizabeth Wilson (1991), some men view the city as *sexual space* in which women are categorized as prostitutes, lesbians, temptresses, or virtuous women in need of protection, based on their sexual desirability and accessibility. Wilson suggests that affluent, dominant group women are more likely to be viewed as virtuous women in need of protection by their own men or police officers. Cities offer a paradox for women: on the one hand, they offer more freedom than is found in comparatively isolated rural, suburban, and domestic settings; on the other, women may be in greater physical danger in the city. For Wilson, the answer to women's vulnerability in the city is not found in offering protection to them, but rather in changing people's attitudes so that they no longer believe they can treat women as sexual objects because of the impersonality of city life (Wilson, 1991).

Michelson (1994) has highlighted another dimension of the vulnerability of women in cities. Women with children are much more likely to be in the paid workforce than they were twenty years ago. When women were more likely to stay home, they spent much of their time in the company of immediate neighbours, and rarely ventured from their neighbourhoods at night without their husbands. Employed women have a much different city experience. Much of their time is now spent with people on the job and they are more often alone outside their immediate neighbourhoods at different hours.

For many women in this situation, travelling to and from work is perceived as dangerous. Michelson cites a Statistics Canada study showing that 80 percent of women fear entering parking garages and 76 percent fear using public transportation after dark. Women feel particularly vulnerable if they have to walk alone after dark because of work or school. Our cities have not yet adapted well to these major social changes in the lives of women.

MICHELSON, FISCHER, AND URBAN CHOICES   Claude Fischer (1976) built on Gans's view of the importance of subgroup values in influencing urban behaviour. Fischer studied the way in which the size of cities and their structural differentiation provided opportunities for the development of urban subcultures. Cities of different sizes and in different locations vary in the kinds of subcultures they support. For example, a city with a large number of manufacturing jobs will support a much more vibrant blue-collar subculture than will a city whose economy is centred on education and financial services. In turn, the latter city will be more likely to have active subcultures focused on the arts, which attract more highly educated people. The diversity of cities creates the opportunity for subgroups to follow a variety of interests which would not be possible in smaller communities. People may be attracted to particular cities because of the subcultural opportunities available to them. The larger and more diverse the city, the broader the range of choices available to its residents. This is one reason large cities continue to attract people. Somali immigrants will feel more at home in Toronto or Ottawa, where there are Somali ethnic subcultures, than they will in Chicoutimi or St. John's, where subcultural supports do not exist.

While Fischer demonstrated the importance of urban institutional structures, William Michelson (1976, 1977) argued that the physical environment of cities (buildings, roads, etc.) also has an impact on behaviour. People make residential choices based on factors such as social class, ethnicity, and stage in the life cycle. These choices, in turn, have an impact on their social relationships and their behaviour. For example, in his research on Toronto, Michelson found that different types of physical environment (high-rise downtown apartments, single-family suburban houses, single-family downtown houses, and high-rise suburban apartments) attracted very different types of residents. The chosen environment did have an effect on behaviour. For example, residents who lived near public facilities and conveniences were more socially active than people of the same social characteristics who lived further from these facilities. An Edmonton study by Kennedy (1978) found that the type of residence people chose played a role in the type and nature of contact they had with their neighbours and relatives.

There is, then, a diversity in the life experience of urban dwellers that depends on a wide variety of factors such as age, social class, gender, marital status, and type of residence. The same is likely true of rural residents; the romantic view of rural society held by the early urban sociologists may have been nostalgia for a mythical past. In reality, urban life is not as bad, nor rural life as good, as Wirth and his colleagues assumed.

DIVIDED INTERESTS: CITIES, SUBURBS, AND BEYOND

Since World War II, a dramatic population shift has occurred in North America as thousands of families have moved from cities to suburbs. Even though some people lived in suburban areas prior to the twentieth century, large-scale suburban development began in the 1950s. Postwar suburban growth was fuelled by the large baby boom families, aggressive land developers, inexpensive real estate and construction methods, better transportation, abundant energy, and liberalized mortgage policies (Jackson, 1985; Palen, 1995).

Regardless of its causes, mass suburbanization has created a territorial division of interests between cities and suburban areas (Flanagan, 1995). While many suburbanites rely on urban centres for their employment, entertainment, and other services, they pay their property taxes to suburban governments and school districts. While Canadian cities are very healthy compared with those in the United States and most other countries, they have not been immune to the problems of poverty, homelessness, unemployment, and urban sprawl. During the recession of the early 1990s Canadian cities were faced with cutting services or raising taxes at a time when the tax base already was shrinking because of migration to the suburbs. As services and urban infrastructures deteriorated, even more middle- and upper-class people moved out of cities, with some businesses following suit.

Montreal in particular has suffered from what has been called the doughnut effect. That is, as people and industry have moved out of the central island of Montreal to surrounding suburban communities, the core has suffered. Urban Montreal has the highest jobless rate of any major North American city, and rates of poverty, homelessness, and infant mortality are all considerably higher than the Canadian average. Despite these very real problems, Montreal is still a vibrant and safe place, and is far more livable than most American central cities. In fact, the Washington-based group Population Action International ranked Montreal first in livability (tied with Melbourne and Seattle) among the world's 100 largest metropolitan areas.

The problems faced by Montreal and several of our other large cities are essentially political. Much of the decline of central cities is caused by a skewed tax system that drives businesses and middle-class residents out to the suburbs. The central cities must provide a wide range of services to their own residents as well as to those who commute downtown from the suburbs. Thus, business and residential property taxes are much higher downtown than in suburban areas. Business taxes in Montreal, for example, are 44 percent higher than in its surrounding municipalities and residential taxes are 30 percent higher (Lalonde, 1996).

The solution to this problem is conceptually simple; develop strong regional governments that would create wider service areas than do existing municipal governments. Regional governments would be responsible for water, sewage, transportation, schools, parks, hospitals, and other public services over a wider area. Revenues would be shared among central cities, affluent suburbs, and suburban municipalities based on the assumption that everyone will benefit if the quality of life is improved throughout the region. Greater Montreal has 102 municipalities ranging in size from Montreal, with 1,017,666 persons in 1991, to Île Cadieux, which had 140 residents in 1991, and only a regional government can avoid the fragmentation this variation produces. London, England, provides an example of how a lack of regional planning and authority can lead to chaos. Traffic in that city is extremely congested, at least partly because each of Greater London's 33 boroughs is responsible for its own transportation policy. Once, most of the Thames River bridges were closed at the same time because the local transportation authorities had not coordinated their maintenance schedules (Drohan, 1996).

If the solution is so simple, why has it not been quickly adopted? The reason is politics. Task force reports in many of our large cities have recommended similar solutions to those described above to the problems of our major cities. However, regionalization has been opposed by politically powerful suburban municipalities whose residents do not want their taxes raised to help the larger community, and urban sprawl continues at the expense of the central city. However, the situation is changing. In 1998 regional governments were established in Toronto and Halifax, though in both cities there is still strong opposition to regionalization. In addition, other cities, including Edmonton and Winnipeg, are also looking at ways of maintaining strong central cities.

POPULATION AND URBANIZATION IN THE FUTURE

As we move into the twenty-first century, rapid global population growth is inevitable. Although death rates have declined in many developing nations, birth rates have not correspondingly decreased. Between 1985 and 2025, 93 percent of all global population growth will have occurred in Africa, Asia, and Latin America; 83 percent of the world's population will live in those regions by 2025 (Petersen, 1994).

Predicting changes in population is difficult. Natural disasters such as earthquakes, volcanic eruptions, hurricanes, tornados, floods, and so on obviously cannot be predicted. A cure for diseases caused by HIV may be found; however,

HIV/AIDS may reach epidemic proportions in more nations. A number of diseases such as tuberculosis, which had been controlled by antibiotics, are now returning in a form that is resistant to the drugs usually used for treatment.

Whatever the impact of disease, developing nations will have an increasing number of poor people. While the world's population will *double*, the urban population will *triple* as people migrate from rural to urban areas in search of food, water, and jobs. Of all developing regions, Latin America is becoming the most urbanized; four mega-cities—Mexico City (20 million), Buenos Aires (12 million), Lima (7 million), and Santiago (5 million)—already contain more than half of this region's population and continue to grow rapidly. By 2010, Rio de Janeiro and Sao Paulo are expected to have a combined population of about 40 million people living in a 350-mile-long **megalopolis—a continuous concentration of two or more cities and their suburbs that have grown until they form an interconnected urban area** (Petersen, 1994). These huge cities will have a profound impact on the environment because of air pollution, greenhouse gas emissions, sewage and waste disposal, and water consumption.

One of the many effects of urbanization is greater exposure of people to the media. In the twenty-first century, increasing numbers of poor people in less developed nations will see images from the developed world beamed globally by networks such as CNN. As futurist John L. Peterson (1994:119) notes, "For the first time in history, the poor are beginning to understand how relatively poor they are compared to the rich nations. They see, in detail, how the rest of the world lives and feel their increasing disenfranchisement." The impact this will have remains an open question.

The speed of social change means that areas that we currently think of as being relatively free from such problems will be characterized by depletion of natural resources and greater air and water pollution (see Ehrlich and Ehrlich, 1991). At the same time, if social and environmental problems become too great in one nation, those who can afford it may simply move to another country. For example, many affluent residents of Hong Kong acquired business interests and houses in the United States, Canada, and other countries in anticipation of Hong Kong's reversion to China in 1997. As people become "world citizens," in this way, their lives are not linked to the stability of any one city or nation. However, this option is limited only to the wealthiest of citizens.

In a best-case scenario for the future, the problems brought about by rapid population growth in developing nations will be remedied by new technologies that make goods readily available to people. International trade agreements such as NAFTA (the North American Free Trade Agreement) and GATT (the General Agreement on Trade and Tariffs) will remove trade barriers and make it possible for all nations to engage fully in global trade. People in developing nations will benefit by gaining jobs and opportunities to purchase goods at lower prices. Of course, the opposite also may occur: people may be exploited as inexpensive labour, and their country's natural resources may be depleted as transnational corporations buy up raw materials without contributing to the long-term economic stability of the nation.

With regard to pollution in urban areas, some futurists predict that environmental activism will increase dramatically as people see irreversible changes in the atmosphere and experience firsthand the effects of environmental hazards and pollution on their own health and well-being. These environmental problems will cause a realization that overpopulation is a world problem, a problem that will be most apparent in the world's weakest economies and most fragile ecosystems. Futurists suggest that as we begin the twenty-first century, we must "leave the old ways and invent new ones" (Petersen, 1994:340). What aspects of our "old ways" do you think we should discard? Can you help invent new ways?

CHAPTER REVIEW

What is demography?

Demography is the study of the size, composition, and distribution of the population.

What demographic processes result in population change?

Population change is the result of fertility (births), mortality (deaths), and migration.

What is the Malthusian perspective?

Over two hundred years ago, Thomas Malthus warned that overpopulation would result in poverty, starvation, and other major problems that would limit the size of the population. According to Malthus, the population would increase geometrically, while the food supply would increase only arithmetically, resulting in poverty and a critical food shortage.

What are the views of Karl Marx and the neo-Malthusians on overpopulation?

According to Karl Marx, poverty is the result of capitalist greed, not overpopulation. More recently, neo-Malthusians have reemphasized the dangers of overpopulation and encouraged zero population growth—the point at which no population increase occurs from year to year.

What are the stages in demographic transition theory?

Demographic transition theory links population growth to four stages of economic development: (1) the preindustrial stage, with high birth rates and death rates, (2) early industrialization, with relatively high birth rates and a decline in death rates, (3) advanced industrialization and urbanization, with low birth rates and death rates, and (4) postindustrialization, with additional decreases in the birth rate coupled with a stable death rate.

What are the three functionalist models of urban growth?

Functionalists view urban growth in terms of ecological models. The concentric zone model sees the city as a series of circular areas, each characterized by a different type of land use; the sector model describes urban growth in terms of terrain and transportation routes; and the multiple nuclei model views cities as having numerous centres of development from which growth radiates.

What is the political economy/conflict perspective on urban growth?

According to political economy models/conflict perspectives, urban growth is influenced by capital investment decisions, power and resource inequality, class and class conflict, and government subsidy programs.

What is the feminist perspective on urbanization?

Feminists feel that different cities have different gender regimes—prevailing ideologies of how women and men should think, feel, and act; how access to social positions and control of resources should be managed; and how relationships between men and women should be conducted.

How do interactionists view urban life?

Interactionist perspectives focus on how people experience urban life. Some analysts view the urban experi-

ence positively; others believe that urban dwellers become insensitive to events and people around them.

Key Terms

central city 626
crude birth rate 607
crude death rate 608
demographic transition 620
demography 606
emigration 609
fertility 606
gentrification 627
immigration 609
infant mortality rate 608
invasion 627
megalopolis 635
metropolis 626
migration 609
mortality 608
population composition 612
population pyramid 613
sex ratio 612
succession 627
urban sociology 624

Internet Exercises

1. Visit the Statistics Canada page (**http://www. statcan.ca**) and go to the Canadian Statistics section. What information can you find about your own community? Now go to the section on the 1996 census. What information has recently been released from this census? How does it benefit you to have direct access to this type of data and information?

2. Many cities have now put themselves online. Using Yahoo! (**http://www.yahoo.com**), search for your city and province. Many countries now have population data available on their Web sites. How is this information useful? Does your city have a Web site? If it does, what type of data does it contain and are these data useful? If not, what would you like it to contain?

3. For an interesting look at Canada's largest city, go to the Virtual Toronto Web Site at **http://www. ryerson.ca/vtoronto**. This site, which has been developed by the School of Applied Geography at Ryerson Polytechnic University, provides a digital atlas and a photo/video gallery. In addition to some technologically fascinating ways of showing us Toronto, the site contains a wealth of sociological information including extensive population data.

The site also has a Literary Landscapes section that includes representations of the female city and the ethnic city.

4. Contemporary cities have been shaped by the automobile. Quickly jot down some of your ideas about how your own city would have evolved differently if no automobiles had been allowed within the city limits. Then go the Carfree Cities Web site at **http://carfree.com** to learn more about this prospect. This is one of the more interesting sites on the Internet and should help you think about how to make urban living more pleasant. Look at some of the pictures of Venice, Italy, and think about what parts of your city are the most people-friendly.

 ## Net Links

Watch the world's population grow on the World Population Clock:

http://www.princeton.edu/popclock

To look up demographic information on births, deaths, and infant mortality, go to the World Factbook at:

http://www.odci.gov/cia/publications/factbook

For the latest revision to world population estimates, go to:

http://www.undp.org/popin/#trends

Questions for Critical Thinking

1. What impact does a high rate of immigration have on culture and personal identity in Canada?
2. If you were designing a study of growth patterns for the city in which you live (or one you know well), which theoretical model(s) would provide the most useful framework for your analysis?
3. What do you think everyday life in Canadian cities, suburbs, and rural areas will be like in 2020? Where would you prefer to live? What, if anything, does your answer reflect about the future of our cities?
4. What is the role of environmental scarcity as a cause of social conflict? How will this scarcity affect the security of developed countries?

Suggested Readings

These texts provide in-depth information on the topics in this chapter:

Roderic Beaujot. *Population Change in Canada: The Challenges of Policy Adaptation.* Toronto: McClelland and Stewart, 1991.

Leo Driedger. *The Urban Factor: Sociology of Canadian Cities.* Toronto: Oxford University Press, 1991.

Peter McGahan. *Urban Sociology in Canada* (3rd ed.). Toronto: Harcourt Brace, 1995.

Wayne W. McVey Jr. and Warren E. Kalbach. *Canadian Population.* Toronto: Nelson Canada, 1995.

The following books discuss global overpopulation and urban growth issues:

Paul Ehrlich and Anne Ehrlich. *The Population Explosion.* London: Hutchinson, 1990.

Thomas Homer-Dixon. *Environmental Scarcity and Global Security.* Foreign Policy Association, Headline Series, Number 300. Ephrata, Penn.: Science Press, 1993.

World Resources Institute. *World Resources 1996–97.* Washington: World Resources Institute, 1996.

Collective Behaviour
  Conditions for Collective Behaviour
  Dynamics of Collective Behaviour
  Distinctions Regarding Collective Behaviour
  Types of Crowd Behaviour
  Explanations of Crowd Behaviour

Social Movements
  Types of Social Movements
  Causes of Social Movements
  Stages in Social Movements

Social Change in the Future
  The Physical Environment and Change
  Population and Change
  Technology and Change
  Social Institutions and Change

A Few Final Thoughts

Clayoquot Sound, located on the west coast of Vancouver Island, is one of the world's last original temperate rain forests. Clayoquot Sound was also the site, in the 1990s, of the latest in a series of bitter struggles fought by Aboriginal peoples and environmental groups to preserve British Columbia's forests. Environmentalists have indicated that the rate at which Canadian firms are clear-cutting forests rivals the devastation in Brazil's Amazon rain forest. Clear-cutting refers to cutting down all the trees in a forested area regardless of their age, size, or species. This practice not only eliminates the trees, but also destroys soil cover, promotes erosion, and damages animal habitats. Journalist Peter C. Newman describes his reaction to the clear-cutting in this area—a reaction that provoked him to support the grassroots environmental movement:

"A few seasons ago, I sailed with three friends around Vancouver Island, a 600-mile journey along some of the intertidal world's most wondrous coastline. An unforgettable incident during that voyage was gliding, late one Sunday evening, into a tiny cove past Meares Island on Clayoquot Sound ... The four of us felt as if we had drifted into a cloistered cathedral. Until the next morning that is. Dawn revealed that the shores of the cove we had gently entered in darkness the previous evening, had been clear-cut. Our cathedral had been desecrated. We found ourselves anchored in a barren, ugly place that resembled nothing so much as the cone of a burned-out volcano. It is from this highly subjective viewpoint that I judge the current controversy about the forestry companies being permitted to cut trees in Clayoquot Sound. They should on no account be allowed to touch a single tree ... It has always been the land—which really means the forests—that has anchored our sense of who we are and what we want to become. The shape and growth of our landscape has been the most potent influence on formation of the Canadian character. Let's not flatten it." (Newman, 1993b:44)

COLLECTIVE BEHAVIOUR AND
SOCIAL CHANGE

Like Newman, many Canadians were sparked out of complacency once they witnessed the devastation of clear-cutting first-hand. In 1993 Clayoquot Sound became a high-profile battleground in which the logging industry was pitted against a coalition of environmental groups including Greenpeace, the Sierra Club, and the Friends of Clayoquot Sound. These environmental activists were seeking social change. *Social change is the alteration, modification, or transformation of public policy, culture, or social institutions over time;* such change is often brought about by collective behaviour. In April 1993, the British Columbia government made the decision to allow clear-cut logging in two-thirds of Clayoquot's old-growth forest. This decision precipitated a social movement that received international attention. The pulp and paper firms involved in this dispute assured the government that this tropical rain forest was renewable—environmentalists disagreed. As Newman explains: "They're wrong for one simple but telling reason. Trees are renewable. Forests are not. It takes literally centuries for bunches of trees to turn themselves into a fully integrated forest. The process involves not just trees, but the quality of the underbrush, natural ponds and the animals that make the forest their habitat. Nature's few original rain forests still remaining on this earth are a precious and highly finite commodity" (1993b:44).

In July 1993, to protest the clear-cutting in Clayoquot Sound, demonstrators created a logging-road blockade at the Kennedy River Bridge. Protesters were joined by high-profile environmentalists including MP Svend Robinson, and Robert Kennedy, Jr., in this effort to save the forests. The Clayoquot protest resulted in the largest criminal prosecution of a nonviolent protest in Canadian his-

tory: over 800 activists were arrested for blocking the road to logging crews. The environmentalists also successfully lobbied several commercial companies in Canada, Britain, and the United States to cancel their contracts with MacMillan Bloedel to protest the Canadian firm's clear-cut logging practices.

In July 1995, the efforts of the environmental activists paid off: the government of British Columbia banned clear-cutting in Clayoquot Sound.

In this chapter, we will discuss collective behaviour, social movements, and social change. Throughout the chapter, we will use environmental activism as an example of all three topics. Before reading on, test your knowledge about collective behaviour, social change, and environmental issues by taking the quiz in Box 20.1.

QUESTIONS AND ISSUES

CHAPTER FOCUS QUESTION: Can collective behaviour and social movements make people aware of important issues such as environmental issues?

What causes people to engage in collective behaviour?

What are some common forms of collective behaviour?

How can different types of social movements be distinguished from one another?

What draws people into social movements?

What factors contribute to social change?

In 1993, the proposed logging of old-growth trees in Clayoquot Sound sparked the largest civil disobedience action in Canadian history.

COLLECTIVE BEHAVIOUR

Collective behaviour is relatively spontaneous, unstructured activity by a large number of people that typically violates established social values and norms. Unlike the *organizational behaviour* found in corporations and voluntary associations (such as labour unions and environmental organizations), collective behaviour lacks an official division of labour, hierarchy of authority, and established rules and procedures. Unlike *institutional behaviour* (in education, religion, or politics, for example), it lacks institutionalized norms to govern behaviour. Collective behaviour can take various forms, including crowds, mobs, riots, panics, fads, fashions, and public opinion.

Conditions for Collective Behaviour

Collective behaviour occurs as a result of some common influence or stimulus that produces a response from a collectivity. A *collectivity* is a relatively large number of people who mutually transcend, bypass, or subvert established institutional patterns and structures. Three major factors contribute to the likelihood that collective behaviour will occur: (1) structural factors that increase the chances of people responding in a particular way, (2) timing, and (3) a breakdown in social control mechanisms and a corresponding feeling of norm-

lessness (McPhail, 1991; Turner and Killian, 1993). A common stimulus is an important factor. For example, in the case of Clayoquot sound, the issue of clear-cut logging was part of a larger issue of environmental destruction. In the words of one commentator, "Clayoquot is a symbol, a cause, one of those local battles that becomes a flashpoint of a larger war" (Fulton and Mather, 1993:20). The clear-cut logging issue came at a time when people were becoming more concerned about social issues and beginning to see that they could empower themselves through grassroots activism.

Timing and a breakdown in social control mechanisms also are important in collective behaviour. Since the 1960s, most urban riots in Canada and the United States have begun in the evenings or on weekends when most people are off work (McPhail, 1971). For example, the 1992 Los Angeles riots erupted in the evening after the verdict in the Rodney King beating trial had been announced. As rioting, looting, and arson began to take a toll on certain areas of Los Angeles, a temporary breakdown in formal social control mechanisms occurred. In some areas of the city, law enforcement was inadequate to quell the illegal actions of rioters, some of whom began to believe that the rules had been suspended. In the aftermath of the Montreal riot following their 1993 Stanley Cup victory, the Montreal Canadiens were protected by hundreds of police officers and a riot squad in an effort to prevent any further breakdown of social control. Similarly, as

BOX 20.1   SOCIOLOGY AND EVERYDAY LIFE

HOW MUCH DO YOU KNOW ABOUT COLLECTIVE BEHAVIOUR, SOCIAL CHANGE AND ENVIRONMENTAL ISSUES?

TRUE FALSE

T	F	1. The environmental movement in North America started in the 1960s.
T	F	2. People who hold strong attitudes regarding the environment are very likely to be involved in social movements to protect the environment.
T	F	3. Environmental groups may engage in civil disobedience or use symbolic gestures to call attention to their issue.
T	F	4. Most sociologists believe that people act somewhat irrationally when they are in large crowds.
T	F	5. People are most likely to believe rumours when no other information is readily available on a topic.
T	F	6. Influencing public opinion is a very important activity for many social movements.
T	F	7. Social movements are more likely to flourish in democratic societies.
T	F	8. Most social movements in Canada seek to improve society by changing some specific aspect of the social structure.
T	F	9. Sociologists have found that people in a community respond very similarly to natural disasters and to disasters caused by technological failures.
T	F	10. People have the capacity to change the environment for better or for worse.

Answers on page 642.

discussed in Box 20.2, hundreds of protesters were arrested at Clayoquot Sound in what law enforcement personnel indicated was an effort to prevent any breakdown in social control.

Dynamics of Collective Behaviour

To better understand the dynamics of collective behaviour, let us briefly examine three basic questions. First, how do people come to transcend, bypass, or subvert established institutional patterns and structures? The *Friends of Clayoquot Sound* initially tried to work within established means through provincial government environment officials. However, they quickly learned that their problems were not being solved through these channels; as the problem appeared to grow worse, organizational responses became more defensive and obscure. Accordingly, some activists began acting outside of established norms by holding protests, establishing blockades, and (on one occasion) storming the B.C. legislature and almost breaking into the assembly. Some situations are more conducive to collective behaviour than others. When people can communicate quickly and easily with one another, spontaneous

behaviour is more likely (Turner and Killian, 1993). When people are gathered together in one general location (whether lining the streets or assembled in a stadium), they are more likely to respond to a common stimulus.

Second, how do people's actions compare with their attitudes? People's attitudes (as expressed in public opinion surveys, for instance) are not always reflected in their political and social behaviour. Issues pertaining to the environment are no exception. The National Opinion Survey of Canadian Public Opinion on Forestry Issues showed that a majority of Canadians believed that "too many trees are being logged." In fact, 71 percent of Canadians disapproved of clear-cut logging and 61 percent indicated that they "get personally upset" when they see the results of clear-cutting (Harding, 1993:456). However, when the Friends of Clayoquot held their first protest session, only 200 people attended. Nevertheless, they assured the media that 1000 people would gather at Clayoquot on Canada Day. Their confidence was unfounded: only 150 supporters appeared (Brunet, 1993).

Third, why do people act collectively rather than singly? Sociologists Ralph H. Turner and

ANSWERS TO THE SOCIOLOGY QUIZ ON COLLECTIVE BEHAVIOUR, SOCIAL CHANGE, AND ENVIRONMENTAL ISSUES

1. **False.** The environmental movement in North America is the result of more than one hundred years of collective action. The first environmental organization in North America was the American Forestry Association (now American Forests), which originated in 1875.

2. **False.** Since the 1980s, public opinion polls have shown that the majority of people in Canada have favourable attitudes regarding protection of the environment and banning nuclear weapons; however, far fewer individuals actually are involved in collective action to further these causes.

3. **True.** Environmental groups have held sit-ins, marches, boycotts, and strikes, which sometimes take the form of civil disobedience.

4. **False.** Although some early social psychological theories were based on the assumption of "crowd psychology" or "mob behaviour," most sociologists believe that individuals act quite rationally when they are part of a crowd.

5. **True.** Rumours are most likely to emerge and circulate when people have very little information on a topic that is important to them. For example, rumours abound in times of technological disasters when people are fearful and often willing to believe the worst.

6. **True.** Many social movements, including grassroots environmental activism, attempt to influence public opinion so that local decision makers will feel obliged to correct a specific problem through changes in public policy.

7. **True.** Having a democratic process available is important for dissenters. Grassroots movements have utilized the democratic process to bring about change even when elites have sought to discourage such activism.

8. **True.** Most social movements are reform movements that focus on improving society by changing some specific aspect of the social structure. Examples include environmental movements and the disability rights movement.

9. **False.** Most sociological studies have found that people respond differently to natural disasters, which usually occur very suddenly, and to technological disasters, which may occur gradually. One of the major differences is the communal bonding that tends to occur following natural disasters, as compared with the extreme social conflict that may follow technological disasters.

10. **True.** One of the goals of most environmental movements is to stress the importance of "thinking globally and acting locally" to protect the environment.

Sources: Based on Worster, 1985; Gamson, 1990; Hynes, 1990; Young, 1990; and Adams, 1991.

Lewis M. Killian (1993:12) say one reason is that "the rhythmic stamping of feet by hundreds of concert-goers in unison is different from isolated, individual cries of 'bravo.'" Likewise, people may act as a collectivity (as was the case for many Clayoquot Sound residents) when they believe it is the only way to fight those with greater power and resources. Collective behaviour is not just the sum of a large number of individuals acting at the same time; rather, it reflects people's joint response to some common influence or stimulus.

Distinctions Regarding Collective Behaviour

People engaging in collective behaviour may be divided into crowds and masses. A *crowd* is a **relatively large number of people who are in one another's immediate vicinity** (Lofland, 1993). In contrast, a *mass* is a large number of people who **share an interest in a specific idea or issue but who are not in one another's immediate vicinity** (Lofland, 1993). To further distinguish between crowds and masses, think of the difference between a riot and a rumour: people who participate in a riot must be in the same general location; those who spread a rumour may be thousands of miles apart, communicating by telephone or through online computer networks.

Collective behaviour also may be distinguished by the dominant emotion expressed. According to sociologist John Lofland (1993:72), the *dominant emotion* refers to the "publicly expressed feeling perceived by participants and observers as the most prominent in an episode of collective behaviour." Lofland suggests that fear, hostility, and joy are three fundamental emotions found in collective behaviour; however, grief, disgust, surprise, or shame also may predominate in some forms of collective behaviour.

Types of Crowd Behaviour

When we think of a crowd, many of us think of *aggregates*, previously defined as a collection of people who happen to be in the same place at the same time but who have little else in common. However, the presence of a relatively large number of people in the same location does not necessarily produce collective behaviour. Sociologist Herbert Blumer (1946) developed a typology in which crowds are divided into four categories: casual, conventional, expressive, and acting. Other scholars have added a fifth category, protest crowds.

CASUAL AND CONVENTIONAL CROWDS

Casual crowds are relatively large gatherings of people who happen to be in the same place at the same time; if they interact at all, it is only briefly. People in a shopping mall or a bus are examples of casual crowds. Other than sharing a momentary interest, such as a watching a busker perform on the street or observing the aftermath of a car accident, a casual crowd has nothing in common. The casual crowd plays no active part in the event—such as the car accident—that would have occurred whether or not the crowd was present; it simply observes.

Conventional crowds are made up of people who specifically come together for a scheduled event and thus share a common focus. Examples include religious services, graduation ceremonies, concerts, and university lectures. Each of these events has established schedules and norms. Because these events occur regularly, interaction among participants is much more likely; in turn, the events would not occur without the crowd, which is essential to the event.

EXPRESSIVE AND ACTING CROWDS

Expressive crowds provide opportunities for the expression of some strong emotion (such as joy, excitement, or grief). People release their pent-up emotions in conjunction with other persons experiencing similar emotions. Examples include worshippers at religious revival services; mourners lining the streets when a celebrity, public official, or religious leader has died; and nonrioting crowds at a sporting event.

Acting crowds are collectivities so intensely focused on a specific purpose or object that they may erupt into violent or destructive behaviour. Mobs, riots, and panics are examples of acting crowds, but casual and conventional crowds may become acting crowds under some circumstances. A *mob* **is a highly emotional crowd whose members engage in, or are ready to engage in, violence against a specific target—a person, a category of people, or physical property.** Mob behaviour in this country has included fire bombings, effigy hangings, and hate crimes. Mob violence tends to dissipate relatively quickly once a target has been injured, killed, or destroyed. Sometimes, actions such as effigy hanging are used symbolically by groups that otherwise are not violent; for example, during the 1990 Oka crisis on the Kanehsatake reserve in Quebec local non-Aboriginal residents burned an effigy of a Mohawk to emphasize their displeasure with the blockade of the Mercier Bridge to Montreal.

Compared with mob action, riots may be of somewhat longer duration. A *riot* **is violent crowd behaviour that is fuelled by deep-seated emotions but not directed at one specific target.** Riots often are triggered by fear, anger, and hostility. This was true of the 1992 Los Angeles riots, which, as has been mentioned, resulted from the announcement of the acquittal of the white police officers involved in the brutal beating of Rodney King, a black. These especially destructive riots caused millions of dollars of damage and thousands of injuries, and left more than fifty people dead. They were followed days later by race riots on the streets of Toronto. However, not all riots are caused by deep-seated hostility and hatred; people may be expressing joy and exuberance when rioting occurs. Examples include celebrations after sports victories such as those that occurred in Montreal following a Stanley Cup win and in Vancouver following a playoff victory.

Panic **is a form of crowd behaviour that occurs when a large number of people react to a real or perceived threat with strong emotions and self-destructive behaviour.** The most

BOX 20.2 CRITICAL THINKING

THE LEGAL RESPONSE TO CIVIL DISOBEDIENCE AT CLAYOQUOT SOUND

At 5:40 A.M., on a logging road near the west coast of Vancouver Island, the sun has begun to tint the sky pink and blue. About 100 demonstrators, mostly under the age 30 and wearing jeans, sweaters, serapes, and windbreakers stand in a wide circle before a bridge that spans the Kennedy River. They chant and sing and listen as the blockade coordinator explains what is about to happen. She warns that when an official acting for the MacMillan Bloedel forestry company, which is logging in the woods nearby, arrives and reads a court injunction banning protests in Clayoquot Sound, they should remain quiet. "The courts will be tougher if there is noise and disrespect." At 6 A.M., a cavalcade of logging vehicles appears and halts several hundred metres away. Now the demonstrators form a blockade in front of the bridge, holding up signs that read "We must take care of her—the earth is our mother."

What follows is nonviolent and very Canadian. The vehicles begin moving down the dirt road. As they approach the bridge, a process server informs the protesters that they should be "off the road before this vehicle has stopped." When some stay put, eight RCMP officers approach, politely explain that the protesters are breaking the law and begin arresting them. Many refuse to be escorted away and have to be carried. "I'm like a tree—you'll have to cut me down," says one woman. She is hauled away by two Mounties. The officers work their way across the bridge and, by 6:30 a.m., the company vehicles—including an explosives truck and four huge logging rigs—rumble across and disappear into the surrounding forest. So goes the almost daily ritual.

The Clayoquot protest resulted in the largest criminal prosecution for nonviolent civil disobedience in Canadian history. Environmentalists and many lawyers have condemned the trials that followed as a government assault on peaceful dissent.

---

common type of panic, known as *entrapment*, occurs when people seek to escape from a perceived danger, fearing that few (if any) of them will be able to get away from that danger. For example, in 1994, a firebomb on a New York City subway engulfed a car in flames. Many people were knocked to the ground by the crush of people (Gonzalez, 1994). Panic sometimes occurs, however, when people attempt to gain access to an event or a location, as was the case at a concert by the British rock group the Who in Cincinnati in 1979. Seating was on a first come–first served basis, and when the doors opened, people surged into the arena and began to fall over one another. Unaware of the press of bodies in front of them, those farther back heard the band warming up and began to panic for fear that they would not get a seat. This type of panic is referred to as *exclusion panic*. When people started to realize what was happening, they experienced an overwhelming emotion of fear. Eleven people were killed in the ensuing pile-up.

Panic also can arise in response to events that people believe are beyond their control—such as a major disruption in the economy. Although instances of panic are relatively rare, they receive massive media coverage because they provoke strong feelings of fear in readers and viewers, and the number of casualties may be large.

PROTEST CROWDS Sociologists Clark McPhail and Ronald T. Wohlstein (1983) added protest crowds to the four types of crowds identified by Blumer. **Protest crowds engage in activities intended to achieve specific political goals.** Examples include sit-ins, marches, boycotts, blockades, and strikes. These sometimes take the form of *civil disobedience*—**nonviolent action that seeks to change a policy or law by refusing to comply with it.** Sometimes, acts of civil disobedience become violent, as in a confrontation between protesters and

BOX 20.2

CONTINUED

When Janet McIntyre travelled to Clayoquot Sound to see the 1500-year-old trees in one of the largest temperate rain forests left on earth, she didn't plan to get arrested. What caused her to act was seeing police take a disabled child from its mother's arms to break up a logging-road blockade. She stepped up to the blockade line and was promptly placed under arrest. At a mass trial three months later, McIntyre and other first-time offenders were convicted of criminal contempt of court, fined $500 each, and sentenced to 21 days in jail. McIntyre, an unemployed youth worker, could not look for a job during the month-long trial. The jail sentence was "enraging," but the fine was even more stressful. According to McIntyre, "Democracy is at an end if we are not allowed to conscientiously object to wrongdoings in our government and in society" (Goldberg, 1994:13). As the arrests, charges,

and criminal convictions of over 800 protesters at Clayoquot Sound demonstrate, civil disobedience has a price—fines for the first 400 arrested ranged from $250 to $3000; one protester (who was arrested twice on the same offence) received a six-month jail sentence. There is no question that preserving one of the last temperate rain forests in the world is a cause worth fighting for. However, given the severity of the criminal justice system's response, it comes as no surprise that many citizens choose not to participate in social movements. How far do you think you would be prepared to go in support of a social movement that is important to you? Would you risk arrest? detention? criminal conviction?

Adapted from Nichols, 1993; and Goldberg, 1994.

police officers; in this case, a protest crowd becomes an *acting crowd*. Such was the case during the Oka crisis, when a police officer was shot and killed and several persons on both sides of the blockade were injured. Apparently, some protests can escalate into violent confrontations even though that is not the intent of the organizers.

As you will recall, collective action often puts individuals in the position of doing things as a group that they would not do on their own. Does this mean that people's actions are produced by some type of "herd mentality"? Some analysts have answered this question affirmatively; however, sociologists typically do not agree with that assessment.

Explanations of Crowd Behaviour

What causes people to act collectively? How do they determine what types of action to take? One of the earliest theorists to provide an answer to

these questions was Gustave Le Bon, a French scholar who focused on crowd psychology in his contagion theory.

CONTAGION THEORY *Contagion theory* focuses on the social-psychological aspects of collective behaviour; it attempts to explain how moods, attitudes, and behaviour are communicated rapidly and why they are accepted by others (Turner and Killian, 1993). Gustave Le Bon (1841–1931) argued that people are more likely to engage in antisocial behaviour in a crowd because they are anonymous and feel invulnerable. Le Bon (1960/1895) suggested that a crowd takes on a life of its own that is larger than the beliefs or actions of any one person. Because of its anonymity, the crowd transforms individuals from rational beings into a single organism with a collective mind. In essence, Le Bon asserted that emotions such as fear and hate are contagious in crowds because people experience a decline in personal responsi-

This crowd is made up of thousands of Canadians from across the country who gathered in Montreal in October 1995 to demonstrate their strong emotions against Quebec separation.

bility; they will do things as a collectivity that they would never do when acting alone.

Le Bon's theory is still used to explain crowd behaviour. However, critics argue that the "collective mind" has not been documented by systematic studies.

SOCIAL UNREST AND CIRCULAR REACTION Robert E. Park was the first U.S. sociologist to investigate crowd behaviour. Park believed that Le Bon's analysis of collective behaviour lacked several important elements. Intrigued that people could break away from the powerful hold of culture and their established routines to develop a new social order, Park added the concepts of social unrest and circular reaction to contagion theory. According to Park, social unrest is transmitted by a process of *circular reaction*—the interactive communication between persons such that the discontent of one person is communicated to another who, in turn, reflects the discontent back to the first person (Park and Burgess, 1921).

CONVERGENCE THEORY *Convergence theory* focuses on the shared emotions, goals, and beliefs many people bring to crowd behaviour. Because of their individual characteristics, many people have a predisposition to participate in certain types of activities (Turner and Killian, 1993). From this perspective, people with similar attributes find a collectivity of like-minded persons with whom they can express their underlying personal tendencies. For example, the 1996 riots at the National Assembly in Quebec City on St. Jean Baptiste Day were believed to have been started by "professional agitators" who were members of the Northern Hammer Skins, a right-wing extremist organization associated with the neo-Nazi Heritage Front. Such groups are known to publish hate propaganda that glorifies rioting and violence against the government. These individuals may have been present at the St. Jean Baptiste Day celebrations with the intent of participating in violence or starting a riot. Although people may reveal their "true selves" in crowds, their behaviour is not irrational; it is highly predictable to those who share similar emotions or beliefs.

Convergence theory has been applied to a wide array of conduct, from lynch mobs to environmental movements. In social psychologist Hadley Cantril's (1941) study of a lynching in the United States, he found that the participants shared certain common attributes: they were poor and working-class whites who felt that their own status was threatened by the presence of successful African Americans. Consequently, the characteristics of these individuals made them susceptible to joining a lynch mob even if they did not know the target of the lynching.

Convergence theory adds to our understanding of certain types of collective behaviour by pointing out how individuals may have certain attributes—such as racial hatred or fear of environmental problems that directly threaten them—that initially bring them together.

Sometimes acts of civil disobedience become violent even though it is not the intent of the parties involved. During what is referred to as the Oka crisis, a police officer was shot and killed and several people on both sides of the blockade were injured.

However, this perspective does not explain how the attitudes and characteristics of individuals who take some collective action differ from those who do not.

EMERGENT NORM THEORY   Unlike contagion and convergence theories, *emergent norm theory* emphasizes the importance of social norms in shaping crowd behaviour. Drawing on the interactionist perspective, sociologists Ralph Turner and Lewis Killian (1993:12) asserted that crowds develop their own definition of a situation and establish norms for behaviour that fit the occasion:

> Some shared redefinition of right and wrong in a situation supplies the justification and coordinates the action in collective behaviour. People do what they would not otherwise have done when they panic collectively, when they riot, when they engage in civil disobedience, or when they launch terrorist campaigns, because they find social support for the view that what they are doing is the right thing to do in the situation.

According to Turner and Killian (1993:13), emergent norms occur when people define a new situation as highly unusual or see a long-standing situation in a new light.

Sociologists use the emergent norm approach to determine how individuals in a given collectivity develop an understanding of what is going on, how they construe these activities, and what

type of norms are involved. For example, in a study of audience participation, sociologist Steven E. Clayman (1993) found that members of an audience listening to a speech applaud promptly and independently but wait to coordinate their booing with other people; they do not wish to "boo" alone.

Some emergent norms are permissive—that is, they give people a shared conviction that they may disregard ordinary rules such as waiting in line, taking turns, or treating a speaker courteously. Collective activity such as mass looting may be defined (by participants) as taking what rightfully belongs to them and punishing those who have been exploitative. For example, following the Los Angeles riots of 1992, some analysts argued that Korean Americans were targets of rioters because they were viewed by Latinos and African Americans as "callous and greedy invaders" who became wealthy at the expense of members of other racial-ethnic groups (Cho, 1993). Thus, rioters who used this rationalization could view looting and burning as a means of "paying back" Korean Americans or of gaining property (such as TV sets and microwave ovens) from those who had already taken from them. Once a crowd reaches some agreement on the norms, the collectivity is supposed to adhere to them. If crowd members develop a norm that condones looting or vandalizing property, they will proceed to cheer for those who conform and ridicule those who are unwilling to abide by the collectivity's new norms.

BOX 20.3 SOCIOLOGY AND TECHNOLOGY

URBAN LEGENDS—DON'T BELIEVE EVERYTHING YOU READ

Consider the following story:

I wish to warn you about a new crime that is targeting business travellers. This ring is well organized, well funded, has very skilled personnel, and is currently in most major cities and recently very active in New Orleans.

The crime begins when a business traveller goes to a lounge for a drink at the end of a work day. A person in the bar walks up to the traveller who is sitting alone and offers to buy them a drink.

The last thing the traveller remembers before waking up in a hotel room bathtub is their body submerged to their neck in ice, sipping that drink. There is a note taped to the wall instructing them not to move and to call 911. A phone is on a small table next to the bathtub for them to call.

The business traveller calls 911 and is told this has become a quite familiar crime. The business traveller is instructed by the 911 operator to very slowly and carefully reach behind them and feel if there is a tube protruding from their lower back.

The business traveller finds the tube and answers yes. The 911 operator tells the business traveller to remain still, having already sent paramedics to help. The operator knows that both of the business traveller's kidneys have been harvested.

This is not a scam or out of a science fiction novel, it is real. It is documented and confirmable. If you travel or someone close to you travels, please be careful.

This story is often accepted as accurate because most people aren't aware of the intricate surgical procedures involved in organ transplants. The story originates in New Orleans during one Mardi Gras celebration, and there were so many calls to the police that a Web site was put up to dispel any more rumours. This rumour is an example of an *urban legend*—an unsubstantiated story, containing a sensational or unusual plot, that is widely circulated and believed. The stories in urban legends are either completely false, or if they do have some basis in fact, the events occurred in the distant past. Urban legends are believed because they call up fears or concerns that are real, because they describe embarrassing situations that we can all

Emergent norm theory points out that crowds are not irrational. Rather, new norms are developed in a rational way to fit the needs of the immediate situation. However, critics note that proponents of this perspective fail to specify exactly what constitutes a norm, how new ones emerge, and how they are so quickly disseminated and accepted by a wide variety of participants. One variation of this theory suggests that no single dominant norm is accepted by everyone in a crowd; instead, norms are specific to the various categories of actors rather than to the collectivity as a whole (Snow, Zurcher, and Peters, 1981). For example, in a study of football victory celebrations, sociologists David A. Snow, Louis A. Zurcher, and Robert Peters (1981) found that, each week, behavioural patterns were changed in the postgame revelry, with some being modified, some added, and some deleted.

Mass Behaviour

Not all collective behaviour takes place in face-to-face collectivities. **Mass behaviour is collective behaviour that takes place when people (who often are geographically separated from**

BOX 20.3

CONTINUED

imagine ourselves in, or because they relate to some aspect of modern life that we accept but find somewhat disturbing. Often, like true stories, they contain a moral.

The urban legend described above is one of the more famous urban legends making its way around the world via the Internet. The Internet has been described as the perfect environment for fostering urban legends. Through e-mail, newsgroups, and the World Wide Web, the Internet provides the medium to share stories with more people, faster than even before.

Why do we believe these outrageous stories? Paul Gilster, author of *Digital Literacy*, explains that for many Internet users any information provided via the computer has instant credibility:

There's lingering public perception ... of the computer's ferocious accuracy: computers don't make mistakes. Couple that with the general public's sense of the Internet as having been developed by the academic–scientific community, under government auspices, as a high level information source, and you do

indeed have some people accepting far too quickly, any information that appears on a computer screen simply because it does appear on a screen. (cited in Ferrell, 1997:4)

Have you received any urgent e-mail lately warning of a deadly virus, or telling you of free Nike shoes in exchange for your dirty, old runners, or free copies of Windows 98 from Bill Gates? These are all Internet urban legends. Some are so believable that they get passed around endlessly. In fact, the world of urban legends is growing so rapidly via the Internet that there are now dozens of Web sites devoted just to debunking these stories. To read about some of the more common urban legends or verify that the e-mail you received about the $250 Neiman Marcus cookie recipe is true, explore some of the following urban legend sites:

http://urbanmyths.com/
http://www.scambusters.org/
　　legends.html
http://urbanlegends.miningco.com/
　　library/blhoax.htm
http://www.snopes.com

Sources: Lanford and Lanford, 1998; and Ferrell 1997.

---

one another) respond to the same event in much the same way. For people to respond in the same way, they typically have common sources of information, and this information provokes their collective behaviour. The most frequent types of mass behaviour are rumours, gossip, mass hysteria, public opinion, fashions, and fads. Under some circumstances, social movements constitute a form of mass behaviour. However, we will examine social movements separately because they differ in some important ways from other types of dispersed collectivities.

RUMOURS AND GOSSIP *Rumours* are unsubstantiated reports on an issue or subject (Rosnow and Fine, 1976). Rumours may spread through an assembled collectivity, but they may also be transmitted among people who are dispersed geographically. Although they may initially contain a kernel of truth, as they spread, rumours may be modified to serve the interests of those repeating them. Rumours thrive when tensions are high and little authentic information is available on an issue of great concern.

People are willing to give rumours credence when no offsetting information is available. Once rumours begin to circulate, they seldom stop unless compelling information comes to the forefront that either proves the rumour false or makes it obsolete.

In industrialized societies with sophisticated technology, rumours come from a wide variety of sources and may be difficult to trace. Print media (newspapers and magazines) and electronic media (radio and television), fax machines, cellular networks, satellite systems, and the Internet facilitate the rapid movement of rumours around the globe. In addition, modern communications technology makes anonymity much easier. In a split second, messages (both factual and fictitious) can be disseminated to thousands of people through e-mail, computerized bulletin boards, and newsgroups on the Internet. For example, despite a publication ban imposed on the media regarding the 1993 trial of Karla Homolka in connection with the brutal murders of Leslie Mahaffy and Kristen French in St. Catharines, Ontario, graphic details of the crimes were available on the Internet. With no official legislation to control the dissemination of information on the World Wide Web, there is also no means to control whether information disseminated on the Net is factually correct. As *Time* magazine reported, "News on the Net may be bogus, error-ridden or just plain wrong" (quoted in Strenski, 1995:33). (See Box 20.3.)

Whereas rumours deal with an issue or a subject, *gossip* **refers to rumours about the personal lives of individuals.** Charles Horton Cooley (1962/1909) viewed gossip as something that spread among a small group of individuals who personally knew the person who was the object of the rumour. Today, this often is not the case; many people enjoy gossiping about people they have never met. Tabloid newspapers and magazines such as the *National Enquirer* and *People*, and television "news" programs that purport to provide "inside" information on the lives of celebrities are sources of contemporary gossip, much of which has not been checked for authenticity.

MASS HYSTERIA AND PANIC *Mass hysteria* is a **form of dispersed collective behaviour that occurs when a large number of people react with strong emotions and self-destructive behaviour to a real or perceived threat.** Does mass hysteria actually occur? Although the term has been widely used, many sociologists believe this behaviour is best described as panic with a dispersed audience. You will recall that panic is a form of crowd behaviour that occurs when a large number

of people react with strong emotions and self-destructive behaviour to a real or perceived threat.

An example of mass hysteria or panic with a widely dispersed audience was actor Orson Welles's 1938 Halloween evening radio dramatization of H.G. Wells's science fiction classic *The War of the Worlds*. A CBS radio dance music program was interrupted suddenly by a news bulletin informing the audience that Martians had landed in New Jersey and were in the process of conquering the earth. Some listeners became extremely frightened even though an announcer had indicated before, during, and after the performance that the broadcast was a fictitious dramatization. According to some reports, as many as 1 million of the estimated 10 million listeners believed that this astonishing event had occurred. Thousands were reported to have hidden in their storm cellars or to have gotten in their cars so that they could flee from the Martians (see Brown, 1954). In actuality, the program probably did not generate mass hysteria, but rather created panic among gullible listeners. Others switched stations to determine if the same "news" was being broadcast elsewhere. When they discovered that it was not, they merely laughed at the joke being played on listeners by CBS. In 1988, on the fiftieth anniversary of the broadcast, a Portuguese radio station rebroadcast the program and, once again, panic ensued.

FADS AND FASHIONS A *fad* **is a temporary but widely copied activity enthusiastically followed by large numbers of people.** Some examples of fads are pet rocks, Tickle Me Elmo dolls, Teenage Mutant Ninja Turtles, hula hoops, and mood rings. Can you think of others? Fads can be embraced by widely dispersed collectivities; news networks such as CNN may bring the latest fad to the attention of audiences around the world. North America has witnessed a number of fads. One especially remembered by faculty who have been on university and college campuses for several decades was the 1970s fad of "streaking"—students taking off their clothes and running naked in public. Regardless of how it may sound, this activity was not purely spontaneous. Streakers had to calculate and plan their activity so that an audience (often including members of the media) would be present. Streaking had no meaning if it was not widely publicized; for this reason, some students chose graduation ceremonies and other highly visible occasions for their streaking

Beanie Babies are one of many fads that have swept North America in recent years. Is advertising a factor in determining what will become a fad?

escapades. Other fads, such as exercise regimes and health practices, tend to be taken more seriously.

Fashion **may be defined as a currently valued style of behaviour, thinking, or appearance that is longer lasting and more widespread than a fad.** Fashion can apply to many areas, including child rearing, education, sports, clothing, music, and art. Sociologist John Lofland (1993) found that language is subject to fashion trends. He examined the terms used to express approval during different decades and found: "Neat!" in the 1950s, "Right on!" in the 1960s, "Really!" in the 1970s, "Awesome!" in the 1980s, and of course, "Cool!" in the 1990s. Most sociological research on fashion has focused on clothing, especially women's apparel (Davis, 1992). In preindustrial societies, clothing styles remained relatively unchanged. With the advent of industrialization, however, items of apparel became readily available at low prices because of mass production. Fashion became more important as people embraced the "modern" way of life and advertising encouraged "conspicuous consumption."

Georg Simmel, Thorstein Veblen, and French sociologist Pierre Bourdieu all have viewed fashion as a means of status differentiation among members of different social classes. Simmel (1904) suggested a classic "trickle down" theory (although he did not use those exact words) to describe the process by which members of the lower classes emulate the fashions of the upper class. As the fashions descend through the status hierarchy, they are watered down and "vulgarized" so that they are no longer recognizable to members of the upper class, who then regard them as unfashionable and in bad taste (Davis, 1992).

Veblen (1967/1899) asserted that fashion served mainly to institutionalize conspicuous consumption among the wealthy. Almost eighty years later, Bourdieu (1984) similarly (but most subtly) suggested that "matters of taste," including fashion sensibility, constitute a large share of the "cultural capital" possessed by members of the dominant class.

Herbert Blumer (1969) disagreed with the trickle-down approach, arguing that "collective selection" best explains fashion. Blumer suggested that people in the middle and lower classes follow fashion because it is *fashion*, not because they desire to emulate members of the elite class. Blumer thus shifts the focus on fashion to collective mood, states, and choices: "Tastes are themselves a product of experience ... They are formed in the context of social interaction, responding to the definitions and affirmation given by others. People thrown into areas of common interaction and having similar runs of experience develop common tastes" (quoted in Davis, 1992:116). Perhaps one of the best refutations of the trickle-down approach is the way in which fashion today often originates among people in the lower social classes and is mimicked by the elites. The mid-1990s so-called grunge look was a prime example of this.

PUBLIC OPINION *Public opinion* **consists of the political attitudes and beliefs communicated by ordinary citizens to decision makers** (Greenberg and Page, 1996). It is measured through polls and surveys, which utilize research methods such as interviews and questionnaires, as described in Chapter 2. Many people are not interested in all aspects of public policy but are concerned about issues they believe are relevant to themselves. Even on a single topic, public opinion will vary widely based on race/ethnicity, religion, region, social class, education level, gender, age, and so on.

Scholars who examine public opinion are interested in the extent to which the public's attitudes are communicated to decision makers and the effect (if any) that public opinion has on policy making (Turner and Killian, 1993). Some political scientists argue that public opinion has a substantial effect on decisions at all levels of governments (see Greenberg and Page, 1993); others strongly disagree. For example, Dye and Zeigler (1993:158) argue that:

> opinions flow downward from elites to masses. Public opinion rarely affects elite behaviour, but elite behaviour shapes public opinion. Elites are relatively unconstrained by public opinion for several reasons. First, few people among the masses have opinions on most policy questions confronting the nation's decision makers. Second, public opinion is very unstable; it can change in a matter of weeks in response to "news" events precipitated by elites. Third, elites do not have a clear perception of mass opinion. Most communications decision makers receive are from other elites—newsmakers, interest-group leaders, influential community leaders—not from ordinary citizens.

From this perspective, polls may create the appearance of public opinion artificially; pollsters may ask questions that those being interviewed had not even considered before the survey.

As the masses attempt to influence elites and vice versa, a two-way process occurs with the dissemination of *propaganda*—information provided **by individuals or groups that have a vested interest in furthering their own cause or damaging an opposing one.** For example, in the Clayoquot Sound protest, the B.C. government and the logging industry used slogans such as "forest renewal," "world-class logging," and "getting greener all the time" (Lam, 1995:24). On the other hand, environmental activists referred to Clayoquot Sound as "the Brazil of the North." Although many of us think of propaganda in negative terms, the information provided can be correct and can have positive effect on decision making.

In recent decades, grassroots environmental activists have attempted to influence public opinion. In a study of public opinion on environmental issues, sociologist Riley E. Dunlap (1992) found that public awareness of the seriousness of environmental problems and support for environmental protection increased dramatically between the late 1960s and the early 1990s. It is less clear, however, that public opinion translates into action by either decision makers in government and industry or individuals (for example, in their willingness to adopt a more ecologically sound lifestyle).

Initially, most grassroots environmental activists attempt to influence public opinion so that local decision makers will feel the necessity of correcting a specific problem through changes in public policy. Although activists usually do not start out seeking broader social change, they often move in that direction when they become aware of how widespread the problem is in the larger society or on a global basis. One of two types of social movements often develops at this point— one focuses on NIMBY ("not in my backyard"), while the other focuses on NIABY ("not in anyone's backyard") (Freudenberg and Steinsapir, 1992). An example of a NIMBY social movement occurred when Toronto proposed the building of a large landfill to handle the city's garbage. Residents of the municipalities identified as possible sites for the landfill protested vigorously and demonstrated the "not in my backyard" approach by counterproposing that the garbage be shipped by rail to abandoned mines in northern Ontario.

SOCIAL MOVEMENTS

Although collective behaviour is short-lived and relatively unorganized, social movements are longer lasting and more organized and have specific goals or purposes. A *social movement* is an **organized group that acts consciously to promote or resist change through collective action** (Goldberg, 1991). Because social movements have not become institutional[ized] [ar]e outside the political mainstream, the[y offer "outsi]ders" an opportunity to have their v[oices heard].

Social movements are [more likely] to develop in industrialized societi[es than in p]reindustrial societies, where accept[ance of tra]ditional beliefs and practices makes [such moveme]nts unlikely. Diversity and a lack [of consens]us (hallmarks of industrialized natio[ns] [contribu]te to demands for social change, a[nd those w]ho participate in social movements typically lack power and other resources to bring about change without engaging in collective action. Social movements are most likely to spring up when people come to see their personal troubles as public issues that cannot be solved without a collective response.

Social movements make democracy more available to excluded groups (see Greenberg and Page, 1993). Historically, people in North America have worked at the grassroots level to bring about changes even when elites sought to discourage activism (Adams, 1991). For example, in the United States the civil rights movement brought into its ranks African Americans who had never been allowed to participate in politics (see Killian, 1984). The women's suffrage movement gave voice to women who had been denied the right to vote (Rosenthal et al., 1985). Similarly, a grassroots environmental movement gave the working-class residents of Clayoquot Sound a way to "fight city hall" and a huge corporation—MacMillan Bloedel.

Most social movements rely on volunteers to carry out the work. Women traditionally have been strongly represented in both the membership and leadership of many grassroots movements (Levine, 1982; Freudenberg and Steinsapir, 1992).

The prototype of the grassroots, locally based environmental group is the homeowners' association formed in the 1970s by some of the residents of the Love Canal neighbourhood in Niagara Falls, New York, whose properties had been contaminated by toxic waste buried on it thirty years earlier by a local chemical company. Action taken by the association included protest marches, demonstrations, press conferences, political lobbying, legal injunctions, and a hostage taking. Finally, in 1980, U.S. president Jimmy Carter declared a state of emergency at Love Canal, and 700 families living close to the canal were relocated at government expense (Gibbs, 1982).

The Love Canal activists set the stage for other movements that have grappled with the kind of issues that sociologist Kai Erikson (1994) refers to as a "new species of trouble." Erikson describes the "new species" as environmental problems that "contaminate rather than merely damage ... they pollute, befoul, taint, rather than just create wreckage ... they penetrate human tissue indirectly rather than just wound the surfaces by assaults of a more straightforward kind ... And the evidence is growing that they scare human beings in new and special ways, that they elicit an uncanny fear in us" (Erikson, 1991:15). The chaos

Erikson (1994:141) describes is the result of technological disasters—"meaning everything that can go wrong when systems fail, humans err, designs prove faulty, engines misfire, and so on." Examples of such disasters include the toxic chemical pollution at Love Canal and the radiation leakage at the Three Mile Island nuclear power plant in the United States, the failure of the nuclear reactor at Chernobyl in the former Soviet Union, the near failure of a reactor in Pickering, Ontario, and the leakage of lethal gases at the pesticide plant in Bhopal, India, which is discussed in Box 20.4.

Social movements provide people who otherwise would not have the resources to enter the game of politics a chance to do so. We are most familiar with those movements that develop around public policy issues considered newsworthy by the media, ranging from abortion and women's rights to gun control and environmental justice. However, a number of other types of social movements exist as well.

Types of Social Movements

Social movements are difficult to classify; however, sociologists distinguish among movements on the basis of their *goals* and the *amount of change* they seek to produce (Aberle, 1966; Blumer, 1974). Some movements seek to change people while others seek to change society.

REFORM MOVEMENTS Grassroots environmental movements are an example of *reform movements*, which seek to improve society by changing some specific aspect of the social structure. Members of reform movements usually work within the existing system to attempt to change existing public policy so that it more adequately reflects their own value system. Examples of reform movements (in addition to the environmental movement) include labour movements, animal rights movements, antinuclear movements, Mothers Against Drunk Driving, and the disability rights movement.

Sociologist Lory Britt (1993) suggested that some movements arise specifically to alter social responses to and definitions of stigmatized attributes. From this perspective, social movements may bring about changes in societal attitudes and practices while at the same time causing changes in participants' social emotions. For example, the civil rights, gay rights, and Aboriginal rights movements helped replace shame with pride (Britt, 1993). Consider the comments of Mohawk

BOX 20.4   SOCIOLOGY IN GLOBAL PERSPECTIVE

ENVIRONMENTAL HAZARDS AS A GLOBAL CONCERN

Nothing seems to help.—Ram Singh Thakur

These four words of Thakur sum up the feelings of frustration and resignation felt by many victims of the 1984 chemical disaster at the Bhopal, India, pesticide plant of Union Carbide, a transnational corporation based in the United States. In what to date is the worst chemical disaster in history, over two thousand people died and many others were injured or blinded when the lethal gas methyl isocyanate seeped from the plant.

More than a decade later, many of the victims still had not received their promised compensation from Union Carbide, and extensive legal wrangling has occurred over whether the ailments people have developed actually were caused by the gas leak. Half a billion dollars has been set aside by the company for compensation; however, only a relatively small percentage has actually reached victims. More than $10 million has been spent in building four hospitals, and another $40 million has been set aside by Union Carbide for building another hospital for medical research and treatment of the victims. Thus far, however,

there is no known antidote for exposure to methyl isocyanate.

At the end of the twentieth century, life goes on near the plant. Many residents have replaced their wooden huts with brick buildings financed by government grants and loans. Some have been able to buy television sets and motorcycles for the first time. Others have moved to new apartments built on the edge of the city by the government. The only difference is that Union Carbide has sold its interest in the plant to Magor Industries group, an Indian corporation.

More recently, the residents of Charleston, West Virginia, became acutely aware that environmental disasters do not stop at national borders. Charleston residents were informed by a dozen of the world's largest chemical companies, which have factories in their area, that methyl isocyanate is one of a number of potentially lethal chemicals being produced in their area. The companies appeared to be moving ahead of an Environmental Protection Agency rule that would require companies that make or use hazardous chemicals to disclose

---

warrior Mike Myers, who participated in the standoff at Oka:

> For the moment, we have to endure persecution. But, in the long course of history, the face of Canada will be politically, socially, economically, and spiritually changed. Back in favour of our people. At least we will be able to leave the earth knowing that while we were here we did all that we could to set in motion a better future for our great-grandchildren. And so for me that's what Kanehsatake is about. (Obomsawin, 1993)

REVOLUTIONARY MOVEMENTS   Movements seeking to bring about a total change in society are referred to as *revolutionary movements*. These movements usually do not attempt to work within the existing system; rather, they aim to remake the system by replacing existing institutions with

new ones. Revolutionary movements range from utopian groups seeking to establish an ideal society to radical terrorists who use fear tactics to intimidate those with whom they disagree ideologically (see Alexander and Gill, 1984; Berger, 1988; Vetter and Perlstein, 1991).

Terrorism is the calculated unlawful use of physical force or threats of violence against persons or property in order to intimidate or coerce a government, organization, or individual for the purpose of gaining some political, religious, economic or social objective. Movements based on terrorism often use tactics such as bombings, kidnappings, hostage taking, hijackings, and assassinations (Vetter and Perlstein, 1991). Over the past thirty years, terrorism has become a global phenomenon. For example, the Irish Republican Army has set off dozens of bombs in England; Mafia terrorists have targeted judges, prosecutors,

BOX 20.4

CONTINUED

to the residents how much of the material they keep on hand and to indicate the potential health risks if it were to escape into the environment through a leak, spill, fire, or explosion. The residents of Charleston now are aware of what a worst-case scenario might look like in their area. However, if they harken back to a journalist's statement in the aftermath of Bhopal, they do not feel a great deal of comfort in their knowledge:

> What truly grips us in these accounts is not so much the numbers as the spectacle of suddenly vanished competence, of men utterly routed by technology, of fail-safe systems failing with a logic as inexorable as it was once—indeed, right up until that very moment—unforeseeable. And the spectacle haunts us because it seems to carry allegorical import, like the whispery omen of a hovering future. (quoted in Erikson, 1994: 155)

Disasters like the tragic accident at the Union Carbide pesticide plant in Bhopal, India, spur many people to join social movements and demand changes they hope will prevent future catastrophes.

Sources: Based on Erikson, 1994; Hazarika, 1994; Holusha, 1994; and Petersen, 1994.

and politicians in Italy; and right-wing militia members committed the 1995 bombing of the Alfred P. Murrah Federal Building, a large government office building in Oklahoma City.

Canada is not immune to terrorist activity. In the late 1960s, the Front de Libération du Québec (FLQ), a small group of extremists on the fringe of the separatist movement, carried out 200 bombings. These incidents ranged from sending mail bombs to the bombing of the Montreal Stock Exchange, in which 27 people were injured. In addition, Sikh separatists are believed to be responsible for the 1985 bombing of an Air India jet that was travelling to India from Canada. This disaster was the biggest mass killing in Canadian history. Of the 329 people who died, 278 were Canadians. Recently, many organizations have sought to prevent terrorism and ensure that

persons who participate in such conduct are punished.

RELIGIOUS MOVEMENTS   Social movements that seek to produce radical change in individuals typically are based on spiritual or supernatural belief systems. Also referred to as *expressive movements*, *religious movements* are concerned with renovating or renewing people through "inner change." Fundamentalist religious groups seeking to convert nonbelievers to their belief system are an example of this type of movement. Some religious movements are *millenarian*—that is, they forecast that "the end is near" and assert that an immediate change in behaviour is imperative. Relatively new religious movements in industrialized Western societies have included the Hare Krishna sect, the Unification Church,

These "pro-lifers" demonstrating outside of the Morgentaler clinic in Toronto are members of a resistance movement. They are seeking to prevent or undo change advocated by another social movement: the "pro-choice" movement.

Scientology, and the Divine Light Mission, all of which tend to appeal to the psychological and social needs of young people seeking meaning in life that mainstream religions have not provided for them.

ALTERNATIVE MOVEMENTS   Movements that seek limited change in some aspect of people's behaviour are referred to as *alternative movements*. For example, in the early twentieth century, the Women's Christian Temperance Union attempted to get people to abstain from drinking alcoholic beverages. Some analysts place "therapeutic social movements" such as Alcoholics Anonymous in this category; however, others do not, due to their belief that people must change their lives completely in order to overcome alcohol abuse (see Blumberg, 1977). More recently, a variety of New Age movements have directed people's behaviour by emphasizing spiritual consciousness combined with a belief in reincarnation and astrology. Such practices as vegetarianism, meditation, and holistic medicine often are included in the self-improvement category. Beginning in the 1990s, some alternative movements have included the practice of yoga (usually without its traditional background in Hindu religion) as a means by which the self can be liberated and union can be achieved with the supreme spirit or universal soul.

RESISTANCE MOVEMENTS   Also referred to as *regressive movements*, *resistance movements* seek to pre-

vent change or to undo change that already has occurred. Virtually all of the proactive social movements previously discussed face resistance from one or more reactive movements that hold opposing viewpoints and want to foster public policies that reflect their own viewpoints. Examples of resistance movements are groups organized to oppose free trade, gun control, and restrictions on smoking. Perhaps the most widely known resistance movement, however, includes many who label themselves as "pro-life" advocates—such as Operation Rescue, which seeks to close abortion clinics and make abortion illegal under all circumstances (Gray, 1993; Van Biema, 1993). Protests by some radical anti-abortion groups in Canada and the United States have grown violent, resulting in the deaths of several doctors and clinic workers, and creating fear among health professionals and patients seeking abortions (Belkin, 1994).

Causes of Social Movements

What conditions are most likely to produce social movements? Why are people drawn to these movements? Sociologists have developed several theories to answer these questions.

RELATIVE DEPRIVATION THEORY   According to relative deprivation theory, people who are satisfied

Among the precipitating factors for environmental movements around the world are technological disasters such as the 1986 meltdown and radiation leak at the Chernobyl nuclear power plant in the Ukraine. Dramatic events like these can move people to take action by reinforcing their generalized beliefs about environmental problems.

decline, such that people have *unfulfilled rising expectations*—newly raised hopes of a better lifestyle that are not fulfilled as rapidly as they expected or are not realized at all.

Although most of us can relate to relative deprivation theory, it does not fully account for why people experience social discontent but fail to join a social movement. Even though discontent and feelings of deprivation may be necessary to produce certain types of social movements, they are not sufficient to bring movements into existence. In fact, sociologist Anthony Orum (1974) found the best predictor of participation in a social movement to be prior organizational membership and involvement in other political activities.

VALUE-ADDED THEORY   The value-added theory developed by sociologist Neal Smelser (1963) is based on the assumption that certain conditions are necessary for the development of a social movement. Smelser called his theory the "value-added" approach, based on the concept (borrowed from the field of economics) that each step in the production process adds something to the finished product. For example, in the process of converting iron ore into automobiles, each stage "adds value" to the final product (Smelser, 1963). Similarly, Smelser asserted, the following six conditions are necessary and sufficient to produce social movements when they combine or interact in a particular situation.

1. *Structural conduciveness.* People must become aware of a significant problem and have the opportunity to engage in collective action. According to Smelser, movements are more likely to occur when a person, class, or agency can be singled out as the source of the problem; when channels for expressing grievances either are not available or fail; and when the aggrieved have a chance to communicate among themselves.
2. *Structural strain.* When a society or community is unable to meet people's expectations that something should be done about a problem, strain occurs in the system. The ensuing tension and conflict contributes to the development of a social movement based on people's belief that the problems would not exist if authorities had done what they were supposed to do.
3. *Spread of a generalized belief.* For a movement to develop, there must be a clear statement of

with their present condition are less likely to seek social change. Social movements arise as a response to people's perception that they have been deprived of their "fair share" (Rose, 1982). Thus, people who suffer relative deprivation are more likely to feel that change is necessary and to join a social movement in order to bring about that change. *Relative deprivation* refers to the discontent that people may feel when they compare their achievements with those of similarly situated persons and find that they have less than they think they deserve (Orum and Orum, 1968). Karl Marx captured the idea of relative deprivation in this description: "A house may be large or small; as long as the surrounding houses are small it satisfies all social demands for a dwelling. But let a palace arise beside the little house, and it shrinks from a little house to a hut" (quoted in Ladd, 1966:24). Movements based on relative deprivation are most likely to occur when an upswing in the standard of living is followed by a period of the problem and a shared view of its cause, effects, and possible solution.

4. *Precipitating factors.* To reinforce the existing generalized belief, an inciting incident or dramatic event must occur. With regard to technological disasters, some gradually emerge from a long-standing environmental threat, while others (such as the Three Mile Island nuclear power plant) involve a suddenly imposed problem.

5. *Mobilization for action.* At this stage, leaders emerge to organize others and give them a sense of direction.

6. *Social control factors.* If there is a high level of social control on the part of law enforcement officials, political leaders, and others, it becomes more difficult to develop a social movement or engage in certain types of collective action.

Value-added theory takes into account the complexity of social movements and makes it possible to use Smelser's assertions to test for the necessary and sufficient conditions that produce such movements. However, critics note that the approach is rooted in the functionalist tradition and view structural strains as disruptive to society. Smelser's theory has been described as a mere variant of convergence theory, which, you will remember, is based on the assumption that people with similar predispositions will be activated by a common event or object (Quarantelli and Hundley, 1993).

RESOURCE MOBILIZATION THEORY Smelser's value-added theory tends to underemphasize the importance of resources in social movements. By contrast, *resource mobilization theory* focuses on the process through which members of a social movement gather, trade, use, and occasionally waste resources as they seek to advance their cause (Oberschall, 1973; McCarthy and Zald, 1977). Resources include money, members' time, access to the media, and material goods such as property and equipment. Assistance from outsiders is essential for social movements. Reform movements, for example, are more likely to succeed when they gain the support of political and economic elites (Oberschall, 1973).

Resource mobilization theory is based on the belief that participants in social movements are rational people. According to sociologist Charles Tilly (1973, 1978), movements are formed and dissolved, and mobilized and deactivated, based on

rational decisions about the goals of the group, available resources, and the cost of mobilization and collective action. In other words, social movements do not develop because of widespread discontent but because organizations exist that make it possible to express discontent by concerted social action (Aminzade, 1973; Gamson, 1990). Based on an analysis of fifty-three U.S. social protest groups ranging from labour unions to peace movements between 1800 and 1945, sociologist William Gamson (1990) concluded that the organization and tactics of a movement strongly influence its chances of success. However, critics of this theory note that this theory fails to account for social changes brought about by groups with limited resources. Concept Table 20.A summarizes the three theories of social movements.

EMERGING PERSPECTIVES Scholars continue to modify resource mobilization theory and to develop new approaches for investigating the diversity of movements. Emerging perspectives based on resource mobilization theory, for example, emphasize the ideology and legitimacy of movements as well as material resources (see Zald and McCarthy, 1987; McAdam et al., 1988).

Recent theories based on an interactionist perspective focus on the importance of the symbolic presentation of a problem to both participants and the general public (see Snow et al., 1986; Capek, 1993). Research based on this perspective is often an investigation of how problems are framed and what names they are given. For example, much of the research on technological disasters points out the ambiguities inherent in naming the problems associated with chemical contamination as contrasted with those associated with natural disasters.

Examples of already existing "new social movements" include ecofeminism and environmental justice movements. Ecofeminism emerged in the late 1970s and early 1980s out of the feminist, peace, and ecology movements. Triggered by the near-meltdown at the Three Mile Island nuclear power plant in the United States, ecofeminists established World Women in Defense of the Environment. *Ecofeminism* is based on the belief that patriarchy is a root cause of environmental problems. According to ecofeminists, patriarchy not only results in the domination of women by men but also contributes to a belief that nature is to be possessed and dominated, rather than treated as a partner (see Ortner, 1974; Merchant, 1983; 1992; Mies and Shiva, 1993).

CONCEPT TABLE 20.A

SOCIAL MOVEMENT THEORIES

KEY COMPONENTS

Relative Deprivation	People who are discontent when they compare their achievements with those of others consider themselves relatively deprived and join social movements in order to get what they view is their "fair share," especially when there is an upswing in the economy followed by a decline.
Value-Added	Certain conditions are necessary for a social movement to develop: (1) structural conduciveness, such that people are aware of a problem and have the opportunity to engage in collective action; (2) structural strain, such that society or the community cannot meet people's expectations for taking care of the problem; (3) growth and spread of a generalized belief as to causes and effects of and possible solutions to the problem; (4) precipitating factors, or events that reinforce the beliefs; (5) mobilization of participants for action; and (6) social control factors, such that society comes to allow the movement to take action.
Resource Mobilization	A variety of resources (money, members, access to media, and material goods such as equipment) are necessary for a social movement; people participate only when they feel the movement has access to these resources.

Another "new social movement" focuses on environmental justice and the intersection of race and class in the environmental struggle. Sociologist Stella M. Capek (1993) investigated a contaminated landfill in the residential community Carver Terrace in Texas. Capek found that residents were able to mobilize for change and win a federal buyout and relocation by symbolically linking their issue to a larger environmental justice framework. Since the 1980s, the emerging environmental justice movement has focused on the issue of *environmental racism*—**the belief that a disproportionate number of hazardous facilities (including industries such as waste disposal/treatment and chemical plants) are placed in low-income areas populated primarily by people of colour** (Bullard and Wright, 1992).

These areas have been left out of most of the environmental cleanup that has taken place in the last two decades (Schneider, 1993). Capek concluded that linking Carver Terrace with environmental justice led to its being designated as a cleanup site.

Stages in Social Movements

Do all social movements go through similar stages? Not necessarily, but there appear to be identifiable stages in virtually all movements that succeed beyond their initial phase of development.

In the *preliminary* (or incipiency) *stage*, widespread unrest is present as people begin to become aware of a problem. At this stage, leaders emerge to agitate others into taking action. In the *coalescence stage*, people begin to organize and to publicize the problem. At this stage, some movements become formally organized at local and regional levels. In the *institutionalization* (or bureaucratization) *stage*, an organizational structure develops, and a paid staff (rather than volunteers) begin to lead the group. When the movement reaches this stage, the initial zeal and idealism of members may diminish as administrators take over management of the organization. Early grassroots supporters may become disillusioned and drop out; they also may start another movement to address some as yet unsolved aspect of the original problem. For example, some environmental organizations—such as the Sierra Club, the Canadian Nature Federation, and the National Audubon Society—that started as grassroots conservation movements currently are viewed by many people as being unresponsive to local environmental problems (Cable and Cable, 1995). As a result, new movements have arisen.

As we have seen, social movements may be an important source of social change. Throughout this text, we have examined a variety of social problems—including suicide, hate crimes, homelessness, sexual abuse, and racial discrimination—that have been the focus of one or more social movements in this century. In the process of bringing about change, most movements initially develop innovative ways to get their ideas across to decision makers and the public. Some have been successful in achieving their goals; others have not. As historian Robert A. Goldberg (1991) has suggested, gains made by social movements may be fragile, acceptance brief, and benefits minimal and easily lost. For this reason, many groups focus on preserving their gains while simultaneously fighting for those they believe they still deserve.

SOCIAL CHANGE IN THE FUTURE

In this chapter we have focused on collective behaviour and social movements as potential forces for social change in contemporary societies. A number of other factors also contribute to social change, including the physical environment, population trends, technological development, and social institutions.

The Physical Environment and Change

Changes in the physical environment often produce changes in the lives of people; in turn, people can make dramatic changes in the physical environment, over which we have only limited control. Throughout history, natural disasters have taken their toll on individuals and societies. Major natural disasters—including hurricanes, floods, and tornados—can devastate an entire population. Even comparatively "small" natural disasters change the lives of many people. As sociologist Kai Erikson (1976, 1994) has suggested, the trauma that people experience from disasters may outweigh the actual loss of physical property—memories of such events can haunt people for many years.

Some natural disasters are exacerbated by human decisions. For example, floods are viewed as natural disasters, but excessive development may contribute to a flood's severity. As office buildings, shopping malls, industrial plants, residential areas, and highways are developed, less land remains to absorb rainfall. When heavier-than-usual rains occur, flooding becomes inevitable; some regions in Canada have remained under water for days and even weeks in recent years. Clearly, humans cannot control the rain, but human decisions can worsen the consequences.

People also contribute to changes in the earth's physical condition. Through soil erosion and other degradation of grazing land, often at the hands of people, an estimated 24 billion tons of the earth's topsoil is lost annually. As people clear forests to create farmland and pastures and to acquire lumber and firewood, the earth's tree cover continues to diminish. As hundreds of millions of people drive motor vehicles, the amount of carbon dioxide in the environment continues to rise each year, possibly resulting in global warming. Scientists from a number of nations issued a report in 1990 pointing out that, if the world's economies continue to follow a "business as usual" approach, the average temperature will rise by five degrees Fahrenheit before the end of the century due to increases in carbon dioxide and other trace gases in the atmosphere (Petersen, 1994).

Just as people contribute to change in the physical environment, human activities also must be adapted to changes in the environment. For example, to decrease the risk of skin cancer we are

The twenty-first century will continue to see passionate debates over the changes people make to the earth's physical condition. Here, members of EarthFirst protest the clear-cutting of trees in hopes of saving the habitat of the endangered spotted owl, while loggers and their families insist that environmental protections threaten their livelihood.

being warned to stay out of the sunlight because of the increased penetrability of the sun's ultraviolet rays, which is a result of the accelerating depletion of the ozone layer. If this prediction is accurate, the change in the physical environment will dramatically affect those who work or spend their leisure time outside.

Population and Change

Changes in population size, distribution, and composition affect the culture and social structure of a society and change the relationships among nations. As discussed in Chapter 19, the countries experiencing the most rapid increases in popula-

tion have a less developed infrastructure to deal with those changes. In Canada, increasing urbanization has provided significant changes with respect to housing, environmental issues, employment, and the demand for social programs.

Immigration to Canada has created an increasingly multiethnic population. The changing makeup of the Canadian population has resulted in children from more diverse cultural backgrounds entering school, producing a demand for new programs and changes in curricula. An increase in the number of women in the workforce has created a need for more child care; an increase in the older population has created a need for services such as home care and placed

Billions of dollars were spent clearing the Y2K problem, which was caused by several generations of computer programmers who allowed only a two-digit field for the year. To their great surprise, the millenium required a change in all four numbers. At Pearson International Airport's air traffic control tower, steps were taken well in advance to ensure the safety of planes and passengers.

increasing demands on programs such as the Canada Pension Plan.

Technology and Change

Technology is an important force for change; in some ways, technological development has made our lives much easier. Advances in communication and transportation have made instantaneous worldwide communication possible but also have brought old belief systems and the status quo into question as never before. Today, we increasingly are moving information instead of people—and doing it almost instantly (Petersen, 1994). Advances in science and medicine have made significant changes in people's lives. The lightbulb, the automobile, the airplane, the assembly line, and the high-tech developments of the late twentieth century—all have contributed to dramatic changes in people's lives. Individuals in developed nations have benefited from the use of the technology; those in less developed nations may have paid a disproportionate share of the cost of some of these inventions and discoveries.

Scientific advances will continue to affect our lives, from the foods we eat to our reproductive capabilities. Genetically engineered plants have been developed and marketed in recent years, and biochemists are creating potatoes, rice, and cassava with the same protein value as meat (Petersen, 1994). Advances in medicine have made it possible for those formerly unable to have children to procreate; women well beyond

menopause now are able to become pregnant with the assistance of medical technology. Advances in medicine also have increased the human lifespan, especially for white and middle- or upper-class individuals in developed nations; they also have contributed to the declining death rate in developing nations, where birth rates have not yet been curbed.

Just as technology has brought about improvements in the quality and length of life for many, it has created the potential for new disasters, ranging from global warfare to localized technological disasters at toxic waste sites. As sociologist William Ogburn (1966) suggested, when a change in the material culture occurs in society, a period of cultural lag follows in which the nonmaterial (ideological) culture has not caught up with material development. The rate of technological advance at the level of material culture today is mind-boggling. Many of us can never hope to understand technological advances in the areas of artificial intelligence, holography, virtual reality, biotechnology, and robotics.

One of the ironies of twenty-first-century technology is the increased vulnerability that results from the increasing complexity of such systems. As futurist John L. Petersen (1994:70) notes, "The more complex a system becomes, the more likely the chance of system failure. There are unknown secondary effects and particularly vulnerable nodes." He also asserts that most of the world's population will not participate in the technological revolution that is occurring in developed nations (Petersen, 1994).

COLLECTIVE BEHAVIOUR AND SOCIAL CHANGE **663**

Technological disasters may result in the deaths of tens of thousands of people, especially if we think of modern warfare as a technological disaster. Nuclear energy, which can provide power for millions, also can be the source of a nuclear war that could devastate the planet. As a government study on even limited nuclear war concluded:

Natural resources would be destroyed; surviving equipment would be designed to use materials and skills that might no longer exist; and indeed some regions might be almost uninhabitable. Furthermore, pre-war patterns of behaviour would surely change, though in unpredictable ways. (U.S. Congress, 1979, quoted in Howard, 1990:320)

Even when lives are not lost in technological disasters, families are uprooted and communities cease to exist as people are relocated. In many cases, the problem is not solved; people simply are moved away from its site.

Social Institutions and Change

Many changes have occurred in the family, religion, education, the economy, and the political system in the twentieth century. As we saw in Chapter 15, the size and composition of families in Canada changed with the dramatic increase in the number of single-person and single-parent households. Changes in families have produced changes in the socialization of children, many of whom spend large amounts of time in front of a television set or in child-care facilities. Although some political and religious leaders have advocated a return to "traditional" family life, many scholars have argued that such families never worked quite as well as some might wish to believe.

Public education has changed dramatically in Canada during the twentieth century. This country was one of the first to provide "universal" education for students regardless of their ability to pay. As a result, Canada has had one of the most highly educated populations and one of the best public education systems in the world. However, some feel that the education ssytem is not meeting the needs of some students, namely, those who are failing to learn to read and write or those who are dropping out. As the nature of the economy changes, schools almost inevitably will have to change, if for no other reason than the demands from leaders in business and industry for an edu-

cated workforce that allows Canadian companies to compete in a global economic environment.

Political systems have experienced tremendous change and upheaval in some parts of the world during this century. Recent events like the fall of the Berlin Wall and the breakup of the Soviet Union, the growing power of religious fundamentalists in many parts of the world, and the passing of the white-supremacist apartheid regime in South Africa have had a dramatic impact on the world. Canada's government seems unable to determine what its priorities should be, even as the country faces serious economic and social problems. As the centralized federal government becomes less able to respond to the needs and problems of the country, federal political leaders likely will seek to decentralize services and programs by putting more of the burden onto provincial and municipal governments. Unfortunately, these governments are no better equipped to deal with problems such as poverty and homelessness, environmental pollution, and decaying infrastructures.

Although we have examined changes in the physical environment, population, technology, and social institutions separately, they all operate together in a complex relationship, sometimes producing large, unanticipated consequences. In the twenty-first century, we need new ways of conceptualizing social life at both the macro- and microlevels. The sociological imagination helps us think about how personal troubles—regardless of our race/ethnicity, class, gender, age, sexual orientation, or physical abilities and disabilities—are intertwined with the public issues of our society and the global community of which we are a part.

A FEW FINAL THOUGHTS

In this text, we have covered a substantial amount of material, examined different perspectives on a wide variety of social issues, and suggested different methods by which to deal with them. The purpose of this text is not to encourage you to take any particular point of view; rather, it is to allow you to understand different viewpoints and ways in which they may be helpful to you and to society in dealing with the issues of the twenty-first century. Possessing that understanding, we can hope that the next century will be something we can all look forward to—producing a better way of life, not only in this country but worldwide.

CHAPTER REVIEW

What is the relationship between social change and collective behaviour?

Social change is the alteration, modification, or transformation of public policy, culture, or social institutions over time; it usually is brought about by collective behaviour, which is relatively spontaneous, unstructured activity that typically violates established social norms.

When is collective behaviour likely to occur?

Collective behaviour occurs when some common influence or stimulus produces a response from a relatively large number of people.

What is a crowd?

A crowd is a relatively large number of people who are in one another's immediate vicinity. Sociologist Howard Blumer divided crowds into four categories: (1) casual crowds, (2) conventional crowds, (3) expressive crowds, and (4) acting crowds (including mobs, riots, and panic). A fifth type of crowd is a protest crowd.

What causes crowd behaviour?

Social scientists have developed several theories to explain crowd behaviour. Contagion theory asserts that a crowd takes on a life of its own as people are transformed from rational beings into part of an organism that acts on its own. A variation on this is circular reaction—people express their discontent to others, who communicate back similar feelings, resulting in a conscious effort to engage in the crowd's behaviour. Convergence theory asserts that people with similar attributes find other like-minded persons with whom they can release underlying personal tendencies. Emergent norm theory asserts that, as a crowd develops, it comes up with its own norms that replace more conventional norms of behaviour.

What are the primary forms of mass behaviour?

Mass behaviour is collective behaviour that occurs when people respond to the same event in the same way even if they are not geographically close to one another. Rumours, gossip, mass hysteria, fads and fashions, and public opinion are forms of mass behaviour.

What are the major types of social movements, and what are their goals?

A social movement is an organized group that acts consciously to promote or resist change through collective action; such movements are most likely to be formed when people see their personal troubles as public issues that cannot be resolved without a collective response. Reform movements seek to improve society by changing some specific aspect of the social structure.

Revolutionary movements seek to bring about a total change in society—sometimes by the use of terrorism. Religious movements seek to produce radical change in individuals based on spiritual or supernatural belief systems. Alternative movements seek limited change to some aspect of people's behaviour. Resistance movements seek to prevent change or to undo change that already has occurred.

What theories do sociologists use to explain the origins of social movements, and why do people join them?

Relative deprivation theory asserts that, if people are discontented when they compare their accomplishments with those of others similarly situated, they are more likely to join a social movement than are people who are relatively content with their status. Value-added theory asserts that six conditions must exist in order to produce social movements: (1) a perceived source of a problem, (2) a perception that the authorities are not resolving the problem, (3) a spread of the belief to an adequate number of people, (4) a precipitating incident, (5) mobilization of other people by leaders, and (6) a lack of social control. Resource mobilization theory asserts that successful social movements can occur only when they gain the support of political and economic elites, without whom they do not have access to the resources necessary to maintain the movement.

How do social movements develop?

Social movements typically go through three stages: (1) a preliminary stage (unrest results from a perceived problem), (2) coalescence (people begin to organize), and (3) institutionalization (an organization is developed and paid staff replaces volunteers in leadership positions).

Key Terms

acting crowds 644
casual crowds 640
civil disobedience 642
collective behaviour 640
conventional crowds 643
crowd 642
environmental racism 659
expressive crowds 643
fad 650
fashion 651
gossip 650
mass 642
mass behaviour 648
mass hysteria 650

mob 643

panic 643

propaganda 653

public opinion 651

riot 643

rumours 649

social change 638

social movement 652

terrorism 654

🕸 Internet Exercises

1. Does collective behaviour exist on the Internet? Check out the newsgroups **alt.internet.folklore** and **news.admin** to find more about some of the behaviours that may be considered "collective." Are these behaviours similar to or different from those described in this book? If they are different, would you still consider them collective behaviours?

2. We have mentioned grassroots movements and their popularity on the Internet. How could someone make effective use of the Internet to help spread the word about his or her movement?

3. How do you think the Internet will affect social change in the future? How is it affecting it now?

🕸 Net Links

The Sierra Club is a public interest organization that concentrates on influencing public policy decisions to conserve the natural environment; go to:

http://www.sierraclub.org

The Canadian Nature Federation is a national voice for the protection of nature, its diversity, and the processes that sustain it. Its site has information of environmental threats, endangered species, community education, and bird conservation; go to:

http://www.cnf.ca/index.html

Web Networks is a nonprofit organization dedicated to serving the needs of the social change community in Canada. This site contains *Web Networks Community*, a comprehensive listing of social change groups and individuals across Canada; go to:

http://www.web.net/noprofit.htm

Questions for Critical Thinking

1. What types of collective behaviour in Canada do you believe are influenced by inequalities based on race/ethnicity, class, gender, age, or disabilities? Why?

2. Which of the four explanations of crowd behaviour (contagion theory, social unrest and circular reaction, convergence theory, and emergent norm theory) do you believe best explains crowd behaviour? Why?

3. In the text, the Clayoquot Sound environmental movement was analyzed in terms of the value-added theory. How would you analyze that movement under the relative deprivation and resource mobilization theories?

4. Using the sociological imagination that you have gained in this course, what are some positive steps that you believe might be taken in Canada to make our society a better place for everyone in the twenty-first century? What types of collective behaviour and/or social movements might be required in order to take those steps?

Suggested Readings

For more in-depth information on collective behaviour and social movements, both of these texts are excellent:

Russell L. Curtis, Jr., and Benigno E. Aguirre. *Collective Behaviour and Social Movements*. Boston: Allyn & Bacon, 1993.

Ralph H. Turner and Lewis M. Killian. *Collective Behaviour* (4th ed.). Englewood Cliffs, N.J.: Prentice-Hall, 1993.

Sociological and historical perspectives on twentieth-century social movements are found in this interesting text:

Robert A. Goldberg. *Grassroots Resistance: Social Movements in Twentieth-Century America*. Belmont, Cal.: Wadsworth, 1991.

This text applies various sociological perspectives to the study of the environment:

Charles L. Harper. *Environment and Society: Social Perspectives on Environmental Issues and Problems*. Englewood Cliffs, N.J.: Prentice-Hall, 1995.

These books provide additional insights on environmental hazards and the social movements that were launched to combat them:

Sherry Cable and Charles Cable. *Environmental Problems, Grassroots Solutions: The Politics of Grassroots Environmental Conflict*. New York: St. Martin's Press, 1995.

Rachel Carson. *Silent Spring*. Boston: Houghton Mifflin, 1962.

Kai Erikson. *A New Species of Trouble: Explorations in Disaster, Trauma, and Community*. New York: Norton, 1994.

GLOSSARY

absolute poverty A level of economic deprivation in which people do not have the means to secure the most basic necessities of life.

achieved status A social position that a person assumes voluntarily as a result of personal choice, merit, or direct effort.

activity theory The proposition that people tend to shift gears in late middle age and find substitutes for previous statuses, roles, and activities.

acute illness Illness of limited duration from which the patient recovers or dies.

age stratification The inequalities, differences, segregation, or conflict between age groups.

ageism Prejudice and discrimination against people on the basis of age, particularly when they are older persons.

agents of socialization Those persons, groups, or institutions that teach people what they need to know in order to participate in society.

aggregate A collection of people who happen to be in the same place at the same time but have little else in common.

aging The physical, psychological, and social processes associated with growing older.

alienation A feeling of powerlessness and estrangement from other people and from oneself.

altruism Behaviour intended to help others and done without any expectation of personal benefit.

analysis The process through which data are organized so that comparisons can be made and conclusions drawn.

animism The belief that plants, animals, or other elements of the natural world are endowed with spirits or life forces that have an impact on events in society.

anomie Emile Durkheim's designation for a condition in which social control becomes ineffective as a result of the loss of shared values and a sense of purpose in society.

anticipatory socialization The process by which knowledge and skills are learned for future roles.

apartheid The policy of the South African government that required the separation of the races.

ascribed status A social position that is conferred on a person at birth or received involuntarily later in life.

assimilation A process by which members of subordinate racial and ethnic groups become absorbed into the dominant culture.

authoritarian leader A leader who makes all major group decisions and assigns tasks to group members.

authoritarian personality A personality type characterized by excessive conformity, submissiveness to authority, intolerance, insecurity, a high level of superstition, a propensity for stereotyping, and rigid thinking.

authoritarian system A political system controlled by rulers who deny popular participation in government.

authority Power that people accept as legitimate rather than coercive.

bilateral descent A system of tracing descent through both the mother's and father's sides of the family.

body consciousness How a person perceives and feels about his or her body; it also includes an awareness of social conditions in society that contribute to this self-knowledge.

bourgeoisie (*or* capitalist class) Karl Marx's term for the class comprised of those who own and control the means of production.

bureaucracy An organizational model characterized by a hierarchy of authority, a clear division of labour, explicit rules and procedures, and impersonality in personnel matters.

bureaucratic personality A psychological construct that describes those workers who are more concerned with following correct procedures than they are with doing the job correctly.

capitalism An economic system characterized by private ownership of the means of production, from which personal profits can be derived through market competition and without government intervention.

caste system A system of social inequality in which people's status is permanently determined at birth based on their parents' ascribed characteristics.

category A number of people who may never have met one another but who share a similar characteristic.

central city The densely populated centre of a metropolis.

charismatic authority Power legitimized on the basis of a leader's exceptional personal qualities.

chronic illness Term applied to long-term or permanent conditions that may or may not be fatal.

chronological age A person's age based on date of birth.

church A large, bureaucratically organized religious organization that tends to seek accommodation with the larger society in order to maintain some degree of control over it.

civil disobedience Nonviolent action that seeks to change a policy or law by refusing to comply with it.

class The relative location of a person or group within a larger society, based on wealth, power, prestige, or other valued resources.

class conflict Karl Marx's term for the struggle between the capitalist class and the working class.

class system A type of stratification based on the ownership and control of resources and on the kinds of work people do.

cohabitation The sharing of a household by a couple who live together without being legally married.

cohort A category of people who are born within a specified period in time or who share some specified characteristic.

collective behaviour Relatively spontaneous, unstructured activity that is engaged in by a large number of people and that typically violates dominant group norms and values.

commonsense knowledge A form of knowing that guides ordinary conduct in everyday life.

comparable worth (pay equity) The belief that wages ought to reflect the worth of a job, not the gender or race of the worker.

complete observation Research in which the investigator systematically observes a social process but does not take part in it.

conflict perspective The sociological approach that views groups in society as engaged in a continuous power struggle for control of scarce resources.

conformity The process of maintaining or changing behaviour to comply with the norms established by a society, subculture, or other group.

conglomerate A combination of businesses in different commercial areas, all of which are owned by one holding company.

content analysis The systematic examination of cultural artifacts or various forms of communication to extract thematic data and draw conclusions about social life.

contingent work Part-time or temporary work.

control group Subjects in an experiment who are not exposed to the independent variable but later are compared to subjects in the experimental group.

core nation According to world systems theory, a dominant capitalist centre characterized by high levels of industrialization and urbanization and a high degree of control over the world economy.

corporate crime An illegal act committed by corporate employees on behalf of the corporation and with its support.

corporation A large-scale organization that has legal powers (such as the ability to enter into contracts and buy and sell property) separate from its individual owner or owners.

counterculture A group that strongly rejects dominant societal values and norms and seeks alternative lifestyles.

credentialism A process of social selection in which class advantage and social status are linked to the possession of academic qualifications.

crime Behaviour that violates criminal law and is punishable with fines, jail terms, and other sanctions.

criminology The systematic study of crime and the criminal justice system, including the police, courts, and prisons.

crowd A relatively large number of people who are in one another's immediate vicinity.

crude birth rate The number of live births per 1000 people in a population in a given year.

crude death rate The number of deaths per 1000 people in a population in a given year.

cult A religious group with practices and teachings outside the dominant cultural and religious traditions of a society.

cultural capital Pierre Bourdieu's term for people's social assets, including their values, beliefs, attitudes, and competencies in language and culture.

cultural imperialism The extensive infusion of one nation's culture into other nations.

cultural lag William Ogburn's term for a gap between the technical development of a society (material culture) and its moral and legal institutions (nonmaterial culture).

cultural relativism The belief that the behaviours and customs of a society must be viewed and analyzed within the context of its own culture.

cultural transmission The process by which children and recent immigrants become acquainted with the dominant cultural beliefs, values, norms, and accumulated knowledge of a society.

cultural universals Customs and practices that occur across all societies.

culture The knowledge, language, values, customs, and material objects that are passed from person to person and from one generation to the next in a human group or society.

culture shock The disorientation that people feel when they encounter cultures radically different from their own.

deductive approach Research in which the investigator begins with a theory and then collects information and data to test the theory.

democracy A political system in which people hold the ruling power, either directly or indirectly.

democratic leader A leader who encourages group discussion and decision making through consensus building.

democratic socialism An economic and political system that combines private ownership of some of the means of production, governmental distribution of some essential goods and services, and free elections.

demographic transition The process by which some societies have moved from high birth and death rates to relatively low birth and death rates as a result of technological development.

demography A subfield of sociology that examines population size, composition, and distribution.

denomination A large, organized religion characterized by accommodation to society but frequently lacking the ability or intention to dominate society.

dependency theory The perspective that global poverty can at least partially be attributed to the fact that low-income countries have been exploited by high-income countries.

dependency theory The perspective that global poverty is at least partially attributable to the fact that low-income countries have been exploited by the high-income countries.

dependent variable A variable that is assumed to depend on or be caused by one or more other (independent) variables.

descriptive study Research that attempts to describe social reality or provide facts about some group, practice, or event.

developed nations Countries with highly industrialized economies, technologically advanced industrial, administrative, and service occupations, and relatively high levels of national and per capita (per person) income.

developing nations Countries undergoing transformation from agrarian to industrial economies.

deviance Any behaviour, belief, or condition that violates cultural norms.

differential association theory The proposition that individuals have a greater tendency to deviate from societal norms when they frequently associate with persons who are more favourable toward deviance than conformity.

diffusion The transmission of cultural items or social practices from one group or society to another.

disability A physical or health condition that stigmatizes or causes discrimination.

discovery The process of learning about something previously unknown or unrecognized.

discrimination Actions or practices of dominant group members (or their representatives) that have a harmful impact on members of a subordinate group.

disengagement theory The proposition that older persons make a normal and healthy adjustment to aging when they detach themselves from their social roles and prepare for their eventual death.

domestic partnership A household partnership in which an unmarried couple lives together in a committed, sexually intimate relationship and is granted the same benefits as those accorded to married heterosexual couples.

dramaturgical analysis The study of social interaction that compares everyday life to a theatrical presentation.

dual-earner family A family in which both partners are in the labour force.

dyad A group consisting of two members.

dysfunctions A term referring to the undesirable consequences of any element of a society.

ecclesia A religious organization that is so integrated into the dominant culture that it claims as its membership all members of a society.

economy The social institution that ensures the maintenance of society through the production, distribution, and consumption of goods and services.

education The social institution responsible for the systematic transmission of knowledge, skills, and cultural values within a formally organized structure.

egalitarian family A family structure in which both partners share power and authority equally.

ego According to Sigmund Freud, the rational, reality-oriented component of personality that imposes restrictions on the innate pleasure-seeking drives of the id.

elder abuse A term used to describe physical abuse, psychological abuse, financial exploitation, and medical abuse or neglect of people age 65 or older.

elite model A view of society in which power in political systems is concentrated in the hands of a small group of elites and the masses are relatively powerless.

emigration The movement of people out of a geographic area to take up residency elsewhere.

empirical approach Research that attempts to answer questions through a systematic collection and analysis of data.

employment equity A strategy to eliminate the effects of discrimination and to make employment opportunities available to groups who have been excluded.

environmental racism The belief that a disproportionate number of hazardous facilities are placed in low-income areas populated largely by people of colour.

epidemics Sudden significant increases in the numbers of people contracting a disease.

ethnic group A collection of people who, as a result of their shared cultural traits and a high level of interaction, regard themselves, and are regarded as a cultural unit.

ethnic pluralism   The coexistence of a variety of distinct racial and ethnic groups within one society.

ethnicity   The cultural heritage or identity of a group based on factors such as language or country of origin.

ethnocentrism   The belief in the superiority of one's own culture compared with that of others.

ethnomethodology   The study of the commonsense knowledge that people use to understand the situations in which they find themselves.

exogamy   Cultural norms prescribing that people marry outside their own social group or category.

experiment   A research method involving a carefully designed test in which the researcher studies the impact of certain variables on subjects' attitudes or behaviour.

experimental group   Subjects in an experiment who are exposed to the independent variable.

explanatory study   Research that attempts to explain cause and effect relationships and to provide information on why certain events do or do not occur.

expressive leadership   Group leadership that provides emotional support for members.

extended family   A family unit composed of relatives in addition to parents and children who live in the same household.

fad   A temporary but widely copied activity followed enthusiastically by large numbers of people.

faith   Unquestioning belief that does not require proof or scientific evidence.

false consciousness   The term used by Karl Marx to indicate that people hold beliefs they think promote their best interests when those beliefs actually are damaging to their interests.

families we choose   Social arrangements that include intimate relationships between couples and close relationships with other couples, and with other adults and children.

family   A relationship in which people live together with commitment, form an economic unit and care for any young, and consider their identity to be significantly attached to the group.

fashion   A currently valued style of behaviour, thinking, or appearance that is longer lasting and more widespread than a fad.

feminism   The belief that all people—both women and men—are equal and that they should be valued equally and have equal rights.

feminist perspective   The sociological approach that focuses on the significance of gender in understanding and explaining inequalities that exist between men and women in the household, in the paid labour force, and in the realms of politics, law, and culture.

feminization of poverty   The trend in which women are disproportionately represented among individuals living in poverty.

fertility   The actual level of childbearing for an individual or a population.

field research   The study of social life in its natural setting: observing and interviewing people where they live, work, and play.

folkways   Informal norms or everyday customs that may be violated without serious consequences within a particular culture.

formal education   Learning that takes place within an academic setting such as school, which has a planned instructional process and teachers who convey specific knowledge, skills, and thinking processes to students.

formal organization   A highly structured group formed for the purpose of completing certain tasks or achieving specific goals.

functional age   A term used to describe observable individual attributes such as physical appearance, mobility, strength, coordination, and mental capacity that are used to assign people to age categories.

functional illiteracy   The condition in which reading and writing skills are inadequate to carry out everyday activities.

functionalist perspective   The sociological approach that views society as a stable, orderly system.

Gemeinschaft (guh-MINE-shoft)   A traditional society in which social relationships are based on personal bonds of friendship and kinship and on intergenerational stability.

gender   The culturally and socially constructed meanings, beliefs, and practices associated with sex differences.

gender bias   Behaviour that shows favouritism toward one gender over the other.

gender identity   A person's perception of the self as female or male.

gender role   Attitudes, behaviour, and activities that are socially defined as appropriate for each sex and are learned through the socialization process.

gender socialization   The aspect of socialization that contains specific messages and practices concerning the nature of being female or male in a specific group or society.

generalized other   George Herbert Mead's term for the child's awareness of the demands and expectations of the society as a whole or of the child's subculture.

genocide   The deliberate, systematic killing of an entire people or nation.

gentrification   The process by which members of the middle- and upper-middle classes move into the central-city area and renovate existing properties.

Gesellschaft (guh-ZELL-shoft)   A large, urban society, in which social bonds are based on impersonal and specialized relationships, with little long-term commitment to the group or consensus on values.

global interdependence   A relationship in which the lives of all people are intertwined closely and any one nation's problems are part of a larger global problem.

goal displacement   A process that occurs in organizations when the rules become an end in themselves and organizational survival becomes more important than achievement of goals.

gossip   Rumours about the personal lives of individuals.

government   The formal organization that has the legal and political authority to regulate the relationships among members within a society and between the society and those outside its borders.

groupthink The process by which members of a cohesive group arrive at a decision that many individual members privately believe is unwise.

Hawthorne effect A term used in research to describe changes in the subjects' behaviour caused by the researcher's presence or by the subjects' awareness of being studied.

health The state of complete physical, mental, and social well-being.

health care Any activity intended to improve health.

hermaphrodite A person in whom sexual differentiation is ambiguous or incomplete.

heterosexism The belief that heterosexuality is the only valid form of sexual behaviour.

hidden curriculum The transmission of cultural values and attitudes, such as conformity and obedience to authority, through implied demands found in rules, routines, and regulations of schools.

homogamy The pattern of individuals marrying those who have similar characteristics, such as race/ethnicity, religious background, age, education, or social class.

homophobia An irrational fear and hatred of people who are not heterosexual.

hospice A homelike facility that provides supportive care for patients with terminal illnesses.

hypothesis In research studies, a tentative statement of the relationship between two or more concepts or variables.

id Sigmund Freud's term for the component of personality that includes all of the individual's basic biological drives and needs that demand immediate gratification.

ideal culture The values and standards of behaviour that people in a society profess to hold.

ideal type An abstract model that describes the recurring characteristics of some phenomenon.

illegitimate opportunity structures Circumstances that provide an opportunity for people to acquire through illegitimate activities what they cannot achieve through legitimate channels.

immigration The movement of people into a geographic area to take up residency.

independent variable A variable that is presumed to cause or determine a dependent variable.

individual discrimination Behaviour consisting of one-on-one acts by members of the dominant group that harm members of the subordinate group or their property.

inductive approach Research in which the investigator collects information or data (facts or evidence) and then generates theories from the analysis of that data.

industrialization The process by which societies are transformed from dependence on agriculture and handmade products to an emphasis on manufacturing and related industries.

infant mortality rate The number of deaths of infants under 1 year of age per 1000 live births in a given year.

infertility A medical term used to describe one year of attempting to achieve pregnancy without success.

informal education Learning that occurs in a spontaneous, unplanned way.

informal structure A term used to describe the aspect of organizational life in which participants' day-to-day activities and interactions ignore, bypass, or do not correspond with the official rules and procedures of the bureaucracy.

ingroup A group to which a person belongs and with which the person feels a sense of identity.

institutionalized racism A term used to describe the rules, procedures, and practices that directly and deliberately prevent minorities from having full and equal involvement in society.

instrumental leadership Group leadership that is goal or task oriented.

interactionist perspective The sociological approach that views society as the sum of the interactions of individuals and groups.

intergenerational mobility The social movement (upward or downward) experienced by family members from one generation to the next.

interlocking corporate directorates A term used to describe members of the board of directors of one corporation who also sit on the boards of one or more other corporations.

internal colonialism According to conflict theorists, a practice that occurs when members of a racial or ethnic group are conquered or colonized and forcibly placed under the economic and political control of the dominant group.

interview A research method using a data collection encounter in which an interviewer asks the respondent questions and records the answers.

intragenerational mobility The social movement (upward or downward) experienced by individuals within their own lifetime.

invasion The process by which a new category of people or type of land use arrives in an area previously occupied by another group or land use.

invention The process of reshaping existing cultural items into a new form.

iron law of oligarchy According to Robert Michels, the tendency of bureaucracies to be ruled by a few people.

job deskilling A reduction in the proficiency needed to perform a specific job that leads to a corresponding reduction in the wages paid for that job.

juvenile delinquency The violation of a law or the commission of a status offence by young people less than a specific age.

labelling theory The proposition that deviants are those people who have been successfully labelled as such by others.

labour union An organization of employees who join together to bargain with an employer or a group of employers over wages, benefits, and working conditions.

laissez-faire leader A leader who is only minimally involved in decision making and encourages group members to make their own decisions.

language   A system of symbols that express ideas and enable people to think and communicate with one another.

latent functions   Unintended functions that are hidden and remain unacknowledged by participants.

laws   Formal, standardized norms that have been enacted by legislatures and are enforced by formal sanctions.

liberation theology   Christian movement that advocates freedom from political subjugation within a traditional perspective and the need for social transformation to benefit the poor and downtrodden.

life chances   Max Weber's term for the extent to which persons have access to important scarce resources.

life expectancy   The average length of time a group of individuals of the same age will live.

looking-glass self   Charles Horton Cooley's term for the way in which a person's sense of self is derived from the perceptions of others.

macrolevel analysis   Sociological theory and research that focuses on whole societies, large-scale social structures, and social systems.

majority (dominant) group   An advantaged group that has superior resources and rights in a society.

manifest functions   Open, stated, and intended goals or consequences of activities within an organization or institution.

marginal job   A position that differs from the employment norms of the society in which it is located.

marriage   A legally recognized and/or socially approved arrangement between two or more individuals that carries certain rights and obligations and usually involves sexual activity.

mass   A large collection of people who share an interest in a specific idea or issue but who are not in another's immediate physical vicinity.

mass behaviour   Collective behaviour that takes place when people (who often are geographically separated from one another) respond to the same event in much the same way.

mass education   Free, public schooling for wide segments of a nation's population.

mass hysteria   A form of dispersed collective behaviour that occurs when a large number of people react with strong emotions and self-destructive behaviour to a real or perceived threat.

master status   A term used to describe the most important status a person occupies.

material culture   A component of culture that consists of the physical or tangible creations (such as clothing, shelter, and art) that members of a society make, use, and share.

matriarchal family   A family structure in which authority is held by the eldest female (usually the mother).

matriarchy   A hierarchical system of social organization in which cultural, political, and economic structures are controlled by women.

matrilineal descent   A system of tracing descent through the mother's side of the family.

means of production   Karl Marx's term for tools, land, factories, and money for investment that form the economic basis of a society.

mechanical solidarity   Emile Durkheim's term for the social cohesion that exists in preindustrial societies, in which there is a minimal division of labour and people feel united by shared values and common social bonds.

medicalization   The process whereby an object or a condition becomes defined by society as a physical or psychological illness.

medicine   An institutionalized system for the scientific diagnosis, treatment, and prevention of illness.

megalopolis   A continuous concentration of two or more cities and their suburbs that have grown until they form an interconnected urban area.

meritocracy   A hierarchy system in which all positions are rewarded based on people's ability and credentials.

metropolis   One or more central cities and their surrounding suburbs that dominate the economic and cultural life of a region.

microlevel analysis   Sociological theory and research that focuses on small groups rather than large-scale social structures.

migration   The movement of people from one geographic area to another for the purpose of changing residency.

minority (subordinate) group   A disadvantaged group whose members, because of physical or cultural characteristics, are subjected to unequal treatment by the dominant group and who regard themselves as objects of collective discrimination.

mixed economy   An economic system that combines elements of a market economy (capitalism) with elements of a command economy (socialism).

mob   A highly emotional crowd whose members engage in, or are ready to engage in, violence against a specific target, which may be a person, a category of people, or physical property.

modernization theory   A perspective that links global inequality to different levels of economic development and suggests that low-income economies can move to middle- and high-income economies by achieving self-sustained economic growth.

monarchy   A political system in which power resides in one person or family and is passed from generation to generation through lines of inheritance.

monogamy   Marriage between two partners, usually a woman and a man.

monotheism   Belief in a single, supreme being or god who is responsible for significant events such as the creation of the world.

mores   Strongly held norms with moral and ethical connotations that may not be violated without serious consequences in a particular culture.

mortality   The incidence of death in a population.

multinational corporations   Large companies that are headquartered in one country and have subsidiaries or branches in other countries.

nonmaterial culture   A component of culture that consists of the abstract or intangible human creations of society (such as attitudes, beliefs, and values) that influence people's behaviour.

nontheistic religion   A religion based on a belief in divine spiritual forces such as sacred principles of thought and conduct, rather than a god or gods.

nonverbal communication   The transfer of information between persons without the use of speech.

normative approach   The use of religion, custom, habit, tradition, or authority to answer important questions.

norms   Established rules of behaviour or standards of conduct.

nuclear family   A family made up of one or two parents and their dependent children, all of whom live apart from other relatives.

objective   Free from distorted subjective (personal or emotional) bias.

occupation   A category of jobs that involve similar activities at different work sites.

occupational (*or* white-collar) crime   A term used to describe illegal activities committed by people in the course of their employment or in dealing with their financial affairs.

oligopoly   The situation that exists when several companies overwhelmingly control an entire industry.

operational definition   An explanation of an abstract concept in terms of observable features that are specific enough to measure the variable.

organic solidarity   Emile Durkheim's term for the social cohesion that exists in industrial societies in which people perform very specialized tasks and feel united by their mutual dependence.

organized crime   A business operation that supplies illegal goods and services for profit.

outgroup   A term used to describe a group to which a person does not belong and toward which the person may feel a sense of competitiveness or hostility.

panic   A form of crowd behaviour that occurs when a large number of people react with strong emotions and self-destructive behaviour to a real or perceived threat.

participant observation   A research method in which researchers collect systematic observations while being part of the activities of the group they are studying.

patriarchal family   A family structure in which authority is held by the eldest male (usually the father).

patriarchy   A hierarchical system of social organization in which cultural, political, and economic structures are controlled by men.

patrilineal descent   A system of tracing descent through the father's side of the family.

patrilocal residence   The custom of a married couple living in the same household (or community) with the husband's family.

peer group   A group of people who are linked by common interests, equal social position, and (usually) similar age.

peripheral nations   According to world systems theory, nations that are dependent on core nations for capital, have little or no industrialization, and have uneven patterns of urbanization.

personal space   The immediate area surrounding a person that the person claims as private.

perspective   An overall approach to or viewpoint on some subject.

pink-collar occupation   Relatively low-paying, nonmanual, semiskilled positions primarily held by women.

pluralist model   An analysis of political systems that views power as widely dispersed throughout many competing interest groups.

polite racism   A term used to describe an attempt to disguise a dislike of others through behaviour that appears to be nonprejudicial.

political crime   Illegal or unethical acts involving the usurpation of power by government officials or illegal or unethical acts perpetrated against the government by outsiders seeking to make a political statement, undermine the government, or overthrow it.

political party   An organization whose purpose is to gain and hold legitimate control of government.

political socialization   The process by which people learn political attitudes, values, and behaviour.

political sociology   The area of sociology that examines the nature and consequences of power within or between societies.

politics   The social institution through which power is acquired and exercised by some people and groups.

polyandry   The concurrent marriage of one woman with two or more men.

polygamy   The concurrent marriage of a person of one sex with two or more members of the opposite sex.

polygyny   The concurrent marriage of one man with two or more women.

polytheism   Belief in more than one god.

popular culture   The component of culture that consists of activities, products, and services that are assumed to appeal primarily to members of the middle and working classes.

population   In a research study, those persons about whom we want to be able to draw conclusions.

population composition   In demography, the biological and social characteristics of a population.

population pyramid   A graphic representation of the distribution of a population by sex and age.

positivism   A belief that the world can best be understood through scientific inquiry.

postindustrial economy   An economy that is based on the provision of services rather than goods.

power   According to Max Weber, the ability of people or groups to achieve their goals despite opposition from others.

power elite   C. Wright Mills's term for a small clique composed of the top corporate, political, and military officials.

prejudice   A negative attitude based on faulty generalizations about members of selected groups.

presentation of self Erving Goffman's term for people's efforts to present themselves to others in ways that are most favourable to their own interests or image.

prestige The respect or regard with which a person or status position is regarded by others.

preventive medicine Medicine that emphasizes a healthy lifestyle in order to prevent poor health before it occurs.

primary deviance A term used to describe the initial act of rule breaking.

primary group Charles Horton Cooley's term for a small, less specialized group in which members engage in face-to-face, emotion-based interactions over an extended period of time.

primary sector production The sector of the economy that extracts raw materials and natural resources from the environment.

primary sex characteristics The genitalia used in the reproductive process.

profane A term used to describe the everyday, secular, or "worldly," aspects of life.

profession A high-status, knowledge-based occupation.

proletariat (or working class) Karl Marx's term for those who must sell their labour because they have no other means to earn a livelihood.

propaganda Information provided by individuals or groups that have a vested interest in furthering their own cause or damaging an opposing one.

public opinion The political attitudes and beliefs communicated by ordinary citizens to decision makers.

punishment An action designed to deprive a person of things of value (including liberty) because of some offence the person is thought to have committed.

questionnaire A printed research instrument containing a series of items to which subjects respond.

race A term used by many people to specify groups of people distinguished by physical characteristics such as skin colour.

racial prejudice Beliefs that certain racial groups are innately inferior to others or have a disproportionate number of negative traits.

racism An organized set of beliefs about the innate inferiority of some racial groups, combined with the power to transform these ideas into practices that can deny or exclude equality of treatment on the basis of race.

random sample A selection in which everyone in the target population has an equal chance of being chosen; in other words, choice occurs by chance.

rationality The process by which traditional methods of social organization, characterized by informality and spontaneity, gradually are replaced by efficiently administered formal rules and procedures (bureaucracy).

rational-legal authority Power legitimized by law or written rules and procedures. Also referred to as *bureaucratic authority*.

reactivity The tendency of experiment subjects to change their behaviour in response to the presence of the researcher or to the fact that they know they are being studied.

rednecked racism Overt racism that may take the form of public statements about the "inferiority" of members of a racial or ethnic group.

real culture The values and standards of behaviour that people actually follow (as contrasted with ideal culture).

reference group A term used to describe a group that strongly influences a person's behaviour and social attitudes, regardless of whether that individual is an actual member.

relative homelessness Being housed in a dwelling that fails to meet basic living standards.

relative poverty A level of economic deprivation in which people may be able to afford basic necessities but still are unable to maintain an average standard of living.

reliability In sociological research, the extent to which a study or research instrument yields consistent results.

religion A system of beliefs, symbols, and rituals, based on some sacred or supernatural realm, that guides human behaviour, gives meaning to life, and unites believers into a community.

replication In sociological research, the repetition of the investigation in substantially the same way that it originally was conducted.

representative sample A selection from a larger population that has the essential characteristics of the total population.

research method A strategy or technique for systematically conducting research.

resocialization The process of learning a new set of attitudes, values, and behaviours different from those in one's previous background and experiences.

respondent A person who provides data for analysis through an interview or questionnaire.

riot Violent crowd behaviour that is fuelled by deep-seated emotions but is not directed at one specific target.

rituals Regularly repeated and carefully prescribed forms of behaviour that symbolize a cherished value or belief.

role A set of behavioural expectations associated with a given status.

role conflict A situation in which incompatible role demands are placed on a person by two or more statuses held at the same time.

role exit A situation in which people disengage from social roles that have been central to their self-identity.

role expectation A term used to describe a group's or society's definition of the way a specific role ought to be played.

role performance How a person actually plays a role.

role strain The strain experienced by a person when incompatible demands are built into a single status that the person occupies.

role-taking The process by which a person mentally assumes the role of another person in order to understand the world from that person's point of view.

routinization of charisma A term for the process by which charismatic authority is succeeded by a bureaucracy controlled by a rationally established authority or by a combination of traditional and bureaucratic authority.

rumour An unsubstantiated report on an issue or subject.

sacred A term used to describe those aspects of life that are extraordinary or supernatural.

sample The people who are selected from the population to be studied.

sanction A reward for appropriate behaviour or a penalty for inappropriate behaviour.

Sapir-Whorf hypothesis The proposition that language shapes the view of reality of its speakers.

scapegoat A person or group that is incapable of offering resistance to the hostility or aggression of others.

second shift Arlie Hochschild's term for the domestic work that employed women perform at home after they complete their workday on the job.

secondary analysis A research method in which researchers use existing material and analyze data that originally was collected by others.

secondary deviance A term used to describe the process whereby a person who has been labelled deviant accepts that new identity and continues the deviant behaviour.

secondary group A larger, more specialized group in which the members engage in more impersonal, goal-oriented relationships for a limited period of time.

secondary sector production The sector of the economy that processes raw materials (from the primary sector) into finished goods.

secondary sex characteristics The physical traits (other than reproductive organs) that identify an individual's sex.

sect A relatively small religious group that has broken away from another religious organization to renew what it views as the original version of the faith.

secularization The process by which religious beliefs, practices, and institutions lose their significance in sectors of society and culture.

segregation A term used to describe the spatial and social separation of categories of people by race/ethnicity, class, gender, and/or religion.

self-concept The totality of our beliefs and feelings about ourselves.

self-fulfilling prophecy A situation in which a false belief or prediction produces behaviour that makes the originally false belief come true.

semiperipheral nation According to world systems theory, a nation that is more developed than peripheral nations but less developed than core nations.

senile dementia A term for diseases, such as Alzheimer's, that involve a progressive impairment of judgment and memory.

sex A term used to describe the biological and anatomical differences between females and males.

sex ratio A term used by demographers to denote the number of males for every hundred females in a given population.

sexism The subordination of one sex, usually female, based on the assumed superiority of the other sex.

sexual orientation A person's preference for emotional–sexual relationships with members of the opposite sex (heterosexuality), the same sex (homosexuality), or both sexes (bisexuality).

shared monopoly A situation in which four or fewer companies supply 50 percent or more of a particular market.

sick role Patterns of behaviour defined as appropriate for people who are sick.

significant others Those persons whose care, affection, and approval are especially desired and who are most important in the development of the self.

simple supernaturalism The belief that supernatural forces affect people's lives either positively or negatively.

slavery An extreme form of stratification in which some people are owned by others.

small group A collectivity small enough for all members to be acquainted with one another and to interact simultaneously.

social bond theory The proposition that the likelihood of deviant behaviour increases when a person's ties to society are weakened or broken.

social change The alteration, modification, or transformation of public policy, culture, or social institutions over time.

social construction of reality The process by which our perception of reality is shaped largely by the subjective meaning that we give to an experience.

social control Systematic practices developed by social groups to encourage conformity and to discourage deviance.

social Darwinism Herbert Spencer's belief that those species of animals— including human beings—best adapted to the environment survive and prosper while those poorly adapted die out.

social devaluation A situation in which a person or group is considered to have less social value than other individuals or groups.

social disorganization According to functionalist theorists, conditions that undermine the ability of traditional institutions (such as family, church, or school) to govern social behaviour.

social distance A term used to describe the extent to which people are willing to interact and establish relationships with members of racial and ethnic groups other than their own.

social facts Emile Durkheim's term for patterned ways of acting, thinking, and feeling that exist outside any one individual.

social gerontology The study of the social (nonphysical) aspects of aging.

social group A group that consists of two or more people who interact frequently and share a common identity and a feeling of interdependence.

social institution A set of organized beliefs and rules that establish how a society will attempt to meet its basic social needs.

social interaction The process by which people act toward or respond to other people.

social marginality The state of being part insider and part outsider in the social structure.

social mobility The movement of individuals or groups from one level in a stratification system to another.

social movement An organized group that acts consciously to promote or resist change through collective action.

social network A series of social relationships that link an individual to others.

social solidarity The state of having shared beliefs and values among members of a social group, along with intense and frequent interaction among group members.

social stratification The hierarchical arrangement of large social groups based on their control over basic resources.

social structure The stable pattern of social relationships that exist within a particular group or society.

socialism An economic system characterized by public ownership of the means of production, the pursuit of collective goals, and centralized decision making.

socialization The lifelong process of social interaction through which individuals acquire a self-identity and the physical, mental, and social skills needed for survival in society.

societal consensus A situation whereby the majority of members share a common set of values, beliefs, and behavioural expectations.

society A large social grouping that shares the same geographical territory and is subject to the same political authority and dominant cultural expectations.

sociobiology The systematic study of how biology affects social behaviour.

socioeconomic status (SES) A combined measure that attempts to classify individuals, families, or households in terms of indicators such as income, occupation, and education.

sociological imagination C. Wright Mills's term for the ability to see the relationship between individual experiences and the larger society.

sociology The systematic study of human society and social interaction.

sociology of family The subdiscipline of sociology that attempts to describe and explain patterns of family life and variations in family structure.

special interest groups Political coalitions comprised of individuals or groups that share a specific interest that they wish to protect or advance with the help of the political system.

split labour market A term used to describe the division of the economy into two areas of employment: a primary sector or upper tier, composed of higher-paid (usually dominant group) workers in more secure jobs; and a secondary sector or lower tier, comprised of lower-paid (often subordinate group) workers in jobs with little security and hazardous working conditions.

state The political entity that possesses a legitimate monopoly over the use of force within its territory to achieve its goals.

status A socially defined position in a group or society characterized by certain expectations, rights, and duties.

status set A term used to describe all the statuses that a person occupies at a given time.

status symbol A material sign that informs others of a person's specific status.

stereotype An overgeneralization about the appearance, behaviour, or other characteristics of all members of a group.

stigma According to Erving Goffman, any physical or social attribute or sign that so devalues a person's social identity that it disqualifies that person from full social acceptance.

strain theory The proposition that people feel strain when they are exposed to cultural goals that they are unable to obtain because they do not have access to culturally approved means of achieving those goals.

street crime All violent crime, certain property crimes, and certain morals crimes.

subculture A group of people who share a distinctive set of cultural beliefs and behaviours that differ in some significant way from that of the larger society.

subliminal racism A term used to describe an unconcious criticism of minorities.

succession The process by which a new category of people or type of land use gradually predominates in an area formerly dominated by another group or activity.

superego Sigmund Freud's term for the human conscience, consisting of the moral and ethical aspects of personality.

survey A research method in which a number of respondents are asked identical questions through a systematic questionnaire or interview.

symbol Anything that meaningfully represents something else.

systemic racism Practices that have a harmful impact on subordinate group members even though the organizationally prescribed norms or regulations guiding these actions initially were established with no intent to harm.

taboo A more that is so strong that its violation is considered to be extremely offensive and even unmentionable.

technology The knowledge, techniques, and tools that make it possible for people to transform resources into usable forms, and the knowledge and skills required to use them after they are developed.

terrorism The calculated unlawful use of physical force or threats of violence against persons or property in order to intimidate or coerce a government, organization, or individual for the purpose of gaining some political, religious, economic, or social objective.

theism A belief in a god or gods.

theory A set of logically interrelated statements that attempts to describe, explain, and (occasionally) predict social events.

total institution Erving Goffman's term for a place where people are isolated from the rest of society for a set period of time and come under the control of the officials who run the institution.

totalitarian system A political system in which the state seeks to regulate all aspects of people's public and private lives.

tracking The assignment of students to specific courses and educational programs based on their test scores, previous grades, or both.

traditional authority Power that is legitimized on the basis of long-standing custom.

transcendent idealism A belief in sacred principles of thought and conduct.

transsexual A person who believes that he or she was born with the body of the wrong sex.

transvestite A male who lives as a woman or a female who lives as a man but does not alter the genitalia.

triad A group comprised of three members.

unemployment rate The percentage of unemployed persons in the labour force actively seeking jobs.

universal health care system System in which all citizens receive medical services paid for through taxation revenues.

unstructured interview A research method involving an extended, open-ended interaction between an interviewer and an interviewee.

urban sociology A subfield of sociology that examines social relationships and political and economic structures in the city.

urbanization The process by which an increasing proportion of a population lives in cities rather than in rural areas.

validity In sociological research, the extent to which a study or research instrument accurately measures what it is supposed to measure.

value A collective idea about what is right or wrong, good or bad, and desirable or undesirable in a particular culture.

value contradiction A situation in which values conflict with one another or are mutually exclusive.

variable In sociological research, any concept with measurable traits or characteristics that can change or vary from one person, time, situation, or society to another.

visible minority Refers to an official government category of nonwhite, non-Caucasian individuals.

wage gap A term used to describe the disparity between women's and men's earnings.

wealth The value of all of a person's or family's economic assets, including income, personal property, and income-producing property.

xenocentrism The belief that the products, styles, or ideas of another society are better than those of one's own culture.

zero population growth The point at which no population increase occurs from year to year.

REFERENCES

Abella, Irving. 1974. *On Strike: Six Key Labour Struggles in Canada 1919–1949*. Toronto: James Lewis and Samuel.

———, and Harold Troper. 1982. *None Is Too Many*. Toronto: Lester and Orpen Dennys.

Aberle, David F. 1966. *The Peyote Religion Among the Navaho*. Chicago: Aldine.

Aberle, D.F., A.K. Cohen, A.K. Davis, M.J. Leng, Jr., and F.N. Sutton. 1950. "The Functional Prerequisites of Society." *Ethics*, 60(January):100–111.

Achenbaum, W. Andrew. 1978. *Old Age in the New Land: The American Experience Since 1870*. Baltimore: John Hopkins University Press.

Achilles, Rona. 1996. "Assisted Reproduction: The Social Issues." In E.D. Nelson and B.W. Robinson (eds.), *Gender in the 1990s*. Scarborough, Ont.: Nelson Canada, 346–364.

Adams, Michael. 1998. *Sex in the Snow*. Toronto: Penguin.

Adams, Owen B. 1990. "Divorce Rates in Canada." In C. McKie and K. Thompson (eds.), *Canadian Social Trends*. Toronto: Thompson Educational Publishing, 146–147.

Adams, Tom. 1991. *Grass Roots: How Ordinary People Are Changing America*. New York: Citadel Press.

Adler, Patricia A., and Peter Adler. 1994. *Constructions of Deviance: Social Power, Context, and Interaction*. Belmont, Cal.: Wadsworth.

Adorno, Theodor W., Else Frenkel-Brunswick, Daniel J. Levinson, and R. Nevitt Sanford. 1950. *The Authoritarian Personality*. New York: Harper & Row.

Agger, Ben. 1993. *Gender, Culture, and Power: Toward a Feminist Postmodern Critical Theory*. Westport, Conn.: Praeger.

Aiello, John R., and S.E. Jones. 1971. "Field Study of Proxemic Behavior of Young School Children in Three Subcultural Groups." *Journal of Personality and Social Psychology*, 19:351–356.

Albanese, Catherine L. 1992. *America, Religions and Religion*. Belmont, Cal.: Wadsworth.

Albas, Cheryl, and Daniel Albas. 1988. "Emotion Work and Emotion Rules: The Case of Exams." *Qualitative Sociology*, 11(4):259–275.

———. 1989. "Aligning Actions: The Case of Subcultural Proxemics." *Canadian Ethnic Studies*, 21(2):74–81.

Albert, Terry, and Gregory Williams. 1998. *The Economic Burden of HIV/AIDS in Canada*. Ottawa: Canadian Policy Research Networks.

Albrecht, Gary L. 1992. *The Disability Business: Rehabilitation in America*. Newbury Park, Cal.: Sage.

Alexander, Jeffrey C. 1985. *Neofunctionalism*. Beverly Hills, Cal.: Sage.

Alexander, Peter, and Roger Gill (eds.). 1984. *Utopias*. London: Duckworth.

Alireza, Marianne. 1990. "Lifting the Veil of Tradition." *Austin American-Statesman* (September 23):C1, C7.

Alix, Ernest K. 1995. *Sociology: An Everyday Life Approach*. Minneapolis: West Publishing.

Allaher, Anton. 1989. *Sociology and the Periphery: Theories and Issues*. Toronto: Garamond.

Allport, Gordon. 1958. *The Nature of Prejudice* (abridged ed.). New York: Doubleday/Anchor.

Altemeyer, Bob. 1981. *Right-Wing Authoritarianism*. Winnipeg, Manitoba: University of Manitoba Press.

———. 1988. *Enemies of Freedom: Understanding Right-Wing Authoritarianism*. San Francisco: Jossey-Bass.

Altman, Dennis. 1982. *The Homosexualization of America*. Boston: Beacon Press.

Alwin, Duane, Philip Converse, and Steven Martin. 1985. "Living Arrangements and Social Integration." *Journal of Marriage and the Family*, 47:319–334.

Amdur, Neil. 1994. "Among Female Athletes, Eating Disorders Are on Rise." *New York Times* (August 1):B9.

Aminzade, Ronald. 1973. "Revolution and Collective Political Violence: The Case of the Working Class of Marseille, France, 1830–1871." Working Paper

#86, Center for Research on Social Organization. Ann Arbor: University of Michigan, October 1973.

Amott, Teresa, and Julie Matthaei, 1991. *Race, Gender, and Work: A Multicultural Economic History of Women in the United States*. Boston: South End Press.

Anderson, Elijah. 1990. *Streetwise: Race, Class, and Change in an Urban Community*. Chicago: University of Chicago Press.

————. 1994. "The Code of the Streets." *Atlantic Monthly* (May):80–94.

Anderson, Gerald F. 1998. *Highlights of the 1998 Multinational Comparisons of Health Care*. New York: The Commonwealth Fund.

Anderson, Karen. 1996. *Sociology: A Critical Introduction*. Scarborough, Ont.: Nelson Canada.

Angier, Natalie. 1993. "'Stopit!' She Said. 'Nomore!'" *New York Times Book Review* (April 25):12.

Annesi, Nicole. 1993. "Like Mother, Like Daughter." In Leslea Newman (ed.), *Eating Our Hearts Out: Personal Accounts of Women's Relationship to Food*. Freedom, Cal.: Crossing Press, 91–95.

Antonius, Andreas, and Robin Crowley. 1986. "The Ownership Structure of the Largest Canadian Corporations, 1979." *Canadian Journal of Sociology*, 11:253–268.

Anyon, Jean. 1980. "Social Class and the Hidden Curriculum of Work." *Journal of Education*, 162:67–92.

Apple, Michael W. 1980. "Analyzing Determinations: Understanding and Evaluating the Production of Social Outcomes in Schools." *Curriculum Inquiry*, 10:55–76.

Appelbaum, R.P., and W.P. Chambliss. 1997. *Sociology* (2nd ed.). New York: Addison-Wesley Longman.

Appleton, Lynn M. 1995. "The Gender Regimes in American Cities." In Judith A. Garber and Robyne S. Turner (eds.), *Gender in Urban Research*. Thousand Oaks, Cal.: Sage, 44–59.

Archibald, Chris P. 1997. "HIV/AIDS— The New 'Great Teacher.'" *Canadian Journal of Public Health*, 88 (January/February):11–12.

Arendt, Hannah. 1973. *The Origins of Totalitarianism*. New York: Harcourt Brace Jovanovich.

Argyris, Chris. 1960. *Understanding Organizational Behavior*. Homewood, Ill.: Dorsey.

————. 1962. *Interpersonal Competence and Organizational Effectiveness*. Homewood, Ill.: Dorsey.

Armstrong Pat. 1993. "Work and Family Life: Changing Patterns." In G.N. Ramu (ed.), *Marriage and the Family in Canada Today* (2nd ed.). Scarborough, Ont.: Prentice-Hall, 127–145.

Armstrong, Pat, and Hugh Armstrong. 1983. *A Working Majority: What Women Must Do for Pay*. Ottawa: Canadian Government Publishing Centre.

————. 1994. *The Double Ghetto: Canadian Women and Their Segregated Work*. Toronto: McClelland and Stewart.

————. 1996. *Wasting Away: The Undermining of the Canadian Health Care System*. Toronto: Oxford University Press.

Armstrong, Pat, Hugh Armstrong, Jacqueline Choiniere, Eric Mykhalovsky, and Jerry P. White. 1997. *Medical Alert: New Work Organizations in Health Care*. Toronto: Garamond Press.

Arnold, Regina A. 1990. "Processes of Victimization and Criminalization of Black Women." *Social Justice*, 17(3):153–166.

Arnup, Katherine. 1995. "We Are Family: Lesbian Mothers in Canada." In E.D. Nelson and B.W. Robinson (eds.), *Gender in the 1990s*. Scarborough, Ont.: Nelson Canada, 330–345.

Asch, Solomon E. 1955. "Opinions and Social Pressure." *Scientific American*, 193(5):31–35.

————. 1956. "Studies of Independence and Conformity: A Minority of One Against a Unanimous Majority." *Psychological Monographs*, 70(9) (Whole No. 416).

Atchley, Robert C. (ed.). 1994. *Social Forces and Aging*. Belmont, Cal.: Wadsworth.

————. 1997. *Social Forces and Aging* (2nd ed.). Belmont, Cal.: Wadsworth.

Audubon. 1994. "Issues in Focus: Issues for the September 1994 UN International Conference on Population and Development." *Audubon* (July/Aug.):56–57.

Aulette, Judy Root. 1994. *Changing Families*. Belmont, CA: Wadsworth.

Austin American-Statesman. 1994. "River City Currents." (August 13):E1.

Axinn, William G., and Arland Thornton. 1992. "The Relationship Between Cohabitation and Divorce: Selectivity or Causal Influence?" *Demography*, 29(3):357–374.

Babbie, Earl. 1992. *The Practice of Social Research* (6th ed.). Belmont, Cal.: Wadsworth.

Backhouse, Constance, Roma Harris, Gillian Mitchell, and Alison Wylie. 1995. "The Chilly Climate for Faculty Women at Western: Postscript to the Backhouse Report." In the Chilly Collective (eds.), *Breaking Anonymity: The Chilly Climate for Women Faculty*. Waterloo, Ont.: Wilfrid Laurier University Press, 118–135.

Bailyn, Bernard. 1960. *Education in the Forming of American Society*. New York: Random House.

Baker, Maureen. 1996. "Introduction to Family Studies: Cultural Variations." In M. Baker (ed.), *Families: Changing Trends in Canada*. Toronto: McGraw-Hill Ryerson, 3–32.

Baker, M., and Donna Lero. 1996. "Division of Labour: Paid Work and Family Structure." In Maureen Baker (ed.), *Families: Changing Trends in Canada*. Toronto: McGraw-Hill Ryerson, 78–103.

Baker, Robert. 1993. "'Pricks' and 'Chicks': A Plea for 'Persons.'" In Anne Minas (ed.), *Gender Basics: Feminist Perspectives on Women and Men*. Belmont, Cal.: Wadsworth, 66–68.

Balakrishnan, T.R., K. Vaninadha Rao, Evelyne Lapierre-Adameyk, and Karol J. Krotki. 1987. "A Hazard Model Analysis of the Covariates of Marriage Dissolution in Canada." *Demography*, 24(3):395–406.

————, Evelyn Lapiere-Adamoyk, and Karol J. Krotk. 1993. *Family and Childbearing in Canada: A Demographic Analysis*. Toronto: University of Toronto Press.

Ballantine, Jeanne H. 1993. *The Sociology of Education: A Systematic Analysis* (3rd ed.). Englewood Cliffs, N.J.: Prentice-Hall.

————. 1997. *The Sociology of Education: A Systematic Analysis* (4th ed.). Englewood Cliffs, NJ: Prentice-Hall.

Ballara, Marcela. 1992. *Women and Literacy*. Prepared for the UN/NGO Group on Women and Development. Atlantic Highlands, NJ: Zed Books.

Baltzell, E. Digby. 1958. *Philadelphia Gentlemen: The Making of a National Upper Class*. New York: Free Press.

Bane, Mary Jo. 1986. "Household Composition and Poverty: Which Comes First?" In Sheldon H. Danziger and Daniel H. Weinberg (eds.), *Fighting Poverty: What Works and What Doesn't*.

Cambridge, Mass.: Harvard University Press.

Banner, Lois W. 1983. *American Beauty.* Chicago: University of Chicago Press.

———. 1993. *In Full Flower: Aging Women, Power, and Sexuality.* New York: Vintage.

Bardwell, Jill R., Samuel W. Cochran, and Sharon Walker. 1986. "Relationship of Parental Education, Race, and Gender to Sex Role Stereotyping in Five-Year-Old Kindergarteners." *Sex Roles,* 15:275–281.

Barer, M.L., R.G. Evans, and C. Hertzman. 1995. *Canadian Journal on Aging,* 14(2):193–224.

Baril, A., and G. Mori. 1991. "Educational Attainment of Linguistic Groups in Canada." *Canadian Social Trends* (Spring):17–18.

Barlow, Hugh D. 1987. *Introduction to Criminology* (4th ed.). Boston: Little, Brown.

Barlow, Maude and Heather-Jane Robertson. 1994. *Class Warfare: The Assault on Canadian Public Education.* Toronto: Key Porter Books.

Barnard, Chester. 1938. *The Functions of the Executive.* Cambridge, Mass.: Harvard University Press.

Baron, Dennis. 1986. *Grammar and Gender.* New Haven, Conn.: Yale University Press.

Baron, Stephen. 1994. *Street Youth and Crime: The Role of Labour Market Experiences.* Unpublished Ph.D. diss., University of Alberta.

Barrett, Stanley R. 1987. *Is God a Racist? The Right Wing in Canada.* Toronto: University of Toronto Press.

Barthel, Diane. 1988. *Putting on Appearances: Gender and Advertising.* Philadelphia: Temple University Press.

Basow, Susan A. 1992. *Gender Stereotypes and Roles* (3rd ed.). Pacific Grove, Cal.: Brooks/Cole.

Bates, Stephen. 1994. *Battleground: One Mother's Crusade, the Religious Right, and the Struggle for Our Schools.* New York: Owl/Henry Holt.

Baxter, J. 1970. "Interpersonal Spacing in Natural Settings." *Sociology,* 36(3):444–456.

Beare, Margaret. 1996a. *Criminal Conspiracies: Organized Crime in Canada.* Scarborough, Ont.: Nelson Canada.

———. 1996b. "Organized Crime and Money Laundering." In Robert A. Silverman, James J. Teevan, and Vincent F. Sacco (eds.), *Crime in*

Canadian Society (5th ed.). Toronto: Harcourt Brace and Co., 187–245.

Beaujot, Roderic. 1991. *Population Change in Canada: The Challenges of Policy Adaptation.* Toronto: McClelland and Stewart.

Beavis, Mary Ann, Nancy Klos, Tom Carter and Christian Douchant. 1997. "Literature Review: Aborginal Peoples and Homelessness." Canadian Mortgage and Housing Corporation. Available: http://www.cmhc-schl.gc.ca/Research/Homeless/F_aborig.html

Becker, Howard S. 1963. *Outsiders: Studies in the Sociology of Deviance.* New York: Free Press.

Beeghley, Leonard. 1989. *The Structure of Social Stratification in the United States* (1st ed.). Boston: Allyn & Bacon.

———. 1996. *The Structure of Social Stratification in the United States* (2nd ed.). Boston: Allyn & Bacon.

Begin, Patricia. 1994. *Child Abuse.* Ottawa: Library of Parliamentary Research.

Bell, Inge Powell. 1989. "The Double Standard: Age." In Jo Freeman, *Women: A Feminist Perspective* (4th ed.). Mountain View, Cal.: Mayfield, 236–244.

Bellan, Ruben. 1978. *Winnipeg First Century: An Economic History.* Winnipeg: Queenston House Publishing.

Belkin, Lisa. 1994. "Kill for Life?" *New York Times Magazine* (October 30):47–51, 62–64, 76, 80.

Belsky, Janet. 1990. *The Psychology of Aging: Theory, Research, and Interventions* (2nd ed.). Pacific Grove, Cal.: Brooks/Cole.

Bendix, Reinhard. 1971. "Charismatic Leadership." In Reinhard Bendix and Guenther Roth (eds.), *Scholarship and Partisanship: Essays on Max Weber.* Berkeley: University of California Press, 170–187.

Benet, Sula. 1971. "Why They Live to Be 100, or Even Older, in Abkhasia." *The New York Times Magazine* (December 26):3, 28–29, 31–34.

Benokraitis, Nijole V. 1993. *Marriages and Families: Changes, Choices, and Constraints.* Englewood Cliffs, N.J.: Prentice-Hall.

Benokraitis, Nijole V. 1997. *Marriages and Families: Cahnges, Choices, and Constraints* (2nd ed.). Englewood Cliffs, N.J.: Prentice-Hall.

Benokraitis, Nijole V., and Joe R. Feagin. 1986. *Modern Sexism: Blatant, Subtle,*

and Covert Discrimination. Englewood Cliffs, N.J.: Prentice-Hall.

Benson, Susan Porter. 1983. "The Customers Ain't God: The Work Culture of Department Store Saleswomen, 1890–1940." In Michael H. Frisch and Daniel J. Walkowitz, *Working Class America: Essays on Labor, Community, and American Society.* Urbana: University of Illinois Press, 185–211.

Bergen, Raquel Kennedy. 1993. "Interviewing Survivors of Marital Rape." In Claire M. Renzetti and Raymond M. Lee (eds.), *Researching Sensitive Topics.* Newbury Park: Sage, 97–211.

Berger, Bennett M. 1988. "Utopia and Its Environment." *Society* (January/February):37–41.

Berger, Peter. 1963. *Invitation to Sociology: A Humanistic Perspective.* New York: Anchor.

———. 1967. *The Sacred Canopy: Elements of a Sociological Theory of Religion.* New York: Doubleday.

Berger, Peter, and Hansfried Kellner. 1964. "Marriage and the Construction of Reality." *Diogenes,* 46:1–32.

Berger, Peter, and Thomas Luckmann. 1967. *The Social Construction of Reality: A Treatise in the Sociology of Knowledge.* Garden City, N.Y.: Anchor Books.

Berliner, David C., and Bruce J. Biddle. 1995. *The Manufactured Crisis: Myths, Fraud, and the Attack on America's Public Schools.* Reading, Mass.: Addison-Wesley.

Bernard, Jessie. 1982. *The Future of Marriage.* New Haven, Conn.: Yale University Press (orig. pub. 1973).

———. 1995. "The Good Provider Role: Its Rise and Fall." In E.D. Nelson and B.W. Robinson, *Gender in the 1990s.* Scarborough, Ont.: Nelson Canada, 156–171.

Bettelheim, Bruno. 1959. "Feral Children and Autistic Children." *American Journal of Sociology,* 64:455–467.

Beyerstein, Barry. 1997. "Alternative Medicine: Where's the Evidence?" *Canadian Journal of Public Health,* 88 (May/June):149–150.

Bibby, Reginald W. 1987. *Fragmented Gods: The Poverty and Potential of Religion in Canada.* Toronto: Irwin.

———. 1993. *Unknown Gods: The Ongoing Story of Religion in Canada.* Toronto: Stoddart.

———. 1995. *Mosaic Madness: The Potential and Poverty of Canadian Life.* Toronto: Stoddart.

———. 1998. "Religion." Pp. 128–152 in Robert J. Brym (ed.), *New Society: Sociology for the 21st Century,* 2nd edition. Toronto: Harcourt Brace Canada.

Bibby, Reginald, and Donald C. Posterskil. 1992. *Teen Trends: A Nation in Motion.* Toronto: Stoddart.

Binder, David. 1993. "As Ethnic Wars Multiply, U.S. Strives for a Policy." *New York Times* (February 7).

Bissoondath, Neil. 1994. *Selling Illusions: The Cult of Multiculturalism in Canada.* Toronto: Penguin.

Bittner, Egon. 1980. *Popular Interests in Psychiatric Remedies: A Study in Social Control.* New York: Ayer.

Blackford, Karen A. 1996. "Families and Parental Disability." In Marion Lynn (ed.), *Voices: Essays on Canadian Families.* Scarborough, Ont.: Nelson Canada, 161–163.

Blau, Peter M., and Marshall W. Meyer. 1987. *Bureaucracy in Modern Society* (3rd ed.). New York: Random House.

Blauner, Robert. 1964. *Alienation and Freedom.* Chicago: University of Chicago Press.

———. 1972. *Racial Oppression in America.* New York: Harper & Row.

Blendon, Robert J., Karen Donelan, Cathy Schoen, Karen Davis, and Katherine Binns. 1998. *1998 Commonwealth Fund International Health Policy Survey.* New York: The Commonwealth Fund.

Bluestone, Barry, and Bennett Harrison. 1982. *The Deindustrialization of America.* New York: Basic Books.

Blumberg, Leonard. 1977. "The Ideology of a Therapeutic Social Movement: Alcoholics Anonymous." *Journal of Studies on Alcohol,* 38:2122–2143.

Blumer, Herbert G. 1946. "Collective Behavior." In Alfred McClung Lee (ed.), *A New Outline of the Principles of Sociology.* New York: Barnes & Noble, 167–219.

———. 1969. *Symbolic Interactionism: Perspective and Method.* Englewood Cliffs, N.J.: Prentice-Hall.

———. 1974. "Social Movements." In R. Serge Denisoff (ed.), *The Sociology of Dissent.* New York: Harcourt Brace Jovanovich, 74–90.

Bogardus, Emory S. 1925. "Measuring Social Distance." *Journal of Applied Sociology,* 9:299–308.

———. 1968. "Comparing Racial Distance in Ethiopia, South Africa, and the United States." *Sociology and Social Research,* 52(2):149–156.

Bolaria, B. Singh, and Rosemary Bolaria. 1994. "Inequality and Differential Health Risks of Environmental Degradation." In Bolaria and Bolaria (eds.), *Racial Minorities, Medicine and Health.* Halifax, N.S.: Fernwood, 85–97.

Bolaria, S., and P. Li. 1988. *Racial Oppression in Canada* (2nd ed.). Toronto: Garamond.

Bolaria, S., B. Singh, and T. Wotherspoon. 1991. "Income, Inequality, Poverty, and Hunger." In B. Singh Bolarie (ed.), *Social Issues and Contradictions in Canadian Society.* Toronto: Harcourt Brace, 464–68.

Boldt, Menno. 1993. *Surviving as Indians: The Challenge of Self-Government.* Toronto: University of Toronto Press.

Bologh, Roslyn Wallach. 1992. "The Promise and Failure of Ethnomethodology from a Feminist Perspective: Comment on Rogers." *Gender & Society,* 6(2):199–206.

Bolton, M. Anne. 1995. "Who Can Let You Die?" In Mark Novak (ed.), *Aging in Society: A Canadian Reader.* Scarborough, Ont.: Nelson Canada, 385–392.

Bonacich, Edna. 1972. "A Theory of Ethnic Antagonism: The Split Labor Market." *American Sociological Review,* 37:547–549.

———. 1976. "Advanced Capitalism and Black–White Relations in the United States: A Split Labor Market Interpretation." *American Sociological Review,* 41:34–51.

Bonger, Willem. 1969. *Criminality and Economic Conditions* (abridged ed.). Bloomington: Indiana University Press (orig. pub. 1916).

Bonner, Raymond. 1994. "Ethnic War Lacerates Former Soviet Resort Area." *New York Times* (June 8):A3.

Borchorst, A., and B. Siim. 1987. "Women and the Advanced Welfare State—A New Kind of Patriarchal Power?" In A. Showstack-Sasson (ed.), *Women and the State.* London: Hutchinson, 128–157.

Bordo, Susan. 1993. *Unbearable Weight: Feminism, Western Culture, and the Body.* Berkeley: University of California Press.

Bourdieu, Pierre. 1984. *Distinction: A Social Critique of the Judgement of Taste.* Trans. Richard Nice. Cambridge, Mass.: Harvard University Press.

Bourdieu, Pierre, and Jean-Claude Passeron. 1990. *Reproduction in Education, Society and Culture.* Newbury Park, CA: Sage.

Bowles, Samuel. 1977. "Unequal Education and the Reproduction of the Social Division of Labor." In Jerome Karabel and A.H. Halsey (eds.), *Power and Ideology in Education.* New York: Oxford University Press, 137–153.

Bowles, Samuel, and Herbert Gintis. 1976. *Schooling in Capitalist America: Education and the Contradictions of Economic Life.* New York: Basic Books.

Boyd, Monica. 1992. "Gender, Visible Minority Status, and Immigrant Earnings Inequality: Reassessing an Employment Equity Premise." In V. Satzewich (ed.). *Deconstructing a Nation: Immigration, Multiculturalism, and Racism in Canada.* Halifax: Fernwood, 279–322.

———. 1995. "Gender Inequality: Economic and Political Aspects." In Robert J. Brym, *New Sociology: Sociology for the 21st Century.* Toronto: Harcourt Brace and Company.

Boyd, Monica, and Doug Norris. 1999. "The Crowded Nest: Young Adults at Home." *Canadian Social Trends* (Spring). Ottawa: Statistics Canada, 2–5.

Boyes, William, and Michael Melvin. 1994. *Economics* (2nd ed.). Boston: Houghton Mifflin.

Bozett, Frederick. 1988. "Gay Fatherhood." In Phyllis Bronstein and Carolyn Pape Cowan (eds.), *Fatherhood Today: Men's Changing Role in the Family.* New York: Wiley, 60–71.

Bradbury, Bettina. 1996. "The Social and Economic Origins of Contemporary Families." In Maureen Baker (ed.), *Families: Changing Trends in Canada.* Toronto: McGraw-Hill Ryerson, 55–103.

Brand, Pamela A., Esther D. Rothblum, and L.J. Solomon. 1992. "A Comparison of Lesbians, Gay Men, and Heterosexuals on Weight and Restrained Eating." *International Journal of Eating Disorders,* 11:253–259.

Branswell, Helen. 1998. "Canada Gets Failing Grade on Treatment of Its Poor." *Canadian Press* (December 3).

Brantingham, Paul J., Shihing Mu, and Aruind Verma. 1995. "Patterns in Canadian Crime." In Margaret A. Jackson and Curt T. Griffiths (eds.), *Canadian Criminology.* Toronto: Harcourt Brace and Company, 187–245.

Braun, Denny. 1991. *The Rich Get Richer: The Rise of Income Inequality in the United States and the World.* Chicago: Nelson-Hall.

Braverman, Harry. 1974. *Labor and Monopoly Capital*. New York: Monthly Review Press.

Briggs, Sheila. 1987. "Women and Religion." In Beth B. Hess and Myra Marx Ferree (eds.), *Analyzing Gender: A Handbook of Social Science Research*. Newbury Park, Cal.: Sage, 408–441.

Brint, Steven. 1994. *In an Age of Experts: The Changing Role of Professionals in Politics and Public Life*. Princeton, N.J.: Princeton University Press.

Brinton, Mary E. 1989. "Gender Stratification in Contemporary Urban Japan." *American Sociological Review*, 54 (August):549–564.

Britt, Lory. 1993. "From Shame to Pride: Social Movements and Individual Affect." Paper presented at the 88th Annual Meeting of the American Sociological Association, Miami (August).

Brod, Harry (ed.). 1987. *The Making of Masculinities*. Boston: Allen & Unwin.

Brooke, James. 1993a. "Attack on Brazilian Indians Is Worst Since 1910." *New York Times* (August 21):Y3.

———. 1993b. "Slavery on Rise in Brazil, As Debt Chains Workers." *New York Times* (May 23):3.

Brooks Gardner, Carol. 1989. "Analyzing Gender in Public Places: Rethinking Goffman's Vision of Everyday Life." *American Sociologist*, 20 (Spring):42–56.

Brooks-Gunn, Jeanne. 1986. "The Relationship of Maternal Beliefs About Sex Typing to Maternal and Young Children's Behavior." *Sex Roles*, 14:21–35.

Brown, Robert W. 1954. "Mass Phenomena." In Gardner Lindzey (ed.), *Handbook of Social Psychology*, vol. 2. Reading, Mass.: Addison-Wesley, 833–873.

Bruce, Steve. 1996. *Religion in the Modern World*. New York: Oxford University Press.

Brumberg, Joan Jacobs. 1988. *Fasting Girls: The Emergence of Anorexia Nervosa as a Modern Disease*. Cambridge, Mass.: Harvard University Press.

Brunet, Robin. 1993. "How to Lose Friends and Influence the Media." *Alberta Report/Western Report* (July, 19):16.

Brym, Robert, and Bonnie Fox. 1989. *From Culture to Power: The Sociology of English Canada*. Toronto: Oxford University Press.

Buchignani, Norman. 1991. "Some Comments on the Elimination of

Racism in Canada." In Ormond McKague (ed.). *Racism in Canada*. Saskatoon: Fifth House, 199–205.

Buchignani, Norman, Doreen M. Indra, and Ram Srivastiva. 1985. *Continuous Journey: A Social History of South Asians in Canada*. Toronto: McClelland and Stewart.

Buckler, Grant. 1996. "Inet '96: Canadian Minister Calls Global Internet a Priority." *Newsbytes News Network* (July 1).

Bullard, Robert B., and Beverly H. Wright. 1992. "The Quest for Environmental Equity: Mobilizing the African-American Community for Social Change." In Riley E. Dunlap and Angela G. Mertig (eds.), *American Environmentalism: The U.S. Environmental Movement, 1970–1990*. New York: Taylor & Francis, 39–49.

Bunis, William K., Angela Yancik, and David Snow. 1996. "The Cultural Patterning of Sympathy Toward the Homeless and Other Victims of Misfortune." *Social Problems* (November):387–402.

Burch, Thomas K., and Ashok K. Madan. 1987. *Union Formation and Dissolution: Results from the 1984 Family History Survey*. Ottawa: Statistics Canada.

Burgess, Ernest W. 1925. "The Growth of the City." In Robert E. Park and Ernest W. Burgess (eds.), *The City*. Chicago: University of Chicago Press, 47–62.

Burke, Mary Anne, Susan Crompton, Alison Jones, and Katherine Nessner. 1994. "Caring for Children." In Craig McKie and K. Thompson (eds.), *Canadian Social Trends*, vol. 2. Toronto: Thompson Educational Publishing Inc.

Burman, Patrick. 1998. *Killing Time, Losing Ground: Experiences of Unemployment*. Toronto: Wall and Thompson.

Burnham, Walter Dean. 1983. *Democracy in the Making: American Government and Politics*. Englewood Cliffs, N.J.: Prentice-Hall.

Burns, Tom. 1992. *Erving Goffman*. New York: Routledge.

Burr, Chandler. 1997. "The AIDS Exception: Privacy Versus Public Health." *The Atlantic Monthly* (June): 57–67.

Burros, Marian. 1994. "Despite Awareness of Risks, More in U.S. Are Getting Fat." *New York Times* (July 17):1, 8.

Burt, Martha R. 1992. *Over the Edge: The Growth of Homelessness in the 1980s*. New York: Russell Sage Foundation.

Busby, Karen. 1999. "LEAF and Pornography: Litigating on Equality and Sexual Representations." In Nick Lansen and Brian Burtch (eds.), *Law in Society: A Canadian Reader*. Toronto: Harcourt Brace.

Busch, Ruth C. 1990. *Family Systems: Comparative Study of the Family*. New York: P. Lang.

Butler, Robert N. 1975. *Why Survive? Being Old in America*. New York: Harper & Row.

———. 1987. "Future Trends." In George L. Maddox, Robert C. Atchley, and Raymond J. Corsini (eds.), *The Encyclopedia of Aging*. New York: Springer, 265–267.

Buvinic, Mayra. 1997. "Women in Poverty: A New Global Underclass." *Foreign Policy* (Fall):38–53.

Byrne, John A. 1993. "The Horizontal Corporation: It's About Managing Across, Not Up and Down." *Business Week* (December 20):76–81.

Cable, Sherry, and Charles Cable. 1995. *Environmental Problems, Grassroots Solutions: The Politics of Grassroots Environmental Conflict*. New York: St. Martin's Press.

Cable News Network. 1997. "Study: Despair Increases Health Risks in Middle-Aged Men." CNN Website: August 26, 1997. Available: www.cnn.com

Cahill, Spencer E. 1986. "Language Practices and Self Definition: The Case of Gender Identity Acquisition." *Sociological Quarterly*, 27(September):295–312.

Calliste, Agnes. 1987. "Sleeping Car Porters in Canada: An Ethically Submerged Split Labour Market." *Canadian Ethnic Studies*, 19:1–20.

———. 1993/94. "Race, Gender, and Canadian Immigration Policy: Blacks from the Caribbean, 1900–1932." *Journal of Canadian Studies*, 28(4):131–148.

Callwood, June. 1995. *Trial Without End*. Toronto: Albert A. Knopf.

Campaign 2000. 1998. *Report Card 1998*. Toronto: Campaign 2000. Available: http://www.campaign2000.ca/main_htm

Campbell, Marian L., Ruth M.F. Diamant, Drian D. Macpherson, and Judy Halladay. 1997. "The Contemporary Food Supply of Three Northern Manitoba Cree Communities." *Canadian Journal of Public Health*, 88 (March/April):105–108.

Canada Mortgage and Housing Corporation. 1998. "Survey of Canadians'Attitudes Toward Homelessness." Available: http://www.cmhc-schl.gc.ca/Research/Homeless/F_public.html

Canadian Centre for Justice Statistics, 1991–1993. *Homicide Survey*. Ottawa: Statistics Canada.

Canadian Committee on Women in Engineering. 1992. "More Than Just Numbers: Report of the Canadian Committee on Women in Engineering." Fredericton: Faculty of Engineering, University of New Brunswick.

Canadian Council on Social Development. 1996. *The Progress of Canada's Children 1996*. Ottawa: Canadian Council on Children Development.

———. 1998. *The Progress of Canada's Children: 1998 Highlights*. Ottawa: Canadian Council on Social Development.

Canadian Education Association. 1999. "Educational Trends in Canada." Available: http://www.acea.ca/trends.html

Canadian Institute of Child Health. 1994. *The Health of Canada's Children* (2nd ed.). Ottawa: Canadian Institute of Child Health.

Canadian Press. 1997. "Health-Care Bill Falls, Report Says." *Winnipeg Free Press* (August 12):A14.

Canadian Public Health Association. 1997. "Position Paper on Homelessness and Health." Available: http://www.cpha.ca/cpha.docs/homeless.eng.html

Cancian, Francesca M. 1990. "The Feminization of Love." In C. Carlson (ed.), *Perspectives on the Family: History, Class, and Feminism*. Belmont, Cal.: Wadsworth, 171–185.

Cancian, Francesca M. 1992. "Feminist Science: Methodologies That Challenge Inequality." *Gender & Society*, 6(4):623–642.

Candland, Douglas Keith. 1993. *Feral Children and Clever Animals: Reflections on Human Nature*. New York: Oxford University Press.

Canter, R.J., and S.S. Ageton. 1984. "The Epidemiology of Adolescent Sex-Role Attitudes." *Sex Roles*, 11:657–676.

Cantor, Muriel G. 1980. *Prime-Time Television: Content and Control*. Newbury Park, Cal.: Sage.

———. 1987. "Popular Culture and the Portrayal of Women: Content and Control." In Beth B. Hess and Myra Marx Ferree, *Analyzing Gender: A Handbook of Social Science Research*. Newbury Park, Cal.: Sage, 190–214.

Cantor, Muriel G., and Joel M. Cantor. 1992. *Prime-Time Television: Content and Control* (2nd ed.). Newbury Park, Cal.: Sage.

Cantril, Hadley. 1941. *The Psychology of Social Movements*. New York: Wiley.

Capek, Stella M. 1993. "The 'Environmental Justice' Frame: A Conceptual Discussion and Application." *Social Problems*, 40(1):5–23.

Carrier, James G. 1986. *Social Class and the Construction of Inequality in American Education*. New York: Greenwood.

Carroll, John B. (ed.). 1956. *Language, Thought, and Reality: Selected Writings of Benjamin Lee Whorf*. Cambridge, Mass.: MIT Press.

Carter, Stephen L. 1994. *The Culture of Disbelief: How American Law and Politics Trivializes Religious Devotion*. New York: Anchor/Doubleday.

Cashmore, E. Ellis. 1996. *Dictionary of Race and Ethnic Relations* (4th ed.). London: Routledge.

Cassidy, Margaret L., and Gary R. Lee. 1989. "The Study of Polyandry: A Critique and Synthesis." *Journal of Comparative Family Studies*, 20(1):1–11.

Castells, Manuel. 1977. *The Urban Question*. London: Edward Arnold (orig. pub. 1972 as *La Question Urbaine*, Paris).

Castles, Stephen. 1995. "Trois Siècles de Dépopulation Amerindienne." In L. Normandeau and V. Piche (eds.), *Les Populations Amerindienne et Inuit du Canada*. Montreal: Presse de l'Université de Montréal.

Cavender, Gray. 1995. "Alternative Theory: Labeling and Critical Perspectives." In Joseph F. Sheley (ed.), *Criminology: A Contemporary Handbook* (2nd ed.). Belmont, Cal.: Wadsworth, 349–371.

Celis, William, III. 1994. "Nations Envied for Schools Share Americans' Worries." *New York Times* (July 13):B4.

Central Intelligence Agency. 1998. *World Factbook*. Available: http://www.odci.gov/cia/publications/factbook/

Chafetz, Janet Saltzman. 1984. *Sex and Advantage: A Comparative, Macro-Structural Theory of Sex Stratification*. Totowa, N.J.: Rowman & Allanheld.

———. 1989. "Marital Intimacy and Conflict: The Irony of Spousal Equality." In Jo Freeman (ed.), *Women: A Feminist Perspective* (4th ed.).

Mountain View, Cal.: Mayfield, 149–156.

Chagnon, Napoleon A. 1988. "Life Histories, Blood Revenge, and Warfare in a Tribal Population." *Science* (February 26):985–992.

———. 1992. *Yanomamo: The Last Days of Eden*. New York: Harcourt Brace Jovanovich (rev. from 4th ed., *Yanomamo: The Fierce People*, by Holt, Rinehart & Winston).

Chalfant, H. Paul, Robert E. Beckley, and C. Eddie Palmer. 1994. *Religion in Contemporary Society* (3rd. ed.). Ithaca, Ill.: Peacock.

Chambliss, William J. 1973. "The Saints and the Roughnecks." *Society*, 11:24–31.

Chandler, Tertius, and Gerald Fox. 1974. *3000 Years of Urban History*. New York: Academic Press.

Chard, Jennifer. 1995. "Factfinder on Crime and the Administration of Justice in Canada." *Juristat*, 15(10). Ottawa: Canadian Centre for Justice Statistics.

Cheal, David. 1991. *Family and the State of Theory*. Toronto: University of Toronto Press.

———. 1996. "Stories About Stepfamilies." In *Growing Up in Canada*. Human Resources Development. Ottawa: Canada and Statistics Canada.

———. 1998. "Poverty and Relative Income: Family Transactions and Social Policy." *How Families Cope and Why Policymakers Need to Know*. Ottawa: Canadian Policy Research Networks, Study no. F02, 1–25.

Chen, M. and N. Zhou. 1994. "The Portrayal of Older People in Canadian Advertisements: Regular vs. Specialized Magazines." In V. Marshall and B. McPherson (eds.) *Aging: Canadian Perspectives*. Peterborough, Ont.: Broadview, 206–18.

Cheney, Peter, Robert Matas, and David Roberts. 1998. "Abuse Claims Against Churches Surge." *The Globe and Mail*. (June 9):A1, A5.

Cherlin, Andrew J. 1992. *Marriage, Divorce, Remarriage*. Cambridge, Mass.: Harvard University Press.

Chernin, Kim. 1981. *The Obsession: Reflections on the Tyranny of Slenderness*. New York: Harper & Row.

Chidley, Joe. 1995. "Spreading Hate on the Internet." *Maclean's* (May 8):3.

Childe, V. Gordon. 1957. "Civilization, Cities, and Towns." *Antiquity* (March):210–213.

Chisholm, Patricia. 1995. "Schooling for the Disabled." *Maclean's* (March 27): 52–54.

———, Sharon Doyle Driedger, Susan McClelland. 1999. "The Mother Load." *Maclean's* (March 1). Available: www.macleans.ca/pub-doc/1999/03/01

Cho, Sumi K. 1993. "Korean Americans vs. African Americans: Conflict and Construction." In Robert Gooding-Williams (ed.), *Reading Rodney King, Reading Urban Uprising.* New York: Routledge, 196–211.

Chon, Margaret. 1995. "The Truth About Asian Americans." In Russell Jacoby and Naomi Glauberman (eds.), *The Bell Curve Debate: History, Documents, Opinions.* New York: Times Books, 238–240.

Chossudovsky, Michel. 1997. *The Globalization of Poverty.* Penang: Third World Network.

Christ, Carol P. 1987. *Laughter of Aphrodite: Reflections on a Journey to the Goddess.* San Francisco: Harper & Row.

Christians, Clifford G.G., Kim B. Rotzoll, and Mark Fackler. 1987. *Media Ethics.* New York: Longman.

Chudacoff, Howard P. 1989. *How Old Are You? Age Consciousness in American Culture.* Princeton, N.J.: Princeton University Press.

Church, Elizabeth. 1996. "Kinship and Stepfamilies." In Marion Lynn (ed.), *Voices: Essays on Canadian Families.* Scarborough, Ont.: Nelson Canada, 81–106.

Church Council on Justice and Corrections. 1996. *Satisfying Justice.* Ottawa: Church Council on Justice and Corrections.

Churchill, Ward. 1994. *Indians Are Us? Culture and Genocide in Native North America.* Monroe, Maine: Common Courage Press.

"Citizen's Forum on Canada's Future: Report to the People and Government of Canada." 1991. Ottawa: Privy Council Office.

Clark, S.D. 1962. *The Developing Canadian Community.* Toronto: University of Toronto Press.

Clark, Warren. 1998. "Religious Observance: Marriage and Family." *Canadian Social Trends.* Autumn 2–7. Ottawa: Statistics Canada.

Clark, Wayne. 1997. "School Leavers Revisited." *Canadian Social Trends.* (Winter) Cat. no. 11-008-XPE. Ottawa: Statistics Canada, 10–12.

———. 1998. "Paying Off Student Loans." *Canadian Social Trends* (Winter). Cat. no. 11-008. Ottawa: Statistics Canada, 24–28.

Clarke, Harold D., Jane Jenson, Lawrence LeDuc, John H. Pammett. 1991. *Absent Mandate: The Politics of Discontent in Canada* (2nd ed.). Toronto: Gage.

Clayman, Steven E. 1993. "Booing: The Anatomy of a Disaffiliative Response." *American Sociological Review,* 58(1):110–131.

Clement, Wallace. 1975. *The Canadian Corporate Elite.* Toronto: McClelland and Stewart.

Cloward, Richard A., and Lloyd E. Ohlin. 1960. *Delinquency and Opportunity: A Theory of Delinquent Gangs.* New York: Free Press.

CNN Interactive. 1998. "Study: Children See Tendency Toward Stereotypes on TV." (May 6):1–3. Available: http://www.cnn.com/showbiz/9805/06/kids.media.ap/

Coakley, Jay J. 1994. *Sport in Society: Issues and Controversies* (5th ed.). St. Louis: Times Mirror/Mosby.

Cohen, Leah Hager. 1994. *Train Go Sorry: Inside a Deaf World.* Boston: Houghton Mifflin.

Cohen, Marjorie Griffin. 1993. "Capitalist Development, Industrialization, and Women's Work." In Graham S. Lowe and Harvey J. Krahn (eds.), *Work in Canada.* Scarborough, Ont.: Nelson Canada, 142–144.

Colby, David C., and Timothy E. Cook. 1991. "Epidemics and Agendas: The Politics of Nightly News Coverage of AIDS." *Journal of Health Politics, Policy and Law,* 16(2):215–249.

Coleman, Richard P., and Lee Rainwater. 1978. *Social Standing in America: New Dimensions of Class.* New York: Basic Books.

Coles, Gerald. 1987. *The Learning Mystique: A Critical Look at "Learning Disabilities."* New York: Pantheon.

Coles, Robert. 1979. *Work Mobility and Participation: A Comparative Study of American and Japanese Industry.* Berkeley: University of California Press.

Collier, Peter, and David Horowitz. 1987. *The Fords: An American Epic.* New York: Summit Books.

Collins, Catherine, and Douglas Frantz. 1993. *Teachers: Talking Out of School.* Boston: Little, Brown.

Collins, Patricia Hill. 1991. "The Meaning of Motherhood in Black Culture." In Robert Staples (ed.), *The Black Family: Essays and Studies.* Belmont, Cal.: Wadsworth, 169–178. Orig. pub. in *SAGE: A Scholarly Journal on Black Women,* 4(Fall 1987):3–10.

Collins, Randall. 1971. "A Conflict Theory of Sexual Stratification." *Social Problems,* 19(1):3–21.

———. 1979. *The Credential Society: An Historical Sociology of Education.* New York: Academic Press.

———. 1982. *Sociological Insight: An Introduction to Non-Obvious Sociology.* New York: Oxford University Press.

———. 1997. "An Asian Route to Capitalism: Religious Economy and the Origins of Self-Transforming Growth in Japan." *American Sociological Review,* 62: 843–865.

Collins, Sharon M. 1989. "The Marginalization of Black Executives." *Social Problems,* 36:317–331.

Coltrane, Scott. 1992. "The Micropolitics of Gender in Nonindustrial Societies." *Gender and Society* 6:86–107.

Comack, Elizabeth. 1996a. "Women and Crime." In R. Linden (ed.), *Criminology: A Canadian Perspective* (3rd ed.). Toronto: Harcourt Brace, 139–175.

———. 1996b. *Women in Trouble.* Halifax: Fernwood Publishing.

———. 2000. "Women and Crime." In R. Linden (ed.), *Criminology: A Canadian Perspective* (4th ed.). Toronto: Harcourt Brace.

Comfort, Alex. 1976. "Age Prejudice in America." *Social Policy,* 7(3):3–8.

Condry, Sandra McConnell, John C. Condry, Jr., and Lee Wolfram Pogatshnik. 1983. "Sex Differences: A Study of the Ear of the Beholder." *Sex Roles,* 9:697–704.

Connelly, Patricia M., and Martha MacDonald. 1990. *Women and the Labour Force,* Cat. no. 98-25. Ottawa: Minister of Supply and Services.

Conrad, Peter. 1975. "The Discovery of Hyperkinesis." *Social Problems* (23) Oct.:12–21.

Conrad, Peter, and Joseph W. Schneider. 1980. "The Medical Control of Deviance: Conquests and Consequences." pp. 1–53 in Julius A. Roth (ed.), *Research in the Sociology of Health Care: A Research Annual (1).* Greenwich, CT: Jai Press.

Conrad, Peter, and Joseph W. Schneider. 1992. *Deviance and Medicalization: From Badness to Sickness.* Philadelphia: Temple University Press.

Cook, Alice H., Val R. Lorwin, and Arlene Kaplan Daniels. 1992. *The Most Difficult Revolution: Women and Trade Unions*. Ithaca, N.Y.: Cornell University Press.

Cook, Ramsay. 1995. *Canada, Quebec and the Uses of Nationalism* (2nd ed.). Toronto: McClelland and Stewart.

Cook, Sherburn F. 1973. "The Significance of Disease in the Extinction of the New England Indians." *Human Biology*, 45:485–508.

Cook, Shirley J. 1969. "Canadian Narcotics Legislation, 1908–1923: A Conflict Model Interpretation." *Canadian Review of Sociology and Anthropology*, 6(1):36–46.

Cookson, Peter W., Jr., and Caroline Hodges Persell. 1985. *Preparing for Power: America's Elite Boarding Schools*. New York: Basic Books.

Cooley, Charles Horton. 1922. *Human Nature and Social Order*. New York: Scribner (orig. pub. 1902).

———. 1962. *Social Organization*. New York: Schocken Books (orig. pub. 1909).

Coontz, Stephanie. 1992. *The Way We Never Were: American Families and the Nostalgia Trap*. New York: Basic Books.

Corelli, R. 1996. "Winter of Discontent." *Maclean's* (February 5):46–48.

Corliss, Richard. 1993. "Who's Bad?" *Time* (September 6):54–56.

Corr, Charles A., Clyde M. Nabe, and Donna M. Corr. 1994. *Death and Dying, Life and Living*. Belmont, Cal.: Brooks/Cole.

Corrado, Raymond R. 1996. "Political Crime in Canada." In Rick Linden (ed.), *Criminology: A Canadian Perspective* (3rd ed.). Toronto: Harcourt Brace and Company, 459–493.

Corsaro, William A. 1992. "Interpretive Reproduction in Children's Peer Cultures." *Social Psychology Quarterly*, 55(2):160–177.

Coser, Lewis A. 1956. *The Functions of Social Conflict*. Glencoe, Ill.: Free Press.

Coughlin, Ellen K. 1993. "Author of Noted Study on Black Ghetto Life Returns with a Portrait of Homeless Women." *The Chronicle of Higher Education* (March 31):A7–A8.

Cowgill, Donald O. 1986. *Aging Around the World*. Belmont, Cal.: Wadsworth.

Cox, Harvey. 1995. "Christianity." In Arvind Sharma (ed.), *Our Religions*. San Francisco: HarperCollins, 359–423.

Craig, Steve. 1992. "Considering Men and the Media." In Steve Craig (ed.), *Men, Masculinity, and the Media*. Newbury Park, Cal.: Sage, 1–7.

Creese, Gillian, and Brenda Beagan. 1999. "Gender at Work: Seeking Solutions for Women's Equality." In Curtis, James, Edward Grabb, and Neil Guppy (eds.), *Social Inequality in Canada: Patterns, Problems, and Policies*. Scarborough: Prentice Hall, 199–221.

Crichton, Anne, Ann Robertson, Christine Gordon, and Wendy Farrant. 1997. *Health Care: A Community Concern?* Calgary: University of Calgary Press.

Crossette, Barbara. 1997. "The 21st Century Belongs to..." *New York Times* (October 19):WK3.

Cumming, Elaine C., and William E. Henry. 1961. *Growing Old: The Process of Disengagement*. New York: Basic Books.

Cunningham, J., and J.K. Antill. 1995. "Current Trends in Non-Marital Cohabitation: In Search of the POSSLQ." In J.T. Wood and S. Duck (eds.), *Under-studied Relationships: Off the Beaten Track*. Thousand Oaks, Cal.: Sage, 148–172.

Currie, Raymond, and John Stackhouse. 1996. "Religious Institutions." In L. Tepperman, J.E. Curtis, and R.J. Richardson (eds.), *Sociology*. Toronto: McGraw-Hill Ryerson, 482–519.

Curtis, James E., Edward Grabb, and Neil Guppy (eds.). 1993. *Social Inequality in Canada: Patterns, Problems, Policies* (2nd ed.). Scarborough, Ont.: Prentice Hall.

———. 1999. *Social Inequality in Canada: Patterns, Problems, Policies* (3rd ed.). Scarborough, Ont.: Prentice Hall.

Curtis, James E., and Ronald D. Lambert. 1994. "Culture." In R. Hagedorn (ed.), *Sociology* (5th ed.). Toronto: Holt Rinehart and Winston, 57–86.

Curtiss, Susan. 1977. *Genie: A Psycholinguistic Study of a Modern Day "Wild Child."* New York: Academic Press.

Cyrus, Virginia. 1993. *Experiencing Race, Class, and Gender in the United States*. Mountain View, Cal.: Mayfield.

Dagg, Alexandra, and Judy Fudge. 1992. "Sewing Pains: Homeworkers in the Garment Trade." *Our Times* (June):22–25.

Dahl, Robert A. 1961. *Who Governs?* New Haven, Conn.: Yale University Press.

Dahrendorf, Ralph. 1959. *Class and Class Conflict in an Industrial Society*. Stanford, Cal.: Stanford University Press.

Dallas Morning News. 1997. "Vagrant Children Are Clinging to Survival on Russia's Streets." *New York Times* (September 26): A40.

Daly, Kathleen, and Meda Chesney-Lind. 1988. "Feminism and Criminology." *Justice Quarterly*, 5:497–533.

Daly, Mary. 1973. *Beyond God the Father*. Boston: Beacon Press.

Darley, John M., and Thomas R. Shultz. 1990. "Moral Rules: Their Content and Acquisition." *Annual Review of Psychology*, 41:525–556.

Darnton, John. 1993. "Western Europe Is Ending Its Welcome to Immigrants." *New York Times* (August 10):A1, A6.

Das Gupta, Tania. 1995. "Families on Native Peoples, Immigrants, and People of Colour." In Nancy Mandell and Ann Duffy (eds.), *Canadian Families: Diversity, Conflict and Change*. Toronto: Harcourt Brace, 141–174.

DaVanzo, Julie, and David Adamson. 1997. "Russia's Demographic 'Crisis': How Real Is It?" *Rand Issue Paper*. Rand Corporation: Center for Russian and Eurasian Studies. Available at: http//www.rand.org/publications/IP/IP162

Davies, Scott. 1999. "Stubborn Disparities: Explaining Class Irregularities in Schooling." In Curtis, James, Edward Grabb, and Neil Guppy (eds.), *Social Inequality in Canada: Patterns, Problems and Policies*. Scarborough, Ont.: Prentice Hall, 138–150.

Davis, Fred. 1992. *Fashion, Culture, and Identity*. Chicago: University of Chicago Press.

Davis, Kingsley. 1940. "Extreme Social Isolation of a Child." *American Journal of Sociology*, 45(4):554–565.

———. 1949. *Human Society*. New York: Macmillan.

Davis, Kingsley, and Judith Blake. 1956. "Social Structure and Fertility: An Analytical Framework." *Economic Development and Cultural Change*, 4(April):211–235.

Davis, Kingsley, and Wilbert Moore. 1945. "Some Principles of Stratification." *American Sociological Review*, 7 (April): 242–249.

Dawson, Rod. n.d. "A Personal Odyssey." *Maturity* (January/February):26–27.

Dean, L.M., F.N. Willis, and J.N. la Rocco. 1976. "Invasion of Personal Space as a Function of Age, Sex and Race." *Psychological Reports*, 38(3) (pt. 1):959–965.

Deaux, Kay, and Mary E. Kite. 1987. "Thinking About Gender." In Beth B. Hess and Myra Marx Ferree (eds.), *Analyzing Gender: A Handbook of Social Science Research*. Newbury Park, Cal.: Sage, 92–117.

Deegan, Mary Jo. 1988. *Jane Addams and the Men of the Chicago School, 1892–1918*. New Brunswick, N.J.: Transaction.

DeKeseredy, Walter S. 1996. "Patterns of Family Violence." In Maureen Baker (ed.), *Families: Changing Trends in Canada*. Whitby, Ont.: McGraw-Hill Ryerson, 249–272.

———, and Katherine Kelly. 1995. "Sexual Abuse in Canadian University and College Dating Relationships: The Contribution of Male Peer Support." *Journal of Family Violence*, 10(1):41–53.

———, and Ronald Hinch. 1991. *Woman Abuse: Sociological Perspectives*. Toronto: Thompson Educational Publishing.

DeMause, Lloyd. (ed.) 1974. *The History of Childhood*. New York: Psychohistory Press.

Denton, Margaret A., and Alfred A. Hunter. 1995. "What Is Sociology?" In Lorne Tepperman and R.J. Richardson (eds.). *The Social World* (3rd ed.). Toronto: McGraw-Hill Ryerson, 1–32.

Denzin, Norman K. 1989. *The Research Act* (3rd ed.). Englewood Cliffs, N.J.: Prentice-Hall.

Department of Justice. 1994. "Minister of Justice Introduces Sentencing Reform Bill." Ottawa: Press Release (June 13).

Derber, Charles. 1983. *The Pursuit of Attention: Power and Individualism in Everyday Life*. New York: Oxford University Press.

Desai, Sabra. 1994. "But You Are Different: In Conversation with a Friend." In Carl E. James and Andrew Shadd (eds.), *Talking About a Difference*. Toronto: Between the Lines, 191–198.

Ditchburn, Jennifer. 1988. "Info-Poor Nations Lose Out, Group Told." *The Globe and Mail*. (August 19):A7.

DiMaggio, Paul. 1987. "Classification in Art." *American Sociological Review*, 52:440–455.

DiMaggio, Paul, and Michael Useem. 1978. "Social Class and Arts Consumption: The Origins and Consequences of Class Differences in Exposure to the Arts in America." *Theory and Society*, 5(2):141–161.

Dollard, John, Neal E. Miller, Leonard W. Doob, O.H. Mowrer, and Robert R. Sears. 1939. *Frustration and Aggression*.

New Haven, Conn.: Yale University Press.

Domhoff, G. William. 1970. *The Higher Circles*. New York: Random House.

———. 1978. *The Powers That Be: Processes of Ruling Class Domination in America*. New York: Random House.

———. 1983. *Who Rules America Now? A View for the '80s*. Englewood Cliffs, N.J.: Prentice-Hall.

———. 1990. *The Power Elite and the State: How Policy Is Made in America*. New York: Aldine De Gruyter.

Doob, Anthony, and Julian V. Roberts. 1983. *An Analysis of the Public's View of Sentencing*. Ottawa: Department of Justice Canada.

Doyle Driedger, Sharon. 1998. "Divorce." *Maclean's* (April 20):39–44.

Driedger, Leo. 1996. *Multi-Ethnic Canada: Identities and Inequalities*. Toronto: Oxford University Press

Driedger, Sharon Doyle. 1997. "Radical Responses." *Maclean's* (July 28):46–47.

Drohan, Madelaine. 1996. "London Traffic Trapped in Carriage Days." *The Globe and Mail* (June 5):A8.

Drucker, Peter. 1994. "The Age of Social Transformation." *The Atlantic Monthly* (November):53–80.

Dube, Francine. 1999. "One in 10 Canadians Plan to Retire on Lottery Winnings." *National Post* (January 15): A1.

Du Bois, W.E.B. 1967. *The Philadelphia Negro: A Social Study*. New York: Schocken Books (orig. pub. 1899).

Dubowitz, Howard, Maureen Black, Raymond H. Starr, Jr., and Susan Zuravin. 1993. "A Conceptual Definition of Child Neglect." *Criminal Justice and Behavior*, 20(1):8–26.

Duff, Robert W., and Lawrence K. Hong. 1984. "Self-Images of Women Bodybuilders." *Sociology of Sport Journal*, 2:374–380.

Duffy, Ann, and Nancy Mandell. 1996. "Poverty in Canada." In Robert J. Brym (ed.), *Society in Question: Sociological Readings for the 21st Century*. Toronto: Harcourt Brace and Company, 96–104.

Duffy, Mike. 1992. "How Life Should Be? TV's Families, Then and Now, Reflect the Ideals of a Society." *Austin American-Statesman* (October 25):5.

Dumas, Jean. 1997. "Report on the Demographic Situation in Canada, 1996." Ottawa: Minister of Industry. Cat. No. 91-209-XPE, 121–186.

Dunlap, Riley E. 1992. "Trends in Public Opinion Toward Environmental Issues: 1965–1990." In Riley E. Dunlap and Angela G. Mertig (eds.), *American Environmentalism: The U.S. Environmental Movement, 1970–1990*. New York: Taylor & Francis, 89–113.

Dunning, Paula. 1997. *Education in Canada: An Overview*. Toronto: Canadian Education Association. Available at: http://www.acea.ca/trends.htm

Durkheim, Emile. 1933. *Division of Labor in Society*. Trans. George Simpson. New York: Free Press (orig. pub. 1893).

———. 1947. *The Elementary Forms of the Religious Life*. New York: Free Press (orig. pub. 1912).

———. 1956. *Education and Sociology*. Trans. Sherwood D. Fox. Glencoe, IL: Free Press.

———. 1964a. *The Rules of Sociological Method*. Trans. Sarah A. Solovay and John H. Mueller. New York: Free Press (orig. pub. 1895).

———. 1964b. *Suicide*. Trans. John A. Sparkling and George Simpson. New York: Free Press (orig. pub. 1897).

———. 1995. *The Elementary Forms of Religious Life*. Trans. Karen E. Fields. New York: Free Press (orig. pub. 1912).

Durning, Alan. 1993. "Life on the Brink." In William Dan Perdue (ed.), *Systemic Crisis: Problems in Society, Politics, and World Order*. Fort Worth: Harcourt Brace, pp. 274–282.

Durrant, Joan, and Linda Rose-Krasnor. 1995. *Corporal Punishment: Research and Policy Recommendations*. Ottawa: Family Violence Prevention Division of Health Canada and the Department of Justice.

Duster, Troy. 1995. "Symposium: The Bell Curve." *Contemporary Sociology: A Journal of Reviews*, 24(2):158–161.

Dworkin, Andrea. 1974. *Woman Hating*. New York: Dutton.

Dyck, Rand. 1996. *Canadian Politics: Critical Approaches* (2nd ed.). Scarborough, Ont.: Nelson Canada.

Dye, Thomas R., and Harmon Zeigler. 1993. *The Irony of Democracy: An Uncommon Introduction to American Politics* (9th ed.). Belmont, Cal.: Wadsworth.

Ebaugh, Helen Rose Fuchs. 1988. *Becoming an EX: The Process of Role Exit*. Chicago: University of Chicago Press.

Eccles, Jacquelynne S., Janis E. Jacobs, and Rena D. Harold. 1990. "Gender Role Stereotypes, Expectancy Effects, and Parents' Socialization of Gender

Difference." *Journal of Social Issues,* 46:183–201.

Economic Council of Canada. 1991. *New Faces in the Crowd: Economic and Social Impacts, Immigration.* Ottawa: Economic Council of Canada.

Eder, Donna. 1985. "The Cycle of Popularity: Interpersonal Relations Among Female Adolescents." *Sociology of Education,* 58 (July):154–165.

Eder, Donna, and Stephen Parker. 1987. "The Cultural Production and Reproduction of Gender: The Effect of Extracurricular Activities on Peer Group Culture." *Sociology of Education,* 60:200–213.

Edgerton, Robert B. 1992. *Sick Societies: Challenging the Myth of Primitive Harmony.* New York: Free Press.

Edsall, Thomas Byrne, with Mary D. Edsall. 1992. *Chain Reaction: The Impact of Race, Rights, and Taxes on American Politics.* New York: Norton.

Edwards, Harry. 1973. *Sociology of Sport.* Homewood, Ill.: Dorsey.

Edwards, Richard. 1979. *Contested Terrain.* New York: Basic Books.

———. 1993. "An Education in Interviewing." In C.M. Renzetti and R.M. Lee (eds.), *Researching Sensitive Topics.* Newbury Park: Sage, 181–196.

Ehrenreich, Barbara. 1989. *Fear of Falling: The Inner Life of the Middle Class.* New York: HarperPerennial.

Ehrenreich, Barbara, and Annette Fuentes. 1981. "Life on the Global Assembly." *Ms.* (January):52–59.

Ehrlich, Paul R., and Anne H. Ehrlich. 1991. *The Population Explosion.* New York: Touchstone/Simon & Schuster.

Ehrlich, Paul R., Anne H. Ehrlich, and Gretchen C. Daily. 1995. *The Stork and the Plow: An Equity Answer to the Human Dilemma.* Connecticut: Yale Universtity Press.

Eichler, Margrit. 1981. "The Inedequacy of the Monolithic Model of the Family." *Canadain Journal of Sociology,* 6: 367–388.

———. 1988a. *Families in Canada Today* (2nd ed.). Toronto: Gage.

———. 1988b. *Nonsexist Research Methods: A Practical Guide.* Boston: Allen & Unwin.

———. 1996. "The Impact of New Reproductive and Genetic Technologies on Families." In Maureen Baker (ed.), *Familes: Changing Trends in Canada.* Toronto: McGraw-Hill Ryerson, 104–108.

———. 1997. *Family Shifts: Families, Policies, and Gender Equality.* Don Mills, Ont.: Oxford University Press.

Eisenstein, Zillah R. 1994. *The Color of Gender: Reimaging Democracy.* Berkeley, Cal.: University of California Press.

Eitzen, D. Stanley, and Maxine Baca Zinn. 1995. *In Conflict and Order: Understanding Society* (7th ed.). Boston: Allyn & Bacon.

Eldridge, N.S., and L.A. Gilbert. 1990. "Correlates of Relationship Satisfaction in Lesbian Couples." *Psychology of Women Quarterly,* 14:43–62.

Elifson, Kirk W., David M. Petersen, and C. Kirk Hadaway. 1983. "Religiosity and Delinquency: A Contextual Analysis." *Criminology* 21:505–527.

Elkin, Frederick, and Gerald Handel. 1989. *The Child and Society: The Process of Socialization* (5th ed.). New York: Random House.

Elliott, D.S., and A. Ageton. 1980. "Reconciling Differences in Estimates of Delinquency." *American Sociological Review,* 45(1):95–110.

Elliott, Jennifer A. 1994. *An Introduction to Sustainable Development: The Developing World.* London and New York: Routledge.

Elliott, Stuart. 1993. "Advertising: The Homeless Give an Anthem New Meaning for the Holidays." *New York Times* (December 24):C14.

Emling, Shelley. 1997a. "Haiti Held in Grip of Another Drought." *Austin American-Statesman* (September 19):A17, A18.

———. 1997b. "In Haiti, It's Resort vs. Reality." *Austin American-Statesman* (September 27):A17, A19.

Engels, Friedrich. 1972. *The Origins of the Family, Private Property, and the States.* Ed. Eleanor Burke Leacock. New York: International (orig. pub. 1884).

Epstein, Cynthia Fuchs. 1988. *Deceptive Distinctions: Sex, Gender, and the Social Order.* New Haven, Conn.: Yale University Press.

Epstein, Ethan B. 1996. "Workers and the World Economy." *Foreign Affairs,* 75(May/June):16–37.

Erikson, Eric H. 1963. *Childhood and Society.* New York: Norton.

———. 1968. *Identity: Youth and Crisis.* New York: Norton.

———. 1980. *Identity and the Life Cycle.* New York: Norton (orig. pub. 1959).

Erikson, Kai T. 1962. "Notes on the Sociology of Deviance." *Social Problems,* 9:307–314.

———. 1976. *Everything in Its Path: Destruction of Community in the Buffalo Creek Flood.* New York: Simon & Schuster.

———. 1991. "A New Species of Trouble." In Stephen Robert Couch and J. Stephen Kroll-Smith (eds.), *Communities at Risk: Collective Responses to Technological Hazards.* New York: Peter Land, 11–29.

———. 1994. *A New Species of Trouble: Explorations in Disaster, Trauma, and Community.* New York: Norton.

Esbensen, Finn-Aage, and David Huizinga. 1993. "Gangs, Drugs, and Delinquency in a Survey of Urban Youth." *Criminology,* 31(4):565–589.

Essed, Philomena. 1991. *Understanding Everyday Racism.* Newbury Park, Cal.: Sage.

Etzioni, Amitai. 1975. *A Comparative Analysis of Complex Organizations: On Power, Involvement, and Their Correlates* (rev. ed.). New York: Free Press.

Evans, Glen, and Norman L. Farberow. 1988. *The Encyclopedia of Suicide.* New York: Facts on File.

Evans, John, and Alexander Himelfarb. 1996. "Counting Crime." In Rick Linden (ed.), *Criminology: A Canadian Perspective* (3rd ed.). Toronto: Harcourt Brace and Company, 61–94.

Evans, Peter B., and John D. Stephens. 1988. "Development and the World Economy." In Neil J. Smelser (ed.), *Handbook of Sociology.* Newbury Park, Cal.: Sage, pp. 739–773.

Eyre, Linda. 1992. "Gender Relations in the Classroom: A Fresh Look at Coeducation." J. Gaskell and A. McLaren (eds.), *Women and Education.* Calgary: Detselig.

Fabes, Richard A., and Carol L. Martin. 1991. "Gender and Age Stereotypes of Emotionality." *Personality and Social Psychology Bulletin,* 17:532–540.

Fagot, Beverly I. 1984. "Teacher and Peer Reactions to Boys' and Girls' Play Styles." *Sex Roles,* 11:691–702.

Fallon, Patricia, Melanie A. Katzman, and Susan C. Wooley. 1994. *Feminist Perspectives on Eating Disorders.* New York: Guilford Press.

Faludi, Susan. 1991. *Backlash: The Undeclared War Against American Women.* New York: Crown.

Farb, Peter. 1973. *Word Play: What Happens When People Talk.* New York: Knopf.

Farley, Christopher John. 1993. "Today Los Angeles, Tomorrow ... " *Time* (July 26):49.

Farley, John E. 1992. *Sociology* (2nd ed.). Englewood Cliffs, N.J.: Prentice-Hall.

Farren, Sandra. 1998. "Money Matters." *The Maclean's Guide to Canadian Universities, 1998*, 44–47.

Fausto-Sterling, Anne. 1985. *Myths of Gender: Biological Theories About Women and Men*. New York: Basic Books.

"The Favoured Infants." 1976. *Human Behaviour* (June):49–50.

Fawcett, G. 1996. *Living with Disability in Canada: An Economic Portrait*, Cat. no. SDDP-020-10-96-E. Ottawa: Canadian Council on Social Development.

Feagin, Joe R. 1991. "The Continuing Significance of Race: Antiblack Discrimination in Public Places." *American Sociological Review*, 56(February):101–116.

Feagin, Joe R., and Clairece Booher Feagin. 1994. *Social Problems: A Critical Power-Conflict Perspective* (4th ed.). Englewood Cliffs, N.J.: Prentice-Hall.

———. 1996. *Racial and Ethnic Relations* (5th ed.). Englewood Cliffs, N.J.: Prentice-Hall.

———. 1997. *Social Problems: A Critical Power–Conflict Perspective* (5th ed.). Upper Saddle River, N.J.: Prentice Hall.

Feagin, Joe R., Anthony M. Orum, and Gideon Sjoberg (eds.). 1991. *A Case for the Case Study*. Chapel Hill: University of North Carolina Press.

Feagin, Joe R., and Robert Parker. 1990. *Building American Cities: The Urban Real Estate Game* (2nd ed.). Englewood Cliffs, N.J.: Prentice-Hall.

Feagin, Joe R., and Hernán Vera. 1995. *White Racism: The Basics*. New York: Routledge.

Featherstone, Mike (ed.). 1990. *Global Culture: Nationalism, Globalization and Modernity*. Newbury Park, Cal.: Sage.

Fennell, Tom. 1993. "What's Wrong at School?" *Maclean's* (January 11):28–34.

Ferguson, John. 1977. *War and Peace in the World's Religions*. New York: Oxford University Press.

Ferree, Myra Marx, and Elaine J. Hall. 1990. "Visual Images in American Society: Gender and Race in Introductory Sociology Textbooks." *Gender & Society*, 4(4):500–533.

Ferrell, Keith. 1997. *Truth, Lies, and the Internet*. CNET (9 October). Available: www.cnet.com/content/Features/Dlife/Truth/index.html

Findlay, Deborah A., and Leslie J. Miller. 1994. "Through Medical Eyes: The Medicalization of Women's Bodies and Women's Lives." In B. Singh Bolaria and Harley D. Dickinson (eds.), *Health, Illness and Health Care in Canada*. (2nd ed.). Toronto: Harcourt Brace, 276–306.

Findlay-Kaneko, Beverly. 1997. "In a Breakthrough for Japan, a Woman Takes Over at a National University. *Chronicle of Higher Education* (June 20): A41–A42.

Fine, Michelle. 1987. "Silencing and Nurturing Voice in an Improbable Context: Urban Adolescents in Public Schools." In Henry A. Giroux and Peter McLaren (eds.), *Schooling and the Politics of Culture*. Albany: SUNY Press.

———. 1989. "Coping with Rape: Critical Perspectives on Consciousness." In Rhoda Kesler Unger (ed.), *Representations: Social Constructions of Gender*. Amityville, N.Y.: Baywood, 186–200.

Finn Paradis, Lenora, and Scott B. Cummings. 1986. "The Evolution of Hospice in America Toward Organizational Homogeneity." *Journal of Health and Social Behavior*, 27:370–386.

Firestone, Shulamith. 1970. *The Dialectic of Sex*. New York: Morrow.

Fischer, Claude S. 1976. *The Urban Experience*. New York: Harcourt Brace Jovanovich.

Fisher, Mary. 1993. "Tap Moral Courage to Mold Opinions." *Masthead*, 45(3):27–30.

Fisher, Luke. 1994. "A Holy War Over Holidays." *Maclean's* (August 12):26.

Fisher-Thompson, Donna. 1990. "Adult Sex-Typing of Children's Toys." *Sex Roles*, 23:291–303.

Fjellman, Stephen M. 1992. *Vinyl Leaves: Walt Disney World & America*. Boulder, Col.: Westview.

Flanagan, William G. 1995. *Urban Sociology: Images and Structure* (2nd ed.). Needham Heights, MA: Allyn & Bacon.

Fleras, Augie, and Jean Leonard Elliott. 1992. *Multiculturalism in Canada*. Scarborough, Ont.: Nelson.

———. 1996. *Unequal Relations: An Introduction to Race, Ethnic and Aboriginal Dynamics in Canada* (2nd ed.). Scarborough, Ont.: Prentice Hall.

Florida, Richard, and Martin Kenney. 1991. "Transplanted Organizations: The Transfer of Japanese Industrial Organization to the U.S." *American Sociological Review*, 56(3):381–398.

Fontana, Vincent J. 1991. *Save the Family, Save the Child: Inside Child Abuse Today*. New York: Dutton.

Forbes. 1998. "The World's Richest People." Available: www.forbes.com/tool/toolbox/billnew/1998.asp

Forcese, Dennis. 1986. *The Canadian Class Structure*. Toronto: McGraw-Hill Ryerson.

Ford, Clyde W. 1994. *We Can All Get Along: 50 Steps You Can Take to Help End Racism*. New York: Dell.

Fox, John, and Michael Ornstein. 1986. "The Canadian State and Corporate Elites in the Post-War Period." *Canadian Review of Sociology and Anthropology*, 23:481–506.

Fox, Mary Frank. 1989. "Women and Higher Education: Gender Differences in the Status of Students and Scholars." In Jo Freeman (ed.), *Women: A Feminist Perspective*. Mountain View, Cal.: Mayfield, 217–235.

Frank, Andre Gunder. 1969. *Latin America: Underdevelopment or Revolution?* New York: Monthly Review Press.

———. 1981. *Reflections on the World Economic Crisis*. New York: Monthly Review Press.

Frankl, Razelle. 1987. *Televangelism: The Marketing of Popular Religion*. Carbondale: Southern Illinois University Press.

Freedman, Lisa. 1985. "Wife Assault." In Connie Bugerman and Margie Wolfe (eds.), *No Safe Place: Violence Against Women and Children*. Toronto: Women's Press, 41–59.

Freidson, Eliot. 1970. *Profession of Medicine*. New York: Dodd, Mead.

———. 1986. *Professional Powers*. Chicago: University of Chicago Press.

Freudenberg, Nicholas, and Carl Steinsapir. 1992. "Not in Our Backyards: The Grassroots Environmental Movement." In Riley Dunlap and Angela G. Mertig (eds.), *American Environmentalism: The U.S. Environmental Movement, 1970–1990*. New York: Taylor and Francis, 27–37.

Frideres, James S. 1993. *Native Peoples in Canada: Contemporary Conflicts* (4th ed.). Scarborough, Ont.: Prentice Hall.

Friedan, Betty. 1993. *The Fountain of Age*. New York: Simon & Schuster.

Friedman, Milton. 1970. "The Social Responsibility of Business Is to Increase Its Profits." *New York Times Magazine* (September 13):33.

Friedman, Thomas. 1998. "The Global Neighbourhood." *Winnipeg Free Press* (July 20): A10.

Friedmann, John. 1995. "The World City Hypothesis." In Paul L. Knox and Peter J. Taylor (eds.), *World Cities in a World-System*. Cambridge, England: Cambridge University Press, pp. 317–331.

Fulton, E. Kaye, and Ian Mather. 1993. "A Forest Fable." *Maclean's* (August 16):20.

Fuse, Toyama. 1997. *Suicide, Individuality, and Society*. Toronto: Canadian Scholars' Press.

Gabor, Thomas. 1994. *Everybody Does It: Crime by the Public*. Toronto: University of Toronto Press.

Gabriel, Trip. 1996. "High-Tech Pregnancies Test Hope's Limit." *New York Times* (January 7):1, 10–11.

Gadd, Jane. 1998. "Young Men Across Canada Earning Less, Report Says." *The Globe and Mail* (July 29):A5.

Gailey, Christine Ward. 1987. "Evolutionary Perspectives on Gender Hierarchy." In Beth B. Hess and Myra Marx Ferree (eds.), *Analyzing Gender: A Handbook of Social Science Research*. Newbury Park, Cal.: Sage, 32–67.

Galloway, Gloria. 1999. "Number of Racist Canadians Falling." *National Post*. Online. Retrieved March 1, 1999.

Gamson, William. 1990. *The Strategy of Social Protest* (2nd ed.). Belmont, Cal.: Wadsworth.

Gans, Herbert. 1974. *Popular Culture and High Culture: An Analysis and Evaluation of Tastes*. New York: Basic Books.

———. 1982. *The Urban Villagers: Group and Class in the Life of Italian Americans* (updated and expanded ed.; orig. pub. 1962). New York: Free Press.

Garber, Judith A., and Robyne S. Turner. 1995. "Introduction." In Judith A. Garber and Robyne S. Turner (eds.), *Gender in Urban Research*. Thousand Oaks, Cal.: Sage, x–xxvi.

Garcia Coll, Cynthia T. 1990. "A Message to a Future Child About the Danger of Gangs." *Austin American-Statesman* (August 17):A6.

Garfinkel, Harold. 1967. *Studies in Ethnomethodology*. Englewood Cliffs, N.J.: Prentice-Hall.

Gargan, Edward A. 1996. "An Indonesian Asset Is Also a Liability." *New York Times* (March 16):17, 18.

Garson, Barbara. 1989. *The Electronic Sweatshop: How Computers Are Transforming the Office of the Future into the Factory of the Past*. New York: Penguin.

Gaskell, Jane. 1994. "Education." In R. Hagedorn (ed.), *Sociology*. Toronto: Harcourt Brace and Company, 469–495.

Gaskell, Jane S., and Arlene Tigar McLaren (eds.). 1987. *Women and Education: A Canadian Perspective*. Calgary: Detselig.

Gaskell, Jane, Arlene McLaren, and Myra Novogradsky. 1995. "What Is Worth Knowing? Defining the Feminist Curriculum." In E.D. Nelson and B.W. Robinson (eds.), *Gender in the 1990s: Images, Realities and Issues*. Scarborough: ITP Nelson, 100–118.

Gatehouse, Jonathon. 1999. *The National Post* (May 19):A1.

Gaylin, Willard. 1992. *The Male Ego*. New York: Viking/Penguin.

Gecas, Viktor. 1982. "The Self-Concept." In Ralph H. Turner and James F. Short, Jr. (eds.), *Annual Review of Sociology, 1982*. Palo Alto, Cal.: Annual Reviews, 1–33.

Gee, Ellen M. 1994. "What Is Family?" In R. Hagedorn (ed.), *Sociology*. Toronto: Harcourt Brace, 369–398.

———. 1995. "Contemporary Diversities." In Nancy Mandell and Ann Duffy (eds.), *Canadian Families: Diversity, Conflict and Change*. Toronto: Harcourt Brace and Company, 79–109.

Geertz, Clifford. 1966. "Religion as a Cultural System." In Michael Banton (ed.), *Anthropological Approaches to the Study of Religion*. London: Tavistock, pp. 1–46.

Gelfand, Donald E. 1994. *Aging and Ethnicity: Knowledge and Services*. New York: Springer.

Gelles, Richard J., and Murray A. Straus. 1988. *Intimate Violence: The Definitive Study of the Causes and Consequences of Abuse in the American Family*. New York: Simon & Schuster.

Gerber, Linda. 1990. "Multiple Jeopardy: A Socio-Economic Comparison of Men and Women Among the Indian, Métis, and Inuit Peoples of Canada." *Canadian Ethnic Studies*, 22(3):22–34.

Gerbner, George, Larry Gross, Michael Morton, and Nancy Signorielli. 1987. "Charting the Mainstream: Television's Contributions to Political Orientations." In Donald Lazere (ed.), *American Media and Mass Culture: Left Perspectives*. Berkeley: University of California Press, 441–464.

Gereffi, Gary. 1994. "The International Economy and Economic Development." In Neil J. Smelser and Richard Swedberg (eds.), *The Handbook of Economic Sociology*. Princeton, NJ: Princeton University Press, 206–233.

Gerschenkron, Alexander. 1962. *Economic Backwardness in Historical Perspective*. Cambridge, Mass.: Harvard University Press.

Gerson, Kathleen. 1993. *No Man's Land: Men's Changing Commitment to Family and Work*. New York: Basic Books.

Gerstel, Naomi, and Harriet Engel Gross. 1995. "Gender and Families in the United States: The Reality of Economic Dependence." In Jo Freeman (ed.), *Women: A Feminist Perspective* (5th ed.). Mountain View, Cal.: Mayfield, 92–127.

Ghosh, Ratna, and Rabindra Kanungo. 1992. *South Asian Canadians: Current Issues in the Politics of Culture*. Montreal: Shastri Indo-Canadian Institute.

Gibbs, Lois Marie, as told to Murray Levine. 1982. *Love Canal: My Story*. Albany: SUNY Press.

Gibbs, Nancy. 1994. "Home Sweet School." *Time* (October 31):62–63.

Gibson, Malcolm D. 1994. "AIDS and the African Press." *Media, Culture, & Society*, 16(2):349–357.

Giddens, Anthony. 1996. *Introduction to Sociology* (2nd ed.). New York: W.W. Norton & Co.

Gideonse, Ted. 1998. "Review: Author Sees Distortion in Marketing of Gays." Available: http://www.salonmagazine.com

Gilbert, Dennis L. 1998. *The American Class Structure in an Age of Growing Inequality* (5th ed.). Belmont, Cal.: Wadsworth.

Gilbert, Dennis, and Joseph A. Kahl. 1998. *The American Class Structure: A New Synthesis* (5th ed.). Belmont, Cal.: Wadsworth.

Gilbert, S.N. 1989. "The Forgotten Purpose and Future of University Education." *Canadian Journal of Community Mental Health*, 8(2):103–122.

Gilbert, S.N., and B. Orok. 1993. "School Leavers." In *Canadian Social Trends*, Cat no. 11–008E. Ottawa: Statistics Canada, 2–7.

Gilder, George F. 1986. *Men and Marriage*. New York: Pelican.

Gilligan, Carol. 1982. *In a Different Voice: Psychological Theory and Women's Development*. Cambridge, Mass.: Harvard University Press.

Gillis, A.R. 1995. "Urbanization." In Robert J. Brym (ed.), *New Society: Sociology for the 21st Century*. Toronto:

Harcourt Brace and Company, 13.1–13.40.

Gilmour, Glenn A. 1994. *Hate-Motivated Violence* (May). Ottawa: Research Section, Department of Justice.

Glaser, Barney, and Anselm Strauss. 1967. *The Discovery of Grounded Theory.* Chicago: Aldine.

———. 1968. *Time for Dying.* Chicago: Aldine.

Glazer, Nona. 1990. "The Home as Workshop: Women as Amateur Nurses and Medical Care Providers." *Gender & Society,* 4:479–499.

The Globe and Mail Report on Business Magazine. 1990. (October):B80.

Goffman, Erving. 1956. "The Nature of Deference and Demeanor." *American Anthropologist,* 58:473–502.

———. 1959. *The Presentation of Self in Everyday Life.* Garden City, N.Y.: Doubleday.

———.1961a. *Asylums: Essays on the Social Situation of Mental Patients and Other Inmates.* Chicago: Aldine.

———. 1961b. *Encounters: Two Studies in the Sociology of Interaction.* Indianapolis, Ind.: Bobbs-Merrill.

———. 1963a. *Behavior in Public Places: Notes on the Social Structure of Gatherings.* New York: Free Press.

———. 1963b. *Stigma: Notes on the Management of Spoiled Identity.* Englewood Cliffs, N.J.: Prentice-Hall.

———. 1967. *Interaction Ritual: Essays on Face to Face Behavior.* Garden City, N.Y.: Anchor Books.

Gold, Rachel Benson, and Cory L. Richards. 1994. "Securing American Women's Reproductive Health." In Cynthia Costello and Anne J. Stone (eds.), *The American Woman 1994–95.* New York: Norton.

Goldberg, Kim. 1994. "Green Relief for Forest Defenders." *Progressive* (March 1):13.

Goldberg, Robert A. 1991. *Grassroots Resistance: Social Movements in Twentieth Century America.* Belmont, Cal.: Wadsworth.

Golden, Carla. 1987. "Diversity and Variability in Women's Sexual Identities." In The Boston Lesbian Psychologies Collective (eds.), *Lesbian Psychologies.* Urbana: University of Illinois Press, pp. 18–34.

Golden, Stephanie. 1992. *The Women Outside: Meanings and Myths of Homelessness.* Berkeley: University of California Press.

Gomme, Ian. 1995. "Education." In Robert J. Brym (ed.). *New Society: Sociology for the 21st Century.* Toronto: Harcourt Brace and Company, 12.1–12.11.

Gonzales, David. 1994. "Frenzied Passengers, Their Hair and Clothes in Flames, Flee Burning Train." *New York Times* (December 22):A12.

Goode, William J. 1960. "A Theory of Role Strain." *American Sociological Review,* 25:483–496.

———. 1976. "Family Disorganization." In Robert K. Merton and Robert Nisbet (eds.), *Contemporary Social Problems* (4th ed.). New York: Harcourt Brace Jovanovich, 511–554.

Goodman, Peter S. 1996. "The High Cost of Sneakers." *Austin American-Statesman* (July 7):F1, F6.

Gordon, David. 1973. "Capitalism, Class, and Crime in America." *Crime and Delinquency,* 19:163–186.

Gordon, Milton. 1964. *Assimilation in American Life: The Role of Race, Religion, and National Origins.* New York: Oxford University Press.

Gordon, Robert M., and Jacquelyne Nelson. 1993. *Census '93: The Report of the 1993 Census of Provincial Correctional Centres in British Columbia.* Victoria: Ministry of the Solicitor General.

Gorey, Kevin, Eric J. Holowaty, Gordon Fehringer, Ethan Laukkanen, Agnes Moskowitz, David J. Webster, and Nancy L. Richter. 1997. "An International Comparison of Cancer Survival: Toronto, Ontario, and Detroit, Michigan, Metropolitan Areas." *American Journal of Public Health,* 87:1156–1163.

Gorlick, Carolyne A. 1995. "Divorce: Options Available, Constraints Forced, Pathways Taken." In Nancy Mandell and Ann Duffy (eds.), *Canadian Families: Diversity, Conflict and Change.* Toronto: Harcourt Brace and Company, 211–234.

Gottdiener, Mark. 1985. *The Social Production of Urban Space.* Austin: University of Texas Press.

———. 1997. *The Theming of America.* Boulder, Col.: Westview.

Gouldner, Alvin W. 1970. *The Coming Crisis of Western Sociology.* New York: Basic Books.

Gower, David. 1990. "Employment Opportunities of Disabled Canadians." In Craig McKie and Keith Thompson (eds.), *Canadian Social Trends.* Toronto: Thompson Educational Publishers, 218–220.

Grant, Karen. 1993. "Health and Health Care." In Peter S. Li and B. Singh Bolaria (eds.), *Contemporary Sociology: Critical Perspectives.* Toronto: Copp-Clark Pitman, 394–409.

Gratton, Bruce. 1986. "The New History of the Aged." In David Van Tassel and Paul N. Stearns (eds.), *Old Age in a Bureaucratic Society.* Westport, Conn.: Greenwood Press, 3–29.

Gray, Charlotte. 1997. "Are We in Store for Some Intergenerational Warfare?" *Canadian Medical Association Journal,* 157:1123–1124.

Gray, Paul. 1993. "Camp for Crusaders." *Time* (April 19):40.

Green, Donald E. 1977. *The Politics of Indian Removal: Creek Government and Society in Crisis.* Lincoln: University of Nebraska Press.

Greenberg, Edward S., and Benjamin I. Page. 1993. *The Struggle for Democracy.* New York: HarperCollins.

Greenhouse, Steven. 1994. "State Department Finds Widespread Abuse of World's Women." *New York Times* (February 3):A1.

Greenspan, Edward. 1982. "The Role of the Defence Lawyer in Sentencing." In Craig L. Boydell and Ingrid Connidis (eds.), *The Canadian Criminal Justice System.* Toronto: Holt, Rinehart and Winston, 200–210.

Greenwald, John. 1993. "Japan: How the Miracle Finally Ended." *Time* (December 13):34–35.

Gregg, Allan, and Michael Posner. 1990. *The Big Picture: What Canadians Think About almost Everything.* Toronto: McFarlane, Walter and Ross.

Griffiths, Curt T., and Simon N. Verdun-Jones. 1994. *Canadian Criminal Justice* (2nd ed.). Toronto: Harcourt Brace and Company.

Grindstaff, Carl F., and Frank Trovato. 1994. "Canada's Population in the World Context." In Frank Trovato and Carl F. Grindstaff (eds.), *Perspectives on Canada's Population.* Toronto: Oxford University Press, 5–23.

Gross, Larry. 1993. *Contested Closets: The Politics and Ethics of Outing.* Minneapolis: University of Minnesota Press.

Grover, K.J., C.S. Russell, W.R. Schumm, and L.A. Paff-Bergen. 1985. "Mate Selection Processes and Marital Satisfaction." *Family Relations,* 34(3):383–386.

Gunn, R., and R. Linden. 1994. "The Processing of Child Sexual Abuse

Cases." In J. Roberts and R.M. Mohr (eds.), *Confronting Sexual Assault: A Decade of Legal and Social Change*. Toronto: University of Toronto Press.

Guppy, Neil. 1995. "Education and Schooling." In L. Tepperman, J.E. Curtis, and R.J. Richardson (eds.), *Sociology*. Toronto: McGraw-Hill Ryerson, 450–478.

Guppy, Neil, Sabrina Freeman, and Shari Buchan. 1987. "Representing Canadians: Changes in the Economic Backgrounds of Federal Politicians, 1965–1984." *Canadian Review of Sociology and Anthropology*, 24:417–430.

Guppy, Neil, and Scott Davies. 1998. *Education in Canada: Recent Trends and Future Challenges*. Ottawa: Statistics Canada.

Haas, J., and W. Shaffir. 1995. "Giving Medical Students a Cloak of Competence." In L. Tepperman and James Curtis (eds.), *Everyday Life*. Toronto: McGraw-Hill Ryerson.

Hackler, James C. 1994. *Crime and Canadian Public Policy*. Scarborough, Ont.: Prentice Hall.

Hadden, Jeffrey K., and Anson Shupe. 1988. *Televangelism: Power and Politics on God's Frontier*. New York: Holt.

Hadden, Jeffrey K., and Charles K. Swann. 1981. *Prime Time Preachers: The Rising Power of Televangelism*. Reading, Mass.: Addison-Wesley.

Hagan, John, and Bill McCarthy. 1992. "Streetlife and Delinquency." *British Journal of Sociology*, 43(4):533–561.

Halberstadt, Amy G., and Martha B. Saitta. 1987. "Gender, Nonverbal Behavior, and Perceived Dominance: A Test of the Theory." *Journal of Personality and Social Psychology*, 53:257–272.

Hall, Edward. 1966. *The Hidden Dimension*. New York: Anchor/Doubleday.

Halle, David. 1993. *Inside Culture: Art and Class in the American Home*. Chicago: University of Chicago Press.

H.A.L.S. 1991. *Health and Activities Limitation Survey*. Cat. no. 82-554. Ottawa: Statistics Canada.

Hamill, Pete. 1993. "How to Save the Homeless—and Ourselves." *New York* (September 20):34–39.

Hamilton, Allen C. and C. Murray Sinclair. 1991. *Report of the Aboriginal Justice Inquiry of Manitoba*, Winnipeg: Queen's Printer, vol. 1. Winnipeg: Queen's Printer.

Hamman, Robin. 1998. "Digital Third Worlds and Barriers to Internet Access." *Cybersociology*, 3. Available: http://hometown.aol.com/Cybersoc/issue3.html

Hamper, Ben. 1992. *Rivethead: Tales from the Assembly Line*. New York: Warner Books.

Hansen, Liane. 1995. "Internet and Cyberspace—Farther Away Than You Think." *Sunday National Public Radio* (November 12):Weekend Edition.

Harding, Jim. 1993. "Ecology and Social Change." In Peter S. Li and B. Singh Bolaria (eds.), *Sociology: Critical Perspectives*. Toronto: Copp Clark Pitman, 439–466.

Hardy, Melissa A., and Lawrence E. Hazelrigg. 1993. "The Gender of Poverty in an Aging Population." *Research on Aging*, 15(3):243–278.

Harlow, Harry F., and Margaret Kuenne Harlow. 1962. "Social Deprivation in Monkeys." *Scientific American*, 207(5):137–146.

———. 1977. "Effects of Various Mother-Infant Relationships on Rhesus Monkey Behaviors." In Brian M. Foss (ed.), *Determinants of Infant Behavior*, vol. 4. London: Methuen, 15–36.

Harman, Lesley. 1989. *When a Hostel Becomes a Home: Experiences of Women*. Toronto: Garamond Press.

———. 1995. "Family Poverty and Economic Struggles." In Nancy Mandell and Ann Duffy (eds.), *Canadian Families: Diversity, Conflict and Change*. Toronto: Harcourt Brace and Company, 235–269.

Harrington Meyer, Madonna. 1990. "Family Status and Poverty Among Older Women: The Gendered Distribution of Retirement Income in the United States." *Social Problems*, 37:551–563.

———. 1994. "Gender, Race, and the Distribution of Social Assistance: Medicaid Use Among the Frail Elderly." *Gender & Society*, 8 (1):8–28.

Harris, Chauncey D., and Edward L. Ullman. 1945. "The Nature of Cities." *Annals of the Academy of Political and Social Sciences* (November):7–17.

Harris, Debbie. 1991. "Violence Against Women in Universities." *Canadian Women's Studies*, 11(4):35–41.

Harris, Diana K. 1990. *Sociology of Aging* (2nd ed.). New York: Harper & Row.

Harris, Marvin. 1974. *Cows, Pigs, Wars, and Witches*. New York: Random House.

———. 1985. *Good to Eat: Riddles of Food and Culture*. New York: Simon & Schuster.

Harrison, Algea O., Melvin N. Wilson, Charles J. Pine, Samuel Q. Chan, and Raymond Buriel. 1990. "Family Ecologies of Ethnic Minority Children." *Child Development*, 61(2):347–362.

Harrison, Trevor, Bill Johnston, and Harvey Krahn. 1996. "Special Interests and/or New Right Economics? The Ideological Bases of Reform Party Support in Alberta in the 1993 Federal Election." *Canadian Review of Sociology and Anthropology* 33(2):159–179.

Hartmann, Heidi. 1976. "Capitalism, Patriarchy, and Job Segregation by Sex." *Signs: Journal of Women in Culture and Society*, 1(Spring):137–169.

———. 1981. "The Unhappy Marriage of Marxism and Feminism." In Lydia Sargent (ed.), *Women and Revolution*. Boston: South End Press.

Hartnagel, Timothy F. 1996. "Correlates of Criminal Behaviour." In R. Linden (ed.), *Criminology: A Canadian Perspective* (3rd ed.). Toronto: Harcourt Brace, 95–137.

———. 2000. "Correlates of Crime." In R. Linden (ed.), *Criminology: A Canadian Perspective* (4th ed.). Toronto: Harcourt Brace.

Hauchler, Ingomar, and Paul M. Kennedy (eds.). 1994. *Global Trends: The World Almanac of Development and Peace*. New York: Continuum.

Hauser, Christine. 1996. "Canada Promises Tough Stand Against Child Labour." *Reuters* (January 13).

Hauser, Robert M. 1995. "Symposium: The Bell Curve." *Contemporary Sociology: A Journal of Reviews*, 24(2):149–153.

Hauser, Robert M., and David L. Featherman. 1976. "Equality of Schooling: Trends and Prospects." *Sociology of Education*, 49:99–120.

Havighurst, Robert J., Bernice L. Neugarten, and Sheldon S. Tobin. 1968. "Disengagement and Patterns of Aging." In Bernice L. Neugarten (ed.), *Middle Age and Aging*. Chicago: University of Chicago Press, 161–172.

Haviland, William A. 1993. *Cultural Anthropology* (7th ed.). Orlando, Fla.: Harcourt Brace Jovanovich.

Hazarika, Sanjoy. 1994. "In India's City of Death, Time Has Healed Little." *New York Times* (December 2):A7.

Health and Welfare Canada. 1998. *Active Health Report: The Active Health Report on Seniors*. Ottawa: Minister of Supply and Services.

Health Canada. 1994. *Suicide in Canada: Update on the Report of the Task Force on*

Suicide in Canada. Ottawa: Health Programs and Services Branch.

———. 1997. *For the Safety of Canadian Children and Youth: From Injury Data to Preventative Measures*, Cat. no. H39-412/1997E. Ottawa: Health Programs and Services Branch.

———. 1998. "How Much Income Do Seniors Have?" *Canada's Seniors at a Glance*. Available at: http://www.hc-sc.ca/seniors-aines

Hedges, Chris. 1997. "In Bosnia's Schools, 3 Ways Never to Learn from History." *New York Times* (November 25): A1, A4.

Hefley, James C. 1976. *Textbooks on Trial*. Wheaton, Ill.: Victor Books.

Heilbroner, Robert. 1985. *The Nature and Logic of Capitalism*. New York:W.W. Norton and Company.

Heinrichs, Daniel. 1996. *Caring for Norah*. Winnipeg: Daniel Heinricks Publishing.

Hendley, Nate. 1998. "Passing the Puck on Child Sex Abuse?" *Eye Magazine* (October 1):10.

Henley, Nancy. 1977. *Body Politics: Power, Sex, and Nonverbal Communication*. Englewood Cliffs, N.J.: Prentice-Hall.

Henry, Frances, and Effie Ginzberg. 1984. *Who Gets Work: A Test of Racial Discrimination in Employment*. Toronto: Urban Alliance on Race Relations and the Social Planning Council of Toronto.

Henry, Frances, Carol Tator, Winston Mattis, and Tim Rees. 1995. *The Colour of Democracy: Racism in Canadian Society*. Toronto: Harcourt Brace and Company.

———. 1996. "The Victimization of Racial Minorities in Canada. In Robert J. Brym (ed.), *Society in Question: Sociological Readings for the 21st Century*, Toronto: Harcourt Brace and Company, 133–144.

Henslin, James M., and Adie Nelson. 1996. *Sociology: A Down to Earth Approach: Canadian Edition*. Scarborough, Ont.: Allyn and Bacon.

Heritage, John. 1984. *Garfinkel and Ethnomethodology*. Cambridge, Mass.: Polity.

Hernandez, Debra Gersh. 1994. "AIDS Fades: The Epidemic Swells But Reporters Complain Editors Have Lost Interest." *Editor & Publisher*, 127(34):16–18.

Heron, Craig. 1993. "The Crisis of the Craftsman: Hamilton's Metal Workers in the Early Twentieth Century." In Graham S. Lowe and Harvey J. Krahn

(eds.), *Work in Canada*. Scarborough, Ont.: Nelson Canada, 4–13.

Herrnstein, Richard J., and Charles Murray. 1994. *The Bell Curve: Intelligence and Class Structure in American Life*. New York: Free Press.

Herzog, David B., K.L. Newman, Christine J. Yeh, and M. Warshaw. 1992. "Body Image Satisfaction in Homosexual and Heterosexual Women." *International Journal of Eating Disorders*, 11:391–396.

Heshka, Stanley, and Yona Nelson. 1972. "Interpersonal Speaking Distances as a Function of Age, Sex, and Relationship." *Sociometry*, 35(4):491–498.

Hesse-Biber, Sharlene. 1996. *Am I Thin Enough Yet? The Cult of Thinness and the Commercialization of Identity*. New York: Oxford University Press.

Hettne, Bjorn. 1995. *Development Theory and the Three Worlds* (2nd ed.). Essex: Longman.

Heywood, Leslie. 1998. *Pretty Good for a Girl*. New York: The Free Press.

Hill, Lawrence. 1994. "Zebra: Growing Up Black and White in Canada." In Carl E. James and Adrienne Shadd (eds.), *Talking About Difference*. Toronto: Between the Lines, 41–47.

Hiller, Harry H. 1995. "Culture." In L. Tepperman, J.E. Curtis, and R.J. Richardson (eds.), *The Social World* (3rd ed.). Toronto: McGraw-Hill Ryerson, 81–113.

Hirschi, Travis. 1969. *Causes of Delinquency*. Berkeley: University of California Press.

Hirschi, Travis, and Michael Gottfredson. 1983. "Age and the Explanation of Crime." *American Journal of Sociology*, 89(3):552–584.

Hochschild, Arlie Russell. 1983. *The Managed Heart: Commercialization of Human Feeling*. Berkeley: University of California Press.

———. 1989. *The Second Shift: Working Parents and the Revolution at Home*. New York: Viking/Penguin.

———. 1997. *The Time Bind: When Work Becomes Home and Home Becomes Work*. New York: Metropolitan Books.

Hodge, Robert W., Paul Siegel, and Peter Rossi. 1964. "Occupational Prestige in the United States, 1925–63." *American Journal of Sociology*, 70 (November): 286–302.

Hodgson, Doug. 1989. "The Legal and Public Policy Implications of Human Immunodeficiency Virus Antibody

Testing in New Zealand." In *Legal Implications of AIDS*. Auckland: Legal Research Foundation, 39–95.

Hodson, Randy, and Robert E. Parker. 1988. "Work in High Techology Settings: A Review of the Empirical Literature." *Research in the Sociology of Work*, 4:1–29.

Hodson, Randy, and Teresa A. Sullivan. 1990. *The Social Organization of Work*. Belmont, Cal.: Wadsworth.

Hodson, Randy, and Teresa A. Sullivan. 1995. *The Social Organization of Work* (2nd ed.). Belmont, Cal.: Wadsworth.

Holland, Dorothy C., and Margaret A. Eisenhart. 1981. *Women's Peer Groups and Choice of Career*. Final report for the National Institute of Education. ERIC ED 199 328. Washington, D.C.

———. 1990. *Educated in Romance: Women, Achievement, and College Culture*. Chicago: University of Chicago Press.

Holmes, Mark. 1998. *The Reformation of Canada's Schools: Breaking the Barriers to Parental Choice*. Montreal: McGill-Queen's University Press.

Holusha, John. 1994. "Bracing for the Worst in Chemicals." *New York Times* (June 4):17, 27.

Homer-Dixon, Thomas. 1993. *Environmental Scarcity and Global Security*. Foreign Policy Association, Headline Series, Number 300. Ephrata, Penn.: Science Press.

Hoover, Kenneth R. 1992. *The Elements of Social Scientific Thinking*. New York: St. Martin's Press.

Hooyman, Nancy R. R., and H. Asuman Kiyak. 1996. *Social Gerontology: A Multidisciplinary Perspective* (4th ed.). Boston: Allyn & Bacon.

Horan, Patrick M. 1978. "Is Status Attainment Research Atheoretical?" *American Sociological Review*, 43:534–541.

Howard, Michael E. 1990. "On Fighting a Nuclear War." In Francesca M. Cancian and James William Gibson (eds.), *Making War, Making Peace: The Social Foundations of Violent Conflict*. Belmont, Cal.: Wadsworth, 314–322.

Howard, Ross. 1998. "No Way Out for Despairing Port Hardy." *The Globe and Mail* (June 15):A4.

Hoyt, Homer. 1939. *The Structure and Growth of Residential Neighborhoods in American Cities*. Washington, D.C.: Federal Housing Administration.

Hughes, Colin. 1995. "Child Poverty Campaign 2000 and Child Welfare

Practice: Working to End Child Poverty in Canada." *Child Welfare*,74:70–79.

Hughes, Everett C. 1945. "Dilemmas and Contradictions of Status." *American Journal of Sociology*, 50:353–359.

Human Resources Development Canada. 1999. *The HRDC Strategic Polict Web Site.* Available: http://www.hrdc-drhc.gc.ca/stratpol/home.shtml

Humphrey, Derek. 1993. *Lawful Exit: The Limits of Freedom for Help in Dying.* Junction City, Ore.: Norris Lane Press.

Humphreys, Laud. 1970. *Tearoom Trade: Impersonal Sex in Public Places.* Chicago: Aldine.

Hunt, Charles W. 1989. "Migrant labor and sexually transmitted diseases: AIDS in Africa." *Journal of Health and Social Behaviour.* 30:353–73.

Hunter, Floyd. 1953. *Copmmunity Power Structure.* Chapel Hill, N.C.: University of North Carolina Press.

Hurst, Charles E. 1992. *Social Inequality: Forms, Causes, and Consequences.* Boston: Allyn & Bacon.

Hurst, Lynda. 1999. "Organ Donations Embarrassing." *Winnipeg Free Press* (March 29):A12.

Huston, Aletha C. 1985. "The Development of Sex Typing: Themes from Recent Research." *Developmental Review,* 5:2–17.

Hyde, Mary, and Carol La Prairie. 1987. "American Police Crime Prevention." Working paper. Ottawa: Solicitor General.

Hymers, Olga. 1997. "Home Is Where the School Is." *Canadian Family* (September/October):31–33.

Hynes, H. Patricia. 1990. *Earth Right: Every Citizen's Guide.* Rocklin, Cal.: Prima Publishing and Communications.

Ibrahim, Youseff M. 1990. "Saudi Tradition: Edicts from Koran Produce Curbs on Women." *New York Times* (November 6):A6.

Innis, Harold. 1984. *The Fur Trade in Canada.* Toronto: The University of Toronto Press (orig. pub. 1930).

Institute for Social Research. Centre for Research in Higher Education. 1995. "York Student Experience Study: Do Private High Schools Make A Difference." *Bulletin* 8 (October 15). Available: http:www.isr.yorku.ca.isr/bulletins/bullet8.asp

Institute National d'Etudes Demographiques. 1995. From Julie DaVanzo and David Adamson. 1997. "Russia's Demographic 'Crisis': How

Real Is It?" *Rand Issue Paper,* July 1997. Santa Monica: Rand Center for Russian and Eurasian Studies.

Isajiw, Wsevolod W. 1999. *Understanding Diversity: Ethnicity and Race in the Canadian Context.* Toronto: Thompson Educational Publishing.

Ip, Greg. 1996. "Shareholders vs. Job Holders." *The Globe and Mail* (March 23):B1.

Jackman, Philip. 1999. "The greying of Canada's sisters and brothers". *The Globe and Mail.* 23 February: A24.

Jackson, Beth E. 1993. "Constructing Adoptive Identities: The Accounts of Adopted Adults." Unpublished masters thesis, University of Manitoba.

Jackson, Kenneth T. 1985. *Crabgrass Frontier: The Suburbanization of the United States.* New York: Oxford University Press.

Jacobs, Gloria. 1994. "Where Do We Go from Here? An Interview with Ann Jones." *Ms.* (September/October):56–63.

Jain, Harish. 1985. *Anti-discrimination Staffing Policies: Implications of Human Rights Legislation for Employees and Trade Unions.* Ottawa: Secretary of State.

JAMA (The Journal of the American Medical Association). 1994. "Heterosexually Acquired AIDS—United States, 1993" (from the Centers for Disease Control and Prevention). *JAMA,* 271(13):975–977.

James, Carl E. 1995. *Seeing Ourselves: Exploring Race, Ethnicity and Culture.* Toronto: Thompson Educational Publishing.

James, Carl E., and Adrienne Shadd (eds.). 1994. *Talking About Difference: Encounters in Culture, Language and Identity.* Toronto: Between the Lines.

Janis, Irving. 1972. *Victims of Groupthink.* Boston: Houghton Mifflin.

———. 1989. *Crucial Decisions: Leadership in Policymaking and Crisis Management.* New York: Free Press.

Jankowski, Martin Sanchez. 1991. *Islands in the Street: Gangs and American Urban Society.* Berkeley: University of California Press.

Jarvis, George K. 1994. "Health, Health Care and Dying." In W. Meloff and D. Pierece (eds.), *An Introduction to Sociology.* Scarborough: ITP Nelson, 342–375.

Jary, David, and Julia Jary. 1991. *The Harper Collins Dictionary of Sociology.* New York: HarperPerennial.

Jenkinson, Edward B. 1979. *Censors in the Classroom: The Mind Benders.* Carbondale: Southern Illinois University Press.

Jewell, K. Sue. 1993. *From Mammy to Miss America and Beyond: Cultural Images and the Shaping of US Social Policy.* New York: Routledge.

Johns Hopkins. 1998. "Can Religion be Good Medicine?" *The Johns Hopkins Medical Letter.* November 3.

Johnson, Earvin "Magic," with William Novak. 1992. *My Life.* New York: Fawcett Crest.

Johnson, Holly. 1990. "Wife Abuse." In Craig McKie and K. Thompson (eds.), *Canadian Social Trends.* Toronto: Thompson Educational Publishing, 173–176.

———. 1996a. *Dangerous Domains: Violence Against Women in Canada.* Scarborough, Ont.: Nelson Canada.

———. 1996b. "Violence Against Women: A Special Topic Survey." In Robert A. Silveimar, James J. Teevan, and Vincent F. Sacco (eds.), *Crime in Canadian Society* (5th ed.). Toronto: Harcourt Brace and Company, 210–221.

Jolis, Alan. 1996. "The Good Banker." *Independent on Sunday.* (May 5):15–16.

Jones, Adele. 1994. "'F' Is for Fired." *NEA Today,* 13(2):23.

Jones, Charisse. 1995. "Family Struggles on Brink of Comfort." *New York Times* (February 18):1, 9.

Joshi, Vijay. 1993. "In Asia, Millions Lose Childhood to Work." *Austin American-Statesman* (September 6):C30.

Juergensmeyer, Mark. 1993. *The New Cold War? Religious Nationalism Confronts the Secular State.* Berkeley: University of California Press.

Jung, John. 1994. *Under the Influence: Alcohol and Human Behavior.* Pacific Grove, Cal.: Brooks/Cole.

Kaihla, Paul. 1991. "Terror in the Streets." *Maclean's* (March 25):78–81.

———. 1994. "Sex and the Law." *Maclean's* (Oct. 24):30.

Kallen, Evelyn. 1991. "Ethnicity and Human Rights in Canada: Constitutionalizing a Hierarchy of Minority Rights." In Peter Li (ed.), *Race and Ethnic Relations in Canada.* Toronto: Oxford University Press, 77–97.

Kanter, Rosabeth Moss. 1977. *Men and Women of the Corporation.* New York: Basic Books.

———. 1983. *The Change Masters: Innovation and Entrepreneurship in the*

American Corporation. New York: Simon & Schuster.

———. 1985. "All That Is Entrepreneurial Is Not Gold." *Wall Street Journal* (July 22):18.

Kaplan, David E., and Alec Dubro. 1987. *Yakuza: The Explosive Account of Japan's Criminal Underworld*. New York: Collier.

Karp, David A., and William C. Yoels. 1976. "The College Classroom: Some Observations on the Meanings of Student Participation." *Sociology and Social Research*, 60:421–439.

Kaspar, Anne S. 1986. "Consciousness Re-evaluated: Interpretive Theory and Feminist Scholarship." *Sociological Inquiry*, 56(1):30–49.

Katzer, Jeffrey, Kenneth H. Cook, and Wayne W. Crouch. 1991. *Evaluating Information: A Guide for Users of Social Science Research*. New York: McGraw-Hill.

Kauppinen-Toropainen, Kaisa, and Johanna Lammi. 1993. "Men in Female-Dominated Occupations: A Cross-Cultural Comparison." In Christine L. Williams (ed.), *Doing "Women's Work": Men in Nontraditional Occupations*. Newbury Park, Cal.: Sage, 91–112.

KCET (Community Television of Southern California). 1992. "Sex, Power, and the Workplace." Los Angeles, CA.

Keegan, Victor. 1996. "A World Without Bosses—Or Workers." *The Globe and Mail* (August 24):D4.

Keller, James. 1994. "I Treasure Each Moment." *Parade Magazine* (September 4):4–5.

Kelly, Gary. 1992. *Sexuality Today: The Human Perspective*. Guilford, Conn.: Dushkin.

Kelman, Steven. 1991. "Sweden Sour? Downsizing the 'Third Way.'" *New Republic* (July 29):19–23.

Kemp, Alice Abel. 1994. *Women's Work: Degraded and Devalued*. Englewood Cliffs, N.J.: Prentice-Hall.

Kendall, Diana, and Joe R. Feagin. 1983. "Blatant and Subtle Patterns of Discrimination: Minority Women in Medical Schools." *Journal of Intergroup Relations* (Summer):21–27.

Kennedy, Leslie W. 1978. "Environmental Opportunity and Social Contact: A True or Spurious Relationship?" *Pacific Sociological Review*, 21:173–186.

———. 1983. *The Urban Kaleidoscope: Canadian Perspectives*. Toronto: McGraw-Hill Ryerson.

Kennedy, Paul. 1993. *Preparing for the Twenty-First Century*. New York: Random House.

Kenyon, Kathleen. 1957. *Digging Up Jericho*. London: Ernest Benn.

Kesterton, Michael. 1999. "Social Studies." *The Globe and Mail* (February 1):A22.

Kettle, John. 1998a. "Death Still Looks Like a Healthy Business." *The Globe and Mail* (May 7):B15.

———. 1998b. "Women Snap Up Prime Jobs." *The Globe and Mail* (March 19).

Kidron, Michael, and Ronald Segal. 1995. *The State of the World Atlas*. New York: Penguin.

Kilbourne, Jean. 1994. "Still Killing Us Softly: Advertising and the Obsession with Thinness." In Patricia Fallon, Melanie A. Katzman, and Susan C. Wooley (eds.), *Feminist Perspectives on Eating Disorders*. New York: Guilford, 395–454.

Killian, Lewis. 1984. "Organization, Rationality, and Spontaneity in the Civil Rights Movement." *American Sociological Review*, 49:770–783.

Kimmel, Michael S., and Michael A. Messner. 1992. *Men's Lives* (2nd ed.). New York: Macmillan.

King, James. 1997. *The Life of Margaret Laurence*. Toronto: Alfred A. Knopf.

Kingsley, Bob. 1996. "Assault." In Leslie W. Kennedy and Vincent F. Sacco (eds.), *Crime Counts: A Criminal Event Analysis*. Scarborough, Ont.: Nelson Canada, 99–113.

Kinsella, Warren. 1994. *Web of Hate: The Far-Right Network in Canada*. Toronto: HarperCollins.

Kirby, Sandra, and Kate McKenna. 1989. *Experience Research Social Change: Methods from the Margins*. Toronto: Garamond.

Kirby, S.L., and A. Robinson. 1998. *Lesbian Struggles for Human Rights in Canada: Report to the Secretary of State on the Status of Women*. Ottawa.

Kirmayer. Laurence J. 1994. "Suicide Among Canadian Aboriginal Peoples." *Transcultural Psychiatric Research Review*, 31:7.

Kitano, Harry, and Iris Chi. 1986–87. "Asian Americans and Alcohol Use." *Alcohol Health and Research World*, 11:42–46.

Kitano, Harry, Iris Chi, Siyon Rhee, C.K. Law, and James E. Lubben. 1992. "Norms and Alcohol Consumption: Japanese in Japan, Hawaii, and California." *Journal of Studies on Alcohol*, 53(1):33–39.

Kitcher, Brigitte, Andrew Mitchell, Peter Clutterbuck, and Marvyn Novick. 1991.

Unequal Futures: The Legacies of Child Poverty in Canada. Toronto: Child Poverty Action Group and the Social Planning Council of Metropolitan Toronto.

Klein, Alan M. 1993. *Little Big Men: Bodybuilding Subculture and Gender Construction*. Albany: SUNY Press.

Klockars, Carl B. 1979. "The Contemporary Crises of Marxist Criminology." *Criminology*, 16:477–515.

Kluckhohn, Clyde. 1961. "The Study of Values." In Donald N. Barrett (ed.), *Values in America*. South Bend, Ind.: University of Notre Dame Press, 17–46.

Knox, Paul L., and Peter J. Taylor (eds.). 1995. *World Cities in a World-System*. Cambridge, England: Cambridge University Press.

Knudsen, Dean D. 1992. *Child Maltreatment: Emerging Perspectives*. Dix Hills, N.Y.: General Hall.

Kohlberg, Lawrence. 1969. "Stage and Sequence: The Cognitive-Developmental Approach to Socialization." In David A. Goslin, *Handbook of Socialization Theory and Research*. Chicago: Rand McNally, 347–480.

———. 1981. "The Philosophy of Moral Development: Moral Stages and the Idea of Justice." *Essays on Moral Development*, vol. 1. San Francisco: Harper & Row.

Kohn, Melvin L. 1977. *Class and Conformity: A Study in Values* (2nd ed.). Homewood, Ill.: Dorsey Press.

Kohn, Melvin L., Atsushi Naoi, Carrie Schoenbach, Carmi Schooler, and Kazimierz M. Slomczynski. 1990. "Position in the Class Structure and Psychological Functioning in the United States, Japan, and Poland." *American Journal of Sociology*, 95:964–1008.

Kolata, Gina. 1993. "Fear of Fatness: Living Large in a Slimfast World." *Austin American-Statesman* (January 3):C1, C6.

Korsmeyer, Carolyn. 1981. "The Hidden Joke: Generic Uses of Masculine Terminology." In Mary Vetterling-Braggin (ed.), *Sexist Language: A Modern Philosphical Analysis*. Totowa, NJ: Littlefield, Adams, 116–131.

Korten, David C. 1996. *When Corporations Rule the World*. West Hartford, Conn.: Kumarian Press.

Kosmin, Barry A., and Seymour P. Lachman. 1993. *One Nation Under God: Religion in Contemporary American Society*. New York: Crown.

Kovacs, M., and A.T. Beck. 1977. "The Wish to Live and the Wish to Die in Attempted Suicides." *Journal of Clinical Psychology*, 33:361–365.

Kozol, Jonathan. 1988. *Rachael and Her Children: Homeless Families in America*. New York: Fawcett Columbine.

———. 1991. *Savage Inequalities: Children in America's Schools*. New York: Crown.

Krahn, Harvey J. 1995a. "Non-standard Work on the Rise." *Perspectives on Labour and Income* (Winter): Ottawa: Statistics Canada, 35–42.

———. 1995b. "Social Stratification." In Robert J. Brym, *New Society for the 21st Century*. Toronto: Harcourt Brace and Company, 2.1–2.31.

Krahn, Harvey J., and Graham S. Lowe. 1993. *Work, Industry, and Canadian Society*. Scarborough, Ont.: Nelson Canada.

———. 1996. *New Forms of Management and Work in Society in Question: Sociological Readings for the 21st Century*. Toronto: Harcourt Brace and Company.

———. 1998. *Work, Industry, and Canadian Society* (3rd ed.). Scarborough, Ont.: Nelson Canada.

Krueger, Lesley. 1997. "Education Report: The Kumon Way." *Canadian Family* (September/October): 23.

Krysan, Maria, and Reynolds Farley. 1993. "Racial Stereotypes: Are They Alive and Well? Do They Continue to Influence Race Relations?" Paper presented at the Annual Meeting of the American Sociological Association, Miami Beach, Florida, August 16.

Kübler-Ross, Elisabeth. 1969. *On Death and Dying*. New York: Macmillan.

Kunen, James S. 1990. "Pop! Goes the Donald," *People* (July 9):29–34.

Kurian, George. 1991. "Socialization in South Asian Immigrant Youth." In S.P. Sharma, A.M. Erwin, and D. Meintel (eds.), *Immigrants and Refugees in Canada*. Saskatoon: University of Saskatchewan.

Kurtz, Lester. 1995. *Gods in the Global Village: The World's Religions in Sociological Perspective*. Thousand Oaks, Cal.: Sage.

Ladd, E.C., Jr. 1966. *Negro Political Leadership in the South*. Ithaca, N.Y.: Cornell University Press.

Lalonde, Michelle. 1996. "The Mayor's Vision." *The Montreal Gazette* (May 4).

Lam, Andrew. 1995. "Beyond Clayoquot Sound." *Earth Island Journal* (June):24.

Lamanna, Marianne, and Agnes Riedmann. 1994. *Marriages and Families: Making Choices and Facing Change* (5th ed.). Belmont, Cal.: Wadsworth.

———. 1997. Marriages and Families: Making Choices and Facing Change (6th ed.). Belmont, Cal.: Wadsworth.

Land, Helen, 1994. "AIDS and Women of Color." *Families in Society: The Journal of Contemporary Human Services,* 75(6):355–362.

Lane, Harlan. 1992. *The Mask of Benevolence: Disabling the Deaf Community*. New York: Vintage Books.

Lanford, Audri, and Jim Lanford. 1998. "Urban Legends: Don't Believe Everything You Read" in *Internet Scambusters*. Available: www.scambusters.org/ Scambusters22.html

Langewiesche, William. 1998. "The Lessons of ValuJet 592." *The Atlantic Monthly* (March).

Lapchick, Richard E. 1991. *Five Minutes to Midnight: Race and Sport in the 1990s*. Lanham, MD: Madison Books

Lapsley, Daniel K. 1990. "Continuity and Discontinuity in Adolescent Social Cognitive Development." In Raymond Montemayor, Gerald R. Adams, and Thomas P. Gullota (eds.), *From Childhood to Adolescence: A Transitional Period? (Advances in Adolescent Development*, vol. 2). Newbury Park, Cal.: Sage.

Larson, Magali Sarfatti. 1977. *The Rise of Professionalism: A Sociological Analysis*. Berkeley: University of California Press.

Lasch, Christopher. 1977. *Haven in a Heartless World*. New York: Basic Books.

Latane, Bibb, and John M. Darley. 1970. *The Unresponsive Bystander: Why Doesn't He Help?* New York: Appleton Century Crofts.

Latouche, Serge. 1992. "Standard of Living." In Wolfgang Sachs (ed.), *The Development Dictionary*. Atlantic Highlands, NJ: Zed Books, pp. 250–263.

Laumann, Edward O., John H. Gagnon, Robert T. Michael, and Stuart Michaels. 1994. *The Social Organization of Sexuality*. Chicago: University of Chicago Press.

Lavigne, Yves. 1987. *Hell's Angels: Taking Care of Business*. Toronto: Ballantine Books.

Law Reform Commission of Canada. 1974. *The Native Offender and the Law*. Ottawa: Information Canada.

Le Bon, Gustave. 1960. *The Crowd: A Study of the Popular Mind*. New York: Viking (orig. pub. 1895).

Lee, Sharon M. 1993. "Racial Classifications in the U.S. Census: 1890–1990." *Ethnic and Racial Studies*, 16(1):75–94.

Leenaars, Antoon A. (ed.). 1991. *Life Span Perspectives of Suicide: Time-Lines in the Suicide Process*. New York: Plenum Press.

Leenaars, Antoon A., Susan Wenckstern, Isaac Sakinofsky, Ronald J. Dyck, Michael J. Kral, and Roger C. Bland. 1998. *Suicide in Canada*. Toronto: University of Toronto Press.

Lefrançois, Guy R. 1993. *The Lifespan* (4th ed.). Belmont, Cal.: Wadsworth.

Lehmann, Jennifer M. 1994. *Durkheim and Women*. Lincoln: University of Nebraska Press.

Lele, J., G.C. Perlin, and H.G. Thorburn. 1979. "The National Party Convention." In H.G. Thorburn (ed.), *Political Parties in Canada*. Scarborough, Ont.: Prentice Hall, 89–97.

Lemann, Nicholas. 1997. "Let's Guarantee the Key Ingredients." *Time* (October 27):96.

Lemert, Edwin M. 1951. *Social Pathology*. New York: McGraw-Hill.

Lengermann, Patricia Madoo, and Ruth A. Wallace. 1985. *Gender in America: Social Control and Social Change*. Englewood Cliffs, N.J.: Prentice-Hall.

Lenski, Gerhard. 1966. *Power and Privilege: A Theory of Social Stratification*. New York: McGraw-Hill.

Lenski, Gerhard, Jean Lenski, and Patrick Nolan. 1991. *Human Societies: An Introduction to Macrosociology* (6th ed.). New York: McGraw-Hill.

Leonard, Margaret A., and Stacy Randell. 1992. "Policy Shifts in the Massachusetts Response to Family Homelessness." In Padraig O'Malley, "Homelessness: New England and Beyond." *New England Journal of Public Policy, Special Issue* (May):483–497.

Lerner, Gerda. 1986. *The Creation of Patriarchy*. New York: Oxford University Press.

LeShan, Eda. 1994. *I Want More of Everything*. New York: New Market Press.

Lester, David. 1992. *Why People Kill Themselves: A 1990s Summary of Research Findings of Suicidal Behavior* (3rd ed.). Springfield, Ill.: Thomas.

Lester, David, and Margot Tallmer (eds.). 1993. *Now I Lay Me Down: Suicide in the Elderly.* Philadelphia: Charles Press.

Letkemann, Peter. 1973. *Crime as Work.* Englewood Cliffs, N.J.: Prentice-Hall.

Leventman, Paula Goldman. 1981. *Professionals Out of Work.* New York: Free Press.

Leviathan, U., and J. Cohen. 1985. "Gender Differences in Life Expectancy among Kibburz Members." *Social Science and Medicine,* 21:545–551.

Levin, Jack, and Jack McDevitt. 1993. *Hate Crimes: The Rising Tide of Bigotry and Bloodshed.* New York: Plenum Press.

Levin, William C. 1988. "Age Stereotyping: College Student Evaluations." *Research on Aging,* 10(1):134–148.

Levine, Adeline Gordon. 1982a. *Love Canal: Science, Politics, and People.* Lexington, Mass.: Lexington Books.

Levine, Murray. 1982b. "Introduction." In Lois Marie Gibbs, *Love Canal: My Story.* Albany: SUNY Press.

LeVine, Steve. 1997. "How to Amuse Rich Russians: Odds on the Horses." *New York Times* (October 15):A4.

Levitt, Kari. 1970. *Silent Surrender: the Multinational Corporation in Canada.* Toronto: Macmillan of Canada.

Levy, Janice C., and Eva Y. Deykin. 1989. "Suicidality, Depression, and Substance Abuse in Adolescence." *American Journal of Psychiatry,* 146(11): 1462–1468.

Lewis-Thornton, Rae. 1994. "Facing AIDS." *Essence* (December):63–130.

Leyton, Elliott. 1979. *The Myth of Delinquency: An Anatomy of Juvenile Nihilism.* Toronto: McClelland and Stewart.

Liebow, Elliot. 1993. *Tell Them Who I Am: The Lives of Homeless Women.* New York: Free Press.

Linden, Rick. 1994. "Deviance and Crime." In Lorne Tepperman, James E. Curtis, and R.J. Richardson (eds.), *The Social World* (3rd ed.). Whitby, Ont.: McGraw-Hill Ryerson, 188–226.

———. 2000. *Criminology: A Canadian Perspective,* 4th ed. Toronto: Harcourt Brace.

Linden, Rick and Raymond C. Currie. 1977. "Religiosity and Drug Use: A Test of Social Control Theory." *Canadian Journal of Criminology and Corrections* 19:346–355.

———, and Cathy Fillmore. 1981. "A Comparative Study of Delinquency Involvement." *Canadian Review of Sociology and Anthropology* 18:343–361.

Linton, Ralph. 1936. *The Study of Man.* New York: Appleton-Century-Crofts.

Lipovenko, Dorothy. 1997. "Older People Looking for Work Often Face Frowns, Study Says." *The Globe and Mail* (November 19):A6.

Lippa, Richard A. 1994. *Introduction to Social Psychology.* Pacific Grove, Cal.: Brooks/Cole.

Lips, Hilary M. 1989. "Gender-Role Socialization: Lessons in Femininity." In Jo Freeman (ed.), *Women: A Feminist Perspective* (4th ed.). Mountain View, Cal.: Mayfield, 197–216.

———. 1993. *Sex and Gender: An Introduction* (2nd ed.). Mountain View, Cal.: Mayfield.

Livingston, D.W., and Meg Luxton. 1995. "Gender Consciousness at Work: Modification of the Male Breadwinner Norm Among Steelworkers and Their Spouses." In E.D. Nelson and B.W. Robinson (eds.), *Gender in the 1990s.* Scarborough, Ont.: Nelson Canada, 172–200.

Lochhead, Clarence, and Richard Shillington. 1996. *A Statistical Profile of Urban Poverty.* Ottawa: Canadian Council of Social Development.

Lofland, John. 1971. *Analyzing Social Settings.* Belmont: Wadsworth Publishing.

———. 1993. "Collective Behavior: The Elementary Forms." In Russell L. Curtis, Jr., and Benigno E. Aguirre (eds.), *Collective Behavior and Social Movements.* Boston: Allyn & Bacon, 70–75.

Lombardo, William K., Gary A. Cretser, Barbara Lombardo, and Sharon L. Mathis. 1983. "For Cryin' Out Loud— There Is a Sex Difference." *Sex Roles,* 9:987–995.

Lorber, Judith. 1994. *Paradoxes of Gender.* New Haven, Conn.: Yale University Press.

Lorch, Donatella. 1993. "With 9% HIV Infection Rate, Uganda Is a Nation of Orphans." *Austin American-Statesman* (Mar. 7):D4.

Loseke, Donileen. 1992. *The Battered Woman and Shelters: The Social Construction of Wife Abuse.* Albany: SUNY Press.

Lott, Bernice. 1994. *Women's Lives: Themes and Variations in Gender Learning* (2nd ed.). Pacific Grove, Cal.: Brooks/Cole.

Lowe, Graham S. 1999. "Labour Markets, Inequality, and the Future of Work." In

Curtis, James, Edward Grabb and Neil Guppy (eds.), *Social Inequality in Canada: Patterns, Problems, and Policies.* Scarborough: Prentice Hall, 113–128.

Luffman, Jacqueline. 1998. "When Parents Replace Teachers: The Home Schooling Option." *Canadian Scoial Trends* (Autumn). Cat. no. 11-008-XPE. Ottawa: Statistics Canada, 8–10.

Lummis, C. Douglas. 1992. "Equality." In Wolfgang Sachs (ed.), *The Development Dictionary.* Atlantic Highlands, NJ: Zed Books, 38–52.

Lupul, M.R. 1988. "Ukrainians: The Fifth Cultural Wheel in Canada." In Ian H. Angus (ed.), *Ethnicity in a Technological Age.* Edmonton: Canadian Institute of Ukrainian Studies, University of Alberta, 177–192.

Lurie, Alison. 1981. *The Language of Clothes.* New York: Random House.

Luttrell, Wendy. 1997. *School-Smart and Mother-Wise: Working-Class Women's Identity and Schooling.* New York: Routledge.

Luttwak, Eugene. 1996. Quoted in Kenneth Kidd, "Social Contracts." *The Globe and Mail Report on Business Magazine* (September):24.

Luxton, Meg. 1980. *More Than a Labour of Love.* Toronto: Women's Press.

———. 1995. "Two hands for the Clock: Changing Patterns of Gendered Division of Labour in the Home." In E.D. Nelson and B.W. Robinson (eds.), *Gender in the 1990s.* Scarborough, Ont.: Nelson Canada, 288–301.

Lynn, Marion (ed.). 1996. *Voices: Essays on Canadian Families.* Scarborough, Ont.: Nelson Canada.

Lynn, Marion, and Eimear O'Neill. 1995. "Families, Power and Violence." In Nancy Mandell and Ann Duffy (eds.) *Canadian Families: Diversity, Conflict and Change.* Toronto: Harcourt Brace and Company, 271–305.

Lyons, John. 1998. "The Way We Live: Central Plains." *Winnipeg Free Press* (June 7):B3.

Maccoby, Eleanor E., and Carol Nagy Jacklin. 1987. "Gender Segregation in Childhood." *Advances in Child Development and Behavior,* 20:239–287.

MacDonald, Kevin, and Ross D. Parke. 1986. "Parental-Child Physical Play: The Effects of Sex and Age of Children and Parents." *Sex Roles,* 15:367–378.

Mack, Raymond W., and Calvin P. Bradford. 1979. *Transforming America: Patterns of Social Change* (2nd ed.). New York: Random House.

Mackie, Marlene. 1995. "Gender in the Family: Changing Patterns." In Nancy Mandell and Ann Duffy (eds.), *Canadian Families: Diversity, Conflict, and Change* (2nd ed.). Toronto: Harcourt Brace, 17-43.

Mackintosh, Maureen M. 1979. "Domestic Labour and the Household." In Sandra Burman (ed.), *Fit Work for Women*. London: Croom Helm.

MacLean, M.J. and R. Bonar. 1983. "The Normalization Principle and the Institutionalization of the Elderly." *Canada's Mental Health*, 31: 16–18.

Maclean's. 1996. "What people are saying." December 2.

———. 1999. (Feb. 15):33.

MacLeod, Jay. 1988. *Ain't No Makin' It: Leveled Aspirations in a Low-Income Neighborhood*. Boulder, Col.: Westview Press.

MacLeod, Linda. 1987. *Battered But NOT Beaten: Preventing Wife Battering in Canada*. Ottawa: Canadian Advisory Council on the Status of Women.

MacSween, Morag. 1993. *Anorexic Bodies: A Feminist and Sociological Perspective on Anorexia Nervosa*. New York: Routledge.

McDonald, Marci. 1996. "The New Spirituality." *Maclean's* (October 10):44–48.

Maggio, Rosalie. 1988. The Non-Sexist Word Finder: A Dictionary of Gender-Free Usage. Boston: Beacon Press.

Malinowski, Bronislaw. 1922. *Argonauts of the Western Pacific*. New York: Dutton.

———. 1964. "The Principle of Legitimacy: Parenthood, the Basis of Social Structure." In Rose Laub Coser (ed.), *The Family: Its Structure and Functions*. New York: St. Martin's Press (orig. pub. 1929).

Malson, Lucien. 1972. *Wolf Children and the Problem of Human Nature*. New York: Monthly Review Press.

Man, Guida. 1996. "The Experience of Middle-Class Women in Recent Hong Kong Chinese Immigrant Families in Canada." In Marion Lynn (ed.), *Voices: Essays on Canadian Families*. Toronto: Nelson Canada, 271–300.

Mandell, N., and A. Duffy (eds.). 1988. *Constructing the Canadian Family: Feminist Perspectives*. Toronto: Butterworths.

Mandell, Nancy, and Julianne Momirov. 1999. "Family Histories." In Nancy Mandell and Ann Duffy (eds.), *Canadian Families: Diversity, Conflict, and Change* (2nd ed.). Toronto: Harcourt Brace, 17-43.

Mann, Patricia S. 1994. *Micro-Politics: Agency in a Postfeminist Era*. Minneapolis: University of Minnesota Press.

Mansfield, Alan, and Barbara McGinn. 1993. "Pumping Irony: The Muscular and the Feminine." In Sue Scott and David Morgan (eds.), *Body Matters: Essays on the Sociology of the Body*. London: Falmer Press, 49–58.

Mao, Y., B.W. Moloughney, R. Semenciw, and H. Morrison. 1992. "Indian Reserve and Registered Indian Mortality in Canada." *Canadian Journal of Public Health*, 83:350–353.

Marble, Michelle. 1995. "Eating Disorders Awareness Week: February 6–12, 1995." *Women's Health Weekly* (February 6):12.

Marchak, Patricia. 1975. *Ideological Perspectives on Canadian Society*. Toronto: McGraw-Hill.

Marcil-Gratton, Nicole. 1993. "Growing Up with a Single Parent, a Transitional Experience? Some Demographic Measurements." In J. Hudson and B. Galaway (eds.), *Single Parent Families with Perspectives on Research and Policy*. Toronto: Thompson Educational Publishing.

Marger, Martin N. 1987. *Elites and Masses: An Introduction to Political Sociology* (2nd ed.). Belmont, Cal.: Wadsworth.

———. 1994. *Race and Ethnic Relations: American and Global Perspectives*. Belmont, Cal.: Wadsworth.

———. 1997. *Race and Ethnic Relations: American and Global Perspectives* (2nd ed.). Belmont, Cal.: Wadsworth.

Marsden, Lorna, and Brenda Robertson. 1991. *Children in Poverty: Toward a Better Future*. Ottawa: Standing Committee on Social Affairs, Science, and Technology.

Marshall, Gordon (ed.). 1994. *The Concise Oxford Dictionary of Sociology*. New York: Oxford University Press.

Marshall, Katherine. 1990. "Women in Professional Occupations: Progress in the 1980s." In Craig McKie and Keith Thompson (eds.), *Canadian Social Trends*. Toronto: Thompson Educational Publishers, 109–112.

———. 1995. "Dual Earners: Who's Responsible for Housework?" In E.D. Nelson and B.W. Robinson, *Gender in the 1990s*. Scarborough, Ont.: Nelson Canada, 302–308.

Martin, Carol L. 1989. "Children's Use of Gender-Related Information in Making Social Judgments." *Developmental Psychology*, 25:80–88.

Martin, James G., and Clyde W. Franklin. 1983. *Minority Group Relations*. Columbus, Ohio: Charles E. Merrill Publishing.

Martin, Nick. 1996. "Aboriginal Speech Dying." *Winnipeg Free Press* (March 29): A8.

Martin, Teresa Castro, and Larry L. Bumpass. 1989. "Recent Trends in Marital Disruption." *Demography*, 26:37–51.

Martineau, Harriet. 1962. *Society in America* (edited, abridged). Garden City, N.Y.: Doubleday (orig. pub. 1837).

———. 1988. *How to Observe Morals and Manners*. Michael R. Hill (ed.). New Brunswick, N.J.: Transaction (orig. pub. 1838).

Martinussen, John. 1997. *Society, State and Market: A Guide to Competing Theories of Development*. Halifax: Fernwood Books.

Marx, Karl. 1967. *Capital: A Critique of Political Economy*. Friedrich Engels (ed.). New York: International Publishers (orig. pub. 1867).

Marx, Karl, and Friedrich Engels. 1967. *The Communist Manifesto*. New York: Pantheon (orig. pub. 1848).

Mason Lee, Robert. 1991. *Death and Deliverance*. Toronto: Macfarlane Walter and Ross.

———. 1998. "I'll Be Home for Christmas." *The Globe and Mail*. 24 December.

Matas, David. 1995. "A Valuable Survey of Canadian Race Controversies." *The Globe and Mail* (July 8):C8.

Matthews, Warren. 1995. *World Religions*. St. Paul, Minn.: West.

Maynard, Rona. 1987. "How Do You Like Your Job?" *The Globe and Mail Report on Business Magazine* (November):120–25.

McAdam, Doug, John D. McCarthy, and Mayer N. Zald. 1988. "Social Movements." In Neil J. Smelser (ed.), *Handbook of Sociology*. Newbury Park, Cal.: Sage, 695–737.

McCall, George J., and Jerry L. Simmons, 1978. *Identities and Interactions: An Explanation of Human Associations in Everyday Life*. New York: Free Press.

McCarroll, Thomas. 1993. "New Star Over Asia." *Time* (August 9):53.

McCarthy, John D., and Mayer N. Zald. 1977. "Resource Mobilization and Social Movements: A Partial Theory." *American Journal of Sociology*, 82:1212–1241.

McCormick, Chris. 1995. *Constructing Danger: The Misrepresentation of Crime in the News*. Halifax: Fernwood Publishing.

McDaniel, S.A. 1994. *Family and Friends*. Ottawa: Statistics Canada.

McDaniel, Susan. 1991. "Feminist Scholarship in Sociology: Transformation from Within." *Canadian Journal of Sociology*, 16:303-312.

McDonald, Marci. 1994. "The New Spirituality." *Maclean's* (October 10):44–48.

McEachern, William A. 1994. *Economics: A Contemporary Introduction*. Cincinnati: South-Western.

McElroy, Ann, and Patricia K. Townsend. 1989. *Medical Anthropology in Ecological Perspective* (2nd ed.). Boulder, Col.: Westview Press.

McGee, Reece. 1975. *Points of Departure*. Hinsdale, IL: Dryden Press.

McGovern, Celeste. 1995. "Dr. Death Speaks." *Alberta Report/Western Report*, 22(January 9):33.

McGuigan, Cathleen. 1993. "Michael's World." *Newsweek* (September 6):34–39.

McGuire, Meredith B. 1992. *Religion: The Social Context* (2nd ed.). Belmont, Cal.: Wadsworth.

———. 1997. *Religion: The Social Context* (4th ed.). Belmont, Cal.: Wadsworth.

McIntosh, Mary. 1978. "The State and the Oppression of Women." In Annette Kuhn and Ann Marie Wolpe (eds.), *Feminism and Materialism*. London: Routledge and Kegan Paul.

McKenzie, Roderick D. 1925. "The Ecological Approach to the Study of the Human Community." In Robert Park, Ernest Burgess, and Roderick D. McKenzie, *The City*. Chicago: University of Chicago Press.

McKie, Craig. 1994. "Population Aging: Baby Boomers into the 21st Century." *Canadian Social Trends*. Toronto: Thompson Educational Publishing, 3–7.

McKie, D.C., B. Prentice, and P. Reid. 1983. *Divorce Law and Family in Canada*. Ottawa: Statistics Canada.

McLanahan, Sara, and Karen Booth. 1991. "Mother-Only Families." In Alan Booth (ed.), *Contemporary Families: Looking Forward, Looking Backward*. Minneapolis: National Council on Family Relations, 405–428.

McLeod, Jonah. 1994. "Helping China Adopt Free Enterprise." *Electronics* (August 8):15.

McPhail, Clark. 1971. "Civil Disorder Participation: A Critical Examination of Recent Research." *American Sociological Review*, 36:1058–1073.

———. 1991. *The Myth of the Maddening Crowd*. New York: Aldine de Gruyter.

McPhail, Clark, and Ronald T. Wohlstein. 1983. "Individual and Collective Behavior within Gatherings, Demonstrations, and Riots." In Ralph H. Turner and James F. Short, Jr. (eds.), *Annual Review of Sociology*, vol. 9. Palo Alto, Cal.: Annual Reviews, 579–600.

McPherson, Barry D. 1998. *Aging as a Social Process: An Introduction to Individual and Population Aging*. Toronto: Harcourt Brace.

McPherson, J. Miller, and Lynn Smith-Lovin. 1982. "Women and Weak Ties: Differences by Sex in the Size of Voluntary Organizations." *American Journal of Sociology*, 87(January): 883–904.

———. 1986. "Sex Segregation in Voluntary Associations." *American Sociological Review*, 51 (February):61–79.

McQuaig, Linda. 1993. *The Wealthy Banker's Wife: The Assault on Equality in Canada*. Toronto: Penguin.

McQuillan, Kevin, and Marilyn Belle. 1999. "Who Does What? Gender and the Division of Labour in Canadian Households." In Curtis, James E., Edward Grabb, and Neil Guppy (eds.), *Social Inequality in Canada: Patterns, Problems, Policies* (3rd ed.). Scarborough, Ont.: Prentice Hall, 186–198.

McVey, Wayne W., and Warren Kalbach. 1995. *Canadian Population*. Scarborough, Ont.: Nelson Canada.

Mead, George Herbert. 1934. *Mind, Self, and Society*. Chicago: University of Chicago Press.

Medved, Michael. 1992. *Hollywood vs. America: Popular Culture and the War on Traditional Values*. New York: HarperPerennial.

Merchant, Carolyn. 1983. *The Death of Nature: Women, Ecology, and the Scientific Revolution*. San Francisco: Harper & Row.

———. 1992. *Radical Ecology: The Search for a Livable World*. New York: Routledge.

Merton, Robert King. 1938. "Social Structure and Anomie." *American Sociological Review*, 3(6):672–682.

———. 1949. "Discrimination and the American Creed." In Robert M. MacIver (ed.), *Discrimination and National Welfare*. New York: Harper & Row, 99–126.

———. 1968. *Social Theory and Social Structure* (enlarged ed.). New York: Free Press.

Miall, Charlene. 1986. "The Stigma of Involuntary Childlessness." *Social Problems*, 33(4):268–282.

Michael, Robert T., John H. Gagnon, Edward O. Laumann, and Gina Kolata. 1994. *Sex in America*. Boston: Little, Brown.

Michels, Robert. 1949. *Political Parties*. Glencoe, Ill.: Free Press (orig. pub. 1911).

Michelson, William H. 1976. *Man and His Urban Environment: A Sociological Approach with Revisions*. Reading, Mass.: Addison-Wesley.

———. 1977. *Environmental Choice, Human Behavior, and Residential Satisfaction*. New York: Oxford University Press.

———. 1994. "Cities and Urbanization." In Lorne Tepperman, James Curtis, and R.J. Richardson (eds.), *The Social World* (3rd ed.). Toronto: McGraw-Hill, 672–709.

Mies, Maria, and Vandana Shiva. 1993. *Ecofeminism*. Highlands, N.J.: Zed Books.

Mihorean, Steve, and Stan Lipinski. 1992. "International Incarceration Patterns, 1980–1990." *Jusistat*, 12(3). Ottawa: Statistics Canada.

Milgram, Stanley. 1963. "Behavioral Study of Obedience." *Journal of Abnormal and Social Psychology*, 67:371–378.

———. 1974. *Obedience to Authority*. New York: Harper & Row.

Miliband, Ralph. 1969. The State in Capitalist Society. New York: Basic Books.

Miller, Casey, and Kate Swift. 1991. *Words and Women: New Language in New Times* (updated). New York: HarperCollins.

———. 1993. "Who Is Man?" In Anne Minas, *Gender Basics: Feminist Perspectives on Women and Men*. Belmont, Cal.: Wadsworth, 68–75.

Miller, Dan E. 1986. "Milgram Redux: Obedience and Disobedience in Authority Relations." In Norman K. Denzin (ed.), *Studies in Symbolic Interaction*. Greenwich, Conn.: JAI Press, 77–106.

Miller, L. Scott. 1995. *An American Imperative: Accelerating Minority Educational Advancement*. New Haven, Conn: Yale University Press.

Mills, C. Wright. 1959a. *The Sociological Imagination*. London: Oxford University Press.

Mills, C. Wright. 1959b. *The Power Elite*. Fair Lawn, N.J.: Oxford University Press.

Mintz, Laurie B., and Nancy E. Betz. 1986. "Sex Differences in the Nature, Realism, and Correlates of Body Image." *Sex Roles*, 15:185–195.

Misztal, Barbara A. 1993. "Understanding Political Change in Eastern Europe: A Sociological Perspective." *Sociology*, 27(3):451–471.

Mitchell, Alana. 1999. "Home Schooling Goes AWOL." *The Globe and Mail* (February 2):A1, A7.

Mitchell, Alanna. 1997a. "Face of Canada Changes." *The Globe and Mail* (November 5):A1.

———. 1997b. "Native Life in Canada: Seed Money for Grassroots Entrepreneurs." *The Globe and Mail* (July 22).

Mitchell, Catherine. 1995. "Expert Takes a Swipe at Spanking." *Winnipeg Free Press* (November 23).

Molotch, Harvey, and Marilyn Lester. 1974. "News as Purposive Behavior: On the Strategic Use of Routine Events, Accidents and Scandals." *American Sociological Review*, 39:101–112.

Monette, Manon. 1996. "Retirement in the 90s: Retired Men in Canada." *Canadian Social Trends* (Autumn):8–11.

Money, John, and Anke A. Ehrhardt. 1972. *Man and Woman, Boy and Girl*. Baltimore: Johns Hopkins University Press.

Moody, Harry R. 1994. *Aging: Concepts and Controversy*. Thousand Oaks, Cal.: Pine Forge Press.

Moog, Carol. 1990. *Are They Selling Her Lips? Advertising and Identity*. New York: Morrow.

Moore, Patricia, with C.P. Conn. 1985. *Disguised*. Waco, Tex.: Word Books.

Moorhead, Caroline (ed.). 1992. *Betrayal: A Report on Violence Toward Children in Today's World*. New York: Doubleday.

Moreau, Joanne. 1994. "Employment Equity." In Craig McKie and Keith Thompson (eds.), *Canadian Social Trends*, vol. 2. Toronto: Thompson Educational Publishers, 147–49.

Morgan, S. Philip, Diane N. Lye, and Gretchen A. Condran. 1988. "Sons, Daughters, and the Risk of Marital Disruption." *American Journal of Sociology*, 94(1):110–129.

Morselli, Henry. 1975. *Suicide: An Essay on Comparative Moral Statistics*. New York: Arno Press (orig. pub. 1881).

Mosher, Steven W. 1994. *A Mother's Ordeal: One Woman's Fight Against China's One-Child Policy*. New York: HarperPerennial.

Mucciolo, Louis. 1992. *Eightysomething: Interviews with Octogenarians Who Stay Involved*. New York: Birch Lane Press.

Mukerji, Chandra, and Michael Schudson. 1991. *Rethinking Popular Culture: Contemporary Perspectives in Cultural Studies*. Berkeley: University of California Press.

Murdock, George P. 1945. "The Common Denominator of Cultures." In Ralph Linton (ed.), *The Science of Man in the World Crisis*. New York: Columbia University Press, 123–142.

Murphy, Emily F. 1922. *The Black Candle*. Toronto: Thomas Allan.

Myles, John. 1999. "Demography or Democracy? The 'Crisis' of Old-Age Security." In Curtis, James E., Edward Grabb, and Neil Guppy (eds.), *Social Inequality in Canada: Patterns, Problems, Policies* (3rd ed.). Scarborough, Ont.: Prentice Hall.

Myrdal, Gunnar. 1970. The Challenge of World Poverty: A World Anti-Poverty Program in Outline. New York: Pantheon/Random House.

NACA. 1992. *The NACA Position on Canada's Oldest Seniors: Maintaining the Quality of Their Lives*. Ottawa: National Advisory Council on Aging, 54–55.

Nader, George A. 1976. *Cities of Canada*, vol. 2. *Profiles of Fifteen Metropolitan Centres*. Toronto: Macmillan of Canada.

Naeyaert, Kathleen. 1990. *Living with Sensory Loss: Vision*. Ottawa: National Advisory Council on Aging.

Nagler, Mark. 1997. *Yes You Can: A Guide for Parents of Children with Disabilities*. Toronto: Stoddart.

Nairne, Doug. 1998. "Good Samaritan Feels That He Was Victimized Twice." *Winnipeg Free Press* (June 4):A4.

Nakhaie, M. Reza, and Robert Arnold. 1996. "Class Position, Class Ideology, and Class Voting: Mobilization of Support for the New Democratic Party in the Canadian Election of 1984." *Canadian Review of Sociology and Anthropology*, 33(2):181–212.

Nancarrow Clarke, Jvanne. 1996. *Health, Illness and Medicine in Canada*. Toronto: Oxford University Press.

Nason-Clark, Nancy. 1993. "Gender Relations in Contemporary Christian Organizations." In W.E. Hewitt (ed.), *The Sociology of Religion: A Canadian Focus*. Toronto: Butterworths, 215–234.

National Cancer Institute of Canada. 1997. *Canadian Cancer Statistics 1997*. Toronto: The Canadian Cancer Society.

National Council of Welfare. 1996. *Poverty Profile 1994*. Ottawa: Minister of Supply and Services Canada.

———. 1998. *Poverty Profile 1996*. Ottawa: Minister of Supply and Services Canada.

National Media Archive. 1997. "TV Coverage Down: Murder Rate Up Slightly." *On Balance*. 10(7). Vancouver: The Fraser Institute.

National Opinion Research Center (NORC). 1993. *General Social Surveys, 1972–1993: Cumulative Codebook*. Chicago: National Opinion Research Center.

National Safety Council. 1992. *Accident Facts: 1992 Edition*. Chicago: National Safety Council.

Navarrette, Ruben, Jr. 1997. "A Darker Shade of Crimson." In Diana Kendall (ed.), *Race, Class, and Gender in a Diverse Society*. Boston, Mass.: Allyn and Bacon, 1997:274–279. Reprinted from Ruben Navarrette, Jr., *A Darker Shade of Crimson*. New York: Bantam, 1993.

Nemeth, Mary, Sharon Doyle Driedger, John DeMont, and Adrienne Webb. 1994. "Body Obsession." *Maclean's* (February 5):44.

Nemeth, Mary, Nora Underwood, and John Howse. 1993. "God Is Alive." *Maclean's* (April 12):32–36.

Nessner, Katherine. 1994. "Profile of Canadians with Disabilities." In Craig McKie (ed.), *Canadian Social Trends*. Toronto: Thompson Educational Publishing Company, 121–124.

Nett, Emily M. 1993. *Canadian Families: Past and Present* (2nd ed.). Toronto: Butterworths.

Nettler, Gwynn. 1984. *Explaining Crime* (3rd ed.). Toronto: McGraw-Hill.

Newman, David M. 1995. *Sociology: Exploring the Architecture of Everyday Life*. Thousand Oaks, Cal.: Pine Forge Press.

Newman, Katherine S. 1988. *Falling from Grace: The Experience of Downward*

Mobility in the American Middle Class. New York: Free Press.

———. 1993a. Declining Fortunes: The Withering of the American Dream. New York: Basic Books.

Newman, Peter C. 1993b. "Trees Are Renewable, But Forests Are Not." Maclean's (August 16):44.

Nichols, Mark. 1993. "The World Is Watching." Maclean's (August 16):22–26.

———. 1999. "Men's Health." Maclean's (February 22):28–29.

Niebuhr, H. Richard. 1929. The Social Sources of Denominationalism. New York: Meridian.

Nielsen, Joyce McCarl. 1990. Sex and Gender in Society: Perspectives on Stratification (2nd ed.). Prospects Heights, Ill.: Waveland Press.

Ng, Edward. 1994. "Children and Elderly People: Sharing Public Income Resources." In Craig McKie (ed.), Canadian Social Trends. Toronto: Thompson Educational Publishing Company, 249–252.

Norland, J.A. 1994. Profile of Canada's Seniors, Cat. no. 96–312E. Scarborough, Ont.: Statistics Canada and Prentice-Hall.

Norris, Mary Jane. 1998. "Canada's Aborginal Languages." Canadian Social Trends (Winter):8–16.

———. 1994. "Alternative Health Care in Canada." In B. Singh Bolaria and Harley D. Dickinson (eds)., Health, Illness, and Health Care in Canada. Toronto: Harcourt Brace, 487–503.

———. 1997. Aging in Alberta. Calgary: Detselig Enterprises.

Northcott, Herbert, C. 1982. "The Best Years of Your Life." Canadian Journal on Aging 1: 72–78

———. 1997. Aging in Alberta. Calgary: Detselig Enterprises

Novak, Mark. 1993. Aging and Society: A Canadian Perspective. Scarborough, Ont.: Nelson Canada.

———. 1995. "Successful Aging." In Aging and Society: A Canadian Reader. Scarborough, Ont.: Nelson Canada.

———. 1997. Aging and Society (3rd ed.). Toronto: ITP Nelson.

Oakes, Jeannie. 1985. Keeping Track: How High Schools Structure Inequality. New Haven, CT: Yale University Press.

Obbo, Christine. 1993. "HIV Transmission: Men Are the Solution." In Stanlie M. James and Abena P.A. Busia (eds.), Theorizing Black Feminisms: The Visionary Pragmatism of Black Women. New York: Routledge, 160–181.

Oberschall, Anthony. 1973. Social Conflict and Social Movements. Englewood Cliffs, N.J.: Prentice-Hall.

Obomsawin, Alanis. 1993. Kanehsatake: 270 Years of Resistance [motion picture]. Montreal: National Film Board of Canada.

O'Brien, Carol-Anne, and Lorna Weir. 1995. "Lesbians and Gay Men Inside and Outside Families." In Nancy Mandell and Ann Duffy (eds.), Canadian Families. Toronto: Harcourt Brace and Company, 111–139.

O'Connell, Helen. 1994. Women and the Family. Prepared for the UN-NGO Group on Women and Development. Atlantic Highlands, N.J.: Zed Books.

O'Connor, James. 1973. The Fiscal Crisis of the State. New York: St. Martin's Press.

Oderkirk, Jillian. 1992. "Food Banks." Canadian Social Trends, 24(Spring):6–14.

Oderkirk, Jillian, and Clarence Lochhead. 1995. "Lone Parenthood: Gender Differences." In E.D. Nelson and B.W. Robinson (eds.), Gender in the 1990s. Scarborough, Ont.: Nelson Canada, 397–405.

Ogburn, William F. 1966. Social Change with Respect to Culture and Original Nature. New York: Dell (orig. pub. 1922).

Ogden, Russell D. 1994. Euthanasia and Assisted Suicide in Persons with Acquired Immunodeficiency Syndrome (AIDS) or Human Immunodeficiency Virus (HIV). Pitt Meadows, B.C.: Perreault Goedman.

Ogmundson, Rick. 1975. "Party Class Images and the Class Vote in Canada." American Sociological Review, 40:506–512.

Ogmundson, Rick, and M. Ng. 1982. "On the Inference of Voter Motivation: A Comparison of the Subjective Class Vote in Canada and the United Kingdom." Canadian Journal of Sociology, 7:41–59.

Oliver, Michael. 1990. The Politics of Disablement: A Sociological Approach. New York: St. Martin's Press.

Orbach, Susie. 1978. Fat Is a Feminist Issue. New York: Paddington.

O'Reilly-Fleming, Thomas. 1993. Down and Out in Canada: Homeless Canadians. Toronto: Canadian Scholar's Press.

Orenstein, Peggy, in association with the American Association of University Women. 1995. School Girls: Young Women, Self-Esteem, and the Confidence Gap. New York: Anchor/Doubleday.

Ortner, Sherry B. 1974. "Is Female to Male As Nature Is to Culture?" In Michelle Rosaldo and Louise Lamphere (eds.), Women, Culture, and Society. Stanford, Cal.: Stanford University Press.

Ortner, Sherry B., and Harriet Whitehead (eds.) 1981. Sexual Meanings: The Cultural Construction of Gender and Sexuality. Cambridge, Mass.: Cambridge University Press.

Orum, Anthony M. 1974. "On Participation in Political Protest Movements." Journal of Applied Behavioral Science, 10:181–207.

Orum, Anthony M., and Amy W. Orum. 1968. "The Class and Status Bases of Negro Student Protest." Social Science Quarterly, 49 (December):521–533.

Osterman, Cynthia. 1995. "Rising Child Poverty in World Worries Health Experts." Reuters (May 30):2.

O'Sullivan, Chris. 1993. "Fraternities and the Rape Culture." In Emile Buchwald et al. (eds.), Transforming a Rape Culture. Minn.: Milkweed Ltd.

Overall, Christine. 1991. "Reproductive Technology and the Future of the Family." In Jean E. Veevers (ed.) Continuity and Change in Marriage and the Family. Toronto: Holt, Rinehart and Winston, 466–477.

Owen, Bruce. 1996. "Harassment Ends in Firings." Winnipeg Free Press (23 March).

Page, Charles H. 1946. "Bureaucracy's Other Face." Social Forces, 25 (October):89–94.

Palen, J. John. 1995. The Suburbs. New York: McGraw-Hill.

Palmore, Erdman. 1981. Social Patterns in Normal Aging: Findings from the Duke Longitudinal Study. Durham, N.C.: Duke University Press.

Palys, Ted. 1997. Research Decisions: Quantitative and Qualitative Perspectives. Toronto: Harcourt Brace.

Palys, Ted, and John Lowman. 1998. "Abandoning 'the Highest Ethical Standards': Research Ethics at SFU." The Bulletin 11(1).

Pammett, Jon H. 1993. "Tracking the Votes." In Alan Frizell et al. (eds.), The Canadian General Election of 1993. Ottawa: Carleton University Press.

Panitch, Leo, and Donald Swartz. 1993. Assault on Trade Union Freedoms (2nd ed.). Toronto: Garamond.

Panzarino, Connie. 1994. *The Me in the Mirror*. Seattle, Wash.: Seal Press.

Parenti, Michael. 1994. *Land of Idols: Political Mythology in America*. New York: St. Martin's Press

Park, Robert E. 1915. "The City: Suggestions for the Investigation of Human Behavior in the City." *American Journal of Sociology*, 20:577–612.

———. 1928. "Human Migration and the Marginal Man." *American Journal of Sociology*, 33.

———. 1936. "Human Ecology." *American Journal of Sociology*, 42:1–15.

Park, Robert E., and Ernest W. Burgess. 1921. *Human Ecology*. Chicago: University of Chicago Press.

Parker, Robert Nash. 1995. "Violent Crime." In Joseph F. Sheley, *Criminology: A Contemporary Handbook* (2nd. ed.). Belmont, Cal.: Wadsworth, 169–185.

Parkinson, C. Northcote. 1957. *Parkinson's Law and Other Studies in Administration*. New York: Ballantine Books.

Parrish, Dee Anna. 1990. *Abused: A Guide to Recovery for Adult Survivors of Emotional/Physical Child Abuse*. Barrytown, N.Y.: Station Hill Press.

Parsons, Talcott. 1951. *The Social System*. Glencoe, Ill.: Free Press.

———. 1955. "The American Family: Its Relations to Personality and to the Social Structure." In Talcott Parsons and Robert F. Bales (eds.), *Family, Socialization and Interaction Process*. Glencoe, Ill.: Free Press, 3–33.

———. 1960. "Toward a Healthy Maturity." *Journal of Health and Social Behavior*, 1:163–173.

Parsons, Talcott, and Edward A. Shils (eds.). 1951. *Toward a General Theory of Action*. Cambridge, Mass.: Harvard University Press.

Patros, Philip G., and Tonia K. Shamoo. 1989. *Depression and Suicide in Children and Adolescents: Prevention, Intervention, and Postvention*. Boston: Allyn & Bacon.

Patterson, Christopher, and Elizabeth Podnieks. 1995. "A Guide to the Diagnosis and Treatment of Elder Abuse." In Mark Novak (ed.), *Aging and Society: A Canadian Reader*. Scarborough, Ont.: Nelson Canada.

Patterson, Naomi. 1998. "Old Dogs Must Learn New Tricks in the Modern Era." *SeniorNet* (Winter/Spring). Available: http://www. Seniornet.org/newsline/olddogs.shtml

Pearce, Diana. 1978. "The Feminization of Poverty: Women, Work, and Welfare." *Urban and Social Change Review*, 11 (1/2):28–36.

Pearson, Judy C. 1985. *Gender and Communication*. Dubuque, Iowa: Brown.

Pedrick-Cornell, Claire, and Richard J. Gelles. 1982. "Elderly Abuse: The Status of Current Knowledge." *Family Relations*, 31:457–465.

Pelzer, Dave. 1995. *A Child Called "It"*. Deerfield Beach, Fla.: Health Communications.

Peplau, Letita Anne. 1991. "Lesbian and Gay Relationships." In John C. Gonsiorek and James D. Weinrich (eds.), *Homosexuality: Research Implications for Public Policy*. Newbury Park, Cal.: Sage.

Perrow, Charles. 1984. *Normal Accidents*. New York: Basic Books.

———. 1986. *Complex Organizations: A Critical Essay* (3rd ed.). New York: Random House.

Perry, David C., and Alfred J. Watkins (eds.). 1977. *The Rise of the Sunbelt Cities*. Beverly Hills, Cal.: Sage.

Peter, Karl A. 1987. *The Dynamics of Hutterite Society*. Edmonton: University of Alberta Press.

Peter, Laurence J., and Raymond Hull. 1969. *The Peter Principle: Why Things Always Go Wrong*. New York: Morrow.

Peters, John F. 1985. "Adolescents as Socialization Agents to Parents." *Adolescence*, 20 (Winter):921–933.

Peters, Linda, and Patricia Fallon. 1994. "The Journey of Recovery: Dimensions of Change." In Patricia Fallon, Melanie A. Katzman, and Susan C. Wooley (eds.), *Feminist Perspectives on Eating Disorders*. New York: Guilford Press, 339–354.

Petersen, John L. 1994. *The Road to 2015: Profiles of the Future*. Corte Madera, Cal.: Waite Group Press.

Peterson's Educational Center. 1996. "Report on Private Secondary Education 1996–97." Retrieved November 23, 1997. Available: http://www.peterson. com/research/reports/privateschools.html

Phaneuf, G. 1990. *Child Sexual Abuse*. Ottawa: National Clearing House on Family Violence.

Pheasant, Valerie Bedassigae. 1994. "My Mother Used to Dance." In Carl E. James and Adrienne Shadd (eds.), *Talking about Difference*. Toronto: Between the Lines, 35–40.

Philbeck, Joyce. 1997. "Seniors and the Internet." *Cybersociology* (2). Available: http://www.socio.demon.co.uk/magazine/magazine.html

Philips, Bruce. 1998. *Privacy Commissioner, 1997–98 Annual Report*. Ottawa: The Privacy Commissioner of Canada.

Philp, Margaret. 1997. "Poverty Crusade Gets Personality." *The Globe and Mail* (September 20):A1.

Piaget, Jean. 1954. *The Construction of Reality in the Child*. Trans. Margaret Cook. New York: Basic Books.

Picot, G., and T. Wannell. 1990. "Job displacement." In Craig McKie and Keith Thompson (eds.), *Canadian Social Trends*. Toronto: Thompson Educational Publishers, 271–275.

Pietilä, Hilkka, and Jeanne Vickers. 1994. *Making Women Matter: The Role of the United Nations*. Atlantic Highlands, NJ: Zed Books.

Piliavin, Jane and Peter Callero. 1991. *Giving Blood: The Development of an Altruistic Identity*. Baltimore: The Johns Hopkins University Press.

Piliavin, Jane, and Hong-wen Charng. 1990. "Altruism: A Review of Recent Theory and Research." In W. Richard Scott and Judith Blake (eds.), *Annual Review of Sociology*. Palo Alto: Annual Reviews Inc., 27–65.

Pillard, Richard C., and James D. Weinrich. 1986. "Evidence of Familial Nature of Male Homosexuality." *Archives of General Psychiatry*, 43(8):800–812.

Pillemer, Karl A. 1985. "The Dangers of Dependency: New Findings on Domestic Violence Against the Elderly." *Social Problems*, 33 (December):146–158.

Pinderhughes, Dianne M. 1986. "Political Choices: A Realignment in Partisanship Among Black Voters?" In James D. Williams (ed.), *The State of Black America 1986*. New York: National Urban League, 85–113.

Pinderhughes, Howard. 1997. *Race in the Hood: Conflict and Violence Among Urban Youth*. Minneapolis, MN: University of Minnesota Press.

Pines, Maya. 1981. "The Civilizing of Genie." *Psychology Today*, 15 (September):28–29, 31–32, 34.

Piot, Peter. 1997. "Why It Is Folly to Feel at All Complacent about AIDS." *The Globe and Mail* (July 24):A15.

Piturro, Marlene. 1994. "Capitalist China?" *Brandweek*, 35(20):22–27.

Podnieks, Elizabeth. 1989. *A National Survey on Abuse of the Elderly in Canada: Preliminary Findings.* Toronto: Ryerson Polytechnical Institute.

Polakow, Valerie. 1993. *Lives on the Edge: Single Mothers and Their Children in the Other America.* Chicago: University of Chicago Press.

Pomice, Eva. 1990. "Madison Avenue's Blind Spot." In Karin Swisher (ed.), *The Elderly: Opposing Viewpoints.* San Diego: Greenhaven Press, 42–45.

Ponting, J.R. 1997. *First Nations in Canada: Perspectives on Opportunity, Empowerment and Self-Determination.* Toronto: McGraw-Hill Ryerson.

Popenoe, David. 1993. "American Family Decline, 1960–1990: A Review and Appraisal." *Journal of Marriage and the Family,* 55(3):527–543.

Popoff, Wilfred. 1996. "One Day You're Family; the Next Day You're Fired." *The Globe and Mail* (March 14):A22.

Porter, John. 1965. *The Vertical Mosaic.* Toronto: University of Toronto Press.

———. 1987. "Education Equality and the Just Society." In J. Porter (ed.), *The Measure of Canadian Society: Education, Equality and Opportunity.* Ottawa: Carleton University Press, 242–280.

Posterski, Donald C., and Irwin Barker. 1993. *Where's a Good Church?* Winfield, B.C.: Wood Lake Books.

Posterski, Donald, and Gary Nelson. 1997. *Future Faith Churches.* Winfield, B.C.: Wood Lake Books.

Pratt, Courtney. 1997. "Business Accountability: Shareholders, Stakeholders or Society?" Address to the Canadian Club of Toronto, September 29.

President's Commission. 1986. *Report of the President's Commission on the Space Shuttle Challenger Accident.* Washington: U.S. Government Printing Office.

Presthus, Robert. 1978. *The Organizational Society.* New York: St. Martin's Press.

Priest, Gordon. 1993. "Living Arrangements of Canada's 'Older Elderly' Population." In Craig McKie, *Canadian Social Trends.* Toronto: Thompson Educational Publishing Company, 183–187.

Prothrow-Stith, Deborah, with Micaele Weissman. 1991. *Deadly Consequences.* New York: HarperCollins.

Quadagno, Jill S. 1984. "Welfare Capitalism and the Social Security Act of 1935." *American Sociological Review,* 49:632–647.

Quarantelli, E. L., and James R. Hundley, Jr. 1993. "A Test of Some Propositions About Crowd Formation and Behavior." In Russell L. Curtis, Jr., and Benigno E. Aguirre (eds.), *Collective Behavior and Social Movements.* Boston: Allyn & Bacon, 183–193.

Queen, Stuart A., and David B. Carpenter. 1953. *The American City.* New York: McGraw-Hill.

Quigley, Tim. 1994. "Some Issues in the Sentencing of Aboriginal Offenders." Cited in Royal Commission on Aboriginal Peoples Report: *1996 Bridging the Cultural Divide.* Ottawa: Minister of Supply and Services Canada.

Quinney, Richard. 1979. *Class, State, and Crime.* New York: McKay.

———. 1980. *Class, State, and Crime* (2nd ed.). New York: Longman.

Quinton, Rhonda. 1989. "Liability of Search and Rescuers." Unpublished paper, Faculty of Law, University of Victoria.

Rabinowitz, Fredric E., and Sam V. Cochran. 1994. *Man Alive: A Primer of Men's Issues.* Pacific Grove, Cal.: Brooks/Cole.

Radcliffe-Brown, A.R. 1952. *Structure and Function in Primitive Society.* New York: Free Press.

Raffalli, Mary. 1994. "Why So Few Women Physicists?" *New York Times Supplement* (January):Sect. 4A, 26–28.

Ramu, G.N. 1984. "Family Background and Perceived Marital Happiness: A Comparison of Voluntary Childless Couples and Parents." *Canadian Journal of Sociology,* 9:47–67.

Rankin, Robert P., and Jerry S. Maneker. 1985. "The Duration of Marriage in a Divorcing Population: The Impact of Children." *Journal of Marriage and the Family,* 47 (February):43–52.

Reckless, Walter C. 1967. *The Crime Problem.* New York: Meredith.

Reed, Christopher. 1998. "No Fingerprints Puts Man Under Society's Thumb." *The Globe and Mail* (April 23):A11.

Reich, Robert. 1993. "Why the Rich Are Getting Richer and the Poor Poorer." In Paul J. Baker, Louis E. Anderson, and Dean S. Dorn (eds.), *Social Problems: A Critical Thinking Approach* (2nd ed.). Belmont, Cal.: Wadsworth, 145–149. Adapted from *The New Republic,* May 1, 1989.

Reiman, Jeffrey H. 1979. *The Rich Get Richer and the Poor Get Prison.* New York: Wiley.

———. 1984. *The Rich Get Richer and the Poor Get Prison* (2nd ed.). New York: Wiley.

Reinharz, Shulamit. 1992. *Feminist Methods in Social Research.* New York: Oxford University Press.

Reinisch, June. 1990. *The Kinsey Institute New Report on Sex: What You Must Know to Be Sexually Literate.* New York: St. Martin's Press.

Reissman, C.K. 1983. "Women and Medicalization: A New Perspective." *Social Policy,* 14:3–18.

Renzetti, Claire M., and Daniel J. Curran. 1992. *Women, Men, and Society.* Boston: Allyn and Bacon.

———. 1995. *Women, Men, and Society* (3rd ed.). Boston: Allyn and Bacon.

———. 1998. *Living Sociology.* Boston: Allyn and Bacon.

Reskin, Barbara F., and Heidi Hartmann. 1986. *Women's Work, Men's Work: Sex Segregation on the Job.* Washington, D.C.: National Academy Press.

Reskin, Barbara F., and Irene Padavic. 1994. *Women and Men at Work.* Thousand Oaks, Cal.: Pine Forge Press.

Richardson, C. James. 1996. "Divorce and Remarriage in Families." In Maureen Baker (ed.), *Changing Trends in Canada.* Toronto: McGraw-Hill Ryerson, 215–248.

Richardson, John G., and Carl H. Simpson. 1982. "Children, Gender and Social Structure: An Analysis of the Content of Letters to Santa Claus." *Child Development,* 53:429–436.

Richardson, Laurel. 1993. "Inequalities of Power, Property, and Prestige." In Virginia Cyrus (ed.), *Experiencing Race, Class, and Gender in the United States.* Mountain View, Cal.: Mayfield, 229–236.

Richardson, R. Jack. 1990. Economic Concentration and Social Power in Contemporary Canada." In J. Curtis and L. Tepperman (eds.), *Images of Canada: The Sociological Tradition,* 341–351.

———. 1992. "Free Trade: Why Did It Happen?" *Canadian Review of Sociology and Anthropology,* 29:307–328.

Richer, Stephen. 1988. "Equality to Benefit from Schooling: The Issue of Educational Opportunity." In D. Forcese and S. Richer (eds.), *Social Issues: Sociological Views of Canada.* Toronto: Prentice Hall, 262–86.

Richler, Mordecai. 1992. *Oh Canada! Oh Quebec!* Toronto and New York: Knopff.

Rifkin, Jeremy. 1995. *The End of Work.* New York: G.P. Putnam's Sons.

Rigler, David. 1993. "Letters: A Psychologist Portrayed in a Book About an Abused Child Speaks Out for the First Time in 22 Years." *New York Times Book Review* (June 13):35.

Riley, Matilda White, and John W. Riley, Jr. 1994. "Age Integration and the Lives of Older People." *The Gerontologist,* 34(1):110–115.

Rinehart, James W. 1996. *The Tyranny of Work: Alienation and the Labour Process* (3rd ed.). Toronto: Harcourt Brace.

Risman, Barbara J. 1987. "Intimate Relationships from a Microstructural Perspective: Men Who Mother." *Gender & Society,* 1:6–32.

Ritzer, George. 1993. *The McDonaldization of Society: An Investigation into the Changing Character of Contemporary Social Life.* Thousand Oaks, Cal.: Pine Forge Press.

Roberts, Julian. 1995a. *Disproportionate Harm: Hate Crime in Canada.* Ottawa: Department of Justice.

Roberts, Keith A. 1995b. *Religion in Sociological Perspective.* Belmont, Cal.: Wadsworth.

Roberts, Lance, and Rodney Clifton. 1990. "Multiculturalism in Canada: A Sociological Perspective." In Peter Li. (ed.), *Race and Ethnic Relations in Canada.* Toronto: Oxford University Press, 120–147.

Robertson, Ian. 1977. *Sociology.* New York: Worth Publishers.

———. 1989. *Sociology: A Brief Introduction.* New York: Worth.

Robertson, Roland. 1992. *Globalization: Social Theory and Global Culture.* Newbury Park, Cal.: Sage.

Robinson, David, Frank J. Porporino, William A. Millson, Shelley Trevethan, and Barry McKillop. 1998. "A One-Day Snapshot of Inmates in Canada's Adult Correctional Facilities." *Juristat,* 18(8). Ottawa: Statistics Canada.

Rockwell, John. 1994. "The New Colossus: American Culture as Power Export." *New York Times* (January 30):Section 2, 1, 30.

Rodgers, Kain, and Rebecca Kong. 1996. "Crimes Against Women and Children in the Family." In Leslie Kennedy and Vincent Sacco (eds.), *Crime Counts: A Criminal Event Analysis.* Scarborough, Ont.: Nelson Canada, 115–132.

Roethlisberger, Fritz J., and William J. Dickson. 1939. *Management and the Worker.* Cambridge, Mass.: Harvard University Press.

Rollins, Judith. 1985. *Between Women: Domestics and Their Employers.* Philadelphia: Temple University Press.

Romaniuc, Anatole. 1994. "Fertility in Canada: Retrospective and Prospective." In Frank Trovato and Carl F. Grindstaff (eds.), *Perspectives on Canada's Population.* Toronto: Oxford University Press, 214–229.

Roof, Wade Clark. 1993. *A Generation of Seekers: The Spiritual Journeys of the Baby Boom Generation.* San Francisco: HarperSanFrancisco.

Roos, Patricia A., and Barbara F. Reskin. 1992. "Occupational Desegregation in the 1970s: Integration and Economic Equity?" *Sociological Perspectives,* 35:69.

Root, Maria P.P. 1990. "Disordered Eating in Women of Color." *Sex Roles,* 22(7/8):525–536.

Ropers, Richard H. 1991. *Persistent Poverty: The American Dream Turned Nightmare.* New York: Plenum.

Rose, Jerry D. 1982. *Outbreaks.* New York: Free Press.

Rosenburg, Michael. 1995. "Ethnic and Race Relations." In L. Tepperman, J.E. Curtis, and R.J. Richardson (eds.), *Sociology.* Toronto: McGraw-Hill Ryerson, 302–344.

Rosenthal, Naomi, Meryl Fingrutd, Michele Ethier, Roberta Karant, and David McDonald. 1985. "Social Movements and Network Analysis: A Case Study of Nineteenth-Century Women's Reform in New York State." *American Journal of Sociology,* 90:1022–1054.

Rosenthal, Robert, and Lenore Jacobson. 1968. *Pygmalion in the Classroom: Teacher Expectation and Student's Intellectual Development.* New York: Holt, Rinehart, and Winston.

Rosnow, Ralph L., and Gary Alan Fine. 1976. *Rumor and Gossip: The Social Psychology of Hearsay.* New York: Elsevier.

Ross, David. 1998. *Child Poverty in Canada: Recasting the Issue.* Ottawa: Canadian Council on Social Development.

Ross, David P. and Paul Roberts. 1997. "Does Family Income Affect the Healthy Development of Children?" *Perception* (21)1:1–5. Ottawa: Canadian Council on Social Development.

Ross, David P., E. Richard Shillington, and Clarence Lochhead. 1994. *The Canadian Fact Book on Poverty.* Ottawa: Canadian Council on Social Development.

Ross, Rupert. 1996. *Returning to the Teachings: Exploring Aboriginal Justice.* Toronto: Penguin Books.

Rossi, Alice S. 1980. "Life-Span Theories and Women's Lives." *Signs,* 6(1):4–32.

Rossi, Peter H. 1989. *Down and Out in America: The Origins of Homelessness.* Chicago: University of Chicago Press.

Rossides, Daniel W. 1986. *The American Class System: An Introduction to Social Stratification.* Boston: Houghton Mifflin.

Rostow, Walt W. 1971. *The Stages of Economic Growth: A Non-Communist Manifesto* (2nd ed.). Cambridge: Cambridge University Press (orig. pub. 1960).

———. 1978. *The World Economy: History and Prospect.* Austin, Tex.: University of Texas Press.

Roth, Nicki. 1993. *Integrating the Shattered Self: Psychotherapy with Adult Incest Survivors.* Northvale, N.J.: Jason Aronson.

Rotheram, Mary Jane, and Jean S. Phinney. 1987. "Introduction: Definitions and Perspectives in the Study of Children's Ethnic Socialization." In Jean S. Phinney and Mary Jane Rotheram (eds.), *Children's Ethnic Socialization.* Newbury Park, Cal.: Sage, 10–28.

Rothman, Robert A. 1993. *Inequality and Stratification: Class, Color, and Gender* (2nd ed.). Englewood Cliffs, N.J.: Prentice-Hall.

Rowe, Patricia. 1992. "Child Abuse Telecast Floods National Hotline." *Children Today,* 21(2):11.

Rowley, Storer H. 1994. "Conference Condemns Mutilation of Female Genitals." *Austin American-Statesman* (September 11):A9.

Royal Commission on Aboriginal Peoples. 1995. *Choosing Life: Special Report on Suicide Among Aboriginal Peoples.* Ottawa: Canada Communications Group Publishing.

Rubin, Lillian B. 1976. *Worlds of Pain: Life in the Working-Class Family.* New York: Basic Books.

———. 1994. *Families on the Fault Line.* New York: HarperCollins.

Russell, Diana E.H. 1986. *The Secret Trauma: Incest in the Lives of Girls and Women.* New York: Basic Books.

Russell, Joel. 1997. "Early Lessons." *Hispanic Business* (June):96–102.

Rutherford, Leanna. 1998. "An Anorexic's Recovery." *Canadian Living* (October): 107–110.

Rutstein, Nathan. 1993. *Healing in America.* Springfield, Mass.: Whitcomb.

Rymer, Russ. 1993. *Genie: An Abused Child's Flight from Silence.* New York: HarperCollins.

Sadker, David, and Myra Sadker. 1985. "Is the OK Classroom OK?" *Phi Delta Kappan,* 55:358–367.

———. 1986. "Sexism in the Classroom: From Grade School to Graduate School." *Phi Delta Kappan,* 68:512–515.

Sadker, Myra, and David Sadker. 1984. *Year 3: Final Report, Promoting Effectiveness in Classroom Instruction.* Washington, D.C.: National Institute of Education.

———. 1994. *Failing at Fairness: How America's Schools Cheat Girls.* New York: Scribner.

Samovar, Larry A., and Richard E. Porter. 1991a. *Communication Between Cultures.* Belmont, Cal.: Wadsworth.

———. 1991b. *Intercultural Communication: A Reader* (6th ed.). Belmont, Cal.: Wadsworth.

Samuelson, Paul A., and William D. Nordhaus. 1989. *Economics* (13th ed.). New York: McGraw-Hill.

Sanger, David E. 1994. "Cutting Itself Down to Size: Japan's Inferiority Complex." *New York Times* (February 6):E5.

Sapir, Edward. 1961. *Culture, Language and Personality.* Berkeley: University of California Press.

Sargent, Margaret. 1987. *Sociology for Australians* (2nd ed.). Melbourne, Australia: Longman Cheshire.

Sass, Robert. 1986. "Workplace Health and Safety: Report from Canada." *International Journal of Health Services,* 16:565–582.

Sassen, Saskia. 1991. *The Global City: New York, London, Tokyo.* Princeton, NJ: Princeton University Press.

———. 1995. "On Concentration and Centrality in the Global City." In Paul L. Knox and Peter J. Taylor (eds.), *World Cities in a World System.* Cambridge, England: Cambridge University Press.

Satzewich, Vic. 1991. "Social Stratification: Class and Racial Inequalities." In B. Singh Bolaria (ed.), *Issues and Contradiction in Canadian Society.* Toronto: Harcourt Brace, 91–107.

Saunders, Eileen. 1999. "Theoretical Approaches to the Study of Women." In Curtis, James, Edward Grabb, and Neil Guppy (eds.), *Social Inequality in Canada: Patterns and Policies.* Scarborough: Prentice Hall, 168–185.

Schafer, A. 1998. *Down and Out in Winnipeg and Toronto: The Ethics of Legislating Against Panhandling.* Ottawa: Institute of Social Policy.

Schellenberg, Grant. 1997. *The Changing Nature of Part-Time Work.* Ottawa: The Canadian Council on Social Development.

Schellenberg, G. and David P. Ross. 1997. *Left Poor by the Market: A Look at Family Poverty and Earnings.* Ottawa: Canadian Council on Social Development.

Schemo, Diana Jean. 1996. "Indians in Brazil, Estranged from Their Land, Suffer an Epidemic of Suicide." *New York Times* (August 25):7.

Schiller, Herbert I. 1989. *Culture, Inc. The Corporate Takeover of Public Expression.* New York: Oxford University Press.

Schmetzer, Uli. 1992. "Across Asia, Slave Trade Prospers—Often for Child Labor of Sex." *Austin American-Statesman* (February 22):J1, J7.

Schmidt, William E. 1993. "A Churchill Draws Fire with Remark on Race." *New York Times* (June 1):A2.

Schneider, Beth E., and Meredith Gould. 1987. "Female Sexuality: Looking Back into the Future." In Beth Hess and Myra M. Ferree (eds.), *Analyzing Gender: A Handbook of Social Science Research.* Newbury Park, Cal.: Sage, 120–153.

Schneider, Keith. 1993. "The Regulatory Thickets of Environmental Racism." *New York Times* (December 19):E5.

Schur, Edwin M. 1965. *Crimes Without Victims: Deviant Behavior and Public Policy.* Englewood Cliffs, N.J.: Prentice-Hall.

———. 1983. *Labeling Women Deviant: Gender, Stigma, and Social Control.* Philadelphia: Temple University Press.

Schwartz, Barry. 1993. "Why Altruism is Impossible ... and Ubiquitous." *Social Service Review,* 67 (September):314–343.

Scott, Joan W. 1986. "Gender: A Useful Category of Historical Analysis." *American Historical Review,* 91(December):1053–1075.

Scully, Diana. 1990. *Understanding Sexual Violence: A Study of Convicted Rapists.* Boston: Unwin Hyman.

Searles, Neil. 1995. *Physician Assisted Suicide in Manitoba.* Manitoba Association of Rights and Liberties.

Seegmiller, B.R., B. Suter, and N. Duviant. 1980. *Personal, Socioeconomic, and Sibling Influences on Sex-Role Differentiation.* Urbana: ERIC Clearinghouse of Elementary and Early Childhood Education, ED 176 895, College of Education, University of Illinois.

Seid, Roberta P. 1994. "Too 'Close to the Bone': The Historical Context for Women's Obsession with Slenderness." In Patricia Fallon, Melanie A. Katzman, and Susan C. Wooley (eds.), *Feminist Perspectives on Eating Disorders.* New York: Guilford Press, 3–16.

Sengoku, Tamotsu. 1985. *Willing Workers: The Work Ethic in Japan, England, and the United States.* Westport, Conn.: Quorum Books.

Serbin, Lisa A., Phyllis Zelkowitz, Anna-Beth Doyle, Dolores Gold, and Bill Wheaton. 1990. "The Socialization of Sex-Differentiated Skills and Academic Performance: A Mediational Model." *Sex Roles,* 23:613–628.

Shadd, Adrienne. 1991. "Institutionalized Racism and Canadian History: Notes of a Black Canadian." In Ormond McKague (ed.), *Racism in Canada.* Saskatoon: Fifth House, 1–5.

———. 1994. "Where Are You Really From?" In Carl E. James and Adrienne Shadd (eds.), *Talking About Difference.* Toronto: Between the Lines Press, 9–15.

Shamai, Shmuel. 1992. "Ethnicity and Educational Achievement: Canada, 1941–1981." *Canadian Ethnic Studies,* 24:43–57.

Shakin, Madeline, Debra Shakin, and Sarah Hall Sternglanz. 1985. "Infant Clothing: Sex Labeling for Strangers." *Sex Roles,* 12:955–964.

Shapiro, Joseph P. 1993. *No Pity: People with Disabilities Forging a New Civil Rights Movement.* Toronto: Time Books/Random House.

Shapiro, Susan P. 1990. "Collaring the Crime, Not the Criminal: Reconsidering the Concept of White-collar Crime." *American Sociological Review,* 55:346–365.

Sharma, Arvind. 1995. "Hinduism." In Arvind Sharma (ed.), *Our Religions.* San Francisco: HarperCollins, 3–67.

Shattuck, Roger. 1980. *The Forbidden Experiment.* New York: Farrar, Straus & Giroux.

Sheley, Joseph F. 1991. *Criminology: A Contemporary Handbook*. Belmont, Cal.: Wadsworth.

Shenon, Philip. 1994. "China's Mania for Baby Boys Creates Surplus of Bachelors." *New York Times* (August 16):A1, A4.

Sherman, Suzanne (ed.). 1992. "Frances Fuchs and Gayle Remick." In *Lesbian and Gay Marriage: Private Commitments, Public Ceremonies*. Philadelphia: Temple University Press, 189–201.

Shillington, E. Richard. 1991. "Estimates of Native Child Poverty: Census 1986." In *Children in Poverty: Toward a Better Future*. Ottawa: Standing Senate Committee on Social Affairs, Science, and Technology.

Shils, Edward A. 1965. "Charisma, Order, and Status." *American Sociological Review*, 30:199–213.

Shilts, Randy. 1988. *And the Band Played On: Politics, People, and the AIDS Epidemic*. New York: Penguin.

Shisslak, Catherine M., and Marjorie Crago. 1992. "Eating Disorders Among Athletes." In Raymond Lemberg (ed.), *Controlling Eating Disorders with Facts, Advice, and Resources*. Phoenix: Oryx Press, 29–36.

———. 1994. "Toward a New Model for the Prevention of Eating Disorders." In Patricia Fallon, Melanie A. Katzman, and Susan C. Wooley (eds.), *Feminist Perspectives on Eating Disorders*. New York: Guilford Press, 419–437.

Shkilynyk, Anastasia M. 1985. *A Poison Stronger Than Love: The Destruction of an Ojibwa Community*. New Haven: Yale University Press.

Shor, Ira. 1986. *Culture Wars: School and Society in the Conservative Restoration 1969–1984*. Boston: Routledge & Kegan Paul.

Shorto, Russell. 1991. "Made-in-Japan Parenting," *Health*, 54 (June):56–57.

Sikorsky, Robert. 1990. "Highway Robbery: Canada's Auto Repair Scandal." *Reader's Digest* (February):55–63.

Silverman, Robert, and Leslie Kennedy. 1993. *Deadly Deeds: Murder in Canada*. Scarborough, Ont.: Nelson Canada

Silverstein, Louise B. 1991. "Transforming the Debate About Child Care and Maternal Employment." *American Psychologist*, 46:1025–1032.

Simmel, Georg. 1904. "Fashion." *American Journal of Sociology*, 62 (May 1957):541–558.

———. 1950. *The Sociology of Georg Simmel*. Trans. Kurt Wolff. Glencoe, Ill.: Free Press (orig. written 1902–1917).

Simon, David R., and D. Stanley Eitzen. 1993. *Elite Deviance* (4th ed.). Boston: Allyn & Bacon.

Simons, Marlise. 1993a. "Homeless Find a Spot in France's Heart." *New York Times* (December 9):A4.

———. 1993b. "Prosecutor Fighting Girl-Mutilation." *New York Times* (November 23):A4.

Simpson, George Eaton, and Milton Yinger. 1972. *Racial and Cultural Minorities: An Analysis of Prejudice and Discrimination* (4th ed.). New York: Harper & Row.

Simpson, Sally S. 1989. "Feminist Theory, Crime, and Justice." *Criminology*, 27:605–632.

Singer, Bennett L., and David Deschamps (eds.). 1994. *Gay and Lesbian Stats*. New York: New Press.

Singh, J.A.L., and Robert M. Zingg. 1942. *Wolf-Children and Feral Man*. New York: Harper & Row.

Sjoberg, Gideon. 1965. *The Preindustrial City: Past and Present*. New York: Free Press.

Sloan, R.P., E. Bagiella, and T. Powell. 1999. "Religion, Spirituality, and Medicine." *The Lancet*. Vol. 353:664–667.

Slugoski, B.F., and Ginsburg, G.B. 1989. "Ego Identity and Explanatory Speech." In John Shotter and Kenneth J. Gergen (eds.), *Texts of Identity*. London: Sage, 36–55.

Smandych, Russell. 1985. "Marxism and the Creation of Law: Re-Examining the Origins of Canadian Anti-Combines Legislation." In Thomas Fleming (ed.), *The New Criminologies in Canada: State, Crime and Control*. Toronto: Oxford University Press, 87–99.

———. 1988. "Social Structure." In Neil J. Smelser (ed.), *Handbook of Sociology*. Newbury Park, Cal.: Sage, 103–129.

Smelser, Neil J. 1988. "Social Structure." In Neil J. Smelser (ed.), *Handbook of Sociology*. Newbury Park, Cal.: Sage, 103–129.

Smith, Adam. 1976. *An Inquiry into the Nature and Causes of the Wealth of Nations*. Roy H. Campbell and Andrew S. Skinner (eds.). Oxford, England: Clarendon Press (orig. pub. 1776).

Smith, Allen C., III, and Sheryl Kleinman. 1989. "Managing Emotions in Medical School: Students' Contacts with the Living and the Dead." *Social Science Quarterly*, 52(1):56–69.

Smith, Dorothy. 1974. "Women's Perspective as a Radical Critique of Sociology." *Sociological Inquiry* (44):7–13.

———. 1985. "Women, Class and Family." In Varda Burstyn and Dorothy Smith (eds.), *Women, Class and the State*. Toronto: Garamond.

———. 1987. *The Everyday World as Problematic: A Feminist Sociology*. Toronto: University of Toronto Press.

Smith, Huston. 1991. *The World's Religions*. San Francisco, Cal.: HarperSanFrancisco.

Smith, Michael D. 1996. "Patriarchal Ideology and Wife Beating." In Robert J. Brym (ed.), *Society in Question: Sociological Readings for the 21st Century*. Toronto: Harcourt Brace, and Company.

Smyke, Patricia. 1991. *Women and Health*. Atlantic Highlands, NJ: Zed Books.

Snider, Laureen. 1988. "Commercial Crime." In Vincent F. Sacco (ed.), *Deviance, Conformity and Control in Canadian Society*. Scarborough, Ont.: Prentice Hall, 231–283.

Snow, David A., and Leon Anderson. 1991. "Researching the Homeless: The Characteristic Features and Virtues of the Case Study." In Joe R. Feagin, Anthony M. Orum, and Gideon Sjoberg (eds.), *A Case for the Case Study*. Chapel Hill: University of North Carolina Press, 148–173.

———. 1993. *Down on Their Luck: A Case Study of Homeless Street People*. Berkeley: University of California Press.

Snow, David A., E. Burke Rochford, Jr., Steven K. Worden, and Robert D. Benford. 1986. "Frame Alignment Processes, Micromobilization, and Movement Participation." *American Sociological Review*, 51:464–481.

Snow, David A., Louis A. Zurcher, and Robert Peters. 1981. "Victory Celebrations as Theater: A Dramaturgical Approach to Crowd Behavior." *Symbolic Interaction*, 4(1):21–41.

Snyder, Benson R. 1971. *The Hidden Curriculum*. New York: Knopf.

Sokoloff, Natalie. 1992. *Black Women and White Women in the Professions*. New York: Routledge.

Soper, Steven Paul. 1985. *Totalitarianism: A Conceptual Approach*. Lanham, Md.: University Press of America.

Sorokin, Pitirim. 1950. *Altruistic Love.* Boston: The Boston Press.

South, Scott J., Charles M. Bonjean, Judy Corder, and William T. Markham. 1982. "Sex and Power in the Federal Bureaucracy." *Work and Occupations,* 9(2):233–254.

Specter, Michael. 1994b. "Soaring Unemployment Is Spreading Fear in Russia." *New York Times* (May 8):A6.

Spencer, Metta. 1993. *Foundations of Modern Sociology* (6th ed.). Scarborough, Ont.: Prentice Hall.

Stackhouse, John. 1996. "Disenfranchised Asian Youth Rage Against Those in Driver's Seat." *The Globe and Mail* (July 31):A7.

———. 1998. "Village Phones Ring Up Profit." *The Globe and Mail* (July 6):A1, A8.

———. 1999. "Foreign Aid Cuts Assailed for Harming Children." *The Globe and Mail* (February 23):A1, A12.

Stamler, Rodney T. 1996. "Organized Crime." In Rick Linden (ed.), *Criminology: A Canadian Perspective* (3rd ed.). Toronto: Harcourt Brace and Company, 423–457.

Stannard, David E. 1992. *American Holocaust: Columbus and the Conquest of the New World.* New York: Oxford University Press.

Staples, Brent. 1994. "Aunt Jemima Gets a Makeover." *New York Times* (October 19):A14.

Stark, Rodney. 1992. *Sociology* (4th ed.). Belmont, Cal.: Wadsworth.

———. 1998. *Sociology* (7th ed.). Belmont: Wadsworth Publishing.

Stark, Rodney, Daniel P. Doyle, and Lori Kent. 1982. "Religion and Delinquency: The Ecology of a 'Lost' Relationship." *Journal of Research in Crime and Delinquency* 19:4–24.

Stark, Rodney, and William Sims Bainbridge. 1981. "American-Born Sects: Initial Findings." *Journal for the Scientific Study of Religion,* 20:130–149.

Starr, Paul. 1982. *The Social Transformation of Medicine: The Rise of a Sovereign Profession and the Making of a Vast Industry.* New York: Basic Books.

———. 1987. "The Sociology of Official Statistics." In William Alonso and Paul Starr (eds.), *The Politics of Numbers.* New York: Russell Sage Foundation.

———. 1992. "Social Categories and Claims in the Liberal State." *Social Research,* 59(2):263–296.

Statham, Anne, Laurel Richardson, and Judith A. Cook. 1994. *Gender and University Teaching: A Negotiated Difference.* Albany: SUNY Press.

Statistics Canada. 1992a. Cat. no. 82-554.

———. 1992b. Minister of Supply and Services. *Labour Force Annual Averages.* Ottawa: Ministry of Industry, Science, and Technology.

———. 1994a. *International Adult Literacy Survey.* Ottawa: Statistics Canada.

———. 1994b. *Women in the Labour Force.* Ottawa: Ministry of Industry, Science, and Technology.

———. 1995a. *Canada at a Glance.* Ottawa: Minister of Supply and Services.

———. 1995b. "Education of Women in Canada." *Canadian Social Trends,* Winter. Cat. no. 11-008-XPE.

———. 1996a. *General Social Survey.* Cat. no. 11–612.

———. 1996c. "Births and Deaths." *The Daily* (May 24). Ottawa: Minister of Supply and Services.

———. 1996d. "Adult Literacy: Canadian Results." *The Daily* (Sept. 12).

———. 1996e. *Canada's Retirement Income Programs: A Statistical Overview.* Ottawa: Ministry of Industry.

———. 1996f. "Percentage Distribution of Total Income of Families and Unattached Individuals by Quintiles, Canada 1951–1996." *Income Distributions by Size in Canada 1996,* Cat. no. 13-207-XPB. Ottawa: Centre for International Statistics of the Canadian Council on Social Development.

———. 1997a. "Breast Cancer Mortality and Mammography." *The Daily* (July 28). Ottawa: Minister of Supply and Services.

———. 1997b. *Canadian Council on Social Development,* Cat. no. 13-569-XPB.

———. 1997c. "Family Income After Separatism." *The Daily* (April 9).

———. 1997d. *National Graduates Survey.* Cat. no. 81-584-XPB. Ottawa: Statistics Canada.

———. 1997e. "1996 Census: Marital Status, Common-law Unions and Families." *The Daily* (October 14), Cat. no. 11-001E.

———. 1997f. "1996 Census: Mother Tongue, Home Language and Knowledge of Languages." *The Daily* (December 2). Ottawa: Minister of Supply and Services. Available:

http://www.statcan.ca/Daily/English/971202/d971202.htm

———. 1997g. "Who Cares? Caregiving in the 1990s." *The Daily* (August 19). Ottawa: Minister of Supply and Services.

———. 1997h. "The Social Context of Young Children." *Canadian Social Trends,* Winter. Cat. no. 11-008-XPE.

———. 1998a. "Canadian Crime Statistics, 1997." *Juristat,* 18(11):12, Cat. no. 85-002-XPE. Ottawa: Statistics Canada.

———. 1998b. "Deaths, 1996." *The Daily* (April 16).

———. 1998c. "Earnings of Men and Women, 1996." *The Daily* (March 23). Ottawa: Minister of Industry.

———. 1998d. "Marriages and Divorce." *The Daily* (January 29). Available: http://www.statcan.ca:80/Daily/English/980129/d980129.htm

———. 1998e. "National Population Health Survey: Cycle 2." *The Daily* (May 29).

———. 1998f. "1996 Census: Aboriginal Data." *The Daily* (January 13).

———. 1998g. "1996 Census: Education, Mobility and Migration." *The Daily* (April 14). Ottawa: Minister of Supply and Services.

———. 1998h. "1996 Census: Ethnic Origins, Visible Minorities." *The Daily* (Feb 17). Ottawa: Minister of Supply and Services.

———. 1998i. "1996 Census: Sources of Income Earnings and Total Income, and Family Income." *The Daily* (May 12). Ottawa: Minister of Supply and Services, 1–22.

———. 1998j. *Report on the Demographic Situation in Canada, 1997.* Ottawa: Statistics Canada.

———. 1998k. "Ten Most Frequent Jobs for Women in Canada, 1996." *The Daily* (March 17). Ottawa: Minister of Supply and Services.

———. 1999a. "Earnings of Men and Women, 1998." Cat. No. 13-217-XPB. Ottawa: Minister of Industry.

———. 1999b. "Enrolment in Elementary and Secondary Schools." Cat. no. 81-229-XPB.Statutes of Canada. 1910 c. 27.

Steiger, Thomas L., and Mark Wardell. 1995. "Gender and Employment in the Service Sector." *Social Problems,* 42(1): 91–123.

Stein, Peter J. 1976. *Single.* Englewood Cliffs, N.J.: Prentice-Hall.

————. (ed.). 1981. *Single Life: Unmarried Adults in Social Context.* New York: St. Martin's Press.

Steinbacher, Roberta, and Helen Bequaert Holmes. 1987. "Sex Choice: Survival and Sisterhood." In Gena Corea et al. (eds.), *Man-made Women: How New Reproductive Technologies Affect Women.* Bloomington: Indiana University Press, 52–63.

Steinback, Robert L. 1993. "The Melting Pot Is Contrary to American Ideal." *Miami Herald* (August 17):B1.

Steinmetz, Suzanne K. 1987. "Elderly Victims of Domestic Violence." In Carl D. Chambers, John H. Lindquist, O.Z. White, and Michael T. Harter, (eds.), *The Elderly: Victims and Deviants.* Athens: Ohio University Press, 126–141.

Stern, Aimee L. 1993. "Managing by Team Is Not Always as Easy as It Looks." *New York Times* (July 18):F5.

Stevenson, Mary Huff. 1988. "Some Economic Approaches to the Persistence of Wage Differences Between Men and Women." In Ann H. Stromberg and Shirley Harkess (eds.), *Women Working: Theories and Facts in Perspective* (2nd ed.). Mountain View, Cal.: Mayfield, 87–100.

Stewart, Abigail J. 1994. "Toward a Feminist Strategy for Studying Women's Lives." In Carol E. Franz and Abigail J. Stewart (eds.), *Women Creating Lives: Identities, Resilience, and Resistance.* Boulder, Col.: Westview, 11–35.

Stier, Deborah S., and Judith A. Hall. 1984. "Gender Differences in Touch: An Empirical and Theoretical Review." *Journal of Personality and Social Psychology,* 47(2):440–459.

Stolker, Paula B. 1992. "Weigh My Job Performance, Not My Body: Extending Title VII to Weight-Based Discrimination." *New York Law School Journal of Human Rights,* 10(1):223–250.

Stoller, Eleanor Palo, and Rose Campbell Gibson. 1997. *Worlds of Difference: Inequality in the Aging Experience* (2nd ed.). Thousand Oaks, Cal.: Sage.

Stone, Leroy O. 1967. *Urban Development in Canada: 1961 Census Monograph.* Ottawa: Queen's Printer.

Stout, Cam. 1994. "Common Law: A Growing Alternative." In C. McKie (ed.), *Canadian Social Trends,* vol. 2. Toronto: Thompson Educational Publishing, 179–182.

Straus, Murray. 1991. "Discipline and Deviance: Physical Punishment of Children and Violence and Other Crime in Adulthood." *Social Problems,* 38, 133–154.

————. 1994. *Beating the Devil out of Them: Corporal Punishment in American Families.* New York: Lexington.

Straus, Murray, Richard Gelles, and Suzanne Steinmetz. 1980. *Behind Closed Doors: Violence in the American Family.* Garden City, NY: Doubleday.

Strenski, James. 1995. "The Ethics of Manipulated Communication." *Public Relations Quarterly,* vol. 40, 09–011993, 33.

Sum Quod Sum Foundation. 1997. *A Report on the Needs Assessment of Senior Gays and Lesbians.* Winnipeg: Sum Quod Sum Foundation Inc.

Sumner, William G. 1959. *Folkways.* New York: Dover (orig. pub. 1906).

Sutherland, Edwin H. 1939. *Principles of Criminology.* Philadelphia: Lippincott.

————. 1949. *White Collar Crime.* New York: Dryden.

Swedish Institute. 1998. "General Facts on Sweden." *Fact Sheets on Sweden.* Stockholm: The Swedish Institute.

Swidler, Ann. 1986. "Culture in Action: Symbols and Strategies." *American Sociological Review,* 51 (April):273–286.

Sytnick, Patricia. 1998. "A District Society in the Tar Sands." *The Globe and Mail* (February 23):A2.

Takaki, Ronald. 1993. *A Different Mirror: A History of Multicultural America.* Boston: Little, Brown.

Tannen, Deborah. 1990. *You Just Don't Understand: Women and Men in Conversation.* New York: Morrow.

————. 1993. "Commencement Address, State University of New York at Binghamton." Reprinted in *Chronicle of Higher Education* (June 9):B5.

————. 1995. "Wears Jump Suit. Sensible Shoes. Uses Husband's Last Name." In E.D. Nelson, and B.W. Robinson (eds.), *Gender in the 1990s: Images, Realities, and Issues.* Scarborough, Ont.: Nelson Canada, 3–7.

Tanzer, Andrew. 1996. "The Pacific Century." *Forbes* (July 15):108–113.

Tavris, Carol. 1993. *The Mismeasure of Woman.* New York: Touchstone.

Taylor, Payl. 1997. "Fatal Viruses Return with a Vengeance." *The Globe and Mail* (April 12):A1.

Taylor, Peter Shawn. 1995. "Grandma! Grandpa! Back to Work." *Saturday Night* (June):18–23, 96.

Taylor, Steve. 1982. *Durkheim and the Study of Suicide.* New York: St. Martin's Press.

Tepperman, Lorne. 1994. *Choices and Chances: Sociology for Everyday Life* (2nd ed.). Toronto: Harcourt Brace and Company.

Terkel, Studs. 1996. *Coming of Age: The Story of Our Century by Those Who've Lived It.* New York: St. Martin's Griffin.

The Economist. 1997. "The Anti-Management Guru." (May 4).

The Hindu. 1998. "The Idea of Human Development." (October 25):25.

Thiam, Awa. 1986. *Speak Out, Black Sisters: Feminism and Oppression in Black Africa.* Dover, N.H.: Pluto.

Thomas, D. 1992. *Criminality Among the Foreign Born: Analysis of Federal Prison Population.* Ottawa: Immigration and Employment Canada.

Thomas, William I., and Dorothy Swaine Thomas. 1928. *The Child in America.* New York: Knopf.

Thompson, Becky W. 1992. "'A Way Outa No Way': Eating Problems Among African-American, Latina, and White Women." *Gender & Society,* 6(4):546–561. Revised article, "Food, Bodies, and Growing Up Female: Childhood Lessons About Culture, Race, and Class." In Patricia Fallon, Melanie A. Katzman, and Susan C. Wooley (eds.), *Feminist Perspectives on Eating Disorders.* New York: Guilford Press, 1994, 355–378.

————. 1994. *A Hunger So Wide and So Deep: American Women Speak Out on Eating Problems.* Minneapolis: University of Minnesota.

Thomson, Elizabeth, and Ugo Colella. 1992. "Cohabitation and Marital Stability: Quality or Commitment?" *Journal of Marriage and the Family,* 54:259–267.

Thompson, Paul. 1983. *The Nature of Work.* London: Macmillan.

Thornberry, T.P., and M. Farnworth. 1982. "Social Correlates of Criminal Involvement." *American Sociological Review,* 47(4):505–518.

Thorne, Barrie, Cheris Kramarae, and Nancy Henley. 1983. *Language, Gender, and Society.* Rowley, Mass.: Newbury House.

Thorne, Barrie. 1993. *Gender Play: Girls and Boys in School.* New Brunswick, NJ: Rutgers University Press.

Thornton, Russell. 1984. "Cherokee Population Losses During the Trail of

Tears: A New Perspective and a New Estimate." *Ethnohistory*, 31:289–300.

Tidwell, Gary L. 1993. *Anatomy of a Fraud: Inside the Finances of the P.T.L. Ministries.* New York: Wiley.

Tilly, Charles. 1973. "Collective Action and Conflict in Large-Scale Social Change: Research Plans, 1974–78." Center for Research on Social Organization. Ann Arbor: University of Michigan, October.

———. (ed.). 1975. *The Formation of National States in Western Europe.* Princeton, N.J.: Princeton University Press.

———. 1978. *From Mobilization to Revolution.* Reading, Mass.: Addison-Wesley.

Time. 1993. "The Week: Schwarzenegger Body Count." (June 28):22.

———. 1997. "An Encouraging Report Card." (June 23):67.

Timpson, Joyce. 1995. "Four Decades of Literature on Native Canadian Child Welfare: Changing Themes." *Child Welfare*, 74:525.

Tiryakian, Edward A. 1978. "Emile Durkheim." In Tom Bottomore and Robert Nisbet (eds.), *A History of Sociological Analysis.* New York: Basic Books, 187–236.

Titmus, Richard. 1971. *The Gift Relationship: From Human Blood to Social Policy.* New York: Vintage Books.

Tittle, Charles W., William J. Villemez, and Douglas A. Smith. 1978. "The Myth of Social Class and Criminality." *American Sociological Review* 43(5):643–656.

Toffler, Alvin. 1980. *The Third Wave.* New York: Bantam.

Tomasevski, Katarina. 1993. Prepared on behalf of the UN-NGO Group on Women and Development. *Women and Human Rights.* Atlantic Highlands, N.J.: Zed Books.

Tong, Rosemarie. 1989. *Feminist Thought: A Comprehensive Introduction.* Boulder, Col.: Westview Press.

Tonnies, Ferdinand. 1940. *Fundamental Concepts of Sociology (Gemeinschaft und Gesellschaft).* Trans. Charles P. Loomis. New York: American Book Company (orig. pub. 1887).

Touraine, Alain. 1971. *Post Industrial Society.* New York: Random House.

Tower, Cynthia Crosson. 1996. *Child Abuse and Neglect* (3rd ed.). Boston: Allyn and Bacon.

Troeltsch, Ernst. 1960. *The Social Teachings of the Christian Churches,* vols. 1 and 2.

Trans. O. Wyon. New York: Harper & Row. (orig. pub. 1931).

Trovato, Frank. 1994. "Mortality Trends in Canada." In B. Singh Bolaria and Harley D. Dickinson (eds.), *Health, Illness, and Health Care in Canada.* Toronto: Harcourt Brace, 22–64.

Tucker, Robert C. (ed.). 1979. *The Marx-Engels Reader* (2nd ed.). New York: Norton.

Tumin, Melvin. 1953. "Some Principles of Stratification: A Critical Analysis." *American Sociological Review,* 18 (August):387–393.

Turcotte, Peter, and Alain Bélanger. 1997. "Moving in Together." *Canadian Social Trends* (Winter). Ottawa: Statistics Canada. Cat. No. 11-008-XPE, 7–10.

Turner, Jonathan, Leonard Beeghley, and Charles H. Powers. 1995. *The Emergence of Sociological Theory* (3rd ed.). Belmont, Cal.: Wadsworth.

Turner, Ralph H., and Lewis M. Killian. 1993. "The Field of Collective Behavior." In Russell L. Curtis, Jr., and Benigno E. Aguirre (eds.), *Collective Behavior and Social Movements.* Boston: Allyn & Bacon, 5–20.

Twenhofel, Karen. 1993. "Do You Diet?" In Leslea Newman (ed.), *Eating Our Hearts Out: Personal Accounts of Women's Relationship to Food.* Freedom, Cal.: Crossing Press.

Underhill, Susan, Victor Marshall, and Sylvie Deliencourt. 1997. *Options 45+: HRCC Survey Final Report.* Ottawa: One Voice.

UNAIDS. 1998. "New World AIDS Day Report Finds Global HIV Infections Increased 10% in 1998." Available: http://www.unaids.org/highband/press/wadep98.html

UNICEF. 1997. *Progress of Nations 1996.* New York: United Nations.

United Nations. 1997a. "Global Change and Sustainable Development: Critical Trends." United Nations Department for Policy Coordination and Sustainable Development. Posted online (January 20).

———. 1997b. *Report of the Workshop on Managing the Social Consequences of Structural Change.* New York: Economic and Social Council.

———. 1998. *Revision of the World's Population Estimates and Projections.* New York: United Nations Population Division.

United Nations Development Programme. 1996. *Human Development Report, 1996.* New York: Oxford University Press.

———. 1997. *Human Development Report, 1997.* New York: Oxford University Press.

———. 1998. *Human Development Report, 1998.* New York: Oxford University Press.

United Nations DPCSD. 1997. "Report of Commission on Sustainable Development, April 1997." New York: United Nations Department for Policy Coordination and Sustainable Development. Posted online.

Ursel, Jane. 1996. *Submission to the Commission of Inquiry into the Deaths of Rhonds LaVoie and Roy Lavoie.* Winnipeg.

U.S. Congress, Office of Technology Assessment. 1979. "The Effects of Nuclear War." Report quoted in Michael E. Howard. 1990. "On Fighting a Nuclear War." In Francesca M. Cancian and James William Gibson (eds.), *Making War, Making Peace: The Social Foundations of Violent Conflict.* Belmont, Cal.: Wadsworth, 314–322.

Vallières, Pierre. 1971. *White Niggers of America.* Toronto: McClelland and Stewart.

Van Biema, David. 1993. "But Will It End the Abortion Debate?" *Time* (June 14):52–54.

Vanier Institute of the Family. 1994. *Profiling Canadian Families.* Ottawa: Vanier Institute of the Family.

———. 1998. "Families: Change and Continuity." Available: http://www.cfc-efc.ca/docs/00000329.htm

Vaughan, Diane. 1985. "Uncoupling: The Social Construction of Divorce." In James M. Henslin (ed.), *Marriage and Family in a Changing Society* (2nd ed.). New York: Free Press, 429–439.

Veblin, Thorstein. 1967. *The Theory of the Leisure Class.* New York: Viking (orig. pub. 1899).

Veevers, Jean. E. 1980. *Childless by Choice.* Toronto: Butterworths.

———. 1991. *Continuity and Change in Marriage and Family.* Toronto: Holt, Rinehart and Wilson.

Verburg, Peter. 1994. *The Alberta Report.*

Vetter, Harold J., and Gary R. Perlstein. 1991. *Perspectives on Terrorism.* Pacific Grove, Cal.: Brooks/Cole.

Vigil, James. 1990. "Cholos and Gangs: Culture Change and Street Youth in Los Angeles." In Ronald C. Huff (ed.), *Gangs in America.* Newbury Park, Cal.: Sage.

Vito, Gennaro F., and Ronald M. Holmes. 1994. *Criminology: Theory, Research and Policy.* Belmont, Cal.: Wadsworth.

Volpe, R. 1989. *Poverty and Child Abuse: A Review of Selected Literature.* Toronto: Institute for the Prevention of Child Abuse.

Wachtel, Andy. 1994. *Child Abuse and Neglect. A Discussion Paper and Overview of Topically Related Projects.* Ottawa: The Circle.

Wagner, Elvin, and Allen E. Stearn. 1945. *The Effects of Smallpox on the Destiny of the American Indian.* Boston: Bruce Humphries.

Waldram, James B., D. Ann Herring, and T. Kue Young. 1995. *Aboriginal Health in Canada: Historical, Cultural, and Epidemiological Perspectives.* Toronto: University of Toronto Press.

Waldron, Ingrid. 1994. "What Do We Know About the Causes of Sex Differences in Mortality? A Review of the Literature." In Peter Conrad and Rochelle Kern (eds.), *The Sociology of Health and Illness: Critical Perspectives.* New York: St. Martin's Press, 42–54.

Walker, Lawrence J. 1989. "A Longitudinal Study of Moral Reasoning." *Child Development,* 60:157–166.

Wallace, Harvey. 1996. *Family Violence: Legal, Medical, and Social Perspectives.* Boston: Allyn and Bacon.

Wallace, Walter L. 1971. *The Logic of Science in Sociology.* New York: Aldine de Gruyter.

Wallerstein, Immanuel. 1979. *The Capitalist World-Economy.* Cambridge, England: Cambridge University Press.

———. 1984. *The Politics of the World Economy.* Cambridge, England: Cambridge University Press.

———. 1991. *Unthinking Social Science: The Limits of Nineteenth-Century Paradigms.* Cambridge, England: Polity Press.

Wannel, Ted, and Nathalie Caron. 1994. "A Look at Employment Equity Groups Among Recent Postsecondary Graduates: Visible Minorities, Aboriginal Peoples and the Activity Limited." Cat. no. 11F0019MPE no. 69. Ottawa: Statistics Canada.

———. 1996. The Gender Earnings Gap Among Recent Postsecondary Graduates, 1984–92, Cat. no. 68 #11F0G19MPE. Ottawa: Statistics Canada.

Ward, Margaret. 1998. *The Family Dynamic: A Canadian Perspective* (2nd ed.). Scarborough: ITP Nelson.

Ward, Mike. 1996. "Firm Fined $6,000 After Man Killed in Unsafe Workplace." *Winnipeg Free Press* (March 7).

Warner, W. Lloyd, and Paul S. Lunt. 1941. *The Social Life of a Modern Community.* New Haven, Conn.: Yale University Press.

Warr, Mark. 1995. "America's Perceptions of Crime and Punishment." In Joseph F. Sheley, *Criminology: A Contemporary Handbook* (2nd ed.). Belmont, Cal.: Wadsworth, 15–31.

Waters, Malcolm. 1995. *Globalization.* London and New York: Routledge.

Watson, Paul. 1997. "Richer, Poorer." *Toronto Star* (August 10):F1, F5.

Watson, Tracey. 1987. "Women Athletes and Athletic Women: The Dilemmas and Contradictions of Managing Incongruent Identities." *Sociological Inquiry,* 57(Fall):431–446.

Webb, Eugene, et al. 1966. *Unobtrusive Measures: Nonreactive Research in the Social Sciences.* Chicago: Rand McNally.

Weber, Max. 1947. *The Theory of Social and Economic Organization.* Trans. A.M. Henderson and Talcott Parsons; ed. Talcott Parsons. New York: Oxford University Press.

———. 1963. *The Sociology of Religion.* Trans. E. Fischoff. Boston: Beacon Press (orig. pub. 1922).

———. 1968. *Economy and Society: An Outline of Interpretive Sociology.* Trans. G. Roth and G. Wittich. New York: Bedminster Press (orig. pub. 1922).

———. 1976. *The Protestant Ethic and the Spirit of Capitalism.* Trans. Talcott Parsons. Introduction by Anthony Giddens. New York: Scribner (orig. pub. 1904–1905).

Weeks, John R. 1992. *Population: An Introduction to Concepts and Issues* (5th ed.). Belmont, Cal.: Wadsworth.

Weigel, Russell H., and P.W. Howes. 1985. "Conceptions of Racial Prejudice: Symbolic Racism Revisited." *Journal of Social Issues,* 41:124–132.

Weinfeld, Morton. 1995. "Ethnic and Race Relations." In R. Brym (ed.), *New Society: Sociology for the 21st Century.* Toronto: Harcourt Brace and Company, 4.1–4.29

Weinstein, Michael M. 1997. "'The Bell Curve,' Revisited by Scholars." *New York Times* (October 11):A20.

Weiss, Meira. 1994. *Conditional Love: Parents' Attitudes Toward Handicapped Children.* Westport, Conn.: Bergin & Garvey.

Weiskel, Timothy. 1994. "Vicious Circles." *Harvard International Review* 16:12–20.

Weitz, Rose. 1993. "Living with the Stigma of AIDS." In Delos H. Kelly (ed.), *Deviant Behavior: A Text-Reader in the Sociology of Deviance* (4th ed.). New York: St. Martin's Press, 222–236.

———. 1995. *A Sociology of Health, Illness, and Health Care.* Belmont, Cal.: Wadsworth.

———. 1996. *The Sociology of Health, Illness, and Health Care: A Critical Approach.* Belmont, Cal.: Wadsworth.

Welsh, Sandy. 1998. "Work and Occupations." In Robert J. Brym (ed.), *New Society: Sociology for the 21st Century* (2nd ed.). Toronto: Harcourt Brace, 295–317.

Wendell, Susan. 1995. "Toward a Feminist Theory of Disability." In E.D. Nelson and B.W. Robinson (eds.), *Gender in the 1990s.* Scarborough, Ont.: Nelson Canada, 455–465.

Weitzman, Lenore J. 1985. *The Divorce Revolution.* New York: Free Press.

Weston, Kath. 1991. *Families We Choose: Lesbians, Gays, Kinship.* New York: Columbia University Press.

Weston, Marianne, and Bonnie Jeffery. 1994. "AIDS: The Politicizing of a Public Health Issue." pp. 721–738 in B. Singh Bolaria and Harley D. Dickinson (eds.), *Health, Illness, and Health Care in Canada* (2nd ed.). Toronto: Harcourt Brace and Company.

Westrum, Ron. 1991. *Technologies and Society: The Shaping of People and Things.* Belmont, Cal.: Wadsworth.

Whitaker, Barbara. 1997. "Earning It; If You Can't Beat Dilbert, Hire Him." *New York Times* (June 29):C12.

Whitaker, Reg. 1991. *Double Standard: The Secret Story of Canadian Immigration.* Toronto: Lester and Orpen Dennys.

White, James. 1987. "Premarital Cohabitation and Marital Stability in Canada." *Journal of Marriage and the Family,* 49:641–647.

White, Merry. 1994. *The Material Child: Coming of Age in Japan and America.* Berkeley: University of California Press.

White, Ryan, and Anne Marie Cunningham. 1992. *Ryan White: My Own Story.* New York: Signet/Penguin.

White, Ralph. 1960. *Autocracy and Democracy.* New York: Harper and Row.

White, Ralph, and Ronald Lippitt. 1953. "Leader Behavior and Member Reaction in Three 'Social Climates.'" In Dorwin Cartwright and Alvin Zander (eds.), *Group Dynamics.* Evanston, Ill.: Row, Peterson, 586–611.

White, Richard W. 1992. *Rude Awakening: What the Homeless Crisis Tells Us.* San Francisco: ICS Press.

Whorf, Benjamin Lee. 1956. *Language, Thought and Reality.* John B. Carroll (ed.). Cambridge, Mass.: MIT Press.

Whyte, William. 1955.

Whyte, William Foote. 1989. "Advancing Scientific Knowledge Through Participatory Action Research." *Sociological Forum,* 4:367–386.

Whyte, William H., Jr. 1957. *The Organization Man.* Garden City, N.Y.: Anchor.

Wickett, Ann. 1989. *Double Exit: When Aging Couples Commit Suicide Together.* Eugene, Ore.: Hemlock Society.

Wieler, Joseph M. 1986. "The Role of Law in Labour Relations." In Ivan Bernier and Andree Lojoie (eds.), *Labour Law and Urban Law in Canada.* Toronto: University of Toronto Press.

Williams, Christine L. 1989. *Gender Differences at Work.* Berkeley: University of California Press.

———. (ed.). 1993. *Doing "Women's Work": Men in Nontraditional Occupations.* Newbury Park, Cal.: Sage.

Williams, Gregory Howard. 1995. *Life on the Color Line: The True Story of a White Boy Who Discovered He Was Black.* New York: Dutton.

Williams, Robin M., Jr. 1970. *American Society: A Sociological Interpretation* (3rd ed.). New York: Knopf.

Williamson, Robert C., Alice Duffy Rinehart, and Thomas O. Blank. 1992. *Early Retirement: Promises and Pitfalls.* New York: Plenum Press.

Wilson, David (ed.). 1997. "Globalization and the Changing U.S. City." *Annals of the American Academy of Political and Social Sciences,* 551. Special issue (May).

Wilson, Edward O. 1975. *Sociobiology: A New Synthesis.* Cambridge, Mass.: Harvard University Press.

Wilson, Elizabeth. 1991. *The Sphinx in the City: Urban Life, the Control of Disorder, and Women.* Berkeley: University of California Press.

Wilson, Everett K., and Hanan Selvin. 1980. *Why Study Sociology? A Note to Undergraduates.* Belmont, Cal.: Wadsworth.

Wilson, William Julius. 1996. *When Work Disappears: The World of the New Urban Poor.* New York: Knopf.

Winn, Maria. 1985. *The Plug-in Drug: Television, Children, and the Family.* New York: Viking.

Wirth, Louis. 1945. "The Problem of Minority Groups." In Ralph Linton (ed.), *The Science of Man in the World Crisis.* New York: Columbia University Press, 38.

Wiseman, Jacqueline. 1970. *Stations of the Lost: The Treatment of Skid Row Alcoholics.* Chicago: University of Chicago Press.

———. 1979. *Stations of the Lost: The Treatment of Skid Row Alcoholics.* Chicago: University of Chicago Press.

Wolf, Daniel. 1996. "A Bloody Biker War." *Maclean's* (Jan. 15):10–11.

Wolf, Naomi. 1990. *The Beauty Myth: How Images of Beauty Are Used Against Women.* New York: Morrow.

———. 1994. "Hunger." In Patricia Fallon, Melanie A. Katzman, and Susan C. Wooley (eds.), *Feminist Perspectives on Eating Disorders.* New York: Guilford Press, 94–111.

Wolfe, David A. 1987. *Child Abuse: Implications for Child Development and Psychopathology.* Newbury Park, Cal.: Sage.

Wolfe, Jeanne M. 1992. "Canada's Livable Cities." *Social Policy,* 23:56–63.

Women for Economic Survival. 1984. *Women and Economic Hard Times: A Record.* Victoria: Women for Economic Survival and the University of Victoria.

Women Working Worldwide (eds.). 1991. *Common Interests: Women Organizing in Global Electronics.* London: Women Working Worldwide.

Wong, Sandra L. 1991. "Evaluating the Content of Textbooks: Public Interests and Professional Authority." *Sociology of Education,* 64:11–18.

Wood, Chris Caragata. 1994. "The Legacy of Sue Rodriquez." *Maclean's* (February 28):22.

Wood, Darryl S., and Curt T. Griffiths. 1996. "Patterns of Aboriginal Crime." In Robert A. Silverman, James J. Teevan, and Vincent F. Sacco (eds.), *Crime in Canadian Society* (5th ed.). Toronto: Harcourt Brace and Company, 222–223.

Wood, Julia T. 1994. *Gendered Lives: Communication, Gender, and Culture.* Belmont, Cal.: Wadsworth.

Wooden, Wayne S. 1995. *Renegade Kids, Suburban Outlaws: From Youth Culture to Delinquency.* Belmont, Cal.: Wadsworth.

Wooley, Susan C. 1994. "Sexual Abuse and Eating Disorders: The Concealed Debate." In Patricia Fallon, Melanie A. Katzman, and Susan C. Wooley (eds.), *Feminist Perspectives on Eating Disorders.* New York: Guilford Press, 171–211.

World Bank. 1996. *World Development Report 1996: From Plan to Market.* New York: Oxford University Press for the World Bank.

World Health Organization. 1998. *Fifty Facts from the World Health Report 1998.* Available: www.who.int/whr/1998/factse.htm

Worster, Donald. 1985. *Natures Economy: A History of Ecological Ideas.* New York: Cambridge University Press.

Wotherspoon, Terry. 1994. "Colonization, Self-Determination, and the Health of Canada's First Nations Peoples." In B. Singh Bolaria and Rosemary Bolaria (eds.), *Racial Minorities, Medicine and Health.* Halifax: Fernwood Publishing, 247–267.

Wouters, Cas. 1989. "The Sociology of Emotions and Flight Attendants: Hochschild's Managed Heart." *Theory, Culture & Society,* 6:95–123.

Wresch, William. 1996. *Disconnected: Haves and Have-Nots in the Information Age.* New Brunswick, N.J.: Rutgers University Press.

Wright, Erik Olin, Karen Shire, Shu-Ling Hwang, Maureen Dolan, and Janeen Baxter. 1992. "The Non-Effects of Class on the Gender Division of Labor in the Home: A Comparative Study of Sweden and the U.S." *Gender & Society,* 6(2):252–282.

Wright, John W. (ed.). 1997. *The New York Times 1998 Almanac.* New York: Penguin Reference Books.

Wu, Z. 1995. "The Stability of Cohabitation Relationships: The Role of Children." *Journal of Marriage and the Family,* 57:231–236.

Wuthnow, Robert. 1996. *Poor Richard's Principle: Recovering the American Dream Through the Moral Dimension of Work, Business, and Money.* Princeton, N.J.: Princeton University Press.

Wylie, Alison. 1995. "The Contexts of Activism on 'Climate' Issue." In the Chilly Collective (eds.), *Breaking Anonymity: The Chilly Climate for Women Faculty.* Waterloo, Ont.: Wilfrid Laurier University Press, 29–60.

Yinger, J. Milton. 1960. "Contraculture and Subculture." *American Sociological Review,* 25 (October):625–635.

———. 1982. *Countercultures: The Promise and Peril of a World Turned Upside Down.* New York: Free Press.

Young, Anthony. 1990. "Television Viewing." In Craig McKie and K. Thompson (eds.), *Canadian Social Trends.* Toronto: Thompson Educational Publishing, 231–233.

Young, Michael Dunlap. 1994. *The Rise of the Meritocracy.* New Brunswick, N.J.: Transaction (orig. pub. 1958).

Yunus, Muhammad. 1997. "Empowerment of the Poor: Eliminating the Apartheid Practiced by Financial Institutions." Paper presented to the State of the World Forum, San Francisco.

Zald, Mayer N., and John D. McCarthy (eds.). 1987. *Social Movements in an Organizational Society.* New Brunswick, N.J.: Transaction.

Zavella, Patricia. 1987. *Women's Work and Chicano Families: Cannery Workers of the Santa Clara Valley.* Ithaca, N.Y.: Cornell University Press.

Zeidenberg, Jerry. 1990. "The Just-in-Time Workforce." *Small Business,* (May):31–34.

Zelizer, Viviana. 1985. *Pricing the Priceless Child: The Changing Social Value of Children.* New Haven, Conn.: Yale University Press.

Zellner, William M. 1978. "Vehicular Suicide: In Search of Incidence." Unpublished M.A. thesis, Western Illinois University, Macomb. Quoted in Richard T. Schaefer and Robert P. Lamm. 1992. *Sociology* (4th ed.). New York: McGraw-Hill, 54–55.

Zimmerman, Don H. 1992. "They Were All Doing Gender, but They Weren't All Passing: Comment on Rogers." *Gender & Society,* 6(2):192–198.

Zipp, John F. 1985. "Perceived Representativeness and Voting: An Assessment of the Impact of 'Choices' vs. 'Echoes.' " *The American Political Science Review,* 60:3:738–759.

Zuboff, Shoshana. 1988. *In the Age of the Smart Machine.* New York: Basic Books.

Zuravin, Susan J. 1991. "Research Definitions of Child Physical Abuse and Neglect: Current Problems." In Raymond H. Starr, Jr., and David A. Wolfe (eds.), *The Effects of Child Abuse and Neglect.* London: Guilford Press, 100–128.

Zurcher, Louis. 1968. "Social-Psychological Functions of Ephemeral Roles: A Disaster Work Crew." *Human Organization,* 27 (Winter):281–298.

———. 1983. *Social Roles: Conformity, Conflict, and Creativity.* Beverly Hills, Cal.: Sage.

PHOTO CREDITS

COPYRIGHT ACKNOWLEDGMENTS

p. 30: Reprinted with permission from *Death and Deliverance*, by Robert Mason Lee (Macfarlane Walter & Ross, Toronto, 1992) 229-231. **p. 36:** Harman, 1989 reprinted by permission. **p. 53:** Lois Zurcher, "Social-Psychological Functions of Ephemeral Roles: A Disaster Work Crew," *Human Organization* 27(Winter 1968):281-98. Reprinted by permission. **p. 56:** Raquel Kennedy Bergen, "Interviewing Survivors of Marital Rape," in Claire Renzetti and Raymond Lee, *Researching Sensitive Topics*. pp. 197-211, copyright © 1993 by Sage Publications, Inc. Reprinted by permission Sage Publications, Inc. **pp. 64-65, 72:** Ross, 1996 from *Returning to the Teachings: Exploring Aboriginal Justice* by Rupert Ross. Copyright © 1996 by University of Saskatchewan. Reprinted by permission of Penguin Books Canada Limited. **p. 74:** Richler, 1991 © 1992 Random House Inc. **p. 82:** Friedman, 1998. Copyright © 1998 by the New York Times Co. Reprinted by permission. **p. 85:** Shadd, 1994 reprinted by permission. **p. 90:** Chagnon, 1992 excerpt from *Yanomamo: The Last Days of Eden* by Napoleon A. Chagnon, copyright © 1992 by Harcourt Inc., reprinted by permission of the publisher. **p. 100:** Pelzer, 1995 reprinted with permission. **p. 124:** Roth, 1993 reprinted with permission. **p. 133:** O'Reilly-Fleming, Thomas, *Down and Out in Canada: Homeless Canadians* © 1993 Canadian Scholar's Press. Reproduced by permission. **p. 138:** Harman, 1989 reprinted with permission. **p. 169:** Owen, 1996 reprinted by permission. **p. 204:** Elliot Leyton, *The Myth of Delinquency: Anatomy of Juvenile Nihilism* © 1979 by Prentice-Hall; reprinted by permission. **p. 207:** Letkemann, 1973 reprinted with the permission of Simon & Schuster from *Crime as Work* by Peter Letkemann. Copyright © 1973 by Prentice-Hall, Inc. **p. 207:** Wolf, 1996 reprinted by permission. **p. 228:** Quigley, 1996 reprinted with permission of the author. **p. 238:** O'Reilly-Fleming, Thomas, *Down and Out in Canada: Homeless Canadians* © 1993 Canadian Scholar's Press. Reproduced by permission. **p. 250:** Jones, 1995. Copyright © by the New York Times. Reprinted by permission. **p. 274:** Lummis, 1992 reprinted by permission. **p. 277:** *The Hindu*, "The Idea of Human Development." Reprinted by permission. **p. 287:** Emling, 1997 reprinted by permission. **p. 302:** Phesant, 1994 reprinted by permission. **pp. 305-306:** *Unequal Relations: An Introduction to Race, Ethnic, and Aboriginal Dynamics in Canada*, Angie Fleras and Jean Leonard Elliot, © 1996, Prentice Hall. Reprinted by permission. **p. 308:** Desai, 1994 reprinted by permission. **p. 309:** James, 1995 reprinted by permission. **p. 309:** James, 1995 reprinted by permission. **p. 318:** Johnson, 1995 reprinted by permission. **pp. 320-321:** Shadd, 1991 reprinted by permission of the author. **p. 326:** James, 1995 reprinted by permission. **pp. 334-335:** Rutherford, 1998 reprinted by permission of the author. **p. 349:** Annesi, 1993 reprinted with permission from "Like Mother, Like Daughter" by Nicole Annesi in *Eating Our Hearts Out*, edited by Leslea Newman. © The Crossing Press. Freedom, CA 95019. **p. 350:**

Reprinted with permission from "Do You Diet?" by Karen Twenhofel in *Eating Our Hearts Out*, edited by Leslea Newman. © The Crossing Press. Freedom, CA 95019. **p. 356:** Susan Bordo, *Unbearable Weight: Feminism, Western Culture, and the Body*. © 1993 The Regents of the University of California. **p. 371:** Dawson reprinted by permission of the author. **p. 378:** Heinrichs, 1996 reprinted by permission. **p. 380:** Terkel, 1996 reprinted by permission of Donadio and Olson, Inc. Copyright © 1964 Studs Terkel. **pp. 382-383:** Patterson, 1998 reprinted by permission of the author. **pp. 387, 389:** Le Shan, 1994 reprinted by permission. **p. 390:** Taylor, 1995 reprinted by permission of the author. **pp. 393-394:** NACA, 1992 reproduced with the consent of the National Advisory Council on Aging (NACA) and the Minister of Public Works and Government Services Canada, 1999. **p. 395:** DaVanzo and Adamson, 1997 reprinted by permission. **p. 401:** Popoff, 1996 reprinted by permission of the author. **p. 404:** Heron, 1993 reprinted by permission of the author. **p. 427:** Luttwak, 1996 reprinted by permission of the author. **p. 437:** *White Niggers of America* by Pierre Vallieres. Used by permission, McClelland & Stewart, Inc. *The Canadian Publishers*. **p. 459:** *Canada, Quebec and the Uses of Nationalism* by Ramsay Cook. Used by permission, McClelland & Stewart, Inc. *The Canadian Publishers*. **p. 468:** Mason Lee, 1998 reprinted by permission of the author. **p. 499:** Church, 1996 reprinted by permission of the author. **p. 524:** Pinderhughes 1986 reprinted by permission of the author. **p. 508:** From "Education Report: The Kumon Way" originally published *in Owl Canadian Family Magazine*, October-November 1997. Copyright © 1997 Lesley Krueger. With permission of the author. **p. 519:** Navarrette, 1993 from *A Darker Shade of Crimson* by Ruben Navarrette Jr. Copyright © 1993 by Ruben Navarrette Jr. Used by permission of Bantam Books, a division of Random House, Inc. **p. 528:** Hymers, 1997 reprinted by permission of the author. **pp. 530-531:** Patricia Chisholm, "Schooling the Disabled," *Maclean's*, March 27, 1995. Reprinted by permission. **p. 541:** Mitchell, 1999 reprinted with permission from The Globe and Mail. **p. 575:** "The Sociology of Health and Health Care" by Karen Grant from *Contemporary Sociology*. Editors: Li and Bolaria. Copyright © 1993 Copp Clark Pitman Ltd. All rights reserved. Reproduced by permission. **p. 580:** White and Cunningham, 1992 from *Ryan White: My Own Story*, by Ryan White and Ann Marie Cunningham. Copyright © 1991 by Jeanne White and Ann Marie Cunningham. Used by permission of Dial Young Readers, a division of Penguin Putnam Inc. **p. 588:** Anderson, 1994 reprinted by permission. **p. 592:** Wendell, 1995 reprinted by permission of the author. **p. 621:** Castels, 1995 reprinted by permission. **p. 652:** Excerpt from *The Irony of Democracy: An Uncommon Introduction to American Politics*, Ninth Edition, by Thomas R. Dye and Harmon Zeigler, copyright © 1993 by Harcourt, Inc., reprinted by permission of the publisher.

INDEX

Aboriginal Canadians, 323–325. *See also*
  Race and ethnicity
  child poverty, 261
  crime, 226
  death rate, 257
  deviance, 203
  families, 502, 503
  healing methods, 588
  health problems, 586–588
  language, 74–77
  self-government, 461–463
Aboriginals. *See* Native Canadians
Absolute monarchs, 443
Absolute poverty, 260, 285
Accommodation, 319
Acculturation, 318
Ace-ace encounters, 151
Ace-bomber encounters, 151
Achieved status, 135, 241
Acoose-Pelletier, Janice, 588
Acting crowd, 643, 645
Activity theory, 387
Acupuncture, 599
Acute illness, 578
Adams, Michael, 78, 83
ADD, 581
Addams, Jane, 16
ADHD, 581
Adler, Freda, 210
Adler, Patricia, 353
Administrative discretion, 228
Administrators, 417
Adolescence, 125, 376
Adoption, 489
Adorno, Theodore W., 309
Adulthood, 125, 126, 376–380
Advertising, 86, 87, 354, 356, 357
Age stratification, 375
Age structure, 373
Ageism, 381
Agents of socialization, 117
Agger, Ben, 365
Aggregate, 166, 643
Aging, 370–399
  age groupings, 375–380
  conflict perspectives, 388, 389
  crime, and, 220
  death/dying, 394–397
  defined, 371
  elder abuse, 385–387
  functionalist perspectives, 387
  future trends, 397, 398

generational war, 390, 391
  health, 582
  historical perspective, 373, 374
  inequalities, 380–387
  interactionist perspectives, 387, 388
  living arrangements, 389–393
  nursing homes, 393
  quiz, 373, 374
  Russia, in, 394, 395
  social significance, 372–374
  support services/homemaker
    services/daycare, 389–393
  trends, 372, 373
  unemployment rates, 422
  wealth/poverty, 240, 261, 262, 384,
    385
Agrarian societies, 343–345
Agricultural societies, 253
AIDS, 574, 575
  Aboriginal Canadians, and, 587
  Africa, in, 596, 597
  media, and, 580, 581
  public health, and, 584, 585
  quiz, 577, 578
  statistics (map), 576
Albas, Daniel and Cheryl, 151
Alienation, 15, 244, 413
Allahar, Anton, 293
Alternative medical practices, 598–600
Altruism, 31, 34, 35
Altruistic Love (Sorokin), 50
Altruistic suicide, 20
Alwi, Tini Heyun, 297
Alzheimer's disease, 582, 583
Analysis, 40
Anderson, Elijah, 205
Anderson, Leon, 57, 134
Animism, 545, 546
Annesi, Nicole, 349
Anomic suicide, 20
Anomie, 14
Anonymity, 57
Anorexia, 339
Anti-intellectualism, 529
Anticipatory socialization, 123
Apartheid, 242
Appleton, Lynn M., 630
Arnold, Regina, 211
Asch, Solomon, 172–174
Ascribed status, 135
Assembly line, 417
Assimilation, 318

Assimilationist, 621
Assisting suicide, 4, 5
Attention deficit disorder (ADD), 581
Attention deficit-hyperactivity disorder (ADHD), 581
Aulette, Judy Root, 470
Authoritarian leaders, 171
Authoritarian personality, 309
Authoritarian systems, 443
Authority, 438–443

Baby boom, 614–617
Baby boom echo, 616
Baby bust, 614, 617
Back stage, 152
Banner, Lois W., 372
Bardolino, Tony, 477
Barendregt, Dick and Joanne, 540
Barnaby, Joanne, 76
Barnard, Chester, 185
Barrett, Stanley, 312
Barter, 403
Bassuny, Aysha, 548
Battered woman, 480
Beanie Babies, 651
Beare, Margaret, 203
Becker, Howard, 208
Beeghley, Leonard, 515
Beliefs, 69
Bell Curve: Intelligence and Class Structure in American Life, The (Herrnstein/Murray), 522
Berdaches, 337
Bergen, Raquel Kennedy, 56
Berger, Peter, 5, 480, 543
Berliner, David C., 517
Bernard, Jessie, 480
Bernardo, Paul, 231
Bertram, Bob, 413
Beyerstein, Barry, 600
Bhopal, India disaster, 654, 655
Bibby, Reginald, 568
Biddle, Bruce J., 517
Bilateral descent, 475
Biological needs, 92
Bissoondath, Neil, 319
Bittner, Egon, 228
Black Candle, The (Murphy), 622
Blass, Michel, 231
Blau, Peter M., 186, 188, 189
Blended families, 498
Blood donors, 47, 48
Blumer, Herbert, 643, 651
Body consciousness, 338
Body image, 335–337
Bodybuilding, 340
Bogardus, Emory, 310
Bomber-bomber encounters, 151
Bonaparte, Napoleon, 181

Booth, Karen, 492
Bordo, Susan, 340, 347
Bouchard, Lucien, 441
Bourassa, Robert, 460
Bourdieu, Pierre, 80, 81, 518, 651
Bourgeoisie, 15
Bridewealth, 343
Brint, Steven, 415
Britt, Lory, 653
Brougham, Lord, 229
Buchignani, Norman, 331
Buddha, 554
Buddhism, 553–555
Buffett, Warren, 274
Bulimia, 339
Bureaucracy
    characteristics, 183, 184
    defined, 181
    Dilbert, 190, 191
    governmental, 457, 458
    informal structure, 184, 185
    management, 417
    oligarchy, and, 189, 190
    quiz, 167, 168
    shortcomings, 185–189
    why it exists, 181, 182
Bureaucratic authority, 441
Bureaucratic personality, 186
Burgess, Ernest W., 627
Business cycle, 413

Callbeck, Catherine, 453
Calliste, Agnes, 322
Calmeadow Foundation, 43
Calvin, John, 549
Campbell, Kim, 453
Canada
    Aboriginal self-government, 461–463
    class structure, 247–251
    constitutional monarchy, as, 445
    core values, 77, 78
    crime rates, 218
    disabled persons, 591
    economy (future trends), 427, 428
    ethnic groups, 323–330
    ethnic origins, 307
    health care, 593–597
    heterogeneous society, as, 85, 88
    immigration, 611, 612, 614, 615
    immigration trends, 329, 330
    language diversity, 74–76
    politics/government, 453–457
    Quebec nationalism, 458–461
    religion, 561–569
    segregation, 320, 321
    skinheads, 89
    social inequality, 254–259
    sociology in, 17
    tolerance of other cultures, 67, 68

vertical mosaic, as, 306
Canadian Uniform Crime Reports (CUCR), 217, 219
Cancian, Francesca, 482
Cantril, Hadley, 646
Capek, Stella M., 659
Capella Papers, A, 527
Capital, 402
Capital flight, 280, 421
Capitalism, 407–410
Capitalist class, 244
Case studies, 54, 55
Caste system, 242, 243
Casual crowds, 643
Category, 166
Census metropolitan area (CMA), 624
Chagnon, Napoleon, 89
Challenger shuttle disaster, 176, 177
Chambliss, William, 208
Change (social change), 660–663
Chaplin, Charlie, 402
Charismatic authority, 438, 439
Charlottetown Accord, 461
Charter of Rights and Freedoms, 441–443
Charter school, 535
Cheal, David, 503
Cherlin, Andrew, 499
Chicago School, 16
Child abuse
    Asia, in, 124, 125
    examples, 100, 101
    historical perspective, 108
    public awareness, 120, 121
    quiz, 103, 104
    reasonable force, 109
    self-concept, and, 111
    what is it, 107
Child-centered education, 525
Childhood, 124, 375
Childless couples, 488
Chilly Climate Report, 352
Chinese Canadians, 327, 328
Chon, Margaret, 523
Chrétien, Jean, 441, 445
Christ, Jesus, 558
Christianity, 553, 558, 559
Chronic illnesses, 578
Chronological age, 372
Church, 559
Church, Elizabeth, 498
Circular reaction, 646
Cities, 624–627. See also Urbanization
City-state, 443
Civil disobedience, 644
Civil inattention, 148
Civil sector, 427
Clark, S.D., 17
Class, 9, 243. See also Social class
Class conflict, 15, 244

Class system, 243, 244
Clayman, Steven E., 647
Clayquot Sound protest, 638–640, 644, 645, 652
Cleghorn, Mildred, 388
Climacteric, 377
Clinton, Bill, 43
Closed-ended questions, 47
Closed system, 241
Cloward, Richard, 204
CMA, 624
Cobain, Kurt, 9
Coercive organizations, 180
Cognitive development, 115, 116
Cohabitation, 482, 483
Cohon, George, 418
Cohort, 373
Cohort approach, 497
Coles, Robert, 191
Collective bargaining, 423
Collective behaviour, 640–652
Collective representations, 547
Collectivity, 640
Collins, Doug, 310, 311
Collins, Randall, 545, 550
Comack, Elizabeth, 211, 503
Commercial capitalism, 407
Commonsense knowledge, 5
Communism, 410
Communist Manifesto, The (Marx), 411
Community, 626
Community corrections, 233, 234
Community justice conferencing, 232
Comparable worth, 360
Compensatory educational programs, 535
Complete observation, 52
Compliance, 172
Computer-assisted telephone interviewing, 46
Comte, Auguste, 12, 13
Concentric zone model, 627
Concrete operational stage, 116
Confidentiality, 57
Conflict perspectives
    aging, 388, 389
    crime/deviance, 209–213
    culture, 92, 93
    defined, 21
    economy and work, 413, 414
    education, 119, 259, 518–521
    families, 477, 478
    gender stratification, 364, 365
    health, 582
    political systems, 449–451
    race/ethnicity, 321–323
    religion, 548–551
    social inequality, 252, 253
    social institutions, 144
    social structure, 134
    socialization, 112
    suicide, 21, 22
    urbanization, 629, 630
Conformity, 172
Confucianism, 553, 555
Conglomerates, 409
Connell, Martin, 43
Conrad, Peter, 581
Conservatives, 453
Constitutional monarchies, 443
Contact cultures, 157
Contact hypothesis, 317
Contagion theory, 645
Containment theory, 205
Content analysis, 51
Contingent work, 419, 420
Continuity, 388
Control group, 41
Control theory, 205, 206
Conventional crowds, 643
Conventional level, 116
Convergence theory, 646
Cook, Ramsay, 464
Cooley, Charles Horton, 108, 167, 650
Core nations, 295
Corporate crime, 214
Corporate responsibility, 431, 432
Corporations, 407
Corsaro, William A., 119
Cosmopolites, 631
Counterculture, 87
Country of destination, 609
Country of origin, 609
Courts, 228, 229
Credentialism, 521
Crime. *See also* Deviance
    age, and, 220
    classification of, 213
    defined, 202
    future trends, 234
    gender, and, 220–222
    Internet, and, 216, 217
    Japan, in, 210, 211
    media, and, 224, 225
    occupational/corporate, 214, 215
    organized, 201, 202, 215
    plea bargaining, 230, 231
    political, 215–217
    race/ethnicity, and, 225–227
    religion, and, 227
    social class, and, 222–225
    statistics, 217–220
    street, 213
Criminal justice system
    community corrections, 233, 234
    courts, 228, 229
    police, 227, 228
    punishment, 229–231
    restorative justice, 231–233
Cross, James, 216
Cross-sectional studies, 40
Crowd, 642
Crowd behaviour, 643–648
Crude birth rate, 607
Crude death rate, 608
CUCR, 217, 219
Cults, 560, 561
Cultural artifacts, 51
Cultural assimilation, 318
Cultural capital, 518
Cultural capital theory, 80
Cultural diversity, 84–89
Cultural imperialism, 96
Cultural lag, 84
Cultural relativism, 92
Cultural transmission, 510
Cultural universals, 69, 70
Culture, 64–99
    components, 70–80
    conflict perspective, 92, 93
    defined, 65
    functionalist perspective, 92
    future trends, 94–96
    ideal vs. real, 78
    interactionist perspective, 93
    material vs. nonmaterial, 68, 69
    popular, 80–83
    society, and, 66–70
    technology, and, 94, 95
Culture shock, 89
Cumming, Elaine C., 387
Currie, Raymond, 568
Cyberculture, 82, 83
Cyclical unemployment, 421
Cyrus, Virginia, 341

Dahrendorf, Ralf, 21, 244
Darley, John, 42–44
Das Gupta, Tania, 502, 503
Das Kapital (Marx), 411
Davis, Kingsley, 106, 251
Davis-Moore thesis, 251, 252
Dawson, Carl A., 17
de facto discrimination, 311
de Guzman, Michael, 214
de jure discrimination, 311
Death and dying, 394–397
Deductive approach, 35
Deference, 156
Degradation ceremony, 127
Deindustrialization of North America, 264, 281
Demeanour, 156
Democracies, 444, 445
Democratic leaders, 171
Democratic socialism, 412
Demographic transition, 620–623
Demography, 606

Dene Yati project, 76, 77
Denis, Solange, 390
Denomination, 560
Density, 609
Dependency theory, 293, 294
Dependent variable, 38
Deprived, 631
Deschamp, Yvon, 437
Descriptive studies, 34
Deskilling, 417
Desmarais, Paul, 451
Deterrence, 229, 230
Developed (high-income) nations, 9, 272
Developing (low-income) nations, 9, 272
Deviance. *See also* Crime
    computer mischief/crime, 205
    control theory (social bonding), 205,
        206
    critical approach, 209, 210
    defined, 200, 201
    differential association theory, 206,
        207
    feminist approaches, 210–213
    future trends, 234
    labelling theory, 207–209
    opportunity theory, 204, 205
    primary vs. secondary, 208
    strain theory, 203
Dictatorships, 443
Differential association theory, 206, 207
Differential exclusion, 620
Diffusion, 84
Digital divide, 430, 431
Digital Literacy (Gilster), 649
Dilbert, 190, 191
Disabilities, 588–592
    contemporary issues, 590–592
    education, 530–532
    historical perspective, 589, 590
    poverty, and, 263
Disability oppression, 589
Discovery, 84
Discretion, 227, 228
Discrimination, 310
Disengagement theory, 387
Disintermediation, 194
Disneyland daddies, 493
Division of labour, 145, 183
Divorce, 496–498
Domestic partnerships, 500
Domestic violence, 49, 480, 494, 495
Domhoff, G. William, 450, 451
Dominant emotion, 643
Dominant group, 307, 308
Double day, 361
Doubling effect, 617
Doughnut effect, 634
Downsizing, 426
Dramaturgical analysis, 151–154

Driedger, Doyle, 498
Drummond, Dwight, 228
Du Bois, W.E.B., 16
Dual-earner families, 486
Dual-labour-market theory, 322
Dunlap, Riley E., 652
Durkheim, Emile, 8, 14, 19, 20, 145, 446,
    476, 515, 544, 547
Dyad, 170
Dyck, Rand, 327, 446
Dye, Thomas R., 447
Dying, 394–397
Dying trajectory, 396
Dysfunctions, 18

Earnings ratio, 358
Eating disorders, 335, 339, 365, 366
Eaton, Emily, 531
Ebaugh, Helen Rose Fuchs, 140
Ecclesia, 559
Ecofeminism, 658
Economic concentration, 407
Economic issues, 455
Economic systems, 407–412
Economy, 402
Economy and work, 400–434
    capitalism, 407–410
    conflict perspective, 413, 414
    contingent work, 419, 420
    functionalist perspective, 412, 413
    future trends, 425–432
    historical changes, 402–407
    interactionist perspective, 414, 415
    labour unions, 422–425
    lower-tier jobs, 418, 419
    managers (management), 417, 418
    mixed economics, 412
    occupations, 415
    professions, 415–417
    quiz, 403, 404
    socialism, 410–412
    unemployment, 420–422
Eddy, Mary Baker, 561
Education, 508–539
    academic standards, 525, 526
    Bosnia, in, 514, 515
    charter schools, 535
    conflict perspectives, 119, 259,
        518–521
    cost of post-secondary education,
        532–534
    defined, 510
    disabilities, students with, 530–532
    dropping out, 524, 525
    functional illiteracy, 526, 527
    functionalist perspectives, 258,
        515–518
    future trends, 534–538
    gender bias, 527–530

    gender socialization, and, 351, 352
    historical perspective, 510–513
    home schooling, 528, 529, 535
    interactionist perspectives, 521–523
    international math/science scores,
        577, 578
    issues/challenges, 523
    Japan, in, 513, 514
    poverty, and, 259
    private vs. public schools, 523, 524
    quiz, 510, 511
    religion, and, 543, 544, 570
    religious holidays, 548, 549
    technology revolution, 536, 537
    women's illiteracy in developing
        nations, 532, 533
Egalitarian family, 475
Ego, 113, 114
Egoistic suicide, 20
Eichler, Margrit, 56, 506
Eightfold Path to Nirvana, 554
Eisenhart, Margaret A., 350
Elder abuse, 385–387
Electronic church, 568, 569
Electronic commerce, 194, 195
Elementary Forms of the Religious Life, The
    (Durkheim), 547
Elite model, 449–452
Elliot, Jean Leonard, 305
Emergent norm theory, 647, 648
Emigration, 609
Emotional labour, 154
Emotions, 154, 155
Empirical approach, 33
Employment equity, 360
End of Work, The (Rifkin), 414
Engels, Friedrich, 364, 477, 619
Entrapment, 644
Environmental determinism, 631
Environmental disasters, 654, 655
Environmental racism, 659
Epidemics, 586
Equalitarian pluralism, 319
Erikson, Erik H., 113–115, 126, 379
Erikson, Kai, 20, 653, 660
Essed, Philomena, 322
Ethical religion, 552
Ethnic group, 305
Ethnic jokes, 308, 309
Ethnic pluralism, 319
Ethnic villagers, 631
Ethnic wars, 320
Ethnicity, 9
Ethnocentrism, 91, 309
Ethnography, 58
Ethnomethodology, 150
Evolutionary approach, 253
Exclusion panic, 644
Executives, 417

Experimental group, 41
Experiments, 41–45
Explanatory studies, 35
Expressive crowds, 643
Expressive leadership, 171
Expressive role, 476
Expressive tasks, 18, 363
Extended family, 471
Eye contact, 157

Face-saving behaviour, 151
Facial expressions, 157
Fad, 650
Faith, 543
False consciousness, 92
Faludi, Susan, 366
Families, 468–506
    adoption, 489
    agent of socialization, as, 117, 118
    cohabitation, 482, 483
    conflict perspective, 477, 478
    deciding to have children, 488, 489
    defined, 470, 471
    descent/inheritance, 475
    divorce, 496–498
    extended/nuclear, 471, 472
    feminist perspective, 478–480
    functionalist perspective, 476, 477
    future trends, 503, 504
    gay/lesbian, 499–502
    housework, 486–488
    interactionist perspective, 480, 481
    intimacy, 481–483
    Japan, in, 484, 485
    marriage, 484, 485
    marriage patterns, 473–475
    native Canadians, 502, 503
    power/authority, 475, 476
    quiz, 472, 473
    remarriage, 498, 499
    reproductive technologies, 489–492
    single parenting, 492, 493
    singlehood, 502
    transitions/problems, 493–499
    wife/child abuse, 494, 495
Families we choose, 470
Family group conferencing, 232
Fashion, 651
Fatalistic suicide, 20
Fausto-Sterling, Anne, 377
Federations, 445
Feeling rules, 154
Female job ghetto, 356
Feminism, 365
Feminist perspectives, 22, 23. *See also*
    Gender
    deviance, 210–213
    families, 478–480
    gender stratification, 365, 366

political systems, 451, 452
race, 322
research, 56
suicide, 23
urbanization, 630
Feminization of poverty, 261, 384
Feral children, 105, 106
Ferree, Myra, 51
Fertility, 606
Fetal sex preselection, 490
Fictive kin, 470
Field research, 52–56
First Nations. *See* Native Canadians
First World countries, 274
Fischer, Claude, 633
Five Constant Relationships, 555
Fjellman, Stephen M., 81
Fleras, Augie, 305
FLQ crisis, 216, 436, 655
Folkways, 79
Fontaine, Phil, 459
Footbinding, 345
Ford, Henry, 417, 427
Fordism, 417
Foreign aid, 282–285
Formal education, 511
Formal norms, 79
Formal operational stage, 116
Formal organization, 142, 176–180. *See also* Bureaucracy
Formal sociology, 16
Four Noble Truths, 554
Frank, Andre Gunder, 293
Free enterprise, 410
Freedman, Lisa, 480
Freeman, Rhonda, 498
French Canadians, 326, 327
Friedan, Betty, 393
Friedman, Milton, 432
Front stage, 152
Frustration-aggression hypothesis, 309
Functional age, 372
Functional illiteracy, 526
Functionalism. *See* Functionalist perspectives
Functionalist perspectives
    aging, 387
    crime/deviance, 203–206
    culture, 92
    defined, 18
    economy and work, 412, 413
    education, 118, 258, 515–518
    families, 117, 476, 477
    gender stratification, 362–364
    health, 577–579
    political systems, 446–449
    race/ethnicity, 318–321
    religion, 547, 548
    social inequality, 251, 252

social institutions, 143
suicide, 19–21
urbanization, 627–629
Fundamental freedoms, 441

Gabor, Thomas, 258, 259
Galton, Francis, 567
Game stage, 110
Gamson, William, 658
Ganhdi, Mohandas (Mahatma), 553
Gans, Herbert, 631
Gardels, Nathan, 426
Gardner, Carol Brooks, 148
Garfinkel, Harold, 150, 151
Gates, Bill, 274, 426
Gautama, Siddhartha, 554
Gay families, 499–502. *See also*
    Homosexuality
Gee, Ellen, 503
Geertz, Clifford, 544
Gemeinschaft, 145, 626
Gender, 334–369. *See also* Feminist
    perspectives
    body image, and, 335–337
    bureaucracy, and, 189
    city life, and, 632, 633
    conflict perspectives, 364, 365
    crime, and, 220–222
    defined, 10, 337
    education, and, 527–530
    feminist perspectives, 365, 366
    functionalist perspectives, 362–364
    future trends, 366, 367
    health, and, 583
    historical perspective, 341–347
    illiteracy (developing nations), 532,
        533
    labour activism, 428, 429
    language, and, 72, 73
    moral development, and, 116, 117
    poverty, and, 261, 262
    prison, and, 231
    religious leaders, as, 567–569
    second shift, 361, 362
    social significance, 339, 340
    socialization, and, 347–355
    touching, and, 157
    unemployment rates, 422
    workplace, and, 355–361
Gender-appropriate toys, 348
Gender-belief systems, 339
Gender bias, 351
Gender identity, 338
Gender role, 338
Gender-segregated work, 356, 357
Gender socialization, 122, 123
Gendered institutions, 339
Gendered racism, 322
General deterrence, 230

Generalized other, 110
Genital mutilation, 345–347
Genovese, Kitty, 41
Gentrification, 627
Gereffi, Gary, 297
Gerontology, 373
Gerstner, Louis V., Jr., 188
Gesellschaft, 146, 626
Gestational surrogacy, 492
Gibbs, Lois, 653
Gifted students, 523
Gilbert, Dennis, 254
Gilbert, S. N., 524
Gilder, George F., 363
Gilligan, Carol, 116, 117
Gilster, Paul, 649
Gini coefficient, 285
Glaser, Barney, 55
Global assembly line, 419
Global cities, 295
Global culture, 95
Global independence, 5
Global political systems, 443–445
Global stratification, 270–301
    consumption and global poverty, 275,
      276
    debt, and, 281, 282
    defined, 272
    dependency theory, 293, 294
    education/literacy, 290
    foreign aid, and, 282–285
    future trends, 297, 298
    Gini coefficient (quality of life issues),
      285, 286
    health, 287, 288
    high-income economies, 280, 281
    human development index, 286, 287
    human poverty index, 286, 288
    levels of development approach,
      275–278
    life expectancy, 286, 287
    low-income economies, 279
    middle-income economies, 279, 280
    modernization theory, 291–293
    new international division of labour
      theory, 296, 297
    quiz, 272, 275
    Three Worlds approach, 274, 275
    world system theory, 295
Globalization of trade, 426–432
GNP, 277, 278
Goal displacement, 186
God a Racist?: The Right Wing in Canada
    (Barrett), 312
Goddess movement, 569, 570
Goffman, Erving, 148
Goldberg, Robert A., 660
Good-boy/nice-girl morality, 116
Good Samaritan laws, 38, 39

Gorbachev, Mikhail, 411
Gossip, 650
Gottdiener, Mark, 630
Gotti, John, 216
Gouldner, Alvin, 154
Governing power, 451
Government, 438
Gower, David, 422
Grameen Bank, 42, 43
Grant, Karen, 575, 596
Graying of Canada, 372, 397
Gross national product (GNP), 277, 278
Grounded theory, 55
Groups, 141–143. *See also* Social groups.
Groupthink, 176, 177
Gujral, I. K., 84
Guyer, Melvin, 121

Hackler, Jim, 229
Hall, Edward, 157
Hall, Elaine, 51
Hall Commission, 595
Hamper, Ben, 413
Hardy, Melissa A., 385
Harlow, Harry and Margaret, 105
Harman, Lesley, 36, 55, 150
Harper, Elijah, 459, 461
Harper, Tom, 563
Harris, Chauncey, 628
Harris, Marvin, 92
Hate crimes, 94, 95
Hawking, Stephen, 589
Hawthorne studies, 184
Hazelrigg, Lawrence E., 385
Health, 574–603
    aboriginals, and, 586–588
    age, and, 582
    alternative approaches, 598–600
    conflict perspective, 582
    defined, 576
    functionalist perspective, 577–579
    future trends, 600, 601
    global inequality, and, 287, 288
    health care (Canada), 593–597
    health care (U.S.), 597, 598
    HIV/AIDS. *See* AIDS
    sex, and, 583
    social class, and, 584–586
    social inequality, and, 256–258
    symbolic interactionist theory,
      579–581
Health care, 576
Heinrichs, Daniel, 378
Henley, Nancy, 157
Henry, William E., 387
Hepburn, Mitchell, 423
Heritage language groups, 76
Hermpahrodite, 337
Heron, Craig, 404

Herrnstein, Richard J., 522
Heterogeneous societies, 85
Heterosexist, 500
Hidden curriculum, 119, 520
Hierarchy of authority, 183
High-income economies, 280, 281
High mass consumption, 292
Hijras, 337
Hill, Lawrence, 304
Hinduism, 552–554
Hirschi, Travis, 205
HIV. *See* AIDS
Hochschild, Arlie, 154, 155, 362, 414,
    486
Holism, 599
Holland, Dorothy C., 350
Home schooling, 528, 529, 535
Homeless, 49, 133
    holidays, and, 152, 153
    Japan/France, in, 158, 159
    panhandling, 146, 147
    possessions, 138
    quiz, 135, 136
    role exit, 141
    social structure, and, 146–148
Homer-Dixon, Thomas, 619, 620
Homeworkers, 419
Homogamy, 485
Homogeneous societies, 84, 85
Homolka, Karla, 231, 650
Homophobia, 492
Homosexuality, 49, 483, 492, 499–502
Hooyman, Nancy, 397
Horizontal corporation, 192–195
Horizontal mobility, 243
Horticultural and pastoral societies, 342,
    343
Horticultural societies, 253
Hospice, 397
Household work, 418, 419
Housework, 361, 486–488
Hoyt, Homer, 628
Hughes, Everett, 17
Human capital, 363
Human development
    biology/society, 103, 104
    psychological theories, 112–117
    sociological theories, 108–112
Human Development Index, 286, 287
Human Development Report, 276
Human ecology, 627
Human Poverty Index, 286, 288
Human relations approach, 185
Human rights
    female genital mutilation, 346, 347
    legal cases, 316, 317
Humphreys, Laud, 59
Hunter, Sue, 120
Hunting and gathering societies, 253, 341

Hutterites, 86, 87
Hymers, Olga, 528
Hypotheses, 33

Id, 113, 114
Ideal culture, 78
Ideal type, 183
Identity politics, 446
Ideological Perspectives on Canadian Society
    (Marchak), 17
Ideologies, 548
Illegitimate opportunity structures, 204
Illiteracy, 526, 527, 532, 533
Illness. *See* Health
Immigration
    baby boom cohort, and, 616, 617
    Canadian, 611, 612, 614, 615
    defined, 609
    media, and, 622, 623
    policies, 620, 621
    quiz, 607, 608
Immigration trends, 329, 330
Impression management, 151
In vitro fertilization, 491
Inclusion programs, 531
Income distribution, 254, 255
Independent variable, 37
Indictable offences, 213
Individual discretion, 228
Individualized education plan, 531
Inductive approach, 35
Industrial capitalism, 407
Industrial cities, 626
Industrial economies, 403–406
Industrial societies, 345–347
Industrial unionism, 423
Industrialization, 11
Industrialized societies, 254
Inequalitarian pluralism, 319
Infancy, 124, 375
Infant mortality rate, 608
Infertility, 488
Inflation, 413
Informal education, 510
Informal norms, 79
Informal sanctions, 79
Informal structure, 184
Ingroup, 167–169
Inner containments, 205
Innis, Harold A., 17
Inquiry into the Nature and Causes of
    Wealth of Nations, An (Smith), 410
Inside game, 447
Institutional behaviour, 640
Institutionalized racism, 314, 315
Instrumental leadership, 171
Instrumental Marxists, 451
Instrumental needs, 92
Instrumental role, 476

Instrumental tasks, 18, 363
Integration, 319
Integrative needs, 92
Interaction order, 148
Interactionist perspectives
    aging, 387, 388
    crime/deviance, 206–209
    culture, 93
    defined, 23
    economy and work, 414, 415
    education, 521–523
    families, 480, 481
    health, 579–581
    prejudice, 309
    race/ethnicity, 317, 318
    religion, 551
    socialization, 112
    suicide, 24
    urbanization, 631–633
Intergenerational mobility, 241
Interlocking corporate directorates, 409
Internal colonialism, 321, 322
Internal migration, 610
International migration, 610–612
Internet
    commerce, 194, 195
    crime, and, 216, 217
    cyberculture, 82, 83
    digital divide, 430, 431
    religion, and, 569
    seniors, and, 382, 383
    third world countries, and, 298, 299
Internet cyberculture, 82, 83
Interview, 46
Intimacy, 482
Intimate distance, 157
Intragenerational mobility, 241
Inuit, 323
Invasion, 627
Invention, 84
Involuntary resocialization, 127
IQ scores, 522
Irizarry, Brenda and Amancio, 249, 250
Iron law of oligarchy, 189
Islam, 553, 558
Isolated children, 106, 107
Itard, Jean-Marc, 105

Jackson, Michael, 121
Jain, Harish, 188
Janis, Irving, 176
Japanese Canadians, 328
Japanese organizational structure,
    190–193
Jewell, K. Sue, 82
Jewish Canadians, 329
Jihad, 558
Job deskilling, 264
Job satisfaction, 415

Johnson, Ervin "Magic," 318
Johnson, Holly, 495
Johnson, Mark, 590
Johnson, Murial, 414
Jones, Jim, 561
Judaism, 553, 555–558
Juvenile delinquency, 202

Kahl, Joseph, 254
Kaihla, Paul, 198
Kanter, Rosabeth Moss, 189
Karma, 553
Karp, David, 52
Kaspar, Anne, 112
Keegan, Victor, 427
Keller, James, 590
Kellner, Hansfried, 480
Kemp, Alice, 363
Kennedy, John, 293
Kennedy, Robert, Jr., 639
Kennedy, Sheldon, 120
Kettle, John, 356
Kielburger, Craig, 125
Kilbourne, Jean, 356
Killian, Lewis M., 642, 647
King, Mackenzie, 615
King, Rodney, 640, 643
Kinsella, Warren, 313
Kinsey, Alfred C., 482
Kirby, Sandra, 34
Kiyak, H. Asuman, 397
Klu Klux Klan, 313
Knowing, 32, 33
Knowledge workers, 426
Kohlberg, Lawrence, 116
Kohn, Melvin, 117
Koresh, David, 561
Kozol, Jonathan, 159
Krahn, Harvey, 420
Kübler-Ross, Elisabeth, 396
Kurtz, Lester, 542

Labelling theory, 207–209, 522, 523
Laboratory experiment, 41
Labour, 402
Labour unions, 422–425
Lachance, Gilles, 231
Laissez-faire leaders, 172
Langewiesche, William, 178
Language, 71–74
LaPiere, Richard, 310, 311
Laporte, Pierre, 216
Latane, Bibb, 42–44
Late adulthood, 378, 379
Latent functions, 18, 517
Latouche, Serge, 278
Laurence, Margaret, 2, 7
Law-and-order orientation, 116
Lawanga, Charles, 596

Laws, 80
Le Bon, Gustave, 645
Learning disabled, 522
Legitimation, 438
Lemert, Edwin, 208
Lenski, Gerhard, 253
Lesage, Jean, 459
Lesbian families, 499–502. *See also*
    Homosexuality
LeShan, Eda, 387, 389
Lévesque, René, 327, 460
Levin, William C., 382
Levitt, Kari, 407
Lewis-Thornton, Rae, 574
Liberal feminism, 210, 365
Liberals, 453
Liberation theology, 569
Liebow, Elliot, 54, 147
Life chances, 240
Life expectancy, 286, 287, 372
Limited monarchies, 443
Linden, Rick, 259
Lips, Hilary M., 340
Living will, 396
Lobbying, 447
Lofland, John, 52, 643, 651
Longitudinal studies, 40
Looking-glass self, 108, 110
Lorber, Judith, 337, 353
Love, 482
Love Canal, 653
Low-income economies, 279
Lower class, 250, 251
Lower-tier jobs, 418, 419
Lower-upper class, 249
Lurie, Alison, 70
Luttrell, Wendy, 519
Luxton, Meg, 479

Macauley, Arnie, 30
Macdonald, John A., 445
MacKay, Sarah, 22
Macrolevel analysis, 23
Mahayana Buddhism, 554
Majority group, 307, 308
Malinowski, Bronislaw, 92
Malthus, Thomas Robert, 617, 619
Managers, 417
Mandatory education laws, 517
Manifest functions, 18, 516
Mann, Patricia, 479
Marchak, Patricia, 17
Marginal jobs, 418, 419
Market economy, 410
Marriage, 473, 484, 485
Marriage patterns, 473–475
Marshall, Katherine, 416
Marshall Plan, 276, 291
Martineau, Harriet, 13, 14

Marx, Karl, 14, 15, 21, 92, 134, 209, 244,
    245, 364, 410, 411, 414, 450, 548, 549,
    619, 629, 657
Mason Lee, Robert, 468, 493
Mass, 642
Mass behaviour, 648–652
Mass education, 512
Mass hysteria, 650
Mass media
    agent of socialization, as, 120–122
    AIDS, and, 580, 581
    crime, and 224, 225
    gender socialization, and, 353–355
    immigration, and, 622, 623
    racism, and, 310, 311
    separatism, 448, 449
Master status, 136, 137
Material culture, 51, 68
Matriarchal family, 475
Matriarchy, 341
Matrilineal descent, 475
McDaniel, Susan, 498
McDonaldization, 406
McEwen, Beth, 415
McIntosh, Mary, 452
McIntyre, Janet, 645
McKenna, Kate, 34
McLachlin, Beverley, 137, 396
McLanahan, Sara, 492
McPhail, Clark, 644
Mead, George Herbert, 16, 17, 109–111
Means of production, 15
Mechanical solidarity, 145
Media. *See* Mass Media
Medicalization, 580
Medicine, 576. *See also* Health
Meech Lake Accord, 460, 461
Megalopolis, 635
Melnitzer, Julius, 214
Menopause, 377
Menstrual taboos, 343
Meritocracy, 252, 521
Merton, Robert K., 181, 186, 190, 203,
    312
Métis, 323
Meyer, Marshall W., 186, 188, 189
Miall, Charlene, 489
Michalik, Steve, 338, 339
Michels, Robert, 189
Michelson, William, 633
Microlevel analysis, 23
Middle adulthood, 377
Middle class, 249, 250
Middle-income economies, 279, 280
Midlife crisis, 377
Migration, 609–612
Milgram, Stanley, 173, 174
Military juntas, 443
Millenarian movements, 655

Mills, C. Wright, 7, 21, 155, 186, 450
Minority group, 307, 308
Mitchell, Mike, 203
Mixed economy, 412
Mob, 643
Modern Times, 402
Modernization theory, 291–293
Monarchy, 443
Money, 403
Monogamy, 473
Monotheism, 546
Moonies, 561, 562
Moore, Patricia, 382
Moore, Wilbert, 126, 251
Moral development, 116, 117
Moral entrepreneurs, 208
Moral restraint, 619
Morals crimes, 213
Mores, 79
Morrison, Nancy, 396
Mortality, 608, 609
Mosca, Gaetano, 449
Mosely, Vincent, 41, 42
Mukerji, Chandra, 83
Mulroney, Brian, 460
Multinational corporations, 408
Multiple nuclei model, 628
Murdock George, 69
Murphy, Emily, 622, 623
Murray, Charles, 522
Myers, Mike, 654
Myths, 6

NAFTA, 430
Nagler, Mark, 531
Naive instrumental hedonism, 116
Naloyev, Daud, 282
Napoleon, 181
Nation-state, 443
Nationalism, 96, 464, 465
Natural experiments, 41
Navarrette, Ruben, Jr., 519
Negative sanctions, 79
Neo-Malthusians, 619
New international division of labour
    theory, 296, 297
New Testament, 558
Newman, Katherine, 244
Newman, Peter C., 638
NIABY (not in anyone's backyard), 652
NIMBY (not in my backyard), 652
Nirvana, 553
Noncontact cultures, 157
Nonmaterial culture, 69
Nontheistic religion, 546
Nonverbal communication, 155–158
Normal accident, 178, 179
Normative approach, 33
Normative organizations, 176–180

Norms, 79
Norris, Mary Jane, 76
North American Free Trade Agreement (NAFTA), 430
North American Indians, 323
Notwithstanding clause, 442, 443
Novak, Mark, 379
Nuclear family, 472
Nunziata, John, 445
Nursing homes, 393

O'Reilly-Fleming, Thomas, 160
Oakes, Jeannie, 519, 520
Obedience to authority, 173, 174
Obesity, 339
Objectification, 335
Objectification of women, 336
Objective, 6
Objective method, 248
Obscenity, 342, 343
Observation, 52, 53, 58
Occupational crime, 214, 215
Occupational gender segregation, 356–358
Occupational socialization, 126
Occupations, 415
Ogburn, William F., 84, 662
Ogden, Russel, 59, 60
Ohlin, Lloyd, 204
Oka crisis, 643, 647
Oligopoly, 408
Oliver, Michael, 589
Open-ended questions, 47
Open system, 241
Operational definition, 38
Opportunity theory, 204, 205
Oral cultures, 74
Organic solidarity, 145
Organization man, 186
Organization structure
    bureaucracy. *See* Bureaucracy
    formal organization, 176–180
    horizontal, 192–195
    Japanese, 190–193
Organizational behaviour, 640
Organized crime, 201, 202, 215
Origin of Family, Private Property and the State, The (Engels), 477
Orok, B., 524
Orum, Anthony, 657
Outer containments, 205
Outgroup, 167–169
Outside game, 447
Overall, Christine, 490, 492

Panhandling, 146, 147
Panic, 643, 644
Panzarino, Connie, 531
Parenti, Michael, 245

Pareto, Vilfredo, 449, 450
Park, Robert E., 16, 627, 646
Parkinson's Law, 187
Parliamentary system, 445
Parole, 230
Parsons, Talcott, 18, 363, 387, 476, 577
Part-time workers, 420
Participant observation, 53
Pastoralism, 342
Patriarchal family, 475
Patriarchy, 23, 341, 440, 478
Patrilineal descent, 475
Patrimony, 440
Pay equity, 360
Payne, Kenneth, 164
Peaks, 413
Pearce, Diana, 261
Peer group, 119, 350
Peer pressure, 119
Péladeau, Pierre, 448
Pelzer, Dave, 100
Peripheral nations, 295
Perrow, Charles, 178, 183, 189
Personal distance, 157
Personal space, 157
Personal troubles, 7
Persons with disabilities. *See* Disabilities
Perspective, 18
Peter Principle, 187
Peters, Robert, 648
Peterson, John L., 635, 662
Phaneuf, Gordon, 112
Pheasant, Valerie Bedassigae, 302
Philadelphia Negro: A Social Study, The (Du Bois), 16
Phillips, Bruce, 217
Physician-assisted suicide, 396
Piaget, Jean, 115, 116
Pillemer, Karl, 386
Pinderhughes, Howard, 524
Pink-collar occupations, 250
Play stage, 110
Plea bargaining, 230, 231
Pluralism, 621
Pluralist model, 446, 447, 451, 452
Police, 227, 228
Polite racism, 314, 315
Political crime, 215–217
Political participation, 456, 457
Political parties, 453–455
Political socialization, 455
Politics, 438
Politics/political systems, 426–467
    Aboriginal self-government, 461–463
    authoritarian systems, 443
    conflict perspectives, 449–451
    democracies, 444, 445
    feminist perspectives, 451, 452
    functionalist perspectives, 446–449

future trends, 463–465
governmental bureaucracy, 457, 458
monarchies, 443
political attitudes, 455, 456
political participation, 456, 457
political parties, 453–455
political socialization, 455
Quebec nationalism, 458–461
quiz, 439, 440
totalitarian systems, 444
Polyandry, 474
Polygamy, 473
Polygyny, 342, 474
Polytheism, 546
Popoff, Wilfred, 400
Popular culture, 80–83
Population
    change, and, 661
    defined, 47, 606
    demographic transition theory, 620–623
    future trends, 634, 635
    Malthusian perspective, 617–619
    Marxist perspective, 619
    neo-Malthusian perspective, 619, 620
    public policy, and, 623, 624
Population composition, 612
Population pyramid, 613
Pornography, 342, 343
Porter, John, 17, 306
Positive checks, 619
Positive sanctions, 79
Positivism, 13
Postconventional level, 116
Postindustrial cities, 626, 627
Postindustrial economy, 406
Poverty
    absolute/relative, 260
    age, and, 240, 260, 261
    Brazil, in, 262, 263
    child, 240
    economic/structural sources, 264, 265
    education, and, 259
    gender, and, 261, 262
    global. *See* Global stratification
    persons with disabilities, 263
    quiz, 242, 243
    race/ethnicity, and, 262, 263
    solutions, 264, 265
Power, 246, 438
Power elite, 21, 450
Powers, Charles H., 515
Pratt, Courtney, 432
Preconventional level, 116
Predestination, 549
Preindustrial cities, 625, 626
Preindustrial economies, 402, 403
Prejudice, 308–310
Prejudiced nondiscriminators, 312

Prejudiced discriminators, 312
Preliterate societies, 510
Prenatal diagnosis, 490
Preoperational stage, 115
Preparatory stage, 110
Prescriptive norms, 79
Presentation of self, 151
Pressure groups, 447
Prestige, 246
Preventive checks, 619
Preventive medicine, 576
Primary deviance, 208
Primary group, 142, 167
Primary sector production, 402
Primary sex characteristics, 336
Principle of legitimacy, 476
Privatization, 411
Probation, 230
Profane, 544
Professions, 415–417
Project Acacia, 299
Proletariat, 15, 244
Property crime, 213
Propaganda, 652
Proportional representation, 444
Proscriptive norms, 79
Protest crowds, 644, 645
*Protestant Ethic and the Spirit of Capitalism,
The* (Weber), 15, 549
Psychoanalytic theory, 113, 114
Psychosocial development, 113–115
Public distance, 157
Public issues, 7
Public opinion, 651, 652
Punishment, 229
Punishment and obedience orientation,
116
Purdah, 344

Quality circles, 193
Quebec nationalism, 437, 458–461. *See
also* FLQ crisis
Questionnaires, 46, 47
Quiet Revolution, 326, 459
Quigley, Tim, 228
Quinney, Richard, 209

R. vs. Butler, 342
Rabbi, 556
Race, 9, 304
Race and ethnicity, 302–333
conflict perspectives, 321–323
crime, and, 225–227
discrimination, 310–312
employment discrimination, 188
environmental racism, 659
ethnic groups in Canada, 323–330
ethnocentrism, 309
feminist perspectives, 322

functionalist perspectives, 318–321
future trends, 330, 331
interactionist perspectives, 317, 318
language, and, 73
majority/minority groups, 307, 308
poverty, and, 262, 263
prejudice, 308–310
racism. *See* Racism
social significance, 305, 306
stereotypes, 308, 309
suicide, and, 22
unemployment rates, 422
Racial prejudice, 308
Racism, 312–315
defined, 313
media, in, 310, 311
quiz, 305, 306
types, 313–315
Radical feminism, 210, 365
Rational-legal authority, 182, 441–443
Rationality, 181
Reactivity, 44
Real culture, 78
Recidivists, 230
Reckless, Walter, 205
Red River floods, 53, 662
Rednecked racism, 313, 315
Reference group, 169
Reform movements, 653, 654
Regressive movements, 656
Rehabilitation, 229
Reich, Robert, 265
Reiman, Jeffery, 258
Reiter, Ashley, 529
Relative deprivation, 657, 659
Relative homelessness, 133
Relative poverty, 260, 285
Reliability, 40
Religion, 540–573
Buddhism, 554, 555
Canada, in, 561–569
categories of, 545, 546
Christianity, 558, 559
church-sect typology, 559, 560
conflict perspective, 548–551
Confucianism, 555
crime, and, 227
cults, 560, 561
defined, 542
ecclesia, 559
education, and, 543, 544, 548, 549,
570
effect of, 566, 567
electronic church, 568, 569
functionalist perspective, 547, 548
fundamentalism, 565, 566
future trends, 569–571
Hinduism, 552–554
interactionist perspective, 551

Internet, and, 569
Islam, 558
Judaism, 555–558
meaning of life, and, 543–545
women in ministry, 567–569
Religious fundamentalism, 565, 566
Religious movements, 655, 656
Religious nationalism, 570
Remarriage, 498, 499
Replication, 40
Representative democracy, 444
Representative sample, 47
Reproductive technologies, 489–492
Republics, 445
Reputational method, 248
Research. *See* Sociological research
Research cycle, 35, 36
Resocialization, 127
Resource mobilization theory, 657–659
Respondents, 46
Restorative justice, 231–233
Retirement, 379, 380
Retribution, 229
Revolutionary movements, 654, 655
*Rich Get Richer and the Poor Get Prison:
Ideology, Class and Criminal Justice, The*
(Reiman), 258
Richer, Stephen, 119
Rifkin, Jeremy, 414, 426, 427
Riot, 643
Risman, Barbara, 493
Rituals, 545
Ritzer, George, 418
Roberts, Keith A., 543
Robinson, Svend, 396, 639
Rodriguez, Sue, 4, 5, 396
Role ambiguity, 139
Role conflict, 139
Role distancing, 140
Role exit, 140
Role expectation, 139
Role performance, 139
Role strain, 140
Role structure, 373
Role-taking, 109
Roles, 138–141
Romantic love, 481
Roof, Wade Clarke, 547
Rosen, John, 224
Ross, Rupert, 64, 72
Rossi, Alice, 126
Rossi, Peter H., 142
Rostow, Walt W., 291
Routinization of charisma, 439
Rules and regulations, 183
Rules of Sociological Method, The
(Durkheim), 14
Ruling class, 450, 451
Rumours, 649, 650

Russell, Diana E.H., 113
Russia, 282, 283

Sacred, 544
Sacred canopy, 543
Sainthood, 50, 51
Sample, 47
Sampling considerations, 47
Sanctions, 79
Sapir, Edward, 71
Sapir-Whorf hypothesis, 71
SARtechs, 30
Sayers, Kathy, 420
Scapegoats, 309
Scared Silent: Exposing and Ending Child Abuse, 120
Schiller, Herbert I., 82
School, 118, 119. *See also* Education
School leavers, 524, 525
School-voucher programs, 535
SchoolNet, 535
Schudson, Michael, 83
Scientific management, 417
Seasonal unemployment, 421
Second shift, 361, 486
Second World countries, 274
Secondary aging, 377
Secondary analysis, 48–52
Secondary deviance, 208
Secondary group, 142, 167
Secondary sector production, 403
Secondary sex characteristics, 336
Sect, 560
Sector model, 628
Secular humanism, 566
Segregation, 319–321
Self-administered questionnaires, 46
Self-concept, 107
Self-fulfilling prophecy, 149, 522, 523
Self-identity, 107
Semiperipheral nations, 295
Senescence, 377
Senile dementia, 582
Sensorimotor stage, 115
Serial monogamy, 473
Service workers, 418
Services, 402
SES, 248
Sex, 9, 336
Sex ratio, 612
Sexism, 340, 341
Sexual harassment, 175
Sexual orientation, 336
Sexual space, 632
Shadd, Adrienne, 85, 320
Shakin, Madeline, 70
Shared monopoly, 408
Sharman, Monica, 593
Shkilnyk, Anastasia, 588

Sick role, 577
Significant others, 109
Sikorsky, Robert, 215
Simmel, Georg, 16, 170, 631, 651
Simons, Rita James, 210
Simple random sample, 47
Simple supernaturalism, 545
Simpson, O. J., 229
Simpsons, The, 478, 479
Sincere fictions, 331
Singer, Ron, 549
Single parenting, 492, 493
Singlehood, 502
Sisters in Crime (Adler), 210
Sjoberg, Gideon, 625
Skinheads, 89
Small group, 170
Smelser, Neal, 657
Smiling, 157
Smith, Adam, 410
Smith, Dorothy, 22, 56
Smith, Sir Donald, 629
Snider, Laureen, 214
Snow, David A., 57, 134, 648
Soap operas, 354
Social bond theory, 205, 206
Social change, 660–663
Social class
    Canadian class-structure, 247–251
    crime, and, 222–225
    criminal justice system, and, 258, 259
    health, and, 584–586
    Internet access, 430, 431
    Marx's views, 244, 245
    political attitudes, 456
    suicide, and, 21, 22
    Weber's views, 245–247
Social construction of reality, 149, 579–581
Social contract orientation, 116
Social control, 200
Social devaluation, 126
Social distance, 157, 310
Social facts, 14
Social gerontology, 373
Social groups, 166–176
    conformity, 172–176
    defined, 141
    groupthink, 176, 177
    leadership, 170–172
    size, 170
    types, 166–169
Social inequality
    Canada, in, 254–259
    conflict perspectives, 252, 253
    evolutionary approach, 253, 254
    functionalist perspectives, 251, 252
Social institutions, 143, 144, 663
Social interaction

defined, 132
    dramaturgical analysis, 151–154
    emotions, 154, 155
    ethnomethodology, 150
    front stage/back stage, 152
    future trends, 159, 160
    meaning, and, 148, 149
    microlevel perspective, 148
    nonverbal communication, 155–158
    social construction of reality, 149, 150
Social isolation, 104–107
Social issues, 455
Social marginality, 134
Social mobility, 241
Social movements
    alternative movements, 656
    causes, 656–659
    defined, 652
    emerging perspectives, 658, 659
    reform movements, 653, 654
    religious movements, 655, 656
    resistance movements, 656
    revolutionary movements, 654, 655
    stages, 659, 660
Social network, 142
Social protection, 229
Social solidarity, 19, 142
Social stratification, 240–244, 265, 266. *See also* Social class
Social structure
    changes in, 144–148
    components, 135–144
    conflict perspective, 134
    defined, 132
    framework, 137
    future trends, 159, 160
    homelessness, and, 146–148
    macrolevel perspective, 134
Socialism, 410–412
Socialist feminism, 211, 365
Socialization, 100–130
    adolescence, 125
    adulthood, 125, 126
    agents of, 117–123
    conflict perspective, 112
    defined, 102
    future trends, 127, 128
    gender, and, 347–355
    importance, 102–107
    infancy/childhood, 124
    interactionist perspective, 112
    peers, and, 349–351
    self, and, 107–117
Societal consensus, 18
Society, 4
Society in America (Martineau), 13
Sociobiology, 103
Socioeconomic status (SES), 248
Sociological imagination, 7

Sociological research, 30–62
case studies, 54, 55
ethical issues, 57–60
experiments, 41–45
feminist research methods, 56
field research, 52–56
multiple methods of, 56, 57
research cycle, 35, 36
secondary analysis, 48–52
steps in research process, 36–41
surveys, 45–48
why necessary, 32–36
Sociology
Canada, in, 17
common sense, and, 5–7
defined, 5
development of, 10–17
early thinkers, 12–16
theoretical perspectives, 18–25
why studied, 4–7
Sociology of family, 476
Sociology of sexuality, 482
Sorokin, Pitirim, 49–51
South Asians, 328, 329
Special interest groups, 446–449
Special Report on Suicide Among Aboriginal Peoples, 22
Specific deterrence, 229
Spencer, Herbert, 13
Split labour market, 322
Split-labour-market theory, 322
Sports, 352, 353
Spouse abuse, 480, 494
Squeegee kids, 147
Stackhouse, John, 568
Stage-based approach, 396
Staples, 407
Stark, Rodney, 181
State, 438
Status, 135
Status attainment research, 246
Status set, 135
Status symbols, 138
Stepfamilies, 498, 499
Stereotypes, 308
Stigma, 134
Stitch rule, 480
Strain theory, 203
Stratification. *See* Global stratification, Social class, Social stratification
Strauss, Anselm, 55
Street crime, 213
Structural assimilation, 319
Structural functionalism. *See* Functionalist perspectives
Structural Marxists, 451
Structural unemployment, 421
Studied nonobservance, 151
Subculture, 85–87

Subjective method, 248
Subjective poverty, 285
Subjective reality, 23
Subliminal racism, 314, 315
Subordinate group, 307, 308
Succession, 627
Suicide
assisted, 4, 5
conflict perspectives, 21, 22
feminist perspective, 23
functionalist perspectives, 19–21
interactionist perspective, 24
international trends, 10, 11
personal trouble, as, 8
public issue, as, 8
quiz, 7, 8
right to die, 396
Suicide (Durkheim), 14
Summary conviction offences, 213
Sun Myung Moon, 560, 561
Superego, 113, 114
Surplus, 403
Surrogate motherhood, 491, 492
Surveys, 45–48
Sutherland, Edwin, 206, 214
Suttee, 345
Swidler, Ann, 68
Swift, Gustavus, 182
Symbol, 23, 70
Symbolic capital, 81, 82
Symbolic interaction, 23, 24
Systemic racism, 315, 316

Tabloid newspapers, 650
Taboos, 79
Take-off stage, 291
Tannen, Deborah, 76
Task-based approach, 397
Taylor, Eli, 75
Taylor, Frederick Winslow, 417
Taylor, Peter Shawn, 390
Taylorism, 417
Tearoom Trade (Humphreys), 59
Technoeconomic base, 341
Technological maturity, 292
Technology, 68
Technology and change, 662, 663
Telephone surveys, 46
Televangelists, 568, 569
Television, 95, 120–123, 354. *See also* Mass media
Tell Them Who I Am (Liebow), 54
Temporary workers, 420
Ten Commandments, 556
Terrorism, 654
Test-tube baby, 491
Theism, 546
Theologians, 543
Theoretical perspectives, 18–25

Theory, 18
Therapeutic social movements, 656
Theravadian Buddhism, 554
Third World countries, 275
Thompson, Becky W., 340, 366
Tilly, Charles, 658
Time-and-motion studies, 417
Timid bigots, 312
Titmuss, Richard, 47, 48
Tonnies, Ferdinand, 145, 146, 626
Total institution, 127
Totalitarian systems, 444
Touching, 157
Tracking, 519
Traditional authority, 439–441
Traditional stage, 291
Traditional surrogacy, 492
Trained incapacity, 186
Transsexual, 337
Transvestite, 337
Trapped, 631
Triad, 170
Triangulation, 56
Trickle down theory, 651
Troeltsch, Ernst, 559
Troughs, 413
Trudeau, Pierre, 460
Trudeau, Yves (Apache), 231
Truman, Harry S., 277, 278
Trump, Donald, 249
Tulloch, James, 593
Turner, Jonathon H., 515
Turner, Ralph H., 641
Typology, 144

Ullman, Edward, 628
Unemployment, 420–422
Unemployment rate, 422
Unfulfilled rising expectations, 657
Unification Church, 560, 561
Union Carbide disaster, 654, 655
Unions, 422–425
Unitary states, 445
Units of analysis, 39
Universal ethical principles, 116
Universal health care system, 594, 595
Unmarried people and childless couples, 631
Unprejudiced discriminators, 312
Unprejudiced nondiscriminators, 312
Unstructured interviews, 55
Upper class, 248, 249
Urban legends, 649, 650
Urban sociology, 624
Urbanism, 631
Urbanization, 624–635
Canadian/U.S. cities, compared, 629
conflict perspectives, 629, 630
defined, 12

divided interests (cities vs. suburbs), 633, 634
evolution of cities, 624–627
feminist perspectives, 630
functionalist perspectives, 627–629
future trends, 634, 635
interactionist perspectives, 631–633
Utilitarian organizations, 180

Vajrayana, 555
Validity, 40
Vallières, Pierre, 436
Value-added theory, 657–659
Value contradictions, 78
Values, 76–78
ValuJet aircraft crash, 178, 179
Variable, 37
Veblen, Thornstein, 186, 651
Vertical mobility, 243
Vertical Mosaic, The (Porter), 17
Victim-offender reconciliation, 232
Victimization surveys, 219
Violent crime, 213
Voluntary resocialization, 127
von Moltke, Marshal Helmuth, 182

Wage gap, 358
Waldron, Ingrid, 583
Wallerstein, Immanuel, 295
War of the Worlds, The, 650

WASPs, 326
Watson, Tracey, 139
Wealth, 246, 255, 256
Weber, Max, 15, 16, 21, 181–183, 189, 240, 245–247, 438–441, 549, 550, 559
Weil-Curiel, Linda, 347
Weiskel, Timothy, 623
Weiss, Meira, 591
Weitz, Rose, 200
Weitzman, Lenore, 262
Wendell, Susan, 592
White, Ryan, 580
White anglo-saxon protestants (WASPs), 326
White-collar crime, 214, 215
White ethnics, 327
White Niggers of America (Vallières), 436
White privilege, 305
White supremacist groups, 313
Who Gets Work? (Henry/Ginzberg), 314
Whorf, Benjamin, 71
Whyte, William H., Jr., 186
Wife abuse, 480, 494
Wilson, Edward O., 103
Wilson, Elizabeth, 632
Wilson, William Julius, 414
Wirth, Louis, 631
Wiseman, Jacqueline, 141, 149
Wohlstein, Ronald T., 644
Wolf, Naomie, 366

Women. *See* Feminist perspectives, Gender
Women and Crime (Simons), 210
Women Ruled by Men, 343
Woods, Tiger, 304
Work. *See* Economy and work
Worker displacement, 421
Working class, 244, 250
Workplace gender segregation, 356–358
Workplace socialization, 126
World system theory, 295
Wright, Patrisha, 590
Wuthnow, Robert, 414

Xaniths, 337
Xenocentrism, 92

Yakuza, 210
Yanomamö, 90
Yoels, William, 52
Young adulthood, 376, 377
Yuen, Peter, 198
Yunus, Mohammad, 42, 43

Zeigler, Harmon, 447
Zellner, William, 59
Zionism, 557
Zurcher, Louis A., 53, 54, 648

NOTES

NOTES

NOTES

NOTES

NOTES

NOTES

NOTES

NOTES

NOTES

NOTES

NOTES

NOTES

To the owner of this book

We hope that you have enjoyed using Diana Kendall, Jane Lothian Murray, and Rick Linden's *Sociology In Our Times*, Second Canadian Edition (0-17-616679-3), and we would like to know as much about your experiences with this text as you would care to offer. Only through your comments and those of others can we learn how to make this a better text for future readers.

School _____ Your instructor's name _____

Course _____ Was the text required? _____ Recommended? _____

1. What did you like the most about the *Sociology In Our Times?*

_____
_____
_____

2. How useful was this text for your course?

_____
_____
_____

3. Do you have any recommendations for ways to improve the next edition of this text?

_____
_____
_____

4. In the space below or in a separate letter, please write any other comments you have about the book. (For example, please feel free to comment on reading level, writing style, terminology, design features, and learning aids.)

_____
_____
_____
_____

Optional

Your name _____ Date _____

May ITP Nelson quote you, either in promotion for the *Sociology In Our Times* or in future publishing ventures?

Yes _____ No _____

You can also send your comments to us via e-mail at **college@nelson.com**

Nelson

0066102399-M1K5G4-BR01

NELSON, THOMSON LEARNING
MARKET AND PRODUCT DEVELOPMENT
PO BOX 60225 STN BRM B
TORONTO ON M7Y 2H1